CHRISTIAN FEAST AND FESTIVAL

Liturgia condenda 12

1. Gerard Lukken & Mark Searle, *Semiotics and Church Architecture. Applying the Semiotics of A.J. Greimas and the Paris School to the Analysis of Church Buildings*, Kampen, 1993
2. Gerard Lukken, *Per visibilia ad invisibilia. Anthropological, Theological and Semiotic Studies on the Liturgy and the Sacraments*, edited by Louis van Tongeren & Charles Caspers, Kampen, 1994
3. *Bread of Heaven. Customs and Practices Surrounding Holy Communion. Essays in the History of Liturgy and Culture*, edited by Charles Caspers, Gerard Lukken & Gerard Rouwhorst, Kampen, 1995
4. Willem Marie Speelman, *The Generation of Meaning in Liturgical Songs. A Semiotic Analysis of Five Liturgical Songs as Syncretic Discourses*, Kampen, 1995
5. Susan K. Roll, *Toward the Origins of Christmas*, Kampen, 1995
6. Maurice B. McNamee, *Vested Angels. Eucharistic Allusions in Early Netherlandish Paintings*, Leuven, 1998
7. Karl Gerlach, *The Antenicene Pascha. A Rhetorical History*, Leuven, 1998
8. Paul Post, Jos Pieper & Marinus van Uden, *The Modern Pilgrim. Multidisciplinary Explorations of Christian Pilgrimage*, Leuven, 1998
9. Judith Marie Kubicki, *Liturgical Music as Ritual Symbol. A Case Study of Jacques Berthier's Taizé Music*, Leuven, 1999
10. Justin E.A. Kroesen, *The Sepulchrum Domini through the Ages. Its Form and Function*, Leuven, 2000
11. Louis van Tongeren, *Exaltation of the Cross. Toward the Origins of the Feast of the Cross and the Meaning of the Cross in Early Medieval Liturgy*, Leuven, 2000

Liturgia condenda is published by the Liturgical Institute in Tilburg (NL). The series plans to publish innovative research into the science of liturgy and serves as a forum which will bring together publications produced by researchers of various nationalities. The motto *liturgia condenda* expresses the conviction that research into the various aspects of liturgy can make a critico-normative contribution to the deepening and the renewal of liturgical practice.

The editorial board: Paul Post (Tilburg), Louis van Tongeren (Tilburg), Gerard Rouwhorst (Utrecht), Ton Scheer (Nijmegen), Lambert Leijssen (Leuven), Charles Caspers (secretary – Tilburg)

The advisory board: Paul Bradshaw (Notre Dame IN), Paul De Clerck (Paris), Andreas Heinz (Trier), François Kabasele (Kinshasa), Jan Luth (Groningen), Susan Roll (New York)

Honorary editor: Gerard Lukken (Tilburg)

Liturgisch Instituut
P.O. Box 9130
5000 HC Tilburg, The Netherlands

CHRISTIAN FEAST AND FESTIVAL

The Dynamics of Western Liturgy and Culture

P. Post, G. Rouwhorst, L. van Tongeren & A. Scheer

PEETERS

LEUVEN - PARIS - STERLING, VIRGINIA

Library of Congress Cataloging-in-Publication Data

Christian feast and festival : the dynamics of Western liturgy and culture / P. Post ...
[et al.], eds.
  p. cm. -- (Liturgia condenda : 12)
Includes bibliographical references.
ISBN 9042910550 (alk. paper)
1. Fasts and feasts. 2. Liturgics. I. Post, Paulus Gijbertus Johannes, 1953-II. Series.

BV43 .C47 2001
263--DC21   2001036640

© 2001, Peeters, Bondgenotenlaan 153, B-3000 Leuven

D. 2001/0602/77
ISBN 90-429-1055-0

CONTENTS

PART I

INTRODUCTION

PAUL POST

LITURGICAL MOVEMENTS AND FEAST CULTURE
A DUTCH RESEARCH PROGRAM

1. DESIGN AND TOPIC

This collection on Christian feast culture is closely connected with the first Dutch national research program, 'Liturgical Movements and Feast Culture', which was conceived and initiated in 1995, and coordinated by the Interuniversity Liturgical Institute, headquartered at Tilburg.[1] This collection marks the conclusion of the program, and through a report of work in progress is intended to present a sort of sampler of Dutch liturgical studies work for an international forum.

In this introduction not only are the plan, arrangement and organization briefly presented (4), but, more importantly, the place of the program is further defined by briefly sketching the context of the Liturgical Institute as the initiator and coordinator of the research program, and also the general position of Dutch liturgical studies (2). Subsequently the program is further characterized through a discussion of the elements which define liturgical movements and feast culture (3).

2. THE SETTING
LITURGICAL STUDIES IN THE NETHERLANDS

2.1. Profiling and positioning Dutch liturgical studies in relation to other disciplines

There is a certain imbalance which strikes one with regard to the renewed interest being experienced in many places for the charter and,

[1] This introduction is in part based on a presentation of the national research program of the Liturgical Institute, located in Tilburg. This program was founded in 1995 as the result of a collaboration of five individuals: Paul Post (coordination and editing), Gerard Rouwhorst, Ton Scheer and Regnerus Steensma; Charles Caspers, coordinator of the Liturgical Institute, provided organizational and secretarial services. The national program was previously described in P. POST: Liturgische Bewegungen und Festkultur. Ein landesweites liturgiewissenschaftliches Forschungsprogramm in den Niederlanden, in *Liturgisches Jahrbuch* 48 (1998) 96-113.

connected with that, the history of liturgical studies as a theological discipline.[2] Explorations, that often have a defensive or polemical

[2] I have in mind articles by Taft (Rome), Winkler and Messner (from Tübingen); the latter two appeal explicitly to the approval of H. Auf der Maur (Vienna), who died suddenly in 1999. For this discussion, see R. TAFT: Reconstructing the history of Byzantine communion rituals. Principles, methods, results, in *Ecclesia orans* 11 (1994) 355-378; G. WINKLER: Über die Liturgiewissenschaft (Glosse), in *Theologische Quartalschrift* 175 (1995) 61-62; R. TAFT: Über die Liturgiewissenschaft heute, in *Theologische Quartalschrift* 177 (1997) 243-255; G. WINKLER & R. MESSNER: Überlegungen zu den methodischen und wissenschaftstheoretischen Grundlagen der Liturgiewissenschaft, in *Theologische Quartalschrift* 178 (1998) 229-243 (it is striking how in this debate particularly Winkler and Messner make an emphatic appeal to the tradition of the discipline for its charter and, through Maria Laach as their source, proclaim Guardini and Baumstark the founding fathers of liturgical studies); R. MESSNER: Was ist systematische Liturgiewissenschaft? Ein Entwurf in sieben Thesen, in *Archiv für Liturgiewissenschaft* 40 (1998) 257-274. Cf. F. KOHLSCHEIN: Liturgiewissenschaft – Selbstverständnis einer "Konzilwissenschaft", in G. KRAUS (ed.): *Theologie in der Universität. Wissenschaft – Kirche – Gesellschaft. Festschrift zum Jubiläum. 350 Jahre Theologie in Bamberg* (= Bamberger Theologische Studien 10) (Frankfurt a.M. 1998) 193-207; B. KRANEMANN: Grenzgängerin zwischen den theologischen Disziplinen. Die Entwicklung einer deutschsprachigen Liturgiewissenschaft im 19. und 20. Jahrhundert, in *Trierer theologische Zeitschrift* [108] 4 (1999) 253-272; A. GERHARDS & A. ODENTHAL: Auf dem Weg zu einer Liturgiewissenschaft im Dialog, in *Liturgisches Jahrbuch* 50 (2000) 41-53; P. POST: Interference and intuition. On the characteristic nature of research design in liturgical studies, in *Questions liturgiques / Studies in liturgy* 81 (2000) 48-65; IDEM: Speelruimte voor heilig spel, in H. BECK, R. NAUTA & P. POST (eds): *Over spel. Theologie als drama en illusie* (Leende 2000) 139-167, esp. 139-146; M. BARNARD: *Liturgiek als wetenschap van christelijke riten en symbolen* (Amsterdam 2000). Cf. also M.E. JOHNSON: Can we avoid relativism in worship? Liturgical norms in the light of contemporary liturgical scholarship, in *Worship* 74 (2000) 135-155; R. TAFT: A generation of liturgy in the Academy, in *Worship* 75 (2001) 46-57. Although there is much more literature from the period preceding this debate in the second half of the 1990s which could be cited, I will confine myself to some references, A. HÄUSSLING: Liturgiewissenschaft zwei Jahrhunderte nach Konzilsbeginn, in *Archiv für Liturgiewissenschaft* 24 (1982) 1-18; IDEM: Liturgiewissenschaftliche Augabenfelder vor uns, in *Liturgisches Jahrbuch* 38 (1988) 94-108; K. KOHLSCHEIN: Liturgiewissenschaft im Wandel? Fragmentarische Überlegungen zur Situation und Zukunft einer theologischen Disziplin, in *Liturgisches Jahrbuch* 34 (1984) 32-49; M. MERZ: 'Liturgiewissenschaft'. Name und Sache über eineinhalb Jahrhunderte. Anlässlich einer Publikation von Franz Kohlschein, in *Archiv für Liturgiewissenschaft* 27 (1985) 103-108; A. GERHARDS & B. OSTERHOLT-KOOTZ: Kommentar zur 'Standortbestimmung der Liturgiewissenschaft', in *Liturgisches Jahrbuch* 42 (1992) 122-138. For a summary of the Dutch position, see G. LUKKEN: *Ontwikkelingen in de liturgiewetenschap: balans en perspectief* (= Liturgie in perspectief 1) (Heeswijk-Dinther 1993); IDEM: Liturgiewetenschappelijk onderzoek in culturele context. Methodische verhelderingen en vragen, in *Jaarboek voor liturgie-onderzoek* 13

undertone, appear to have as a common background the fact that the historical (comparative, source-oriented) method which has been traditional in the discipline has come under pressure from the now dominant practical-theological orientation or from rising ritual studies alliances. Moreover, it strikes one how certain blind spots have arisen: for instance, fundamental theoretical-methodological reflections from women's studies in theology and liturgical studies are hardly noted, and German and English language literature completely dominates the field. In addition to important French literature – for instance, an exploration with regard to the "systematic" approach in liturgical studies and theology of liturgy failed to integrate references to the important work of Louis-Marie Chauvet[3] – Dutch liturgical studies too are notable primarily by their absence. Although we are conscious of the limitations in terms of the number of researchers and institutions, and particularly of the restricted circulation of materials published in Dutch, the limited presence of Dutch liturgists among those being cited in international circles can nonetheless be characterized as a shortcoming. After all, for some time now it has been precisely Dutch liturgical studies which has been emphatically involved in reexamining the charter of the discipline and in renewal in the areas of theory and method. Only once is Lukken mentioned by name,[4] or is there a conspicuous selection from Dutch authors listed.[5] As has already been said, one of the intentions lying behind this collection is to bring the research tradition in Dutch liturgical studies onto the international

---

(1997) 135-148; IDEM: *Rituelen in overvloed. Een kritische bezinning op de plaats en de gestalte van het christelijk ritueel in onze cultuur* (Baarn 1999); P. POST: Zeven notities over rituele verandering, traditie en (vergelijkende) liturgiewetenschap, in *Jaarboek voor liturgie-onderzoek* 11 (1995) 1-30 (for Winkler and Taft: pp. 10ff); IDEM: De synthese in de huidige liturgiewetenschap. Proeve van positionering van De weg van de liturgie, in *Jaarboek voor liturgie-onderzoek* 14 (1998) 141-172 (for Winkler and Taft: pp. 161-164); IDEM: Interference and intuition; IDEM: Speelruimte; BARNARD: *Liturgiek als wetenschap*; J. LAMBERTS: Liturgical studies: a 'marginal phenomenon' in *Questions liturgiques / Studies in liturgy* 81 (2000) 151-154. See further our note 6. In our introductory essay in part II of this collection we will return to this matter.

[3] Cf. R. MESSNER: Was ist systematische Liturgiewissenschaft?; L.-M. CHAUVET: *Symbole et sacrement. Une relecture sacramentelle de l'existence chrétienne* (Paris 1988) = *Symbol and sacrament. A sacramental reinterpretation of Christian existence* (Collegeville 1995).

[4] Lukken, in MESSNER: Was ist systematische Liturgiewissenschaft? 267, n. 36.

[5] In TAFT: Über die Liturgiewissenschaft heute, Groen, Brouwer, De Blaauw and Post are listed.

stage. Therefore it is fitting that in this introduction we devote some explicit attention to the discipline in The Netherlands and its tradition.[6]

[6] A good picture of Dutch liturgical studies research over the past years can be obtained from the annual *Jaarboek voor liturgie-onderzoek* that has been appearing since 1985, published by the Institute for Liturgical Studies at Groningen and the Liturgical Institute at Tilburg. Further, reference can be made to the following series, journals and periodicals: Liturgia condenda (Tilburg, Liturgical Institute; international series; published by Peeters, Louvain; Liturgie in perspectief (Tilburg; until 1999; Liturgical Institute; national series, published by Gooi en Sticht, Baarn); Meander (since 2000; Liturgical Institute; national series, published by Gooi en Sticht, Kampen); the series Levensrituelen (Louvain: KADOC); reports from the biennial international liturgical studies colloquia at Louvain (a cooperative project of the Liturgical Institute, Keizersberg Abbey and the Faculty of Theology, Catholic University Leuven: usually issued in Dutch as part of the Nikè-series (Louvain/Amersfoort) and in English or French as a special issue of *Questions liturgiques/Studies in liturgy* (Louvain); *Tijdschrift voor liturgie* (Affligem/Louvain); series Religie en kunst, Institute fot Liturgical Studies (Groningen). To supplement these, although with more of a pastoral-liturgical orientation, there is also the *Werkmap [voor] liturgie* (Baarn: Gooi and Sticht, 1966ff), which since 1997 has been succeeded by the series Liturgie in beweging (Baarn/Kampen: Gooi en Sticht). See also the retirement tribute for H. Wegman: C. CASPERS & M. SCHNEIDERS (eds): *Omnes circumadstantes. Contributions towards a history of the role of the people in the liturgy* (Kampen 1990). See likewise: G. ROUWHORST: Onderzoeksactiviteiten en -plannen op het terrein van de liturgiewetenschap in Nederland, in *Jaarboek voor liturgie-onderzoek* 1 (1985) 173-181; IDEM: Recente ontwikkelingen op het terrein van de liturgiewetenschap en hun mogelijke betekenis voor de liturgische praktijk, in *Tijdschrift voor liturgie* 72 (1988) 382-394; P. POST: Wetenschappelijk grensverkeer tussen disciplinevorming en ontdisciplinering, in *Verslag STEGON symposium 'Uitdagingen aan de theologie', 27 april 1990* (The Hague 1990) 33-43 (= *Jaarboek voor liturgie-onderzoek* 6 (1990) 65-81); H. WEGMAN: Ontwikkelingen in de liturgiewetenschap, in *Tijdschrift voor liturgie* 74 (1990) 232-242; H. BOON-SCHILLING *et al.* (eds): *Liturgievernieuwing in een veranderende wereld. Terugblik en toekomstperspectief* (= Mededelingen van de prof.dr. G. van der Leeuw-Stichting 66) (Amsterdam 1991); G. LUKKEN: *Ontwikkelingen in de liturgiewetenschap. Balans en perspectief* (= Liturgie in perspectief 1) (Heeswijk 1993); G. LUKKEN: Liturgiewetenschap in Nederland. Naar aanleiding van een onderzoekbeoordeling, in *Jaarboek voor liturgie-onderzoek* 47 (1995) 57-76. More in bibliographical surveys, A. SCHEER: Liturgiewetenschap. Cultus en cultuur in dialectiek, in *Praktische theologie* 22 (1995) 80-99; P. POST: Liturgische bewegingen: een literatuurbericht, in *Praktische theologie* 24 (1997) 59-80; IDEM: Rijke oogst: literatuurbericht liturgiewetenschap, *Praktische theologie* 26 (1999) 94-117. IDEM: Personen en patronen. Literatuurbericht liturgiewetenschap, in *Praktische theologie* 28 (2001) 86-110. See also the discussion of the position of the recent Dutch Protestant liturgical manual: POST: De synthese in de huidige liturgiewetenschap. Proeve van positionering van De weg van de liturgie, in *Jaarboek voor liturgie-onderzoek* 14 (1998) 141-172. See now also: BARNARD: *Liturgiek als wetenschap*.

2.2. Today's situation: researchers

Although Dutch liturgical studies do not wholly coincide with Dutch language liturgical research, nevertheless we do include the Flemish research that is concentrated in and from Louvain (Liturgical Institute and Faculty of Theology of the Catholic University Leuven) within the domain discussed here. With regard to the institutional settings for Dutch liturgical studies, a quick random list of institutions (to which only the names of permanent full-time staff are added) may afford a first picture:

- Louvain: Liturgical Institute; Faculty of Theology, Catholic University Leuven (L. Leijssen; J. Lamberts)
- Groningen: Institute for Liturgical Studies, Faculty of Theology and Religious Studies, State University of Groningen (J. Luth; R. Steensma)
- Kampen: Theological University Kampen (N. Schuman; D. Dijk)
- Utrecht: Faculty of Theology, Utrecht University (G. Immink); also related to this Faculty: Old Catholic Seminary (K. Ouwens) and Evangelical Lutheran Seminary (M. Barnard)
- Utrecht: Catholic Theological University of Utrecht (G. Rouwhorst)
- Amsterdam: Faculty of Theology, Vrije Universiteit (N. Schuman)
- Nijmegen: Faculty of Theology, Catholic University, Nijmegen (A. Scheer; with: Institute for Eastern Christianity, Nijmegen: B. Groen)
- Tilburg: Liturgical Institute, Tilburg Faculty of Theology (Ch. Caspers, P. Post, L. van Tongeren, A. Vernooij; emeritus: G. Lukken).

With regard to professorships, the situation now cannot precisely be called rosy. Leaving out of consideration the two chairs in Louvain (Leijssen and Lamberts), The Netherlands has only five chairs in liturgical studies, two part places on the Protestant side (Schuman and Barnard) and three full time on the Roman Catholic side (Rouwhorst, Scheer and Post).

2.3. Characteristics of the discipline

At the inception of the national research program mentioned above a descriptive profile of the discipline of liturgical studies was drawn up, of which we will offer a resumé here. In general, the relative disciplinary profile of liturgical studies, particularly in the context of the theological and religious studies curriculum, can be defined by four accents. The point of departure is that a tetrad of definitive elements *together* make up the irreplaceable identity or property of the discipline and autonomy of liturgical studies as a theological *disciplina principalis*.[7] These four are, respectively, the object or research terrain, the fields of research or themes (1); the manner in which the questions are posed, methods, techniques and ways of approaching research (2); point of view and objective (3); and the tradition of the discipline (4).

2.3.1. *Terrain or object of research*

It is primarily through its object and themes that the discipline of liturgical studies distinguishes itself from other disciplines practiced in the theological departments of universities; this is likewise true for ritual studies with a strong multi- or interdisciplinary orientation. Liturgical studies concentrate on fields of research that have to do with Christian liturgy or worship understood in their widest sense, in the past, present and future. This includes all rituals that one encounters within Christian churches and confessions, which in one way or another express the faith of the community. More specifically, among these are the sacraments and *sacramentalia*, services of the Word and their components such as homilies and sermons, the Divine Office, all celebrations which are connected with the church year, Christian rites of passage, pilgrimages and processions.[8]

Since the discipline arose, the following fields of research have been developed: anthropology of liturgy; the *artes* in relation to liturgy; history of liturgy; theology of liturgy, including sacramental theology; and themes from contemporary liturgical practice.[9] In principle, this canon

---

[7] Cf. P. POST: Zeven notities; see also IDEM: Interference and intuition.

[8] This characterization implicitly acknowledges that in a general sense liturgical studies are ecumenical in character, which of course does not exclude that in a more pointed sense one can more closely delimit the object in research. Regarding the call for ecumenical liturgical studies, see T. BERGER: Prolegomena für eine ökumenische Liturgiewissenschaft, in *Archiv für Liturgiewissenschaft* 29 (1987) 1-18; A. HÄUSSLING: Was heißt: Liturgiewissenschaft ist ökumenisch?, in K. SCHLEMMER: *Gottesdienst - Weg zur Einheit. Impuls für die Ökumene* (= Quaestiones disputatae 122) (Freiburg etc. 1989) 62-88; F. LURZ: Für eine ökumenische Liturgiewissenschaft, in *Trierer theologische Zeitschrift* [108] 4 (1999) 273-290. Cf. BARNARD: *Liturgiek als wetenschap*.

[9] Terminology regarding theology of liturgy/liturgical theology, etc., is in many regards diffuse and confusing. For an initial bibliographical orientation to the literature (not an analysis), see MESSNER: Was ist systematische Liturgiewissenschaft? 259ff, esp. the literature in notes 9, 10, 11, 13. As partial supplements we can also list P. FERNANDEZ: Liturgia y teologia. Una cuestion metodologica, in *Ecclesia orans* 6 (1989) 261-283; B. NEUNHEUSER: Liturgiewissenschaft: Exakte Geschichtsforschung oder (und)

of domains remains open and welcomes enrichment by new insights and developments.

2.3.2. Research methods and formulating questions

In the course of the 20th century, and particularly over the past decades, liturgical studies have undergone a number of radical developments, more so than other theological disciplines or subdisciplines. In the past the discipline was for many years rather exclusively focused on practice and – in the Roman Catholic tradition – moreover directed strongly toward juridical matters. Education in theological institutions was oriented toward the acquisition of practical liturgical skills and carrying out the instructions in the rubrics. Gradually a broadening of focus took place, especially under the influence of the Liturgical Movement. To an increasing degree there arose an interest in the history of liturgy, as well as for the pastoral aspects with which the celebration of liturgy was connected, and for the questions in systematic theology which these raised. The last decades, however, one can sense that there has been a further reorientation of liturgical studies, and in this The Netherlands has most certainly taken a high profile role, seen from an international perspective. This reorientation expresses itself in two ways:

(1) To an increasing degree people have become conscious of the complexity of the object of liturgical studies, of Christian ritual as a verbal and non-verbal phenomenon. The realization has grown that rituals, including Christian rituals, can have a wider range of meanings and functions than people previously had generally assumed. Moreover, the realization has penetrated more deeply than before that on the basis of their relation with Christian worship various *artes*, forms of art such as church music, church architecture, images in the church building, body movement, literary forms, can and should be subjects for research in liturgical studies.

(2) There is also a sense of a growing interest in rituals with a non-official character (one can think here of rituals in popular or folk religion, but also of other forms of new or 'emerging rituals'[10]) that received

Theologie der Liturgie?, in *Ecclesia orans* 4 (1987) 87-102; J. HERMANS: L'étude de la liturgie comme discipline théologique. Problèmes et méthodes, in *Revue théologique de Louvain* 18 (1987) 337-360. See further my introduction in part II of this collection.

[10] Cf. R.L. GRIMES: *Reading, writing, and ritualizing. Ritual in fictive, liturgical, and public places* (Washington DC 1993) 23-38; N. MITCHELL: Emerging riuals in contemporary culture, in *Concilium* 3 (1995) 121-129. Cf. the "re-inventing of ritu-

little or no attention in older liturgical studies (history of liturgy) publications. These involve forms of liturgy that are not specified in the official books, or are performed in ways differing from what is indicated in these books. There is also attention being given to the combination of liturgy and 'piety' or forms of religious expression past and present.

This realization of the complexity of the object of research, and its accompanying expansion, has led to the insight that justice can only be done to this object by undertaking interdisciplinary contacts with disciplines and subdisciplines such as the social sciences, cultural history, art history, musicology, archaeology, linguistics, semiotics, anthropology and European ethnology, comparative religion, and recently, especially in the field of what are being termed 'ritual studies', creating a forum where elements of these disciplines can encounter one another.[11] Thus

als" (esp. of rites of passage): R. GRIMES: *Deeply into the bone. Re-inventing rites of passage* (Berkeley/Los Angeles/London 2000). See also J. PIEPER & P. POST: Rituele veranderingen met betrekking tot de huwelijkssluiting. Een onderzoeksvoorstel, in *Jaarboek voor liturgie-onderzoek* 12 (1996) 136-165; P. POST, J. PIEPER & R. NAUTA: Om de parochie. Het inculturerende perspectief van de rituele marginaliteit. Verkenning van een onderzoeksperspectief, in *Jaarboek voor liturgie-onderzoek 14* (1998) 113-140.

[11] 'Ritual studies': increasingly this term denotes a field of research that includes elements from religious studies, cultural studies and the social sciences. The connecting element is the often theoretical concern with rituals, in which particularly cross-cultural and comparative aspects are central. By way of examples, see the studies of Ronald Grimes, R.L. GRIMES: *Beginnings in ritual studies* (Washington DC 1982); IDEM: *Ritual criticism. Case studies in its practice, essays on its theory* (Columbia 1990); IDEM: *Reading, writing, and ritualizing*; IDEM: *Marrying & burying. Rites of passage in a man's life* (Boulder etc. 1995); IDEM: *Deeply into the bone.* Further (chronologically), T. GERHOLM: On ritual. A postmodernist view, in *Ethnos* 3-4 (1988) 190-203; C. BELL: *Ritual theory, ritual practice* (New York/Oxford 1992); H.-G. HEIMBROCK: *Gottesdienst – Spielraum des Lebens. Sozial- und kulturwissenschaftliche Analysen zum Ritual in praktisch-theologischem Interesse* (= Theologie & empirie 15) (Kampen/Weinheim 1993); T. ASAD: Toward a genealogy of the concept ritual, in T. ASAD: *Genealogies of religion. Discipline and reasons of power in Christianity and Islam* (Baltimore 1993) 55-79; C. HUMPHREY & J. LAIDLAW: *The archetypal actions of ritual. A theory of ritual illustrated by the Jain rite of worship* (= Oxford studies in social and cultural anthropology) (Oxford 1994); J. PLATVOET & K. VAN DER TOORN (eds): *Pluralism and identity. Studies in ritual behaviour* (= Studies in the history of religions 67) (Leiden 1995); M.B. AUNE & V. DeMARINIS (eds): *Religious and social ritual. Interdisciplinary explorations* (New York 1996); C. BELL: *Ritual. Perspectives and dimensions* (Oxford 1997); B.C. ALEXANDER: Ritual and current studies of ritual – Overview, in S.D. GLAZIER: *Anthropology of religion. A handbook* (Westport 1997) 139-160; the posthumously published standard work R.A. RAPPAPORT: *Ritual and religion in the*

liturgical studies live by the grace of methodological plurality, and use is made there – in an autonomous manner – of methods which are employed in these disciplines and subdisciplines.

These developments make it possible right now to distinguish the following approaches and lines of research in The Netherlands, all of which can be recognized in this collection:[12]

- the historical approach (liturgical history, which now can have various profiles, i.e., strongly source-oriented and/or comparative in the tradition of Anton Baumstark, anthropological history, etc.);
- the biblical-theological approach (with 'Bible', not only the historical but also theological aspects are included in the discussion);
- the anthropological approach (cf. anthropology of liturgy, anthropology of Christian rites and symbols);

making of humanity (= Cambridge studies in social and cultural anthropology 110) (Cambridge 1999), which does, however, employ definitions of 'liturgy' and 'liturgical' the content of which diverges from those used here; M.D. STRINGER: *On the perception of worship. The ethnography of worship in four Christian congregations in Manchester* (Birmingham 1999); N. MITCHELL: *Liturgy and the social sciences* (Collegeville 1999). Little noted has been K. FLANAGAN: *Sociology and liturgy. Re-presentations of the holy* (Houndmills/London 1991). See also the bibliography in POST: De synthese 141-172 and POST: Liturgische Bewegungen 99, notes 6, 7. A rather limited view on ritual studies was offered recently by Schillebeeckx in the context of his project on modern sacramental theology. See E. SCHILLEBEECKX: Naar een herontdekking van de christelijke sacramenten: ritualisering van religieuze momenten in het alledaagse leven, in *Tijdschrift voor theologie* 40 (2000) 164-187. Issues surrounding the connections between liturgical studies and ritual studies were not unimportant in sparking off the debate about the charter of liturgical studies. For this, see the views of Taft, Winkler and Messner already cited (cf. for instance MESSNER: Was ist systematische Liturgiewissenschaft? 270, n. 46!). A provocative view here was given by D. STRINGER: Liturgy and anthropology. The history of a relationship, in *Worship* 63 (1989) 503-521. Concerning defensive movements to stake out territory, parallels can be drawn with the rise of and discussions surrounding another specifically domain-oriented discipline, 'cultural studies'. On this, see the special issue of the journal *Cultural studies* 12,4 (1998): a special issue on "The institutionalization of cultural studies". If there could be an up-to-date version of H. AUF DER MAUR: Das Verhältnis einer zukünftigen Liturgiewissenschaft zur Religionswissenschaft, in *Archiv für Liturgiewissenschaft* 11 (1968) 327-343 (as urged by Messner, for instance; see MESSNER: Was ist systematische Liturgiewissenschaft?), then I believe that it could only come from this broad ritual studies perspective. See also T. JENNING: Ritual studies and liturgical theology. An invitation to dialogue, in *Journal of ritual studies* 1 (1987) 35-56.

[12] Only in a few cases the approaches can be provided with names, projects or studies in the terrains referred to.

- the semiotic approach;[13]
- the pastoral-liturgical approach;
- associated with that, the empirical-liturgical approach, in close dialogue with the social sciences;[14]
- the approach from the *artes* (image-iconography, music, space-architecture, physical expression-dance);[15]
- the approach from systematic theology (cf. theology of liturgy, including sacramental theology);
- other approaches, for instance from women's studies[16] and spirituality.[17]

It is important to see this listing of approaches as open and its components as complementary.

In liturgical studies research attention is focused both on description, classification and sketching various Christian rituals and the reconstruc-

---

[13] It should be noted that this approach is not of the same order as the others listed here; for this approach in the general sense see the work of Lukken, for example the section of semiotic studies in G. LUKKEN: *Per visibilia ad invisibilia. Anthropological, theological and semiotic studies on the liturgy and the sacraments*, ed. by L. VAN TONGEREN & CH. CASPERS (= Liturgia condenda 2) (Kampen 1994) 239-394.

[14] A. SCHEER: Empirische liturgiek, in *Jaarboek voor liturgie-onderzoek* 6 (1990) 83-90; first samples of empirical liturgical studies are M. GERTLER: *Unterwegs zu einer Fernsehgemeinde. Erfahrung von Kirche durch Gottesdienstübertragungen* (= dissertation Nijmegen) (Cologne 1998); A. MULDER: *Geloven in crematieliturgie. Een pastoraalliturgisch onderzoek naar hedendaagse crematieliturgie in rooms-katholieke context* (= dissertation Nijmegen) (Nijmegen 2000); in part P. POST & J. PIEPER & M. VAN UDEN: *The modern pilgrim. Multidisciplinary explorations of Christian pilgrimage* (= Liturgia condenda 8) (Louvain 1998).

[15] The relatively wide attention paid to liturgy and *artes* in Dutch liturgical studies is striking; notice of iconography, liturgical music, architecture, literature and poetry recurs regularly in the work of Barnard, (De Blaauw), Caspers, Luth, Ouwens, Post, Schuman, Steensma, Van Tongeren and Vernooij.

[16] I am thinking here of the work of M. Geurtsen (Utrecht) and D. Dijk (Kampen). Cf. the dissertation by Denise Dijk: D. DIJK: *Een beeld van een liturgie. Verkenningen in vrouwenstudies liturgiek, met bijzondere aandacht voor het werk van Marjorie Procter-Smith* (= dissertation Kampen) (Gorinchem 1999).

[17] For a first specimen of systematic academic integration of spirituality and liturgical studies, see the *expositio missae* of A. DE KEYZER: *Om voor Gods gelaat te staan. Een expositio missae* (= dissertation Nijmegen) (Baarn 1998). For this line previously, see C. VAGAGGINI: *Liturgia e storia della spiritualità. Un campo di indagine*, in A. BUGNINI: *Introduzione agli studi liturgici* (Rome 1962) 225-267; K. WAAIJMAN: Spiritualiteit en liturgie, in *Tijdschrift voor liturgie* 76 (1992) 222-238; cf. IDEM: *Spiritualiteit. Vormen, grondslagen, methoden* (Gent/Kampen 2000).

tion of their origins and development, but also on an analysis of the linguistic and non-verbal meanings and symbols that lie within them and the various functions which these fulfill. The research focuses not only on the rituals as such, but also on their reception, appropriation and how they are experienced by believers, as well as on the relation with their cultural context, with which they are in constant interaction. The description and analysis of the liturgical rituals is the point of departure for theological and pastoral-liturgical reflection which on the one side is oriented to renewal of the theology of liturgy (including sacramental theology), and on the other to improvement of contemporary liturgical practice.

It is, finally, characteristic of liturgical studies that use is commonly made of comparative method in its investigations. Depending on the contexts and objects, this can be a matter of historical, typological, theological or symbolic comparison. Especially since Anton Baumstark, who laid the foundations of 'comparative liturgical studies', mutual comparisons across liturgical traditions – from different churches and different periods in the history of liturgy – has commanded considerable attention.[18] On the one hand, this comparative method is used with a purely liturgical-historical intention, namely as a means for reconstructing the course taken in the development of liturgical history; on the other hand, it also appears fruitful for theological and pastoral-liturgical reflection on worship. We thus consciously see the comparative way as broader than the comparisons that are endorsed by means of an appeal to Baumstark in the ongoing debate on the charter of liturgical studies.[19]

Although a number of methods and techniques are thus established in the tradition of the discipline, and through their individual applica-

---

[18] Cf. the pioneering work of Baumstark, which is again the centre of interest, A. BAUMSTARK: *Liturgie comparée: conférences faites au Prieuré d'Amay* (Chevetogne 1939); *Liturgie comparée: principes et méthodes pour l'étude historique des liturgies chrétiennes*, 3e ed. rev. par B. BOTTE (Chevetogne 1953); a now much used English version of the latter publication has also appeared: *Comparative liturgy* (London 1958). On Baumstark and what is termed 'comparative liturgical study', see F.S. WEST: *Anton Baumstark's comparative liturgy in its intellectual context* (= Ph.D. Diss. Notre Dame University, 1988); see also the fine little book F.S. WEST: *The comparative liturgy of Anton Baumstark* (Joint liturgical studies 31) (Nottingham 1995); A. CAMERON-MOWAT: Anton Baumstark's comparative liturgy, in *Questions liturgiques / Studies in liturgy* 76 (1995) 5-19; see further POST: Zeven notities.

[19] See particularly the articles by Winkler, Winkler & Messner and Messner cited above. For the expansion, see POST: Zeven notities.

tion and development have come to be thought of as "typical of liturgical studies", nevertheless from the open and broad description of the field presented above and the likewise open and broad range of approaches, it must be clearly understood that liturgical studies are characterized by a multiplicity of complementary methods. Depending on the object of research selected and the manner of approach, diverse research methods and techniques are employed. This means liturgical studies are in principle multidisciplinary. The content connected with this can, with Sible de Blaauw, be described as a way of working which is characterized by an effort to get to know the method or methods from the traditions of other disciplines and assimilate them, in order to digest the results independently and integrate them into a new whole.[20] Being multidisciplinary in this sense is elsewhere sometimes considered as inter- or even intradisciplinary. To us, working with 'multi-' appears adequate and, for the time being, the most feasible option.

2.3.3. Point of view and objective

Underlying liturgical studies research, as this is conducted in The Netherlands with the aid of various methods and from diverse approaches, is a certain vision of the discipline that binds the researchers together and brings them into dialogue with one another.

The study of Christian rituals takes place with a threefold objective:

(1) The enlargement of insight into the phenomenon of the Christian service of worship, which must be situated in the tensions between tradition and modernity (or postmodernity), continuity and change, cultus and culture, provision and reception.

(2) The development of criteria for a responsible theology of liturgy. On the one side this should contribute to theological reflection on worship; on the other side, liturgy is an irreplaceable *locus theologicus*, and as such it is an important contribution for reflection in systematic theology.

(3) The improvement of current liturgical practice.

---

[20] S. DE BLAAUW: *Cultus et decor. Liturgie en architectuur in laatantiek en middeleeuws Rome* (= dissertation Leiden) (Delft 1987) proposition 8; an application of the perspective is found in S. DE BLAAUW: Architecture and liturgy in Late Antiquity and the Middle Ages. Traditions and trends in modern scholarship, in *Archiv für Liturgiewissenschaft* 33 (1991) 1-34; on programmatic application of methodological plurality in liturgical studies, see, in summary P. POST: Wetenschappelijk grensverkeer; IDEM: Interference and intuition, and my introduction to part II of this volume.

2.3.4. Tradition of the discipline and the place of liturgical studies in academic theological curriculum

As with every academic discipline, a not unimportant part of its identity is derived from and defined by its tradition. Both in The Netherlands and internationally one can point to a series of individual institutions, professional journals, manuals,[21] conferences, research, training and educational curricula, academic-liturgical studies involvement with liturgical books and practices, etc.[22]

---

[21] Particularly manuals play a key role in the discipline's tradition. In recent years one senses there has been a remarkable blossoming of this genre in liturgical studies; for instance, in the German language area A. GERHARDS: Die Kunst, Liturgie zu lehren und lernen, in *Theologische Revue* 92 (1996) 181-194; J. LAMBERTS: Twee belangrijke Duitse handboeken liturgiewetenschap, in *Tijdschrift voor liturgie* 81 (1997) 442-448. See likewise P. POST: De synthese in de huidige liturgiewetenschap. Proeve van positionering van De weg van de liturgie, in *Jaarboek voor liturgie-onderzoek* 14 (1998) 141-172; see also the regular surveys in *Archiv für Liturgiewissenschaft*. For the Dutch language area, one is referred to the following manuals: H. WEGMAN: *Riten en mythen. Liturgie in de geschiedenis van het christendom* (Kampen 1991); J. LAMBERTS: *Hoogtepunt en bron. Inleiding tot de liturgie* (= UTP-studies) (Averbode/Helmond 1991); P. OSKAMP et al. (eds): *De weg van de liturgie. Tradities, achtergronden, praktijk* (Zoetermeer 1998); LUKKEN: *Rituelen in overvloed*; M. BARNARD & P. POST (eds): *Ritueel bestek. Antropologische kernwoorden van de liturgie* (Zoetermeer 2001).

[22] In contrast to other areas (particularly German-speaking countries), there has still been little systematic attention given to its peculiar tradition in the discipline in The Netherlands. For possible, and very divergent, diagnoses for this lacuna, see POST: De synthese. This lacuna is particularly striking in the area of the history of the Liturgical Movement and the Second Vatican Council. Yet the field is not entirely fallow. There is a fundamental study by K. JOOSSE: *Eucharistische gebeden in Nederland. Een documentaire studie over de ontwikkeling van de vertaalde Romeinse en 'eigen' Nederlandse eucharistische gebeden (1963-1979)* I-II (Tilburg 1991); see also various articles on the history of the Liturgical Movement in Dutch-speaking areas by J. LAMBERTS. Further, reference can be made to J. WILDERBEEK: Professor Prein en de Gemeenschapsmis in het Utrechtse, in *Jaarboek voor liturgie-onderzoek* 10 (1994) 31-71, and the sketches of the life and work of Wegman and Lukken, G. ROUWHORST: Herman Wegman. Een terugblik op zijn leven en werk, in *Jaarboek voor liturgie-onderzoek* 12 (1996) 6-20; Inleiding, in H. WEGMAN: *Voor de lange duur. Bijdragen over liturgie en spiritualiteit* (Baarn 1999) 7-16; L. VAN TONGEREN: Rite and Signs. Some bio-bibliographical notes, in G. LUKKEN: *Per visibilia* 9-22. Of a strongly historiographic character is G. LUKKEN: *Ontwikkelingen in de liturgiewetenschap. Balans en perspectief* (= Liturgie in perspectief 1) (Heeswijk-Dinther 1993). Sometimes smaller biographical sketches afford fine historical perspectives, such as G. LUKKEN: Augustinus Hollaardt: een lang leven in dienst van de liturgie, in *Tijdschrift voor liturgie* 83 (1999) 298-307. For Germany see F. KOHLSCHEIN & P. WÜNSCHE (eds): *Liturgiewissenschaft - Studien zur Wissenschaftsgeschichte* (= Liturgiewissenschaftliche Forschungen und Quellen 78)

As has already been implicitly acknowledged in the preceding description of the objective of liturgical studies, this discipline fulfills multiple and important functions in theological faculties and universities. In a very special way, the study of Christian rituals affords insight into the faith, and the experience of faith, in the Christian community. In a more general sense, it can be affirmed that, as is increasingly acknowledged, rituals are an important key for the study of culture in its various religious and social dimensions. Moreover, as previously said, many theologians consider liturgy as an irreplaceable *locus theologicus*.[23] Finally, it is generally acknowledged that insight into and familiarity with the various liturgical traditions is of eminent importance for theological students preparing for a career in the church.

(Münster/Maria Laach 1996); see further the good overview with extensive bibliography, B. KRANEMANN: Grenzgängerin zwischen den theologischen Disziplinen. Die Entwicklung einer deutschsprachigen Liturgiewissenschaft im 19. und 20. Jahrhundert, in *Trierer theologische Zeitschrift* [108] 4 (1999) 253-272. The previously mentioned studies by TAFT, MESSNER and POST: De synthese, provide a summary of the international picture. On the Protestant side, numerous studies in liturgical history also indirectly offer starting points. I will list only J. LUTH: *De 25, 26 en 11 andere psalmen door Jan Utenhove*, 4 vols. (Brasschaat 1997ff); J. SMELIK: *Eén in lied en leven. Het stichtelijk lied bij Nederlandse protestanten tussen 1886 en 1938* (= Nederlandse cultuur in Europese context, long series 9) (The Hague 1997); L. WESTLAND: *Eredienst en maatschappij. Een onderzoek naar de visies van A.A. van Ruler, de prof.dr. G. van der Leeuw-stichting en de beweging Christenen voor het Socialisme* (The Hague 1985); F. DE JONG & K.W. DE JONG: Van forme naar formulier. Het ontstaan en de ontwikkeling van het klassieke gereformeerde doopformulier in de Nederlandse reformatie, in *Jaarboek voor liturgie-onderzoek* 14 (1998) 7-60.

[23] Cf. T. BERGER: Liturgy - a forgotten subject-matter of theology?, in *Studia liturgica* 17 (1987) 10-18; G. LUKKEN: La liturgie comme lieu théologique irremplaçable, in *Questions liturgiques* 56 (1975) 97-112; P. DE CLERCK: 'Lex orandi lex credendi'. The original sense and historical avatars of an equivocal adage, in *Studia liturgica* 24 (1994) 178-200. We will also return to this question in the contributions in part II (with supplementary bibliography). Regarding this matter in general, see also the influential collection K. RICHTER *et al.* (eds): *Liturgie - ein vergessenes Thema der Theologie?* (= Festschrift E.J. Lengeling) (= Quaestiones disputatae 107) (Freiburg etc. 1986); cf. recently W.M. MÜLLER: 'Lex orandi, lex credendi'. Wo Systematik und Liturgiewissenschaft heute zusammenarbeiten können, in *Münchener Theologische Zeitschrift* 49 (1998) 145-154; P. DE CLERCK (ed.): *La liturgie, lieu théologique* (= Sciences théologiques et religieuses) (Paris 1999), and therein especially P. DE CLERCK: La liturgie comme lieu théologique 125-142; H. VORGRIMLER: Liturgiewissenschaft: für Theologie und Kirche lebensnotwendig, in *Trierer theologische Zeitschrift* [108] 4 (1999) 319-324; P. DE CLERCK: Lex orandi, lex credendi. Un principe heuristique, in *La Maison-Dieu* 222 (2000) 61-78.

2.4. The (Interuniversity) Liturgical Institute
Profile and aims

At the initiative of the Tilburg Faculty of Theology, the Liturgical Institute started in 1992.[24] The aim of the Institute, in light of the above background of developments in liturgical studies in The Netherlands, is to coordinate, stimulate and further expand research in the field of liturgical studies.

Through de facto developments in the academic world, Dutch liturgical studies research was, and is, threatened with marginalization within The Netherlands. As has been reported briefly above, the profile of the discipline has now become open and pluralistic in nature; in the theological enterprise it has more and more taken on the status of an interdisciplinary study, such as, say, women's and gender studies. That contributes to a certain atomization.[25] The marginalization mentioned is extremely unfavorable for the theological enterprise in The Netherlands. Starting the Liturgical Institute was an important step in maintaining and expanding the new open profile for the discipline, and countering further marginalization.

For this general objective the organization of a national program of research was important, in which as much as possible all liturgical research in The Netherlands (that is to say, both Catholic and Protestant) should be brought together and coordinated by the Institute. Thanks to the structure of an institute, the terrain of the discipline can also be more clearly presented to other scholars than those strictly involved in liturgy. Depending on the theme chosen and the method followed, non-liturgists (one thinks here of theologians and scholars in religious studies and humanities, philologists, historians, anthropologists, European ethnologists and researchers in the psychology and sociology of religion) may be invited to participate in the Institute's projects. One sees that effort reflected in this collection. Furthermore, the

---

[24] The official opening of the Liturgical Institute was on December 4, 1992. In 1996 the Institute acquired the status of an Interuniversity Institute. It is supported by the Catholic Theological University Utrecht, the Faculty of Theology of the Catholic University Nijmegen, and the Tilburg Faculty of Theology. The latter institution is also the headquarters, and provides secretarial support. The Institute cooperates closely with the Institute for Liturgical Studies, Groningen, and the Liturgical Institute, Louvain.

[25] For this atomization, see POST: Wetenschappelijk grensverkeer.

Institute is a structure which makes it possible to present Dutch liturgical studies on the international stage.[26]

2.5. Current challenges

Although this introduction is not the place for speaking on behalf of
Dutch liturgical studies in the revitalized international debate on the
charter of liturgical studies, already mentioned briefly above, several current tendencies that to some extent are heard through this collection,
are relevant to it. By these current tendencies I am chiefly referring to
several challenges with which we are confronted.

(1) First I would list a challenge in the terrain of theory and method.
Liturgical studies must develop a well thought-through research design,
both from the continuing fundamental perspective of liturgical inculturation, as well as from the multidisciplinary perspective already outlined. I will say nothing more on this matter at this point, but only refer
to the work of Lukken and Wegman, who each in their own way provide a strongly innovative dimension in the realm of theory and
method. Rather, in my introduction to the general systematic and disciplinary part of this collection (II) I will return to this question of
research design.

(2) Within this general overall attention for theory and method in
the discipline there is, more specifically, the challenge of giving shape to
liturgical studies as a ('systematic') theological discipline. An important
part of the profile of Dutch liturgical studies that a 'theology of liturgy',
which increasingly encompasses sacramental theology as a part of classic
systematic theology, is linked with ritual-orientated lines of analysis that
we have already listed several times previously (especially the anthropological, ethnological, historical, *artes*, empirical and biblical-theological
approaches). One could speak here of an integral or integrated liturgical
studies approach. That has a programmatic background that is increasingly under pressure. For instance, the theological component of liturgical studies research of this sort is often ignored, or denied and misun-
derstood, or, as another example, with increasing frequency researchers
again work with disastrous subdivisions in relatively autonomous theological subdisciplines, so that the theological dimension of the liturgical

---

[26] This takes place, for example, through the international series *Liturgia condenda*
(Louvain: Peeters).

study is relegated exclusively to the realm of dogmatics or systematic theology, with the result that a sacramental theology once again arises that stands almost apart from liturgy as a ritual practice. The fact that scholars will sometimes pursue a certain approach to the extent that it dominates all others or competes with others, disrupting the integral interplay, also plays a part. Further there are the more preliminary aspects of ecclesiastical-theological nature, such as the *anabasis* and *katabasis* in liturgy which sometimes play off against each other, or imputations against what has been called the *anthropologische Wende*, which has so stimulated the discipline since the 1960s (see above). In general terms, Dutch liturgical studies are faced with the challenge of maintaining an integral study of liturgy in which there is not a de facto situation in which liturgical studies occupies itself with actual rites and rituality, and a sacramental theology as a component of systematic theology that occupies itself with a theology of liturgy. The research design for liturgical studies mentioned above must have a 'theological heart' which expresses itself in the fact that the search for the identity of Christian rituality and sacramentality ultimately is what is most central to the discipline.

In relation to this, I will explicitly mention a recent book by Lukken that is essentially a – to my mind – very successful specimen of this profile of the discipline in the way it succeeds to hold together anthropology and theology of liturgy.[27] This fundamental perspective is also in essence the central concern of this collection, in which 'feast' is employed as the concept linking empirical, anthropological, ethnological, historical and theological spheres.

(3) Within this integral, open and multidisciplinary profile of the discipline there is, further, the important task of giving the discipline its own recognizable position in the whole of ritual studies.

(4) Connected with this, but nonetheless a separate task and challenge, is the development and, especially, the exemplary application in specific studies, of what is being termed empirical liturgics. There has been a call for this for some time, but there are still very few thematic applications.[28]

---

[27] LUKKEN: *Rituelen in overvloed*, particularly the final chapter 10. See also the programmatic opening contribution in this collection for part II.

[28] A first exemplary exploratory beginning is provided by M. GERTLER: *Unterwegs*; POST, PIEPER & VAN UDEN: *The modern pilgrim*; MULDER: *Geloven in crematieliturgie*.

3. THE RESEARCH PROGRAM: GENERAL

3.1. Points of departure

One of the important ways of giving shape to the coordination, stimulus and profiling of Dutch liturgical studies discussed above was providing the impetus for a national research program. This found shape in the program 'Liturgical Movements and Feast Culture', which ran from 1995 to 2000. Subsequently a second, follow-up program has been started (2001-2005), under the title 'Liturgical Movements II: Persons and Patterns'. Two important points of departure were that the program would be welcoming, as well as assisting in creating a profile for the discipline. Through the national research program the discipline of liturgical studies, in many respects friable and divided, attains and maintains a face; the program could thus be characterized as being a platform or podium. The program includes projects that also play a role elsewhere in other connections, from institutes, schools, networks and programs, etc.; by bringing them in onto the podium of this liturgical studies program the open, broad and multi-disciplinary character of the discipline of liturgical studies in The Nether-lands is assured and extended. The program also emphatically strove for internationalization, and is open and interconfessional in nature.

3.2. Short description

Before elaborating the elements of liturgical movement and feast culture that define this program and this collection, some short general notes on the nature and organization of the program are called for.

3.2.1. Topic and theme

Under the title 'Liturgical Movements and Feast Culture' the national liturgical studies research program has, as its central and general concern, the processes of change in relation to Christian rituals. In a series of crucial eras, or periods of focus, the process of ritual change is considered in diverse cultural contexts. In a general sense this element is the topic of all of the participating projects.

This general supporting parameter of liturgical movement in the constant interplay of cultus and culture is subsequently more specifically worked out through a common theme: changing feast culture in the year and through life.

3.2.2. Periods of focus

Both the general supporting concern of ritual change (in the general program) and the theme of feast culture (sub-program) focus on cultural phenomena that have developed through time and space in accordance with processes of cultural history. Christian ritual culture in general and feast culture in particular are placed in the line of liturgical history through a series of periods which function as a sort of reference points. Reference points should be understood broadly here, as we are actually dealing with periods of focus. Despite the express intention of primarily making room for a diachronic aspect, for the longer term, and also for connections between periods, and always fully involving the broad context in the investigation, nevertheless a choice has been made for a series of crucial periods with regard to liturgical movement; these also in part provide the structure for this collection.

(1) The transitional period of the early Church (1st - 4th century), with the Christianizing of both Jewish and Hellenistic rituals. This period of focus runs through to and issues into the process of homogenization that rather generally, with regard to Christian liturgy in the East and West, took place in the second half of the 4th century.

(2) The transitional period of the early Middle Ages, when liturgy in the West began to undergo shifts in a specific cultural and political context (i.e., from a Roman to a Frankish-Germanic liturgy, 7th - 8th century).

(3) The transition in the late Middle Ages, around the 15th and 16th century, followed by the Reformation and the Roman Catholic Counter-Reformation.

(4) The period of the 17th and 18th century.

(5) The 20th century, which, especially in the second half, forms an important period of focus for change and movement, especially also linked with and based on the effects of liturgical shifts beginning in the 19th century.

In addition there is space created in the program, with or without a tighter or looser connection with the periods of focus, for a more general methodological, theoretical component, as well as for a component that concentrates on *liturgia condenda* (liturgy in the making) as its period of focus, as it were, and provides a place for current reflection on concerns and themes, particularly linked with inculturation.

3.2.3. Lines of research or manners of approach

Following from what has been said above regarding pluralism in methods and diversity in manners of approach, an effort was made in the program to afford as roomy a place as possible for various lines of research and approaches. More specifically, the following approaches are found in the program, as means of working out the lines sketched above:

(1) Anthropology of liturgy, in which projects focus on rituals undergoing change and where attention, among other things, is given to: the form and structure of rituals; their functions and meanings; the element of repetition which is characteristic of rituals; the way in which rituals, despite their repetitive nature, develop in interaction with changing contexts; the experience of space and time in rituals; the use of language and of non-verbal forms of expression; the relation between rituals and art forms. Important themes such as tradition, shifts in sacred zones, and ritual experts are also covered here.

(2) Liturgy and *artes*, in which investigation of the relation between liturgical movements and various art forms finds its place. In the program this primarily involves music in service of the liturgy, church architecture, iconography and literary forms. In this collection, which comprises a special emphasis on feast and festival, this approach, which is so important in The Netherlands, comes somewhat less to the fore.

(3) History of liturgy, a line of research that by its choice of a series of periods of focus is self-evidently included. Attention here focuses on the changes that Christian rituals have undergone through the periods in the history of the Church listed above, and on the social, cultural and religious factors that have played a role in these changes. Special attention is given to the relation between rituals and their reception, and the way believers in various groups in the church and social strata (from 'high' to 'low') experience and appropriate these rituals. One will encounter this line particularly in part III.

(4) Theology of liturgy, in which liturgy in motion is the subject of theological reflection. The objective is to arrive at renewal of the theology of liturgy. The impetus for renewal can be sought in the biblical-theological and exegetical foundation of the theology of liturgy, in theological reflection on the relation between the anthropology of liturgy and the theology of liturgy, in semiotics, or in a renewed vision of sacramental theology and the history of liturgy and clearer insight into contemporary liturgical practice.

(5) Contemporary liturgical practice; this line of investigation aims to develop and apply instruments for both qualitative and quantitative research into liturgy in its current and future performance and setting. In principle, the subjects of research encompass the full scope of liturgical occurrences, the preparation, performance and effects of rituals. This line will be found in part IV.

3.3. Liturgical movements

The research program focuses on the complex relation between Christian rituals – which, because one is dealing with rituals, are often considered as changeless and timeless – and changes in the religious, cultural and social fields. In order to clarify this relation, research must be directed toward the meaning and function of religious rituals. In addition, particular attention is bestowed on the origin and development of Christian rituals, and the transformations these have undergone during crucial periods in the history of the Church and the alterations to which they are subject in the current situation as a consequence of profound social and cultural shifts. In order to obtain a good picture of these movements and changes, attention must also be paid to the tension that has existed in both the present and past between, on the one hand, the prescribed rituals and, on the other, their reception and how various categories of believers experience them (there being a continual interplay between the changes which the rituals themselves undergo and the shifts that one can discover in the field of experience).

Here the important aspect of past and tradition comes into play in the process of change.[29] What role is played by an idealized, created or imagined past, or, especially, a past considered to be normative? How, and to what extent, is a movement or change a transformation or renewal? After all, every religion and religious current can be termed a 'tradition'; it is the product of historical development. Its anchor in the

---

[29] Tradition, the past and appeals to the past are again very vital themes in liturgical studies. I will here mention only P. POST: Het verleden in het spel? Volksreligieuze rituelen tussen cultus en cultuur, in *Jaarboek voor liturgie-onderzoek* 7 (1991) 79-124; IDEM: De creatie van traditie volgens E. Hobsbawm, *ibidem* 11 (1995) 77-101; IDEM: Rituals and the function of the past. Rereading Eric Hobsbawm, in *Journal of ritual studies* 10 (1996) 91-108; MESSNER: Was ist systematische Liturgiewissenschaft? 267-270. In our introduction to part II we will return to this at greater length, with additional bibliography.

past has precipitated institutions, rituals, scriptures and customs. Tensions often arise between this inheritance and the present situation in which the traditions stand. The conceptions and forms passed down are constantly subject to the influence of changes in society and culture. Thus religions and religious currents are characterized by continuity on the one hand and discontinuity on the other. In addition to the plurality and identity of ritual traditions and repertoires, the call for inculturation is also played out against this background.

The following summary notes may be of help in situating the use of 'liturgical movements':

(1) Although an indirect but conscious allusion is being made to what we from both the Roman Catholic and Protestant sides in the course of the 19th and 20th centuries label the 'Liturgical Movement', this program decidedly does not focus only on specific liturgical reform and/or renewal movements of this sort. There is also only an indirect link with today's liturgical movements, among them the program of liturgists who underscore the continuity of the Liturgical Movement,[30] and the feminist liturgical movement that is gaining influence, chiefly in the United States. In her richly documented survey article on the American Feminist Liturgical Movement, Denise Dijk has correctly demonstrated how 'movement' in this case principally evokes the qualities of a social movement. The 'movement' here first of all arises from dissatisfaction, and is characterized by reforming activity, forming groups of 'kindred souls', and can be followed in organizations and interacting networks.[31]

It is true that movements of this sort are included in the national research program, but primarily and more generally by the use of 'movements' it seeks to find a fundamentally open, broad and neutral term for

---

[30] Cf. L. VAN TONGEREN: Liturgie in context. De vernieuwing van de liturgie en de voortgang ervan als een continu proces, in *Tijdschrift voor liturgie* 81 (1996) 178-198; G. LUKKEN: *Inculturatie en de toekomst van de liturgie*; IDEM: Inculturation de la liturgie: théorie et pratique, in *Questions liturgiques / Studies in liturgy* 77 (1996) 10-39 (issue contains a report of the International Colloquium on Liturgy of the Liturgical Institute at Louvain, October, 1995, on inculturation).

[31] D. DIJK: De Feministisch Liturgische Beweging in de Verenigde Staten van Amerika, in A.-M. KORTE *et al.* (eds): *Proeven van vrouwenstudies theologie* IV (= IIMO Research Publication 44) (Utrecht 1996) 63-118, for 'movement': 65ff; see also D. DIJK: Developments in feminist liturgy in the Netherlands, in *Studia liturgica* 25 (1995) 120-128; cf. IDEM: Een beeld van een liturgie 21-90.

what could also be designated as liturgical changes or developments. Referring to the ample literature available on the theme of ritual change in general, and that on liturgical change in particular, 'movements' is a gesture toward including liturgical developments in an open and general manner, especially directing attention to the aspect of inculturation – in short, to the theme of the interplay of cultus and culture, which again is the centre of interest.[32]

(2) With all of this there is the realization that liturgy is always in motion, always changing, always inculturating. Rites are by nature dynamic, even if it is simply because of the fact that they always involve a new and unique performance each time. They are always a new play, *in actu*, despite the factors of being written down, of tradition, monitoring, reproducibility, scripts, scenarios and rubrics. That liturgy is dynamic and in motion, and also continues to develop through space and time, has now, as we have said, become an important point of departure in the discipline of liturgical studies. The perspective of continuity and a fixed tradition has generally now yielded to that of change, discontinuity and contingency.

The historical development of liturgy allows the dynamic of tradition to be seen. It is true that there are various elements and aspects and diverse persons and institutions to which one can point, which steer and influence this dynamic, but developments also take place through contingent processes. Through new interpretative frameworks an effort is made to seek out the reasons that inspire and explain liturgical change, movement and transformation over the course of time. For example, with regard to each phase in the development, the question presents itself of to what degree the past is (or was) normative or prescriptive for the future. For liturgy today this means a hermeneutic approach to the history of liturgy (which means in this case, for instance, the principle of 're-sourcing', much employed since Vatican II).

(3) Thus the term 'movements' covers processes of liturgical change in general. One of the intentions behind this is not to privilege any one particular type of process above others before the fact. There is a variety of processes through which liturgy develops: there are marginal adaptations, inarticulate or defensive movements, great transformations involving whole new creations. For the rest, it is interesting to see precisely

---

[32] Cf. C. BELL: Ritual, change, and changing ritual, in *Worship* 63 (1989) 31-41 and the references to the work of Anton Baumstark in note 18.

how this range of changes at the same time determine the diverse definitions and descriptions of liturgical inculturation![33]

(4) Also, the general and grammatically plural 'movements' is not conceived beforehand as applying to only a certain phase or pause in the development process. By examining various locations and multiple periods of focus one gets a picture of both enervating and innovating impulses and trend-setting paradigms, such as moments when things become fixed, are standardized or homogenized, as we encounter for instance in the second half of the 4th century and perhaps also, par excellence, in the second half of the 20th century.

(5) With all this, it must be acknowledged that 'movements' is often a relative diagnosis or construction. People strive to create 'movements', or they can be identified within their period itself, or perceived and reconstructed by historians. Much depends, then, on the point of view of the observer. In fact, liturgical movements do not always run synchronously with movements which interest scholars. Examples of this can be found, for instance, in the attention devoted to rites in religious popular culture, or the realm of women in liturgy. Liturgical movement is a very complex and stratified process; many factors and stimuli, varying from internal liturgical to external cultural, play their roles. We seek to keep the whole range in mind.

(6) In this way, via a series of specific studies spread out across periods of focus, in the research program we intend to study processes of change in liturgy in their context. How is the change shaped? What factors play a part in this? In the background – and sometimes in the foreground – two points play a role, a role to which reference has been made already in the description of the discipline. First, there is the

---

[33] In general here see the work of A. CHUPUNGCO and G. LUKKEN. The extremes here are, for instance, the definitions of CHUPUNGCO in *Cultural adaptation of the liturgy* (New York 1982) and A. SHORTER: *Toward a theology of inculturation* (New York 1988). See also the literature mentioned in note 30; a summarizing survey with extensive bibliography is found in G. LUKKEN: *Inculturatie en de toekomst van de liturgie* (= Liturgie in perspectief 3) (Heeswijk-Dinther 1994) and IDEM: Inculturatie van de liturgie: theorie en praktijk, in J. LAMBERTS (ed.): *Liturgie en inculturatie* (= Nikè-series 37) (Louvain/Amersfoort 1996) 15-56 = Inculturation de la liturgie. Théorie et pratique, in *Questions liturgiques / Studies in liturgy* 77 (1996) 1-39. A recent applied study concerning liturgical inculturation is H. BAUERNFEIND: *Inkulturation der Liturgie in unsere Gesellschaft. Eine Kriteriensuche - aufgezeigt an den Zeitzeichen Kirche heute, Esoterik/New Age und modernes Menschsein* (= Studien zur Theologie und Praxis der Seelsorge 34) (Würzburg 1998).

consideration that research of this sort can provide building blocks for the 'period of focus' of the *liturgia condenda*, and secondly the perspective that through research like this a contribution can ultimately be made to a new form of *liturgie comparée*: that there are perhaps patterns of movement which will emerge, per period or on a more general plan.[34]

Whatever the end result, the concept or term 'movements' serves as framework and organizing principle for this program.

3.4. Feast in the year and in life

3.4.1. *Historiographic impressions*

These general concerns, which also structure the program, are focused and developed in the theme 'feast in the year and through life', which is of central interest in many of the humanities and social sciences. Through this, not only are points of contact established with international developments,[35] but especially also with the lines of investigation

---

[34] In the general introduction to parts III and IV of this collection an effort will be made to shed light on such patterns.

[35] For the international perspective, see A. SCHILSON: Fest und Feier in anthropologischer und theologischer Sicht, in *Liturgisches Jahrbuch* 44 (1994) 3-32. For the more liturgical studies 'feast-perspective', to supplement Schilson we would add (the work of CORNEHL is already mentioned in his *Nachtrag*, 31ff): B. KRANEMANN: 'Feiertags kommt das Vergessene...'. Zur Deutung und Bedeutung des christlichen Festes in moderner Gesellschaft, in *Liturgisches Jahrbuch* 46 (1996) 3-22; K.-H. BIERITZ: Nächstes Jahr in Jerusalem. Vom Schicksal der Feste, in *Jahrbuch für Liturgik und Hymnologie* 35 (1994/95) 37-57; P. POST: Alle dagen feest, of: de ritencrisis voorbij, in P. POST & W.M. SPEELMAN (eds): *De Madonna van de Bijenkorf. Bewegingen op de rituele markt* (= Liturgie in perspectief 9) (Baarn 1997) 11-32; T. WALTHER-SOLLICH: *Festpraxis und Alltagserfahrung. Sozialpsychologische Predigtanalysen zum Bedeutungswandel des Osterfestes im 20. Jahrhundert* (= Praktische Theologie heute 29) (Stuttgart 1997) (good survey of feast theory on 17-94); POST: *Liturgische bewegingen*; P. POST & L. VAN TONGEREN: Het feest van de eerste communie. Op zoek naar de identiteit van het christelijk ritueel, in: K. MERKS & N. SCHREURS (eds): *De passie van een grensganger. Theologie aan de vooravond van het derde millennium* (Baarn 1997) 249-266 (see the revised English version in this collection, part IV); T. MICHELS & P. POST: Huwelijk: dynamiek van feest en sacrament, in *Tijdschrift voor liturgie* 81 (1997) 327-343; P. POST: Pleidooi voor de liturgische ruimte als feestzaal, in IDEM (ed.): *Een ander huis. Kerkarchitectuur na 2000* (= Liturgie in perspectief 7) (Baarn 1997) 25-27; P. POST: Een idyllisch feest. Over de natuurthematiek in Brabantse oogstdankvieringen, in A. MULDER & A. SCHEER (eds): *Natuurlijke liturgie*) (= Liturgie in perspectief 6) (Baarn 1996) 118-139; LUKKEN: *Ri-*

in research programs in Dutch liturgical studies, previously mentioned.[36]

With regard to a survey of feast research, one can build upon the overview that was offered by Arno Schilson in 1994, which in turn is built upon a previous, more thematic, case-study oriented survey in 1992.[37] By way of reference and supplement, and particularly with the liturgical studies perspective employed since about 1994 in view, we can here identify the following dynamics:

(1) One can say unreservedly that there has been a singular interest in the subject of festivity over the past decades. Schilson demonstrates how the theme of feast is conspicuous all across the full range of the humanities and social sciences (philosophy, sociology, psychology, anthropology, phenomenology of religion or history of religion and comparative studies of religion, history). The general background appears to be that researchers coming from the fields of philosophy, sociology, psychology and history have discovered how, through this ritual category, one can delve deeply into a culture, either in the past or in the present.

(2) Reviewing the boom in feast studies, one is struck by a strong conceptual, theoretical interest that once again is connected with a

---

tuelen in overvloed 84-86, 303-306; P. POST & L. LEIJSSEN: Huwelijksliturgie. Inculturatie van een levensfeest, in R. BURGGRAEVE, M. CLOET, K. DOBBELAERE & L. LEIJSSEN (eds): *Het huwelijk* (= KADOC-Studies 24, series Levensrituelen) (Leuven 2000) 179-196; P. POST: *Het wonder van Dokkum. Verkenningen van populair religieus ritueel* (Nijmegen 2000) 127-133; BARNARD & POST (eds): *Ritueel bestek* s.v. Feest (P. Post), 171-180.

[36] We are thinking here for instance of the lines of earlier research programs such as 'Heortological contributions' (Utrecht) and 'Festa chori, festa fori' (Tilburg). See for a historiographical sketch of Dutch heortological research in the second half of the 20th century, the introduction to part III.

[37] SCHILSON: Fest und Feier; cf. IDEM: Aus Festen leben. Religionsgeschichtliche und grundsätzliche Überlegungen, in *Erbe und Auftrag. Benediktinische Monatschrift* 68 (1992) 293-311. IDEM: Vom Sinn christlicher Feste. Geschichtliche und liturgietheologische Hinweise im Blick auf Weihnachten und Epiphanie, *Ibidem* 452-470. A good supplement with a short and able survey of anthropological, philosophical, sociological, historical and European ethnological studies is also to be found in P. HUGGER: Einleitung. Das Fest - Perspektiven einer Forschungsgeschichte, in P. HUGGER et al. (eds): *Stadt und Fest. Zur Geschichte und Gegenwart europäischer Festkultur* (= Fs. Phil. Fakultät I der Univ. Zürich, 2000 J. Jubil. Stadt Zürich) (Stuttgart 1987) 9-24; and G. ROOIJAKKERS: Vieren en markeren. Feest en ritueel, in T. DEKKER, H. ROODENBURG & G. ROOIJAKKERS (eds): *Volkscultuur. Een inleiding in de Nederlandse etnologie* (Nijmegen 2000) 173-230.

sharply increased multidisciplinary perspective. It goes without saying that this academic 'cross-border' traffic is a conspicuous feature in the stream of more theoretically oriented publications on feast, although of course the traces of each author's own discipline are to be seen in the approach and references. That Schilson concludes that the theological disciplines clearly lag behind in feast research has to do with theology's rather limited participation in such academic cross-border traffic. The same can also be noted in the realm of religious popular culture.[38]

(3) It is necessary here to introduce the nuance, that a distinction must be made between the period of the 1960s and '70s, and the 1980s and '90s, and that we are now going to concentrate on the latter two decades. In the 1960s and '70s the theme of feast was connected with the attention bestowed on the element of play in culture and ritual, so high on the agenda of the humanities and social sciences. In those same decades, this dimension also received ample attention in theology and liturgical studies.[39] In the present context, we will not be further developing this very specific and dated direction for feast research. By now, the playful has been accepted as a self-evident element in the anthropological-ritual foundation of liturgy. Naturally, this dimension of play is always assumed or taken up by citation and developed in later feast theory.

(4) One can note a certain distinction between conceptually and theoretically oriented studies on the one hand and more thematic, empirically oriented studies on the other.[40] One of the important devel-

---

[38] See P. POST: Religieuze volkscultuur en liturgie. Geïllustreerd pleidooi voor een benadering, in J. LAMBERTS (ed.): *Volksreligie, liturgie en evangelisatie* (= Nikè-series 42) (Louvain/Amersfoort 1998) 19-78, here 21-40; = Religious popular culture and liturgy. An illustrated argument for an approach, in *Questions liturgiques / Studies in liturgy* 79 (1998) 14-59, here 21-36; POST: *Het wonder van Dokkum.*

[39] J. Huizinga's book *Homo ludens* (1938) and Harvey Cox's *Feast of fools* (1969) were highly influential in this. On this, see H. MERTENS: De ludische en feestelijke mens, in *Tijdschrift voor liturgie* 56 (1972) 53-60; G.J. HOENDERDAAL: *Riskant spel. Liturgie in een geseculariseerde wereld* (The Hague 1977) 65-78; H. RAHNER: *Der spielende Mensch* (Einsiedeln 1978); M. MALINSKI: Weltliche und religiöse Feste, in H. VORGRIMLER (ed.): *Wagnis der Theologie* (Freiburg i.Br. 1979) 537-552. Through several prominent authors like Pieper (see note 40) and Cox we also evoke this line for the decades of the 1980s and '90s. See now also the collection BECK, NAUTA & POST (eds): *Over spel*; BARNARD & POST (eds): *Ritueel bestek.*

[40] The citations here will all reflect the theoretical approach. The following may be accounted good examples from over a longer period in a number of disciplines: R.G. KLOTE: *Ordnung und Fest. Eine Vorstudie zum philosophisch-anthropologischen Verständnis des Festes* (Mainz 1954); J. PIEPER: *Zustimmung zur Welt. Eine Theorie des Festes* (Munich

opments in feast research as it has begun to flourish, is that this distinction has begun to narrow. With increasing frequency, theoretical explorations are being linked with specific empirical studies, and in their design, analysis and evaluation case studies of specific feasts in the past or present are more and more carried out on the basis of the ample theoretical literature available. Particularly the interchanges among philosophy, anthropology and sociology, European ethnology and historical disciplines have had advantageous results here.[41]

(5) Thus, in a general sense, the bloom in feast research has everything to do with the rise of multidisciplinary work in which, as we have said, theology in general (and liturgical studies in particular) initially did not share. An inward-looking, strongly heortologically determined the-

---

1963); IDEM: *Über das Phänomen des Festes* (Cologne 1963); C. VERHOEVEN: *Inleiding tot de verwondering* (Utrecht 1967) 198-206 (on feast, reception and experience); B. NEF: *Die Bedeutung von Fest und Feier in Erziehung und Heilerziehung* (Bern/Stuttgart/Vienna 1969); H.-G. GADAMER: *Die Aktualität des Schönen. Kunst als Spiel, Symbol und Fest* (Stuttgart 1977); K. KERÉNYI: Vom Wesen des Festes, in IDEM: *Antike Religion* (Munich/Vienna 1971) 43-67; IDEM: *Über das Phänomen des Festes* (= Arbeitsgemeinschaft für Forschung des Landes Nordrhein-Westf. Geisteswiss. 113) (Cologne-Opladen 1963); G.M. MARTIN: *Fest und Alltag. Bausteine zu einer Theorie des Festes* (= Urban-Taschenbücher 604) (Stuttgart etc. 1973); J. DUVIGNAUD: *Fêtes et civilisations* (Paris 1973); IDEM: *Le don du rien. Essai d'anthropologie de la fête* (Paris 1977); J.-J. WUNENBERGER: *La fête, le jeu et le sacré* (Paris 1977); J. MOLTMANN: *Die ersten freigelassenen der Schöpfung. Versuche über die Freude an der Freiheit und das Wohlgefallen am Spiel* (= Kaiser Traktate 2) (Munich 1971²); H. COX: *The feast of fools. A theological essay on festivity and fantasy* (Cambridge 1969); W. GEBHARDT: *Fest, Feier und Alltag. Über die gesellschaftliche Wirklichkeit des Menschen und ihre Deutung* (Frankfurt a.M. 1987); IDEM: Der Reiz des Außeralltäglichen. Zur Soziologie des Festes, in B. CASPAR & W. SPARN (eds): *Alltag und Transzendenz* (Munich 1992) 67-88; O. MARQUARD: Kleine Philosophie des Festes, in U. SCHULZ (ed.): *Das Fest. Eine Kulturgeschichte von der Antike bis zur Gegenwart* (Munich 1988) 413-420 = IDEM: Moratorium des Alltags. Eine kleine Philosophie des Festes, in W. HAUG & R. WARNINK (eds): *Das Fest* (= Poetik und Hermeneutik. Arbeitsergebnisse einer Forschungsgruppe 14) (Munich 1989) 684-691; WALTHER-SOLLICH: *Festpraxis*; J. ASSMANN & T. SUNDERMEIER (eds): *Das Fest und das Heilige. Religiöse Kontrapunkte zur Alltagswelt* (Gütersloh 1991).

    [41] However, when it comes to certain disciplines, interchange of this sort also has limits. For example, to this day the rich field of the particularly German-language European ethnological 'Festforschung' remains rather isolated. A classic example of such a study is I. WEBER-KELLERMANN: *Saure Wochen. Frohe Feste. Fest und Alltag in der Sprache der Bräuche* (Munich/Lucerne 1985), and for an overview the reader is further referred to A.C. BIMMER: Brauchforschung, in R.W. BREDNICH (ed.): *Grundriß der Volkskunde. Einführung in die Forschungsfelder der Europäischen Ethnologie* (Berlin 1988) 311-328, particularly 320ff.

ory of feast (or perhaps better: feast orientation) very much its own prevailed in liturgical studies; together with the theological context, not
particularly oriented to multidisciplinary perspectives, this did not contribute to intensive acquaintance with the flourishing feast research in
the humanities and social sciences. Only in the recent past have contacts
been made between theoretical perspectives on feast and the classic lines
of research on ecclesiastical feasts on the axes of the year and of life. The
podium of ritual studies which has since arisen and claimed such interest certainly plays an important role here, although it is striking that,
when we look at survey studies in the case of rituality there, the subject
of festivity does not form a dominant theme.[42]

(6) In addition to the aspect of academic cross-border traffic and mul-
tidisciplinarity, the strong separation between theoretical and case-study
also, and chiefly, has to do with the fact that through the concept or
theme of festivity various layers of research come into the picture, which
vary from very specific feasts as they are celebrated to the meta-level of 'the
feast'. We will further develop that separately, because in this collection
these layers repeatedly recur as research perspectives (in combination!).[43]
For the present, in summary, it can be said for our collection that in its
design we tried to make a contribution to the interplay between a case-
study oriented and a more general theoretical approach to feast.

(7) Within theoretical feast research there appears to be a sort of
small canon of studies, to which reference is all the time made and on
which authors continuously fall back. This involves a series of individual 'classics',[44] but also – and that is closely connected with the repeatedly stressed multidisciplinary character of feast research – a number of
influential collections.[45] Particularly collections which were produced by

---

[42] See, for instance, the studies listed in our note 11. As another example, the subject heading 'feast' is absent from the very full index in RAPPAPORT: *Ritual and Religion*.
Do see, however, BELL: *Ritual. Perspectives and dimensions*, part II, 120-128.

[43] For this, see H. GERNDT: Festkultur als Forschungsfeld, in *Ethnologia Flandrica* 7
(1991) 7-29.

[44] To take just the more liturgically oriented studies of feast as a reference point, it
is striking that, for instance, in recent studies by Kranemann, Bieritz, Post and Walther-
Sollich (see our note 35) on feast theory, a nearly identical list of references may be
found (for instance, in BIERITZ: Nächstes Jahr 37, note 2). As examples of this 'small
canon', from the list in note 40, I would like to cite the studies of Pieper, Martin, Cox,
Gebhardt and Marquard.

[45] Cf. the collections (chronologically) E. OTTO & T. SCHRAMM: *Fest und Freude* (=
Kohlhammer Taschenbücher, Bd. 1003, Biblische Konfrontationen) (Stuttgart etc.

broadly composed study groups or symposia appear to be productive platforms for interchange and fruitful encounters among various disciplines. By this means, for example, contributions by specialist authors can receive attention from far outside their actual discipline. A still more current example here is the work of the Egyptologist-Semitist Jan Assmann.[46] Apart from that, I have the impression that it is particularly these collections which have decreased the fissure between general theoretical and more case-history oriented studies.

(8) At several points, which chiefly involve certain disciplines such as European ethnology and anthropology, certain language areas (Dutch!), case studies, the picture concerning theology, and particularly the period after 1994, Schilson's survey must be supplemented. I could provide many additions for anthropology, European ethnology and historical studies.[47] I will merely refer here to earlier presentations of the research

---

1977); G.K. KALTENBRUNER (ed.): *Grund zum Feiern. Abschaffung und Wiederkehr des Festes* (Freiburg etc. 1981); C. BIANCO & M. DEL NINNO (eds): *Festa, antropologia e semiotica. Relazioni presentate al Convengno di studi 'forme e pratiche della festa'* (Florence 1981); A. KOSTER *et al.* (eds): *Feest en ritueel in Europa: antropologische essays* (Amsterdam 1983); HUGGER *et al.*: *Stadt und Fest*; A. BLIJLEVENS *et al.* (eds): *Feest: gelegenheidsverkondiging* (= UTP-Studies 9) (Averbode/Apeldoorn 1988); U. SCHULZ (ed.): *Das Fest. Eine Kulturgeschichte von der Antike bis zur Gegenwart* (Munich 1988); W. RAIBLE (ed.): *Zwischen Festtag und Alltag* (Tübingen 1988); W. HAUG & R. WARNING (eds): *Das Fest* (= Poetik und Hermeneutik 14) (Munich 1989); J. ASSMANN & T. SUNDERMEIER (eds): *Das Fest und das Heilige. Religiöse Kontrapunkte zur Alltagswelt* (Gütersloh 1991); J. BOISSEVAIN: Nieuwe feesten: ritueel, spel en identiteit, in IDEM (ed.): *Feestelijke vernieuwing in Nederland?* (= Cahier van het P.J. Meertens-Instituut 3) (Amsterdam 1991); *Feste und Feiern im Mittelalter: Paderborner Symposion des Mediävistenverbandes* (Altenburg 1991); B. CASPAR & W. SPARN (eds): *Alltag und Transzendenz* (Munich 1992); P. CORNEHL, M. DUTZMANN & A. STRAUCH (eds): *"...in der Schar derer, die da feiern." Feste als Gegenstand praktisch-theologischer Reflexion* (Göttingen 1993); *Feesten* = special issue *Jota* 17,4 (1993) (there particularly: R. NAUTA: Het feest als voorsmaak van de eeuwigheid, 5-21); POST & SPEELMAN (eds): *De Madonna van de Bijenkorf*; T. ANDREE *et al.* (eds): *Feesten vieren in verleden en heden; visies vanuit vijf wereldgodsdiensten* (Zoetermeer 1997).

[46] Regarding Assmann, see particularly his coupling of feast - ritual - collective memory and feast and the two-dimensional man: J. ASSMANN: Der zweidimensionale Mensch: das Fest als Medium des kollektiven Gedächtnisses, in ASSMANN & SUNDERMEIER (eds): *Das Fest* 13-30. See SCHILSON: Fest und Feier 24ff. In the context of ritual studies Messner does speak of the theme of "kulturelle Gedächtnis" and anamnesis, but does not mention Assmann's name; see MESSNER: Was ist systematische Liturgiewissenschaft? 270, n. 46. We return to Assmann in our introduction to part II.

[47] I am thinking particularly of studies from the perspective of anthropology and European popular culture on the revitalization of feast culture, J. BOISSEVAIN: Nieuwe

program,[48] and for The Netherlands cite a practical theology-homiletic collection from 1988,[49] and further concentrate on supplementing for the period after Schilson's survey.

(9) It would appear that within the humanities and social sciences mentioned, the period of greatest interest for the theme has peaked. No collections that really leap to mind have appeared there since around 1994. One can certainly assert, however, that theology and its subdisciplines have been making up for lost time. A *Nachtrag* added by Schilson at the last moment to his survey has already served to introduce this.[50] After about 1994 feast more and more became a theme in theology, yet not in the sense of Schilson's desired 'theology of feast' (the 1988 work of Francesco Taborda, oriented toward sacramental theology, remains a notable exception),[51] but rather in terms of practical theology and liturgical studies connections.[52] Here too the strongly programmatic-theoretical input as well as the multidisciplinary context is conspicuous. Moreover, feast is welcomed as an entry point into an analysis and diagnosis of the current position of rituality and religiosity in modern and postmodern culture. The comparison of Christian feast with modern

feesten; IDEM (ed.): *Revitalizing European rituals* (London 1992). See further the report including several recent case studies: POST: Religieuze volkscultuur 24, note 9 = Religious popular culture 18, note 9; additions in P. POST: Van paasvuur tot stille tocht. Over interferentie van liturgie en volksreligieus ritueel, in *Volkskundig bullletin. Tijdschrift voor Nederlandse cultuurwetenschap* 25 (1999) 215-234; IDEM: *Het wonder van Dokkum*. An interesting recent study of processes of ritual continuity and change is H. TAK: *South Italian festivals. A local history of ritual and change* (Amsterdam 2000).

[48] See the presentations of the program in the *Jaarboek voor liturgie-onderzoek* and the *Liturgisches Jahrbuch*. Cf. our note 1.

[49] A. BLIJLEVENS *et al.* (eds): *Feest*.

[50] SCHILSON: Fest und Feier 31ff, where the practical-theological collection CORNEHL, DUTZMANN & STRAUCH: *"...in der Schar"* is discussed as a sterling example of the current significance of the theme of feast culture for theology.

[51] Fr. TABORDA: *Sakramente: Praxis und Fest* (Düsseldorf 1988). Of course, there are smaller and larger contributions to a theology of feast to be found in a number of sources. For instance, the recent studies listed above by Kranemann, Bieritz, Post and Walther-Sollich expressly contribute such building blocks, and there are also good things to be found elsewhere, such as, for instance, R. TAFT: Toward a theology of the Christian feast, in: IDEM: *Beyond East and West. Problems in liturgical understanding* (Washington DC 1984) 1-13. Further, one can site the somewhat older A. KIRCHGÄSSNER: Umrisse einer Phänomenologie und Theologie des christlichen Festes, in *Liturgisches Jahrbuch* 12 (1962) 175-180.

[52] Exemplary studies of this nature, from those which have already been cited, are Cornehl, Kranemann, Bieritz, Walther-Sollich, Post and Post & Speelman.

secular festivity, often in a critical perspective, is ultimately the topic there. A certain dependence on the classic heortological line of research remains, although bridges are constructed, as in the dissertation of Tilman Walther-Sollich.[53] In cases of sporadic more concrete elaborations in liturgical studies considerations of feast, it is striking how feasts on the axis of the year, including Sundays, are placed in the spotlight, and feasts on the axis of life are taken up to a much lesser degree. The present collection is intended to provide a certain counterbalance to this by not only dealing with annual feasts (and Sundays) in both historical and contemporary explorations, but also life feasts such birth-baptism, first communion and marriage.[54]

(10) Not unimportant among the factors through which feast has come to stand higher upon the agenda of liturgical studies is a wider interest in religious popular culture. Especially in the context of liturgical inculturation and critical reflection on liturgical renewal, people have again become deeply aware of the qualities of the repertoire of popular religious ritual. The aspect of festivity is always high on the short list of the classic general anthropological-cultural qualities of this repertoire, along with, for instance, physicality, a sense of drama and expression.[55] This point is taken up again in a pastoral-liturgical perspective and a connection is made between festivity as a dominant ten-

---

[53] WALTHER-SOLLICH: *Festpraxis*.

[54] For 'rituals of life' see, for instance, the inculturating explorations G. LUKKEN: Die Taufe: ein unersetzbares Sakrament, in *Per visibilia ad invisibilia* 158-183; IDEM: Theology and baptism after Vatican II. Shifting accents and lacunae, *ibidem* 184-195; IDEM: This is a great mystery. A theological reflection on the sacrament of marriage, *ibidem* 196-205; IDEM: Funérailles et marginalité, *ibidem* 205-223; A. SCHEER: Peilingen in de hedendaagse huwelijksliturgie. Een oriënterend onderzoek, in *Tijdschrift voor liturgie* 62 (1978) 259-317. This broad contextual approach to feasts on the axis of life is found primarily with birth-baptism and death-burial-cremation, and to a lesser extent with marriage. As a good example of this, see also the recent collection G. LUKKEN & J. DE WIT (eds): *Nieuw leven. Rituelen rond geboorte en doop* (= Liturgie in beweging 1) (Baarn 1997) (particularly here Lukken's opening contribution, 9-31), and the consistently multidisciplinary and contextually broadly planned series Levensrituelen van KADOC: K. DOBBELAERE, L. LEIJSSEN & M. CLOET (eds): *Levensrituelen. Het vormsel* (= KADOC-Studies 12) (Louvain 1991); L. LEIJSSEN, M. CLOET & K. DOBBELAERE (eds): *Levensrituelen. Geboorte en doopsel* (= KADOC-Studies 20) (Louvain 1996); BURGGRAEVE et al. (eds): *Het huwelijk*. Cf. also GRIMES: *Deeply into the bone*.

[55] See the overview, with extensive bibliography, POST: Religieuze volkscultuur = Religious popular culture, and IDEM: *Het wonder van Dokkum*.

dency in our culture,[56] the phenomenon of 'feast Christians' (Christian people come in contact with liturgy only through feasts in the year –Christmas!– and the course of life), and the *liturgia condenda*.[57] A important contribution to liturgical feast research is provided by the flourishing research into pilgrimage. For instance, among the things offered by the large-scale inventory project 'Places of Pilgrimage in The Netherlands', unique in the international perspective, is a basis for numbers of diachronic and comparative investigations into saints' feasts.[58]

(11) Approaching the close of these historiographic impressions, we will now pause briefly to consider the fact, already mentioned, that feast has traditionally belonged to the heart of the classic canon of liturgical studies research. In this, the theme of feast was chiefly, and sometimes almost exclusively, linked to the ecclesiastical year and feast calendar. Under the influence of the perspectives of the Liturgical Movement and liturgical inculturation, this field of interest also took on a strongly pastoral slant.[59] This strongly, sometimes strictly heortological approach still to an important degree defines feast research in liturgical studies. This is emphatically reflected in the handling of the theme of feast in

---

[56] See, for instance, W. LIPP: Feste heute. Animation, Partizipation und Happening, in HAUG & WARNING: *Das Fest* 663-683.

[57] Cf. P. CORNEHL: Christen feiern Feste. Integrale Festzeitpraxis als volkskirchliche Gottesdienststrategie, in *Pastoraltheologie. Monatsschrift für Wissenschaft und Praxis in Kirche und Gesellschaft* 70 (1981) 218-233. Also indirectly instructive is P. MALLOY: The re-emergence of popular religion among non-Hispanic American Catholics, in *Worship* 72 (1998) 2-15. For the rest, it is striking how here in theological circles diverse points of view are heard regarding feast, feast Christians and popular religious strategies. Cornehl is positive and generous regarding the feast dimension in the 'Volkskirche', Kranemann and Bieritz instead critical, calling for critical reflection, catechesis and mystagogy.

[58] P.J. MARGRY & C. CASPERS (eds): *Bedevaartplaatsen in Nederland*, Vol. 1: *Noord-en Midden-Nederland* (Hilversum/Amsterdam 1997); Vol. 2: *Noord-Brabant* (1998); Vol. 3: *Limburg* (2000); for this project see P.J. MARGRY & P. POST: The 'Places of Pilgrimage in The Netherlands' Project. An orientation, in POST, PIEPER & VAN UDEN: *The modern pilgrim* 49-88. POST: *Het wonder van Dokkum*.

[59] For instance, one of the classic documents here is J.A. JUNGMANN: Das kirchliche Fest nach Idee und Grenze, in IDEM: *Liturgisches Erbe und pastorale Gegenwart. Studien und Vorträge* (Innsbruck etc. 1960) 502-526 [= original article in Festschrift F.X. Arnold (Freiburg 1958) 164-184]. Cf. also A. HÄUSSLING: Heute Feste feiern? Zu einigen Schwerpunkten heutigen Verständnisses der kirchlichen Feste, in *Theologisch-Praktische Quartalschrift* 126 (1978) 122-128.

manuals and reference works.[60] One of the great challenges before us is to connect this traditional line of liturgical studies feast research with the broader feast research briefly sketched here. In a general sense, one might consider this as the intent of this collection. One could speak of a 'relativization' of liturgical feast research, in the sense of establishing a relation with adjacent research.

Two important stimuli work to the advantage of the discipline here. First there is the large role of academic cross-border traffic in modern liturgical studies (see above), and second the heavy emphasis on contextual soundings and analysis from the perspective of liturgical inculturation. Both stimuli contribute to 'feast' coming to stand high on the agenda of liturgical studies research, as feast is an important theme in research in the social sciences and humanities, and is considered as one of the important typifying dimensions of our modern and postmodern culture. The classic canon of liturgical studies is thus enriched. It is this specific liturgical studies line of feast research that we therefore recognize in the now flourishing feast studies in the domain of liturgical studies. It is in this line that we intend this collection to stand.

In summary, we may now list the following as key points:

(1) seeking to link up with the broad philosophical, phenomenological, social sciences and humanities tradition of feast research;

(2) establishing links between conceptual, theoretically oriented and case study feast research;

(3) from these lines, striving for an enrichment and expansion of the classic heortological liturgical studies track;

---

[60] There the theme of 'feast' is generally dealt with in the heortological sense (feast in the liturgical year), or is not dealt with at all (as in J. DAVIES (ed.): *A new dictionary of liturgy and worship* (London 1994⁴)). A good exception is the reasonably broadly conceived article 'feest' in the *Liturgisch Woordenboek* I (1958-1962) 738-746; when we compare this entry with, for instance, that in the *Dictionnaire d'archéologie chrétienne et de liturgie* (s.v. 'Fêtes (chrétiennes, les)' t. 5,1 (1922) 1403-1452), it is striking how, thanks to the above mentioned attention for feast, ritual and play, the strictly heortological perspective has expanded. The article has five successive sections: (1) general characteristics (phenomenological, history of religions), with as the definitive qualities of 'the feast' the exceptional, new, communal, anamnestic ('the going-to-its-end'); (2) feast in Scripture; (3) feast in liturgy; (4) deeper significance of the liturgical feast; (5) liturgical regulations regarding feasts. Kranemann offers an overview of feast in recent liturgical manuals, KRANEMANN: Feiertags 4, note 5.

(4) extending liturgical studies feast research to cover rituals through the course of life.

We would like to develop these central concerns further at several points. For the collection this involves such essential fields of interest as elaborating in greater specificity a working definition of 'feast', the distinctions and, more important, the coherence among the three levels of research into feast and its culture, the current perspective of the dynamic of feast culture in connection with the flourishing of and crisis in rituals, and the challenge to gather building blocks for a theology of feast.

3.4.2. Further specification (a working definition)

Without entering here into an overview of the definitions and characterizations of feast which are circulating today, a working definition has been developed for the design of the research program and this collection.

By 'feast' we refer to the moment in which, or the occasion on which people, in the structuring of time and the course of an individual's life cycle, as groups or as a society, give special (that is to say, in a way which breaks through the everyday) ritual form to occurrences that mark personal and social existence, doing so from faith, a religious, philosophical or ideological orientation which makes sense of life.

3.4.3. Levels of research

By connecting 'feast' in the program and collection with liturgical movement and change, feast becomes particularly feast culture. This approach brings together three levels of research that elsewhere in research into feast and rituals are rather often encountered in isolation. These levels, which involve the general subject of research, can be distinguished as follows:[61]

(1) First, there is the level of the *individual* feast or ritual, in the past or present.

(2) Next there is at a somewhat higher and more general plane the level of *feast culture*.[62] Here a broader terrain is covered, because individual cases are seen in connection. This level particularly supports possibilities for both diachronic and comparative work.

---

[61] Cf. H. GERNDT: Festkultur als Forschungsfeld, in *Ethnologia Flandrica* 7 (1991) 7-29.

[62] GERNDT: Festkultur.

(3) At a still higher plane is the meta-level. Here the subject is *the* feast, ritual itself. Here too work is done on the theory of feast. It is here that a philosophy of feast (see, for example, the startling closing essay by Odo Marquard in the collection *Das Fest*, where he presents 'a brief philosophy of feast'),[63] or the theology of feast to which for instance Schilson summons us,[64] or a psychology,[65] or a pastoral or religious sociology of feast[66] can be found. Although we in no way make a pretense that this collection presents a meta-approach of this sort, nevertheless this interest can be heard coming through somewhat in the first series of more systematic articles (part II).

Now, by explicitly opting for 'feast culture', these levels can be brought into connection with one another, a process in which the second level fills a key role as the vital intermediary between the first and third levels.

Especially through the theme of feast culture we can also go a way toward fulfilling the desire to bridge the gap between theory and empirical case study, as well as the desire to involve the reception of the rite in the research, precisely because feast culture is borne by the interplay of cultus and culture, of public and religious rites, and particularly because large groups from society participate in the ritual repertoires of feast culture. In many cases in our present postmodern society, it is only through feasts in the year and the course of life that people still come in contact with liturgy. It is in light of this that the term 'feast Christians' has been coined. On the other hand, many researchers consider festivity as a defining characteristic of our postmodern culture. Here we encounter an important pastoral-liturgical point of departure that can be elaborated in all sorts of ways.[67] In this context is it also interesting to see, on the basis of specific studies, to what comparisons between ecclesiastical-Christian, general religious and profane-secular feast culture in the year and in life can lead. What

[63] O. MARQUARD: Kleine Philosophie des Festes.

[64] SCHILSON: Fest und Feier; see our note 51.

[65] See, for instance, R. NAUTA: *Ik geloof het wel. Godsdienstpsychologische studies over mens en religie* (Assen 1995) 107-109 (primarily a resumé of Gebhardt and Marquard). See also his contribution to part II in this collection.

[66] G. VAN TILLO: De religieuze dimensie van feesten, in A. BLIJLEVENS *et al.* (eds): *Feest: gelegenheidsverkondiging* (= UTP-studie 9) (Averbode/Apeldoorn 1988) 10-32.

[67] See, for instance, the works by Walther-Sollich, Kranemann, Bieritz and Cornehl, already cited several times.

are the similarities and differences here?[68] It is striking how many authors show a certain preference for making this pastoral-liturgical and comparative aspect a theme through the consideration of Sunday as a feast day.[69] This theme recurs several times in this collection too, in the contributions by Rouwhorst and Van Tongeren in parts III and IV.

3.4.4. Relevance: festive change and the paradox of the crisis in rites

Especially in today's world the connection between the theme of feast culture and liturgical dynamics can be linked with a wide selection of topics of interest in the study of man and culture. After all, liturgical change appears to be a part of the broader context of changes in festivity. Researchers have noted a process of change in a rather general sense in the area of feast and ritual that, according to many scholars (particularly in the social sciences), has been taking shape on an unprecedented scale in Europe since the 1960s.[70] It is, of course, a question to what extent these changes in ritual culture are really new or unprecedented, and whether and how these developments perhaps are in part connected with changes in the researchers' own agendas. But however that may be, many investigators call attention to striking changes in the European culture of rites and feasts. It would appear from a series of diverse case studies which have become available that it is particularly in the public feast culture at a regional and local level that these changes are taking shape. These changes coincide particularly with the remarkable blossoming of what can be termed 'traditional' feast culture. It will be sufficient to refer the reader to what is rather generally denoted 'revitalization' and what is termed the paradox of the crisis in rites.[71] While

[68] See here once again the studies by Schilson, Bieritz, Kranemann and Post. For a programmatic and critical view regarding the divergence and convergence between Christian and secular feast, see KRANEMANN: Feiertags 14ff. I further refer to WALTHER-SOLLICH: Festpraxis, and particularly to CORNEHL, DUTZMANN & STRAUCH (eds): "...in der Schar?"; see also P. CORNEHL: Liturgische Zeit und Kirchenjahr. Sinn, Gestalt und neue Gestaltungsmöglichkeiten aus evangelischer Sicht, in *Gemeinsame Arbeitsstelle für Gottesdienstliche Fragen* 23 (1995) 39-73.

[69] Cf., for instance, GEBHARDT: Der Reiz, 68ss.; see also the cited studies by Kranemann and Bieritz.

[70] Summarized in BOISSEVAIN: Nieuwe feesten; IDEM: *Revitalizing European rituals*. See also TAK: *South Italian festivals*.

[71] For rites and the crisis in rites in general, see G. LUKKEN: *Geen leven zonder rituelen. Antropologische beschouwingen met het oog op de christelijke liturgie* (Hilversum 1988³); IDEM: *De onvervangbare weg van de liturgie* (Hilversum 1984²); see also the collection of

within many church walls feast and ritual, in spite of all liturgical renewal, appear to be crumbling away (an interesting change too, for that matter!), outside them feast culture is flourishing. There are also signs which point to a new rapprochement between liturgy and public feast culture. There are both examples of a folklorization of liturgy and of a liturgization of public feast culture.[72] Village feasts, devotions, pilgrimages, processions, harvest thanksgiving festivals, carnivals, Christmas markets, guild feasts, feasts of patron saints, the interesting competition in The Netherlands between St. Nicholas on the evening of December 5 and the Anglo-Saxon Santa Claus on Christmas,[73] Palm Sunday processions: these are just a random sample from a Western ritual culture that is abundantly alive and in motion.

As we have already noted, to an increasing degree these ritual repertoires have now become the object of research in various disciplines. An enormous stimulus for this was the fact that scholars in religious studies, history, anthropology and European ethnology, among others, discovered how especially feast and ritual can be exceedingly productive as heuristic tools. As said before, through feast and ritual one can enter the field of cultural research in an extremely purposeful manner. Social anthropology thus is increasingly really becoming cultural anthropology, and numerous historians are discovering the realm of feast studies. Here, in the context of the national research program, liturgical studies can make its connections.

The time seems ripe for confrontations and comparisons. For instance, in the field of Dutch feast culture of the 19th and 20th centuries a series

work by LUKKEN: *Per visibilia ad invisibilia,* particularly 45-236. Cf. GRIMES: *Deeply into the bone.* In connection with feast culture, see POST: *Alle dagen feest.* See also now: G. LUKKEN: *Rituelen in overvloed* (Baarn 1999).

[72] A summary, with extensive bibliography, POST: *Alle dagen feest;* P. NISSEN: *De folklorisering van het onalledaagse* (Tilburg 1994) and P. POST: *Ritueel landschap: over liturgie-buiten* (= Liturgie in perspectief 5) (Heeswijk/Baarn 1995) = *Paysage rituel: liturgie en plein air* I-II, in *Questions liturgiques / Studies in liturgy* 77 (1996) 174-190; 240-256. See further WALTHER-SOLLICH: *Festpraxis,* passim; P. POST: *Een idyllisch feest. Over de natuurthematiek in Brabantse oogstdankvieringen,* in A. MULDER & A. SCHEER (eds): *Natuurlijke liturgie* (= Liturgie in perspectief 6) (Baarn 1996) 118-139; IDEM: *Van paasvuur tot stille tocht;* IDEM: *Het wonder van Dokkum.*

[73] See the contributions of Helsloot (the feast of St Martin) and Roll (Christmas) in this collection; for Christmas and Santa Claus in The Netherlands, see *Sinterklaas en de kerstman: concurrenten of collega's? Rituelen - commercie - identiteiten* (= *Volkskundig bulletin. Tijdschrift voor Nederlandse cultuurwetenschap* 22, 3 (1996)) (Nijmegen 1996).

of case studies could form the basis for an examination focusing on the patterns by which particularly developments outside its strictly internal ecclesiastical liturgical framework are confronted with liturgical change within the church.[74] Here would also be the place for a comparison with the much less investigated feast culture on the axis of life. Eastern and Sunday are discussed in this collection in parts III and IV.

3.5. Toward a theology of feast?

In 1994 Schilson called attention to the fact that theological disciplines lagged strikingly behind others in feast research. While numerous anthropological and sociological studies on 'feast and ritual' appeared, theological studies played hardly any role. Through its multidisciplinary character, liturgical studies can fulfill an important pioneering function within theology. We have already mentioned the challenge of arriving at a theology of liturgy. At a number of points in this collection it is shown that the search for building blocks for a theology of feast can make a contribution to this larger theology of liturgy. Only rarely is the attempt made now to clarify the meaning of feast theologically, and in so doing to involve the anthropological foundation and the cultural context (the feast culture). This is all the more remarkable because it concerns a human event that plays a central and irreplaceable role in the mediation of meaning for both the individual and society. This is equally true, and perhaps still more radical, for the Christian process of discovering meaning. It is therefore extremely important to further reflect on the theme of 'feast' theologically. Starting points for this are found in a number of places in this collection, including but not limited to the contribution by Wiel Logister in part II.

---

[74] See here, for instance, G. ROOIJAKKERS: *Rituele repertoires* (= Memoria) (Nijmegen 1994); C. WIJERS: *Prinsen en clowns in het Limburgse narrenrijk. Het carnaval in Simpelveld en Roermond 1945-1992* (= Publikaties van het P.J. Meertens-Instituut 22) (Amsterdam 1995); J. HELSLOOT: *Vermaak tussen beschaving en kerstening. Goes 1867-1896* (= Publikaties van het P.J. Meertens-Instituut 24) (Amsterdam 1995); as well as the many specific studies in the field of rites in religious popular culture, summarized with bibliography in P. POST: *Ritueel landschap* sub 4.1. 23-28 note 54; IDEM: Thema's, theorieën en trends in bedevaartonderzoek, in J. PIEPER, P. POST & M. VAN UDEN (ed.): *Bedevaart en pelgrimage. Tussen traditie en moderniteit* (= UTP-katernen 16) (Baarn 1994) 253-302; POST, PIEPER & VAN UDEN: *The modern pilgrim*; POST: Van paasvuur tot stille tocht. For rituals through life, see our note 54. Cf. ROOIJAKKERS: Vieren en markeren.

4. Plan of the collection

Against the broader background briefly sketched out above and the theme of liturgical movements, the dynamic of cultus and culture, Christian feast culture in the year and in life forms the central theme of this collection. A number of choices have had to be made as this developed.

In the first place, the collection nearly exclusively focuses on Western Christian rituality, in which, within that Western perspective, broader ritual contexts are continually brought into the discussion. The perspective of Eastern liturgy only comes into the picture in the diachronic contribution of Groen on the feast of the Presentation in part III. The Western perspective is left behind in order to present the characteristic outlook of comparative cultural anthropology and religious studies (Droogers and Beck, in part II; see also Jewish and non-Western Christian contexts in the contribution on the Early Church by Rouwhorst in Part III).

The content of 'feast' is further somewhat more restricted than in the research program; for example, funerals, burial and cremation are not directly considered 'feast';[75] this is done for the sake of familiarity and coherence, and also reflects the necessary limits of the size of the collection. Nevertheless, this boundary is crossed at least three times: Speelman discusses the memorial rites after the death of princess Diana as an example of ritual-liturgical movement; in the contributions by De Jong on Good Friday, and particularly by Steensma the aspect of suffering is central. In modern religious art (or, better, in surveying religious themes in modern visual arts), this theme is dominant, even when modern art takes its place in liturgy in feasts on the axis of the year.

The collection is divided into four parts. In addition to this introduction (I) to situate the topic, part II contains a series of systematic, theoretical explorations which present a series of diverse but also converging disciplinary approaches, generally illustrating them as well. Part III comprises the historical explorations, in which the periods of focus recur to the greatest extent possible. Part IV comprises studies in contemporary liturgical practice, including the *liturgia condenda*.

---

[75] Cf. J. POTEL: Les funerailles, une fête?: que célèbrent aujourd'hui les vivants? (Paris 1973); cf. LUKKEN: Overvloed, 85s.

Each of the parts II-IV, has a preface in which it is not only intro-duced, but in which an effort is also made to offer some lines of syn-thesis and evaluation.

An effort has been made, as much as possible, to treat a concrete case study in each contribution (see above), thus working in a way which provides an example of the deductive research process within the per-spectives emphasized above. The approaches and liturgical studies tracks discussed above in this introduction also return in as far as this was fea-sible.

Although we are looking toward an international audience, this col-lection does arise out of a Dutch research program. Particularly in the more current part IV this collection concerns itself more and more exclusively with The Netherlands and Dutch issues. Sometimes, as the result of the case study, the context can be said to be specifically Dutch, as in the contribution of very specific liturgical repertoire by Smelik. On the other hand Roll's contributions include comparative material about Belgium and the USA. In any case, it is our conviction that the broader perspective of feast culture is still present there.

The editor's main task was chiefly and particularly to guarantee the coherence of the collection. Individual editors bore specific responsibil-ity for various parts: Post (I, II); Rouwhorst and Van Tongeren (III), Scheer (IV). General coordination and secretarial services were provided by Ch. Caspers, assisted by M. Schneiders. The contributions of Caspers, Hoondert, Lukken, Post, Scheer, Smelik, and Van Tongeren, were translated into English by D. Mader.

PART II

MULTIDISCIPLINARY PERSPECTIVES

PAUL POST

INTRODUCTION AND APPLICATION:
FEAST AS A KEY CONCEPT IN A LITURGICAL STUDIES RESEARCH DESIGN[1]

1. MULTIDISCIPLINARY PERSPECTIVES

As has already been said in the general introduction, this collection opens with a series of programmatic and systematic contributions from a range of disciplines. This is intended to expressly reflect a well-defined vision of the multidisciplinary profile of liturgical studies. In this first contribution, also intended as an introduction to this second part, this profile will be further developed by presenting a model for research. At the same time, the concept of feast is subsequently allocated a role, indeed, an important role, in this presentation.

This opening contribution bears two faces: it is to be an introduction to a series of multidisciplinary programmatic contributions, and at the same time offers a similar programmatic contribution from the perspective of liturgical studies. If it had not also included this introductory objective, it would perhaps have been better placed as the last of the contributions in this series.

Because of the open, contextual and multidisciplinary practice in liturgical studies, to be described in more detail here, the discipline lives by grace of interchanges across academic boundaries and alliances with a whole series of other disciplines. In this process there is nothing approaching a fixed list of disciplines which can be engaged. The possibilities are entirely open. Still, when feast is central to the study, there will be certain disciplines which will come into the picture rather than others. Feast and ritual have for a long time been weighty themes in fields such as cultural anthropology and religious studies (history of

[1] A previous version of this contribution was submitted to Gerard Lukken. In a detailed letter he offered his commentary on this version, touching on a series of fundamental issues. The contribution received its final focus and form partly in response to his reaction. Although it is unpublished, at several points I shall be citing Dr. Lukken's response as LUKKEN: Response (1999).

religion, comparative religion). In this part we wish to evoke this multidisciplinary perspective through our selection from adjacent disciplines that are concerned with the themes of feast and ritual.

Selection has been involved in this, in which we have stayed relatively
close to theological and religious disciplines. We have opted for
approaches from cultural anthropology (André Droogers), history of
religion (Herman Beck), psychology of religion (Rein Nauta), sociology
of religion (Gérard van Tillo), systematic theology or dogmatics (Wiel
Logister), biblical theology (Jan Holman) and pratical theology and aesthetics (Marcel Barnard). Many other approaches were possible, and
perhaps even desirable, among them, specifically, philosophy of religion
and feminist theology.

I would note that as a criterion for our selection we have looked primarily toward historiography: a series of disciplines have been chosen in
which the concept of feast has acquired a certain place in the research
tradition, and from which, moreover, fruitful contacts with liturgical
studies have developed. Despite this criterion, the selection is still arbi-
trary, since if tradition and historiography form the point of departure,
philosophy of religion, for instance, would certainly come into the picture. It remains therefore a selection the primary purpose of which is to
rough out a sketch of research perspectives today.

I would wish to point out, however, that certain approaches which
are absent here are certainly represented elsewhere, albeit indirectly. For
instance, the multidisciplinary perspective is expressed by the contributions brought together in this second part, and, for example, this perspective will be explicitly underlined in this opening contribution
through the work of Assmann and Taborda. Through Assmann the
alliances with phenomenology of religion can make their contribution,
and through Taborda those with systematic and liberation theology,
while the contributions of biblical theology are also represented again
through the latter.

2. STRUCTURE AND ISSUES: ON METHOD IN LITURGICAL STUDIES

Liturgical studies are central in this first contribution to the series of
programmatic and systematic perspectives. I will tentatively develop a
general research model for liturgical studies, and demonstrate how the
concept of 'feast' can fulfill a key role in it. After having briefly discussed

liturgical inculturation and the provision of critical-normative perspectives for the *liturgia condenda* as general concerns of liturgical studies, the various phases of a qualitative investigation are presented. The tradition of Dutch research in this field is a starting point for the development for the design. More particularly, the work of Lukken and Wegman serves as a point of reference. The concept of 'feast' will serve to draw our attention to elements in, and guide the working out of a relatively complex research matrix. The role of the concept will be further specified and also, finally, illustrated through a phenomenological and liturgical-theological development of the feast paradigm, using the example of Christian marriage ritual.

This contribution must be placed against the background of fundamental reflections regarding theory and method in liturgical studies which, as discussed in our Introduction (I), have recently again become concerns commanding great interest.[2] It would serve the purpose of clarity to state briefly here, in advance, several related stimuli which have spurred this flowering of the discussion of theory and method in liturgical studies:[3]

(1) First, there is the realization of essential contextuality. In part connected with what has been termed the *anthropologische Wende* (the anthropological turn), the radical change that took place in the discipline in the 1960s in the broader ritual-liturgical framework of liturgical renewal, the fundamental realization began to grow that liturgical study ought to be taking seriously both the basic human data regarding a ritual, and also its complex, multilayered context. It was recognized that every liturgical study was at the same time both an anthropological and a cultural study. In connection with this, the consciousness also

---

[2] For the discussion on theory and method in liturgical studies and the scholarly charter of the discipline, see our Introduction (I), section 2, note 2 and P. POST: Interference and intuition. On the characteristic nature of research design in liturgical studies, in *Questions liturgiques / Studies in liturgy* 81 (2000) 48-65.

[3] Recently published manuals for liturgical studies are an interesting source for the discussion; for a summary, see P. POST: De synthese in de huidige liturgie-wetenschap. Proeve van positionering van *De weg van de liturgie*, in *Jaarboek voor liturgie-onderzoek* 14 (1998) 141-172; additions: B. TESTA: Die Sakramente der Kirche (Paderborn 1998) (= AMATECA: Lehrbücher z. Kath. Theol. 9); G. LUKKEN: *Rituelen in overvloed. Een kritische bezinning op de plaats en de gestalte van het christelijke ritueel in onze cultuur* (Baarn 1999); D. POWER: *Sacrament. The language of God's giving* (New York 1999); M. BARNARD & P. POST (eds.): *Ritueel bestek. Antropologische kernwoorden van de liturgie* (Zoetermeer 2001).

arose of the necessity for a broad, contextual 'integral approach' to the liturgical object. New questions, themes and perspectives challenged the discipline to use new sources and new methods, and to forge new academic alliances.[4]

(2) This change meant that the discipline was no longer historical-philological, or, more generally, that the tradition of literary-critical research was no longer dominating. Recent repeated pleas concerning the place and appreciation of the historical-comparative method, in particular those by Taft and Winkler, which constantly call upon Anton Baumstark in a manner that is, to my mind, almost defensive, essentially merely demonstrate how modern liturgical studies is still wrestling with the fact that as a discipline it inescapably lives by the grace of methodological plurality.[5]

In stead of playing off methodological traditions and alliances against one another, such as the social sciences (anthropological) versus the historical-comparative approach, the discipline would be better served by devoting the same energy to developing a general, 'systematic'[6] framework or program for research in liturgical studies, in which various methods and techniques could all be accommodated.[7] An academic, theoretical perspective of this nature is the focus of my contribution.

Several parameters can be formulated in a general sense for this in advance, which I will also briefly summarize:

(1) The systematic, general program in question will have to do justice to liturgical studies as a theological discipline. That does not have to mean that the ultimate goal can consist only of what might be termed a

---

[4] For the *anthropologische Wende*, see the summary sketch in G. LUKKEN: *Ontwikkelingen in de liturgiewetenschap. Balans en perspectief* (Heeswijk-Dinther 1993) (= Liturgie in perspectief 1) 14-17.

[5] For the arguments around the historical-philological method, see particularly the works by Taft and Winkler cited in the Introduction (I), note 2. For Baumstark's comparative method, with a bibliography of recent studies, see in summary, P. POST: Zeven notities over rituele verandering, traditie en (vergelijkende) liturgiewetenschap, in *Jaarboek voor liturgie-onderzoek* 11 (1995) 11ff. n. 27.

[6] This slogan of a 'systematic' study of liturgy, derived from Guardini, is echoed with his own peculiar accents in: R. MESSNER: Was ist systematische Liturgiewissenschaft? Ein Entwurf in sieben Thesen, in *Archiv für Liturgiewissenschaft* 40 (1998) 257-274; cf. R. GUARDINI: Über die systematische Methode in der Liturgiewissenschaft, in *Jahrbuch für Liturgiewissenschaft* 1 (1921) 97-108.

[7] See our Introduction (I), section 2, regarding fundamental methodological plurality in liturgical studies.

derived, more or less comprehensive 'liturgical theology' – a term which, for that matter, can give rise to many misunderstandings – more or less inspired by systematic theology.[8] It is, I think, not a matter of chance that recent attempts to create a model for a comprehensive, systematic liturgical studies are theological in nature (cf. Wainwright,[9] Chauvet,[10] and in a very individual way, Stock too[11]). I would, however, want to explore another direction in order to give the critical-normative dimension a solid place in the design of the investigation and the eventual theological orientation, and to do justice to the question of the identity of Christian rituality and sacramentality. In this context, wrestling with the normative nature of the past and the concept of tradition takes centre stage and there is further the question of the primary and secondary *loci theologici*. Debates around the stubborn adage of Prosper of Aquitania, *lex orandi, lex credendi*, still offer timely input into this question of *theologia prima* and *theologia secunda*.[12]

---

[8] For discussion of the diverse proposed content of the program for a theology of liturgy or liturgical theology, I list here: A. KAVANAGH: *On liturgical theology* (New York 1984) (= The Hale Memorial Lectures of Seabury-Western Theological Seminary 1981); J. RATZINGER: *Das Fest des Glaubens. Versuche zur Theologie des Gottesdienstes* (Einsiedeln 1981); T. JENNINGS: Ritual studies and liturgical theology. An invitation to dialogue, in *Journal of ritual studies* 1 (1987) 35-56; M. KELLEHER: Liturgical theology. A task and a method, in *Worship* 62 (1988) 2-25; K. IRWIN: *Liturgical theology. A primer* (Collegeville 1990); G. LATHROP: *Holy things. A liturgical theology* (Minneapolis 1993); K. IRWIN: *Context and text. Method in liturgical theology* (Collegeville 1994); D.W. FAGERBERG: *What is liturgical theology? A study in methodology* (Collegeville 1992); apart from that, see our Introduction (I), section 2 (cf. note 9). More explicitly within systematic theology: G. WAINWRIGHT: *Doxology. The praise of God in worship, doctrine and life. A systematic theology* (Westminster 1982[2]); L.-M. CHAUVET: *Symbole et sacrement. Une relecture sacramentelle de l'existence chrétienne* (Paris 1988) = *Symbol and sacrament. A sacramental reinterpretation of christian existence* (Collegeville 1995). Cf. POWER: *Sacrament* and LUKKEN: *Rituelen in overvloed*. See also our note 12.

[9] WAINWRIGHT: *Doxology*.

[10] CHAUVET: *Symbole et sacrement*.

[11] A. STOCK: *Poetische Dogmatik. Christologie. 1. Namen; 2. Schrift und Gesicht; 3. Leib und Leben* (Paderborn 1995-1998).

[12] For the liturgy as primary source and the adage of *lex orandi, lex credendi*, see P. DE CLERCK: 'Lex orandi, lex credendi'. Sens originel et avatars historiques d'un adage équivoque, in *Questions liturgiques* 59 (1978) 193-212, later in a somewhat revised English version: Lex orandi, lex credendi. The original sense and historical avatars of an equivocal adage, in *Studia liturgica* 24 (1994) 178-200; G. LUKKEN: De liturgie als onvervangbare vindplaats van de theologie. Methoden van theologische analyse en verificatie, in H. BERGER et al. (eds.): *Tussentijds. Theologische Faculteit Tilburg. Opstellen bij*

(2) The broader framework of postmodern theories of science is also influential. Together with the rising methodological plurality came not only the demand for a comprehensive or integral research program, but also a demand for a practice in the discipline that could rightly be designated as scientific, or 'exact' and 'certain'. Here, as in numerous adjoining fields of study, there are many routes possible. One can here point to 'harder' or 'softer' traditions. It is important to point out that the two lines, the 'hard' and the 'soft', do not exclude each other. Lukken demonstrates how in relationship to an open and soft design, during the phase of source and context analysis, for instance, harder empirical or semiotic methods can have their place.[13] In this connection, a one-sided opposition of qualitative and quantitative research can put us on the wrong track. For instance, recent pilgrimage research has attempted to link the two lines of research with one another.[14]

(3) Finally, liturgical inculturation is the common and supporting perspective of almost every modern liturgical studies program. By this

---

gelegenheid van haar erkenning (Tilburg 1974) 317-332; G. LUKKEN: Pleidooi voor een integralere benadering van de liturgie als theologische vindplaats. Een uitdaging voor heel de theologie, in W. LOGISTER et al. (eds.): *Twintig jaar ontwikkelingen in de theologie. Tendensen en perspectieven* (Kampen 1987) 194-204 (cf. La liturgie comme lieu théologique irremplaçable. Méthodes d'analyse et de vérification théologiques, in L. VAN TONGEREN & C. CASPERS (eds.): *Per visibilia ad invisibilia. anthropological, theological and semiotic studies on the liturgy and the sacraments* (= Liturgia condenda 2) (Kampen 1994) 239-255; B. CARDINALI: Per un approccio dinamico al mistero. La mediazione delle lex orandi, in *Rivista liturgica* 79 (1992) 576-587; MESSNER: Was ist systematische Liturgiewissenschaft? 265-267 (with a critical note on Lukken's approach on p. 267, n. 36. Messner appears to base this on G. LUKKEN: In der Liturgie wird der Glaube auf unersetzbare Weise Wirklichkeit, in *Concilium* (German edition) 9 (1973) 86-93); W.M. MÜLLER: "Lex orandi, lex credendi". Wo Systematik und Liturgiewissenschaft heute zusammenarbeiten können, in *Münchener theologische Zeitschrift* 49 (1998) 145-154; H.-J. SCHULZ: Der Grundsatz "Lex orandi – lex credendi" und die liturgische Dimension der "Hierarchie der Wahrheiten", in *Liturgisches Jahrbuch* 49 (1999) 171-181; P. DE CLERCK (ed.): *La liturgie, lieu théologique* (= Sciences théologiques et religieuses) (Paris 1999), see esp. 125-142; H. VORGRIMLER: Liturgiewissenschaft: für Theologie und Kirche lebensnotwendig, in *Trierer theologische Zeitschrift* [108] (1999) 319-324; LUKKEN: *Rituelen in overvloed* 311-334; P. DE CLERCK: Lex orandi, lex credendi. Un principe heuristique, in *La Maison-Dieu* 222 (2000) 61-78.

[13] In addition to the studies by Lukken already cited, I refer in general to the collection of his work: *Per visibilia ad invisibilia*, ed. by VAN TONGEREN & CASPERS.

[14] P. POST, J. PIEPER & M. VAN UDEN: *The modern pilgrim. Multidisciplinary explorations of Christian pilgrimage* (Leuven 1998) (= Liturgia condenda 8); P. POST: *Het wonder van Dokkum. Verkenningen van hedendaags populair religieus ritueel* (Nijmegen 2000).

I refer again to the previously formulated anthropological, contextual and fundamental theological dimension of liturgical studies and link this with the concern for a living liturgy and the normative-critical theological dimension.[15] This perspective lends the research design a particular direction. It is important to emphasize the dynamic of liturgical inculturation. From the perspective of Christian liturgy, this always involved a double movement: on the one side, it involves the new design of Christian faith, life and celebration and ritual from the particular surrounding rituality and culture, but also, on the other side, the transformation of the particular rituality and culture by the Gospel.[16] This perspective of liturgical inculturation introduces two fundamental elements to any liturgical studies research design. First, the model is always borne and defined by an expressly open, broad, integral contextual approach to liturgy, an approach which always is acutely aware of the dynamic of cultus and culture. Subsequently, through this basic intertwining of Christian ritual and culture, it poses the central question regarding the continuity or discontinuity of tradition. As we shall see below, both elements introduce both a dynamism and a complexity into the research model.[17]

---

[15] For the explosion of literature with regard to liturgical inculturation I list first the survey with an ample bibliography, by G. LUKKEN: Inculturatie van de liturgie. Theorie en praktijk, in J. LAMBERTS (ed.): *Liturgie en inculturatie* (= Nikè-reeks 37) (Leuven/Amersfoort 1996) 15-56 = Inculturation de la liturgie. Théorie et pratique, in *Questions liturgiques / Studies in liturgy* 77 (1996) 1-39, complemented by the surveys of Stauffer (most recent: S.A. STAUFFER: Worship and culture. A select bibliography, in *Studia liturgica* 27 (1997) 102-128); LUTHERAN WORLD FEDERATION: Chicago statement on worship and culture. Baptism and rites of passage, in *Studia liturgica* 28 (1998) 244-252; A.M. TRIACCA & A. PISTOIA (eds.): *Liturgie et cultures* (Rome 1997) (= Bibliotheca Ephemerides Liturgicae 90); A.M. TRIACCA: 'Inculturazione e liturgia'. Eventi dello Spirito Santo. A proposito di alcuni principi per il progresso dell'approfondimento degli studi su liturgia e cultura, in *Ecclesia orans* 15 (1998) 59-90; H. BAUERNFEIND: *Inkulturation der Liturgie in unsere Gesellschaft. Eine Kriteriensuche, aufgezeigt an den Zeitzeichen Kirche heute, Esoterik/New Age und modernes Menschsein* (= Studien zur Theologie und Praxis der Seelsorge 34) (Würzburg 1998); apart from these, see our Introduction (I), note 33.

[16] For an exemple of this dynamic, see the development in: LUTHERAN WORLD FEDERATION: Chicago statement, as in note 15.

[17] The choice could be made for a separate, preliminary conceptual analysis or research phase in which a critical discussion of the concept of tradition could be given a place; the concept of 'culture' might also receive such treatment.

3. General contours of the research design

The next step is now to work out this general perspective into a model usable for research. As a step toward trying to do this – and at that, merely establishing the general contours – I will follow in the tradition of such research at Tilburg, particularly as it has been shaped by Gerard Lukken, and in recent publications by him further articulated, nuanced and corrected (the latter, in part, after critique by Herman Wegman).[18] The central question is how, with an eye to liturgical inculturation, the fundamental dynamic of cultus and culture and the essential question of continuity and discontinuity of the liturgical tradition, which it calls up, can be translated into a research design for liturgical studies as a multi-disciplinary (Lukken also speaks of 'inter- or intradisciplinary') theological discipline.[19]

Following Lukken, the scheme of the design can, in the first instance, be worked out through four points of particular interest. First he pauses to consider the concept of culture, which particularly emphasizes the structural interrelationship of disparate sectors such as politics and cultus. Liturgical research is always therefore a study in both ritual and culture. Next comes the question of the identity of the liturgical tradition in varying cultural settings, which we have already mentioned. The question of the continuity and discontinuity of the tradition must be given a place in the research model. Here Lukken sees possibilities for

---

[18] With regard to Lukken's research model, I would emphasize the importance of the following studies, listed chronologically: G. Lukken: In der Liturgie; Idem: De liturgie als onvervangbare vindplaats; Idem: *De onvervangbare weg van de liturgie* (Hilversum 1984[2]); Idem: Pleidooi; Idem: *Geen leven zonder rituelen. Antropologische beschouwingen met het oog op de christelijke liturgie* (Hilversum 1988[3]); Idem: *Ontwikkelingen in de liturgiewetenschap*; Idem: *Inculturatie en de toekomst van de liturgie* (= Liturgie in perspectief 3) (Heeswijk-Dinther 1994); Idem: La liturgie comme lieu théologique (= supplemented version of De liturgie als onvervangbare vindplaats); Idem: Inculturatie van de liturgie; Idem: Liturgiewetenschappelijk onderzoek in culturele context. Methodische verhelderingen en vragen, in *Jaarboek voor liturgie-onderzoek* 13 (1997) 135-148; further I refer once again to the collection: *Per visibilia ad invisibilia*, ed. by Caspers & Van Tongeren. See now Lukken: *Rituelen in overvloed* esp. 129-143 on the method of 'comparative ritual and theological verification' and 311-334 on the identity of Christian ritual. For a schematic overview of the research design, see Post: Interference and intuition 65.

[19] We will here leave aside the discussion about the terms multi-, inter- and even intradisciplinary. As we justified and discussed in the Introduction, we have opted for 'multidisciplinary'; cf. our Introduction (I), section 2.

the way of comparative ritual and theological verification. Lukken
develops this basic methodological model further.[20] It comprises a pair
of interlinked research phases attuned to one another: the primary careful analysis of the integral (and note, 'integral' is a key word here.
Here too it is a matter of the complete repertoire in context) ritual order of
past or present with regard to form and content, which issues into the
confrontation of these primary ritual sources, opened in context, with
secondary sources of theological and liturgical reflection (and note
again, the metaphor of 'opening' is significant here; one could also
speak of 'decoding'). It is here that we encounter a key moment in the
design. How can this confrontation or comparison be done soundly, in
a way that can be verified and checked? Here, after all, all of the aspects
of the normative nature and identity of tradition we mentioned above
are at stake. Lukken sees comparative ritual and liturgical verification as
a process of mutual clarification and critique of disparate theological
sources, the course of which is not a literal, formal search for identity
and correspondence, as much as for congruence, a point which, for the
rest, he developed in 1997 in a semiotic manner.[21] In this way the question of continuity and discontinuity with tradition, called up by the task
of liturgical inculturation, can be met. Against this, Wegman argues the
fundamental ambiguity, contingency and contextualization of liturgical
tradition,[22] while Lukken believes he has found safe ground in semiotics, which, because it is certain and verifiable, can serve as a scientific
aid enabling one to trace and compare deep structures. The ultimate
dynamic of verification is essentially 'anamnetic' in nature: it involves a
creative process that both acknowledges vital liturgical praxis as the primary source, analyzing it at the level of deep structure and employing it
critically and normatively for the *liturgia condenda*, while being prepared to acknowledge liturgical tradition as the touchstone and guide

---

[20] For this verification model, see especially LUKKEN: De liturgie als onvervangbare
vindplaats; IDEM: Pleidooi; IDEM: Liturgiewetenschappelijk onderzoek. The model was
approached critically by Wegman, see H. WEGMAN: Liturgie en lange duur, in L. VAN
TONGEREN (ed.): *Toekomst, toen en nu. Beschouwingen over de ontwikkeling en de voortgang van de liturgische vernieuwing* (= Liturgie in perspectief 2) (Heeswijk-Dinther
1994) 11-38; to an important degree, LUKKEN: Liturgiewetenschappelijk onderzoek, is
again a reaction to this.

[21] LUKKEN: Liturgiewetenschappelijk onderzoek 142-144; cf. IDEM: *Rituelen in
overvloed* 129-133, 135-143.

[22] WEGMAN: Liturgie en lange duur.

for the present and future. These two lines meet each other in the liturgical links among past, present and future, with the Paschal tetrad of the suffering, death, resurrection and second coming of Christ as the fundamental deep structure.

Finally, to this description of the design Lukken adds some notes about the necessity of restricting the contextual analysis, and on the role of the researcher, who him or herself always is part of the cultural whole and thus to some extent always injects interpretation and evaluation into the analysis.

I would want to adopt the general organization of Lukken's model, subsequently nuancing, supplementing and developing some of its components. It is an open design and distinguishes itself from other models through its breadth and integral approach, the power of its synthesis, the comparison and verification dimension, and the built in methodological plurality, which is decidedly more than a conversation or dialogue with other disciplines.[23] I would likewise intend to refine the model and make it more dynamic, and, especially, want to develop the testing phase, involving confrontation and verification. It seems to me that by a qualitative elaboration of the research phase that Lukken describes in his verification model, the positions of Lukken and Wegman can be linked and developed, opening up wider perspectives.

4. FURTHER DEVELOPMENT OF THE RESEARCH DESIGN FOR LITURGICAL STUDIES

4.1. Qualitative interference

The first major elaboration or sharpening of the design involves the analysis or 'opening' of the primary and secondary sources mentioned, with regard to their form and content. It is now of importance to indicate the complexity of this analysis. There is decidedly more at stake than a confrontation of primary and secondary sources or of prescribed order and celebrated practice. Moreover, I have the impression that both Lukken and Wegman rather exclusively focus on the confrontation between past and present. Precisely because of the complexity of the liturgical analysis, still to

---

[23] As MESSNER: Was ist systematische Liturgiewissenschaft? appears to suggest; see our Introduction (I).

be indicated, I would want to work with series in the research to trace *qualities* that are successively involved with each other in a process of critical *interference*, thus leading to inculturating qualities. Working with qualities is closely connected with a clear trend in ritual studies, while the notion of interference points to reciprocity and a 'two way traffic' more clearly than confrontation or comparison do. I will briefly develop both terms.

4.1.1. Qualities[24]

An interesting development has taken place recently in the broad field of research into rituals. In the multidisciplinary realm termed 'ritual studies' there is an increasing tendency to set aside the search for theoretical constructions and definitions with regard to rituality.[25] In place of theoretical exercises, what is termed the ritual market is now approached and described in an open, indicative and sometimes narrative manner. Although the phrase itself is not employed by everyone, this rising approach in ritual studies could be termed an approach through 'qualities of rituality'. I would propose to bring this 'qualitative' approach into the general research design sketched earlier.

The term 'quality of ritual' was introduced by the influential work *Ritual criticism* by Ronald Grimes.[26] Initially 'quality' was used in very close connection with the search for a definition or characterization of ritual; Grimes tries to determine the calibre of ritual through a series of qualities. The list of qualities functions as a sort of working tool in this process. Later the qualities were used more openly and indicatively, even by Grimes himself. Qualities now came to be seen not so much as a theoretical instrument for determining ritual calibre, but more generally as tendencies or characteristics through which ritual repertoires could be described and categorized. Through series of qualities researchers attempt to catch tendencies in rituality in a certain cultural or religious context, a process in which the focus is on basic anthropological dimensions, including the functions and effects, or rites and their anchorage in culture.

---

[24] Working with qualities is further elaborated upon in: P. POST: Leidende kwaliteiten in het spel. Over liturgisch voorgaan, in H. BECK & R. NAUTA (eds.): *Over leiden. Dynamiek en structuur van religieus leiderschap* (Tilburg 1999) 57-80.

[25] For the platform of what are termed ritual studies see our Introduction (I), section 2, note 11.

[26] R. GRIMES: *Ritual criticism* (Columbia SC 1990) 13ff; see further M. AUNE: The subject of ritual. Ideology and experience in action, in M. AUNE & V. DEMARINIS (eds.): *Religious and social ritual. Interdisciplinary explorations* (Albany NY 1996) 147-173, on 148-150.

Without introducing an etymological digression here, it is important to indicate that in this specific context quality may not be simply equated with the positive-normative connotation that adheres to the term, and so dominates our general use of the word. In its origins, the Latin *qualitas* (genitive, *qualitatis*), as derived from *qualis* (what sort of?) and *qui* (who, which?), points in a neutral sense to traits or characteristics. That line does continue in most modern languages (French, German, English, Dutch), with, as mentioned, a general tendency toward the positive connotation of 'good characteristic' or 'virtue'. In the broad context of ritual studies qualities are in the first place the identity-determining characteristics, traits, dimensions or tendencies in a ritual repertoire. In our model, soon to be developed further, both the more neutral usage to mean characteristic, and the more normative connotation, will enter the picture.[27]

I believe that, in a general sense, despite their by now widespread and undoubtedly diffuse usage, in qualities we have an interesting heuristic instrument for ritual studies in general and liturgical studies in particular. Undoubtedly the concept must be developed further. Particularly a further distinction and characterization of qualities and a more specific tailoring for use in liturgical studies research subjects deserves attention. Here I will content myself with these general notes, and state my conviction that the necessary further development will perhaps best be carried out gradually, in the course of studies, by working with the concept.

4.1.2. Interference[28]

Interference is a term that chiefly has its roots in physics, especially in connection (with movements) of vibrations of light and sound waves, where

[27] For further elaboration, see POST: Leidende kwaliteiten.

[28] For 'interference', see, for instance, *The new encyclopaedia britannica* (1998[15]) Vol. 6, 341s., and the general definition in *Van Dale groot woordenboek der Nederlandse taal* (Utrecht/Antwerp 1993) 1289f, which offers as basic meanings: 1) Meddling, intervention; 2) Interruption; 3) Simultaneous working of two movements which can intensify or impede and disrupt each other; 4) Disruption; 5) Mutual influence; 6) Suppression, as for instance of one virus by another. For cultural applications, see W. FRIJHOFF: *Heiligen, idolen, iconen* (Nijmegen 1998) 46ff. and passim. Cf. in the analysis of celebrations, the divergence and convergence between Christian and modern secular feasts, although not explicitly termed interference, B. KRANEMANN: 'Feiertags kommt das Vergessene…'. Zur Deutung und Bedeutung des christlichen Festes in moderner Gesellschaft, in *Liturgisches Jahrbuch* 46 (1996) 3-22, here 14ff. It does appear that among various authors there are certain differences in emphasis in the interpretation of interference. We would emphasize the reciprocity in the interaction.

it denotes the reciprocal effects of the movements on one another. This interaction or reciprocal effect can hinder or disrupt, but can also reinforce and enrich. With that in mind, the term has been taken over into the humanities in order to denote reciprocal influence, borrowings and effects, and especially to indicate the dynamic of a back-and-forth movement. At the same time, the term has a normative-critical implication. Through the foundational perspective of inculturation (see above), we employ interference for enhancement, and not for effects or interactions which disrupt or impede. In the model used by Lukken and Wegman, qualitative interference thus includes confrontation, comparison and verification. Moreover, this perspective refines the application of interference and renders it more complex. In the model for analysis proposed here it involves successively the interactions of (1) cultus and culture, (2) primary and secondary sources, (3) designation and appropriation, and (4) past and present. Together, these four domains form the research matrix.

4.1.3. Cultus and culture

We have already mentioned the interference of cultus and culture as a general dynamic of inculturation. The analysis of liturgical sources will always have to be confronted with the broad general context which encompasses both basic anthropological and cultural dimensions.

4.1.4. Primary and secondary loci[29]

Next, in this connection, there is the interference of qualities of the primary and secondary sources opened up. Primary or direct *loci* involve the primary witness regarding God in the praxis of the Church. They can be both the practice of faithful Christian life and the practice of Christian ritual acts. Thus primary sources in a broad sense comprise expression with regard to God in word, action, celebration and life. Secondary or indirect *loci* speak about God at a second level of authority. These involve, for instance, the pronouncements of theologians and doctrine. They are thus reflective witnesses, including especially scholarly reflection in liturgical studies, systematic theology and catechesis.

4.1.5. Designation and appropriation

The interference between the two series of sources now takes on a multi-layeredness which both introduces nuance into the confrontation and

---

[29] I here reprise more precise definitions as provided by LUKKEN: Response 2.

makes it more complex. With increasing frequency ritual repertoires are being seen in the context of designation and appropriation processes.[30] This significant research perspective, which can be traced back to the Jesuit De Certeau via Chartier, relativizes the perspective of 'designation' that often dominates research – that is to say, the perspective of how culture and culture elements are viewed and described from outside – and focuses also on the specific manner of dealing with culture that lies rooted in the social group or community itself, i.e. appropriation. Essentially, the emphasis in the research shifts from top-down to bottom-up, in which the community is the central *locus* in which culture takes its shape. Rather than a one-sided accent on designation by, for instance, academic or ecclesiastical authorities, the accent shifts to the broad process of production, distribution and consumption of culture, from prescribed order to lived, celebrated, sung practice. These shifts of focus in research are other and more than just paying attention to the reception side. In addition to the expansion of context already mentioned, this new research perspective means that, for instance, a feast is not viewed merely as a ritual offering, or designated by ecclesiastical guidelines and instructions, but primarily as a bearer of meaning in the process of interpretation and conferring significance, through which groups or individuals experience and flesh out for themselves a liturgical repertoire handed down to them. In this, the question must always be investigated from the inside, in various contexts, of which elements play a role in the appropriation process (i.e. creation of traditions, identities, group cultures, etc.).

Although a direct connection exists between primary sources and appropriation on the one side and secondary sources and designation on the other, in neither case are the two elements congruent with each other.

4.1.6. Past and present, continuity and discontinuity

The final field of interference of qualities introduces a depth into the research matrix through the interaction between past and present, and

---

[30] Cf. the good overview in W. FRIJHOFF: Toeëigening: van bezitsdrang naar betekenisgeving, in *Trajecta* 6 (1997) 99-118; cf. R. CHARTIER: *Cultural history between practices and representations* (Cambridge 1988); IDEM: Popular culture. A concept revisited, in *Intellectual history newsletter* 15 (1993) 3-13; M. DE CERTEAU: *The practice of everyday life* (Berkeley, Los Angeles & London 1984); W. FRIJHOFF: Foucault reformed by Certeau. Historical strategies of discipline and everyday tactics of appropriation, in *Arcadia. Zeitschrift für allgemeine und vergleichende Literaturwissenschaft* 33 (1998) 92-108.

via the mentioned aspect of inculturation: the future, the *liturgia condenda*. As we will soon see, this involves a field that is extremely important when it comes to the testing dimension in the research model. At this point, Lukken's verification model has recently undergone revision. Initially the emphasis strongly lay on the normative qualities which were inherent in the past and in tradition; recently Lukken corrected this by emphasizing the dynamic (or, as I would say, the interference) between past and present.[31] One can now say that there is a testing not only of the present by the past, but equally of the past by the present. Moreover, this is true for both the past and present in inculturated *loci*.[32]

4.2. Testing interference: control, criteria

At the end of the process, series of qualities under the central perspectives of liturgical inculturation, mentioned above, and basic Christian *anamnesis* are involved with one another. This interference brings into play the inculturation of liturgical tradition and its identity, that is to say the qualities that already function as guides and norms for the interference in a general sense, together with the general depth structures of Christian *anamnesis*. The interference thus has a testing, normative dimension.[33]

The interference of qualities is inseparably linked with a 'criteriology', and with the question of its control and testing. This will involve, for instance, the making of necessary choices in the research. After all, our research matrix is extremely broad and complex. For instance, the interplay of primary and secondary *loci*, in all their complexity, with the

---

[31] See here especially the contrast between the original verification scheme, in LUKKEN: De liturgie als onvervangbare vindplaats, and the scheme as revised in LUKKEN: Liturgiewetenschappelijk onderzoek.

[32] Cf., concisely, LUKKEN: Liturgiewetenschappelijk onderzoek 143f (original in Dutch): "One has here a creative process which takes contemporary liturgical enunciative praxis with utmost seriousness, further analyzes it in depth, and employs it normatively in a critique of the past, but on the other hand also is prepared to take the past seriously as a touchstone. Thus it is a matter of a dynamic theological verification that neither seeks its point of departure exclusively in the past, nor in the present, but that in constant ongoing dialogue does justice to the tension of time with its inescapable triad of past, present and future."

[33] With regard to this normative point, it is interesting to refer briefly to the study of liturgical inculturation by Bauernfeind, BAUERNFEIND: *Inkulturation der Liturgie in unsere Gesellschaft.*

anthropological context, is very sweeping. How will we make choices here? Is it a matter purely of choice, or an intuitive process? The need for criteria that can control and give the choice direction is still more pressing with regard to the choice of suitable inculturating qualities from the interference of series of qualities. Are there parameters which can offer guidance here? Can one be satisfied with 'taming' subjectivity and intuition by, for instance, striving for a certain measure of intersubjectivity?

Consciously or unconsciously, various criteria will play a role here in liturgical analysis. For instance, certain designative qualities of primary or secondary *loci*, such as massive ecclesiastical doctrinal authority or *editiones typicae*, are often advanced. Heavy appeals to Scripture are not unknown: the 'biblical' criterion, for instance, by which liturgy is derived directly from the New Testament in certain churches of the Reformation. In circles more oriented to pastoral liturgy, contextual qualities sometimes appear to be overwhelmingly decisive. In connection with the designative qualities mentioned earlier, there is then indeed a formulation that views liturgy in the opposition of selling out or rigorism. These criteria often lead to a very neatly ordered confrontation of qualities, but we must see that the contextual perspective has disappeared here. Furthermore, in place of interference there is now a one-sided confrontation in which all attention for appropriation is missing. At the very least, our matrix demonstrates that the opposition between selling out and rigorism, or of supply and demand, is one-sided and ultimately misleading.

In Lukken's verification model, as critically annotated by Wegman, the testing, guiding function of tradition is brought to the fore and considered critically. We also intend to give this point a place in our model.

4.3. Tradition

As we have said, the interaction of past and present plays an important role in our model, the matrix we have constructed. Part of the process of testing in liturgical studies analysis, with an eye to (Lukken prefers to speak of 'in the service of') the *liturgia condenda*, takes place through the comparative search for congruence with the liturgical tradition. Although, as we have argued, it is not exclusively a one-way process – this being one of many interferences – our ways of celebrating, to be contextualized, are tested against tradition, against the past. Translated into our elaboration of the research design, the interference of qualities is thus subjected to norms and guidance by liturgical tradition. At this point Lukken's original verification model needed adaptation and elaboration. Wegman quite correctly began his critique of Lukken with regard to this appeal to the past.[34] It must be admitted that neither the test of congruency nor calling on deep structures from tradition to illuminate the preset qualify as wielding a massive, confrontational concept of tradition. Interference is not eliminated. The question is, however, how, and particularly where this congruency or deep structure can be found. How can tradition be a point of reference? Translated in terms of the model we have been using thus far: Does this not locate tradition, as a suggested independent touchstone, too much outside the inculturation process, outside the dynamic of cultus and culture, as a separate element, while in reality it is precisely an inextricable part of it? It is fundamental that the continual dynamic of the process is seen. Liturgical tradition is itself constantly the product of interference. Thus an accurate perception of tradition is crucial for the interference of qualities. Only when that is the case, the call upon liturgical tradition can take a sound place in the research model.

Therefore a brief, separate look at the concept of tradition is fitting at this point. By its nature, in ecclesiastical and theological circles tradition almost always appears to be given a normative, controlling significance. In liturgical studies one becomes increasingly conscious of this through the intensive contacts with adjoining disciplines in the humanities that deal with tradition and appeal to the past in a more open and detached manner. I have developed this aspect elsewhere.[35] I would like to cite

---

[34] WEGMAN: Liturgie en lange duur.

[35] P. POST: The creation of tradition. Rereading and reading beyond Hobsbawm, in J.W. VAN HENTEN & A. HOUTEPEN (eds.): *Religious identity and the invention of tradition. Papers read at a NOSTER conference in Soesterberg, January 4-6, 1999* (= Studies in theology and religion 3) (Assen 2001) 41-59; of the bibliography listed and used there I would here single out the following for citation, P. POST: Het verleden in het spel? Volksreligieuze rituelen tussen cultus en cultuur, in *Jaarboek voor liturgie-onderzoek* 7 (1991) 79-121, esp. 104ff; IDEM: De creatie van traditie, in *Jaarboek voor liturgie-onderzoek* 11 (1995) 77-102; IDEM: Rituals and the function of the past. Rereading Eric Hobsbawm, in *Journal of ritual studies* 10 (1996[1998]) 85-107. I consider the following important for the perspective of an open concept of tradition, L. BOEVE: Erfgenaam en erflater. Kerkelijke traditie binnen de traditie, in H. LOMBAERTS & L. BOEVE (eds.): *Traditie en initiatie. Perspectieven voor de toekomst* (Leuven/Amersfoort 1996) (= Nikè-reeks 36) 43-78; LUKKEN: *Rituelen in overvloed* 129-143; POST: *Het wonder van Dokkum* 72-88.

here particularly the major contribution made by Herman Wegman to relativizing the classical concept of tradition in the research model in liturgical studies.[36] To my mind, with his critical discussion of Lukken's verification model, Wegman provides an important contribution for our research model. Lukken also acknowledges that.[37] Wegman relativizes the massive directive and verifying potential of liturgical tradition. After all, liturgical tradition is always the result of a prior process of inculturation in which qualities of designation and appropriation interfered in a specific context. In a positive sense, he further develops the fundamental congruence also cited by Lukken, particularly by pointing to the long life of narratives, images and experiences. Translated into terms of our research model, to my mind that implies that the involvement with each other of the qualities found in the analysis must be guided by concepts which are rooted in this evocative, narrative, experience-oriented tradition of liturgical 'long standing'. Thus Lukken and Wegman meet each other in the normative function of a liturgical deep structure found over the long term, and thus in the criterion of tradition.

Yet it must be asked if Wegman does sufficient justice to the dynamic and complexity of the research model that we have constructed in this contribution. In the end, Wegman makes the primary liturgy of past and present, and in particular that in the form of appropriation, into the ultimate deep structure, without allowing that liturgy to interfere in the analysis on the other fronts of *loci* and contexts, precisely in order to discover this definitive deep structure. In doing so, a new imbalance is created.[38]

In order to include this open multiplicity of interferences of qualities as much as possible in the opening of sources, a critical signalizing function should be able to be derived from certain concepts that guide the analysis in question. Here, as the next step in the development of the research design, I would want to introduce what are termed 'concepts in between'.

4.4. Concepts in between

The research platform and the various qualitative interferences demand guidance for the research pragmatic and setting norms for verification.

---

[36] H. WEGMAN: Liturgie en lange duur. See now also the collection H. WEGMAN: *Voor de lange duur. Verzamelde artikelen en toespraken* (ed. L. VAN TONGEREN & G. ZUIDBERG) (Baarn 1999).

[37] Cf. LUKKEN: Liturgiewetenschappelijk onderzoek; IDEM: Response.

[38] Cf. LUKKEN: Response 4f.

Here, connected with and in addition to the anamnetic deep structures already mentioned, what are being termed 'concepts in between' could serve as heuristic instruments. This terminology[39] denotes that there are certain concepts that already encompass within themselves the links between qualities, and at the same time transcend them. Using concepts of this sort, a focused search can be conducted for inculturating qualities. The term 'concept in between' has a certain tradition in the humanities (cf. Barbara Bender), theology, spirituality, the visual arts and architecture as a marker for interferences. A 'concept in between' transcends existing standpoints or poles by 'involving the in-between'. It is therefore an innovative, enriching concept which moves us ahead. It can also be characterized as paradoxical and reconciling. In the words of Buber, concepts of this type are always sustained by meeting, contact and dialogue. Although their application, designation and development can be extremely diverse (Paul Klee: 'die mediale Zone';[40] Martin Buber: 'das Reich des Zwischen';[41] Barbara Bender: 'concept in between';[42] Aldo van Eyck: 'the in-between' or 'twin phenomenon'[43]), such concepts can also be employed in our experimental design, particularly in the light of what we said with Wegman regarding the long term as providing direction. Thus they critically approach cult and context, primary and secondary *loci*, dimensions of designation and appropriation, and are focused on past and present.

Such concepts take various forms. In essence, 'ritual' is such a concept. After all, in general terms, rituality enables the researcher to push forward productively in all the fields in our complex matrix. The general 'qualities of ritual' discussed earlier can now, through the interferences, guide the search for definitive inculturating perspectives by drawing our attention to them. 'Concepts in between' thus particularly embody a critical potential for pointing beyond themselves.

Translated into our attempt at setting forth a research model, plastic, narrative and experience-oriented 'anamnetic' concepts qualify for the

---

[39] For a summary and application, see P. POST: *Ritueel landschap. Over liturgie-buiten* (Heeswijk-Dinther 1995) (= Liturgie in perspectief 5) 16 = Paysage rituel. Liturgie en plein air I, II, in *Questions liturgiques / Studies in liturgy* 77 (1996) 174-190; 240-256, here 181. See also POST: *Het wonder van Dokkum* 89-135.

[40] P. KLEE: *Pädagogisches Skizzenbuch* (Munich 1925; Reprint Mainz 1966).

[41] M. BUBER: *Das Problem des Menschen* (Heidelberg 1982[5]; originally 1943).

[42] For landscape as a concept in between in Bender, see POST: *Ritueel landschap* 16.

[43] For Aldo van Eyck and the in-between, F. STRAUVEN: *Aldo van Eyck. The shape of reality* (Amsterdam 1998) 354ff.; cf. J. HARDY, in *FORUM* 8 (1959) 249.

role of 'concepts in between' discussed above, which can give direction to the interference of diverse qualities. They also always serve as further thematization in the fundamental 'concept in between' of ritual. After previously employing '(ritual) landscape' as such a concept and exploring the potential of the interferences there,[44] as Willem Frijhoff also recently did with the concepts of 'saint', 'idol' and 'icon',[45] and Susan Roll with the metaphor 'journey'[46]. I would now want to examine and employ 'feast' as such a 'concept in between' par excellence.[47]

5. FEAST AS A GUIDING INTERFERENTIAL CONCEPT

For the further development of festivity as a key to interference of qualities, we are not beginning with a *tabula rasa*. Already the theme of feast and feast culture can rejoice in a wide interest on the part of a number of disciplines. The paradigm of feast therefore does not have to be opened up *in extenso* in a separate phase of conceptual investigation. Even for the reasonably less well off realm of theology (as Schilson rightly observes[48]), one can most certainly fall back on good syntheses. I would here want to open up the paradigm in two steps on the basis of existing synthesizing studies, with the intention of thus formulating their critical signalizing potential. I will first address the phenomenology of the subject via the work of the influential Egyptologist and Semitist Jan Assmann, and then approach it theologically-liturgically via the standard work of Francisco Taborda.

---

[44] POST: *Ritueel landschap.*
[45] FRIJHOFF: *Heiligen.*
[46] S.K. ROLL: A feminist approach to liturgical time, in: *Proceedings of the North American Academy of Liturgy* (1997) 95-107, here 105-107.
[47] Cf. already P. POST: De uitslag van de Rotterdamse prijsvraag. Typen en thema's, balans en perspectief, en een afsluitend pleidooi, in IDEM (ed.): *Een ander huis. Kerkarchitectuur na 2000* (Baarn 1997) (= Liturgie in perspectief 7) 18-29; T. MICHELS & P. POST: Huwelijk. Dynamiek van feest en sacrament, in *Tijdschrift voor liturgie* 81 (1997) 327-343; P. POST & L. VAN TONGEREN: Het feest van de eerste communie. Op zoek naar de identiteit van het christelijk ritueel, in K. MERKS & N. SCHREURS (eds.): *De passie van een grensganger. Theologie aan de vooravond van het derde millennium* (Baarn 1997) 249-266; see also the contribution of P. Post and L. van Tongeren in part IV of this collection.
[48] Schilson offers this assessment in closing: A. SCHILSON: Fest und Feier in anthropologischer und theologischer Sicht, in *Liturgisches Jahrbuch* 44 (1994) 4-32; see our Introduction (I), section 3 with bibliography in notes 35-75.

5.1. Opening the feast paradigm as signalizing concept

5.1.1. Phenomenology

In various contributions Assmann presents feast as a central ritual, because it represents a cultural-ritual point of convergence: the feast is the locus of cultural memory (*Gedächtnis*).[49] To my mind, his development of the paradigm of feast provides an accurate synthesis of existing theoretical conceptions regarding festivity. The key lies in contrast. Feast exists by grace of a necessarily sought and cherished contrast with the everyday.[50] This contrast can be elaborated in three domains:

(1) While the cadence of everyday life is dominated by the unstructured, the chance and the contingent, to which an attitude of care, alertness and seeking to avert danger are appropriate responses, feast exists by grace of the prescribed, the planned, the non-chance. A feast is *festgelegt*.

(2) Everyday life is ruled by shortage and want (of food, of meaning), to which work, struggle and searching are the fitting responses; in feast there is utopian abundance. In place of labour and struggle, peace, satisfaction and rest are appropriate for feast.

(3) The everyday is further matter-of-course, grey and monotonous, banal and oriented to basic patterns of behaviour. Feast transcends this perspective, and orients itself to what are really fundamental matters. Feast picks up that which is suspended or reduced in the everyday. This neutralizing of the mundane takes place through great gestures and emotions.

Assmann emphasizes that humans are two-dimensional beings, that they live in two time frames: the everyday and feast. The holy, that

---

[49] Cf. J. ASSMANN: Kollektives Gedächtnis und kulturelle Identität, in J. ASSMANN & T. HOLSCHER (eds.): *Kultur und Gedächtnis* (Frankfurt a.M. 1988) 9-19; IDEM: Der zweidimensionaler Mensch. Das Fest als Medium des kollektiven Gedächtnisses, in IDEM (ed.): *Das Fest und das Heilige. Religiöse Kontrapunkte zur Alltagswelt* (Gütersloh 1991) (= Studien zum Verstehen fremder Religionen 1) 13-30; IDEM: *Kult, Kalender und Geschichte. Semiotisierung von Zeit als kulturelle Konstruktion* (Tübingen 1997) (= Ars semeiotica 20,1-2); IDEM: *Das kulturelle Gedächtnis. Schrift, Erinnerung und politische Identität in frühen Hochkulturen* (Munich 1997² 1992¹). For our sketch we have used particularly the 1991 survey article. For Assmann, see also MESSNER: Was ist systematische Liturgiewissenschaft? 270, n. 46 (on 'kulturelle Gedächtnis' and *anamnesis*, without however mentioning Assmann by name) and SCHILSON: Fest 24f.

[50] Lukken underlines the dimension of joy, cf. LUKKEN: *Rituelen in overvloed* 84-86.

which rises above the mundane, comes into the picture through feast. Two forms of memory are connected with the two dimensions: communicative and cultural memory. Cultural memory, and thus feast, is indispensable for a culture. It is in feast that group cultures find their meaning and identity; there lies the underlying order of society: consensus, solidarity, justice. This cultural *anamnesis* is not simply contained in myths, but is passed on in the feast ritual. Assmann speaks here of festive circulation. Through the rites of the feast the memory is presented, made contemporary.

Assmann thus presents a paradigm of feast that affords a creative synthesis of modern feast phenomenology, and furthermore – and this is of great importance for us – his elaboration, focusing as it does on *anamnesis*, is closely allied with more liturgical-theological theories surrounding feast.

I would briefly strike a balance here by formulating six notes:

(1) The great strength of Assmann's feast phenomenology lies in the synthesis. Without much difficulty it appears to fall into a line with authors from Durkheim, Mol, Douglas to Taborda.

(2) In the paradigm of feast, cultural memory takes centre stage. This gives feast an anamnetic character.[51] With the term *anamnesis* I am deliberately evoking a religious (though not exclusively Christian), liturgical context. Although not explicitly formulated that way, a two-dimensional person is a religious person. Feast and the collective, cultural memory lying within it, is a holy performance in which past, present and future are linked with one another. This aspect is closely connected with what has been said about tradition and custom and the long term.

(3) The next central element is the group. Feast as a medium of *anamnesis* is linked to group culture.

(4) Feast also receives what I would call a 'sacramental' elaboration. Feast is not just a reference to other dimensions and times, but this other time is brought into the present in ritual, made present in the ritual performance.

(5) Finally, according to Assmann there is an unmistakable critical-normative dimension. Marginalizing feast affects the 'anamnetic connection' of a culture. The reduction of mankind to one dimension is

---

[51] J.G. DAVIES (ed.): *A new dictionary of liturgy and worship* (London 1994⁴) under *anamnesis* 18.

thus a constant threat, past and present. This marginalization is continually taking place in two ways: Through the absolutizing of the everyday or through the reduction of the feast to the mundane, on the one hand, or through the absolutizing of feast and the elevation of the everyday to feast on the other. In the final analysis, one can read Assmann as a highly relevant defense of feast.

(6) In closing, it is still well to recall the dynamic of feast. The metahistorical and metacultural character of Assmann's synthesis can suggest a static image of feast. This, however, deserves correction, as will happen in other contributions to this collection. Assmann himself alludes to this already when he speaks of the threats to feast or of the dynamic of changing ritual performances. Feasts contextualize themselves and change constantly. The feast dimension constantly attaches itself in new places in a culture. In the final pages of the collection *Das Fest und das Heilige*, planned and edited by Assmann, Ratschof reflects on changes in feast in our present secularized world.[52] He ends the book with the following diagnosis:

> Freilich ist das Fest in einer säkularisierten Welt bedroht, denn alle Feste haben am ihrem religiösen Grundzusammenhang ihr Lebenselixer. Wo die Anerkenntnis dieses religiösen Lebensgrundes aus Unbedachtheit und Überbeschäftigung zurücktritt, da bleiben die Alltage ohne den sie vollendenden Sonntag, da gerät die Menschheit außer Atem, denn es fehlen die Feste zum Atemholen. Dies schafft einen gefahrvollen Übergang. Doch schon melden sich überall die religiösen Unausgefülltheiten – wenn auch vorerst wirr und unverständlich – zu Worte. Sie führen eine neue Festkultur und damit eine neue lebendige Sittlichkeit herauf.[53]

Assmann's anamnetic, ritual-liturgical, and also critical-normative elaboration provides a sound basis for the liturgical-theological development or 'upgrading' of feast as a guiding 'concept in between'. For its dynamic lines I will fall back upon the theological study of feast by Francisco Taborda, still fundamental today.[54] Before briefly introducing that material, I would again want to underscore the suitability of feast as a 'concept in between', precisely because, in the paradigm just presented, the

---

[52] C.H. RATSCHOF: Die Feste. Inbegriff sittlicher Gestalt, in ASSMANN (ed.): *Das Fest und das Heilige* 234-246.

[53] *Ibidem* 245f.

[54] F. TABORDA: *Sakramente. Praxis und Fest* (Düsseldorf 1988). For other theological literature on feast, see our Introduction (I) with literature.

inculturating interference is, as it were, implicit in the concept of feast. Feast can only be described as a twin phenomenon. By its nature, feast is connected with everyday life, is always dependent on the constant dynamic of cultus and culture. But it also brings together antitheses such as past and present and conflict and celebration. It is not mere chance that both Assmann and Carlos Mesters speak of the 'twins feast and struggle'.[55]

5.1.2. Liturgical-theological

The paradigm of feast worked out immediately above in terms of phenomenology can also be introduced onto a liturgical-theological platform.[56]

First, there is the fundamental connection between feast and sacramentality. Taborda develops a doctrine of the sacraments on the basis of feast. I will not elaborate upon all the various dimensions here, but only refer in general to the important insight of what is termed *synkatabasis* that he advances as an important perspective, which he calls upon to justify the coupling of feast and sacrament. The Greek concept of *synkatabasis* stems from John Chrysostom, and ultimately defies translation.[57] That is undoubtedly also the reason why Vaticanum II's Constitution *Dei Verbum* (13 with note 17) does not directly arrive at a Latin translation of this legacy from the Greeks, but allows the Greek word to stand. One might literally translate the term as "to descend to someone at the point at which he or she is". A willingness to do this is ascribed to God, and can thus be designated as God's turning toward mankind. Linking feast with the category of sacrament then is not to tailor something divine to purely human affairs and deliver it up to them, but is on the contrary to cherish a God who turns to mankind: God turns toward mankind with means that are accessible and fitting for men! In feast the general ritual milieu and the sacramental milieu come together.

---

[55] Cf. ASSMANN: Der zweidimensionale Mensch 14; C. MESTERS: Zes dagen in de kelders van de mensheid (Den Haag 1980) 90.

[56] See also the fine article G. BRÜSKE: Die Liturgie als Ort des kulturellen Gedächtnisses. Anregungen für ein Gespräch zwischen Kulturwissenschaften und Liturgiewissenschaft, in Liturgisches Jahrbuch 2001 no. 3 or 4 (forthcoming).

[57] Synkatabasis is a key concept in the anthropocentric-anthropomorphical theology of John Chrysostom. Cf. JEAN CHRYSOSTOME: Sermons sur la Genèse, ed. L. BOTTIER (= Sources chrétiennes 433) (Paris 1998) II, 110, with a bibliographical note on p. 376s.

Subsequently, against this general background of sacramentality, by way of a normative-critical perspective four dynamics can be formulated as the qualities or dimensions of feast:

(1) In a general and inclusive summary, there is the dimension of contrast with regard to the everyday: feast is other, it stops the rat race, it is a refuge.

(2) Feast lives by the grace of memory: something or someone is remembered and therefore there is something or someone to celebrate. This is the myth of feast, the content.

(3) Feast is a ritual. The memory is kept going through a ritual setting. The anamnetic and sacramental dimensions are linked in the ritual performance: feasting is something you *do*, performed in word and action.

(4) Feast is inseparably linked with group culture. Feast stands or falls with group solidarity: feasting is done *together*.

These four dimensions of feast can now be critically employed to discover qualitative interference. We will conclude our contribution with an example of their application. For this, marriage ritual has been chosen.[58]

6. AN APPLICATION AS EXAMPLE: MARRIAGE AS FEAST[59]

Each of the four pillars formulated from the phenomenological and liturgical-theological perspectives on feast now serves as an impetus for

---

[58] For a previous application, see materials listed in note 47.

[59] In the following I reprise a previous exploration of marriage, to be found in MICHELS & POST: Huwelijk, and J. PIEPER & P. POST: Rituele veranderingen met betrekking tot de huwelijkssluiting. Een onderzoeksvoorstel, in *Jaarboek voor liturgie-onderzoek* 12 (1996) 136-164. On marriage and marriage ritual, see A. BLIJLEVENS & E. HENAU (eds.): *Huwelijkssluiting: gelegenheidsverkondiging* (Averbode 1985) (= HTP-studies 7), esp. A. BLIJLEVENS: Het huidige romeinse ritueel van de huwelijkssluiting tijdens de eucharistieviering, 42-73; A. BLIJLEVENS & G. LUKKEN (eds.): *In goede en kwade dagen. Beschouwingen over huwelijksliturgie en modellen van huwelijksvieringen uit 20 jaar werkmap Liturgie (1966-1985)* (Baarn 1991); L.-M. CHAUVET: Le mariage. Un sacrement pas comme les autres, in *La Maison-Dieu* 127 (1976) 64-105; IDEM: Parler du sacrement de mariage aujourd'hui, in *Pastorale Sacramentelle. Points de repère. Commentaires et guide de travail. I. Les sacrements de l'initiation chrétienne et le mariage* (= Liturgie. Collection de recherche du centre national de pastorale liturgique 8) (Paris 1996) 182-205; A. GOOSSENS: Spreken over huwelijksliturgie, in *Tijdschrift voor liturgie* 73 (1989) 259-274; B. KLEINHEYER: Riten um Ehe und Familie, in *Sakramentliche Feiern II* (= Gottesdienst der Kirche 8) (Regensburg 1984) 67-156; M. KUNZLER: *Die Liturgie der*

critical reflection on qualities traced in a liturgical studies analysis of the marriage ritual. In this connection we are going to pass over the actual research, which brings the various qualities to light in the various domains of the research design matrix.[60] What concerns us here is to show how the dimensions of feast indicate and critically direct the interference of qualities. Apart from that, this must also be understood as a tentative sketch in which certain qualitative directions are suggested.

6.1. The solidary group

However much we still continue to yearn for and seek after a feeling of fellowship and solidarity in community, with increasing frequency, on the contrary, our community is often being divided by our rites. More than ever before there appears to be a development in the direction of ritual repertoires oriented toward parts of the community and target audiences. Rites for rich and poor, young and old, the sick and the well, seem to be becoming rarer. Even the Christian *Ecclesia* is being divided up through her rites into sector liturgies, into rites for groups of believers: for children, youth, young adults, the elderly, the sick, etc. Many people are disappointed in the rites of the Church at precisely this

Kirche (= AMATECA: Lehrbücher zur katholischen Theologie 10) (Paderborn 1995) 449-460; G. LUKKEN: De nieuwe Romeinse huwelijksliturgie, in *Werkmap voor liturgie* 12 (1978) 337-367; L. MEURDERS: Mijmeringen bij huwelijksvieringen, in *Tijdschrift voor liturgie* 70 (1986) 227-242; IDEM: 'Zoals alle anderen huwen zij.' Enkele grepen uit de lange geschiedenis van huwelijksriten, in *Tijdschrift voor liturgie* 81 (1997) 310-326; F.-J. NOCKE: *Sakramententheologie. Ein Handbuch* (Düsseldorf 1997) 258-277; P. PAS: *De zeven sacramenten op de drempel van het derde millennium* (Leuven 1999) 185-250; P. POST: Huwelijksliturgie tussen aangereikte liturgische ordo en gevierde rituele praktijk, in J. STAPS (ed.): *Tot zegen aan elkaar gegeven. Over huwelijksliturgie en huwelijkspastoraat* (= Liturgische Handreikingen) (Breda 2000) 5-30; P. POST & L. LEIJSSEN: Huwelijksliturgie. Inculturatie van een levensfeest, in R. BURGGRAEVE, M. CLOET, K. DOBBELAERE & L. LEIJSSEN (eds.): *Het huwelijk* (= KADOC-studies 24, series Levensrituelen) (Leuven 2000) 179-196; M. PROBST: Das neue Trauungsrituale der katholischen Bistümer des deutschen Sprachgebietes, in *Liturgisches Jahrbuch* 42 (1992) 203-218; M. PROBST & K. RICHTER: *Die kirchliche Trauung* (Freiburg 1994); K. RICHTER (ed.): *Eheschliessung – mehr als ein rechtlich Ding?* (Freiburg etc. 1989) (= Quaestiones disputatae 120); IDEM: Die Theologie der kirchlichen Trauung, in *Heiliger Dienst* 52 (1998) 244-253; T. SCHEER: Peilingen in de hedendaagse huwelijksliturgie: een oriënterend onderzoek, in *Tijdschrift voor liturgie* 62 (1978) 259-317. Cf. the contribution of Scheer in part IV.

    [60] Cf. RICHTER: Die Theologie der kirchlichen Trauung; NOCKE: *Sakramententheologie* 258-277 with bibliography; G. LUKKEN: This is a great mystery. A theological reflection on the sacrament of marriage, in LUKKEN: *Per visibilia* 196-204.

point, and flee to charismatic groups where this community solidarity can indeed be felt. Feast and ritual supported by a true solidary community are rare. Is this perhaps the power of attraction that Taizé has? With regard to the marriage ritual, the questions arise: How private has our marriage ritual really become? What group supports the celebration? What is the relation between the Church community, the parish and the family, district or neighbourhood? How personal and individually tailored can and may a celebration be? In the case of the liturgy for marriage, what is it which reveals the active participation, the covenantal dimension? Is there support from the community? What, in the symbolic actions, demonstrates that?

This signalizing and critical element of feast thus raises for discussion what might be called the ecclesial or Church dimension. In contrast to the repertoire of the past, from before Vatican II, the ecclesial dimension, entering into marriage *in facie ecclesiae*, receives scant recognition. Hardly ever, if at all, is there a presence of the broader Church community, or its representatives, actively involved in the ritual performance. Despite theological developments, the ritual of Christian marriage thus remains to an important extent a matter for family and friends, and the public-ecclesial element is concentrated primarily on the pastor.

Although the questions and ecclesial and ecclesiological perspectives may be clear, the interferences can also introduce other accents. For instance, marriage practices in the early Church are cause to nuance the quality of group solidarity. There Christians married in the closed circle of the family, with the realization that they "marry in the Lord" (Eph. 5, 25-32). The nucleus of the wedding was the mutual assent of the parties being married.[61]

6.2. Ritual performance

The ritual dimension also helps in finding direction in the interplay of qualities. First, there is the fact that marriage is deeply anchored in the culture by its festive character. We have here therefore an important contextualizing and inculturating fact. But in connection with that, the question certainly must be asked regarding the actual 'ritual calibre' of that festive ritual repertoire. For instance, celebrations are often no

---

[61] Cf. G. LUKKEN: De geschiedenis in vogelvlucht, in BLIJLEVENS & LUKKEN (eds.): *In goede en kwade dagen* 41.

longer mythic collective performances, but performances into which
more and more distance is incorporated, performances in the sense of
education, productions carried out by some and watched by others.
People are also often wrestling with the sensory dimensions of feast and
ritual. Even the leaders in our rites adopt an attitude of distance,
explaining, speaking *about* the ritual. In general, in our postmodern culture 'mythic' celebration of feasts has, by way of folklore, been consigned to the realm of the museum and theatre, or even to the world of
commerce and the picturesque, as a lovely old local or national tradition. Marriage ritual appears to share something of this fate: there is
increasingly often distance and watching rather than participation. It is
romantic theatre which is viewed seated, and explained. To some degree
this is related with the absence of a generally shared symbolic 'code',
while it is precisely marriages that 'suddenly' bring together people from
many sectors of life, often people who have drifted far from the repertoire of Christian feasts.

6.3. The reason why: the myth behind the rite, the content

And then there is the heart of feast and ritual: the reason behind it. This
signalizing dimension sets us on the trail of the *anamnesis,* which we
have already discussed. A feast is supported by a delicate web bringing
together past, present and future. Something out of the past – a person
or event – is commemorated in the present, with an eye to the future. If
the ritual memory or *anamnesis* decays, then the celebration becomes
hollow and empty, and the door to the anti-feast of bread and circuses
stands wide open. Seen from this perspective, feast and celebration is
always a critical, dangerous game. It is a critical activity, a subversive act.
And thus marriage, seen from the perspective of feast, steers the interference towards specific, substantive anamnetic qualities. This is a counterweight against other, often dominant qualities from the general context of rituality and festivity, such as immediate emotion and the 'high'
it produces. After all, memory is often subordinated to the rite of the
emotional 'high', or a cause, a suitable memory, is created or even
invented. Often too those involved are happy to 'civilize' the memory,
eliminate its dangerous dimensions, and with them the risk, to provide
a temporary flight from everyday life, with nothing problematic about
it. Here too distance wins out over engagement; there is performance
and memory, viewers and hearers. It is at this point that Taborda rightly

takes up the critique of feast spoken by the Old Testament prophets.[62]

This critical, substantive perspective can now be focused in on the sacramental celebration of marriage. What qualities do we see emerge from the interference of actual liturgical practice and existing theologies? What is being celebrated here? A romantic theatre piece, a background for a lovely day, or a sacrament full of mythical *anamnesis*, a true "marriage in the Lord"?

In this context, then, a series of qualities come up for discussion on the interferences between designation and appropriation and between primary and secondary *loci*, which we in this connection can only briefly summarize.[63] I will mention the accent which more and more comes to be placed on marriage as an interpersonal relationship, and the expressions of that in the ritual. Then there is the idea of covenant. This particularly involves the question of whether and how Christian theology of marriage, or marriage ritual, sees in marriage the covenant between Christ and His Church, and if and how this aspect is experienced in the ritual. I would also explicitly mention themes such as vows for better or worse, and the asking and receiving of God's blessing, and especially the specific quality of the 'long haul' which is implicit in this sacrament: a lasting yes to a indissoluble pact that, from general experience and the context all around us, appears to be extraordinarily vulnerable.[64]

6.4. A double contrast

Finally, there is also the double contrast effect of feast and ritual. There is first the tension between feast and everyday. Feast lives, exists by the grace of the contrast with the course of the everyday. This dimension appears to be a quality sought in contemporary rituality. In our era and culture we also assiduously seek opportunities to stage feasts: Feasts as

---

[62] Taborda does that at various points in his books, see for instance TABORDA: *Sakramente* 55ff.

[63] For these dimensions of sacramental theology in marriage I would summarily refer to G. LUKKEN: This is a great mystery; KUNZLER: *Die Liturgie der Kirche* 449-460; RICHTER: Die Theologie der kirchlichen Trauung; NOCKE: *Sakramententheologie* 258-277, with bibliography.

[64] It is important to see how, on the part of many liturgists and theologians, this practical observation of the vulnerability of marriage seems to be directing the qualitative interference and proposals for a new, inculturating liturgical praxis. For a summary and statement of the problem, see RICHTER: Die Theologie der kirchlichen Trauung.

carefully nurtured rituals through which we can step off of the daily treadmill, feast as the excuse, par excellence, for a break. Feast exists by the grace of a balance between feast days and everyday days. Regarding the very real threats posed by both the onward march of 'every day a feast day' and the omnipresent everydayness of life in our 24-hour, 365-day economy, I cannot say more here.[65]

A second important element of contrast touches the very core of rituality. In contrast to our other actions, in which we are increasingly led by calculation, interests, rationality, functionality, benefit and profit thinking, ritual play is useless – though not senseless or meaningless –, disinterested, gratuitous play. In the interferences, this dimension of feast points us towards those ritual qualities that are detached from calculation, and their potential for inculturation and their necessity. Liturgy is essentially 'useless', and real inculturation of liturgy demands that we discover and do justice to this dimension of contrast in feast and celebration. That means that there will inevitably be objections from many quarters, and contrasts with contemporary trends. We do not have to legitimate liturgy, justify it, or make it plausible. Against the meta-ritual of explanation and justification, we must insist that liturgy, like every mythic feast and ritual, contrasts with useful and functional actions of this sort. Liturgy is useless, serves no ends, is a waste of time, is just playing before God. In a critical essay on postmodern rituals, Nauta, invoking Guardini, turned his sights on this aspect.[66] According to Guardini, liturgy, purposeless but full of meaning, is "eine in sich ruhende Welt des Lebens". Liturgy is like the movement of angles, the play of a child. Because the playing child seeks only to be himself, the play is full of harmony, naturally beautiful, clear in form.[67]

It is my belief that through rites of life like marriage, anchored deep in the culture's general sense of feast, there is still plenty of chance to ultimately give a place to these ritual qualities as inculturating qualities.

---

[65] Reference was made to this aspect above, in the discussion of Assmann; it also forms the essence of a fine small philosophy of feast by Marquard, O. MARQUARD: Kleine Philosophie des Festes, in U. SCHULTZ (ed.): Das Fest. Eine Kulturgeschichte von der Antike bis zur Gegenwart (Munich 1988) 413-420.

[66] R. NAUTA: Rituelen als decor. Over het geheim van de leegte, in P. POST & W.M. SPEELMAN (eds.): De Madonna van de Bijenkorf. Bewegingen op de rituele markt (Baarn 1997) (= Liturgie in perspectief 9) 73-94; cf.: R. GUARDINI: Vom Geist der Liturgie (Freiburg 1953[7]).

[67] GUARDINI: Vom Geist der Liturgie 56.

7. CONCLUSION

As I emphasized earlier, this contribution was programmatic in nature. There are already various explorations which have been done in which feast has been employed in critical interference as a 'concept in between'. In a general sense, we see this whole collection in that light. The exploration of feast offered here, can likewise be considered as an introduction to the chosen theme of feast and the organization of this project. The studies included in this collection can therefore also, to an important degree, be read in light of a critical 'concept in between' in which, by continuation, interference of qualities of cultus and culture, primary and secondary *loci*, designation and appropriation and past and present are brought to light.

ANDRÉ DROOGERS

FEASTS: A VIEW FROM CULTURAL ANTHROPOLOGY

If one wishes to discuss feasts from the perspective of cultural anthropology, one must first state that a feast is a cultural event. This starting
point allows several aspects to come into view. Thus the relevance of
culture for the understanding of celebrations must be taken into
account (section 2). In addition, the concept of ritual, which is what the
anthropologist would think of first in connection with feasts and is central to this collection's definition of feast, must be reviewed (section 3).
Also, some reference must be made to the ludic or playful aspect, which
is by no means reserved for the exclusive attention of anthropologists
but about which they, from the perspective of their discipline, can say
something (section 4). But first I would like to present a significant case
(section 1), or, as Fernandez would put it, "a revelatory incident",[1]
which can serve to illustrate and test the more abstract generalizations.
This carries with it the risk of making easy generalizations on the basis
of only one case, but it may also enliven the discussion. Though the case
is not European, it concerns descendants of European immigrants and
may serve for purposes of comparison. In any event, it will be helpful in
developing the cultural anthropological issues.

1. A SIGNIFICANT CASE[2]

While doing fieldwork in the small town of São Martinho (not its real
name) in the Brazilian state of Espírito Santo, one Sunday I witnessed
the 66th annual church feast of the local Lutheran parish. The feast was
held around or on the date on which the parish church had been inau-
gurated. Although Brazil has the largest number of Catholics in the

---

[1] James W. FERNANDEZ: *Persuasions and performances. The play of tropes in culture*
(Bloomington 1986) xi.
[2] This case was described earlier in André DROOGERS: De kerk viert feest... Een
leerzame zondag in een Braziliaans stadje, in Peter KLOOS (ed.): *Antropologie. Een juweel
van een vak* (Assen/Maastricht 1992) 25-32.

world, the majority of the local population of São Martinho is Lutheran. This is a result of massive emigration to this region in the 1860's by Pomeranians from what is now Northwest Poland. Even today the Pomeranian dialect is still used, next to high German and of course Portuguese, Brazil's national language. These languages are used not only in everyday conversation but also, for example, in church life and during the annual church feast. Some church services are still held in Pomeranian, including the sermon, which is delivered in that language by pastors who are of Pomeranian descent. The ancestors of today's Lutheran population of São Martinho and the surrounding rural area came to Brazil with the dream of farming land that they themselves owned. Many of them had worked as tenants in Pomerania but were evicted when the landowners decided to mechanize agriculture and to employ Polish day labourers. Other Pomeranians had gone to the United States and to other parts of Brazil.

For many the dream became a nightmare. They did not succeed in the new environment and had to sell their land to local businessmen, also of German descent, who in time became the large landowners of the region. In many cases the former owners continued as tenants on the land. Recently, the large landowners have started to evict their tenants, hiring cheap day labourers from the neighbouring state of Minas Gerais. History is repeating itself.

Although at the present virtually all São Martinenses of Pomeranian descent have Brazilian citizenship, many still think of themselves as Pomeranians, and view outsiders as Brazilians. This way of positioning themselves is reinforced by a self-imposed isolation that has marked the region for decades. Contacts with the Brazilian economy and politics were mediated by the local businessmen. Only recently, with improved transportation facilities, has the population become more mobile. More outsiders are coming in and tourism is a fledgling business, interestingly exploiting the Pomeranian folklore of the region.

As often happens in the case of immigrants, not only their language but also their religion helped the Pomeranians to maintain their cultural identity amidst the radical changes they have had to undergo. Yet the Lutheran church remained at a distance from large parts of the population for a long time, partly because, as in economics and politics, the local business elite dominated the church council. Moreover, until the seventies the pastors who served the parish were German and used high German as the language of the church, a language that the local elite families knew but in which the majority of the church members could not express themselves well. An illustration of the influence of the elite families is that their adult members were often asked to be godparents to the new-born children of the people who were dependent on them. When a child was baptized the family would often be accompanied by the godparents who served as translators. Through this practice the elite organized and reproduced its network of dependence.

But not all German pastors lived in harmony with the elite members of the church council, as both contested ownership of the parish. Brazilian pastors who worked in the parish of São Martinho and neighbouring towns during the last decades have introduced a more nationally oriented type of Lutheranism. Moreover, many of them were adepts of the theology of liberation that became typical of large parts of the Latin American Catholic church as well as some of the traditional Protestant churches. This entailed that they opposed the local economic elite, the same people who had traditionally served as mediators between laity and clergy. From the pulpit they condemned the excessive interest rates the businessmen imposed on customers who were not able to pay directly. The same businessmen's selfish role in the transfer of local agricultural products to state markets was also criticized. The double dependence of people on merchants who sold consumer products on credit at high interest rates and at the same time bought agricultural products from their debtors at self-determined low prices was condemned. The new pastors defended the rights of tenants and helped small landowners in legal disputes over land rights. Their sermons were intended to make the flock conscious of the class struggle of which their church members were a part and they used paradigmatic stories from the Bible, such as the exodus from Egypt, to make their point. Soon there were only a few members of the elite families left in the church council. One of the unintended consequences of the pastors' discourse was that middle-class church members started to worry about whether they belonged to the rich or to the poor. Yet, a significant portion of the membership assimilated the new religious views and changed their view of social, economic and political life. With this support, the pastors organized a successful campaign for the election of a progressive mayor of São Martinho, thus producing a situation in which for the first time in the town's history the economic elite was no longer politically dominant. Interestingly, the pastors' candidate was the grandson of one of the last German pastors who had had a long history of conflicts with the most dominant of elite families. His father, though employed as a civil servant, came from one of the other elite families.

The church feast is held in this setting. The Sunday begins with a church service in which the three languages, Portuguese, German and Pomeranian, are used. It is not as well attended as the usual Sunday services, since many parishioners are already preparing the activities that take place after the church service, a large bazaar with a bingo game as the main attraction, intended to raise funds for the maintenance of parish life, including the pastor's salary, house and car. Interestingly, one of the most influential members of the elite – and one of the few remaining upper-class members of the church council – is in charge of the central cashier's desk. The games on which one can spend money are varied. One, shuffleboard, is known as the Dutch game, *jogo holandês*, apparently introduced by Dutch immigrants in the region. Food and drinks are sold and at noon a full meal is served. During the day snacks are sold, among them *churrasquinho*, a modest version of the *churrasco*, the barbecue for which the gaucho south of Brazil is known. Pastors from the south who have worked in São Martinho are said to have introduced this part of the feast. Among the beverages is the locally distilled rum. A sound system is installed and used intensively for announcements but also for playing records. Virtually the whole population of the town, whether Lutheran or not, is present. Busses bring people from parishes from all over the state of Espírito Santo. São Martinho is one of the oldest centers of the Pomeranian immigration and from here many people have populated other parts of the state. Parish feasts are good opportunities to meet relatives and several such church feasts are announced via the sound system. About 2000 people are present at the bingo game. A special feature in the day's program is the uniformed brass band of church members. As on other Sundays the band accompanies the hymn singing during the church service. Later on, on the bandstand outside the church building, the band plays sacred music for a time but then switches to secular tunes of German origin but performed with a slight Brazilian accent. Brazilians from outside the region consider this brass band to be one of the typical aspects of the Pomeranian character and the band is presented as a tourist attraction. It also performs at other feasts in São Martinho.

The sermon in the church service is in Pomeranian, with a summary in Portuguese and its message is different from that of the bazaar and the bingo game. Its theme is mercy, both divine and human. Parish life should be characterized by mercy and members have to be merciful towards each other. Oppression and exploitation are condemned.

The activities after the service are not based on mercy but on chance and greed. In order to win and leave the feast richer than when one came, chance is needed. For the poor, the bingo game offers an opportunity to obtain a consumer product that is beyond their reach. A small amount of money may lead to an expensive product. The poor have little to spend and the rich have a greater chance statistically, because they can buy more tickets. Whereas the sermon represents the utopia of an alternative society, the bazaar and the bingo game mirror reality. To many lay people chance and not the class struggle explains the difference between poor and rich. The typical elite member would add that in addition to chance hard work is also important, suggesting that poor people do not work sufficiently hard. Moreover, the prizes at the bazaar and the bingo game have in part been donated by the local shop owners, who thus generate publicity and reinforce their position in local and church life. In general, the ambience during the bazaar is one of reproducing the existing social reality. People meet relatives and friends. Patrons from the elite families meet their clients, godfathers meet their godchildren. The local politicians, including the progressive mayor, are emphatically present and walk around, entertaining their network participants with drinks or buying them chances at attractions. As if to please the champions of social justice, chance has it that the bingo's first prize, a motorcycle, is won by a lower-class woman from a village near São Martinho. She and her husband are Catholics of non-Pomeranian descent and are neither white nor black. It is announced on the public sound system that they are tenants and the name of their landowner is mentioned, suggesting that he is part of their identity. At the end of the day the help of 'the friends from the Catholic religion' is publicly acknowledged. In a few months' time the small Catholic parish will have its annual feast and then the Lutheran majority will certainly come to participate. At sunset the feast is over, leaving a dozen men drunk. Some start a fight which is readily stopped by more sober bystanders.

2. A CULTURAL EVENT

The Lutheran church feast described above is not just a church event. It is a religious feast but it takes place in a specific societal context and has a particular form that can in part be traced back to church feasts in 19th-century Germany. The feast has Pomeranian elements, at least as preserved by the descendants of nineteenth-century's immigrants. But there is also a strong similarity to the feasts for the patron saint, celebrated annually in Brazilian Catholic parishes. The public reflects the region's history of migration streams. The use of high German, Pomeranian and Portuguese mirrors the multicultural situation in which the feast takes place. Moreover, it is a showcase of social relations such as those between godparents and godchildren as well as those between rich and poor. The contrast between the church service on the one hand and the bazaar and the bingo game on the other expresses the tension between the pastors and the elite. The emphasis on chance corresponds to the elite's ideology. The strong resilience of tradition obliges the pastors to comply with a feast that is in fact contrary to their message. Moreover, the feast is essential to the financial situation of the parish, including that of its pastors.

In the feast we observe a rather complex constellation of religious, social, ethnic, political, economic and also artistic and ludic aspects. Almost all dimensions of culture are present but each to their own degree and with differentiated connections between them. The constellation is even more complex because of the different (sub)cultural influences. Despite the complexity, people are very efficient in dealing with such a situation. They easily find their way through such a festive day. One may ask what enables them for such a task. The answer from cultural anthropology might be that culture is an exclusively human characteristic and that it exists due to the human gift of producing meaning. In the case described above people are able to decipher meaning in the feast because of their cultural capacity. They know at least why they go and what to expect.

But the concept of culture is two-sided. First, as in the concrete example given above, 'culture' stands for the localized customs and habits that are typical of a population group, in this case, people of Pomeranian descent. Reality is more complex, since there are elements from cultures other than that of the Pomeranians that play a role: several 'cultures' are involved, such as the Brazilian culture or, to be more specific, that of the non-Pomeranian Catholic inhabitants of São Martinho, and even Dutch and gaucho cultural elements are present. Because the local cultures operate in a wider context, they can be called subcultures. In any case, culture has a localized meaning. There are many such cultures. In this first sense culture has both a plural and a singular meaning. In the second sense 'culture' has only a singular meaning. It refers to something all human beings have in common, a capacity that leads to different results (many cultures) but is basic to human nature. Culture then refers to something like the capacity to give meaning to objects, persons, space, and time. In this sense culture always operates in a context that is cultural in the first sense. Nobody starts from scratch in building a culture. All people are socialized in some way so that they can function with some degree of efficiency and success. So the capacity to produce meaning operates within an already existing framework. Many meanings and parts of tradition are established and to avoid them demands effort on someone's part. Thus the pastors, even though they do not like the role that chance and greed play in the bazaar and the bingo game, are unable to abolish this part of the church anniversary feast. Pastors can be considered professional meaning-producers and yet they are not able to change the feast nor are they capable of producing another type of local society. What they were developing with some degree of success was a new type of faith, a new interpretation of the Christian message. There is usually a margin of freedom for those who find reason to change the current appreciation of objects, persons, space or time. The act of emigrating from Pomerania to Brazil is an example of such a change in the appreciation of space, of land, of dependence. In a situation where more cultural influences make themselves felt and people of different ethnicity and religion live together, the human gift of meaning-making and understanding is used to make one 'fluent' in more than one context. Catholics know how to behave at a Lutheran feast and vice versa. Non-Pomeranians do not feel that they are prohibited from participating in a typical Pomeranian activity. All persons have a whole repertoire of behavioural types that they activate when necessary.

The double characteristic of identity, whether religious, ethnic or political, on the one hand supports a more or less permanent profile, whereas on the other hand it is flexible and can be adapted as it becomes visible. It reflects the double meaning of culture, as a set of specific characteristics, typical of a category of people but also as a gift for understanding different cultural expressions, for changing accepted meanings and developing new ones. A participant in the Lutheran feast described in section 1 has, consciously or unconsciously, a set of meanings regarding the constellation of aspects and elements that is this particular feast.

Participation in a cultural setting is not at all homogeneous. Each category has its own identity and acts accordingly. Thus the pastors are active during the church service but do not play a significant role in the program of the rest of the day. They more or less tolerate the program after the church service. To many members the church service that opens the day is not the most essential element. This is also because they may be busy preparing the program for the rest of the day. The brass band changes roles when the service ends. The poor have another view of the feast than the rich. The local businessmen and politicians have their own interests when they support the feast and participate in it. To young people the feast may serve as a marriage market. The possibilities go on. And next year people may come with sets that are different from those of this year.

This case also shows that feasts cannot be understood without taking into account the power relations between the people present. Power can be described as the capacity to influence other people's behaviour, even against their will. During the church service the pastors' power is exercised, especially in the field of the production of meaning, whereas it almost disappears after the service. Then the lay organisers make their power felt with the objective of making the feast a financial success. Through their public appearance members of the local economic and political elite reproduce their power relations with their clients. The tenant woman who wins the motorcycle is publicly introduced as dependent on a landowner. The drunks who want to start a fight must submit to the power of those who prevent their quarrel.

3. FEAST AND RITUAL

It is interesting that the term feast is rarely used by anthropologists, with the possible exception of studies on Latin America where no fieldworker can escape the fiesta. In contrast to folklore studies, indexes of books in the anthropology of religion, whether textbooks or monographs, rarely feature the term. What is very much part of the anthropological vocabulary is the term 'ritual'. The terms feast and ritual do not coincide completely. The particularity of their discipline's vocabulary, linked with a field of study that for a long time was limited to 'exotic', non-literate, tribal cultures, led anthropologists to treat feast and ritual as almost synonymous, as if every ritual in tribal cultures is a feast and every feast a

ritual. It seems useful to research the differences. The editors of this collection prefer a definition of feast in which the term ritual appears as an
essential element: a feast is a moment or occasion on which people,
within the temporal order and at various stages in their lives, either individually or as a group or as a society, go beyond everyday life and in the
form of a ritual give expression to events that mark the personal and
social existence by means of a believing, religious or worldview orientation on meaning.[3]

The key elements in this definition refer to the connection of a feast
with time, the individual or social context of the feast, the extraordinary,
ritual form of the feast, and as a frame of reference for attributing meaning to it. A feast is a time-related, social, ritual event that takes place in
connection with beliefs of some sort. With regard to the term ritual, it
is clear that an emphasis is put on the exceptionality of the event. It goes
beyond everyday life. It seems that the special character of the feast also
refers to the fact that it is a celebration, an occasion for joy. Therefore
burial rituals and Good Friday rituals are excluded from the category
'feast': Not all rituals are feasts.

The implicit question when reference is made to ritual is, of course,
how ritual is defined. There has been much debate on this question.
One issue is whether the concept of ritual refers only to religious events
or also includes secular ceremonies. Admittedly, this point has been a
matter of a long debate in anthropology and religious studies, in which
there was a growing consciousness of the cultural constraints on the art
of defining. In a few words: Ritual exists because scholars from the
western academic subculture use the term, which is no guarantee that
it exists in reality (if there is such a thing as reality...). This has even
led some authors to abandon the term ritual altogether.[4] Others simply

[3] P. POST: Liturgische beweging en feestcultuur. Een landelijk onderzoeksprogramma, in *Jaarboek voor liturgie-onderzoek* 12 (1996) 21-55, p. 35. See also Part I of
this collection.

[4] A summary of the debate on the concept of ritual can be found in Barbara
BOUDEWIJNSE: The conceptualization of ritual. A history of its problematic aspects, in
Jaarboek voor liturgie-onderzoek 11 (1995) 31-56. Important recent contributions are
Catherine BELL: *Ritual theory, ritual practice* (New York and Oxford 1992); IDEM: *Ritual. Perspectives and dimensions* (Oxford 1997); Ronald GRIMES: *Ritual Criticism. Case
studies in its practice, essays on its theory* (Columbia SC 1990); Caroline HUMPHREY &
James LAIDLAW: *The archetypal actions of ritual. The theory of ritual illustrated by the Jain
rite of worship* (Oxford 1994). An influential article is Talal ASAD: Toward a genealogy
of the concept of ritual, in Talal ASAD: *Genealogies of religion. Discipline and reasons of*

distinguish between religious and secular rituals. To the degree of academic self-consciousness, there is almost a consensus that ritual should not be restricted to religious events. The reference to 'worldview' in the above-mentioned definition of feast is of course a very ample one, but should the focus in the discussion on what is a feast be limited to religion, it can again be stated that not all rituals are feasts. What else can be called typical of ritual? One recurring defining characteristic of the term 'ritual' is that it is behaviour of a standardized, formal and therefore repetitive type. This characteristic suggests that it has its own exclusive time and place. Its formality is a consequence of another supposed feature of ritual: the use of symbols with a more or less fixed meaning and which are part of a supposedly all-encompassing symbol system,[5] even though each performance can be shown to include minimal or more important changes, as I discovered in my Ph.D. research on male initiation rites of a Congolese tribe.[6]

A special feature of the use of symbols in ritual that is often mentioned is the use of inversion and reversal, an aspect that was emphasized by Victor Turner.[7] The issue is the alleged functionality of ritual that is sometimes considered sufficiently essential to include it in definitions of the concept. Although ritual's instrumentality is then often viewed as non-technical and based on symbolism (there is a difference between a ritual for a good harvest and the normal activities of the agricultural calendar), rituals are supposed to serve some goal, whether set by the performers or unknown to them, such as healing, controlling nature, reducing anxiety, solving a conflict, promoting social integration or guaranteeing the legitimization of power relations. The idea of a goal implies that a ritual is behaviour that is meant to communicate something either to the participants themselves, to outsiders or (in religious rituals) to spiritual beings of some kind: God, gods, spirits, saints etc.

power in Christianity and Islam (Baltimore and London 1993) 55-79. The most recent study is the posthumously published book of Roy A. RAPPAPORT: *Ritual and religion in the making of humanity* (Cambridge 1999).

[5] Some authors prefer not to include this symbolic dimension since they wish to include types of animal behaviour as ritual (e.g. RAPPAPORT: *Ritual and religion in the making of humanity* 25).

[6] André DROOGERS: *The dangerous journey. Symbolic aspects of boys' initiation among the Wagenia of Kisangani, Zaire* (The Hague, Paris and New York 1980).

[7] See e.g. Victor W. TURNER: *The ritual process, structure and anti-structure* (London and Chicago 1969).

With regard to instrumentality a distinction must be made between the emic goals that the performer and his or her audience formulate from within, and the researcher's etic goals as formulated from the outsider's point of view. Both perspectives on instrumentality have given rise to typologies of ritual, such as rites of passage, of affliction, of healing, of reconciliation, life cycle rituals, year cycle rituals, purification rituals, political rituals, and several more. In the above-mentioned doctoral thesis, I criticized the over-serious quest for social functions and defended the idea that a ritual can also be performed for the fun it brings.[8] Scholars seem to suffer from the temptation to turn that which is celebrated into something serious. In the next section I will return to the ludic aspect of feasts and rituals.

As to the comparison between feast and ritual, we may now ask what can be learned from this definitional exercise. If ritual is such a characteristic element of the definition of feast, as the editors of this collection want us to believe, what does the debate on the definition of ritual contribute to the understanding of feasts? The exceptionality that was presented as typical of the feast was also noted in the discussion on ritual. Though not mentioned explicitly in the above definition of feast, the role of symbols has been acclaimed in studies of feasts.[9] The use of the word meaning in that definition also points in that direction. The reference to time and the life cycle is similar to the attention given in ritual studies to rites of passage, especially as linked to the human biography. In other respects, the definition is not overly instrumental, which does not exclude the possibility that a feast may have one of the functions mentioned in the preceding paragraph. It seems that ritual and feast are terms that above all reflect different disciplinary and other parochial preferences, even though there is certainly some interdisciplinary contact and an overlap of citation. The field that is chosen for research influences the terminology used and the typologies that are developed. Therefore, it seems wise not to try to attempt any kind of uniformity but to explore the complementarity of the two approaches. This might be combined with a family resemblance use of definitions, accepting that exemplars differ and need not have all the characteristics that are succinctly put into a definition. It seems preferable to use definitions primarily in a heuristic manner, as a means of drawing attention

---

[8] DROOGERS: *The dangerous journey* 359-367.
[9] See e.g. Francisco TABORDA: *Sakrament: Praxis und Fest* (Düsseldorf 1988) 60-88.

to significant aspects and characteristics. Concepts should not become goals in themselves but remain subservient to actual research efforts. Therefore, I will not add to the amount of definitions that has already been produced. It appears to be more fruitful to draw the map of the options in this landscape full of pitfalls.

In the light of this general discussion of feast and ritual we might test the ideas developed so far through a reflection on the case of the Lutheran church feast. I have called it a feast, but is it a feast? Is it a ritual? What characteristics of feast and ritual that have been discussed above can be recognized in this case? Would a family resemblance approach work?

Following the characteristics of feast as defined above, it is clear that the anniversary of a church building's inauguration represents an occasion in time. It is also evident that it is a social event, not only for the members of the parish but also for the Catholics in the region, and for relatives from all over the state of Espírito Santo. The festivity of the occasion is very much present, though the joy is not so much caused by the fact that the church building has survived sixty-six turbulent years, nor, as the pastor would have it in his sermon, that God's mercy has been with the church members. The church feast is much more a fixed point on the calendar just as there are other festivities in São Martinho during the year, all justified by their exceptionality. The routine of everyday life is interrupted. It is an occasion to have fun, to spend some money and perhaps have the pleasure of winning something, whether it be some worthless gadget or the first prize of the bingo game. Ritual was among the terms mentioned in the definition, but I will discuss that aspect in a moment.

A form of belief, the last key word mentioned, is also present in this case of Lutheran modality. Yet the role Lutheran beliefs played during the day varied. They were emphatically present in the church service in the liturgy, in the hymns and prayers, and in the pastor's sermon. Yet the change in the role of the brass band, when it switched from hymns during the church service to secular music at the band stand, was representative of the rest of the feast. The church provided the occasion for the feast and reaped the financial benefits. But for the rest it was much more representative of the local society, including its ideology of success and chance. The feast also served as a platform for all the social, economic and political categories of actors that populate São Martinho and surroundings. The church thus served not only its own financial survival by organizing the feast, but also helped to reproduce the predominant social structure. In sum, in an idiosyncratic way the church feast was a feast that obeyed the definitional parameters the editors of this book developed.

What about ritual? The feast is repeated annually, following a more or less fixed scenario, starting with a church service, and afterwards continuing with a program of attractions, including bingo and its prizes. Space is used in a prescribed way: inside the sacred space of the church the service is held, outside and in the rooms and halls around the church the more secular part of the program takes place. This seems to indicate that in this case the ritual is religious as well as secular. The fact that the brass band starts playing sacred music after the church service but then moves on to secular tunes is an interesting example of a gradual transition between the religious and the secular parts of the program.

The use of symbols with a more or less fixed meaning, carrying a reference to something other than the symbol itself, can also be observed in the case of the São Martinho church feast, not only in the liturgy of the church service, a place so obviously symbolic that it needs no elaboration, but also, though less evidently, during the secular part of the feast. The brass band's uniform was an indication of the musicians' special status, and both in the church and outside they had a reserved place. The type of music they played was adapted to the phase of the day. The people who came to the feast were generally wearing their best clothes, indicating the festive character of the day. Even so these clothes functioned as indicators of differences in status and wealth. Money was spent in a different way, i.e. in the interest of the church's finances, and was therefore a token of the nature of the feast. Yet although money was easily spent, there was still the hope of winning more than what was spent. Money represented a strange mixture of charity and self-interest. The way drinks were offered was symbolic of the type of social relation. Despite a certain ambience of equality and brotherhood, dependence was present and reciprocity certainly not general. 'Can I offer you a beer?' may be an invitation to reproduce a relation of dependence. The gift carries obligations. The bingo game can be seen as an explicit symbol of consumerism. The Lutheran ownership of the feast is indirectly symbolized by the polite way in which at the end of the feast the non-Lutherans, especially Catholics, are thanked for their presence.

Another aspect of ritual concerns its non-technical functionality. The church feast corresponds to this non-technicality. The primary purpose is the celebration of an anniversary and in a more general sense an occasion to relax, to break from daily economic work. The church service is one way to celebrate and, for example, the hymns are chosen to emphasize this festive side. Although during the rest of the day a great deal of money is spent, nothing is produced or bought, even though economic values make themselves felt, as in the consumer's desire to win a prize, and also in the explicit purpose to reinforce the parish's finances. But most of the participants, even the poorest, are ready to spend money without expecting to gain something in return. The instrumentality of the feast takes on other forms, as we observed already, depending on the category the participant belongs to. But several serve their own social, political or economic purposes. Nonetheless, for all an important motivation for participating is to have fun, and this can hardly be called instrumental.

In sum, it seems that feast and ritual go hand in hand, though each term draws attention to different aspects. When looking at the church feast, the two main stages of the feast differ, but as such they contain elements that are proper to either feast or ritual. The family resemblance approach and a corresponding heuristic use of concepts seem valid.

4. THE LUDIC

A few words must be said about the ludic, an aspect that feast and ritual share and that also seems to play an important role in the Lutheran church feast.[10] I have defined the ludic as "the capacity to deal simultaneously and subjunctively with two or more ways of classifying reality".[11] The participants in the church feast share the ambience of the feast but know that there is another reality outside and after the feast. 'Simultaneously' refers to the player's 'double awareness',[12] combining different or even opposite perspectives and contexts. 'Subjunctively' is a term taken from Victor Turner, who distinguishes between the indicative

---

[10] The present discussion is based on ideas elaborated in two earlier publications, André DROOGERS: Turner, spel, en de verklaring van religie, in *Antropologische verkenningen* 13/4 (1994) 31-45; IDEM: Methodological ludism. Beyond religionism and reductionism, in Anton van HARSKAMP (ed.): *Conflicts in social science* (London 1996) 44-67.

[11] DROOGERS: Methodological ludism 53.

[12] P.W. PRUYSER: *A dynamic psychology of religion* (New York 1976) 190.

(the 'as is') and the subjunctive mood (the 'as if'),[13] thus characterizing the human gift of play to evoke another reality. In the last decades, a number of scholars have drawn attention to this aspect. *Homo ludens* was depicted by the Dutch historian J. Huizinga as a cultural being.[14] Myth and ritual are areas in which the ludic is very much present. Huizinga emphasized that playfulness has its own time and place and stands outside normal life yet fully occupies the player. Play does not serve a material interest and is not economic in nature. The non-technicality of ritual instrumentality was already mentioned earlier. According to Huizinga, play creates its own perfect order, even though it has an inbuilt uncertainty because of the element of chance. It has an important social function, uniting people in the same activity.[15] Through the evocation of another reality, the child's play, adult's play and religion are closely related.[16] It is clear that Huizinga was one of the first to emphasize the elements of exceptionality and non-technicality in play, as well as their relationship with feast and ritual. In the church feast we have shown the elements of chance, uncertainty and sociality. In addition, the feast had its own order, its own rules.

The cultural anthropologist Victor Turner showed how the marginal phase in rites of passage, between the separation and integration phases, is characterized by playfulness and inversion and therefore by innovation. This is possible because of the human "ludic capacity, to catch symbols in their movement, so to speak, and to play with their possibilities of form and meaning".[17] It is remarkable that Turner does not make a strict separation between work and play. Whereas play allows for all combinations of variables, work limits itself to the rational combinations that adapt means to goals. But to Turner ritual is a combination of work and play.[18] In his view the marginal phase is characterized by *communitas*, an absence of hierarchical social-structural relationships. As we saw, the church feast's *communitas* was not sufficiently strong to make the social hierarchy invisible. On the contrary, the feast contributed to

---

[13] Victor W. TURNER: *The anthropology of performance* (New York 1988) 25, 169.

[14] J. HUIZINGA: *Homo ludens. Proeve eener bepaling van het spel-element der cultuur* (Haarlem 1952).

[15] HUIZINGA: *Homo ludens* 5-14.

[16] HUIZINGA: *Homo ludens* 25.

[17] Victor W. TURNER: *From ritual to theatre. The human seriousness of play* (New York 1982) 23.

[18] TURNER: *From ritual to theatre* 34-35.

the reinforcement of dependence: *communitas* seems to be a matter of degree.[19] The ritual combination of work and play was visible in the secular part of the church feast.

The Dutch anthropologist of religion Jan van Baal has pointed to the similarity between play, religion and art.[20] All three bring a solution to the basic human problem of belonging and yet being separated, from reality, from fellow human beings, from nature.[21] Through play people create a separate but consciously fictitious world with which they can identify themselves; religion offers the possibility of communicating with another reality, taken to be real even though it can not be proven to exist; in art reality is presented as beautiful and therefore as enjoyable. Of these three the Lutheran church feast contained the elements of play and religion. The unproven reality that is central in the church service is matched by the fictitious reality that the attractions of the bazaar evoked.

The complex constellation of different frames of reference that was characteristic of the church feast forced the visitors to use their human gift to orient themselves simultaneously toward several orders for classifying the world. This capacity has been highlighted by scholars from cognitive anthropology, especially those who in the last decade have applied connectionist ideas to the field of culture.[22] Connectionism is an approach in cognitive studies that presents the thinking process as the simultaneous consultation of different generic archives in the human brain. These archives are connected by the person who is thinking. Verbalization seems to point to so-called sentential logic with just one frame of reference and with people thinking the way they speak. Connectionism suggests that different trails of thought can be followed simultaneously. Above I spoke about playfulness as a simultaneous combination of different ways of classifying reality. It is clear that the connectionist model shows that such a human capacity exists. People participating in

[19] Similar criticism can be found in J. EADE & M. SALLNOW (eds.): *Contesting the sacred. The anthropology of Christian pilgrimage* (London and New York 1991).

[20] J. VAN BAAL: *De boodschap der drie illusies. Overdenkingen over religie, kunst en spel* (Assen 1972).

[21] A similar insight can be found in D.W. WINNICOTT: *Playing and reality* (London 1971).

[22] For an overview see Roy G. D'ANDRADE: *The development of cognitive anthropology* (Cambridge 1995) esp. ch. 6. A more detailed account can be found in Claudia STRAUSS & Naomi QUINN: *A cognitive theory of cultural meaning* (Cambridge 1997).

a feast play with several archives, even though the feast can be so absorbing that the merrymakers forget their lives before or after the party. In any event, connectionism reinforces the idea of the important role of playfulness in a feast or, *mutatis mutandis*, in a ritual.

In this light it can be understood why symbols are essential to feast and ritual. The connectionist model of human thought corresponds with the basic idea that a symbol stands for something else. In other words: a person using a symbol refers simultaneously to the thing that serves as a symbol, and to the meaning or meanings it has.[23] Thus the cross on the church's bell tower is a construction of two metal bars but it refers to a whole christology, either sophisticated and with a plethora of meanings as in theological discourse or simple as in a believer's statement that the cross saves one from death. Two realities, with their corresponding archives, are connected. Symbols are a typical human propriety and the connectionist way of understanding human thinking clarifies how symbols work and why they are important in settings where playfulness is present as well. All three sectors that Van Baal mentioned – play, religion and art – depend for their functioning on symbols. Although the visitors to the church feast might have been as surprised to hear that they are constantly decoding symbols as Molière's protagonist was when he heard that he had been speaking prose during his whole life, it is clear that their behaviour had this background.

To end this section on a somewhat lighter note: It may be that multidisciplinary work on feast, festival and ritual demands a scholarly playfulness, switching from one concept to the other, from one disciplinary paradigm to another. Scholars, being as human as the people they study, share the gift for play and for a connectionist use of classifications of reality with the people who are the objects-subjects of their research. Here is another reason to follow not too unilateral a course and to be a member of the family that works along lines of family resemblance.

5. Conclusion

The concrete example of a Lutheran church feast in a small Brazilian town has helped us to make a summary inventory of the aspects that may be activated when using terms like feast and ritual. Feast and ritual

---

[23] See FERNANDEZ: *Persuasions and performances.*

were presented primarily as cultural phenomena. A plea was made for a certain degree of tolerant and multidisciplinary use, viewing terms more as means than as goals in themselves. In following this approach it was shown that contributions from different disciplines can be combined to reach a more encompassing understanding of feast and ritual. The dimension of play was given separate attention in order to clarify its role in both feast and ritual.

HERMAN L. BECK

CHRISTMAS AS IDENTITY MARKER
THREE ISLAMIC EXAMPLES

1. INTRODUCTION

"Meaning is in the eye of the beholder." With these words an Indian
participant opened his argument criticizing a paper on ritual at a congress of the International Association for the History of Religions at
Hildesheim, Germany, May 22-25, 1998. He illustrated his point by
referring to his first experience of Christmas. He had been invited by
Canadian friends to celebrate Christmas at their home. As a participant
observer, he was surprised by the rituals performed during the Christmas celebration. He could hardly reconcile them with the rules of
Christianity he had become acquainted with in India. Being a Hindu
himself, he had associated the observed rituals with Hinduism rather
than with Christianity. He gave some examples. The placing and decoration of an evergreen tree could be connected with what he knew as the
tree of life or with a vegetation or fertility cult. The gifts laid under the
tree and the carols sung near it could be thought of as offerings. The
lighting of candles in the Christmas tree reminded him of the lighting
of lamps during the Divali festival of Hinduism.[1]

This description of Christmas, half in jest, by a Hindu Indian cultural
anthropologist makes it convincingly clear that a religious phenomenon
takes its meaning, at least partly, from its beholder and his or her frame
of reference. Someone unfamiliar with Christianity will interpret Christmas rituals in another way than a person familiar with Christianity. I take
this outsider's interpretation of Christmas as the point of departure of this
contribution: What significance might an outsider attribute to the celebration of Christmas? Through this approach, it will become clear that
the meaning(s) attributed to Christmas by outsiders can differ in important ways from the meaning(s) it usually has in the eyes of Christian

---

[1] See, e.g., Robert JACKSON: Hindu Festivals, in Alan BROWN (ed.): *Festivals in
world religions* (London/New York 1986) 104-139, pp. 134-135.

believers or it has been credited with by scholars studying Christmas as a religious phenomenon. To make clear the difference between the insider's view of Christmas and that of the outsider, I take the example of some past and present views of orthodox Muslim religious scholars on Christmas. However, I will begin by summarizing some of the best-known results of the science of religion regarding Christmas, its meaning(s) and its social significance. Then, I will give three examples of Muslim reactions towards Christmas in the course of history. Finally, I will conclude that, by taking the outsider's position *vis-à-vis* Christmas, its role as identity marker between different religious communities becomes much clearer than by studying it only from the insider's point of view.

2. CHRISTMAS AND THE SCIENCE OF RELIGION

Most people accept without any hesitation the fact that the common Christian believer celebrates Christmas in remembrance of the birth of Jesus Christ. However, the reason why Christmas is celebrated on December 25, and the question of what can be considered the essential nature and function of Christmas, are central themes of many a study in the field of the science of religion. The results of these studies differ according to the approach taken as a starting point. In the science of religion, Christmas is generally studied along three lines, i.e., the historical, phenomenological, and anthropological approaches.[2]

Roughly speaking, it can be said that the historical approach in religious studies, as far as Christmas is concerned, was focused on the reconstruction of the origin and development of Christmas on the basis of written sources. Many historians of religion were especially interested in tracing pre-Christian and non-Christian elements in the celebration of Christmas. The celebration of the winter solstice and the birthday of *Sol Invictus* by the Romans were favourite examples to prove the celebration of Christmas on December 25 to have been influenced by the environment in which early Christians lived.[3] One of the most impor-

___

[2] Recently, Susan Roll has given a survey of some well-known historical, phenomenological, and anthropological studies on Christmas, Susan K. ROLL: *Toward the origins of Christmas* (= Liturgia condenda 5) (Kampen 1995).

[3] To mention only two examples, Friedrich HEILER: *Erscheinungsformen und Wesen der Religion* (Stuttgart 1961) 156 (although Heiler is a phenomenologist of religion rather than a historian of religion); Catherine BELL: *Ritual. Perspectives and dimensions*

tant reasons, according to some historians of religion, to celebrate Christ's birthday on the festival of the official Roman state god *Sol Invictus* was the wish of the Church to keep Christians from participating in this non-Christian feast.[4] A second explanation of the celebration of Christmas on December 25 is the so-called calculation theory according to which the conception of Christ took place on the same date as his death, which occurred on March 25, which implied that he was born nine months later on December 25.[5]

Some other favourite Christmas themes that have attracted the attention of both historians of religion and cultural anthropologists are, e.g., the evergreen tree which, like many other Christmas symbols, is very often linked with the original pre-Christian and non-Christian cultures from which the Christians originated,[6] and Santa Claus, whose origin is connected with various personalities, such as the shaman[7] and St Nicholas of Myra.[8] The gifts presented to children at Christmas are another theme which reveals pre-Christian and non-Christian influences on the feast. They are regarded as a transformation of the offerings once given to the deceased.[9] Presenting gifts to the children is even seen as one of the most essential elements of the celebration of Christmas.[10]

(New York and Oxford 1997) 104 (although Bell is a cultural anthropologist rather than a historian of religion).

[4] Cf., e.g., ROLL: *Origins* 53.

[5] Cf. ROLL: *Origins* 87 ff.

[6] See, e.g., Roger D. ABRAHAMS: The language of festivals. Celebrating the economy, in Victor TURNER (ed.): *Celebration. Studies in festivity and ritual* (Washington, D.C. 1982) 161-177, p. 175; Marko KERŠEVAN: Das slowenische Weihnachtsfest. Zur Volksfrömmigkeit in Jugoslawien, in Michael N. EBERTZ & Franz SCHULTHEIS (eds): *Volksfrömmigkeit in Europa. Beiträge zur Soziologie populärer Religiosität aus 14 Ländern* (Munich 1986) 177-186.

[7] To mention only one example: Tony van RENTERGHEM: *When Santa was a shaman. The ancient origins of Santa Claus and the Christmas tree* (St. Paul, MN, 1995).

[8] To mention only one example, John RANKIN: Christian festivals, in BROWN (ed.): *Festivals in world religions* 74-103, p. 84.

[9] KERŠEVAN: Das slowenische Weihnachtsfest 186.

[10] Wolfhart PANNENBERG: Mythos und Dogma im Weihnachtsfest, in Walter HAUG & Rainer WARNING (eds): *Das Fest* (Munich 1989) 53-63, p. 61. Pannenberg's position is very close to Ratschow's view who states that feast and offering are inseparably linked, see Carl Heinz RATSCHOW: Die Feste. Inbegriff sittlicher Gestalt, in Jan ASSMANN (ed.): *Das Fest und das Heilige. Religiöse Kontrapunkte zur Alltagswelt* (Gütersloh 1991) 234-246, p. 241.

Looking after the essence of a religious phenomenon can be considered a characteristic of the phenomenological approach in the science of religion. To reveal the 'true' nature of Christmas, it has been studied by phenomenologists as a feast separate from its historical and social context. Attention has especially been paid to Christmas as being originally a time of feasting, a 'time out of time',[11] rather than as a feast itself.[12] As 'time out of time', Christmas falls into the category of 'sacred time', which is an essential feature of Christmas, according to some phenomenologists.[13] Sacred time is inseparable from the myth of the origin of the feast. Accordingly, participants in a feast are living in the sacred time of the myth of the feast.[14]

Thus, another aspect belonging to the essentials of every feast is to remind its participants of the reason why the feast and its rituals were instituted, by telling its myth over and over again.[15] Through the myth and rituals of the feast, its participants remember what must not be forgotten, neither culturally nor religiously. The aspect of remembrance has become an important theme in studies of the feast. The feast has even been labelled the 'place of cultural remembrance'.[16] As for the Christian feast, and this is also true of Christmas, it is stated that it always revolves, in some way or other, around the commemoration of the Easter mystery.[17] The feast reminds its participants of their original

---

[11] The expression 'time out of time' was coined by Falassi: Alessandro FALASSI (ed.): *Time out of time. Essays on the festival* (Albuquerque 1987). Cf. G. VAN DER LEEUW: *Phänomenologie der Religion* (Tübingen 1970³) 439-445: "Das Fest ist das *tempus kat' exochén*, die aus dem Ganzen der Dauer als besonders mächtig 'herausgenommene' Zeit"; and also HEILER: *Erscheinungsformen* 150ff.

[12] Van der LEEUW: *Phänomenologie* 439-445: "... Weihnachten, ursprünglich nicht ein Fest, sondern eine Festzeit..."

[13] Mircea ELIADE: *Traité d'histoire des religions* (Nouvelle édition entièrement revue et corrigée. Paris 1975) 326ff. However, see Roll's critique of Eliade, ROLL: *Origins* 20f.

[14] E.g., Karl KERÉNYI: Vom Wesen des Festes, in Karl KERÉNYI: *Antike Religion* (Stuttgart 1995) 33-51, p. 41.

[15] KERÉNYI: Vom Wesen des Festes 44.

[16] A translation of Jan Assman's "... das Fest als ein... 'Ort' kultureller Erinnerung". See Jan ASSMANN: Der zweidimensionale Mensch. Das Fest als Medium des kollektiven Gedächtnisses, in Jan ASSMANN (Hrsg.): *Das Fest und das Heilige. Religiöse Kontrapunkte zur Alltagswelt* (Gütersloh 1991) 13-30, p. 13.

[17] Benedikt KRANEMANN: "Feiertags kommt das Vergessen..." Zu Deutung und Bedeutung des christlichen Festes in moderner Gesellschaft, in *Liturgisches Jahrbuch* 46 (1996) 3-22, p. 6.

religious identity. By celebrating the feast, the participants find their individual and communal identity consolidated. They experience community spirit, solidarity, continuity of their shared history and heritage, and cultural and religious unity.[18] Because the feast creates a sense of community among the participants and confirms their identity, it is often thought that adherents of other religions should not participate in the feast.[19]

In the anthropological approach to the feast, identity and solidarity have also always been pivotal themes. However, this was not discovered through the aspect of remembrance but, primarily, by paying special attention to the rituals and ceremonies of the feast.[20] Like ritual the function of a feast is to consolidate the community and its identity over and over again, both on the individual and communal levels. In general, it can be said that, in the anthropological approach to the feast, priority was given to the function of the feast and its social significance over its symbolic meaning(s). A recent study of Christmas mumming in Newfoundland is an appropriate example of an anthropological approach focusing on the social significance of the celebration of Christmas. The importance of Christmas mumming for the intensification of collective solidarity is stressed. It is shown that these kinds of rituals are closely linked with the wish to distinguish "between the inside of the community, its social relationships, and the strangerhood that lies beyond it".[21] This search for the social significance of the feast is a rewarding exercise, in particular when applied to the study of the position of minorities in a situation of religious pluralism. Therefore, I will now turn to three examples of Muslim reactions to Christmas in the course of history.

---

[18] Cf., e.g., ASSMANN: Der zweidimensionale Mensch 22; Winfried GEBHARDT: Der Reiz des Ausseralltäglichen. Zur Soziologie des Festes, in Bernhard CASPER & Walter SPARN (eds): *Alltag und Transzendenz. Studien zur religiösen Erfahrung in der gegenwärtigen Gesellschaft* (Freiburg/München 1992) 67-88, p. 76; Helge GERNDT: Festkultur als Forschungsfeld, in *Ethnologia Flandrica* (1991) 7-24, p. 18.

[19] Francisco TABORDA: *Sakramente. Praxis und Fest* (Düsseldorf 1988) 90.

[20] To mention only one example, Herman TAK: Feest en ritueel; enkele theoretische kanttekeningen, in Trees ANDREE & Cok BAKKER (eds): *Feesten vieren in verleden en heden. Visies vanuit vijf wereldgodsdiensten* (Zoetermeer 1997) 11-17.

[21] Don HANDELMAN: *Models and mirrors: Towards an anthropology of public events* (New York/Oxford 1998; first published 1990) 144.

3. THREE EXAMPLES OF MUSLIM REACTIONS TO CHRISTMAS

Again and again, it turns out that Muslims, in particular those living as a minority in a non-Muslim, so-called Christian country, struggle to decide on their attitude towards Christmas and its celebration.[22] In the Netherlands, this struggle emerges most prominently with regard to Muslim children attending Christian and so-called 'encounter' schools. The question is frequently raised of whether or not they can be forced to participate in the celebration of Christmas.[23] An imam in Amsterdam has recently tried to resolve the question of whether or not Muslims in the Netherlands should attend Christmas celebrations by issuing a *fatwa*, a religious advice, in which he declared attendance forbidden.[24] However, this struggle is not a recent phenomenon. In the course of the history of Islam, the celebration of Christmas seems to have held great attraction for Muslims. It has been tried to dissuade Muslims from participating in the celebration of Christmas in several ways. Three examples from different periods of Islamic history and different regions of the Muslim world will be given to show in which ways Muslims have reacted to the celebration of Christmas.

(1) The first example of the way Muslims have reacted to Christmas is opposing it by celebrating the *mawlid al-nabi*, the birthday festival of Muhammad, the prophet of Islam.[25] The celebration of Christmas is said to have had some influence on the origin of the birthday festival of Muhammad. This opinion is expressed in the following way:

> The Christmas festival with its humming markets, country fairs, gifts, flowers, candles and, above all, its jostling gay crowds not only became an important social event in the life of popular Islam but also supervened on

---

[22] E.g., Yvonne Yazbeck HADDAD & Adair T. LUMMIS: *Islamic Values in the United States. A comparative study* (New York - Oxford) 93 ff.

[23] To mention only one example, Gé SPEELMAN: Kerstfeest in een interreligieuze school: de Juliana van Stolbergschool uit Ede, in *Begrip* 106 (17 [1991]) 16-21.

[24] I owe this information to an oral communication by Prof. P.S. van Koningsveld of Leiden University.

[25] For the early history and development of Muhammad's birthday festival, see N.J.G. KAPTEIN: *Muhammad's birthday festival. Early history in the central Muslim lands and development in the Muslim West until the 10th/16th Century* (Leiden etc. 1993).

a native tendency to glorify in comparable terms and almost mythify the Prophet of Islam in the form of what is known as the *Maulid* festival, celebrated in commemoration of the birthday of Muhammad.[26]

Apparently, the celebration of Christmas in certain regions of the Muslim world, sometimes became so popular that Muslim officials felt the urge to take measures to counterbalance its appeal. A splendid example is the case of Abu 'l-'Abbas al-'Azafi (1162-1236), cadi of Ceuta.[27] This North Moroccan city was known for its Christian inhabitants from different origins, who(se families) had lived in Ceuta at least since the beginning of the twelfth century. Some Christians were Genoese traders or Catalonian merchants, others belonged to the powerful Christian militia stationed in the city.[28] The feasts celebrated by the Christians of Ceuta seemed to have exerted great attraction for many a Muslim fellow townsman, just as Muslims in al-Andalus were said to have been attracted to the Christian feasts celebrated in Muslim Spain.[29] Now, cadi Abu 'l-'Abbas al-'Azafi is believed to have introduced the celebration of Muhammad's birthday festival in the western part of the Muslim world as a reaction to the participation in Christmas celebrations by his Muslim fellow townsmen. He legitimized this introduction by writing that he wanted "… to counteract the custom adopted by the Muslims of the Straits, of participating in the Christmas celebrations of the local Christian population, including the Christmas Eve revel".[30] To give his deci-

---

[26] Muhammad Umar MEMON: *Ibn Taimiya's struggle against popular religion. With an annotated translation of his Kitab iqtida' as-sirat al-mustaqim mukhalafat ashab al-jahim* (The Hague/Paris 1976) 2.

[27] KAPTEIN: *Muhammad's birthday festival* 76.

[28] IBN ABI ZAR': *Al-Anis al-mutrib bi-rawd al-kirtas fi akhbar muluk al-Maghrib wa ta'rikh madinat Fas* (Rabat 1973) 249-254; H. TERRASSE: *Histoire du Maroc des origines à l'établissement du Protectorat français* I-II (Casablanca 1949-1950) I 248; H.R. SINGER: Ceuta, in *Lexikon des Mittelalters* II (München/Zürich 1983) 1643-1644.

[29] I owe this information to A. LJAMAI who is preparing a PhD thesis entitled *Ibn Hazm et la polémique Islamo-Chrétienne dans l'histoire de l'Islam*. In a discussion regarding these Christian feasts celebrated by Muslim women, Prof. P.S. van Koningsveld (Leiden University), A. Ljamai, and I agreed that it is, probably, not too bold a proposition to suppose that the Muslims of al-Andalus and Ceuta were participating in Christmas celebrations and other Christian feasts not only because of their cheerfulness and sociability but, in particular, because of the existing family ties between Muslims and Christians in these regions.

[30] P. SHINAR: Traditional and reformist Mawlid celebrations in the Maghrib, in Myriam ROSEN-AYALON (ed.): *Studies in memory of Gaston Wiet* (Jerusalem 1977) 371-413, p. 376.

sion a well-founded basis, Abu 'l-'Abbas al-'Azafi claimed that the plan had been inspired by God.[31]

The celebration of the *Mawlid al-nabi* in Eğirdir, a small town in contemporary Turkey, has also been studied from the perspective of counterweighing Christmas. Muslims living in this region of Turkey around 1920 were confronted with Greek Orthodox Christians in relation to whom they had to define their own identity. However, in defining their own identity, these Muslims adopted many Christian elements. This became clearest in the celebration of Muhammad's birthday festival and the panegyrical poems recited in honour of the Prophet. Both Muhammad's birthday festival and the content of the panegyrical poems are considered to be Muslim transformations of Christmas and of Christian stories revolving around Jesus and his mother.[32]

(2) The second example of the way Muslims have reacted to Christmas is opposing it by proving it to be a heresy for Muslims. As a result, Muslims had to keep themselves separated from Christmas. The best-known representative of this view in Islamic history is the eminent and influential Hanbali theologian and jurisconsult Ibn Taymiyya (1263-1328), who spent his life partly in Syria and Egypt.[33] Ibn Taymiyya was an indefatigable champion of the orthodox Muslim values and standards. In his many writings, he denounced the religious and social abuses he observed among his fellow believers. One of the evils threatening the purity and integrity of the Muslim community was, according to Ibn Taymiyya, the enormous magic Christian feasts possessed for Muslims. However, what he was fighting "was not so much a question of Muslim participation in primary acts of worship, which, apart from walking in popular processions on occasions of Christians feasts, does not seem to have occurred", but "Muslim participation in the secondary events which surround the feasts".[34]

---

[31] KAPTEIN: *Muhammad's birthday festival* 83.

[32] Nancy TAPPER & Richard TAPPER: The birth of the Prophet. Ritual and gender in Turkish Islam, in *Man* 22 (1987) 69-92. Although I concur with the Tappers' view that the celebration of the *mawlid al-nabi* has something to do with the wish of the local Muslims to define their identity *vis-à-vis* the Greek Orthodox Christians, I share a great deal of the severe criticism regarding their article by Nadia ABU-ZAHRA: *The pure and powerful. Studies in contemporary Muslim society* (Reading 1997) 41-49.

[33] For Ibn Taymiyya, see H. LAOUST: Ibn Taymiyya, in *The Encyclopaedia of Islam. New edition* s.v.

[34] Thomas F. MICHEL: *A Muslim theologian's response to Christianity. Ibn Taymiyya's Al-Jawab al-Sahih.* Edited and translated by Thomas F. Michel (Delmar/New York 1984) 82.

In fact, Ibn Taymiyya condemned the celebration of Christmas only in passing, for example, in his treatise against popular religion. In this work, he defended the opinion that except for the two official festivals acknowledged by the Islamic Law, the Festival of Breaking the Fast and the Festival of Sacrifice, all other festivals were to be rated among popular religion. These kinds of festival phenomena can be defined, according to Ibn Taymiyya, on the basis of the elements of time, location, and rites.[35] By means of these elements, he showed Christmas to be un-Islamic. He concluded, with regard to Christmas:

> The ceremonies undertaken by many people during winter on 24 December, which they claim to be the birthday of Jesus,… Kindling fires, preparing foods, lighting candles – in short, all practices of this day are disreputable. Making a festival out of this birthday is a Christian cult and has no basis in Islamic faith.[36]

Ibn Taymiyya not only forbade his fellow believers to participate in the celebration of Christmas or to imitate its ceremonies,[37] he also stated that Muslims should not support Christians celebrating Christmas in one way or another, for example, by selling them "… anything needed for the feast or giving them presents".[38] By his very rigid stance, Ibn Taymiyya wanted to prevent the Islamic community from becoming contaminated with heresies through Christianity. In fact, he advised Muslims to separate themselves from Christians in order not to become infected with unbelief. The danger was the greater as the Christian festivals were very popular among Muslims.[39] However, for the record, it is worthwhile mentioning that Ibn Taymiyya and, in the course of history, many orthodox Muslim scholars also condemned the celebration of Muhammad's birthday festival as a heresy.[40]

(3) The third example of the way Muslims have reacted to Christmas is opposing it by forbidding Muslims to attend Christmas celebrations by way of a *fatwa*, a religious advice. Actually, the third example is very close to the second one. A very instructive example is the case of the

---

[35] MEMON: *Ibn Taimiya's struggle* 11ff.
[36] MEMON: *Ibn Taimiya's struggle* 222.
[37] MEMON: *Ibn Taimiya's struggle* 219, 243.
[38] MICHEL: *A Muslim theologian's response* 82.
[39] MICHEL: *A Muslim theologian's response* 83, 85.
[40] MEMON: *Ibn Taymiyya's struggle* 13.

fatwa issued by the Indonesian Council of Religious Scholars in March 1981.[41]

Indonesia is not an Islamic state, although 87 percent of its inhabitants are Muslims, making it the country with the largest Muslim population on earth. Next to Islam, four other religions have been officially recognized by the Indonesian government since the mid-1970s, viz. Protestantism, Catholicism, Hinduism, and Buddhism. The Protestants and Catholics form a Christian minority of some 9 percent with proportionately much stronger economical and political powers than the Muslim majority. This is partly a heritage of the Dutch colonial period. Indonesian Muslims often have the feeling that they are the minority instead of the Christians.[42] The Christians live under continuous suspicion, especially since the abortive coup of September 30, 1965, because they are suspected by the Muslims of wanting to christianize Indonesia completely.[43] The Christians are accused of taking advantage of the poverty and ignorance of many illiterate Muslims, urging them to convert to Christianity by promising education, rice, and all kinds of material goods.[44]

The celebration of Christmas in Indonesia is given a disproportionate amount of public attention compared to the number of Christians living in the country. During the month of December, some Indonesian cities are a match for cities in England and the United States as to their Christmas decorations. Christmas carols are heard everywhere and the Christmas mood permeates social life. Muslims are invited on a large

---

[41] See Mohammad Atho MUDZHAR: *Fatwa-Fatwa Majelis Ulama Indonesia: Sebuah Studi tentang Pemikiran Hukum Islam di Indonesia 1975-1988 / Fatwas of The Council of Indonesia Ulama. A study of Islamic legal thought in Indonesia 1975-1988* (Jakarta 1993) 117-123/101-106; Mohamad Atho MUDZHAR: The Council of Indonesian 'Ulama' on Muslims' attendance at Christmas celebrations, in Muhammad Khalid MASUD, Brinkley MESSICK & David S. POWERS (eds): *Islamic legal interpretation. Muftis and their Fatwas* (Cambridge, MA/London 1996) 230-241.

[42] Herman Leonard BECK: *De Islam en Nederland. Romancing religion?* (Tilburg 1992) 5f.

[43] Two examples of influential books written by prominent Muslims, Lukman HAKIEM (ed.): *Fakta dan data usaha-usaha kristenisasi Indonesia* (Jakarta 1991); M. NATSIR: *Islam dan Kristen di Indonesia* (Jakarta 1969). Cf. also MUDZHAR: The Council of Indonesian 'Ulama' 231.

[44] Muhammad RASJIDI: The role of Christian missions in the Indonesian experience, in *International review of mission* 65 (1976) 427-438, p. 429ff. Cf. also MUDZHAR: The Council of Indonesian 'Ulama' 232.

scale to attend the celebrations of Christmas, an invitation which is often happily accepted for various reasons. One of the reasons is the wish of many Indonesians to live in a harmonious way with their fellow countrymen, or, stated negatively, the wish not to be accused of intolerance against the Christians.[45] Another reason is the fact that it is not an uncommon phenomenon in Indonesia to have families with members belonging to different religions, without this intermingling causing any problem. Usually, the family members attend each other's religious feasts and festivals.

The *fatwa* issued by the Indonesian Council of Religious Scholars in March 1981 has to be understood against the background of the information given in the preceding two paragraphs. Since Christmas was becoming increasingly popular both in family and public life, the Muslim authorities in Indonesia feared it to be a strong temptation for Muslims attending its celebration. Misunderstanding the theological and ritual value of the Christmas celebration, they might inadvertantly violate the provisions of the Islamic law or forget the doctrines of the Islamic faith. However, the greatest danger lay in the risk of Muslims becoming seduced by attending Christmas celebrations into conversion to Christianity.[46] Basically, Christians were suspected of using Christmas as part of their conversion strategy.

According to the *fatwa* of the Indonesian Council of Religious Scholars, the tide could only be turned by declaring the attendance of Christmas celebrations completely forbidden for Muslims. The Council put forward some interesting theological arguments in support of its interdiction. The ban was underpinned by a number of Koran verses on the status of Jesus according to Islam. Jesus is considered a messenger and prophet of God. Muslims have to hold Jesus in high esteem, but in no way are they allowed to believe Jesus to be God or the son of God. God is the One and the Only. The Christian belief in the Trinity is condemned as polytheism and unbelief.[47] The significance of this *fatwa* for the Council of Indonesian Religious Scholars emerged from the fact that it refused to revoke or withdraw the *fatwa*, notwithstanding the

[45] MUDZHAR: *Fatwas* 118/101; MUDZHAR: The Council of Indonesian 'Ulama' 233.
[46] MUDZHAR: *Fatwas* 118/101; MUDZHAR: The Council of Indonesian 'Ulama' 233.
[47] MUDZHAR: *Fatwas* 119ff/103ff; MUDZHAR: The Council of Indonesian 'Ulama' 238ff.

strong pressure exerted by the Indonesian government claiming it to be a dangerous threat to the stability of the country by harming the inter-religious harmony of Indonesian society.[48]

4. CHRISTMAS AS IDENTITY MARKER

Although both well-known scholars of the science of religion and ordi-nary lay persons claim that the celebration of Christmas does not cause any problem for Muslims, history and contemporary daily practice prove the opposite, as is shown by the three examples in the preceding section.[49] The experiences at the Christian and so-called 'encounter' schools in the Netherlands, the *fatwa* of the Amsterdam imam and many other cases only confirm the view that "Of all the widely cele-brated holidays…, Christmas seems to provide the greatest dilemma for Muslim families".[50]

Indeed, the celebration of Christmas causes enormous problems for Muslims living in modern non-Muslim countries. In many places, Christmas has lost a great deal of its religious significance and has changed into an important social and commercial event with a great attraction for non-Christians. To participate in this event is sometimes considered to be a symbol of modernity and a token of integration into the host society for Muslims living in a non-Muslim country. Especially when children are involved and Christmas has become a family affair,[51]

---

[48] MUDZHAR: *Fatwas* 122ff/105ff; MUDZHAR: The Council of Indonesian 'Ulama' 236ff.

[49] As an example of a well-known scholar of the science of religion I mention Geof-frey PARRINDER: *Worship in the world's religions* (London repr. 1974) 187: "Today Mus-lims will say that Christians have no monopoly of Jesus and there is no reason why a Muslim should not celebrate Christmas". As an example of a lay person, I quote a high positioned official of the Palestinian Department of Education as rendered by Caroline de GRUYTER: De vrolijke school, in *NRC Handelsblad* (20.02.1999) Z6: "Here, hun-dreds of Muslim families celebrate Christmas and the feast of St Nicholas. As for Cairo, the city is one huge Christmas tree during the month of December. In this part of the world, there is no need for people to be afraid that their children will mix up the two cultures, because their identity is clear".

[50] HADDAD & LUMMIS: *Islamic values* 93.

[51] See, e.g., the very interesting case of Turkish Muslim labour migrants in Germany who conflate New Year's Eve celebration and its firework displays with Christmas: Lale YALÇIN-HECKMANN: Are fireworks Islamic? Towards an understanding of Turkish migrants and Islam in Germany, in Charles STEWART and Rosalind SHAW (eds.): *Syn-*

it is almost impossible not to take a stand regarding Christmas. Muslims could participate in its celebration in an adapted and transformed form, in a way that makes it crystal clear that they want to be considered integrated into the host society without, however, sacrificing their original social and religious identity. This seems to be the case with the Christmas celebration of some Sikh and Hindu Punjabi families living in the West London suburb of Southall.[52]

The three examples of the preceding section, the experiences at the Christian and so-called 'encounter' schools in the Netherlands, the *fatwa* of the Amsterdam imam and many other cases show that orthodox Muslim religious scholars are not inclined to allow their fellow believers to participate, neither in Christmas celebrations nor in an adapted or transformed Muslim version of this Christian feast. Christmas is celebrated by Christians in remembrance of (the birth of) Jesus Christ who is believed to be God and the Son of God. This is an affront to the Islamic faith, according to which Jesus is only a human being, albeit an esteemed prophet of God. From this point of view, the celebration of Christmas leads to unbelief and polytheism. Besides, Christmas is not included into the feasts officially recognized by the Islamic law. From this point of view, celebrating Christmas is a heresy. Therefore, to opt for participation, adaptation, or transformation as far as Christmas is concerned means, according to orthodox Muslim religious scholars, a violation of both the Islamic faith and the Islamic law. It would damage the purity and integrity of the community of believers which they consider to be the core of the social identity of the Muslim. Because the social identity is the most important component of the human self-concept,[53] of which it is feared that it will become irreparably broken as a result of a damaged community of believers, it is understandable why orthodox Muslim religious scholars, past and present, were and are opposed to Christmas asd its celebration. Participation of Muslims in Christmas celebrations would ruin their Islamic identity.

---

cretism/anti-syncretism. The politics of religious synthesis (London/New York 1994) 178-195, p. 184ff. It is important to pay attention to the view of Pannenberg who believes that Christmas owes its continuing popularity probably to the fact that it is a family feast: PANNENBERG: Mythos und Dogma 56.

[52] Gerd BAUMANN: Ritual implicates 'others'. Rereading Durkheim in a plural society, in Daniel de COPPET (ed.): *Understanding rituals* (London/New York 1992) 97-116.

[53] William B. GUDYKUNST & Young Yun KIM: *Communicating with strangers. An approach to intercultural communication* (Second edition, New York etc. 1992) 67ff.

The study of a religious phenomenon from an outsider's point of view reveals elements of this phenomenon which, otherwise, would stay undiscovered, underexposed, or underestimated. To study Christmas and its celebration from the perspective of orthodox Muslim religious scholars validates, on the one hand, the opinion that the function of the celebration of Christmas is to bind together the community of its Christian participants and to consolidate their identity again and again. On the other hand, however, the severe opposition of orthodox Muslim religious scholars to the participation of their fellow believers in Christmas celebrations shows that Christmas also serves as an identity marker for non-Christians. In the case of Islam, to participate or not in the celebration of Christmas marks, according to orthodox Muslim religious scholars, the difference between those believers who want to keep the purity and integrity of the Muslim community entirely intact and thus to maintain their Islamic self-concept and social identity, and those Muslims who are inclined to give up their pristine Islamic identity. In fact, Christmas serves as an identity marker in several ways as far as Islam is concerned. It not only differentiates between the adherents of Islam and Christianity, but also between Muslims themselves.

Rein Nauta

THE OTHER SIDE OF PARADISE
BOREDOM AND DISAPPOINTMENT AS THREATS TO FESTIVITY

For a psychologist of religion the study of festivity is particularly rewarding because the ambiguous nature of any party or feast[1] can only be understood in the context of faith and doubt, of hope and disappointment. Hoping to transcend the frustrations of every day life, longing for a glimpse of paradise, people engage in all kinds of festivity, but too often festal celebrations result in the opposite of what they intend to perform.[2] Frustration and boredom constitute the other side of paradise, a paradise so eagerly sought when the routines of ordinary life are forgotten in the flush of festivity. As a consequence, although the hope for a better life may never be stilled, people become scared of the unavoidable disappointment inherent in any trial to escape the imperfections and deficiencies of life as it is lived. But it is perhaps only in reflection on this boredom and disappointment, that the essence of festivity may be found to be an act of faith. Whenever and wherever feasts are celebrated and people are willing to throw a party, the practice of faith must be essential to any such form of festivity. Festivity is always concerned with the 'as if', with pretention, with belief against all evidence of the opposite of what will be believed. It is from this perspective of festivity as a performative act[3] that the religious dynamic of festivity in its ambiguous expression is studied in this contribution.

---

[1] 'Festivity' is used as a general reference to any festive gathering. The term 'feast' is commonly used in relation to some ecclesiastical celebration or to the banquet given in the context of such an occasion. In this paper several alternatives are used (fête, festal, festive, celebration etc.) when it is deemed necessary to avoid the familiarity or banality of 'party' or the too religious and nutritional connotations of 'feast'.

[2] E.g. D. KORSCH: Weihnachten – Menschwerdung Gottes und Fest der Familie – systematisch-theologische Gedanken zu gelebter Religion, in *International journal of practical theology* 2 (1999) 213-228.

1. To celebrate

Festivity represents the extraordinary. In their exuberance and abundance, fêtes and festivals constitute a break with the commonplace. The festal merry-making transforms us into a new person, causes us to be born again. When celebrating singing and dancing are required, food and drink should be plentiful, decorations and happiness must abound, all in order to express excess and ecstasy.[4]

Whereas exuberance characterizes the outward appearance of any festive gathering, transcendence constitutes the essence of festivity. When celebrating we step out of the transitoriness of everyday life. Parties and feasts break through the limits of the here and now. They are linked to creation and have no end. Parties are endless, they transcend finality.[5]

Celebrating a party is not to flee the commonplace; the ordinary is not denied but rather confirmed, albeit conditionally, as provisional and transitory. By occasionally enjoying oneself at some party or another, the ordinary is made bearable. To be able to share in any festive joy and revelry requires an act of faith and of trust. Festivity can best be compared to an act of common prayer. One can only start praying if one believes the prayer will be heard, but only when actively praying can one accept that this is not the case. This same pragmatic ambiguity also characterizes festivity. In surrendering oneself to the festal and festive, what appeared to be self-evident is subjected to criticism. Festivity both criticizes and makes the ordinary possible by transcending the commonplace. Festal parties are signs of hope. Because feasts are celebrated, the commonplace can be accepted as imperfect, as fragmentary – not just as a ruin of failed expectations, but as a promise of fullfilment in the future to come.[6]

[3] Cf. H.M. Kuitert: Ervaring als toegang tot de religieuze werkelijkheid, in *Nederlands theologisch tijdschrift* 32 (1978) 177-198. A performative act is an act which validates or even constitutes a reality by its reaction to that reality, examples may be found in the domain of faith and love, and also in that of festivity. Cf. R. Nauta: *Ik geloof het wel* (Assen 1995) 33.

[4] O. Marquard: Kleine Philosophie des Festes, in U. Schulz (ed.): *Das Fest* (Munich 1988) 413-420; G.H. Martin: *Fest und Alltag – Bausteine zu einer Theorie des Festes* (Stuttgart 1973); G.H. Martin: Fest und Feiertage – ethisch, in *Theologische Realenzyklopädie* XI (Berlin 1983) 132-134.

[5] K. Albert: Metaphysik des Festes, in *Zeitschrift für Religion und Geistesgeschichte* 19 (1967) 140-152.

[6] H. Luther: *Religion und Alltag. Bausteine zu einer praktischen Theologie des Subjekts* (Stuttgart 1992) 170.

2. RISK AND DANGER

However, for those invited to share in a celebration, participation is a risky business. Because of the intensity of togetherness and interaction in a festive occasion, the balance between community and loneliness, between freedom and obligation, will be disturbed. Festal happenings bolster the public order, but threaten the individual existence. Although parties are celebrations of *communitas*, they do so by drawing boundaries distinguishing the initiates from the excluded. In a sense, parties may transcend the mundane only in secret, since an all too openly exclusive festivity would arouse envy and resentment among those who have been excluded from participation. If this is the case, the party only confirms everyday inequality rather then transcending it. This transcendence, so essential to the meaning of festivity, seems only possible where the party is public and participation is based on a free choice of the guests. In fact, only spectators' games like the football world championship or Wimbledon tennis matches, or lotteries that are broadcasted on television, make public transcendence and general participation possible. At the same time, it provides food for thought that such inclusive parties are often a glorification of materialism and violence, the incorporated sense of community being one of a collection of separate individuals.

But even where there is active participation, it turns out that parties are not just a source of delight but can also be the cause of much hidden sorrow. Besides the exclusive, excluding aspects, the Swedish ethnologist Bringéus[7] discusses some other sad and tragic effects of what should be considered to be a festive drama.

(1) A party is demanding – it just appears to express freedom and non–commitment. A Dutchman who stands a round in a pub expects free drinks for the rest of the evening. At a party, too, (reflexive) reciprocity is the norm: it is the old *quid pro quo*. Parties also require the right dress. Anyone wearing the wrong suit or the wrong dress will feel displaced, or, as in the Biblical parable of the royal wedding meal (Matthew 22:12-13), will be cast into the outer darkness. At a party, freedom is celebrated, but at the same time, a variety of behavioural rules apply, the observance of which shows that one knows how to

---

[7] N.-A. BRINGÉUS: Bitte kein Feier – oder das Fest als Trauma, in *Hessische Blätter für Volk– und Kulturforschung* N.F. 7/8 (1978) 35-49.

behave and, therefore, that one belongs. Rather than liberating their existence, a party reinforces the pressure of norms on the party-goers. It is part of the game to be happy at parties, hence happiness is required. This is a norm that at quite a number of family gatherings leads to considerable hidden sadness. Not everybody can withstand that pressure – being alone at Christmas, at one's own birthday evokes feelings of guilt rather than feelings of regret or sorrow. That which deviates from the norm is experienced as personal failure.

(2) A party coerces – party-goers are necessary for the party, which is why guests must be invited to festive occasions. The consequence of this is that some are ruined by a party – materially by the large debt incurred for the celebration, mentally by the toil and the drudgery required for its organization. The party also forces persons to adopt a new role. When celebrating a birthday the hero or heroine of the feast is the focus of everybody's attention, which forces them to expose themselves to criticism. Presents, flowers, and the number of guests are the visible signs of their prestige. A discrepancy with their own expectations or with their public self-image hurts and embarrasses; this is why some people shun parties: the jubilee is celebrated while on holiday; at the funeral no flowers are expected and speeches are forbidden. The party pressure also asserts itself when an invitation cannot be turned down: when newly-weds are expected to spend Christmas at the parental home where grandparents also are forced to attend; as in the staff party to which participants are expected to bring their partners. The party pressure is a pressure to adapt. The food must be delicious, the music great. It is unbecoming at a party to sit down in a corner to read a book or to refuse an invitation to dance.

(3) A party discriminates – togetherness is characteristic of a party, but parties divide as much as they unite. Social dividing lines that are hardly noticed in everyday life turn out to constitute unbridgeable gulfs at festive occasions: Mother's Day for children without a mother, or for women with no children; Christmas for immigrant workers from the Islamic world. Festivity unites, but at the same time emphasizes potential differences. The lustre radiating from the Holy Family is tragically broken when family members fall out at Christmas over the question who will attend the midnight mass. The reception at which everybody is cosily chatting away is a social purgatory for the lonely guest. For the girl no one wants to dance with, the dancing hall turns into a battlefield

of self-confidence. The party divides. At feasts of reversal and fraterniza-
tion, i.e., the carnival, differences between social categories become
quite clear when the higher classes have their get-togethers in the privacy of their own clubs, while the rank and file give themselves over to
public celebration in the streets, lanes and alleys of the town. The
Queen's Honours List used to emphasize distinctions in the nation, in
that medals and orders corresponded more precisely with income and
function than with achievement rewarded.[8] In addition, the Honours
List serves primarily the greater glory of the Majesty, who on the occasion of her royal birthday benevolently confers distinctions upon some
of her subjects, more so at least than any one of her honoured and distinguished subjects, who is just one among many.

(4) The party punishes – parties are not always rewarding, but sometimes occasions for inflicting punishment. Quite innocently at the
Dutch feast of *Sinterklaas,* the saint well known for his mercifulness, by
his black servant *Zwarte Piet,* but on other festive occasions in a more
covert but also more malicious manner. Time and place of the party
supply information about the status, or lack thereof, of those involved –
a wedding ceremony on a cheap day at the registry office; a burial in a
grave without a tombstone. Parties are occasions for self-presentation,
and therefore entail risks. If the guests do not show up, the host loses
face. The reports given by the paparazzi allow everybody to enjoy the
risky party-habits of the privileged few. The party is a popularity barometer, the purpose of which is to satisfy the guests. At the party, the guests
call the shots – it is their judgement on frugality or abundance that can
make or break the name of the host. However, what arouses admiration
and awe in one, is resented as waste and provocation by another: for
example, the parties of the lower classes which were regarded as a form
of resistance against elitist attempts at disciplining their life style and
behaviour.[9]

Parties do disappoint. Their inherent dialectic of essence and existence
affects the participants where they are most vulnerable. Our hopes for a
better life run up against the party turning out, unexpectedly, to be nothing but what was already known: determined by rules and regulations

[8] K. BRUIN: *Kroon op het werk. Onderscheiden in het Koninkrijk der Nederlanden*
(Meppel 1989).
[9] R. VAN DÜLMEN: *Kultur und Alltag in der frühen Neuzeit* I-II (München 1990-
1992).

and driven by competition and rivalry. Instead of creating openness and abandon, festivity increases insecurity, insecurity about one's own value and about the supporting strength of the community one belongs to. What was expected to confirm existence by transcending it, makes life suspicious out of disappointment. What seemed to be an invitation to renewal and transformation, is in fact experienced as a threat of loss.

The idea that the essence of festivity is found in the transcendence of what exists, is undermined in two ways. On the one hand, there is the fear of the emotional, the unordered, the chaos of feelings that are out of control. This is a fear that causes the party to be postponed and put at a distance, so that what turned out to be uncontrollable becomes controllable again. Feelings are threatening, unless they can be controlled. Therefore, parties are suspicious because excess and ecstasy are inherent to any form of festivity. This ecstacy is threatening because it can not be controlled. Sometimes, this ecstasy is an effect of the atmosphere and rhythm of the party,[10] sometimes it is artificially generated or purposefully effected – the transgression of taboos around sexual decency or the expression of violence is not just an unforeseen side effect of the festive mood, but may be in stead the determining condition of any festive celebration. Transcendence belongs to the essence of festivity. The surrender to transcendental ecstasy is threatening and terrifying in ordinary life, where order and discipline are the norm, but sought and found in any party as an expression of the extraordinary.

Apparently opposed to this fear of feelings is the need for continuous stimulation, for ever new and different emotions. Although people always want to have new experiences, they do not want to run the risk of being undone by them. This need, too, has its basis in the desire for control and mastery. What is sought are emotions that can be examined and tested on their value. The great upsurge in theme parties and of theme parks where a variety of props, design, and scenery determine the mood of festivity, may attest to an ambivalent longing for the exotic that is only attractive when it is controllable. This need is fatal to festivity. Parties exist by virtue of the spontaneous, the unexpected, the transcendence of the mundane, of a loss of control. Whereas the fear of disappointment

---

[10] Cf. A. JACKSON: Sound and ritual, in *Man* N.S. 3 (1968) 293-300; B. LEX: The neurobiology of ritual trance, in C.D. D'ACQUILLY *et al.* (eds.): *The spectrum of ritual* (New York 1979) 117-152; B. LEX: Voodoo death. New thoughts on an old explanation, in *American anthropologist* 76 (1974) 818-824.

means that any festive entertainment will be postponed and kept at a distance, the longing for ever new, different experiences eventually causes the party to die in boredom. In either case, it is impossible for the participants to forget the ordinary and mundane and to free themselves from the commonplace. It remains to be seen whether in modern society festivity is still possible if the party-goers are beginning to feel fearful of the festive occasion and no longer dare or want to celebrate.

3. FEAR OF DISAPPOINTMENT AND POSTPONEMENT

Parties are uncontrollable and therefore frightening. They are no longer the places where people relax and take a break from ordinary life, but instead contribute to the everyday stress themselves. They are taken for granted as markets and arenas of power and prestige, of profit and loss. Self-preservation thus causes parties to be avoided, postponed, trivialized, reduced, consumed, turned into a spectacle. A year long, preparations are made for a holiday; the shopping done for Christmas becomes the main determinant of the festive atmosphere; a career becomes more important than the work itself. In this way, although the risk of disappointment is reduced, the essence of festivity is lost. Thus, parties and feasts become an illusion cherished by individuals who are unable to share the joy for fear of being hurt. Festive intimacy is threatening because in it time and space are uncontrollable, chaos and exuberance being glorified instead.

The fear of risk and freedom explains why the party is celebrated as leisure, as an interruption of ordinary time and commonplace. In the consumption of leisure, experienced as a less risky alternative to the drama of festivity, the role relations between the participants are purely functional. It just so happens that one needs other players to play football, tennis, or billiards. These players will present no surprises since their role is prescribed and therefore known. Any discussion is determined by the parameters of the game. This makes it comprehensible why art and culture are *en vogue* again. Concerts, operas, museums, and exhibitions enable one to join in an innocent, non-threatening, individualistic implementation of communality.

If any celebration takes place at all, it is done from duty, perfunctory, by the book, as work. For most participants, the business dinner or the public reception are not even an interruption of the commonplace. Even ordinary people, neighbours, acquaintances, friends, when bumping into each other, will say, 'we really ought to organize a party one of these days' – postponement and instrumentality caught in one phrase. And if once in a time a feast is celebrated, it looks as if its professionalization works against its intimacy, causing *communitas* to be lost. Instead of trusting their own powers and abilities, people come to depend on outside experts. Chefs, clowns, waiters, musicians have to take care of the festive atmosphere; drugs, drinks, and pills take care of the right festal mood. Thus, the attitude towards festivity becomes a metaphor of the alienated society of everyday. Instrumental effect and expected utility replace the assignment of meaning and the creation of community. Parties no longer criticize the existing order, but just reflect the mundane.

4. BOREDOM AND THE DESIRE FOR NEW STIMULI

Although they fear intimacy and uncontrollable emotions in which they run the risk of losing themselves, modern people are just as much driven by an insatiable desire for ever new stimuli. They constantly seek the thrill and surprise of the strange and alien[11]. In the domain of religion such a need for excitement expresses itself in a fascination for the exotic and irrational, as a desire for variation and change. The combination of fear of injury and the need for ever new experiences creates a culture in which horror and spectacle dominate entertainment, a culture that has also, less challenging been characterized as an *Erlebnisgesellschaft*.[12] The good life seems to have become a matter of taste. The German theologian Wilfried Engemann[13] distinguishes a number of characteristics of this orientation towards the experiential. No matter how closely they are connected to the desire for feeling good, all are contrary to the festive experience:

---

[11] Cf. A. VAN HARSKAMP: De zingeving van de Celestijnse belofte, in *In de marge* 5 (1996) 17-25; R. NAUTA: Rituelen als decor. Over het geheim van de leegte, in P. POST & W.M. SPEELMAN (eds): *De Madonna van de Bijenkorf. Bewegingen op de rituele markt* (= Liturgie in perspectief 9) (Baarn 1997) 73-94, on 83.

[12] G. SCHULZE: *Die Erlebnisgesellschaft. Kultursoziologie der Gegenwart* (Frankfurt/Main 1995).

[13] W. ENGEMANN: Der 'moderne' Mensch – Abschied von einem Klischee, in *Wege zum Menschen* 48 (1996) 447-458; cf. M. KLESSMANN: Religiöse Sprache als Ausdruck und Abwehr, in *Wege zum Menschen* 34 (1982) 32-42.

(1) The dominance of feeling – Everything that is experienced or encountered is judged on its emotional value. Thus, articles of everyday consumption like soap and tobacco, shirts and trousers, food and drink, but also more durable and less commonplace things like cars and houses, operas and church services, are mainly given a functional assessment in terms of the quality of feeling, their smell, taste, texture and form. Whatever is consumed deteriorates into a mere source of experience. On account of its transience, the fear of boredom prevents us from really relishing the enjoyment of that experience; instead, the subsequent feeling is already envisaged. The search for enjoyment is forever threatened by the risk of disappointment. If experiencing becomes the most important occupation in life, a loss of meaning is risked when enjoyment fails to materialize. Not to be able to feel anything anymore constitutes the ultimate meaninglessness, a form of nonexistence which must be avoided by continuously seeking new stimuli and change.

(2) Variation – Experiencing requires discrimination. We only realize that we are (still) alive when there is something to experience. And something can only be experienced if it is different from everything we have experienced before. To validate the feeling of being alive, therefore, life must be characterized by permanent variation. But if one is continuously confronted with the new, then also the new becomes repetitive, is a form of repetition, and boredom becomes unavoidable. At the frontier of experience, there is the threat of a lack of feeling, the fear that the senses become dulled and one no longer feels anything in whatever can be experienced.

(3) Introverted orientation – The quality of experiencing is determined by the question whether we like what we feel. Weighing the pros and cons, we must, however, always suspect that in experiencing whatever is happening now, we are missing out on even more pleasant or interesting experiences. Such a restriction makes abandonment impossible. While we concentrate on feeling, the only feeling that remains to be experienced is one of disappointment and insecurity, of jealousy and envy of others who are having a better time.

(4) Choosing – If experience is central, the important thing is to make the right choice. We must choose the most enjoyable experiences. In such a perspective, creating a culture is subordinate to the cultural experience, which merely requires a choice between various options. If there is action, than it is purely for reasons of avoiding boredom. However, there is a danger that, because of the indifference to the nature of

the experience (the only thing that counts is freshness and novelty), the motivation to act will gradually disappear. Each choice becomes trivial. The ultimate consequence of giving priority to experience over behaviour is that the possibility to remain true to oneself eventually will be lost. The choice for experience requires relinquishing the determination and restriction of the I, the human faculty of control and will.

(5) Perception – If experiencing is dominant, than the importance of that what is perceived also disappears. The subject itself then becomes the primary object of perception, because everything is reduced and instrumentalized to what can be experienced. Paradoxically, such a preoccupation with perception by the subject simultaneously leads to a loss of the subjective, because what is perceived no longer has any meaning while the only thing that counts is personal enjoyment. All other interests disappear and development becomes impossible.

(6) Memory – If feeling prevails, then the past is rejected. The present is no longer considered as a continuation of what went before, so that the uniqueness and exceptionality of the experience is guaranteed. In an *Erlebnisgesellschaft*, history is not valued, and identity no longer depends on whatever biographical reconstruction is made. Thus, experiences lose their foundation and life is lost in pursuing what can be felt.

(7) Kitsch – If a person constantly wants to experience life as a show, this will effect the mundane to be transformed into the aesthetic. As a consequence a way of living will result in which the celebration of kitsch is predominant. Kitsch is to be understood as the desire to accept that which is not good as beautiful and to believe that what is not beautiful must be good.[14] Such aestheticism only knows of harmony and misses out on the tragic: it allows kitsch to prevail over art.

The consequences for the festive mood of such a dominance and primacy of feeling are disastrous. Indeed, where a state of feeling good is for ever pursued but at the same time any possible experience of that state must be distrusted, it is no longer possible to indulge in what appears to exist. Festive celebrations after all presuppose the reality of the transcendent, the possibility of overcoming, be it temporarily, the fragmentary nature of existence. Despite the unavoidable fact of the necessity to accept, and live with, all our personal deficiencies, physical, as well as social and mental, festivity infuses us with hope. However, if the experiential consequences prevail in everything we do, even in what we want to call fêtes, feasts, festivals or even parties, then the release promised by such a festal entertainment will prove to be a fata morgana. Festivity can not be calculated, it is not instrumental but intended to be without consequences. Festivity is celebrated in the here and now. However if we want to live by virtue of feeling and experience, variation must become the principle of existence. We will need a new experience every moment. We will expect a party every day. But if this becomes the way to celebrate, the party will be transformed into a routine occasion and boredom ensues. The constant search for new feelings and experiences will inevitably lead to tedium. In boredom, every party loses its lustre, life becomes grey, the festive mood forgotten. Parties do not offer passive pastime. They exist by virtue of action, they require effort and excess. Festivity constitutes the opposite of an existence in which enjoyment consists of being entertained, a passive way of living that kills meaning and motivation.

5. THE ILLUSION OF FESTIVITY AND THE NECESSITY TO LIE

Distancing and boredom are symptoms of what is called the narcissistic personality. It is not remarkable that those who suffer from this cultural pathology of individualism are not able to celebrate and play. Their whole world is focused on satisfying their need for recognition and acceptance. Others are just instrumentalized into vehicles for sustainment of the self that is publicly presented. It seems as if, in a narcissistic culture, festivity is no longer possible because gratuite but expressive involvement with other people, so characteristic of any festive occasion, causes anxiety and is therefore absent. Parties are instrumentalized or postponed, because the emotions inherent to the festive occasion are feared while they expose the participants in their vulnerability to others who may profit from that exhibition. In a narcissistic culture fear of exposure, of being used, of failure to live up to one's public image is damaging to the selfconcept, even selfdestroying. In such a culture, even religion does not offer a solace anymore. Is not the liturgy, too, subject to the powers of darkness, however masked as an enlightened spirit, when the festivity disappears and adaptation to the dictates of the times make the good feeling win out over meaning and expression?[15] But also where order and rules govern the party,

[14] M. KUNDERA: *The unbearable lightness of being* (New York 1984).
[15] R. GUARDINI: *Vom Geist der Liturgie* (Freiburg 1957).

where feelings are controlled, we must suspect that in such denial and repression of the spontaneous, in the negation of feeling, festivity similarly fails to be appreciated. Both the relentless pursuit of the good feeling, of feeling good, and the denial of any feeling at all are central but paradoxical concerns of modern man. Distrust of what one experiences and repression of any emotional involvement are the two main threats to the festive mood, to the celebration of festivity.

How can festivity survive in such a culture of distrust and denial? Where parties, festivitiy can be considered to be foremost a celebration of community, an answer to that question may be found in an analysis of intimacy. Not only feasts and festivity but also passion and love are feared as dangerous because of their connotation of abandonment and selfloss, for putting selfhood at risk. When a person is afraid of getting overwhelmed by feeling and emotion, when emotions are suspect because one is not sure of their ultimate truth and is waiting for ever new and more and better experiences, love is delegated to the partner[16] who is subsequently reproached for being deficient in expressing what is required, so that it becomes possible to demand that the relationship should be worked through in order to restore the balance of contributions and effects, of profits and expenses. Such work offers security, provides control, whereas love given freely requires surrender and implies a loss of control. A person in love rejoices in the togetherness with the beloved, without any expectation of reward or compensation, hoping that that which is offered will be welcomed. However when feelings are suspect, love is transformed into work. In order to retain control over affects that are unruly and strong, people prefer to sacrifice themselves in the service of others in order to earn love because it is safer to believe that to be loved is to be needed. When love is transformed into work, in order to maintain a stable relation and some satisfaction of the need for love, reciprocity is required to settle the bill of subservience. Such exchange of work for love forces the partner to repay in kind and transforms an amorous relation into competitive cooperation for a common good. When and where emotions cannot be controlled, feelings are masked and the threat of too much emotionality is warded off by opting for reasonableness and adaptation. Creativity and imagination are thus transferred into functionality and instrumentality. Where feelings make a person weak and vulnerable, togetherness is feared. Every intimate relation is avoided.

---

[16] W. SCHMIDBAUER: *Die Angst vor Nähe* (Reinbek bei Hamburg 1985) 62.

When as a consequence of fear of feelings, personal relations deteriorate into sacrificial enterprises, festivity is likewise at risk. Festivity implies shared intimacy. If intimacy is transferred into work, festivity too will fail and disappear. Where parties are postponed, in order to prevent disappointment, feelings are spared by denying them. A denial that makes invulnerable, however, also maims. If feelings are denied and repressed, a dividing wall is put up inside one's inner self while what is aimed for is simply to build a defense against the outside world. To become invulnerable to that reality, a lie is perhaps a better means than negation, deception better than denial. The lie is after all a helpless attempt to win space for one's own feelings in a "nahefeindliche Welt".[17] To avoid disappointment at a party, we must lie that we are having fun. Lies do recognize the ambivalence of existence and also respect human vulnerability. If intimacy demands openness and festivity merrymaking, if people must be always outspoken and always cheerful, then they can only spare each other by lying, by acting as if. A party does not survive any demand for distance and postponement, for adaptation and performance, but like in love it requires an exercise in lying, a training in appearances, in order to develop a self-convincing belief in the reality of whats is festal. A festival of anticipation is thus consummated in the celebration of the illusion. Celebration really requires faith, and also a real faith.

Perhaps parties can only be celebrated when the threats inherent to them are acknowledged instead of denied or repressed. The acknowledgement of ambivalence however makes the return of paradise, a return always so eagerly sought and sometimes wishfully found when parties are thrown, to an illusionary event. However, to turn that illusion into reality lies are needed. The illusion must be made real by lying. To celebrate, to have fun, to experience something of the essence of humanity, it is better to lie, that is to recognize the ambivalence of festivity but to act as if it is possible to overcome the dark sides of what promised to be paradise, than to deny any ambivalence and to prefer to remain ignorant about the fragmentary nature of existence. To celebrate one must accept the illusionary nature and transient character of any festive occasion, in order to deny ourselves the capacity to celebrate at all.

---

[17] SCHMIDBAUER: *Die Angst vor Nähe* 140-152.

GÉRARD VAN TILLO

SOCIOLOGICAL ANALYSIS OF LITURGICAL CELEBRATIONS

1. INTRODUCTION

Hitherto the sociology of religion has paid relatively little attention to liturgical festivals. One reason may perhaps be that two important characteristics of liturgical celebrations, namely the religious and the ritualistic aspect, have been seen as being more closely related to other disciplines such as theology and anthropology than to the sociology of religion. However, this is not a correct interpretation as both aspects also have an important sociological relevance. Not only the form but also the meaning of liturgical celebrations change over time and vary from place to place and are also dependent on the interpretation of the participants. Liturgical celebrations and other festive occasions where people express their feelings in a collective way, say a lot about the time and place in which they occur. They not only reflect the religion of a community but also say something about the way of thinking, about the roles played in daily life and about customs and choices.

In this study I focus on the sociological approach to liturgical celebrations in The Netherlands, especially to the worship in the Roman Catholic Church. Special consideration is given to the different approaches within sociology and to the question of what aspects of liturgical rituals they can clarify. Liturgical celebrations frequently are a part of festivals and consist themselves of festive expressions so that this study in some way also focuses on the sociology of feasts.[1] What aspect of celebrations is emphasized in sociological studies is largely dependent on the sociological methodology applied. One methodological approach particularly appropriate to the analysis of liturgical aspects is semiotic analysis. An important reason is that liturgy in all its different aspects is a symbolic presentation of a hidden reality. Another reason is that this

---

[1] Gérard VAN TILLO: De religieuze dimensie van feesten. Een bijdrage van de godsdienst- en pastoraalsociologie, in A. BLIJLEVENS et al.: Feest: gelegenheidsverkondiging (= HTP-studie 9)(Averbode-Apeldoorn 1988) 10-33.

approach brings to the fore the ambivalence and tensions in the celebration of liturgy. Semiotic analysis focuses precisely on the symbolic
meaning of texts and rituals. This is why this approach will be explained
in a separate section. The study will finish with a description of some
tensions and ambivalences that are revealed when liturgy is subjected to
sociological research.

2. APPROACHES

Despite the great variety of sociological theories and approaches, it is
possible to distil four main types, derived from the basic characteristics
of social phenomena. All social phenomena have four characteristics in
common. In the first place all social phenomena have a specific *structure*. For instance, the celebration of the Eucharist consists of the service
of the word and the service of the sacrifice. In the same way the administering of the baptism sometimes takes place both at the altar and at the
baptismal font. Likewise, in the case of a funeral prayers may be said
and ceremonies performed both in the church and at the cemetery.
Another characteristic that all social phenomena have in common is that
they are always subject to processes of *change*. This is also true of phenomena that have a very stable structure over time, such as marriage,
war and family life. Another common characteristic is the fact that people are always involved in *interpretation* of their own role in their social
environment. In this way every liturgical ceremony is performed by
human actors, who add something of their own to the formal framework of the ceremony by the way in which they interpret their role. A
last common feature of social phenomena is their *symbolic meaning*.
Besides the official or denotative meaning social phenomena also commonly have the capacity to invoke associations and refer to meanings
that are entirely separate from the denotative ones. This could be illustrated by the case of members of a sports club who associate the chalices
used in liturgical ceremonies with a sporting trophy.

Depending on which of the four aspects of social reality is the focus of
attention, sociology may be structural, dialectical, interpretative (phenomenological) or semiotic. Because the four basic features of social phenomena are interrelated, it is often found that although one approach is
primary it overlaps with the other features used in the research. Each of
the four main sociological approaches has a theoretical basis.

Structural sociology is characterized by a positivistic approach of the kind that is also applied in the natural sciences. This involves the measurement of external features, often in a quantitative manner. In this framework important methodological approaches are the different types of functionalism that have characterized sociology from the outset. In the case of rituals this approach involves investigating their functions, variations in forms, components and participation in them. This approach has produced the well-known sociological surveys in the field of religion.

Dialectical sociology is characterized by a focus on change; dialectics is seen as the motor of change. This type of sociology is primarily directed to the origin and historical development of social phenomena. Also, some types of sociology have change as a goal of their research. Critical sociology was applied to the renewal of liturgy in the period after the Second Vatican Council, a process in which the emancipation of laity was an important argument.

Interaction sociology, or interpretative sociology, is characterized by a phenomenological approach. The founding father of this sociology is Max Weber who pointed out that the individual intention of the actor plays a major role in human behaviour. In relation to liturgical celebrations this sociology is primarily concerned with how the meaning of liturgical rituals differs for the various actors involved in the rituals, for example the organisers, the participants and the celebrants.

Semiotic sociology is characterized by a structuralistic approach.[2] Structuralism originated when well-known structuralists such as Louis Althusser applied the historical materialism of Karl Marx to the superstructure of culture. In the process, greater attention was paid to the fact that every opposition can generate change. In the writings of Marxists and critical sociologists this was mainly confined to the economic sphere. A structuralistic approach is therefore especially concerned with the origin and development of phenomena, a process that is understood as dialectical. But this structuralism is strongly allied to semiotics, in particular the notion, as propounded by Edmund Leach, that meanings are also created through their unconscious oppositions, and that signs and symbols are only to be understood within the systems to which they

---

[2] Gérard VAN TILLO: Semiotische systemen. Ontwikkelingen, varianten, thema's, in Wiel SMEETS & Gérard VAN TILLO: *Religie als systeem van tekens en symbolen. Naar een semiotische godsdienstsociologie* (Heerlen 1993) 19-48.

belong.[3] The semiotic approach is an adequate method of studying feasts and liturgy, because it covers not only the denotative but also the associative meanings.

3. SOCIOLOGY OF LITURGICAL FESTIVALS

After this brief explanation of the different sociological approaches I will now consider how liturgical elements can be analysed in the different approaches.

3.1. Structural analysis

As in the natural sciences positivistic sociology makes use of models. Such a model indicates the underlying question used to investigate reality, in our case liturgical celebrations. The most frequently applied models of structural sociology are function, exchange and conflict. The function model is used to examine the functions of liturgy for totalities such as belief, church and society, and for their different parts. This can be done in a fairly theoretical way, for example the method employed by Talcott Parsons in what is termed structural functionalism, or in a more practical way in relation to specific social questions, for example the approach taken by Robert King Merton.[4] Alternatively, a more experimental method can be employed: this involves studying the effects of replacing specific elements by more simple solutions, as is done in system theory, the so-called *Equivalenz Funktionalismus*, which makes frequent use of computer simulations. The exchange model traces the investments made by the different participants in liturgy and what they get in return for these investments. This method resembles the function model. The conflict model identifies the various interest groups and the mechanisms that play a part in advancing these interests and in reconciling the different positions in order to guarantee the functioning of the system.

---

[3] E. LEACH: *Culture and communication. The logic by which symbols are connected. An introduction to the use of structuralist analysis in social anthropology* (= Themes in the social sciences) (Cambridge etc. 1976) 20.

[4] Nicholas S. TIMASHEFF: *Sociological theory. Its nature and growth* (New York 1964) 221-231.

Hitherto, relatively little sociological research has been undertaken in the field of liturgy. Sometimes liturgy has, however, been included as an aspect of broader research into religious change and church management. Such research is often characterized by a functional approach and addresses such issues as the function of liturgy or a particular liturgical festival for church, society, the initiated and the participants. In this research a distinction is still often made between different types of function, for example non-functions that are purely ritualistic, integrating functions and disintegrating functions, manifest and latent functions and so forth.

These different functions are put forward in research which investigates not only the participation and motivation of the worshippers but also their social position and how they try to look after their own interests. The method of structural sociology consists in explaining their behaviour and social roles on the basis of their social position and the interests involved. In this way, the research of the sociology of religion has identified a relationship between the interests of the middle class and a high degree of group integration, which is precisely something that is promoted by the church. This has meant that in its liturgy and teaching and even in its interpretation of values the church has tended to focus on the middle class, thereby accelerating the exodus of other social groups such as the labourers and intellectuals.

3.2. Historical perspective

Prompted by the liturgical renewal after the Second Vatican Council, the sociology of religion has taken a renewed interest in liturgical change, once again usually in the context of relatively large research projects. It should be noted in this respect that often only a subtle difference exists between historical research proper and historical-sociological research. The sociological elements that characterize historical-sociological research are dependent on the underlying type of sociology. A general characteristic of historical-sociological research is that the social context is involved in a more systematic way in the investigation. For example, research into liturgical change will take account of the extent to which this is connected with religious and societal change. Structural historical-sociological analysis tries not only to trace separate changes but also to relate them to the context that influences these processes and to classify them in types and sequences. A recent study of Roman

Catholicism in the post-war period in The Netherlands thus distinguished four phases, namely stabilization (1945-1960), renewal (1960-1970), polarization (1970-1985) and new consciousness (1985 to the present-day).[5] In these phases the liturgy of the Roman Catholic Church in The Netherlands is classified as Roman-orthodox liturgy in the period of reconstruction after World War II, experimental liturgy in the sixties, polarized liturgy with various opposing forms in the years 1970-1985 and a more spiritual and ecumenical liturgy from 1985 onwards. The sociology of change puts less emphasis on these structural elements and more emphasis on the antitheses behind these changes, for instance the opposition between right and left in the sixties, the opposition between Rome and The Netherlands in the next period, the opposition between conservative and progressive Catholics in later years and, more recently still, the contrast between an electronically managed information society and the spiritual dimension of human existence. In phenomenological sociological historiography change is viewed mainly as the product of the changeable human spirit and the intentions of individual actors. As the work of M. Foucault shows, the structuralist method involves examination of cross-sections of particular periods and describes the transformation from one era to another. As I hope to show below, the four sociological approaches described above are fully integrated in this method.

All this shows how different types of sociology can be intertwined. Sociology always focuses to some extent on the structural aspect of social reality. It follows that this structural element is present in every approach, including the phenomenological and semiotic ones. As the sociology of change comprises structural elements, neither phenomenological nor semiotic sociology is conceivable without an element of change, because consciousness is always involved in a process of change and, as we shall see, the meaning of symbols is continuously changing.

The research into liturgical change may focus on the performance of certain liturgical rites in a given period, but it may equally well examine the changed place of ritual in the context of church and society in a given period, the origin and development of rites as such and how they influence liturgy, or the different elements that comprise liturgical ritual. For example, there has been research into the origin and development of

---

[5] W. GODDIJN, J. JACOBS & G. VAN TILLO: *Tot vrijheid geroepen. Katholieken in Nederland 1945-2000* (Baarn 1999).

liturgical texts, the changes in applying texts to specific liturgical ceremonies, liturgical buildings (e.g. churches) and their interior decoration,
liturgical dress, the music during liturgical ceremonies etc. Much of this
research is performed by other disciplines. A sociological element arises
as soon as the people somehow involved in the choices and the realization of liturgy influence one another in such a way that the routine
becomes dependent on the interpretations, behaviour, choices and interests of the actors concerned or on the institutional patterns that come to
existence over time.

3.3. Phenomenological analysis

The phenomenological or interpretative interaction approach in sociology is adequate for the study of liturgy since this clearly involves different roles, and meaning and interpretation are highly dependent on
how the participants interpret their own role. An important aspect of
the phenomenological analysis of liturgical elements is the extent to
which the participants deviate from the prescribed liturgical roles, for
the official significance of a liturgical festival often differs from the way
in which it is primarily interpreted by the participants. For the interpretative sociological study of liturgy this is a structural situation. In
the Catholic world all kinds of events and circumstances are commemorated by celebration of the Eucharist. The intention of the participants, for example people gathered to celebrate a silver wedding
anniversary celebrated in a Eucharist ceremony, is then connected with
the original meaning of the Eucharist. Although the clergy often try to
reconcile these different meanings, a wide gap often remains between
them. Examples are the celebration of Eucharist to mark the start of
the hunting season or carnival. These clearly show that the cultural
context has a major influence on the meaning and form of liturgical
celebrations.

Widely differing interpretations of the meaning of the liturgy can
occur among different groups of participants, who may therefore have
very different reasons for participating. Where a silver wedding
anniversary is celebrated in the course of the Eucharist on a Sunday, it
may well be that some of the congregation want only the holy mass
and not the wedding sermon. Similarly, the interpretation of the liturgy
may well differ among individual participants too. For instance, relatives of the bride and bridegroom may be present not really out of a

desire to participate in the rites or attend the celebration but in order to keep up appearances or to avoid a quarrel.

Another difference in the interpretation of the liturgy may result from a difference in the way in which people believe. For example, orthodox, Rome-oriented Catholics in The Netherlands greatly appreciate the performance of traditional rites, which play a major role in their religious experience, but these rites are of less importance to progressive Catholics. The progressive Catholics prefer to experiment with forms of liturgy and to adapt them to their own culture and situation and are inclined to put the rules of the Roman liturgy in perspective.

Where there is a large measure of agreement about its interpretation, a liturgical ceremony will be relatively stable and less susceptible to change. But where there are differences of opinion about its interpretation, there is a greater likelihood of changes in the liturgical ceremony. For instance, its form may be modified to satisfy as many groups of participants as possible. Otherwise, there is a chance that dissatisfied participants may stay away.

In addition to all these different interpretations, liturgical ceremonies have an intrinsic meaning. This can be inferred from the basic meaning that festivals always have, namely to provide an opportunity to pause and reflect on special events. Liturgy may therefore be seen as providing an opportunity to reflect on the important secrets of belief. The ritual form expresses something of the eternal values as confirmed and constantly revived by liturgy. The most central values around which the other religious values are grouped are, as far as the Roman Catholic Church is concerned, the seven sacraments.

3.4. Semiotic analysis

The semiotic analysis of liturgical celebrations may be performed at two levels. First, liturgical ceremonies may be examined as representatives of a certain period, culture or community. At this level liturgy is seen as a symbol referring to a certain reality concerning church and society. An example of this could be the differing interpretations of the liturgy of the Roman Catholic Church in The Netherlands since the sixties as a symbol of the polarization that has characterized the Roman Catholic Church. Secondly, it is possible to examine the symbolic meanings of the buildings, objects, actions and texts used in liturgy. We can distinguish between the official symbols that have a fixed meaning, for example the bread and wine in the Eucharist that refer to the body and blood of Jesus Christ, and the unofficial meaning of behaviour, objects and texts that occur in the framework of a liturgical celebration and are also accorded a symbolic meaning. Additional distinctions can be made between expressions intended to be liturgical and those not so intended. For example, the celebrant can support the meaning of the liturgy by his behaviour and body language, but this may equally well indicate an attitude that is non-liturgical or even anti-liturgical. For example, hurrying through the liturgical celebration or displaying an attitude of indifference may detract from the official meaning of the liturgy.

Signs and symbols tend to be constantly redefined not only by each academic discipline but also by most authors within a given discipline. In this respect I will confine myself to an indication of the traditional semiotic theory in which a symbol refers to another reality. A distinction is made in sociology between symbols and signs. Symbols are understood as simply signifiers, and signs are treated as referents intended to elicit a reaction. For example, worshippers regard the blessing pronounced by the priest at the end of the celebration as a symbol of priestly power and, when he makes the sign of the cross, they view this as confirmation that the celebration is at an end and that they may go home.

A different approach to signs and symbols has emerged since the end of the sixties. This has been due in particular to the approach to linguistics adopted by the French philosopher Jacques Derrida, who argued that signs and symbols are not referring to another reality but were an inadequate replacement, or a kind of surrogate for an absent reality. The symbol derives its relevance precisely from the absence of the signified. The symbol is said to be inadequate since it can never represent the signified in a believable way. The reality is a shadow that is always ahead of the symbol and therefore never coincides with it. It follows that the symbol is always wearing out and must in the long run be replaced by a new symbol better able to conceal the absence of the signified.[6] An example of this is a photograph. A photograph of a person has a function in a situation in which the subject is not present or may indeed even have died. The photograph refers to the subject, but does not adequately replace him or her. In the long run this inadequacy may become so bothersome that the need is felt for another photograph that

[6] J. DERRIDA: *Of grammatology* (Baltimore 1974) 269-316.

is better able to suggest the presence of the pictured person simply because it is new and different.

A relationship exists between the character of signs and symbols and their functioning. This functioning was described by Edmund Leach in two premises: (1) Signs and symbols are only to be understood within the context in which they belong. (2) Signs and symbols derive their meaning from their antitheses, although people are not normally aware of them.[7] The relationship between the character and the functioning of symbols exists in the perception that the presence of anything has its strongest contrast in its absence. In other words: symbols show to their full advantage when they refer to something that does not exist. A good example of this is advertising. Advertising is not needed for a product that is known to everyone and is universally perceived as fulfilling all requirements. But if it is unknown or if, above all, it has deficiencies, advertising can help to publicise the product and cover up its deficiencies. In this way, social symbols are the facades that suggest the presence of something, or in other words hide what does not exist.

This approach to symbolism is important to the analysis of religious phenomena and liturgy because religious symbols are used precisely to represent an absent reality, i.e. a reality that is not visible. That is why it is important that such symbols should represent an invisible reality in a credible way. Where religious symbols fail in this respect, they too may be changed, firstly through interpretation and later by replacement. From the moment when literal interpretation of the Transubstantiation in the Roman Catholic Eucharist no longer satisfied believers, the meaning of the symbol was gradually shifted to put the emphasis on the celebration of the community (the Holy Communion). Now that people are starting to tire of the notion of the host as a symbol of a meal, we see that in many places worshippers are being given the opportunity to dip the host in the chalice or to drink from the chalice to complete in this way the symbolism of the fellowship meal.

The semiotic approach to liturgical celebrations is fruitful because it makes it possible to trace the unintended blending of symbolism in its social and religious meanings. In other words: this analysis of ritual symbols can reveal not only the absence of a religious reality, but also the absent religious commitment. That is why it is always insisted upon religious sermons that people should live according to their beliefs as

---

[7] LEACH: *Culture and communication* 9-16.

expressed in the celebrations. To the extent that this is not the case, liturgy itself becomes a facade concealing the non-religious attitude of the participants.

Since, as mentioned above, the object that is to be the subject of the structuralistic-semiotic analysis is seen as the result of a dialectical process, this approach focuses in particular on the underlying interests and contrasts that play a part in the organization and celebration of liturgy. From this point of view liturgy can be regarded as a supermarket in which the different role-players look after their own interests and, in the process, reach a compromise – the result of all the different objectives. The official aim of liturgy is to enable the congregation to celebrate the religious rites together, but since liturgy is for the most part the domain of priests and those designated by them it provides above all an opportunity for them to confirm their authority and convey their expressive qualities.

The participants in liturgical celebrations express religious choices through their presence. As suggested earlier, however, their presence may also be due to other motives and interests. Business people in predominantly Catholic or Protestant districts often participate in church celebrations in order to retain the confidence of their customers. In parishes with many pastors worshippers often have a favourite pastor whose celebrations they prefer to attend. Likewise there may be pastors whom they tend to avoid. Such preferences may be related to the way in which the celebrations are performed, but also to entirely unrelated sympathies and antipathies.

4. CLOSE-UP OF THE SEMIOTIC ANALYSIS OF LITURGICAL CELEBRATIONS

The research model of semiotic-sociological analysis is derived from the way in which Claude Lévi-Strauss analysed ancient myths.[8] In this analysis he used a research design consisting of three phases, which can be described as phenomenological-historical analysis (phase 1), structuralistic analysis (phase 2) and sociological analysis (phase 3). In the first phase the interpretation of meanings is derived from the research object's different origin and development. In the second phase, the structure of the interpreted meanings is identified, for instance through

---

[8] C. LÉVI-STRAUSS: *Structural anthropology* (New York 1979) 206-236.

the categorization of binary oppositions, different dimensions or, specific configurations. The structures are regarded not as empirical findings but as meta-empirical classifications discovered by the researcher in the data. In the third phase, the researcher tries to establish connections between the meanings classified in the above manner and the socio-cultural context in which they occur.

A classical example of the application of this method can be found in Victor Turner's analysis of different rituals of the Ndembu tribe in Zambia. In his book *The ritual process* he analyses in turn a fertility ritual, a ritual concerning twins and the ritual installation of a tribal chief, all of which are rites of passage.[9] In the first phase of his research, Victor Turner begins by trying to discover the origins of the rituals and to trace the changes they have undergone over time. The next step in this first phase is to register exactly the meanings attributed to every aspect of the ritual acts, places and ingredients and how they interrelate. In practice, these meanings always correspond to the prevailing meanings in society, for example jumping as a sign of joy, hard and tough trees and boughs as symbols of strength and durability, heat and fire as symbols of death, coolness as a symbol of life, and water as a symbol of fertility. Turner emphasizes that the various symbols may be accorded different meanings by individuals or groups or indeed by the community as a whole.

In the second phase of his research project Turner tries to discover the structures on the basis of which the meanings are created. Although Turner identifies himself in this research as a follower of Lévi-Strauss, the approach he adopts in this second phase differs from that taken by Lévi-Strauss in his analysis of ancient myths. What Lévi-Strauss did was to reveal the cosmology of a given culture as expressed in mythological cycles, and then to explain the rituals as expressions of the structural models found in the myths. As the Ndembu do not have any myths or coherent cosmological stories Turner adopts the opposite approach and starts by analysing the building blocks of their view of the world, namely the ritual symbols, and thus constructs the model by which these symbols are seen as bearers of the elements of their view of the world. In the ritual symbolism of the Ndembu three triads stand out as the basis of the meaning. These triads refer to (1) the sphere of the witches and the spirits of the ancestors, (2) the sphere of religious symbolism and, (3) the sphere of social life. The world of the spirits and the

---

[9] V. TURNER: *The ritual process* (Chicago 1969).

world of social life meet and are reconciled with each other at the level of religious symbols, which together form a three-dimensional classification structure of mutually intersecting binary oppositions. Within a given level of classification, each symbol represents one of the poles of a binary opposition and has as such only one meaning. However, since there are several intersecting levels of classification, most of the symbols and binary oppositions have a totally different meaning at the other levels of classification. The symbols and pairs of symbols also often have a tying function, in other words tying together different intersecting classifications. Moreover, different levels of classification may refer to different situations. Turner cites as an example the contrast between black and white which, depending on the ritual and classification involved, may refer to the man-woman opposition or to entirely different oppositions such as meat and meal.

By constructing the ritual symbols of the Ndembu in this way, Turner has no difficulty in the third phase of the analysis in identifying connections between this symbolism and the society and culture of the Ndembu. Owing to the connecting function of ritual symbolism this link is largely established by the symbolism itself. The world of symbols, classified by clear-cut oppositions, replaces and has a psychological effect on a reality that is not always so well-ordered. The crises created by the social norms are resolved by the meaningful expression of the values from which the social rules are derived. The fundamental inadequacy of the signs is supplemented by supernatural powers in such a way that there is no need to change the system of symbols itself. This is possible because the system of classification is multi-dimensional. This allows different interpretations at the same time, and also transformations of meaning along the axis of time.

The advantage of this type of analysis over other approaches is not only that it allows profound historical and phenomenological analysis of the meanings of rituals, but also that it shows how different meanings are classified in several interrelated dimensions and can be explained by the socio-cultural context of the community. That is why the semiotic approach may also be used to good effect in the analysis of western Christian rituals.

As an example I outline a notional semiotic analysis of the remarkable phenomenon that while church attendance has declined sharply in recent decades, there has been an explosion of interest in the Christmas mass. This outline is not concerned with precise empirical data. Instead I use this example as an experiment of ideas to demonstrate what extra dimensions a semiotic approach can produce.

When people are asked for their motives for participation in the Christmas night mass, a variety of motives arise. Only a relatively small number of people have religious motives. They frequently mention nostalgic memories from their youth that momentarily prompt residual feelings of religion. For other participants the Christmas mass is something of a cultural event: an opportunity to soak up the seasonal atmosphere. Other reasons mentioned by respondents include the possibility of playing an active role in the liturgical ceremony, for example as a member of the local church choir, or of escorting other members of the family, acquaintances etc. Most participants appear in fact to have several interrelated motives, although it is usually not clear which of them is decisive. How the participants interpret the symbolism of the night mass depends on their personal motives for attendance.

The aim of semiotic analysis of the night mass ritual should therefore be to detect the different related meanings given to the Christmas mass, to find out how these meanings are structured, and to determine what explanations are to be found in the socio-cultural situation of the participants.

Furthermore, it is almost certain that such an analysis would reveal several dimensions of intersecting meaning. Such intersections form the connection between layers of meaning which are in principle separate from one another and which might not – without the existence of these connections – have motivated the people to attend the night mass. This is similar to the case of the Ndembu world, in which witches and the spirits of the ancestors combine with social symbols to provide the religious meaning of the ritual. Since the Westerners are in this case less deeply religious than the members of the African tribe in the sixties, this linking element should perhaps be sought in the need they feel for communal experience of a cultural event, which evokes memories from their own past and culture. In other words, the cultural and season-bound pattern of going out, the sentimental feelings and memories of youth evoked by the atmosphere of Christmas carols, the decorations and the coloured lights in the darkness of the Christmas night all come together and are fulfilled in the religious ceremony of Christmas mass.

5. AMBIVALENCE AND TENSIONS

It is perhaps clear from the above that sociological research into liturgical rituals and festivals is particularly useful in revealing underlying ambivalence and tensions. In the structural approach, the focus is on the latent functions which the celebration of liturgy fulfils for the different groups and persons, giving liturgical rituals an ambivalent character. The dialectical approach can help to explain to what extent the way in which liturgy is celebrated and the manner of participation in the ceremonies are the result of interacting forces. The interpretative approach is able to make clear the difference between on the one hand individual intentions and group intentions in celebrating liturgy and on the other its official place and meaning in church and belief. Finally, the semiotic approach is able to reveal what is behind the facade provided by the celebration of liturgy and what interests are served by this. In this final section I will discuss some important ambivalences and tensions that can occur in relation to the celebration of liturgy. As the methodological approach has already been sufficiently discussed above, we will disregard this subject in explaining these approaches and confine ourselves to the substance of the question regarding tensions and ambivalences.

Some factors that give rise to significant tensions and ambivalence too in relation to the celebration of liturgy are: (1) supply and demand, (2) openness and closedness, (3) competencies to play liturgical parts and credibility of liturgical celebration, (4) religious and profane motivations, (5) the question of money and (6) the tension between science and religion.

5.1. Supply and demand

The supply of liturgical celebrations is basically governed by church rules and classifications that stipulate the form of the celebrations and often, in earlier times, the obligation to participate as well. In the Protestant churches the governing organization is responsible for liturgy and authorises the clergy to implement it. In the Roman Catholic Church liturgy is the responsibility of the individual bishops, who are naturally bound by the church precepts and rules mentioned above. Responsibility for the performance of liturgy is delegated to the local pastors appointed by the bishop. Since celebrants and liturgical groups have in practice a fair degree of freedom to give their own form and content to the basic design of the liturgical ritual, a rich variation has arisen. In the Roman Catholic Church this freedom has been fostered by the Second Vatican Council, in particular by the decision to celebrate liturgy in the vernacular and to give laity the possibility of taking an active part. But most liturgical celebrations also contain obligatory parts such as the use of Eucharistic prayers approved by the Catholic Church. It is not possible, however, to monitor these prescribed parts except in special circumstances, for example where the rites are more public, as in the case of the celebration of the Eucharist on television. This sometimes leads to a conflict with the bishops. Apart from the lack of monitoring, there is also a lack of celebrants and, above all, a lack of priests. This gives laymen two motives for taking charge: first, the encouragement to participate in an active way and, secondly, the lack of ordained or professionally trained clergy.

This has given rise to a situation in which a wide variation in norms may also be accompanied by more structural changes of meaning. A far-reaching change for instance has been that the individual confession of sins has gradually receded into the background, its significance being blurred by the communal rite of penitence. Yet another gradual change has been the administration of the sacrament of extreme unction in an early stage of illness. As a result, it has ceased to accompany the process of dying and is now administered in the course of terminal illness. In old peoples homes extreme unction is sometimes administered to Catholic residents communally as a form of spiritual care for the elderly. Structural changes of this kind are frequently discussed by theologians, with the result that every structural change has given rise, as it were, to a new theology that legitimises the change.

Religious change becomes visible first and most clearly in the sphere in which religiousness is best expressed, namely in liturgy. This is why polarization in The Netherlands has occurred mainly in relation to the renewal of the liturgy, and why new directions and movements have often resulted from conflicts about liturgy.

5.2. Openness and closedness

A structural tension exists between the openness and closedness of liturgy. An important part of liturgy is preaching – the proclamation of belief being a basic function of liturgical celebrations. This contributes to the universal character of liturgy. In principle, nobody is excluded from attending a religious service. On the contrary, the religious message is often at its most effective when the listeners are unfamiliar with the proclaimed message. In order to put across the message, it is therefore better for the liturgy to be open and externally oriented. In the Catholic Church, this applies only to the demand side, not the supply side. The Roman Catholic Church does not lead the way when it comes to ecumenical cooperation designed to win humankind for Christianity. On the contrary the Roman Catholic Church still claims to be the only true church with the only true message, which has to be preached to as many people as possible.

In its celebratory aspect liturgy tends to focus more on existing Catholic parishioners. The way in which liturgy is celebrated is at the same time a proclamation and confirmation of the identity of the group. But liturgy also emphasises the identity of the group in relation to groups that do not wish to form part of the church. The student *ekklèsia* of Amsterdam, which operates outside the responsibility of the local bishop, is a clear example of this. The way in which liturgy is celebrated may even become a weapon in the struggle of those concerned to show that they are in the right.

5.3. Competencies to play liturgical parts and credibility of liturgical celebration

An ambivalent aspect of liturgical celebrations related to the above concerns the issue of competences. Formerly, liturgical ceremonies were led only by ordained priests. As a result of two circumstances already mentioned – the competences of laymen and the lack of priests – an ambivalent situation has arisen in this context. The ambivalence consists in the fact that although laymen are allowed to officiate at celebrations of word and communion, this is usually confined to situations in which no priest is available to celebrate the Eucharist. In other words: the advances made by laity in the celebration of the liturgy have been possible mainly for want of better. Moreover, it is a limited advance within narrow constraints. These constraints are that the administration of the sacraments is, with some exceptions, reserved for ordained priests, and the great majority of the population (i.e. all women and married men and, in principle, divorced men whose former wife is still alive) are excluded from the priesthood.

This distinction between priests and laity in relation to officiating at liturgical ceremonies also reflects adversely on the competences of the large group of volunteers in the Roman Catholic Church. Owing to the restrictions imposed on the laity in officiating at ceremonies, these volunteers remain a kind of underclass, who are allowed to make the preparations and make themselves useful in other ways, but are barred, as it were, from careers in the church and may not officiate in liturgical celebrations.

A special ambivalence concerns the role of women in the church, especially in liturgy. Here women are suspect and constrained in two ways. First, women can never be ordained as priests in the Roman Catholic Church because ordination is reserved to men. In addition, women are often seen as posing a threat to the small number of priests active in the church because although there is a degree of a tolerance about relations between women and priests, the latter cannot marry. However, the lack of priests has become so acute that in many respects a more tolerant policy is being pursued.

5.4. Religious and profane motivations

As the example of the Christmas mass clearly shows, non-religious motives may play a big role in the liturgy. This is true not only for the congregation but also for the celebrants. Those who officiate at liturgical ceremonies are usually intellectuals who have a critical and often scholarly attitude. Most of them have positions as religious leaders, sometimes in combination with roles in education, upbringing and research. That is to say, they are generally in the position of being encouraged to know rather than to believe. The custom of confining their atheistic views to the discipline in which they are working at a given moment and of relinquishing it when they play their religious role does not provide a certain guarantee of their religious involvement in liturgy. In practice it is much easier to give up a belief than a position, especially in cases where they can still suggest sufficient belief to warrant retaining their religious roles, since they may well have had to make major sacrifices to obtain them and be dependent on them for their living and status. In such cases an ambivalence arises between the attitude towards belief required by the role of celebrant in a liturgical ceremony and his lack of belief in the religious meaning of the ceremony.

As we have seen earlier, profane motives may also play a role in the case of the congregation. Where this is the case, members of the congregation may also have to simulate a degree of belief in order to justify attendance at the ceremony in a credible way. This gives rise to a situation in which not only the celebrant but also the members of the congregation are creating the pretence of a belief in religious meanings that does not exist in reality. Nonetheless, the rites remain possible as long neither party is aware of the real thoughts of the other. As long as this is not the case, the situation stays in balance and it is possible to continue the ritual in a credible way. The function of the ritual for both parties is then to confirm a non-existent belief, thereby making it possible for them to keep their roles and the positions and advantages they confer. This situation is not entirely hypothetical as priests and laymen alike tend to be more interested in the production of religion than its consumption. This is why churches sometimes resemble theatres in which those present are putting on a play for the benefit of an empty hall.

5.5. The question of money

There is also a tension between the spiritual values of liturgy and the material conditions for it. This is the case where worshipers pay beforehand for the holy services, for example in the case of baptism or marriage and a mass celebrated for a special intention. Money can also play a role during liturgical celebrations as collections are often held and some of the liturgical actors are paid.

How money is gathered differs widely from parish to parish and church to church. Nor are there fixed prices for the holy services of the church. In parishes the members usually pay a fixed amount every year. This entitles them to certain rights as a parishioner, for example the free blessing of their marriage and a free funeral. However, separate charges are sometimes made for these services, especially where the clients do not pay the yearly church taxes.

Similarly, a charge is made for a mass celebrated for a special intention. Formerly, such masses were almost always commissioned by a single individual, who paid the full amount. Later, when fewer masses were celebrated these special masses tended to be commissioned by groups of believers who had a collective intention and paid jointly for one and the same mass. From then on the prices fell from, say, 25 guilders to 15 or even 10 guilders, the charge sometimes being dependent on the solemnity of the celebration (e.g. with or without a choir). This practice has been frequently criticised by worshippers, who have indicated that they would never again commission a mass since its benefits have to be shared with too many people.

As mentioned above, collections are part of most liturgical celebrations. They are regarded as an important part of the celebrations, because they constitute an important additional source of income for many churches (alongside the annual contributions). This extra income is needed for the functioning and services of the parish or church concerned and provides an opportunity to obtain extra money for special purposes such as missions, diaconal projects, the construction of a new church or the upkeep of an existing one. The attention of the congregation is drawn to the collection in a variety of ways. Often the amount donated in the previous collection and the special goals of the present collection are announced beforehand. Usually, the celebrant waits until the collection is ended before resuming the service. The official reason for this is the shared conviction that business is incompatible with the holiness of the celebration. A latent function of this separation between the sacred and the profane is that special attention is focused on the collection and ample opportunity provided for it. Sometimes celebrants try to give the collection a more sacred character by establishing a connection between the offering made by the congregation and the holy offering at the altar. At any rate the collection seems to be one of the most stable parts of the celebration. During the liturgical renewal many elements of the liturgy were changed, but the collection was one of the parts never called into question.

Sometimes tensions arise in connection with the payments to those who officiate at liturgical celebrations. In principle, those who officiate professionally, for example the celebrant, the organist, the conductor and the verger, are paid for their work. Indeed, the verger generally has a fixed contract. The fees are fixed by the diocese and vary greatly from one diocese to another. When the churches try – as they often do – to reduce these fees, this can lead to tensions and quarrels.

5.6. The tension between science and religion

Liturgy therefore serves a facade that conceals conflicting interests and ideas. Research can strip away this facade, clearly revealing the basic sociological structure that underlies every religion, namely the conflict between power and submission, and the arena in which this power-struggle is continuously fought out. This opposition, which is a common feature of religion in general, highlights the basic tension and ambivalence of liturgy. Because in the liturgy the power of God is represented by parts acted by people who exhort others to show the submission that can equally be expected of themselves.

WIEL LOGISTER

A SMALL THEOLOGY OF FEASTING

At the end of the fourth century John Chrysostom complains in his noto-
rious sermons *contra-Judaeos*, that for many Christians the Jewish liturgy
is much more attractive than the Christian one.[1] Whoever has witnessed
Jewish people celebrating a feast like 'the Rejoicing of the Law', will
understand that attraction: amidst boisterous song and dance, the scrolls
of the Thora fly, literally, through the air. The Christian liturgy is in comparison a tedious affair, at least in the West. It has taken over the style of
the serene introversion and seriousness with which the monks of
Solesmes or of Santo Domingo de Silos perform Gregorian chant. Not
even the Alleluia's are able to break through this atmosphere. A lot can be
said about this celebration of the *Mysteriengegenwart* (O. Casel), but it
cannot be said that it is full of exuberance. Everything is organised and
ritualised and takes place in harmonious order. That the feast of eternity
is characterised, according to Augustine, by rest and through the absence
of unruly desires and passions, already casts its shadow here.

   Has the fact that the Jewish feasts are so excessively earthy, anything
to do with the realisation that for the Jews the messianic era is much
further away than for the Christians? I suspect that is not the reason.
The quieting down of rejoicing in the latin liturgy is not specifically
Christian, because African Christians are certainly not less exuberant
than the Jews. Yes, even in Western-Europe it happens that people loose
their heads during processions and other so-called paraliturgical rituals,
incomprehensible as it may appear to many a theologian. From where
does this incomprehension come? Has it only to do with the fact that
many theologians have a clerical and semi-monastic background and
that their culture corresponds completely with a liturgy which is regulated and programmed down to the last details? Is that the only reason
that theologians shy away from festive exuberance? Or do the roots go
much deeper and do they also have other backgrounds?

---

[1] R.L. WILKEN: *John Chrysostom and the Jews. Rhetoric and reality in the late fourth
century* (Berkeley 1983).

The attitude of theology with regard to exuberant joy and big celebrations has become, in the last decades, even more aporetic. That at present – as Arno Schilson[2] remarks – systematic theology shows hardly any interest in the nature and the meaning of feasting, has probably more to do with a feeling of unease than with neglect. Are we allowed at all to celebrate in a time and a culture where there is such dramatic suffering, as in Ruanda, Bosnia and Kosovo? Two theologians as different as Hans Urs von Balthasar and Johann Baptist Metz, find the starting point for their reflections in the mood that prevails on Easter Saturday, on the borderline between death and life, in the stillness of sadness and in somewhat fearful expectations. When the shadow of darkness and death falls over the world, then exuberant joy is not fitting and we can only hope in fear and trembling for a change. Auschwitz has become the chiffre for this dark undertone in contemporary theology. That bleak feeling has a lot to do with the issues articulated in the theodicee with which theology is already wrestling for several centuries and which rests upon her heart like a stone of lead. Do faith and hope really have a foundation and a content, seen against the background of such an overwhelming deluge of suffering and evil? Are faith and hope better at home in the quiet hiddenness of underground churches than in the ceremonies of a Christian empire and an official state church, with all their ambiguous certainties? Should not the theology of feasting remain small?

So as not to engage in all kinds of other-worldly considerations, I begin this little theology of feasting with a consideration of the problem voiced in the theodicee (1). These remarks I will then try to connect with the festive mood in the kerygma of Jesus (2). Following that I try to make clear how the festive character of the Christian existence finds its place in the point of connection between suffering and hope (3). Then, starting from the doctrine of the trancendentals, I will try to come to a set of criteria of what is authentic joy and what is an authentic feast (4). Finally, I will say something about the flaw in feasts in honor of gods like Baal and I suggest that that criticism should not lead to curbing all exuberance in our culture of feasting (5).

---

[2] A. SCHILSON: Fest und Feier in anthropologischer und theologischer Sicht, in *Liturgisches Jahrbuch* 44 (1994) 3.

1. Feasts after Auschwitz

From 1970 onwards, Auschwitz has become *the* chiffre in theology for the question whether, in a world full of enormous disasters and killing parties on a grand scale, belief in God is still possible, for the question what we should hope for, if we are at all entitled to entertain hope,[3] for the question of the legitimacy of joy and feasting. The complaint of Job does not come any longer from time to time from the mouth of a single individual or a couple of people, but has entered deeply into the sentiment of culture as a whole. It can be heard among Jews and Christians, in Europe and Japan, after the dramatic genocide in Ruanda and elsewhere in Africa. And who can forget what happened 500 years ago to the Indians in America at the time of Columbus etc. Ideas and ideologies, that seemed to have been buried forever, have come to life again, under the pressure of the problem articulated in the theodicee: the flight into a collective suicide from an evil world, the idea that the world is the playing field in a contest between a good god and an evil god, Manichaean gloom, the distaste for the earth and the looking forward to a life in heaven after death as the only hopeful perspective. In any case, there seems to be no place anymore for joy and feasting. At the most, in a purely sceptical sense: let us eat and drink, for tomorrow we will be dead. But can one really speak of feasting from that perspective?

'Auschwitz' silences the theologians; they seem to be unable to go beyond the 'Good-Friday' atmosphere. The certainty with which not so long ago one talked jubilantly about God and about hope and progress, has changed into a mood of hesitation and reticence. Exuberance and joyfulness have become suspect. The eschatological reserve has become so great, that there is very little left to celebrate and to feast. Many a theologian reacts therefore in a bitter and cynical way when confronted with the exuberant joy in charismatic circles and keeps his silence when sympathisers of New-Age go back to the song of the sixties "Let the sunshine in" from the musical Hair. The gloomy frame of mind of many Christians, theologians included, reminds one of the man who remains dejectedly behind in the highlands of Jordan and Hermon, while others are full of joy on their way to Jerusalem (Ps 41-42). In 1974 Metz speaks about the difficulty to say yes and to rejoice, because of the

---

[3] F.-W. MARQUARDT: *Was dürfen wir hoffen, wenn wir hoffen dürften. Eine Eschatologie* 1-3 (Gütersloh 1993-1996).

fragility of Christian joy and because of the history of suffering in the world.[4] Many are unable to play anymore and have, like the exiles in Babel of old, hung their citers on the willows (Ps 137). They lack the spontaneity to really celebrate and do not see a reason anyway. The one thing left is a one-sided stress on ethics, even though the realisation is growing that our actions will not bring about paradise on earth.

Of course, it is not only in modern times that great disasters and killing sprees have happened. In former time there was also groaning and lamentation. But this did not take the form of the modern question as put in the theodicee, with its completely defeatist tenor. That does not happen even when in the 20th century the Armenian people are being decimated. Despite that great suffering and the many tears, they did not fundamentally despair of God, of humanity and the value of human life. The question being asked in the theodicee, with its radical scepsis and atheistic tendency, belongs apparently to a specific culture, where typical backgrounds play an important role. It concerns a culture in which the expectation was rife that paradise could be established on earth, certainly from the moment that the lofty human intellect had liberated itself from the dark Middle Ages and science and technology were expected to bring an end to sickness and suffering. Did not God create the human being just for that reason? A great optimism existed in the Renaissance and certainly during the Enlightment. The period of tutelage was over, once and for all. Trust in science and technology was practically without limit. At the background of this expectation we probably find the conviction of a scholastic theology that we are able on basis of dialectic and logic to penetrate more and more into the secrets of God and of our world, and that on that basis we can develop strategies for acting and behaviour that will lead us (back) to paradise. God was seen as the architect par excellence, more powerful and wiser than ever before.

When this world view and this theological concept were confronted with disasters which could not be interpreted as a small and transient breakdown, the whole world collapsed, literally and metaphorically. The modern times are as never before confronted with traumas which are brought about by this belief in progress and these unrealistic eschatological expectations. This does not mean that resignation was the last

---

[4] J. B. METZ: Von der Freude und der Trauer, von der Heiterkeit und der Melancholie und vom Humor, in *Concilium* 10 (1974) 307-309.

and only answer. At first God who had proven to be unable to prevent all this, was pushed aside as an illusion. On top of that it was assumed that faith in God was the scapegoat of the sand in the engine of progress and that humankind could go on under its own steam, provided it dared to trust in its own positive possibilities. A new faith in progress was the answer to the death of God. That is the reason why the French Revolution started full of hope with a new era. Utopian socialism believed in the possibility to create a world without suffering and oppression, even if entire nations and generations had to be sacrificed for the time being on the altar of salvation history.[5] Even though national-socialism saw in communism its biggest opponent, it still cherished just as much belief in progress, centered around its own race and its own nation and culture, around an all-wise *Führer*. When first national-socialism collapsed and some decades later with the Berlin Wall the communist dream also fell apart, capitalism lost no time to fill up the gaping hole with its own faith in progress. And still we are unable to get rid of it, despite the great poverty and the many environmental disasters. Still, the elect are feasting as never before, while at the same time their growing mass disguises the fact that the number of victims is increasing even more acutely. The problems are being repressed, even if their feasts are becoming more and more trivial, their bellies simply being filled and use is being made of psychedelic means to fill up the emptiness. But those who see through what is happening, are not able any longer to enjoy this consolation with its transitory character. The hedonist sinks into the bottomless pit of finiteness and deficit. A sceptic reading of the book of Ecclesiastes is very appropriate here! The reality of the world and of ourselves does not correspond to what we think and expect of it. She is different, possibly less.

Does not the same apply to God? Is God perhaps different from the grand ideas and spheres of omnipotence in which modern times have clothed God? Modern times demand that God only exists if he is the answer to all questions. God has to prove his omnipotence. If not, God does not exist. It is very important to see through the dated character of this apparent water-tight reasoning. Schobert states correctly that the

---

[5] K. LÖWITH: *Meaning in history* (Chicago 1952). Löwith rejects in this book faith in progress and prefers the classical theory of circular movement. In a certain way I am looking in this article for a third possibility and I try to situate there the place of feasting.

problem voiced in the theodicee comes into existence at the moment
that reason claims the fundamental insight into the whole of reality. It is
"a dilemma of Reason itself".[6] God is summoned before the tribunal of
reason. The fact is denied that God, and therefore also our life, is a
secret (Job). The claim of reason does not only lead to atheism, but also
to a deep sense that life is pointless. Up until the sixties optimism still
returned a few times and the situation was not perceived as hopeless.
After that it led to an almost incurable defeatism.

　　Theology let itself be seduced by this trick of reason. Is it still possible for us to go back to the biblical notion of a hidden God, "who is not
the guarantor of a meaningfully ordered an rationally transparent
world"?[7] If so we will have to leave the deep waters of the nominalistic
concept, that God is utterly incomprehensible in his absolute power.
Not that God cannot be understood, rather it is recognised that ultimately the world cannot be understood. On the other hand, God points
at his creative power: against the onslaught of chaos, which forces itself
upon us time and again in our experience of the world, God makes
himself known as the one to whom we owe the fact that we live.[8] This
does not do away with suffering and pain, but it creates "the space
where they are not thrown back upon themselves, but are open to the
future of God".[9] From this perspective it is not proper to speak either
about God's defenselessness or defenseless supremacy or just to draw all
kinds of conclusions from the confession of God's omnipotence. This
does not mean however that now in turn we lay all pain, suffering and
evil at the door of human sinfulness. We are only human beings and not
everything is transparant to us.

　　Should not many questions be left as questions? We are learning
again the hard way that God cannot be handled as a clear and pure idea.
We are, simply on basis of what we know, unable to penetrate into the
transcendence of God. Whoever speaks about God, speaks about a Presence that cannot be pin-pointed and for whom we have no adequate
terms. Gradually and carefully, hesitantly and timidly, people here and
there take leave of the dominant ideology and search for a new life style
and a new world view. Not by running faster towards the future but by

---

　　[6] W. SCHOBERT: Gottes Allmacht und das Leiden, in W.H. RITTER: Der All-
mächtige. Annäherungen an ein umstrittenes Gottesprädikat (Göttingen 1997) 55.
　　[7] SCHOBERT: Gottes Allmacht 61.
　　[8] SCHOBERT: Gottes Allmacht 63.
　　[9] SCHOBERT: Gottes Allmacht 64.

returning to old insights and by listening carefully to the poor and the victims who in the midst of all their need and misery display an infectious human dignity and humanity, without glorifying suffering and misery. It is very well possible that the West has developed a culture which leads more to destruction than to progress, which suppresses the human person more than that it enables him to walk tall.

2. JOY AND FEASTING IN THE VISION OF JESUS

To explore in more depth this last suggestion, I draw attention to the way Jesus went about life. The circumstances in which he appeared were very miserable. In the little towns, villages and hamlets he visited, the mood was gloomy and many walked head down. Galilea in the first century resembled quite a bit the description given in Isaiah 9 of that area: "the land in the shadow of death". Jesus does not deny that at all but neither does he allow it to be the final word. In his prayerful contact with God and with God's word in the Scriptures of Israel, he found the energy and the courage to shoulder this deformed existence. "The Kingdom of God is near with its possibilities and opportunities. That is a reason for hope and joy." Jesus invited people to change towards that direction and to look there for the foundation for a new style of life (cf. Mc 1, 15-15). No one should bury any longer his talent, everyone has at least one talent. Everyone should consider himself as a human being, created out of joy by God. While he wandered about with this message, Jesus saw himself as the bridegroom gathering his friends and inviting them to a feast. He certainly was a realist, not a pessimist. In that he differed from the Baptist, to such an extent even that people characterised him as a bonvivant and drunkard (Lc 7, 34). He wanted to give a chance for the best in human beings to come out, even though he realised very well that some people curtailed their joy in life by limiting their vision to their family, their level in society and their well-to-do colleagues. If one looks at life as a feast in such a narrow-minded way, one undermines the deepest reason for feasting: that we are born naked and for that very reason addressed, encouraged and loved by God. By giving the greatest wretch a place in life, we acknowledge how much we ourselves depend on the sympathy and empathy of friends and strangers and ultimately of God.

Jesus began to realise more and more how much pain and effort was needed to let God's creative insistence penetrate in life. His identification with the mysterious figure of the suffering servant (Isa 53) points into that direction. He comes to perceive in a more and more radical way that his vocation and destiny are to be found in selfless solidarity, even if because of it he will experience in his life oppression and dejection. That makes his life hard and his fate bitter, but deep in his soul a tone of gratefulness, hope and joy will keep sounding. That becomes clear in the account of the synoptic gospels about the last supper. John points in the same direction with the story of the washing of the feet (John 13) and with the whole tenor of the words of farewell (John 14-17). Jesus with his life in danger shows, according to John 13, 1, in a more intense way than ever his devotion to and care for his disciples, who function here as the representatives of the whole of Israel and the whole of humankind. "I have told you all this (and done for you) to share with you my own joy, and so to make your joy complete (= to make it at last possible). This is my commandment: that you love each other with the love with which I have loved you. The greatest love one can show his friends, consists in giving your life for them." (John 15, 11-13). In his joy, Jesus refuses to let misfortune and betrayal have the final word, without giving in to frivolity or superficiality. The very last horizon of this joy is for Jesus the realisation "that the Father has given everything into his hands and that he had come from God and that he would return to God" (John 13, 3).

This joy is not just there simply for the asking. She has a surprising structure. The supporting elements are: the notion of being created, a sense of responsibility, gratitude, confidence, courage. The circumstances are very serious here: Jesus is facing death. The space here is not egocentric, but is determined by care for others. God plays his part here, but we do not find here an all-embracing and completely transparant systematic-theological concept of God. God is much more a space filled with fragments of stories, sayings, hymns, a love story (Song of Songs) and prayers and also with people who following in those footsteps have gone their own way. No easy roads. Often paved with lamentations, but also leading to songs of jubilation, sometimes hardly heard, at other times proudly sung. With peace on their lips, but also with the bitter-sweet taste of vinegar mixed with gall.

That is the way Paul envisages Jesus when he writes: "we are like mourners who always rejoice, as poor who enrich many, as beggars who own everything" (2 Cor 5, 10). In the same spirit the apostle writes elsewhere: "Always rejoice in the Lord. Again: rejoice. Let your good sense be obvious to everybody. The Lord is near. Never worry about anything;

but tell God all your desires of every kind in prayer and petition" (Phil 4, 4-6). The kindness referred to is somewhat peculiar. The greek term (*epieikès*) points to a very typical combination of royal pride and modesty; this attitude is in the context of the letter to the Philippians based on God's selfless presence to people who are laboriously seeking their own real form and shape. In such a proud-modest way, Jesus was a cheerful person and he radiated a stimulating effect. When at Easter he, the living one, fills his disciples with joy, then the holes of the nails are still in his hand and his side is open after the stabbing with the spear (John 20, 19-29). Only if he is seen and recognised in this way, will stammering words like "My Lord, my God", be uttered. For "power is at full stretch in weakness" (2 Cor 12, 9). And exactly on basis of this specific form of weakness, life is becoming a feast. Paul points repeatedly to the paradoxical connection between joy and negative experiences. In the same way a *Laetare Jerusalem* will sound in the midst of a sober Advent and a *Gaudete* in the midst of Lent. The cares and the burdens should not do away with joy, while joy by no means obscures or denies the many negative experiences. This joy gives the courage to fight against the negative. As long as joy is not there for everyone, those who do rejoice, should at times do as if they do not (1 Cor 7, 30), i.e. they should be able to cry with those who cry (Rom 12, 15) in the fervent hope that one day all tears will be wiped away: "May the God of hope fill you with all joy and peace in your faith, so that in the power of the Holy Spirit you may be rich in hope" (Rom 15, 13). His contact with the Corinthians gives Paul a deep joy, despite all his difficulties (2 Cor 7, 4). This joy is not a kind of superficial sentiment because "the kingdom of God is justice, peace and joy in the Holy Spirit" (Rom 14, 7). The joy over the return of the Prodigal Son, should be matched by doing justice and bringing about peace. The way Jesus has become the living figure of the messenger of joy (Isa 40, 9), is therefore quite complicated. He shows a singular and specific entwining of suffering and joy, of sadness and hope. All cheap positions are purified here. All megalomanic claims are tempered here. All big mouths are shut here. His joy has passed through testing and temptations and is quite different from superficial joy. But on the other hand, it is not silent, retiring and purely internal. It breaks through into the open. "The Lord advances like a hero, like a warrior he rouses his fire. He shouts, he raises the war cry, he shows his might against his foes" (Isa 42, 13). Jesus does not fight with the sword or similar weapons, but he does not lack fierceness and commitment, when he takes the side of the crushed reed and the faltering wick (Isa 42, 3). Joy that does not engage in battle, remains stuck halfway. She wants to fight, even though her armor is nothing but good words, writing in the sand, visiting a publican who is looked down upon, taking the hand of a sinner who is excommunicated. As messenger of joy Jesus does not deny the deeply felt suffering, but he does not speak the last word about it. Amazingly, despair – at times strangling – is not the last perspective. He believes in God. What God? The God who has heard the cry of his people in Egypt. Who passes by, while his voice speaks of compassion and sympathy (Ex 34, 6). Whose voice is heard from time to time in a prophet or in a truly wise man. This is the God Jesus believes in. What may we, human beings, expect from this God? There are probably hardly any words for this. But the one who believes, knows that he is not alone, not useless. Executioner and death do not rule supreme. Thank God. A 'thank-you' uttered probably with hesitation, but it can also rise up – as in the biblical psalms of supplication – into a song of praise and joy. In honor of God, who, also in his revelation to earthly beings, remains hidden. Not hidden because of being exalted or because of apathy. Hidden, because this God is so different, at first glance even as practically nothing in the midst of all violence, until he is discovered again with a laugh and a tear in a fearless closeness, full of hope.

3. THE POINT OF CONTACT BETWEEN SUFFERING AND HOPE

This feeling of joy is not lost in the first generation of Christians, not even when the fulness of salvation or the coming of the Lord do not materialise immediately.[10] The apostles do not appear in a minor key, but full of frankness (Acts 4, 13.31). Frankness is characterised, according to 1 Timothy 3, 13, by a basic attitude full of joy, an attitude not thrown off balance by anything or anyone. Even the weight of time does not temper this joy because joy, built upon God's near-

---

[10] The problem of the delay of the parousia is according to me a modern creation. The first generations of Christians experienced therefore less frustration than should have happened in modern eyes. The similarity with the problem of the theodicee is remarkable. Cf. W. LOGISTER: 'Hij zal komen in macht en majesteit'. De vreemde wereld van de christelijke parousieverwachting, in *Tijdschrift voor theologie* 35 (1995) 373-396.

ness which is full of promise, is the ground for hope and patience. The order in which in Galatians 5, 22-23 the fruits of the Spirit are mentioned is striking: love, joy, peace, patience, friendliness, goodness, trust, gentleness, self-control. Love tends towards joy and peace, but with a lot of patience and without becoming fanatic. That flies against the face of normal logic and testifies to a great audacity. The account hope wants to render (1 Pet 3, 15) does not happen over against the demands of reason, but is the actual answer to God and his promise. In that sense Jesus lived as the future human being or as the new Adam. That was the foundation for his joyful message about the kingdom of God and his grateful jubilation over the fact that God had removed the veil. "I bless you, Father, Lord of heaven and earth, for hiding these things from the learned and the clever and revealing them to little children" (Mt 11,25). The high christology of the New Testament indicates this order: Jesus and his will are completely determined by God's promise, that is his support, he does not live on the basis of experiences that can be verified. Belief is born out of listening to prophets and wise men rather than out of reasoning on basis of clearcut experiences. That the promise in him who carries it, is born with labour pains in his own body and soul, is "for Jews/Jewish Christians an obstacle and for pagan/pagan Christians madness" (1 Cor 1, 23). That is why it is so difficult for the Risen One to free his disciples from their fear and to break open their closed doors. They have to begin living in a way that is completely at odds with everything human beings dream of. The joy of the Easter faith makes one brave and vulnerable at the same time.

A feast from within this perspective is something completely different from superficial exuberance, sheer fun or psychedelic elation. It has another foundation and another duration. It is full of seriousness, but this seriousness differs radically from the cynical remoteness of the modern intellectual with his question from the theodicee. This combination of seriousness and exuberance was rediscovered by the liberation theologians among the poor in the slums. The face of the suffering Christ evokes hope in these people, even though they deny neither his suffering nor theirs. With Christ and like him, they take the cross on their shoulders in the power of the promise. In this way the Procession in which the Passion is remembered, becomes a feast that encourages to rise up against injustice and oppression. "This prophetic-subversive dimension of the liturgy calls into question the

spiritual-liturgical traditions and the trancendentalistic or immanen-
tistic reductionism."[11] A celebration is not just a messianic intermezzo
(Van Ruler); then it would still be too much of an incident. It is an
expression of messianism that wants to stretch its wings.

This structure is also present in the hymn *O sacrum convivium* which
is sung during Corpus Christi. In plain terms reference is made to the
passion of Jesus (*memoria recolitur passionis eius*). A correct vision of his
suffering is of fundamental importance here. Jesus did not try to escape
suffering and accepted fully the hard consequences of his commitment.
He did not deny it, did not take flight before it, did not glorify in it
either, but accepted it as a consequence of his joy which he had found
in the space of God. The joy of the kingdom of God presses ahead in a
world full of violence. This joy is not tempered in the midst of violence,
but is hardened. The sentimental and romantic sides disappear from joy.
It comes of age. Its feature is serious, without becoming resigned or
measured. Something similar we find in Ecclesiastes. In a cynical way,
he often seems to give the last word to the pessimist: even with wine,
beautiful women and riches there seems little to be gained under the
sun. At the same time however, he suggests another point of view: the
fear of the Lord and keeping the commandments is the only true wisdom (Eccl 12, 12); they cure us from depression and make it possible to
take pleasure in every day (Eccl 11, 8), and also in wine, in beautiful
men and women and in riches. This joy gives to the human person the
strength of youth, which is not related primarily to a certain age but to
an attitude in life. In this sense Hieronymus translates Psalm 43, 4 as
follows: "I go to the altar of God, to God who gives joy to my youth."
God keeps human life vital. In this sense the more literal translation of
the psalm verse mentioned applies: "God, my only joy" or "the God of
my joyful exultation". This special entwining of seriousness and joy is
precisely what is at stake in the passion and death of Jesus, as the traditions of the last supper show us. And that is caught by others in the celebration of the eucharist. Whoever passes through suffering in this way,
has an unprecedented gracefulness and courage to face life, which other
people find contagious (*mens impletur gratia*). They find without effort
or cramp a way of life in which a real future dawns (*futurae gloriae nobis
datum pignus*). This should be properly understood. That future wants

---

[11] M. PUGA: Het collectief gedenken in de liturgie van de basisgemeenschappen in
Latijns-Amerika, in *Concilium* 31,3 (1995) 78.

to impart already now gracefulness and courage. It challenges people to commit themselves already here and now in the fight against injustice and tyranny. It is precisely in this entwining that joy reveals its true nature. In the same way Christ and the saints are brought by heavenly joy into solidarity with the so-called suffering Church and the Church Militant.[12]

In no way is suffering repressed or denied here. It is a question of *recolitur*: the fact that suffering exists, is being recalled, relived again, not repressed, truly perceived and cultivated or made public. It should not be minimalised or its harshness denied. That a new future is waiting for us, should not be sung too quickly. But the one who can only see suffering and is completely determined by it, fails equally. Suffering can be endured, but probably only those who experience and share it in their own body are able to say this in an authentic way. We should not speak in a cheap way about grace. Only poor and oppressed people with their high-spirited courage and their proud resistance are the bearers of salvation and promise, according to liberation theology and the Bible. Even though poor people sometimes escape to hope and feasts, their cheerfulness is often permeated with a real sense of solidarity, patience and endurance. In that way they become real witnesses of the connection between passion that is not suppressed, gracefulness that enters life, and glory that dawns. Gracefulness and glory do not do away with suffering, but they are the positive force that make it possible to live through suffering. As when Jesus, at death's door, celebrated his positive attitude with his disciples. As when in concentration camps minuscule pieces of bread were broken under the very eyes of the enemies. The gracefulness of the moment is the essence of all feasts: not frivolous, but neither dejected. It rises from a power hidden in the soul and from there comes to light proudly, courageously and joyfully. Because this gracefulness breaks through the cycle of suffering and sorrow, it swings and sings at certain moments. As a challenge and a condemnation of the accomplices of evil. As a helping hand for those who are still burdened under injustice and cynicism, in the sense John 16, 22 says: "You are sad now, but one time your heart will be full of joy, and that joy no one shall take from you." Gracefulness anticipates what has not yet been fully, or possibly only very inchoatively, been accomplished. That is why

---

[12] Buddha becomes in the same way, after his enlightenment, a Boddhisatva, i.e. someone who helps human beings.

it displays a certain discretion. Whether a sense of anticipation or of restraint should dominate, cannot be determined once and for all. At one moment the wealth of possibilities has to be celebrated, at the other caution is called for.

The relation between the three moments in *O sacrum convivium* (the remembrance of the suffering, joyfully finding courage and gladly going towards a new future) is therefore not fixed once and for all. The tensions between the moments appear time and again, but one should not gain the upper hand at the cost of the others. The suffering of the world is never absent but is, in the remembrance of Jesus, surrounded by inflexible hope and by joy because of the opportunities that are there, not to bow one's head in resignation, whatever the situation may be. Encouragement is given not to be crushed by suffering, but to gracefully raise one's head. So that we may become free human beings and so that it may become clear how much pride God takes in these people (cf. Ireneus: *gloria Dei, vivens homo*). It is only then that we can speak properly about a feast. In the face of suffering and death. Ratzinger aptly remarks: "A feast presupposes the mandate to generate joy; this mandate is only convincing if it stands up against death."[13] In the face of death Israel traditionally celebrates Pesach, singing about the hand of the Lord who has smitten the enemy (Ex 15, 6). And the primitive Church sings with Isaiah 25, 8 and Hosea 13, 14: "Death has been swallowed up, the victory is gained! Death, where is your victory? Death, where is your sting?" (1 Cor 15, 54-55).

Is this stressed sufficiently in the way Jesus is celebrated by the Church? Is not too much emphasis put on the internal process of assimilation? Should not joy become more extrovert? No doubt, the stimulating and joyful power of God wants to stir the human person inwardly. But when Paul speaks about the inner human nature which is renewed day by day, and about the invisible (2 Cor 4, 16-18), then he refers to a power which is not subject to the wear and tear of a trivial existence. That power should come to the surface and should be manifested openly. It should become visible. Not through screaming but in a realistic way. Inner nature refers here to the point from where the human being "with all your heart, with all your soul, with all your strength and with all your mind" should follow the active and living word of God

---

[13] J. RATZINGER: *Das Fest des Glaubens. Versuche zur Theologie des Gottesdienstes* (Einsiedeln 1981) 58.

and so transform life. Therefore Paul says: "In my inmost self I dearly love God's law" (Rom 7, 22). Both in liturgy and life we are dealing with the inner side and the outside, with leaping up inwardly and then moving outwardly. The promise or the future do not have us wait until after this mortal existence. It wants to penetrate already now all the dimensions of life. The feast of the gospel therefore reaches further than the liturgical celebration within the Church. If the feast is limited to just that, too much of the dynamism in all the doings of Jesus is disregarded. The present moment is too small and transubstantiation, transfinalisation and transformation too restricted. Then also the cry *Maranatha* becomes too thin, too unworldly, not revolutionary enough. What Jesus did in every day life, should not be placed too readily in the Temple, with the danger that it remains in the Holy of Holies. The Jesus present in such a liturgy is a different Jesus, even though that liturgy may be very solemn. It is much more a Greek deity, than the Messiah who enters life. With the result that the sanctification is not messianic enough. The liturgy with her beautiful form is not hard enough, materially speaking. The eucharist wants to restructure the sometimes abstract longing for wholeness and fullness into a much more earthy way of dealing with life, looking up at him whom they have pierced. The eucharist like the sabbath stands at the meeting point of suffering (Good Friday), falling silent (Holy Saturday) and heartened rising (Easter Sunday). It finds its culmination at the moment that communion with Jesus leads to communion with those from whom we were separated up to then. Is that not what is lacking in our liturgy? Has it not imprisoned the Spirit in the aesthetics of the rite? Is that not why it is lacking the character of a real feast? God, Jesus and the Spirit aim at a transformation which embraces everything. Where that begins, the feast is really beginning.

The Scriptures speak about God and see God present at the meeting point of hope and sorrow, of *theologia crucis* and *theologia gloriae*. The creative force of all that exists, must be sought and found there. If you do not look for it there, you will never find God. Whoever fails to find it there immediately, should not take flight straightaway to another place. God in his hidden heavenly majesty wants to become the shining optimistic edge around suffering people and a groaning world, close to a people wandering through the desert, close to a widow burying her son. That is why Jesus is literally concerned about the destiny of a divided society. That is why the disciples immediately after the vision of the Ascension have to make present the glory of Jesus in the town of humankind. Luke 24, 52 says that the disciples returned to Jerusalem full of joy. As messengers of joy they must speak to the heart of Jerusalem: "Cry to her that her period of service is ended, that her guilt had been atoned for" (Isa 40, 2) "and speak to the towns of Juda: 'Here is the Lord God. He is coming in power; his arms maintain his authority; his reward is with him, and his prize precedes him'" (Isa 40, 10). When God appears, life becomes a feast. Not life in general, but the life of those people who have been visited by the devil, have tears in their eyes, have lost heart, have capitulated.

It is important for the theology of feasting that we resist the temptation to differentiate between God's essence and God's existence. Jüngel emphasises that the existence or the place of God, tells everything about God's essence. We can only say something about God, if we follow God's ways. "Doing theology is pre-eminently being carried along."[14] This applies even more to faith. It is in the strict sense of the word peripatetic, following the specific path of life of God. False prophets prophesy a future where the power of the center and of the rulers is consolidated. This amounts in the eyes of Elijah to giving JHWH the features of Baal. That is the reason why David in 2 Samuel 7 is forbidden to give God a permanent place in his capital. Because of the way God moves, Paul says: "walk in love" (Eph 5, 2) and "look carefully how you walk" (Eph 5, 15). No strolling, not becoming forgetful, not becoming introvert but radically taking new roads. Not going around, despairingly and dazed like the disciples on the road to Emmaus (Lc 24, 17), but going the road of humility, gentleness, patience and tolerance (cf. Eph 4, 1-2). "He who says that he is united with God, should walk (*peripatein*) in the same way as Jesus walked (*peripatein*)" (1 John 2, 6). The way Jesus lived as a *Wanderprediger*, a nomad, tells a lot about the way he perceived and experienced God: as a space of compassion and solidarity, who in a very specific way turns life into a feast.

4. FEASTING IN THE LIGHT OF THE TRANSCENDENTALS

Belief in God, as seen in Israel and in Jesus, makes one look at the world and deal with life in a particular way. To clarify this specific experience

---

[14] E. Jüngel: *Gott-Geheimnis der Welt* (Tübingen 1977) 20b.

and vision of God, I revert to the articulation of God's presence in the doctrine of the transcendentals. God's presence should not be sought outside the wonder over the fact that things exist at all, not outside the impulse to seek truth (trustworthiness, endurance), not outside the pursuit of goodness, the search for unity and the rediscovery of beauty. When God becomes present, the nature and quality of a being (*ens*) becomes clear, it is freed from abandonment and dispersion, relations with other beings (*unum*) arise, it finds or finds again its meaning and finds a sure footing (*verum*), it enters into the space of justice and peace (*bonum*) and it shows a special radiance (*pulchrum*). There is no static presence of God in phenomenons and events; neither is his presence necessarily given therein, nor always equally intense or explicit. This applies especially to that part of reality 'the human person', to the way human beings deal with the whole of reality and especially to the way people live with each other. Everything in our world that can be named and pin-pointed, participates in truth, goodness, unity and beauty. But this happens in people more than anywhere else, in a way that is contingent, not necessary, and therefore frail. People are not necessarily pure and good. Precisely for them, God is present not in a static way but in a dynamic, affirmative, judging, condemning and disturbing way. That is why the reality, truth, unity, goodness and beauty of phenomenons and events are such an exciting affair for people. Sometime the transcendentals are still painfully absent, sometimes they are also happily given as a source of joy that wants to grow into a feast.

Our reality is surrounded by a promise; yes, it permeates our reality to a larger or lesser degree. The transcendentals provide us with a map so that we may discover, how reality – in principle good – is doing, what has become of it and what it still can become. Beauty that fails to open the eyes for still existing injustice, is make-believe. Justice in the sense of *do ut des* or 'an eye for an eye and a tooth for a tooth' does not break through the cycle of evil and keeps isolation alive. If the pursuit of justice leads to inquisition, persecution and intolerance or totalitarian demands, then no real unity is founded. The richness of being and the vocation or destiny of the whole world is denied, if the desire for unity does not go any further than one's own tribe, nation or church. The same happens when everyone is forced into the same mold, after the model of Mao or Pol Pot.

The transcendentals complement each other, are in line with each other, presuppose and clarify each other. Anyone who does not take to heart the interrelation between the different transcendentals, prevents

God from becoming fully present and deforms the vision of God. God should not be reduced to the mysterious ground of created reality, because he is present in everything, enticing and provoking. God should not be considered in a merely positivistic way as source of knowledge, because his truth wants to encourage people to show caring attention. As source of goodness God is asking that the richness of being and the nature of being of all forms of reality, should be respected. As source of unity God wants that the richness of being of everything and everyone may be unfolded. As source of beauty God offers resistance when only the exterior is seen and when the suffering of the disfigured face fails to awaken compassion.

Feasting is, from this theological perspective, only authentic if the transcendentals emerge somehow in their singularity and in their interwoveness, in the midst of our so often suffering and groaning world. Authentic means here also that during a feast, one way or another and to a greater or lesser degree of intensity, a connection with the different transcendentals must become apparent. Joy over being alive and the disposition of someone because of his birth, birthday or jubilee, should imply that the party goers recognise this human being in his richness and need and that in this way a person himself creates space for others. Rejoicing over peace should not mean to put the spotlight on one's own tribe or nation while at the same time belittling the enemy, but it means to break down the walls between tribes and nations. Joy because someone is saved from perdition and has found again his identity, should open the eyes for the lack of radiance on the face of others and open the hands to transform this situation. In a feast God's manifold and dynamic presence is celebrated, that means: recognised, praised and accepted as a challenge. Not simply speculatively, but with all the strength of body, psyche and spirit (cf. Deut 6, 5). In a feast the sphere of the mere tangible and the mere practical is surpassed and transcended. Another, more intensive experience of time and space comes into being. The presence and absence of God comes into prominence. It is experienced in relation to the presence and absence of possible richness of being, truth, justice, unity and beauty, in life in and around us. A feast becomes in this way a peak experience. But at the same time it may imply a crisis and lead to a new way of looking and judging. A feast creates new and challenging certainties that are self-evident.

Feasts can and should be celebrated, when life is set free and rises again from being enclosed in itself and from its sinfulness and when a new space of gratuity is coming into existence. Also when someone no longer tries to silence his own contingency, is not tempted by his fragility to despondency or aggressiveness, but accepts himself in his creaturely actuality. When fear of the others disappears and sympathy arises with both the strength and the weakness of others. In all those moments a certain restfulness is realised and existence reflects a certain lightness of being. Then hurry and agitation disappear and real time is won. Then 'eternal rest' is dawning, a rest which according to Augustine has to do with the absence of negative passions and the presence of positive emotions. These are descriptions, every one of them, of *mens impletur gratia* and of *futurae gloriae pignus*. A certain abundance is seen here, something is brimming over. That is why guests are invited for a feast, why a chair stands ready for the stranger and why expansiveness predominates. Solipsism and individualism are not appropriate for a feast. This very sin is being overcome. And that gives joy, lightness, radiance. But at the same time others are sometimes intensely missed or one's own deficit is acutely felt. Longing springs up, sometimes with all the pain that involves. Also this makes clear that during a feast we anticipate what is not yet fully in existence. Therefore sometimes a collection is made during a feast for a good cause. A feast creates in this way abundance, a flowing over, communicativeness.

This becomes clear in the way Jesus behaved when he was invited to a feast. He did not adapt himself to the table manners of the rich. When he ate and drank at the table of the well-to-do, he always mentioned that there was still no place for the poor and the needy. He took part as a jester and behaved as a kind of outsider. Only when the publicans and the sinners also would participate, would there be a real cause to celebrate. A real feast has always something to do with breaking and sharing, with being what is impossible, doing what is unthinkable. In the same way, Paul raises an objection against party goers who are not prepared to share their bread with the poor (1 Cor 11, 20-22). Whoever does not believe in the possibility of genuine feasting, bows to the power of circumstances, tyrants and scoffers. Then feasting becomes a cynical affair and life is pushed even further into the abyss. The perspective of "this world upside down, that those who mourn will laugh", as a modern Dutch church hymn sings, must therefore be present in one form or another during a feast. The new world breaks through, when we do recognise weakness and sorrow, failure and deficit, sin and guilt, but refuse to give them the final word. Then being really comes into its own, becomes a force for goodness, begins to forge unity and radiance comes over it. The poor and humble person leaps up, grabs the hand of others, starts to dance and maybe to

give kisses and speaks in word and deed of peace. Transcendence is breaking through here. *Ubi caritas et amor, Deus ibi est!*

5. FEASTS OTHER THAN THOSE IN HONOR OF BAAL

The preceding considerations make clear why Israel agitated against the
feasts in honor of Baal. During the feasts in honor of Baal, vitality and the
life instinct occupied centre stage. All attention was directed towards these
realities, in fear and trembling. In the religion of Canaan attempts were
even made in times of crisis, to manipulate life by means of sacrifices of
children and to arouse life energy through temple prostitution. In times of
need, prayers were offered in order that the cycle of nature (rain and sunshine, autumn and spring) would be restored. When feasts were celebrated, then it was a matter of the eternal return of the same, including
the same social system with its apparently necessary phenomenons like
violence, suspicion and repression. Those suppressed received bread and
games as a compensation and to keep the social-political order balanced.
No question here of transformation and revolution, of a new future.

Israel recognises that the sun and other natural phenomenons sing the
praises of God. But Israel's interpretation here is only correct, when it
according to Psalm 19, keeps its eyes directed towards the Thora and submits itself to an examination of conscience. Then natural phenomenons
and other happenings are not seen as divine, but testify in their richness
and poverty of a creating Presence and Benevolence. In this sense the seasons of the year do have a theological dimension: richness and poverty in
being, beauty in varying forms, goodness and deficit, illuminating and
obscuring the truth, growing together and falling apart. The mistrust
with regard to the feasts of Baal is the result of the revelation in which
God appears as the one who breaks through the cycle of existing relations. To glorify God and extol and praise him, is fitting for human
beings, provided they listen to God and his prophets. The seemingly eternal return of the same in nature should not lead to the suggestion, that
life is just the way it is, including all oppression, tyranny and arrogance,
including also the victims made through the system. In Israel we are dealing with another form of perceiving existence, appreciating beauty,
another sense of justice, longing for unity and search for truth and support. The festivities in Canaan were an abomination for JHWH, because
the promise of God has disappeared here, a promise out of which flowed

the relationship based on the covenant and on obedience. Apparently the adagium applies here: tell me when, where and how you celebrate your feasts and I will tell you who and what God is for you.

When we abolish or change a feast or create a new feast, we touch the notion of God and intervene in the vision of life. Israel and Christianity have transformed feasts in honor of the solstice or spring and imbued it with salvation-historical dimensions (the exodus from Egypt, the epiphany of the Messiah, the resurrection of the Messiah etc). The feast became surrounded by other forms of spirituality and ethics. In Canaan feasts were held in honor of the existing order in nature, politics and culture. In Israel on the other hand, the natural phenomenons loose their fascination during a feast, the political power is confronted with the critical word of prophets and questions are asked regarding the wisdom of the existing culture. When this happens, a lot of certainties begin to be undermined and we are not sure anymore where we are heading to. This probably explains the hesitation to participate in feasts where prophetic people or texts play a role, who state that our tendency first of all to play safe and to opt for security, is an obstacle to our full development. In this way the celebration of the last supper ends with a difficult mission. We usually try to avoid that, because we are afraid to loose control and direction. The confrontation with another vision and perception of God, my own existence and that of others, unity, goodness, truth, beauty is confusing.

This does not mean that there is no place for feasting and exuberance. Prophets, wisdom figures and messiah's point to new possibilities in dealing with nature, life and human existence. The wonder over the gratuitous nature of existence, over the light of the sun, over love and affection, over moments when peace dawns and everyone is coming into his or her own, provides quite a few reasons to celebrate. The promise breaks through and we are encouraged, despite dissatisfaction, disappointment and alienation. This future makes sometimes such a profound impression on us during the great feasts of Easter and Pentcost that we even put on new clothes. On days we celebrate the saints, it becomes clear that the promise can come to fulfillment in human beings, each in his or her own way. That is worth an Alleluia and should be celebrated. A feast wants to lift us up beyond restraint and hesitation.

Unfortunately, too great an emphasis on ritual and liturgy has curtailed the scope and meaning of many a feast. Church and theology operate still too much from the opinion that the real feast takes place within the walls of the temple and within the castle of the soul. The Kingdom of

God does not want to be present among us in that way only and certainly does not want to be limited to those spaces. It wants to break through in everyday life, in human relationships, in our contact with nature, in politics and culture. Even if we do not succeed completely, life should not be situated primarily in sorrow and gloom. It is relevant in this respect to remember the fact, that some of the deportees celebrated feasts in Auschwitz and elsewhere in view of their enemy. They refused to let go of their human dignity, of their mutual solidarity, of their belief that ultimately injustice cannot be victorious. Many have refused to be robbed of their belief in God. Not in God as the great architect or watchmaker, but the God who speaks in and through the stories of the Scriptures and who comes to light in the simple gesture of a man or a woman, Jew or Christian, heterosexual or homosexual, believer or pagan, town dweller or gypsy. All this is not simply something cheap and self-evident. Whoever dares to live and to believe in this way, will nearly always have to go through trial and error, beseeching and groaning, fear and doubt. Courage is not drawn from an all-explaining theology. We are talking here of a theology which is much weaker than the self-evident certainties, coming from a revelation-positivistic, ecclesiastical setting. This theology is born in moments of small surprises, in the joy over a dandelion between the bars of a prison, in the happiness over a melody which – though played on improvised instruments in the barracks of a concentration camp – gives a completely different joy than the pleasure with which the camp bullies listened to records of Mozart or Beethoven.

The complication with a feast lies in the difference with superficiality, the place of quiet, the measure of exuberance and the connection with the ethical-missionary task. A moment of quiet reserve, like in classical liturgy and in Gregorian, is undoubtedly necessary to prevent superficiality. But something is missing if that quiet reserve is not expressed with a certain exuberance. This goes undoubtedly hand in hand with the seriousness of a mission, in which the ethical demand is taken up in the possibility given. Theology should not suppress too much the explosive character of feasting by stressing onesidedly the importance of seriousness. Hope, cheerfulness and optimism are characteristic for believers. That gives them a sharp eye for pain and suffering, but they will not be downcast. Every moment something can be celebrated and that opportunity is not missed. As long as this happens "under the eyes of the enemy" (Ps 23, 5) and is accompanied by endurance, tolerance and patience, there is nothing wrong here.

Jan Holman

AN APPROACH FROM BIBLICAL THEOLOGY OF THE PASSOVER
A CRITICAL APPRAISAL OF ITS OLD TESTAMENT ASPECTS

1. Biblical Theology

An approach from biblical theology raises the question: what do we understand by 'biblical theology'? Two answers are known, one from scholars with an Anglo-Saxon cultural background, and the other from experts from the European, German-speaking area.[1] The English usage sets 'biblical theology' off against doctrinal and philosophical theology. Moreover, it distinguishes 'theology of the Old Testament' and 'theology of the New Testament' as two distinct *species* within the one *genus* 'biblical theology'. German-speaking exegetes consider 'biblical theology' as *one* single theology comprising the whole *Christian Bible* i.e. of both the Old and the New Testament. In order to avoid misunderstanding, in texts written in English, one may call this German type of biblical theology 'pan-biblical theology'. Apart from their 'biblical theology', i.e. pan-biblical theology, Germans acknowledge the existence of a separate individual theology of the Old Testament and one of the New Testament. But even there in such an exclusive Old Testament theology of German origin, the authors quite often allow the New Testament to play an important role. Besides, it is characteristic of German writers that their dogmatic persuasion (Lutheran, Calvinistic, Roman Catholic) comes through even in their specific Old Testament theologies. A typical recent instance of this is Otto Kaiser's *Der Gott des Alten Testaments*, which shows definite Lutheran features.[2]

The English terminology seems to me clearer and more respectful towards the proper value and dignity of the Old Testament than the German option, which too often makes the Old Testament tacitly

---

[1] James BARR: *The concept of biblical theology* (London 1999) 1.

[2] Otto KAISER: *Der Gott des Alten Testaments. Theologie des Alten Testaments* 1-2 (= UTB 1747; 2024) (Göttingen 1993-1998).

subservient to the New Testament and to Christian dogmatics. I therefore prefer the English usage in order to mark off my field of work. Within the borders of this concept of Old Testament theology I focus on the phenomenon 'feast' illustrated by the example of the *pascha* (Easter). *Pascha* offers a natural, well defined object, being an eminent case in the development of the theology of the Old Testament, for an exemplary, heuristic approach. Dynamics of culture and cult, transformation in context and appropriation by the liturgical community can here aptly come to the fore.

2. FEAST

The term 'feast' derives from the Latin *festus,* in which we recognize the root *fes-*, which means 'ceremony', 'rite'. A feast carries three characteristics: it is something extraordinary, it is a social event and it synthesizes past, present and future. I will deal briefly with these three elements.[3]

A feast is extraordinary because it interrupts the series of ordinary days in order to commemorate a joyful fact of a cosmic or historic nature. The effect of the fact under consideration can be present all the time and everywhere. But the festival celebration sets such a fact apart in time and space in order to give it special attention. For this purpose, a feast marks out a certain time (feastday) and room (a temple). For example, the beneficial effect of the sun on the human body is present every day, but it is celebrated explicitly on the feast of the solstice. We daily enjoy the freedom fought for so hard in 1945. Nevertheless, we feel a need to observe the 5th of May as a feastday commemorating our liberation. The extraordinary feature of a feast does not depend on the recurrence of a

---

[3] For a reflection on the phenomenon 'feast' defined by *four* elements: (1) a feast is an interruption of the course of time; (2) a feast has an occasion or object; (3) a feast has a shape of its own; (4) a feast is carried by a community, see the article by Paul POST and Louis VAN TONGEREN: The celebration of the First Holy Communion, in part IV of this collection. The elements 1 and 2 we combine under the *extraordinary* character of a feast, since the interruption of time always is an interruption 'filled' by a concrete motive. In the same way, we take together 3 and 4 under the title *community character,* because a festive shape is never disconnected from the community from which it receives its composition. Feast as a synthesis of past-present-future, or its anamnetic function, embedded in the co-ordinates of time with the necessity of fencing off the feast from its environment, does not occur explicitly in the four dimensions just mentioned.

certain date, but on the fact that is called to remembrance. Often this will be the beginning or the newness of a happening in nature (for example spring) or in history (the birth of an important person as celebrated on Christmas day). The exceptional character of a feastday is expressed by people dressing up for the occasion, getting together, having meals together, holding speeches, and engaging in music and dance. A feast carries a social character. It has something that brings people together. People meet around that which binds them together. People toiling away on their own are in imminent danger of being absorbed by their restless labour and of getting stuck. A feast draws them out of the isolation brought about by their monotonous working days. By a communal celebration, the commemoration of the happening itself receives more emphasis and relief. People usually experience this type of social gathering as wholesome. It adds a dimension to the individual human existence. Virtually all the means mentioned earlier which underline the exceptional character of a feast play a part in expressing the community aspect of a feast: clothing, meeting, meal, speech, song and dance. A feast synthesizes past, present and future. From the present, a feast looks commemoratively to the past, and at the same time it is oriented towards the immediate future as a delimitation of the festivity. This marking out is necessary in order both to emphasize the exceptional, social character of the celebration and to intensify the pleasure it brings. Therefore, it is a special art to end a feast at the right moment and in the correct manner, so that it does not fizzle out like a damp squib. Moreover, we may here apply the observation of the philosopher J. Peters: "The past is accepted there, not to become a slave of it, but in order to complete it according to its deepest sense at present and tomorrow. Because the true past is future... And there is the awareness that the future is prepared by the past."[4] A feast celebrates the reconciliation of past and future in the present time, which is filled by both.

3. FEASTS IN THE OLD TESTAMENT

Feasts are constitutive of a religion. This holds good of Israel as well. For the people of God, feasts are a matter of course. Initially they were

---

[4] J. PETERS: Het ondeelbaar ogenblik, in *Studia Catholica* 28 (1953) 274-287, esp. 286.

connected with various phenomena in the world of nature (Ex 23, 14-17). Later on, Israel fills up its most important feasts by the great historic events to which it ows its existence: Easter (liberation from slavery in Egypt), Pentecost (covenant on Mount Sinai), the Feast of Tabernacles (journey through the desert; Lev 23, 4-44). These feasts consisted of rest, a religious gathering and, on the three main festivals just mentioned, a visit to the temple to offer a sacrifice. Characteristic feature of all feasts was 'festive joy' manifesting itself in a banquet 'before the Lord your God' (Dt 12,7). The technical Hebrew term for 'feast' is *chag* which evokes associations with the verb *ch-g-g* 'round dancing' an expressive image of festive joy. From the criticism of religion by the prophets Isaiah, Amos, Hosea and Micah, who were contemporaries (from 750 BC), it appears that celebrations did not always take place in a correct way. These prophets denounce the three classic temptations of the liturgy. They are: (1) the misunderstanding that in a cultic celebration, God's grace becomes available in a commercial manner; (2) the separation of cultic festivals from ethics, as if cultic celebrations can function in a meaningful way independently of moral behaviour; (3) apostasy from YHWH by mingling elements from other religions.[5] The most rabid criticism of religious practices we find in Amos 5, 21-24:

> I hate, I despise your feasts, and I take no delight in your solemn assemblies. Even though you offer me your burnt offerings and cereal offerings, I will not accept them and the peace offerings of your fatted beasts I will not look upon. Take away from me the noise of your songs; to the melody of harps I will not listen. But let justice roll down like waters, and righteousness like an everflowing stream.

In the beginning of the twentieth century this type of texts was a reason in Protestant circles to reject liturgical celebrations as customary in the Roman Catholic church. It was suggested that a prophetic, pure religion 'in spirit and truth' is found in the churches of the Reformation. Nowadays it is virtually *communis opinio* that this view on liturgy has been a misunderstanding. Prophetic criticism of religion is directed towards abuses in the cult of Israel and not against its festive variegated cultic celebrations as such.

---

[5] Cf. Am 2, 8; 4, 4f; 5, 4-6; 14f 21-27; Hos 2, 15; 4, 4ff; 5, 1ff.;5, 1ff; 6, 6; 8; 9, 1-7; 10, 1-2; Mi 1, 2-7; 3, 9-12; 5, 12f; 6, 6-8; Isa 6, 16-21; 7, 14, 11f; Mal 1, 10; Isa 66, 1-4.

4. Survey

After these introductory remarks we are hopefully equipped to a sufficient degree for an examination of the Old Testament Easter. The specific nature of my contribution consists in a critical analysis of modern scholarly publications on liturgy from the point of view of an Old Testament student. We will see how four specialists in liturgical matters deal with the Old Testament Easter feast and we will infer from that survey suggestions for a future biblical theology of Passover.[6] Between these two themes I place a modest, unassuming piece of scenery on the question *How historical is the Passover of the Exodus?*, which serves as background information for both of them.

4.1. Raniero Cantalamessa

In 1971, Raniero Cantalamessa of the Catholic University of Milan published *La Pasqua della nostra salvezza, le tradizioni pasquali della bibbia e della primitiva chiesa.*[7] The book presents itself as an attempt to give a new biblical and patristic basis to Easter catechesis. For this purpose, Cantalamessa distinguishes between: (1) "The Passover of the Lord", which is the salvific passing by of YHWH during the night of the departure of the people of God from Egypt; (2) "The Passover of the Jews", which is the liturgical actualization of the 'The Passover of the Lord' by the reminiscence of countless interventions of God in salvation history in favour of the chosen people; (3) "The Passover of Christ", which is "his hour (...) to depart out of this world to the Father" (John 13, 1) through his passion, death and resurrection; (4) "The Passover of the church", which is the renewal in the liturgy of the "Passover of Christ". This distinction between a twofold *historical* Easter of the Old and New Testament respectively on the one hand, and the

---

[6] Those authors who are not dealt with here did publish important contributions to the study of Passover, but they do not go into the Old Testament in such a manner that a separate analysis by me is due. I mention Wolfgang HUBER: *Passa und Ostern. Untersuchungen zur Osterfeier der alten Kirche* (Berlin 1969); Gerard ROUWHORST: *Les hymnes pascales d'Ephrem de Nisibe* 1-2 (= Supplements to Vigiliae Christianae 7, 1-2) (Leiden 1989).

[7] Raniero CANTALAMESSA: *La pasqua della nostra salvezza. Le tradizioni pasquali della bibbia e della primitiva chiesa* (Milano 1971). Translations: IDEM: *La pâque dans l'église ancienne* (Bern 1980); IDEM: *Ostern in der alten Kirche* (= Traditio Christiana 4) (Bern 1981). I take the original Italian text as my starting point.

twofold *liturgy* of Easter of the Old and New Testament severally on the other hand, has been taken for granted by Christian authors from antiquity. In the heading of his introduction, Cantalamessa calls these different Easter celebrations "The four seasons of Easter". He presents this appealing quadripartite division in two pieces. The first part of his book, entitled "The Passover of the Bible", deals with the first three of the four 'seasons': the Passover of the Exodus, the Passover of the liturgy of Israel, and the Passover of Christ.[8] The whole of the second part, "The Passover of the church", is devoted to the fourth 'season', i.e. the Passover of the church,[9] as one might expect from the superscription. I limit myself here to the first two chapters of the first part concerning the Old Testament. The first chapter, "The historical Passover of the Exodus", offers an inventory of Old Testament texts on the first Easter night (Ex 12, 1-14 and Dt 16, 1-8) in a section called "The night in which YHWH 'passed over'". Cantalamessa analyzes their origins and their literary genres. These ten pages make up a concise, clear overture. But then follows a second section "What does this rite mean?" Here a difficulty shows up. I understand where it comes from; nevertheless I cannot let it pass by tacitly. I had already started to smell a rat in the introduction of the quadripartite division of Easter where we meet the heading "The Passover of the *Jews*" as a description of the liturgical actualization of the Passover in the Old Testament... The terms 'Jews' and 'Jewish' come into use after the end of the Babylonian Exile (537 BC). They do not refer to biblical texts dating from the time before the exilic period. Like other Christian authors who are keen on interesting theological ideas rather than on doing justice to their sources, Cantalamessa sweeps everything that is not New Testament, such as the Mishna and Midrash, on one almost timeless heap with the label 'Old Testament'. Without much ado and summarily, Cantalamessa jumps from the books of Exodus and Deuteronomy, commonly supposed to date from before the Babylonian Exile, to the Mishna treaty *Pesachim* from the the second century AD and the *Haggada* of Easter belonging to the *Midrashic* genre.[10] Subsequently Cantalamessa turns from Deuteronomy 26, 5-10 to the Easter liturgy of the time of the coming about of the New Testament. An Old Testament scholar will not draw

---

[8] CANTALAMESSA: *La pasqua* 11-106.
[9] CANTALAMESSA: *La pasqua* 107-232.
[10] CANTALAMESSA: *La pasqua* 23.

special delight from this jumping chronology and that partially under a false flag ('Jewish'). Finally, the author dishes up a small 'genealogy' of central ideas in connection with Passover. In it the theme of Israel's being the chosen people of God (Dt 7, 6-9) plays a decisive role. Already in Ex 15, 16 the idea of 'redemption' is connected with this 'election'. 'Redemption' in its turn is linked explicitly to the notion of 'creation' in Isa 44, 24. According to the author this bond between creation and redemption can be found in 'the late Jewish' (Cantalamessa) *Haggada* and even in the *Exsultet*. It is not clear to me which historical profile Cantalamessa uses in establishing the chronological sequence of books of the Bible, if he has one at all. His concise *ideengeschichtliche* (concerning the history of ideas) exposé is somehow attractive to preachers because of its simple clarity. Unfortunately, I cannot call this a scholarly underpinned presentation. The third section of the first chapter is labelled: "Pesach: history of a name". These pages, written around 1971, contain a survey of different etymological hypotheses of the Hebrew noun *pesach,* none of them convincing. This compendium appeared ten years after the publication of James Barr's classical dissertation *The semantics of Biblical language.*[11] The main thesis of this book is that it does not do to base theology on etymologies of biblical words, even if they are correct. This view has been generally accepted for some time now. As a result the usefulness of the highly praised *Theologisches Wörterbuch zum Neuen Testament* by Gerhard Kittel (eleven substantial volumes) is strongly diminished. The fact is, we are still groping in the dark as far as the meaning of *pesach* is concerned. It sounds awkward but the four and a half pages of Cantalamessa dedicated to the etymology of *pesach* are just an exercise in futility. He presents interesting etymological details but after reading them, one is hardly any the wiser, since they are no longer a source of theological knowledge and since so little is certain about the origin of the term *pesach*.

The objections raised against section 2 of the first chapter apply in a fuller measure to the whole of the second chapter "The liturgical Passover of Israel".[12] This gives me an opportunity to formulate my difficulties in a more comprehensive way.

The second chapter of "The Passover of the Bible" is supposed to deal with "The liturgical passover of Israel". It consists of four sections. The

---

[11]   James BARR: *The semantics of Biblical language* (Oxford 1961).
[12]   CANTALAMESSA: *La pasqua* 32-66.

first section is entitled "The witness of the Holy Books" and fills three pages or, if one deducts the introduction, little more than two pages.[13] The remaining 32 (!) pages are concerned with Easter in *extra-biblical* sources, taken from the rabbinic and apocryphal literature. Cantalamessa is thoroughly aware of the difference between canonical books of the Old Testament and the extra-biblical Jewish sources just mentioned.[14] Still he does not live up to his knowledge. True, there is nothing against an elaborate exposé on what the discipline called *judaica* (Jewish studies) has to say on the Easter festival. There is, however, an objection against the suggestion that the study of *judaica* produces *biblical* data on Passover, presuming tacitly that extra-biblical Jewish writings present a concrete filling in of the biblical instructions on the celebration of Easter and that therefore they are of equal standing with Scripture. In this connection, some scholars parade ill-defined *uraltes Material* ('ancient material') in extra-biblical sources. This is a clear case of pollution of trade. The fact is that the Old Testament has *two* heirs: one Jewish (rabbinical writings) and one Christian (the New Testament). As we realize nowadays, it does not do to consider the New Testament's 're-lecture' of the Old Testament as *the* exegesis of the Old Testament; it is not right to deal with rabbinical and apocryphal writings as sources of *the* interpretation of the Old Testament either. It is true that the study of *judaica* in Christian circles has assumed enormous proportions and rightly so. It is, however, a persistent and widespread fallacy that Jewish studies throw the ultimate light on the Old Testament. In fact, *judaica* produce more useful information for the exegesis of the New Testament than for the understanding of the Old Testament. We have mentioned two heirs to the Old Testament. But that does not mean they have the same theological value. For Christians, the New Testament is a *normative* source, whereas the extra-biblical *judaica* are not. This looks like forcing an open door, but Cantalamessa's writings show that this remark is not superfluous.

A concrete cause of 'trade pollution' between Old Testament exegesis and Jewish studies lies in the enthusiasm over the discovery of a supposedly lost manuscript of the complete Jerusalemite *Targum* by the Spaniard Alejandro Diez Macho MSC. He found out that this Jerusalemite *Targum* was registered mistakenly under the name of the competing *Targum Onkelos* in the library of the Casa dei Neofiti, a

---

[13] CANTALAMESSA: *La pasqua* 33-35.
[14] CANTALAMESSA: *La pasqua* 32, last section.

Roman house for converted Jews (1542-1962), and was transferred to the Vatican under the lastmentioned name.[15] For the study of the Passover in the *Targum* of Jerusalem R. Le Déaut's solid dissertation, *La nuit pascale*,[16] has been of special importance. Le Déaut draws attention to the *Targum* of Exodus 12, 42 in that Jerusalemite *Targum* which presents a beautiful fourfold poetical 'holistic' explanation of the Passover night. The first night is that of creation, the second is the night of the the fulfilment of the promise made to Abraham by the birth of Isaac, the third is the night of the Exodus story, the fourth night is that of the messianic salvation marking the end of the world. It is quite understandable that Cantalamessa wants to benefit from this rich Jewish theology of the Easter night. Le Déaut is therefore his most frequently quoted author. There is nothing wrong with this enthusiasm of Cantalamessa and others. But my objection against their presenting the *Targum* as a *biblical* source of Passover theology with all the theological weight of normative Sacred Scripture, stands.

4.2. Hansjörg Auf der Maur

As careless as Raniero Cantalamessa is in dealing with the usual distinctions of the Old Testament discipline and related subjects (*judaica*), so responsible is Hansjörg Auf der Maur.[17] His exposé consists in seven short sections (A-G) on ample seven (!) pages, presenting exactly what their superscriptions announce. I have not yet met a better concise survey of the question 'Easter in the Old Testament'. Already the title of section A (on the name *pesach*), "The origin of the word is shrouded in darkness", ("Der Ursprung des Wortes liegt im Dunkeln"), inspires confidence in Auf der Maur's scholarly quality from the outset. Auf der Maur does not hesitate to give full credit to those older authors who have contributed in a significant and seminal way to the study of the Passover feast in the Old Testament.[18] Regarding Auf der Maur's survey

---

[15] Piet VAN BOXEL: *Rabbijnenbijbel en Contrareformatie* (Hilversum 1983) 14-17.

[16] R. LE DÉAUT: *La nuit pascale* (= Analecta biblica 22) (Rome 1963).

[17] Hansjörg AUF DER MAUR: *Feiern im Rhythmus der Zeit 1. Herrenfeste in Woche und Jahr* (= Gottesdienst der Kirche. Handbuch der Liturgiewissenschaft 5) (Regensburg 1983) 56-63.

[18] Leonhard ROST: Weidewechsel und altisraelitischer Festkalender, in *Zeitschrift des Deutschen Palästina-Vereins* 66 (1943) 205-216; Joseph HENNINGER: *Les fêtes de printemps chez les Sémites et la Pâques israélite* (= Etudes bibliques) (Paris 1975).

as a whole, I want to make just one remark. Germanspeaking authors show a tendency to present a chronological sequence of biblical books and texts on the basis of their form-critical research with a certitude that does not always exist in reality. Especially the positiveness with which they present *detailed* layers of edition (*Redaktionsschichten*) and ancient material (*uraltes Material*) could do with some more nuances. By way of illustration, I quote from section B (the *pesach* of the nomadic period): "Yet the oldest yahwistic layer of edition of the account of pesach (Ex 12, 21-30) shows an ancient layer (V.21.22a.23b.27b), which reaches back into the pre-yahwistic nomadic period. But also the later P-Edition (Ex 12, 1-14) contains ancient material." Such a jaunty, self confident language one does not often hear nowadays outside the German language territory in the Old Testament discipline. As an excuse, I point to the fact that Auf der Maur wrote his book before 1983.

4.3. Anscar Chupungco

Shaping the Easter Feast by the Filippino Chupungco is a revised edition of *The cosmic elements of Christian Passover*.[19] His book consists of six chapters, in which there are three sections of importance for my approach. They are, in Chapter I, the paragraph "The Jewish antecedents of Easter";[20] in Chapter IV "The Jewish background";[21] and, in Chapter VI, again "The Jewish background".[22] The suspicion that Chupungco plays the same trick (a sort of 'ringing the changes') as Cantalamessa is confirmed in the three sections mentioned. The sting is in the fact that 'Jewry', 'Jewish' may refer to texts of the canonical Old Testament dating from after the Babylonian Exile (537 BC). But they can also point to the extra-biblical writings of the intertestamentary period and of the beginning of our Christian era (rabbinica). Having said this, I see that Chapter I "The Jewish antecedents of Easter", deals with strictly Old Testamentary texts (Exodus, Leviticus, Deuteronomy) but then wrongly under the Jewish flag ('Jewish Antecedents'). In Chapter IV, everything hinges on Jewish extrabiblical literature (Philo of

[19] Anscar CHUPUNGCO: *Shaping the Easter feast* (= NPM Studies in Church Music and Liturgy) (Washington DC 1992); IDEM: *The cosmic elements of Christian Passover* (= Studia Anselmiana 72) (Rome 1977).

[20] CHUPUNGCO: *Shaping the Easter feast* 12-16.

[21] CHUPUNGCO: *Shaping the Easter feast* 61-63.

[22] CHUPUNGCO: *Shaping the Easter feast* 87-90.

Alexandria, the Book of Jubilees). The Jewish flag covers an essentially different cargo from that in Chapter I. The same holds good for Chapter VI "The Jewish background", which centers around the treaty of the Talmud *Pesachim*. I suspect that with Chupungco the real reason for his interest in Jewish extrabiblical literature lies in his enthusiasm for Le Déaut's dissertation, *La nuit pascale,* mentioned above, just as with Cantalamessa. Their keenness, however, should not go so far as to mix up biblical and extrabiblical sources. Theologically speaking this is unacceptable.

4.4. Karl Gerlach

How totally differently from all the foregoing authors Karl Gerlach approaches the Easter feast![23] It is true, this Lutheran theologian from the United States spends only a few pages on the Old Testamentary basis of the Passover festival.[24] But they are really worth reading. They are entitled "From Rite to Text: the Genesis of Exodus 12". Careful analysis prompts me to make the following remarks. Firstly, Gerlach practices, alongside a diachronic reading, also a synchronic reading of the texts. This has advantages in comparison with the one-sided diachronic exegesis by Gerlach's predecessors in their study of Passover.[25] Secondly, Gerlach is fully alive to the proper features of his sources. Thirdly and in contrast with authors mentioned earlier, except for Auf der Maur, Gerlach does not try to adorn extrabiblical witnesses with the importance of the canonical books of the Bible. Fourthly, there is no mention of a kind of postulated, rectilinear, genealogical dependence of various ritual customs on the original celebration of the Passover festival. Whereas with earlier authors the wish is the father of the thought that all later elements of the Easter feast are a development of an embryonic biblical Passover (Ex 12), Karl Gerlach thinks rather that new data in Easter texts are the result of a *re-interpretation* of Easter, inspired by the changing circumstances of life. Their link with the seminal Easter texts of the Bible is often very thin. Karl Gerlach tries to reach back as far as the time before Exodus 12 by entering into a discussion

---

[23] Karl GERLACH: *The Antenicene Pascha. A rhetorical history* (= Liturgia condenda 7) (Leuven 1998).

[24] GERLACH: *The Antenicene Pascha* 26-30.

[25] For an explanation of the difference between 'diachronic' and 'synchronic', see Jan HOLMAN: De kernboodschap van Jesaja. Omvang en betekenis van de inclusie van Jes. 1-2,4 met 65-66, in *Tijdschrift voor theologie* 36 (1996) 3-17, on p. 3.

with the classical publications of Leonhard Rost and Joseph Henninger.[26] According to Henninger, a German cultural anthropologist, who elaborates on the ideas of Rost, Easter is strictly speaking not a feast, but a nomadic custom in connection with the change of pastureland during spring. It consists in an apotropaeic usage. A lamb or a buck is slaughtered at the beginning of the dry season in order to ward off dangers and demons before shepherds drive their cattle to cultivated areas. Henninger states that this custom has developed into a feast with the following typical salient features.[27] It is a springtime festival celebrated in the family, during which not a priest but the head of the family officiates. The central rite is the sacrifice of the first-born animal of the flock. The principal three rubrics surrounding this sacrifice are the following. A tentpole or the housedoor is smeared with the blood of the animal. Its meat is eaten during a sacred meal. No bone of the animal may be broken. As said before, the smearing with blood serves to ward off evil. The eating of the meat means taking part in the sacrifice. The specific prohibition to break even one bone, according to Henninger, is related to the belief in a 'revival' (*Wiederbelebung*) of the animal by the godhead, either as a real return to life in the world hereafter or as a symbolic living on in the fertility of the flock.[28]

Henninger reaches the conclusion that the Old Testamentary Passover as narrated in Exodus 12 almost certainly is a direct continuation of a common Semitic custom, a springtime festival of shepherds, which Israel shares with other nomadic tribes. Nomadic and seminomadic traditions already appear to contain the typical features of the Easter feast of the Old Testament. During the full moon of the springtime month, the beginning of the new year, an animal is killed. The doorposts of the house or the tentpoles are smeared with blood. Then a sacred meal follows consisting of a roasted animal, unleavened bread and bitter herbs, during which not a single bone of the animal may be broken. Nothing of the food may be kept till the next day.

In contrast with Henninger, Gerlach takes the stand that "Kerygma supersedes rituals (...)".[29] From the beginning, that is from the origin of the basic biblical text of Exodus 12, ancient Semitic rituals are subordinated to the message of Easter which has to be preached. This holds

---

[26] See our note 18.

[27] HENNINGER: *Les fêtes de printemps* 61-77.

[28] Cf. herewith John 19,36 ("For these things took place that the scripture might be fulfilled, 'Not a bone of him shall be broken'").

[29] GERLACH: *The Antenicene Pascha* 5.

good of the possible dependence of the biblical Passover on a preceding nomadic springtime festival, but also of extrabiblical Jewish Easter rituals taken up in the celebration of Easter prescribed by the Bible to the people of Israel. It appears possible that the Easter lamb, initially central to the Passover festival, disappears altogether from the celebration of Easter after the destruction of the Second Temple (70 AD) without prejudice to the Easter character of the customary Jewish Passover meal which has been in use till today. "Anamnesis shifts to other objects, but the dynamic remains unchanged", Gerlach concludes.[30]

On the grounds of my study of the Old Testamentary priesthood, I am inclined to support Gerlach. The striking flexibility of that priesthood in adapting to the ever changing historical circumstances shows that 'the pastoral need' is more important than fidelity to an institutional past.[31] In such a theological climate, a conservative rigidity with a fixation on the past and a paralysing absence of creativity is not to be expected as a norm in moulding the Easter liturgy.

5. How historical is the Passover feast of the Exodus?

Modern Old Testament scholarship is very sceptical about the historical value of biblical traditions describing the Exodus.[32] As early as 1988 Niels Peter Lemche from Denmark wrote: "It is generally acknowledged by scholars that the traditions about Israel's sojourn in Egypt and the *exodus* of the Israelites are legendary and epic in nature (...) There is accordingly no real reason even to attempt to find a historical background for the events of the Exodus."[33] The Old Testament scholar J. Alberto Soggin, emeritus professor of the Pontifical Biblical Institute in Rome, thinks that the Exodus narrative is a fictitious retroprojection of the exodus from the Babylonian Exile.[34] Philip R. Davies, a British

---

[30] GERLACH: *The Antenicene Pascha* 30.

[31] Jan HOLMAN: Het priesterambt onderworpen aan een kijkoperatie, in *Tijdschrift voor geestelijk leven* 51 (1995) 359-375.

[32] J.C. DE MOOR: *The rise of Yahwism* (= Bibliotheca Ephemeridum theologicarum Lovaniensium 91) (Leuven 1997²) 208-209.

[33] N.P. LEMCHE: *Ancient Israel. A new history of Israelite society* (Sheffield 1988) 109.

[34] J.A. SOGGIN: Gedanken zur Vor- und Frühgeschichte Altisraels und -Judas, in *Near Eastern Studies. Festschrift for H.I.H. Prince Takahito Mikasa* (Wiesbaden 1991) 391.

agnostic, Old Testament scholar of the University of Sheffield, England, jettisons the supposedly historical alloy of the Old Testament completely.[35] He maintains: 'Ancient Israel' is a scholarly construction. What we do have is the literary 'Israel' of the Bible text. Without this text, it is questionable whether there would ever have been talk of 'Ancient Israel', since neither historiography nor archeology give rise to this. The only real Israel, without quotation marks, which can be traced with certainty, is called the 'Northern kingdom' in the jargon of exegetes of the Bible. It consists of a piece of territory in the Northern and central hilly country of Palestine between 800 and 700 BC. But the 'Ancient Israel' which is supposed to be the basis of the Books of Exodus, Joshua and Judges, is neither a historical nor a literary reality. Scholars have made of the product of their own line of thought an object of historical research. But what is even worse, they have elevated 'Ancient Israel' to the rank of creator of Bible texts. If, however, 'Ancient Israel' never existed, who then wrote the texts of the Bible, to which *literary* 'Israel' owes its existence? Davies is aware he can only give a beginning of an answer. The whole of the Old Testament was written, according to Davies, between 500-200 BC by writers in the service of the ruling class. This élite left its own imprint on much of the older text material which admittedly was included in the Bible as well. The purpose of this was to create a national consciousness amongst a population that hung very loosely together. The fiction of the existence of one Israel in the distant past plays an important role in this context. According to the will of the ruling élite, the authors of the national literature, our well-known Old Testament, deduce everything from this fiction (their own origin, the cult of Yahweh and their intstitutions). As can be expected, Old Testament scholarship did not accept this frontal attack without a reply. A 'Catholic' reaction written by myself can be found in the jubilee volume of the Theological Faculty Tilburg 1997.[36] Johannes de Moor (Kampen, the Netherlands) presents a balanced position concerning the historicity of the book of Exodus by evaluating the arguments against its historical value carefully and by presenting some new data which are possibly in

---

[35] Ph.R. DAVIES: *In search of 'Ancient Israel'* (= Journal for the study of the Old Testament, Supplement series 148) (Sheffield 1995²).

[36] Jan HOLMAN: Heeft de katholieke kerk een boodschap aan het Oude Testament, in K.W. MERKS & N. SCHREURS (eds): *De passie van een grensganger* (Baarn 1997) 73-91, esp. 84.

favour of it. He rightly points to the tricky character of the argument from silence frequently used by the opponents of the historicity of the Exodus.[37] In the meantime scholars everywhere are busily engaged in the search for extrabiblical facts which can confirm the historical value of the Old Testament. I think that the pendulum which has swung to the far left by Philip Davies' publications will go back to the middle. But we will never know the exact course of events during the Exodus from Egypt, unless an archaeological miracle happens.

6. BIBLICAL THEOLOGY OF THE PASSOVER FEAST

We have stated as a typical feature of any feast that it carries in itsef a synthesis of the past, the present and the future. This characteristic we see verified in an exceptional way in the Passover festival. The ritual points to the past. Various elements are connected with the events of the Exodus narrative. This also holds for the feast of the Unleavened Bread. But there is a difference. The feast of the Unleavened Bread is a reminder of a divine benefit in the past: "And it shall be to you as a sign on your hand and as a memorial between your eyes, that the law of the Lord may be in your mouth; for with a strong hand the Lord has brought you out of Egypt" (Ex 13, 6). The Easter feast, on the other hand, serves as a *zikkaron*, as a 'memorial day' (Ex 12, 14) of a divine redemptive intervention, which according to the book of Exodus still has to happen at the moment of the institution of the Passover festival. Only later on will it point back in time as a memory of the liberation by YHWH. Moreover, the Easter feast is not just a 'memorial day' but a kind of sacramental presentation of what happened then and there during the exodus from Egypt. By the celebration of Easter, salvation realized in the past becomes present here and now. But Easter also looks to the future. This looking forward is a national characteristic of Israel. The coming of the Messiah is expected during the Passover feast. During the last few centuries before Jesus Christ, the eschatological aspect of Easter comes to the fore. Precisely because Israel lives on divine promises, it lives on the past. The past is being continuously cultivated and deepened in a creative manner under the ever changing circumstances of life. So the past presents a guarantee for the future. Past and

---

[37] DE MOOR: *The rise of Yahwism* 209-214.

future together make the present. We can summarize the theological meaning of Easter in terms of renewal, passing over and liberation. The Easter festival is celebrated in spring, which is the time of the renewal of creation, conmemorating the passing over of God for the benefit of Israel's children and to the detriment of the firstborn Egyptians. Moreover, it is a remembrance of the liberating exodus from the slavery in Egypt.

So far we are within the framework of traditional biblical theology, which loves drawing main lines throughout the history of God's people and operates with all-embracing schemes of salvation history. In the case of the Easter feast, a connection is made between the ritual of Exodus 12 and later celebrations of Passover. If one accepts the German view on biblical theology, which I myself do not, the Easter of the Church of the New Testament is the *terminus ad quem* of these main lines and schemes. Students of liturgy often prefer to go a few steps further, as we have seen. They like to integrate the findings from the treasuries of the Jewish people AD into their reflections and love to add them to the biblical line. [38]

This approach has lately become the target of implicit criticism. Well-known postmodern thinkers argue for a break with the great narratives. The French philosopher Jean-François Lyotard gained followers by his proclamation of 'the death of the great stories'. He and with him Jacques Derrida draws attention to the things the text tends to make the reader forget. They point to the repressed thoughts, which had to be forgotten in order to create the illusion of one big transparent, maneagable and coherent whole. Derrida set himself the task of putting in the centre that which the text had marginalized. Instead of stressing the similarities between the ancient Semitic spring festival and the biblical Passover feast of Exodus 12 and all the other Easter celebrations known from both the Old and New Testament and from rabbinic literature, a comparative study with a keen eye for the differences could lead to a view of the Easter feast in which the traditional boundaries are shifted. From this approach, one could successively analyse the Semitic nomadic springtime festival, the Passover of Exodus 12, the Easter feast as an agricultural celebration (Jos 5, 10-12; Ez 45, 21; 2 Chron 30), the centralisation of the Passover

---

[38] CANTALAMESSA: *La pasqua* 6-8. For instance on p. 7: "Tale visione unitaria del mistero pasquale, raggiunta dalla Chiesa fin dalle origini, è una conquista per sempre della teologia."

(Dt 16, 1-8), the Easter feast after the Exile, and the Jewish Easter differentiated into a biblical and into a rabbinical part.

7. PERSPECTIVES

There is a rich variety of methods to tackle such a project. This multicoloured fan of procedures has its raison d'être. Every exegetical method has its advantages and disadvantages.[39] My personal preference is for the semiotic approach adopted by the Paris School of A.J. Greimas. I have argued in favour of this method in an article entitled "Can the Old Testament be enclosed in a theology? Westermann's 'Theologie' and the Procrustean Bed".[40] In any case, when approaching the study of the Passover feast in this new way I advocate, one should beware of the danger which I have expressed in the following quote.

> A respectable theology of the Old Testament cannot aim to reduce itself to a documentary, summarizing description of the "message" in the style of the traditional "positive theology". The matter at issue is rather to scan the Bible in order to discover how a specific meaning is brought about in various texts of Scripture by a perspective on God and man of their own so as to realize a fresh theological understanding.[41]

The advantages of a semiotic approach of different Easter celebrations to find out what their deepest intentions are, may be the following. The semiotics of the Paris School works on the principle of *text immanence*, which has been described by the adage 'outside the text there is no salvation'. A semiotician leaves information from outside the text out of consideration as much as possible. He/she does not want to interrupt the text by that which one believes to know beforehand. A semiotician does not want to put up a sound-isolation screen to stop the text's own voice. I am thinking of the line of salvific history on which tradition assigns a place to different Passover feasts. It leads irrevocably to *gleichschalten* (levelling). This verb, laden with nasty associations for people of my generation, meant during the occupation of the Netherlands by

---

[39] See the 'editio typica' of COMMISION BIBLIQUE PONTIFICALE: *L'interprétation de la Bible dans l'Église*, in *La documentation catholique*, 2 janvier 1994. Almost all current exegetical methods pass in revue with an analysis of their strengths and weaknesses.

[40] In *Tijdschrift voor theologie* 35 (1995) 217-235.

[41] HOLMAN: Can the Old Testament be enclosed in a theology 234.

Nazi Germany (1940-45) the elimination of all that was typically Dutch in subservience to the Great German Empire of all Teutons. My interest is focussed on the specific element of the texts, on highlighting the newness of the text as clearly as possible. Reading, in the Paris School of Semiotics, also means letting oneself become bewildered, disconcerted by the text. A second good feature of semiotics à la Greimas is that it has a keen eye for 'the form of the contents' of the text. This is to be distinguished from interest in 'the form of the expression', which is engaged with the 'outside' such as the division into sections, strophes and so on. 'Form' is used in this context in the sense of the Latin *forma*, known from Aristotelian logic. 'Form' is that which is at stake, the heart of the matter. 'Form of the contents' is that which guarantees durability and identity of the object. Precisely by its interest in the particularity of a text or of a ritual, a semiotic approach can be of use when we attempt to restore their individuality to the various Passover feasts.

Where this semiotic operation has come to a conclusion on the basis of a thorough analysis, the study of Easter rituals in the spirit of Jean-François Lyotard and Jacques Derrida can start with special attention for that which has been marginalized in the single Easter texts and rituals. On the basis of this, a history of the theology of marginalization of elements in the Passover feast can be traced. This could contribute, as far as Easter is concerned, to a new insight into the dynamics of culture and cult, its transformations in context and its appropriation by the community. This is exactly what the present volume envisages and to which my bible theological reflections, within the boundaries of its limited scope, have hopefully contributed.

MARCEL BARNARD

SECULAR FEAST AND CHRISTIAN FEAST IN SCHLEIERMACHER'S *PRACTICAL THEOLOGY* AND *AESTHETICS* A THEORETICAL CONTRIBUTION TO THE STUDY OF LITURGY AND THE ARTS[1]

1. INTRODUCTION

The study of liturgy sees itself confronted by the recognition that its object is very complex and can not be studied apart from its context. One of the aspects of liturgy is art. Church architecture, poetry and prose, paramentics, the visual and plastic arts, dance, music and drama are among other things aspects of the liturgy. But those aspects can not be understood apart from such forms of art in their non-religious or cultural manifestations. Culture can be defined as a symbolic order, and liturgy is a part of it. Cultus or liturgy is a manifestation of culture, even when the former has a negative relation to the latter. In other words liturgy has to be studied in the context of culture. Therefore art history and aesthetics must be included in liturgical discourse.

Although theological research on the arts is part of the study of liturgy, a method of research has not yet been developed in Protestant theology. That lack of methodology is due to the fact that the arts have for long been neglected by Protestant theologians. So we have to begin from the scratch. Our proposal is that Schleiermacher could be helpful in developing a method for such research. The two most important notions of worship are, according to Schleiermacher, art and religion.[2] His entire theology is from the outset a cultural theology in the sense of being deliberately adapted to contemporary culture. His famous *Speeches* of 1799 are directed towards the *cultured despisers* of religion. Also his *Practical theology* is a cultural one, as we will see in this contribution.

---

[1] I would like to thank dr Martin Walton for his comments on the English of this contribution. Citations from Schleiermacher's *Praktische Theologie* and *Ästhetik* are given in my own English translation.

[2] *Die praktische Theologie nach den Grundsätzen der evangelischen Kirche in Zusammenhange dargestellt* (Berlin 1850) 76.

The question answered in this contribution is how Schleiermacher's *Practical theology* and *Aesthetics* can be made fruitful for research on the relation of liturgy and the arts? An answer is found in seeing liturgy and the arts as representations (*Darstellung*) of affections (*Erregungen*), whether religious or not, that need the context of festival and feast to flourish. Festival and Christian feast are the dynamic context in which the arts (or culture) and worship (or cultus) flourish and of which they are a part. Such insights bring us close to what is nowadays called ritual studies. We will see that Schleiermacher's contribution is relevant to contemporary discussions on ritual.

There is a connected question. The study of liturgy is included in the department of practical theology in Protestant faculties and universities of theology, and Schleiermacher is generally considered to be the founding father of Protestant practical theology. As we have said, in Protestant theology a method of research on the arts and liturgy has not yet been developed. In trying to develop such a method we also need to ask the encyclopaedic question how such research on the relation between arts and liturgy is to be positioned in contemporary practical theological discourse? A characteristic of liturgical studies and of aesthetics will be found in the aimlessness of liturgical ritual and artistic representation. Further, just as pastoral sciences are related to psychology, Christian education to pedagogics, church development to sociology, so are liturgics related to cultural anthropology.

2. METHOD AND COMPOSITION: DEFINITIONS

In this contribution we will investigate Schleiermacher's most important publications on liturgy and art. We will pay attention to two books in which Schleiermacher is explicitly concerned with those topics, *Practical theology* and *Aesthetics*. In those two works we expect to find the core of Schleiermacher's thought on our question.[3] When necessary, we will make excursions to other works.

---

[3] Between 1821/1822 and 1833 Schleiermacher lectured six times on practical theology. On the ground of Schleiermacher's own notes and eleven lecture notes of students, Jacob Frerichs edited in 1850 the *Praktische Theologie*. Also the *Aestetics* are based on lectures, in 1819, 1825 and 1832/1833. Schleiermacher's own notes from 1819 and 1825 are edited. On Schleiermacher and liturgy, see Chr. ALBRECHT: *Schleiermachers Liturgik. Theorie und Praxis des Gottesdienst bei Schleiermacher und*

Feast and festival are the starting point of our research, as they are keynotes in both Schleiermacher's *Practical theology* and in his *Aesthetics* (§3). In general 'festival' and 'feast' are used as synonyms in this contribution, which finds its main reason in the fact that there is only a gradual difference between both notions according to Schleiermacher (see §§3.4 and 3.5).

We will study his definition of feast and compare it to that of the Dutch research program. Then Schleiermacher's analogy of feast and liturgy will be enumerated in four comparisons. In the sub-paragraphs that follow those four points will be explained and discussed (§3.1-3.4). Once the complex relation between art and liturgy has been made clear, we will consider how Schleiermacher's thinking on feast and festival and on arts and liturgy can be made fruitful for contemporary research on the arts and liturgy. In this concluding paragraph also the position of this research within the practical theological field is discussed (§4).

The aim of this contribution is to formulate methods of research for analysing liturgy and art. So we will not seek to comprehend Schleiermacher in his historical context, but as a theorist of (practical) theology or, more precisely, of liturgics. Consequently, this contribution has a theoretical character. Nevertheless, its perspective is the analysis of liturgical and cultural praxis.

Liturgy refers in this contribution to the public and private worship of Christian community. Schleiermacher's terminology is not always unequivocal. He himself prefers the word 'cultus' to liturgy. And his study of cultus includes homiletics and liturgical science.[4] Public worship is "a union of individuals, that constitutes a Christian parish and that occupies a particular space".[5] When he uses the term liturgy, Schleiermacher sometimes distinguishes it from prayer and singing, sometimes only from preaching.[6] A definition of feast will be discussed in the next paragraph.

---

ihre geistesgeschichtlichen Zusammenhänge (Göttingen 1963); Th.M. VIAL: Friedrich Schleiermacher on the central place of worship in theology, in *Harvard theological review* 91 (1998) 59-73; M. BARNARD: *Liturgiek als wetenschap van christelijke riten en symbolen* (= inaugural lecture Universiteit van Amsterdam) (Amsterdam 2000) 14-15, 19.

[4] *Praktische Theologie* 67.
[5] *Praktische Theologie* 69.
[6] *Praktische Theologie* 124-125; ALBRECHT: *Schleiermachers Liturgik* 90.

3. FESTIVAL AND CHRISTIAN FEAST

We first will pay attention to Schleiermacher's definition of feast *(Fest)*. He introduces his definition in the first chapter of the first part of his *Practical theology*. That first part is devoted to worship.[7] In the introduction to the first chapter – *Der Cultus* – Schleiermacher discusses the nature of worship. As his entire theology is a dialogue with culture, he wonders what worship is in relation to common and individual life. In other words, Schleiermacher does not speak of worship apart from culture. Cultus can not be studied as an isolated phenomenon, but only in its dynamic relation to culture and to people. He finds the core of his definition of worship in the notion of an interruption of the rest of life. As worship is an interruption of daily life, it stands in a certain opposition to it. Civil and economic activities are interrupted. But this negative notion of interruption is rooted in a positive notion of the gathering of people in larger groups. These essential notions on the nature of worship have a secular analogy *(Ähnlichkeit* or *Analogie)* in feast.[8] Schleiermacher defines feast as follows: "When people break the continuity of labour and business and gather in larger groups for a common activity, we speak of a feast."[9] He adds that one can only speak of a feast when its origin lies in a community sense *(Gemeingeist)* and a historical cause. An imposed feast, by government, for example, is no feast. In other words, feast implies a certain degree of spontaneity.

When we compare this definition to that of the research program of the Dutch *Liturgical Institute*, the modernity of Schleiermacher's definition is striking. The research program's definition is: "the moment or occasion at which people, in the order of time and during the life-circle, as individual, in groups or as society, give a particular, that is an everyday-life interrupting, ritual shape to events that mark individual and social life with a faithful, religious or ideological meaning."[10] There are agreements and differences between the two definitions, although we shall see that the agreements prevail. We call attention to three aspects of both definitions, namely (1) the interruption of continuity;

---

[7] *Praktische Theologie* 64.
[8] *Praktische Theologie* 70.
[9] *Praktische Theologie* 70.
[10] P. POST: Liturgische bewegingen en feestcultuur. Een landelijk liturgiewetenschappelijk onderzoeksprogramma, in *Jaarboek voor liturgie-onderzoek* 12 (1996) 21-55, citation on p. 35.

(2) individuality and collectivity, and (3) the kind of activity that comprises a feast.

The most notable agreement is the notion of an interruption (ad 1). Schleiermacher relates the interruption to labour and business, while the institute's definition relates it to every-day life. The latter apparently reckons with the fact that only part of the population is employed in paid labour and that the economy more and more seems to be an incessant business. Connected to this point is the difference between the possible size of the participating groups (ad 2). Schleiermacher speaks of "larger groups" whereas the institute's definition refers to individuals, groups or society. As Schleiermacher proposes, feast always entails a larger group, although the individual is quite important as we will demonstrate below and as we already have seen in the definitions. Schleiermacher defines cultus as a gathering of individuals. The notion of the individual is essential. The third notion that we call attention to is that of "common activity" (ad 3). In his definition Schleiermacher does not specify that activity. The institute speaks of a "ritual shape" with "faithful, religious or ideological meaning". We will see, however, that measure and rule are important aspects of Schleiermacher's view on the arts and thus on liturgy. They are also central notions in ritual. Religious and artistic expression form a *cycle* or order of myths and symbols. In that mythological and symbolic order meaning, religious or non-religious, is comprehended because the order is the expression of feeling, religious or not.

After studying Schleiermacher's definition of feast and comparing it to that of the Dutch research-program, we will now turn our attention to the analogy of feast and worship. Schleiermacher proposes four points of correlation and difference between feast and worship. In the sub-paragraphs that follow, those four points will be discussed and related to modern discussions. (1) The first analogy we want to discuss is in Schleiermacher's enumeration the last one. Feast and liturgy originate from the same source, namely, from a self-consciousness set free (*das Selbstbewußtsein [wird] frei gelassen*), in other words from human activity in which inwardness enters into an outward manifestation (*das innerliche will auch aüßerlich in die Erscheinung heraustreten*).[11] Self-consciousness is usually captured in civil and economic activities, but when feast and liturgy interrupt those activities, self-consciousness is set free. (2) The

---

[11] *Praktische Theologie* 72.

outward manifestation is only possible by means of art. Worship and feast are always to a greater or lesser degree compositions of artistic elements such as speech, music, singing and decoration. (3) A third analogy is connected to the former two. The essence of all art is its manifestation, just as everything that seeks only to be a manifestation or representation is art. The heightened consciousness attains its end in its manifestation. Representative activity (*Darstellende Tätigkeit*) rests in itself and is nevertheless common, i.e., shared by community.[12] In as much as worship and art are pure expressions and worship includes elements of art, worship is an end in itself. That means, according to Schleiermacher, that acting in worship and in the arts does not serve any aim or end. In practical theology acting is often seen as an intentional activity. For liturgics that understanding can not be upheld. (4) The fourth aspect is a difference, as analogy implies both likeness and difference. The difference between liturgy and feast is the religious character of the former, as Schleiermacher says.[13] We will see, however, that a distinction between religious and non-religious art is more complicated. In the next four sub-paragraphs we will further explain and discuss these four aspects. We will also relate them to modern debates on liturgy and ritual.

3.1. Heightened consciousness and stimulated affection

Schleiermacher's terminology is not always unequivocal, and related terms sometimes have different meanings. This is the case with consciousness and self-consciousness (*Selbstbewußtsein*). The last term is employed in the *Christian faith*, where it is the consciousness of the pure self in relation to God. That consciousness is the feeling (*Gefühl*) of dependence upon God, that is to say, on a single and absolute infinity.[14] Humankind is not self-dependent; in a person's consciousness there is

---

[12] *Praktische Theologie* 71. "In der Kunst ist alles bloßer Ausdruck und völlig zwecklos. Also aus sich selbst heraus erfunden, in Bezug auf die Totalität aber zwecklos, ist das eigenthümliche Wesen der Kunst." *Aesthetik (1819/25). Über den Begriff der Kunst (1831/32)* herausgegeben von Thomas LEHNERER (= Philosophische Bibliothek 365) (Hamburg 1984) 120.

[13] *Praktische Theologie* 72.

[14] *Der christliche Glaube* (1821/1822) §9, cf. *id.* (1830) §§4 and 5. Cf. also G.J. HOENDERDAAL: *Religieuze existentie en aesthetische aanschouwing. Een studie over het misverstand omtrent het aesthetische element in Schleiermachers wezensbepaling der religie* (Arnhem 1948) 49-52.

an empty space that hides itself from reflection. There infinity (or God) reveals itself, and that infinity can not be analyzed in finite factors.[15] The same can also be said of affection. But consciousness (*Bewußtsein*) and feeling (*Gefühl*) can also function as categories of the reason or even as psychological terms. The terms consciousness and feeling in other words are not exhausted in their transcendental definiteness.[16]

Religiosity is a relationship. But the relation is not an isolated one. The person whose consciousness is being dominated by the idea of God is a religious person. The idea of the godhead dominates all human functions, including reason and affection in their non-metaphysical meaning. Artistic representation results from a heightened consciousness (*erhöhtes Bewußstsein*) or from a stimulated feeling (*aus dem [...] erregten Gefühl*).[17] Its representation has a non-metaphysical function. Nevertheless, it can be a result of a consciousness that is heightened by the affection of dependency on God. In other words, every object of art can be a representation of a religiously heightened consciousness or, what is the same, of a religiously stimulated affection.[18] And reversely, every human function can be a manifestation of human religiosity.

In his *Aesthetics* Schleiermacher refines his description of the manifestation of a stimulated affection.[19] He there says that a direct identity of affection and representation lacks measure and rule. Measurelessness and lack of rules are the distinguishing marks of artlessness. Schleiermacher offers the examples of a jump for joy, a rage or a cry of terror, which are direct representations of affections, but are not art. Art presupposes reflection or inhibition between the stimulated affection and its representation. It requires a reflection in which any direct identity is abolished, and measure and rule become operative. Arts and liturgy imply order and rhythm. A symbolic order comes in that is inseparably connected to ritual. Measure and rule are effected by the prototype (*Typus*, *Urbild*). Between stimulation (*Erregung*) and representation (*Darstellung*) in art there is always a prototype. In short, this is an ideal model of representation. Beautiful is what corresponds to that ideal.[20] Art is not the

---

[15] I owe this sentence to Rev. Heleen Zorgdrager (Leersum, the Netherlands), who introduced me to Schleiermacher's *Der christliche Glaube*.
[16] HOENDERDAAL: *Religieuze existentie* 70-71.
[17] *Ästhetik* 37.
[18] *Praktische Theologie* 87-88.
[19] *Ästhetik* 12f. An impulse to this refinement in *Praktische Theologie* 78f.
[20] *Ästhetik* 33ff.

identity of stimulation and representation, but of stimulation and prototype. One stimulation can lead to two or more prototypes and to one, two or more representations.

But even the intermission of a prototype is an oversimplification of the creative process. Schleiermacher thus proposes one more intermediate stage, namely, the mood (*Stimmung*). Art is founded in an innerly heightened affection, in other words in an inner stimulation of the affection.[21] That is not necessarily religious. There is a subjective knowledge of the world, and thus stimulation from the world, that activates the imagination to create images. Art is religious when rooted in a religiously stimulated affection. The affection need not be momentary, but can be durable. A lasting affection is a frame of mind or mood. This mood thus is the constant of the affection. This can be said of religious as well as non-religious affection. The mood mitigates the stimulation and generates the prototype, although itself will not appear in the representation.

The process can be pictured in a diagram as follows:

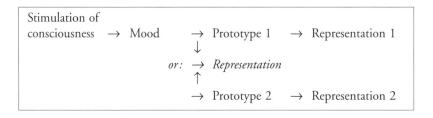

The stimulated or heightened consciousness is set free, i.e., is made manifest and represents itself via the prototype. The notion of consciousness is therefore a dynamic one. The heightened consciousness is in itself an activity, namely the activity of being made manifest. In other words, there is no heightened or stimulated consciousness that is not manifested, as there is no activity of the heightened consciousness without the act of representation.

Schleiermacher's reflections on representation of the inner life are quite similar to what Catherine Bell in present times has called a "new paradigm" in ritual, namely ritual as expression.[22] Within that paradigm

---

[21] *Ästhetik* 23-31.
[22] C. BELL: *Ritual. Perspectives and dimensions* (New York/Oxford 1997) 241.

the ritual and symbolic order is no time-honoured tradition or "heavenly ordained worship", but an expression of a (religious) feeling. Bell stresses that in the new paradigm of ritual community and society are defined "in terms of the self rather than in terms of the community".[23] The same can be said from the point of view of Schleiermacher's thoughts on expression, that in the first place is always an individual expression (see §3.3). But the negative dimension of the paradigm that Bell stresses, does not hold for Schleiermacher: nowadays ritual as expression is seen as a hindrance for 'good sense and good taste', whereas Schleiermacher is explicitly concerned with the aesthetic dimension of ritual and rejects the artless.[24] That points us to the next sub-paragraph.

We will make one more remark in this sub-paragraph, anticipating §3.2. Feast and worship originate from the same source, i.e., a heightened consciousness. Schleiermacher sees feast and worship as representations of that consciousness. On the other hand such consciousness flourishes in an atmosphere that stimulates the process of heightening and representation, i.e., an atmosphere of feast and worship. So, reversibly, feast and worship stimulate the heightening of consciousness and its manifestation. In other words there is an oscillation between on the one hand feast and worship and the heightening of consciousness on the other hand. This remark provides a natural transition to the next sub-paragraph.

3.2. Liturgy and elements of art

The arts and church presuppose each other, as there is no cultus without representation of a stimulated affection. Art is the form by which the affection is represented. From this general rule two questions arise. The first is which artistic forms play a role in worship? The second is which art is religious art? We need not go very deep into the first question, as Schleiermacher's answer is much determined by his historical and personal (Moravian) circumstances. The real power of Christianity he finds in the Word, and thus, for him the sermon is the core of worship. As a consequence he considers symbolic acting of less importance. Roman Catholicism is therefore for Schleiermacher "a reduced Christianity".[25] Speech (*Rede*) is thus the most important art in worship.

---

[23] BELL: *Ritual* 241.
[24] BELL: *Ritual* 241.
[25] *Praktische Theologie* 108.

Mimic art accompanies speech.[26] Poetry in the sense of metre, should only be present in the singing of the parishioners, just as music is only for accompanying the singing. There should be no independent instrumental music![27] Schleiermacher admits the importance of churcharchitecture, but plastic arts serve only to prevent a possible distraction of thoughts.[28]

In our opinion the other forms of arts have an almost equal importance for worship. However, their relation to the Word is not a subject of this contribution. Of more interest here is the second question, concerning the religious character of art. As we have said, every work can be a representation of a heightened consciousness. But when is such an art *religious* art? Does a religious style exist at all? Schleiermacher arrives at a formal definition, based on the notion of composition. Composition implies oneness and multiplicity (*Einheit und Vielheit*). The essence of a work is to be found in a certain oneness, its manifestation in a certain multiplicity (*die Einheit des Wesens und die Vielheit der Erscheinung*).[29] In a religious representation or work of art the multiple is seen in the perspective of God, that is, of an absolute oneness. It does not rest in itself. So in religious art multiplicity is a means to an end, to oneness. Reality obtains a religious value as it points to oneness. Thus, the multiplicity of reality refers to infinity. In religious art reality becomes a sign that is directed toward infinity. In non-religious art the single element receives emphasis. To be sure, the difference between religious and non-religious art is not absolute, but gradual.[30] But before discussing this thesis, we will make three remarks. First, whether a work of art is actuated by a *religiously* stimulated affection or not can not be seen in the work itself. A religiously heightened consciousness can generate a non-religious work just as a non-religious consciousness can generate a religious work. Two examples will illustrate this thesis. The title of Barnett Newman's *Cathedra* (in the Stedelijk Museum, Amsterdam) refers to a religious background of the abstract painting. It 'pictures' the throne of God. But presumably the work is usually not seen as a religious painting. On the other hand, *Psalm 122* of the jazz-musician and composer Willem

---

[26] *Praktische Theologie* 109-112.
[27] *Praktische Theologie* 112-113.
[28] *Praktische Theologie* 114-116.
[29] *Praktische Theologie* 86.
[30] *Ästhetik* 24-27.

Breuker is often experienced as a highly religious work, although the composer declares himself to be an atheist. Second, what is represented in, for example, a painting does not actuate its religiosity. An *Annunciation* is not necessarily religious, and a landscape-painting not necessarily irreligious. Third, whether a work of art is religious or not, does not depend upon the interpretation of the spectator, as there is a formal and in that respect objective criterion.

The aim of this contribution is to formulate methods of research for analysing forms of liturgy and art. We have found a formal criterion to determine if a liturgical – and thus aesthetical – form or work of art is religious. How can this formal criterion be made operational?

Now we will discuss how Schleiermacher's formal criterion for religious art can be made operative. We borrow our thoughts from a study of Inken Mädler, *Kirche und bildende Kunst der Moderne. Eine an F.D.E. Schleiermacher orientierter Beitrag zur theologischen Urteilsbildung.*[31] Mädler tries to distinguish the case between church and modern plastic art. She does so by combining the theology and aesthetics of Schleiermacher with insights of semiotics. As Schleiermacher's *Speeches* were the beginning of modern theology in a strict sense, so the paintings of his contemporaries Caspar David Friedrich and Philipp Otto Runge were the beginning of modern art.

Pre-modern art can be described as an iconographic system in which the significans (*signifiant, Bezeichnendes*) and significat (*signifié, Bezeichnetes*) are held together by fixed codes. There is a semantic unequivocality. In modern art such fixed codes no longer exist. Images or iconic signs embody their own iconic code, that regulates their interpretation. The iconic signs decode the conditions of their perception. Pre-modern art can be described in conceptions, modern art only in functions or as an act. In that act productivity and receptivity are inseparably connected.

At this point Schleiermacher's thinking is comparable to semiotics. Art and religion are – as we have seen – understood as *darstellendes Handeln*, as representative acting. In worship as well as in art the mood generates a free production. Beauty is found in an act. That consists of three moments, namely stimulation, generation of the prototype via the mood and representation. Mood implies passivity just as production

---

[31] Tübingen 1997. Cf. my review of the book in *Kerk en theologie* 50 (1999) 353-355.

implies activity. Passivity and activity are both aspects of the same process. Productivity and receptivity differ only in degree. The consequence is that the artist and whoever enjoys art differ only in degree. A judgement of taste provides an impulse to produce, while on the other hand the judgement of taste is formed by means of what is produced.[32] Productivity and receptivity can both be traced back to the mood. More precisely, art is rooted in the mood that generates a free production.[33] All religious feast life and all liturgy is rooted in a reciprocity between the receptive mood on the one hand and productive and spontaneous representation on the other.[34]

Mädler explains her theory by reference to what is probably Friedrich's most famous canvas, the *Tetschener Altar* or *Das Kreuz im Gebirge*. Although it was painted as an altarpiece, it was never accepted as such. It found a home in a museum; its religious content was denied. That single example is part of a broader phenomenon of the nineteenth century: the museum became a sacred temple of art; the church became a museum of religious architecture. What religiosity does the *Tetschener Altar* exhibit? We see a rock, grown over with pines. On the top a crucifix stands, that we see slanting from behind. The red clouded air is intersected by broad streaks of light. Nature is a mystic reflection of God. In pre-modern art the sign 'cross' would be identified with the historic event of Jesus' death on the cross and its significance for salvation. A cross on a mountain refers to the possible meaning of the fact of someone's *vision* of Christ's death on the cross. The memorial cross correlates to the meaning 'cross' as a religious experience. That experience in turn possibly correlates to the meaning of 'crucifixion of Christ' as an historic event. In other words, there is a non-fixed stream of meanings. There is only an indirect reference to Jesus or God. The canvas of Friedrich has a strict, geometric composition, with three axes. The three axes prevent the eye and the conception of whoever views the painting to focus on either a detail or its multiplicity. God becomes imaginable in an image that breaks through its own fixation.

A landscape with a cross on a mountain here has a religious meaning in this case, although the meaning is not found in the fixed image of the landscape, but in the stream of meanings that the sign 'cross on a

---

[32] *Ästhetik* 3.
[33] *Ästhetik* 17f.
[34] *Ästhetik* 22.

mountain' initiates and in the moving of the eye and mind along the three axes. In short, the religiosity is found in a unity that surpasses all details.

3.3. Manifestation

The third analogy of feast and worship is that they are pure expressions. That means that they are only 'representation' – in German: *Darstellung* – of a heightened consciousness. Representation is the essence of all art. Everything that does not want to be anything else than representation, is art. Also, the festive can only appear in art. Two points call for attention.

First, *Darstellung* can in an immediate sense only ensue from an individual, but presupposes a common understanding. A feast implies a like-mindedness as it is a common activity of people. The expression of individual feelings is only understandable when there is a understanding community, or – as Schleiermacher says – 'an identity of life'.[35] The communal aspect implies measure and rule, which are characteristic marks of art.[36] There is a symbolic order of which the liturgy and the arts are a part. The contrast between non-communicable, i.e., individual prototypes on the one hand and their representation by means of their communication on the other, is not absolute, but relative. Community and order are intertwined and are the conditions of any understanding of art and liturgy and of the communicability of ideas.[37] It is necessary to belong to a group or nation to participate in a feast. For that reason, art only really flourishes in a unifying feast *life*. Schleiermacher offers two examples: the Hellenistic and the Renaissance era.[38] Feast life is – what Paul Post has called – a 'feast culture'. In the sense of Schleiermacher that means a culture that is focused on the expression of a stimulated feeling in a common spirit. Thus an expression that is focused on order, on forming a cycle or system, i.e., a symbolic order that includes most aspects of a culture. Here we note difference with our own 'feast culture', which is splintered into many various cultures. When Schleiermacher defines a feast as an "interruption of the continuity of labour

---

[35] *Ästhethik* 12.
[36] *Ästhethik* 12; *Praktische Theologie* 173.
[37] *Ästhethik* 29.
[38] *Ästhethik* 18, cf. 21.

and business and the gathering of people in larger crowds", we can understand that as an act that fosters culture. Festival and feast create culture and are at the same time the expression of a culture. Participating in culture and creating of culture are reciprocal notions. Schleiermacher formulates the purpose of religious community as the circulation of religious interest (*die Circulation des religiösen Interesse*).[39] A religiously heightened consciousness does not exist apart from its communication of itself; it is an intrinsic part of the stimulated feeling. Such communication is in turn the aim of a religious community. In Schleiermacher's words, the aim of the cultus is "the representative communication of a more stimulated religious consciousness" (*die Darstellende Mitteilung des starker erregten religiösen Bewußtseins*).[40] The communication of the heightened consciousness of the preacher heightens the consciousness of the hearers, but that aim is only attained when the preacher has no other aim than the communicative representation and the representative communication. The effectivity of the religious leader depends on the pureness of the representation.[41] That means, his or her religious activity in worship is in fact void of any aim.[42] It is a pure work, it has no end except to be representation.[43] The paradox is that only by not pursuing any end, a possible *effect* is attained. Liturgy, ritual and even a sermon are never means to an end. That is not to deny that they have a certain effect, but to realize that an effect can only be achieved by not pursuing it. Between the leader of worship and the hearer there must be a pureness of the medium.[44] Liturgy and ritual and art have no aim, no end. In fact, long before Guardini Schleiermacher formulated this famous rule of liturgy![45]

What about the hearer? First, we recall Schleiermacher's notion of representation as acting, in which passivity as well as activity, productivity and receptivity, differ only in degree. At the same time, worship consists of both a distance and a union of sender and receiver. That relative opposition is mediated in a general self-activeness (*die allge-*

---

[39] *Praktische Theologie* 65.
[40] *Praktische Theologie* 75.
[41] *Praktische Theologie* 43.
[42] *Praktische Theologie* 75.
[43] *Ästhethik* 42, *Praktische Theologie* 37.
[44] *Praktische Theologie* 43.
[45] R. GUARDINI: *Vom Geist der Liturgie* (= Herder Taschenbuch) (Freiburg 1957) 89-105, esp. 102f.

meine Selbsttätigkeit).[46] That self-activeness expresses a dynamic relation, which can be characterized as the relation between the progressive consciousness of the hearer and a willingness of the preacher.[47]
The activity of the hearer appropriates the activity of the leader, in
such a manner that the religious consciousness of the hearer is heightened. In the same way the liturgy (including not only liturgical formulas, but also the ecclesiastical feast cycle) and the hymns of the
church are mediated. The same holds for the feast cycle and stimula-
tions from culture. Individual appropriation of the religious occurs by
means of listening to the individual expression of the heightened consciousness of the leader, by the singing of hymns and participation in
the liturgy of the church, and also by the admission of secular conditions that might heighten religious consciousness. So basically, worship
is a union of individuals who are dynamically related to each other, to
church and culture.[48] Those individuals are engaged in mediation,
between themselves and the leader, themselves and the religious community, themselves and the church, and themselves and culture. There
is a dynamic relation, beginning with the individual and including the
individual and the religious leader, the community, the church and
society.

In light of contemporary discussion on the relationships of religion,
subject and society it is important to note that the individual is constituted in his dependency upon God or the infinite. Identity is not
obtained through acceptance in society, but in the experience not to
be ultimately dependent upon that acceptance. Schleiermacher's position surpasses that of Habermas and is closer to that of Henning
Luther.[49]

The second point requiring our attention when we speak of manifestation, is that Schleiermacher distinguishes between an unconditioned and a conditioned manifestation. An illustration is provided by
Christian feast. An unconditioned expression is directly related to life
in its development.[50] It is a spontaneous process. But there also is
an outer cause to the (religious) feeling and its expression, e.g., a

---

[46] *Praktische Theologie* 132.
[47] *Praktische Theologie* 69.
[48] *Praktische Theologie* 69.
[49] H. LUTHER: *Religion und Alltag. Bausteine zu einer praktischen Theologie des Subjekts* (Stuttgart 1992) 34f.
[50] *Praktische Theologie* 128.

(Christian) feast. A Christian feast causes a modification of the religious feeling, because it is determined by the remembrance of a happening in the history of salvation.[51] Every Christian feast has a special atmosphere. The approach of the feast stimulates the consciousness and consequently we prepare for it. But secular feasts can also function as conditions for a religious feeling and its expression; e.g., a new year, a harvest feast, memorial day, etc. The difference between conditioned and unconditioned expression is, similar to that between a receptive and creative mood, only gradual.

3.4. The religious or non-religious character of art

Just as there is a gradual difference between religious and non-religious art, so also between secular feast and Christian feast. We do not want to delve into the difference between religious and non-religious art very deeply. The origin of a feast, for example Christmas, is a moment that is important to that religion. Christmas commemorates the birth of Christ, the founder of the religion. The origin of a feast can likewise be of importance for a nation. Liberation Day in the Netherlands commemorates the liberation from German occupation in May of 1945. The story – the myth – connected with the feast or festival is different and may or may not be religious.

We reflect once more on the notion that liturgy and feast are both expressions of a heightened consciousness, or, more precisely, of an affected mood. The religious mood is expressed in a more subjective and in a more objective manner. The objective manner is that of reflection in dogma's which are ordered in a system. The subjective manner is that of expression in artistic forms. In their own way, they also form a cycle or system, namely a mythological or symbolic circle. Similarly, feast and festival form an order, a cycle, which can be analysed, according to Schleiermacher. We suggest that that circle is comparable to what is presently called the ritual or ritual order. Whether a feast or festival, or its ritual, is religious or not is a matter of degree. In modern ritual studies a secular, a profane and a sacred domain are discerned. Those domains can be investigated using the same method. Secular feast and Christian feast can be analysed on the same level.

---

[51] *Praktische Theologie* 128f.

4. SCHLEIERMACHER AND CONTEMPORARY RESEARCH ON ARTS AND LITURGY: SOME METHODOLOGICAL REMARKS

In conclusion, we make some remarks on how to employ the insights of Schleiermacher's *Practical theology* and *Aesthetics* in contemporary liturgical research. Two questions were to be investigated. How can Schleiermacher's *Practical theology* and *Aesthetics* be made applicable to the research on the relation of liturgy and arts? And: how is that research to be positioned in contemporary practical theological discourse?

Arts and liturgy are both to be seen as expressions of affections. Schleiermacher emphasizes the necessity of investigating them in the context of festival and feast, i.e., as symbolic orders. Ritual and myth are keynotes in that order. From our perspective we can say that Schleiermacher studied liturgy and arts with the tools of ritual studies and semiotics. The merely gradual difference between a secular and a Christian feast, and between liturgical and secular art, corresponds to what is now understood as the distinction between the secular, the profane and the sacred domains. The social science closest to liturgical study is cultural anthropology. In short, arts and liturgy have to be investigated as symbolic orders in the dynamic context of culture. And we should be alert to the fact that in our days we must speak in the plural sense: in the contexts of cultures.

Two possible misunderstandings are to be discerned. The first misconception is that expressions of feelings might be exhaustively investigated by methods of social sciences. Expression in itself is always a psychological or rational notion. But the expression is a disclosure of a stimulated feeling or heightened consciousness. In that feeling there is an empty space where God or infinity reveals itself. Feeling is not merely a psychological notion. It requires a theological method. The second possible misunderstanding is that expressions should not be corrected by aesthetical considerations. Expression is not a pure disclosure of an inner feeling; there is no identity of affection and representation, but of prototype (*Urbild*) and representation. Art and thus liturgy imply reflection and inhibition between the affection and its expression. Reflection provides the prototype and mood by which an identity of expression and feeling is precluded. Measure and rule enter in, and duration as well. Ritual and myth should be understood in terms of repetition, regularity and duration; they are never pure impulses. Expressions have to be rooted in lasting affections. They shape an order and are not just a contingent bunch of symbols.

In short, Schleiermacher is no advocate of the contemporary paradigm that expression places good sense and good taste on a subordinate level. Expression and aesthetics go hand in hand.

The cultural context of liturgy and arts makes it possible to communicate symbols, rites and myths. But the starting point of Schleiermacher's thinking is the individual subject, constituted in its dependency on God. But the thus constituted individual stands in a dynamic relation with others, church and culture. The church is a religious communion. The communion of feelings is inseparably connected to the nature of the inner feelings and their manifestation. But the concrete manifestation of a feeling is also conditioned by the context of the individual. Starting from the individual subject Schleiermacher comes to a delicate balance between individual and community. Art and liturgy have to be studied in the context of that delicate equilibrium.

Such an equilibrium is connected to Schleiermacher's understanding of art. An individual expression can not be seen apart from its cultural context, in a particular festival or feast. That context stimulates a feeling just as it conditions the expression of the feeling. In other words, there is a conditioned and an unconditioned expression, as there is a creative and a receptive mood. But they differ only in degree. The artist and he who enjoys art, creativity and passivity, making art and taking pleasure in art are basically the same. Both are processes that can not be understood as conceptions, but only as functions or acts of the symbolizing mood. The act or function can, as we explained, be investigated with the methods of semiotics. Semiotics can clarify whether feelings are directed toward a single detail or are taken to a higher unity in which all details serve as symbols. When that is the case, we can in the sense of Schleiermacher, speak of religious art.

Arts and liturgy have no aim. The praxis that is the object of practical theology, is usually understood as intentional praxis and with a strategic claim[52] (although there are exceptions under practical theologians[53]). In the Netherlands in state universities and Protestant faculties

---

[52] E.g., G.D.J. DINGEMANS: *Manieren van doen. Inleiding tot de studie van de praktische theologie* (Kampen 1996) 43, 50 and 52; G. HEITINK: *Praktische theologie. Geschiedenis, theorie, handelingsvelden* (Kampen 1993) 195-211; J.A. VAN DER VEN: *Entwurf einer empirischen Theologie* (= Theologie und Empirie 10) (Kampen 1990) 96-101, cf. 69-88.

[53] E.g., M. DEN DULK: *Heren van de praxis. Karl Barth en de praktische theologie* (Zoetermeer 1996) 78-91.

or universities of theology, liturgical studies are part of the department of practical theology. That does not create difficulties, as long as the study of the liturgy can claim an own position within the realm of practical theology. The sciences closest to liturgics are cultural anthropology and semiotics.

Art and liturgy have no aim. Do they also have no effect on people? On the contrary. But Schleiermacher has taught us that a possible effect is only achieved when it is not pursued. The pureness of the medium – that is, of the expression of a stimulated affection, reflected on by the mood, and of obedience to the aesthetic rules – provides the only way of achieving a possible effect. That corresponds again to Schleiermacher's opinion that creative and receptive association in art differ only in degree.

PART III

HISTORICAL EXPLORATIONS

Gerard Rouwhorst & Louis van Tongeren

HISTORICAL RESEARCH ON CHRISTIAN FEASTS AND FESTIVALS IN THE NETHERLANDS AND CURRENT APPROACHES AND SUBJECTS: AN INTRODUCTION TO THE HISTORICAL EXPLORATIONS

From the moment that liturgical studies developed into a separate discipline in the 19th and, particularly, the 20th century, feasts have always been an important subject of investigation. This involved both heortological research into the feasts of the calendar, as well as study of the life-cycle liturgies as these are chiefly celebrated in the sacraments. Feast has always occupied a central place in research by Dutch liturgists too.

By way of introduction to Part III, which includes ten studies that afford insight into present historical research on Christian feasts and festivals in The Netherlands, a brief historiographic sketch of Dutch liturgical/historical research into feasts will first be given. In it the accent will be on drawing attention to the developments, shifts and changes in paradigms that have occurred over the previous half century. Subsequently, on the basis of the various subjects and approaches dealt with in the different contributions in this section, several general trends within present historical research into Christian feasts will be delineated.

1. HISTORIOGRAPHIC SKETCH

In the first half of the 20th century liturgical studies research in The Netherlands was performed primarily in some monasteries and in the many seminaries of the dioceses and the various orders and congregations. Through the merger of these seminaries into several university-level institutions in the 1960s, education and research in theology and liturgical studies was structurally put on an academic footing. Within the academic milieu of these theological training programmes, liturgical studies in The Netherlands developed further, and it was there that the present generation of researchers were, to an important degree, shaped. Through their teachers they achieved competence in the philological and historical/critical study of early Christian and medieval liturgical sources, and in terms of method they followed the path opened by Anton Baumstark, who had introduced and elaborated comparative liturgical studies. Most of them completed their training with a dissertation in which they studied the historical dimensions of a feast according to this method. The dissertation of Hansjörg Auf der Maur dealt with Easter, Herman Wegman studied the Easter Octave, Anton Scheer performed research into the Feast of the Annunciation, and Gerard Lukken studied the theology of original sin in early Christian baptismal liturgy, among other sources.[1] The last three of these men completed their dissertation in Rome under the guidance of the Dutch Jesuit Herman Schmidt, who himself also counted heortology to his field of research, a fact to which his massive publication on Holy Week, among others, bears witness.[2]

The classic philological approach to sources and the texts for feasts in the year and life cycle they contain, has been of incalculable value for the reconstruction of the history of the development of liturgy. Such historical studies gave an important impetus to the liturgical renewal of Vatican II, which would not have been possible without the insights that the cataloguing and study of sources produced. One of the points of departure for this renewal was resourcing. The renewal sought – and shaped – was one which as much as possible was rooted in the practice of the early Church, because this was regarded as the most original and authentic. According to the vision of history which lay behind this view, tradition was understood as continuity. The historical development which was uncovered through the increasing number of sources being published, and studies of them, was valued from the perspective of the oldest available data. Later developments and contemporary practice were related to that.

This – from a methodological perspective, classic – philological and historical/critical approach is still practised by Dutch liturgical histo-

---

[1] HJ. AUF DER MAUR: *Die Osterhomilien des Asterios Sophistes als Quelle für die Geschichte der Osterfeier* (= Trierer theologische Studien 19) (Trier 1967); H. WEGMAN: *Het paasoktaaf in het Missale Romanum en zijn geschiedenis* (Assen 1968); A. SCHEER: *De aankondiging van de Heer. Een genetische studie naar de oorsprong van de liturgische viering op 25 maart* (Baarn 1991); G. LUKKEN: *Original sin in the Roman liturgy. Research into the theology of original sin in the Roman sacramentaria and the early baptismal liturgy* (Leiden 1973).

[2] H. SCHMIDT: *Hebdomada sancta* 1-2 (Roma 1956-1957).

rians,[3] but at the same time they have begun to pose new and different questions to their sources, in part under the influence of stimuli within historical disciplines. Following on the rising study of intellectual and cultural history, attention shifted to a more contextual approach, with increasing attention for the religious and cultural matrix of the feasts celebrated. An initial impetus for this shift of perspective can be recognized in the two heortological monographs by Auf der Maur in which he was the first (albeit yet modestly and in smaller type) to also focus attention on folk customs and how feasts were anchored in culture.[4] This search for new orientations and an expansion of the paradigm for liturgical/historical research also resulted in Wegman's choice, in his manual, to frame the description of the development of liturgy on the basis of facts and sources in the broader cultural and religious context.[5] According to him, the history of liturgy could no longer be studied in isolation; he expressed this still more explicitly in the subtitle that he gave to the revised version of his manual, and which indeed became the main title for the German edition.[6] Wegman worked out the orientation to new paradigms in historical investigation of Christian feasts further in a research programme entitled 'Heortological contributions'. Attention for the broader religious context was here expressly taken into account; the presentation of the question was in part focused on the mentality of faith and the piety of those who celebrated liturgical feasts annually.

[3] See for instance G. ROUWHORST: *Les hymnes pascales d'Ephrem de Nisibe. Analyse théologique et recherche sur l'évolution de la fête pascale chrétienne à Nisibe et à Edesse et dans quelques Eglises voisines au quatrième siècle* 1-2 (Leiden etc. 1989); L. VAN TONGEREN: *Exaltation of the Cross. Toward the origins of the Feast of the Cross and the meaning of the Cross in early medieval liturgy* (= Liturgia condenda 11) (Leuven 2000); E. ROSE: *Communitas in commemoratione. Liturgisch Latijn en liturgische gedachtenis in het Missale Gothicum (Vat.Reg.lat. 317)* (Utrecht 2001).

[4] HJ. AUF DER MAUR: *Feiern im Rhythmus der Zeit 1. Herrenfeste in Woche und Jahr* (= Gottesdienst der Kirche. Handbuch der Liturgiewissenschaft 5) (Regensburg 1983); IDEM: Feste und Gedenktage der Heiligen, in PH. HARNONCOURT & HJ. AUF DER MAUR: *Feiern im Rhythmus der Zeit 2/1* (= Gottesdienst der Kirche. Handbuch der Liturgiewissenschaft 6/1) (Regensburg 1994) 65-358.

[5] H. WEGMAN: *Geschiedenis van de christelijke eredienst in het westen en in het oosten. Een wegwijzer* (Hilversum 1983²) (= *Christian worship in East and West. A study guide to liturgical history* (New York 1985)).

[6] H. WEGMAN: *Riten en mythen. Liturgie in de geschiedenis van het christendom* (Kampen 1991) (= *Liturgie in der Geschichte des Christentums* (Regensburg 1994)).

Among others, this programme produced monographs on the feasts of Corpus Christi and the Exaltation of the Cross.[7] This meant that the research question shifted from the reconstruction of the genesis and developmental history of feasts and rituals to the role and position of the people. This thematic and methodological reorientation in liturgical/historical research was worked out in diverse ways by Dutch liturgists in the collection which was presented to Wegman on his retirement.[8]

By studying the celebration of the feasts and the piety connected with that within the broad context of culture, the distinction between sacred and profane and between being inside and outside the church was integrated into the research; no longer was attention devoted exclusively to the *festa chori*, but also to the *festa fori*. This meant that the question of reception and the relation between cultus and culture came to lie more within the realm of study. Anthropological and ethnological approaches began to be part of heortological studies, both in regard to the past[9] and the present.[10] Following on this development, the theme of inculturation has since become central in the liturgical studies agenda, in part prompted by questions arising from contemporary liturgical practice. In historical research into liturgical feasts this theme has, however, not yet been worked out into a central focus.

The shifts observed with regard to method, the formulation of research questions and the objects of historical research were coupled with an altered vision of history. Researchers began to have more of an eye for change, discontinuity and contingency. The pluriformity of the past was evaluated differently. Contingency of developments in the past nuances the claim of the past to absoluteness, making a reconsideration

---

[7] C. CASPERS: *De eucharistische vroomheid en het feest van sacramentsdag in de Nederlanden tijdens de late Middeleeuwen* (= Miscellanea neerlandica 5) (Leuven 1992); VAN TONGEREN: *Exaltation of the Cross*. Cf. also R. KURVERS: *Ad faciendum peregrinum. A study of the liturgical elements in the Latin peregrinus plays in the Middle Ages* (Frankfurt am M. 1996), although this study is not part of the programme.

[8] C. CASPERS & M. SCHNEIDERS (eds): *Omnes circumadstantes. Contributions towards a history of the role of the people in the liturgy* (Kampen 1990).

[9] Such as research into the processional culture, connected with feasts in The Netherlands in the 19th century: P.J. MARGRY: *Teedere quaesties. Religieuze rituelen in conflict. Confrontaties tussen katholieken en protestanten rond de processiecultuur in 19e-eeuws Nederland* (Hilversum 2000).

[10] P. POST & J. PIEPER: *De Palmzondagviering. Een landelijke verkenning* (Kampen/Amsterdam 1992).

of the meaning of tradition necessary, and demanding a reassessment of a vanished pluriformity.[11]

The study of the sacraments and the feasts of the life cycle from an historical perspective has had less attention in the past decades in The Netherlands than has been given to the feasts of the calendar. In addition to a study of sacramental celebrations according to the ritual in the 17th and 18th century, more detailed studies have appeared on the historical development of extreme unction and marriage, and on baptism, with regard to original sin and godparents.[12] The change of paradigm described, and the reorientation with respect to method and formulating research questions within heortological research, have taken place in a comparable manner with regard to research on feasts lying on the axis of life. After a strongly systematic and dogmatic/theological approach, through anthropological interest the stress has shifted to the position of those involved, the meaning for participants, and the ritual aspects of these feasts. But this new formulation of the questions has not yet been worked out for an historical approach to the celebration of life-cycle feasts. With regard to these feasts, the accent has, from the very beginning, lain on the study of contemporary practice (see part IV).

2. INTRODUCTION TO THE CASE STUDIES

The ten papers collected in this historical part have several things in common. Apart from the fact that all of them are related to the central theme of this book, their authors share the conviction that research on the history of Christian liturgy could benefit from a broadening of its perspective and a renewal of its methods. Challenged by this idea, they want to explore new ways for studying Christian rituals, in particular

---

[11] Cf. H. WEGMAN: De la pesanteur de la liturgie catholique romain, in *Praxis juridique et religion* 4 (1987) 168-175; IDEM: Liturgie en lange duur, in L. VAN TONGEREN (ed.): *Toekomst, toen en nu. Beschouwingen over de ontwikkeling en de voortgang van de liturgievernieuwing* (= Liturgie in perspectief 2) (Heeswijk-Dinther 1994) 11-38.

[12] F. SPIERTZ: *De katholieke liturgie in de Noordelijke Nederlanden in de zeventiende en achttiende eeuw* (Nijmegen 1992); B. GROEN: *Ter genezing van ziel en lichaam. De viering van het oliesel in de Grieks-Orthodoxe Kerk* (= Theologie en empirie 11) (Kampen/Weinheim 1990); J. VAN DE VEN: *In facie ecclesiae. De katholieke huwelijksliturgie in de Nederlanden, van de 13de eeuw tot het einde van het Ancien Régime* (= Miscellanea neerlandica 22) (Leuven 2000); LUKKEN: *Original sin*; P. OSKAMP: *Doopborgen. Profiel en profijt* (Den Haag 1988).

Christian festivals. On the other hand, when reading the different contributions one is struck by the great variety of issues as well as by the differences in approach. Several reasons may be adduced to account for this fact. To begin with, the heterogeneity can be explained to a large degree by the complexity of the history of Christian festivals and Christian feast culture, which easily might provide sufficient material for several thick volumes. Next, the fact that the authors come from different disciplines and ecclesiastical backgrounds certainly has played an important role as well. Last but not least, it should be acknowledged that the search for a more integral approach to Christian rituals and liturgy just has started, and that therefore the ten case studies under consideration inevitably have a tentative and experimental character, and this certainly adds to their heterogeneity as well.

In spite of the divergence of approaches and subjects dealt with, while reading the ten case studies a number of contours soon become visible. It appears possible to discover some convergent lines and tendencies. On the other hand, it cannot be denied that several lacunae also become apparent, which call for further investigation. It seemed to us useful to indicate some of the threads running through the different contributions, hoping that in this way some modest conclusions and also a number of perspectives for future research will emerge.

2.1. Christian feasts?

A first observation we want to make concerns the *character of Christian festivals*. As has been observed by Paul Post, three levels of investigation may be distinguished in research into feast and rituals: that of the individual feast analysed in its own social, cultural and religious context; that of the feast culture which encompasses several feasts and types of feast; and that of feast itself. There is no doubt that the ten case studies may be quite easily categorised under one or two of these headings. Most of them explicitly deal with individual feasts, although in several contributions an attempt is made to widen the perspective by establishing diachronic developments and employing the comparative method which has been so much in vogue in the study of the history of liturgy since Baumstark. This being said, the question may be raised as to whether the contributions collected in this section do not invite us to distinguish a fourth level, namely that of the feast as it takes shape in a specific religious tradition, in this case that of Christianity. Every Christian feast has its own typical features, and at the same time it has elements in common with non-Christian feasts. On the other hand, Christian feasts as such exhibit some common characteristics which are more or less peculiar. Perhaps the specific Christian conception of feast and celebration most clearly emerges from the phenomenon of Christian Sunday. The combination of its weekly recurrence and the custom of reading from Scripture on the one hand – both elements being borrowed from Judaism – and the focus on the death and resurrection of Christ on the other hand give this 'feast' a specifically character of its own which is more or less unparalleled. Further, the focus on the reading of Scripture and on the death of Christ or the saints, in particular the martyrs, have profoundly marked annual festivals as well. Naturally, the question may be raised as to what extent these elements have impinged upon the Christian feasts and festivals celebrated outside the official liturgy and the church building, and it goes without saying that many other traditions and influences have left their mark on this category as well. Yet it would be premature to deny or play down beforehand the effect that these specifically Christian ideas and practices – which in part are also Jewish – may have had on the Christian feast culture in the broader sense of the term. On the contrary, there is a wealth of evidence pointing to the existence of an uninterrupted tension and interaction between these two poles. An illustrative example of this tension is the debate about the relation between the seasonal cycle centred on Christ and the Paschal mystery on the one side, and, on the other side, the sanctoral cycle. Closely related to this is the discussion about the question of to what extent the weekly Sunday, a specifically Christian 'feast', should have precedence over feasts belonging to the annual cycle. These issues have been a matter of debate both in Protestantism, in particular in the period of the Reformation, as well as in Roman Catholicism, especially since the rise of the Liturgical Movement and during the liturgical reform of the Second Vatican Council (see the contribution by Lamberts).

In this connection some remarks are in order with regard to the selection of the concrete themes and festivals. The choice of the different feasts that are dealt with in this section is the result of both conscious planning and more or less fortuitous circumstances. On the one hand, our primary intention has been to give a representative overview of both the different types of festivals and the most crucial periods in the history of Christian liturgy. On the other hand, the number of scholars who were able to collaborate, as well as their specialisms, unavoidably involved serious limitations. The result was a kind of compromise. A relatively wide range of feasts derived from very different periods ranging from the first centuries till the second half of the 20th century has been selected, and as for the period after the Reformation, the choice of the issues betrays an ecumenical intention, in so far as both Protestant and Roman Catholic traditions are represented. On the other hand, we frankly admit that very important lacunae exist. Apart from the fact that some essential historical periods do not receive the attention they certainly would deserve (see below), it might be rightly objected that insufficient attention is paid by far to the liturgical traditions of Eastern Christianity (the only exceptions being the contribution of Groen and, to some extent, that of Rouwhorst). In addition, it cannot be denied that with regard to the later periods, a strong focus is upon the development in The Netherlands, especially upon Dutch Protestantism (but one might hardly expect otherwise in a volume edited and written by Dutch scholars!).

2.2. Processes of transformation

One of the aims of this historical section is to give a rough idea of the genetic development of festivals during the different phases of the history of Christianity, and in particular of the complex *processes of transformation* which have taken place during the history of Christian liturgy, especially in the pivotal periods at which Christianity in general (and therefore also its rituals) were subject to radical and far-reaching changes. What was the character of the changes taking place in these periods in the field of liturgy? To what degree did these changes involve a radical break with the past? Or is the whole idea of a radical change rather misleading and the result of an optical illusion to which historians living in a later period always risk falling victim? Would it not be more correct to talk about gradual shifts which were prepared for at a much earlier time coming to the surface quite suddenly, but which would take more time to be really implemented than is commonly assumed?

One should not expect to find here final and peremptory answers to all these questions. In fact, the studies collected only have an exploratory character. Nevertheless, some conclusions emerge from them almost automatically. The first observation we want to make is that it proves to be highly problematic to make a distinction between an allegedly unchangeable essence of Christian liturgy and its changing forms of manifestation, as was done by Baumstark in his seminal book *Liturgie comparée*.[13] As a matter of fact, it is possible to talk about the specific character peculiar to Christian liturgy and festivals, as we have done ourselves in the foregoing. But it should be kept always in mind that every attempt to describe this character cannot be more than a tentative working definition, and never entirely covers the heterogeneous historical data on which it is founded. More in particular, it should be emphasised that the type of Christian liturgy evoked by such a characterisation never will be found in a pure form in any phase in history. Thus, for instance, it is not to be identified with a very early phase of Christian worship, for instance that of the period of its origins, as too many liturgical scholars have tended to do in the past. From numerous critical studies about the origins and the earliest development of Christian worship, it has become unmistakably clear that there was change and variety of ritual forms from the very beginning, and scholars who tend to ignore this and try to reconstruct a pure, original liturgy can be sure of falling into the trap of what Wayne Meeks has called the "Golden Age fallacy",[14] which usually goes hand in hand with theological and confessional prejudices (see the contribution by Rouwhorst). Next, as for the later periods, one of the principal conclusions that can be drawn from our case studies is that liturgical changes often occur in a less flowing and homogeneous way than is suggested by many of the classical overviews of the history of liturgy. With hindsight, liturgical scholars and historians often prove to have fallen victim to the tendency to streamline processes of change, to make them look more smooth than they were in reality, and to underestimate or even overlook factors like stagnation. On the other hand, they also tend to overlook sudden accelerations, as well as regional and local diversity and variety which may have existed long before and after the change described. A fine example of the complicated processes that the institution of a feast may involve, and that may precede its final breakthrough and its broad acceptance by the community of the believers, is to be found in the study by Caspers of the feast of Corpus Christi and the processions that gradually became its main characteristic feature.

[13] A. BAUMSTARK: *Comparative liturgy*, revised by B. BOTTE (London 1958).

[14] See W. MEEKS: The Christian beginnings and Christian ethics. The hermeneutical challenge, in *Bulletin ET. Zeitschrift für Theologie in Europa* 9 (1998) 171-181, esp. 172-173.

Another case that may be mentioned in this regard is the reception of Sabbath in early Christianity and its final though still partial replacement by the Christian Sunday (see Rouwhorst).

2.3. *Crucial periods*

This being said, it may be observed that the ten papers have in common that they deal with some of the most *crucial periods* in the history of liturgy, i.e. periods that have proven to be pivotal in the sense that they marked the beginning of developments which implied a certain break with the past, turned out to have a lasting effect on the practice and the experience of Christian rituals, and moreover were clearly related to deeper religious, cultural and social processes.

The contribution written by Rouwhorst is devoted to the period of the origins, and especially to the question of to what extent the Christian way of celebrating the weekly recurring festival has been influenced by and is beholden to Jewish Sabbath practice. It thereby raises one of the most crucial and debated issues connected with the origins of Christian liturgy, that of the complicated relationship between early Christian and Jewish rituals. Naturally this question is part of a much broader complex of problems, which is connected with the relationship between Judaism and Christianity as well as to the origins of Christian anti-Judaism, and which constitutes the specific theme of a research programme of the Catholic Theological University of Utrecht, of which Rouwhorst is a member.

A second historical period that has notoriously been of crucial importance for the further development of Western liturgy is that of the early Middle Ages. The main focus is here on the regions which in the period under consideration belonged to Gaul or to the Frankish territories, and later on became part of the Carolingian empire. Both Rose and Van Tongeren try to map the transformations that liturgical traditions and in particular the Calendar underwent in that area between roughly the sixth and the ninth century. While reading the two papers one after the other, one gets a vivid picture of the development of the liturgy, especially of the calendar and the veneration of saints in that period: on the one hand a rise of an original local Gallican cult, namely that of Saint Martin, which succeeded in obtaining an important place in the Gallican liturgical books (and even in the Roman ones!), and on the other hand the Romanisation of Gallican and Frankish liturgical traditions resulting in the introduction of Roman feasts, but also in the elimination of a great number of indigenous feasts from the official calendar and, more in general, a far-reaching transformation of the Gallican and Frankish festal practices and customs. A considerable part of the contribution by De Blaauw is likewise devoted to this phase of history, with this difference however, that its author explicitly concentrates on the liturgical traditions of Rome. Lastly, it may be remarked that the liturgical development in this period, both in the East and the West, has an important place in Groen's comparative study on the feast of the Presentation of the Lord in the Byzantine and the Roman rites.

Quite a few liturgical scholars and church historians tend to view the second half of the Middle Ages as a rather uninteresting phase in the history of Christian liturgy in which, all told, only very little happened. There is a quite widespread tendency to consider this period in its liturgical aspects as a continuation of the early Middle Ages, and to that extent as an era of stagnation. On the other hand, it is often depicted as a period in which the official liturgy obtained an almost exclusively clerical character and, as a corollary, the individual piety of the believers started to go its own way, resulting in a steadily growing gap between liturgy and piety (which the Reformers and adherents of the Liturgical Movement, in their turn, attempted to bridge again). This seems to be the main reason why surveys of the history of liturgy often move very rapidly from the Merovingian and Carolingian period to the Reformation and the Council of Trent. That such views are one-sided and do not do justice to historical reality, clearly emerges from the contributions by Caspers and Dauven-van Knippenberg, which discuss two phenomena that are typical of the development of late medieval liturgy, i.e. the rise of what is commonly called 'liturgical theatre' – more specifically Easter drama – and the emergence and growing popularity of processions on Corpus Christi.

With regard to both these papers, it may be remarked that the phenomena described by the authors testify to a remarkable tendency which to some degree should be considered characteristic of the development of late medieval Christian rituals, namely the tendency to loosen the ties with the official liturgy and to move away from the church building to the streets of the city or the marketplace. In some cases, this development might imply a secularisation of the liturgical rituals involved and, for instance, go hand in hand with an evolution from rite to popular entertainment, as becomes apparent from Dauven-van Knippenberg's study on the Easter offices and the Easter plays. In other cases, this tendency is much less obvious or even simply absent. Further, it certainly would be a simplification to consider this development as a sign of the decline of the liturgy and of a growing alienation of lay people from the official liturgy, as some 20th century proponents of the *actuosa participatio* certainly might be inclined to do. A more open-minded and less prejudiced and negative assessment would be possible, even from the point of view of the *actuosa participatio*. The most important thing here, however, is not to judge this development according to modern pastoral liturgical standards, but to take it seriously as a historical phenomenon.

Two contributions have been included that deal with liturgical developments in the 19th century. Both of them give an idea of liturgical life and rituals in Dutch Protestantism, which in general is characterised by profound Calvinist influences and comprises a great number of different churches varying from very orthodox to markedly liberal. De Jong sketches a picture of a discussion on a liturgical issue, the way of celebrating Good Friday, which for a considerable time continued to agitate one of the largest Dutch protestant churches, namely the *Gereformeerde Kerken* which separated from the national protestant church, the *Nederlandse Hervormde Kerk*, in the 19th century. Smelik in his contribution deals with a specifically Protestant type of festival which existed until the Second World War, exerted a considerable attraction on several Protestant denominations, and was in particular concerned with the missionary task of Christians.

Finally, Lambert's study of the reform of the Roman Calendar provides a bird's-eye view of the development of the sanctoral cycle from the beginning until its recent reform in the Roman Catholic Church. His main focus, however, is on the last half of the 20th century. Thereby this contribution functions in a sense as the closing part of this section, while at the same time forming a kind of transition to the next part, which comprises a number of explorations dealing with contemporary developments and changes.

It will have become evident from this brief survey that attention is paid to a number of the most pivotal periods and turning points in the history of Christian feasts and festivals. In all fairness, however, it should be admitted that some very crucial periods of transition are lacking. In our view, at least two of them should not remain unmentioned, in the hope that in future publications and in writings of other scholars they will receive the attention they deserve.

First of all, a period which certainly should not be skipped in an overview that aims at some degree of completeness – once more, this part does not have that pretence – is that of the fourth and fifth century, when Christianity received general recognition and even became a state religion, which had the effect that Christian rituals and feasts more and more took on a public character. In our view, it would be hard to over-estimate the importance of that development. It should be examined from a double perspective. On the one hand, it might be considered as a far-reaching inculturation of Christian liturgy and Christian ways of celebrating feasts and festivals. On the other hand, this process might be looked at as a Christianisation of pre-Christian rites and festal prac-tice.[15] Several examples might be adduced here of studies taking their departure from one of these different angles which, for the rest, have to be considered as complementary. Both approaches, however, still might open up numerous perspectives for further promising research.

Another period of which we deeply regret that it has not received its due attention in this book, is that of the Protestant Reformation. It could be a very challenging and fascinating task to follow the processes of transformation medieval festivals and feast culture underwent in the time of the Protestant Reformers and in the period thereafter when the Protestant churches developed and institutionalised their own ritual tra-ditions. Authors who would accept that challenge, might consider E. Duffy's *The Stripping of the Altars*, which deals with the situation in England, as a source of inspiration, and try to apply his methodological approach to other countries.[16]

2.4. Feasts and the identity of communities

While reading the ten studies, one will soon discover that most of them have some themes in common. Mentioning all of them here would lead

---

[15] See for these processes for instance F. TROMBLEY: *Hellenic Religion & Christian-ization c.370-529* (Leiden 1995) esp. vol. I, 98-186; R. MACMULLEN: *Christianity & paganism in the fourth to eighth centuries* (New Haven/London 1997) and several of P. Brown's publications. Of course, this list might be easily expanded with numerous other titles.

[16] E. DUFFY: *The stripping of the altars. Traditional religion in England c. 1400-c. 1580* (New Haven/London 1992). See further for instance also J. BOSSY: *Christianity in the West 1400-1700* (Oxford 1985); E. MUIR: *Ritual in early modern Europe* (Cambridge 1997).

us too far afield. For the rest, we have already pointed to some issues that appear in more than one of the ten contributions. Nonetheless, one of those issues stands out in particular because of the frequency with which it recurs, namely the prominent role festivals and feasts may fulfil in strengthening the sense of belonging to a certain community, religious or otherwise, and in marking the boundaries of groups. In some of the contributions this motif plays a role only in the background. In some of them, however, it becomes manifest in a much more explicit manner. All in all, however, it turns out to be one of the threads running through this historical section. That is the reason why, to conclude our introduction, we will give special attention to it.

To begin with, it becomes obvious from Rouwhorst's study on the reception of the Sabbath that one of the main intentions of early Christian polemics against the observance of this day, as well as of the emphasis laid on the Sunday, was to mark the identity of the early Christian communities vis-à-vis Judaism. This conclusion will hardly appear surprising to anyone who is familiar with research on early Christian liturgy. What is, however, perhaps more noticeable is that the idea modern scholars themselves have of Jewish Sabbath and early Christian Sunday is in reality much less objective than one might expect at first sight. Despite all the differences by which they distinguish themselves from early Christians, these modern scholars as well show a tendency to sketch a picture of Jewish Sabbath and early Christian Sunday that may serve to justify the ritual practices of the communities to which they belong, and in so far may contribute to mark the boundaries of these communities. Next, that festivals may play an important role in strengthening the cohesion of a community becomes especially apparent from Smelik's description of the Protestant *zendingsfeesten*. One of the functions of these festive meetings in the open air obviously was a social one and consisted in binding together different denominations and overcoming, at least for a while, the internal divisions which characterised and continue to characterise Dutch Protestantism. Moreover, it helped these denominations to form a united front against all kinds of external dangers that were believed to threaten their identity and even their survival, such as secularisation, liberal theology and so on. Next, one of the main conclusions of De Jong's paper is that communities may express their identity not only by celebrating certain feasts, but, conversely, also by refusing to celebrate feasts that are taken to be characteristic of other groups, for instance churches from which they want to distinguish themselves. Thus it appears that one of the reasons why in general the *Gereformeerde Kerken* were averse to liturgical services on Good Friday, and in any case fiercely rejected the administration of the Lord's Supper on that day, was that these practices were viewed as peculiar to the national *Hervormde Kerk* and in particular, that they were associated with certain liberal tendencies in that church as well as with Roman Catholicism (although, as a matter of fact, the latter does not celebrate the Eucharist on Good Friday). Finally, both from the study of De Blaauw and from that of Caspers, it becomes apparent that especially processions (and comparable phenomena like parades, marches and so on) constitute an ideal means of expressing and demonstrating group cohesion. For the rest, they do not only manifest the unity of the community as a whole and mark, so to speak, their external boundaries. The behaviour of the participants, and in particular the way in which they are lined up, may also have the function of emphasising internal boundaries, for instance stressing the position of the ordained clergy or members of the hierarchy over against the laymen. In this respect, the distinction De Blaauw makes between a letania and a cortège is very illuminating.

GERARD ROUWHORST

THE RECEPTION OF THE JEWISH SABBATH IN EARLY CHRISTIANITY

Among the enormous variety of festivals encountered in the religions of humanity the Jewish Sabbath has a very peculiar and even unique position. There is no doubt, this weekly day of rest and worship shares several striking characteristics with the festivals which in Judaism are celebrated during the year especially in the spring and in the autumn, and more in general with many religious feasts and holidays of non-Jewish religions and societies. Just like many of those Jewish and non-Jewish festivals it has a sacred character, in the sense that it represents a segment of time clearly marked off from the routine of daily life and work and set apart for religious and communal activities. Likewise, its joyful atmosphere unmistakably adds to its festive character. On the other hand, in several respects it is a very atypical festival, and in a sense the question might be raised whether it should be considered a festival at all. One of the reasons why it is such an atypical festival lies in its independence from the cosmic and 'natural' rhythms of the sun and the moon. Equally abnormal is the frequency with which it is celebrated. In a sense, festivals owe their existence and subsistence to the fact of not being celebrated too frequently. The weekly recurring Sabbath, however, seems to ignore this rule. Finally, the way in which this day is celebrated clearly deviates from what is current in most festivals and certainly differs from what was customary in Antiquity among non-Jews, for example Greeks, Romans, Egyptians. At least two things must have struck non-Jews as being abnormal: first the Sabbath-halakha, the numerous and detailed rules regarding what was allowed and forbidden on the weekly day of rest and worship and, secondly, the type of celebration that came into development in the Synagogue, which did involve neither sacrificial rituals nor festive processions or dancing and singing, but basically consisted of reading and studying a holy book, that is to say the Torah and the Prophets, which – probably in a later stage (end first or during the second century C.E.)[1] – was com-

---

[1] See further, section 2.

bined with the communal recitation of the so-called statutory prayers, like the Shema and the Eighteen Benedictions.

From a very early period on, Christians have taken an ambivalent position towards the Sabbath. On the one hand, they mostly agreed that the so-called Ten Words or Ten Commandments were not exclusively intended for observation by the Jews and, moreover, they did not consider them to apply only for a limited period of time, that is to say until their abolishment by Christ (such, in their view, was the case for the ceremonial laws, like the circumcision, the rules of purity and the dietary rules). In general, they believed in the universal meaning and validity of those commandments for both Jews and Christians. On the other hand, the attitude Christians took during the centuries towards two among those commandments must be qualified as rather ambiguous, since these were not accepted straightforwardly by many of them and moreover gave rise to theological discussions and debates. I mean the prohibition to make graven images which by some Christian traditions was interpreted more strictly than by others, and the fourth one (or, according to another way of counting, the third one) prescribing the observance of the Sabbath. As for the latter commandment, some Jewish Christian and Sabbatarian movements took it literally, but the majority of them did not. On the other hand, the commandment to remember and observe the Sabbath has unmistakably left its traces in the history of Christianity and in particular from the fourth century onwards it has influenced the way in which Christians and Christian communities spent their Sunday and, to a lesser degree, sometimes also the Saturday.

The reception of the Jewish Sabbath in Christianity, the different and sometimes contradictory views and reactions it provoked among Christians and the impact it had on Christian ritual and festal practices, constitutes a fascinating subject which has already given rise to numerous monographs and other publications.[2] One of the most intriguing and equally crucial periods in the history of the Christian reception of the Sabbath is that of the beginning, that is to say of the first four centuries. It is this period that I will deal with in this article.

---

[2] See apart from the publications that will be examined in the following (Rordorf, Mosna and Bacciocchi) esp. P. GRELOT: Du sabbat juif au dimanche chrétien, in *La Maison-Dieu* 123 (1975) 79-107 and 124 (1975) 14-54; D. CARSON (ed.): *From Sabbath to Lord's Day. A biblical, historical, and theological investigation* (Grand Rapids 1982).

The choice of this subject might cause some surprise among those who are familiar with the numerous publications that have already been written about it. Is it still possible, one might ask, to add something new to what already has been said and written about this theme? In fact, I agree that a lot of very valuable work already has been done, but at the same time I think there are some valid reasons for taking up the subject once again. First of all, it has to be admitted that the publications of the most authoritative and influential authors did not lead in all respects to a consensus on the subject and that several questions related to it have remained unresolved and are still open to debate. At the same time, it may be remarked that those publications date to the sixties and the seventies of the twentieth century, while on the other hand since that period the research on the development of the Jewish Sabbath at the beginning of the Common Era has made a considerable progress (thanks, inter alia, to the publications of all the documents of Qumran). I think this may change the perspective from which we look at the reception of the Sabbath by Jesus and by early Christianity, at least on some points. Finally, scholarly research is always affected – at least to some extent – by the specific views and preoccupations of the scholars. This in particular holds true for the research on early Christianity which in general is held to be of particular relevance for actual debates about religious and ecclesiastical issues, but for that same reason runs a particular risk of being coloured by the theological convictions and preferences of the scholars. Nobody can be blamed for his personal involvement in his research on early Christianity. On the other hand, the high degree of involvement which is rather common among scholars working in this field, requires a particular alertness and at least it justifies other scholars to devote new studies to old issues starting from their own perspectives, to try to balance once more the most relevant questions and to throw some new light upon them.

In light of the foregoing observations it seems evident that the best way to start a new publication on the Christian reception of the Sabbath will be to have a look at the available secondary literature. Ideally, I would have to give an overview of the content of the publications of the last decades, but this is not possible within the scope of this contribution. I will, therefore, limit myself to a survey of the content of three doctoral dissertations which deal with the question of Sabbath and Sunday. All of them have been written during the sixties and seventies of the twentieth century and have, moreover, played a crucial role in the debate about this issue until recently. In this way we will get an idea of the way the subject has been dealt with in the most influential publications which are of concern to us and at the same time also of the major questions to which the subject (still) gives rise.

1. VIEWS AND THEORIES CONCERNING THE RELATIONSHIP BETWEEN SABBATH AND SUNDAY

One of the leading and certainly most influential scholars who has published on the subject, is without any doubt the Swiss Church historian Willy Rordorf. In 1962 he published a thoroughgoing doctoral dissertation entirely devoted to the Sunday in which he deals especially with the origins of this Christian weekly day and enters in particular at great length into its relationship with the Sabbath.[3] Since then he has regularly come back to this issue in several publications in which he has repeated and developed the basic ideas and intuitions encountered in his doctoral dissertation.[4]

It is first of all important to remark that Rordorf has very specific ideas about the Jewish Sabbath. In his view, the pre-Israelite origins of this day remains more or less obscure but, as far as the Israelite Sabbath is concerned, Rordorf is convinced that originally, in the oldest layers of the Pentateuch, that is to say in the pre-exilic period, it was an exclusively *social* institution.[5] Its only function was to give the necessary rest

---

[3] W. RORDORF: *Der Sonntag* (Zürich 1962).

[4] W. RORDORF: *Sabbat und Sonntag in der alten Kirche* (Traditio christiana 2) (Zürich 1972 (French and Italian edition, Torino 1972); IDEM: Le dimanche, jour du culte et jour du repos dans l'Eglise primitive, in *Le dimanche* (= Lex orandi 39) (Paris 1965) 91-112; IDEM: Origine et signification de la célébration du dimanche dans le christianisme primitif. Etat actuel de la recherche, in *La Maison-Dieu* 148(1981) 103-122. Reprint in W. RORDORF: *Liturgie, foi et vie des premiers chrétiens. Etudes patristiques* (= Théologie historique 75) (Paris 1986) 29-48; IDEM: Ursprung und Bedeutung der Sonntagsfeier im frühen Christentum. Der gegenwärtige Stand der Forschung, in *Liturgisches Jahrbuch* 31 (1981) 145-158. Reprint in W. RORDORF, *Lex orandi. Lex credendi. Gesammelte Aufsätze zum 60. Geburtstag* (= Paradosis 36) (Freiburg Schweiz 1993) 1-14; IDEM: Domenica, in *Dizionario patristico e di Antichità cristiane* (Roma 1983); IDEM: Sunday, in *Dictionary of Christian spirituality* (London 1983); IDEM: Dimanche, in *Dictionnaire encyclopédique du christianisme ancien 1* (Paris 1990) 690-693. See also Rordorf's recension of C. Mosna, Storia della domenica dalle origini fino agli inizi del V secolo, in *Zeitschrift für Kirchengeschichte* 82 (1971) 383-385, as well as his recension of S. Bacciocchi: From Sabbath to Sunday, in *Zeitschrift für Kirchengeschichte* 91 (1980) 112-116.

[5] *Der Sonntag* 46.

and relief to the slaves and the animals who had worked during the whole week. The Sabbath was intended for the working men, women and animals, not for God. It was not a holy nor a cultic day and there were no religious or liturgical meetings. Furthermore, the Sabbath was not yet associated with the idea of the creation or with the Exodus-motif, as is the case in Exodus 20 and Deuteronomium 5. These ideas which provided a new foundation for the observance of the Sabbath, were the work of the priestly upper class.[6] Especially the fact that the observation of the Sabbath became one of the distinctive features, one of the identity markers, of the Jewish people – a view encountered inter alia in Ex. 31, 12-16 – gave rise to what Rordorf calls the later "Sabbath casuistry", which in his view was a "labyrinth from which Judaism never found the way out"[7] and became a heavy burden for the Jews.

Furthermore, a considerable part of Rordorf's dissertation is devoted to the deeply debated question raised by the attitude of (the historical) Jesus towards the Sabbath.[8] Rordorf here rejects decidedly the idea, defended among others by scholars like Rudolf Bultmann, that the passages of the Gospels referring to discussions between Jesus and the Jews, in particular the Pharisees, would not go back to the historical Jesus, but would exclusively mirror discussions which would have taken place after the death of Jesus between Jews and Christians or between Christians amongst one another. In his view it is possible to reconstruct a reliable historical nucleus underlying these Gospel stories which gives us valuable and solid information about the behaviour and the views of the historical Jesus with regard to the Sabbath observance. One of the most striking characteristics of the personality of the historical Jesus as reconstructed by Rordorf was that he was strongly aware of being sent by God and, more in particular, of being the 'Lord of the Sabbath'.[9] This attitude resulted in a very free and provocative behaviour during the Sabbath. He allowed his disciples to pluck ears of corn – a scene considered as essentially historical[10] – and he healed people who were ill, but whose life was not threatened (if their life was seriously at risk, the Jewish halakhah permitted transgressions of the Sabbath rules, but not in the case of chronic diseases). In this way, Jesus undermined not only rules

[6] *Der Sonntag* 47-54.
[7] *Der Sonntag* 53.
[8] *Der Sonntag* 55-79.
[9] *Der Sonntag*, esp. 68-71.
[10] *Der Sonntag* 59-63.

regarding the Sabbath observance, but the 'Old Testament priestly' commandment itself and that is why this practice was abolished in early Christianity. Rordorf adds, however, that the Sabbath did not disappear immediately and completely.[11] Many Jewish Christians stuck to it – which according to Rordorf was permitted to them from a Christian point of view, though they were not obliged to do so – and some Judaising gentile Christians felt attracted to it, a development which is judged by him very negatively. Moreover, during the third and fourth century it was – or it became – customary to have special liturgical celebrations on Saturday, but this custom did not imply an observation of the Sabbath rest (and that is the reason why Rordorf is rather positive about it).[12]

Next, there is the question of the Sunday, in particular in relation to the Sabbath. Rordorf's position is well-known among liturgical scholars. Therefore I want to limit myself to mentioning the most essential points.[13] These may be summarised as follows:

(1) The Sunday is an originally Christian creation that cannot be traced back to any pre-Christian tradition. It did not have its origins in the transmission of the Jewish Sabbath to the first day of the week. Nor is there a relationship to any supposed pre-Christian veneration of the Sun (by adherents of the Mithraic cult or by Essenes and so on).

(2) The Sunday has very ancient roots and goes back to the oldest Jewish-Christian communities.

(3) For the early Christians Sunday was not a day of rest, but the day in which they assembled for the rite of the 'breaking of the bread', that is the 'Lord's Supper' or the 'Eucharist'. This rite took place not on Sunday morning, neither on Saturday evening, but on Sunday evening.

(4) The celebration of the breaking of the bread on Sunday evening had its roots in the meals which according to some passages from the Gospels – especially according to Luc. 24, 13 vv. – had taken place during some first days of the week after the resurrection of Christ and during which the risen Lord had appeared to his disciples.

(5) The introduction of the Sunday as the official day of rest for the whole Roman Empire by the Emperor Constantine was primarily

---

[11] *Der Sonntag* 117-140.
[12] *Der Sonntag* 144-146.
[13] See *Der Sonntag* 174-268 and the other publications of Rordorf mentioned in note 4.

inspired by political and social considerations and possibly the Emperor's solar piety, but not by specifically Christian motives. For the rest, Rordorf stresses the fact that Christians only gradually started justifying the observation of the Sunday as a day of rest by appealing to the Old Testament Sabbath commandment.

Finally, it should be noticed that for Rordorf his reconstruction of the disappearance of the Sabbath and the rise of the Sunday in early Christianity has outspoken theological and pastoral implications.[14] He admits that the early Christian way of celebrating the Sunday cannot be simply transplanted to modern Christianity. On the other hand, he claims that modern theological and pastoral decisions concerning the Sunday practice cannot be simply deduced from what is current in modern society and culture, but should *also* be based upon continuity with the history and upon confrontation with the Bible. This implies, on the one hand, a relativization of the Sunday as a day of rest. Although Rordorf is not in favour of abolishing the Sunday as a weekly rest day in societies where it functions as such, he emphasises that it should not be considered as a Christian Sabbath and that it should not be motivated by an appeal to the Old Testament Sabbath commandment. On the other hand, he holds a strong plea for the Sunday as a liturgical day in which Christians assemble to read from the Scripture and in particular to celebrate the Lord's Supper.

The second work we want to mention, is the doctoral dissertation of C. Mosna which was defended at the Pontifical Gregorian University in Rome some years after Rordorf published his monograph and which is devoted to the origins and the development of the Christian Sunday in the first five centuries.[15]

Although not primarily dealing with the Sabbath and its reception in Christian tradition, Mosna does not fail to express his ideas about this issue (which, of course, is very closely tied up with the emergence of the Sunday). These prove to basically concord with those of Rordorf. In his view the Sabbath[16] is a creation of pre-exilic 'Yahwist' religion and has no direct parallels in non-Israelite tradition. Originally, it was a weekly day of rest which fulfilled a social function. In and after the Babylonian

---

[14] See for the following in particular *Der Sonntag* 289-301.
[15] C. MOSNA: *Storia della domenica dalle origini fino agli inizi del V secolo* (= Analecta Gregoriana 170) (Roma 1969).
[16] See for Mosna's view on the Sabbath: *Storia* 168-171.

exile it also obtained a cultic function and in the post-exilic period the Sabbath commandment increasingly became the object of extremely rigid interpretations which Mosna qualifies as being 'insopportabile'[17] and for which he holds responsible in particular groups of zealous Jews, like those of Qumran, and the Sadducees (while the Pharisees rather tried to make those regulations more acceptable by means of casuistry). The discussions between Jesus and the Jews about the Sabbath observance in the Gospels are basically considered 'historical', that is to say not primarily reflecting the ideas of the first Christian communities, but essentially those of the 'historical' Jesus himself. This historical Jesus behaved in a sovereign way as the Lord of the Sabbath and did not hesitate to transgress the existing regulations in order to do good works. In this way Jesus placed the Sabbath in a new perspective and inspired the first Jewish Christian communities to stop observing the Sabbath in a rabbinic way (although at first they did so only hesitantly and timidly, as still appears from some passages of the Gospels).[18]

Mosna's main issue, however, is not the Sabbath, but the rise and development of the Sunday. Here his ideas diverge considerably from those of Rordorf.[19] In several respects he agrees with the latter, in particular as far as he considers the Sunday to go back to a very early period and to have been devoted from the very beginning to the commemoration of the Resurrection.[20] He equally holds that from the time of its origins a celebration of the Eucharist was part of it.[21] However, he is very critical about Rordorf's attempt to prove that the first Christian communities assembled on Sunday evening and to bring these Sunday evening celebrations in relation with traditions concerning the appearance of the risen Lord during meals at that time and even to explain their origins by those traditions.[22] According to Mosna, the first Christian communities assembled on Sunday morning and they did not commemorate the appearances of the risen Lord, but the Resurrection itself which in the Gospel stories is situated in the night after the Sabbath.

As for the observance of the Sabbath in early Christianity, Mosna's view concords in its broad outlines with that of Rordorf. The first Jewish

---

[17] *Storia* 170.
[18] *Storia* 171-178.
[19] *Storia* 1-60.
[20] *Storia* 42-60.
[21] *Storia* 72-90.
[22] *Storia* 48-57.

Christians went on observing the day, but Mosna suggests a process of inner dissociation from this practice might have started at a very early stage.[23] The Hellenists, that is to say the Greek-speaking Jews whose leader was Stephen, opted for a much more radical stance and radically broke with the law and therefore also with the Sabbath. As a matter of fact, the Christians from paganism followed suit and in line with the abandonment of the Sabbath commandment by the majority of Christians, the Church fathers developed an 'allegorical-typological-spiritual' exegesis of this commandment.[24] Like Rordorf, however, Mosna points to the fact that there were some exceptions to this rule. There were particular groups of 'fanatical' Jewish Christians, like the Ebionites, who refused to give up the observance of the Sabbath.[25] Moreover, some Christians from paganism felt attracted to it (according to Mosna "also for superstitious reasons").[26] Finally, apart from these particular categories of Christians, there are indications that some kind of veneration of the Sabbath never disappeared entirely in early Christianity. The main evidence adduced by him comes from some writings of Tertullian – also (briefly) discussed by Rordorf – who mentions Christians refusing to bend their knees both on Sundays *and on Saturdays* and who himself, at least in his Montanist period, opposed the custom of fasting on Saturday (which is known to have existed at some places from the second century onwards).[27] For the later period (fourth century) he refers to several sources attesting some kind of liturgical celebration of the Saturday (especially in some Churches of the East).[28] Mosna argues that some kind of historical continuity must exist between the Sabbath observance of the early Jewish Christians, the practices as alluded to by Tertullian and the fourth century liturgical celebration.[29]

On the other hand, Mosna's view on the institution of Sunday as a general day of rest considerably differs from the picture sketched by Rordorf. Both agree that the Emperor applied certain legislative rules related to pagan festivals and holidays on Sunday and moreover that the Sabbath commandment played no role. Contrary to Rordorf, however,

---

[23] *Storia* 178-185.
[24] *Storia* 187-201.
[25] See in particular *Storia* 182, 188.
[26] *Storia* 183-184.
[27] *Storia* 203-205. Cf. RORDORF: *Der Sonntag* 140-143.
[28] *Storia* 202-203, 243-244.
[29] *Storia* 205-206.

Mosna stresses the specific Christian and sincere motivation of the Emperor who, in his view, certainly was not exclusively inspired by political motives neither by his alleged syncretistic 'solar religion'.[30] Moreover, he argues that the idea of Sunday as a day of rest was more or less in line with the celebration of this day in the first three centuries, in so far as every "joyful cultic celebration of a community tends to expand to a complete holiday" (210). Therefore Mosna emphatically rejects the idea that the institution of the Sunday would have been the beginning of a process of paganisation and he quotes with approval Jean Gaudemet who characterised the introduction of the Sunday as a day of rest as follows: "In this way Constantine went beyond sheer tolerance or religious mentality. With him the official transformation of the world of Antiquity in a Christian society takes shape."[31]

A very different picture of the development of Sabbath and Sunday in early Christianity has been sketched by the Adventist scholar S. Bacciocchi in his doctoral thesis which he defended at the Pontifical Gregorian University in Rome some years after Rordorf and Mosna published their dissertations.[32] While making use of globally the same sources as the last-mentioned scholars, he arrives at conclusions which are radically different from theirs, in particular from that of Rordorf.

Bacciocchi's view of the Jewish Sabbath presents a very clear similarity to those of his two colleagues. He has in common with them a very negative attitude toward the Sabbath as it developed in the post-exilic period. In his view as well, the institution of the weekly day of rest fell victim to all kind of regulations which he calls "casuistic" and "legalistic" and which in his eyes led to a "perversion" of the day.[33] On the other hand, he puts a high value on the Sabbath as it was intended by God, namely as a "time to cease from secular activities in order to experience the blessings of creation-redemption by worshipping God and by acting generously toward needy people".[34] It is therefore more than only a social institution fulfilling a social function – as Rordorf claims with regard to the Sabbath of the pre-exilic period – but it basically has a religious and

---

[30] *Storia* 221-227, especially 224.
[31] *Storia* 227. Cf. J. GAUDEMET: La législation religieuse de Constantin, in: *Revue historique de l'Eglise de France* 33 (1947) 44.
[32] S. BACCIOCCHI: *From Sabbath to Sunday. A historical investigation of the rise of Sunday observance in early Christianity* (Rome 1977).
[33] *From Sabbath to Sunday* 36-37.
[34] *From Sabbath to Sunday* 9, 54-55.

spiritual character. For the rest, Bacciocchi does not speculate about the historical development in the pre-exilic period.

As for Bacciocchi's reconstruction of Jesus' attitude to the Sabbath, he differs from most other scholars dealing with the question but especially with Rordorf in that he does not make an attempt to distinguish between passages which might go back to the 'historical' Jesus and those reflecting the ideas and the preoccupations of the earliest Christian communities. Generally speaking, he seems to take for granted the historical character of the relevant passages of the Gospel. Second, basing himself on the passages of the Gospels he argues that from none of them it may be inferred that Jesus transgressed the Sabbath commandment or that he had the intention to abolish the Sabbath or to replace it by another day (the Sunday). On the contrary, the only thing he did was to restore the day of which he was the Lord, to its original meaning (against the 'distortions' of post-exilic Judaism).[35]

Still more remarkable is Bacciocchi's view on the two related questions raised by the survival of the Sabbath in early Christianity and the emergence of early Christian Sunday. His view on these issues radically deviates from those of the two other authors (and, for the rest, of those of practically every specialist of early Christianity). Bacciocchi claims there is no evidence in the New Testament of a regular Sunday observance. In one of the chapters of his book[36] he argues at great length that no probative value can be drawn from the three New Testament references commonly adduced by the adherents of this generally accepted position, namely 1 Cor. 16, 2; Acts. 20, 7-12 and Rev. 1, 10. In his view the first passage refers to a private fund-raising plan and the second one to an extraordinary, irregular gathering of the believers of Troas with Paul before his departure on the 'first day of the week'.[37] The 'Lord's Day' to which Rev. 1, 10 alludes, is interpreted as the day of Christ's judgement and parousia.[38] Starting from these conclusions, Bacciocchi tries to demonstrate that the first generations of Christians, in particular the early Jerusalem community, continued to meet during the Sabbath and were completely unknown with any form of Sunday worship[39]

---

[35] *From Sabbath to Sunday* 26-63, 69-73.
[36] Ch. IV, p. 90-131.
[37] *From Sabbath to Sunday* 90-101.
[38] *From Sabbath to Sunday* 111-131.
[39] *From Sabbath to Sunday* 131-164.

(though he seems to reckon with the possibility that from a certain period onwards (but since when?) Christians extended their Sabbath celebration in the evening of the next day, the first day of the week).[40] As for the Sunday observance in the proper sense of the word (that is to say the worship during Sunday itself, in particular on Sunday morning), he claims that it did not exist prior to 135 C.E., but arose only in the middle of the second century, starting from the city or Rome.[41] In his view its emergence was influenced by two main factors, namely anti-Judaism which prompted Christians to differentiate themselves from Judaism and caused a widespread devaluation and repudiation of the Sabbath[42] and, on the other hand, the influence of pagan Sun-worship which early in the second century would have caused the advancement of the day of the Sun to the position of the first day of the week and on the other hand provided a fitting symbolism that had parallels in Judaeo-Christian tradition and, moreover, proved helpful to explain to the pagan world fundamental Christian themes, such as the creation of the world and the resurrection commemorated on that day.[43]

It may be added that Bacciocchi does not pay any explicit attention to the institution of Sunday as a day of rest by the Emperor Constantine. For him this fact is of minor relevance because his main concern is to prove that Sunday observance does not rest on a foundation of biblical theology and/or of apostolic authority.[44] It suffices therefore for him to unravel the process which led to the abandonment of the Sabbath and its replacement by the Sunday. What happened after that crucial and in his view wrong and fatal decision is of less importance to him.

So far, our summary of the three doctoral dissertations. At first sight, it may seem a little bit exaggerated to have dealt with them at such a great length and to have followed their line of reasoning so closely. I think, however, that there was good reason to do so. In fact, from a rather detailed analysis of these works at least two things may be deduced. First of all, the three dissertations are characterised by a remarkable

---

[40] From Sabbath to Sunday 283-285, 300-301.

[41] From Sabbath to Sunday 165-212.

[42] From Sabbath to Sunday 169-185, 213-235.

[43] From Sabbath to Sunday 237-269, 301.

[44] See esp. From Sabbath to Sunday 309: "This means, to put it bluntly, that Sunday observance does not rest on a foundation of Biblical theology and/or of apostolic authority, but on later contributory factors which we have endeavored to identify in our present study."

internal coherence and this certainly may be considered as one of their merits. On the other hand – and this aspect is more problematic – their internal coherence is very closely related to the confessional background of the authors. It may be that some scholars will answer that this holds especially true for the work of Bacciocchi and to a much lesser degree for the other two authors. But to what extent, one might ask, should this judgement be due to a one-sided perception, to the fact that Adventists form a minority among Christians, certainly in comparison with Roman Catholics and Lutheran or Calvinist protestants? In fact, it is obvious that Bacciocchi arrives at conclusions which suspiciously fit in with Adventist liturgical practice. On the other hand, while dealing with specific aspects of Sabbath or Sunday or while discussing the inter- pretation of certain crucial texts, he makes ample use of arguments developed by numerous other generally acknowledged specialists. Next, if it is true that a certain theory may raise suspicion because it fits in too well with a specific ecclesiastical position or practice, this argument could also be invoked against the way in which Mosna and Rordorf attempt to reconstruct the development of Sabbath and Sunday in early Christianity. In fact, the picture Rordorf sketches of that development strikingly matches the view of the protestant Church reformers, for instance of Calvin who in the third chapter of his *Institutes* argues that Christ has abolished the Sabbath and that the Sunday should not be considered as a new Sabbath, but on the other hand emphasises that Christians need some specific days on which they assemble in order to listen to the Word, to break the holy Bread and to pray together and who admits that servants and labourers need a day on which they can rest from their work (social function of the Sunday as a day or rest, GR).[45] As for Mosna, the idea that the first Christians almost from the very start would have celebrated the Eucharist on Sunday morning, not on Sunday evening, to commemorate and to celebrate the resurrection of Christ, remarkably fits in with the liturgical practice of many Chris- tians, in particular Roman Catholics as well as Eastern Orthodox Chris- tians. As a matter of fact, all this does not mean that the arguments invoked by Mosna and Rordorf are without value or should not be taken seriously. Neither does it mean that the reconstruction proposed by Bacciocchi is the most convincing one. The only conclusion that may be drawn from it is that hidden agendas may be hidden every-

---

[45] *Institutes* II, 8, 32.

where and that therefore caution and even suspicion are in order with regard to every publication dealing with the subject, whatever their theological or ideological background may be.

Apart from alerting us to the presence of eventual hidden agendas, the summary of the three dissertations is helpful still for another reason. It permits us to gain an idea of the main issues which play a role in the discussion about the reception of Sabbath in early Christianity. These issues are:

(1) the observance of the Sabbath by the Jews, in particular in the post-exilic period;
(2) the attitude Jesus took towards this observance and more in general, towards the Sabbath;
(3) the (eventual) survival of the Sabbath in early Christianity during the first three centuries and
(4) the role of Constantine.

In the rest of my article I will attempt to go deeper into these crucial questions, taking into account the arguments that have been put forward by the three aforementioned authors (and eventually by other scholars) and occasionally adding supplementary considerations which may contribute to placing old questions in a new perspective.

2. JEWISH OBSERVANCE OF THE SABBATH IN THE POST-EXILIC PERIOD

Every attempt to answer the question as to whether the Sabbath survived in one way or the other in early Christianity, is unavoidably and considerably determined by the picture one has formed of this day, especially as it was observed and celebrated at the beginning of the Common Era. A scholar who starts from a negative view concerning that day, will usually be inclined to assume early Christians were also opposed to it and he will be apt to minify and to explain away eventual traces of its survival in early Christianity. Conversely, it may be expected that Christian scholars who take a more positive and sympathetic attitude towards this day, will be more inclined to reckon with the possibility that the observance of the Sabbath continued in early Christianity in one way or the other. It is therefore important to briefly sketch a picture of the Sabbath at the beginning of the Common Era and to sum up its most characteristic features.

It is generally agreed that, from the very start the Sabbath was a day of rest on which everybody, both freemen and slaves as well as foreigners and even animals interrupted their work. This institution has a positive aspect in the sense that everybody has the possibility to 'rest', but it has also negative implications in the sense that it is forbidden to do 'any' work at all (Ex. 20, 10; Deut. 5, 14). This prohibition in itself is rather general and vague and lends itself to multiple interpretations, but already in the Tenach itself some specifications are given as to the activities that fall under the category of forbidden work. It is not allowed to kindle fire in the homes (Ex. 35, 3), to gather wood (Num. 15, 32-36), to plough and to harvest (Ex. 34, 21), to leave one's home or abode (Ex. 16, 29; Is. 58, 13), to conduct trade (Is. 58, 13).[46] From the post-exilic period onwards the rules became increasingly elaborated and this led to what is called the Sabbath-halakha which certainly already existed at the time of Jesus and the first Christians. In order to rightly understand this phenomenon and the attitude Jesus may have taken towards it, it is important to realise that there was no general agreement among the Jews and the different Jewish groups about the precise interpretation of the different rules and that both extremely rigorous and less strict approaches existed. Recently, L. Doerig has convincingly argued that globally speaking two main halakhic schools may be distinguished, namely a priestly one that took a very strict position with regard to the observance of the Sabbath rules and, next, a non-priestly one which was more apt to take into consideration the concrete situation and the reality of life and, therefore, to accept some 'transgressions' of the rules and to give priority in some cases to principles that were considered more important than the commandments and prohibitions related to the Sabbath (saving of life; celebration of certain festivals that coincided with the Sabbath).[47] To the former school belonged, among others, the book of the Jubilees, the community of Qumran and the Sadducees and to the latter Philo and Josephus, but also the Pharisees and the early Tannaitic teachers. As for the latter category, the early Tannaites, a

---

[46] See for the Sabbath observance in the Tenach/Old Testament for instance: H. DRESSLER: The Sabbath in the Old Testament, in CARSON (ed.): *From Sabbath to Lord's Day* 22-41.

[47] L. DOERIG: *Schabbat. Sabbathalacha und -praxis im antiken Judentum und Urchristentum* (= Texts and studies in ancient Judaism 78) (Tübingen 1999) esp. 576.

distinction has to be made between the 'house of Shammai', which stuck to the older more strict traditions and to a literal interpretation, and to the 'house of Hillel', which rather emphasised the intention of the rules.[48] In the period after the destruction of the Second Temple (70 C.E.), the Yavneh period, the development of the halakhah in a Hillelite direction led to the mitigation of some Sabbath-rules.[49] The question finally may be raised as to whether the various commandments and rules were followed by all Jews, both in Palestine and in the Diaspora. It is very unlikely this was everywhere the case. Philo makes mention of extreme 'allegorists' who only seem to be interested in discovering and deciphering the deeper spiritual messages hidden in the Biblical Sabbath commandments, but not in their actual observance.[50] Furthermore, there are indications that there were Jews who celebrated the Sabbath in a more or less non-halakhic way, that is to say, in principle they refrained from work but they were rather indifferent to all kinds of halakhic rules and certainly had no problem in transgressing certain rules if in their opinion circumstances obliged them to do so.[51] Briefly, one should not make the mistake to assume that the ideals and the guidelines of the rabbis were followed by everyone.[52]

Originally, the Sabbath was first and foremost a day of rest. There is no evidence that at an early stage, for example in the first centuries after the Exile, special types of worship took place on that day, but in so far they did exist, they remained restricted to the temple in Jerusalem and to some religious rituals that were performed there by the Temple officials but not by the ordinary people. In the centuries prior to the beginning of the Common Era the situation changed. From that period onwards, it became common practice to assemble on the Sabbath for liturgical meetings in Synagogues. The emergence and the early development of this practice still always give rise to scholarly debates, but there can be no doubt that it certainly had gained acceptance around the beginning of the Common Era – and even earlier – both in Palestine

---

[48] DOERIG: *Schabbat* 528-532.
[49] DOERIG: *Schabbat* 532-535.
[50] PHILO: *De migratione Abrahami* 89-93. Cf. DOERIG: *Schabbat* 347-348; D. HAY; Philo's references to other allegorists, in *Studia Philonica* 6 (1979-1980) 41-75, esp. 47-49.
[51] DOERIG: *Schabbat* 396-397.
[52] DOERIG: *Schabbat* 397.

and in the Diaspora.[53] In addition, there is little question that the oldest nucleus of these 'liturgical' meetings was constituted by the reading and the study of the Torah, which very soon must have been combined with the reading (and the explanation or study) of a text taken from one of the Prophets.[54] More complicated is the question as to whether these gatherings comprised some form of communal prayer.[55] That this was the case at least to some degree becomes apparent from the mere fact that the oldest attested Greek word for 'synagogue' is *proseuche* which means 'prayer', 'house of prayer'.[56] On the other hand, in so far as communal prayer was part of the Synagogue gatherings, this certainly had not yet obtained the developed form it possessed or received in the second and third century C.E., let alone in later times. There is no evidence that the reading of the Torah and the Prophets on Sabbath morning was already preceded by a fully developed and standardised morning prayer. The regular recitation of psalms definitely was not yet part of the

---

[53] See for instance L. LEVINE: *The ancient Synagogue. The first thousand years* (New Haven/London 2000) esp. 135-159. Cf. also S. SAFRAI: The Synagogue, in S. SAFRAI & M. STERN: *The Jewish people in the first century* 2 (= Compendia Rerum Iudaicarum ad Novum Testamentum) (Assen/Philadelphia 1987) 908-944. Recently, the fact that the Sabbath was a day of communal Jewish worship at this period has been called into question by H. McKay who argues there is no evidence that the Sabbath fulfilled this function before 200 C.E. (H. MCKAY: *Sabbath & Synagogue. The question of Sabbath worship in ancient Judaism* (Leiden 1994). This thesis, however, has been convincingly criticised and refuted by P. VAN DER HORST (Was the Synagogue a place of Sabbath worship before 70 C.E., in S. FINE (ed.): *Jews, Christians and Polytheists in the ancient Synagogue* (London/New York 1999) 18-43). The most strong argument raised by Van der Horst against McKay's theory is that starting from a too narrow definition of worship, she wrongly disregards the "typically Jewish nature of studying the Torah as a holy and cultic activity"(36). Moreover, Van der Horst rightly points to a certain tendency to play down the evidence that does not fit in with her thesis (31).

[54] See for instance LEVINE: *The ancient Synagogue* 135-151 and moreover C. PERROT: The reading of the Bible in the ancient Synagogue, in M. MULDER (ed.): *Mikra. Text, translation, reading and interpretation of the Hebrew Bible in ancient Judaism and early Christianity* (Assen/Philadelphia 1988) 137-159; L. SCHIFFMANN: The early history of public reading of the Torah, in S. FINE: *Jews,Christians and Polytheists* 44-56; G. STEMBERGER: Schriftlesung II. Judentum, in: *Theologische Realenzyklopädie* 30 (Berlin/New York 1999) 558-563.

[55] See for the views taken by different scholars (especially E. Fleischer and S. Reif) on this question: LEVINE: *The ancient Synagogue* 151-159. Cf. S. REIF: *Judaism and Hebrew Prayer* (Cambridge 1993) 54, 82-85.

[56] P. VAN DER HORST: Was the Synagogue a place of sabbath worship 31-32.

meetings under consideration.[57] Furthermore, we cannot be sure that the 'statutory prayers' like the Amidah of which several older versions must have existed at a very early period, already had been incorporated in the Synagogue gatherings on Sabbath. As we shall see further on, for a correct understanding of the relationship between Jewish and early Christian liturgy and also of the reception of the Sabbath in early Christianity, this fact is not unimportant.

Apart from the rituals in the temple and the meetings in the Synagogue, the Jews spent a considerable part of the Sabbath in their houses. We do not have any information about the way the day was observed or eventually celebrated at home in the centuries before the beginning of the Common Era, whether for example some specific domestic customs and rituals existed at that period. If they would have existed, it should be noted that the available sources do not make mention of them. There is, however, no doubt they did exist at the beginning of the Common Era. Both Jewish and pagan sources make mention of the Jewish custom of lighting the lamps on Friday evening[58] which apparently was more than a merely ordinary and functional act. We also know for sure that the meals that were held on the Sabbath, especially that of Friday evening, had a particularly festal character and that it was for example customary to drink wine at that occasion.[59] It may be added that meals, especially meals with a more or less festal character, entailed some ritual elements, such as blessings pronounced over the wine and the bread and a prayer of thanksgiving at the end. There is no doubt those elements were also part of the meals held during Sabbath.[60] Furthermore, it is very likely that already in the period in which Christianity emerged, the meal on Friday evening was preceded by a special Sabbath blessing, the central theme of which was the sanctification of the day of the Sabbath

---

[57] See J. MAIER: Zur Verwendung der Psalmen in der synagogalen Liturgie, in H. BECKER & R. KACZYNSKI: *Liturgie und Dichtung. Ein interdisziplinäres Kompendium* I (St. Ottilien 1983) 55-90.

[58] See the poet Persius (34-62 C.E.), *Satires* 5, 176-184; Seneca, *Ad Lucillium epistula morales* 95.47; Josephus: *Jewish Antiquities* 4, 212; *Against Apion*, 2, 282. Cf. McKAY: *Sabbath & Synagogue* 104; L. FELDMAN: *Jew and gentile in the Ancient World* (Princeton 1993) 165-166.

[59] See Persius: *Satire* 5, 176-184; Plutarchus: *Quaestiones convivales* 4.6.2.

[60] See for instance G. ROUWHORST: Bread and cup in early Christian Eucharist celebrations, in C. CASPERS, G. LUKKEN & G. ROUWHORST (eds): *Bread of heaven* (= Liturgia condenda 3) 11-40, esp. 13-17.

(qiddush). Most probably, the oldest nucleus of the so-called *havdalah* prayer which marked the end of the Sabbath, equally dates back at least to this period. The oldest sources referring to both these rites are the tractates *Berakhoth* of the Mishna and the Tosefta which make mention of disputes between the houses of Hillel and Shammai about the precise moment when they should be recited.[61] It is, however, very unlikely that they would have come into existence just prior to the redaction of these sources (beginning third century C.E.). They must have been considerably older.

This being established, we may return to the question already raised at the beginning of this article, the question namely as to whether the Sabbath may be considered as a festival. It should be admitted that in the eyes of many pagan authors who have written about the Sabbath, it was not. In fact, it is striking that a great number of them call the Sabbath a 'fast'[62] (an idea which according to most scholars is due to a misinterpretation[63]). The majority of the Jews, however, definitely did not see it in this way. Particularly revealing in this regard is the fact that in the Hebrew Bible the Sabbath is mentioned at several places in close conjunction with the big Jewish festivals (and the new moons).[64] In addition, several sources underline the joyful character of this day[65] and it was connected with the commemoration of markedly joyful events, as the creation of the world and the liberation from Egypt. For the rest, according to a great number of sources it was explicitly forbidden to fast on Sabbath.[66] Finally,

---

[61] See Mishna, Berakhot, ch. 8 and Tosefta, Berakhot, ch. 5:25-32. Cf. T. Zahavy: *The Mishnaic law of blessings and prayers. Tractate Berakhot* (Brown Judaic studies 88) (Atlanta 1987) 109-117; D. Houtman: *Mishnah und Tosefta* (= Texts and studies in ancient Judaism 59) (Tübingen 1996).

[62] See for the relevant sources Feldman: *Jew and gentile* 161-164.

[63] For an overview of other possible explanations presented by different scholars, see R. Goldenberg: The Jewish Sabbath in the Roman world up to the time of Constantine the Great, in *Aufstieg und Niedergang der römischen Welt* (Berlin 1947) 411-447, here 439. Goldenberg himself leaves open the possibility of a Sabbath-fast among certain groups of Jews.

[64] See esp. Lev. 23 and Num. 28-29. For an enumeration of the other relevant passages of the Hebrew Bible, see McKay: *Sabbath & Synagogue* 26-28.

[65] See esp. Is. 58, 13-14 and further Philo: *On the life of Moses* II, 211. See for other relevant passages from Qumran and rabbinic texts Doerig: *Schabbat* 350 (note 317), 382-383.

[66] See in particular *Book of Jubilees* 50, 12 and several other Jewish texts enumerated by Doerig (*Schabbat*) 105-107.

the festal character of the meals certainly will have contributed to its joy-ful and festive character.

In addition, it is quite common to associate festivals with a certain degree of 'sacredness', in the sense that they are clearly distinguished from the days belonging to the 'Alltag', to 'ordinary' time.[67] If sacred-ness, understood in this way, may be considered as an essential charac-teristic of festivals, it should be noted that the Sabbath has this festive aspect in common with 'festivals'. In the Ten Commandments, as trans-mitted both by Ex. 20 and Deut. 5, it is explicitly called a 'holy day', set apart for and devoted to the Lord (cf. especially Ex. 31, 12-17). It may be added that its holy character also becomes apparent from the way in which it was celebrated and ritualised. Very revealing in this regard are for instance the rites that marked the beginning and the end of the day and had the effect of setting the Sabbath apart, of separating it from the other days of the week.[68]

So far, the main characteristics of the Sabbath as it was observed and celebrated at the beginning of the Common Era. If we confront this short description with the view our three authors have of the Sabbath, we cannot but conclude that their approach is one-sided and biased. First of all, it is remarkable that they have almost exclusively focussed on the halakhic rules. The festive and joyful aspects of the Sabbath have got much less attention. In addition, these halakhic rules have been inter-preted by them in a very massive, undifferentiated and polemical way. They are uniquely depicted as examples of extravagant casuistry and the phenomenon of the Sabbath-halakha as such is represented as an outra-geous, heavy and even inhuman burden. In addition, almost no atten-tion is paid to the differences in interpretation which are to be found in

[67] See for example J. ASSMANN (ed.): *Das Fest und das Heilige. Religiöse Kontrapunkte zur Alltagswelt* (Gütersloh 1991), especially the essay written by ASSMANN: Der zweidi-mensionale Mensch. Das Fest als Medium des kollektiven Gedächtnisses, pp. 13-31. Cf. also A. SCHILSON: Fest und Feier in anthropologischer und theologischer Sicht, in *Litur-gisches Jahrbuch* 44 (1994) 4-32.

[68] The idea of 'holiness' has been particularly stressed by the priestly tradition who defended the stricter type of halakhah and associated the 'sanctity' of the Sabbath with that of Mount Sinai and therefore tended to apply the purity rules that Moses had to observe before climbing this holy Mount to the Jews observing and celebrating the Sab-bath (and therefore prescribed sexual abstention during that day). For the rest, it should be remarked that this idea, and especially, that of sexual abstention, was rejected by later rabbinic tradition. Cf. for this question DOERIG: *Schabbat*, in particular 79-83, 169-175, 238-242, 570-572, 575-576.

the various Jewish groups. The most striking thing, however, is that they look at the Sabbath exclusively from the viewpoint of (Christian) outsiders and do not undertake any attempt to understand this phenomenon from inside, that is to empathise with people belonging to a different religion and with the religious mentality from which this halakha derived. Did the majority of the Jews really experience the Sabbath observance only as a heavy burden? Most probably, the verdict of the three scholars on the observance and celebration of the Sabbath would have become less severe and more subtle, if they only had seriously raised that question. And probably, several other related issues would then have appeared in a different light as well.

3. DID JESUS WANT TO ABOLISH THE SABBATH?

It has become very evident from our summaries of the monographs of Rordorf, Mosna and Bacciochi that all the three of them draw important arguments for their view on the Sabbath from the alleged behaviour of the 'historical' Jesus, from his attitude towards the Sabbath which they try to reconstruct with all possible means. The problem, however, is that they arrive at almost opposite conclusions. According to Rordorf, Jesus wanted to radically abolish the Sabbath. Mosna argues that Jesus was only opposed to the rabbinic way of observing the Sabbath. Bacciocchi seems to agree on this point with Mosna, but he definitely more strongly emphasises Jesus' *positive* attitude towards the Sabbath.

The complete lack of consensus between the three authors does not come as a surprise. As we already noted, the three authors have very different views on issues such as the meaning of Sabbath, Sunday, festivals, holidays. Given the fact that they ascribe a more or less normative value to the behaviour of Jesus during the Sabbath, it is not really surprising that their views of this behaviour considerably diverge. Moreover, this lack of unanimity is more or less representative of the state of the research done by New Testament scholars on this issue. In fact, almost every theoretically conceivable position has found adherents and moreover continues to do so.[69] On the one side of the spectrum of views

---

[69] See for an overview of the different positions defended DOERIG: *Schabbat* 398-400.

defended we encounter the radical position of scholars who, like Rordorf, assume Jesus wanted to abolish and to reject not only a special way of observing the Sabbath, but simply the Sabbath as such. On the other side of the spectrum there is the view of exegetes who maintain that Jesus did not even deviate from the most common halakhic Sabbath rules (starting from the idea, of course, that he followed the less strict, non priestly and not the severe, priestly type of halakha). Between these two opposites we encounter all kind of less radical intermediate varieties. There are, for instance, scholars who take Jesus to have been a non-halakhic or a low-halakhic Jew who did not call into question the Sabbath as such, but was not interested in halakhic rules or was opposed to exaggerated casuistry (as it would, for instance, have been developed by the Pharisees).

It is impossible to deal exhaustively here with this very complicated question, let alone of proposing a solution to it and this all the more so since I am not a New Testament scholar. I will limit myself, therefore, to some brief remarks which are mainly of a methodological character.

(1) First of all, there is every reason to be suspicious of each attempt to reconstruct the position of the historical Jesus with regard to the Sabbath. How to distinguish between earlier and younger strata in the text of the Gospels, between authentic Jesus material and traditions reflecting views and discussions of the first Christian communities? The problem is that, apart from the Gospels themselves, we have no external evidence regarding Jesus' attitude towards Sabbath observance which might enable us to verify or to falsify our conclusions. This makes it very difficult to escape the risk of circular reasoning and, moreover, it offers ample opportunity to fall victim to theological hidden agendas. In fact, someone who is convinced from the very start that Christian worship is based on completely different principles than Jewish ritual traditions, will be inclined to legitimise this point of view by ascribing every passage containing a polemic against Sabbath observance to the historical Jesus. Conversely, a scholar holding a more positive view on the Jewish Sabbath, will tend to assume more easily that Jesus kept that day and respected the commonly accepted rules regarding its observance and he will be inclined to attribute all polemical passages to the influence of early Christian communities, who in that case must be supposed to have taken a different stance.

(2) It is very likely that in the first Christian communities the Sabbath observance became time and again a matter of discussion. This certainly happened from the time many non-Jews became Christians, as is testified by some passages of the letters of Paul. Most probably, however, those discussions already started at an earlier period and it is very likely that they have affected the transmission of the traditions regarding Jesus' behaviour on Sabbath. Thus it may be that, as several exegetes have argued, the pericope on plucking grain on Sabbath was mainly or even entirely a creation of the early Church.[70] It should, however, be admitted that it remains difficult to go beyond formulating plausible presumptions.

(3) It seems difficult to me to radically deny the historicity of all the passages describing Jesus' behaviour on Sabbath. Here one may appeal to the well-known adage 'where there is smoke there is fire'. There is smoke, that is to say there are Gospel passages describing discussions between Jesus and other Jews, in particular the Pharisees, about Sabbath observance. So there must have been fire, that is to say either Jesus himself or otherwise the first Christian communities must have been involved in discussions about this subject and have advocated some more or less liberal position with regard to this issue. Next, even if these passages primarily would reflect discussions among Christians after Jesus' death, one might raise the question why a number of early Christians apparently felt entitled to appeal to Jesus' behaviour and attitude if he never had acted on certain Sabbaths in a way that could have given rise to discussion in the Jewish milieu of his time or if he never had pronounced himself about certain issues that constituted a matter of debate in his environment.

(4) On the other hand, one should be very cautious in drawing too far reaching conclusions from this observation. First of all, there is no hard evidence that Jesus ever contravened any written rule of the Torah concerning the Sabbath. In this regard it should be observed that his way of healing during a Sabbath as described by the synoptic Gospel for which, according to those Gospels, he was blamed by the Pharisees, did not imply any form of work that was forbidden

---

[70] Thus for instance already R. BULTMANN: *Die Geschichte der synoptischen Tradition* (FRLANT 29, 9) (Göttingen 1979⁵) esp. 14. See also E. SANDERS: *Jesus and Judaism* (Philadelphia 1985) 264-267 and DOERIG: *Schabbat* 408-438.

on Sabbath.[71] There was no rule, also no halakhic rule, forbidding the laying on of hands. The situation would be different for the disciples of Jesus if indeed they had picked grain during the Sabbath and in that case one might argue that their behaviour had been encouraged by Jesus. It may, however, be remarked that it is the historicity of precisely this Sabbath story that is the most debated one and that a large number of exegetes assume that it was composed in the light of debates about the Sabbath after Jesus' death (between Jews and Christians or between Christians amongst each other).[72] Next, supposing that Jesus did indeed engage in discussions about Sabbath observance and did pronounce himself on this issue at several occasions in a controversial way, it may not be deduced that he had the intention to undermine or to abolish Sabbath observance in its entirety. Discussions about all kinds of issues related to the Torah and its observance and in particular also to the Sabbath were a very common thing in the Jewish world of that period (as well as of later periods). Suffice it to refer to the differences between the strict, priestly and the less severe non-priestly approach we have distinguished. Even hypothesising, that Jesus would have advocated a very liberal position or had been a non-halakhic or a low-halakhic Jew – something that in my opinion remains difficult to substantiate –, this would not mean that he was opposed to Sabbath observance in its entirety.

(5) There is no question that several Gospel passages depict Jesus as calling himself 'Lord of the Sabbath' and claiming a big sovereignty and freedom as regards the observance of that day. Whether these passages go back to certain sayings or actions of the historical Jesus or not, will probably remain a matter of debate among exegetes. The most essential thing for us, however, is that it cannot be deduced from them that Jesus intended to put an end to the institution of the Sabbath. Remarkable in this regard is also the fact that apparently, as we shall see in the next paragraph, the first (Jewish) Christian communities did not draw that conclusion, as has been rightly pointed out by several exegetes, in particular also by Rordorf (who, however, interprets this fact – wrongly, in my view – as the result of a hesitancy to accept Jesus' radical and revolutionary position in this respect).

---

[71] See SANDERS: *Jesus and Judaism* 266.
[72] See note 70.

It goes almost without saying that one should not make too much from these observations. It would be a simplification to straightforwardly conclude on their basis that the Sabbath observance remained mandatory for Christians from paganism. The question as to whether this observance still was of relevance – and if so, in what sense and to what degree – for those Christians cannot be detached from larger issues such as the relevance of the Torah or the Ten Commandments for them. On the other hand I am convinced that a balanced view on Jesus' attitude towards Sabbath, which places him in the (Jewish) context of his time, makes it impossible to appeal to him in order to denounce every trace of the survival of the Jewish Sabbath observance that may be found in the history of Christianity, as being in contradiction with his radical intention.

4. Traces of Sabbath observance in first-century Christianity

The next question that logically arises, is to what extent the Jewish Sabbath and Sabbath observance actually did leave traces in early Christianity. For the sake of clarity, I will start by making clear that my concern here is not with the spiritual interpretation or exegesis of the Sabbath commandment – neither in a moral, an eschatological nor a Christological sense – by Christian authors. That the passages of the Old Testament dealing with the Sabbath have been interpreted in such a way is a well established fact on which there is no need to insist. The issue I will examine and discuss is here whether there are traces to be found of a continuing Sabbath *practice* in early Christianity. While dealing with this subject, I will at first limit myself to the first century C.E. and reserve the discussion of the data pertaining to the second and third centuries for the next paragraph. Moreover, as for this early period, there are two main issues which, though being interrelated, should be distinguished and be dealt with separately, namely the survival of the Sabbath observance as such and, next, the relationship between the Sabbath and the 'first day of the week', Sunday.

4.1. Sabbath observance

It is very difficult to obtain a clear picture of the Sabbath observance of the first generations of Christians. This holds in particular true for those communities which consisted for the main part of Jewish Christians.

In fact, there is no doubt that, generally speaking, Gentile Christians did not keep the Sabbath (although we know from the letters of Paul that Sabbath observance had an appeal for some of them). However, what about the Jewish Christians? Did they go on keeping Sabbath and, if so, in what way?

First of all, it should be remarked that there are clear indications that at least large groups of them indeed remained faithful to Sabbath observance. It may, for instance, be deduced from the fact that Jewish Christian communities of later times, like those of the Ebionites, also did and there is no serious reason to hypothesise that they would have introduced this custom in a later period, as the result of secondary rejudaising tendencies. Further, one may refer to a passage of the Gospel of Matthew (24, 20) in which Jesus exhorts his disciples to pray to God that they will not have to flee in the winter or 'on the Sabbath'. It is likely that this sentence presupposes a situation in which the Sabbath is observed by Christians (and therefore is no favourite day for fleeing, although in a case of necessity it would be allowed to do so).[73]

On the other hand the discussions between Jesus and the Jews/Pharisees and the scene of the disciples picking ears of grain on the Sabbath that are described in the Synoptic Gospels definitely point to the fact that Sabbath observance must have been a matter of debate in the first Christian communities in one way or the other. Either, these passages have a historical kernel and then it would be very surprising if they would not have left any echo in those communities and given rise to discussions about the Sabbath observance. In that case, it certainly might be expected that they would have incited certain Christians to call into question this institution. Or those scenes reflect discussions that would have taken place among Christians – and maybe this is the most plausible solution – but in that case there is all the more reason to assume that the Sabbath actually was a matter of dispute. The next question that has to be answered is why those disputes arose. Should they, as some scholars have argued, be accounted for primarily as being the result of the increasing number of Gentile Christians? Given the early date of the relevant Gospel passages this does not seem very likely. Other developments, for example discussions about the person of Jesus, about his messianic titles, his relation to the Torah and so on, may have

---

[73] Cf. DOERIG: *Schabbat* 402-403.

played a role as well. To enter into these complicated questions, however, would take us too far afield. We will confine ourselves to concluding that the first Christians continued to keep Sabbath, but that on the other hand this institution became a matter of dispute. As regards the last-mentioned observation, however, it should be emphasised that prudence is in order and that one should avoid drawing premature conclusions from it. As far as I can see, there is no evidence of early Christian attempts, dating prior to the rise of Gentile Christianity, to abolish the Sabbath as an institution for both Jews and Jewish Christians.[74] One of the implications of this conclusion is that the Sabbath observance of Jewish Christians cannot be conceived as the result of a tendency to return to or – as some scholars would say in a anti-Jewish and polemical way – to fall back into Jewish patterns and customs (that had been abolished by Jesus).

4.2. Sabbath and the 'first day of the week'

Even if there can hardly be any doubt that Sabbath observance continued in early Christianity for a certain time, namely in those communities that consisted of Jewish Christians or in which Jewish Christians constituted the majority, it is a well established fact that from a certain period onwards both Jewish and Gentile Christians assembled for liturgical meetings on another day of the week, on the day following on the Sabbath, the first day of the week. This development begs the question as to whether there is a relationship between the Sabbath and the Christian 'first day of the week' and, if so, how this relationship may be characterised, for instance, what aspects of Sabbath celebration have left some traces in early Christian Sunday.

To find an answer to this question, it will be necessary to first clarify some issues related to the emergence of Sunday in early Christianity. As will have already become apparent from our surveys of the studies of Rordorf, Mosna and Bacciocchi, the origin and early development of this day is surrounded with numerous problems for which very varying solutions have been proposed. Discussing in detail all the issues related

---

[74] Against Rordorf and Mosna it should be asserted that there is no clear indication that the so-called Christian 'Hellenists' following Stephen (Acts 6) would have called into question or abolished the Sabbath observance. Thus rightly BACCIOCCHI: *From Sabbath to Sunday* 141-142, esp. also note 20. Cf. also DOERIG: *Schabbat* 406.

to it and the solutions that have been advanced would lead us too far afield. We will be forced to limit us to some general remarks about the different theories proposed and to formulate a tentative and prudent hypothesis regarding the origins of Sunday that, let us announce it in advance, will not bring something basically new.

To begin, it should be observed that convincing arguments have been advanced against Bacciocchi's theory according to which Sunday observance arose only in the second century and more precisely starting from Rome.[75] It has been rightly objected that the earliest references certainly come before 115 C.E. and moreover are not associated to the city of Rome. The existence of Sunday is for example unmistakably attested by sources such as the Didache, the letter of Barnabas, Pliny and Ignatius which all have in common that they date of a somewhat earlier period (end of the first/beginning of the second century) and have no Roman background. In addition, Bacciocchi's interpretation of the expression κυριακη ἡμερα in Rev. 1, 10 as referring to the eschatological Day of the Lord, is based on very weak arguments and cannot be considered convincing.[76] Given the fact that there are neither good arguments for the view it refers to Easter Sunday[77] as has been argued by some scholars, the only possibility left is that it refers to the 'first day of the week'. Likewise, Bacciocchi's attempt to dismiss Acts 20, 7 as being an allusion to a regular liturgical meeting on the 'first day of the week' cannot be considered convincing. The main problem with his theory is that he wrongly interprets the expression 'breaking the bread' as simply meaning 'eating', 'taking dinner' without referring to a special ritual meal, that is to say to a celebration of the Eucharist.[78] In fact, there is no evidence to substantiate this interpretation. On the contrary, the use that is made of this expression elsewhere in the Acts as well as in other early Christian sources, makes it clear that it has a much more pregnant meaning and designates a ritual action taking place at the beginning of this meal and which in early Christianity soon became considered as one of the most crucial

---

[75] See in particular S. WILSON: *Related strangers. Jews and Christians 70-170 C.E.* (Minneapolis 1995) 234-235 and R. BAUCKHAM: Sabbath and Sunday in the Post-Apostolic Church, in: CARSON (ed.): *From Sabbath to Lord's Day* 251-298, esp. 270-273.

[76] See BAUCKHAM: The Lord's Day 221-250, esp. 225-227, 232.

[77] See BAUCKHAM: The Lord's Day 230-231.

[78] BACCIOCCHI: *From Sabbath to Sunday* 108-110.

moments of the Eucharist.[79] More generally speaking, it may be objected against Bacciocchi's interpretation that he proceeds from a conventional, but problematic and much too narrow idea of the early Christian Eucharist and wrongly assumes that this rite should have always followed the pattern of the Last Supper (and that every ritual meal deviating from this pattern should be considered a 'normal' meal or eventually an agape).[80] If, however, the expression 'to break the bread' refers to a celebration of the Eucharist, be it not in the way we are most familiar with, the suggestion that in Acts 20, 7 allusion is made to a regular, extraordinary meal at Troas, loses much of its plausibility. It becomes more probable that the passage refers to an already existing custom which consisted in gathering on the first day of the week for a kind of celebration of the Eucharist. This implies that such a practice must have existed in Luke's time at the latest. Finally, a supplementary argument in favour of an early origin of the first day of the week as a regular day of Christian worship may be drawn from the fact that no evidence is available of discussions regarding this day. If, for example, it would have been the result of a somewhat later innovation introduced by Gentile Christians, one might have expected some Jewish Christians to have called it into question. That there is no trace to be found of any sort of protest against this day, may be considered an indication of its antiquity and its rather early Jewish Christian roots.

On the other hand, it should be remarked that Rordorf and Mosna are inclined to make too much out of some vague or even hypothetical allusions to a celebration of the first day of the week in other – partly earlier – passages of the New Testament. In particular, the fact that in 1 Corinthians 16, 2 reference is made to the first day of the week as the day on which money was set aside and collected, is in itself interesting but even assuming that it presupposes some sort of Sunday observance, it must be concluded that it is singularly uninformative about the origins and the character of that Christian day.[81] Next, as for Rordorf's reconstruction of the emergence of Sunday, it must be concluded that some of his ideas are highly speculative or even simply cannot stand the test of criticism. It is very well possible that a Eucharistic celebration

---

[79] See G. ROUWHORST: La célébration de l'Eucharistie dans l'Eglise primitive, in *Questions liturgiques* 74 (1993) 89-112, esp. 96-99 and IDEM: Bread and Cup, esp. 24-26.

[80] *Ibidem.*

[81] Thus rightly WILSON: *Related Strangers* 230.

was part of Christian Sunday observance, but it remains difficult to ascertain that this was the case from the very start (naturally this argument may also be advanced against Mosna). One aspect of his theory, however, is in particular open to question, namely his suggestion that these Eucharistic meals would have taken place on Sunday evening. The evidence for this theory is meagre and, in particular, it must be stressed that it heavily depends on the assumption that the author of Acts, mentioning in ch. 20:7 the 'first day of the week', would have followed the Roman computation which reckoned the day from midnight to midnight and not from evening to evening as the Jewish way of reckoning did. Bacciocchi, following other scholars, has rightly objected to this hypothesis that the indications of time used by the author of Acts to mark the beginning of a day are rather vague and ambiguous but that in particular the evidence for a Roman time reckoning is weak and cannot be substantiated by the indications of time used elsewhere in the Acts. All in all, the most plausible solution seems therefore to be that the gathering at Troas took place in the night from Saturday to Sunday and that this was conform the practice with which Luke was familiar.

This being established, what can be said with some certainty about the origins of Christian Sunday? I think that at least the following conclusions are sufficiently well-founded to constitute a sound starting point for a comparison with Sabbath observance.

(1) There is hard and irrefutable evidence that Sunday observance was generally accepted by Christians from different regions at the latest at the end of the first century. It may be much older and in fact it is not unlikely that it really was and that it dated back to the period prior to the Gentile mission.

(2) On the basis of the scarce evidence available it seems the most plausible to assume that the liturgical meetings to which several sources refer, took place in the night from Saturday on Sunday and not on Sunday evening. The precise moment of the night (evening or morning and so on) remains a matter of conjecture.

(3) Whatever the contents of those early Christian gatherings may have been, they at least have comprised the rite of the 'breaking of the bread'. This was neither simply a communal meal nor a classical celebration of the Eucharist following the pattern of the Last Supper. One may hazard the guess that it will have looked like the Eucharistic celebration described in the Didache or that at least it will have had a number of elements in common with that ritual meal.

(4) Every attempt to find an explication for the origins of Christian Sunday necessarily remains speculative. One may, however, speculate with good reason that the Christian meetings on the first day of the week arose as an extension of the Sabbath service to Saturday evening.[82] It may be guessed – and not more than that – that this date first of all was chosen because there was a pragmatic need for regular gatherings accessible to both Jewish and Gentile Christians. Moreover, it is very likely that the first day of the week was associated with Jesus' resurrection at a very early period. There is no hard evidence to substantiate this view, but the sole fact that all the Gospel stories associate stories about the resurrection of Jesus with the first day of the week, the day after the Sabbath, point in that direction.

What conclusions can be drawn from the foregoing about the relationship between Sabbath and Sunday in this early period? Can we rightly speak of some sort of continuity between both days or should our conclusion rather be that we are dealing with two completely different and unrelated phenomena?

To begin, it should be emphasised that the differences between both days are more conspicuous than their similarities and the elements they have in common. Sunday was certainly no day of rest. We do not find any unambiguous trace of a regular reading of the Torah and the Prophets or of any other part of Scripture (though it should admitted this is an argument from silence). Likewise, in the available sources no mention is made of any rite or ritual gesture specifically related to the celebration of the Sabbath at home, such as a version of the *qiddush*.

To put these data in the right perspective, it should be added that we hardly might have expected otherwise, provided we assume that the Sunday dates back to an early period in which Jewish Christians were in the majority. Jewish Christians continued observing the Sabbath and an additional Sabbath or a partial reprise of that day was completely superfluous for them. As for the Gentile Christians, they will not have missed the Sabbath or elements taken from it, no more than they had done before their conversion.

---

[82] This thesis was developed and defended in particular by H. RIESENFELD: The Sabbath and the Lord's Day in Judaism. The preaching of Jesus and early Christianity, in: H. RIESENFELD: *The Gospel tradition* (Oxford 1970) 111-137, see esp. 125-137. Cf. also BACCIOCCHI: *From Sabbath to Sunday* 283-285, 300-301 and MOSNA: *Storia della domenica* 46, 59.

Nonetheless one may note three things Sabbath and Sunday had in common from the very start:

(1) Both days had in common that their celebrations occurred every week. It should be emphasised once again that this was very exceptional in Antiquity.

(2) It seems that, at the time when Christianity emerged, more or less ritualised meals were part of both days. One might object that, as far is the Christian Sunday is concerned, this may be exclusively accounted for either by the tradition regarding the Last Supper or by stories about the meals the risen Lord had held with his disciples. This argumentation, however, seems to me untenable. First, it would be a serious mistake to conceive of the Eucharistic celebrations of this period as copies of the Last Supper. Even the idea that they were primarily celebrated to commemorate the death of Jesus is heavily subject to discussion.[83] In addition, that the celebrations of the Eucharist were a continuation of the meals of the risen Lord cannot be more than a speculative hypothesis. Further, even supposing that the first Christian Eucharistic celebrations were connected in one way or the other with either the passion and death of the Lord or with his resurrection – which almost certainly was the case – it should not be overlooked that the most crucial ritual actions connected with these celebrations such as the breaking of the bread and probably certain meal berakhoth connected with the bread and/or the wine derive from Jewish meal traditions that admittedly were not unique to the Sabbath meals but anyhow were part of these.

(3) Sabbath and Sunday had in common their joyful character. In a sense, they were weekly recurring festivals. Scholars polemically insisting on the legalistic character seem to be inclined to overlook this fact. They are, however, wrong.

5. TRACES OF SABBATH IN THE SECOND AND THIRD CENTURIES C.E.

There is no question that from the second half of the first century the observance of the Sabbath rapidly declined.[84] It becomes evident from

---

[83] See ROUWHORST: La célébration de l'Eucharistie; IDEM: Bread and cup.

[84] Cf. for the following also BAUCKHAM: Sabbath and Sunday in the Post-Apostolic Chuch.

numerous sources, such as the writings of Paul, Justin, Irenaeus, Ignatius of Antioch that this observance was in principle restricted to Jewish Christians and it is well known that their number drastically decreased in the period under consideration. This, however, does not mean that every trace of the Sabbath became completely erased. Apart from the above-mentioned features the Christian Sunday has in common with Jewish Sabbath and which most probably have been borrowed from the latter day, one may mention certain phenomena that will be best explained as traces or as echoes of the Sabbath.

I will start by observing that some of the historical facts that are sometimes adduced in the secondary literature – amongst others by Rordorf and Mosna – as indications of the survival of the Sabbath in Christianity, are subject to discussion and most probably are better accounted for in another way. I think this holds at least true for the custom of fasting on Saturday which is testified for Western Christianity by Tertullian and by some other sources.[85] This practice can probably be better explained to be due to an extension either of the existing weekly Friday fast to Saturday or of the yearly fast of Saturday before Easter to every Saturday during the week. One even cannot exclude the possibility that this Saturday fast has an anti-Jewish background and originated as a kind of protest against the celebration of the Sabbath.[86] This presumption is reinforced by the fact that, according to Epiphanus, the Marcionites fasted on the Sabbath to express their hatred against the Creator of the world.[87] One might hazard the guess that this practice was not restricted to the Marcionites but that the latter had taken it over from 'orthodox' Christians and subsequently given it a typically Marcionite twist. In that case, the relationship between the Christian fast on

---

[85] TERTULLIAN: *On fasting* 14, 3; HIPPOLYTUS: *Commentary on Daniel* 4, 20. Tertullian and Hippolytus criticise this custom (see also TERTULLIAN: *On fasting* 15). It is, however, defended by the Synod of Elvira (can. 26), by AUGUSTINE: *Ep.* 36, 14, 32, VICTORIN OF PETTAU: *De fabrica mundi* 5, and by INNOCENTIUS I: *Ep.* 25, 4, 7. Cf. further for the discussion about the Saturday fast in the early Church AUGUSTINE: *Epistle* 36 (to Casulanus) and 55 (to Januarius) and JOHN CASSIAN: *Institutes* 3, 10.

[86] Cf. BACCIOCCHI: *From Sabbath to Sunday* 188-194. This author speculates that the Sabbath might have been transformed in Rome from a day of feasting and joy to a day of fasting and mourning in order to degrade it and to enhance the Sunday worship. This solution in the way it is presented by Bacciocchi is problematic, in so far as it is related to his very debatable view on the rise of the Sunday, but it might have an element of truth.

[87] *Panarion* 42.3, 3-4. See also TERTULLIAN: *Against Marcion* 4, 12.

Saturday and the Sabbath observance should be characterised as a very antagonistic and polemical one, the former practice being a kind of counter-observance resulting from a protest against the latter.[88]

The situation seems to be less clear for another practice which is equally attested by Tertullian as existing among some groups of Christians and which consisted in not kneeling on Saturday (just as it was customary to refrain from kneeling on Sunday and during the Pentecost).[89] This custom might, as has been argued by some scholars, betray a particular estimation of the Saturday, but this remains difficult to prove. In any case, we are dealing here not with a Jewish, but with a specifically Christian practice that has been extended from the Christian Sunday or from the Christian Pentecost to the Saturday.

Having inferred that no solid conclusions may be drawn from these disputable and ambiguous data with regard to the survival of the Sabbath in early Christianity, it should be observed that there are other indications of the influence of the observance and celebration of this day that seem much more reliable and cannot be put aside so easily.

The first hard fact that is explicitly mentioned and dealt with by both Rordorf and Mosna, but not by Bacciocchi, is the reading of passages from the Bible – that is to say from the Old Testament and the New Testament – in the first part of the Sunday Eucharist, a custom that is attested for the first time by Justin's first Apology (ch. 65-67) and has gained general acceptance in early Christianity at a quite early stage. Several scholars, the most famous of which are H. Lietzmann, G. Dix and J. Jungmann, have posited that this liturgical practice usually situated on Sunday *morning* has its roots in the Scripture reading in the Synagogue which takes places on the Sabbath after the morning prayer.[90] It appears that this solution which is adopted by Rordorf and Mosna, in itself is open to question if only for the reason that we cannot be sure that a combination of the reading of Torah and Prophets with the morning prayer at Sabbath had already gained general acceptance in the Synagogue at that time (and if so, that it did already exist for a longer period).

---

[88] In that case the Sabbathfast might compare with the fast of the Quartodeciman Passover which more or less coincided with the Jewish Passover meal.

[89] *On Prayer* 23, 1-2.

[90] H. LIETZMANN: *Messe und Herrenmahl* (Berlin 1926) 211; G. DIX: *The shape of the liturgy* (London 1978) (1945[1]) 36-37; J. JUNGMANN: *Missarum sollemnia* I (Wien 1952[3]) 25-26.

Moreover the objection might be raised that the way the Scripture was read in the Church of Justin certainly deviated considerably from the traditions of the Synagogue. On the other hand, one should not overlook the fact that the mere idea of reading from a holy Book was borrowed by the Christians from no other institution or tradition than that of the Synagogue. It seems therefore very obvious that there must have been some sort of continuity between the early Christian Liturgy of the Word, the first part of the Sunday Eucharist as described by Justin, and the reading from the Torah and the Prophets in the Synagogue, especially on the Sabbath.[91]

Another phenomenon that should not remain unmentioned in this regard is the liturgical celebration of Saturday as attested by several Christian sources who all have in common that either they originate from the East or at least refer to practices existing in Eastern regions and mention the Eucharist as one of the main elements of the celebration.[92] Both Rordorf and Mosna hypothesise the existence of some type of historical continuity between this phenomenon and early forms of Christian Sabbath observance as they are known to have existed in the first and in the beginning of the second centuries. They argue that it should be considered as a specifically Eastern trace of the survival of the Sabbath (the Western variant being the fast on Sabbath). Rordorf even speculates that there is some link with the traditions of Gentile Christians of Asia Minor who would have introduced practices related to the Sabbath for 'suspect' reasons (imitations of Jewish customs; astrological superstition). These 'dubious' traditions, however, might have gradually lost their superstitious aspects and this would have finally resulted in a joyful and purely liturgical celebration which meets Rordorf's approval.[93]

---

[91] See also G. ROUWHORST: *The reading of Scripture in early Christian liturgy*, in Festschrift G. Foerster (Leuven 2001), forthcoming.

[92] The main witnesses are EPIPHANIUS: *De fide* 24, 7 (*GCS Epiphanius III* 525); SOCRATES: *Ecclesiastical history* 5, 22; SOZOMENOS: *Ecclesiastical history* 5, 22 en 7, 19; JOHN CASSIAN: *Institutes* 3, 2; Council of Laodicea, canon 16; *Apostolic Constitutions* II, 59, 3; VII, 23, 3; VIII, 33, 2 (cf. also VII, 36); Ethiopic version of the *Traditio apostolica*, ch. 22 (see for the origin and date of this source the observations we will make further on). Cf. RORDORF: *Der Sonntag* 145-146; H. AUF DER MAUR: *Feiern im Rhythmus der Zeit* I (= Gottesdienst der Kirche 5) (Regensburg 1983) 33-34.

[93] RORDORF: *Der Sonntag* 146-149.

I think against this theory several serious objections may be raised:

(1) First, as I have tried to demonstrate before, it is very doubtful whether the Sabbath fast as it certainly has existed in the West, can be accounted for as a trace of the Jewish Sabbath.

(2) Rordorf and Mosna seem to assume that at least one of the witnesses of the liturgical celebration of the Saturday may be traced back to the beginning of the third century, namely the Ethiopian version of the so-called 'Apostolic Tradition' of Hippolytus (ch. 22).[94] This assumption, however, is certainly unfounded. Apart from the whole question raised by the origins of this document and by the authorship of Hippolytus that has become again open to scholarly debate,[95] there can be no doubt that the passage under consideration is due to a recent insertion that is lacking in the other variants.[96] Incidentally, the reference to the celebration of the Sabbath is in obvious contradiction to the Roman origins which Rordorf and Mosna appear to suppose, given the fact that the Christians of Rome knew the custom of fasting on Saturday.

(3) Rordorf's ideas about the continuity between Gentile Christian 'sabbatisers' and the liturgical celebration of Saturday make a highly speculative impression and the fact that the sources he adduces as witnesses of a survival of the Sabbath observance or celebrations have to be discarded, makes his theory still more speculative.

This being said, several questions arise almost automatically. Was the liturgical celebration of Saturday the result of an innovation of the fourth century or did it have nonetheless roots in earlier Christian traditions? Further, if it was a fourth century innovation, what was the reason of its introduction? On the other hand, if it was not the result of an innovation – or if it was so only partially – what was the character and the provenance of these traditions? With what type of communities were

---

[94] See the reconstruction (and translation) of the Traditio apostolica by B. BOTTE: *La tradition apostolique de saint Hippolyte* (= Liturgiewissenschaftliche Quellen und Forschungen 35) (Münster 1989[5]) 60-61.

[95] See esp. M. METZGER: Nouvelles perspectives pour la prétendue Tradition apostolique, in *Ecclesia orans* 5 (1988) 241-259; IDEM: Enquêtes autour de la prétendue 'Tradition apostolique', in *Ecclesia orans* 9 (1992) 7-36; P. BRADSHAW: Redating the Apostolic Tradition. Some preliminary steps, in N. MITCHELL & J. BALDOVIN (eds.): *Rule of prayer, rule of faith. Essays in honor of Aidan Kavanagh O.S.B.* (Collegeville 1996) 3-17.

[96] See also AUF DER MAUR: *Feiern im Rhythmus der Zeit* 34.

they connected? Did mainly Jewish Christians or Gentile Christians follow them?

It should be emphasised that about many aspects of this phenomenon we remain in the dark. There is, however, one source, dating from the end of the fourth century, that maybe permits us to lift a corner of the veil at least with regard to one specific region, namely the surroundings of Antioch. Several passages of the Apostolic Constitutions, a document originating from this areas, testify to a very high appreciation of the Sabbath. The most remarkable thing, however, is that the seventh book contains an elaborate blessing of the Sabbath (VII, 36). While reading this text and consulting the secondary literature concerned, one is struck by two things.[97] First, it is an undisputed fact that it must be characterised as a (Christianised) version of the Amidah of the Sabbath (that instead of eighteen contains only seven benedictions). On the other hand, it is striking that the text of the prayer explicitly emphasises the superiority of the Sunday vis-à-vis Saturday-Sabbath. How to explain these facts? Elsewhere I have developed an hypothesis that might provide a satisfactory explanation and that I will content myself to resuming here briefly.[98] In fact, we know among others from the *Didascalia Apostolorum* (ch. 26) that in the region under consideration there were many Christians, most probably Jewish Christians, who continued to observe the Sabbath and even held the Sabbath higher than the first day of the week.[99] Starting from these facts, I have suggested that the Sabbath blessing incorporated in the Apostolic Constitutions did not derive directly from a Jewish Synagogue – as has been argued frequently – but from Jewish Christian groups. The practices of these groups must have given rise to debates and conflicts with other (Gentile Christian) communities. The author of the Apostolic Constitutions, now, attempted to find a compromise between Jewish and Gentile Christians by meeting his opponents, the Jewish Christians, part of the way, that is

---

[97] See for example D. FIENSY: *Prayers alleged to be Jewish. An Examination of the Constitutiones Apostolorum* (Brown Judaic studies 65) (Chico 1985) esp. 129-144, 165-187.

[98] See G. ROUWHORST: Jewish liturgical traditions in early Syriac Christianity, in *Vigiliae christianae* 51 (1997) 72-93, esp. 85-87. Cf. IDEM: Continuity and discontinuity between Jewish and Christian liturgy, in *Bijdragen* 54 (1993) 72-83, esp. 78-81.

[99] Ed. A. VÖÖBUS: *The Didascalia Apostolorum in Syriac* II (CSCO 407/408) (Louvain 1979) 251 (233).

to say by emphasising the importance of the Sabbath celebration and on the other hand by simultaneously stressing that Sunday was more important than the Sabbath.

The implication of this explanation might be that the liturgical celebration of Saturday, at least in certain regions, originated from an attempt to integrate minorities of Christians who had remained faithful to some type of Sabbath observance into the larger Gentile Christian communities. I do not pretend to say that this theory provides the final solution for the emergence of the Christian celebration of Saturday. Moreover, I admit that one has to reckon very seriously with the possibility that in other regions in the East things developed differently and that other factors may have played a decisive role there. Nonetheless, as far as the surroundings of Antioch are concerned, this appears to be a very plausible and attractive hypothesis.

For the rest, a further argument in favour of this explanation may be drawn from what we know about the reading of the Bible during the first part of the Eucharist in this region. It is precisely the Churches East of Antioch that are known to have preserved the custom of regular reading from the Torah and the Prophets during the Eucharist, a custom that is not explicitly attested by sources derived from other regions.[100] The question may be raised as to how this liturgical tradition came into existence. The most natural explanation seems to be that it was transferred at a certain moment from the Sabbath to Sunday. Admittedly, based on the available data we can only guess how this process took place. Were the Christians once used to reading from the Torah and the Prophets on the Sabbath? And if so, how did they celebrate Sunday? Did their Sunday Eucharist comprise a liturgy of the Word from the outset? Was the reading of the Torah and the Prophets combined with passages from the New Testament and if so, since when? And assuming that a reading from the Torah and the Prophets on the Sabbath remained customary amongst (some) Christians living in this region, till when did it continue to exist and when was it transposed to the Sunday Eucharist? All these questions must remain unanswered. Nonetheless, there are strong indications that the reading from the Torah and the Prophets persisted for a considerable time among a number of Churches with a more or less Jewish background and that this practice finally had a bearing on the liturgical traditions of Gentile Christianity, both on their celebration

---

[100] Cf. ROUWHORST: The reading of Scripture; IDEM: Continuity and discontinuity.

of the Saturday/Sabbath as on their way of reading from the Bible in the Sunday Eucharist.

6. THE FOURTH CENTURY: THE SUNDAY BECOMES A DAY OF REST

Leaving aside the question whether the Jewish Christian communities continued to observe the Sabbath as a day of rest and, if so, till when – unfortunately it must remain unanswered for want of reliable sources –, it can be asserted that during the first three centuries C.E. the Christian Sunday did not function as a weekly day of rest. At least the Gentile Christians were not familiar with such a day, no more than non-Christian Greeks and Romans were (for the sake of clarity, it might be added they did not continue their work all the time, but they enjoyed a considerable number of holidays and festal days during the year on which everybody had time off). Christians assembled on Sunday either in the evening or in the morning or eventually at both times to read from the Bible, to celebrate the Eucharist and/or an agape and to pray together, but during the day they continued their professional activities.

It is well known that due to an initiative of the Emperor Constantine this situation changed at the beginning of the fourth century. In 321 C.E. Constantine promulgated two laws preserved by the Codex of Justinian and the Codex of Theodosius that were of decisive importance in this regard.[101] Given the fact that they are discussed in all the relevant publications,[102] we can confine ourselves to briefly summarising their basic thrust. The first law dating from 3 March requires public rest from work "on the most honourable day of the Sun" for judges, the population of the cities and all craftsmen. It makes, however, an exception for farmers living in the countryside who are heavily dependent on the unpredictable caprices of the weather. The second law promulgated on 3 July explicitly forbids legal procedures on Sunday but it exempts from

---

[101] *Codex Justinianus* III, 12, 2 (see RORDORF: *Sabbat und Sonntag* no. 111); *Codex Theodosianus* II, 8, 1 (RORDORF: *Sabbat und Sonntag* no. 112). See also Eusebius: *The life of Constantine* 4, 18-19 (ed. F. WINKELMANN: *Über das Leben des Kaisers Konstantins. Eusebius I/1* (GCS) (Berlin 1992²). See for a recent translation (with introduction and commentary) of the last-mentioned work CAMERON & HALL: *Eusebius. Life of Constantine* (Oxford 1999).

[102] See RORDORF: *Der Sonntag*, 160-165; MOSNA: *Storia della domenica*, 216-220; BAUCKHAM: Sabbath and Sunday in the Post-Apostolic Church 280.

the ban vows and legal actions leading to the manumission of slaves. One may wonder how strictly these laws were followed by the Christians of the fourth century. It seems, at least, that several Church fathers were somewhat ambivalent towards the idea of refraining from work on Sunday and feared the dangers of idleness.[103] Nonetheless, there is no doubt that Constantine's laws were gradually put into practice and that the Sunday ended up by becoming a generally recognised Christian day of rest.

This being established, several questions may be raised that are of particular relevance for our subject. They may be subdivided in two categories, namely those that are strictly historical and those that are rather theological. On the one hand, one may try to retrace the factors that contributed to the introduction of Sunday as a day of rest and to its acceptance by Christians. On the other hand, there is the question as to how this development should be valued, whether it should for instance be considered as a rupture with an older and more authentic conception of Christian Sunday or as a legitimate and more or less natural adaptation to the changing ecclesiastical situation of the fourth century. It is obvious that those questions often tend to be intertwined in the secondary literature. It is, however, essential to distinguish them as carefully as possible.

To begin with the historical factors, there is general agreement that at first the appeal to the Sabbath observance did not play a role of importance neither in the decision of the Emperor nor, as far as we know, in the motivation of the Christians who refrained from work on Sunday. The 'sabbatisation' of the Sunday in the sense that the Sabbath was understood as a model for the Christian Sunday as a day of rest, came into development only gradually after the fourth century, in the fifth and especially in the sixth century.[104] As for Constantine, it is indisputable that he based himself for his legislation on existing Roman regulations that were applied to pagan holidays and not on the prescriptions and prohibitions connected with the Old Testament. The sole fact that farmers were exempted from the ban on work, might suffice to prove this, since this was in conformity with pagan practice, but in plain contradiction with the Old Testament Sabbath rules. Furthermore, it is striking that the Church Fathers of the fourth century do not draw

---

[103] See RORDORF: *Der Sonntag* 165-166.
[104] See RORDORF: *Der Sonntag* 165-171; MOSNA: *Storia della domenica* 349-362.

argument from the Old Testament Sabbath to substantiate the idea of Sunday as a day of rest. On the contrary, they rarely appeal to the Sabbath as a model for the Sunday and if they do so, their focus is not on the abstention from work, but on the aspect of worship that apparently remains the most essential for them. As for the aspect of rest, references to it are quite rare in Christian sources of the fourth and even the fifth century and, moreover, some authors prove to be afraid of the idleness that the abstention from work entails and to fear that the devil will find work for empty hands. On the other hand, it cannot be denied – and in fact nobody denies – that from a certain period onwards the Sabbath, viewed both as a day of worship and as a day of rest, starts serving as a model for Christian Sunday. And there is no doubt that this development is due for a considerable part to Constantine's decision to turn the early Christian Sunday in a public day of rest, which meant a decisive step in the process of 'sabbatisation' of the Sunday.

So far, there is general agreement among the scholars who have written about this subject. It should, however, be noted that there are some issues related to it that remain a matter of debate. Among those issues the most disputed and at the same time the most difficult one is probably constituted by the motivation of the Emperor Constantine. What motives did he have for choosing the Christian day of worship as a public day of rest? Taking for granted that his decision was not motivated by barely strategic political considerations – in that case his political strategy would have been very risky even if from the perspective of a later period it may appear differently – but at least in part by a religious conviction, the question still may be raised whether his motivation may be qualified as specifically Christian or whether it was rather due to his so-called solar piety. As we have noticed above, the opinions of different scholars, in particular of Rordorf and Mosna, diverge on this point. The latter depicts the Emperor as a sincere Christian who by his regulation above all wanted to favour the Christians, but the former seriously reckons with the possibility that his main intention would have been to unify the empire by a monotheistic religion of the Sun.

It is impossible to gain access to the inner motivations of a dead Emperor. The earliest and most essential data related to the introduction of the Sunday as a day of rest do not contribute very much to solving the riddle, but rather add to the confusion. Whereas the laws preserved by the Codex of Justinian and that of Theodosius use only the term 'day of the Sun', Eusebius in his *Life of Constantine* clearly prefers

more explicitly Christian indications like the 'day of the Lord and Saviour' and the 'day of Salvation' and he refers to the terms 'Light Day'
and 'Sun Day' only in order to explain the former indications.[105] Of
course, one might try to account for the terminology used in the *Life of
Constantine* by the indisputably Christian background of its author and
by his theological intentions. On the other hand, it would be equally
legitimate to attempt to explain the terms encountered in both laws by
the fact that they were not exclusively intended for Christian, but
equally for pagan citizens. For the rest, the question may raised if Rordorf is not too much inclined to depict Constantine as a half-informed
syncretist and half-hearted Christian.[106] Moreover, it may be asked to
what extent Rordorf's critical and sceptical attitude towards Constantine's motives for introducing Sunday as a day of rest is somehow
related to his negative stance towards Sabbath observance. On the other
hand, assuming that Constantine's motivation was sincerely Christian,
as Mosna tends to believe, this in itself does not yet mean that his decision was a fortunate one from a theological point of view or that it
might be adduced as an argument in favour of the Sunday as a rest day
(admittedly, Mosna does not explicity draw that conclusion, but his
positive and benevolent approach of Constantine's legislation eventually
might be explained in this sense).

This brings us to the next issue we will have to deal with, the theological appreciation of the Sunday rest. Much will depend here on the
theological position one holds with regard to the place of Scripture and
tradition. Basically two options may be defended: either one may ascribe
a highly normative role to Scripture or to early Christianity, be it of the
New Testament period or of the period prior to Constantine, or one
may put less stress on the normative character of the period of the origins and start from the conviction that the further development of liturgical tradition may be legitimate even if it does not appear to be immediately in line with the practice of the first or of the first three centuries.
In the latter case, one most probably will be inclined to attach more
importance to anthropological knowledge concerning the functioning of

---

[105] See *Life of Constantine* 4,18-19 (see also: CAMERON & HALL: *Eusebius* 319).

[106] See for the person of Constantine and the numerous questions raised by his
political career, his personal piety, his theology and his relation to the Church. S. HALL:
Konstantin I in *Theologische Realenzyklopädie* 19 (Berlin/New York 1990) 489-500. See
further CAMERON & HALL: *Eusebius* 34-46, in particular with regard to the genuineness
of his Christianity, p. 44-46.

rituals and festivals than adherents of the former option will do. Personally I am rather in favour of the second position that some might with some reason qualify as typically Roman-Catholic. In my view, the theological value of the Sunday as a day of rest does not only depend on its existing or not in the first or second century and even not on the position Jesus took with regard to the Sabbath, as long as there is no evidence that he straightforwardly rejected this institution outright. One should also take into account the role Sunday has played in the course of history, whether or not it has contributed to a modest degree of humanisation of society, for example in the Middle Ages or in the period of the industrial revolution.[107] In addition, I think a further reflection is needed on the more or less intrinsic relationship between feast and celebration on the one hand and interruption of work on the other hand. If Sunday can be described as a celebration of the resurrection – and therefore as a weekly festival (feast) –, was it then not very natural that as soon as it became possible Christians stopped working on Sunday because feast and work do not easily combine? An additional reason why in the fourth century the Sunday became a day of rest, so one may add, was that in that period the existing generally recognised holidays were tied up with paganism and were therefore unacceptable to Christians, while at the same time collective holidays were a necessity, as they were and are in every society both in the past and in modern times. On the other hand, it has to be admitted that the New Testament and the early Church remain of particular relevance for everyone who wants to form a theologically founded judgement about the meaning of Sunday and I can imagine that someone else will emphasise this aspect more than I do. But then the question immediately rises as to what are the implications of a less biased view on the Jewish Sabbath and on the position Jesus appears to have taken towards this institution. Supposing he did not reject it radically, the fact that Jewish Christians remained faithful to the observance of the Sabbath as well as the fact that Gentile Christians took over some elements from the Jewish observance, as soon as the political and religious situation permitted it, appears in a different light, even if one holds to the (more or less) normative character of early Christianity. And of course, this also will have implications for the position one will take with regard to the question of Sunday observance in a

---

[107] See for example H. HECKMANN: *Arbeitszeit und Sonntagsruhe* (Essen 1986) and R. BECK: *Histoire du dimanche de 1700 à nos jours* (Paris 1997).

modern secularised society, in the sense that it will become less easy to defend the abolition of Sunday as a day of rest by an appeal to the early Church and to the behaviour and the sayings ascribed to the historical Jesus.

7. CONCLUSION

The conclusion of this article can be brief. Our primary purpose was to sketch a picture of the complicated relationship between Sabbath as a weekly recurring Jewish 'festival' and Christian Sunday, especially in the first four centuries of Christianity. In general, our conclusion can be that there was more continuity than Christian scholars are sometimes inclined to believe and the rupture that undeniably took place in the first and second century was not as drastic as often is suggested, not even in Gentile Christianity and most probably not everywhere to the same degree. Moreover, there are no convincing reasons for Christians to place the influence that the Sabbath unmistakably exerted on the Sunday observance in later periods beforehand in a negative light. They would do better to consider this process in a more objective way. This would have a double advantage. First of all, it might benefit Jewish Christian dialogue and mutual understanding between Jews and Christians. In addition, it could help Christians to better understand their own weekly celebration of the resurrection which, just as the Sabbath, should be a weekly feast.

ELS ROSE

CELEBRATING SAINT MARTIN IN EARLY MEDIEVAL GAUL*

It is incredible how many people gathered for St. Martin's funeral. The entire city hastened to meet the body. All inhabitants of the country and of the villages were present, as well as many from neighbouring towns. What grief for all of them! What laments, particularly from the deeply distressed monks. About two thousand are said to have gathered on that day, in honour of Martin alone [...] This crowd accompanied the body of the blessed man to the site of the tomb while singing heavenly hymns [...] Martin is applauded with divine psalms, Martin is honoured with celestial hymns.[1]

Despite lamentations and tears, the funeral of Martin, bishop of Tours between 371 and 397, was coloured not only by the tones of mourning. The procession accompanying Martin's dead body was marked by something festive as well. In the above quoted letter to his mother-in-law Bassula, Martin's hagiographer Sulpicius Severus (after 355-after 420) compared the events of 11 November 397 to the triumphant arrival of a prince into his city rather than to a funeral as such. Indeed Martin, tormented until the end by the temptations of the Adversary, could not be defeated by death, but kept his soul out of the devil's claws and was finally saved in Abraham's bosom.[2]

* I would like to thank Hans Peterse and Iain Ward-Campbell for the time they spent in correcting this contribution. Abbreviations: Bo: Bobbio missal (see note 53); *CSEL: Corpus scriptorum ecclesiasticorum Latinorum* (Wien 1886-); Go: *Missale Gothicum* (see note 45); *MGH: Monumenta Germaniae historica, AA: Auctores antiquissimi, SRM: Scriptores rerum Merovingicarum* (Hannover/Köln/München 1826-); *SChr: Sources Chrétiennes* (Paris 1941-).
    [1] SULPICIUS SEVERUS: *Epistola* III.18-21. Ed. J. FONTAINE: *SChr* 133 (Paris 1967) 342-344: "In obsequium uero funeris credi non potest quanta hominum multitudo conuenerit. Tota obuiam corpori ciuitas ruit, cuncti ex agris atque uicis multique de uicinis etiam urbibus adfuerunt. O quantus luctus omnium, quanta praecipue maerentium lamenta monachorum! Qui eo die fere ad duo milia conuenisse dicuntur, specialis Martini gloria [...] Haec igitur beati uiri corpus usque ad locum sepulchri hymnis canora caelestibus turba prosequitur [...] Martino diuinis plauditur psalmis, Martinus hymnis caelestibus honoratur."
    [2] SULPICIUS SEVERUS: *Epistola* III.14, 16.

One of the most peculiar features of St. Martin's commemoration is, that it is celebrated not on the day of his demise, on 8 November, but of his burial. Although the bishop of Tours was already at an advanced age and foresaw his own death, he could not ignore the troubles in one of the villages of his see, Candes, where the clergy was involved in an internal discord. Martin set off to restore peace. The success of this journey became the crowning glory of his episcopal work. After achieving the reconciliation, the beloved bishop felt his strength decrease and died.[3]

Although Martin's disciples, the monks and virgins, as well as the citizens of Tours, felt like a flock without a shepherd, they firmly believed that their protector did not sleep for ever, but lived on in heaven. Had not Martin's face changed immediately after his demise into the face of an angel, representing the holy one's participation in the glory of the resurrection?[4] Therefore the people of Tours, while singing "divine psalms and heavenly hymns", turned Martin's burial into a commemoration festival.

This study is an attempt to reconstruct the celebration of the commemoration of St. Martin in Gaul during the Merovingian period, as it is attested by both hagiographical and liturgical texts.

Martin's triumph over the forces of eternal death would not have been the only reason for the people's delight at the *receptio* of his body in their own town. The presence of the bishop's body in Tours promised nothing but good things for the city. As in the late antique and early medieval world a holy person, once dead, was supposed to live on close to God, his or her strength on earth remained unbroken. The saint's tomb was not a dwelling place of death, but rather a place where heaven touched the earth with life-giving strength. It is not surprising that the inhabitants of Tours honoured their patron on his body's return with all the ceremony belonging to the traditional *adventus* of the emperor or his representative to a city. As the *adventus* of a secular ruler celebrated his presence *in situ* – though indicating at the same time that his power was not bound to that particular place[5] – the arrival of St. Martin's body to Tours promised his *presentia* in that town, the clearest possible

---

[3] SULPICIUS SEVERUS: *Epistola* III.6-17.
[4] SULPICIUS SEVERUS: *Epistola* III.17.
[5] Raymond VAN DAM: *Leadership and community in late antique Gaul* (Berkeley 1985) 140.

evidence of God's mercy.[6] The *presentia* of a saint's body, or part of it in the form of relics, was a linking power in late antique and early medieval society, ensuring protection and solidarity.[7]

The importance of having the saint's tomb within the city wall is expressed very clearly by one of St. Martin's most faithful admirers, Gregory of Tours, bishop of the city between 573 and ca. 594. Apart from the four books on the miraculous feats of his great predecessor, Gregory also paid much attention to Martin in his more general writings, such as his ten books of history and the *Liber in gloria confessorum*. In *Historiae* I.48, Gregory describes how Martin's body was brought back to Tours after his death in Candes. The citizens of both Poitiers and Tours were present at the holy bishop's death bed. In Poitiers Martin had spent a large period of his life as a monk, before he was elected bishop in Tours. This caused the inhabitants of both cities to start a quarrel over the body as soon as Martin had breathed his last. The people of Poitiers considered the body their property, as they had only lent out 'their' Martin to the see of Tours. The inhabitants of Tours however argued:

> [...] You must know, that he performed more miracles with you than with us. Leaving his other miracles aside, with you he raised two persons from the dead, with us only one [...] He therefore must, now that he is dead, complete what he has not finished with us during his lifetime.

As they did not come to an agreement, the decision was finally made by God, "who did not want the city of Tours to lose her patron saint". The inhabitants of Poitiers fell asleep, so that the people of Tours could carry the body home across the river Loire in secret triumph.[8]

1. THE DEVELOPMENT OF THE CULT

Both the cult of St. Martin and the celebration of his festival were initially concentrated around the saint's tomb. As one of the best documented

---

[6] Peter BROWN: *The cult of the saints* (Chicago 1981) 91-92.

[7] Neatly expressed in the *Vita Martini* of Paulinus of Périgueux (see our note 14), VI l. 366-367, where the poet describes the yearly celebration of Easter around the saint's tomb: *Omnis adest, vacuae resident custodibus aedes / et cunctis alterna fides penetralibus adstat.* Also BROWN: *The cult of the saints* 94.

[8] GREGORY OF TOURS: *Historiarum libri X*, I.48. Eds. B. KRUSCH & W. LEVISON: *MGH, SRM* I.1 (Hannover 1937-1951).

cults of early medieval saints, quite a clear picture can be drawn of its development.[9]

First of all, the veneration of the Gallic saint was expressed in written form. The *Vita sancti Martini*, written by Sulpicius Severus, was finished during its hero's lifetime. In hagiography this is a rare phenomenon, as usually a saint's biography finds its climax in the holy person's death. Sulpicius, when visiting the already famous bishop, was so impressed by Martin's dignity and many other virtues,[10] that he could not keep the bishop's admirable and exemplary way of life to himself.[11] The *Vita Martini*, the first product of the hagiographical genre in the West, soon became very popular, not only in Gaul but also far abroad: Sulpicius' friend Postumianus described the Roman booksellers' delight in this profitable book.[12] The *Vita* was completed by three letters, of which the second and third describe Martin's deathbed and burial. Shortly after 400, Sulpicius wrote three books of *Dialogues*, in which the author and his friends Gallus and Postumianus reminisced about the life of their beloved master and friend.[13]

The works of Sulpicius provided material for two versions in verse. In the second half of the fifth century, Paulinus of Périgueux wrote his *De vita sancti Martini libri VI*.[14] Paulinus used the material of Sulpicius' *Vita* and *Dialogi* for the first five books of his work, whereas the last book contains contemporary miracle stories. These stories were written down at the request of Perpetuus, bishop of Tours at that time (461-491). Especially book VI is a very old source for the pilgrimage to Tours and the people's veneration of the holy places where Martin spent his life.

The sixth century saw the production of many works on the holy bishop. Apart from the abovementioned writings of Gregory of Tours, Gregory's friend Venantius Fortunatus wrote a second version in verse

---

[9] Eugen EWIG: Der Martinskult im Frühmittelalter, in *Archiv für mittelrheinische Kirchengeschichte* 14 (1962) 11-30; G. OURY: Culte et liturgie de saint Martin, in *L'ami du clergé* 71 (1961) 641-650; Raymond VAN DAM: *Saints and their miracles in late antique Gaul* (Princeton 1993) 13-28.

[10] SULPICIUS SEVERUS: *Vita sancti Martini* 25. Ed. J. FONTAINE: *SChr* 133-135 (Paris 1967-69).

[11] SULPICIUS SEVERUS: *Vita* 1. On Sulpicius and his *Vita Martini*, see Clare STANCLIFFE: *St. Martin and his hagiographer. History and miracle in Sulpicius Severus* (Oxford 1983).

[12] SULPICIUS SEVERUS: *Dialogi* I.23. Ed. C. HALM: *CSEL* I (Vienna 1886).

[13] SULPICIUS SEVERUS: *Dialogi*. Ed. C. HALM: *CSEL* I (Vienna 1886).

[14] PAULINUS OF PÉRIGUEUX: *De vita Martini libri VI*. Ed. M. PETSCHENIG: *CSEL* 16 (Vienna 1888) 16-159.

of the *Vita Martini*.[15] The Italian poet, educated in Ravenna where he was schooled in classical rhetoric and grammar, claimed to be cured from blindness at Martin's intercession.[16] Fortunatus considered his coming to Gaul as a pilgrimage to the tomb of the saint,[17] although elsewhere he mentioned the search for a new *Maecenas* as a second reason for his journey to the North.[18] The *Vita* of Fortunatus as a whole is based on the writings of Sulpicius: book I and II are a revision of Sulpicius' *Vita*; book III and IV of his *Dialogi*. Fortunatus' *Vita* therefore does not contain any information on the celebration of Martin's festivals. Fortunatus' poems, however, are an important source for the contemporary veneration of the great saint by the people as well as the Merovingian kings and queens.

In addition to the writings of these famous authors, an important source of information is formed by the collection of anonymous *Vitae* of Merovingian saints. Although only a few of many saints' lives were written down in the Merovingian period – most of the lives of Merovingian saints are transmitted by Carolingian writers – these few ones provide some interesting information as regards the development of the celebration of St. Martin in the early period.

In Sulpicius' writings, Martin appears as a stern ascetic, a bishop without secular ambitions. Sulpicius characterized Martin as more of a monk than a bishop.[19] Martin himself felt that his *virtus* had decreased after he was, against his own wish, put on the episcopal seat of Tours.[20] According to Sulpicius, Martin was not held in high regard by his episcopal contemporaries.[21] Among the Gallic bishops, originating from ancient local aristocratic families, Martin, averse to worldly power and properties, must have been an outsider.[22] As Sulpicius made no secret of

---

[15] VENANTIUS FORTUNATUS: *De Vita sancti Martini libri IV*. Ed. F. LEO: *MGH AA* IV.1 (Berlin 1881) 292-370.

[16] VENANTIUS FORTUNATUS: *Vita* IV l. 689-701. For a biography of Fortunatus, see B. BRENNAN: The career of Venantius Fortunatus, in *Traditio* 41 (1985) 49-78.

[17] VENANTIUS FORTUNATUS: *Carmina*. Ed. F. LEO: *MGH AA* IV.1 (Berlin 1881) VIII.1.

[18] BRENNAN: The career of Fortunatus 58.

[19] SULPICIUS SEVERUS: *Vita* 10.1-2. Also Raymond VAN DAM: Images of saint Martin in late Roman and early Merovingian Gaul, in *Viator* 19 (1988) 1-27, esp. 3-4.

[20] SULPICIUS SEVERUS: *Vita* 9-10 on Martin's election; *Dialogi* II.4 on his decreasing *virtus*.

[21] SULPICIUS SEVERUS: *Dialogi* I.26.

[22] STANCLIFFE: *St. Martin and his hagiographer* 265-296.

his critical attitude towards the ecclesiastical rulers of his days,[23] it is not surprising that the Gallic bishops were not the first ones to encourage the 'monastic' bishop's cult. The cult of St. Martin was initially promoted by his disciples and followers, such as Sulpicius and his friend Paulinus of Nola.[24]

The first bishop who made an effort at a worthy celebration of St. Martin was Perpetuus, bishop of Tours in the second half of the fifth century. The most important impulse Perpetuus gave the cult of St. Martin was the building of a large basilica as a new sanctuary to hold the saint's body. The basilica replaced the poor small church, erected by Martin's successor Brictius. The latter building, a lumpish structure according to the inscription which Sidonius Apollinaris made for the new church at the request of Perpetuus, was a disgrace compared with the character of the man whose burial place it was.[25] According to the writings of Gregory of Tours, Perpetuus built this church mainly because of the many miracles that took place close to St. Martin's tomb.[26] The body of the saint was transferred to the new church on the day of his ordination as a bishop, 4 July. Henceforth, this day was a triple festival, on which Martin's ordination, the dedication of the church and the translation of the saint's relics were celebrated. The monks who transferred the body set the tone: they celebrated mass and held a banquet.[27]

Apart from building the basilica, Perpetuus contributed to the celebration of the liturgy in the saint's city by drawing up a list of fasts and vigils, to be celebrated either in St. Martin's church or in the cathedral. This list is transmitted in Gregory's *Historiae* (X.31). Both festivals for the patron saint, 11 November and 4 July, were preceded by a vigil, celebrated in the saint's basilica. The contemporary authors on St. Martin do not give any information on the liturgy of these celebrations as such. Paulinus, in his sixth book of the *Vita Martini*, described the innumerable pilgrims coming to Tours to receive health and delivery

---

[23] SULPICIUS SEVERUS: *Vita* 20.1; *Dialogi* I.24 and 26.
[24] PAULINUS OF NOLA: *Epistolae* XXII. Ed. G. DE HARTEL: *CSEL* 29 (Vienna 1894).
[25] SIDONIUS APOLLINARIS: *Epistulae* IV.18. Ed. C. LUETJOHANN: *MGH AA* VIII.69 (Berlin 1887).
[26] GREGORY OF TOURS: *Historiae* II.14.
[27] GREGORY OF TOURS: *Libri IV de virtutibus sancti Martini episcopi* I.6. Ed. B. KRUSCH: *MGH SRM* I.2 (Hannover 1885) 584-661.

from possession. The people delighted in decorating the saint's tomb and church. On the tomb they placed a crown, commemorating St. Martin's merits, and representing the crown of righteousness the saint had received from Christ.[28] The entry of the church was embellished with beautiful columns.[29] For the citizens of Tours, Easter also became a festival of St. Martin. The people then travelled to Marmoutier, the monastery Martin founded outside the city when he became bishop of Tours.[30] There the people, singing, weeping and praying, visited and venerated the holy places where the bishop had lived. All the inhabitants of Tours, of all ages and both sexes, took part in this pilgrimage, which was headed by the bishop.[31]

2. THE CELEBRATION OF ST. MARTIN IN SIXTH-CENTURY TOURS

More detailed information about the content of St. Martin's festivals can be found in the writings of Gregory of Tours. As many cures Gregory described in his miracle books took place on festivals of the saint, Gregory's four books of miracles are a particularly important source providing information on the saint's feast days.

In the miracle books, Gregory often speaks of the many people who came to visit Tours during St. Martin's festivals on 4 July and 11 November. Pilgrims came to Tours to celebrate these special days in the saint's city itself. Not only the common man joined in this devotion, but also people of high birth, as well as episcopal (II.44; IV.13) and secular (IV.6) rulers made the pilgrimage. "Once the blessed Germanus, bishop of Paris, came to the festival of the glorious bishop."[32] The festivals were preceded by vigils (II.12, 31, 34, 42; III.50). On the day itself, a mass was celebrated, during which the *vita* was recited while the faithful listened (II.49). The congregation received the communion (II.47).

During the celebration of the mass, many cures took place. Hence, mass was often interrupted by the cries of pain and joy of the cured (II.14). Sometimes these cures came about three days before (III.57) or

---

[28] PAULINUS OF PÉRIGUEUX: *Vita* VI l. 226-229. On the *corona justitiae*, see 2 Tim. 4, 8.

[29] PAULINUS OF PÉRIGUEUX: *Vita* VI l. 265-268.

[30] SULPICIUS SEVERUS: *Vita* 10.3-4.

[31] PAULINUS OF PÉRIGUEUX: *Vita Martini* VI l. 351-368.

[32] II.12 (translation VAN DAM: *Saints and their miracles* 233).

after the festival (II.54, III.2, 14, IV.45). Miraculous cures were often accompanied by vigils, praying and fasting (III.19, IV.4).

The recitation of the *vita* during mass had its own power, as the miracles often took place actually during this recitation. On the saint's summer festival, for instance, two blind men from Bourges were cured during the recitation while a flash of light was visible (II.29). On the day of Easter, Martin's tomb was washed.[33] The water that was used for this event was collected, as it had healing powers (III.34).

It was not only through the recitation of the *vita* that the people in the churches of Tours got to know the miracles of St. Martin. The saint's beneficial miraculous works, made concrete, as it were, during the celebration of his festivals, were also depicted on the walls of both the cathedral and St. Martin's basilica.[34] The paintings in the cathedral, which was restored by Gregory after it had burnt down in 558[35], were accompanied by seven *tituli* written by Gregory's friend Venantius Fortunatus.[36] In these little poems Fortunatus described the most important deeds of the great saint: how he kissed the leper and divided his cloak, how he gave his tunic to a poor man before celebrating mass, how he raised the dead and chopped the holy pine-tree, how pagan idols were pulled down and a false martyr was exposed. Obviously, these famous miracle stories, told by Sulpicius and told again by Paulinus, Gregory and Fortunatus, and painted on the walls of the church, surrounded the faithful when they attended mass.

Among the many poems of Fortunatus in which St. Martin is a subject of veneration, *Carmen* X.7, written for the queen regent Brunhild (d. 613) and her son Childebert (575-596), is a document in verse showing the special veneration with which the Merovingian princes honoured St. Martin. Since Childebert's great-grandfather Clovis, baptized around 500 by bishop Remigius of Reims, had chosen St. Martin as his favourite saint, the holy man of Tours held a dominant position in the Merovingian royal family.[37] Clovis' widow Clothild searched for

---

[33] This custom seems to be an extending development of the Easter pilgrimage mentioned by Paulinus of Périgueux in his *Vita Martini* VI. Others suggest that the tomb was washed on Maundy Thursday (L. PIETRI: *La ville de Tours du IVe au VIe siècle: Naissance d'une cité chrétienne* (Rome 1983) 447).

[34] VAN DAM: Images 18-19.

[35] GREGORY OF TOURS: *Historiae* X.31.

[36] VENANTIUS FORTUNATUS: *Carmina* X.6.

[37] GREGORY OF TOURS: *Historiae* II.37.

shelter at the saint's tomb after her husband had died;[38] their son Clothar, when he felt that death was near, made a pilgrimage to Tours to confess his sins.[39] In the late seventh century, the basilica of St. Martin in Tours, grown into a complex of various monasteries and churches, had become a strategic political stronghold. Queen Balthild (d. circa 680), widow of Clovis II (638-657), made an effort to keep the monasteries in the so-called *Martinopolis* under royal authority. Thus she tried to enlarge her influence on this breeding ground of Christian civilization and education.[40] The royal patronage of St. Martin survived the Carolingian assumption of power, as the new rulers adopted the patron saint of their predecessors.[41]

To return to Fortunatus' poem – that the Merovingian rulers did indeed venerate St. Martin as their special patron as early as the sixth century, becomes clear from the verses Fortunatus dedicated to the royal visit to St. Martin's festival in Tours:

> O kings, this Martin, whom you honour as your patron
> on earth, remembers you in heaven [...]
> he whom you venerate and whose festivals you celebrate.[42]

3. The liturgical celebration of St. Martin's festivals

In the first part of this study, the sources have made clear how the cult of St. Martin developed around his tomb in Tours, what festivals were celebrated in honour and remembrance of the saint, and who participated in these celebrations. The stories of Gregory show something of

---

[38] GREGORY OF TOURS: *Historiae* II.43, III.28.

[39] GREGORY OF TOURS: *Historiae* IV.21.

[40] *Vita sanctae Balthildis* 9. Ed. B. KRUSCH: *MGH SRM* II (Hannover 1888) 475-509. Arnold ANGENENDT: *Das Frühmittelalter* (Stuttgart 1990) 187-188; EWIG: Der Martinskult 17-18. Van Dam is less convinced that St. Martin was the favourite of the sixth century Merovingian kings; he remarks that in this century, only the weak and shunned persons of the dynasty visited the tomb of the saint (*Saints and their miracles* 22-24). However, Van Dam fails to consider in this context Fortunatus' poem to Brunhild and Childebert.

[41] EWIG: Der Martinskult 24 and 30; J. VAN DEN BOSCH: *Capa, basilica, monasterium et culte de Saint Martin de Tours* (Nijmegen 1959).

[42] VENANTIUS FORTUNATUS: *Carmina* X.7 l. 31-32, 38: *Hunc quoque Martinum colitis quem, regna, patronum / Vos hunc in terris, vos memor ille polis... Quem vos hic colitis vel pia festa datis.*

the way in which people took part, what they got to hear and see during the services in church, and what their attendance of mass and vigils
brought about. In the second part of this study, the liturgical texts written for the festivals of St. Martin in early medieval Gaul will be at the
centre. In Gregory's miracle books on St. Martin, a story is told of a
paralysed girl who was cured on a festival of St. Martin, not during the
recitation of the saint's life, but during the celebration of the eucharist
itself:

> When, during the celebration of the most holy ceremony, I was reciting
> the *contestatio* on the holy lord's miracles, suddenly she began to cry out
> and to weep, indicating that she was being tormented.[43]

On this torment the cure followed, while the people were singing the
Sanctus. Gregory's story of this paralysed girl seems to suggest that not
only the recitation of the *vita*, but also the liturgical prayer texts, presented the saint's *virtus* in such a way that people were cured and liberated from illness and possession on site. It is therefore interesting to take
a close look at the prayer texts, in order to determine whether these texts
reflect any aspect of the picture of the celebration of St. Martin drawn
above.

It is easier to ask this question than to find a correct method to answer
it. The Gallican liturgy of the early medieval period is a difficult field,
marked by many uncertainties. Whereas the hagiographical and historiographical sources considered in the first part of this study give some
impression of the celebration of St. Martin's festivals in the fifth and
sixth century, the earliest liturgical manuscripts are not found until the
second half of the seventh century. Moreover, it is hardly possible to talk
about the Gallican liturgy as a unity.[44] Since there was no specific ecclesiastical centre in Gaul during the first centuries of Christendom, the
local churches and their bishops were relatively independent. The manuscripts in which liturgical texts have been transmitted are not only comparatively late, but also very scarce. Unfortunately, most of them seem to

---

[43] GREGORY OF TOURS: *Liber de virtutibus* II.14: *Cumque nos rite sacrosancta solem-
nia celebrantes, contestationem de sancti domini virtutibus narraremus, subito illa vociferare
coepit et flere, indicans se torqueri.*

[44] Yitzhak HEN: Unity in diversity. The liturgy of Frankish Gaul before the Carolingians, in R.N. SWANSON (ed.): *Unity and diversity in the Church* (Oxford 1996) 19-
30; W.S. PORTER: *The Gallican rite* (= Studies in eucharistic faith and practice 4) (London 1958) 47.

originate from the same region of Gaul, namely Burgundy, so that only a limited part of liturgical Gaul is mapped out. Besides, it is often very difficult to find out for which particular church or monastery a specific book was written. Nevertheless, despite all these unanswered questions, the liturgical texts as they are transmitted make their own contribution to the picture of the celebration of St. Martin in the early period.

3.1. Missale Gothicum

The oldest Gallican sacramentaries provide three masses for St. Martin's *natale* on 11 November. The first one worth considering is found in the *Missale Gothicum*, one of the most important books of the Gallican liturgy.[45] This sacramentary, written around 700, presumably for the church of Autun, contains both an elaborate *Temporale* and a large number of saint's masses. In the *Sanctorale*, commemorating twenty seven (groups of) saints and martyrs, biblical, Roman and Gallic saints occur alike.

The *Missa sancti Martini episcopi* consists of five prayers. At first sight, the first four prayers are not particularly special. They could have been used for any martyr or confessor. Yet there are some peculiarities. In the first and second prayer the celebration is explicitly indicated by the word *depositio*, burial. This reminds us of the fact that St. Martin is commemorated on the day of his funeral, not his death. In the second place Martin is pointed to as *pater noster*, our father. In the *Missale Gothicum*, this is a very rare manner of addressing a saint, which is used in only one other prayer, concerning pope Gregory (352). This is an indication of the special patronage of the Merovingian saint *par excellence* that Martin was. The prayer in the *collectio* asking Martin to obtain through his prayers, what the faithful cannot achieve with theirs (*tribue, quaesomus, ut quod nostris obtinere praecibus non possumus, ipsius meriamur obtinere suffragiis* 473), seems to be rather general. Still it is also an almost literal parallel with the prayer of Sulpicius in his letter to the deacon Aurelius: "This one hope, however, remains, this ultimate one: that we will merit through Martin's prayer for us, what we cannot obtain by ourselves."[46]

---

[45] Ed. L.C. MOHLBERG: *Missale Gothicum (Vat. Reg. lat. 317)* (Rome 1961). Revised edition in E. ROSE, *Communitas in commemoratione. Liturgisch Latijn en liturgische gedachtenis in het Missale Gothicum (Vat.reg.lat. 317)* (Diss. Utrecht 2001).
[46] SULPICIUS SEVERUS: *Epistola* II.18: *Spes tamen superest illa sola, illa postrema, ut quod per nos obtinere non possumus, saltim pro nobis orante Martino mereamur.*

Of greatest interest in this mass is the *immolatio*, or *contestatio*, terms which in the Gallican liturgy designate the preface, the prayer preceding the *Sanctus*. This text makes clear that, apart from the recitation of the *vita* and the mural paintings, there is a third way through which the faithful got to know St. Martin and his beneficial works: the liturgical prayers themselves. In the *immolatio*, St. Martin's deeds of faith and charity are presented in a poetic way. In the prayer, most attention is paid to Martin's best known act: how he shared his cloak with the beggar of Amiens.[47] The prayer focuses on the second part of this story, the night that followed on the meeting at the town gate of Amiens. In that night, Christ appeared to Martin, dressed in the cloak which the soldier shared with the poor man, and proclaiming: "Martin, still a catechumen, covered me with this vestment."[48] The prayer praises Martin, who was worthy not only to clothe,[49] but even to see God (...*tanta erat gloriacio passionis, ut per quantitate uestis exiguae et uestire deum meruit et uidere* 476). Then other great feats of the saint are called to mind: how Martin resisted the attacks of the Arian heresy;[50] how he received the episcopate and how his way of life made him a worthy successor of the apostles.[51]

"La grande préface" as André Wilmart, not without reason, called the *immolatio* of the *Missale Gothicum*, was not only a recurrent feature throughout the precarolingian liturgy of St. Martin, but even reached the 13th century collection of saints' legends, the *Legenda aurea*.[52]

3.2. Missale Bobbiense

As far as the liturgical books are concerned, the text of the *immolatio* is found in the *Missa sancti Martini episcopi* of the *Missale Bobbiense*.[53] The manuscript, named after the monastery Bobbio where it was found by the 17th century scholar Mabillon, is a mixture of Gallican and Roman elements. The mass formulas betray a close relationship to the *Missale*

---

[47] SULPICIUS SEVERUS: *Vita* 3.
[48] SULPICIUS SEVERUS: *Vita* 3.3: *Martinus adhuc catechumenus hac me ueste contexit.*
[49] Cf. Matth. 25, 36: "[For I was] naked, and ye clothed me."
[50] SULPICIUS SEVERUS: *Vita* 6.4.
[51] SULPICIUS SEVERUS: *Vita* 20.1: *In solo Martino apostolica auctoritas permanebat.*
[52] André WILMART: Saint Ambroise et la Légende dorée, in *Ephemerides liturgicae* 50 (1936) 169-206, esp. 201-203.
[53] Ed. E.A. LOWE: *The Bobbio Missal. A Gallican mass-book* (London 1917-1924).

Gothicum. The *contestatio* in the Bobbiense is roughly similar to the text in the Gothicum, although it may differ in some details, which will remain undiscussed here.

The four other prayers differ from the corresponding prayers in the Gothicum. The first prayer (363) concentrates on Martin's bloodless martyrdom, which is referred to by Sulpicius in his letter to Aurelius:

> For although the nature of this time was not able to give him martyrdom, yet the glory of a martyr will not be lacking to him, for through his wish and his virtue he both could and wanted to be a martyr.[54]

This thought is concisely expressed in the Bobbiense, as follows:

> Without any doubt he is a martyr in heaven who was a confessor under the sun, as we know that Martin was not lacking in martyrdom, but the martyrdom was lacking in Martin.[55]

The same prayer occurs in the mass formula for the protomartyr Stephen in the *Missale Gothicum*, where the faithful ask to be able to imitate this attitude:

> Grant [...] that we are proved not to be lacking in martyrdom, but martyrdom to be lacking in us.[56]

The second prayer, *collectio*, refers to the raising of the dead Martin achieved according to the *Vita*:

> We humbly beseech thee, o God, that your church that is in tribulation, may be considered worthy of the defence of him, whom thou hast given abundant faith, even to raise the dead.[57]

In Sulpicius' *Vita* it can be read, how Martin raised two dead people who died before their time: a catechumen who had not been baptized yet, and a young servant who had taken his own life by hanging himself.[58]

---

[54] SULPICIUS SEVERUS: *Epistola* II.9: *Nam licet ei ratio temporis non potuerit praestare martyrium, gloria tamen martyris non carebit, quia uoto atque uirtute et potuit esse martyr et uoluit.*

[55] Bo 363: *Dubium enim non est ut sit martyr in celo qui fuit confessor in saeculo cum sciamus non martinum martirium sed martirium defuitse martinum.*

[56] Go 33: *Tribue [...] ut probemur non nos martyrio, sed nobis defuisse martyrium.*

[57] Bo 364: *...supplices exoramus, ut aeclesiam tuam conuersantem in tribulacione dignetur defendere cui a te satis larga pietate concessum est, etiam mortuos suscitare.*

[58] SULPICIUS SEVERUS: *Vita* 7 and 8.

The prayer *post nomina* and the prayer *ad pacem* are both concerned with the intercession of the saint.

As the *Missale Bobbiense* does not only give the prayers for the mass, but also the lections, we can get an impression of what was read during the mass of St. Martin's commemoration. Unfortunately, the Bobbiense does not contain a lection from the *Vita Martini*, but only three biblical passages. The first one is taken from the prophet Jeremiah:

> Blessed is the man that trusteth in the Lord, and whose hope the Lord is. For he shall be as a tree planted by the waters… (Jer. 17, 7-14).

As the epistle 2 Tim. 4 is read, where the apostle encourages the reader to fight the good fight, in order to obtain the *corona iustitiae*. Finally, the gospel tells the parable of the man who received five talents, and gained five more (Matth. 25). Thus Martin appears in these biblical readings as the *Beatus uir*, whose trust is in God, the fountain of living waters; as the *uir apostolicus*, who has fought the good fight and has now received the crown in heaven, as visualized by the citizens of Tours in the days of bishop Perpetuus, and as the good servant of the heavenly kingdom, who did not hide his talents, but made the most of them.

"La grande préface" continued to play a part in the Gallican liturgical books of the eighth century, the so-called eighth century Gelasiana. However, these books will not be the centre of attention in this article, as they cannot be considered as representatives of the *Merovingian* liturgy.

3.3. Irish Palimpsest Sacramentary

The third manuscript representing the Gallican liturgy in its pre-carolingian stage is surrounded by even more enigmas than the *Missale Bobbiense* is. The so-called *Irish Palimpsest Sacramentary* was found as a palimpsest in a manuscript of the Münchener Staatsbibliothek at the beginning of the 20th century.[59] The book, written according to insular practice, holds a number of masses which clearly betray the Gallican character of the compilation. Apart from a close relationship with the other Gallican sacramentaries, influences of the contemporary Spanish

---

[59] A. DOLD & L. EIZENHÖFER: *Das irische Palimpsestsakramentar im CLM 14429 der Staatsbibliothek München* (Beuron 1964).

liturgical tradition are visible as well. The *immolatio* for the commemoration of St. Martin is one of these Spanish derivatives, as it is also found in the Spanish *Liber mozarabicus sacramentorum*.[60]

From the first two prayers of the severely damaged *Ordo missae Martini* only the opening sentences remain. The third prayer, *post nomina*, of which only the second half is legible, could be reconstructed with the help of the almost identical *post nomina* in the mass for the fourth day in the Easter week in the Gothicum (Go 294). This, then, is a general prayer, not specifically related to the person or celebration of St. Martin. After the long *immolatio* two prayers follow: *post sanctus* and *ante orationem domini*. Both, again, are general prayers.

The only text of interest to the question of this study is the *immolatio*, a major example of the superiority of Spanish over Gallican eloquence in the field of liturgy. The *immolatio* in the Irish Palimpsest Sacramentary is the best example of the retelling of a saint's life in a liturgical prayer. In this text the main facts of Martin's life are reviewed. After a laudatory introduction, in which Martin is called a "praiseworthy pledge" (*uenerandum pignus*) – a word common in the context of the Eucharist –, the "height of sanctity and righteousness" (*emenendissimum culmen sanctitatis adque iustitiae*), an "intercession and remedy for our sins" (*peccatorum nostrorum intercessionem adque remedia*), the core of the eulogy is found in the quality *uitae sacerdotalis exemplum*: Martin as a model for priestly life. The image of St. Martin as the ideal priest and bishop is, as has been expounded above, the thread through the *Vita Martini* of Sulpicius, and was even Sulpicius' main spring for writing down Martin's life.[61] This image is elaborated in the *immolatio*: "At the beginning of his blessed life, this man, still bearing arms in secular service, became a priest in his heart."[62] This thought is expressed in Sulpicius' *Vita* 2.7: "In those days already (i.e. when Martin served in the imperial army), he was considered a monk, rather than a soldier."[63]

This priestly attitude was, according to the *immolatio*, accompanied by the full dedication and devotion of the young Martin to God as his

---

[60] DOLD & EIZENHÖFER: *Das irische Palimpsestsakramentar* 103*-104*.

[61] SULPICIUS SEVERUS: *Vita* 1.6.

[62] *(...) qui inter ipsa beatae uitae suae primordia etiam sub armis militiae saecularis iam sacerdos animae suae factus.*

[63] *(...) ut iam illo tempore non miles, sed monachus putaretur.*

judge,[64] which is put in Sulpicius' *Vita* 2.4: "And soon he was in a remarkable way fully converted to the work of God."[65]

The *immolatio* extensively reports on the way in which Martin eventually accepted the episcopate (Sulpicius' *Vita* 9.1), when, in spite of his efforts to hide himself in his monastery, in the words of the *immolatio* "the good odour of his life and the good reputation of his just works could not remain concealed".[66] Martin "did not take up the episcopate as an opportunity to seize power, but took upon him the form of a servant",[67] as is expressed by Sulpicius in the *Vita* 10.1-2. In the following the *immolatio* enumerates the miraculous and beneficial works of St. Martin: how he restored sight to the blind, chased away demons from the possessed, returned health to the cripple and raised the dead through his prayer. All these miraculous feats are found in the *Vita* 7-8, 16-17, and in the *Dialogi* II.4, III.6-9.

On Martin's daily life, the *immolatio*, following Sulpicius' *Vita* 26, declares that he never broke his conversation with God, but was sunk in prayer day and night.[68] The *immolatio* then terminates with a praise of this blessed man, the treasure of Mother Church (*Haec sunt gaudia quibus aeclesia mater exsultat*), whose company was searched for by angels (*angelo comes*; cf. Sulpicius' *Vita* 14.5, 21.1), who shared in the dignity of the apostles (*consors apostolicae dignitatis*; cf. Sulpicius' *Vita* 20.1, *Dial.* II.13), who finally found his reward in the promised *corona iustitiae*.

3.4. The liturgical celebration of 4 July

So far, the Gallican sources give an impression of the liturgical celebration of St. Martin on his commemoration day 11 November in the Merovingian period. None of the early sacramentaries gives a formula for the celebration of Martin's summer festival. The only book in which a mass for the triple commemoration of 4 July is found, is the

---

[64] *Totum se deo iudici consecrauit adque tradidit.*

[65] *Mox mirum in modum totus in Dei opere conuersus.*

[66] *(...) cuius odor bonus uitae bona iustorum operum fama (...) quam et dum beatus totis uiribus occultare uoluerit toto tamen terrarum orbe deffusa est.*

[67] *(...) quia non occasione exercendae potestatis suscipit sacerdotii principatum, sed formam serui suscipisse cognouit*; cf. Phil. 2, 7.

[68] *(...) quia solus soli deo uacans non diebus non noctibus a conloquis dei et oratione cessabat.*

Sacramentarium Engolismense, belonging to the group of the eighth century- or young Gelasiana.[69] Although the eighth century Gelasiana, all going back to a lost archetype which must have been written around 750, under the reign of Pepin III, are actually beyond the scope of this study, the mass for 4 July in the sacramentary of Angoulême, unique in precarolingian Gaul,[70] is too interesting to be left unmentioned.

The local character of the prayers (as is evident from phrases like *Deus qui [...] Martinum [...] declaratum ad toronicae ciuitatis episcopalem cathedram summum pontificem et magnum patronum populo tuo ordinare uoluisti* 1100; *praesta nobis petentibus huius patroni suffragantibus precibus* 1101) as well as the fact that the formula returns in some post-carolingian sacramentaries for the city of Tours, seem to indicate that the mass was originally written for the church of Tours.[71] In the prayers, much attention is paid to Gregory's story on the translation of the saint's relics to the new basilica (*VM* I.6). The preface is a more general ode to the patron saint, his merits and his miracles.

3.5. Conclusion

In addition to mural paintings and the recitation of the *vita*, the earliest Gallican sacramentaries provide a third possibility to get to know the saint whose festival is celebrated. Especially the *immolatio*, or *contestatio*, gives a detailed summary of the saint's life. In the other prayers, important features of the saint in question are singled out. Remarkable characteristics of Martin's life, underlined in the liturgical texts, are his bloodless martyrdom, his unusual but exemplary interpretation of the episcopate, his power over illnesses and death, as well as his conversations with angels and saints and his fight for the orthodox doctrine, all of which makes him a *uir apostolicus*. Especially the *immolatio* is seized as an opportunity to make known the great miracle deeds of the saint. Not only in the recitation of the saint's life, but also in the *immolationes* of the Gallican sacramentaries the *virtus* of the saint is brought to the fore during the celebration of the Eucharist. I therefore disagree with Van Dam's translation of Gregory's story of the paralysed girl quoted

---

[69] Ed. P. SAINT ROCH: *Liber sacramentorum Engolismensis*, CCSL 159C (Turnhout 1987).

[70] SAINT ROCH: *Liber sacramentorum Engolismensis* xiii-xiv.

[71] G. OURY: Les messes de Saint Martin dans les sacramentaires gallicans, romano-francs et milanais, in *Études grégoriennes* 5 (1962) 73-97, esp. 82-83.

above. Where Gregory says he recites, on the saint's festival, the *contestationem de sancti domini virtutibus*, Van Dam translates: 'I recited the prefatory prayer about the miracles of our holy Lord'.[72] By this translation, Van Dam suggests that the *contestatio* contains the miracles of the Saviour, not of the lord (with small l) Martin. This is, as has been demonstrated above, not the case. On the saint's festival, it is St. Martin who is the main figure of all the prayers. Even in the core of the Gallican eucharistic celebration, the great deeds of the celebrated saint seem to obtain more attention than the eucharistic ritual itself.[73]

4. EPILOGUE: SERMO IN LAUDE SANCTI MARTINI

Now that both hagiographical and liturgical texts have been reviewed in order to reconstruct the celebration of St. Martin in early medieval Gaul, there is one genre left: the sermon. The last source therefore, which can complete the picture as it is achieved so far, is a sermon for the saint's festival: *Sermo in laude sancti Martini*. This text, incomplete as a result of water damage, was found for the first time in an 11th or 12th century Beneventan manuscript, and was edited by its finder, A. Mai, in 1852. More than a century later, Bernard Peebles found a much better and complete copy in a 10th or 11th century manuscript, also Italian, which he edited in 1961.[74] Lambert, to whom the earlier copy found by Peebles was not yet available, quite positively dated the text to the early sixth century,[75] whereas Peebles for his part does not regard as impossible a dating after the 6th century.[76]

As regards the genre, the *sermo* stands as it were between the hagiographic texts and the liturgical prayers. But also in respect of content the text can be seen as a link between the two groups of texts, as it is a rich source in which the main themes of both Martin's cult and celebration are collected in a nutshell.

---

[72] VAN DAM: *Saints and their miracles* 235.
[73] Cf. PORTER: *The Gallican rite* 50.
[74] Ed. B.M. PEEBLES: An early "Laudatio sancti Martini". A text completed, in *Saint Martin et son temps* (Rome 1961) 237-249. An English translation can be found in VAN DAM: *Saints and their miracles* 304-307.
[75] A. LAMBERT: Le premier panégyrique de saint Martin, in *Bulletin de saint Martin et de saint Benoît* 32 (1924) 316-320.
[76] PEEBLES: An early "Laudatio" 242-243.

The sermon actually begins with a detailed description of the importance of the festival for the community. *Laetemur in Domini, fratres dilectissimi, omni laetitia spiritalis gaudii...*; these are the words with which the preacher adresses himself to his audience. In the first place, the saint's festival gives cause for joy and spiritual gladness. "This is the day in which the entire catholic church, spread all over the world, takes great pleasure."[77] The saint's festival is a means of unification. Its unifying function, however, is not confined to the boundaries of the church, but it also connects the citizens of the earth with the celestials, all enjoying the celebration of the same saint.[78] And there is no division between the people either, for all ages and both sexes are invited to celebrate.[79] The attention of the faithful is caught through an appeal for obedience in pious devotion, as this will please the saint.[80] The sermon refers briefly to the book on the saint's life, which became famous particularly for its signs and wonders.[81] This book is said to be spread throughout the whole world, so that it is unknown to no reasonable creature.

The city of Tours is in the centre of the sermon's attention. Just as Rome is the *Caput mundi* because it was enlightened by Peter and Paul, Tours is the *caput totius Gallicae regionis*, as it merited to be the great saint's earthly dwellingplace as well as merits to hold his tomb. Here the sermon makes clear the great importance of a saint's tomb to a community of which I spoke above. The saint's presence brings fertility, not only for the benefit of the multitude gathered in the city, but also of the entire region.[82] The saint in heaven is invoked to intercede, to accept the prayers of the faithful and to bring them to the Saviour. The saint is asked to help the people, entangled in the distress of their sins, and to defend them against the attacks of unspecified enemies.

Better than any other text, this sermon, the final touch to the picture of the celebration of St. Martin in the early Middle Ages, makes clear

---

[77] *Haec est etenim dies in qua sancta ecclesia catholica, longe lateque per orbem diffusa, multiplici exultatione tripudiat.*

[78] *Haec est (...) dies hominibus celebrabilis, angelis collaudabilis.*

[79] *(...) omnis aetas, omnis sexus, omnisque condicio (...) celebremus.*

[80] *(...) obsequio tamen piae deuotionis condelectatur benignitas proprii pastoris.*

[81] *Hic namque pastor beatissimus quantis in mundo claruerit insignibus, liber eius uitae indicat, qui tam mirandis signorum descriptionibus effulget.*

[82] *Per cuius meritum et benedictionis imbrem, non solum irrigantur mentes hominum, sed etiam terra adiacens accumulatur fertilitate fructuum. His vero omnibus felicior atque sublimior ille credendus est locus qui ipsius est sacratissimi corporis tumulo tam gloriose decoratus.*

how the saintly idol of Merovingian Gaul was the centre of attention on which all eyes were focused, guided by the festivities around the saint. The observance of the saint's festival helped the entire flock, both the monastic and those living secularly, to complete the capricious journey of their lifetime through the threats of illness and disaster. The celebration of the saint thus provided solidarity, and protection against the attacks of the devil, so that all might eventually enjoy the fruits of righteousness in the heavenly City, celebrating a festival without end.

LOUIS VAN TONGEREN

TRANSFORMATIONS OF THE CALENDAR IN THE EARLY MIDDLE AGES

1. INTRODUCTION

1.1. Liturgical unification

The Carolingian period is a crucial link in the development of the Western liturgy. Before the Carolingians came to power in the middle of the eighth century, in the regions where Christianity had spread diverse local and regional liturgical traditions had grown up, such as those of Rome, North Africa, Southern Italy, Northern Italy, Spain, Gaul and Ireland.[1] It is true that these traditions were in accord with one another in many respects, but various theological, ecclesiastical and political spheres of influence, and likewise differing national characters, had contributed to each developing in its own manner. The process which would bring an end to this liturgical pluriformity began in the course of the eighth century.[2] The Carolingians furnished an important and decisive impetus for

---

[1] See A. KING: *Liturgies of the primatial sees* (London 1957); IDEM: *Liturgies of the past* (London 1959); J. PINELL: La liturgia gallicana, in S. MARSILI e.a.: *La liturgia. Panorama storico generale* (= Anàmnesis 2) (s.l. [Roma] 1983ʳ) 62-67; J. PINELL: La liturgia celtica, *ibidem* 67-70; IDEM: La liturgia ispanica, *ibidem* 70-88; A. TRIACCA: La liturgia ambrosiana, *ibidem* 88-110; J. PINELL: Libri liturgici gallicani, *ibidem* 185-190; IDEM: Libri liturgici ispanici, *ibidem* 190-201; A. TRIACCA: Libri liturgici ambrosiani, *ibidem* 201-217; H. MEYER: *Eucharistie. Geschichte, Theologie, Pastoral* (= Gottesdienst der Kirche. Handbuch der Liturgiewissenschaft 4) (Regensburg 1989) 152-164; H. WEGMAN: *Liturgie in der Geschichte des Christentums* (Regensburg 1994) 128-129; 183-189; G. RAMIS: Liturgical families in the West, in A. CHUPUNGCO (ed.): *Introduction to the liturgy* (= Handbook for liturgical studies 1) (Collegeville 1997) 25-32.

[2] Th. KLAUSER: Die liturgischen Austauschbeziehungen zwischen der römischen und der fränkisch-deutschen Kirche vom achten bis zum elften Jahrhundert, in *Historisches Jahrbuch* 53 (1933) 169-189; C. VOGEL: Les échanges liturgiques entre Rome et les pays francs jusqu'à l'époque de Charlemagne, in *Le Chiese nei regni dell' Europa occidentale* (= Settimane di studio del centro italiano di studi sull' alto medioevo 7) (Spoleto 1960) 185-295; IDEM: la réforme cultuelle sous Pepin le Bref et sous Charlemagne (deuxième

this process. When the Frankish territories came under their rule, they developed a strategy for bringing uniformity to the existing multiform liturgical practice, which was denoted by the collective term Gallican liturgy.[3] This strategy was aimed toward the introduction of the same liturgy everywhere, to be achieved through the distribution of uniform liturgical books. The new books which had to be compiled for this were based on the local liturgy of the city of Rome, which itself, however, was not uniform. The liturgy conducted by the Pope differed from the liturgy in the parish churches (*tituli*) of the city. Initially the Franks oriented themselves both to the liturgy as it was celebrated in the Roman *tituli* as well as to the Papal liturgy, but soon primarily the latter would serve as their model. The new liturgical books were not, however, purely copies of Roman models. Usages and texts from their own indigenous tradition were taken over during the Frankish editing, and new elements were added. Still, this introduction of new books did lead to the elimination of existing, indigenous traditions as such. Because to a great extent the new Frankish books were patterned on Roman models, this process of making the liturgy uniform was also a process of Romanization. This process continued after the Carolingian period, and the liturgy, which by that time had evolved into a Franco-Roman liturgy, would also come to eclipse other indigenous traditions. The ultimate result, in the second millennium, would be the uniform Western, Latin liturgy.

1.2. Frankish liturgical books

Two significant events can be distinguished in the earliest phase of this process, events which not only were of great import and influence at the moment, but which also determined subsequent developments. These

moitié du VIIIe siècle et premier quart du IXe siècle), in E. PATZELT: *Die Karolingische Renaissance* (Graz 1965[2]) 171-242; WEGMAN: *Liturgie in der Geschichte* 166-169 and 189-194.

[3] E. GRIFFE: Aux origines de la liturgie gallicane, in *Bulletin de littérature ecclésiastique* 52 (1951) 17-43; IDEM: *La Gaule chrétienne à l'époque romaine* 3. *La cité chrétienne* (Paris 1965) 164-213; W. PORTER: *The Gallican rite* (= Studies in eucharistic faith and practice 4) (London 1958); KING: *Liturgies of the past* 77-185; Th. VISMANS: Oud-gallicaanse liturgie, in L. BRINKHOFF e.a. (eds.): *Liturgisch woordenboek* 1 (Roermond 1958-1962) 2084-2094; PINELL: La liturgia gallicana; Y. HEN: Unity in diversity. The liturgy of Frankish Gaul before the Carolingians, in R. SWANSON (ed.): *Unity and diversity in the Church* (Oxford 1996) 19-30; IDEM: *Culture and religion in Merovingian Gaul A.D. 481-751* (= Cultures, beliefs and traditions 1) (Leiden/New York/Köln 1995).

were the composition of a new sacramentary around 750 and the intro-duction of a Roman sacramentary around 800. Various versions of the former were in circulation in the second half of the eighth century. Diverse liturgical traditions come together in sacramentaries of this type, generally termed the Frankish Gelasian or the Gelasian Sacramen-tary of the Eighth Century.[4] To a great extent it is based on two sacra-mentaries, or their predecessors or representatives, that were associated with Roman parish churches: the Old Gelasian, and a type of sacra-mentary that is preserved in the *Paduensis*; elements and usages from the indigenous tradition were added to this. This sacramentary did not long function, as about two generations later, around the year 800, Charle-magne, after having asked several times, received another sacramentary from the Pope. This was an example of a Gregorian sacramentary, termed the *Hadrianum*, which reflected the liturgy as it was celebrated by the Pope in Rome at the end of the eighth century.[5] Charlemagne had this Roman book transcribed into multiple copies and distributed. However, it proved to be incomplete, because the Papal liturgy did not provide for all the Sundays and feasts which were a part of Frankish liturgical practice. In order to fill the lacunae and adapt the book to its new circumstances a supplement was added, which was completed between 831 and 835.[6] The editors provided materials themselves and

---

[4] See B. MORETON: *The Eighth-Century Gelasian Sacramentary. A study in tradition* (Oxford 1976); J. DESHUSSES: Les sacramentaires. État actuel de la recherche, in *Archiv für Liturgiewissenschaft* 24 (1982) 39-40; A. CHAVASSE: *Le sacramentaire dans le groupe dit 'Gélasiens du VIIIe siècle'. Une compilation raisonnée. Étude des procédés de confection et synoptiques nouveau modèle* 1-2 (= Instrumenta patristica 14 A-B) (Steenbrugge/Den Haag 1984); C. VOGEL: *Medieval liturgy. An introduction to the sources* (revised and translated by W. STOREY and N. RASMUSSEN) (Washington D.C. 1986) 70-78; A. CHAVASSE: Évangéliaire, épistolier, antiphonaire et sacramentaire. Les livres romains de la messe au VIIe et au VIIIe siècle, in *Ecclesia orans* 6 (1989) 243-249; E. PALAZZO: *Le Moyen Age. Des origines au XIIIe siècle. Histoire des livres liturgiques* (Paris 1993) 69-72.

[5] See for the Gregorian Sacramentary DESHUSSES: Les sacramentaires 28-46; VOGEL: *Medieval liturgy* 79-102; J. DÉCRÉAUX: *Le sacramentaire de Marmoutier (Autun 19 bis) dans l'histoire des sacramentaires carolingiens du IXe siècle* 1. *Étude* (= Studi di anti-chità cristiana 38) (Roma 1985); CHAVASSE: Évangéliaire 197-211; PALAZZO: *Le Moyen Age* 72-78; L. VAN TONGEREN: *Exaltation of the Cross. Toward the origins of the feast of the Cross and the meaning of the Cross in the early Middle Ages* (= Liturgia condenda 11) (Leuven 2000) 44-48.

[6] See VOGEL: *Medieval liturgy* 85-92; DESHUSSES: Les sacramentaires 41-42; DÉCRÉAUX: *Le sacramentaire de Marmoutier* 1, 215-232; VAN TONGEREN: *Exaltation of the Cross* 48.

drew from their own indigenous traditions, but for the most part they made use of the Gelasian Sacramentary of the Eighth Century. Thus the Frankish-Carolingian period is an important link in the mediation of the Roman liturgy from the fifth to eighth centuries to the generally distributed and uniform Western liturgy. Although predecessors of Roman sacramentaries had already circulated earlier in Merovingian Gaul, the phase described here, between about 750 and 835, can be considered as the first great crucible of Western liturgy. Multiple traditions come together and material from these traditions is selected, edited, joined together and supplemented with indigenous Frankish material. Perhaps the eighth-century Gelasians did not function for very long,[7] but they represent the first implementation of Roman liturgy outside of Rome. Moreover, they formed in part the basis for the supplemented *Hadrianum* which furnished the basic model for the liturgy in following centuries.[8]

Because multiple traditions are mixed together in this period, comparisons among the Frankish, Roman and Gallican sources yield a good insight into the changes in the field of liturgy which occurred in the eighth and ninth centuries. What was maintained from the various traditions and what was eliminated? To what degree are elements and content transformed by editorial interventions, and what is the peculiar Frankish contribution? Subsequently one can ask the question of to what degree the Frankish editors were intermediaries for other indigenous traditions, such as the North Italian, Visigothic and Celtic, because they had been influenced by them, and in part allowed themselves to be inspired by them.

Other liturgical books also underwent the same development as has been briefly described here with respect to sacramentaries. In the case of

---

[7] However, some time would still have elapsed before the *Hadrianum* was distributed. The transcription of enough copies was a time-consuming task, and furthermore it first had to be edited, and provided with its supplement. The old and new would have coexisted side by side for some time; see VOGEL: La réforme cultuelle 194. This means that, while the process of creating a uniform liturgy may have begun in the eighth century, Frankish liturgy was still characterized by diversity and pluriformity in the Carolingian period. Regionalism was a vital aspect of Carolingian history. See R. SULLIVAN: The Carolingian age. Reflections on its place in the history of the Middle Ages, in *Speculum* 64 (1989) 267-306, esp. 290-297; R. McKITTERICK: Unity and diversity in the Carolingian Church, in SWANSON: *Unity and diversity* 81-82.

[8] For the influence of the Hispanic and Gallican traditions on the feast of the Exaltation of the Cross, see VAN TONGEREN: *Exaltation of the Cross* 253-274.

lists of Bible pericopes, and for the song books too, various arrangements, choices, selections and creations from the different traditions came together in the Frankish period and were edited into new entities.

1.3. Transformation of the calendar from the Frankish perspective

With the changes all these liturgical books underwent, the calendar which was built into or derived from these books and their related documents was also transformed. Because this transformation was radical, and moreover occurred within a rather short time, it must have had far-reaching consequences for the Franks. Therefore this developmental phase in the history of the calendar deserves particular attention, all the more because heortological studies generally concentrate on the origins and the genesis of individual feasts and feast cycles, which leads to the Carolingian period being viewed only as a part of the total development.[9] A specific approach to the liturgical calendar from a Frankish perspective can clarify what this change meant for the celebration of the various feasts. A comparison of the Frankish feast calendar with indigenous Gallican and Roman calendars can shed light on the extent to which the Carolingians preserved or transformed their own heritage with regard to the feasts, or gave it up in favour of the Roman tradition. The image which will arise from such a comparison will afford a perspective on shifts in feast practice in the second half of the eighth and the beginning of the ninth century. For this comparison, study must first be made of the scale and structure of calendars in Gallican and Frankish books. Next, these must be compared with Roman arrangements. Because it is not possible to discuss all feasts sep-

---

[9] See, for instance, the great survey studies of K. KELLNER: *Heortologie oder das Kirchenjahr und die Heiligenfeste in ihrer geschichtlichen Entwicklung von der ältesten Zeit bis zur Gegenwart* (Freiburg i. Br. 1911³); J. PASCHER: *Das liturgische Jahr* (München 1963); A. MARTIMORT (ed.): *L'église en prière. Introduction à la liturgie 4. La liturgie et le temps* (Paris 1983); Hj. AUF DER MAUR: *Feiern im Rhythmus der Zeit 1. Herrenfeste in Woche und Jahr* (= Gottesdienst der Kirche. Handbuch der Liturgiewissenschaft 5) (Regensburg 1983); IDEM: Feste und Gedenktage der Heiligen, in Ph. HARNONCOURT & Hj. AUF DER MAUR: *Feiern im Rhythmus der Zeit* 2/1 (= Gottesdienst der Kirche. Handbuch der Liturgiewissenschaft 6,1) (Regensburg 1994) 65-358; M. AUGÉ *et al.*: *L'anno liturgico. Storia, teologia e celebrazione* (= Anàmnesis 6) (Genua 1988). The study of the sanctoral cycle in the eighth-century Gelasian Phillipps Sacramentary is an exception; see P. JOUNEL: Le sanctoral du sacramentaire de la collection Phillipps, in P. DE CLERCK & E. PALAZZO (eds.): *Rituels* (Paris 1990) 347-356.

arately in a study of this size, I will then examine the differences between the traditions with respect to the feasts of saints. Analysis and comparison of the content of the texts for the various feasts in the different sources also falls outside the scope of this contribution. This does not in any sense minimize the fact that the transformation of the calendar through the confrontation of the various traditions also affected the content of the feasts. That will finally be given central attention when, on the basis of several feasts as examples, reference is made to shifts in motifs.

There are many sources available for the study of the liturgical feasts which together comprise the calendar. In addition to liturgical sources, pronouncements and prescriptions of councils and synods, sermons and church historical writings by authors of the early Middle Ages contain much useful information; that is also true for calendars which are included in computistic treatises. It will be necessary, however, to leave aside these sources which are not strictly liturgical, while indeed the liturgical sources themselves cannot be exhaustively discussed here. The emphasis will be chiefly, though not exclusively, on the sacramentaries of the various traditions. With regard to the Gallican tradition these are the Gothic Missal (GaGo), the Bobbio Missal (GaBo), the Old Gallican Missal (GaV) and the Frankish Missal (GaF).[10] For the sake of a more complete image, we will add to these the Lectionary of Luxeuil and surveys of other Gallican lectionaries included in the edition of the Luxeuil

[10] L. MOHLBERG: *Missale Gothicum (Vat. Reg. lat. 317)* (= Rerum ecclesiarum documenta. Series Maior. Fontes 5) (Roma 1961); E. LOWE: *The Bobbio Missal. A Gallican mass-book (ms. Paris. lat. 13246)* (= Henry Bradshaw Society 58) (London 1920); L. MOHLBERG: *Missale Gallicanum Vetus (Cod. Vat. Palat. lat. 493)* (= Rerum ecclesiasticarum documenta. Series Maior. Fontes 3) (Roma 1958); IDEM: *Missale Francorum (Cod. Vat. Reg. lat. 257)* (= Rerum ecclesiasticarum documenta. Series Maior. Fontes 2) (Roma 1957).

Although a predecessor of the Old Gelasian perhaps had circulated in Gaul and therefore underwent Gallican influence, it would be going too far to classify this sacramentary among the Gallican books, as is done by HEN: *Culture and religion*. Following A. CHAVASSE: *Le sacramentaire gélasian (Vaticanus Reginensis 316). Sacramentaire presbytéral en usage dans les titres romains au VIIe siècle* (= Bibliothèque de Théologie 4,1) (Tournai 1958), and in harmony with the *communis opinio*, I regard the Old Gelasian as a Roman sacramentary; cf. VOGEL: *Medieval liturgy* 64-70; PALAZZO: *Le Moyen Age* 68-69; C. FOLSOM: The liturgical books of the Roman rite, in CHUPUNGCO: *Introduction to the liturgy* 248-249.

Secondly, reference will be made to several other Gallican arrangements of feasts, such as the Calendar of Willibrord.

Lectionary.[11] The study of the Frankish sources will concentrate on the eighth-century Gelasians, for which the Sacramentary of Gellone (GeG) is the starting point,[12] and the Supplement to the *Hadrianum* (GrSp).[13] Because of the comparison between the different traditions and their continued effect in the Frankish books, among the Roman books it will be primarily the Old Gelasian (GeV)[14] and the *Paduensis* (GrPa),[15] which functioned as the source for the eighth-century Gelasian, that will be consulted, and the *Hadrianum* (GrHa),[16] which was augmented and distributed in Frankish territory in the early part of the ninth century.

2. SIZE, STRUCTURE AND ORDER

2.1. The Gallican and Frankish calendars

There was no uniform liturgical calendar in the Frankish region prior to the assembly of the eighth-century Gelasian Sacramentary around 750. It is true that Gallican sources do include various shared feast days, but the mutual differences among them point to a non-standardized calendar. The information from the Gothic Missal, the Bobbio Missal and in

---

[11] P. SALMON: *Le lectionnaire de Luxeuil. Édition et étude comparative* (= Collectanea biblica latina 7) (Roma 1944). For the comparison with other lectionaries see the survey, *ibidem* ci-cxxiii.

[12] A. DUMAS & J. DESHUSSES: *Liber sacramentorum Gellonensis. Textus* (= Corpus christianorum. Series latina 159). *Introductio, tabulae et indices* (= Corpus christianorum. Series latina 159A) (Turnhout 1981). The Sacramentary of Gellone is taken as the primary reference point because it is the most authentic representative of an archetype of the eighth-century Gelasians assembled around 750 in Flavigny, the archetype itself not being preserved; see IDEM: *introductio* vii and xxv; MORETON: *The Eighth-Century Gelasian Sacramentary* 13-17; VOGEL: *Medieval liturgy* 73-76. When other Frankish Gelasians are not in conformity with the Sacramentary of Gellone, these will also be cited.

[13] J. DESHUSSES: *Le sacramentaire grégorien. Ses principales formes d'après les plus anciens manuscrits. Edition comparative* 1. *Le sacramentaire, le supplément d'Aniane* (= Spicilegium Friburgense 16) (Fribourg 1971) 349-605.

[14] L. MOHLBERG: *Liber sacramentorum Romanae aeclesiae ordinis anni circuli (Cod. Vat. Reg. lat. 316 / Paris Bibl. Nat. 7193, 41/56)* (= Rerum ecclesiasticarum documenta. Series Maior. Fontes 4) (Roma 1960).

[15] DESHUSSES: *Le sacramentaire grégorien* 607-684.

[16] DESHUSSES: *Le sacramentaire grégorien* 83-348.

the Lectionary of Luxeuil is the most extensive.[17] All three of these sources make mention of Advent,[18] Christmas, Stephen, John (and James), Holy Innocents, Circumcision, Epiphany, Mary, Cathedra Perti, Quadragesima,[19] Maundy Thursday, Good Friday, Easter, Rogation Days, Ascension, Pentecost, the *natale* of John the Baptist, Peter and Paul, and the *passio* of John the Baptist. The feasts and periods listed here seem to form the core of the Gallican liturgical calendar, because in addition to these days shared in common there were still other Sundays and feast days celebrated, but these are not listed in all the sources. These were apparently not generally observed, and reflect local or regional differences. These involve feast days of saints and Sundays that are linked to a feast day, such as Sundays after Easter or the celebration of an octave. The Gallican liturgical books thus show us calendars that vary among themselves, but moreover none of them cover the whole year.

[17] Because various sources have only survived in incomplete form, the extent of the calendar cannot always be determined, and mutual comparisons among calendars are of course unsatisfactory. This is true especially for the Old Gallican Missal, which is comprised of various incomplete manuscripts. The first part contains a mass-set for Bishop Germanus and two *benedictiones*, after which follow two fragments with regard to preparation for baptism (*traditio* and *expositio symboli*). More substantial pieces for the celebration of Sundays and feast days are included in the third and largest fragment: two formularies for Advent, followed by Christmas; a series of texts with regard to preparation for baptism during Lent; the period from Maundy Thursday through Easter Week, the Sunday *clausum Paschae* and two more Sundays after Easter, and finally two series of prayers *in rogationibus*. With respect to the calendar the Frankish Missal is less relevant because in the main it contains benedictions, formulas for consecrations and *commune*-formularies; with regard to calender, it only notes the celebration of the *natale* of Hilary, and that, as it is, without a date (GaF 80-91).

[18] Advent is missing in the Gothic Missal and in the Lectionary of Luxeuil because the manuscripts are incomplete, but it apparently was included there in the missing sections which precede Christmas. In the Lectionary of Luxeuil Advent apparently comprised six Sundays, according to SALMON: *Le lectionnaire de Luxeuil* 1; the epistolary of Sélestat even records seven Sundays: see *ibidem* civ. Because the Old Gallican Missal has two Sundays for Advent and the Bobbio Missal three, the period of preparation for Christmas in Gaul could thus vary from two to seven Sundays. According to Caesarius of Arles (d. 542), Advent comprised a period of from ten to fifteen days, and according to the Council of Mâcon (581-583) this period began on St. Martin's day (November 11), according to HEN: *Culture and religion* 61.

[19] The Lectionary of Luxeuil reports only the beginning of Quadragesima, but the other Sundays were included in a missing portion of the manuscript, according to SALMON: *Le lectionnaire de Luxeuil* 77-79.

A calendar with an order completely worked out for the whole year was first introduced into Frankish territory through the Gelasian Sacramentary of the Eighth Century. In this calendar every Sunday of the year was given a title and provided with a formulary. Moreover, an extensive series of feasts linked to particular dates and the feast days subsidiary to them was included, and likewise a large number of saints' feasts on fixed dates. The year received a much more emphatic cyclic order, with an established weekly rhythm from Sunday to Sunday. In the Sacramentary of Gellone coherent periods of the calendar are concentrated around Christmas, Theophany or Epiphany, Easter and Pentecost. The calendar begins with Christmas, which is accompanied by two Sundays. Advent, which comprises five Sundays (four Sundays *ante natale domini* and a *dominica vacat*), is not at the beginning of the book, preceding Christmas, but at the end of the calendar. After the celebration of Theophany on January 6 follows a period of six Sundays, the first of which is an octave celebration.[20] Next, Easter forms the hub of a period which begins with the Sundays Septuagesima, Sexuagesima, Quinquagesima and six Sundays in Quadragesima, and after which comes Easter Octave, four Sundays related to the Easter Octave, Ascension, the Sunday after Ascension, and finally Pentecost. After Pentecost, which also has an octave, 32 weeks after Pentecost are counted,[21] the last five of which have a double designation because these formularies are at the same time the formularies for the five Sundays of Advent. This rhythm from Sunday to Sunday is intermixed with an extensive series of feast days and saints' feasts on fixed dates, for which 146 formulas are provided.

A fully worked out and comprehensive calendar like this was new for the Franks. The Gallican liturgy indeed had had a cyclic arrangement around Christmas and Easter, but these comprised smaller periods of time; not all the Sundays of the year had their own formularies. The year was less elaborately structured according to successive Sundays, and also the feasts with fixed dates were considerably fewer in number. The size of the calendar in Gallican sources is thus considerably smaller than later in Frankish sources. The cause of this lies not only in the number

---

[20] According to DESHUSSES: *Liber sacramentorum Gellonensis. Introductio* xv and xxvii, the copyist has forgotten the fourth Sunday after Epiphany.

[21] An error in the calculation is made from the 12th to the 28th Sunday; see DESHUSSES: *Liber sacramentorum Gellonensis. Introductio* xvi and xxvii-xviii.

of feasts being much smaller, but also through the as of yet more modest contexts surrounding many feasts. Christmas is linked with Advent, which can vary from two to seven weeks.[22] The calendar begins with Advent in all Gallican sources, while Christmas is at the beginning in the Sacramentary of Gellone, and Advent moves to the end. In several Gallican lectionaries Christmastide is lengthened with a Sunday after Christmas, an octave (or Circumcision, or January 1), and a Sunday after the octave, or after Circumcision. A second, larger unit of Sundays and feast days related to one another includes Quadragesima, Easter, Ascension and Pentecost. However, the period after Easter is still worked out less uniformly than will be the case in the later Frankish Gelasian. The Old Gallican Missal has an Easter week which is closed off by the *clausum Paschae*, followed by a Sunday after Easter and a Sunday before Ascension. In the Gothic Missal the mass-set *clausum Paschae* closes Easter week and there are no formularies for the other Sundays between Easter, Ascension and Pentecost, although these are indeed found in the Lectionary of Luxeuil.[23] A further differentiation of the year and a small expansion in the number of Sundays is found only in a few lectionaries which provide one, two or five Sundays after Epiphany;[24] in addition, the Lectionary of Luxeuil also has three Sundays after Cathedra Petri and one Sunday after Pentecost, and one evangeliary notes a fifth Sunday after the Assumption of Mary.[25] With this differentiation, many Sundays did not stand alone, and their connection with specific feast days afforded a particular coherence and dynamic for a larger part of the annual cycle. Moreover, we may assume that the feast days which had the effect of structuring the time around them were of greater significance. In addition to Christmas and Easter these are Epiphany, Cathedra Petri and the Assumption of Mary. Also, as compared with the Frankish Gelasian, the number of feasts with a vigil and/or an octave is quite limited in the Gallican liturgy. Only Christmas, Epiphany and Easter have a vigil,[26] and according to one lec-

---

[22] See our note 18.

[23] Albeit that the formularies for the first three Sundays and the beginning of the fourth Sunday *post clausum Paschae* cannot be traced because the pages involved are missing from the manuscript, according to SALMON: *Le lectionnaire de Luxeuil* 135.

[24] SALMON: *Le lectionnaire de Luxeuil* cvii and cix.

[25] SALMON: *Le lectionnaire de Luxeuil* cix.

[26] The origin of the vigil with Epiphany perhaps lay in Gaul (GaGo 64-81; see also SALMON: *Le lectionnaire de Luxeuil* 27-57), and from there went on to receive a place in the Roman books, according to AUF DER MAUR: *Feiern im Rhythmus der Zeit* 160.

tionary, also Pentecost,[27] while the observance of an octave is limited to Christmas and Easter.[28] This number is expanded considerably in the Sacramentary of Gellone; not only Christmas, Epiphany and Easter have both a vigil and an octave, but there is also a vigil provided for the feasts of Ascension, Pentecost, Gervase and Protase (June 6), John the Baptist (June 24),[29] John and Paul (June 26), Peter and Paul (June 29), Lawrence (August 10), the Assumption of Mary (August 15), Matthew (September 21), Simon and Jude (October 28) and Andrew (November 30). Moreover, of these, the feasts of Peter and Paul, Lawrence and Andrew are expanded with an octave.

The Gallican sources make a not entirely consistent distinction between the temporal cycle and the sanctoral cycle. They reveal a sort of mix of a separate sanctoral and a telescoping of the temporal and the sanctoral. Of the feasts of saints that are not given a date in the Gallican books, a number are included between Christmas and Epiphany: Stephen, John (and James) and Holy Innocents;[30] here the Lectionary of Luxeuil also includes the feast of Genovefa. Next, between Epiphany and Lent, a Marian feast (Assumption) and Cathedra Petri are noted; in the Gothic Missal a whole series of saints' feasts are included at this point as a sort of small sanctoral cycle. These, in addition to the Assumption of Mary and Cathedra Petri, are the feasts of Agnes, Cecilia, Clement, Saturninus, Andrew the Apostle, Eulalia, and the Conversion of Paul.[31] Next, the Gothic Missal alone includes the feast of John the Apostle and Evangelist between the Finding of the Cross

---

[27] SALMON: *Le lectionnaire de Luxeuil* cxvii.

[28] Only two lectionaries speak of an octave after Christmas, which is also celebrated as January 1; in most sources, however, this day refers to Circumcision: *in circumcisione domini*; see SALMON: *Le lectionnaire de Luxeuil* cvi-cvii. Easter Octave, also termed *clausum Paschae*, is noted in the Gothic Missal (GaGo 312-316), in the Old Gallican Missal (GaV 242-245) and in several lectionaries; see SALMON: *Le lectionnaire de Luxeuil* cxii-cxiii.

[29] At least that is how I interpret the mass-set *in ieiunio sancti Iohannis Baptistae* on June 23 in GeG 1143-1148. In Rome this feast had already had a vigil in the sixth century; see AUF DER MAUR: Feste und Gedenktage 119.

[30] In the Old Gelasian, which has a separate sanctoral cycle, these feasts are included in the temporal cycle. For the rest, in the various traditions the feasts in the week after Christmas are remarkably consistent.

[31] If the feasts listed were also actually celebrated between Epiphany and Lent, then a divergent practice existed in Gaul, because various of these feasts were celebrated on other dates in both the Frankish Gelasians and in the *Hadrianum* and the *Paduensis*.

and Rogation Days. After the last feast of the temporal cycle (Pentecost), all the sources present a list of saints' feasts, although they are not all mutually in agreement. In the Gothic Missal (where it is a sort of second sanctoral) this sanctoral includes the feasts of Ferreolus and Ferrucio, John the Baptist, Peter and Paul, the *passio* of John the Baptist, Sixtus, Lawrence, Hippolytus, Cornelius and Cyprian, John and Paul, Symphorian, Maurice and companions (*et socii*), Leodegar, and Martin. The Bobbio Missal and the Lectionary of Luxeuil have fewer saints' feasts. Both note the *natale* and *passio* of John the Baptist, and the feast of Peter and Paul, all three of which are also listed in the Gothic Missal. In addition the Bobbio Missal also has mass-sets for the feasts of Sigismund, Martin and Michael. Incidental mentions of still several other saints' feasts are found in various lectionaries. Apart from the feasts that are also found in the Gothic Missal, the Bobbio Missal and the Lectionary of Luxeuil, those noted are Peter, the Holy Machabees, Sigismund, Martin, Andrew, Thomas, Paul, Matthew and Zacharia. Finally, for the sake of completeness, the feasts of Hilary and Germanus must be mentioned, which are included only in the Frankish Missal and the Old Gallican Missal, respectively.

Many of the saints' feasts are found in only one source. This points to the regional character of the veneration of many saints, and the local character of the liturgical sources. Common feasts had a wider geographic distribution, and transcended local or regional boundaries. On the basis of the Gallican sources discussed here these involve the feasts of Stephen, John (whether with James or not), Holy Innocents, the Assumption of Mary, Cathedra Petri, the *natale* and *passio* of John the Baptist, Peter and Paul, and Martin. These common feasts are also retained in the Frankish Gelasian. There are various of the other, less widely distributed feasts, that do not return. For instance, the Sacramentary of Gellone does not take over the feasts of Saints Hilary, Germanus, Eulalia, Genovefa, Ferreolus and Ferrucio, Symphorian, Leodegar, Sigismund and Zacharia.

2.2. The Frankish and Roman calendars

The comparison between the structure, order and extent of the calendar in the Gallican books and in the eighth-century Gelasian brought to light several differences. The calendar which was assembled and distributed in the second half of the eighth century was in many respects new when compared with the calendar that the Franks knew from Gallican books. This should not be surprising, because to a great extent the Frankish editors based their work on Roman books. But that next raises the question of to what degree the editors were oriented toward Rome: to what extent are the Roman Gregorian and Gelasian tradition recognizable in the Frankish calendar, and in what points these Roman calendars differ from the Gallican, with which the Franks had originally been familiar?

The two types of Roman sacramentaries that each in part served as a foundation for the eighth-century Gelasian did not reflect a uniform Roman practice, but referred to two different liturgical traditions. The books that represented these traditions each had their own distinctive organization, and structured the calendar in two different ways. The Old Gelasian is divided into three books. With regard to the calendar, it is the first two of these which are of greatest importance. The first is comprised to a great extent of the temporal cycle, and the second of the sanctoral cycle. There is a double system, which meant that for daily use one had to switch back and forth between the books. In the *Paduensis* the temporal and sanctoral are integrated into one continuous calendar. Because in the Frankish Gelasians the Sundays and feast days and the saints' feasts alternate with one another in accord with the calendrical arrangement of the year, with regard to organization and structure these sacramentaries are most akin to the *Paduensis*. The size of the calendar in the eighth-century Gelasian also corresponds more closely with the size of the calendar in the *Paduensis*. Each Sunday is provided with a mass-set in both of these sacramentaries, in contrast to the Old Gelasian, which lacks mass-sets for the Sundays between Christmas and Septuagesima and between the octave of Pentecost and Advent, which, for the rest, is not included with the temporal in the first book, but at the end of the second book, after the mass-sets for the feasts of the saints.

Although the organization and the size of the calendar in the Frankish Gelasian accords best with the calendar in the *Paduensis*, the two calendars also differ from each other in various respects. For both Advent and the Sundays after Christmas the *Paduensis* has one mass-set less; in the Sacramentary of Gellone Advent comprises five Sun-

---

[32] In this Gellone agrees with the Old Gelasian, which also has five mass-sets for Advent (GeV 1120-1156).

days,[32] while the *Paduensis* counts four (three Sundays *de adventu* and one *dominica vacat*), and after Christmas Gellone gives two mass-sets, against one in the *Paduensis*. Gellone is also somewhat more full in the period after Epiphany: in contrast to the five Sundays in the *Paduensis* it counts six Sundays, and furthermore provides an octave. In regard to the period around Easter there are not many differences, the chief being that in Gellone Ascension and Pentecost are expanded with a vigil, which, for the rest, is also the case for the Marian feast on August 15. The two books vary the most with regard to the division of the period between Pentecost and Advent. Gellone here counts 32 Sundays after Pentecost,[33] while the *Paduensis* introduces several discrete units: these are, successively, the five Sundays after Pentecost, five Sundays after the octave of the feast of the Apostles Peter and Paul,[34] five Sundays after the feast of Lawrence, the Ember Week in the seventh month followed by a *dominica vacat*, and finally eight Sundays (nine weeks) after the feast of the Archangel Michael. Such a differentiated division, in which a series of Sundays are connected with a feast (or saint's feast), is also to be found in several Gallican lectionaries;[35] nevertheless, the Franks did not take these over into the eighth-century Gelasian. Although the feasts of Peter and Paul, and that of Lawrence, are provided with both a vigil and octave in Gellone, these feasts, like that of Michael too, apparently were no longer of such central importance that they could function as a principle for structuring the calendar.

The calendars of the two Roman predecessors of the eighth-century Gelasian share many feasts in common, but they are not entirely congruent. All feasts in the two calendars return in the Frankish Gelasian, as if they have been telescoped together,[36] but there are also several feasts

---

[33] The first of these is Pentecost octave, and the last five coincide with the Sundays of Advent.

[34] It is true that the *Paduensis* has a collective vigil for Peter and Paul on June 28, but the feasts of the two Apostles are split to, respectively, June 29 and 30.

[35] The Lectionary of Luxeuil has three Sundays after Cathedra Petri, and in one evangeliary there is mention of a fifth Sunday after the feast of the Assumption of Mary; see SALMON: *Le lectionnaire de Luxeuil* cviii-cix.

[36] The only exception are the saints Audifax and Abacus, who on January 20 in the Old Gelasian are part of a mass-set for several saints, including also Sebastian and Mary and Martha (GeV 815-818). Neither of the two martyrs are taken over into the Frankish Gelasian.

added, such as a number of saints' feasts and the Rogation Days.[37] The Frankish calendar is thus more extensive.

When, at the beginning of the ninth century, the Carolingians assembled the Supplement to the Hadrianum in order to fill in the lacunae in this Roman Gregorian, they made use of the eighth-century Gelasian for the purpose. In this manner too the calendar introduced from Rome was brought into concordance with the arrangement of Sundays and feast days in this Frankish sacramentary. The Supplement included mass-sets for two Sundays after Christmas, six after Epiphany, four after Easter Octave, one after Ascension and 24 after Pentecost. From the collection of prefaces that is included in the Supplement it would appear that the number of Sundays after Pentecost was expanded to 27 and that Advent spanned five Sundays.[38] The number of feasts of saints is also rounded out in the Supplement,[39] which is to say that the Supplement includes a preface for several feasts that are absent from the *Hadrianum*. Nevertheless, the size of the calendar of saints in the *Hadrianum* in combination with the Supplement is smaller than that in the eighth-century Gelasian. Moreover, a number of feasts are celebrated on other dates.

When we compare the Frankish calendar, as it is found in the eighth-century Gelasians and the Supplement, with the calendars in the Roman books (the Old Gelasian and the Gregorian *Hadrianum* and *Paduensis*), then it is clear that the Frankish calendar is modelled on the Roman, and particularly the Gregorian version of the type that is represented by the *Paduensis*, albeit that they are not identical. The number of Sundays is somewhat expanded by the Franks, and the Sundays after Pentecost are arranged differently. Greater differences present themselves with respect to the sanctoral cycle.

3. THE SANCTORAL

Although the Frankish books were composed on the basis of the Roman, the calendars for the saints are not identical with one another.

---

[37] See VOGEL: *Medieval liturgy* 73-74. I will return to the saints' feasts below. The observance of Rogation Days preceding Ascension Day is of Gallican origin, and is already mentioned by Gregory of Tours and by the Synod of Orleans (511). After these *Rogationes* were included in the Frankish Gelasian, they were introduced in Rome around 800; see AUF DER MAUR: *Feiern* 121-122; HEN: *Culture and religion* 63-64.

[38] The Supplement does not provide mass sets for the vigils of Ascension and Pentecost, although a *benedictio* is included for the latter (GrSp 1761).

[39] See VOGEL: *Medieval liturgy* 89.

The Frankish books have more feasts than the Roman. When compared with the Gallican books, the Frankish calendar also lists more saints' feasts.[40] In comparison with the Frankish Gelasian, the following feasts are lacking in the Roman books:[41] Emerentiana and Macarius (January 23); Praiectus (or Prix, January 25); Conversion of Paul (January 25); Zoticus, Irenaeus, Iacinthus (February 10); Zeno (February 14); Cathedra Petri (February 22); Leo the Great (April 11); Primus and Felician (June 9); Basilides (June 12);[42] Benedict the Abbot (July 11); James the Great (July 25); Bartholomew (August 24); Augustine of Hippo (August 28); vigil and feast of Matthew (September 20-21); Maurice *et socii* (September 22); Jerome (September 30); Luke (October 18); vigil and feast of Simon and Jude (October 27-28); Damasus (December 12).

Through their inclusion in the Frankish books, these feasts were to spread throughout the West. However, this is not to say that they were all new. Various of the feasts were already known elsewhere and had Eastern origins, or had their roots in Gaul. The last is the case, for instance, for the feast of the Conversion of Paul (January 25), which was already a part of the Gothic Missal (GaGo 143-147), and is also included in the Calendar of Willibrord.[43] It is apparently of Gaulish origin, but the impetus behind its origins and for the date is unknown.[44]

---

[40] The difference between the Frankish and Gallican calendars is highlighted still further when we realize that because of the predominantely local character of the veneration of saints in Merovingian Gaul, various saints' feasts did not pass on through to the Frankish books.

[41] The Supplement adds a preface for various saints' feasts not present in the *Hadrianum*. These are not new feasts, however, when compared to the eighth-century Gelasian Sacramentaries, so reference to the Frankish Gelasian will suffice here. The basis for references to this sacramentary here is Gellone. Other representatives of the eighth-century Gelasians will only be cited when their sanctoral diverges from Gellone. For the differences among them see: MORETON: *The Eighth-Century Gelasian Sacramentary* 150-157, and for the feasts which are peculiar to the Phillipps Sacramentary, JOUNEL: Le sanctoral 351-356.

[42] Nazarius will not be considered here. Only in Gellone this Milanese martyr is added to the celebration of the vigil of Gervase and Protase on June 18, which is otherwise present in both the Old Gelasian and in the eighth-century Gelasian. The feast of Nazarius is celebrated together with that of Basilides, Cyrinus and Nabor on June 12.

[43] H. WILSON: *The Calendar of St. Willibrord* (= Henry Bradshaw Society 55) (London 1918) 3.

[44] See P. JOUNEL: *Le culte des saints dans les basiliques du Latran et du Vatican au douzième siècle* (= Collection de l'école française de Rome 26) (Rome 1977) 218-219, IDEM: Le sanctoral 348-349. This feast is absent from Gellone but does appear in the

The feasts of Augustine and Luke were also already mentioned in Willibrord's Calendar, but they are probably African or Eastern in origin, and not Gaulish.[45]

Although the feast of Cathedra Petri is not found in the Roman books, the feast had very old roots in Rome. As early as the fourth century there was a memorial celebration for Peter on February 22 (*natale Petri de cathedra*). This was connected with the classic memorials for the dead in the *Parentalia* and *Cara cognatio*, falling at the end of the year according to the calendar then in use,[46] which began with March 1. This feast shortly also spread beyond Rome and was known in Africa, Gaul and Spain. In contrast to the Roman liturgical books, the feast is noted in various Gallican sources, which, however, are not at one with regard to the date; both January 18 and February 22 are found.[47] The Calendar of Willibrord even lists both days, the first of which coincides with *adsumptio sanctae mariae*.[48] The Gothic Missal, which notes no dates, places Cathedra Petri (GaGo 148-157) immediately after Conversio Pauli, so that a date in February would seem to be obvious. In contrast, the Bobbio Missal situates Cathedra Petri (GaBo 115-121) between Epiphany and the feast of Mary,[49] so that here January is the likely date. This is also true for the Lectionary of Luxeuil, which places the commemoration celebration for Peter immediately after the feast of Mary, and moreover follows it by three Sundays post Cathedra Petri. These first serve to give extra weight to the feast, but also imply a date in January, because after February 22 there would be no more Sundays available before the beginning of Lent.[50] The Frankish Gelasians place

eighth-century Gelasians; see, for instance, the Sacramentary of St. Gall (GeSg 169-172; K. MOHLBERG: *Das fränkische Sacramentarium Gelasianum in alamannischer Überlieferung (Codex Sangall. No. 348)* (= Liturgiewissenschaftliche Quellen und Forschungen 1/2) (Münster 1971³)) and the Sacramentary of Angoulême (GeAn 181-184; P. SAINT-ROCH: *Liber sacramentorum Engolismensis. Manuscrit B.N.lat. 816. Le sacramentaire gélasien d'Angoulême* (= Corpus christianorum. Series latina 159C) (Turnhout 1987)).

[45] WILSON: *The Calendar* 10 and 12. Cf. JOUNEL: *Le culte des saints* 281 and 298.

[46] See AUF DER MAUR: Feste und Gedenktage 82, 137, 148, 232, 252.

[47] KING: *Liturgies of the past* 142 places the feast on January 16, without support for doing so.

[48] WILSON: *The Calendar* 3-4, 18 and 22.

[49] There were even two mass-sets offered for this: *sanctae Mariae sollemnitate* (GaBo 122-128) and *adsumpcione sanctae mariae* (GaBo 129-133).

[50] SALMON: *Le lectionnaire de Luxeuil* cvi-cix, 64 and 66; See also JOUNEL: *Le culte des saints* 225-226; IDEM: Le sanctoral 348.

the feast on February 22 (GeG 234-237), as also happens in the Supplement (GrSp 1541).[51] Only in the course of the tenth and eleventh centuries would Cathedra Petri (again) be celebrated as a feast in Rome.[52]

The feast of James the Great is also mentioned in Gallican books earlier than in their Roman counterparts.[53] As with the oldest witness from the fourth century,[54] in Gaul it is celebrated on December 27 together with the feast of his brother John. Various Eastern rites have various dates for the feast of James the Great. The feast is placed on July 25 in the Frankish liturgy, where it has since remained, also after it was introduced into Rome in the tenth century.[55]

The feasts listed at the beginning of this section as appearing in the Frankish sacramentaries and not in the Roman only found their way to Rome in the course of the second millennium. Thus it is remarkable that for a part they involve martyrs and saints – although sometimes very obscure – who are specifically linked with Rome: Emerentiana, Zoticus, Irenaeus, Iacinthus, Zeno, Peter, Pope Leo the Great, Primus, Felician, Basilides and Damasus.[56] It is true that Rome had a feast for Pope Leo the Great, but not on April 11. This date is an erroneous report in the *Liber pontificalis* of the actual date of the death of Leo the Great, November 10, 461.[57] The correct date is indeed stated in the Calendar of Willibrord,[58] but the eighth-century Gelasian took over April 11 as the date, whereupon the error spread. There was, however, still another feast of Leo the Great, which was connected with the translation of his body to the Vatican basilica by Pope Sergius I on June 28,

---

[51] The eighth-century Gelasians actually do make use of Roman texts from the Old Gelasian for the mass-set, but, as it happens, those from the feast of Peter on June 29 (GeV 918-920), supplemented by a preface which is also included in the Supplement. The Phillipps Sacramentary is the only one of the Frankish Gelasians to which a celebration of Cathedra Petri on January 18 has been added; see JOUNEL: Le sanctoral 351-352.

[52] JOUNEL: *Le culte des saints* 225-226.

[53] GaGo 37-45; GaBo 94-100; for an evangeliary of the eighth century, see SALMON: *Le lectionnaire de Luxeuil* cvii; WILSON: *The Calendar* 14 and 45.

[54] See JOUNEL: *Le culte des saints* 260.

[55] See JOUNEL: *Le culte des saints* 260-261.

[56] See JOUNEL: *Le culte des saints* 217-218, 244, 245, 323; IDEM: Le sanctoral 349-350.

[57] L. DUCHESNE: *Le liber pontificalis. Texte, introduction et commentaire* 1 (Paris 1955) 239.

[58] WILSON: *The Calendar* 13.

688. Since then this feast, which is noted in the Calendar of Willibrord[59] and is included in the Roman *Hadrianum* (GrHa 586-588), has been celebrated on June 28.[60]

Only a few of the saints can be placed in a specifically Frankish context. This is especially the case for Praiectus (Prix), who is not easy to identify.[61] It is most likely that Praiectus was the Frankish bishop who died as a martyr around 676 and whose remains were transported around 765 to the monastery at Flavigny named for him, which is also conjectured to have been the site of the compilation of the eighth-century Gelasian.[62] The origins of the feast of Maurice *et socii*, which for the rest is not in Gellone, must also be sought in Frankish territory. He was put to death with several thousand companions at Agaunum, in Burgundy, at the end of the third century. Because of its presence in the Gothic Missal (GaGo 419-424) and in the Calendar of Willibrord,[63] the roots of this feast reach back further than the Frankish liturgy.[64] A Frankish context is somewhat less evident for the feast of Benedict, but is also possible insofar as the date of July 11 is prompted by the translation of his relics to Fleury (Saint-Benoît-sur-Loire).[65] Gellone even provides two mass-sets in honour of St. Benedict (GeG 1233-1236; 1237-1240). What is further striking is that the number of feasts of apostles spread over the year is expanded: Paul (Conversion), Cathedra Petri, James the brother of John, Bartholomew, Matthew, Simon and Jude are added.[66]

Several more must be added to the feast days listed. These involve several feasts of saints that are indeed included in the *Hadrianum*, but their presence in the eighth-century Gelasian implies that they were

---

[59] WILSON: *The Calendar* 8.
[60] JOUNEL: *Le culte des saints* 231.
[61] MORETON: *The Eighth-Century Gelasian Sacramentary* 14.
[62] VOGEL: *Medieval liturgy* 73-74; JOUNEL: Le sanctoral 349.
[63] WILSON: *The Calendar* 11.
[64] JOUNEL: *Le culte des saints* 290 dates the introduction of the feast in Rome to the twelfth century, overlooking the fact that it is already included in the Paduense (GrPa 672-675), though with a mass-set that, except for a preface of its own, is precisely the same as the mass-set for Lucia and Geminianus on September 16 (GrHa 699-701).
[65] See MORETON: *The Eighth-Century Gelasian Sacramentary* 15, and JOUNEL: Le sanctoral 351. In addition to July 11, the Calendar of Willibrord also notes March 21; see WILSON: *The Calendar* 5, 9 and 34.
[66] These are also all included in the Calendar of Willibrord, see WILSON: *The Calendar* 3, 4, 9, 10, 11 and 12.

already known in Frankish territory before the *Hadrianum* was distributed there in the course of the ninth century. One feast for which this is the case is that of Pope Gregory the Great, on March 12, which is also already noted in the Calendar of Willibrord.[67] Furthermore, the mass-set in the Frankish Gelasian (GeG 243-246) is not the same as in the *Hadrianum* (GrHa 137-139). The martyrs Lucia and Geminianus also have a mass-set in the *Hadrianum*. Their feast on September 16 coincides, as it does in the eighth-century Gelasian, with the feast of the martyr Euphemia.[68] It is true that in Rome midway through the seventh century there was a feast of Lucia on September 16, but she figures there alone with Euphemia.[69] The combination of Lucia and Geminianus is peculiar to the *Hadrianum* and the Frankish Gelasians. Moreover, this is not a matter of indigenous saints: Pope Gregory the Great must be chiefly located in Rome, Lucia in Syracuse, and the origin of Geminianus is unknown.

Finally, from this comparison of the saints' feasts in the various calendars, it can be observed that several of the feasts were not celebrated everywhere on the same date. The following shifts are found in Gellone when compared with Roman sources: Felix (January 15; in GeV, GrHa and GrPa, January 14); Mary and Martha (January 19; in GeV, January 20); Juliana (February 16; in GeV, February 17); George the Martyr (April 24; in GrHa, April 23); Vitalis (April 29; in GrHa and GrPa, April 28); Nicomedes (May 31; in GrHa and GrPa, June 1); Simplicius, Faustinus and Beatrice on July 28 and Felix on July 29 in GeG, while the *natale* of all four of these saints is collectively celebrated on July 29 in GrHa and GrPa; the octave of Andrew (December 8; in GeV, December 7); Thomas (December 22; in GeV, December 21; the latter date also in GrSp).

The expansion in the calendar of saints in Frankish liturgical books in comparison with their Roman counterparts, as described here, is linked with the tremendous growth that the cult of saints underwent in Gaul during the Merovingian period. On the basis of five reconstructions of local or regional cycles of saints' feasts in Gaul from various periods, Y. Hen has demonstrated the increase in the number of saints' feasts, and

---

[67] WILSON: *The Calendar* 5.

[68] In both the Roman and Frankish sources Lucia has another feast on December 13, which need not be considered here.

[69] This involves the evangeliary PI, of about 645; see Th. KLAUSER: *Das Römische Capitulare Evangeliorum. Texte und Untersuchungen zu seiner ältesten Geschichte. 1. Typen* (= LQF 28) (Münster 1972²) 38.

reveals the religious and social significance of the cult of the saints.[70] His reconstructions involve Arles, Chelles, Auxerre, Poitiers and Utrecht, and span a period from the first half of the sixth to the first half of the eighth century. Still another series of feast days from a somewhat earlier period, described by Gregory of Tours (d. 594) in his *Histories* (10,31), which he says he derived from a written instruction of Bishop Perpetuus (461-491) which was at his disposal, can be added to these.[71] The sizes of all these calendars diverge considerably, varying from about a dozen to slightly over 100 saints' feasts. In actuality the number would have been greater, because the sacramentaries also contained *commune* mass-sets that were intended for other saints' feasts. Because the later calendars are more extensive, the number of saints' feasts rises with the passage of time. The vast majority of the feasts involve local Gallican saints, various of whom were immediately connected with local monasteries or churches. The cult of saints was a very locally oriented activity. As the number of new local saints who were absorbed into the local sanctoral cycles was growing from the fifth to the middle of the eighth century, there existed no unity and no generality with regard to the sanctoral cycle in Merovingian Gaul.[72] Because of their local character, there are strong differences among the lists with saints' feasts. That is also the case when we compare them with Gallican liturgical books. Although some of the feasts do indeed appear in two or more of the calendars we have listed here, it is virtually only the feasts in honour of the apostles that they have in common; in the calendar from Arles all these feasts have obtained a place. In addition, it seems that particularly the feasts of John the Baptist and Martin were widespread. The Calendar of Willibrord, from the start of the eighth century, is an exception with respect to these lists of saints' feasts. The number of sanctoral feast-days there is by far the largest. Moreover, the Calendar of Willibrord distinguishes itself by the fact that of the 110 saints' days, not one is related to a local saint.[73] In this respect

[70] HEN: *Culture and religion* 89-107.
[71] MIGNE: *Patrologia latina* 71, 566-567.
[72] HEN: *Culture and religion* 84.
[73] HEN: *Culture and religion* 105, explains this by the fact that Utrecht was a new diocese, and that in this region, in contrast to for instance Auxerre and Arles, there were still no local martyrs and saints. There is, however, a question of whether the Calendar of Willibrord had specific reference to Utrecht. Through its agreements with other insular calenders, it would appear that Willibrord's Calendar is anchored in the Anglo-Irish tradition, according to *ibidem*: 106.

the Calendar of Willibrord can be considered as a transition from the indigenous calendars to the calendars of the Frankish liturgical books. The number of saints' feasts in these would also be considerable, but the feasts of local Gallican saints would assume only a modest place there.

4. SOME SHIFTS IN EMPHASIS IN CONTENT

Up to this point attention has been devoted primarily to the size, organization and distribution of the calendar. These elements are the external expression of the content. In order to trace the religious significance and theological content of the feasts, analysis of the liturgical text material is essential. At the same time, on the basis of this a picture can be drawn of what shifts with reference to content took place when the Frankish liturgical books were compiled. This analysis provides insight into the ways in which themes and motifs from the different liturgical traditions from the early Middle Ages are handled in the content by the Frankish editors of the liturgy in the eighth and ninth centuries. Careful study can pick out Gallican traces within the Frankish liturgy, the main currents of which are based on Roman sources. Because it is impossible in this setting to analyze and discuss all the material from the different sources for the separate feasts, I will here by way of example refer to several shifts in emphasis with regard to several feasts that in some way are connected with Christmas. Hopefully they will make it sufficiently clear that in the compilation of the Frankish liturgical books, while the Roman tradition indeed was dominant, the indigenous Gallican tradition, with which people in Frankish territory had until then been familiar, was so deeply anchored that elements of it were taken over and so preserved.

4.1. Advent

Of the motifs which can be distinguished in the euchological text material for Advent, two advance to the foreground: the incarnation, or first coming, and the parousia or second coming. These motifs appear in all the sources, Roman, Gallican and Frankish alike, which is in keeping with the hypothesis of A. Chavasse that the textual material from these traditions in part goes back to a common source.[74] It is striking here

---

[74] CHAVASSE: *Le sacramentaire gélasien* 412-426 and esp. 641-643.

that in the ten prefaces and benedictions that the Supplement to the *Hadrianum* has included for Advent, the motif of the parousia is present with particular prominence.[75] Apparently the Franks wished to emphasize the second coming in glory, when men and the world would be judged.

4.2. January 1

In the various traditions the celebration of January 1 has a multiplicity of themes. Because the date falls precisely a week after Christmas, by arithmetic it is the octave, and that is indeed how the celebration is designated in both the Roman and Frankish sacramentaries: *(in) octova(s) Domini*. The celebration on the eighth day takes up again the celebration of Christ's birth, which is where, in terms of content, the accent lies in the mass-set in the Old Gelasian, which returns in full in the eighth-century Gelasian (GeV 48-53 = GeG 76-81). In addition Gellone, like some of the Frankish Gelasians, also includes a second mass-set *de octabas Domini* (GeG 82-87). This is the sum of two mass-sets from the *Hadrianum* being added to one another: the mass-set for the octave (GrHa 82-84), and a part of the mass-set for *Hypopante* on February 2 (GrHa 123, 125, 127). Although the mass-set for the octave from the *Hadrianum* can be characterized as Marian,[76] this is expressed only in the first oration, which implores the intercession of Mary.[77] It cannot be excluded that in Rome the celebration of the *natale* of Mary on January 1 represents an older layer than the celebration of the octave of Christmas.[78] Little more of this can be found in the sacramentaries, however. The final prayer of the second mass-set for January 1 in Gellone does not so much have Mary as its theme, but emphasizes the octave through mention of Simeon, who, with the presentation of Jesus in the Temple,

---

[75] Cuius primi adventus mysterium (…) ut secundum valeamus exspectare (GrSp 1695); inveniat secundus eius adventus (GrSp 1700); Iustificetque in adventu secundo, qui nos redemit in primo (GrSp 1704); ita iustificet cum ad iudicandum venerit manifestus (GrSp 1708); illi tremendi examinis diem exspectetis interriti (GrSp 1768); Ut qui de adventu redemptoris nostri secundum carnem (…), in secundo cum in maiestate venerit (GrSp 1769).

[76] DUMAS: *Liber sacramentorum Gellonensis. Textus* note on p. 10-11.

[77] Deus qui salutis aeternae beatae mariae virginitate fecunda, humano generi praemia praestitisti, tribue quaesumus ut ipsam pro nobis (aput te) intercedente sentiamus, per quam meruimus auctorem vitae (nostrae) suscipere (GeG 82 = GrHa 82).

[78] AUF DER MAUR: *Feiern* 171-172.

saw the fulfillment of his wish to witness before he died the coming of the Lord (Luke 2, 25-32).[79] This theme is in keeping with Gallican sources, in which in the main the central themes for January 1 are the presentation of Jesus in the Temple, and particularly his circumcision,[80] which according to Luke 2, 21-24 took place on the eighth day after his birth; counting from Christmas, that is January 1, the octave. This motif of the presentation in the Temple, the circumcision and the encounter with Simeon, dominant in Gallican sources, returns briefly in the preface of the first mass-set in Gellone as a part of an elaborate summing up of the marvellous events with regard to Jesus' birth (GeG 79).

At first sight it would appear that the sources in the various liturgical traditions pass over the celebration of January 1 as the beginning of a new year. Since antiquity the beginning of a new year has been celebrated with all sorts of festivities and customs. Various synods and Christian authors campaigned against these practices and made attempts to bend the pagan practices into customs with Christian meanings.[81] The antithesis in the last oration of the mass-set for the octave in the Old Gelasian can be seen as an allusion to these festivities.[82] The context of the *missa prohibendo ab idolis*, which following the example of the Old Gelasian is also placed after Christmas octave in the Frankish Gelasian (GeV 54-56 = GeG 88-90), also becomes clearer against this background. It is true that this mass-set does not mention the new year, but nevertheless it expresses the abhorrence of the profane and demonic. A connecting link between this mass-set *ad prohibendum ab*

---

[79] (…) qui iusti symionis expectationem implisti, ut sicut ille mortem non vidit. This oration comes from the Gregorian mass-set for February 2: GeG 87 = GrHa 127.

[80] Here the feast is also called *circumcisio Domini*; see GaGo 51-63, GaBo 101-107, and various lectionaries as reported in SALMON: *Le lectionnaire de Luxeuil* cvi-cvii. The origin of the feast of the Circumcision apparently also lies in Gaul, according to R. SCHWARZENBERGER: Die liturgische Feier des 1. Januar. Geschichte und Pastoralliturgische Desiderate, in *Liturgisches Jahrbuch* 20 (1970) 223, or in the East, according to J.-C. SCHMITT: *Bijgeloof in de Middeleeuwen* (Nijmegen 1995) 85-86.

[81] See SCHWARZENBERGER: Die liturgische Feier des 1. Januar 218-222; M. MESLIN: *La fête des kalendes de janvier dans l'empire romain. Étude d'un rituel de Nouvel An* (= Collection Latomus 115) (Bruxelles 1970) 95-118; D. HARMENING: *Superstitio. Überlieferungs- und theoriegeschichtliche Untersuchungen zur kirchlich-theologischen Aberglaubensliteratur des Mittelalters* (Berlin 1979) 121-145; HEN: *Culture and religion* 164-170.

[82] Omnipotens sempiterne deus, qui tuae mensae participes a diabolico iubes abstinere conuiuio, da, quaesumus, plebi tuae, ut gustum mortiferae profanitatis abiecto puris mentibus ad aepulas aeternae salutis accedat (GeV 53 = GeG 81).

idolis and the pagan customs surrounding the New Year is possibly provided by the Gallican liturgy. The Gallican feast of the Circumcision would appear to be intended as a counterweight to the pagan celebration of January 1.[83] In both the Gothic Missal and the Bobbio Missal the celebration of the Circumcision is transformed into a spiritual sense. As Jesus is physically circumcised, so are the believers spiritually circumcised without a wound in the flesh; circumcision of the 'foreskin of the heart' extirpates the paganism that cleaves to us, the heathenish error with which we are covered.[84] The salvific meaning of the Circumcision is twice expressed in the Bobbio Missal as the destruction of the sway of idolatry.[85] In the Gallican books this terminology and this imagery is linked with the celebration of January 1. This use of the term *idola* also returns in the title of the mass-set in the Old Gelasian and in Gellone.[86] Perhaps these are reminiscences of the festivities which surrounded January 1. The selection of the first two readings for the feast of Circumcision in the Lectionary of Luxeuil also appears to be intended to offer a counterbalance against the celebration of New Year.[87]

4.3. Epiphany

The celebration of Epiphany on January 6, which arose in the East, in the Roman liturgy is modelled around the theme of the adoration by

---

[83] According to SCHMITT: *Bijgeloof in de Middeleeuwen* 86, this role of the Gallican celebration of the Circumcision is beyond dispute.

[84] (...) Circumcisus est in carne corporis nostri, ut nos per uerbum spiritus sui in corde purgati sine carnis uulnere circumcideremur in spiritu, ut utrique sexui proficeret circumcisio spritalis (...) (GaGo 55); (...) Cordis nostri praeputia, quae gentilibus uitiis excreuerunt, non ferro, sed spiritu circumcidat (...) (GaGo 51); (...) quos error gentilitatis inuoluit (...) (GaGo 52).

[85] (...) omnia idola destruxit (...) (GaBo 103); (...) rignum idolatriae distruxit... (GaBo 104).

[86] In the Veronense Sacramentary the prayers of this mass-set are part of the collection of prayers for the months of July and December,; see L. MOHLBERG: *Sacramentarium Veronense (Cod. Bibl. Capit. Veron. LXXXV [80]* (= Rerum ecclesiasticarum documenta. Series Maior. Fontes 1) (Roma 1955-1956) nos. 515, 517, 1304. The term *idola* is, however, unknown in the vocabulary of the Veronense.

[87] Is. 1, 10-20 and I Cor. 10, 14-31. The third reading involves the presentation in the Temple, the circumcision and the encounter with Simeon (Luke 2, 21-40); see SALMON: *Le lectionnaire de Luxeuil* 21-23.

the Wise Men, as described in Matthew 2.[88] More motifs can be distinguished in non-Roman traditions. So too in the Gallican, where in addition to the adoration of the Wise Men orations also touch on the themes of the baptism in the Jordan (Matt. 3) and the wedding at Cana (John 2) (GaGo 64-93; GaBo 110-114). Both of these latter themes are frequently found in the readings.[89] The Frankish sacramentaries follow the Roman line and reduce the threefold motif to the adoration by the Wise Men. The only exception is the benediction which is included in the Supplement to the *Hadrianum* for Epiphany, in which reference is made to the guiding star of the Magi, the Spirit which descended upon the Son as a dove, and the water which turned to wine at Cana.[90] The vigil of Epiphany probably arose in Gaul and from there was taken up into the Roman liturgy, and from thence came into the Frankish books.[91]

4.4. Marian feasts

Lastly, several Marian feasts briefly require our attention. The four feasts in honour of Mary which are part of the Roman books also return in the Frankish Gelasian: February 2, March 25, August 15 and September 8. All these feasts come from the East and were apparently introduced into Rome in the seventh century;[92] in any case, they were known in the time of Pope Sergius (687-701), because the *Liber pontificalis* reports that during his pontificate a procession was held at each of the four feasts involved.[93] In terms of content, the oldest Marian feasts

---

[88] See, in connection with the origin and spread of Epiphany, AUF DER MAUR: *Feiern* 156-159.

[89] SALMON: *Le lectionnaire de Luxeuil* cvi-cvii; 27-60.

[90] Deus lumen uerum, qui unigenitum suum hodierna die stella duce gentibus uoluit reuelare, sua uos dignetur benedictione ditare. Amen. Quo exemplo magorum mystica domino iesu christo munera offerentes, spreto antiquo hoste, spretisque contagiis uitiorum, ad aeternam patriam redire ualeatis per uiam uirtutum. Amen. Detque uobis ueram mentium innocentiam, qui super unigenitum suum spiritum sanctum demonstrari uoluit per columbam, eaque uirtute mentes uestrae exerceantur ad intellegenda diuinae legis archana qua in chana galileae lympha est in uinum conuersa. Amen. (GrSp 1744).

[91] So AUF DER MAUR: *Feiern* 160.

[92] R. HESBERT: *Antiphonale missarum sextuplex* (Bruxelles 1935) lxxx; AUF DER MAUR: *Feste und Gedenktage* 123-130.

[93] DUCHESNE: *Liber pontificalis* 1, 376.

are connected with the incarnation,[94] so that it should not be surprising that various Marian feasts have received a place in the immediate vicinity of Christmas. This applies to February 2 and March 25,[95] to which January 1 (the octave of Christmas) can also be added, as apparently the oldest Marian feast in Rome.[96]

Before these feasts were introduced into Frankish territory via the Roman books there was only one Marian feast known there, which is both generally designated as *missa sanctae Mariae sollemnitate* (GaBo 122-128) and *in festivitae sanctae Mariae*,[97] but the content of which is also specified more precisely as *adsumptio sanctae Mariae* (GaBo 129-133, GaGo 94-105 and the Calendar of Willibrord).[98] No date is stated in these liturgical books. The Gothic Missal places the feast between Epiphany and the feast of Agnes; in the Bobbio Missal, which has two mass-sets, the feast is situated between Cathedra Petri and the beginning of Lent, and the Lectionary of Luxeuil places it immediately before Cathedra Petri. Since the feast of Cathedra Petri was celebrated in Gaul on January 18 (and February 22),[99] this points in the direction of mid-January. On the basis of the Calendar of Willibrord, among other sources, the celebration of the Marian feast in Gaul can be more or less precisely dated to January 17, 18 or 19.[100] In the Frankish books, following their Roman counterparts, the Assumption of Mary receives a place on August 15, and the general Marian feast seems to have disappeared.

Yet there are several indications that the Gallican Marian feast in January has left traces in the Frankish liturgy. The antiphonal of Senlis,

---

[94] Auf der Maur: Feste und Gedenktage 124, 126.

[95] This is true for March 25 to the extent that it is related to Christmas by way of the Annunciation. In addition this date is of course also related to the spring equinox and to Easter; see Auf der Maur: *Feiern* 192-193; Th. Talley: *The origins of the liturgical year* (New York 1986) 91-103; A. Scheer: *De aankondiging van de Heer. Een genetische studie naar de oorsprong van de liturgische viering op 25 maart* (Baarn 1991) esp. 55-63 and 307-336.

[96] Auf der Maur: *Feiern* 171-172; Idem: Feste und Gedenktage 125.

[97] Salmon: *Le lectionnaire de Luxeuil* 64-65.

[98] Wilson: *The Calendar* 3. Aside from this, the Calendar of Willibrord also notes Marian feasts for August 16 and September 9; for the information and commentary with regard to the variant data, see *ibidem* 10-11, 36-37 and 39.

[99] See below.

[100] See Salmon: *Le lectionnaire de Luxeuil* 64. To the degree that the Assumption was the theme, the date may have been inspired by the Egyptian calendar, which celebrated the *adsumptio* on January 16, according to Auf der Maur: Feste und Genktage 127 and 129.

from the ninth century, calls January 19 the *natale sanctae mariae*.[101] The eighth-century Gelasian celebrates the *natale* of Mary and Martha on the same date (GeG 152-155). At first sight the relationship with the Old Gelasian, which specifies January 20 for the *natale* of Sebastian, Mary, Martha, Audifax and Abachus (GeV 815-818), appears great. However, what is involved there is not the sisters Mary and Martha, but the martyrs Marius and Martha and their two sons, who would later receive a place in the calendar on January 19.[102] Also, in terms of content the mass-set for Mary and Martha in Gellone is not consonant with this mass-set in the Old Gelasian. It is to a great extent the same as a *commune* mass-set (GeV 1091-1093), which has as a consequence the fact that the content of the prayers does not specifically relate to the subject, but only speaks of saints in general terms. One might find a possible connection between this feast in the Frankish Gelasian and in the Gallican liturgy through the gospel reading for one of the Marian feasts in the Bobbio Missal (GaBo 130): Jesus' visit to Mary and Martha (Luke 10, 38-42). Combining the data makes the following reconstruction possible: the celebration of the Assumption follows Cathedra Petri in the Bobbio Missal, which points to January 19; when, under the influence of the Roman books the Assumption was moved to August 15, the Marian feast continued to live on (as indicated in the antiphonal of Senlis), and under the influence of the original gospel reading broadened out into a feast of Mary and Martha.

5. CONCLUSION

Exploring the calender from a Frankish perspective brings various aspects to light and calls up questions which deserve further study and reflection. In the eyes and experience of the Franks, the calendar must have undergone radical changes during the transitional period from the eighth to the ninth centuries. Although the whole process of transition, of which several facets have been described here, did not take place overnight, and also did not occur at the same pace everywhere, but must

---

[101] HESBERT: *Antiphonale sextuplex* 31, no. 23bis. Three other antiphonals report this same feast for January 1, *ibidem*: lxxxi-lxxxii and 22-23, no. 16bis.

[102] See A. FRUTAZ: Marius und Martha, in J. HÖFER & K. RAHNER (eds): *Lexikon für Theologie und Kirche* 7 (Freiburg i. Br. 1962²) 89; JOUNEL: *Le culte des saints* 215.

have lasted for some generations, it would still seem more fitting to speak of a revolution than of natural evolution. The changes were more extensive and sweeping than would have been justified by the relatively short time in which they were carried through.

In summary, the most important changes come down to this. The calendar was not only expanded, but also rearranged and restructured in different ways. Diversity, which arose from the local nature of the previous calendars, made way for uniformity. Through this, people were confronted with many new feasts, and many familiar feasts fell into disuse. The composition of the new calendar was to a great extent based on Roman liturgical books, but not all the feasts were taken over uncritically. Feasts or elements from the indigenous tradition were added, and some feasts were moved to other days.

This means that the Frankish calendar shows both continuity and discontinuity with respect to its Gallican predecessors, particularly with respect to the saints' feasts, where the differences appear greatest. They show that the popular devotion to the saints and their cults, which characterized the piety of Merovingian Gaul, persisted into the Carolingian period.[103] But the cult of the saints, which appears to be one of the most prominent and significant aspects of cultural life in Merovingian Gaul,[104] was at the same time radically transformed. Local or regional boundaries were transcended and increasingly left behind by the introduction of an almost uniform calendar, achieved through the distribution of the Frankish books.[105] Only a few feasts from the indigenous calendars were retained. The history of the oldest liturgical books reveals that already, before the eighth century, there was also some degree of mutual interchange between the liturgy of the Roman and Gallican traditions. Before the Carolingians exerted their influence to streamline the liturgy and produce a uniform result, Roman books with a more extensive calendar had already circulated in Gaul, but apparently there yet existed no need at the time to take them over integrally. For that, an incentive from a higher authority would be necessary. This came particularly from Pepin the Short (741-768) and Charlemagne (768-814).

---

[103] Cf. HEN: *Culture and religion* 88.

[104] So HEN: *Culture and religion* 82.

[105] The manifest homogenization of the calendar nonetheless in no way detracts from the fact that in principle, until the Council of Trent, only calendars for individual provinces and dioceses existed; see Ph. HARNONCOURT: Der Kalender, in AUF DER MAUR & HARNONCOURT: *Feiern* 49.

The involvement of the rulers in the revision of the liturgical books also explains why the transformation of the calendar described here could take place in such a relatively short span of time. But at the same time, one can ask if the practices surrounding feasts also developed this quickly, and if they remained in a balanced relation to the transformation of the calendar.

When Christianity made its appearance, the existing calendar, based on cosmic patterns and corresponding to the rhythm of nature, was brought into accord with the needs of Christian liturgy. The pivotal dates in the annual cycle were marked by liturgical feasts. The rhythm of liturgy became an important factor in arranging the year, and corresponded in some respects to the agrarian cycle that defined life in the early Middle Ages.[106] The calendar with its feasts thus had a regulatory function with regard to the ordering and structuring of time. For the calendar to function in this way as a time-control supposes that the cycle of feasts is rooted in religious and cultural life pattern, because the calendar is a reflection of the relation with the cultus on the one side and with the culture and nature on the other. This relationship implies that a change in the calendar will be accompanied by a simultaneous change in the feast culture. Whether there was a simultaneous change of this sort in the time of the Carolingians can be doubted. The transformation of the calendar was rather an attempt to eliminate the differences in existing feast practice and regulate, streamline and make it more uniform, or to further Christianize existing feasts.

The meaning of the saints' feasts and the way in which they were celebrated must also have changed through the changes in the calendar. The degree of involvement in the feasts would have been influenced by the disappearance of local saints, and because people became further removed from the saints not only in terms of identification with familiar places, but also in terms of time. In the period when indigenous Gallican calendars were functioning, people celebrated the feasts of saints who had sometimes lived in the regions involved only a couple of generations earlier. Further, however popular the cult of the saints was, the considerable growth can only have had an inflationary effect. Where in some cases the sanctoral cycle counted over 100 feast days, in addition to those of the temporal cycle, it can only have had the result that not

---

[106] See A. GURJEWITSCH: *Das Weltbild des mittelalterlichen Menschen* (München 1986) 108-109, and HEN: *Culture and religion* 85.

all were celebrated with equal intensity. Because of the mainly small-scale agrarian form of livelihood, the concept of working time perhaps functioned differently than in our present post-industrial context with its peculiar economic patterns, but even then it would have been impossible to celebrate over one third of the days of the year lavishly as feast days,[107] for which rest from labour and attendance at Mass were required.[108] The calendar in the Frankish liturgical books no longer reflects the same feast practice as that which had been customary in Merovingian Gaul. There all feasts were observed similar to the feasts celebrated at Christmas, Easter or any other feast from the temporal cycle. They began with a long night vigil which probably took all night.[109] In the morning, a Mass was celebrated, and that celebration continued outside the church. These festivities, in which people from all strata of society participated, were coupled with singing, drinking and dancing.[110] In the eighth century and later there would still be feasts which were celebrated in this way, but it is beyond the realm of possibility that this happened an average of two or three times a week. There would also have been saints' feasts which would have been much more popular than any of the temporal feasts,[111] but a certain degree of gradation will have been introduced, so that not all feasts were not celebrated as massively and lavishly. Therefore it seems obvious to situate the transformation of the calendar in the monastic milieu, where the liturgical books were also edited and copied out. The structuring of time through an extensive calendrical arrangement of feasts fits in with the rhythm of life in the monasteries, where intensive celebration of the liturgy defines the rhythm of the day, week and year. It is notable that in addition to the monasteries, the expanded calendar was also followed in the episcopal churches in the cities. It would seem that for the parishes, rising in importance in that era,[112] the intensity of feasts assumed by the calendar was as yet aiming too high.

---

[107] Cf. GURJEWITSCH: *Das Weltbild* 304-305.

[108] HARNONCOURT: Der Kalender 52.

[109] So HEN: *Culture and religion* 85. However, we have seen above that the Gallican liturgical books only specify a vigil for Christmas, Epiphany, Easter and Pentecost.

[110] HEN: *Culture and religion* 85-88.

[111] As HEN: *Culture and religion* 88 concluded with regard to Merovingian Gaul.

[112] See PALAZZO: *Le Moyen Âge* 198.

SIBLE DE BLAAUW

FOLLOWING THE CROSSES:
THE PROCESSIONAL CROSS AND THE TYPOLOGY OF
PROCESSIONS IN MEDIEVAL ROME

1. PROCESSION TYPES

A simple inscription on the marble slab covering the tomb of the
Roman John, who lived in the fifth or sixth century, commemorated the
deceased as a *stauroforus*.[1] Evidently, in his days carrying the cross in a
procession was an honourable duty in Roman liturgy. Also other early
Christian testimonies from East and West bear witness to the prestige of
the crosses and of those whose task it was to carry them. The emperor
Justinian (527-565) stressed the importance of the orderly use of the
"holy crosses" in urban processions even in his legislation.[2]

Processions in medieval cities and monasteries were frequent and
manifold. Yet a coherent system of intentions and corresponding
forms underlay this colourful and seemingly heterogeneous custom.
This allows the classification of processions into two main types: per-
sonage-centred and participatory processions.[3] The first category is

---

[1] (Some abbreviations used in the notes, are explained at the end of this contribution.) *Locus iohanNIS STAUROFORI Se vivo fecit*: G.B. DE ROSSI: *Inscriptiones Christianae Urbis Romae* I-II (Roma 1857-1888) I, 232 n. 544; IDEM: Coperchio di sarcofago
rinvenuto presso Ravenna con scultura effigiante una croce cereofora, in *Bullettino di
archeologia cristiana* (Serie V) II (1891) 105-115, esp. p. 113.

[2] TH. MOMMSEN, P. KRÜGER & R. SCHÖLL et al. (eds): *Corpus iuris civilis* I-III
(Dublin/Zürich 1970-1972) III: Novellae 123.32, p. 617: "Sed etiam honorandas
cruces, cum quibus in letaniis ingrediuntur, non alibi nisi in venerabilis locis reponi, et
si quando opus vocaverit ad letanias celebrandas; tunc solum ipsas sanctas cruces
accipere eos qui consuete eas portare solent, et cum episcopo et clericis letanias celebrari." For general discussions of processional crosses, see e.g. J. TURNER (ed.): *Dictionary of art* (London/New York 1996) s.v. Cross; *Enciclopedia dell'Arte Medievale* V
(Rome 1994) s.v. Croce; *Reallexikon zur Byzantinischen Kunst* V (Stuttgart 1991) s.v.
Kreuz; Karl A. SANDIN: *Middle Byzantine bronze crosses of intermediate size: Form, use
and meaning* (= PhD dissertation Rutgers University 1992).

[3] I use the terms of John F. BALDOVIN: *The urban character of Christian worship. The
origins, development, and meaning of stational liturgy* (Roma 1987) 234-238.

characterized by the progress of an important personage, the second
by a circuit traversed by a group of people, often with supplicatory or
penitential overtones. In the former, the number of participants is
strictly limited and the most important objective is that of display
towards spectators. In the latter, collective participation is intended,
and therefore these processions have a distinctly popular component.
The first may be designated as a *cortège*, the second as a *participatory
procession*.

In Roman liturgical sources, both types are easily recognizable, but
a coherent terminology is lacking. The word *processio* and its deriva-
tions are in use for both categories. Terms like *litania / letania* or *collecta* are used in relation to the second type, but, strictly speaking, they
indicate only specific elements in the sequence of ceremonies.[4] The
notion *letania* covers the processional movement from or to a gathering which can be defined as a *collecta*. From the eleventh century
onwards, the former term in the sense of procession gradually disappeared from ritual language. The only meaning of *letania* that
remained was that of a series of petitions, the 'litany', usually sung during these processions.

The cortège may be seen as inherent to the Roman stational system. In order to travel to and from the stational church, the pope and
the clerics and functionaries involved in the celebration would
progress through the city in a formalized way. By contrast, the *letania*
was not necessarily linked to the stational organization. *Letaniae*
could be organized on specific occasions that had nothing to do with
papal celebrations or the stational calendar. One of the earliest examples in Rome are the sevenfold *letaniae* announced by Gregory the
Great in the face of plague epidemics.[5] Yet it is clear from the early
medieval liturgical books that the *collecta* soon became firmly established within the stational system as a penitential exercise that preceded the stational Mass on fast days and on some other days of the
ecclesiastical year.[6]

---

[4] *Ibidem* 158-166.
[5] *Ibidem* 158-159.
[6] Victor SAXER: L'utilisation par la liturgie de l'espace urbain et suburbain: l'exemple de Rome dans l'antiquité et le haut moyen âge, in: *Actes du XIe Congrès International
d'Archéologie Chrétienne. Lyon, Vienne, Grenoble, Genève et Aoste (21-28 septembre 1986)*
I-III (Città del Vaticano 1989) II, 917-1033.

The different intentions and content of the two types of procession found their expression in widely divergent formal characteristics.[7] In the cortège, the dominant mode of progression was equestrian. The pope – as the principal personage of the ceremony – closed the cavalcade, which followed the principle 'the higher in rank, the closer to the pope'. The participatory procession, on the other hand, moved on foot, irrespective of the status of the participants. When the pope and the higher clergy participated, which was not essential to the *letania* – in obvious contrast to the cortège –, the supreme pontiff, surrounded by the clergy, would open the procession and be followed by the people. Clearly, he was not the culmination of the procession, but a prominent participant and the highest intercessor for his people.

The deviations in ritual and form should not mask the fact that both types of procession were essentially liturgical events. The cortège was an intrinsic part of the Roman stational organization. It was the outdoor and 'urban' part of the ceremonial entrance procession of pontifical Mass celebrations. While riding, the pope would wear a vestment appropriate to the Mass, the planet or chasuble.[8] Even in the twelfth century, when the ideological concept of equivalence between pope and emperor had become highly topical in papal ceremonial appearances, the cavalcade to the stational churches retained its traditional liturgical character. Wearing the papal crown in almost twenty processions a year, the pope would still make use of the chasuble and refrain from all too obvious emulation of imperial forms. On the other hand, the *letania* clearly was a more independent liturgical act in itself. It had an established programme of liturgical texts to be sung by the participants for the entire duration of the procession, stressing its supplicatory and penitential intents.

The divergencies between the two main processional forms are reflected in the gradations in the use and significance of the cross as a conspicuous attribute in each type of procession. In this study, the functional characteristics of the processional cross will be discussed on the basis of the ritual directories in the Roman ordines and ceremonials of the early and high Middle Ages.

---

[7] The 'typology' of Roman processions is the theme of my article (based on an analysis of twelfth-century sources) Contrasts in processional liturgy. A typology of outdoor processions in twelfth-century Rome, in: *Actes du colloque Art et Liturgie au Moyen Age* (Lausanne / Fribourg), forthcoming.

[8] This is true for the twelfth century, but apparently not for the early Middle Ages, when after the ride the pope completely changed vestments in the sacristy: OR I 33-35.

2. Early Medieval Stational Liturgy

Two functions of processional crosses may be distinguished regarding their position in the order of the procession: one directly related to the central personage, and the other of opening the procession in a more collective sense. The former function appears to be essential in the papal cavalcade to and from the stational churches. The oldest source directly referring to a specific cross with this purpose is a notice regarding the renewal of a gold cross by pope Leo IV (847-855). It is said that this cross, decorated with gold, silver and jewels, was borne by a subdeacon ahead of the pope's horse "according to ancient custom".[9] The reference to the riding pope clearly distinguishes it from another gold cross listed among Leo's donations.

Leo IV's second cross was a substitute for an older one, donated by Charlemagne.[10] The Carolingian cross, which had the Lateran basilica as its home base, had been robbed a couple of decades after its donation. The memory of this present by the first medieval Roman emperor had remained alive, but only Leo IV saw to its replacement. Leo's new cross of gold encrusted with pearls and jewels, jacinths and prases was explicitly intended to be carried like its predecessor "preceding the holy pontiff during the *letaniae*".[11] Apparently two different crosses were used in the two distinct types of procession, both of precious materials, both carried directly in front of the pope, but

[9] *LP* 105 c. 28: "Fecit (…) crucem auream a noviter, et ipsa crux, ut mos antiquitus, a subdiaconibus manibus ferebatur ante equum praecessorum pontificum, Deo iubente, in auro et in argento in gemmis melius renovavit."

[10] *LP* 98 c. 25: "Item, in basilica Salvatoris domini nostri, quae appellatur Constantiniana, obtulit crucem cum gemmis yacinthis, quam almificus pontifex in letania procedere constituit, secundum petitionem ipsius piisimi imperatoris (…)."

[11] *LP* 105 c. 17: "crucem ex auro purissimo gemmis ornatam, quam Karolus (…) imperator (…), in basilica Salvatoris (…) Constantiniana temporibus domni Leonis (…) tertii papae obtulerat, quae mos erat ut in letaniis ante sacratissimum pontificem ipsa praecederet, et sic permansit usque ad tempus (…) Paschalis papae, unde diabolica suggestione atque instigatione a malis exorta est et eandem a latronibus nocte furtim ablata est, et nullus deinceps praecessorum pontificum, tam domnus Paschalis quam domnus Eugenius, sive domnus Valentinus seu domnus Gregorius necnon et domnus Sergius, recordatus fuit ut eam restauraret et ad usum sanctae Dei ecclesiae Romanae pararet, isdem praefatus et magnificus praesul fecit eam ex auro purissimo, et mirae magnitudinis margaretis et gemmis iacinctinis et prasinis utiliter ornavit, et ad usum pristinum sanctae Dei Romanae ecclesiae mirifice paravit."

definitely not interchangeable: one was destined for the *equitatio*, the other for the *letania*.[12]

Both crosses were clearly personage-centered, since they were meant to go ahead of the supreme pontiff. This use of a processional cross as an attribute of the most important person in the ranks of participants is attested since the mid-sixth century as a widespread custom.[13] The Roman liturgical directories indicate this function in a description of the *letania* on the feast of the Purification from Sant'Adriano to Santa Maria Maggiore, in which the pope is preceded by two candlebearers, a servant with the thurible and two men carrying crosses.[14] The same scheme underlies the Greater Litany, a supplicatory procession on April 25th. Again, the pope is preceded by two candles, the thurible and by two crosses, carried by subdeacons.[15] The candles and the thurible are also part of the usual entrance procession of the stational Mass, but the two crosses directly in front of the pope are only referred to in the case of these solemn *letaniae*. A 'papal' cross in the cortège preceding the stational Mass is not explicitly mentioned in the early medieval ordines, but the above-quoted allusion to 'ancient custom' with regard to such a cross illustrates that it was in use in the *equitatio* as well.

Not the crosses carried in front of the pope during processions, but another category was designated as *cruces stationales* or *stacionariae*. The earliest mention of "crosses that are borne through the stations" is in a guidebook for pilgrims of the second quarter of the seventh century: these crosses are said to be kept in the church of Sant'Anastasia at the foot of the Palatine hill.[16]

---

[12] DUCHESNE: *LP* II, p. 38 note 37 and p. 135 note 9, p. 136 note 16 confuses the functions of Leo's crosses. Cf. ANDRIEU: *OR* III, 242 note 3, who has doubts about Duchesne's interpretation, but equally fails to note the obvious typological distinction made in the source. I myself erroneously followed these authors in: Sible DE BLAAUW: *Cultus et decor. Liturgia e architettura nella Roma tardoantica e medievale: Basilica Salvatoris, Sanctae Mariae, Sancti Petri* I-II (Città del Vaticano 1994) 70, 84.

[13] E.g. concerning bishop Samson of Dol in Brittanny (died 565), and certainly reflecting an established usage: Vita Samsonis Dolensis 2.10, R. FAWTIER: *La vie de St. Samson* (Paris 1912) 165-166: "imago crucis quae ante eum ferri semper solebatur, quamque benedixerat, quae denique auri atque argenti gemmarumque venustatibus circumfuerat sociata".

[14] OR XX 7 (about 770-790).

[15] OR XXI 10; candlebearers OR XXI 18 (about 770-790).

[16] De locis martyrum: Roberto VALENTINI & G. ZUCCHETTI (eds.): *Codice topografico della città di Roma* I-IV (Roma 1940-1953) II, 120: "ubi cruces servantur quae portantur per stationes".

Sant'Anastasia's crosses may be identified with the set of seven processional crosses mentioned in some Roman ordines of the eighth century. One text refers to the same *letania* of the Purification in which two crosses were carried directly in front of the pope. This procession opened with "the seven crosses" borne by functionaries still enjoying the title of their fifth-century predecessor John: *stauroforus*. The crossbearers were "surrounded by people".[17] Between this front group and the pope proceeded the priests and the deacons, whereas the singers of the *schola cantorum* followed behind the pope. Another ordo describes the Greater Litany, with a corresponding order, while giving more details.[18] The procession is opened by painted wooden crosses, carried by the occupants of the *xenodochia*. Since these were paupers or strangers, their role gives a remarkable social colour to the ceremony.[19] Behind them follow the seven "stational crosses", carried by *staurofori*. It is specified that the stational crosses had three burning candles attached to each of them. Hence, the stational crosses are clearly distinguished from the 'papal' crosses, which could be used in the same procession, but in a different position and therefore with a different function.

The seven crosses appear also in the context of the stational Mass. *Ordo Romanus* XV points out that the crosses are brought to the church and set up there to the right side of the presbytery during the Mass.[20] A frame of two timber beams arranged crosswise served as a stand for the crosses. The famous *Ordo Romanus* I for the papal Mass does not mention any cross in the cortège preceding the eucharist, but does speak of crossbearers, now referred to in Latin as *cruces portantes*, among the lower functionaries forming a two-row guard of honour in front of the

---

[17] OR XX 7: "permixti cum populo".

[18] OR XXI 10.

[19] Cf *LP* 94 c. 4 (752-757): the four hostels existing of old are restored and three new ones are founded. The new *Xenodochium in Platana* (later S. Eustachio) is said to have been destined for a hundred "of Christ's poor" and to have been provided with food for them every day. I am not convinced by the alternative interpretation of the *pauperes* as "Heiligtumshüter" by Angelus A. HÄUSSLING: *Mönchskonvent und Eucharistiefeier. Eine Studie über die Messe in der abendländischen Klosterliturgie des frühen Mittelalters und zur Geschichte der Messhäufigkeit* (Münster 1973) 130, 195-196, in relation to the Roman situation.

[20] OR XV 12: "(…)procedunt crocis septem cum psallentio et veniunt ad ecclesiam ubi stacio denunciata fuerit et ponunt ipsas super dua materia in cruce posita, prope gradu in dexteram partem."

choir of the stational church.[21] In both cases, it is implied that the crosses were brought to the church on days that did not have a *collecta* and *letania*, but on which the Mass was directly preceded by a cortège. This means that the seven crosses were used both in the *letania* and in the stational Mass on days without a *letania*.

However, their presence at the stational Mass need not imply that the seven crosses were also part of the papal cortège from the Lateran palace to the stational church. Indeed, there are two circumstances that seem to exclude this possibility. First, their home church far from the Lateran is hardly reconcilable with the cortège having the Lateran as its starting point. The cross bearers would sooner have brought them directly from Sant'Anastasia to the stational church. Secondly, *Ordo Romanus* XV says that the seven crosses proceeded to the church where the *statio* had been announced, "with psalm-singing", a feature alien to the cortège, but characteristic of the *letania*. Hence the procession with the seven crosses may have represented an abbreviated form of the *collecta* liturgy, independent of the cortège that took place more or less simultaneously. Indeed, the ordo seems to include "the rest who carry the crosses" among those who went to the appointed station at daybreak and had "to await the pontiff in the church".[22]

The set of seven crosses made an appearance also in the ceremonial reception of important personages in the city.[23] Crosses, banners and candles or torches were the standard attributes employed in the ritual of solemn *adventus* of the exarch or a friendly ruler.[24] The military chiefs with their banners rode out thirty miles for the first welcome, while other groups with the "venerable crosses" went to a place closer to the city – probably because they were unmounted – to meet the high guest and to accompany him into the city. The crosses are referred to as *signa*.[25]

---

[21] OR I 24, 126.

[22] OR I 24; among these are also the bearers (*baiuli*) of the utensils brought to the stational church from the Lateran vestry.

[23] Louis DUCHESNE: Les régions de Rome au Moyen-Age, in *Mélanges d'archéologie et d'histoire* X (1890) 126-149 [also in: IDEM: *Scripta minora* 1973] esp. pp. 130-131; Achim Thomas HACK: *Das Empfangszeremoniell bei mittelalterlichen Papst-Kaiser-Treffen* (Köln 1999) esp. pp. 325-330.

[24] The reception with torches and crosses is attested as early as 523/525 for the reception of pope John I in Constantinople: *LP* 55 c. 3.

[25] E.g. *LP* 97 c. 35/36 on the reception of Charlemagne under pope Hadrian in 774: "direxit in eius occursum universos iudices ad fere XXX milia ab hac Romana urbe, in loco qui vocatur Nobas: ibi eum cum bandora susceperunt. Et dum adpropinquasset

They may have been ensigns of the seven ecclesiastical districts of the city at that time.[26] They are distinct from the *signa* carried by the *milites draconarii* or *signiferi*: their ensigns were military banners. Both categories played a role in the ceremony, but only the crosses were honoured with the epithets "venerable" and "most holy". Like the seven crosses, also the banners were carried to the stational Mass, but the standard-bearers stood within the chancel enclosure, whereas "those who carry the crosses" stood outside it.[27] The descriptions of *adventus* ceremonies confirm that neither the seven crosses, nor the banners were attributes of the clergy.[28]

The character of a fixed set of seven makes it probable that the above-mentioned objects were identical with those referred to about 856, when pope Benedict III had a set of seven silver crosses restored "that in former times customarily went in procession through all the catholic churches". They were in a sorry state "owing to their great antiquity", and were restored "to their former shape".[29] It seems that these ancient crosses had not been in use for a long time, and the notice can even be read in the sense that they were restored for historical reasons and not with the purpose of returning them to their old function.

Other references to supplicatory processions in the early Middle Ages suggest that the use of a set of special crosses was a characteristic feature of this type of liturgical event. In the monastic liturgy of the abbey of Saint-Riquier in Centula (northern France), described by abbot Angilbert shortly after 800, a group of seven crosses preceded the *leta-*

---

fere unius miliario a Romana urbe, direxit universas scolas militae una cum patronis simulque et pueris qui ad didicendas litteras pergebant, deportantes omnes ramos palmarum adque olivarum, laudesque illi omnes canentes, cum adclamationum earundem laudium vocibus ipsum Francorum susceperunt regem; obviam illi eius sanctitas dirigens venerandas cruces, id est signa, sicut mos est exarchum aut patricium suscipiendum, eum cum ingenti honore suscipi fecit." Cf. *LP* 104 c. 9. *Signon* in Greek: SANDIN: *Middle Byzantine bronze crosses* 6-7.

[26] DUCHESNE: Les régions 129-130; ANDRIEU: *OR* III, p. 70-71 note 2; Th. NOBLE: *The republic of St. Peter. The birth of the Papal State, 680-825* (Philadelphia 1984) 235-236.

[27] OR I 126.

[28] Cf. HACK: *Das Empfangszeremoniell* 326-327 and note 180. Cf. DUCHESNE: Les régions 129-131.

[29] *LP* 106 c. 28: "fecit cruces argenteas 7, quae per olitana tempora per omnes catholicas ecclesias more solito procedebant, prae nimia vetustate confracte fuerant, isdem praeclarus et sanctissimus praesul a noviter restauravit et in pristino statu iterum erexit, qui pens. simul lib. 51 et semis."

niae on the Rogation days.[30] They may have represented the different churches and chapels of the monastery complex, since the central cross was that of the Saviour, from one of the main cult centres of the abbey church. Further back in the procession followed the *cruces forinsecae* of the surrounding villages, also seven in number. The distinguished role of the crosses is underlined by Angilbert's use of the expression "following the crosses" for this type of participatory procession.[31] One is inclined to draw a parallel between the first seven crosses and the Roman stational crosses. The second group of crosses was 'foreign' to the liturgical corporation of the actual monastery and may constitute a parallel to the crosses of individual churches in Rome, which could operate individually and apart from the stational organization. Their existence is documented in sources from the twelfth century, but perhaps also the wooden crosses of the Roman *xenodochia* belonged to this category.

3. *EQUITATIO* AND *LETANIA* IN THE HIGH MIDDLE AGES

The crucial role of the cross in the cortège of the Roman pontiff is corroborated by the privileges in which the popes of the Reform period granted a limited number of bishops the right to use the white horse, to wear the pallium and to have the processional cross carried in their equestrian processions. Evidently, the cross was considered to be one of the insignia of solemn papal appearances. It is said to "face" the pontiff during the cavalcade; in other words, it was clearly set in a specific relation-

---

[30] ANGILBERTUS: *Institutio* 9 in K. HALLINGER et al. (eds.): *Initia consuetudinis benedictinae: Consuetudines saeculi octavi et noni* (= Corpus consuetudinum monasticarum 1) (Siegburg 1963) 296-299. On other occasions the group might be reduced to three, e.g. *ibidem* 11, p. 300.

[31] *Ibidem* 11, p. 300: "cruces sequi". Cf. the expression "crucem portare et litanias facere" in the contemporary *Supplex libellus* 19, in *Initia consuetudinis* (above, note 30), p. 326. Cf. also HRABANUS MAURUS: *Homiliae de festis* 19 (822-825), J.P. MIGNE: *Patrologia Latina* CX, 38: "In Litaniis: Cum autem sanctae cruces et sanctorum reliquiae cum litaniis a clero exportantur, ipsi non insistunt precibus, neque sequuntur vexillum sanctae crucis cum laudibus, sed super phaleratos resiliunt equos, discurrunt per campos, ora dissolvunt risu, alterutrumque se praecurrere gestiunt (…)". The Early Christian roots of the essential role of "cruces sanctae" in letaniae are visible in the *Corpus iuris civilis*, above, note 2. *Cross* as a synecdoche for *procession* in more recent language: Peter Jan MARGRY: *Teedere Quaesties: Religieuze rituelen in conflict. Confrontaties tussen katholieken en protestanten rond de processiecultuur in 19e-eeuws Nederland* (Hilversum 2000) 61-62.

ship to the principal actor of the procession (fig. 1).[32] Moreover, the priv-
iliges underline the significance of the processional cross as a symbol of

Fig. 1. Pope on horseback preceded by cross-bearer, intaglio with inscription
INAEMA (Innocentius ascendit equum mitratus alte?). Florence, Palazzo
Pitti, Museo degli Argenti, inv.no. 319.

triumph in using the term "the Lord's standard".[33] In the ceremonial
texts of the sixteenth century, it is specified that only in processions with
the presence of the pope or a privileged bishop will the cross be borne
with the crucifix facing the central figure.[34]

---

[32] E.g. the privilege for Trier 975, J.P. MIGNE: *Patrologia Latina* CXXXVII, 322: "crux
ante eumdem, sicut et ante Ravennatum archipraesulem, ubi ubi geratur"; for Bamberg
1146, J. VON PFLUGK-HARTTUNG (ed.): *Acta pontificum romanorum inedita* I-III
(Stuttgart 1881-1888) III, 83-84: "(...) ante faciem tuam crucem portari concedimus".

[33] E.g. Innocent II to bishop Syrus of Genoa 1133, VON PFLUGK-HARTTUNG: *Acta*
II, 274: "(...) in processionibus uti et crucem, vexillum videlicet dominicum, per
subiectam vobis provinciam portandi tibi tuisque successoribus damus."

[34] Agostino FIVIZZANI: *De ritu sanctissimae Crucis romano pontifici praeferendae com-
mentarius* (Romae 1592) 73. This was a long-standing custom in papal liturgy, witness the
Ceremonial of Patrizi Piccolomini (1488): Marc DYKMANS: *L'oeuvre de Patrizi Piccolomini
ou le Cérémonial papal de la première Renaissance* I-II (Città del Vaticano 1980-1982), nn.
1065 (addition in note) and 1320.

The cross that in the ninth century is mentioned as having for many centuries been carried ahead of the pope on horseback, is referred to in the twelfth-century ordines as the *crux domini pontificis* or *crux papalis*. It was used during the stational celebrations (fig. 2). Inside the church

Fig. 2. Pope in procession with cross and banners, detail from: The translation of St. Clement's relics, fresco, late eleventh century. Rome, San Clemente, lower church (copy after J. WILPERT: *Die Römischen Mosaiken und Malereien der kirchlichen Bauten vom IV. bis XIII. Jahrhundert* (Freiburg 1916) IV, Taf. 239).

it was carried at the head of the entrance procession from the sacristy to the altar; outside the church, it was the only cross specified in the cavalcade.[35] The bearer of the cross was a young subdeacon of the Lateran palace, which confirms the character of the papal cross as one of the insignia of the pope in function.[36] In the Lateran, even a department of four clerics was formed as the *schola crucis*, presumably consisting of the subdeacon of the papal cross and other functionaries responsable for the ceremonial.[37] The papal subdeacon, holding the cross, rode at the head of the procession, while just in front or just behind him came the military standard-bearers on horseback, who carried the twelve *vexilla* or *bandora* representing the twelve wards or *regiones* into which the city had been divided since the tenth century.[38] These clearly were the successors of the old *milites draconarii*. Even if the cross was carried at some distance of the pontiff, separated from him by several clerical groups, it was clearly one of his attributes. This is confirmed not only by its name and ritual context, but also by high medieval representations of the pope, in which he is frequently depicted in the close company of a subdeacon bearing the papal cross (fig. 3).[39]

In the ordines of the first half of the twelfth century, the designation for the principal attribute of the *letaniae* is *crux stationalis*. The term is identical with that applied in the early Middle Ages to a group of seven silver crosses, which had multiple functions but were not used in the papal cortège. Nothing is heard of the set of seven silver crosses after their restoration in the 850s. This may have to do with the disappearance of the ancient seven districts and the formation of twelve military wards. The twelfth-century stational cross is a solitary object, carried directly in front of the pope, and used only in the *letania*. In this sense, it is the successor both of the above-mentioned, precious, ninth-century cross said to have preceded the pope in the *letania*, and of the seven silver crosses.

[35] Entrance procession: OR Ben 17.

[36] OR Cenc 7.

[37] OR Cenc 4; cf Gaetano MORONI: *Dizionario di erudizione storico-ecclesiastica* (103/6 vols. Venezia 1840-1879) XVIII (1843) 252.

[38] OR Ben 21 / OR Cenc 7.

[39] E.g. two scenes of the Legend of St. Alexius in the lower church of S. Clemente (the same gemmed cross as was carried in the procession with the relics of St. Clement in the narthex), our figs. 2-3; the Presentation of the Tiara in the Cappella di San Silvestro, SS. Quattro Coronati. Cf. a similar use of the patriarch's cross in Middle Byzantine liturgy in Constantinople: SANDIN: *Middle Byzantine bronze crosses* 84-88.

Fig. 3. The legend of S. Alexis, fresco, late eleventh century. Rome, San Clemente, lower church (copy after WILPERT: *Römische Mosaiken* IV Taf. 242).

It seems that the twelfth-century stational cross was not a single object, but that various churches owned a special cross that might be elected to assume this role in the *letania*. For the simple *collecta* and procession to the stational church on the weekdays of Lent and the Ember days, the cross of St. Peter's served as the stational cross.[40] Peter Mallius brings this fact to the fore in his propagandistic treatise on the Vatican basilica of the third quarter of the twelfth century, in order to emphasize the primacy of St. Peter's among the churches of the city.[41]

Like the papal cross in the cortège, the stational cross was always carried by a subdeacon; however, it was not a member of the papal palace, but the prior of the *subdiaconi regionarii* who performed this function in the *letania*. He, the coordinating officer in charge of the execution of the stational liturgy, was in fact the central figure of the supplicatory processions by virtue of his bearing the cross and singing the litany. This illustrates the different contexts of the two crosses: the papal cross belonged to the sphere of the papal court, whereas the stational cross was a symbol of the collectivity of Roman churches, united in the stational system. Yet the fact that the latter was carried directly in front of the pope gives it a connotation different from that of the early medieval silver crosses. The stational cross, however, significantly differed from the papal cross in that it was not dependent on the pope's presence: it was also used in the frequent *letaniae* without papal participation.[42]

The dominating role of the stational cross does not rule out the presence of the papal cross in the *letania* with the pope. There are some reasons to suspect that the eighth-century tradition of carrying two crosses in front of the pope by the twelfth century had been reinterpreted so as to have the stational and the papal cross precede the pontiff in the *letania*.[43] In contemporary representations of pontifical ritual, a pair of processional crosses is sometimes depicted in the context of a procession on foot.[44]

Apart from the stational and possibly the papal cross, the crosses of individual churches might be carried in *letaniae*, at the head of the

---

[40] OR Ben 10.

[41] DBV 38, 40, pp. 422-423, 424.

[42] OR Ben 74.

[43] The twelfth-century Roman Ordo in Basel reports the use of both crosses together: "Et sic induti procedunt, sicut mos est, cruce domini pape et stationali cruce precedente", Bernhard SCHIMMELPFENNIG: *Die Zeremonienbücher der römischen Kurie im Mittelalter* (Tübingen 1973) 374.

[44] E.g. the Translation of St. Magnus's relics in the crypt of the cathedral at Anagni (13th c.). Cf. a letania in Constantinople depicted in the chronicle of Skylitzes (12th c.), Madrid Biblioteca Nacional Virt. 26-2, f. 210v: John A. COTSONIS: *Byzantine figural processional crosses* (= Dumbarton Oaks Byzantine Collection publications 10) (Washington D.C. 1994) 23.

respective sections of the laity or clergy participating in the procession. This was the case, for instance, with the chapters of the patriarchal basilicas in the Greater Litany. They were an integral part of the procession with the pope.[45] The crosses of the individual churches, *cruces Romanae civitatis*, were used in a parallel procession on the same day, both processions ending up at the stational Mass in St. Peter's.[46] Here papal clerks would record which of the almost three hundred churches had sent their cross, in order to pay them a gratuity.[47] The crosses of the churches were also used in the small processions from the respective churches to the collective point of departure of the *letania* proper.[48] These parallel processions were identifiable by the crosses and, on three Marian feasts, by the images of the Virgin carried by the eighteen deaconries.[49] In the church of gathering, all the groups with their respective crosses would in turn proceed to the high altar to pray and then line up for the *collecta* service and the collective procession to follow.[50]

There can be no doubt, however, about the central role of the stational cross in the ritual. It was set beside or on top of the high altar during the *collecta* service and taken up by the first regional subdeacon as a sign to begin the procession.[51] On some occasions at least, the cross was carried out from the *collecta* church in a special way. The regional subdeacon seems to have held the cross directly in his hands, resting it horizontally on his arms so that it could be kissed by the congregation. Only from the start of the outdoor procession was the cross held in an upright position.[52] Usually, the procession ended with the singing of the

---

[45] OR Ben 57, OR Cenc 64.

[46] OR Ben 56: "Eodem die [in letania maiore] omnes cruces Romane civitatis cum clero et populo honorifice cum processione procedunt ad S. Marcum."

[47] OR Cenc 65, 67.

[48] OR Ben 56, OR Cenc 6. Probably the crosses of the churches had also taken over the role of the ancient stational crosses in the reception of rulers, see e.g. Ordo XVII 1, R. ELZE (ed.): *Ordines coronationis imperialis. Die Ordines für die Weihe und Krönung des Kaisers und der Kaiserin* (= MGH Fontes iur. Ger. ant. 9) (Hannover 1960) 62: "Cum rex in imperatorum electus pervenerit ad portam Collinam (…) recipiatur honorifice a clero urbis cum crucibus et thuribulis, et processionaliter deducatur usque ad gradus basilice sancti Petri (…)"

[49] OR Alb 11.

[50] OOL 194, pp. 95-96, OOL 198, pp. 98-99.

[51] OR Ben 29.

[52] OR Ben 29, 57.

litany by the same 'leader' of the ceremony, as he proceeded with the cross to the altar of the stational church.[53]

The *letania* was subject to significant changes in the second half of the twelfth century. The most striking shift was that the pope moved to the tail of the clerical part of the procession, which had never been the case in the *letania*.[54] The *crux stationalis* virtually disappears from the descriptions of papal ceremonial. Its role in the *letania* with the pope was taken over completely by the papal cross, which was not carried directly in front of the pope, but at the beginning of the section with the higher and curial clergy, in an order not unlike that of the cortège.[55] Probably, it was only at this reorganization that the *schola crucis* was created.[56]

The development of the Good Friday procession may illustrate the shift. At the beginning of the twelfth century, the role of the stational cross in this procession from the Lateran to Santa Croce was twofold. It would have been recognizable for everybody in its usual function of processional cross – and indeed, it was carried by the regional subdeacon, as in each *letania*. But the particular way in which it was carried moreover made it an object of veneration: the bearer did not hold it aloft on a staff, but held it directly to his breast, and – on this occasion – it was covered with a veil.[57] By the last decades of the century its two functions

---

[53] OR Ben 29, 34.

[54] This is illustrated by the position of the *schola cantorum* in the processional order: traditionally it followed the pope, now it went ahead of him: OR Cenc 12, 15.

[55] OOL 193, p. 95. A century later, a similar scheme is given in the Ceremonial of Gregory X (1273): Marc DYKMANS: *Le cérémonial papal de la fin du moyen âge à la renaissance* I-IV (Bruxelles 1977-1985) I, 217 n. 293, with some variants.

[56] See OR Cenc 64, where "one of the *scola crucis*" sings the litany, traditional task of the subdeacon-crossbearer (e.g. OR Ben 57). This implies that the *schola crucis* combined the remaining duties of the subdeacon *regionarius* in the letania with the papal-cross duties of the palace subdeacon in processions with papal participation (cf. above, note 37).

[57] OR Ben 42. Cf. the eighth-century ritual of OR XXIII 11, in which the cruciform gemmed reliquary of the palace chapel was borne in the procession, a custom that reappeared later in the twelfth century (OR Cenc 28). I nevertheless would not identify the particular stational cross of the Good Friday procession as described by OR Ben with the gemmed relic cross of the Sancta Sanctorum: OR Ben 74 clearly distinguishes the cross reliquary from the *crux stationalis* in the liturgy of the Exaltation of the Cross, where both are used. Moreover, the *Descriptio* of the Lateran of the late 11th century refers to the relic cross of the palace chapel as used in the procession of the Exaltation only: VALENTINI & ZUCCHETTI: *Codice topografico* III, 356.

had been split up. As a processional cross, it had been replaced by the papal cross. The fact that this was carried by a regional subdeacon still was reminiscent of the earlier situation. On the other hand, as an object of veneration, it was superseded by the relic cross from the Sancta Sanctorum, held by a cardinal.[58]

The occasional use of a processional cross as an object of veneration seems to have been typical for the *crux stacionalis*. The epithet 'venerable' applied to it in the eighth century may be recalled here. It suggests the presence of a relic in the crosses used for this function, a well-known phenomenon in the genre of processional crosses from early times.[59] However, unequivocal evidence for Rome is lacking.[60] Be this as it is, the custom of venerating a processional cross is no longer documented after the mid-twelfth century. As we have seen, the *crux papalis* appeared as the principal processional cross around the same time. This merely was a processional prop, never used for veneration. At least two versions of the papal cross existed. In the *letania* the plainer of these will have been used, as it is said that in the Great Litany the 'everyday' cross was carried: the *crux cotidiana domini papae*.[61] Probably a more 'solemn' papal cross was used in the cortège and entrance procession on the high feasts of the year.

The specific stational function of the cross of St. Peter's did remain alive, but it was now simply called *crux Sancti Petri*. On Ash Wednesday it would be carried in the procession together with the papal cross, but it still had priority over the latter in the stational church, Santa Sabina, where – according to tradition – the cross of St. Peter's was brought to the altar.[62] The different functional context of the two crosses was evident also from their bearers: the traditional prior of the regional sub-

---

[58] OR Cenc 28.
[59] E.g. Cyril MANGO: La croix dite de Michel le Cérulaire et la croix de Saint-Michel de Sykéôn, in *Cahiers archéologiques* 36 (1988) 41-49, esp. p. 41; COTSONIS: *Byzantine figural processional crosses* 28: here a distinction has to be made between cruciform reliquaries that could be carried in a procession and processional crosses with a relic container.
[60] A surviving example of a processional cross with relics at its intersection in Lazio is the late thirteenth-century silver-gilt cross from Casamari abbey with a crucifix on the obverse and a Cross relic and evangelists on the reverse (87 x 56 cm), in the Tesoro of the Cathedral of Veroli: Luisa MORTARI: La croce nell'oreficeria del Lazio dal Medioevo al Rinascimento, in *Rivista dell'Istituto Nazionale d'Archeologia e Storia dell'Arte* S. III 2 (1979) 229-345, esp. p. 251.
[61] OR Cenc 63.
[62] OR Cenc 15-16.

deacons for the cross of St. Peter's and a 'papal' subdeacon for the cross of the pope. This seems a typical case of the survival of old liturgical traditions on the most eminent moments of the ecclesiastical year.[63]

4. PHYSICAL AND FORMAL CHARACTERISTICS OF ROMAN PROCESSIONAL CROSSES

The first, scarce Roman examples that allow a confrontation with the documentary sources date from the sixth century. A uniquely preserved piece is the gemmed cross donated by the Eastern emperor Justin II (565-578).[64] It was heavily restored even at an early date, but some features still indicate its use as a processional cross. Its height of 41 cm is in keeping with the usual size of Byzantine processional crosses of the time.[65] It has a double-sided decoration, and it seems to have had a pin for fixing it onto a pole for carrying. A similar type of gemmed cross is depicted on a fresco datable to the sixth or seventh century, in the catacomb of Pontian on the Via Portuense. It is a Latin cross with slightly flaring ends; its lateral arms have *pendelia* in the shape of the letters Alpha and Omega and are surmounted by brackets with burning candles.[66] Both the tangible and the painted cross are difficult to relate to any documented category of cross, other than the processional cross. As for the sources, some texts indeed speak of candles atop crosses used in processions.[67] This use is corroborated in Rome by an eighth-century notice on the stational crosses (see above). This type, which seems to have disappeared in the high Middle Ages, may have been specific for the use in *letaniae*.

Of special relevance in the context of processional crosses are those crosses designed to stand close to the altar (figs. 4-5). Leo III donated

---

[63] Baumstark's "Gesetz der Erhaltung des Alten in liturgisch hochwertiger Zeit", cited in Theodor KLAUSER: *Kleine abendländische Liturgiegeschichte* (Bonn 1965) 56.

[64] Tesoro di San Pietro, see Anatole FROLOW: *La relique de la Vraie Croix: Recherches sur le développement d'un culte* (Paris 1961) 180-181; *Reallexikon zur Byzantinischen Kunst* V (Stuttgart 1991) 152-153.

[65] MANGO: La croix 41-43.

[66] DE ROSSI: *Inscriptiones* I, 107, 113-114.

[67] E.g. GREGORIUS TURONENSIS: *In gloria confessorum* 78, B. KRUSCH (ed.): *Monumenta Germaniae historica. Scriptores rerum Merovingicarum* I, 1 (Hannover 1884) p. 796: "Adsumpta igitur palla de beati sepulchro, conponunt in modum feretri; accensis super cruces cereis atque cereferalibus, dant voces in canticis, circumeunt urbem cum vicis." Cf. ANDRIEU: *OR* III, p. 241.

Fig. 4. Procession approaching church, miniature from 'Stuttgart Psalter', Northern France, first half ninth century. Württembergische Landesbibliothek, Stuttgart Fol. 23, f. 118v (Bildarchiv Foto Marburg).

Fig. 5. Altar with processional cross attached to it, miniature from 'Stuttgart Psalter', Northern France, first half ninth century. Württembergische Landesbibliothek, Stuttgart Fol. 23, f. 130v (Bildarchiv Foto Marburg).

two different silver crosses to stand next to St. Peter's high altar: an adorned *crucifix* of 52 pounds of pure silver and a *crux maior* of 22 pounds, silver-gilt.[68] The terms suggest that the latter was an aniconic cross, the former a cross bearing an image of the crucified Christ. After the sack of Rome by the Saracens, Leo IV donated a gilt silver crucifix of 77 pounds with gems, perhaps as a replacement for Leo III's crucifix.[69] He also provided a fine gold cross with jewels and precious stones, to stand on a silver support on the right-hand side of St. Peter's high altar.[70] This must have been the successor of the earlier *crux maior*. The staff that supported the cross was "renewed" by Leo IV, who added silver plating to it with a dedicatory inscription.

The crosses flanking the altar seem to have belonged to different types. The crucifix with its specific iconographical message suggests a permanent association with the eucharistic altar, and thus it was the predecessor of the later altar cross. Conversely, the other cross may have been removed occasionally to serve as a processional cross.[71] The rod may have provided an adjustable fitting which allowed its removal. Indeed few processional crosses are known in the Christian world of the early Middle Ages with a representation of the crucified Christ. The standard design was a double-sided aniconic decoration, preferably with precious stones.[72] The first known processional crosses with a crucifix in the Roman area date from the later twelfth

[68] *LP* 98 c. 48: "fecit crucifixum ex argento purissimo, qui stat iuxta altare maiore, mire magnitudinis decoratum, pens. lib. 52." *LP* 98 c. 87: "Fecit et crucem maiorem ex argento purissimo deaurata, qui stat iuxta altare maiore, pens. lib. 22." Cf. the donations for S. Paolo of one gemmed gold *crux maior* (42 lib.?) and a pure silver *crucifix* (52 lib.): *LP* 98 c. 60 / 97.

[69] *LP* 105 c. 46: my arguments are the relative uniqueness of silver crucifixes in the *LP* donation lists and the correspondence in weight. Cf. the other silver crucifix provided by Leo IV for St. Peter's and placed between the columns of the nave, also as a replacement for a predecessor donated by Leo III: *LP* 105 c. 89 and *LP* 98 c. 39.

[70] *LP* 105 c. 56: "Obtulit (…) crucem ex auro purissimo ex diversis gemmis, iaquintinis, albis, exmaragdis, mirae magnitudinis ornata, quae stat parte dextra iuxta altare maiore; in qua etiam noviter renovavit virga et deargentavit eam, in qua predicta cruce continetur, pens. lib. argenti 11 et semis, legente de nomen domni Leoni quarti papae."

[71] Cf. Joseph BRAUN: *Das christliche Altargerät in seinem Sein und in seiner Entwicklung* (München 1932) 467-469, 478-480. Pairs of (processional) crosses standing close to the altar are represented in several miniatures from the eleventh-thirteenth centuries, see Peter SPRINGER: *Kreuzfüße. Ikonographie und Typologie eines hochmittelalterlichen Gerätes* (Berlin 1981), figs. A12-A14.

[72] Cf. COTSONIS: *Byzantine figural processional crosses* 42-46.

century.[73] On the other hand, the image of the crucified Christ did not exclude the cross being adorned with gems, as Leo IV's donation proves.

The specific tradition of the crosses flanking the altar of St. Peter's is still tangible in the twelfth century. Leo IV's bejewelled gold cross to the right is said to have been robbed in 1130 and between 1138 and 1143 to have been replaced by Innocent II with a large silver-gilt cross. Innocent also renewed the "stational cross, that went through the stations".[74] This was obviously not the *crux maior* standing to the right, but like it, it is mentioned in the context of the high altar. This must have been "the Lord's cross, taken from St. Peter's most holy altar to lead the people in penitence to the stations during Lent", referred to by Mallius.[75] And so it was the *crux Sancti Petri* that still functioned in the tradition of the stational cross in the later twelfth century.[76] Even in the fifteenth-century inventories of the basilica, a tall silver *crux stationaria* is listed.[77] Another tall cross of gold and silver, adorned with precious stones is referred to as *crux Constantini*.[78] This designation is applied also to a processional cross in the Lateran (see below).

Towards the end of the thirteenth century, a crucifix must have become the standard type of the Roman processional cross. The 1295 inventory of the papal treasury lists three crosses to be carried "in front of the pope",

[73] E.g. the Cross of the Santuario di Vallepietra, 31 x 24 cm, engraved gilt copper, with a figure of the dead Christ in the round, once in the Tesoro of the Cathedral at Anagni: MORTARI: La croce 230-232.

[74] *LP* II, p. 380 (Boso); DBV 56, p. 436: "Innocentius papa II ad ornatum altaris beati Petri fecit fieri magnam crucem argenteam pensantem .c. libras, et deauratam posuit iuxta altare beati Petri manu dextera. Renovavit etiam crucem stationalem, quae vadit per stationes, et beati Petri altare optimis et deauratis vestibus vestivit."

[75] DBV 38, p. 422-423: "sumitur de sanctissimo altari Beati Petri crux domnica, quae praecedat populum paenitentem per totam quadragesimam ad stationes euntem. Quae nimirum crux stationalis ob Christi et eius Apostoli reverentiam in tanta veneratione a cunctis est habita, quod, sicut cantores et regionarii asserunt, hac cruce non delata, immunes ab statione saepe recedant."

[76] OR Cenc 15.

[77] Inventarium S. Petri 1436, E. MÜNTZ & A.L. FROTHINGHAM: Il tesoro della basilica di S. Pietro in Vaticano dal XIII al XV secolo, con una scelta di inventari inediti, *Archivio della Società romana di storia patria* 6 (1883) 1-137, esp. p. 54: "Crux magna de argento alba, que stationaria dicitur." Cf. Inventarium S. Petri 1454-1455, *ibidem*, p. 89: "crux processionalis".

[78] Inventarium S. Petri 1454-1455, *ibidem*, p. 89: "Crux Constantini magna de auro et argento, cum lapidibus, et pede ligneo coperto de argento."

which must be three versions of the *crux papalis*.[79] They are said to have the image of the crucified Christ on one side, "in relief". One cross is of gold, the others are of gilt silver. The associated "apples" will be knops with an opening for the tang of the cross, and a spherical attachment to fit over the top of the staff.[80] Only one of these crosses is still specified as a processional cross in the inventory of 1311: it is the silver one with the crucifix in relief, of which we now hear that the reverse has the Lamb of God in the centre and the evangelists at the ends, a well-known iconographical scheme for double-sided crosses since the twelfth century.[81]

The only surviving specimen of a Roman processional cross from the period is the famous silver cross of the Lateran with a narrative cycle of the Book of Genesis in relief.[82] Probably dating from the first decades of the fourteenth century, it may have been designated to serve as the processional cross of the recently founded secular chapter of the basilica. The absence of a crucifix and the emphasis on an extensive figural programme make it a remarkable piece. In later centuries, this cross was associated with the emperor Constantine, founder of the basilica. Even in the eighteenth century it was carried in processions through the city, by "robust men", together with a late Gothic processional cross of the crucifix type containing a relic of the True Cross.[83]

[79] Inv. Thesauri Sedis Apostolicae 1295, Émile MOLINIER: Inventaire du trésor du Saint-Siège sous Boniface VIII (1295), in *Bibliothèque de l'École des Chartes* 1882-1888, 1-140, esp. pp. 50-51, nn. 434-436: "Item unam crucem de auro que portatur coram papa in qua est [ex] una parte Crucifixus. Item unam crucem ad portandum coram domino de argento deaurato cum Crucifixo relevato et pomo cum canulo longo iii digitis; pond. vi m. Item, unam aliam crucem similem isti, pro consimili officio; pond. v. m."

[80] *Ibidem*, n. 437: "duo poma de argento deaurata cum duobus cruciculis simplicibus; pond. ii m. et v. unc." Cf. COTSONIS: *Byzantine figural processional crosses* 112-113.

[81] Inv. Thesauri Ecclesiae Romanae 1311, CLEMENS V: *Regestum (...) cura et studio monachorum ordinis sancti Benedicti* (8 vols. Roma 1885-1888), Appendices 1892, pp. 384-385: "aliam crucem de argento, deauratam, cum crucifixo relevato, que consuevit portari ante papam in asta; et sunt in parte superiori lictere Ihesus Nazarenus rex iudeorum; a parte posteriori est agnus dei in medio, et in quatuor angulis sunt quatuor evangeliste, ponderis duarum librarum quinque unciarum et dimidie." For a preserved example of this type, see the cross of Vallepietra, mentioned above, note 73.

[82] Ulrike KOENEN: *Das "Konstantinskreuz" im Lateran und die Rezeption frühchristlicher Genesiszyklen im 12. und 13. Jahrhundert* (Worms 1995).

[83] FIVIZZANI: *De ritu* 51; DE BLAAUW: *Cultus et decor* 316 note 264; KOENEN: *Das "Konstantinskreuz"* 28-29. On imperial connotations of processional crosses and an early assocation with Constantine in Constantinople: COTSONIS: *Byzantine figural processional crosses* 8-11.

Other processional crosses are listed in the inventories of churches, for instance in S. Maria Maggiore in the later fifteenth century. A tall cross "that is carried in *letaniae*" is described as a wooden construction covered with silver, on one side decorated with an image of the Virgin, on the other side with the crucifix, and having relics in its "foot".[84] These clearly are successors of the chapter and church crosses referred to in the high medieval *letaniae*.

The documentary evidence suggests that until the thirteenth century both the papal and the stational crosses were aniconic crosses of considerable size, made of precious metal and frequently adorned with gems. This image corresponds well with high medieval depictions of liturgical scenes.

There may have been no essential difference between the Roman stational cross and the Byzantine *litanikos stauros* as depicted in the Menologion of Basil II, about 1000: a tall Latin cross with precious stones and small *pendelia*, a cleric holding it by its tang.[85] The fact that the Roman stational cross had to be carried both in a horizontal and an upright position, suggests the existence of a short staff or only a tang on the cross itself. The representations in the Roman area from the late eleventh century onwards depict only the papal cross. It is always carried on a long staff, ranging from a modest to a relatively tall size (translated into reality approximately 30 to 60 cm long), aniconic, apparently made of metal and decorated with precious stones and frequently attached to the staff by means of a knop. Even if it depicts a procession on foot, the late-eleventh-century relic-translation fresco in the lower church of San Clemente probably shows the attributes of the cortège: a tall processional cross with gems on a high staff and several staffs topped with a golden cross beneath which hangs a length of red, white-speckled cloth, presumably the military banners (fig. 2).[86]

---

[84] Paolo De Angelis, *Basilicae S. Mariae Maioris de Urbe (…) descriptio et delineatio* (Romae 1621), p. 136 (Inventory 1480 c.): "Crux una magna de ligno cooperta argento, quae portatur per litanias, in medio ipsius ab uno latere est imago Virginis Mariae, ab alio latere est Crucifixus, et cum nonnullis reliquiis in pede et quibusdam imaginibus in capite, pede et lateribus."

[85] COTSONIS: *Byzantine figural processional crosses* 20-24. The Byzantine influence on the development of processional crosses in Rome may be worth a specific study.

[86] The red colour of the banners is confirmed by thirteenth-century sources: Pontificale romanae curiae (saec. XIII) xiii B 34: Michel ANDRIEU (ed.): *Le pontifical romain au moyen-âge* I-IV (Città del Vaticano 1938-1941) II, 376.

5. CONCLUSION

Functional differentiations that may be made regarding the crosses used in Roman processional liturgy have two aspects. On the one hand, a cross was an attribute, appropriate to either a person or a group. On the other, a cross was a requisite in a specific type of procession.

The papal cross was an attribute of the pontiff, and it could be used in both the cortège and the *letania* (if the pope participated in the latter). The seven stational crosses were an attribute of the Christian community of the city, organized in districts. They could only be used in processions of the *letania* type, appropriate as they were to the *letania*'s participatory character. The painted wooden crosses of the *xenodochia* also belong to the category of collective attributes used in the *letania*. The stational crosses, however, clearly enjoyed a higher and more official status. The Roman stational crosses were employed as a group, and were stored collectively in one church. This distinguishes them from crosses that could be carried individually at the head of specific groups in processions from different directions. Their functional unity seems to have converged in the single stational cross that was employed in the high medieval *letaniae*.

The high medieval stational cross no longer bore any relationship to the districts, but seems to have represented the entire Roman community of churches. It stood literally closer to the pope, but its use depended in no way on the pope's actual presence. Although during *letaniae* with participation of the pope its liturgical use coincided more and more with that of the papal cross, its special significance must still have been sensed. The stational cross was a symbol of the stational system, the papal cross only an attribute of the principal actor. The papal cross was a sign of papal presence in the procession, whereas the stational cross was an object with a real liturgical function.

Crosses had a more essential function in the *letania* than in the cortège. The stational cross could be venerated; the crosses of the churches were the symbols of the constituent parts of the Christian community of Rome. The crosses might even be regarded as the subject of the processions: the crosses proceed, people and clergy follow. The crosses were objects of piety, and at the same time a means of corporative propaganda.

Common to all the various types of the participatory procession is the concept of 'following'. The ranks of participants followed the stational cross, the icon of Christ, or the ensigns of the Roman churches. The principle of the *letania* was often paraphrased as "following the crosses", and indeed this was quite the opposite of the cortège, which culminated in the principal character at its end. When the old *letania* tradition faded in the second half of the twelfth century, the papal cross took over the central role of the stational cross in the few *letaniae* still practised at the urban level and with papal participation. The crosses of the individual chapters and churches continued to be employed in supplicatory processions, but exclusively as attributes of their own groups of participants in processions of a limited scale. The monopoly of the papal cross symbolized the growing importance of the doctrine of universal papal power and marked the end of the old concept of urban liturgy.

Abbreviations

DBV	Descriptio basilicae Vaticanae: Roberto Valentini / G. Zucchetti eds, *Codice topografico della città di Roma*, 4 vols. Roma 1940-1953, III (1946)
LP	Liber Pontificalis: Louis Duchesne ed., *Le Liber Pontificalis. Texte, introduction et commentaire*, 2 vols. Paris 1886-1892; *Additions et corrections*, C. Vogel ed., Paris 1957
OOL	Ordo Officiorum Lateranensis, by Bernardus: *Bernhardi cardinalis et Lateranensis Ecclesiae prioris Ordo officiorum*, L. Fischer ed., München 1916
OR	Ordo Romanus: Michel Andrieu ed., *Les ordines romani du haut moyen-âge*, 5 vols. Louvain 1931-1961
OR Alb	Ordo Romanus of Albinus: Paul Fabre / Louis Duchesne eds, *Le Liber Censuum de l'Église romaine*, 2 vols. Paris 1910, 1952, II
OR Ben	Ordo Romanus of Benedictus Canonicus: Fabre - Duchesne, *Liber Censuum*, II
OR Cenc	Ordo Romanus of Cencius Camerarius: Fabre - Duchesne, *Liber Censuum*, I

BERT GROEN

THE FESTIVAL OF THE PRESENTATION OF THE LORD: ITS ORIGIN, STRUCTURE AND THEOLOGY IN THE BYZANTINE AND ROMAN RITES

The Festival of the Presentation of the Lord is known to most of us only as a small one in the church year.[1] Between Christmas and Epiphany on the one side and Lent and Easter on the other, it is not very conspicuous. In the Byzantine rite it belongs to the cycle of the Twelve Festivals – the main ones in the liturgical year – but is hardly celebrated. Nevertheless, it is an important one in the Epiphany cycle. Besides, Simeon's words, "Let now Your servant depart in peace, Lord ...", are a central part of evening prayer: vespers in Byzantine and compline in Roman rite.

I will confine myself to the Festival of the Presentation of the Lord in the Byzantine and Roman rites. However, one should realise that both rites have integrated many elements from other liturgical centres and have thus become syntheses. The Roman rite has been mixed, notably with Frankish-Germanic elements and in the Byzantine synthesis quite a few Syrian and Palestinian elements can be found.[2] Further, only a few phases of the festival's history and theology in these two rites will be dealt with. The celebration of the festival in other churches, in particular the Protestant and the Anglican churches, must remain outside consideration.

First, I will discuss the origin of the festival; secondly, its structure and contents in the Byzantine and Roman rites; and thirdly, some aspects of its theology.

In the course of Christian liturgical history, both in the Byzantine and in the Roman rite, the Festival of the Presentation has undergone many changes. The festival's history is a dynamic process. One can also observe

---

[1] The author wishes to thank Mr Ulrich Berges for his comments on an earlier version of this article and Mrs Ania Lentz-Michaelis for her help in revising the English text.

[2] See e.g. H. WEGMAN: *Riten en mythen. Liturgie in de geschiedenis van het christendom* (Kampen 1995²) 127-129, 182-193, 254-264.

a strong link between cult and culture. The festival has not only been affected by the culture in which it was celebrated but has formed it as well.

1. ORIGIN

The Festival of the Presentation of the Lord only came late into being. As far as we know, the early Christians of the first three centuries did not celebrate it. It originated in Jerusalem. Because of the many pilgrimages and the establishment of festivals to commemorate historical facts from the life of Jesus, the liturgy there was of great influence in the development of festivals in the yearly cycle of the whole Church.[3]

Before we look at the festival's origin in some detail we must take into consideration the development of doctrine and the changed position of the Christian Church during the fourth and fifth centuries. The Arian controversy on the relation between the Son of God, Jesus Christ, and His Father led to the definition of the Son's consubstantiality with the Father at the First Council of Nicaea (325). The First Council of Constantinople (381) affirmed that Father, Son and Holy Spirit are coeternal and consubstantial. At the same time preachers gradually transferred terms, such as *despotês* (master), *hupsistos* (highest) and *pantokratôr* (almighty), to Christ. The victory of Christianity in becoming a permitted religion, then the favoured and finally the official religion of the Roman Empire promoted the emphasis on the greatness and glory of Christ.[4] Other factors are the pastoral endeavour to impregnate the great number of new converts with the image of Christ's majesty so that they would behave in a decent manner and the underdevelopment of anthropological thought of the Church fathers.[5] The consequence of all

---

[3] J. BALDOVIN: *The urban character of Christian worship. The origins, development, and meaning of stational liturgy* (= Orientalia Christiana analecta 228) (Rome 1987) 45-104; P. WALKER: Jerusalem and the Holy Land in the 4th century, in A. O'MAHONY, G. GUNNER & K. HINTLIAN (eds.): *The Christian heritage in the Holy Land* (London 1995) 22-34.

[4] P. COLEMAN-NORTON: *Roman State and Christian Church. A collection of legal documents to A.D. 535. Vol. I* (London 1966) 30-35, 353-356. Cf. B. GROEN: Nationalism and reconciliation. Orthodoxy in the Balkans, in *Religion, state & society* 26 (1998) 111-128, p. 112-113.

[5] A. VAN DER AALST: Het oosterse Christusbeeld. De byzantijnse kerk, in *Tijdschrift voor theologie* 15 (1975) 237-254.

this was a strong stress on the divinity of Jesus Christ. Although the Council of Chalcedon (451) declared that Jesus Christ is not only truly God but also truly man, in liturgy, spirituality, art and political thought Jesus' divine character got more attention than his human aspect. Moreover, the mariological discussion, the definition of the Council of Ephesus (431) of the 'Holy Virgin' as the *theotokos* (Mother of God) and popular apocryphal writings, such as the *'Protevangelion* of James' (see §§2.1.1 and 2.1.3) and the 'Assumption of the Virgin', led to an exaltation of Mary in doctrine and devotion. All of these phenomena exercised a great influence on the shape and content of worship, in particular of the great festivals including the Festival of the Presentation.[6]

1.1. Early liturgical and homiletic evidence

It is well conceivable that Bishop Cyril of Jerusalem (died 386 or 387), the great propagator of the mysteriological and topographical liturgical year in his 'holy city', introduced the Festival of the Presentation.[7] However, the first certain piece of evidence of the existence of this festival comes from the famous traveller Egeria. In her travel report on the liturgy in Jerusalem at the end of the fourth century (381-384), she mentions that the fortieth day after Epiphany (*quadragesimae de epiphania*) was celebrated with the greatest honours. Epiphany was celebrated in Jerusalem on January 6, on which date one also commemorated the birth of Christ. The fortieth day thus fell on February 14, and, according to Egeria, people gathered in the Anastasis sanctuary. Everything is as festive as at Easter. All the priests and the bishop preach on the gospel which speaks of the Presentation of the Lord. Then the mysteries are celebrated (*aguntur sacramenta*).[8]

Another important source is the so-called Armenian Lectionary. This is not just one lectionary, but there are divers manuscripts during the

---

[6] The Councils' definitions can be found in *Conciliorum Oecumenicorum decreta* (Bologna 1973[3]) 5 (Nicaea I), 24 (Constantinople I), 58-59 (Ephesus), 86 (Chalcedon). See also H. WYBREW: *Orthodox feasts of Jesus Christ & the Virgin Mary. Liturgical texts with commentary* (Crestwood N.Y. 2000) 7-14.

[7] K. DEDDENS: *Annus liturgicus? Een onderzoek naar de betekenis van Cyrillus van Jeruzalem voor de ontwikkeling van het 'kerkelijk jaar'* (Goes 1975). Cf. G. DIX: *The shape of the liturgy* (Westminster 1945[2]) 349-353.

[8] P. MARAVAL: *Égérie. Journal de voyage (Itinéraire)* (= Sources chrétiennes 296) (Paris 1997[2]) 254-257; H. PÉTRÉ: *Éthérie. Journal de voyage* (= Sources chrétiennes 21) (Paris 1948) 206-207. Maraval renders *processio* with gathering, Pétré with procession.

first half of the fifth century (probably 417-442) with translations from
the Greek liturgy in Jerusalem into Armenian.[9] The Armenian Lectionary confirms the Festival of the Presentation on February 14, " the
fortieth day of the birth of our Lord Jesus Christ". People come together
in the Martyrium basilica and read psalm antiphons on the glorious
manifestation of the Lord (Ps 97, 3b. Alleluia: Ps 95).[10] They also listen
to an epistle from the Letter to the Galatians on the discipline of the
Law and on being children of God through belief in Christ (Gal 3, 24-
29) and to the gospel verses according to St. Luke.[11]

Maybe the oldest known sermons on this festival are by the priest
Hesychios of Jerusalem, who also lived during the first half of the fifth
century. Three of these, which are both eloquent and unsophisticated,
have been passed down to us.[12] Hesychios calls this festival *heortê
katharsiôn*, the Festival of Cleansing, and also the "feast of feasts, Sabbath of Sabbaths, holy festival of holy festivals, in which the entire mystery of the incarnation of Christ is expressed".[13] He explains Luke's

---

[9] Three important manuscripts are Jerusalem arm. 121 (J), Paris B.N. arm. 44 (P)
and Erevan 985. Critical edition by A. RENOUX: *Le codex arménien Jérusalem 121. I.
Introduction aux origins de la liturgie hiérosolymitaine. Lumières nouvelles; II. Édition comparée du texte et de deux autres manuscrits* (= Patrologia orientalis 35, 1 and 36, 2) (Turnhout 1969 and 1971). Renoux dates ms. J between 417-439 and ms. P between 439-442.

[10] The numeration of the Psalms in this study is according to the Septuagint and the
Vulgate. Ps 95, 8b, which speaks of an offering for the Lord, may have been the reason
for the choice of this psalm. However, according to one manuscript, viz. codex Paris
B.N. arm. 44, the Alleluia is only vs. 2b.

[11] RENOUX: *Le codex arménien Jérusalem 121. II. Édition comparée* 176, 228–229.

[12] Two authentic Greek sermons can be found in M. AUBINEAU: *Les homélies festales
d'Hésychius de Jérusalem. I. Les homélies I-XV* (= Subsidia hagiographica 59) (Brussels
1978) 1-75. Sermon I deals with Lk 2, 22-35 and sermon II with the verses 35-38.
According to AUBINEAU LXV-LXVI, sermon I dates from the first years of Hesychios'
career and the chronology of sermon II is uncertain. See also R. CARO: *La homiletica Mariana Griega en el siglo V* (= Marian library studies N.S. 3-5) (Dayton Ohio 1971-1973)
53-58; cf. 130-148, 176-187, 592-622, 646-649 (sermons on the Presentation by posterior writers and conclusions). This author, who focuses on mariological thought, thinks
that Hesychios' first homily – the only one on the Presentation he discusses – is a later
adaptation of a commentary (by Hesychios) on St. Luke's text for the liturgical festival.
There exists also a Georgian translation from another sermon by Hesychios on this
festival. Critical edition and translation into Latin by G. GARITTE: L'homélie géorgienne
d'Hésychius de Jérusalem sur l'Hypapante, in *Le Muséon* 84 (1971) 353-372.

[13] *Heortôn... heortên, sabbatôn sabbaton, hagiôn hagian ...holon gar anakefalaioutai
to tês sarkôseôs tou Christou mustêrion.* See AUBINEAU: *Homélies festales d'Hésychius* 24.
The name *hupapantê* in the sermons' titles is probably a later addition; cf. *ibid.* 5-6. In

account and discloses the meaning of the cleansing, Mary's virginity, Simeon's righteousness and his prophecy as well as Anna's devout life and her words. Moreover, he states that on the occasion of His presentation, Jesus entered Jerusalem for the first time – no doubt an interesting theme for a Jerusalem audience. According to Hesychios, God became Man, was carried as a baby and offered Himself for the elevation and salvation of men. Here the festival is primarily a feast of the Lord, not yet of the Mother of God. Further, it is highly likely that Hesychios used the system of readings laid down in the Armenian Lectionary.

A later stage in the festival's historical development is reflected in the so-called Georgian Lectionary. Here too we have different manuscripts with translations from the Greek liturgy in Jerusalem but this time into Georgian.[14] The incorporated descriptions range from the fifth to the eighth centuries. In this lectionary the festival is called Festival of the Meeting (*Hypapante*). However, because here the Meeting is celebrated forty days after Christmas and the date of Christmas is December 25, the date of the Meeting festival is February 2. This lectionary also lays down a more developed structure than the Armenian Lectionary.[15] On February 1 the prophetess Anna is commemorated – together with Father Ephraim. On the eve of the Festival of the Meeting there is a service in which the readings deal with circumcision (Col 2, 8-15 on the fullness of life in Christ and on spiritual circumcision, and Lk 2, 21 on the circumcision of Jesus). The psalm verses that accompany these readings deal with the Lord's triumph and the King's majesty (Ps 97, 3b, 2 on the victory of the Lord and Ps 44, 13-15 on the princess and virgins who are led to the King). At the eucharistic liturgy of the festival there are no less than five readings. Two are from the wisdom literature: one from the Proverbs regarding a pure heart and knowledge (Prov 22, 11-18) and one from the Wisdom of Solomon on the righteous and old age (Wis 4, 8-12). The third reading is from Isaiah and describes how Egypt is confounded by the Lord (Isa 19, 1-4). The fourth and fifth lessons

GARITTE: L'homélie géorgienne 361, the festival is called "the mother of all festivals". The name *hypapante* can only be found in the title, which again may be a later addition.

[14] An important manuscript is codex Paris B.N. georg. 3. Critical edition and translation into Latin by M. TARCHNISCHVILI: *Le grand lectionnaire de l'Église de Jérusalem (Ve-VIIIe siècle)* (= Corpus scriptorum Christianorum Orientalium 188-189, 204-205) (Louvain 1959 and 1960).

[15] TARCHNISCHVILI: *Le grand lectionnaire*, Vol. 189, 34-36.

(Gal 3, 24-4:7; Lk 2, 22-40) are almost the same as in the Armenian Lectionary. The psalm chant is similar to that at the eve of the festival (Ps 97, 3b, 2; Ps 44, 11-12).

1.2. *Occursus domini*

Cyril of Scythopolis (died c. 558) reports an interesting fact in his Life of St. Theodosios (written in 530; Theodosios Koinobiarches died in 529). According to Cyril, a devout lady, Hikelia, introduced the custom that "the meeting (*hupapantêsis*) with our saviour God would take place with candles".[16] Hikelia, who may have been a noble Byzantine Greek lady, had founded the Kathisma church along the road between Bethlehem and Jerusalem. Her initiative was probably taken during the second half of the fifth century. We may connect the information on Hikelia's innovative custom with the journey that was probably made by the clergy and faithful of Jerusalem on the day of the festival from the holy city southward in the direction of Bethlehem (from where Jesus had once come for His presentation in the temple). The goal of this trip was to meet the Lord, an *occursus domini*, comparable to the honours given to civilian and ecclesiastical dignitaries visiting a city (*adventus principis, parousia*) when authorities and inhabitants of the city used to come out in order to solemnly meet the coming prince and accompany him to the city. After the 'meeting with the Lord' the procession probably went back to the city, where the main service of the day was celebrated.[17] It is not unlikely that on their way north to the city the monks from the Kathisma, with candles in their hands, joined the participants of the procession coming southward from town.

Certainly, the Festival of the Presentation was not the first with a ritual departure from the holy city to meet the Lord. As early as in Egeria's travel report, two 'encounter processions' are described.[18] On Palm Sunday the faithful, including the bishop, gathered on the Mount of Olives,

---

[16] *(...) meta kêriôn ginesthai tên hupapantêsin tou sôtêros hêmôn theou.* See E. SCHWARTZ: *Kyrillos von Skythopolis* (= Texte und Untersuchungen zur Geschichte der altchristlichen Literatur 49, 2) (Leipzig 1939) 235-241, p. 236.

[17] Convincing evidence in H. BRAKMANN: Hê hupapantê tou Kuriou. Christi Lichtmess im frühchristlichen Jerusalem, in H.-J. FEULNER, E. VELKOVSKA & R. TAFT (eds.): *Crossroad of cultures. Studies in liturgy and patristics in honor of Gabriele Winkler* (= Orientalia Christiana analecta 260) (Rome 2000) 151-172.

[18] PÉTRÉ: *Éthérie* 216-223; MARAVAL: *Égérie* 268-275. See also BRAKMANN: Hupapantê 164-166.

where a service was held in the Eleona church and then another on top of the mountain. Afterwards all the people slowly escorted the bishop back to the city, viz. to the Anastasis. There a final assembly was held (lucernarium evening service and a prayer to the Cross). The biblical inspiration for this procession was undoubtedly the description of Jesus' entry into Jerusalem in the Gospel of St. John, according to which the crowd went out to meet Jesus (Jn 12, 12-19). The second procession took place on the day before Palm Sunday. Then it was customary to go to the place near Bethany where the sisters of Lazarus had met the Lord (Jn 11, 20, 29-30).[19] There all the monks met the bishop and a short service was held. Subsequently everyone went to the Lazarium, where another service was celebrated. Finally, people returned to the city and participated in the lucernarium in the Anastasis. Incidentally, another New Testament inspiration for an 'encounter procession' may have been the story in the Gospel of St. Matthew about the bridesmaids who went out to meet the groom (Mt 25, 1-13. Cf. Mt 8, 34; Lk 17, 12; 1 Thess 4, 17).

A sermon from the mid-fifth century, that wrongfully used to be attributed to Cyril of Jerusalem, presupposes the Presentation procession. The faithful are exhorted by the preacher to go out to meet (*hupantaô*) the Lord, who is the Creator and Commander of heaven and earth. The Child comes from Bethlehem to Jerusalem, the almighty God enters into Zion. The preacher tells the people to bring candles and lights with them. Joy and praise must prevail. This rhetorical sermon focuses upon Christ's majesty and *parousia* and is entirely christological.[20] Patriarch Sofronios of Jerusalem (died 638 or 639) also held a sermon on the festival, in which he exhorts his audience to go to meet the Lord and carry lights with them.[21]

2. STRUCTURE AND CONTENT

2.1. Byzantine rite

Constantinople adopted the festival under the Emperor Justin (518-527). Initially, its date of celebration was February 14. However, under

---

[19] Egeria mentions only Mary.
[20] J.P. MIGNE (ed.): *Patrologia Graeca* 33, 1187-1204; CARO: *Homiletica Mariana* 596-599.
[21] H. USENER: *Sophronii de praesentatione Domini sermo* (Bonn 1889) 8-18.

the Emperor Justinian (527-565), the date was changed to February 2 so that it would fall precisely forty days after Christmas.[22]

The illustrious hymnographer, Romanos Melodos (died after 555), wrote a popular kontakion about the Presentation. In a highly theological language, he describes the paradoxes of the virgin birth and of the inaccessible God laying in the arms of human beings. He also narrates Simeon's awe at these events and the old man's wish to be released from earthly life.[23]

I will only briefly mention two stages in the historical development of the festival and then concentrate upon the present-day celebration in the Greek Orthodox Church.[24]

2.1.1. A patriarchal typikon

A tenth-century manuscript of the typikon[25] of the Great Church of Constantinople lays down that on February 2 the Festival of the Meeting (*Apantêsis*) is celebrated and on the next day the commemoration of "St. Simeon, the Righteous, who received the Lord in his arms and Anna, the Prophetess".[26] On the eve of the festival, the patriarch descends to the Chalkoprateia church, where vespers are held. There are three readings. One is from Genesis and narrates God's revelation to Jacob by way of the ladder (Gen 28, 10-17). The second lesson from Ezekiel is about the offerings by the priests, the reason why the

---

[22] BRAKMANN: Hupapantê 152; W. PAX & H. BRAKMANN: Hypapante, in *Reallexikon für Antike und Christentum* 16 (1994) 946-956; G. BEKATOROS: Hupapantê, in *Thrêskeutikê kai Ethikê Egkuklopaideia* 11 (1967) 951-953.

[23] J. GROSDIDIER DE MATONS: *Romanos le Mélode. Hymnes. II. Nouveau Testament (IX-XX)* (= Sources chrétiennes 110) (Paris 1965) 163-197. An English translation can be found in *Kontakia. On the life of Christ. St. Romanos the Melodist*, transl. Ephrem Lash (Sacred literature series) (San Francisco 1995) 25-34.

[24] Cf. K. STEVENSON: The origins and development of Candlemas. A struggle for identity and coherence? in J. NEIL ALEXANDER (ed.): *Time and community. In honor of Thomas J. Talley* (Washington D.C. 1990) 43-76, p. 53-56 (= *Ephemerides liturgicae* 102 (1988) 316-346).

[25] Book containing liturgical directions and sometimes (in case of monastic typika) also instructions on everyday life in the monastery or convent.

[26] J. MATEOS: *Le Typicon de la Grande Église. Ms. Sainte-Croix n° 40, X° siècle. I. Le cycle des douze mois* (= Orientalia Christiana analecta 165) (Rome 1962) 220-227. Many elements of the festival's description in ms. Jerusalem Hag. Stavrou gr. 40 can also be found in the mid-9th-century ms. Patmos gr. 266. Cf. H. DELEHAYE: *Propylaeum ad Acta sanctorum novembris. Synaxarium ecclesiae constantinopolitanae e codice sirmondiano nunc berolinensi* (Brussels 1902) 156, 439.

east gate of the temple remains shut and the Lord's glory in his temple
(Ezek 43, 27-44, 4). The theme of the closed temple gate through
which the Lord God of Israel will enter (Ezek 44, 2)[27] had, in earlier
periods, already been applied by the preacher Hesychios and the poet
Romanos to the virgin birth[28] and may still be an important motive in
the tenth century. Finally, the third lesson is from Proverbs and praises
the house and the appeal of wisdom (Prov. 9, 1-11). Also a troparion
praising the Mother of God and Simeon – the present-day apoly-
tikion, viz. the main troparion of a feast day – is sung.[29] Matins are
again held in the Chalkoprateia. The prokeimenon proclaims the
Lord's mercy and revelation to Israel and the gentiles (Ps 97, 2)[30],
whereas the gospel narrates Mary's visit to Elisabeth and her song of
praise (Lk 1, 39-49, 56).[31] At the same time a procession including the
patriarch goes from the Great Church[32] to the Blachernae church;
there is a stop at the Forum of Constantine, where the deacon says
intercessions and the choir sings the troparion. According to one manuscript – from Cyprus, dating from the fourteenth century – the procession is led by the Emperor, who carries a procession candle. The
procession described in the tenth-century manuscript is certainly not
an exclusive characteristic of the Festival of the Presentation, because
at that time there were numerous liturgical processions in Constantinople, often with participation of the Emperor and with more or less
the same development. Liturgical processions were important 'public
events'.[33] The eucharist is celebrated in Blachernae and is attended by
the imperial court.[34] The readings are the same as those used in the

---

[27] The LXX applies the future tense.

[28] AUBINEAU: Homélies festales d'Hésychius 28-31; GROSDIDIER DE MATONS: Romanos
le Mélode 184-185.

[29] Chaire kecharitômenê ..., but without the words ho Hêlios tês dikaiosunês.

[30] The stichos, viz. the second verse, is vs. 3ab.

[31] The references to the prokeimenon and the gospel can be found in a supplement
to the typikon. See J. MATEOS: Le Typicon de la Grande Église. Ms. Saint <sic> -Croix
n°40, Xe siècle. II. Le cycle des fêtes mobiles (= Orientalia Christiana analecta 166) (Rome
1963) 180-183.

[32] Viz. the Hagia Sophia. Chalkoprateia is not far from the Hagia Sophia, Blachernae is situated near the northeast corner of the city.

[33] BALDOVIN: Urban character 190-204, 209-214, 292-303; R. JANIN: Les processions religieuses à Byzance, in Revue des études byzantines 24 (1966) 69-88.

[34] R. JANIN: La géographie ecclésiastique de l'empire byzantin. I. Le siège de Constantinople et le patriarcat oecuménique. Tome III. Les églises et les monastères (Paris1969²) 170.

Byzantine rite at present (see §2.1.3). The prokeimenon is taken from
the Magnificat (Lk 1, 47),[35] the Alleluia chant from the Presentation
story itself (Lk 2, 29-30, 32). The great number of references to Mary
and the fact that both Blachernae and Chalkoprateia have the Mother
of God as their patron show that by now the festival has a strong
Marian character.

The next day's synaxis of St. Simeon is celebrated in the chapel of
the Brother of the Lord, St. James, situated within the atrium of
Chalkoprateia.[36] After the said troparion has been sung, a passage from
the Letter to the Hebrews on the purification of conscience by Christ,
the high priest, and the gospel verses on Simeon and Anna are read
(Heb 9, 11-14 and Lk 2, 25-39).[37] Moreover, on October 23, the feast
day of St. James, the commemoration of "Simeon, the Righteous" is
held again, this time without Anna but together with "St. Zechariah,
the Priest".[38] The combination of these two men should come as no
surprise in view of the contents of the influential *Protevangelion* of
James (see §2.1.3).

2.1.2. *A monastic typikon*

A further development can be found in a twelfth-century typikon
(1131) written for a monastery in Messina and used there until the sixteenth century.[39] On February 1, besides the commemoration of St.
Tryphon, the forefeast of our festival is celebrated with special troparia.
The Festival of the Meeting itself (*Hupapantê*) has many specific
troparia, too, including a canon.[40] During vespers there are three readings (Ex 13, 1ff; Isa 6, 1ff; Ezek 2, 2ff or 3, 24ff).[41] In matins three

---

[35] Stichos: vs. 48.

[36] The relics of St. Simeon were kept in the crypt of Chalkoprateia. After the capture and sacking of the imperial city by western crusaders the relics were partly taken to
Zadar in 1243 and, during the fourteenth century, partly to Milan. JANIN: *Géographie
ecclésiastique* 254.

[37] The prokeimenon is Ps 63, 11 (stichos: 2). The stichos of the Alleluia chant is Lk
2:29. The communion chant is Ps 32, 1 ("righteous").

[38] MATEOS: *Typicon de la Grande Église. T. I* 74-75.

[39] M. ARRANZ: *Le Typicon du monastère du Saint-Sauveur à Messine. Codex messinen-
sis gr 115 A.D. 1131* (= Orientalia Christiana analecta 185) (Rome 1969).

[40] A canon is a sequence of hymns that are originally based on nine scriptural canticles and are sung during matins.

[41] With the exception of the third one, these lessons might be the same as those cur-
rently used (see §2.1.3).

psalms that concentrate on thankfulness and praise to the Lord for his mercy and manifestation are sung as antiphons (Ps 135; the *Polueleos* Psalm, Ps 97, together with Ps 99; Ps 148). Besides non-scriptural readings from the works of Methodios of Patara[42] and Leo, "the Master", there is again the gospel lection from St. Luke with a preceding prokeimenon, the same as in the typikon of the Great Church (Ps 97, 2[43] and Lk 2, 25-32). The divine liturgy has again three antiphons on gratitude and God's majesty (Pss 91, 92 and 94). Its readings are identical with those used nowadays: Heb 7, 7ff (epistle) and Lk 2, 22ff (gospel). The prokeimenon is Lk 1, 47,[44] the Alleluia chant Lk 2, 29 and the communion chant Ps 115, 4. The procession mentioned in the Great Church's typikon is missing, probably because it belongs to the stational liturgy of Constantinople.

On February 3, it is "the righteous Simeon, who received the Lord", who is commemorated. Anna is lacking in the title of today's festival. Simeon is honoured with a special canon and a set of readings. The epistle is taken from the Letter to the Hebrews (Heb 9, 11ff) and the gospel, of course, from St. Luke's narrative (Lk 2, 25-32).[45] On St. James' feast day, Simeon is not commemorated again; that day's commemoration was probably a typically Constantinopolitan usage. Further, an octave has been added to the Festival of the Meeting, culminating in an afterfeast on February 9; on that day the service of the festival is repeated, but only in matins.[46] During the octave, on the festival itself and on the preceding day, monks should not make any penitential prostration, neither in the church nor in their cells. There are special regulations if the period of the Meeting festival coincides with the beginning of Lent.

It is interesting to note that the author of this typikon regards the Festival of the Meeting as a feast of the Lord, not as one of the Mother of God. Both the typikon of the Great Church and the Messina typikon demonstrate clearly that the Festival of the Meeting had by then become one of the great feasts of the liturgical year.

---

[42] Viz. Pseudo-Methodios of Olympos. See J.P. MIGNE (ed.): *Patrologia Graeca* 18, 348-381.

[43] Stichos: vs. 3ab.

[44] Stichos: vs. 48.

[45] Prokeimenon: Ps 63, 11 ("righteous"); (stichos: 2). Alleluia chant: Lk 2, 29. The communion chant (Ps 111, 6b) contains the word "righteous" too.

[46] ARRANZ: *Typicon du monastère* 8 (R 46).

2.1.3. Current practice

We will now take a giant step and arrive at the end of the twentieth century. This is not only for reasons of limitation but also because – contrary to Roman rite – the service books in the Greek Orthodox church have not been radically revised by the ecclesiastical hierarchy during the second millennium.

In the present-day Greek Orthodox Church as well as in the Eastern-Catholic Church of the Byzantine rite, the festival examined in this study is known as the "Meeting of our Lord and God and Saviour Jesus Christ". It is still held forty days after Christmas, on February 2. The specific liturgical texts for the festival are to be found in the Menaion (Month Book) for February.[47] There are texts for the small and great vespers, orthros (matins) and for the divine liturgy, i.e. the eucharist. Because of its significance, the festival has a forefeast (on February 1) and an afterfeast (on February 9).[48] Further, on February 3, a special festival in commemoration of two protagonists, viz. Simeon and Anna, is celebrated.

Just as its twelfth-century predecessor from Messina, the current typikon lays down how the Meeting festival is to be celebrated. It also provides for directions in case the festival and its accompanying minor festivals fall after the beginning of the Lenten triodion or on a Sunday, etcetera.[49] The regulation that the Patriarch of Constantinople has to take part in the services in his church on February 2, as on all major festivals, sheds clear light on the significance of the festival.[50]

The views of contemporary Greek Orthodox theologians on the question of whether the festival should be considered as a festival of the Lord or as a Marian feast are divergent. Two examples must suffice here. Fr. Konstantinos Papayannis, a renowned liturgiologist, asserts that it is a festival of the Lord, although according to the typikon it is a festival

---

[47] *Mênaion tou Februariou*, Apostolikê Diakonia (Athens 1966) 12-20. An English translation can be found in *The Festal Menaion*, transl. Mother Mary and Kallistos Ware (London 1969) 406-434; cf. 44, note 2; 60. See also WYBREW: *Orthodox feasts* 19-20, 81-91.

[48] *Mênaion tou Februariou* 5-11 (forefeast). In the afterfeast, almost the entire liturgy of February 2 is repeated but without readings. Depending on the starting date of Lent one may shorten or omit the afterfeast.

[49] G. VIOLAKIS: *Tupikon tês tou Christou Megalês Ekklêsias* (Athens s.a.) 169-181, 449-450.

[50] VIOLAKIS: *Tupikon* 428.

of the Mother of God and of the Lord.[51] The British scholar, Bishop Kallistos Ware, opts in favour of the Marian character but also leaves the possibility of a Lord's festival open.[52] So this confusion about the nature of the festival is not an exclusive privilege of the Roman rite.

I will now put forward various elements of the services. There are three readings in the great vespers. The composition of the first reading is somewhat complex. According to the Menaion, it is from Exodus. However, it is a cento consisting of Ex 12, 51-13, 3b, 10-12a, 14-16a; Lev 12, 2b-4, 6, 8; Num 8, 16-17. One of its main themes is the offer of all first-born sons to the Lord, as they belong to God. A second theme deals with the forty days' impurity of the mother of a new-born boy and the offers she must bring the priest so that she may be cleansed. The second lesson concerns the appearance of the Lord of Lords to the Prophet Isaiah in the temple, as well as the prophet's cleansing and mission (Isa 6, 1-12). The third, also from Isaiah (Isa 19, 1, 3a-5, 12, 16, 19-21), describes how Egypt trembles before the Lord, sets up an altar to Him and recognises Him. The criteria for the choice of the last two readings is the appearance of God, on the one hand to the prophet and the resulting cleansing, on the other to the heathen Egyptians and their trembling recognition of the God of Israel. The reflexive relationship to Epiphany is obvious.

As usual, matins has a lesson from the gospel, in this case the presentation of Jesus from St. Luke (Lk 2, 22-40). This can also be found in the eucharist. There too can be found a reading from the Letter to the Hebrews on the polemics with respect to the Law and on Christ's priesthood as opposed to that of the Levites (Heb 7, 7-17).

One of the significant things in the Byzantine liturgy is that basic themes of the festival appear meditatively in the many hymns suggested by the lessons. This is also the case with the troparia at the Festival of the Meeting

In the hymns, the poets often use paradoxes. The paradox is well-loved in liturgical poetry, not only as a stylistic means, but also, and in particular, because in this way one is better enabled to approach the mystery of God becoming man. The following themes and paradoxes can be found:

---

[51]   See his work *Leitourgikê-Teletourgikê. Boêthêma dia tous hierospoudastas mesôn kai anôterôn hieratikôn scholôn* (Athens 1973) 109, 113, 279.

[52]   *Festal Menaion* 41; T. WARE: *The Orthodox Church* (Harmondsworth 1993³) 299.

Today (*sêmeron*), the Holy Mother goes to the sanctuary to offer the Creator of the world and the Lawgiver there according to Moses' law. He who once gave Moses the Law, now submits to the provisions of that law. The pure God, a holy child that opened the pure and maiden womb, offers Himself to God in order to bring salvation from the curse of the law (*katara tou nomou*).

Simeon, an old man and a priest, holds an infant in his hands; this is the Logos, exalted above all things. The servant holds the master. He who holds the universe in His hands and who is feared by the heavenly hosts, meets the old man and lies in his arms. Moses once saw only God's back and heard God's voice in storm and darkness, but Simeon sees Him. Therefore Simeon is also the receiver of God: *Theodochos*. It is striking that the face to face encounters between God and Moses (Ex 24, 9-11; 33, 11. Cf. Ex 3; 20, 21; 24, 18; 33, 14-23; 34) are not mentioned in the Byzantine festival.

Simeon prays for "deliverance from the chains of the flesh" – meaning life on earth – and for entry to eternal life. He who carries everlasting life in his hands, wishes to be freed from mortal life.

The darkness of the ungodly will be dispelled. The light that knows no darkness has come. Christ appears. He is the living coal of fire (Isa 6, 6-7). In this Byzantine typological imagery, Mary is the pair of tongs. Christ is also the sun of justice risen from the Maiden. The godly is united with the human. All this comes about for our sake, for the saving of our souls. God shows His benevolence, His *sugkatabasis*. Consequently, we must rejoice.

A short reference to the figure of Simeon is important here. Simeon is a priest of the old covenant. According to the *Protevangelion* of James – a very wide-spread and influential document, probably written in the second half of the second century – he was not only priest but also, after the murder of Zechariah, the new high priest.[53] In later times there was, however, also opposition to Simeon's alleged priesthood. For instance, Hesychios of Jerusalem denied that Simeon was in holy orders.[54] However, for others, such as the fifth-century Pseudo-Cyril of Jerusalem (see

---

[53] E. DE STRYCKER: *La forme la plus ancienne du Protévangile de Jacques. Recherches sur le papyrus Bodmer 5 avec une édition critique du texte grec et une traduction annotée* (= Subsidia hagiographica 33) (Brussels 1961) 186-189. Cf. H.R. SMID: *Protevangelium Jacobi. A commentary* (Assen 1965) 166-167.

[54] AUBINEAU: *Homélies festales d'Hésychius* 34.

§1.2) the priestly office was something obvious.[55] It is not unlikely that the view that Simeon was a priest also arose because of a confusion of names, viz. confusion with the person of Simon, the Maccabee, Jewish "leader and high priest forever until a reliable prophet would arise" (1 Macc 14, 41).[56] Further, Simeon receives God in his arms and recognises Him. This priesthood, his reception and his hymn are probably the reasons for his being the centre of attention while the prophetess Anna is hardly mentioned. Joseph too hardly plays a role in this festival.

2.1.4. Icons

In the Orthodox liturgy, icons play an important part. They belong to the celebration. Besides prayer with lips and minds, there is prayer with the eyes.[57] There is also a didactical aspect: icons tell biblical and hagiographical stories. Because to many faithful the rites remain obscure and the liturgical language, which in Greece is ancient Greek and in Russia Church Slavonic, is hardly intelligible, icons, frescos and mosaics can tell details which the rites themselves are unable to relate. Further, believers who honour the icons, honour those pictured there: Christ, the Mother of God, saints, etc. So it is not surprising that during the services of the Presentation of the Lord, the icon of this festival is especially honoured. In the festival icon, Simeon, the Child and Mary are mostly in the centre, in front of an altar with a canopy. Joseph and Anna stand to the side; Joseph carries the two doves, Anna sometimes a scroll with the words "This infant has made heaven and earth secure".[58] In the background one discerns temple buildings.[59] Just as on many Russian Presentation

[55] J.P. MIGNE (ed.): *Patrologia Graeca* 33, 1197.

[56] For the full story on the high priest Simon, see 1 Macc 13-16. On the relation between Simeon and Simon, see K. KOK: Simeon en Hanna. Over Lukas 2, vers 22-40, in *Maandbrief voor leerhuis & liturgie* 5 (2000) no. 10, 5-7.

[57] J. BAGGLEY: *Festival icons for the Christian year* (Crestwood N.Y. 2000) 4-8, 13-14; cf. 40-47 (various liturgical texts and iconography of the Festival of the Presentation).

[58] *Touto to brefos ouranon kai gên estereôsen.*

[59] G. PASSARELLI: *Die Ikonen zu den grossen byzantinischen Festen* (Zürich/Düsseldorf 1998) 129-146; K. ONASCH & A. SCHNIEPER: *Ikonen. Faszination und Wirklichkeit* (Luzern/Freiburg 1995) 105; cf. 214-225, 287; *Treasures of Mount Athos* (Thessalonica 1997) 131-132; *Gouden licht. Meesterwerken der ikonenkunst* (Gent 1988) 109; F. KONTOGLOU: *Ekfrasis tês Orthodoxou Eikonografias. Tomos prôtos. Technologikon kai eikonografikon* (Athens 1993³) 161-162; cf. 224, 264, 305; *Tomos deuteros. Pinakes* (Athens 1993³) plates 79, 88-90.

icons, on a sixteenth-century icon from Pskov, Simeon and Mary bend
towards the Child and also towards each other. The new and the old
covenant meet. Mary's and Simeon's hands are covered with cloths out of
reverence for Christ. The Child stretches his arms towards Simeon and
blesses him with His right hand (see plate 1).[60] There are also several
Byzantine and Russian icons with only Simeon and the Child as a close-
up of the Meeting.[61]

2.1.5. Patron's feast and folklore

In present-day Greece, only a few churches are dedicated to the Festival
of the Meeting of Christ, such as the parish of the *Hupapantê tou Christou* in the centre of Thessalonica. Besides the official liturgical programme outlined above, the annual patron's feast may consist of even
more liturgical services, such as vigils and a celebration of the anointing
of the sick (as a penitential rite and for well-being)[62] and a procession
with the icon in the streets. Of course there are markets, music, eating,
drinking and dancing too. An important church that has the Meeting of
Christ as its patron's feast is the cathedral of the diocese of Messenia in
Kalamata, southern Peloponnese. Here the celebrations and festivities
even last from January 27 till February 9.[63]

For people in the country the Festival of the Presentation has long
served as a significant date for the planning of work, the expectation of
weather conditions and fertility. Many Greek mothers still feel close to
Mary because, just as they did, she too submitted to the cleansing rite
forty days after giving birth. However, many pregnant women used to
believe that if they worked on the 'feast days of Simeon' (*Sumogiorta*), as

---

For reasons of space I will not examine here the historical development of the Presentation icon. See H. MAGUIRE: The iconography of Symeon with the Christ Child in
Byzantine art, in *Dumbarton Oaks papers* 34-35 (Washington DC 1980-1981) 261-269;
H. LECLERCQ: Chandeleur, in *Dictionnaire d'archéologie chrétienne et de liturgie* III, 1
(1913) 207-210; K. WESSEL: Darstellung Christi im Tempel, in *Reallexikon zur byzantinischen Kunst* I (1966) 1134-1145.

[60] M. ALPATOV & N. RODNIKOVA: *Pskovskaja ikona XIII-XVI vekov* (Leningrad
1990) plate 86. See also BAGGLEY: *Festival icons* 40-47; plates 7, 8a.

[61] *Gouden licht* 142; *Ikonen und ostkirchliches Kultgerät aus rheinischem Privatbesitz.
Katalog zur Ausstellung im Schnütgen-Museum* (Cologne 1990) 116-117.

[62] B. GROEN: '*Ter genezing van ziel en lichaam.*' *De viering van het oliesel in de
Grieks-Orthodoxe kerk* (= Theologie & empirie 11) (Kampen 1990) 113, 134-135.

[63] *Diptucha tês Ekklêsias tês Hellados. Kanonarion-Epetêris 2000* (Athens 1999) 646,
656.

Plate 1. Icon of the 'Meeting of the Lord', 16ᵗʰ century, Pskov.

the first three days of February were called, their child would be handicapped. Here the name of Simeon was identified with the Greek word *sêmadi* (sign, mark).[64]

2.1.6. 'Churching'

According to canon 18 of the Canons of Hippolytus from the mid-fourth century, a new mother who has given birth to a son should not enter the church for forty days and, in case of a girl, not even for eighty days. When she re-enters the church she should pray with the catechumens.[65] However, when a Byzantine special ritual for 'entering the church forty days after birth' develops it is the newborn child, not the mother that is the centre of attention. In the famed eighth-century *codex Barberini graecus 336* a prayer for this occasion can be found. It asks for growth of the child so that it may take part in the initiation sacraments.[66] The ritual is intended to bring the child (mostly not yet baptised) to the church and present it to God. An important change occurs during the eleventh century: prayers that stress the uncleanliness of the new mother and ask for her cleansing are added to the ritual. Since then the purification of the mother ever more overshadows the presentation of the newborn child to God. 'Churching of the child' becomes 'churching of the mother'.[67]

In his popular work on Orthodox faith and worship, *Dialogos en Christôi* etc., the Archbishop of Thessalonica, Simeon (died 1429), writes that this ritual intends to cleanse the mother and offer the child to God. Only if the child is baptised it is carried around the altar. Simeon does not discriminate between boys and girls in this matter.

---

[64] D. LOUKATOS: *Sumplêrômatika tou Cheimôna kai tês Anoixês* (= Laografia-Paradosê 5) (Athens 1985) 110-112; A. KURIAKIDOU-NESTOROS: *Hoi dôdeka mênes. Ta laografika* (Athens/Thessalonica 1982) 30-33.

[65] R.-G. COQUIN: *Les Canons d'Hippolyte. Édition critique de la version arabe, introduction et traduction française* (= Patrologia orientalis 31, 2) (Paris 1966) 374-375.

[66] S. PARENTI & E. VELKOVSKA: *L'Eucologio Barberini gr. 336 (ff. 1-263)* (= Bibliotheca "Ephemerides liturgicae" "Subsidia" 80) (Rome 1995) 97-98.

[67] P. TREMBELAS: *Mikron Euchologion. Tomos A. Hai akolouthiai kai taxeis Mnêstrôn kai Gamou, Euchelaiou, Cheirotoniôn kai Baptismatos kata tous en Athênais idia kôdikas* (Athens 1950) 259-317, 327-335; A. DMITRIEVSKIJ: *Opisanie liturgičeskich rukopisej chranjaščichsja v bibliotekach pravoslavnogo vostoka. T. II. Euchologia* (Kiev 1901 and Hildesheim 1965); J. GOAR: *Euchologion sive Rituale Graecorum* (Venice 1730², Graz 1960¹) 267-271.

Further, he states that only after the cleansing ritual the mother may again attend the sacramental celebrations.[68]

At the beginning of the third millennium, in the Orthodox Balkan states – especially in the country, less so in the cities – many mothers stick to the ritual of 'churching', in Greek called *sarantismos* (fortieth-day rite). Usually the priest reads four prayers in the narthex. The first and second prayers – the younger ones – ask "to cleanse the woman from the stains of body and soul"; the second prayer also asks for the blessing of the child.[69] In the third and fourth prayers, that are older, growth, protection and the blessing of the child are the central themes. These two prayers also refer to the events of the presentation in the temple. Then, just as Simeon carried the Infant Jesus, the priest blesses the child, takes it into his arms, goes into the nave and presents the child to God. Boys are carried around the altar, girls stay outside. This discrimination of sexes has occurred ever since the sixteenth century. It was also possible that girls were only carried around three quarters of the altar (not on the front side). Most euchologia[70] from the Byzantine period, however, do not make a distinction between the sexes.[71]

Not only the present-day rite of churching but also the Orthodox prayers "for the new mother" that are nowadays used[72] stress the unclean-liness and sin of the new mother. Several Greek Orthodox theologians raise protests though. The professor of liturgiology, Ioannis Fountoulis, states that not the physical functions of the human body but dead works make a person unclean.[73] According to Anastasios Kallis, the faith of the Church is deformed and mothers are insulted by these prayers.[74]

---

[68] J.P. MIGNE (ed.): *Patrologia Graeca* 155, 209-212.

[69] *Katharison apo pasês hamartias kai apo pantos rupou* (from the first prayer); *apoplunon autês ton rupon tou sômatos kai ton spilon tês psuchês* (from the second prayer). See *Mikron Euchologion*, Apostolikê Diakonia (Athens 1981[8]) 51-56 (quotations: 52-53).

[70] An euchologion is a book for the clergy containing liturgical texts, such as the sacraments and blessings.

[71] On the Byzantine ritual of 'churching', see also I. FOUNTOULIS: *Apantêseis eis lei-tourgikas aporias. I (1-150)* (Athens 1988[3]) 166-167, 179-181; Idem: *Apantêseis eis lei-tourgikas aporias. IV (301-400)* (Thessalonica 1982) 13-14, 178-179, 225-242.

[72] *Mikron Euchologion* 43-47.

[73] FOUNTOULIS: *Apantêseis IV* 238.

[74] He says that this is a "Gestalt…, die den Glauben der Kirche entstellt und die Frau als Mutter grob beleidigt". In his edition of the prayers at the occasion of the birth of a child, gratefulness and asking for blessing are the main themes. In 'his' ritual of going to church after forty days, the "defilement of the body and the impurity of the

Konstantinos Kallinikos does not protest but discerns four 'moods' that in his opinion are characteristic of the ritual of churching: the need for cleansing from physical and spiritual uncleanliness, gratitude for the birth of a child, thankfulness that the mother has been saved and the need for divine protection.[75]

2.2. Roman rite

Just as in the examination of the Byzantine rite only several significant phases from the development of the festival in Roman rite can be discussed here.[76]

2.2.1. Procession of light

The Festival of the Presentation was probably only introduced in Rome around the middle of the seventh century or shortly after.[77] From the very beginning a procession of light belonged to it. Maybe this procession was a christianisation of the Roman Amburbale, a cleansing and penitential procession around the city, held at the beginning of February every five years. Our knowledge about its exact practice, however, is uncertain.[78] The theory that the introduction of the Presentation festi-

soul" of the new mother is out of the question. See A. KALLIS: *Akolouthia tou Baptismatos tês Orthodoxou Ekklêsias. Taufgottesdienst der Orthodoxen Kirche. Griechisch-Deutsch* (= Doxologie 3) (Münster 1999) IX-XIII, 2-39 (quotation: X).

[75] K. KALLINIKOS: *Ho Christianikos Naos kai ta teloumena en autôi* (= Hapanta Kônstantinou Kallinikou 7) (Athens 1969³) 379-380.

[76] See also STEVENSON: Origins and development of Candlemas 56-69; I DEUG-SU: La festa della purificazione in Occidente (secoli IV-VIII), in *Studi medievali*, 3rd series, 15 (1974) 143-216; J. ADRIAANSE: Lichtmis, in *Liturgisch woordenboek* II (1965-1968) 1535-1540; H. AUF DER MAUR: *Feiern im Rhythmus der Zeit I. Herrenfeste in Woche und Jahr* (= Gottesdienst der Kirche. Handbuch der Liturgiewissenschaft 5) (Regensburg 1983) 176-179.

[77] J. DESHUSSES: *Le Sacramentaire Grégorien. Ses principales formes d'après les plus anciens manuscrits. I. Le Sacramentaire, le Supplément d'Aniane* (= Spicilegium Friburgense 16) (Fribourg 1971) 53-54, 56-57; IDEM: *Le Sacramentaire Grégorien. III. Textes complémentaires divers* (= Spicilegium Friburgense 28) (Fribourg 1982) 61-63. Deshusses asserts that the Hypapanti Mass can not have been composed before Pope Theodorus (642-649) and that the texts of the festival have been added to the Gregorian Sacramentary before about 660-670. See also the argumentation in A. CHAVASSE: *Le sacramentaire Gélasien (Vaticanus Reginensis 316). Sacramentaire presbytéral en usage dans les titres romains au VIIe siècle* (= Histoire de la théologie 1) (Tournai 1958) 375-402.

[78] W. PAX: Amburbale, in *Reallexikon für Antike und Christentum* I (1950) 373-375.

val in Rome was intended as a christianisation of the Roman Lupercalia must be discarded. The Lupercalia, which were held around the Palatine on February 15, were seemingly both cathartic and for the promotion of fertility, but there is no convincing evidence for a connection between these and the Presentation.[79] Maybe the processional practices of Constantinople and Jerusalem influenced Rome. Apart from the possible interrelatedness of festivals, one can point out that fire and light from candles and torches are a general characteristic of cleansing rites.

A sure piece of evidence of the existence of the festival in Rome is a statement in the *Liber Pontificalis*. It says that Pope Sergius I (687-701), a Syrian, prescribed that on the day "of St. Simeon, which the Greeks call Ypapanti," a procession should leave from St. Hadrian's church in the Forum (the former Curia) and that the people should meet at St. Mary's (Maria Maggiore). Similar processions and gatherings should be held on the days of the Annunciation, the Dormition and the Birth of Mary; three Marian festivals that were introduced in Rome somewhat later than the Presentation festival.[80] The Pope himself participated in these processions, major elements of the Roman stational liturgy. Throughout the year, from the sixth century onwards, there were numerous liturgical processions in Rome and they were basically penitential.[81] Further, it is significant to note that the festival is listed here together with the three (other) festivals of the Mother of God, something that may have reinforced its Marian character.

In his work *De temporum ratione liber* dating from 725, the Venerable Bede confirms the procession on the "day of St. Mary" (*die sanctae Mariae*) in Rome, although he does not indicate its exact route. During this procession, in which the clergy also participated, people sang and carried burning candles, given to them by the Pope.[82]

More details about the procession can be found in two eighth–century descriptions in the *Ordines Romani*, books that contain liturgical

[79] C. SCHÄUBLIN: Lupercalien und Lichtmess, in *Hermes* 123 (1995) 117-125; D. BAUDY: Lupercalia, in *Der neue Pauly* 7 (1999) 509-510. See also D. BAUDY: Lustratio, in *Der neue Pauly* 7 (1999) 520-522 ('lustratio' as a cleansing ritual circumambulation).

[80] *Constituit autem ut diebus Adnuntiationis Domini, Dormitionis et Nativitatis sanctae Dei genetricis (…) ac sancti Symeonis, quod Ypapanti Greci appellant, letania exeat (…)*. See L. DUCHESNE: *Le Liber pontificalis* I (Paris 1955²) 376.

[81] BALDOVIN: *Urban character* 122, 137-138, 158-166, 234-238.

[82] Corpus Christianorum. Series Latina 123B (Turnhout 1977) 322-323. See also vol. 122 (Turnhout 1955) 128-133, containing a sermon on the festival by Bede in which he explains Lk 2, 22-35. This sermon was held between 730-735.

directions. The most extensive one calls our festival the "cleansing of St. Mary" (*in Purificatione sanctae Mariae*),[83] the other one, which is probably older, still speaks of *Ypapanti*.[84] In the early morning of the Purification festival all the people assemble at St. Hadrian's with burning candles. The Pope and the deacons put on black (penitential) vestments (other interpretations of the black colour are that it stands for the impurity of Mary[85] or for the sword that will pierce Mary's soul (Lk 2, 35) and her ensuing grief). Then the Pope distributes candles and says the prayer in front of the altar. All proceed with candles, together with incense and crosses, to the church of the Mother of God.[86] Near this shrine the litany is sung three times.

Contrary to Byzantine liturgical usage, the Roman rite develops no octave of the Presentation festival.

2.2.2. Sacramentaries

From Rome the celebration of the festival spread over Western Europe. In the Gregorian Sacramentary one finds the papal liturgy mixed with Gallican, Visigothic, Milanese and other texts that were added after the Sacramentary's diffusion in the Carolingian Empire. Important manuscripts of this book which date from the beginning of the ninth century also contain prayers for the service of the festival.[87] Here it has retained its Greek name *Ypapanti*. The prayers presuppose the procession and served originally, as their titles say, for the assembly in St. Hadrian's and for Mass in St. Mary's.[88] Several of them emphasise the inner, spiritual meaning of the events in the temple for those living now. Characteristi-

---

[83] M. ANDRIEU: *Les Ordines Romani du haut moyen âge. III. Les textes (suite) (Ordines XIV-XXXIV)* (= Spicilegium sacrum Lovaniense 24) (Louvain 1961) 229-236. This is *Ordo Romanus XX* dating from c. 780-790.

[84] ANDRIEU: *Ordines Romani* 113-114. This is a section from *Ordo Romanus XV*. The Ordo itself dates from c. 750-878.

[85] H. LECLERCQ: Présentation de Jésus au temple, in *Dictionnaire d'archéologie chrétienne et de liturgie* XIV, 2 (1948) 1722-1729, k. 1729.

[86] According to *OR XX*, only the schola and the clergy sing the antiphon, whereas according to *OR XV*, all people sing together.

[87] Date of composition of the primitive Gregorian Sacramentary: c. 600-650. For a summary of the complex textual history of the Gregorian Sacramentary, see DESHUSSES: *Sacramentaire Grégorien* I, 50-75; C. FOLSOM: The Liturgical books of the Roman rite, in A. CHUPUNGCO (ed.): *Handbook for liturgical studies. I. Introduction to the liturgy* (Collegeville Minn. 1997) 245-314, p. 251-254.

[88] DESHUSSES: *Sacramentaire Grégorien* I, 123-124; cf. 616.

cally, the almighty God is beseeched, that, even as today (*hodierna die*) Christ is offered in the temple as of our flesh, we might be offered to God in a pure spirit (*nos facias purificatis tibi mentibus praesentari*). In a supplement by Benedict of Aniane (died 821) one also finds a special preface about the new spiritual light and an episcopal blessing which accentuates the spiritual meaning of the festival and at the same time exhorts us to doing good works. In both the preface's and the blessing's titles *In purificatione sanctae Mariae*, Mary's cleansing is now the point of special interest but the texts themselves do not yet pay particular attention to her.[89]

Another important sacramentary, the so-called Gelasianum (composition date: between 628-715; date of the manuscript: around 750), presents a mixture of both papal and presbyteral liturgy from Rome to which Gallican elements have been added. Here too special Mass prayers are provided for. These have been borrowed – with adaptations – from the Christmas festival in the Gregorian Sacramentary and in the Gelasianum itself. In spite of the title of the festival, which is *In purificatione sanctae Mariae*, the prayers again do not refer to Mary.[90] The Gelasianum also provides for a Mass for the Christmas octave on January 1, a previous date for a festival of the Mother of God. In the octave Mass not only Christ's birth but also his circumcision, the presentation in the temple and the encounter with Simeon are commemorated.[91] Also interesting here is the theme of 'pure minds' (*purificatae mentis ... puris mentibus*). This theme occurs in services on other occasions, too, of course, but here it is very appropriate.

In the Carolingian empire the Gelasian and Gregorian sacramentaries were combined and other, mainly Gallican and monastic texts were

[89] DESHUSSES: *Sacramentaire Grégorien* I, 505, 580. See also another preface in IDEM: *Le Sacramentaire Grégorien. II. Textes complémentaires pour la messe* (= Spicilegium Friburgense 24) (Fribourg 1979) 346. Interesting are here, firstly, the paradox that the Maker of Law submits to Law and, secondly, the identification of Simeon, a man, and Anna, a woman, with the two human sexes.

[90] L. MOHLBERG: *Liber sacramentorum Romanae Aeclesiae ordinis anni circuli (Cod. Vat. Reg. lat. 316 / Paris Bibl. Nat. 7193, 41/56) (Sacramentarium Gelasianum)* (Rerum ecclesiasticarum documenta. Series maior. Fontes IV) (Rome 1960) 133; cf. 270; CHAVASSE: *Sacramentaire Gélasien* 307, 375-402.

[91] MOHLBERG: *Liber sacramentorum* 13-14; CHAVASSE: *Sacramentaire Gélasien* 211-212, 382-383; A. CHAVASSE: *Textes liturgiques de l'Église de Rome. Le cycle liturgique romain annuel selon le sacramentaire du "Vaticanus Reginensis 316"* (= Sources liturgiques 2) (Paris 1997) 216-219.

added. The result of this was the 'Eighth-Century Gelasianum' or 'Frankish Gelasianum', which existed in many variations. Several important manuscripts show uniformity as to the name given to the festival: day "of St. Simeon". As usual the spelling varies: *Sancti Symonis* according to the Gellone Sacramentary,[92] *Sancti Simeonis* according to the 'Phillipps' or Autun Sacramentary[93] and the St. Gallen Sacramentary,[94] *Sancti Symeoni* according to the Angoulême Sacramentary[95] and *Simonis* according to the Rheinau Sacramentary.[96] However, in the Monza Sacramentary, which also contains Ambrosian material, the title is *purificatio sanctae Mariae*.[97] A special case of interest is the Triplex Sacramentary (compiled c. 1000), in which one finds not only Gregorian and Gelasian texts but Ambrosian as well. Here the Gregorian title is used: *Yppapanti* in the Triplex spelling.[98]

The titles in the martyrology (calendar) attached to several sacramentaries are different again. The Gellone Sacramentary speaks of "solemnity

[92] A. DUMAS & J. DESHUSSES: *Liber sacramentorum Gellonensis* (= Corpus Christianorum. Series Latina 159 and 159A) (Turnhout 1981), Vol. 159, 24-25; cf. 10-11. See also the episcopal blessing with its paradoxes on p. 289. Date of composition of the sacramentary: c. 760-770; date of the manuscript: 790-800.

As to the relations between the texts of the different sacramentaries, see A. CHAVASSE: *Le sacramentaire dans le groupe dit "Gélasiens du VIIIᵉ siècle". Étude des procédés de confection et synoptiques nouveau modèle*. T. I-II (= Instrumenta patristica XIV A-B) (Steenbrugge/The Hague 1984) 130-131 (Vol. I), 111 (Vol. II); A. CHAVASSE: *La liturgie de la ville de Rome du Vᵉ au VIIIᵉ siècle. Une liturgie conditionnée par l'organisation de la vie in urbe et extra muros* (= Studia Anselmiana 112) (Rome 1993) 179-182, 223, 269-271.

[93] O. HEIMING: *Liber sacramentorum Augustodunensis* (= Corpus Christianorum. Series Latina 159B) (Turnhout 1984) 25-26; cf. 12, 264.

[94] K. MOHLBERG: *Das fränkische Sacramentarium Gelasianum in alamannischer Überlieferung (Codex Sangall. No. 348)*. St. Galler Sakramentar-Forschungen I (= Liturgiegeschichtliche Quellen 1/2) (Münster 1918) 27-28; cf. 12-13.

[95] P. SAINT-ROCH: *Liber sacramentorum Engolismensis. Manuscrit B.N. Lat. 816. Le Sacramentaire Gélasien d'Angoulême* (= Corpus Christianorum. Series Latina 159C) (Turnhout 1987) 27-28; cf. 11-12.

[96] A. HÄNGGI & A. SCHÖNHERR: *Sacramentarium Rhenaugiense. Handschrift Rh 30 der Zentralbibliothek Zürich* (= Spicilegium Friburgense 15) (Fribourg 1970) 94; cf. 83-84.

[97] A. DOLD & K. GAMBER: *Das Sakramentar von Monza* (= Texte und Arbeiten. I. Abteilung, 3. Beiheft) (Beuron 1957) 8*, 108*-109*; cf. 5*.

[98] O. HEIMING: *Corpus Ambrosiano Liturgicum I. Das Sacramentarium Triplex. Die Handschrift C 43 der Zentralbibliothek Zürich. I. Teil. Text* (= Liturgiewissenschaftliche Quellen und Forschungen 49) (Münster 1968) 44-45; cf. 28-29.

of Saint Mary, when she presented the Lord in the temple"[99] and the Rheinau Sacramentary simply of *Purificatio sanctae Mariae virginis*.[100]

2.2.3. *Epistle lists, gospel lists and antiphonaries*

Before the introduction of the feast in Rome, the gospel narrative of St. Luke on the circumcision and presentation was read during the Christmas octave Mass just mentioned. This Mass was celebrated in *Sancta Maria ad Martyres*, the former Pantheon.

According to gospel lists from the eighth century, so after the introduction of the festival, this reading was kept in use. The gospel lesson par excellence for the festival itself is almost the same passage, this time without reference to the circumcision. Here too variations in the festival's name can be noted: *Ypapanti, Purificatio sanctae Mariae* and even no name at all.[101]

The epistles vary. Because the *Comes* of Würzburg (c. 700 or c. 730) is based on a Roman list from c. 600, an entry for our feast is still lacking. The *Comes* of Murbach, dating from the end of the eighth century, has an epistle from Jesus Sirach about the praise of wisdom for the Festival of the *Purificatio sanctae Mariae* (Sir 24, 23-31) and an epistle from the Letter to Titus about God's manifestation for the Christmas octave Mass (Titus 2, 11ff). The gospel readings are, of course, Lk 2, 22-32 for the festival itself and Lk 2, 21ff for the Christmas octave.[102] In the *Comes* of Alcuin from the beginning of the ninth century, "at the day on which the blessed Virgin presented Christ in the temple" (*in die qua beata uirgo offerebat Christum in templo*), we meet with the verses from Malachi that will be read throughout the later Roman history of the fes-

---

[99] *Solemnitas sanctae mariae quando dominum in templum representavit.* See HEI-MING: *Corpus* 493.

[100] HÄNGGI & SCHÖNHERR: *Sacramentarium Rhenaugiense* 295.

[101] Th. KLAUSER: *Das römische Capitulare Evangeliorum. Texte und Untersuchungen zu seiner ältesten Geschichte. I. Typen* (= Liturgiegeschichtliche Quellen und Forschungen 28) (Münster 1935) 13, 17-18, 59, 63, 102, 105, 141, 144, 173-174. This author distinguishes four types. Type II, which is purely Roman, dates from c. 645 and has only the Christmas octave gospel reading (Lk 2, 21-32). Type Λ (purely Roman, c. 740), type Σ (purely Roman, c. 755) and type Δ (Roman-Frankish, after 750) contain both the octave reading and the reading from February 2 (Lk 2, 22-32). Type Δ provides also for a second festival reading, viz. Lk 2, 28-40.

[102] A. WILMART: Le Comes de Murbach, in *Revue bénédictine* 30 (1913) 25-69, p. 36-37.

370 BERT GROEN

tival (Mal 3, 1-4). Its themes are the coming of the Lord to His temple, cleansing and offering.[103]

Besides prayers and readings, there is chanting. In various important antiphonaries from the eighth and ninth centuries[104] one finds two originally Greek antiphons translated into Latin. These are *Ave gratia plena*, viz. the troparion on the Mother of God and Simeon that we encountered in the tenth-century typikon, and *Adorna thalamum tuum Sion* (Adorn your bridal chamber, Zion), unfortunately poorly translated.[105] Further, the Introit and Gradual sing of God's mercy in the temple (Ps 47, 9-11) and the Alleluia sings of adoration of God in His sanctuary (Ps 137, 2). In the Offertory "grace on your lips" is the theme (Ps 44, 2-4) and the Communion chant is about Simeon (Lk 2, 26).

In these antiphonaries, the name of the festival varies again: *Natale sancti Simeonis, In sancti Simeonis* or *Purificatio sanctae Mariae*.

2.2.4. Blessing of candles

A new element at the end of the ninth and the beginning of the tenth centuries is the blessing of the candles. In the Romano-Germanic Pontifical dating from c. 950-963 and written in Mainz, the blessing of the candles has grown into an elaborate ritual with seven prayers. A main theme in the second, third and fourth prayers is that the dark powers will be driven away through the blessed candles. After the exorcising, blessing, sprinkling and censing of the candles they are lit and distributed. Then the procession is held, during which antiphons are sung. Finally, Mass is celebrated.[106]

During the high and late Middle Ages the faithful attached great value to the blessing of the candles. It was thought that the blessed candles chased away the devil and all evil and that through the light of the candles

[103] A. WILMART: Le Lectionnaire d'Alcuin, in *Ephemerides liturgicae. Analecta historico-ascetica* 51 (1937) 136-197, p. 152.

[104] R.-J. HESBERT: *Antiphonale Missarum sextuplex* (Brussels 1935) 36-39; cf. LXXX-LXXXII, LXXXVII-LXXXIX.

[105] Viz. the words *hautê bastazei ton Basilea tês doxês, nefelê fôtos huparchei hê Parthenos* ("She carries the King of Glory, a cloud of light is the Virgin"), rendered into Latin with *ipsa enim portat Regem gloriae novi luminis: subsistit Virgo*.

[106] C. VOGEL & R. ELZE: *Le Pontifical Romano-Germanique du dixième siècle. Le texte. II* (= Studi e testi 227) (Vatican City 1963) 5-10. This text can also be found in M. ANDRIEU: *Les Ordines Romani du haut moyen âge. V. Les textes (suite) (Ordo L)* (= Spicilegium sacrum Lovaniense 29) (Louvain 1961) 89-99.

dark powers disappeared. Moreover, wax candles changing into flame served as symbols for the eucharistic transubstantiation.[107] The significance of the blessing and of the procession of light was comparable, on the one hand to the blessing of the ashes on Ash Wednesday and that of the palms on Palm Sunday, on the other to the processions on Palm Sunday and Ascension Day. So both the blessing of candles and the lights procession became the festival's principal features and for that reason it is called Candlemas, Chandeleur, Maria Lichtmess, etc. in Western Europe to this day.

2.2.5. Council of Trent

The new liturgical books initiated by the sixteenth-century Council of Trent aim at maintaining the ecclesiastical traditions in a uniform way.

According to the Roman breviary, the Roman missal and the Roman ritual of Trent, the festival is called "The Cleansing of Mary" (*Purificatio B.M.V.*). The festival of the Lord has now officially become a festival of Mary. Thus the reform of Trent confirms a long development during the Middle Ages that increasingly accentuated the Marian character of the festival. It is a double feast of the second class, i.e. the lowest level of the higher feasts. I shall first deal with the position of the festival in the breviary. This prescribes the general formulary for festivals pertaining to the Mother of God. There are also, however, specific readings, prayers and hymns which are more in the character of a festival of the Lord.[108]

With the exception of matins, the readings in all the services of the breviary are from Malachi (Mal 3, 1-4 or only one verse). There are no readings from Isaiah. Matins has nine lessons, three per nocturn. The first readings are from Exodus and Leviticus (Ex 13, 1-2, 11-13; Lev 12, 1-5; Lev 12, 6-8). After that there are three readings from the thirteenth *Sermo de Tempore* by Augustine, in which he describes how, as Simeon recognises and worships the Child, he is rejuvenated and renewed. Then, as in the Byzantine matins, there is a reading from St. Luke's gospel (Lk 2, 22-32). This is followed by part of Ambrose's commentary on St. Luke, according to which Simeon wishes to be released from his earthly life and

---

[107] C. CASPERS: Leviticus 12, Mary and wax. Purification and churching in late medieval Christianity, in M. POORTHUIS & J. SCHWARTZ (eds.): *Purity and holiness. The heritage of Leviticus* (Leiden 2000) 295-309, p. 298-300, 306-307.

[108] *Breviarium romanum ex decreto sacrosancti concilii tridentini restitutum S. Pii V pontificis maximi jussu editum aliorumque pontificum cura recognitum Pii papae X auctoritate reformatum. Pars hiemalis* (Malines 1931) 955-963.

reunited with Christ. According to Ambrose, whoever wishes to be released from earthly life should await Christ, accept the Word of God and embrace it, both with works and with the arms of belief.[109]

As it is a Marian feast, praises to the Mother of God are sung at length. She is the renowned maiden, the King's gateway, She who feeds Him who has made Her. She is entreated to lead the sinners and the blind, to ward off all evil and to intercede for all men. Some Christmas themes are also heard.[110] Just as in the Byzantine feast, in which Simeon plays a dominant role, the old man is often mentioned in the Roman liturgy. Old Simeon carried the Child, it is also said, but the Child ruled over him;[111] a paradox, as in the Byzantine rite. A central place is for the prayer from the Gregorian Sacramentary on being offered in a pure spirit.

The Missale Romanum of Trent provides special texts both for the Mass and for a candlelight blessing and procession.[112] In a violet cope, a sign of penance, the priest says five prayers at the altar to bless the candles (however, after the procession he puts on white vestments, which changes the mood of the service). The main themes in the prayers are: for health of body and soul; and that we should be offered in the temple of God's glory, cleansed of all sin, acknowledge Christ and reach the everlasting light. With the exception of the first prayer, all the prayers emphasise the illumination and inner cleansing of the participants. The third, fourth and fifth prayers also have a pneumatological character: Illumination is brought about by the Holy Ghost. The 'bridal chamber' stichiron mentioned above (see §2.2.3) and verses from St. Luke's gospel are sung as antiphons. By way of Introit and Graduale, the choir sings of God's mercy in His temple (Ps 47). The readings are, as one may expect, from Malachi and Luke (Mal 3, 1-4 and Lk 2, 22-32). The Mass prayers are almost literally the same as in the Gregorian Sacramentary.[113]

---

[109] The first part of this section serves as homily, its second and third parts are the last two readings.

[110] E.g. the antiphon *O admirabile commercium*.

[111] *Senex Puerum portabat, Puer autem senem regebat.*

[112] *Missale romanum ex decreto sacrosancti concilii tridentini restitutum S. Pii V pontificis maximi jussu editum aliorum pontificum cura recognitum a Pio X reformatum et ssmi d.n. Benedicti XV auctoritate vulgatum. Editio VII juxta typicam vaticanam* (Regensburg 1923) 498-502.

[113] Two changes are that the first prayer in the Gregorian Sacramentary, *oratio collecta ad sanctum Hadrianum*, begins with *erudi (…) plebem tuam* (teach Your people) and in the missal of Trent with *exaudi (…) plebem tuam* (hear Your people) and that the Gregorian book has an extra prayer. See DESHUSSES: *Sacramentaire Grégorien* I, 123-124.

It must be emphasised that these texts point more to a festival of Christ, with the Epiphany accent, than to a Marian festival, although that is what it purports to be.

2.2.6. Western portrayal of the festival

Before dealing with the Vatican II rite, a short look at western art: here the portrayal of the festival is very varied. I shall give only a few examples.[114] In Chartres Cathedral, viz. on the right in the west porch, the so-called Royal Portal, the Presentation scene (between c. 1145-1155) has a central place, compared to the Annunciation, Visitation and the Birth of Christ (see plate 2). The Child stands on an altar and is offered by the Mother of God and Simeon. Joseph carries the doves but offerings are also brought by other figures symbolising the Church. In the total programme of illustrations in Chartres, this representation probably also refers to the presence of Christ in the eucharist: the Child is identical with the host that is offered on the altar. The sculptures of Chartres show the indissoluble link between Christ, in whom Godhead and manhood are united, and the Mother of God, Mary, too.[115] Further, in the central porch of the north transept façade (built between c. 1210-1220), among twelve Old and New Testament saints one finds a statue of Simeon holding the Infant Jesus in his hands. He is regarded as one of the key figures in the history of salvation.[116]

At the beginning of the seventeenth century, Rubens painted a baroque Presentation on a triptych for Antwerp Cathedral (plate 3). Simeon, dressed in priestly robes, offers the Child to God. The young Mary reaches out to him. Light falls upon the Child, Simeon and Mary.

Rubrics for the procession can also be found in the Roman Ritual. See *Rituale romanum Pauli V pontificis maximi jussu editum aliorumque pontificum cura recognitum atque auctoritate ssmi d.n. Pii papae XI ad normam Codicis Juris Canonici accommodatum. Editio juxta typicam vaticanam* (Malines 1926) 360-365.

[114] More information in D. SHORR: The iconographic development of the Presentation in the Temple, in *The art bulletin* 28 (1946) 17-32; L. GOOSEN: *Van Andreas tot Zacheüs. Thema's uit het Nieuwe Testament en de apocriefe literatuur in religie en kunsten* (Nijmegen 1992) 264-268; E. LUCCHESI & L. HOFFSCHOLTE: Darbringung Jesu im Tempel, in *Lexikon der christlichen Ikonographie* I (1968) 473-477; F. TSCHOCHNER: Darbringung Jesu im Tempel. IV. Kunstgeschichte, in *Marienlexikon* 2 (1989) 144-147.

[115] A. KATZENELLENBOGEN: *The sculptural programs of Chartres cathedral. Christ, Mary, Ecclesia* (Baltimore 1959) 7-26, 37-49, plates 2, 9, 10; N. LÉVIS-GODECHOT: *Chartres im Lichte seiner Skulpturen und Fenster* (Würzburg 1988) plates 13, 15.

[116] KATZENELLENBOGEN: *Sculptural programs* 53-78, 91-102, plates 43, 44, 51.

Plate 2. The Presentation of the Lord (middle). Chartres Cathedral,
Royal Portal.

Plate 3. The Presentation of the Lord P.-P. Rubens, Antwerp Cathedral.

Joseph kneels with the pigeons in his hand. Old Anna looks tenderly at the Child. Amongst the witnesses there is also a friend of Rubens.[117] Rembrandt, a Protestant, loved the theme and used it often in paintings and etchings, but his works did not serve a liturgical aim. However, because many seventeenth-century Dutch patricians liked to look at biblical scenes and contemplate on them, notwithstanding the fact that the Calvinist Church was hostile to liturgical religious images, paintings of biblical scenes hang in many Dutch mansions.

2.2.7. Second Vatican Council

Now I will again take a giant step and deal with the liturgy reforms of the Second Vatican Council. The festival was once more revised. The name was altered to: "Festival of the Presentation of the Lord" (*Praesentatio Domini*). From being a Marian festival it returned to being a festival of the Lord.

The new Book of Hours, the Liturgia Horarum, provides its own material for the festival.[118] Several psalms and antiphons emphasise the radiation of light, Israel's expectation of the Lord (Ps 129) and the arrival and renown of the King (e.g. Ps 44). Also God's entry of the temple (after Ezekiel) is sung. Some of the readings from the Roman breviary of Trent remain, others have been replaced. In the new Book of Hours, there are excerpts from Exodus (on the first-born), now also from Isaiah, Malachi, the Gospel of St. John, the Epistle to the Hebrews, as well as a fragment of the said sermon by the Jerusalem Patriarch Sofronios. The details are as follows: The lessons in the Office of Readings are Ex 13, 1-3a, 11-16. In this office the Sofronios fragment can be found too. The short readings in the other hours are Isa 8, 14; 12, 5-6; 42, 13; Mal 3, 1; Heb 4, 15-16; 10, 5-7. During the vigil Jn 1, 1-18 or Jn 3, 16-21 is read. The prayer from the breviary and missal of Trent on *our* presentation in a pure spirit has been kept and is prescribed for all hours and the eucharist. New are the intercessions in vespers and matins. Among others, the prayers are that our eyes shall see

[117] J. VAN BRABANT: *Onze-Lieve-Vrouwkathedraal van Antwerpen. Grootste gothische kerk der Nederlanden. Een keur van prenten en foto's met inleiding en aantekeningen* (Antwerp 1972) 265, 267. Cf. J.R. MARTIN: *Rubens. The Antwerp altarpieces* (London 1969).

[118] *Liturgia horarum iuxta ritum romanum. III. Tempus per annum, Hebdomadae I-XVII*, editio typica (Vatican City 1977) 1099-1115, 1611-1613.

the salvation by God and that those who do not yet know Christ may be illuminated. Paradox has been retained in the hymns and some of the antiphons, as for instance: He who rules over the angels and created heaven and earth now submits to the Law of Moses.[119] In the vigil, the canticles speak of the arrival of the Prince of Peace, of justice and peace in Zion, of comfort and joy in Jerusalem (Isa 9, 2-7; 26, 1-4, 7-9, 12; 66, 10-14a). The new Book of Hours thus emphasises the anticipation and appearance of the Lord, as well as the joy over His coming.

Characteristic for the new Mass is that, as in the Trent missal, there is still a procession and a blessing of candles.[120] However, the ritual of the blessing has become simpler. There is now only one prayer of blessing. Instead of a procession, a solemn entry suffices. The aspect of joy is stressed. The priest wears white instead of violet robes. The main theme is the meeting between Christ and the believers. In his address to the people, the priest emphasises that Jesus, at His presentation today, outwardly complies with the Law, but in reality meets His faithful people and that, as those of yore recognised and acknowledged the Lord, we too will go forward to Christ and acknowledge Him in the breaking of bread. The theme of meeting is also heard in the summons to the procession (*Procedamus … ad occurendum Domino*), in the preface (*…nos, Salutari tuo in gaudiis occurentes*) and in the prayer after communion (*…nos, in occursum Domini procedentes*).

In addition to the readings from Malachi and St. Luke's gospel (Mal 3, 1-4 and Lk 2, 22-40 or 22-32) there is a lesson from the Epistle to the Hebrews about Jesus becoming equal to men (Heb 2, 14-18).[121] The responsorial psalm deals with the arrival of the King of Glory (Ps 23, 7-10). The Alleluia verse is again from Luke (Lk 2, 32).

2.2.8. 'Churching' in Roman rite

Just as in Byzantine Orthodox culture, in Western and Central Europe too, going to church forty days after giving birth was customary. Especially

---

[119] *Legis sacratae sanctis caeremoniis subiectus omnis calamo Mosaico dignatur esse, qui regit perfulgidos in arce Patris ordines angelicos, caelumque, terram fundavit ac maria* (first strophe of the hymn of the Office of Readings).

[120] *Missale romanum ex decreto sacrosancti oecumenici concilii vaticani II instauratum auctoritate Pauli pp. VI promulgatum*, editio typica (Vatican City 1975²) 522-526.

[121] *Ordo lectionum missae*, editio typica (Vatican City 1969) 215; *Lectionarium. III. Pro missis de sanctis, ritualibus, ad diversa, votivis et defunctorum*, editio typica (Vatican City 1972) 38-41.

during the late Middle Ages 'churching' was a popular rite, in which the new mother, relatives and friends participated. The service's prayer to take away the mother's impurity and bless her was considered a contribution to her recovery.[122] Contrary to many diocesan rituals,[123] the Rituale Romanum from 1614 does not contain a prayer for cleansing the new mother but expresses gratitude.[124] However, during the twentieth century 'churching' gradually died out in the Catholic West because it became an isolated ritual, which was more and more felt to be an indignity for women.

The blessing of mothers in the new Roman Book of Benedictions from 1984 and in the German Catholic *Benediktionale* from 1978 – in both without reference to the forty days period – emphasises thankfulness and the protection of mother and child.[125]

3. MAIN ELEMENTS IN THE THEOLOGY OF THIS FESTIVAL

In summarising the main elements of the liturgical forms of this festival examined here, it is clear that the festival of the Presentation of the Lord has, in the course of history, not only changed its name but also a variety of its accents and structures. This again draws attention to the fact that the liturgy is not only affected by historical processes but forms them as well.

Here I would like to mention five elements of the theology of this festival: Epiphany and illumination; encounter between God and Man; cleansing; continuity between the old and the new covenant; paradoxes.

---

[122] CASPERS: Leviticus 12, Mary and wax.

[123] B. KLEINHEYER: Riten um Ehe und Familie, in B. KLEINHEYER, E. VON SEVERUS & R. KACZYNSKI: *Sakramentliche Feiern II* (= Gottesdienst der Kirche. Handbuch der Liturgiewissenschaft 8) (Regensburg 1984) 67-156, p. 152-156.

[124] *Rituale romanum* 290-293.

[125] *De benedictionibus*, editio typica (Vatican City 1984) 92-99: *Ordo benedictionis mulieris post partum*; DIE LITURGISCHEN INSTITUTE SALZBURG, TRIER & ZÜRICH (eds): *Benediktionale. Studienausgabe für die katholischen Bistümer des deutschen Sprachgebietes* (Einsiedeln-Zürich and Freiburg-Vienna 1978) 91-95: *Muttersegen nach der Geburt*. Cf. R. SCHWARZENBERGER: Der Muttersegen nach der Geburt, in A. HEINZ & H. RENNINGS (eds.): *Heute Segnen. Werkbuch zum Benediktionale* (Freiburg 1987) 279-284.

3.1. Epiphany and illumination

The first element is the idea of the presentation in the temple as a historical fact in the life of Jesus, when God reveals Himself and submits to Jewish law in Jesus. The revelation of God is not something abstract but takes place in actual history. The Festival of the Presentation celebrates God's revelation to the people in Jesus and that Jesus is the Light of the World. It is after all no coincidence that this festival is the last in the Epiphany cycle. The light shines and illuminates the people who acknowledge it. Both the Byzantine and the Roman liturgy accentuate this.

A key word in both rites is 'today'. The festival is not only a commemoration of past events but also aims at our reliving these events and becoming participants in them.[126] The liturgical 'today' contains past, present and future.

In the Festival of the Presentation a basic dimension of the Christian liturgy is illuminated, viz. the celebration of the appearance of light,[127] as Christmas is thought of as bringing light to the world; as the Festival of the Transfiguration of the Lord on August 6 focuses attention on the shining of the Lord's light; and as in Emmaus the eyes of the disciples are opened so that they see the Lord.

3.2. Encounter between God and Man

The Festival of the Presentation is a commemoration of the meeting of God, the source of light, and Man. The liturgy of Vatican II in particular accentuates the aspect of contact. The Byzantine liturgy, too, emphasises that Jesus Christ, when at His presentation He meets Simeon and Anna, and in them the people of Israel and the gentiles, also meets us today. There is not only contact between Christ and the participants but also among the participants themselves.

Contact between God and Man is not confined to the church service. There is also the liturgy after the liturgy.[128] In the dismissal, the partic-

---

[126] Cf. *The Lenten Triodion*, transl. Mother Mary and Kallistos Ware (London and Boston 1978) 57.

[127] Also K.-B. MÜLLER: Im Licht Christi geborgen. Gedanken zur Lichtfeier am Fest der Darstellung des Herrn und zum Blasiussegen, in *Heute Segnen* 192-200; F. RECKINGER: Unterwegs mit dem Licht. Die Lichtfeier am Fest der "Darstellung des Herrn", in W. MEURER (ed.): *Volk Gottes auf dem Weg. Bewegungselemente im Gottesdienst* (Mainz 1989) 101-103.

[128] Cf. I. BRIA: *The liturgy after the liturgy. Mission and witness from an Orthodox perspective* (Geneva 1996).

ipants are called to help their neighbours and relieve the needs of the world, to meet others and in this way to become for others a sacrament of God's love.

3.3. Cleansing

The encounter between God and Man also includes the aspect of cleansing, as is emphasised in Byzantine, Western medieval and Tridentine-Roman liturgy in particular.[129] Cleansing also encompasses rectifying individual or collective wrongdoings when the faithful stray from the path of serving God or one's neighbour. According to the Constitution *Lumen Gentium* of the Second Vatican Council, the Church is also an *ecclesia semper purificanda*, ever striving for repentance and renewal.[130] Cleansing enables the Church to be joy and hope (*Gaudium et Spes*) for its people in their need.

Mary's cleansing after forty days of impurity after giving birth, viz. because of the blood lost during giving birth, is, like the presentation of Jesus as first-born, part of St. Luke's gospel and promoted the rite of 'churching' of new mothers, both in the Byzantine East and in the Catholic West. At the same time the different historical stages of this ritual and its divers meanings in both parts of Christendom are a good example of the liturgy being subject to historical processes.

3.4. Continuity between the old and the new covenant

The Presentation of the Lord proves the continuity between the old and the new covenant. The revelation to Israel is not revoked at the Presentation of Christ, but is enlarged throughout the world and set into a liturgy. The God of Israel appeared to His people and all nations, appears to the world in Jesus and still manifests Himself today. However, in many liturgical texts, especially in the Byzantine rite, the old and new covenants are opposed and the redemption by God's Son from the old covenant, symbolised by Simeon and Anna and in the laws of

---

[129] STEVENSON: Origins and development of Candlemas 66-69, argues also in favour of the 'bitter' character of the festival and deplores its disappearance in modern Catholic liturgy. See also his suggestions on p. 73 (note 87).

[130] *Ecclesia (…) sancta simul et semper purificanda, poenitentiam et renovationem continuo prosequitur.* See *Conciliorum Oecumenicorum decreta* 855.

the Torah, is proclaimed. In my opinion one should be cautious of all substitution theories that reduce Israel and its scriptures to a historical prelude to the coming of Jesus and thus do not give due attention to the continuity of God's appearance throughout the Bible.

3.5. Paradoxes

This festival shows that paradoxes are essential elements in speaking of God. Mysticism and the apophatic way are basic dimensions of liturgical theology. In the Byzantine liturgy in particular paradoxes have an important place. This raises the question whether the present-day Western Church, which, after the Enlightenment, is indebted to human reason in a special way, gives enough space to the ineffable and the secret. After all, in the liturgy becoming susceptible to the mystery of God and staying susceptible to it is at stake.

CHARLES M.A. CASPERS

HOW THE SACRAMENT LEFT THE CHURCH BUILDING THEOPHORIC PROCESSIONS AS A CONSTITUENT OF THE FEAST OF CORPUS CHRISTI[1]

1. INTRODUCTION

In the period of the late Middle Ages, the Sacrament of the Eucharist assumed a place in religious life and the practice of the Church which was more important than it had ever been before, or would be since. Particularly the introduction of the elevation of the Host in the Mass (after the words of the Lord's institution of Eucharist were spoken) at the beginning of the 13th century, and the formulation of the dogma of transubstantiation by Pope Innocent III several years later in 1215, at the fourth Lateran Council, had as their consequence a significantly increased regard for this sacrament as compared with the preceding centuries. Practising believers, particularly women, often underwent ecstatic or mystic experiences in the vicinity of the altar or around the moment of communion. For them, but also for all other baptized individuals who had reached the age of discretion, preparation for communion and its reception, through which one might be united with Christ in many possible manners, was the most important act of faith which could be performed in this earthly life. Partaking of communion was possible in a sacramental manner (that is to say, by means of receiving the Host) in the church and during Mass, but also in a spiritual manner (without partaking of the Host), independent of time and place.[2] The latter implied that the Sacrament was continually

[1] This study is a revision of a part of the author's doctoral dissertation, *De eucharistische vroomheid en het feest van Sacramentsdag in de Nederlanden tijdens de late Middeleeuwen* (= Miscellanea Neerlandica 5) (Louvain 1992), chiefly p. 75-101, updated and revised to emphasize its relevance to the theme of this collection. The English translation has been made possible in part by a financial contribution of Vertaalfonds KNAW/Stichting Reprorecht.
[2] For both forms of communion, however, the condition applied that one must be 'worthy' for it to be efficacious in achieving salvation; see Charles M.A. CASPERS: *Meum summum desiderium est te habere.* L'eucharistie comme sacrement de la rencontre avec Dieu pour tous les croyants (ca. 1200 - ca. 1500), in André HAQUIN: *Fête-Dieu (1246-*

and universally present in a certain way, wherever there were Christians. To be sure, the parish church remained a privileged holy place and collective worship, the Mass, a privileged holy moment, but the universality of the Sacrament, as mentioned, certainly detracted a bit from the exclusivity of these privileges. For instance, during the late Middle Ages representations referring to the Passion and salutary work of Christ were placed in the landscape – and many individuals also had such depictions in their private possession – for the purpose of providing a visual aid in achieving spiritual communion among viewers.[3]

In this contribution I will be devoting attention to a very concrete manifestation of the Sacrament 'breaking through' the church walls: the first theophoric processions, that is, processions in which a consecrated Host was carried in the procession, and thus in this case, outside the church building. Of all the theophoric processions it is the procession of the Sacrament accompanying the feast of Corpus Christi which most appeals to the imagination. The origin and development of this procession has fascinated many, first of all because it did not coincide with the introduction of the feast itself – in 1246 in the diocese of Liège and after 1264 gradually throughout the whole of the Western Church – but was only later added to it, and then at that locally and in various forms; and secondly because this procession completed the long history of development of Corpus Christi as a 'feast of joy'.

In historiography other theophoric processions are often discussed only to the degree that they can be considered as predecessors of the procession on Corpus Christi; as a result, various authors have also designated various predecessors. This discussion is summarized below, and brief comments are made on it; five types of theophoric processions are presented, including the first Corpus Christi processions in the 13th and early 14th centuries.[4] Then elements from the presenta-

1996), I. Actes du colloque de Liège, 12-14 septembre 1996 (= Publications de l'Institut d'Études Médiévales 19/1) (Louvain-la-Neuve 1999) 127-151.

[3] See Charles M.A. CASPERS: Het laatmiddeleeuwse passiebeeld. Een interpretatie vanuit de theologie- en vroomheidsgeschiedenis, in *Nederlands kunsthistorisch jaarboek* 45 (1994) 161-175.

[4] The later development of the Corpus Christi procession in the 14th and 15th centuries into what is probably the most triumphal expression of faith that the Western Church has ever known, as well as its relation to Corpus Christi Cycles, confraternities, the contributions of urban citizens, rhetoricians and national authorities (the 'general processions'), etc., fall outside the scope of this paper. See CASPERS: *Eucharistische vroomheid* 101-124.

tion will be discussed further with a double purpose: to obtain a more concrete image of the 'universalization' of the Sacrament mentioned above, from inside to outside the church walls; and to obtain more insight into the process by which Corpus Christi became a 'feast of joy'.

2. THE THEOPHORIC ASPECT

Various types of theophoric processions already existed in the 13th century: the first Corpus Christi processions; the procession on Maundy Thursday; the procession on Palm Sunday; the 'small processions' in which the priest brought the viaticum to the home of a sick person; and processions during a Sacrament of Miracle feast. According to Peter Browe (d. 1950), who in the decades before the Second World War devoted several studies to the history of eucharistic devotion, the procession on Corpus Christi, which would only become widespread in Western Christianity after about 1350, is to be distinguished from these five types of processions.[5] The peculiarity of the Corpus Christi procession was, in his view, that it was unconcealedly theophoric, which permitted the believers to publicly view the Sacrament (a consecrated Host). In the period from about 1200 to about 1350 it would otherwise have only been possible for them to do so during the elevation of the Host in the Mass. According to Browe this unconcealed aspect was a total innovation that made the Sacramental procession into an event through which the faithful were enabled to concentrate entirely on the eucharistic presence of Christ. According to him, that was not the case in the five older types; the covering of the Sacrament blocked not only direct eye contact, but at the same time obstructed the inward surrender to the eucharistic Christ. Thus the distinction between the concealed and unconcealed theophoric was not a matter of degree, but a fundamental difference. Because here, as has been said, we have an innovation, none of the older processional types, despite their similarities, can be considered to be the predecessor or source of inspiration for the later Corpus Christi procession.

---

[5] Peter BROWE: Die Entstehung der Sakramentsprozessionen, in *Bonner Zeitschrift für Theologie und Seelsorge* 8 (1931) 97-109; Peter BROWE: *Die Verehrung der Eucharistie im Mittelalter* (München 1933) 26-28, 89-115.

It would appear that we are dealing here with a personal, somewhat exaggerated view, but it is one that has had considerable implications for the subject of this study. By connecting an innovation of about 1200 (the unconcealed display of the Host during the Mass) and one of about 1350 (the display of the unconcealed Host in the Corpus Christi procession), this author in fact implies that it took a century and a half before it was possible to venerate the Sacrament outside of the church building in a way equivalent to that possible inside it. Only then could Corpus Christi be celebrated as a 'feast of great joy', a characteristic that was the chief reason for Pope Urban IV to place Corpus Christi on the calendar of universal feasts.[6]

Browe's view has had considerable influence on the work of later authors. The distinction which he introduced between two types of Corpus Christi processions – the clerical procession in which the concealed Sacrament was carried along within the church building or within the clerical immunity (see §3.1), and the 'lay' procession in which the Sacrament was carried around with a number of honours through cities and villages – has been taken over in studies on religious life and/or feast culture, in which likewise the middle of the 14th century is taken as the turning point.[7] The radical dimension in his view (i.e., the distinction between 'concealed' and 'unconcealed' and the implications this has for Corpus Christi as a feast) has however been found insufficiently convincing by various scholars. Thus a discussion arose in which the last word has not yet been spoken. Following up on this debate, in the subsequent subsections an attempt will be made to 'measure' the theophoric content of the five types of processions listed above, by relating them to the two 'innovations' also mentioned.

---

[6] The already existing commemoration of the institution of the Sacrament, Maundy Thursday, did not come into consideration for being characterized in this way, because as a component of Holy Week it referred to the suffering and death of Christ. See also our note 8.

[7] See CASPERS: *Eucharistische vroomheid* 69-70 (esp. note 29); Sabine FELBECKER: *Die Prozession. Historische und systematische Untersuchungen zu einer liturgischen Ausdruckshandlung* (= Münsteraner theologische Abhandlungen 39) (Altenberge 1992) 207. An anomalous position is taken by G.J.C. SNOEK: *Medieval piety from relics to the Eucharist. A process of mutual interaction* (= Studies in the history of Christian thought 63) (Leiden etc. 1995) 267, 277, who sees the Corpus Christi procession as gradually evolving from the procession of relics.

3.1. The first Corpus Christi processions and the processions on Maundy Thursday

Upon the introduction of the feast of Corpus Christi into the universal calendar in 1264 it was indeed decreed by Pope Urban IV that this feast should be celebrated with great exuberance, but he does not say a word about processions.[8] The oldest information presently known regarding a Corpus Christi procession – possibly the first which was ever held – dates from 1275-1277 and involves the Church of St. Gereon in Cologne. In the directions for the celebration of Corpus Christi, among other things it is instructed that prior to the High Mass the Body of Christ, together with the two most important relics of the Church of St. Gereon (the head of St. Gereon and the crown of Empress Helen) should be brought to the Church of St. Christopher in procession. Thus the procession remains inside the clerical immunity. In the following decades processions of the Host were introduced elsewhere, albeit very slowly, which show great similarities with that of the Church of St. Gereon.[9] Only in the course of the 14th century would the 'triumphalist' procession of the Host begin to penetrate urban life.

According to Th. Schnitzler the first Corpus Christi procession in Cologne can be considered as a variant of what is termed an 'Asperges-procession' that was held every Sunday prior to the High Mass.[10] The new element – carrying along the Sacrament – was, according to him, inspired by another already long existing liturgical tradition, namely the old Roman custom of taking away the Sacrament in procession after the Mass on Maundy Thursday. The canons of the Church of St. Gereon would not, then, have been intending to begin something new with

---

[8] Ezio Franceschini: Origine e stile della bolla "Transiturus", in *Aevum* 39 (1965) 218-243.

[9] Theodor Schnitzler: Die erste Fronleichnamsprozession. Datum und Charakter, in *Münchener theologische Zeitschrift* 24 (1973) 352-362; cf. Otto Nussbaum: *Die Aufbewahrung der Eucharistie* (Bonn 1979) 155-156, where the oldest Corpus Christi processions are mentioned from Benediktbeuern (1286), Würzburg (1298), the St. Gotthard monastery at Hildesheim (1301), and several other places.

[10] Schnitzler: Erste Fronleichnamsprozession 361. The term *Asperges* is derived from Psalm 50, 9 and denotes the custom of blessing the believers present before the solemn Sunday Mass with Holy Water. See Terence Bailey: *The processions of Sarum and the Western Church* (Toronto 1971) 98-106. According to this author the custom of holding the *Asperges* procession each Sunday would only become established in the 12th century.

their procession. It could even be said there was a "(…) nahtlosen über-
gang von den frühmittelalterlichen Verehrungsformen der Eucharistie
zum hochmittelalterlichen Fronleichnamsglanz."[11]

This last, static characterization is, to my mind, inaccurate. For
instance, the Maundy Thursday procession was indeed already very
old at the end of the 13th century, but distinctly had not remained
unchanged until that time. The actual ritual development of this procession took place only after the 12th century, thus in the decades
directly preceding the introduction of the first Corpus Christi processions. Moreover, this growth in rituals occurred under the influence of
the doctrine of the *praesentia realis* and transubstantiation formulated
by the Church, and the greater honours due to the Sacrament as a
result of this.[12] In fact, Schnitzler's view raises more questions than it
answers; there is no way whatsoever in which one can speak of a
'seamless' continuation of forms of devotion from the early Middle
Ages.

From its similarities with the Sunday *Asperges*-processions and the
translatio-procession on Maundy Thursday it is certainly clear that in
terms of design the first Corpus Christi processions were not drawn
from thin air. With the new procession the people of Cologne and elsewhere likewise tightened the logical connection between the two feasts
in which the institution of the Eucharist was commemorated.[13]
Undoubtedly the link between the two feasts was part of what encouraged the later inclusion of elements referring to Jesus's suffering in 14th
and 15th centuries Corpus Christi processions, such as the carrying
along of the *arma Christi* and the singing of hymns that one would associate more with Holy Week than with Corpus Christi.[14]

[11] SCHNITZLER: Erste Fronleichnamsprozession 360.

[12] Hans NIEDERMEIER: Über die Sakramentsprozessionen im Mittelalter. Ein Beitrag
zur Geschichte der kirchlichen Umgänge, in *Sacris Erudiri* 22 (1974-1975) 401-436,
esp. 402-406; Hansjörg AUF DER MAUR: *Feiern im Rhythmus der Zeit*, I. *Herrenfeste in
Woche und Jahr* (= Gottesdienst der Kirche, Handbuch der liturgiewissenschaft 5)
(Regensburg 1983) 106. A familiar example of a *translatio*-procession on Maundy
Thursday, arising after what is termed the Second Eucharistic Controversy (the controversy between Berengar of Tours and the ecclesiastical authorities) is that of Rouen; see
JOANNES ABRINCENSIS: *Liber de officiis ecclesiasticis*, in J.-P. MIGNE: *Patrologia Latina*
147 (Paris 1879) 50.

[13] See CASPERS: *Eucharistische vroomheid* 54-56, on the Office of the Sacrament, *Sacerdos in aeternum*, of Thomas Aquinas. Cf. SNOEK: *Medieval piety* 263-264.

[14] CASPERS: *Eucharistische vroomheid* 77-78.

Questions must be raised, however, about the theophoric content of the first Corpus Christi processions. Despite the complications introduced by the eucharistic discourse, bearing the Sacrament did not function exclusively as a tribute to Christ, who was present in the Sacrament, but to a great degree also as a dramatic representation of an episode from Jesus' Passion. The information that Schnitzler provides indeed contributes to greater understanding of the theophoric processions, but does not affect Browe's proposition. On the contrary, the strong link that it demonstrates between the two feasts of the Lord, makes this proposition all the more convincing.

3.2. The Palm Sunday procession

More than once in the literature attention has been devoted to the question of whether the Palm Sunday processions, as these existed in England and Normandy after the end of the 11th century, were the most important source of inspiration for later Corpus Christi processions. According to Browe this question must be answered in the negative. The Host was indeed carried along during the procession on Palm Sunday, in a closed pyx, but it certainly would not have been the centre of attention. In addition to a statue of the Saviour, the Gospelbooks, and possible relics of saints, it would have been only one of the objects worthy of veneration that were being processed.[15]

However, from a frequently used processional order for Palm Sunday which Lanfranc of Bec had promulgated, it can be clearly seen how central a place the Sacrament occupied. In the procession as prescribed there were indeed also two crosses and two texts of the Gospels carried along, but these acts are subordinate to the bearing of the Body of Christ.[16] The reason that Lanfranc attached importance to this processional order, which he possibly assembled himself,[17] would have been

---

[15] BROWE: *Verehrung* 89-90. For an iconographic survey of 'Christ on the donkey', the statue that was borne in the Palm Sunday procession, see Marijke BROEKAERT: Kristus op de palmezel. Bijdrage tot een kultuurhistorische en ikonografische betekenis van een processiebeeld, in *Oostvlaamse Zanten* 60 (1985) 125-144, 215.

[16] David KNOWLES: *Decreta Lanfranci monachis Cantuariensibus transmissa* (Siegburg 1967) 23-25. On the authority of Lanfranc's *Decreta pro ordine Sancti Benedicti*, see Theo STEMMLER: *Liturgische Feiern und geistliche Spiele. Studien zu Erscheinungsformen des Dramatischen im Mittelalter* (Tübingen 1970) 196, n. 111.

[17] STEMMLER: *Liturgische Feiern* 199.

that he wanted to provide a clear and visible answer to the heresy of Berengar (d. 1088), who contended that Christ was only present in the Sacrament in a symbolic manner.[18] Among other things, the Sacrament is preceded by men bearing banners, is honoured by genuflection as it passes, and is set on a *mensa* whenever the procession comes to a halt at a station. These are all clear agreements with the later Corpus Christi procession as Browe has it in mind.[19] According to Th. Stemmler, thanks to the Palm Sunday procession the population of England and Normandy would already have been familiar with theophoric processions long before Corpus Christi existed. And thanks to the joyful and triumphant Palm Sunday procession, in these regions the tableaus displayed and the plays performed on Corpus Christi would have been in service of the theophoric character, or more precisely, of bringing homage to the eucharistic Christ. In contrast, on the continent, save for Normandy, in the Corpus Christi procession more emphasis was placed on the Passion of Christ. Thus in England, much earlier than in the rest of Europe, there was an answer to the call of Pope Urban IV to make Corpus Christi a feast of joy.[20]

The English Corpus Christi Cycles indeed exude a different, more exuberant atmosphere, and deliver a different message than many European processions of the Sacrament in which, for instance, the *arma Christi* were accorded such an important place.[21] This points to the peculiar situation in Normandy and England. But at the same time it is clear that the Palm Sunday procession cannot be considered as predecessor or source of inspiration for the later processions of the Sacrament on the European mainland, over the greatest part of which Western Christendom extended at that time.

---

[18] STEMMLER: *Liturgische Feiern* 196, with reference to Gerhard MATERN: *Zur Vorgeschichte und Geschichte der Fronleichnamsfeier besonders in Spanien. Studien zur Volksfrömmigkeit des Mittelalters und der beginnenden Neuzeit* (Münster 1962) 43.

[19] Particularly STEMMLER: *Liturgische Feiern* 195-196, points to the great similarities between these two processions. More recent, but more concise, are Miri RUBIN: *Corpus Christi. The Eucharist in late medieval culture* (Cambridge 1991) 244 and SNOEK: *Medieval piety* 261-262.

[20] STEMMLER: *Liturgische Feiern* 206-208. It is remarkable that at the same time that the Corpus Christi procession became better established in England, the Palm Sunday procession began to lose its theophoric character. The theophoric Palm Sunday procession survived the Middle Ages in only a few places; see NIEDERMEIER: Sakramentsprozessionen 421.

[21] STEMMLER: *Liturgische Feiern* 167-180.

3.3. Bringing the viaticum

According to S. van Dijk and J. Walker the roots of the Corpus Christi procession are, to a large extent, to be found in a pastoral practice of the Middle Ages, namely of the pastor bringing the viaticum to the home of a sick person.[22] They point out that the Corpus Christi procession is not liturgical, because it is not part of the Office or the Mass. Therefore it could not have been created on the basis of the Palm Sunday or any other liturgical procession. The Corpus Christi procession deserves, rather, to be considered as a independent expression of piety, directed toward the Son of God in the form of the Bread. Such a procession could only really have started after the 'medieval mind' had become accustomed to a liturgical feast specifically in honour of the Sacrament. Following these two authors further, at the earliest this precondition could have been fulfilled after the first quarter of the 14th century. The only custom then existing which could be considered as serving as a model for the Corpus Christi procession was, as has been said, the bringing of the viaticum. In the course of the 13th and 14th centuries ecclesiastical authorities at the diocesan level had issued numerous instructions for the conduct of both the pastor and the individual believers involved during this 'small procession', as it is called.[23] A favourite theme in these was the way in which respect for the Sacrament must be expressed. Thus when believers had become accustomed to the idea of a feast in honour of the Sacrament, thanks to the 'small procession' they were also familiar with the idea of a procession in which the idea of the Sacrament was central.

The argument put forward by Van Dijk and Walker is overstated; the strict separation that they introduce between liturgical processions and the 'non-liturgical' Corpus Christi processions, on the ground of which the bringing of the viaticum must be considered as the predecessor of

---

[22] S.J.P. VAN DIJK & J. Hazelden WALKER: *The myth of the aumbry. Notes on medieval reservation practice and eucharistic devotion* (London 1957) 80-83. Cf. FELBECKER: *Prozession* 196-197.

[23] Among others who use the expression 'small procession' is O.F. TER REEGEN: De Sacramentsprocessie. Onderzoek naar de bronnen van het processie-ceremonieel in het *Caeremoniale Episcoporum*, in *Sanctissima Eucharistia* 47 (1956) 189-254, esp. 193. This term is particularly applicable for the Low Countries and adjoining areas. The use of the term *processio* to denote the bringing of the viaticum in the 13th century appears to have been restricted to the dioceses in this area.

the Corpus Christi procession, is not convincing.[24] Through this all too facile selection, the 'pastoral' procession with the viaticum comes to the fore as the only candidate for inspiring the later magnificent Corpus Christi procession. There are other authors who also refer to this function as a model, but they always do this with some qualifications.[25] What makes the discourse of this pair of authors especially relevant for this paper is, however, their argumentation regarding the 'medieval mind', which needed so much time to become used to a feast in honour of the Sacrament – an argument that in terms of content, and time span, is in harmony with Browe's view. It is because of this that the historical consideration of the procession bringing the viaticum will be somewhat more extensively discussed than that of the types of procession already considered.

As Van Dijk and Walker already emphasized, from the 13th century councils and synods paid increasing attention to the bringing of the viaticum.[26] Until that time there was little worthiness surrounding this custom, although both priests and believers regarded it as of the greatest importance. Being able to provide the viaticum in good time was even, from the 12th century, given as a motive for founding parishes.[27] In taking up this new issue, ecclesiastical gatherings followed a trend which had begun within the milieu of the Cistercians, according to whom the consecration during the Mass and the bringing of the viaticum were of the same order. For example, in 1201 the Cistercian cardinal, Abbot Guido, determined that henceforth the ringing of a church bell would serve to indicate that the people in the church must kneel from the elevation of the Host through the blessing of the chalice, and that also each time that the Body of Christ was brought to the home of an ill person this should be indicated by the ringing of the

---

[24] For example, the two authors suggest without any justification that the 13th century processional order of the Church of St. Gereon in Cologne, which is part of the liturgy, never even existed; VAN DIJK & WALKER: *Myth* 81.

[25] TER REEGEN: Sacramentsprocessie 5, 24-25; MATERN: *Vorgeschichte* 58-71; Joseph AVRIL: La pastorale des malades et des mourants aux XIIe et XIIIe siècles, in Herman BRAET & Werner VERBEKE (eds): *Death in the Middle Ages* (Louvain 1983) 88-106, esp. 99.

[26] For the way in which the viaticum had been dealt with before the late Middle Ages, see SNOEK: *Medieval piety* 115-131 (see also 263); for the historical development of the bringing of the viaticum, see BROWE: Die Sterbekommunion im Altertum und Mittelalter, in *Zeitschrift für katholische Theologie* 60 (1936) 1-54, 211-240.

[27] AVRIL: La pastorale 88-106, esp. 93.

bells, so that the people, both at home and in the streets, could adore Christ.[28]

In the synodical statutes of Paris from the early 13th century, Bishop Eudes de Sully (who was also the initiator of the elevation of the Host during the Mass) laid down a number of stipulations with regard to the bringing of the viaticum, therein termed the *corpus Domini, corpus Christi*, or *Eucharistia*, making it into an elaborate ceremony. Eudes prescribed that:[29]

- it is not permitted for a deacon to bring the Body of Christ to the ill, unless no priest is available;
- because of the danger of a fall, the pyx must be securely sealed;
- the bringing of the viaticum must occur *cum laterna precedente*;
- both going and coming the priest must sing the seven penitential psalms;[30]
- if it was a long way, the priest must add fifteen psalms and other prayers to these, in order to invite bystanders to express the requisite honour to God;
- the laity must be admonished, everywhere, that they witness the Body of Christ being carried past, to genuflect at once and pray with folded hands.

Several years later the bringing of the viaticum would receive still another upgrade in status, this time to be credited to Pope Honorius III. In a letter of 1220, directed to the bishops of Ireland, Honorius determined that the priest should frequently instruct the faithful that they must bow in respect when, during the celebration of the Mass, the Host was elevated, and that they must do the same when the priest brought the Host to the sick, because piety must be multiplied among all.[31]

It is striking how Honorius places the bearing of the Sacrament in the small procession on the same level with the elevation in the Mass,

---

[28] J. STRANGE (ed.): *Caesarii Heisterbacensis monachi Ordinis Cisterciensis Dialogus miraculorum* II (Köln etc. 1851) 206; BROWE: *Verehrung* 35.

[29] Odette PONTAL (ed.): *Les statuts synodaux français du XIIIe siècle, précédés de l'historique du synode diocésain depuis ses origines* I. *Les statuts de Paris et le synodal de l'Ouest* (Paris 1971) 58-60.

[30] Cf. MATERN: *Vorgeschichte* 300-302, regarding the old Corpus Christi procession on Majorca.

[31] Ioannes D. MANSI: *Sacrorum Conciliorum nova, et amplissima collectio* XXII (Venice etc. 1778) 1100.

only a few years after the latter action was introduced into the Church in the West. From the formulation it likewise appears to what a great degree the custom was already established that people should direct their attention to the Host in inward prayer during the elevation. Honorius, as before him the Abbot Guido, evidently wanted to introduce a new form of devotion, one which was linked to the small procession. He wanted to expand, in terms of time and place, that short moment that believers had to adore Christ in the Sacrament. Henceforth there were to be two occasions: the elevation *and* the small procession.[32]

In the further course of the 13th century the ceremonial was increasingly further expanded. The statutes that Guiard de Laon, Bishop of Cambrai and one of the spiritual fathers of the feast of Corpus Christi, issued between 1238 and 1247 with regard to the bringing of the viaticum set the stage for later synodical legislation in many dioceses.[33]

– When a sick person wishes to receive communion, the priest must first visit him without the Body of the Lord and, if the situation still permits it, carefully receive a confession from him. Then the priest returns to the church, but before he is ready to bring communion to the sick person, the bell must be rung for some time so that the faithful, being warned, come to the church in order to respectfully follow the priest who bears their Lord and, on the way there and back, reverently say the prayers, which they know, for the benefit of the ill. Both going and returning the priest says the seven psalms and the litany and other prayers. Preceded by a lantern-bearer, the priest enters the home of the sick person, while the faithful wait outside for him. When the sick person has received communion, they return to the church, following the priest who bears the Body of Christ. The return is performed in the same manner as the way there. Believers who participate in this act of penitence and contrition receive for each, both the going and the coming, five days indulgence (...).

---

[32] That we are here dealing with two forms of the same devotion we find illustrated once again in the *Dialogus miraculorum* of Caesarius of Heisterbach, in the same chapter (51) which contains references to the stipulations of Abbot Guido, see STRANGE (ed.): *Caesarii Heisterbacensis (...) Dialogus miraculorum* 206, "Miles quidam in Francia fuit tantae devotionis, ut quotienscumque Christi corpus elevari sive deferri videret, prostratus illud adoraret."

[33] Joseph AVRIL (ed.): *Les statuts synodaux français du XIIIᵉ siècle, IV. Les statuts synodaux de l'ancienne province de Reims (Cambrai, Arras, Noyon, Soissons et Tournai)* (Paris 1995) 41-43.

– If there is a danger that the sick person will vomit up the Body of Christ, it is better that this will not be administered to him, but if he believes sincerely, he will communicate spiritually. Before the priest permits the sick person to communicate, he asks him if he believes that under this form the bread is the same as the Body of Christ, who was born of the Virgin, suffered on the cross, and rose on the third day (...).

– When the Body of the Lord is carried past, the faithful standing in the area must kneel if possible, beat themselves on the breast, and pray with head bowed and hands folded. Knights must not esteem themselves too highly to descend from their horses and adore Him, who descended from heaven for them.[34]

Like Guido, Bishop Guiard, noted as *doctor eucharisticus*,[35] sought to fix the attention of the faithful on the Sacrament by means of the ringing of the church bells. About the same time the custom was being introduced into the parishes of ringing the church bell during the elevation in the Mass, "to summon the spirits of the faithful to prayer".[36] The stipulations from Cambrai would in the course of the 13th century be taken over by other dioceses, most extensively by Munster (1279), Cologne (1280) and Liège (1288).

Aside from the theophoric aspect, there exist several remarkable similarities between the procession with the viaticum developed in the 13th century and the later Corpus Christi procession. These include the possibility for believers to earn indulgences by their participation, and the notable role accorded to light (candles, lanterns) carried in the procession. Still more remarkable, however, is the parallel between the Body of Christ in the Mass and the Body of Christ in the small procession.

The history of the small procession fits in readily with the views of Van Dijk and Walker with regard to the 'medieval mind' that very gradually became accustomed to the Sacrament outside the church building. On the other hand, their unjustified separation of liturgical processions,

---

[34] Cf. Phil. 2, 10. See also our note 39 regarding Berthold of Ratisbon.

[35] P.C. BOEREN: *La vie et les oeuvres de Guiard de Laon, 1170 env. - 1248* (La Haye 1956) 86-87; Ephrem LONGPRÉ: Eucharistie et expérience mystique, in *Dictionnaire de spiritualité* IV (Paris 1960) 1586-1621, esp. 1598.

[36] PONTAL (ed.): *Statuts de Paris* 101; cf. note 28 regarding the Cistercian Guido. In the Cistercian order the sounding of the bells before the consecration was already customary in 1152; see Hans Bernhard MEYER: Die Elevation im deutschen Mittelalter und bei Luther, in *Zeitschrift für katholische Theologie* 85 (1963) 162-217, esp. 166.

already noted above, and the distinction which they introduce between pastoral actions and liturgy are thrown into sharp relief. It is clear that to the degree that the ceremonial aspects of the small procession developed further, ever more attention was also given to the Sacrament in this 'pastoral' duty, and ever less to the sick person. If the bringing of the viaticum in the period before the 12th century (in the monastic world) and the 13th century (in public life) had been an integral part of pastoral care of the ill,[37] after that point the small procession became autonomous while extreme unction receded into the background in the interest of bishops and theologians. In this way, the death of a fellow Christian became an occasion to venerate the Eucharist. The conciliar regulations that the priest must take care that on the way back to the church from his visit to the sick person, he also has in his possession a consecrated Host are significant here; with regard to earning indulgences, the return is just as important as going there. The view of some authors that the public small procession must primarily be considered as a testimony to the familiarity with physical death that people in the Middle Ages had, cannot be sustained on the basis of the foregoing.[38]

The way in which the clergy could acquaint believers with the importance of the small procession and their obligations in regard to it is arrestingly illustrated in a sermon by the Franciscan missionary preacher Berthold of Ratisbon (d. 1272).[39] With requisite pathos he rehearses how the faithful, when they see that the priest brings Him (God) to the sick, must kneel on both knees:

> Before an earthly lord one goes down on one knee, because such a lord has power only over the body. Before the Lord of heaven one goes down on both knees, because he has given us body and soul. Men must kneel and

[37] Cf. AVRIL: Pastorale 90, 98, regarding Reginon of Prüm. Cf. also Bert WIRIX: The viaticum. From the beginning to the present day, in Charles CASPERS, Gerard LUKKEN & Gerard ROUWHORST (eds.): *Bread of heaven. Customs and practices surrouding Holy Communion. Essays in the history of liturgy and culture* (= Liturgia condenda 3) (Kampen 1995) 247-259, esp. 250-253.

[38] Gerhard JARITZ: Der öffentliche Tod. Gedanken zum Sterben in Spätmittelalter und früher Neuzeit, in James HOGG (ed.): *Zeit, Tod und Ewigkeit* (Salzburg 1987) 108-124, esp. 113-114.

[39] Franz GÖBEL (ed.): *Die Predigten des Franziskaners Berthold von Regensburg* (Regensburg 1929) 407-424, the passage summarized here, p. 420-421. Apart from this, Berthold also preached at the request of Pope Urban IV; see J. VAN HERWAARDEN: Middeleeuwse aflaten en Nederlandse devotie, in D.E.H. DE BOER & J.W. MARSILJE (eds.): *De Nederlanden in de late Middeleeuwen* (Utrecht 1987) 31-68, esp. 44.

bare their heads without hesitation, even if this means to kneel in the mire.[40] Many, however, remain standing, without even removing their hats. These impious persons would do well to take a lesson from the Old Testament, which tells of men who were struck dead because they did not conduct themselves with respect for the Ark with the manna in it, which refers to the pyx with the viaticum.[41] One must call upon Him regarding everything which distresses body and soul, and ask to nevermore be separated from Him. One must ask Him for forgiveness, for now and for that moment when the body and soul shall be parted. When someone conducts themselves in that way, each and every time that a priest passes with Him, day or night, they will receive from Him eternal honour.[42]

This sermon is not isolated. There arose in the 13th century a whole genre of narratives about respect (or disrespect) shown for the viaticum, or the priest who bore it, and the potential consequences that such acts or omissions had for one's eternal happiness.[43] Although in these stories – as in Berthold's sermon – connections were often indeed made between respect for the Sacrament and the destination of the soul after earthly death, the sick person, to whose house the procession made its way, usually played no role at all.

In the administration of the viaticum as prescribed by Guiard and later bishops it is also noticeable that the attention shifts from the sick person to the Sacrament. First, there is the remarkable credo, concentrated on the *praesentia realis*, that is different from and less balanced than the confession of faith that the dying pronounced in earlier times. This 'eucharistic credo' arose in the second half of the 11th century inside the walls of monasteries, and was intended to emphasize the

---

[40] With respect to kneeling in the mire, see the last statute of Guiard de Laon, regarding knights who should dismount from their horses. Cf. also STRANGE (ed): *Caesarii Heisterbacensis [...] Dialogus Miraculorum* II, 206 (dist. 9, cap. 51); BROWE: Sterbekommunion 42-43; MEYER: Elevation 170.

[41] Cf. François BOESPFLUG, Olivier CHRISTIN & Benoît TASSEL (eds.): *Molanus, traité des saintes images* I (Paris 1996) 226-227, where those who mock the sacrament that is being carried are compared with Michal, who was disgusted with David's dancing before the Ark (II Sam. 6, 20).

[42] Other mendicant friars in the 13th century also preached views on the Eucharist which in general terms agreed with those of Berthold; cf. D.L. D'AVRAY: *The preaching of the Friars. Sermons diffused from Paris before 1300* (Oxford 1985) 85-89.

[43] For example, a legend, drawn upon by Peter Paul Rubens, among others, connects the respect that Rudolf I of Hapsburg showed for the Sacrament in 1264 with the good fortune that his dynasty experienced thereafter; see Luc DUERLOO & Werner THOMAS: *Albrecht & Isabella 1598-1621* (Turnhout 1998) 233-235.

identity of the Sacrament of the Altar with the historic Christ, and at the same time to censure the heresy of Berengar which was then agitating the Church.[44] It was already laid down in the 12th century rituals of the Cistercians that the priest must display the Host to the sick person and then must ask him if he believed that all salvation resided in it alone.[45] From the beginning of the 13th century, outside of the world of monastics and clerics, starting in the diocese of Cambrai, the making of such a declaration would begin to play an increasingly important role in the pastoral care of the sick.[46] Although the 'threat' posed by Berengar then had already long become a thing of the past, the eucharistic credo continued to exist as a sort of declaration of loyalty to the Church and her dogmas, in opposition to those of different views.[47] Secondly, there is the stipulation that if the sick person is no longer able to partake of the Host, he can communicate spiritually, provided that he believes what the Church (through the pastor) proclaims about the Eucharist.[48] On the one hand this stipulation testifies to an understanding for the condition in which the sick can find themselves; on the other hand this generous gesture serves to make it clear

[44] Friedrich BAUMKIRCHNER: *Das Credo beim Sterben in der Spiritualität des Mittelalters* (Salzburg 1983) 197-198.

[45] BAUMKIRCHNER: *Das Credo* 106-110.

[46] BROWE: Sterbekommunion 213.

[47] Cf. W. NOLET & P.C. BOEREN: *Kerkelijke instellingen in de Middeleeuwen* (Amsterdam 1951) 257, who arrive at a completely wrong assessment of the situation by interpreting the credo on the sickbed (as it was formulated by the 1288 synodical statutes in Liège) as an ultimate attempt made by the priest to teach believers that it was not always necessary to communicate under both forms. What makes this mistake somewhat understandable is the fact that in many dioceses in the 13th century it was still customary that the faithful received ablution wine after their annual communion (at Easter). See Jacques TOUSSAERT: *Le sentiment religieux en Flandre à la fin du Moyen-Age* (Paris 1963) 161-180.

[48] The statutes of Guiard de Laon evidently form the oldest source with guidelines for spiritual communion in lay pastoral care. These guidelines at the same time provide evidence that spiritual communion had taken its place in popular piety much earlier than has been accepted in the literature. Cf. Heinz R. SCHLETTE: *Die Lehre von der geistlichen Kommunion bei Bonaventura, Albert dem Grossen und Thomas von Aquin* (München 1959) 214: 'Für die Früh- und Hochscholastik gilt gleicherweise, dass die manducatio spiritualis als theologisches Problem bedacht wird, nicht als Frömmigkeitspraxis [...] Die Methoden der geistlichen Kommunion als Frömmigkeitspraxis in diesem Sinne werden erst in der Mystik das 14. bis 16. Jahrhunderts im einzelnen entwickelt'. See also Louis DE BAZELAIRE: Communion spirituelle, in *Dictionnaire de spiritualité*, II (Paris 1953) 1294-1300, esp. 1297.

that communion – be it sacramental, or be it spiritual alone – is indispensable for acquiring eternal salvation.

After the above digressions, the bringing (and administration) of the viaticum comes yet more to the fore as the place outside the Mass where the faithful also learned to venerate the Sacrament. It is clear that for Guido, Eudes, Honorius III, Guiard, Berthold and those who followed their exhortations, the theophoric character of the small procession was not something secondary. They already had in mind what according to Browe was realized only in the 14th century with the carrying of the 'unconcealed' Sacrament in the procession of Corpus Christi.

3.4. Sacraments of Miracle

Already before the introduction of the feast of Corpus Christi in the diocese of Liège, there existed cults in the region of Western Christendom which had arisen as a result of a miracle involving the Sacrament, the so-called 'Sacraments of Miracle'. These cults multiplied sharply in number during the same period that the feast of Corpus Christi began to expand – i.e., from the second half of the 13th century. With regard to many institutions in honour of the Sacrament (particularly chapels), it is not clear whether it was Corpus Christi, or a Sacrament of Miracle, which lay behind their founding.[49] In some places miraculous Hosts or blood-marked corporales, which were considered to be tangible evidence of such miracles, were from time to time displayed to the populace. Normally the Host or corporale was contained in a reliquary or (later) a monstrance for this purpose.

To the question of whether these cults had already, in the 13th century, familiarized the Christian population in one way or another with the veneration of the Sacrament outside of the Mass, we can answer: no. The first reason is that the theophoric processions (on a certain day of the year) became connected with these cults relatively late, generally only after the 'triumphant' type of the Corpus Christi procession had already become a familiar phenomenon.[50] A second and more funda-

---

[49] Peter BROWE: Die Ausbreitung des Fronleichnamsfestes, in *Jahrbuch für Liturgiewissenschaft* 8 (1928) 107-143, esp. 111-113; vgl. Ludwig REMLING: *Bruderschaften in Franken. Kirchen- und sozialgeschichtliche Untersuchungen zum spätmittelalterlichen und frühneuzeitlichen Bruderschaftswesen* (Würzburg 1986) 215.

[50] Occasioned by a miracle involving the Sacrament, before 1300 there were processions which did take place now and then, but these were never repeated on a regular

mental reason for a negative answer is that Sacrament of Miracle cults were in fact corrosive to the universalizing of the Sacrament which was promoted in the small procession and the Corpus Christi procession, because, in view of the peculiar circumstances and special manifestations involved, such a cultus distinguishes itself from the Sacrament that is present at the Mass everywhere and was carried to the sick daily in countless places. Moreover, with every Sacrament of Miracle it is a knotty problem to determine whether it was an example of eucharistic devotion, or of veneration of a relic in which Christ was not (or was no longer) present.[51] Many of these cults did indeed have a certain place in eucharistic piety, but often only as a reference to the Mass. For example, the still existing Sacrament of Miracle at Meerssen arose out of a divine sign by which it was indicated that Peter Cantor had an incorrect view on transubstantiation.[52]

4. A NEW HYPOTHESIS

This contribution recapitulates and poses anew a much discussed component of the history of the feast of Corpus Christi, namely the significance of the 13th century theophoric processions. The point of departure for this was Browe's argument that only after the introduction of

schedule. An example of such a procession can be found in the report that Rupert of Deutz makes of the fire that struck Deutz in 1128. The only attempt known to me to organize an annual eucharistic procession during the 13th century in honour of a Sacrament of Miracle involves Daroca in Spain. There are at least 47 eucharistic miracles known from Spain from before 1300. For more information and references to the literature, see CASPERS: *Eucharistische vroomheid* 100, note 156.

[51] According to Browe the clergy in the late Middle Ages was quite divided about the veneration of miraculous Hosts and corporales. Some clergy held the view that Christ remained sacramentally present in a Sacrament of Miracle, while others vigorously denied that presence, and still others reckoned the miraculous Hosts, etc., to the *summae reliquiae*; see Peter BROWE: *Die eucharistischen Wunder des Mittelalters* (Breslau 1938) 198. Cf. also Charles ZIKA: Hosts, processions and pilgrimages. Controlling the sacred in fifteenth-century Germany, in *Past and present* no. 118 (1988) 25-64; CASPERS: *Eucharistische vroomheid* 231-264.

[52] Jaap VAN MOOLENBROEK: *Mirakels historisch. De exempels van Caesarius van Heisterbach over Nederland en Nederlanders* (Hilversum 1999) 251-256; Charles CASPERS & Jan VAN HERWAARDEN: Meerssen, in Peter Jan MARGRY & Charles CASPERS (eds.): *Bedevaartplaatsen in Nederland [Places of Pilgrimage in the Netherlands]* II. *Provincie Limburg* (Amsterdam-Hilversum 2000) 562-582, esp. 567.

the carrying of the 'unconcealed' Sacrament in the Corpus Christi procession, about 1350, this feast did become what it had been intended to be at its introduction in 1264, to wit, a 'feast of joy'. It was only then that the mentality of the faithful enabled them to adore Christ in the Sacrament in a way which was of a similar nature and equal to that of the elevation during the Mass. The moment of joy was defined by the possibility of beholding Christ in the form of the Bread, source of all grace. This was the green light for honouring the Saviour with music and dance and theatre, consonant with the wish of Pope Urban IV. Corpus Christi, with its triumphalistic procession and elaborate performances, so characteristic for religious life in the late Middle Ages, was born.

As a result of this contribution, Browe's views have come under fire, since it has been established that devotion to the Sacrament outside of the Mass did not develop later, but contemporaneous with the devotion to the Sacrament during the Mass, and that both forms of devotion were promoted by the same individuals and considered as being of the same order. An extra motive for them was that the devotion in question at the same time implied a declaration of loyalty to ecclesiastical doctrine on the *praesentia realis* (cf. the 'eucharistic credo'). These motives can chiefly be illuminated on the basis of the discussion of what is termed the 'small procession', in which the viaticum is brought to the home of a sick person. It would appear from the many exhortations to its adoration that the fact that during the small procession the Sacrament was carried in a 'concealed' manner formed no obstacle to such devotion. It is true that the bishops decreed that the Sacrament must be well encased during the small procession; the rationale for this was not, however, that the Host might not be seen but that it must be well protected against potential accidents.[53]

From all this we can only conclude that the explanation which Browe gives for the late origin of Corpus Christi as a 'feast of joy' is no longer adequately founded. The question which remains, however, is what then was indeed the impetus for this new, joyful dimension for Corpus Christi? Pointing to the small procession as the predecessor of the Corpus Christi procession does have some ground, in view of the similarities between the two types of procession, but an all too direct derivation is still problematic. All things considered, the small procession was not

---

[53] See our note 29.

joyful, as the instruction that penitential psalms are to be prayed alone testifies.

On the basis of the historiographic considerations offered I would still, by way of hypothesis, lay out a new explanation. First, I would want to change something in the stereotypical succession of events: starting with the elevation of the Host in the Mass, followed by the first theophoric processions, and at the close the later, 'unconcealed' theophoric procession.

Eucharistic devotion inside and outside the Mass arose at the same time, at least within the public domain of the church (i.e., parishes). Within the world of the monasteries – particularly the Cistercian milieu has been mentioned several times – a development had however already been under way much earlier with regard to the administration of the viaticum. It is from this fact that I would propose a different succession of events, for clarifying the 'universalization' of the Sacrament: first came the moment at which the Host was shown to the sick individual who thereupon recited an 'eucharistic credo'; next there came the display of the Host to the faithful during the Mass, the elevation; and finally there was the 'unconcealed' theophoric procession in which the Host was displayed to everyone. This new succession, from individual to universal, perhaps has nothing binding about it, but it does imply the possibility that the later Corpus Christi procession does not necessarily have to rest on older theophoric processions. Put more strongly, it makes it possible for us to see these processions as an obstacle to the breakthrough of the 'unconcealed' theophoric procession. The eucharistic devotion which arose in the beginning of the 13th century, from its very inception had influence on the already existing processional practices, as we have seen in the case of the processions on Maundy Thursday and Palm Sunday. The first Corpus Christi processions took over important elements from these, but they were at the same time impeded, or at any rate delayed, in their own development by them. In the early decades of the 13th century the Western Church wanted to take rapid strides in ushering its congregants into an *orbis eucharisticus*, but it would necessarily take considerable time before this new *orbis* was integrated within the already long-standing liturgical tradition. That the 'feast of joy' ultimately experienced its breakthrough was despite, rather than thanks to, the then existing processional practices. The transition from the concealed theophoric to the unconcealed theophoric procession can thus still be seen as an important innovation. In this way the feast is liberated from older feasts with their 'privileges'. The believers in the cities and countryside were now at last enabled to combine the devotion with which they had so long been familiar with the token of homage toward the eucharistic Christ that arose from their own initiatives. The joy involved sprouted not only from the papal intentions proclaimed with the initiation of the feast in 1264, but also from the emancipation of the feast itself, and the believers who celebrated it.

CARLA DAUVEN-VAN KNIPPENBERG

DRAMATIC CELEBRATION OF THE EASTER FESTIVAL[1]

1. INTRODUCTION

In a contribution to a compendium in the field of liturgical studies it may seem superfluous to begin with the statement that in the Catholic tradition Easter, the celebration of Christ's resurrection, is the most important festival of the church's year. This is however the correct starting point for this article, since the Easter festival was frequently elaborated with historicising rituals which had a wide and long-lasting influence. The Easter rite is reflected in the religious and secular drama of the middle ages, indeed the roots of mediaeval drama as a whole are closely bound up with the theatrical representation of the resurrection.

Older scholarship believed in an evolutionary theory of the development of medieval religious drama, the nucleus of which was the Easter trope. It was thought to have developed in stages via simple Easter celebration, complex Easter office and Easter play to Passion play. The Christmas plays were held to have developed in similar fashion by analogy. Careful consideration of the extant texts however revealed that the Easter and Christmas offices are not simpler forms of the corresponding plays. The plays should rather be regarded as independent products with a definite didactic purpose, never associated with the liturgy.[2]

Starting out from extant texts from the German-speaking dioceses of the Holy Roman Empire[3] we will show the way in which the visual

---

[1] With thanks to John Tailby of the University of Leeds for translating my German text.

[2] The chief representatives of the outdated evolutionary theory are Edmund K. CHAMBERS: *The medieval stage* (Oxford 1903), and Karl YOUNG: *The drama of the medieval church* (Oxford 1933). It was refuted by Osborne B. HARDISON: *Christian rite and Christian drama in the Middle Ages* (Maryland 1965).

[3] The emphasis of this article lies in the drama of the German-speaking area, since the author is herself a German drama specialist. For an overview of the genre in the French language area, see Charles MAZOUER: *Le théâtre français du Moyen Age* (Paris

representation of the resurrection contributed to the celebration of Easter day. A review of the centuries up to the Reformation will then by discussion of selected dramatic texts illustrate the movements from rite to popular entertainment and indeed to satire, alongside this we find also the contrary tendency to tie the texts once more more closely to the rite.

If we accept the report of the late 4th-century pilgrim Etheria, the Easter offices were accompanied by commemorative rituals from an early date.[4] The travel diary of this high-born nun on her pilgrimage to Jerusalem survives only in an incomplete 11th-century manuscript, lacking beginning and end, and with several other pages missing.[5] The surviving sections however provide significant information about liturgical practices in Jerusalem at that date. They make clear that whereas in the west the emphasis was on the mystery of salvation, in Jerusalem the liturgy overall had a strong historicising tendency. The liturgical texts matched the place and time of the historical events and therefore the offices were a historical reconstruction of episodes in the process of salvation.[6] Thus during the Easter vigils baptismal candidates were led in procession with the bishop to the Anastasis, the great rotunda around the Holy Sepulchre erected by Constantine (d. 337). According to her report as soon as the procession entered the brightly illuminated church a priest sang a psalm and the whole congregation the response; this was repeated twice more, before the Cave of the Sepulchre was censed; from there the bishop then read the Easter gospel, appropriately enough from Matthew 28.[7]

1998), and for the English drama, see Richard BEADLE (ed.): *The Cambridge companion to medieval English theatre* (Cambridge 1994). A brief survey of recent research in the various language areas is to be found in Eckehard SIMON (ed.): *The theatre of medieval Europe. New research in early drama* (Cambridge 1991).

[4] The lady is known by various names: Egeria, Etheria, Aetheria and Silvia. For an edition, and translations, see Hélène PÉTRÉ (ed.): *Ethérie, Journal de voyage. Texte latin, intro. et traduction* (Paris 1948), contains Latin text with French translation on facing page; German translation by Karl VRETSKA: *Die Pilgerreise der Aetheria, eingeleitet und erklärt von Hélène Pétré* (Vienna 1958); English translations: John H. BERNARD: *The pilgrimage of S. Silvia of Aquitania to the holy places (circa 385 AD)* (= Palestine Pilgrims' Text Society) (London 1891); and J. WILKINSON: *Egeria's travels* (London 1971); see also E.D. HUNT: *Holy Land pilgrimage in the Later Roman Empire, AD 312-460* (Oxford 1982).

[5] The extant text does not include her name, which is deduced from a letter written by Abbot Valerius of Bierzo (d. 695).

[6] VRETSKA: *Die Pilgerreise der Aetheria* 59.

[7] *Ibidem* 91.

2. EASTER TROPE

These vivid, strongly historicising practices recalling the act of redemption appeared first of all in the West in graphic art, specifically in that iconographic type which showed the three Marys at the Tomb with thuribles. From the Carolingian period onwards this became the literary topos of the *Visitatio sepulchri*. In the liturgical rite the historicising representation of the act of redemption is made tangible in the Easter trope, the content of which is the alternatim sung *quem quaeritis*.

Tropes are musical highlights with free prose text known throughout the Middle Ages and intended to heighten the celebratory mood of the mass. The Catholic church abolished them at the Council of Trent (1545-63) because of possible abuses. They apparently came into being to provide a textual basis for extremely melismatised singing, to assist the singer in keeping to the extremely long series of notes all belonging to a single syllable.[8]

It is scarcely possible to pinpoint the origin of this elaboration of the liturgy since this *quem quaeritis* trope is first found in the mid 10th century almost simultaneously in widely scattered locations: St Gall, Winchester, Limoges, Mainz, Bamberg and Northern Italy.[9] It can be exemplified by the theoretical 'perfect' version reconstructed by Carl Lange:

Angels: 1. Quem queritis in sepulchro, o christicolae?
Women: 2. Jhesum Nazarenum crucifixum, o caelicolae.
Angels: 3a. Non est hic, surrexit, sicut predixerat.
    3b. Ite, nuncite, quia surrexit
Women: 4. Surrexit ... (Proclamation in various versions)[10]

The content of the Easter trope is based on the synoptic gospels. As an optional part of the liturgy, it did not have a fixed position, though two preferred points for its inclusion become apparent: a) as Introit to the

---

[8] A melisma is a long melody on a single syllable, very popular as a musical elaboration in the Middle Ages. See Ulrich MEHLER: Osterfeiern, III. Musik, in *Die deutsche Literatur des Mittelalters. Verfasserlexikon* 7 (Berlin/New York 1989) 101-108, p. 103.

[9] On this see Helmut DE BOOR: *Die Textgeschichte der lateinischen Osterfeiern* (Tübingen 1984) 24; Hansjürgen LINKE: Osterfeiern I-II, in: *Die deutsche Literatur des Mittelalters. Verfasserlexikon* 7 (Berlin/New York 1989) 92-101, esp. 93.

[10] See Carl LANGE: *Die lateinischen Osterfeiern. Untersuchungen über den Ursprung und die Entwicklung der liturgisch-dramatischen Auferstehungsfeier* (München 1887) 18; here quoted from DE BOOR: *Textgeschichte.*

Easter mass, and b) – because associated with the early morning – in combination with the so-called *Visitatio sepulchri* in the Mattins for Easter Day immediately before the *Te deum laudamus*. It was usual to locate the gospel for that day's mass in the final responsory at the end of Mattins.[11] For the Easter mass the reading[12] was Mark 16, 1-7, beginning: "1. Et cum transisset sabbatum Maria Magdalene et Maria Jacobi et Salome emerunt aromata ut venientes unguerunt eum. 2. Et valde mane una sabbatorum veniunt ad monumentum orto iam sole…"[13] After this responsorially sung proclamation of the Easter gospel the Mattins of Easter Eve/Night closes with the singing of the *Te deum laudamus*, creating the opportunity to include the festive trope before it.

3. EASTER OFFICE

Initially the trope was sung by two half choirs, but later by individuals.[14] In relation to the visual representation this was a significant moment since it provided the opportunity for an action which represented and no longer only symbolised.[15] German scholarship designates this kind of presentation of the *Visitatio sepulchri* as Easter office (*Osterfeier*) (by this term implying that it is not a play, see below §4). A significant role in the transition from singing by half choirs to individual voices was played first by the early addition of the Marys' question, based on Mark 16, 3, as to who will roll away the stone for them; and secondly the sequence *Victimae paschali laudes* by Wipo (d. 1050), court chaplain to two Holy Roman Emperors, Conrad II (d. 1039) and his son Henry III

[11] See YOUNG: *Drama of the medieval church* vol. 1, 44-75.

[12] Maura O'CARROL: The Lectionary for the proper of the year in the Dominican and Franciscan rites of the thirteenth century, in *Archivum Fratrum Praedicatorum* 49 (1979) 79-103, here p. 93.

[13] Robertus WEBER (ed.): *Biblia sacra iuxta Vulgatam versionem* (Stuttgart 1975).

[14] The oldest surviving text is in Aethelwold's *Regularis concordia*.

[15] The question as to the relationship of ritual and representational presentation to 'theatre' has most recently been addressed by Jan-Dirk MÜLLER: Mimesis und Ritual. Zum geistlichen Spiel des Mittelalters, in Andreas KABLITZ & Gerhard NEUMANN (eds): *Mimesis und Simulation* (Freiburg 1998); IDEM: Realpräsenz und Repräsentation. Zur Ausdifferenzierung von Theatralität im geistlichen Spiel, in Hans-Joachim ZIEGELER (ed.): *Ritual und Inszenierung. Conference proceedings* (in the press). See also Rainer WARNING: *Funktion und Struktur. Die Ambivalenzen des geistlichen Spiels* (München 1974) (Coming soon in English translation at Stanford UP).

(d. 1056). It begins with praise of the risen Christ and continues with the question addressed to Mary apparently by the disciples, as to what she has seen, followed by her answer, proclaiming the resurrection.[16] This sequence has continued until the present as part of the festive liturgy for the whole of Easter week, being sung immediately before the reading of the gospel.

The Easter offices[17] are conventionally divided into three types:

(1) The *Visitatio sepulchri* alone – the three Marys visit the tomb early on Easter morning with the intention of anointing Christ's body. They find the tomb empty, and one or more angels proclaim the resurrection.

(2) The *Visitatio sepulchri* followed by the 'race' between the Apostles Peter and John to the empty tomb. After the announcement of the resurrection to the women, they report to the disciples what they have seen and these two race to the tomb to see for themselves.

(3) The *Visitatio sepulchri* followed by the appearance of the risen Christ to Mary Magdalene, the so-called *hortulanus* scene, with or without the 'race'. This scene must have had a tremendous effect, given that the risen Lord himself appears.

These three types do not constitute stages in an evolutionary process; they all occur alongside one another from the start, with regional preferences discernible.[18] The office took place within the framework of the Easter liturgy. Its purpose was to praise God. Its language was Latin, the performers were all – both angels and Marys – clergy, i.e. men, with only a few exceptions.[19] Various liturgical costume devices were used to differentiate characters, such as "the three Marys vested in copes". The stage properties such as containers for ointment or grave clothes were the equipment for the liturgy. Christ's tomb might be the altar or some alternative such as a crypt or a copy of the Holy Sepulchre. Since the Easter offices were essentially theocentric and served only as an elaboration of

---

[16] The text of the sequence does not make it clear whether Mary Magdalene alone or the three Marys together are being addressed. In Easter offices and plays both posibilities occur.

[17] The standard edition of the Easter offices and plays is that by Walther LIPPHARDT: *Lateinische Osterfeiern und Osterspiele* 1-9 (Bern 1975-1990).

[18] See DE BOOR: *Textgeschichte* 67.

[19] As such exceptions we may note Prague between 12th and 15th centuries; Essen 14th century; Gernrode – Southeast of Göttingen – 15th century; Nottuln – West of Münster – circa 1500; and Münster circa 1600.

the divine service, further elaborations are almost unknown. The various forms of the Easter office remained in the Easter rite until the Council of Trent (1545-1563), when, as mentioned above, the tropes and with them all such elaborations as the offices were removed from the liturgy.[20]

4. EASTER PLAYS

In the period roughly between 1200 and 1500 besides Easter tropes and offices we also find Easter plays, both vernacular and Latin. German scholarship continues to be preoccupied with defining terminology and separating off 'Easter offices' (*Osterfeiern*) from 'Easter plays' (*Osterspiele*). De Boor sees the difference not in content or form but in purpose. The office thus includes everything devised for use as part of the church service. Church usage has by definition space only for the holy. A play, by contrast, for him encompasses everything which does not belong in a liturgical context, be it in Latin or the vernacular, whether still performed by clerics within the church, or including the laity as performers and is performed in the open air. The liturgical sphere does not admit spoken portrayal of worldly scenes, even those mentioned in the Bible, e.g. those with *unguentarius*, tomb guards, Jews and Pilate. On the other hand Hansjürgen Linke sees the difference between 'offices', where the acts of salvation are called to mind, and 'plays', where they are re-enacted; the 'office' is theocentric, the 'play' anthropocentric.[21]

Easter plays seem to be associated with the third type of Easter office, but have the potential for a larger number of scenes including posting the guards around Christ's tomb, the harrowing of Hell, the three Marys' purchasing ointment, and on the road to Emmaus, in English usually called *Peregrinus* scenes.[22] Here too there is no progression from the simple to the complex, we find the simple and the elaborate alongside one another from the start.

The most marked difference to the liturgically orientated Easter offices is the elaboration of the worldly scenes, with the inclusion of

[20]   See MEHLER: Osterfeiern 103.

[21]   See DE BOOR: *Textgeschichte* 5; LINKE: Osterfeiern 99.

[22]   On the Latin Peregrinus plays see now Robert G.A. KURVERS: *Ad faciendum Peregrinum. A study of the liturgical elements in the Latin Peregrinus plays in the Middle Ages* (Frankfurt 1996).

guards for the tomb, the ointment vendor (in English usually called *mercator* or *unguentarius*) with his henchmen, devils and Jews, which shifts the whole emphasis to the didactic level. This didactic slant also moved the plays into a wider context, the target group was no longer the narrow circle of those participating in the liturgy and praising God inside the church but a wider lay public who sought the opportunity to learn and comprehend the message of salvation. This makes it very unsurprising that vernacular Easter plays appeared very quickly.

The oldest extant German Easter play is the 'Muri Easter Play', probably written down between 1240 and 1260.[23] What survive are a series of parchment strips, since as with many old play texts the manuscript was later cut up and used to reinforce the binding of other mansucripts considered more valuable. When first discovered the play was taken as evidence of a tradition of German religious drama from the 13th-century courtly period which had later been displaced by a tradition using a mixture of Latin and German. Recent scholarship suggests that what we have is the prompt copy of the German texts from an Easter play.[24]

This novel theatrical presentation of the events of Eastertide came into being separate from both liturgical context and church building. The mendicant orders[25] were often behind the visual presentation of the process of redemption in whole or in part, since it was their aim to make the doctrine of redemption comprehensible to all. With this they combined teaching about the Christian life. The plays were to teach the audience both about doctrine and about right Christian living. To this latter end both positive and negative images were presented. The dramatic action reflected the cosmic tension between heaven and hell, with the earth as the location of the conflict between the forces of good and evil. The outdoor acting area was usually the market place or church square, on which scaffolds (*loca*) were erected, in which the performers remained throughout the action, visible to the spectators who

---

[23] Basic edition, Friedrich RANKE: *Das Osterspiel von Muri nach den alten und neuen Fragmenten herausgegeben* (Aarau 1944).

[24] See Rolf BERGMANN: Interpretation und literaturgeschichtliche Stellung des Osterspiels von Muri, in *Internationales Archiv für Sozialgeschichte der deutschen Literatur* 9 (1984) 1-21.

[25] On the relationship between the preaching of mendicant orders and religious drama see my article in *Mittelalterliches Schauspiel. Festschrift für Hansjürgen Linke zum 65. Geburtstag* (= Sonderband der Amsterdamer Beiträge zur älteren Germanistik 38-39 [1994]) 143-160.

surrounded the acting area. The distribution of the *loca* matched the principle of division into good and evil: the Christians were on one side, the earthly opponents of God on the other.[26]

From the early 14th century onwards the Easter play was also incorporated into more elaborate Passion plays.[27] The custom was soon established of performing these plays, which lasted several days, during Holy Week, arranging for the action of Easter Day to be performed on Easter Sunday. While remaining under clerical supervision these elaborate performances soon developed into major civic undertakings, just as likely to be put on at Whitsuntide or Corpus Christi. Such a Passion play could encompass the whole history of mankind from creation to doomsday and therefore was likely to include the events of Easter. For this section authors might well adapt the corresponding sections from an Easter play and build them into their text. Nevertheless the section recognisable as the 'Easter play' by the relatively fixed set of scenes involved, retained its function of increasing the mood of rejoicing at the resurrection.[28]

An Easter play usually included the following scenes:[29]

(1) Besides those scenes found in Easter offices, i.e. *Visitatio sepulchri*, 'race' between Peter and John and *hortulanus* scene, it included scenes with the guards at the tomb. These were concerned with hiring knights to prevent Jesus' followers from stealing the body and also with their report to Pilate that Jesus has indeed risen from the dead. They provided the authors and adaptors with the opportunity to make fun of knights; bragging and singing coarse drinking songs, swearing and squabbling are commonplace. These scenes provided the urban audience with a comforting feeling of not belonging to this knightly class.

(2) A further stereotyped addition was the elaboration of the words in Mark 16, 1-8: "Maria Magdalena et Maria Jacobi et Salome emerunt aromata." The Eastertide spectators were presented with a real market scene, with bargaining, swearing, fighting and flirting – when the spice

---

[26] This simultaneous staging is a characteristic feature of medieval drama.

[27] E.g. in the early Passion play from the Rhineland which is preserved in St Gall (*St. Galler (Mittelrheinisches) Passionsspiel*) dating from the first half of the 14th century.

[28] For discussion of one such case see Anthonius H. TOUBER: Das Osterspiel im Donaueschinger Passionsspiel – Text und Musik, in Max SILLER (ed.): *Osterspiele. Texte und Musik* (Innsbruck 1994) 203-209.

[29] The term 'scene' is used in the context of medieval drama but should be understood as meaning the relevant biblical 'episode.'

merchant's wife tries to get off with his servant.[30] The believer now celebrating the resurrection was here given the opportunity after the long strict lenten abstemiousness to gain release through his *risus paschalis*.[31]

(3) The laughter was doubtless rather more apprehensive in the scene where Lucifer instructs his devils to scour the world for suitable candidates to repopulate hell now that the patriarchs have been freed by the risen Christ. This turned into a review of the social scene: priest, miller, baker, butcher, innkeeper, each must in turn account to Lucifer for his lifestyle and submit to appropriate punishment. This section was both didactically and theatrically effective and must have made a strong impression on the audience.

(4) Another common extension of the material is the appearance of the risen Christ to doubting Thomas. This scene was employed on the one hand to exemplify how Christ does not turn away from the weak and unbelieving; on the other hand it was also used to criticise the garrulous nature of women. God had taken advantage of this to proclaim the resurrection, but it was also the reason why the message had not been believed.[32]

(5) The final possible addition was the *Peregrinus* scene on the road to Emmaus, which on the basis of the narrative in Luke 24 provided a further opportunity to include a scene in a tavern.[33]

The elaboration of the scenes on earth brought about an inevitable secularisation of the material being portrayed, but one must bear in mind that the depiction of mankind's 'bestial' nature was to be understood in

---

[30] This is most marked in the plays from Tyrol. Little has been written on these in English, but see now John TAILBY: Drama and community in South Tyrol, in Alan HINDLEY (ed.): *Drama and community. People and plays in Medieval Europe* (Turnhout 1999) 148-160. It should be noted that from this episode in the Easter plays the 'doctor' plays among the Shrovetide or Carnival plays originate.

[31] Their justification based on Luke 24, 15: "et factum est dum fabularentur (...)", from the 15th century especially in Bavaria 'Easter tales' are incorporated into the sermons, to provide additional entertainment for the congregation after the long lenten fast, to allow them to express their joy at redemption and the conquest of evil. See Max WEHRLI: Christliches Lachen, christliche Komik?, in *From Wolfram and Petrarch to Goethe and Grass. Studies in Literature in Honour of Leonard Forster* (Baden-Baden 1982) 17-32.

[32] As in the text of the Passion play from Brixen (now officially in Italian Bressanone), ll. 4248ff: "Whatever you do not want to be kept quiet about, you should tell a woman. God took that into account in showing himself to a woman." Text in J.E. WACKERNELL: *Altdeutsche Passionsspiele aus Tirol* (Graz 1897) 424.

[33] See KURVERS: *Ad faciendum Peregrinum*.

terms of the doctrine of salvation and found its justification therein. The intention was to emphasise the good by contrast with the sinful: the guards at the tomb are to be understood as the foolish counterparts to the *miles christi*, the spice merchant or apothecary with his ointments and coarse behaviour as the crass contrast to Christ the healer of souls, the repopulation of hell as an ambivalently amusing *memento mori*.

But the tendency towards secularisation does not only affect the extensions to the basic Easter play. Scenes added to the 'central' episodes, such as the disciples' race and the *hortulanus* scene were remotivated to humorous effect. In the first of these Peter and John do now really race one another to the tomb. Peter as the older man is portrayed as hobbling, tripping over his own feet and calling out for breathers before reaching the tomb after John. One of the clearest examples of this realignment is the *hortulanus* scene in the so-called third Bozen Easter play (Bozner Osterspiel III).[34] It mixes languages, with the Latin being the text of the *Visitatio sepulchri*, transmitted with musical notation showing it to have been sung. As usual the vernacular, German sections follow on from the Latin text but the continuation deviates very rapidly from the expected. *Hortulanus* sings line 278 "Mulier, quid ploras, quem queritis", but the spoken line 279 continues in German with

---

[34] The fragmentary text of the Easter play from Bozen (Bolzano) survives in the manuscript collection of the Bozen schoolmaster and choirmaster Benedikt Debs (d. 1515) which he bequeathed to the Sterzing (Vipiteno) painter Vigil Raber. The most famous 'old manuscript' (*alte Scarteggn*) containing 15 play texts has been edited by Walther LIPPHARDT and Hans-Gert ROLOFF as Vol I in the series 'Die geistlichen Spiele des Sterzinger Spielarchivs', Bern et al. 1986 (2. verbesserte Auflage), this play on pp. 251-286. Unfortunately even the revised 2nd edition of 1986 is not error free. Just as unfortunate is the inconsistency in the designation of this play. In the article under 'Debs, Benedikt', in *Die deutsche Literatur des Mittelalters. Verfasserlexikon* 2 (Berlin/New York 1980) 59-61 the play which Raber in the manuscript notes as "another Easter play 8 folios long, with Jews", is referred to as third Bozen Easter play (Bozner Osterspiel III) whereas in the above edition it is called "Bozen Easter play (IV) – visitatio". Further, in Rolf BERGMANN: *Katalog der deutschsprachigen geistlichen Spiele und Marienklagen des Mittelalters* (München 1986), the indispensible catalogue of the play manuscripts, it has the same title as in the *Verfasserlexikon*, entry no 137. The confusion is completed by the note in Professor Linke's article on this manuscript, Hansjürgen LINKE: Die Osterspiele des Debs-Codex, in *Zeitschrift für deutsche Philologie* 104 (1985) 104-129, where he confirms that the text in question does indeed constitute a fourth Easter play in the manuscript. Overall it should be noted that the two standard works of secondary literature, the *Verfasserlexikon* and BERGMANN's *Katalog*, aim to standardise nomenclature and their usage is to be followed.

"*Salvete, salvete*, said the wolf to the bull". The initially chummy state-ments rapidly become coarse and offensive until it is apparent that this '*hortulanus*' is not the unrecognised risen Lord but a real gardener, who takes Mary Magdalene to task for trampling down the herbs from which he was wanting to make an ointment. This '*hortulanus*' does not hide his recipe from the audience, but it is a joke recipe for a thrashing oint-ment (*Prügelsalbe*). As soon as this gardener and his assistant have left, the 'genuine' *hortulanus* appears and the action continues in serious vein with the recognition of the risen Christ by Mary Magdalene.

The examples of the extension of the text of Easter plays cited here make it clear that the Middle Ages did not distinguish so sharply between religious and secular as we do today. Laughter was just as per-missible in a religious context. Here we can see how the herald speaking the epilogue to Vigil Raber's Tyrolean Easter play of 1520 calls on the spectators to rejoice at the resurrection and enjoy themselves, though not excessively, after the restraints of Lent.[35]

> Darumb ain yeder mensch soll freyen sich
> Diser össterlichen zeyt,
> Die allen Christn gross freuden geit,
> Dann gwoncklich kumpt freuden nach grossm klagn.
> Darumb will ich euch kundtthoen von den fladen,
> Die man isst alls heut am Ostertag.
> Darzue ain yeder auch woll mag
> Air, fleisch, gsotn oder gepratn essn.
> Doch sollt ier euch daran nit vergessn,
> Als ainst ainem paurn pschach
> Dem nach fleisch auch war so gach.
> (ll. 502 – 512)

(Therefore everyone should rejoice at this Eastertide, which brings all Christians great joy, for joy generally comes after great sorrow. Therefore I want to let you know that there are flat breadcakes to eat this Easter day and everyone can eat with them eggs and meat, be it boiled or roast. But you should not overdo it, as a peasant once did who was too keen on meat.)

As a cautionary tale there then follows the story of a peasant who returns from Easter mass and gobbles down a calf's stomach, having previously

---

[35] In BERGMANN: *Katalog* entry number 140, "Tyrolean Easter play" ("Tiroler Oster-spiel"); in the edition by Walther LIPPHARDT and Hans-Gert ROLOFF: *Die geistlichen Spiele des Sterzinger Spielarchivs, Bd. III*: it is called "Ludus Pascalis de Resurrectione Domini 1520", 299-325.

asked his wife to stuff it with thirty eggs and boil it for him. Unfortunately the wife has not yet done so and consequently the peasant suffers from consuming the uncleaned, uncooked stomach. The herald explains:

> Zimlicher schwanckh ist nit zu vil
> An disem osterlichen tag.
> Darumb ain yeder Christ wol mag
> Sich freuenn diser heyligen zeytt
> ...
> Dann wier endtlediget sind vonn des teufls panden.
> (ll. 584-589)

(A suitable tale is always appropriate on this Easter day. Therefore every Christian can rejoice at this holy season, for we are freed from the devil's bonds.)

The plays ends with the singing of *Christ ist erstanden* ('Christ is risen') which makes it clear that this is a serious religious context.

5. CONTRARY TENDENCIES

From as early as the 14th century a contrary development, working against the tendency towards secularisation, can be discerned, which persists right through until the 17th century. Throughout this period we find in increasing numbers mixed language Easter plays alongside the exclusively vernacular ones. Apparently because the often lighthearted tone of some of the Easter plays did not suit all tastes, increasing attempts were made to bring the plays closer to the liturgy again. The liturgical Latin texts become once more the framework on which the vernacular parts base themselves through translation and paraphrase, preserving a serious note throughout. We here can see that mixed-language texts are not an intermediate stage between Latin and vernacular versions but a deliberate pulling back towards liturgical plays in church and away from vernacular texts performed outdoors.[36] Although these

---

[36] See Hansjürgen LINKE: Drama und Theater, in Ingeborg GLIER (ed.): *Die deutsche Literatur im späten Mittelalter. 1250-1370. Zweiter Teil: Reimpaargedichte, Drama, Prosa* (Munich 1987) 153-233, here pp. 182f. (= Helmut DE BOOR & Richard NEWALD (eds): Geschichte der deutschen Literatur von den Anfängen bis zur Gegenwart III, 2). As examples Linke cites the Wienhaus Easter play (fragment from end of 14th century) and the Trier Easter play (15th century).

serious mixed-language texts give the impression of being close to the liturgy, this does not mean they were necessarily used in such a context. Cases can sometimes be identified where a play text has been deliberately separated from performance and turned into edifying reading material, as with the 'Wienhäuser Easter play fragment'.[37]

A textual fragment discovered in 1953 in the former Cistercian convent of Wienhausen – Southeast of Celle, Northeast of Hannover – was identified as part of an Easter play. It is datable to the late 14th century and begins in the middle of the scene where Mary Magdalene meets the risen Christ, i.e. a *hortulanus* scene. On folio 4r a later hand has added a brief 'doubting Thomas' scene, immediately before the start of the sequence *Victimae paschali laudes*, the Latin text of which has musical notation. Each line of Latin is followed by the German paraphrase. The sequence probably formed the end of the Easter play, as the text ends half way down a side which has remained empty. Art historian Horst Appuhn deduced for Wienhausen a possible dramatised version of the events of passion and Easter, of which the surviving fragment constituted part.[38] In doing so he took as his starting point the holy sepulchre and the figure of the risen Christ both preserved in the convent. He integrated both these in a rite which he believed could be modelled along the lines of a set of instructions for deposition and burial of Christ from the neighbouring monastery of Prüfening. However, recent research has revealed the two sculptures as objects revered as religious symbols with the implication that this was not confined to the Passion and Easter seasons but went on throughout the year.[39] This in turn has implications for the use to which the fragment of play text was put.

In determining what was the purpose behind the tiny pamphlet containing the text from the Easter play, the holy sepulchre is crucial, but not in the way in which Appuhn envisaged. This sepulchre is a wooden shrine/reliquary with a pointed roof; the roof and one side wall can be opened. On the inner sides of the roof the story of salvation from the

[37] Walther LIPPHARDT: Das Wienhäuser Osterspielfragment, in *Daphnis* 1 (1972) 120-129 (with facsimile of ms.).

[38] Horst APPUHN: Der Auferstandene und das Heilige Blut in Wienhausen, in *Niederdeutsche Beiträge zur Kunstgeschichte* 1 (1969) 73-139.

[39] Kerstin HENGEVOSS-DÜRKOP: *Skulptur und Frauenklöster. Studien zu Bildwerken der Zeit um 1300 aus Frauenklöstern des ehemaligen Fürstentums Lüneburg* (= ARTEfact 7) (Berlin 1994).

Annunciation to Pentecost is portrayed in sequence.[40] It can be looked at when the roof is folded open and the buried Christ inside is visible (see fig. 1). This figure contained holy relics and is considered one of the convent's most venerable objects. This makes it highly probable that the nuns were very well acquainted with the paintings inside the roof of the reliquary.

But the wooden shrine could also be used to represent the empty Easter tomb.[41] For this purpose the pointed roof could be folded shut, so that the figure of Christ was no longer visible. Then the two small doors in the long side could be opened, to reveal an empty space inside, the empty Easter tomb (see fig. 2). The inside of the left hand door has a painting of Christ appearing to Mary Magdalene as the gardener, the *hortulanus* figure's scroll of text has the words "quid ploras, quem queris", while Mary Magdalene's has the words "tulerunt dominum meum et nescio ubi posuerunt eum".[42] Here the play text and the state of the tomb in its Easter day position are identical. But the parallel goes even further, as the right hand door depicts doubting Thomas, the scene which the play fragment has as a marginal addition. Here too scrolls of text identify and locate the figures: Christ says to Thomas "mitte manum tuam et cognosce loca clavorum", Thomas replies "dominus meus et deus meus".[43] It is in no way surprising that the elaboration of the play text matches the situation with the tomb.

The closer connection to Easter is thus made by the ordering of the material on the inner sides of the tomb doors. Furthermore the occurrence of the same sequence of scenes with the same texts on their scrolls appears on the series of paintings of the history of salvation visible when the roof surfaces have been opened (which means the side wall is obscured if not closed). This fact shows how the play-text fragment could be used in a way extending beyond the limitations of the liturgical year and associated with the cult of the Holy Sepulchre. It may well have aided the nuns to reach a profounder level of absorption in their

---

[40] For a full description, see Konrad MAIER: *Die Kunstdenkmäler des Landkreises Celle im Regierungsbezirk Lüneburg. Teil II. Wienhausen. Kloster und Gemeinde* (= Die Kunstdenkmäler des Landes Niedersachsen 34, Teil II) (Hannover 1970).

[41] Cf. Justin E.A. KROESEN: *The Sepulchrum Domini through the ages. Its form and function* (= Liturgia condenda 10) (Leuven 2000).

[42] Renatus-Johannes HESBERT (ed.): *Corpus Antiphonalium Officii* (Roma 1970) (here number 7128).

[43] The quotations are according to MAIER: *Die Kunstdenkmäler.*

contemplation of the reliquary: the play text as devotional reading, as an aid to contemplative consideration of one of the convent's chief objects of veneration, no longer tied exclusively to Eastertide.[44]

My final textual example also does not relate immediately to the celebration of Easter, but it does derive from the tradition of Easter plays. This is Chapter 13 in the chapbook of the *Adventures of Till Eulenspiegel* entitled "How Eulenspiegel put on a play in the mass at Easter, so that the priest and his housekeeper scrapped and fought with the peasants".[45] The priest gives Eulenspiegel the task of arranging the play for Easter eve, with the priest himself playing the risen Christ, his housekeeper – who is apparently capable of speaking the Latin text – the angel at the tomb, Eulenspiegel and two peasants the three Marys. He is to teach the peasants their lines and does so in his typical fashion. As the reply to the angel's question *quem queritis* he teaches them to reply: "We are looking for an old one-eyed priest's whore." This leads during the Easter mass to a general punch-up, during which Eulenspiegel slips away. This parody of a *Visitatio sepulchri* is only meaningful if the target group is familiar with the real version. It might well be that this imaginary *Visitatio sepulchri* – which one can envisage being of 'type one' – was to be understood as a polemical pamphlet, propaganda against the over-secularised Easter plays which had turned into popular entertainment.[46]

6. CONCLUSION

As the series of examples has shown, it was possible to vary tremendously the stress which was put on the dramatic presentation of Easter even within one and the same functional context. The elaborations of

[44] In greater detail on the purpose to which this manuscript was put see my article Ein Schauspiel für das innere Auge? Notiz zur Benutzerfunktion des Wienhäuser Osterspielfragments, in Christa TUCZAY, Ulrike HIRHAGER & Karin LICHTBLAU (eds): *Ir sult sprechen willekomen. Festschrift für Helmut Birkhan zum 60. Geburtstag* (Bern 1998) 778-787.

[45] Wolfgang LINDOW (ed.): *Ein kurtzweilig Lesen von Dil Ulenspiegel, nach dem Druck von 1515* (Stuttgart 1997). It is now generally accepted that Hermann Bote was the author of Eulenspiegel.

[46] This thesis latches onto the observation that Bote's work as a whole shows him to be a moralist with a traditional world view. See Herbert BLUME: Bote, Hermann, in Walther KILLY (ed.): *Literaturlexikon. Autoren und Werke deutscher Sprache* (München 1988-1993) vol. 2, 1128-1130.

the Easter rite by means of trope and *visitatio* had originally been confined to the context of the liturgy but when they made the transition in the area of educating the laity they were combined with the presentation of the negative world, which is to be rejected and does not lead to eternal life. There was no room for the dramatic presentation of these worldly scenes as extensions of the Easter story in the liturgical context. Nor was liturgical language necessary, indeed it became a positive hindrance to the didactic effect if its use obscured understanding. In dramatic terms the inclusion of worldly scenes provided a golden opportunity to develop theatrically effective plays.[47] Nevertheless liturgical connections were maintained through echoes of the mass, such as inclusion of a *Visitatio sepulchri* or other elements from the Easter office, communal singing of hymns, performance of ritual actions such as blessing or breaking bread. This made for a striking mixture of seriousness and entertainment. Overemphasis of this latter aspect, which evolved especially in certain regions, led to the discredit of the whole genre and made it an easy target for reformation attacks. This in turn led to banning or purging. Decrees of the Council of Trent banned embellishment of the rite with tropes or offices. Yet this could not remove the popularity of the dramatic representation of the Easter story. We still today at Eastertide have Easter offices and Easter plays, for some an added component in their joy at the resurrection, for others an aesthetic pleasure, though no longer part of the liturgy.

---

[47] This amalgamation of liturgical Easter Office and non-liturgical Easter play shows clearly that the latter is based on or incorporates the former.

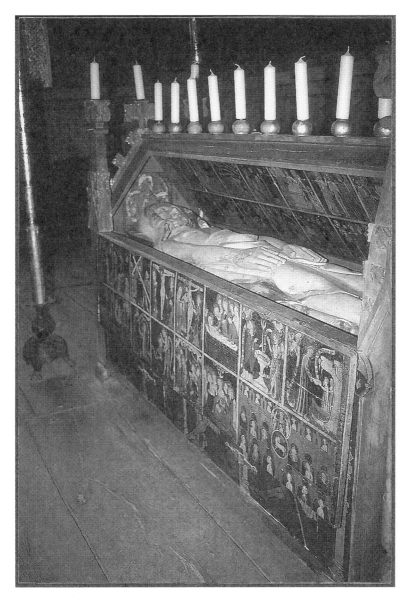

Fig. 1. The Holy Selpulchre of the Cistercian convent of Wienhausen showing the Burial of Christ and the story of the salvation from the Annunciation to Pentecost.
Photograph: W. Brandis, Klosterarchiv Wienhausen.

Fig. 2. The Sepulchre in its Easter play position.
Photograph: W. Brandis, Klosterarchiv Wienhausen.

KLAAS-WILLEM DE JONG

OPPOSITION TO A FESTIVE CELEBRATION OF GOOD FRIDAY IN THE *GEREFORMEERDE KERKEN IN NEDERLAND* AND THEIR PREDECESSORS[1]

In 1854 the synod of the *Christelijk Afgescheidene Gereformeerde Kerk* declared Good Friday "under no account to be celebrated festively".[2] This decision typifies the attitude towards Good Friday that is found amongst some orthodox reformed churches and many of their members in the 19th century. It differs from the conviction then expressed by the majority of protestants in The Netherlands, especially by many in the *Nederlandse Hervormde Kerk*. In this contribution I intend to describe the attitude itself, its backgrounds, development and influence.

1. HISTORICAL BACKGROUNDS

The National Synod of Dordrecht in 1618-19 sanctioned in its church-order five official holidays: Christmas, Circumcision, Easter, Ascension Day and Whit Sunday. In most places services on Good Friday had already been abolished during or shortly after the Reformation period. In some congregations, however, this old custom continued to exist. In the city of Utrecht, for example, on Good Friday the Calvinists still met for even several services until at least 1647, whereas in the surrounding countryside these occasions had already died out at that time.[3] After some time services remained intact only in some regions: in the province of Friesland, where the church did not confirm most resolutions of the

---

[1] I want to thank G.W. van der Brugge and N. Joosse for their efforts to correct the English text of this article.

[2] Cf. that this day "volstrekt niet feestelijk gevierd worde" (*Hand. syn. Chr. Afgesch. Geref. Kerk* 627; for this and other abbreviations see the scheme used in *Biografisch Lexicon voor de Geschiedenis van het Nederlandse Protestantisme*).

[3] J. KOELMAN: *Reformatie nodigh ontrent de feest-dagen, naaktelijk vertoont ende beweezen* (Rotterdam 1675) 22f.

Synod of Dordrecht, and probably also in some congregations in the
(north-)eastern part of the country.[4] In doing so, the congregations concerned did not act according to ecclesiastical law, but – strictly speaking
– did not go against it either. Apart from this a custom to commemorate
Christ's suffering on the seven Sundays before Easter came into being all
over the country in the 17th century.

This situation lasted until the end of the 18th century, when in the city
of Delft protestants of Walloon origin founded a religious society and considered how to improve the traditional liturgy.[5] Their aim was to relate
their services directly to christian life. For them this implied revalueing
Good Friday and administering the Lord's Supper in the evening of this
day, to relive the memory of His death and to strengthen their faith. To
our knowledge the administration of the sacrament on this day had been
an unknown phenomenon in the protestant churches until this moment.
Therefore it seems unlikely that the group in Delft followed any example
in this matter. In the Reformed Church too the awareness grew that the
traditional liturgy had to be renewed. After a thorough reorganisation of
the church in 1816, again a national synod was installed, the first after the
assembly of Dordrecht. The synod of what now was called the *Nederlandse
Hervormde Kerk* was asked to reflect on the liturgy of the church, and so
it did in the summer of 1817. It wanted services to be more "edifying"
and "solemn".[6] Among other things it prescribed ministers to preach on
the "Friday before Easter", "the day of death of Him, who is both our life
and the life of the world": there should be held "a service in remembrance
of this great event".[7] About the administration itself of the Lord's Supper
on this day the synod kept silent.[8] Notwithstanding the fact that in quite
a few places believers opposed the decision of preaching on Good Friday,

---

[4] Cf. K.W. DE JONG: Naar oude gewoonte. Een vergelijking tussen Friesland en
Zuid-Holland van enkele aspecten van de protestantse eredienst in de 1/e eeuw, in *Jaarboek voor liturgie-onderzoek* 7 (1991) 1-24, p. 10, 17f; F.J.J.A. JUNIUS: *Geschiedenis en
belangrijkheid der lijdensprediking (…)* I (Tiel 1853) 248f., 256.

[5] Cf. R.A. BOSCH: Rouwsluier over de Tafel van de Heer? Over de herkomst van de
avondmaalsviering op de Goede Vrijdag, in *Eredienstvaardig* 15 (1999) no. 1, 7-11.

[6] C. HOOIJER: *Kerkelijke wetten voor de Hervormden in het Koningrijk der Nederlanden* (Zaltbommel 1846) 361 ("stichtelijke", "plegtige").

[7] HOOIJER: *Kerkelijke wetten* 364 ("Vrijdag vóór Paschen", "de dag des doods van
Hem, die ons leven, en het leven der wereld is", "eene Godsdienstoefening, ter gedachtenis van die groote gebeurtenis").

[8] A proposition in this direction was made by its member, the rev. A. Goedkoop
(*Hand. Syn. Ned. Herv. Kerk* 1817 60f).

it became a highly valued service all over the country in the next decades. In 1818 in at least one congregation the minister did not only rehabilitate the Good Friday service, but also initiated the celebration of the Lord's Supper in this service. In the fourties a growing number of especially liberal congregations urged the synod to promote Good Friday as an official holiday as well as to set rules for the administration of the Lord's Supper on this day. Initially the highest assembly of the church hesitated, but it met these wishes in 1853. In a letter to the church councils the synod recommended a dignified celebration of Good Friday as a whole, i.e. as a day of rest that includes a church service. If possible, the Lord's Supper should be administered.[9] A comparison of the decision-making in 1817 and 1853, shows some interesting differences in its approach of the matter (compulsive versus inviting and appealing), origin (deliberations in the synod itself versus requests from congregations and ministers), means of memorial (preaching only versus sanctifying the day and administering the Lord's Supper too) and address (ministers versus church councils). To understand the synodal point of view in 1853, the growing influence of the liberal theology should be taken into account. Because its spokesmen stressed Jesus' human nature, His death appealed more to their imagination than His resurrection. Rather than being a sacrament, the Lord's Supper was a meal in remembrance of Jesus' death, which should be held on the evening of his crucifixion. Though quite a lot of congregations welcomed the synodal proposals, more orthodox circles opposed it.[10] They indeed valued the service on Good Friday, but they wished to abide by old customs, for example the administration of the Lord's Supper at Easter. In the course of the next decades some of them still changed their minds, while others kept refusing to adapt their liturgy to the new standards. We may well suppose that at the turn of the century the celebration of the Lord's Supper was common practice in large parts of the *Nederlandse Hervormde Kerk*.[11]

---

[9] Cf. K.W. DE JONG: *Ordening van dienst. Achtergronden en ontwikkelingen in de eredienst van de Gereformeerde Kerken in Nederland* (Baarn 1996) 31 and the references given there.

[10] Cf. *Kerkelijke Courant* 1855, no. 21 (26th May); cf. also the nos. 17 (28th April), 20 (19th May), 27 (7th June), 31 (4th August). Even the moderate D. Chantepie de la Saussaye questioned the administration of the Lord's Supper on Good Friday (*Ernst en Vrede* 6 (1858) 165).

[11] Cf. the orthodox E.F. KRUIJF: *Liturgiek. Ten dienste van dienaren der Nederlandsche Hervormde Kerk* (Groningen 1901) 243; *Christelijke encyclopaedie voor het Nederlandsche volk* 2 (Kampen n.d.) 368.

2. OPPOSITION IN THE CHURCH OF THE SEPARATION OF 1834

In 1834 a few ministers and a comparatively small group of believers separated from the *Nederlandse Hervormde Kerk*. They rejected the church organisation of 1816 and fell back on the classical reformed confessions, liturgy and church-order which had been established by the Synod of Dordrecht in 1618-19. They unanimously claimed therefore to be the continuation of the old Reformed Church, but the new church occurred to be very heterogeneous and heavy conflicts were bound to happen. At their synods held in Amsterdam in 1836 and in Utrecht in 1837, some wanted to preserve existing traditions while others wished to reform church life in accordance with the Scriptures. Though initially the latter group appeared to have won, at the synod of Amsterdam in 1840 the former group was in the majority and decided to have the church-order of Dordrecht unaltered. We may suppose these traditionalist congregations gathered for services on at least Sundays and the (above mentioned) prescribed holidays.[12] For want of facts we do not know their point of view towards Good Friday.

More can be said about the minority which rejected the compulsory celebration of holidays. Its most important representatives, the ministers A. Brummelkamp (and A.C. van Raalte) working especially in the provinces of Gelderland and Overijssel, and H.P. Scholte (and G.F. Gezelle Meerburg), serving in the province of Noord-Brabant, in the south-eastern part of Zuid-Holland and initially also in Zeeland, alienated themselves from the mainstream of the church.[13] Each of them

---

[12] Hendr. de Cock, one of the leaders of the secession of 1834, belonged to the mainstream of the new church, but still put into perspective the meaning of the holidays (cf. H. de Cock to H.J. Budding, without date [Dec. 1837/Jan. 1838], in J.H. GUNNING J.Hzn.: *H.J. Budding. Leven en arbeid* (Rhenen 1909²) 562).

[13] In the province of Zeeland the self-willed minister H.J. Budding must be mentioned too, who soon after the separation went his own way. Until 1851 facts are lacking. But judging by his positive position towards the church-order of Dordrecht he will not have paid any attention to Good Friday initially (cf. C. DEKKER: *Gereformeerd en evangelisch. Ontstaan en geschiedenis van de Buddinggemeente te Goes en haar plaats in het Nederlandse Protestantisme in de periode 1839-1881* (Kampen [1992]) 27ff). His diary shows, that certainly from 1851 he called together the congregation of Goes every Friday before a Sunday on which the Lord's Supper was administered (which according to the church-order of Dordrecht preferably took place at Christmas, Easter and on Whit Sunday). But in the meetings on Good Friday no special reference seems to have been made to Christ's suffering and death. This didn't change after 1859, when Budding started to break the bread every Sunday. Only in 1875 he notes a short sermon on the occasion of the special meaning of the day (cf. DEKKER: *Gereformeerd* 531-582).

founded a school. Their questioning of the holidays goes back to the so-called *Nadere Reformatie*, a 17th-century reform movement of puritans and pietists. They did not only feel affinity with its theology, but also identified with its treatment by the church and by the government at that time. Some of its spokesmen were suspended from their ministry, a fate which happened to Scholte even twice: in 1834, and again in the new denomination of the separatists in 1840. The latter event confirms his decreasing influence.

We restrict our attention to one representative of the *Nadere Reformatie*, J. Koelman, whose works were known by Scholte and more fragmentarily also by Brummelkamp.[14] On December 26, 1672, Koelman preached about Galatians 4, 9-11. Later on he elaborated this sermon and published it under the title of *Reformatie nodigh ontrent de feestdagen, naaktelijk vertoont, ende beweezen*.[15] Its careful line of reasoning and the passion with which it was written, still impress the modern reader. Koelman wasn't the first to fight the holidays. He refers to other representatives of the *Nadere Reformatie*, especially to his teacher G. Voetius, but also to other reformed theologians and discusses their views. Koelman states that the holidays are typical of the papacy and that observing them diverts from the essentials in christian faith. Therefore they should be abolished. He founds his conviction on a long range of arguments, of which the biblical ones form the basis. He tries to prove all holidays were abolished in the New Testament. Celebrating holidays threatens the observation of the one day of rest which is given each week, Sunday. He even considers it against the fourth commandment, in which six days of labour are ordered. Koelman's stressing this point must be seen in the broader context of the debate about the character of the Sunday in the decades before. In the second part of his book Koelman discusses the matter from the point of view of ecclesiastical law. He is not impressed by the rules of the church-order of Dordrecht. The prescription of five holidays is against the Scriptures and therefore illegal. Though a lot of other pros and cons are given, this remains the basis of his point of view. He argues that a previous Synod of Dordrecht (1574) decided the church should be satisfied with the Sunday only,

---

[14] Cf. L. OOSTENDORP: *H.P. Scholte. Leader of the Secession of 1834 and Founder of Pella* (Franeker 1964) 84ff, 195. Cf. also H. IMMINKHUIZEN: *De Nadere Reformatie. Primaire bibliografie van de 19de-eeuwse uitgaven* (Den Haag 1985) 113 (s.v. Scholte, H.P.); M. TE VELDE: *Anthony Brummelkamp (1811-1888)* (Barneveld 1988) 292f.

[15] KOELMAN: *Reformatie*.

that some rules (as the one in question) are of no use, that difficult rules should be pushed aside if that should uplift a congregation, that a lot of rules have fallen into disuse, etc. In the end he shows to be aware of the fact that abolishing traditional holidays can cause a lot of problems to the minister concerned. He seems to point to himself then. Officially his refusal to use the liturgical forms was the cause of his suspension in 1674, but his view about holidays and other opinions was probably also taken into account.

As stated above, Brummelkamp, Scholte and others seemed to have won the synods of Amsterdam in 1836 and Utrecht in 1837 for their alterations of the church-order of Dordrecht. In the case of the holidays the influence of the *Nadere Reformatie* can be clearly recognised, when the Synod of Amsterdam stated: celebrating holidays is not prescribed in the Bible and therefore cannot be imposed on anyone, nor in any way be compared with observing the day of rest. Services should be held on the prescribed holidays, but no one is obliged to observe these days.[16] The latter provision is weakened in 1837. It is only said then, that those who do not work on the holidays should spend their days in edification.[17] After the reintroduction of the traditional church-order of Dordrecht and the suspension of Scholte in 1840 most congregations in the province of Noord-Brabant went their own way. Three years later Scholte's companion Gezelle Meerburg edited a revised church-order. In the case of the holidays it is less definite and more ecclesiastical than its predecessor of 1837: not the individual, but the church (!) is free in its choice to celebrate the holidays; it is not the responsibility of the individual, but of the ministers to prevent idleness on holidays.[18] For Gezelle Meerburg personally this meant a change of mind. From another source we know he had completely rejected the holidays in the past. To show this publicly he once ordered his maid to clean the front windows of the parsonage on Christmas Day.[19]

Taking all the facts into account we may suppose, that in the first decades of the *Christelijk Afgescheidene Gereformeerde Kerk* – as the

---

[16] *Hand. syn. Chr. Afgesch. Geref. Kerk* 53.
[17] Cf. *Hand. syn. Chr. Afgesch. Geref. Kerk* 136f, 1148.
[18] Cf. *Hand. syn. Chr. Afgesch. Geref. Kerk* 1190f.
[19] Cf. H.E. Verschoor to J.D. Janssen dated Dec. 31st 1835 (in *Archiefstukken betreffende de Afscheiding van 1834* III (Kampen 1942) 21). It is said that Gezelle Meerburg also opposed having a service on Good Friday, but no evidence is given (cf. *Christelijke encyclopaedie* 2, 367).

majority of those who had left the *Nederlandse Hervormde Kerk* in 1834 called their church – Good Friday was considered an average workday even when a minister preached on its evening. Only the Sunday (and, depending on the region, some holidays prescribed in the church-order of Dordrecht) should be sanctified as a day of rest.

At the Synod of Zwolle in 1854 a period of internal squabbles and mutual estrangement was closed, though not all differences were solved. The synod reacted unanimously upon the decisions of the synod of the *Nederlandse Hervormde Kerk* concerning Good Friday in the way already quoted: Good Friday is "under no account to be celebrated festively".[20] This decision can be understood in two ways: Good Friday should not be celebrated at all, or it should not be celebrated festively. The congregation at Schiedam for example chose the latter interpretation.[21] After some hesitation its church council decided to meet for a service in the evening, but it added explicitly that the Lord's Supper was not to be celebrated on Good Friday, but at the traditional time of Easter. We suspect this position was not uncommon.[22] *De Bazuin*, an influential weekly, published since 1854 in favour of the Theological School in Kampen, started to publish meditations under the title 'Good Friday' in 1861. In the case of holidays in general, however, the old differences remained, though accents changed. F.A. Kok, minister and representative of the traditional school, the so-called *Drentse richting*, chose a legal approach: a good Dutch citizen observes the holidays because the law forces him, a good reformed adherent in addition also because the church-order of Dordrecht prescribes so.[23] Hel. de Cock, son of Hendr.

---

[20] Cf. also articles in *De Bazuin* 2 (1854) nos. 36 and 43. The proposal to take a stand in the matter of Good Friday was made by the congregations in the province of Drente (credentials dated 9th May 1854 – Public Records Office Utrecht, Synodal Archives of the *Gereformeerde Kerken in Nederland* no. 40). We note that there was a strong movement to promote Good Friday in the *Nederlandse Hervormde Kerk* precisely in this province.

[21] A. VAN DER BLOM & J.J. DONKERS AZN.: *De Geschiedenis van de Gereformeerde Kerk van Schiedam* (n.p. n.d.) 68.

[22] Cf. P. HUISMAN: *Een dorpsgemeente onderweg. Gereformeerd Hazerswoude 1864-1989* (n.p. [1989]) 23: "In het voorjaar werd het Avondmaal meermalen op het Paasfeest gevierd" (period 1864-1869). Cf. also the confession of faith in the congregation at 's-Hertogenbosch on the 3rd of April 1874 (= Good Friday) (announcement of P.F. Dillingh in Dordrecht). This was probably followed by the Lord's Supper at Easter.

[23] *De Bazuin* 2 (1855) no. 26 (cf. the contribution of J.A. Smeedes in *De Bazuin* 2 (1855) no. 36).

de Cock, one of the leaders of the separation in 1834, took up an ambivalent and pragmatical position in his lectures in Kampen.[24] In his view a minister, in the choice of the text for his sermon, somehow has to take into account the ecclesiastical year and its holidays, because it influences the mood of the congregation present. Still De Cock has his doubts about Good Friday, especially about the way it is observed in the *Nederlandse Hervormde Kerk*. In spite of these reservations in the province of Friesland with its long tradition of celebrating Good Friday there was at least one congregation with even two services on Good Friday.[25] The comparatively progressive Brummelkamp still repeatedly took a stance against holidays in general and Good Friday in particular, using a broad range of arguments.[26] He refers to several New Testament texts arguing that the celebration of holidays is not necessary from a biblical point of view, and warns that it is forbidden to impose these human creations (Matth. 15, Acts 15:10, Rom. 14:5 and 6a, Gal. 5:1, Col. 2:16, 23); he points to older Dutch church-orders, in which holidays are put into perspective or even turned away on principle; he mentions spokesmen of the *Nadere Reformatie*, who are of the same opinion as he is (A Brakel, Voetius); he describes the situation in foreign countries such as Scotland and America where certain Calvinist branches do not observe any holidays at all. It should be noticed that theologically the traditional school stood much closer to 'old writers' as A Brakel and Voetius, but did not follow them in respect to the holidays.[27] It appears Brummelkamp's arguing that he did not only have the *Nederlandse Hervormde Kerk* in his mind, but also the Roman Catholic Church. In 1853 the episcopal hierarchy had been re-established in The Netherlands, which was considered a serious threat to church and society by large sections of the protestant population. Brummelkamp for example criticised cabinet ministers who had given their officials a day off, because it was Good Friday. He was afraid it could be used as a precedent by Roman Catholics claiming a legal status for their special holidays. Within the sphere of influenceof Brummelkamp hardly any service is to be held on

[24] Cf. DE JONG: *Ordening* 55. The lectures of De Cock were held in 1877.

[25] R.A. Bosch in Maastricht gave me a sermon of his great-grandfather W. Bosch, said on Good Friday 1886 in Workum. The sermon suggests the existence of a service in the morning as well as one in the evening.

[26] *De Bazuin* 2 (1854) no. 43. Cf. *De Bazuin* 11 (1863) no. 7; 14 (1866) nos. 18 and 24; 20 (1872) no. 34.

[27] Cf. TE VELDE: *Anthony Brummelkamp* 292f.

Good Friday. In Winterswijk for example this situation lasted until 1893, when the two existing reformed congregations united (see section 4).[28] In the former work area of Gezelle Meerburg and Scholte a similar situation can be observed. A letter of a concerned believer shows us that in the *Gereformeerde Kerk* of Hardinxveld in 1920 a service on good Friday was not known yet.[29] But it also suggests the introduction of such a service is only a matter of time. The author of the letter blames ministers for promoting this development.

3. OPPOSITION IN THE CHURCHES OF THE SEPARATION OF 1886

Before continuing with the 20th century we must take a view at the second separation, which took place in the *Nederlandse Hervormde Kerk*. In the fifties and sixties of the 19th century the orthodox reformed movement in this denomination grew slowly but surely. Abr. Kuyper became one of its most important spokesmen and had a leading role in the separation, which took place in 1886. As well as in 1834 the preservation of the orthodox reformed tradition was the aim, but this separation was more deliberate and based on well-considered ecclesiological and juridical principles. In his first ('Nederlandse Hervormde') congregation, Beesd, Kuyper followed the orthodox tradition of administering the Lord's Supper at Easter. In some of his earlier meditations about Good Friday and Easter, published in *'Dagen van goede boodschap'*, Kuyper gives the impression he approves of celebrating the Lord's Supper on Good Friday.[30] In the preface, dated March 1, 1888, on the other hand he forcefully rejects breaking up the connection between crucifixion and resurrection by administering the sacrament on Good Friday. Therefore in his view the Lord's Supper should take place at Easter.[31] But having a service on Good Friday (without the Lord's Supper) still seems obvious to him.

---

[28] Cf. J.P. RUITINGA: *In en om de Zonnebrink 1841-1991. Uit de geschiedenis van de Gereformeerde Kerk van Winterswijk* (Winterswijk [1992]) 53.

[29] W.H. Swet to H. Bouwman dated 2nd March 1920, published in *De Bazuin* 68 (1920) no. 11 (12th March). Swet refers to his mother, who in this matter was educated by W.H. van Leeuwen in Werkendam (minister in this congregation from 1858 to 1863).

[30] A. KUYPER: *'Dagen van goede boodschap.' II. De Paaschmorgen (Met Goede Vrijdag)* (Amsterdam 1888) 55, 58, 83.

[31] KUYPER: *'Dagen (…)'* preface; cf. also 122.

W. van den Bergh, a follower of Kuyper in his struggle for a truely reformed church, was of another opinion. In both the congregations he served, Schaarsbergen and Voorthuizen, he stopped preaching on Good Friday.[32] He referred to the Scriptures (Gal. 2, 11-19, Col. 2, 19f), the church-order of Dordrecht and the *Confessio Belgica* (art. 25). He argued that new customs and holidays were human inventions and typical of liberal theology in imitation of the Roman Catholic Church. It was a sign of the denial of the authority of the Bible. Van den Bergh especially opposed the administration of the Lord's Supper on Good Friday. He saw it as a contempt of the sacrament, because it was not valued as such when celebrated on this day. The Lord's death should be commemorated personally every day, and in particular when the Lord's Supper was administered. We note that Van den Bergh stressed the sacramental and dogmatical side of the issue. This had been of less importance to the followers of the separation of 1834, who paid more attention to the ethical question whether Good Friday should or should not be a day of rest.[33] Van den Bergh's more specific approach may have been caused by the fact, that in the eighties the administration of the Lord's Supper had been become more current in orthodox circles, from which he wanted to distinguish clearly.

Van den Bergh's radical measures hardly met with any response. The first provisional synod of the new denomination took a position strategically. Having a service on Good Friday is a matter of the local church council, it declared in 1887, but the Lord's Supper shall not be administered.[34] Some church councils wanted more guidance. In the assembly of the region ('classis') of Franeker there were severe doubts as to having a service on Good Friday, but delegates were not really able to convince

---

[32] P.L. SCHRAM: *Willem van den Bergh 1850-1890* (Amsterdam 1980) 83, 112f; G. VAN ZEGGELAAR: *Wat God deed met Zijn Kerk te Voorthuizen* (Barneveld [1904?]) 88. Cf. W. van den Bergh to Abr. Kuyper dated 28th April 1884 (Kuyper Archive no. 3308, Historisch Documentatiecentrum voor de Geschiedenis van het Nederlands Protestantisme (1800 - heden), Free University (VU), Amsterdam). According to his edition of the church-order of Dordrecht Van den Bergh also principally rejected Circumcision Day and Ascension Day, because their observance was made dependant on the simple fact that they were held in most cities and provinces (cf. *De Dordtsche kerkenorde. Met verklaring van vreemde woorden en enkele bepalingen uit de Post-Acta. Uitgegeven door W. van den Berg & G.H. van Kasteel* (Nijkerk [1893]⁴) III and 23).

[33] Cf. *De Bazuin* 2 (1854) no. 36, where an unknown author deals with the Lord's Supper on Good Friday.

[34] *Acta Nederd. Geref. Kerken* 85 (art. 51).

one another of either point of view.[35] In Winterswijk another question rose: how should believers spend Good Friday?[36] The synod had to speak out again and concluded there was a principal difference between Good Friday and the Sunday, because only the latter is established by God as a day of rest. Therefore working on Good Friday is allowed. The synod also stipulated that a service should not be encouraged. But, so it added diplomatically, should a service already exist and should the congregation be attached to it, then this issue should be handled carefully. It could continue, but the congregation had to be instructed that the remembrance of Christ's death should not take place on Good Friday exclusively. It belongs to the heart of everyday christian life.[37] In this last sentence we sense the influence of the pietist Van den Bergh. The basis for the approach as a whole, however, had been layed by Abr. Kuyper in a rational proposal in his weekly *De Heraut* some months before.[38] He was convinced that a good explanation to the congregation concerned would soon end the need to attend a service on Good Friday. In the meantime, a church council was free to call the congregation for a service in the evening, as it was free to do on any other day.

4. ACCOMMODATION

After an insecure period of sometimes tough negotiations the two churches, separated in 1834 and in 1886, united in 1892; the 'Gereformeerde Kerken in Nederland' came into being. It seems Good Friday was no longer an issue. Having a service on this day was optional: not compulsory but not prohibited either. Especially for those originating from the separation of 1886 it would have been difficult to abandon the old custom. They had been used to it for many decades in the *Nederlandse Hervormde Kerk*. All members of the new denomination were

---

[35] Cf. 'Classis Franeker' (H.R. Nieborg) to the General Synod dated? – Public Records Office Utrecht, Synodal Archives of the *Gereformeerde Kerken in Nederland* no. 212. Cf. minutes dated 13th and 14th June 1889, 11th September 1889, 12th March 1890 – Public Records Office Leeuwarden, Archive of the 'classis Franeker' no. 10.

[36] Cf. church council of Winterswijk (H. Fransen?) to the General Synod dated 7th June 1890 – Public Records Office Utrecht, Synodal Archives of the *Gereformeerde Kerken in Nederland* no. 212.

[37] *Acta Nederd. Geref. Kerken* 300f (art. 65).

[38] Cf. *De Heraut* no. 640 (30th March 1890).

convinced Good Friday should be observed as a normal working day.[39] This is confirmed by some personal research in oral history.[40] There were villages where members of the *Gereformeerde Kerken* ostentatiously worked on Good Friday: while other Christians solemny walked to their church, women scrubbed the doorstep and the pavement, and men wheeled manure.

Yearly directories show us, how the observation of Good Friday slowly developed and changed. Among a lot of other things these directories contain calenders with some practical data. Until 1911-12 the calenders only give the official holidays of the church-order of Dordrecht. In some years before Good Friday is also mentioned, but it seems only by accident. From 1911-12 the date of Good Friday is consistently published.[41] In church papers on the other hand the local correspondents and the editors did not choose a clear attitude. They precisely published which minister took a service on a particular Sunday or holiday.[42] Services on New Year's Eve, not even mentioned in the church-order of Dordrecht, are consistently mentioned and appear to be held almost everywhere. Services on Good Friday on the other hand are rather carelessly dealt with. According to the church papers they were absent in some congregations, though on the basis of some combined data we may suppose they really were held in most cases.

In the twenties, a service on Good Friday was widely spread in the *Gereformeerde Kerken*, though the attendance of these services left a lot to be desired.[43] Because members of the *Gereformeerde Kerken* were regular churchgoers, this indicates the service on Good Friday was considered not essential by many of them. The resistance to celebrating this day as a holiday calmed down in these years, though the old principles towards its observation didn't change. K. Schilder in the weekly *De Reformatie*, for

---

[39] Cf. Abr. Kuyper criticising a movement in the 'Zaanstreek' to establish Good Friday as an official holiday (*De Heraut* no. 795 (19th March 1893)).

[40] I refer to three letters in my possession (from N.N. without date; from R.S. dated 8th September 1998; from W.D. dated 17th September 1998). Cf. also M.A. VRIJ-LANDT: *Liturgiek* (Delft [1987]) 116 ("mestkruien").

[41] Cf. *Jaarb. Chr. Geref. Kerk* (from 1911) and *Handb. Geref. Kerken* (from 1912).

[42] I studied *Friesch Kerkblad. Orgaan voor de Officieele Berichten der Gereformeerde Kerken in Friesland; Friesche Kerkbode. Weekblad voor de Gereformeerde Kerken in Friesland; Noord-Hollandsch Kerkblad. Weekblad voor de Gereformeerde Kerken in Noord-Holland;* and *Geldersche Kerkbode. Weekblad voor de Gereformeerde Kerken in Gelderland.*

[43] Cf. Joh. JANSEN: *Korte verklaring van de kerkenordening* (Kampen 1923¹) 290.

example, still opposes to Good Friday as a holiday and incites his readers to meditate on the facts of Christ's substitute suffering in everyday life.[44] He sees this orthodox attitude endangered by liberal denominations, because in the Good Friday service superficial and fleeting feelings are played on. This kind of subjectivism threatens the objective reformed approach.

We conclude, that the observance of Good Friday as such is not brought up for discussion anymore. Another minister, K. Fernhout, even supported an interdenominational movement, which sought to ask the government to give Good Friday the same rights as the Sunday.[45] Fernhout was a minister in the capital, in Amsterdam. Nowhere more than in a city like this, Good Friday was not observed as a day of rest. Fernhout must have sensed and seen the decreasing influence of christian faith on society. In this environment making Good Friday a public holiday could be seen as a proclamation of the faith. It is characteristic of the changing opinion in the *Gereformeerde Kerken* that the authoritative weekly *De Heraut* in 1932 openly questioned the arguments of Van den Bergh, which were called to mind again by the church council of his congregation in Voorthuizen.[46] The council fought a rearguard action and surrendered in 1949 when it decided to have a service on the evening of Good Friday.[47] It probably was the last church council in the *Gereformeerde Kerken* to make this move. During a thorough revision of the church-order in 1958, the national synod finally decided to prescribe church councils to call their congregation together for a service on Good Friday.[48] Because this had

---

[44] Cf. *De Reformatie* 5 (1924-25) 218f. Cf. also Tj. HOEKSTRA: *Gereformeerde homiletiek* (Wageningen 1926) 263, where the author mentions Good Friday without any critical remark. The traditional arguments and a subtle evaluation can be found in H. BOUWMAN: *Gereformeerd kerkrecht* 2 (Kampen 1934) 443 and 493 (cf. also 352; *De Bazuin* 68 (1920) no. 11 (12th March)); and JANSSEN: *Korte verklaring* 292-294.

[45] Cf. *De Heraut* no. 2828 (3rd April 1932); *Christelijke encyclopaedie* 2, 365-369.

[46] Cf. *De Heraut* no. 2828 (3rd April 1932). Cf. also Joh.C. FRANCKEN: *Veel vragen... één antwoord. Een keur uit de onderwerpen in het vragenuurtje der N.C.R.V. behandeld* (Kampen 1940) 345-348.

[47] G. KUYPERS: *Iets goeds uit Voorthuizen? Amsterdam en de moederkerk der Doleantie* (Kampen 1985) 161.

[48] Cf. *Acta Gen. Syn. Geref. Kerken* 1955-56 (Leeuwarden) art. 377 and 495; 1957-58 (Assen) art. 347 and 348. Cf. also: *Rapport van de Deputaten voor de Herziening van de Kerkorde, aangeboden aan de Generale Synode van de Gereformeerde Kerken in Nederland, welke D.V. samenkomt te Leeuwarden in Augustus 1955* 16: "Wat artikel 72 betreft, zij opgemerkt dat deputaten zich aangesloten hebben bij de in onze kerken langzamerhand gegroeide praktijk om ook op den Goeden Vrijdag een kerkdienst te houden."

already become common practice, hardly any objections were made. In the same year even the traditional K. Dijk, professor in Kampen, seems to suggest people should work as little as possible on Good Friday.[49] Though he was influential in his church, in this case he didn't find any considerable support. The wish to observe Good Friday as a day of rest faded away in other denominations. The differing opinions of the past approached each other now.

As in the next decades the number of ecumenical contacts of the *Gereformeerde Kerken* increased, the appreciation of liturgy and the liturgical year grew. More Calvinist customs such as the seven Sundays before Easter with sermons in remembrance of the suffering of Christ, lost popularity. In the seventies and eighties a more Catholic, ecumenical approach was welcomed in a growing number of congregations of both the *Nederlandse Hervormde Kerk* and the *Gereformeerde Kerken*: a (liturgical) period of lent including six instead of seven Sundays, services on Maundy Thursday (in remembrance of the institution of the Lord's Supper), Good Friday and Easter Saturday. On Good Friday only the Passion is read and prayers are said, there is no sermon, not to mention the administration of the Lord's Supper. These developments are typical of a certain shyness towards the person of Jesus Christ and towards an orthodox reformed theme as reconciliation once and for all. In the past His suffering and its meaning were at the heart of reformed faith and preaching. Nowadays for many believers the accent has moved to reflection on their relationship with God and their personal ethics.

5. REFLECTION

In his dissertation *De emancipatie van de Gereformeerden* J. Hendriks paints a picture of the history of the members of the *Gereformeerde Kerken* and its predecessors from a sociological point of view. He characterizes it as an emancipatory movement. He distinguishes between several periods.[50] Before c. 1860 their only claim is to be able to arrange

---

[49] Cf. *Christelijke encyclopedie* 3 (Kampen 1958[2]) 271: "Wel dringt de overtuiging hoe langer hoe meer door, dat op G. [Goede Vrijdag] zo weinig mogelijk moet gewerkt worden". Cf. also K. DIJK: *De dienst der prediking* (Kampen 1955) 309-313 and 339f.

[50] J. HENDRIKS: *De emancipatie van de Gereformeerden. Sociologische bijdrage tot de verklaring van enige kenmerken van het huidige gereformeerde volksdeel* (= Serie maatschappijbeelden 8) (Alphen a/d Rijn 1971) 241-245 (cf. 234f).

their personal and religious life as they want. From c. 1860 to c. 1880 they strife for emancipation of their group and the re-christianization of society, trying to cooperate with other protestant movements. In the next period they strengthen their internal organization, slowly reaching the goal of emancipation, more or less giving up the aim of re-christianization. From c. 1920 the isolation intensifies, the life of the *Gereformeerde Kerken in Nederland* freezes. The thought is cherished that they are the only true church. After World War II, from c. 1950 cracks become visble in their bastion. Relationships with other groups and churches develop slowly but surely. The *Gereformeerde Kerken* have become a denomination between other denominations. The emancipation is completed.

This theory deepens our insight in Good Friday in the *Gereformeerde Kerken* and their predecessors as a cultural phenomenon, which developed in close interaction with other denominations. The participants of the separation of 1834 united in their opposition to innovations in the *Nederlandse Hervormde Kerk*, from which in most regions a compulsory service on the Friday before Easter is one. They wanted to organize church life as they saw fit, which in most cases will have meant without any service on Good Friday. This was, however, not only a matter of conviction, but also of distinction from the *Hervormde Kerk* they had left and also from others with whom they turned their backs on the *Hervormde Kerk*. In both cases it strengthened the profile of the own group. After a period of passionate arguments the different groups of the new denomination reached a consensus in the fifties with respect for minor differences. In the case of Good Friday a compromise was found: having a service on Good Friday is tolerated, but observing Good Friday as a day of rest is rejected fiercely. It distracts from what are thought to be the essentials of christian faith – as all holidays tend to do according to a minority. We also see a new contra-argument coming up, which originates in the re-establishment of the episcopal hierarchy in 1853, and also must have appealed to other protestants: tolerating Good Friday as a day of rest may give elbow-room to the introduction of special Roman Catholic holidays into official state law. Abr. Kuyper seems initially not to have opposed the administration of the Lord's Supper on Good Friday, probably not to alienate kindred spirits from him. When around 1880 this cooperation ended in deception, he adopted a more strict, though still pragmatical attitude towards Good Friday. If in view of the needs of the believers a service is necessary, it can be held, because a church council can organize a service on any day. The Lord's Supper, however, should not be administered on Good Friday, but at Easter. On that festive day both His death and resurrection should be celebrated in the sacrament. Kuyper did not take up such a radical position as Van den Bergh, member of a younger generation, did. Van den Bergh wanted to abolish Good Friday completely. In his opinion it only did harm. Kuyper on the other hand, known for his tactical insight, recognized he had to meet his followers half way. They had been used to attending one or even two services on Good Friday for many, many decades. Taking all this away at once would not have been understood. Kuyper was aware of the ambivalence of the day, but did not want to exaggerate its more negative sides.

Although Kuyper principally opposed to the observation of Good Friday as a day of rest, his both legal and pragmatical approach openened the possibility to integrate a service on this day into reformed church life. We get the impression, that after the union of 1892 this became a fact in most congregations within a few decades. It strikes us that in the period of isolation, from c. 1920 until c. 1950, the service on Good Friday is hardly an issue of importance anymore. The special reformed approach didn't seem to need any sort of justification or defense anymore. It had become obvious, so obvious that no further discussion was necessary. Even the thought of observing Good Friday as a day of rest came into the picture and was cautiously allowed.

The church-order of 1958 shows having a service on Good Friday is officially accepted in the *Gereformeerde Kerken*: it obliges church councils to organize one. The practice in the *Hervormde Kerk* and the *Gereformeerde Kerken* started to resemble one another more and more. Even in some *Gereformeerde* congregations the Lord's Supper was celebrated on Good Friday, though it never became common.[51] On the one hand the aim to observe Good Friday as a day of rest was received with more sympathy in the *Gereformeerde Kerken*, on the other hand it lost popularity in other denominations. In the end the thought died out slowly, probably also because of the more modest position of the church in society. In the *Gereformeerde Kerken* the need to stress the own identity

---

[51] See e.g., *Centraal Weekblad* 6 (1958) 351; 8 (1960) 117; 9 (1961) 307. A protest from the *Gereformeerde Werkgroep voor Liturgie* shows that the popularity of this ritual grew after some years (cf. minutes of meetings on 5th January, 31st March, 31st August 1970 and 4th January 1971 – Public Records Office Utrecht, Archive of the *Gereformeerde Werkgroep voor Liturgie* no. 290; cf. also nos. 294 and 317).

decreased, the openness towards other churches and traditions grew. This resulted in an ecumenical layout of the service on Good Friday. The view can be defended that the *Gereformeerde Kerken* and their predecessors didn't exert any influence at all with their opinion towards Good Friday. Apart from the fact that initially it was not their aim to have any influence, it must be admitted that it is more the other way around: others influenced them, for example in the 19th century representatives of the *Nadere Reformatie* and in the last decades ecumenicals. Still it should be considered a theoretical possibility that without the *Gereformeerde Kerken* Good Friday would have been declared an official holiday in The Netherlands. In reaction to several requests to do so the synod of the 'Hervormde Kerk' as well as the government stated that the support among other denominations was too small.[52] Without any doubt, apart from the Roman Catholic Church of this group the *Gereformeerde Kerken* were the most important.

---

[52] *Christelijke encyclopaedie* 2 (Kampen n.d.), 368; *Christelijke encylopedie* (Kampen 1958²) 3, 271.

JAN SMELIK

THE NATIONAL PROTESTANT MISSION FESTIVALS IN THE NETHERLANDS, 1863-1939

During the nineteenth century there was great interest in 'domestic mission' and 'foreign mission'. 'Domestic mission' meant more than what is presently termed 'evangelisation'. The term also encompassed all sorts of charitable activities which were intended to effect the restoration or consolidation of Christian life.[1] 'Foreign mission' was understood to mean mission among the heathen in non-Western lands. The deep commitment to foreign missions took concrete form in all sorts of activities such as the founding of mission societies and dispatching missionaries to 'barbaric' heathens in distant countries that – according to the views of the time – waited longingly for the saving word of the Gospel.

The interest in mission also had its impact on Protestant feast culture. For instance, based on British models and stimulated by the *Nederlandsch Zendeling Genootschap*,[2] in 1798 prayer meetings were initiated, held once a month on a weekday, in support of missionary activities.[3] These gatherings never really proved popular. According to the Groningen professor E.F. Kruyf, as early as 1800 the attendance figures were disappointing.[4] Complaints about the low number of participants rose sharply after 1850.[5]

The *Christelijk Nationaal Zendingsfeest* (National Christian Mission Festival), which arose in the second half of the 19th century and

[1] S.D. VAN VEEN: *Eene eeuw van worsteling* (Groningen 1904) 721.

[2] Regarding the Nederlandsch Zendeling Genootschap (later also called Het Nederlandsche Zendelinggenootschap and Nederlandsch Zendinggenootschap), see E.F. KRUYF: *Geschiedenis Nederlandsche Zendelinggenootschap en zijne zendingsposten* (Groningen 1894); J. BONESCHANSKER: *Het Nederlandsch Zendeling Genootschap in zijn eerste periode* (Leeuwarden 1987).

[3] For an extended treatment of these prayer meetings, see KRUYF: *Geschiedenis Nederlandsche Zendelinggenootschap* 268-270; BONESCHANSKER: *Nederlandsch Zendeling Genootschap* 84-88.

[4] KRUYF: *Geschiedenis Nederlandsche Zendelinggenootschap* 268-270.

[5] C.F. GRONEMEIJER: De zendings-werkzaamheden der gemeente, in *Stemmen voor waarheid en vrede* 13 (1876) 1315-1316.

continued to exist until the eve of the Second World War, proved to have more allure.[6] This study will examine the mission festival as an outstanding specimen of a typical Protestant feast. At the outset of this, it is wise to note that Dutch Protestantism was decidedly not a homogenous entity. The Netherlands accommodated disparate Protestant groups. Since the Reformation the Calvinist church, after 1816 calling itself the *Nederlandsche Hervormde Kerk* (Netherlands Reformed Church), had been the official and privileged denomination. Other groups such as the Lutherans and Mennonites represented a minority and were more or less tolerated. Orthodox Calvinist groups, who preferred to term themselves *gereformeerd*, split off from the Netherlands Reformed Church in 1834 (the *Afscheiding*) and again in 1886 (the *Doleantie*). Further splits in turn occurred within these separatist groups. As will be discussed below, the mission festival was a celebration which bound Protestants together, despite all these denominational divisions.

After examining the prehistory and origins of the mission festival, attention will be focused on the participants in the festival as a group. In this, not only the size, but also the social and denominational composition of the group will be examined. Then I will describe the organisation and content of the festival. In part on the basis of this data, an examination of the background and objectives of the mission festival will follow. The study will be rounded off with a concluding section.

1. PREHISTORY AND ORIGINS

The national mission festivals were patterned on foreign models. Among the models which can be listed were the American 'camp meetings', which were being held in rural areas from about 1800 onward, reports of which reached The Netherlands.[7] The German *Missionsfest*

---

[6] Regarding the mission festivals, see also I.H. ENKLAAR: De christelijk nationale zendingsfeesten op Middachten (1868-1937), in *Mededelingen van de Oudheidkundige Kring "Rheden-Rozendaal"* 61 (maart 1977) 2-7; I.H. ENKLAAR: *Kom over en help ons! Twaalf opstellen over de Nederlandse zending in de negentiende eeuw* (Den Haag 1981) 145-155; S.J. SEINEN: *Zendingsfeesten en Veenkloosterbos 1877-1987* (Kollumerzwaag/Zuidhorn 1987) 26-33; H. REENDERS: *Alternatieve zending. Ottho Gerhard Heldring (1804-1876) en de verbreiding van het christendom in Nederlands-Indië* (Kampen 1991) 357-361.

[7] See e.g. M. COHEN STUART: Wolfhezen, in *Stemmen voor waarheid en vrede* 1 (1864) 723.

was also familiar to the Dutch. That can be seen from, among other things, the enthusiastic reports that O.G. Heldring[8] wrote during the 1850s about these German mission festivals in *De Vereeniging: Christelijke Stemmen.*[9]

The mission days that the *Broedergemeente* (Moravians or *Hernhutters*) had been holding in Zeist since 1793 on a Wednesday in September were of particular importance for the origins of the Dutch mission festivals. This refugee community, originally from Bohemia, which had formed around Count Nikolaus Ludwig von Zinzendorf, were fervent missionaries. The Moravians had settled in The Netherlands in the first half of the 18th century, under the patronage of Princess Maria Louise. In 1745 they were given the old castle at Zeist, around which they constructed various buildings in the years which followed. After initial opposition from the Protestant status quo, the ideals of the Moravians at Zeist, whose membership declined during the 19th century from 328 to 170, began to claim increasing attention from Dutch Protestants.

The Moravians' mission days were primarily held to foster love for missionary work.[10] It was customary that missionaries who were on leave reported at length on their efforts. There were also lectures by prominent church and lay figures. Very quickly after their founding, the mission days in Zeist fell into a regular pattern. In the morning a worship service took place which was generally led by a Moravian minister. In the afternoon there was a festive gathering which included many orations. A love feast in honour of the missionaries was connected with this gathering. The proceedings were conducted in German. Only the

---

[8] O.G. Heldring (1804-1876) was the Netherlands Reformed minister at Hemmen from 1827 to 1867. The crying social needs with which his congregation was confronted brought him to increasingly devote himself to charity work. For example, in 1848 the Asyl Steenbeek was opened at Zetten, a refuge for 'penitent fallen women'. In 1857 'Talitha Kumi', a home for neglected children from five to sixteen years of age, was set up. Six years later Heldring founded 'Bethel', an institution for neglected girls over sixteen years of age. The focus of the institutions in Zetten was the 'Vluchtheuvel' (Hill of Refuge) Church, built in 1867. In that year Heldring became minister of the Vluchtheuvel congregation and director of the institutions he had established in Zetten.

[9] See e.g. *De Vereeniging: Christelijke Stemmen* 10 (1856) 102-106; 14 (1860) 229-237.

[10] Regarding the Moravian community in Zeist and their mission festivals, see Hartmut BECK: Kanttekeningen bij de geschiedenis van het Zeister Zendingsgenootschap, in A. DE GROOT & P. PEUCKER (eds): *De Zeister Broedergemeente 1746-1996. Bijdragen tot de geschiedenis van de Hernhutters in Nederland* (Zutphen 1996) 166-184.

evening gathering, which closed off the mission festival, was commonly conducted in Dutch.

Among the characteristics of the Moravian mission days was the fact that they were attended by members of various Dutch Protestant denominations. Interest in the Zeist mission days was found particularly in the Dutch *Réveil*, a regeneration movement not connected with any specific church, which had arisen in the first half of the 19th century and which had its strongest support among persons from the higher social classes in the population. People visited the days "to hear the mighty acts of God proclaimed, to enjoy the inspirational music and the frank hospitality among 'the quiet in the land' [Ps. 35, 20], but most of all to pray together those mighty words, 'Lord, Thy Kingdom come.'"[11]

Around 1860 the number of visitors to the Moravian mission festivals rose steeply. Chiefly because the number of missionary societies had expanded sharply during the 1850s, many more people had become actively involved with missionary work. The festival in Zeist afforded a good opportunity for the friends of missionary activities to meet one another. Furthermore, the expansion of the rail network which took place after 1860[12] made visits to the mission festival possible for many more people. In 1861 and 1862 special trains were chartered to bring visitors to the Zeist mission day from Amsterdam and Rotterdam.

This enormous flood – more than 2000 people – was not really appreciated by the Moravians. Organisational difficulties arose: the church building could not hold the number of visitors, and holding of the love feast was greatly complicated by the number of participants.[13] Moreover, the Moravians were of the view that many of the visitors were attending the mission day out of the wrong motives: many came only for diversion, and not out of love for the Gospel. This last was contested by the Netherlands Reformed minister S.H. Buytendijk,[14]

---

[11] S.H. Buytendijk: *Het veertigjarig bestaan van het Christelijk Nationaal Zendingsfeest* (Utrecht 1903) 6.

[12] In 1860 the Dutch government took responsibility for the construction of railways. The increase in rail traffic demanded the passage of the Railway Act (1865).

[13] A. de Groot: Hernhutters in de wereld van het negentiende-eeuwse Nederlandse protestantisme, in De Groot & Peucker (eds): *De Zeister Broedergemeente 1746-1996* 207.

[14] Simon Hendrik Buytendijk (1820-1910) was a coachman until 1853. He studied theology at Utrecht from 1853 to 1858. He served as minister of various congregations, retiring in 1898.

among others. He was, however, understanding of the organisational problems with which the Moravians had to contend.

This brought him to the happy thought of organising an alternative mission festival the following year somewhere along the Rhine railway. He succeeded in realising his plan in 1863, although not without a last minute hitch which threatened the event because of a difference of opinion between the organising committee and the Ministry of Justice. What was at stake was the question of whether or not the mission festival was in conflict with a section of the law that made religious gatherings of more than twenty persons illegal. The organisers relied on Article 167 of the Constitution, which said that "all public religious exercises within buildings and enclosed places" were permitted. Because the festival was to take place in the open air, the point of contention was over the words "enclosed places": did the intended site, an estate near Arnhem, indeed qualify as an "enclosed place"? Even the Minister of Justice himself became personally involved in the dispute. Ultimately permission was given for the mission festival to be held.[15] Beginning with that date, in addition to the Moravians' mission day this annual mission festival took place almost every year through 1939.[16] These festivals were organised by the *Vereeniging Christelijk Nationaal Zendingsfeest*, and were held at 23 different locations in the provinces of Gelderland, Utrecht, North Holland and South Holland. Access by rail was essential in the selection of places where the festivals were to be held. The location had to be within walking distance of a railway station.

2. THE AUDIENCE

Interest in the festivals was enormous. To give some impression: an estimated 6,000 people came to the first festival; in 1872 there were more than 17,000 visitors. After 1872 the numbers declined. The reason for this is that after that date separate mission festivals were organised in the northern and southern provinces. The Northern Mission Festival was

[15] Cf. P.J. MARGRY: *Teedere quaesties. Religieuze rituelen in conflict. Confrontaties tussen katholieken en protestanten rond de processiecultuur in 19ᵉ-eeuws Nederland* (Hilversum 2000).

[16] No mission festivals were held in 1866, 1915, and 1917-23, inclusive.

held for the first time in 1872.[17] The first Southern Mission Festival took place in 1873.[18]

The numbers who attended the mission festivals are also reflected in the print runs of the programme brochures which were on sale at various book shops around the country in the weeks preceding the mission festival, and also served as an admission ticket.[19] For instance, the Board of the *Christelijk Nationaal Zendingsfeest* decided in 1877 that the edition of programme brochures would henceforth be 9,000 copies.[20] In comparison with the 17,000 attendees of five years before, the decline is clearly to be seen.

The decline in the number of visitors also had to do with the fact that the novelty of the festival wore off after a couple of years. Another cause possibly lay in the *Doleantie*, the exodus from the Netherlands Reformed Church of a group of critical orthodox Calvinists, which took place under the leadership of Abraham Kuyper in 1886. At least, in 1888 A.W. Bronsveld[21] pointed to the *Doleantie* as the cause for the lower number of visitors.[22] Whatever the case, according to Bronsveld the 25th anniversary mission festival in 1888 was still attended by over 12,000 people.[23] But it was apparently the anniversary character of the mission festival that had a positive effect on the number of visitors.

[17] SEINEN: *Zendingsfeesten.*

[18] J. HELSLOOT: *Vermaak tussen beschaving en kerstening* (Amsterdam 1995) 185-194.

[19] Almost all the programme brochures are to be found in the former Library of the Hendrik-Kraemer Institute, in Oegstgeest (now: Utrecht). The only programme brochures I was unable to locate were those for the first and second mission festivals, 1863 and 1864. The songs which were sung during the first mission festival were, however, reported in *Het eerste Algemeen Evangelisch Nationaal Zendingsfeest* (n.p. 1863).

[20] *Notulen Vergadering van het moderamen van het Bestuur Christelijk Nationaal Zendingsfeest, 8 augustus 1877* (Zendingsarchief Hendrik Kraemer-instituut te Oegstgeest, dossier 22).

[21] Andries Willem Bronsveld (1839-1924) studied theology in Utrecht, where he received his doctorate in 1862. He served various congregations in the Netherlands Reformed Church. After 1875 Bronsveld was the only editor of the journal *Stemmen voor waarheid en vrede*. He wrote many articles and reviews which appeared in it. In the column 'Kroniek' he also give his views on countless events and situations in the religious, cultural, social and political spheres. In addition, Bronsveld occupied various other functions. He was, among other things, a member of the Board of the Christelijk Nationaal Zendingsfeest. He wrote two extensive studies on Reformed hymn books, one of which was published posthumously.

[22] A.W. BRONSVELD: Kroniek, in *Stemmen voor waarheid en vrede* 25 (1888) 740.

[23] *Ibidem* 779.

The mission festivals were attended by people from all classes of society. In regard to the eleventh mission festival (1874), Bronsveld wrote, "We were struck by the diversity that was to be discerned among those present. All layers of society were represented."[24] In 1903 Bronsveld recollected that most of the visitors had "belonged to the prosperous middle-class, and to the working class. Of course there were also clergymen, evangelists, Christian teachers, together with deaconesses, for the most part present in large numbers."[25]

According to the Netherlands Reformed professor J.I. Doedes,[26] a mission festival could be qualified as a 'national celebration,' in which no distinctions existed between the common people on the one hand and the wealthy and highly placed on the other. It is the characteristic of a national celebration that it should unite the whole of a nation, without any distinction regarding status, birth or wealth. According to Doedes the mission festival distinguished itself from other popular celebrations on this point. The difference between the eminent and the little people falls away at the mission feast, "because there it is as the body of Christ, certainly distinguished into limbs and organs, but all limbs and organs of one and the same body, and all in the same Spirit!"[27]

Not only social distinctions but also denominational differences fell away at mission festivals. The mission festivals were organised and attended by members of various Protestant denominations and groups, with the exception of the liberals.[28] The Salvation Army, which became active in The Netherlands in 1887, was also present at the mission festivals from 1888 onward.[29]

This interconfessional character of the mission festivals is remarkable, given the rising pluriformity in the Protestant world in the period from

[24] A.W. BRONSVELD: Kroniek, in *Stemmen voor waarheid en vrede* 11 (1874) 966.

[25] A.W. BRONSVELD: Uit de geschiedenis van het Christelijk Nationaal Zendingsfeest, in *Stemmen voor waarheid en vrede* 40 (1903) 730.

[26] Jacobus Isaac Doedes (1817-1897) studied theology at Utrecht; from 1847 to 1859 he was a Netherlands Reformed minister in Rotterdam. After 1888 he was a professor at the university at Utrecht.

[27] J.I. DOEDES: Een zendingsfeest, voor christenen het heerlijkst feest. Openingsrede, den 3 Juli 1872 te Wolfheze uitgesproken, in *Stemmen voor waarheid en vrede* 9 (1872) 791-792.

[28] Individuals from various denominations were members of the Vereeniging Christelijk Nationaal Zendingsfeest. For a list of the members from the period 1863 through 1903, see BUYTENDIJK: *Het veertigjarig bestaan* 42-44 (Bijlage 3).

[29] BRONSVELD: Kroniek (1888) 780. Cf. SEINEN: *Zendingsfeesten* 91.

1866 to 1938; not only were there splits in existing churches, but there
were also various new religious sects being imported into The Netherlands, primarily from Anglo-Saxon countries. It is, moreover, striking
because during the course of the 19th century denominational differences manifested themselves with increasing strength precisely in attitudes involving foreign missions.

As it was, during the 1840s an intense discussion had arisen about
the question of whether the *Nederlandsch Zendeling Genootschap* was still
true to its principles, the foundation of which was summarised concisely
but powerfully in the motto "Peace through the blood of the cross".
Among its critics were, for instance, the *Réveil* figures Groen van Prinsterer,[30] O.G. Heldring, Isaac da Costa and Nicolaas Beets.[31] The
Genootschap, where those in charge were increasingly followers of the
more liberal evangelical 'Groningen theology,' was accused of no longer
being orthodox enough, and of undermining essential Christian truths.
Dissatisfaction with the *Genootschap* led to the setting up of various
new, orthodox mission organisations in the period from 1850 to 1860,
such as the *Java-Comité* (1855), the *Nederlandsche Zendingsvereeniging*
(1858), the *Utrechtsche Zendings-Vereeniging* (1859) and the *Nederlandsche Gereformeerde Zendingsvereeniging* (1859).

In 1861 the *Afgescheiden Christelijk Gereformeerde Kerken*[32] were
the first to begin denominational mission work. They took the standpoint that Christ's missionary commission[33] was given to the church,
and that mission work was therefore fully a concern of the church.[34]
Missionary activity must not be left to a private organisation of
activists.

---

[30] I.H. ENKLAAR: Groen van Prinsterer en het NZG, in J. VAN DEN BERG (ed.):
Aspecten van het Réveil (Kampen 1980) 89-105.

[31] KRUYF: *Geschiedenis Nederlandsche Zendelinggenootschap* 472-483.

[32] This denomination was established in 1834 when critical members of the
national church left it because of dissatisfaction with the prevailing theological views
and the way in which the church was governed.

[33] Matthew 28, 19-20a: "Go ye therefore, and teach all nations, baptising them in
the name of the Father, and of the Son, and of the Holy Spirit, teaching them to observe
all things whatsoever I have commanded you" (KJV).

[34] For further discussion of the missionary activities of the Christelijk Gereformeerden, see H. HIDDING: *De zending van de Christelijk (Afgescheiden) Gereformeerde Kerk
1860-1892* (Kampen 1977); H. BOUMA: Het begin van de zendingsaktie door de
afgescheiden kerken, in D. DEDDENS & M. TE VELDE (eds): *Afscheiding-Wederkeer.
Opstellen over de Afscheiding van 1834* (Haarlem 1984) 243-264.

There were initially objections against the mission festivals in the denominations which had separated from the Netherlands Reformed Church. The Directors of the separatist Theological School at Kampen officially rejected participation.[35] The most important objection was the interconfessional character of the mission festivals. Nevertheless, A. Brummelkamp (1811-1888) lent his support to the festivals from the beginning.[36] Later the secessionist groups abandoned their reservations.[37] They participated in the mission festivals on through into the 20th century. Various *Gereformeerde* ministers were members of the *Vereeniging Christelijk Nationaal Zendingsfeest*.

The initial objection of the separatists, that the mission festivals were interconfessional, was precisely what was regarded as positive by persons of other denominations. In 1863 Heldring wrote:

> There is, in the great Mission Festivals, something that reminds us in an exceptional way of the great community of saints that exists, more than any denominational festival can express.

According to M. Cohen Stuart[38] the mission festivals were evidence of the mounting need for union and rapprochement, and visitors left with the feeling that a living community existed transcending the existing churches in The Netherlands.[39]

Doedes, who was mentioned above, said in his opening address to the ninth mission festival:

> The [mission festival] is not a festival of the church, which always allows one or another schism to show through, not a celebration at which there can be any place for slogans such as "I belong to Paul", "I belong to Apollos", "I

---

[35] M. TE VELDE: *Anthony Brummelkamp 1811-1888* (Barneveld 1988) 296, 384.

[36] Brummelkamp was lecturer at the Theologische School at Kampen. From 1870 to 1887 he was member of the Vereeniging Christelijk National Zendingsfeest. Brummelkamp appeared as a speaker at the mission festivals in 1863, 1868, 1869, 1871, 1883 and 1884 (see the programme brochure for the 50th Zendingsfeest, Raaphorst 1913, 34). For more regarding Brummelkamp's attitude toward the mission festivals, see TE VELDE: *Anthony Brummelkamp* 383-385.

[37] See also W.H. GISPEN: *Eenige Brieven aan een Vriend te Jeruzalem* (Kampen 1903) 124.

[38] Martinus Cohen Stuart (1824-1878) studied theology at the Remonstrant Seminary at Amsterdam. After his retirement in 1873 he occupied himself with, among other things, all sorts of domestic and foreign mission concerns which were stimulated by the Réveil.

[39] M. COHEN STUART: Wolfhezen, in *Stemmen voor waarheid en vrede* 1 (1864) 725, 726.

belong to Peter", or even a sectarian "I belong to Christ". The only question here is, if you love Jesus, and in Him love mission, and for His sake love the supreme Sender. Your YES to this question is your ticket of admission here.[40]

3. ORGANISATION AND CONTENT

On the site where the mission festival was held there normally were four rostrums. Near each rostrum a couple of benches were set up for the benefit of "the weak, elderly and women". Other listeners could remain standing, sit on the ground or hire folding chairs. In the morning and afternoon addresses were given by more than fifteen different, prominent individuals from church and society. Among the speakers were generally one or more missionaries who were on leave in The Netherlands. When at the end of the 19th century there arose an increasing interest in The Netherlands for its colonial territories,[41] the number of speakers at the mission festivals who were working in Dutch colonies also increased. Naturally, the central topic was the work of mission in all its facets. But there were also subjects chosen for the addresses that involved the advancement of Christian life in The Netherlands.

A prominent component of the mission festivals, in which the visitors were active participants, was the singing of inspirational hymns. As in other situations, the songs here functioned primarily to deepen and affirm Christian faith within and beyond their own circle. In addition to information about the speakers and their subjects and the arrival and departure times of the trains, the programme brochures contained the texts of the songs which were to be sung (the "festival songs"). These songs – about 20 or 25 of them – were selected by the Directors of the *Vereeniging Christelijk Nationaal Zendingsfeest*. In addition to mission hymns there were also many songs selected and sung which had little or nothing to do with mission. The mission festivals functioned as a conduit through which new songs were spread across the country and across denominational lines. In the programme brochures which appeared through 1872 it is possible from the headings above the songs to know at precisely what point in the programme they were sung. The books further divide the songs up to serve as *voorzang*, *tusschenzang* and *nazang* for

---

[40] DOEDES: Een zendingsfeest 792.
[41] Cf. J.C.H. BLOM & E. LAMBERTS (eds): *Geschiedenis van de Nederlanden* (Amsterdam 1994) 454.

the addresses. For instance, in the programme brochure for the fifth mission festival, of July 29, 1868, it is indicated that at 2:00 p.m., after the main noon break, the hymn *Laat Uw zegen nederdalen* is to be sung. The first verse is sung before the appearance of the first series of speakers (*voorzang*), the second verse after they have finished and before the appearance of the second series of speakers (*tusschenzang*), and the final verse after the second series of addresses were over (*nazang*).

Beginning in 1873 the programme brochures no longer indicated when the songs were supposed to be sung. That was done to permit the speakers more freedom in choosing the songs to accompany their addresses. It may be assumed that the songs continued to function as opening, intermediary or closing songs.

Actually, this practice was familiar to Protestants from their church services.[42] That brings me to the fact that the festivals were similar to church services. In church services the *tusschenzang* was sung as an interlude during the sermon (also sometimes termed a "rest of attention").[43] The hymns which were sung before and after the sermon were frequently termed *voorzang* and *nazang*.[44]

The *collecten* were likewise familiar from church services. These too were standard elements at mission festivals. There were collections at the various rostrums, and at the exit from the site. There were also collection boxes placed here and there around the site. The proceeds were used exclusively for mission, and divided among the various mission societies.

As was the case for church services, the mission festivals were closed with a benediction and the singing of a closing hymn. It was customary to close the mission festivals with Psalm 72 (verse 11: "His Name must eternal honour receive") and Hymn 96 from the *Evangelische Gezangen*: *Halleluja! eeuwig dank en eere.*[45]

---

[42] Regarding Protestant church services in the 19th century, see K.W. DE JONG: *Ordening van dienst. Achtergronden van en ontwikkelingen in de eredienst van de Gereformeerde Kerken in Nederland* (Baarn 1996).

[43] E.F. KRUYF: *Liturgiek* (Groningen 1901) 102, 265 note 1.

[44] Cf. L.H. VAN LENNEP: Het gezang in de kerk, in *Stemmen voor waarheid en vrede* 47 (1910) 929-931.

[45] The singing of the eleventh verse of Psalm 72 at missionary gatherings appears to have a long tradition. The psalm was also sung as the closing during the prayer meeting on December 1, 1800, in the Gasthuis Church in Gouda (BONESCHANSKER: *Nederlandsch Zendeling Genootschap* Bijlage F, 213-218). On the songs which were sung during this prayer meeting, see R.A. BOSCH: *En nooit meer oude Psalmen zingen. Zingend geloven in een nieuwe tijd 1760-1810* (Zoetermeer 1996) 268-270.

In summary, the mission festivals can be characterised as Protestant 'open-air services.' That they were indeed seen as church services is also confirmed by the fact that in 1863 Buytendijk expressly states that people did not come to Wolfheze to meet, but "to hold religious exercises".[46]

The festival-goers not only sang hymns at the mission festival, but also during the train trips to and from the festival. To judge from our sources, the quality of the singing must have been rather poor.[47] As one example, I can give the description provided by Bronsveld of his trip to the fifth mission festival, in 1868. He writes that he sat in a train compartment:

> (…) the front part of which was occupied by a host so devoted to singing that the constant clack-clack of the train was drowned out by their bawling. When the train stood still the song rose up with new fury, and by the time we arrived in Middachten there were many, particularly women by the sound of it, who could almost sing no more. The hoarse, dismally out of tune noise caused one to shudder, and was anything but inspirational. People must learn to moderate their zeal.[48]

Indeed, by the 20th century the bad quality of the singing caused the directors of the *Vereeniging Christelijk Nationaal Zendingsfeest* to regularly print the following notice in the programme brochures: "It is forbidden to sing in the festival trains while they are standing in stations." It would appear there was good reason for such an annual admonition.

There are more positive reports known of the singing during the festivals. Buytendijk quotes a friend, not further identified, who offers his opinion on the first mission festival in 1863. The singing crowds reminded him of the Israelites' procession up to the Temple in Jerusalem, and for him was a prophecy of the community that awaits us at the Second Coming of Christ. According to Buytendijk, this was the general impression.[49] Fidelio (pseudonym of A.W. Bronsveld) responded positively to the singing. He found that there was something moving and uplifting about the singing at the mission festivals. In the woods,

---

[46] S.H. BUYTENDIJK: *Bladen uit mijn levensboek* (Nijkerk 1911) 272-273.
[47] Jan SMELIK: *Eén in lied en leven. Het stichtelijk lied bij Nederlandse protestanten tussen 1866 en 1938* (= Nederlandse cultuur in Europese context. Monografieën en studies 9) (Den Haag 1997) 204-209.
[48] A.W. BRONSVELD: Kroniek, in *Stemmen voor waarheid en vrede* 5 (1868) 871.
[49] BUYTENDIJK: *Bladen* 275.

under the open sky, it sounded so majestic and so full. There was something heartening and consoling in it.[50] These positive assessments did not involve any aesthetic judgement on the mass singing. One is always impressed by the numbers, by the fact that thousands of people are singing together in the open air. The quality of the singing was no better at the mission festivals.

The poor quality of the singing would often have been caused by the fact that it was not always led by brass accompaniment. Apparently there was at least one rostrum where the mass singing was accompanied by a brass band.[51] For a long time this task was undertaken by the 'Obadja' (Dutch for 'Obadiah') musical society of Rotterdam.[52] During the noon intermission this society frequently performed a number of instrumental works. In addition to arrangements of hymns and compositions by famous Protestant composers of the day, on more than once occasion there were arrangements of selections from opera on the programme. For instance, the 1913 programme lists works by Giuseppe Verdi ("Ernani - Fantasie") and Richard Wagner ("Lohengrin - Fantasie"). In view of the fact that the Protestant world at that time viewed the phenomenon of opera with some suspicion, this is rather remarkable. Apparently it was acceptable when the Protestants themselves performed operatic music and did that in an emphatically Christian context, such as in the home or at mission festivals.[53]

In addition to brass bands, from their inception choral societies also regularly lent their assistance to the mission festivals.[54] From the notes of the Board of the *Vereeniging Christelijk Nationaal Zendingsfeest* from 1890, it appears that performances by choral societies during the mid-day intermission were a subject of discussion. For some of the board members, there was a question of whether such performances fit with the character and the objective of the mission festivals. Did performances by choral societies not encourage the impression that the

[50] FIDELIO: Uit de geschiedenis van het christelijk nationaal zendingsfeest, in *Stemmen voor waarheid en vrede* 40 (1903) 732.
[51] FIDELIO: Uit de geschiedenis 733-734. See also: BUYTENDIJK: *Bladen* 278.
[52] This musical society appeared for the first time during the 25th mission festival in 1888. In the programme brochure for the 40th mission festival (June 17, 1903), there is mention of "Mr. H. Snel, who for many years has accompanied our songs with the brass band of the Christian Youth Association 'Obadja,' of Rotterdam".
[53] SMELIK: *Eén in lied en leven* 65-66, 315.
[54] The Noordelijk Evangelische Zendingsfeesten also made use of bands and choral societies. See SEINEN: *Zendingsfeesten* 40, 63, 71, 79, 96, 97, 101, 103, 105.

emphasis in the festivals was coming to lie more on profane recreation than on the nurturing of faith? During the Board meeting of October 24, 1890, Buytendijk argued that the Christian character of the feast must be preserved. But, according to Buytendijk, appearances by choral societies[55] did not have to undermine this character, because these were, after all, Christian societies.[56] As a result of the discussion in the Board, after 1891 choral societies regularly performed during the mission festivals. For the rest, it is striking that the Christian character of the choral societies, and not the repertoire that they performed, was the argument advanced for accepting the assistance of these groups. Apparently some of the Board were of the opinion that the Christian repertoire sung by the societies – even at the mission festivals – did not or could not promote the 'nurturing of faith'. Singing in the context of a choral society was seen in itself as a form of recreation, which did not harmonise with the nature and objectives of the mission festival.

4. BACKGROUND

During the 19th century Protestantism was a river of many currents, with numerous denominations and groups, in all sorts of gradations varying from orthodox Calvinist to liberal. Therefore it is remarkable that the mission festivals were attended by people with varying church backgrounds (see section 3). The motivation for this cooperation was the identification of collective enemies, the struggle against which was taken up with complete dedication under the banner of 'foreign missions'.

Secularisation was seen as one collective enemy. One of the things to which one can point in connection with this is Heldring's 1863 statement about mission festivals: "Mission festivals are the Christian antithesis to the worldly pleasure trains, festivals conducted in a more glorious, more becoming, really Christian sphere."[57] The mission festivals were a Christian counterpart to 'worldly amusement'. They were at

---

[55] Specifically, the discussion at this meeting concerned cooperation with the Bond van Christelijke Zangvereenigingen.

[56] *Notulen Bestuursvergadering Christelijk Nationaal Zendingsfeest, 24 oktober 1890* (Zendingsarchief Hendrik Kraemer-instituut te Oegstgeest, dossier 22).

[57] *De Vereeniging: Christelijke Stemmen* (1863) 99-100.

the same time a Protestant alternative for the liberal festivals, against which Protestants had serious objections.[58]

This can be seen, for example, in the opening address by the Netherlands Reformed professor G.H. Lamers,[59] at the twelfth mission festival in 1875.[60] Lamers found that the people's love for the mission festivals had been gained:

> Do not ask with the malcontents, what do these thousands mean against such a mass of people as Leiden recently saw flow together through its gates [on the occasion of the festivities marking the 300th anniversary of the University of Leiden; J.S.] – but acknowledge rather with thankfulness – the courageous developers of the plan for the mission festivals in our midst shall not be the last to do so – that a splendid victory has been achieved in the in many respects so narrow-minded, and with regard to that which comes on this side, sometimes so suspicious Netherlands. In this respect too the nation has clearly made its feeling obvious.

And that feeling consisted of this: that people wished to demonstrate that in "our fatherland" *one* missionary community existed, that recruited its members from various denominations, and which also desired to see "the fruit of the Gospel displayed in this century of expositions."

In a time in which, according to Lamers, the Protestant character of The Netherlands was being undermined, it was of great importance that Dutch Christians "wished to preserve the fruit that had been cultivated with such difficulty, with so many tears, on the soil of the fatherland". In this sense the mission festivals were of great importance for the nation's development of religious and church life, and for the sorely needed elevation of national strength and national courage. Lamers therefore called upon Dutch Christians to hold their national virtues in esteem.[61]

Among the collective enemies were also all sorts of religious and ideological currents which were considered to be opponents of Christen-

---

[58] HELSLOOT: *Vermaak* 149-150.
[59] Gijsbert Hendrik Lamers (1834-1903) studied theology in Utrecht, where he received his doctorate in 1858. Lamers was assistant director of the Zendelinghuis in Rotterdam. In 1874 he became professor at Groningen. Nine years later he was named professor at Utrecht.
[60] G.H. LAMERS: Toespraak ter opening van het twaalfde Christelijk Nationaal Zendingsfeest, gehouden te Boekenrode, den 7den Juli 1875, in *Stemmen voor waarheid en vrede* 12 (1875) 757-775.
[61] LAMERS: Toespraak 766-769.

dom. H.V. Hogerzeil[62] observes that the mission festivals must be a protest against pernicious efforts to push aside the Gospel of Christ in all sorts of areas.[63] By this he, and others, would have had in mind particularly the modern theology of the second half of the 19th century, which opened to question such essential orthodox Christian truths as the divine inspiration of the Bible, the historicity of the life and work of Jesus, and belief in miracles. The success of the mission festivals was seen as a victory against modernism and as a proof that orthodoxy was still alive and vital. Buytendijk wrote of the mission festival of 1863 that orthodoxy celebrated "her triumph openly" in this first mission festival.[64] In 1873 Bronsveld stated:

> The mission festivals stand there, strong and thriving, like real Dutch linden trees. To a high degree, they have earned the love of our people. They bring to light the good elements of The Netherlands, and reinforce them. We are still a Christian nation! The modernists can organise all their popular amusements, but not festivals like these. Just let them try! It is said in truth: when it comes to strength, orthodoxy wins in this land.[65]

Thus the connection was made between the festivals, the promotion of the objectives of foreign mission work, and the place of Protestantism in Dutch society.

The struggle against common enemies and the militancy of Protestantism was also expressed in the repertoire of songs sung in the course of the mission festivals. One is struck by the frequent use of military terminology in the texts of the songs sung in the mission context, terms that are generally connected with notions such as spreading the kingdom of God[66] and God's almighty rule.[67] In these, the distinction

---

[62] Hendricus Vredenrijk Hogerzeil (1839-1907) studied theology at Utrecht and in 1866 became director of the Nederlandsche Zendingsvereeniging in Rotterdam, a function he filled for two years.

[63] H.V. HOGERZEIL: Onze zendingsfeesten. Openingsrede, den 1 Juli 1874 te Middachten gehouden, in *Stemmen voor waarheid en vrede* 11 (1874) 937.

[64] BUYTENDIJK: *Bladen* 275. See also F.W. GROSHEIDE, J.H. LANDWEHR (eds.): *Christelijke Encyclopaedie voor het Nederlandsche volk* 5 (Kampen 1925-1931) 789.

[65] A.W. BRONSVELD: Kroniek, in *Stemmen voor waarheid en vrede* 10 (1873) 892.

[66] The 'Kingdom of God' was understood to include the recognition of God as king by all men, who would then keep His commandments. The Kingdom of God is "the royal sovereignty of God over humanity, so that they enthrone Him in their hearts, and willingly serve Him with their whole heart, and subject themselves to Him out of love." F.W. GROSHEIDE (ed.): *Korte Christelijke Encyclopaedie* (Kampen [1934]) 611.

[67] For a more extensive treatment of this, see SMELIK: *Eén in lied en leven* 221-239.

between The Netherlands and 'heathen lands' falls away, for Protestants were convinced that God's rule must be established and confirmed in every corner of the world – and therefore in The Netherlands too.

A characteristic example is found in the mission hymn *Fahre fort, Fahre fort,* highly popular in that day. Although used in The Netherlands in Dutch translation, the first and last stanza of the original German reads:[68]

Fahre fort, fahre fort,	Halte aus, halte aus,
Zion, fahre fort im Licht;	Zion, halte deine Treu,
mache deinen Leuchter helle,	Laß doch ja nicht lau dich finden.
Laß die erste Liebe nicht,	Auf, das Kleinod rückt herbei;
Suche stets die Lebensquelle;	auf, verlasse, was dahinten;
Zion, dringe durch die enge Pfort,	Zion, in dem letzten Kampf und Strauß
Fahre fort, fahre fort!	halte aus, halte aus!

A further motivation for organising the mission festivals was that they were a form of 'recreation' which was acceptable to Protestants, even as the "hours of prayer for mission" in the first half of the 19th century were commended as a means of "providing the people with nobler diversion".[69] This aspect is already mentioned in sources in connection with the Moravian mission festivals in Zeist. On various occasions Buytendijk remarks that these festivals were attended for reasons in addition to purely religious motives. People also came to enjoy the inspirational music and the surroundings of the park and woods.[70] The national mission festivals similarly had a recreational aspect. At the mission festivals, one could enjoy nature in abundance, although for someone like J.P. Hasebroek[71] that could not be separated from the ultimate purpose of the festival: promoting mission.

---

[68] The hymn "Fahre fort, Fahre fort" by J.E. Schmidt (1669-1745) comes from the *Geistreichem Gesangbuch* (1704/14) of J.A. Freylinghausen, and was translated into Dutch by C.F. Gronemeijer. See for the German text: *Evangelisches Kirchengesangbuch* (Gütersloh) hymn 213.

[69] "Over eenige volks-uitspanningen en vermakelijkheden, die voor eene christelijke natie betamelijk en, met name ook op het platte land, uitvoerlijk zijn", in *Waarheid in liefde* (1845) 209-211.

[70] BUYTENDIJK: *Het veertigjarig bestaan*; BUYTENDIJK: *Bladen* 270.

[71] Johannes Petrus Hasebroek (1812-1896) studied theology at Leiden. In addition to prose, he wrote various songs. Through Nicolaas Beets and Willen de Clerq Hasebroek came into contact with the Réveil.

The mission festivals enabled Protestants to escape from the daily routine. One could get out for a day and enjoy oneself in a responsible Christian manner. The festivals also afforded the chance for Christians to be active culturally. As was described in section 3, vocal and instrumental music (mass singing, choral societies and brass bands) were an important component of the festivals. Except for reading books, journals and the like,[72] making music – and especially singing religious songs – was the primary form of cultural participation among Protestants. Singing was a natural, daily activity, both at home and in gatherings. The creation and flourishing of choral societies is also typical of a blooming culture of singing.[73] In addition to its pedagogic aspects and providing religious training, such music-making in all sorts of contexts also had definite recreative purposes.

From the background as it has been described here it will appear that the mission festivals had goals beyond quickening enthusiasm for foreign missions. There were also goals related to domestic mission. In 1864 M. Cohen Stuart wrote that the actual dispatch of missionaries was not the central purpose of the mission festivals. He suggested that the festivals were a contribution to a new reveille, an awakening to conversion.[74]

Other authors, such as Doedes[75] and Hogerzeil[76] also brought to the fore that the mission festivals first and foremost had the purpose of advancing domestic mission objectives. Looking back over a decade of mission festivals, the programme brochure for the 1873 festival stated:

> missionary spirit has been quickened and promoted; many there became convinced of their eternal calling, and began to seek those things which are heavenly; they were always pleasant gatherings contributing to the refreshment of the spiritual life; the communion of the saints was practised and many enjoyed a foretaste of the joy that awaits the children of God above.[77]

---

[72] For a more extensive treatment of this, see R.G.K. KRAAN (ed.): *Omzien met een glimlach. Aspecten van een eeuw protestantse leescultuur* (Den Haag 1991); J. DANE: *De vrucht van bijbelsche opvoeding. Populaire leescultuur en opvoeding in protestants-christelijke gezinnen circa 1880-1940* (Hilversum 1996).

[73] SMELIK: *Eén in lied en leven* 66-72.

[74] COHEN STUART: Wolfhezen 724, 728.

[75] DOEDES: Een zendingsfeest 790.

[76] HOGERZEIL: Onze zendingsfeesten 935.

[77] Programma *Christelijk Nationaal Zendingsfeest* 1873 te Boekenrode (near Haarlem) 4.

5. CONCLUSION

From this contribution it becomes clear that the mission festivals were a mixture of cultus and culture – one might even say leisure culture. In their organisation, the festivals were strongly modeled on church services. All the more because the mission festivals were held in the open air and seemed to be organised like church services, they can be seen as a 19th century variant of the field preaching of the 16th century.

The most essential elements of the festivals were the addresses and the songs. Both were intended to be positive influences on the religious life of those in attendance. There was of course considerable attention for the work of foreign missions, but, as we saw in section 4, the theme of "converting the heathen in distant lands" was deeply linked with the conversion and instruction of "baptised heathen" in The Netherlands itself.

The mobilisation of the Protestant portion of the Dutch population, and providing a demonstration of its strength, was also among the motives for organising mission festivals on a mass scale. In a time in which Protestants felt threatened from all sides – rising secularism, liberal thought and non-Protestant ideologies – they found such events that contributed to the reinforcement of their mutual bonds no unnecessary luxury.

In addition to all kinds of exalted religious motives for organising and attending the festivals, more 'worldly,' cultural motives also played a role. These festivals fulfilled the purpose of providing recreational activity, and for the lay membership of the Protestant churches were a responsible form of relaxation in the open air. One of the cultural aspects of the festivals was the involvement of brass bands and choral societies. Although the repertoire performed, particularly by the choral groups, was overwhelmingly religious, their performances were still regarded as a recreational element.

In short, the national mission festival as a new celebration in Protestant feast culture in the 19th century chiefly arose as a reaction to, and indeed counter to, developments of all sorts that were taking place in The Netherlands in both the social and ecclesiastical spheres.

Jozef Lamberts

THE REFORM OF THE ROMAN CALENDAR

In May 1969, there was some commotion in the normally peaceful town of Londerzeel, situated about twenty kilometres from Brussels. The centuries old little statue of St. Christopher, the parish patron saint, had disappeared from its place in the parish church. After a few days it became obvious that the 'robbery' was a stunt of the local students' club to express their displeasure about the fact that Christopher had been 'eliminated' from the revised Roman calendar. When Christopher is no longer recognised as a saint, what then is the sense of the yearly blessing of cars and bicycles? Drivers and cyclists were considered to be under the special protection of Christopher by this blessing. This celebration had been experienced as one of the summits of the festivities in the little town. Does it no longer make sense to have a medal of Christopher in your car? Was this the end of a particular devotion? Would it be better for parents to stop giving the name of Christopher at baptism? Should the organisers look for another name for their yearly cycle race, which until then had been called 'Great St. Christopher's Prize'?

Indeed, on May 9, 1969, at a press conference in Rome, Pierre Jounel, one of the authors, had presented the new calendar and the General norms.[1] During the following days journalists had given more attention to the saints who had been 'eliminated' or 'reduced to second rank' than to the principles governing the revised calendar.

In this contribution we would like to discuss the principles of the revised calendar. First we need to put the revision in a broader historical context and in line with the decisions of the Second Vatican Council. Herein we only deal with the liturgical calendar, and speak neither about a possible reorganisation of the weeks and months during the year nor about a revision of the date of Easter, which is the centre of the liturgical year.

---

[1] Conferentia Rev. Prof. Jounel ad Scriptores diariorum et periodicorum, in *Notitiae* 5 (1969) 295-298.

1. Historical background

In our historical overview we seek to focus on the relation between the sanctoral cycle and the seasonal cycle. From the very beginning, the reason for the gathering together of Christians was to celebrate the Paschal mystery of the Lord, and this especially on the Lord's Day. An annual Passover soon followed and gradually developed into the Easter cycle with its period of preparation and festive continuation. The annual commemoration of the birth of Jesus likewise developed. These two cycles are still the supporting pillars of the liturgical year. The intervening weeks, which are called 'ordinary time', are devoted to the mystery of Christ in all its aspects. All together they are known as the temporal or 'proper of seasons'. As such, the emphasis during the entire year is on the Paschal mystery in a broad sense. But in addition to the seasonal cycle, the sanctoral cycle, i.e. the celebration of the feasts of the saints, gradually developed and sometimes even overshadowed it in people's experience. That is why the Church has needed to intervene several times through history in order to safeguard the pre-eminence of the Paschal mystery. The last time that the Church reorganised the liturgical year in this context was at the occasion of Vatican II.

1.1. The beginning of the veneration of the saints

Christians started to venerate the saints about the middle of the second century.[2] The first to be venerated were those Christians who gave their lives and thus became witnesses to Christ in a unique way. They were called martyrs, derived from the Greek μάρτυς = witness. Bishop *Polycarp*

---

[2] Peter Brown: *The cult of the saints. Its rise and function in Latin Christianity* (Chicago 1981); Pierre Jounel: The veneration of the saints, in Aimé-Georges Martimort: *The Church at prayer. Volume IV: The liturgy and time*, trans. Matthew J. O'Connell (Collegeville 1986) 108-129; Hansjörg Auf der Maur: Feste und Gedenktage der Heiligen, in Philipp Harnoncourt & Hansjörg Auf der Maur: *Feiern im Rhythmus der Zeit II/1* (= Gottesdienst der Kirche. Handbuch der Liturgiewissenschaft 6,1) (Regensburg 1994) 65-357; Philipp Harnoncourt: *Gesamtkirchliche und teilkirchliche Liturgie. Studien zum liturgischen Heiligenkalender und zum Gesang im Gottesdienst unter besonderer Berücksichtigung des deutschen Sprachgebiets* (Freiburg im Breisgau 1974); Jacques Dubois: Les saints du nouveau calendrier. Tradition et critique historique, in *La Maison-Dieu* 100 (1969) 157-178; Henri Delehaye: *Les origines du culte des martyrs* (= Subsidia hagiographica 20) (Brussels 1912, 1933²); Jozef Lamberts: *Op weg naar heelheid. Over bedevaart en liturgie* (Leuven-Amersfoort 1997).

of Smyrna (d. 155) was probably the first martyr to be given such veneration by his community, since the faithful of Smyrna decided to gather each year and remember him "in joy and gladness".[3] This veneration was mainly the same as the cult paid to the dead in general. It also took place at the tomb. One great difference, however, was that this veneration was paid not only by the family, but by a communion of believers, who became one family of brothers and sisters of the martyr in faith. Secondly, the Christians did not celebrate the martyr's earthly birthday but the day of his/her death, which was seen as the day of rebirth, the day of entry in the Kingdom of Heaven. Further, the martyrs were quickly experienced as intercessors with God. Eventually, the Eucharist was celebrated at the tomb. In this way, a link was established between the Eucharist and martyrdom. The celebration of the Paschal mystery gave meaning to the self-sacrifice of the martyr. His/her entrance in the Paschal mystery of Christ through baptism was now fulfilled and completed in his/her martyrdom.

Still during the age of persecutions, this veneration was extended to the 'confessors': those who had not been put to death for their faith but suffered torture, imprisonment, forced labour, or exile. Once the persecutions came to an end, ascetics and virgins came to be honoured as 'confessors', since ascetic life was seen as a substitute for martyrdom, as *John Chrysostom* (d. 407) explained: "Mortify and crucify your body and you too will receive the crown of the martyrs."[4] Virginity consecrated to the Lord was then esteemed as a high form of asceticism.[5] Gradually also the apostles came to be venerated as the official witnesses who had been appointed by the Lord himself.

1.2. The composition of lists with the names of the martyrs

As early as the third century, each local community of Christians started keeping a list containing the names of their confessors of the faith, as

---

[3] *Martyrium Polycarpi*, 18; Herbert MUSURILLO (ed.): *The acts of the Christian martyrs* (Oxford 1972) 2-21; Boudewijn DEHANDSCHUTTER: *Martyrium Polycarpi. Een literair-kritische studie* (= Bibliotheca Ephemeridum theologicarum Lovaniensum 52) (Leuven 1979).

[4] John CHRYSOSTOM: In Epist. ad Hebraeos homiliae II, 3, in J.P. MIGNE: *Patrologia Graeca* 63, 93.

[5] The concentration on the martyrs may be the reason why there is no clear evidence of Marian feasts during the first three centuries. Many of these feasts from the fourth century on arose in the East and were soon adopted in the West.

well as the date of their *dies natalis* and the place of their tomb. The oldest extant list is to be found in the *Chronograph* of 354, compiled by
Furius Dionysius Filocalus for the use of a rich Christian named *Valentinus*.[6] The document contains two lists of anniversaries: one of the burials of bishops (*Depositiones episcoporum*) and the other of the burials of
martyrs (*Depositiones martyrum*). The former gives, in calendar
sequence, the names of the bishops of Rome who were not martyrs,
from Lucius (d. 254) to Sylvester (d. 335). The latter first gives the
natale of Christ and then a list of the martyrs celebrated in Rome.
Although the terminology includes two different meanings (*dies natalis*
as the birthday of Christ and *dies natalis* as the death-day of the martyrs) the play upon words points to the christocentric interpretation of
the veneration of the martyrs. Christ is seen here as the source of all life
and holiness.

The fact that the difference between the two types of anniversaries as
given in the *Chronograph* must have been rather vague in liturgical practice may partially explain the veneration of bishops as saints. In any
case, we may see in this list a draft of the first Christian calendars. Even
when some local communities had several martyrs to celebrate, their
feast days were experienced as real 'feasts', this means as special or exceptional days in the course of the year, during which they celebrated what
we now call the temporal cycle. Next to the 'calendars' for the local
Churches, 'martyrologies' were composed for a larger spread of the
memories of the increasing number of saints without providing a liturgical celebration for them. In this way, an exchange of the memories of
the saints between the local Churches took place.

While originally the cult of the saints was paid at their tombs, we see
in the *Chronograph* Rome celebrating the *natale* of the African martyrs
Cyprian, Perpetua, and Felicity. The *Calendar of Nicomedia*, composed
in Greek ca. 363, preserved today in a Syriac version dated 411, reports
martyrs' commemorations for the entire Church.[7]

Around the beginning of the sixth century the main liturgical celebration took place at the basilica, which was built over or in the neighbourhood of the tomb. But at the same time, other city churches also

[6] Noële Maurice DENIS-BOULET: *The Christian calendar*, trans. P. Hephurne-Scott
(= Twentieth-century encyclopaedia of Catholicism 113) (New York 1960) 51-55.

[7] Bonaventura MARIANI (ed.): *Breviarum Syriacum seu martyrologium saec. IV iuxta
cod. Sm. Musaei Britanici add. 12150* (= Rerum ecclesiasticarum documenta, Series
minor, Subsidia studiorum 3) (Rome 1956).

celebrated the feast. In the Roman sacramentaries of the seventh century we find how the celebration of the saints was organised in the apostolic city. When these sacramentaries were spread over Europe in the Carolingian epoch and supplanted the local liturgies, the names and the cult of the Roman martyrs were spread at the same time.

1.3. The translation of the relics

The renown of some saints, for instance the Apostles Peter and Paul, is undoubtedly an important reason for the extension of their cult. Other saints, however, began to be celebrated because of the spread of their relics.[8] People believed that the place of a saint's relics was also his/her 'home', and he/she could be venerated there. Since Constantinople did not possess tombs or remains of the martyrs, the eastern emperors did not raise objections against the digging up (*elevatio*), the transfer (*translatio*), and even the dismembering (*dismembratio*) and sharing of relics. Constantius, for instance, let the relics of Timothy and the apostle Andrew be transferred to the *Hagia Sophia* in 358-359. When the remains of Stephen were discovered in 415, a parcel of them reached Hippo.[9] Since such translation, however, was against the Roman law, Rome only tolerated to use objects that had been in physical contact with a martyr's tomb (*brandea*).[10] In the eighth century, however, due to the Lombard invasions, Pope Paul I (d. 767) decided to transfer the remains of the martyrs and other saints from the extra-urban cemeteries into the city of Rome in order to defend them from the invaders. New churches were built to house the relics or they were shared among the extant churches. In this way, the veneration of the saints took another turn. Any church that had the smallest relic of a saint felt obliged to celebrate that saint's *dies natalis*. Churches that possessed several relics attracted many faithful and became places of pilgrimage. Where before

---

[8] Arnold ANGENENDT: *Heiligen und Reliquien. Die Geschichte ihres Kultes vom frühen Christentum bis zum Gegenwart* (München 1994); Paolo MOLINARI *et al.*: *I santi e il loro culto* (= Collectanea spirituali 9) (Rome 1962).

[9] This relic worked miracles in Hippo as is testified by AUGUSTINE: De civitate Dei XXII, 8, in *Corpus Christianorum, Series Latina* 48, 825-827.

[10] See, for instance, the reaction of Pope Gregory I (d. 604) on a request of the Byzantine empress to send the head of the apostle Paul for a new church consecrated to Paul. GREGORIUS I: Registrum epistolarum, Liber IV, 30, in *Corpus Christianorum, Series Latina* 140, 249.

an altar was placed over a martyr's tomb to celebrate the Eucharist on the *dies natalis*, now the relics were placed beneath the permanent altar in churches. Soon it became impossible to dedicate a church without placing relics beneath the altar, and thus the search for relics increased. This gave rise to the theft of relics, commerce in pseudo-relics, and eventually even the 'invention' of pseudo-saints.

1.4. Hagiographic literature

To be sure of having an 'authentic' relic, one needed a *vita*, a description of a saint's life, demonstrating that he or she really lived as a saint. This is to be connected with a tradition by which the hagiographic literature also contributed to the spread of a saint's cult.[11] The Acts of the martyrs are the most valuable documents in this context. More difficult to appraise are the passion stories. The first *vitae* or lives of the saints are from an early date: the oldest is that of Saint Cyprian. Important in this regard are the lives of the Dessert Fathers and the monastic founders.

1.5. The canonisation of the saints

The conviction that the saint is present in his/her relics incited the faithful not only to veneration, but also to asking the saint for help and favours. The most important favour they were asked for was health. Some saints were experienced as specialised in the cure of distinct diseases. While during the preceding centuries, indeed, the saints were not only venerated as examples for Christian life to be imitated, but also as intercessors, during the Middle Ages they were seen as almost autocratic miracle-workers. There was a real danger that the saints no longer brought people to Christ, but that they were sought for themselves and for their favours. Moreover, some needs could even 'create' new saints. In order to counteract such an evolution, the Church developed a process of canonisation. Although such canonisation originally belonged to a bishop's authority, it gradually became a papal prerogative.[12]

---

[11] We may say: happy are those who had a biographer. So for instance, it is mainly due to Pope Gregory the Great that Saint Benedict became so important. DUBOIS: Les saints du nouveau calendrier 176.

[12] The canonisation of bishop Ulric of Augsburg by Pope John XV in 993 was the first one. It is only from the twelfth century that it became a papal prerogative.

1.6. The further development of the Roman calendar

The second part of the twelfth century was an important step in the development of the Roman calendar insofar a process that started in the ninth century came to its completion and determined the sanctoral until Vatican II.[13] Indeed, the Roman-Frankish sacramentaries had brought together the various local traditions of Rome. Their calendar contained, along with those saints included in the Gelasian and Gregorian sacramentaries, the feasts of all the apostles, Popes Leo the Great and Gregory the Great, Augustine and Benedict, as well as the feast of All Saints. It was the Ottonians who brought the Roman-Frankish-Germanic liturgy to Rome, where under Pope Gregory VII (d. 1085) it was adopted and then gradually prescribed for the Western Church.

When we compare the *Lateran calendar* of the twelfth century with for instance the sanctoral of the *Sacramentarium Gregorianum Hadrianum* of the eighth century, we first notice a strong increase of the feasts of the saints: from 95 names to 254. While in the latter almost all martyrs mentioned belong to the local church, in the former 23 are from Rome, 29 from other parts of the West, and 18 from the East. In other words, the Lateran calendar had already become a 'universal' calendar. The number of doctors of the Church and of the great models of monastic life increased. Characteristic for the Lateran calendar is the emphasis on papal feasts: from 12 popes in the *Hadrianum* (8 martyrs and 4 confessors) to 40 in the calendar.[14] The increase of the number of other saints is less important (most of them being bishops). Another characteristic of the calendar is the common celebration of apostles and evangelists. A very remarkable aspect is the adoption of Thomas Becket, who had been murdered in 1170: the calendar seemed to be open to contemporary saints!

In the period before the Council of Trent the calendars continued to be basically particular calendars, for which the bishops were responsible. Nevertheless, they were no longer local calendars in the original sense of the word. The number of saints continued to increase, and insofar as all

---

[13] Pierre JOUNEL: *Le culte des saints dans les basiliques du Latran et du Vatican au douzième siècle* (= Collection de l'école française de Rome 26) (Rome 1977).

[14] The religious reform movement of the late 10th and early 11th centuries probably wanted to hold up to the morally and religiously desolate papacy the examples of the ancient Roman martyr-bishops, see JOUNEL: *Le culte* 169-181. Later it became an instrument to propagate esteem for the Roman papacy.

the free days became feasts of the saints, the temporal cycle was largely obscured by their veneration. People no longer experienced the central place of Christ in salvation history. Not only were the ferial days of Lent and Advent oppressed, but even the Lord's Day. Popular practices surrounding the cult of the saints went their own way. Already since the end of the 14th century some theologians, bishops and synods reacted against this situation, but with no lasting success.[15] In the 16th century, the Reformers questioned the practice of the veneration of saints. They acknowledged the example of the saints for a good Christian life, but denied their intercession.

1.7. The Tridentine calendar

The Council of Trent (1545-1563) approved of the invocation of the saints with the clarification "in order to obtain favours from God through his Son, Jesus Christ our Lord, who alone is our redeemer and saviour".[16] Because there were divergent views on the subject, no reform of the calendar could be effected and the decision was made to entrust the reform to the Pope. In 1564 Pope Pius IV (d. 1572) appointed a reform commission for both the breviary and the missal, which he promulgated in 1568 and 1570 respectively. With both books a new *Calendarium Romanum* was published. For the first time in history this calendar was seen as universal, at least for the Latin Church. The bull that accompanied the promulgation of the Roman missal stipulated that all local churches had to adopt the revised liturgy, except those that could prove that their own rites had been in use for over two hundred years.[17] Most of the dioceses and orders adopted the revised liturgical books, but combined the Roman calendar with their own calendar. In this way, the aim of the reform was not obtained. Moreover, the general rubrics of the new breviary and missal allowed some feasts, which are not in the Roman calendar: the commemora-

---

[15] So e.g. Radulph of Rivo (d. 1403), John Gerson (d. 1429), Nicholas of Cusa (d. 1464). In the 13th century the Cathari and Waldenses already reacted strongly to the notion of intercession by the saints.

[16] H. DENZINGER & P. HÜNERMANN: *Enchiridion symbolorum definitionum et declarationum de rebus fidei et morum = Kompendium der Glaubensbekenntnisse und kirchlichen Lehrentscheidungen* (Freiburg im Breisgau etc. 1991[37]) 578-573 (No. 1821).

[17] The bull *Quo primum tempore* of September 15, 1570 is to be found in all the editions of the missal until Vatican II.

tion of the dedication of a church, the feast of the local patron, feasts of the saints whose relics are conserved in a church,[18] and feasts of saints that have a local tradition.[19]

The aim of the reform commission was clearly to safeguard the precedence of the celebration of the Christ-mystery in the temporal cycle. Since some saints had to be celebrated on the same day, there remained 164 ferias or days without a feast, vigil or octave of a saint. February, March, April and December had particularly few feasts of the saints because of the need to emphasise Lent and Advent.[20] The Lord's feasts were also safeguarded by a new rubrical classification of the liturgical days (duplex, semi-duplex, simplex, commemoratio).

When compared with the *Lateran calendar*, 38 names were removed and 43 were introduced. We now find the great saints of the thirteenth century, including theologians like Thomas Aquinas and Bonaventure, as well as Francis and Dominic or even King Louis IX. The list also includes saints whose legends had made them popular, as for example Christopher.[21]

1.8. The evolution until the beginning of the 20th century

During the following period, notwithstanding the initial aim, the calendar experienced excessive growth. About 120 feasts were added to the Roman calendar, while several diocesan calendars added over 100 feasts of their own.[22] A close reading demonstrates the influence of the different devotions throughout that period, but also of the endeavour of the different orders to have their own saints on the universal calendar – this

---

[18] "Festa sanctorum... ubi habetur corpus vel insignis reliquia sancti de quo agitur".

[19] "Festa sanctorum, qui apud quasdam ecclesias, religiones, vel congregationes consueverunt solemniter celebrari, etiamsi praedicta festa in Kalendario non sunt descripta". These feasts, however, are only mentioned in the rubrics of the breviary and not in those of the missal.

[20] Carolus Borromeus (d. 1584) for instance made Lent and Sundays free from whatever feast of a saint for the Church of Milan.

[21] A. VAUCHEZ: *La sainteté en Occident aux derniers siècles du Moyen Age d'après les procès de canonisation et les documents hagiographiques* (= Bibliothèque des Écoles Françaises d'Athène et de Rome 241) (Rome 1981).

[22] A list with the number of new saints added by the different Popes is given in Pierre JOUNEL: Les développements du sanctoral romain, de Grégoire XIII à Jean XXIII, in *La Maison-Dieu* 63bis (1960) 74-81.

could be interpreted as having a higher rank among the saints –, as well as of the personal preferences of the Popes.[23] It is quite striking that only during the papacy of Benedict XIV (1740-1758) no saint was added to the universal calendar.

This points to the fact that there was also some reaction during the period between Trent and the beginning of the 20th century. Prosper Lambertini (*1675), before becoming Pope Benedict XIV, was a liturgical scholar.[24] In line with his scientific work he wanted to stress the priority of the Sunday celebration over the veneration of the saints.[25] But, since he was not a fighter, he could not completely realise his important visions. In any case, he further reduced the number of the feasts *de praecepto*: before Pope Urban VIII in 1642 had reduced their number to 37, the faithful had to attend Mass and to abstain from work on fifty feast-days in addition to the 52 (53) Sundays.[26] Although there was strong opposition, Pope Benedict XIV allowed several dioceses to reduce the number of the feasts *de praecepto* to seventeen or fifteen. On the other feast-days, however, the faithful still had to attend Mass. Pope Clement XIV abolished these 'half-feast-days' in 1772. Accordingly, the idea of a 'feast' devalued: now there existed *festa fori*, namely the real feasts that were liturgically and publicly ('on the market-place') celebrated, and *festa chori* that were only celebrated in the choir, within the walls of the church. In this way, a 'wall' was erected between liturgy and life.[27]

Pope Benedict XIV is not only to be situated in the line of the liturgical scholars of the late 17th and 18th centuries who began to discover the ancient liturgy, but also in the context of the Enlightenment. In the same line we meet some of his ideas in the work of Ludovico Muratori: *Della regolata devozione dei cristiani* (1747).[28] The Synod of Pistoia (1786) not only opposed abuses and exaggerations in the veneration of the saints but also stipulated that no feasts of the saints may be cele-

---

[23] Even as late as 1960, Pope John XXIII introduced saint Gregory Barbarigo, a bishop of his own diocese Bergamo, into the Roman calendar.

[24] Jo HERMANS: *Benedictus XIV en de liturgie. Een bijdrage tot de liturgiegeschiedenis van de Moderne Tijd* (Brugge-Boxtel 1979) [with a summary in English].

[25] See his *De servorum Dei beatificatione et beatorum canonizatione* 1-4 (Bologna 1734-1738).

[26] Pope Urban VIII's bull *Universa per orbem* dated September 13, 1642.

[27] HARNONCOURT: *Gesamtkirchliche und teilkirchliche Liturgie* 86-87.

[28] This work was first edited under the pseudonym Lamido PRITANIO.

brated on the Lord's Day.[29] Likewise, the so-called Neo-Gallican liturgies wanted to safeguard the Lord's Day by avoiding celebrating the feasts of saints on Sunday.[30] The consequences of the French Revolution (1789) and the Restoration movement of the 19th century brought an end to these initiatives. Pilgrimages to the Holy Land and to the shrines of saints regained their attraction. Together with an abolition of the Neo-Gallican liturgy and the restoration of the uniform Roman liturgy in France, Dom Prosper Guéranger (d. 1875) also promoted the veneration of the saints.[31] Twenty-three canonisations date from the 19th century, twelve of them were promulgated by Pope Leo XIII (d. 1903). At the end of the 19th century, an emerging generation of liturgical scholars paved the way for the rediscovery of the central place of the Paschal mystery in liturgy. They, however, were sometimes blamed as *les dénicheurs de saints*.[32]

1.9. The calendar reform by Pope Pius X

Pope Pius X (d. 1914) aimed to free the temporal cycle, especially the Lord's Day and the divine office on the ferial days, in order to emphasise the Christ-mystery in the liturgy. He expressed his plan for an overall reform of the liturgy of the divine office and of the Mass in his Apostolic constitution *Divino afflatu*, dated November 1, 1911.[33] For example, a

---

[29] Jozef LAMBERTS: The Synod of Pistoia (1786) and popular religion, in *Questions liturgiques – Studies in liturgy* 76 (1995) 86-105. Charles A. BOLTON: *Church reform in 18th-century Italy (The Synod of Pistoia, 1786)* (= International archives of the history of ideas 29) (The Hague 1969).

[30] Jozef LAMBERTS: Een interessante bladzijde uit de liturgiegeschiedenis: de Neo-Gallicaanse liturgieën, in *Tijdschrift voor liturgie* 79 (1995) 197-209.

[31] He had no problems to identify Saint Denis with Dionysius the Areopagyt, who should have taken his head into his hands after his decapitation, see Prosper GUÉRANGER: *Institutions liturgiques II* (Paris 1841) 42.

[32] Pierre JOUNEL: Le culte des reliques et son influence sur l'art chrétien, in *La Maison-Dieu* 170 (1987) 29-57, p. 42.

[33] *Acta Apostolicae Sedis* (= *AAS*) 3 (1911) 633-638. Some concrete decisions by the Congregation of the Rites followed, such as: Rubricae servandae ad normam constitutionis apostolicae 'Divino afflatu', in *AAS* 3 (1911) 639-650; Litterae Circulares quoad propria officiorum dioecesana, in *AAS* 4 (1912) 376; Instructio seu responsium ordinariis postulantibus kalendarii proprii reformationem, in *AAS* 4 (1912) 538; Instructio super kalendariis propriis reformandis, in *AAS* 5 (1913) 67-70; Decretum generale SCR, in *AAS* 5 (1913) 457-464; Decretum generale circa propria officiorum et Missarum, in *AAS* 6 (1914) 316.

distinction was made in the local calendars between *festa propria sensu stricto* and *festa aliquibus locis ex mero indulto S. Sedis concessa*. Only feasts of the first category should take precedence over the feasts of the universal calendar having the same rank, except privileged Sundays, ferial days, octave days, and vigil days, as well as feasts with the rank of double of the first class of the universal calendar. Another example is that the feast of the dedication of the cathedral is to be celebrated in all the churches of a diocese. In other words, the 1911 document may be seen as the first step towards organised local calendars. The following year, however, Pope Pius X had to recognise that his dream about an overall reform of the liturgy was unrealistic and that it would take at least thirty years to realise his plan.[34] In 1913, in his motu proprio *Abhinc duos annos*, he pointed to the necessity of long and sustained scientific research.[35] Accordingly, he began a gradual reform, which was hindered by his sudden death and by World War I.[36] The concrete results are to be found in the calendar of the *editio typica* of the *Breviarum Romanum* (1914) and of the *Missale Romanum* (1920). By suppressing supplementary offices as daily obligations not only the weekly recitation of the psalter was restored, but also the priority of the temporal cycle over the sanctoral. The number of feasts *de praecepto* was reduced to ten.[37] A reduction in the number of the feasts of the saints in the calendars of dioceses and religious orders was sought for, but not in the general calendar. Pius X himself, however, introduced two new feasts in the general calendar and despite his measures the next decades saw the introduction of new feasts into the general calendar as well as into the particular calendars.

1.10. The endeavour of the Liturgical Movement

From an early stage the Liturgical Movement of the twentieth century sought the precedence of the Lord's Day and the Lord's feasts, the centrality of the Paschal mystery in liturgy. Dom Odo Casel (1886-1948) may be seen as the most important and influential protagonist of the discovery and the experience of the liturgical year as the celebration of

---

[34] Litterae circulares 376.

[35] *AAS* 5 (1913) 449-451.

[36] Jozef LAMBERTS: Paus Pius X en de actieve deelneming, in *Tijdschrift voor liturgie* 71 (1987) 293-306.

[37] *Codex Iuris Canonici 1917*, c. 1247 §1.

the Christ-mystery.[38] Aemiliana Löhr pointed to the celebration of the Christ-mystery as the very centre in the liturgical year, which she called "the Lord's Year".[39] Thus also did Pius Parsch (1884-1954) when he spoke about the "the Year of Salvation".[40] Several articles were written about Sunday as the Lord's Day. To give only one example, Dom Albertus Van Roy, from 1924 until 1946 chief-editor of the Belgian liturgical review co-founded by Dom Lambert Beauduin in 1910, *Tijdschrift voor liturgie*, in 1944 wrote an article 'Each Sunday is a Christ-Day'.[41] The topic of the second national liturgical congress of the French *Centre de Pastorale Liturgique*, which was held in Lyons in 1947, dealt with the Lord's Day and demanded to focus on Sunday as the weekly celebration of the Paschal mystery.[42] Dom Odilo Heiming, at the occasion of the First International Liturgical Conference in the abbey of Maria Laach (Germany) on July 12-15, 1951, argued for a fundamental revision of the calendar in order to secure the predominance of the Lord's feasts over the feasts of the saints.[43] These endeavours, already before the beginning of the Second Vatican Council resulted into two documents of the Congregation of the Sacred Rites, which intended to give priority to the temporal cycle over the sanctoral.[44] As a result, a great number of the feasts of the saints lost their octave: in this way Sundays and several days of Lent and Advent were safeguarded. In any case, the necessity of a thorough reform became obvious. It is important to note that the idea of a (gradual) reform acquired definite shape when the historical section

[38] Among his numerous books and articles, see Odo CASEL: *Das Gedächtnis des Herrn* (Freiburg 1918); IDEM: Das Mysteriengedächtnis der Messliturgie, in *Jahrbuch für Liturgiewissenschaft* 6 (1926) 113-204; IDEM: Mysteriengegenwart, in *Jahrbuch für Liturgiewissenschaft* 8 (1928) 145-224; IDEM: *Das christliche Kultmysterium* (Regensburg 1932).

[39] Aemiliana LÖHR: *Das Herrenjahr. Das Mysterium Christi in Jahreskreis der Kirche* (Regensburg 1934).

[40] Pius PARSCH: *Das Jahr des Heiles* (Klosterneuburg 1923). This work started as a small liturgical directory, but very soon it became a book in three volumes; it had 14 editions and has been translated into nine languages.

[41] Albertus VAN ROY: Iedere zondag een Christus-dag, in *Tijdschrift voor liturgie* 29 (1944-45) 1-8.

[42] The proceedings are to be found in *La Maison-Dieu* 13 (1948).

[43] Odilo HEIMING: Gedanken zur Kalenderreform, in *Liturgie und Mönchtum* 9 (1951) 34-51.

[44] Decretum generale de rubricis ad simpliciorem formam redigendis, in *AAS* 47 (1955) 218-224; Codex rubricarum breviarii ac missalis Romani, in *AAS* 52 (1960) 597-685.

of the Sacred Congregation of Rites met the wishes of Pope Pius XII, uttered in 1946.[45] A plan for such renewal was proposed as *Memoria sulla riforma liturgica* in 1948. Two aspects were somewhat developed in this document: the liturgical year and the divine office. On May 28, 1948, a commission for liturgical reform was appointed, better known as the 'Pian' Commission. This commission, which prepared some of the liturgical renewals under Pope Pius XII, as for example the restoration of the Paschal Vigil in 1951, also paved the way for the renewal that was demanded for by the Second Vatican Council.[46] Also the questionnaire on reform of the missal, breviary, calendar, martyrology, and other liturgical books sent by the editors of the review *Ephemerides liturgicae* on January 28, 1948, to some liturgical scholars supported further research in prospect of a possible reform.

2. THE DECISIONS OF THE SECOND VATICAN COUNCIL

Whereas the Council of Trent entrusted the revision of the Roman calendar to the Pope, the Second Vatican Council itself formulated some clear theological principles and practical guidelines. The constitution on the sacred liturgy, *Sacrosanctum Concilium,* not only has a complete chapter on the liturgical year (chapter 5 = art. 102-111), but also has other articles that formulated important elements for the revision of the calendar.

2.1. Some general elements

To start with the latter, art. 5-8 interpret the entire liturgy as the celebration of the memorial of the Paschal mystery. Art. 23 states that theological, historical, and pastoral investigations are necessary into each part of the liturgy to be revised, while the experience derived from recent (i.e. just before the Council) liturgical reforms and from the indults conceded must be taken into account. Art. 34 states that "the rites should be marked by a noble simplicity; they should be short, clear,

---

[45] The complete name of this section, which Pope Pius XI installed by his *motu proprio Già da qualche tempo* of February 6, 1930, is *Per le cause storiche dei servi di Dio e l'emendazione dei libri liturgici,* see *AAS* 22 (1930) 87-88.

[46] Annibale BUGNINI: *The reform of the liturgy. 1948-1975* (Collegeville 1990) 7-10.

and unencumbered by useless repetitions; they should be within the people's powers of comprehension and as a rule not require much explanation". Art. 37-40 recognise that "the Church has no wish to impose a rigid uniformity", that "provided the substantial unity of the Roman rite is preserved, provisions shall be made for legitimate variations and adaptations", and that "it shall be for the competent, territorial ecclesiastical authority to specify adaptations".

This principle of the particular Churches is also recognised by the dogmatic constitution on the Church, *Lumen gentium*:

> Moreover, within the Church particular Churches hold a rightful place. These Churches retain their own traditions without in any way lessening the primacy of the Chair of Peter. This Chair presides over the whole assembly of charity and protects legitimate differences, while at the same time it sees that such differences do not hinder unity but rather contribute toward it. (LG 13)

In chapter seven, the constitution links the pilgrim Church with the heavenly Church, and thus offers a theological basis for the veneration of the saints. In chapter eight, Mary's role in salvation is also interpreted in conjunction with the mysteries of Christ and his Church.

2.2. The conciliar norms about the liturgical year

Chapter five of *Sacrosanctum Concilium*, dealing with the liturgical year, can be divided into two parts. The first one (art. 102-105) is a theological introduction to the meaning of the liturgical year and its composition. The second one (art. 106-111) is a practical part that deals with the renewal of the liturgical year.[47]

In close connection with art. 5-8, art. 102 states that the Church has to celebrate the Paschal mystery "by devoutly recalling it on certain days throughout the course of the year". That leads to the predominance of Sunday as the weekly celebration of the Paschal mystery in such a way

---

[47] The schema that was proposed at the Council consisted of a theological introduction and two parts. The first part was entitled: *De anno liturgico instaurando*, and consisted of six articles (art. 80-84), respectively about Sunday, the liturgical year in general, the proper of time, Lent, the restoration of the praxis of penance, and the fact that the feasts of the saints may not predominate the feasts of the mysteries of salvation. The second part was about the revision of the calendar (art. 85-86), but during the Council it became the appendix to the constitution.

that "other celebrations, unless they be truly of greatest importance, shall not have precedence over the Sunday, the foundation and core of the whole liturgical year" (art. 106). It is important to note that during the conciliar discussions several fathers asked for a better description of the Sunday as that was given in the schema.[48] Also the feasts of the Lord on which the different aspects of the overwhelming Paschal mystery are celebrated throughout the year have to come to the foreground. "Therefore, the proper of seasons shall be given the precedence due to it over the feasts of the saints, in order that the entire cycle of the mysteries of salvation may be celebrated in the measure due to them" (art. 108). Article 107 also points to the specific character of the liturgical seasons, "so that they duly nourish the devotion of the faithful who celebrate the mysteries of Christian redemption and above all the Paschal Mystery".[49] The concluding sentence of this article ("If certain adaptations are considered necessary on account of local conditions, they are to be made in accordance with the provisions of art. 39 and 40") is an addition to the schema. In this way, it is recognised that the general rules for the accommodation of the liturgy are also valid for the reform of the calendar: the conference of bishops have to make decisions in this domain.

Chapter 5 sees the feasts of Mary ("who is joined by an inseparable bond to the saving work of her Son", art. 103)[50] and of the saints ("the Church proclaims the Paschal Mystery achieved in the saints", art. 104) in close connection with the mystery of salvation and not as separated festivities. That is why art. 111 states that "the feasts of the saints cannot take precedence over the feasts commemorating the very mysteries of salvation". The same article 111 honours the particular or local Churches (see art. 22, 37-40, and LG 13) and leads to a decentralisation of the feasts of the saints: "many of them should be left to be celebrated by a particular Church or nation or religious family". This article also formulates an important rule that, when really brought into practice, may have far reaching consequences: "those [feasts of the saints] only should be extended to the universal Church that commemorate saints of truly universal significance". It clearly underscores that only those feasts

---

[48] The art. 80 of the schema was completely rewritten and, as an *emendatio maioris momenti*, had to be put to a vote: 2049 pro, 10 con, and 1 null.

[49] This sentence was put to a vote: 2071 pro, 11 con, 3 null.

[50] Also the first sentence of art. 103 is an *emendatio maioris momenti* that was put to a vote: 2217 pro, 15 con.

of the saints can have a place on the liturgical calendar which "proclaim the wonderful works of Christ in his servants and display to the faithful fitting examples for their imitation".[51] In this way, it becomes possible to rediscover the function of the liturgical calendar, which in fact is not a catalogue with the names of all the saints.[52] Moreover, insofar we may speak about a *Calendarium Romanum generale*, only those saints who have a truly universal significance for the celebration of the *mysteria salutis* in the Christian congregations belonging to the *Romana* can have a place on it. Insofar as the liturgical calendar is supposed to be at the use of a particular Church room can be made for the celebration of those saints who, for the faithful of a particular Church, are indeed fitting examples for imitation. We may conclude that *Sacrosanctum Concilium* decided for a fundamental change, which wants to replace the unfortunate uniformity and central organisation of the calendar under Pope Pius V by a particular arrangement responding to the original tradition of the veneration of the saints in the Church.

As characteristic for chapter 5 of *Sacrosanctum Concilium* we may point to three main decisions: the precedence of Sunday as the Lord's Day over other celebrations, the precedence of the proper of seasons over the feasts of the saints, and the decentralisation of the liturgical celebration of the saints.

2.3. The first decrees on the way toward the reform of the calendar

Pope Paul VI, through his *motu proprio Sacram liturgiam* of January 25, 1964, installed a postconciliar commission that would implement the liturgical constitution.[53] A letter of the Secretariat of the State, dated February 29, 1964, described the responsibilities of the commis-

---

[51] The introductory sentence of this article ("the saints have been traditionally honoured in the Church and their authentic relics and images held in veneration") as the result of the discussions is an addition to the schema and was put to a vote as an *emendatio maioris momenti*: 2057 pro, 13 con, 1 null.

[52] A further distinction can be made in 'name-day calendars', wall or pocket calendars, academic calendars, football-calendars or calendars proper to whatever purpose. It seems no longer to be appropriate to take the liturgical calendar as the basis for other calendars as this was experienced in previous times.

[53] *AAS* 56 (1964) 139-124.

[54] *Documents on the liturgy. 1963-1979. Conciliar, papal, and curial texts* (Collegeville 1982) 77 no. 613 (hereafter DOL).

sion that received the name "Consilium for the Carrying out of the Constitution on the sacred liturgy" (*Consilium ad exsequendam Constitutionem de sacra liturgia*).[54] The names of the forty-two members of the *Consilium* were published in the *Osservatore Romano* on March 5, 1964.[55] In its first general meeting on March 11, 1964, the working method of the *Consilium* and the forty-two study groups or *coetus* were established. The study group in charge of revising the calendar, because it was considered to be the basis on which the celebrations of the Mass and the liturgy of the hours are organised, was put first in the list of *coetus*. A. Bugnini became relator, A. Dirks was secretary, and the members were: R. van Doren, J. Wagner, A.-G. Martimort, P. Jounel, A. Amore, and H. Schmidt. On October 14, 1966, P. Jounel was appointed relator.[56] As to the proper of saints, the first report to the *Consilium*, discussed on April 25, 1965, stated that care must be taken that the cult of the saints continues but also that priority is given to the mysteries of Christ. In order to bring out the universality of holiness in the Church, the introduction of feasts of saints of the various parts of the world in the universal calendar was suggested. At the same time a suggestion was made that several saints could be commemorated on the same day, with celebrants free to celebrate any one of them.

On March 5, 1967, the Congregation of Rites edited the instruction *De musica in sacra liturgia*.[57] In its number 32, this document offered the possibility, instead of the official texts of the *introitus-, offertorium-* and *communio*-songs, of using other songs that better correspond to the liturgical season. This way the temporal cycle could better come to the foreground. Also when the Second Instruction for the right application of the Conciliar constitution on the liturgy, *Tres abhinc annos*, officially recognised the use (*ad experimentum*) of a new arrangement of the pericopes for the weekdays, an important step was made towards a revaluation of the temporal cycle.[58]

---

[55] The list was not published in the *Acta* until June: *AAS* 56 (1964) 479. The number of members changed during the work of the *Consilium*. For the names of the members, as well as of the consultors and the advisors, who were appointed by the *Consilium*, see BUGNINI: *The reform* 942-952.

[56] BUGNINI: *The reform* 305.

[57] *AAS* 59 (1967) 300-320; *Notitiae* 3 (1967) 87-105.

[58] *AAS* 59 (1967) 442-448; *Notitiae* 3 (1967) 169-194 (with comment). Remark the reference to Pius X's motu proprio *Abhinc duos annos* (1913), see our note 36.

3. A CRITICAL EVALUATION OF THE REVISED CALENDAR

The new calendar was published on May 9, 1969, by the decree *Anni liturgici ordinatio* of the Congregation of Rites, dated March 21, 1969, after Pope Paul VI had approved it in his *motu proprio Mysterii paschalis* of February 14, 1969. The complete document of 180 pages contains, next to the *motu proprio* and the decree, the General norms for the liturgical year and the calendar, the General Roman calendar, the interim calendar for 1970, the litany of the saints, and an unofficial commentary on the calendar.[59] Nos. 49-57 of the General norms give precise rules for particular calendars of individual Churches and families of religious. For the transition period the Sacred Congregation for Divine Worship[60] published on June 26, 1969, an *Instructio de calendariis particularibus ad interim accomodandis*.[61] The final *Instructio de calendariis particularibus atque officiorum et Missarum propriis recognescendis*, dated June 24, 1970, instructed all the competent authorities to let their individual calendars and texts be revised by a body of experts, to approve it and to send to Rome for confirmation within a period of five years after the publication of the missal and breviary.[62]

3.1. The precedence of Sunday as the Lord's Day

The restoration of Sunday as the celebration of the paschal mystery[63] on the first day of the week so that it is really the Lord's Day – a restoration which started under Pope Pius X and continued under Pope John XXIII – is consistently elaborated. The Sundays of the Easter season henceforth take precedence over all solemnities and feasts, as was already the case for the Sundays of Advent and Lent (General norms 5). The fact that the feasts of the Holy Family and of the Baptism of the Lord

---

[59] *Calendarium romanum* (Vatican 1969).

[60] By the Apostolic constitution *Sacra Rituum Còngregatio* of May 8, 1969, Paul VI had replaced the Congregation of Rites by two new congregations: the *Sacra Congregatio pro Culto Divino* that should incorporate the *Consilium* after the completion of the liturgical reform, and the *Sacra Congregatio pro Causis Sanctorum*, see *AAS* 61 (1969) 297-305.

[61] This instruction was not published in *AAS*. See *DOL* 480, nos. 3991-3994.

[62] *AAS* 62 (1970) 651.

[63] It is important to note that the *motu proprio* begins with the words: *Mysterii paschalis celebrationem*.

as well as the solemnities of the Holy Trinity and of Christ the King are to be celebrated on a Sunday, however, obfuscates the general rule that "by its nature, Sunday, excludes other celebration's being permanently assigned to that day" (GN 6). As such, the situation is made worse than in the 1914 calendar of Pius X![64] Three of these feasts are even 'idea-feasts' and thus should not have the same importance as the celebration of the Lord's Day.[65] As for example the solemnity of Christ the King it could be argued that one had better recognised Epiphany as the real feast of Christ the King in liturgy.

The stipulation that the solemnities of Epiphany, Ascension, and Corpus Christi, in those places where they are not observed as days of obligation, are assigned to a Sunday (GN 7), is not only a harming of the Sundays, but also a devaluation of those feasts themselves. Why then not also create this possibility for Christmas?! Don't we give the governments a pretext to cancel or to move the public holidays since the Church replaces its solemnities without problems?[66]

3.2. The priority of the temporal over the sanctoral

The abolition of pre-Lent and of the octave of Pentecost contributed to a more obvious profile of Lent and of the Easter season. The second part of Advent (December 17-24) and Lent regained their proper character by the basic rule that no feasts or memorials of the saints may be celebrated then. But this principle is not completely realised in such a way that some saints now, indeed, are celebrated or commemorated on another date, while others are not as for example the solemnity of saint Joseph.[67]

---

[64] The feast of the Holy Family was generally prescribed and celebrated on the first Sunday after Epiphany only in 1921. The feast of the Baptism of the Lord was introduced in 1955 and celebrated on the octave day of Epiphany. The solemnity of Christ the King was introduced in 1925 and celebrated on the last Sunday of October.

[65] Notice the great reserve toward 'idea-feasts' and 'devotion feasts' expressed in the (unofficial) commentary on the calendar, *Calendarium Romanum* 66-67.

[66] HARNONCOURT: *Gesamtkirchliche und teilkirchliche Liturgie* 123.

[67] For example, the memorial of Thomas Aquinas was changed from March 7 to January 28, the feast of Benedict from March 21 to July 11, and the feast of Thomas the Apostle from December 21 to July 3. "The solemnity of Saint Joseph, except where it is observed as a holy day of obligation, may be transferred by the conference of bishops to another day outside Lent." *GN* 56f. The Neo-Gallican calendars already transferred the feast of Saint Joseph as husband of Mary to Advent, to January or to the end of April, see Pierre JOUNEL: *L'organisation de l'année liturgique*, in *La Maison-Dieu* 100 (169) 139-156, 153.

The shift of the previous feasts of the third class into memorials for the liturgy of the hours as well as for the eucharistic celebration, however, in a certain sense has restored the proper of seasons, making those days again ferial days. Indeed, most of the previous feasts of the saints are no longer 'feasts', but *memoriae* either obligatory or optional. In this way, the 'feasts' become again exceptional days in the course of the liturgical year, while the 'memorials' are in a certain sense officially selected or proposed nominations of some saints, taken from the martyrology, during the liturgy of that particular day.

A positive factor is that as a principle the memorial of the saints is brought to the date of their death,[68] which is seen as their 'birthday' (*dies natale*) into the Kingdom of the resurrected Lord. This principle, however, can only be brought into practice during the *tempus per annum* and accordingly, as mentioned already, some saints are celebrated on another day, for example on the anniversary of the translation of their relics. In this way, the Paschal mystery is respected and the cult of saints is better integrated in the celebration of the Christian mystery. Indeed, during ordinary time no specific aspect of the mystery of Christ is celebrated, but rather the mystery of Christ in all its aspects[69]. So we may then remember those saints who for our local community[70] are real examples of how we can live the Christian mystery.

3.3. Decentralisation of the calendar of the saints

The desire of the Constitution on the sacred liturgy to decentralise the calendar with the feasts of the saints (art. 111) is not completely realised. The bishops and heads of religious orders did not really obtain the competency to organise their own calendar of the saints to be celebrated. On the contrary, the principle of the reform of Pius V is maintained insofar

---

[68] *GN* 56. So for example, the memorial of Polycarp of Smyrna is changed from January 26 to February 23. The principle is not always applied in a rigid way: so for example the memorial of Martin of Tours remained on November 11, although he died on November 8.

[69] *GN* 43.

[70] 'Local' does not only indicate here a diocese: "There is no reason why some celebrations may not be observed with greater solemnity in some places than in the rest of the diocese or religious community" (*GN* 54). A good example is the memorial of Saint Martin: a solemnity may be celebrated in the numerous parishes in Belgium that have him as their parish patron.

that the calendar of the saints is organised in a central way and the particular calendars are only additions to it. All local churches still have to celebrate a great number of saints, which are seen as having universal significance and since they have their place in what is called the General calendar. As an extension to this calendar they also may celebrate those saints who have only a national, regional, or local significance.

This is the inverse of *Sacrosanctum Concilium* 111: "those [feasts of the saints] only should be extended (*iis tantum extensis*) to the universal Church that commemorate saints of truly universal significance." The unofficial commentary nevertheless declares: "The Constitution on the sacred liturgy stated that in the General calendar should be conserved (*servanda esse*) the feasts that commemorate those saints having universal importance." It further explains: "If the mandate of the Constitution on the sacred liturgy had been taken literally and followed to the letter, only a few saints of truly universal importance would have been retained in the General calendar. Such a procedure seemed unsuitable and extreme; it would have caused great astonishment and offence. That is why another way is chosen."[71] Ph. Harnoncourt correctly remarks that with such reflection whatever task to reform the liturgy as this was given to the *Consilium* could have been rejected.[72]

The conciliar wish of truly universal significance of a particular saint is changed into the universality of the calendar. Since it was seen to be very difficult to determinate those saints who really have a universal significance, a new principle was chosen. Next to a critical historical examination[73] of those saints to be put on the calendar, a historical and geographical balance was sought in such a way that the calendar should witness to the universality of holiness in both time and space.[74] In this way – insofar

---

[71] *Calendarium Romanum* 68.

[72] HARNONCOURT: *Gesamtkirchliche und teilkirchliche Liturgie* 126.

[73] The principle applied here is that people of our day want "their devotion to the saints to be based on historical truth". On the basis of the science of hagiography a number of 'saints' are no longer retained. The principle however is not always followed as for example in the case of Saint Cecilia. See DUBOIS: Les saints du nouveau calendrier 162-164.

[74] The unofficial commentary provides an overview of the geographical as well as of the chronological spread of the saints who are listed in the calendar. A close reading shows that there is still a preponderance of European saints, especially from Romance countries, as well as of some centuries. Maybe, one can defend the 'universal significance' of the martyrs of the first centuries, but what makes the saints of the 16th and 17th centuries so important?

as this is really possible – saints from all times and all peoples, but also representing the different types of holiness lived by the people of God were sought.[75] This principle is translated in the General norms, article 49, as: "of those saints having universal significance (…) or of saints who show the universality and continuity of holiness within the people of God." In other words, the 'only' (*tantum*) of *Sacrosanctum Concilium* 111 has become 'of.. or of' (*tum… tum*). This may lead to a further misunderstanding of the calendar as a kind of a martyrology since it is not really experienced as a feast-calendar. This leads to a disappointment of those who do not find their favourite saints in the General calendar. It also fosters the endeavour of local churches and religious families to have their saints on the General calendar or even to give them a higher rank becoming obligatory memorials or even feasts. Indeed, this endeavour has proved to be successful for some in the years after the promulgation of the General calendar.[76] In other words, on this domain the revised calendar fell short of the expectations that were awakened by the Constitution on the sacred liturgy.

3.4. The number of saints in the General calendar

The number of the feasts and memorials of the saints, either obligatory or optional, remains surprisingly high. In addition to the Marian feasts and memorials, the 1969 calendar contains 168 saints' days, and this number even increased in the following years. As to the principle of "the universal significance", it can be demonstrated that for the greatest part those saints who received an obligatory memorial do not have that qualification. Although one may argue that a great number of the memorials are optional and in every case are no longer detrimental to the temporal, they give the General calendar such an important value that it becomes very difficult to construct a real particular calendar. Such a particular calendar then is experienced as a mere extension of the general one instead of making it the proper indication of those days on which the diocesan community of faithful or the religious order or congregation gather together to celebrate their saints, their own great examples of holiness and true Christian faith.

[75] *Calendarium Romanum* 66 and 70; Carolus BRAGA: De anno liturgico et calendario generali instauratis, in *Ephemerides liturgicae* 83 (1969) 183-201, 190; JOUNEL: Conferentia 297; BUGNINI: *The reform* 321.
[76] For example, the memorial of Saint Benedict (July 11) became a feast in 1980 as was also the case for Saints Cyril and Methodius (February 14) in 1981. The optional memorial of Saint Stanislaus (April 11) became an obligatory memorial in 1979.

The adoption of the many optional memorials in the General calendar may well be seen as honouring the particular churches by giving the entire Romana the possibility of remembering their most important saints. But this can never be the aim of a 'General' calendar, namely to be the repercussion and norm of the established celebrations. Because of the optional character of so many memorials, one can never *in concreto* express the universality of the church as she is assembling at this particular place. Once again, these saints whose memorial is optional according to the General calendar must have their place in the particular calendars, which can give testimony to their own celebrations based on their proper tradition.[77]

4. CONCLUSION

As a positive result of the 1969 revision of the calendar we may point to the centrality which is given back to the celebration of the Paschal mystery, especially by the precedence of the Lord's Day and the proper of seasons. We have formulated some serious criticism about the place of the veneration of the saints in the so-called General calendar and about the step-motherly fashion the particular calendars are treated in. This is not to say that the particular calendars have to become lists with, on each day, the name of a saint that the local church wants to commemorate. On the contrary, these calendars must mention those saints a local community wants to celebrate by a real feast-day in the sense of the *festa fori* and not only as *festa chori*. We cannot celebrate a feast every day, since this is the opposite of a 'feast': feast-days are landmarks, highpoints, marked days among the other days, days on which all involved can be free of other engagements to gather together in order to celebrate what unites them. A further reduction of the calendar of saints seems to be necessary as well as a further revalorization of the martyrology, which also is a liturgical book. From it the names of the saints whose anniversaries occur on a given day can be read during the liturgy of the hours. Catholics have to realise that no saint is driven from heaven by a further reform of the liturgical calendar, but that a liturgical calendar has another function than the martyrology.

---

[77] Augustinus HOLLAARDT: De nieuwe liturgische kalender en de heiligen, in *Tijdschrift voor liturgie* 58 (1974) 200-206, 203.

PART IV

CONTEMPORARY EXPLORATIONS AND PERSPECTIVES

TON SCHEER

CONTEMPORARY EXPLORATIONS AND PERSPECTIVES

1. INTRODUCTION

The twelve studies that have been brought together in the fourth part of the collection all deal with important aspects of liturgical ritual life in The Netherlands, in particular during the second half of the 20th century, at the transition to the third millennium. As such they provide true-to-life 'snapshots' of the situation in which liturgy in Dutch-speaking areas finds itself today. Of course, this image is not complete, but is certainly typical for this relatively small region, of which friend and enemy, insider and outsider alike know that very intense and profound processes of development have occurred there. Frequently enough these developments have attracted attention from the rest of the world, particularly in the centre of the world Church, and met with criticism, because what happens in a geographically small area can have considerable consequences and stir up influences outside its borders. Two factors have played a particular role in this: the development of consciousness in the church, and the secularisation of social cultural life.

2. DEVELOPMENT OF CONSCIOUSNESS IN THE CHURCH

Until the middle of the 20th century the development of consciousness in the church was driven by a strong urge for emancipation and equality. In particular the Catholic portion of the nation strove for full participation in social life, in response to the great social disadvantages that had built up during the centuries since the arrival of the Reformation. A comprehensive system of Catholic and Protestant social

[1] Cf. J. THURLINGS: *De wankele zuil. Nederlandse katholieken tussen assimilatie en pluralisme* (Deventer 1970); E. SIMONS & L. WINKELER: *Het verraad der Clercken. Intellectuelen en hun rol in de ontwikkelingen van het Nederlandse Katholicisme na 1945* (Baarn 1945).

institutions was created in the fields of politics, education, health care, media, art, sports, labour unions, etc., resulting in the typically Dutch phenomenon termed *verzuiling* ('columnisation')[1]. The spirit of this emancipatory revival among the Catholics in The Netherlands was strongly defined by ultramontane tendencies, and the region was to a great extent led according to the model of an hierarchically structured Catholicism.

These processes reached their completion around 1950, and since then a stormy spiritual and institutional reversal has taken place in the Dutch church, and particularly Dutch Catholicism. The phoenix, arisen from its ashes, now took free flight. From the Dutch side, the striving for autonomy and religious maturity and responsibility – the consciousness of being reborn in freedom – found its voice at the Second Vatican Council through Cardinal Bernard Alfrink (1900-1987) and others, and in the following decades dominated ecclesiastical and religious life in The Netherlands. Not the least of the spheres in which it found expression was a liturgical revival, when for the first time in history liturgy displayed a physiognomy of its own in terms of content and form. To this very day a measure of intractability characterises the ecclesiastical and religious consciousness of the Dutch, and to a certain degree marks the Dutch attitude to ritual and liturgy.

3. SECULARISATION OF SOCIAL AND CULTURAL LIFE

The second factor which has given the religious situation in The Netherlands its peculiar character can be called the secularisation of social cultural life. Until beyond the middle of the 20th century The Netherlands was the model of a religious, and particularly Christian nation. Countless aspects of religiosity permeated almost all sectors of society, not in the least everyday life in the family. The furnishings and ornaments in the home, the regularly recurring activities that took place at home or at school, the names given to children and the very landscape – particularly in Catholic regions – bore witness to an ubiquitous religious consciousness, which for that matter equally manifested itself at the macro-level of society in politics, media and economic life, as described above.[2]

---

[2] O. SCHREUDER & L. VAN SNIPPENBURG (eds.): *Religie in de Nederlandse samenleving. De vergeten factor* (Baarn 1990); G. DEKKER, J. DE HART & J. PETERS (eds.): *God in Nederland 1966-1996* (Amsterdam 1997).

It is therefore all the more remarkable that in the 1960s this religious consciousness in The Netherlands suddenly and quickly tipped in the direction of a secular outlook on life. To be sure, this collapse did run parallel with other social/cultural upheavals, particularly in Western Europe, but in The Netherlands it particularly affected the position of the religious, Christian attitude toward life in social and political respects. This development could be illustrated by countless examples. In this part of the collection it will be referred to regularly. Here we particularly want to focus attention on the consequences for liturgical life. One might assume that liturgy has begun to take a less obvious and less frequent place not only in public life, but also in the personal lives of Dutch Christians, and that the ties of the Dutch with rituality as it has been handed down – and thus with the symbolic and metaphorical universe that it provides – has gradually become less tight, but also less oppressive. In The Netherlands at the moment, among almost all who are disposed to the church at all, to a certain degree an ecumenical climate holds sway; there is a rising awareness of the presence and significance of non-Christian religions, and there exists a multiplicity of views and interpretations on religious concerns, almost as a matter of principle. Moreover, the phenomenon of cultural Christendom has by now taken root, which is at loggerheads with the institutions of the church, and which sets itself sharply apart with a secular way of life that is premised on primarily socio-economic and technological bases. The implications of these shifts in perspective in society, however, are the subject of a permanent and sometimes heated debate. One can think, for instance, of the problems which have arisen around the beginnings and the ending of life.

4. THE CONTRIBUTIONS IN GENERAL

The background sketched above is reflected in almost all the studies in this fourth part of the collection. To a certain extent they can also be characterised as 'historical' studies: more or less detailed interpretations that attempt to understand liturgy (and matters related to it) today, from a very specific past. That does not detract from the fact that all the studies have been undertaken with the intention to describe and clarify the contemporary situation for liturgy. One can trace the similarities among them along various lines.

First, each author has chosen as a starting point a specific aspect or component of what one could term the liturgical 'programme'. This programme reveals a very wide spectrum, as broad as liturgical reality itself. We hope that despite their selective limitations, the twelve subjects will still, together, sketch an image of the Dutch liturgical situation today.

Secondly, the studies are similar because they view liturgy as rituality, which is related to the celebration of 'feast', in agreement with the thematic orientation of the whole collection. The experience of celebration is understood in a broad sense, but at the same time implies that other kinds of experiences of liturgy, including conflict, gravity, suffering, loss, wrong and parting – just as essential to liturgical life – are not discussed, or only dealt with tangentially. W.M. Speelman's study on the funeral of Princess Diana is an exception to this. Choice means selection, and selection means limitation as well as focus.

In the third place, we want to note that all studies are extrapolations of the 'basic structure' of the liturgical order. Some are part of cyclic ritual, in the cases of the celebrations of St. Martin, Christmas and Easter. Others are part of the rhythmic rituality peculiar to the celebration of milestones in life, when they discuss birth, First Communion, marriage and death. Still others are part of the spiritual dimension of liturgical reality, such as the considerations devoted to the manner in which meaning has been assigned to Gregorian chant, to contemporary artistic representations, particularly of Christ, in a ritual context, to the experience of Sunday and to experiences on the pilgrimage route to Santiago de Compostela. Finally, others belong to the realm of incidental rituality, when attention is devoted to the peculiar manner of reception and communication that occurs in liturgical rituality presented by the media, and in the perception of liturgical music.

In the fourth place, the studies in this part of the collection are all in harmony because the authors have not limited themselves to the description of ritual phenomena and contemporary liturgical practice, nor to the analysis of historical backgrounds and contextual sources, but have at the same time, and particularly, set out their own position with regard to the issues that they are examining. In several cases this position is defined by their methodological position and by explicit justification of the method with which they have worked. In general, the methodological considerations are not the strongest aspect of the studies included. Possibly on this point the views of the authors vary considerably. However, one can detect great similarities in the attitude with which they approach ritual phenomena. Those working in liturgical studies in The Netherlands are almost unanimous in their critical view of ritual developments that are ongoing today and have not yet crystallized. In this part of the collection they demonstrate an openness to ritual change and renewal. Finally, it is noteworthy that the studies have to a limited extent made a contribution to a further conceptual clarification of the basic concept of 'feast'. Perhaps the authors have grasped that "not everything that glitters is gold", as both Dutch and English proverbs have it.

5. THE CONTRIBUTIONS IN PARTICULAR

We conclude this introduction with a short description of the contributions.

J. Helsloot, ethnologist, offers an analysis of the rituality of the feast of St. Martin during the 20th century in The Netherlands, and alerts us to the variety of systems of interpretation that have determined the meaning of children's rituals of this sort.

S. Roll, liturgist, briefly describes the origin and development of the symbolism that forms the foundation for the high feasts of Christmas and Easter, and subjects this symbolism to critique from a feminist perspective.

G. Lukken, liturgist, sketches the fundamental issues surrounding liturgical rituals for birth and distinguishes two pastoral strategies in The Netherlands and Flanders. He wonders whether expanding the rituality surrounding birth is not the proper course in a time of liturgical deinstitutionalisation.

P. Post and L. van Tongeren, liturgists, offer a contextual description of the feast of First Communion and apply the characteristics of the basic concept of 'feast' to this case study of a child/family celebration. Fundamental questions surrounding this practice demand a rejuvenated mystagogy as well as a widening in the time.

A. Scheer, liturgist, investigates the impact of marriage ritual on the participants, with regard to fostering their religious identity and communication in and through the ritual actions. To that end, he analyses the practice of official Catholic marriage ritual, and discovers a number of ambivalences.

M. Hoondert, liturgist, reports on an historical investigation into the renewal in the theory and practice of Gregorian chant since the 19th century, and in particular discusses its reception in The Netherlands since the beginning of the 20th century. The spiritual depth of this music makes its way thanks to – and in spite of – strategies of appropriation.

R. Steensma, theologian, describes several case studies in a Protestant setting in which works of religious art (paintings), whether centred around a particular theme or not, are displayed in church buildings, for example. The seeing of the image and the hearing of the word, art and ritual, appear to be components which in their interplay actualise and deepen religious experience.

L. van Tongeren, liturgist, sketches the fundamental development that attitudes and practices involving Sunday have undergone in Dutch society, with far-reaching consequences for religious experience and liturgical practice. He makes an argument for the significance of Sunday as a "window on the transcendent" and offers suggestions for preserving and promoting it.

A. Mulder, J. Pieper, R. van Uden, religious studies scholars, report on the dossiers of two pilgrims who travelled to Santiago de Compostela. Systematic analysis of the dossiers raises a number of questions about the experience of pilgrims itself and the experience of pilgrimage as a festive event.

M. Gertler, media theologian, reports from his personal experience and academic study on the peculiar manner of communication that occurs in liturgy presented by media. He notes that liturgy on television imposes special demands on the medium, but that in particular theology and church institutions must reassess the traditional concepts of *communicatio* and *communio*.

W.M. Speelman, liturgist, offers a personal but at the same time semiotically coloured analysis and reflection on the funeral rituals that were broadcast on television after the death of Diana, Princess of Wales. The aesthetic (musical) and ritual (textual) aspects of this event, seen worldwide, can be conceived as catalysts for an authentic religious experience, on the personal level as well, on the part of viewers and listeners.

John Helsloot

AN ELEMENT OF CHRISTIAN LITURGY?
THE FEAST OF ST MARTIN IN THE NETHERLANDS IN THE 20TH CENTURY

1. Introduction: liturgy and popular culture

The problem of the relationship, in all its complexity, between liturgy and religious popular culture is a theoretical concern to both liturgists and (European) ethnologists. Increasingly during the last decades, this has been perceived as a common problem, requiring an interdisciplinary approach. Although liturgists have taken account in their analyses of ethnological models, concepts and data – and *vice versa*, a truly integral perspective, as Paul Post noticed recently, in the study of ritual in a Christian context has only rarely been realized.[1] Still, researchers combining at least in their person an initimate knowledge of both disciplines have made some remarkable statements concerning this relationship.

Such was the case, for instance, in the early 1980s when Dietz-Rüdiger Moser revolutionized the view on the Roman-Catholic carnival. Contrary to the commonly accepted view that the Church was opposed to this festival, he argued – referring to hitherto neglected theological statements, the practice of liturgy, in particular the reading during services of prescribed parts of the bible (pericopes), and sermons based on these readings – that the Church actually welcomed carnival as fulfilling an important catechetic role in the dissemination of religious doctrine. When this function became obscured, it was natural – only then! – that the Church opposed the feast.[2] There are, as

---

[1] P. Post: Religieuze volkscultuur en liturgie. Geïllustreerd pleidooi voor een benadering, in J. Lamberts (ed.): *Volksreligie, liturgie en evangelisatie* (Leuven/Amersfoort 1998) 19-77, p. 21-40; P. Post: Van paasvuur tot stille tocht. Over interferentie van liturgisch en volksreligieus ritueel, in *Volkskundig bulletin* 25 (1999) 215-234, p. 215-217.

[2] D.-R. Moser: *Fasnacht, Fasching, Karneval. Das Fest der "verkehrten" Welt* (Graz/Wien/Köln 1986); D.-R. Moser: Perikopenforschung und Volkskunde, in *Jahrbuch für Volkskunde* 6 (1983) 7-52. See the discussion in *Jahrbuch für Volkskunde* 5-7 (1982-1984).

can be readily imagined, various problems with this bold and provocative model, on an empirical as well as a theoretical level. These include
foremost the likely discrepancies between the supposed intentions of
the Church and their appropriation by those participating in carnival.
Perhaps even more important in this respect is the sweeping claim of
the model, that was soon extented by Moser, often with equally surprising claims, to other elements of popular culture in the liturgical
year as well.[3]

Despite its novelty at first sight, there was, on a higher level of
abstraction, a familiar ring to the model. Well into the 1950s, ethnologists were prone to ascribing pre-Christian ('pagan') origins to all
kinds of (religious) popular customs. The contribution of ethnology
consisted in making people aware of these long-forgotten, 'unconscious', connections. As in the 1960s due to the efforts of German ethnologists the ideological impetus behind this line of reasoning became
apparent and also on factual grounds – there are no facts, except on a
simple phenomenological level, to corroborate this continuity – the
model was definitely dismissed, only to linger on at the level of popular lore. It would be unfair to apply directly the same kind of criticism
to Moser's more sophisticated model. Moreover, although there is room
for debate, he does adduce factual sources to support his theses. But
their implication shows a striking similarity to the previously mentioned, 'pre-Christian' model. As a result of the steady erosion of Christian knowledge, people nowadays are more and more unconscious of
the originally Christian grounds and motives behind all sorts of popular rituals and festivals. It is up to the ethnologist to uncover these
underlying layers of meaning and to make them known again.[4] In so
doing, the banner of continuity is raised a second time and participants
are made, perhaps against their will, unconscious enactors of Christian
liturgy. It may well be, however, that some of these, after reading
Moser's studies, actually welcome and internalize his message, thereby

---

[3] D.-R. MOSER: *Bräuche und Feste im christlichen Jahreslauf. Brauchformen der
Gegenwart in kulturgeschichtlichen Zusammenhängen* (Graz 1993).

[4] "Der christliche Kalender enthält also eine Fülle von Hinweisen auf heils-
geschichtliche und theologische Zusammenhänge, die erst dann wirksam werden können, wenn man sich ihrer bewußt wird." It was his aim "'verlorengegangene Selbstver-
ständlichkeiten' wieder ins Licht zu heben". For: "Es handelt sich bei ihnen [the
elements of religious popular culture (Bräuche) treated by him] um nichts anderes als
um Ausdrucksformen christlicher Religion", MOSER: *Bräuche und Feste* 23, 286.

eventually confirming – in terms of Hans Moser's *Rücklauf* – the validity of the interpretation.[5]

Another example of this comprehensive incapsulation of religious popular culture is provided by the similar model of the ethnologist, specialising in religious popular culture, Wolfgang Hartinger. Drawing on a large number of examples from Central Europe from the Middle Ages to the present, he also concludes that the liturgy of the Catholic Church was of paramount importance in shaping religious popular culture. And again, it is to the secularization of recent times that he attributes the evaporation of the knowledge regarding this connection.[6]

On theoretical grounds Paul Post, also a scholar well versed both in ethnology and the study of liturgy, has objected to this model of liturgical primacy. In several theoretical and empirical studies[7] he has advanced the perspective of the very complex nature of the relationship, or more precisely the interference, between liturgy and religious popular culture – to the point of considering by now these interferences in themselves the object of study. It is, as Post claims, on the dynamic interplay of ritual and cultural elements and attitudes that one should concentrate, on their congruence, convergence or divergence, on shifts in contexts, quotations and borrowings.[8] A consequence of this view is that efforts at defining the precise nature of religious popular culture become somewhat less urgent.

Although on sure theoretical basis – because his model was tested and elaborated in various empirical studies, Post has called for new investigations, preferably case studies into the vast domain of feasts and

---

[5] H. MOSER: *Volksbräuche im geschichtlichen Wandel. Ergebnisse aus fünfzig Jahren volkskundlicher Quellenforschung* (München-Berlin 1985) 359-360; H. BAUSINGER: Für eine komplexere Fastnachtstheorie, in *Jahrbuch für Volkskunde* 6 (1983) 101-106, p. 105-106.

[6] "Ideenlieferant für alles brauchtümliche Geschehen", W. HARTINGER: *Religion und Brauch* (Darmstadt 1992) 240-241; 244. See the summary and critical assessment of his book, in POST: *Religieuze volkscultuur* 40-47; POST: *Paasvuur*, 219-223.

[7] A fine example is P. POST: "An excellent game…". On playing the mass, in C. CASPERS, G. LUKKEN & G. ROUWHORST (eds): *Bread of heaven. Customs and practices surrounding Holy Communion. Essays in the history of liturgy and culture* (Kampen 1995) 185-205.

[8] POST: *Paasvuur* 219, 229. Cf. P. POST: Het rituele perspectief, in A. VAN HARSKAMP et al.: *De religieuze ruis in Nederland. Thesen over de versterving en de wedergeboorte van de godsdienst* (Zoetermeer 1998) 47-55; P. POST: Rituele dynamiek in liturgisch perspectief. Een verkenning van vorm, inhoud en beleving, in *Jaarboek voor liturgie-onderzoek* 15 (1999) 119-141.

rituals, to try it again.[9] The purpose of this study is to answer this call – merely from the point of view of an ethnologist – by offering a cursory sketch and interpretation of some developments in the celebration of the feast of St. Martin's in the Netherlands in the 20th century.

2. PROBLEM, PERSPECTIVE, SOURCES AND OUTLINE

The question to be addressed here in particular concerns the nature of this feast. In discussing the field of 'folklorized liturgy' – i.e. rituals originating in liturgy which are being appropriated by secular festive culture; the term interference refers to the same phenomenon – Post mentions as an example: out-door "processions with more or less 'liturgical content'", like those of children at the feast of St Martin's.[10] This hesitance in calling these processions liturgical is not surprising – and puts us into the heart of the problem, for it shows an implicit assumption that there are grounds for engaging in this effort.

This is not unimportant. When one holds a particular point of view, one usually has little difficulty in finding 'facts' that will substantiate this view. This will only be achieved by neglecting competing readings or interpretations of the same facts or by ignoring other facts. Against this one might argue that, in particular in the social sciences, the *raison d'être* of the researcher's effort lies in the assumption that in the end he knows best – or at least better than the people he studied. Unconscious motives as objects of study play a deciding role here. To those who would object that these considerations are irrelevant in this context, one could point to the frequent use of precisely this term unconscious when the interference of ritual and religious popular culture is at issue, both in scholarly publications, as mentioned above, and in the popular press.[11] The term acts as a convenient metaphor indicating the many layers of meaning attached to a ritual. It is the researcher's task, however, not so much to 'uncover' these meanings as to monitor the arena of competing definitions and interpretations projected onto a ritual and appropriated – in all its modalities – by participants and commentators

---

[9] POST: Paasvuur 224-226.

[10] P. POST: *Ritueel landschap. Over liturgie-buiten. Processie, pausbezoek, danken voor de oogst, plotselinge dood* (= Liturgie in perspectief 5) (Heeswijk-Dinther 1995) 21.

[11] E.g.: "children honour him [St Martin] *unconsciously* [italics added] with a fantastic procession of lanterns", *Het Binnenhof* 10-11-1948.

in their different strands and in precise historical situations. In this arena his own interpretation plays a role on equal footing with those of others.[12] The outcome of these various debates not infrequently has resulted, as is well known, in adaptations of form and content of the ritual concerned – again triggering off new interpretations.[13]

This ongoing and complex process is best grasped at the level of a detailed case study. Bearing the above considerations in mind, however, here a different approach is used: presenting a tentative sketch of the history of St Martin over the course of about a century and in the country as a whole. What is lost in depth may be gained in taking a broader, historical perspective. My main sources are newspaper cuttings on St Martin's day from the archives of the Meertens Instituut and the Nederlands Openluchtmuseum (collection Van der Ven). Ethnological questionnaires (EQ) 4 (1938) 18-27 and 68 (1997) of the Meertens Instituut were also consulted.[14]

This contribution is divided in three sections each dealing with ideological systems that have sought to interpret, to influence and to mould the outward forms of and meanings attributed to the folklore of St Martin's day: those of the discipline of folklore itself, of the peace movement and of organized Catholicism. In the conclusion the findings are confronted with the abovementioned theses on the relationship of folklore and liturgy.

3. ST MARTIN'S DAY: THE IMPACT OF THE DISCIPLINE OF FOLKLORE

The basis of the St Martin's day folklore, in the Netherlands and in many other European countries, is the tradition that, on the feast day of this saint (11th November in the Roman-Catholic liturgical calendar),

---

[12] In this respect Hartinger's position is ambiguous, for, while sharing this view in principle (HARTINGER: *Religion und Brauch* 41-43) and in the analysis of cases (e.g. the *Sternsingen* (ibid.: 47, 204-206), his final conclusion still is comparable to that of D.-R. Moser.

[13] Newspaper journalists may play a similar role; see the interesting study of C.A. NORMAN: 'Annual well-dressing – another brilliant success – finest work for many years' (by our own correspondent), in Th. BUCKLAND & J. WOOD (eds): *Aspects of British calendar customs* (Sheffield 1993) 137-146.

[14] For an assessment of the purpose and value of this type of source see A.J. DEKKER: Inleiding, in *De Volkskundevragenlijsten 1-58 (1934-1988) van het P.J. Meertens-Instituut* (Amsterdam 1989) 1-27.

children are given special freedoms and privileges. In this respect, the feast shows some resemblance to Halloween in the United States. During two hours or so after nightfall, children roam the streets and ring at doors, carrying lanterns and singing St Martin songs.[15] Usually their appearance is rewarded by the distribution of some coins, fruits or candy. I shall focus here on this characteristic and more or less unique element of the feast and leave aside the St Martin's bonfire.[16]

The very nature of the children's action – expecting a gift as an uncertain reward for their singing or quasi threatening the adults (as in the song: "give me something now and I won't be around till next year") – contained an element of dependence that led in the first half of the 20th century to its overall description as begging. For poor children (with their parents sometimes in the background) the St Martin's singing was an occasion to gain some extra income in winter. This practice was looked down upon by the better sort. They would only allow their children to be treated simply with some sweets by their relatives and acquintances, their social equals, at a few addresses nearby.

In the 1920s and 1930s ethnology as an academic discipline began to take shape in the Netherlands. Congresses and lectures were organized, folkloristic festivals were held and textbooks and schoolbooks were published.[17] Accounts of all this were disseminated in the press and more and more ordinary people became aware of 'folklore' as a distinct subject matter. It changed their perception of what they were participating in or witnessing in their vicinity. This also extended to the customs on St Martin's day. From then on, they came to be seen as a part of 'folklore', that

---

[15] On these songs, see G. HELMER: Het Sintmaartenslied in Nederland, in *Volkskunde* 57 (1956) 1-21; M.J. FRANCKEN: Het Sint-Maartenszingen in Noord-Holland, in *Noord-Holland* 8 (1963) 141-160. See also D. SAUERMANN: Westfälische Martinslieder nach den Sammlungen des Atlas der deutschen Volkskunde, in *Rheinisch-westfälische Zeitschrift für Volkskunde* 16 (1969) 70-104; D. SAUERMANN: Martinslied, in R.W. BREDNICH et al. (eds): *Handbuch des Volksliedes. I. Die Gattungen des Volksliedes* (München 1973) 391-417.

[16] J.J. VOSKUIL & A.J. DEKKER: De jaarvuren in Nederland omstreeks 1938, in *Volkskunde* 71 (1970) 204-210, p. 205-207.

[17] E.g. R. VAN GINKEL: Illusies van het eeuwig onveranderlijke. Volkskunde en cultuurpolitiek in Nederland, 1914-1945, in *Volkskundig bulletin* 24 (1998) 345-384; R. VAN GINKEL: *Op zoek naar eigenheid. Denkbeelden en discussies over cultuur en identiteit in Nederland* (Den Haag 1999) 107-111. In the series *Volkskundig leesboek voor de lagere scholen* (Groningen 1931) attention was paid to St Martin's in the volumes on *Nederland* (41-49), *Groningen* (59-68), *Drenthe en Overijsel* (24-27), *Limburg en Noord-Brabant* (47-51).

is untainted by the connotation of social inequality. The idea of real begging receded into the background and the procession with lanterns and
the accompanying singing attracted the participation of children of all
social strata; or that was the image one preferred to perceive.[18] This
process entailed, on the one hand, that gifts in money were considered
less appropriate, and on the other hand that poorer families too were
now frequented by the St Martin's singers. By the 1950s their action was
described as "decent begging", executed by "pseudo-poor children".[19] In

Fig. 1. St Martin's singers besieging a confectioner's shop in the 1930s.

[18] E.g., "children of the rich and the poor, of all denominations, of the village
[Spaarndam] as a whole", *Haarlemsch Dagblad* 12-11-1938.
[19] *Nieuwe Noordhollandse Courant* 15-11-1948; *Trouw* 7-11-1957. Still, in the town
of Haarlem, there was even in the 1970s some hesitance on the part of parents of the
more well-to-do, Tj.W.R. DE HAAN: Sint Maarten in Haarlem, in *Jaarboek Haerlem*
1974, 285-296, p. 289.

the 1960s the real begging was only remembered as something of a distant past.

That was not to say that negative associations surrounding the custom remained altogether absent. On the contrary, some of them even increased as a result of the 'folklorizing' operation. The probably larger number of children participating and their freeer, that is more demanding, attitude, led to their behaviour being considered more and more as a nuisance. Ordinary people found it hard enough to answer the doorbell several dozen times that evening. It was worse for shopkeepers such as grocers and bakers. They felt besieged by scores of noisily singing children, not daring to turn them down, particularly because they were their customers' children. It was understandable that terms like "a mess" and even "begging in disguise" turned up again in this connection. The superintendent of police in the town of Alkmaar for instance, referring to complaints of shopkeepers, in 1938 felt that "an ancient custom, well-meant in its origin" had become "degenerated" because of "a wrong sense of sympathy" on the part of adults. In the same manner, the children themselves elsewhere were blamed for their "wrong conception" of the nature of the custom.[20] Perceptions like these paved the way for intervention.

This negative attitude was further enhanced by the riot-like events that accompanied St Martin's day in the later hours of the night in some towns and villages in the provinces of North-Holland and Friesland (such as Zaandam, Enkhuizen, De Rijp and Bolsward) in the 1930s and in the 1950s and 1960s. When half-grown youths threw firecrackers at the police or kindled small fires, this was seen as wantonness: "with folklore this row has nothing in common".[21] As ethnologists have remarked in similiar cases, it was not so much the appreciation of folklore itself that was in question as its form and function in new circumstances.[22] The simultaneous folklorization of St Martin's day, that is its

---

[20] Quoted in *Alkmaarse Courant* 8-11-1951; Ethnological questionnaire 4 (1938) 20/F 66.

[21] *De Zaanlander* 12-11-1934. Cf.: "This way De Rijp demonstrates its misunderstanding of the feast of St Martin", *Nieuw Noord-Hollands Dagblad* 13-11-1947.

[22] D. SAUERMANN (ed.): *Weihnachten in Westfalen um 1900. Berichte aus dem Archiv für westfälische Volkskunde* (Münster 1976) 28; H. SCHWEDT: St. Martin, vorwärtsreitend. Zur Transformation und Diffusion eines Brauchkomplexes, in A. LEHMANN & A. KUNTZ (eds): *Sichtweisen der Volkskunde. Zur Geschichte und Forschungspraxis einer Disziplin* (Berlin-Hamburg 1988) 257-266, p. 258, 262.

narrowing down to an innocent feast especially for small children, may have contributed to a sense of unfair exclusion on the part of youths from about twelve years and up. When these tried to get some candy too, they were described as 'St Martin's poachers' and 'dissonants'.[23] By throwing firecrackers they showed off their anger, in a sense making mock of the childrens' idyllic lanters. This, of course, was a serious offence to those with new and different views on the meaning of this folklore. It seemed that some force was needed to put these into effect.

Bringing order to feasts of the lower classes and reducing their perceived excesses had a tradition dating back at least to the Enlightenment.[24] From the 1920s on this urge gained a new impetus.[25] It affected the tradition of St Martin too. In the 1930s and after the war in the 1950s, there was a ready climate for intervention. To meet the demand of a spectacle of proper and decent folklore, in the wake of the diffusion and popularization of academic folkloristics, it was deemed self-evident to lend tradition a hand.[26] Adults took over the free wandering of the children by organizing it on their own terms. The moments of the start and end of the procession as well as its route were fixed and publicly announced, the children were lined up orderly and a musical band was engaged. In order to attract the participation of the children, prizes were put up for the most beautiful or original lanterns. When the procession had come to an end, the children received some sweets or fruit from the hands of the organizing committee. After that they were supposed to be well satisfied and go home.

Along this basic pattern a wide array of committees and associations took it upon themselves to organize and thereby civilize the former begging and singing. It stood to reason that those in close connection with small children took the lead, such as teachers in primary schools and kindergartens. They explained the figure of St Martin to their pupils and passed on their knowledge of the folklore of that day, they

---

[23] *De Typhoon* 12-11-1959.

[24] E.g. B. HEIDRICH: *Fest und Aufklärung. Der Diskurs über die Volksvergnügungen in bayerischen Zeitschriften (1765-1815)* (München 1984); P. BAILEY: *Leisure and class in Victorian Britain* (London 1978); J. HELSLOOT: *Vermaak tussen beschaving en kerstening. Goes 1867-1896* (Amsterdam 1995).

[25] F. GROOT: *Roomsen, rechtzinnigen en nieuwlichters. Verzuiling in een Hollandse plattelandsgemeente, Naaldwijk 1850-1930* (Hilversum 1992) 187-188.

[26] H. SCHWEDT: St. Martin – Ein reformierter Brauch! Bräuche – Geschichte und Theorie, in *Volkskultur an Rhein und Maas* 11 (1992) 9-18.

had the children fabricate their lanterns out of mangolds or other materials, and rehearsed with them the songs to be performed in the procession. A special role was played by Catholic youth organizations (see below). But also associations organizing all kinds of festivities in their town or village took part, as well as associations specifically dedicated to the promotion of folklore.[27] To organisations operating on a very local level, that of neighbourhoods in towns and villages alike, the feast clearly had a special attraction. This was even reinforced when, as a result of the internal migration in the first decades after the war, new housing areas became populated with people from all over the country. Some of these newcomers introduced the tradition of St Martin's from regions where it was customary (the provinces of Groningen, Friesland, Drenthe, North-Holland and parts of North-Brabant and Limburg) into areas where it was unknown before. Their initiative seems to have been generally welcomed and may in part account for the growing popularity and spread of the custom in the 1970s and 1980s.[28]

By the very organization of the procession, the children were largely reduced to passive ornaments for the amusement of adult spectators, whose active role in the tradition was decreased as well. This didn't preclude, however, groups of children singing on their own initiative before and after the organized procession. Sometimes they were even explicitly allowed to do so, attesting to the relative fluidity between the boundaries of spontaneous and organized folklore. Still, the organized processions seem to have contributed to an increased involvement on the part of adults – and in the end of the local community as a whole – in their conception of the tradition of St Martin.[29]

---

[27] Such as 'The Society for Archeology and Folklore' in Doesburg, *Zutphensche Courant* 12-11-1936. In the same spirit in Koog aan de Zaan in the 1930s the children were dressed up – explicitly to "curb the wantonness of overgrown boys" – in traditional local custumes in the St Martin's procession, Ethnological questionnaire 4 (1938) 21a/E 85.

[28] Ethnological questionnaire 68/3. Cf. on this process H. & E. SCHWEDT: *Bräuche zwischen Saar und Sieg. Zum Wandel der Festkultur in Rheinland-Pfalz und im Saarland* (Mainz 1989) 120.

[29] D. TILLMANN: Dörfliche Festkultur am Großstadtrand, in *Kieler Blätter zur Volkskunde* 29 (1997) 147-160, p. 152-153; Th. LUDEWIG: Politische Gruppierungen und das Martinsfest, in H. SCHWEDT (ed.): *Brauchforschung regional. Untersuchungen in Rheinland-Pfalz und im Saarland* (Stuttgart 1989) 71-86, p. 81-85; S.J. VAN DER MOLEN & P. VOGT: *Onze folklore* (Amsterdam-Brussel 1980) 160, 162.

The influence of this conception showed itself also in another aspect of the custom. Folklorists and the general public were fascinated, particularly in the 1930s, by the idea that in the lanterns and bonfires of St Martin's day one could see – as in so many other elements of popular culture – the vestiges of ancient pagan rituals. These were supposedly held to beg the sungod for his return or to bring thanks to Wodan for the harvest.[30] The effect of this kind of theorizing was, as it became more widely known, to confer on the contemporary custom the status of something vaguely sacred, or meaningful – because very old. This in turn demanded, from those who knew, a reverent or at least respectful attitude, for the feast "was religious in origin".[31] The participants were seen, and probably sometimes saw themselves, as staunch upholders of tradition, thereby even proving their moral quality.[32]

As is well known, conservatism is an aspect of this attitude. This became manifest in particular in views on the proper shape of the lanterns carried along by the children in their processions. With the benefit of hindsight, it was fortunate that an ethnological questionnaire was sent out in 1938, at a time the folklorization of the custom was being consolidated. Numerous correspondents noticed that most children carried paper lanterns. This was a phenomenon that in their view only recently had come into fashion. They contrasted this practice unfavourably – e.g.: "I consider this to be a loss"[33] – to earlier times when children made their lanterns out of all kinds of beets. Chance remarks that paper lanterns were seen as something for the rich or life in the cities are indications that the adoption of these new attributes was part of the general process of modernization of the countryside during the inter-war years.[34] It is safe to assume that aversion or resistance of others to this process found expression, in a slightly distorted way, in

---

[30] E.g. *De Telegraaf* 11-11-1931; *Nieuwe Rotterdamsche Courant* 11-11-1935.

[31] *De Zaanlander* 9-11-1935.

[32] E.g.: "in old folk customs the sound spirit of our ancestors becomes apparent", *Culemborgsche Courant* 11-11-1949; "We welcome the maintenance of the tradition of St Martin's. Folklore is of great value to all who are Dutchmen to the backbone", *Eems-bode* 13-11-1953. See for the general background of this mood e.g. J.H. KRUIZINGA: *Levende folklore in Nederland en Vlaanderen* (Assen 1953) 200; J. VOS: *Democratisering van de schoonheid. Twee eeuwen scholing in de kunsten* (Nijmegen 1999) 145-146.

[33] Ethnological questionnaire 4 (1938) 20/E 45.

[34] See on this process e.g. A. SCHUURMAN: Plattelandscultuur in de negentiende en vroege twintigste eeuw. Modernisering en glocalisering. Een essay, in *Jaarboek Nederlands Openluchtmuseum* 5 (1999) 270-301.

the denunciation of the paper lantern as "not so beautiful", because simply bought, "for convenience's sake". People felt unable to admire lanterns like these and showed this even by receiving the children carrying them with ridicule![35] Also a burning real candle was deemed an essential requisite. Otherwise one couldn't speak of truly celebrating St Martin's.

What was going on was, of course, a cultural battle around the notion of the authenticity of folklore. Echoing the dominant model in scholarly studies, newspapers too maintained that the countryside was the true *locus* of folklore.[36] St Martin was "one of the few old customs not yet swept away by modern civilisation" or by the "general trivialisation and encroaching influence of modern times". In small villages one could still come upon these customs, "unknown to city-dwellers".[37] Concomitant with this diagnosis was the conviction that the authenticity of the custom was best preserved when the children were stimulated to fabricate the lanterns by themselves. That way they could testify to their "unconscious ties to the folklore (*volkscultuur*) of their own village or region". Not surprisingly, this view was preached by the staunch promotor of all things folklore, Dirk Jan van der Ven.[38] Pedagogical ideas, developed from the 1920s onwards and gaining ground after the war, on the moral and social value of children expressing themselves artistically, coincided and reinforced the preference for this kind of lantern.[39] In kindergartens they were eagerly seized upon.

When, as a logical consequence, kindergartens and various local associations made the children show their lanterns in organized processions this collided, however, with the professed authenticity of the custom – as emanated in the self-fabricated lanterns. There was "something

---

[35] Ethnological questionnaire 4 (1938) 20, esp. E 45, C 88, C 75, C 176, C 99, E 35, G 12a. "A produce of one's own yields more", a child confirmed, DE HAAN: Sint Maarten in Haarlem 290.

[36] With respect to material culture e.g. G. ROOIJAKKERS: 'De tot vorm gekomen persoonlijkheid van het volk'. Volkskunst als cultuurdiagnose, in *Volkskundig bulletin* 23 (1997) 89-105, p. 92-95.

[37] *Nieuwe Rotterdamsche Courant* 11-11-1935; *De Tijd* 11-11-1938; *De Telegraaf* 12-11-1936.

[38] *Alkmaarse Courant* 8-11-1951. On Van der Ven, see VAN GINKEL, Illusies 348-351; T. WAGEMAKERS: Het Vaderlandsch Historisch Volksfeest. Over D.J. van der Ven, massatoerisme en de moderne folklore, in *Jaarboek Nederlands Openluchtmuseum* 2 (1996) 170-187.

[39] VOS: *Democratisering* 108-167.

unnatural" in an organized procession, its "emotional value" was different (Van der Ven) and also "detrimental to the atmosphere (*gezelligheid*) of the old folk custom".[40] Such puritanism did not gain much support.[41] In the 1960s the attitude towards the lanterns became more relaxed and tolerant. Increasingly no contradiction was felt between organization and celebrating folklore.

4. St Martin's Day: the Impact of the Peace Movement

This malleability of popular culture became manifest in the late 1920s. The coincidence of the dates of the feast of St Martin and of Armistice Day (November, 11, 1918) was seized upon by the proponents of world peace. Defining St Martin's as "a children's feast of light", that "for many people had lost its meaning", the Dutch branch of the International Women's League for Peace and Freedom (*Vrouwenbond voor Vrede en Vrijheid*) sought to give it "a new content" to those willing "to overcome the forces of darkness". Joined by similar organizations with progressive Protestant leanings and with the support of schoolteachers in several larger and smaller towns, mainly in the northern part of the country, processions were organized in the 1930s of children carrying lanterns with peace emblems or symbols – like the bells, the dove, the angel of peace and banners with peace slogans – and singing peace songs like 'Children of one Father' and 'Never again war'. Afterwards slogans were shouted and meeting were held to discuss peace and disarmament.[42]

This initiative met with a mixed reception. Surprisingly, the influential folklorist Van der Ven at the time welcomed the idea of filling old forms with new meanings. It testified to the "indestructible vitality" of folklore. By participating in the celebration, on St Martin's day, of world peace, the disappearance of confessional and social divisions, "party politics and chauvinism" would certainly ensue.[43] This way he

---

[40] *Alkmaarse Courant* 8-11-1951; *De Volkskrant* 11-11-1959. Cf. KRUIZINGA: *Levende folklore* 192-193.

[41] Looking at newspaper photographs of processions one is, in the same vein, struck by the still continuing presence of paper lanterns.

[42] *Nieuwe Rotterdamsche Courant* 22-10-1931; *De Telegraaf* 11-11-1931; *Leeuwarder Nieuwsblad* 11-11-1930; 13-11-1936, *De Zaanlander* 11-11-1934; Ethnological questionnaire 4 (1938) 20/E 77, 20/F 179.

[43] Offprints of *Agrarisch Nieuwsblad* c. 1930, 1936, archive NOM.

harmonized the idea of peace, acceptable to all, with his view on the a-political nature of popular culture. It is not quite clear how the children reacted to this restyling of the feast. When, for instance, it was reported from the town of Groningen they were not much attracted to the peace procession, this was probably because they disliked the idea of an organized procession as such.[44] Some adults, of course, were more outspoken. "This was an ill-conceived action. The character of a St Martin's procession got completely lost and a tradition of many years was destroyed. This is unpleasant for those keen on traditions." The disappearance of typical St Martin's songs was also deplored.[45] After World War II commemorating the Armistice Day of 1918 lost its appeal in The Netherlands. Pacifists made no new attempts to appropriate the lanterns of St Martin. Their interference proved to be only an incident.

In passing, it may be mentioned that, contrary to expectation,[46] the Nazi's seem to have kept aloof from St Martin's day. During the occupation of The Netherlands the processions of the lanterns were not allowed because of the general black-out of the country. Whereas in Germany St Martin's day was used for propaganda meetings during the war in towns like Dortmund and Düsseldorf[47] and St Martin was also instrumentalized to benefit the *Winterhilfe*,[48] I have not yet come across similar examples for The Netherlands.

---

[44] *Nieuwsblad van het Noorden* 12-11-1930.

[45] Letter to the editor from a person in Edam, newspaper cutting 1938, archive Meertens Institute; S.J. VAN DER MOLEN: *De Friesche kalenderfeesten. Volksgebruiken van Westerlauwersch Friesland, het geheele jaar rond* (Den Haag 1941) 89. Curiously, Van der Ven in later years changed his opinion and wrote that the old tunes had been "drowned" by the "pedagogical St Martins'-peace songs", *Helmondsche Courant* 5-11-1955.

[46] On their appropriation of carnival and Christmas, see D.-R. MOSER: National-sozialistische Fastnachtsdeutung. Die Bestreitung der Christlichkeit des Fastnachtsfestes als zeitgeschichtliches Phänomen, in *Zeitschrift für Volkskunde* 78 (1982) 200-219; E. GAJEK: Weihnachten im Dritten Reich. Der Beitrag von Volkskundlern an den Veränderungen des Weihnachtsfestes, in *Ethnologia Europaea* 20 (1990) 121-140.

[47] M. HAPP: Die Martinslegende als ein religionsgeographisches Problem, in M. BÜTTNER & K.-H. ERDMANN (eds), *Geisteshaltung und Umwelt – Stadt und Land. I. Beiträge zum Geographentag in Bonn 1997* (Frankfurt am Main 1998) 59-88, p. 84 n. 69.

[48] D. SAUERMANN: Neuzeitliche Formen des Martinsbrauches in Westfalen, in *Rheinisch-westfälische Zeitschrift für Volkskunde* 14 (1967) 42-67, p. 66.

5. ST MARTIN'S DAY: THE IMPACT OF ORGANIZED CATHOLICISM

Obviously, as St Martin was a Christian saint, the abovementioned pagan interpretation of the St Martin's ritual could only be partial. Newspaper accounts of the custom pointed, often in the same breath, to the christianization of orginally pagan practices in later times. "In the early Middle Ages St Martin was such a popular saint and his feast coincided so luckily with the end of the season, that the pagan feast without any difficulty was brought into the Christian sphere."[49] This interpretation, repeated over and over again in the popular press, must have gained very wide currency indeed, perhaps even up to the point of becoming the accepted truth in the minds of those participating in the custom.

Its cogency can be measured by the relative disinclination to accept the interpretation of St Martin as a "purely Christian feast". This view was already put forward in 1937 – undoubtedly inspired by Karl Meisens' book on St Nicholas that advocated the same kind of interpretation[50] – by the influential student of folklore Jan de Vries in his popular textbook *Volk van Nederland.*[51] Although later repeated in similar textbooks, it apparently sounded less attractive.[52] Contributing to this was the fact that even in Roman-Catholic circles the pagan interpretation continued to be passed on. This was mainly due to the equally influential textbook on Dutch folklore of the Roman-Catholic scholar Jos Schrijnen. In his view it was "undeniable" that present-day customs originated in Germanic pagan feasts. Saints like St Martin later simply had taken over the role of chthonic deities.[53]

---

[49] *Limburgs Dagblad* 10-11-1956.

[50] See W. MEZGER: *Sankt Nikolaus. Zwischen Kult und Klamauk. Zur Entstehung, Entwicklung und Veränderung der Brauchformen um einen populären Heiligen* (Ostfildern 1993) 45-48.

[51] J. DE VRIES: *Volk van Nederland* (Amsterdam 1937) 228. His view was only seldom echoed in the press.

[52] S.J. VAN DER MOLEN: *Levend Volksleven. Een eigentijdse volkskunde van Nederland* (Assen 1961) 18-19; VAN DER MOLEN & VOGT, *Onze folklore* 160. Cf., probably also by Van der Molen: "It is out of the question that this day is a christianized pagan feast", *Leeuwarder Courant* 7-11-1953. Only incidentally one finds: "Not a single Germanic feast can be found on or about November 11th", *Alkmaarse Courant* 11-11-1961.

[53] J. SCHRIJNEN: *Nederlandsche Volkskunde.* Tweede herziene druk. I (Zutphen 1930) 139, 129-130. On Schrijnen and De Vries e.g. T. DEKKER: De blik omlaag gericht. Over koerscorrecties in de volkskunde, in *Volkskundig bulletin* 21 (1995) 351-369, p. 354-355; T. DEKKER: Ideologie en volkscultuur. Een geschiedenis van de Nederlandse

If few were inclined to regard St Martin's day as a purely Christian feast, there was even less room for seeing it as a typically Roman-Catholic event. On the contrary, St Martin was widely seen as only 'nominally' a Roman-Catholic saint and the feast in his honour – just like that of the very popular St Nicholas – as 'non-confessional' or 'national' in character. This could be plain to all, as it was celebrated not only in the Catholic southern provinces, but also in parts of the predominantly Protestant North and West of the country. Against the devotion towards a real saint of the people (*volksheilige*) the Reformation was powerless.[54] Comments in newspaper accounts suggest that this wishful and ideological view on folklore's ability to overcome religious divisions in society found resonance, particularly in the 1930s.[55] Indeed, Protestants were generally not unsympathetic to the children singing in praise of St Martin at their doorsteps. Perhaps they were even unaware of the Catholic ring of the custom.[56]

However, in the back of some Catholic minds may equally have lingered thoughts of a less distant – that is: medieval – past when the whole of Holland was still Catholic and saints like St Martin were venerated by all. Admittedly this situation no longer persisted. Narrowing down the perspective (and so contrary to the view mentioned earlier), one was prone to point to the Catholic south where St Martin and his feast were still, that is continuously, kept sacred. Elsewhere in the country these had "fallen into disuse" or were "on the brink of dissapearing" – the, in the discipline of folklore familiar, vocabulary of *Folklorismus*.[57] This called for their revitalisation. By organizing the traditional feast of

---

volkskunde, in T. DEKKER, H. ROODENBURG & G. ROOIJAKKERS (eds): *Volkscultuur. Een inleiding in de Nederlandse etnologie* (Nijmegen 2000) 13-65, p. 36-42; VAN GINKEL: Illusies 353.

[54] E.g. *Nieuwe Haarlemsche Courant* 10-11-1930; *Leeuwarder Nieuwsblad* 14-11-1939; *De Nieuwe Dag* 9-11-1949; *Alkmaarse Courant* 8-11-1951. Cf. W. FRIJHOFF: *Heiligen, idolen, iconen* (Nijmegen 1998) 25.

[55] Still, when in 1953 the figure of St Martin was depicted on the new 25 guilders note not all protestants were pleased. In the Lower House an orthodox protestant member objected to this, in his view, typical papist (*rooms*) image. Other protestants, however, denounced his action as "narrow-minded anti-papist bigotry", *De Volkskrant* 11-11-1953.

[56] VAN DER MOLEN & VOGT: *Onze folklore* 163

[57] E.g. *Gooise Klanken* 14-11-1949; *Maas- en Roerbode* 8-11-1947. On folklorization e.g. R. BENDIX: *In search of authenticity. The formation of folklore studies* (Madison-London 1997) 176-187; P. NISSEN: *De folklorisering van het onalledaagse* (Tilburg 1994).

St Martin one could uphold the memory of St Martin as a "national figure", "the same way this was done in earlier centuries".[58] The dominant motive behind this revitalizing effort, as allways, was to stress and to promote he distinctive features of, in this case, Catholic culture in the present.[59]

In 1936 in Utrecht an attempt was made, by an organisation of Catholic young girls, to honour St Martin publicly by laying a wreath at an image of the saint and singing a special song. Because St Martin was, already in pre-Reformation times, the patron saint of that city, an inclusive strategy was followed. St Martin was hailed as "the patron of Utrecht's Catholics and non-Catholics, christians and non-christians" alike. This could not, however, soften the attitude of the municipality towards the plan. Precisely its motivation as a "purely religious" occasion will have led them to forbid the outward aspects of the manifestation. The children were only allowed to pay a tribute to the saint by marching past the image in silence. The organizers acquiesced in this – "we Catholics of the northern provinces have been accustomed to confine our Catholic traditions within the walls of our churches" – but hopes were expressed for better times in the future.[60] They were not disappointed.

After the war Catholics succeeded in actively promoting the public cult of St Martin. Imitating the example of St Martin's processions in Germany, particularly the Rhineland,[61] a live St Martin already from the 1930s onwards occasionally figured in processions. He was mounted and usually dressed up as a Roman soldier, wearing a conspicuous red mantle. This allowed the staging, during the procession or at its close, of the scene for which St Martin is most well known. After meeting a shivering beggar, the saint draws his sword, cuts his mantle in two and gives half to the beggar. A huge bonfire, sometimes lit by

[58] *De Nieuwe Limburger* 10-11-1955; *Biltse Courant* 12-11-1948.

[59] E.g. W. FRIJHOFF: Traditie en verleden. Kritische reflecties over het gebruik van verwijzingen naar vroeger, in *Jaarboek voor liturgie-onderzoek* 7 (1991) 125-136, p. 133-134.

[60] *Utrechtsche Courant* 11-11-1936. On these 'unofficial' processions at the time, P.J. MARGRY: *Teedere quaesties: religieuze rituelen in conflict. Confrontaties tussen katholieken en protestanten rond de processiecultuur in 19e-eeuws Nederland* (Hilversum 2000) 412-413, 606 n. 24.

[61] D. PESCH: *Das Martinsbrauchtum im Rheinland. Wandel und gegenwärtige Stellung* (Diss. Münster 1969) 58. This was in the style of 'historical parades' of earlier decades, SAUERMANN: Neuzeitliche Formen 62.

the mayor, constituted the solemn and spectacular end of the events of the day. These theatrical aspects understandably appealed a great deal to Catholic organizations looking for ways and means to express themselves.[62]

Within the already elaborate and refined network of Catholic youth organizations in 1947 the 'Boys Guild' (*Jongensgilde*) was founded. Originating from the diocese of Den Bosch in Brabant, it became a more or less national organization. In 1955 it fused with the kindred youth movement of Young Holland (*Jong Nederland*), that from 1944 on had operated exclusively in the diocese of Roermond in Limburg. Their joint name became Guild Young Holland, later simply Young Holland. The Guild resembled the boy scouts, but was based, as its name indicated, on quasi-medieval notions and ideas. Under the slogan 'Be prepared' (*Sta klaar*) the boys were to devote themselves to Christ, the Church, the fatherland and their fellow human beings. In doing so they would become "fine Catholic boys and in later life vigorous Catholic men".[63]

As patron saint for the Guild, St Martin was chosen. Because he was a figure of both martial and religious qualities he was considered fit to appeal to impressionable young hearts. Having a patron saint, of course, called for the celebration of the patron's day. The effects of this were considered beneficial to the organization itself: "beautiful traditions will guarantee the continued existence of our movement".[64] To all local branches in the mid-1950s booklets were distributed containing stories of the saint's life and various ideas on how to keep the feast. The performance of plays like 'The miracles of Saint Martin' by Henri Ghéon or 'The good bishop' by C.A. Bouman was encouraged.[65] This was seen

[62] "Our catholic youth organizations are so busy looking for a theme for their festive calendar. (…) it is in the feast of St Martin that they will find exactly what they are looking for", *De Volkskrant* 6-11-1937.

[63] J.W. DINJENS: *Jong Nederland. Ontstaan en ontwikkeling van een jeugdbeweging* (Utrecht 1981). See also: *Sta klaar. Het Jongensgilde van de Katholieke jeugdbeweging* ('s-Gravenhage 1954); *Het programma van het Jongens Gilde* (S.l. [c.1955]); *Rakkers. Het Jongensgilde van de Katholieke Jeugdbeweging* ('s-Gravenhage 1956), 9; *Sta klaar. Handleiding voor Jong Nederland* ('s-Gravenhage [c.1958]); *Jong Nederland. Schets van een methodiek* (Utrecht 1973).

[64] *Leidersblad* 1954, 181.

[65] *De mantel van Sint Maarten. Gilde – Jong Nederland. Katholieke Jeugdbeweging* ('s-Gravenhage 1956) 70; see also: "We celebrate St Martin", in *Leidersblad* 1952, 186-187; *Leidersblad Jong Nederland* 1958, 24-25; *Leidersblad* 1953, 194.

as part of a general effort to 'restore' all over the country the tradition of celebrating the feasts of the liturgical year. "Folklore and observances outside the church proper", however, were explicitly included in this.[66]

Fig. 2. St Martin cutting his mantle before the beggar in a procession of the Guild Young Holland in the 1950s.

[66] *De Volkskrant* 12-11-1949; *Het programma van het Jongens Gilde* 7.

From the late 1940s onwards the Guild, often with the aid of other local Catholic youth clubs, celebrated St Martin's day with great fervor. In Amsterdam in 1949, for instance, after having attended Mass in the morning, the Boys Guild organized a splendid procession in the evening, with its flag in front, buglers and drummers, a group of mounted Roman soldiers escorting St Martin, in the outfit of a Roman officer and surrounded by beggars, and other members carrying lanterns. In the outskirts a bonfire was lit, with the boys dancing and singing around. As it died down, the chaplain chanted the *In manus tuas*, his example followed by all attendants. In conclusion a 'St Martin's message' was read exhorting the boys to unity, mutual love in the family and to follow the example of their patron saint.[67] Along similar lines in the 1950s equally impressive processions were held in various other towns (like The Hague, Rotterdam, Utrecht, Tilburg). In smaller towns and villages in the southern provinces groups of Young Holland were active till about the mid-1960s. Medievalism as source of inspiration was renounced in 1958.[68] In the course of the 1960s Catholic organizations began to lose their grip on the young and their active involvement in the feast of St Martin was increasingly shared or taken over by other local groups, as indicated above.

Although it was sometimes deemed necessary to carry a banner with the words 'St Martin' to explain to the public what was happening,[69] Catholic youth organizations were rather successful in appropriating the folk custom through their organizational effort. Also their flags, uniforms and sometimes the presence of a chaplain or their parading before the local bishop (as in Rotterdam, Roermond) brought this easily home to outsiders. These did not fail to respond. A liberal Protestant newspaper expressed the hope, referring to the Catholic parade on St Martin's day in Utrecht in 1953, that "this revival will not expand much further". The march looked like a disguised effort to hold a – still officially prohibited – religious procession. "What is to become of Utrecht when, through its innocent patron, it were to develop gradually into a papist (*rooms*) city?" Objecting to similar views supposedly expressed in Amsterdam – "a papist horror" – the leading Catholic newspaper of the city pointed to the entry, gaining every year in importance, of St Nicholas

---

[67] *De Volkskrant* 12-11-1949; *De Nieuwe Dag* 10-11-1949, 12-11-1949.
[68] DINJENS: *Jong Nederland* 60.
[69] *Het Binnenhof* 13-11-1956 (The Hague); sometimes even a loud-speaker was used to clarify the meaning of the ritual, *Maas- en Roerbode* 11-11-1952 (Roermond).

and his greyhorse. There was clearly no evidence that these figures acted as the Trojan Horse of a Catholic take-over![70] Still, organizers of a St Martin's procession may have felt satisfied: they had unequivocably made their point.

An exclusive claim to St Martin, however, was not granted to them. Already in 1948 and 1952, for example, the city centre of Utrecht had seen mass rallies of Catholic organizations on St Martin's day. In the mid-1950s there seems to have been a Protestant reaction to this too conspicuous Catholic appropriation of the saint, in line with the general view that he was of a nonconfessional nature. Now processions of hundreds of children with lanterns were organized by a joint committee of both Catholic and Protestant boy scouts. They were addressed by the mayor and his wife and received from their hands a 'traditional St Martin's cake'. Moreover, during their procession the children had collected fruits that were delivered later on to children's hospitals or money for UNICEF – an element, so obvious in respect to St Martin, that was absent in Catholic processions.[71] In later years implicit tensions like these seem to have subsided as the custom grew more and more popular, explicit Catholic involvement became attenuated and religious identity increasingly lost its power as a marker in social life.[72]

Uniting the boys (and the adults surrounding them) in their Catholic associations and ultimately in the Church itself was the main impetus behind the revitalization of these St Martin's processions. It was one of the many ritual means used to reinforce the cultural identity of young Catholics. In contrast, the Catholic impact on the meaning(s) attributed to the custom was rather poor. Not surprisingly, the pagan connotation surrounding the feast was not altogether absent. For instance, when Young Holland in the Limburgian village of Born organized its annual procession in 1950, it was explained to the boys in advance that "the feast of St Martin had evolved from pagan-Germanic autumn- and har-

---

[70] *Nieuwe Rotterdamse Courant* 12-11-1953; *De Tijd* 12-11-1953. For similar views of orthodox protestants in Germany, G. ANGERMANN: Das Martinsbrauchtum in Bielefeld und Umgebung im Wandel der Zeiten, in *Rheinisch-westfälische Zeitschrift für Volkskunde* 4 (1957) 231-256, p. 253. Cf. also MARGRY: *Teedere quaesties* 416-418.

[71] *Nieuw Utrechts Dagblad* 11-11-1955; *Het Centrum* 12-11-1956; *Nieuwe Rotterdamse Courant* 12-11-1957; *Trouw* 13-11-1957; *Utrechts Dagblad* 11-11-1958. Cf. on this type of involvement of protestants, ANGERMANN: Das Martinsbrauchtum 251.

[72] Cf. S. TOP: Das Martinssingen in Mecheln und Umgebung 1982 und 1983, in W. DEUTSCH & W. SCHEPPING (eds): *Musik im Brauch der gegenwart* (Wien 1988) 189-211, p. 208.

vestrituals". Rather frivously elsewhere it was stated that apparently "the old heathen was still not dead yet".[73]

On the other hand some efforts were made by the leadership of Young Holland to impart a purely Christian meaning. In their guidelines it was emphasized that the feast of their patron saint was "not only a folkloristic event. Its religious celebration is primary".[74] Indeed, the feast often began with a Mass in the morning or the evening before. Although mention was also made of the explanatory legend, echoed many times in the press, of the villagers looking at night with lanterns for St Martin's lost donkey, one was "of a different opinion" as regards its value. The emphasis was on another interpretation of the lanters carried by the children. "I cannot understand", it was written in the journal for their leaders, "why diligent researchers of the treasure of our folk customs exclusively point to the pagan origin of the many traditions of St Martin's day." Wouldn't is be more plausible, it was rhetorically asked, to trace their origin back to the "gospel of light" or "the gospel according to St Martin": Jesus' admonition in Luke 11, 33-36 not to hide one's light under a bushel? "We consider it of eminent importance to take this motive of light as the point of departure for our celebrations, also in their outward form."[75] Presumably, the boys were instructed with this meaning of the lanterns. However, contrary to the various other interpretations, this specifically Catholic one found hardly any echo in the press, neither at the time nor in later years.

Although the bonfires at St Martin's day could be interpreted as "a symbol of the burning *charitas* of which St Martin, splitting his soldier's mantle, set the noble example",[76] only weak attempts were made to impart this meaning on the participants of the processions in which this scene was dramatized. It was regarded by the leadership of the Guild as "a splendid point of contact with our boys to transpone the life of St Martin into their own ways of thinking and imaginative faculties. Not to moralize, but simply as a living example of his sainthood."[77] Still, it was on the moral aspects of his deed that emphasis was layed in the annual 'messages of St Martin', issued from headquarters and read aloud

---

[73] *Limburgs Dagblad* 8-11-1950; similarly, *Bisdomblad* 15-11-1974; *Brabants Nieuwsblad* 10-11-1956.

[74] *Sta Klaar* 62.

[75] *Leidersblad* 1953, 193, 183; *De mantel van Sint Maarten* 14, 61-62.

[76] *De Tijd* 11-11-1947.

[77] *Leidersblad* 1953, 192.

at the feast of each local branch, and less on the practical. For as the boys nowadays didn't wear a soldier's mantle, it was impossible for them to give away half of it. "But you can give a part of yourself to another person. Instead of putting your own interests first you must be ready for him." By imitating St Martin the boys would become "adequate men and adequate christians".[78] As they were seldom followed by concrete acts, e.g. making a collection for a charity, such highminded words remained just that. When catholic youth clubs withdrew from organising St Martin's processions, these ideas in later years were no longer repeated, or only in very general terms like 'love of one's neighbour'.

Compared to its (recent) involvement in and generally positive attitude to other elements of 'folklorized liturgy', such as children disguising themselves as the Three Kings and singing in the streets at Twelfth Night, the folklore of the palms and even carnival,[79] the Church itself seems to have kept rather aloof from the feast of St Martin. In contrast to the German Rhineland, in The Netherlands the procession of the lanterns only incidentally – unless my documentation is incomplete – entered the church or was part of some special service for children.[80] His feast was not moved to a Sunday, which would have facilitated a possible liturgical incapsulation.

6. CONCLUSION

My aim in sketching above the history of the St Martin's feast in the Netherlands, of its outward forms and the impact on them of various systems of interpretation, was to provide some materials to enable an evaluation of theses regarding the interference of liturgy and popular culture.

---

[78] *Leidersblad* 1951, 265; 1954, 195. Texts of messages for other years in *Leidersblad* 1952, 195; 1953, 183; 1955, 199, 1957, 179.

[79] G. ROOIJAKKERS: Vieren en markeren. Feest en ritueel, in DEKKER, ROODENBURG & ROOIJAKKERS (eds): *Volkscultuur* 173-230, p. 201-204; P. POST & J. PIEPER: *De Palmzondagviering. Een landelijke verkenning* (Kampen-Amsterdam 1992) 53-54, 58; C. WIJERS: *Prinsen en clowns in het Limburgse narrenrijk. Het carnaval in Simpelveld en Roermond 1945-1992* (Amsterdam 1995) 24-26. See on the history of Twelfth Night in the Netherlands in the 20th century, closely parallelling that of the feast of St Martin, P. SPAPENS & P. HORSTEN: *Driekoningenzingen. Een lange en levende traditie* (Utrecht 1996).

[80] P. POST: Het verleden in het spel? Volksreligieuze rituelen tussen cultus en cultuur, in *Jaarboek voor liturgie-onderzoek* 7 (1991) 79-124, p. 105.

One of the most outspoken statements in this respect has been made by Dietz-Rüdiger Moser. The dominating impulse behind customs like that of St Martin's day was and is to provide a marker for a "christliche Gesamtlebensordnung". The rituals of popular culture testify to "eine religiöse Haltung, die keineswegs ins Diffusen verborgen blieb, sondern über die Liturgie mit ihren vorgeschriebenen Lesungen unmittelbar auf das Verhalten der Gläubigen einwirkte". This liturgical imprint was provided by the lecture of Luke 11, 33f that was found in the *Missale Romanum* from the 13th century onwards and generally prescribed after Trent, until 1969. This lecture inspired the carrying of lanterns – the process was defenitely not the other way round – that spread "das 'Licht' (des Glaubens) [...], auf das am Martinstag so konkret wie möglich hingewiesen werden soll". Another lecture, that of Mt 25, 40 (*pauperi datum, Deo datum*), related the legend of St Martin to liturgy and exhorted to love of one's neighbour. In a world alienated nowadays from its religious roots, it was up to the researcher to revive the public consciousness of these connections.[81]

Despite its reliance on historical sources, this is essentially an a-historical view. Werner Mezger accepts D.-R. Moser's interpretation of the lanterns on the one hand as highly probable, but also makes some critical comments that make sense. It is unlikely that the participants in St Martin's processions were conscious of the theological connotations of their lanterns. Whether or not this was the case, certainly after the Enlightenment the custom became more secularized. Its Christian meaning was even lost to theologians. Only when the custom was reorganized, particularly in the course of the 20th century, this led "natürlich auch zu einer verstärkten Rückbesinnung auf den religiösen Kontext und dadurch wiederum zur katechetischen Vertiefung der Botschaft des Heiligen".[82] This way the Christian interpretation becomes historicized.

---

[81] MOSER: *Bräuche und Feste* 36, 32; cf. 24. "Ein wirklicher Fund", according to H. TRÜMPY: Kirchlicher Einfluß oder christliches System?, in *Jahrbuch für Volkskunde* 6 (1986) 88-90, p. 89. See also J. KÜSTER: *Wörterbuch der Feste und Bräuche im Jahreslauf. Eine Einführung in den Festkalender* (Freiburg im Breisgau 1985) 124; J. KÜSTER: *Bräuche im Kirchenjahr. Historische Anregungen für die Gestaltung christlicher Festtage* (Freiburg im Breisgau 1986) 103-105. See also the comment of K. MEISEN: Sankt Martin im volkstümlichen Glauben und Brauch, in *Rheinisches Jahrbuch für Volkskunde* 19 (1968) 42-91, p. 91.

[82] W. MEZGER: "Brenne auf mein Licht...". Zur entwicklung, Funktion und Bedeutung der Brauchformen des Martinstages, in W. GROß & W. URBAN (eds): *Martin von Tours. Ein Heiliger Europas* (Ostfildern 1997) 273-350, p. 309 and also 319, 329, 343.

As generally accepted nowadays, this course is the most wise to take. The meaning(s) of elements of popular culture are always contingent. They come into being as a result of a complex process of negotiation and appropriation between all kinds op interest groups. They can, however, never be fixed. As circumstances change, there will equally be a propensity to develop new meanings.[83] Konrad Köstlin rightly observes, *nota bene* in the *Festschrift* for D.-R. Moser:

> Historische Bräuche, ihre Muster und ihr Sachinventar können in der Moderne auf ganz verschiedene und oft widersprüchliche Weise genutzt und eingesetzt werden. Ihr ausdrückliches Zitieren ist oft Bestandteil einer Strategie, gegenwärtige Anliegen und Deutungen aus dem Fundus der Historischen und des ausdrücklich Eigenen zu stützen und so zu legitimieren. Dabei gibt es kein Gebrauchsmusterschutz, und auch keinen warnenden Hinweis.[84]

The Christian interpretation and appropriation of St Martin's day – at least in the 20th century – were only an incident at a very specific moment in its history. Gertrud Angermann witnessed its incipience in Germany in the early 1950s and was probably right in concluding: "Damit war zum erstenmal seit der Reformation der hl. Martin bewußt gefeiert worden." That is, in a Christian sense, referring particularly to the idea of *caritas*.[85] In The Netherlands this Christian meaning, although not altogether absent in the 1950s, seems to have been only

---

[83] E.g. P. NISSEN: Percepties van sacraliteit. Over religieuze volkscultuur, in DEKKER, ROODENBURG & ROOIJAKKERS (eds): *Volkscultuur* 231-281, p. 242, 247-248; ROOIJ- AKKERS: Vieren en markeren; MEZGER: *Sankt Nikolaus* 283-291 ('Perspektiven der Brauchanalyse'); H. SCHUHLADEN: Auf der Suche nach Geschichte – Selbstfindung im Mythos. Zu Neuschöpfungen steirischer Nikololäufe, in B. PÖTTLER *et al.* (eds): *Innovation und Wandel. Festschrift für Oskar Moser zum 80. Geburtstag* (Graz 1994) 377-395; W. BRÜCKNER: Brauchforschung tut not, in *Jahrbuch für Volkskunde* 21 (1998) 107-138; R. JOHLER: Volkskunde – und doch wieder Bräuche. Das Scheibenschlagen, der Funken- und der Hollepfannsonntag, in F. GRIESHOFER & M. SCHINDLER (eds): *Netzwerk Volkskunde. Ideen und Wege. Festgabe für Klaus Beitl zum siebzigsten Geburtstag* (Wien 1999) 655-666.

[84] K. KÖSTLIN: Sternsingen, Christkind und Eintöpfe. Brauch-Transformationen in die Moderne, in M. SAMMER (ed.): *Leitmotive. Kulturgeschichtliche Studien zur Traditionsbildung. Festschrift für Dietz-Rüdiger Moser zum 60. Geburtstag am 22. März 1999* (Kallmünz 1999) 553-561, p. 560.

[85] ANGERMANN: Das Martinsbrauchtum 248-249. Sauermann made similar observations. He also pointed to the tendency that the feast in the 1960s had become "offen für neue Sinngebungen", SAUERMANN: Neuzeitliche Formen 67.

weakly developed. One is tempted to infer that scholars like D.-R. Moser have taken the feast of St Martin's as they encountered it in the 1950/60s for the normal or even normative practice. This is, as research on the popular understanding of the idea of 'tradition' has shown,[86] a very common phenomenon. When this normative conception is threatened by new developments, a defensive attitude usually is the result. Pointing to new evidence to substantiate the original view may be part of this strategy. Of course, each view plays a role in the arena of meanings. As this game is neverending, however, no one is entitled to claim a final victory.

---

[86] A. ERIKSEN: "Like before, just different". Modern popular understandings of the concept of tradition, in *ARV. Nordic yearbook of folklore* 50 (1994) 9-23. Cf. B. BLEHR: On ritual effectiveness. The case of Constitution Day, in *Ethnologia Scandinavica* 1999, 28-43, p. 35-36.

Susan K. Roll

CHRISTMAS: THE MIRROR REFLECTING US BACK TO
OURSELVES

Christmas of 1999 hardly presented a typical example of the festal interaction between the holidays of Christmas and New Year's, due to the
deafening roar of the oncoming Millennium. Global television coverage
beginning December 31st depicted a 24-hour-long succession of New
Year's celebrations, beginning from the Pacific Islands, moving through
a succession of hourly midnights into Asia, then into Europe – the festivities at the London Millennium Dome and the fireworks over the
Thames, the striking light display on the Eiffel Tower in Paris – then on
to the American continent, the dropping of the crystal ball at midnight
over Times Square in New York City, and so forth. Several years beforehand travel companies, hotels and commercial tourist attractions had
booked special events for the millennial New Year's, many of which had
to be cancelled in the last month due to a poor showing of consumer
interest. Large-scale disruption of the social infrastructure due to computer failure when 1999 rolled over into 2000 had been predicted, and
massive investment in computer adjustments by those who could still
manipulate the older programs (the 'COBOL cowboys') as well as public concern led to months on the edge of general panic. Households
stocked up on water and non-perishable foods to ride out the apocalyp-
tic crisis to come when the year turned over 2000. At the fateful hour,
as it happened, there were only a few tiny glitches here and there. January 1, 2000 was simply the day after December 31, 1999. Apocalypse
did not happen. Nor did the 'Y2K bug.'
    The contrast between the Christian feast of Christmas and the civil
feast of New Year's seven days later provides an interesting study in the
interplay of festal behavior particularly in secularized North Atlantic
societies in which the (nominally) religious feast of Christmas takes on
a strongly social/cultural character, and the secular New Year's (particularly this time around) might assume sometimes disconcertingly religious overtones. In this study we will examine first the general structure and dynamics of the festal period November through January in

the culture of the Low Countries along with that of North America as
a point of contrast. We will then explore how the concept of inculturation applies to Christmas both in its distant past and today, and
finally raise a number of related issues in the contemporary cultural
embedding of Christmas.

1. 'THE HOLIDAYS'

The place of Christmas in its environment of surrounding feasts differs
markedly between North America and the Low Countries.[1] 'The holidays,' or 'the holiday season,' generally begins with Thanksgiving (late
November in the U.S.),[2] and extends until New Year's. New Year's tends
to recede in importance behind the high point of Christmas, and is
marked at most by one evening of festivity. In Belgium by contrast 'the
holidays' would begin with St. Nicholas' Day, 6 December, Christmas is
celebrated with more reserve, and New Year's stretches to a month-long
season in its own right. In the Low Countries people send New Year's
cards, not Christmas cards often with religious motifs as in North
America. While in North America it would be a social gaffe if one's
Christmas cards arrive after the 25th of December, here New Year's
wishes can be exchanged right through January. In the U.S. giving gifts,
while increasingly lavish, is confined to Christmas; in Belgium by contrast gift-giving is diffused among St. Nicholas for children, Christmas,
and again on New Year's customarily after children present their parents
and godparents with a letter thanking them for everything they have
done for the children all year. In Belgium Christmas tends to be seen as
a low-key religious feast day, 'just for the family,' and 'just for going to
church,' while the most elaborate and exuberant celebrations are
reserved for New Year's. Several Epiphany folk customs persist in Belgium while in North America a feast of Epiphany is entirely unknown
outside of church.

---

[1] *Sinterklaas en de kerstman. Concurrenten of collega's? Rituelen–commercie–identiteiten* (= Volkskundig bulletin 22/3) (Amsterdam 1996).
[2] We should add that in the 1990's the significance of Halloween has increased
greatly in North America, as measured by the number of households decorating with
orange lights and various ghoulish motifs, costume/fancy dress parties, horror films and
so forth. One could argue that Halloween has become in fact the first major feast in the
sequence which concludes with New Year's.

For example, one time a Belgian research assistant in theology invited an American colleague for a New Year's meditation vigil and party. When the American asked to be excused due to fatigue, saying that in the U.S. many people simply go to bed as usual on New Year's, the Belgian was aghast: "But everyone knows that New Year's is more important than Christmas! You can't possibly stay home alone tonight!"

Here were two well-trained Catholic theologians talking, in the context of at least a nominally Catholic culture. Yet the issue was not whether one Christian feast was more important than the other, nor one secular holiday more important than the other, but rather a comparison between a Christian feast and a purely secular one. Strictly on a socio-cultural level the Belgian was right – even in traditionally Catholic Flanders, New Year's was indeed more important, at least for adults.

The curious irony is that in Belgium the centrality which could be claimed by the feast of the incarnation shifted on the social-experiential level to two surrounding holidays, that of a very minor if not legendary saint on one side, and the totally secular New Year's holiday on the other. Yet in North America Christmas has achieved a legitimacy of its own in the culture, independent of the Christian church as such, and has become a primary vehicle of yearly spiritual renewal on a broad scale, even for the many who would not express any religious or spiritual preference otherwise. The Gospel infancy narratives and the liturgy of the churches for the most part no longer function as determinative for the social-cultural Christmas holiday.

In the aforementioned conversation both a religious and a secular 'timescape' were operative in the same time period, and they shifted back and forth according to a cultural, not a religious set of priorities. In the process the distinction between feasts of religious and of secular origin became blurred, even among theologians. There was more than one scale of priorities operating, and more than one way to estimate the significance of each feast day.

2. THE HISTORICAL ORIGINS OF CHRISTMAS ARE ECHOED IN THE PRESENT

The ancient evidence for the origin of Christmas sets up a sort of case study in the interaction between Christian festal practice and its social-cultural context not entirely dissimilar to the embedding of the feast of

Christmas in a contemporary techno-consumer culture just described. The feast of the Nativity of Christ represents a relatively late addition to the festal calendar of the early church. The first calendar notation appears in 336, the earliest suggestion of Christian liturgical celebration dates from 361, and the feast was apparently unknown in the East until around 380. There are two major competing theories to explain its origins, which remain highly speculative in spite of considerable scholarly research and debate in the first three decades of the 20th century and another spurt of interest in the 1980's.[3]

In spite of the fact that we have no historically reliable attestation of the birth date of Jesus, by the fifth century church fathers and apologists such as Augustine had neatly schematized the significant festal dates in a balanced structure which purported to prove how perfect and inscrutable the eternal designs of God were. There was a feast to correspond with each of the four climatic turning points of the year: Christ was born at the winter solstice, when the sun was at its lowest point and the days at their shortest in the northern hemisphere; and by way of balance, the birth of John the Baptist was celebrated on June 24th, at the summer solstice. In this theory John was supposed to have been conceived after the annunciation to his father Zachariah when Zachariah returned home from acting as high priest in the Temple at the September High Holydays (however he had served as a priest of the order of Abijah, not high priest – this is a flaw in the theory). Christ in turn was believed to have been conceived on the anniversary of his passion, which coincided with the Jewish Passover feast (or one day either side of it, depending on whether one reads the Synoptic gospels or John). To this day Christians mark the feast of the Annunciation to Mary on March 25th, and Christ's birthday on December 25th –

---

[3] See Susan K. ROLL: *Toward the origins of Christmas* (Kampen 1995), especially chapter 2 on the calculation hypothesis, and chapter 3 on the history of religions hypothesis. Thomas J. TALLEY: *The origins of the liturgical year*, second edition (Collegeville 1990) is the foremost contemporary proponent of the calculation hypothesis, historically the minority opinion. A selection of authors associated with the one or another form of the history of religions hypothesis include Bernard BOTTE: *Les origines de la Noël et de l'Épiphanie* (=Textes et études liturgiques 1) (Louvain 1932); Hieronymus FRANK: Gründe für die Entstehung des römischen Weihnachtsfestes, in Theodor BOGLER (ed.): *Weihnachten heute. Der Weihnachtsfest in der pluralistischen Gesellschaft* (Maria Laach 1966) 36-49; Adrian NOCENT: *Célébrer Jésus Christ. L'année liturgique* (Paris 1975) 20-22.

precisely nine months later.[4] The date of Christ's conception was also popularly believed to have been the anniversary of the creation of the world, or alternately the fourth day of creation, and this coincided with the spring equinox and with the Passover, the constitutive founding-event of the Jewish people.[5]

Augustine and others found Scriptural support for this schema in John 3, 30, the words of the Baptist, "He must increase, but I must decrease." In the northern hemisphere, the hours of daylight begin to increase after the winter solstice, the birth date of Christ, which in the old Julian calendar was marked not on the current December 21st but on December 25th; and correspondingly, daylight begins to decrease after the summer solstice, the birth of John the Baptist, June 24th. So here was a neat little square structure of feasts linked tightly with nature and the cosmos, already in place in the fifth century.

Yet if Christmas had remained only a feast conceived in the intellect, extracted from the cosmic year with mathematical precision if not logic, and forcibly imposed upon reluctant local worshiping communities (as indeed it was in the late fourth century in the East)[6] it could hardly have put down deep roots in the religious psyche of European Christians. To draw a common thread between the past and the present, the most useful paradigm may be that of the inculturation of the liturgical year in an informal sense which refers to the ethnic, cultural /social, climate, and gender embedding of particular Christian feast days, and Christian festal practice in general.

The strictly formal sense of the term 'inculturation of the liturgy,' would refer to the process by which certain adaptations of a Roman rite may be made on a national or regional level. For our purposes however inculturation can also refer to the way in which core Christian events, ideas and values are expressed in the thought forms, vocabulary and cultural structures of a given defined society or subgrouping. This gradual, natural inculturation process owes as much or more to religious practice as it takes shape at the grassroots than to planned implementation with a particular vision or goal in mind. Over a period of time it might seep its way upward into the theological formulation or

---

[4] Augustine of Hippo: *Sermon 287*, in J.P. MIGNE: *Patrologia Latina* 38, 1302.

[5] Anscar CHUPUNGCO: *The cosmic elements of Christian Passover* (Rome 1977) (= Studia Anselmiana 72, = Analecta liturgica 3) 40.

[6] This is evident in John CHRYSOSTOM's sermon *In diem natalem*, in J.P. MIGNE: *Patrologia Graeca* 49, 351-362.

policy-making structure of the church: a process of inculturation from below, as it were.

Perhaps no other feast on the Christian calendar has found itself so thoroughly inculturated in contemporary North Atlantic nations, nor with such ambivalent and controversial results. The roots of this inculturation, and interestingly of the ambivalence as well, go back to its very start. The predominant school of opinion concerning the origins of Christmas points to a series of intriguing, if not conclusive, parallels between the Nativity feast of Christ and certain phenomena in fourth-century Roman culture:

(1) the fact that the winter solstice on the old Julian calendar, December 25th, had been celebrated among the adherents of the cult of Mithras as the birth of Mithras, their sun-god, and later beginning in 275 as the *Natalis Solis Invicti*, the birth of the Invincible Sun, when the sun-god was placed at the head of the Roman pantheon by the emperor Aurelian;

(2) the fact that scholars' most reliable conjectures for the time-period of the origin of the Nativity feast coincide with the rise of state-sponsored sun worship in the Roman Empire;

(3) the factor which ties these together are the numerous instances of analogies made between Christ and the sun among patristic writers both in the West and the East beginning in the same period. While these parallels do not in themselves prove that Christmas came about as a direct result of the influence of Roman non-Christian culture of the time, they do lay a foundation for understanding the contemporary inculturation of the Christmas feast not as an aberration nor as an encroachment of 'the secular world' or even 'the pagan world' upon Christian civilization, but as progressively integrated elements which influence each other.

3. ISSUES IN THE INTERPLAY BETWEEN CHURCH AND CULTURE AT CHRISTMAS

Examining the broad spectrum of contemporary issues draws the observer deeper and deeper into a complex of cultural templates overlaid upon the religious Nativity feast (and sometimes the other way around). Applying a critical analytical eye to these issues is almost certain to shatter any lingering naïve hope of retrieving a child's simple wonderment at Christmas. Nonetheless the contemporary North Atlantic Christmas provides a wealth of fascinating possibilities for exploring cultural / festal interaction.

3.1. Incarnation and the body

Part of the enduring attraction of the infancy narrative is the idea that Christ was born into circumstances representing the most tenuous human existence thinkable. His parents were on the road in spite of his mother's advanced pregnancy, unable to find decent shelter even at such a crucial time, so that he was born in a dirty stable under unhygienic and makeshift conditions. Christ identifies himself with the lowest-ranking homeless persons on the face of the earth.

To choose to give over power, to empty oneself and become self-less, is a radically different existence from the deep-rooted internal poverty and emptiness of those who never had a self to begin with – persons oppressed on racial, gender or economic grounds who can hardly imagine personal dignity or legitimate empowerment. Sacrificing one's self is a meaningless concept to those who never had a self to lose.

So one significant aspect of the idea of incarnation is the affirmation that one's self is created and loved by God, loved so much that God also freely took on a human self. The immediate complement of this aspect is the ongoing, dynamic nature of incarnation: if incarnation pertains only to one specific time-period and one geographic location, then the Nativity feast might be today simply a historical topic, perhaps a notation on a pious calendar, but hardly a feast capable of marshalling the interest and involvement even of post-Christians.

More immediately 'incarnation' signifies a profoundly sensate, bodily reality: not only the Christian doctrine that God took on human flesh, but the idea that human flesh, glorious in its sensuality yet frighteningly vulnerable and prone to decay, is somehow holy. This is consistent with new thinking particularly among feminist theologians on the goodness of the body and its centrality as a locus of knowing.[7] Incarnation levels out hierarchy and domination/submission paradigms by proposing a continuum between body and spirit.

---

[7] See especially the work of the Dutch national research program in Jonneke BEKKENKAMP & Maaike DE HAARDT (eds): *Begin with the body. Corporeality, religion and gender* (Leuven 1998).

3.2. The relation of Advent and Christmas

The distinction between Advent and Christmas can be set up several ways. Churchgoers mark the liturgical season of Advent most concretely by lighting one candle on the Advent wreath for each of the four Sundays, ritually measuring the four weeks preceding Christmas. Meanwhile outside the church walls the commercial season of Christmas has been steadily gaining momentum by a relentless buildup of civic decorations, an array of merchandise for gifts and home decorations in the shops, and inescapable Christmas music both broadcast and in live performance. This is exemplified by the German *Weihnachtsmarkt* which draws numbers of Dutch and Belgian shoppers and has spawned similar markets in towns of the Low Countries with all of the commercial potential of the German markets, if usually less of the charm. In North America Christmas merchandise appears row upon row in the shops already in September, and the front page of the daily newspaper counts off the number of shopping days before Christmas.

The two contiguous liturgical seasons of Advent and Christmas parallel the secular (pre)-Christmas season and the secular post-Christmas, all four of which pivot on the same turning point, Christmas Day itself. The season of Advent prepares for, but does not as such thematically participate in Christmas because it has a character of its own, unlike the way in which the secular (pre)-Christmas season represents a continual and steadily intensifying Christmas-process, as it were.

Four distinct overlapping seasons with markedly separate characteristics are visible here: one might term them cultural pre-Christmas (which in fact constitutes most of the Christmas season outside the church), religious pre-Christmas (Advent), secular Christmas and religious Christmas. When transferred into the liturgical rhythm the cognitive dissonance induced by shifting back and forth from one timescape to another literally at the church door can lead to a blurring of the two. Realistically the secular timeframe tends to prevail in priority over the religious, or at least exert considerable pressure.[8]

---

[8] Frank C. SENN: The Christmas cycle. Historical origins, traditional practices, and contemporary possibilities, in *Currents in theology and mission* 8 (1981) 330, applies to the contemporary experience of Christmas H. Richard Niebuhr's categories of "Christ against culture" (the frenetic pre-Christmas activities), "Christ of culture" (acceptance of the secular on its own terms), "Christ above culture" (the reactive attitude of many church leaders, unworkable because of the diminishing influence of Christianity upon

Epiphany as the liturgical end-point of the religious Christmas season introduces more difficulties precisely because of its problematic nature and lack of a compelling festal object in either the rationale and readings for the church feast, or for the most part in contemporary folk customs in much of the West. Some old folk customs persist in Germany and the Low Countries: the marking of doorjambs with the year and "C[aspar] + M[elchior] + B[althasar]," as well as the custom of children dressing as the Three Kings and collecting money. By and large however Epiphany fails to capture the imagination or inspire much depth of reflection among Anglo-Saxon Christians, and functions simply as a marker on a certain calendar day that the religious Christmas season has come to a close.

3.3. Christmas and marginal or nominal Christians

Generally when persons baptized and raised as Christians leave the church, whether through a sudden break in anger or outrage, or a gradual process of drifting away due to indifference or disengagement, Christmas seems to be one of 'the last things to go'. Even those who hold on to bitterness toward the church of their youth tend to return, if at all, on Christmas Eve, far more than at Easter, and because the season of the year triggers an old and deep association in their lives. Marginal Christians crowd into the masses at Christmas, particularly Christmas Eve, less as participants than as spectators, to retrieve something of their childhood sense of belonging. Hearing the familiar Christmas story serves the comforting repetitive function known all too well to parents of toddlers who demand that the parent read the same story exactly the same way, over and over. All the sensory aspects of the Christmas liturgy engage the imagination and call up associations which operate beyond the level of cognition and touch them more deeply than the pain or emptiness which propelled them away from the church – smells of pine and incense, evocative and heartrendingly familiar Christmas music, poetic lyrics, mysteriously flickering candles in a hushed crowd obscured in darkness, and above all of these, a sense of a mysterious presence and a depth of beauty and meaning which evades words.

the culture), "Christ and culture in paradox" (which affirms the pressure many Christians are under while caught between the two, but does not encourage any change for the better), and "Christ the transformer of culture" (in Senn's view the only practical alternative to an unworkable counter-cultural stance regarding Christmas).

One factor which might account for the intensely magnetic draw which Christmas exercises on marginal, often alienated Christians, could be the integration of compelling birth/life symbolism with the greatest beauty in music, decor and text that the parish can muster, as an aesthetic experience. Another aspect is simply the pervasiveness of the socio-cultural season of Christmas and the effect this may have both of de-ecclesiasticizing the feast so that it might not present a threatening face – a point crucial especially to those dealing with traumas such as clergy abuse – but also to make it possible to let down one's guard, to give in to one's affective side. Christmas gives permission, as it were, to express feelings not otherwise considered quite socially acceptable or appropriate – sentimentality, nostalgia, or simple optimism.

3.4. The geography of Christmas

By no accident did Christmas as a feast of light develop in the Northern hemisphere entangled with deep pre-Christian roots of midwinter Jul-feasts or solstice vigil bonfires. Against the background of frigid, dark, damp, often snowy winter weather, the turning at the winter solstice promised long-term hope for the future, not only as psychological encouragement but the hope of plain survival in agrarian societies. The sharp clash between the traditional Christmas symbolism rooted in the cold dark Northern hemisphere and the totally opposite climatic conditions of late December in the Southern hemisphere, reflects a compelling credibility gap between practice and reality in the South. In Australia for example, when Christmas occurs during summer vacation and many families escape the heat at the beach, shops still play "Jingle Bells" and "White Christmas" as background music. In Rio de Janeiro, Christmas cards with cute snowy village scenes typical of Europe are sold in 35ºC weather.

One liturgical scholar suggests changing the date of Christmas only in the Southern hemisphere to their midwinter to maintain the link between Christmas and (relatively) cold weather.[9] However although there is no historical evidence to establish 25 December as the birth date of Jesus, this fact bears little relevance to the contemporary experience

---

[9] Anscar CHUPUNGCO: The adaptation of the liturgical year. A theological perspective, in Giustino FARNEDI (ed.): *Traditio et progressio* (Rome 1988) (= Studia Anselmiana 95, = Analecta liturgica 12) 149-161, p. 158-160.

of Christmas because of its deep-rootedness in the civil as well as liturgical calendar, as well as fragmenting the worldwide festal calendar into local calendars. Yet the present situation can easily be interpreted as a form of liturgical imperialism of the North over the South, since the lived reality of those in the South is radically separate from the dominant symbols characteristic of Christmas.

The theme of light, whether exemplified in the liturgy or by the winter solstice, remains a primary experiential evocation of Christmas – but specifically under the climatic conditions prevailing in the Northern hemisphere. In northern Europe the streets are lit with dazzling delicate white lights strung in designs and hung as an archway of brilliant light down the street. In the United States and Canada individual homes are customarily strung with multicolored lights draped around trees, edging roofs and window frames, blinking furiously, illuminating garish plastic manger scenes or Santa figures. Almost in a spirit of neighborhood competition one house may splash around all of these at the same time in a riotous blast of color and light, at once exuberant, joyful and totally overdone.

Clearly humans respond to the sharp contrast of light against darkness. Similarly, traveling through a winter night buffeted by bitter winds, slipping on icy pavement or gingerly steering one's car on treacherous roads, can be a profound and frightening experience, ending in relief by finally arriving in a warmly heated, brightly lit building or safe at home. The sensory associations linked to the Christmas holiday in a northern climate, together with a realistic sense of danger, potentially evoke a sort of ground-level spirituality, if nothing else a sense of dependence on the clemency of the power which governs the universe.

As above however, the beauty and the evocative power of these contrasts have to do with specific climatic conditions in a particular region at a particular time of year. The inculturation issues provide ample cause to relativize the symbolic configurations too long presented as determinative for the feast, and to permit a greater openness for Christians celebrating the same feast with the same themes, at the same time of the year, but in a vastly different climate, to express the character of the feast in terms of their own lived environmental reality.

3.5. Dualism and racism

The metaphor of light shining in the darkness, whether drawn from the scripture texts read at Christmas liturgies or from the solstice, need not automatically evoke the association of light with all that is positive, and darkness with all which is negative. Along with the generally positive symbolic connotations of light, more negative ones exist: intense sunlight can mean unbearable heat, sun-blindness, sunburn, even eventual skin cancer, linked to the global warming trend and the 'greenhouse effect'. By the same token, darkness need not always signify something evil or frightening: darkness could also suggest safety or protection; peace, stillness; mystery, excitement, intrigue; infinite unknown depths or heights; or the all-enveloping environment of the womb.

The motif of the sun as identified with Christ provided a way for patristic-era bishops and preachers both to co-opt the popular and familiar figure of the sun, and to employ it within the parameters of Christianity. Those patristic-era preachers whose sermon texts linking Christmas and intra-Christian doctrinal controversy have survived, applied the metaphor of light polemically to their own particular doctrinal stance. Yet in increasingly multi-racial European societies the uncritical use of a simplistic light=good, dark=bad paradigm might not inconceivably promote discrimination against dark-skinned persons.

The very act of setting up an absolute dichotomy in itself exposes the terms of the dichotomy to a ranking in regard to value or goodness: a dualism becomes valuational, almost automatically. The value assigned to each of the terms depends upon who has the power to define the categories, and in whose interest such a definition would operate. Human beings exist with light skin, dark skin, or any of a range of variations, shades and undertones in between. Yet the deeply-rooted, pervasive and enduring nature of racism indicates that on some deep level of consciousness light skin is considered better, more highly-valued, perhaps even cleaner, purer and less susceptible to sin and evil than dark. Compare Psalm 51, "Cleanse me of sin… wash me, and I shall be whiter than snow."

3.6. Commercialism and pragmatism

The easiest target for an uninspired preacher at Christmas is its accelerating commercialization and plain greed, exemplified by the replacement of the lovely legend of St. Nicholas by the ubiquitous Santa Claus. Yet one could argue that the extensive commodification of Christmas arises precisely from the fact that this one Christian feast has managed to retain its relevance in pluralistic or post-Christian Western societies. In a highly technologized society, function operates as the primary value, while questions of meaning are relegated to the private sphere. Christmas however also manages to serve some pragmatic functions in a capitalistic society:

(1) as a legal holiday which, like vacation time, provides an opportunity for rest and recreation before one plunges back into the 'really important' work of producing and consuming;[10]
(2) as a means of promoting the health of the consumer sector of the economy by stimulating the purchase of gifts and the increased consumption of goods;
(3) by promoting vacation travel and tourism;
(4) to recall societal values, as shown in the fact that heads of state take the opportunity to deliver an inspiring or value-reaffirming address to their people.

The down side of acknowledging the functional virtues of the Nativity feast is the reluctant recognition that not only marginal Christians but also often those involved in the church tend to carry over a passive consumerist attitude fostered by the social normativity of market values. In the same way that marginal Christians might show up at the church office to request a wedding or a funeral much as they would call the plumber to fix a leak, the liturgy of Christmas can be misinterpreted as a sort of consumer service, produced by the church and available upon demand. This misperception of the nature of the church as a commercial provider of custom services tends to perpetuate a relationship between such persons and the church community characterized by both dependency and disengagement. Detached from the ongoing life of the church and its people and lacking a personal commitment of their own, the infrequent contacts with the church initiated by these people leave them unable to participate fully because they simply don't know what is going on.

3.7. 'Producing' Christmas in the family

A more specific and more widespread concern regarding the ethos of Christmas is simply the degree to which Christmas as a feast accompa-

---

[10] As D.A. SEEBER: Plädoyer für Weihnachten, in Sigrid BERG: *Weihnachten. Materialien und Entwürfe für den Religionsunterricht* (Stuttgart and Munich 1978) 50-56, p. 55, points out, leisure time itself becomes a product to be consumed which truncates the possibility to experience a feast as a gratuitous open space.

nied by its associated customs, visual images, music and practices, represents a product in itself, manufactured to specifications by often strenuous and exhausting human efforts at that time of the year. Not only the pressure of shopping, decorating, writing cards and letters, baking, producing (or consuming) Christmas concerts and other programs, paying attention to shut-ins or distant relatives, but more deeply, the pressure to produce the ideal Christmas can turn into a vicious trap, particularly for women. Understandably parents feel a certain obligation to 'produce' a memorable Christmas for their children precisely because this will form part of their lifelong store of treasured memories: the special foods and decorations, the excitement, the anticipation. Recognizing the extent to which celebrating Christians themselves work unconscionably hard every year to manufacture Christmas as a product for private and short-term consumption should mitigate the all too easy condemnation of the advertising industry or the retail sector. The production of Christmas contradicts probably the single relatively uncontaminated value inherent in the deep core of the feast: that of the grateful and humble reception of a gratuitous gift.

3.8. Gender and power

The fundamental iconic image identified with Christmas is that of a mother and baby. In the vast majority of societies throughout recorded history this visual image expresses a conventional role, even the normative role, of women as such. On the positive side Christmas can contribute a regular symbolic affirmation of the dignity of childbearing as well as a public reaffirmation of the importance of human relationality. However there is another insidious dualism operative here: the splitting and stereotyping of human traits and behaviors as characteristic of one gender or the other, with those traits associated with the female downgraded in importance. When the role of mother is sentimentalized and domesticated, women as such are less likely to be taken seriously as full human persons distinguishable from their primary relationships.

A strong comparison can be set up with the polemic denunciations often made against the contemporary commercialized Christmas holiday: too shallow, childish and emotional; too busy, too focused on material trivialities; too small-scale, privatized and family centered and not enough involved in hard social realities. All of these echo some of the most damaging stereotypes of women perpetuated in patriarchal societies. Ironically both the dismay at the commodified Christmas, and the deep psychological credibility of Christmas as the celebration of God's incarnation, are derived directly from the same general constellation of characteristics and values which have been invoked to argue the inferiority and dependency of women, and to justify the disempowerment of women.

The perduring popularity of Christmas even in non-religious and non-supportive contemporary cultures testifies to the authenticity and importance of the deeper underlying human values it brings to the surface, and suggests that in spite of all the rhetoric concerning the abuses of the contemporary Christmas, its basic instinct is on target. What is fundamentally important however is that a constructive, fearless and wise interpretative process be undertaken upon the distinctively 'feminine' character of the feast by women-identified women, in other words those who have themselves undergone a journey of progressive consciousness. When accompanied by a healthy, realistic and appropriately critical hermeneutic, the icon of mother and baby which epitomizes Christmas could serve as a springboard for reclaiming the feast as, in one aspect, a celebration of God as Mother.

3.9. The male savior in the manger

The historical evolution of the analogy of the sun with the exercise of power and the godlike status of the emperor, and the way in which all of these formed the conceptual context for the growing Christian church of the same era is relatively easy to document.[11] Linking these elements further with the feast of Christmas is slightly more speculative. Sufficient patristic homiletic evidence exists to connect Christmas with the sun, and the sun with Christ, but the cultural background conducive to sun-worship is what serves to tie all these with the governmental paradigm which exalts domination and centralized power. Exploring the same mental terrain from a psychological approach is even more speculative in nature, but reveals some interesting dimensions of the entire problematic.

One valid starting-point can be the image of the baby in the manger scene. A new baby not only absorbs virtually all the parents' energy and much of their sleep in its first few months, but draws attention like a

[11] See ROLL: *Christmas,* esp. chapter 3.

magnet from all visitors. The new baby is showered with gifts and affection, sometimes much to the chagrin of its older siblings. From a psychological standpoint the central triad of the traditional creche, Mary, Joseph and the baby Jesus, form a perfect idealized family configuration, taken from the egocentric standpoint of the child. The baby is the undisputed center of the manger scene, the cornerstone of the entire structure, surrounded by the parents on each side, or a few shepherds or magi bringing lavish gifts, all kneeling before the baby in utter adoration while angels sing his praise from above. This baby has no siblings which might constitute a threat to the baby's totalizing absorptive power – the idea that Mary was a virgin would permanently exclude such competition in any case. The baby is a wanted child, cherished as a gift of God both to his adoring parents and to the entire universe, for all time.[12]

One could hardly consciously design a visual representation more immediately appealing to the common human longing to be a wanted child, to be unfailingly loved and adored, and on a more immature level, to have all one's needs promptly and generously met and to be the permanent center of attention. The subtle psychological working of the celebration of a feast which centers around the gratification of ego needs on such a basic level is obvious. What might be less obvious is the healing potential of meditation on the image for those carrying deep psychological scars from their own childhood rooted precisely in the lack of such deep love and respect represented in the manger scene. The nostalgic desire to return to an idealized warm, safe naïvety of childhood which characterizes especially the Anglo-Saxon Christmas, a trait so easy to ridicule and to belittle, could for many people point up a legitimate need for long-term psychological healing.

The exclusive use of the male pronoun to refer to the baby in the discourse above is not accidental, nor is it meant to refer only to the Christ child. The centrality of the baby functions with the self-evident understanding that this most highly valued baby is of course a male. In traditional patriarchal societies the birth of a boy is a cause for special rejoicing. His birth confirms the father's masculinity, and secures the

---

[12] Arnold ULEYN: Kerstmis, het feest van het kind, in A. ULEYN: Religiositeit en fantasie (Baarn 1978) 18-30, p. 22; also Manfred GÖRG: Kindlicher Gott – Gottliches Kind, in Diakonia 19/6 (November 1988) 393-397; Johannes SCHLOSSER: Urbilder – Schlüssel zum Kirchenjahr (Regensburg 1980) 32-35; André GOOSSENS: Oerbeelden en liturgisch jaar, in Tijdschrift voor liturgie 76 (1992) 314-315.

mother's position and prestige in the home as well as her future economic security in widowhood. The son would carry on the family name, receive the inheritance and perpetuate the future lineage of the family. The application of these cultural realities to the birth of Jesus is reflected in the scriptural titles recited at Christmas: the Christ child is a prince in the line of King David, the Prince of Peace, the Savior of his people, the Anointed One, promised through the ages, the only Son of the Most High, the Almighty Father. Christ as the 'Sun of Justice' in patristic texts was automatically a male power-figure. The male titles give enormous strength and force to the entire paradigm, when the unspoken common understanding is that a male child is more wanted because he is infinitely more valuable than a female.

Potentially to the contrary, celebrating incarnation could point more authentically to the viability of a radically different non-dominative model of leadership. Such a model draws its credibility from an emerging awareness of the fundamental value of human dignity, human rights and mutuality in relations of justice. Ideally this should break an uncritical identification of the image of the all-powerful heavenly Father God with an analogously powerful human male dominator, individual or collective, who is not God. Opening a space for perceiving God among the powerless opens up the deep inner dynamic of the incarnation: the ongoing coming-to-dwell-with-us of the God who, in the words of the Philippians hymn, was "made in human likeness".

4. CONCLUSION

Christmas, for good or ill, reflects us back to ourselves at twice life size. The earliest Christmas feast of late antiquity, to the extent we can judge from the extant sermon texts, reflected its own cultural embedding in a rapidly fragmenting society in which the imperial power of the Emperor, assimilated to the sun-god, could no longer secure peace within the borders of the Roman Empire. In turn, contemporary Northern/Western technological societies exhibit their own progress or regress, their own characteristics, norms and conceptual structures. One prominent characteristic, one with an intense impact upon individuals and social groups, is global commercialization and the normativity of a market-oriented society.

The commercialization of Christmas is, to paraphrase a film cliché, "inculturation from hell". This consumer Christmas is well adapted to the contemporary operative values of the geographic regions in which it first flourished, firmly established in its socio-cultural environment, on the environment's terms. The massive production, advertising and marketing essential to the retail sector of the economy in developed countries serves as a predominant secular form of the feast, the content of which derives not only from the incarnation in the salvation history of Christian belief, but even beyond Christianity in a complex of climatic change, folklore, custom, art, familial bonding, common values and personal and collective memories. The Gospel story of the birth of Christ secures the base meaning, the original core and point of reference, yet the story does not alone determine what Christmas is. The feast has long since taken on a life of its own.

Susan K. Roll

EASTER: FROM DEATH TO NEW LIFE

The water splashed and formed bubbles on the surface of a shallow pool, and below the ripples one could make out a mosaic in the form of a Jerusalem cross. In this setting, the immersion pool for baptism in the sanctuary of a working-class parish in Texas, ten candidates for initiation were invited, one by one, to step into the pool of water where the priest was already waiting, barefoot and with the skirts of his vestments dragging in the water. The priest called Kathy, the first of the candidates with the words, "Step into the tomb of Christ to be reborn!", and reached out to clasp her hands. He asked Kathy, "Do you believe in God the Father Almighty...", inviting her to profess her new faith in the ancient words of the Apostles' Creed. Then Kathy knelt in the water as the priest bent over, placed his right hand on her forehead and his left on her back, and called out, "I baptize you in the name of the Father...", suddenly plunging her headfirst into the pool of water, "...and of the Son...", dunking her a second time, "...and of the Holy Spirit..." By now Kathy's head went fully under the water and flew back up, splashing droplets into the air and on the crowd gathered around the edge. The assembly sang a joyous "Alleluia" refrain, Kathy beamed and dripped and glowed with happiness as she stepped out of the pool. The catechumenate director and Kathy's godparents wrapped her in a dry sheet over the wet sheet and the bathing suit she was wearing. And the priest reached across the water to the following candidate, Kim, "Do you believe in God the Father Almighty..." Kim reported afterward, "The water was so warm, and so inviting, and so embracing. It was so powerful. I just wanted to get into it so bad."

Shortly afterward the ten newly baptized stood in a row for their confirmation. A tall carafe of blessed oil was held over each candidate's head. The fragrant yellow oil poured in a silent, stately slender rivulet over Kathy's tightly braided hair, as the priest gently spread it by hand over her hair, her temples, her cheeks, as he did with each one in turn. The oil, in Kim's words, was "warm, beautiful. It ran all down my face. I could taste it, I could smell it, I could feel it."

When the video reached its end and the final credits began to roll, adult students in the evening sacraments class sniffled and blinked, red-eyed, trying not to show that they had been touched to tears by what they had seen.[1]

By way of contrast, consider the conventional associations with the Easter holiday: Easter eggs, Easter baskets, Easter bunnies, fuzzy Easter chicks. Masses of spring flowers brightening homes indoors and dispersing sweet fragrance in the mild outdoor air. Candy. More candy.

According to a survey conducted by the Dutch broadcasting service NOS in 1996, less than half of the respondents could accurately identify the original Christian meaning of the Easter feast: 44% knew that Easter celebrated the resurrection of Jesus. By contrast some 80% knew that Christmas celebrated the birth of Christ, one-third knew that Good Friday marked the crucifixion of Christ, and one-quarter could identify the origin of Pentecost. Not unsurprisingly, persons with a religious upbringing fared better in recognizing the original rationale for these feasts, those with more education better than the less educated, and older persons better than youth. Only 13% of young people knew what Good Friday was.[2]

In this study we will explore the massive gulf which exists between the envisioned religious meaning of the celebration of Easter so eloquently depicted in the above-described video presentation of a parish Easter Vigil baptismal liturgy, and Easter's festal reverberations among the population at large. After a glance at the third-century celebration of baptism at the Easter Vigil, we will explore more deeply the baptismal link with Easter and the place of Easter in the liturgical year, then raise several other issues pertinent to the contemporary Easter feast and its liturgical celebration in North Atlantic societies.

1. THE LITURGICAL CELEBRATION OF EASTER

The renewal and rescheduling of the night Easter Vigil in the Catholic liturgical calendar in 1951 went hand in hand with the restoration of

[1] Gabe HUCK (producer): *This is the night* (Chicago 1992).

[2] Wim WYLIN: Paasfeest (commentary on a survey by the Dienst Kijk- en Luisteronderzoek of the NOS), broadcast by Radio Vlaanderen Internationaal on 8 April 1996. The author added that the results of this survey would apply also to Flanders, although the process by which secularization was steadily eroding the influence of Christian culture on public life was taking place "with a delay of some ten years" in Belgium compared to the Netherlands.

the adult catechumenate as the normative process by which unbaptized adults become Catholic Christians. The Easter Vigil, the "mother of all vigils", summarizes the pillars of the Christian faith and celebrates them by setting the death and resurrection of Christ in a profound, deeply anchored and richly sensuous ritual setting. The vision of one great feast, the high point of the entire liturgical year, with the potential to renew powerfully the commitment of all baptized persons within revitalized worshiping communities, is gradually being realized here and there in different countries, or in individual parishes, though relatively little in regions in which infant baptism remains a dominant cultural custom or in which a nominal Christianity maintains a toehold on popular culture in the face of increasing secularization, pragmatism and consumerism.

The three liturgical events of the Triduum – Holy or Maundy Thursday, Good Friday, and Easter – commemorate successively the final meal of Jesus of Nazareth with his disciples, his arrest, trial and execution, and two days later his disciples' powerful experience that he was in fact alive and continued to appear among them. The apostle Paul in the mid-first century had exhorted Christians saying, "Our paschal lamb, Christ, has been sacrificed. Therefore let us keep the festival [...] with the unleavened bread of sincerity and truth."[3] This indicates the Hebrew roots of the symbolic link between Christ's sacrificial death at or near the Passover, and the Paschal Lamb. While early Christians of Jewish ancestry may or may not have continued to celebrate some form of Pesach, the extant documentation concerning the Christianized Paschal feast has been strongly colored by its rhetorical and anti-Judaic use.[4] By the late second century a sizeable group of Christians in Asia Minor staunchly celebrated Easter on the Jewish Passover date, the fourteenth day of the first spring month of the Hebrew lunisolar calendar or its equivalent on the local solar calendar[5] regardless of the day of the week. Known as Quartodecimans, their practice was at odds with that attested among Western Christians of rotating the feast to the following Sunday which was more consistent with the significance of the Sunday

<hr/>

[3] I Corinthians 5, 7, New Revised Standard Version.

[4] According to Karl GERLACH: *The Antenicene Pascha. A rhetorical history* (= Liturgia condenda 7) (Leuven 1998) 399: "(...) a christianized Pesach, with some or all rituals intact, did not survive into the second century except perhaps in isolated Jewish-Christian groups for whose ritual life there are almost no literary remains."

[5] Thomas J. TALLEY: *The origins of the liturgical year* (Collegeville 1991) 8-9.

proto-eucharistic gathering of the assembly. The latter practice, which took as its object the first post-resurrection appearances of Christ on the first day of the week, prevailed as the principle of setting the date of Easter: to this day Easter is celebrated among Western Christians on the first Sunday following the first full moon following the spring equinox, in other words sometime between March 22 and April 25.

By the third century Easter consisted of a ritual sequence of a preparatory fast, a concluding celebration, and a nocturnal vigil as the transition in between, which culminated in the Eucharist. An extensive text in the *Apostolic Tradition* of Hippolytus in the early third century attests to the procedure for baptizing candidates at the Easter Vigil:

> And they shall spend the whole night in vigil; they shall be read to and instructed...
> At the time when the cock crows, first let prayer be made over the water. Let the water be flowing in the font or poured over it... They shall take off their clothes. Baptize the little ones first.... Then baptize the men, and lastly the women, who shall have loosened their hair, and laid down their gold and silver ornaments.[6]

The text sets forth instructions for blessing the oil of thanksgiving and the oil of exorcism, the ritual words to be said at the anointing with the oil of exorcism, then the procedure for baptism by the bishop or priest: in the words of the Apostles' Creed, the candidate was first to profess faith in God the Father,

> And the giver, having his hand placed on [the candidate's] head, shall baptize [the candidate] once. And then he shall say: "Do you believe in Christ Jesus, the Son of God, who was born from the Holy Spirit..." And when [the candidate] has said, "I believe," [the candidate] shall be baptized again. And he shall say again: "Do you believe in the holy Spirit and the holy Church and the resurrection of the flesh?" Then [the one] who is being baptized shall say, "I believe," and thus [the candidate] shall be baptized a third time.[7]

Following the triple immersion baptism each one was anointed by the priest with the oil of thanksgiving, clothed, brought into church where the bishop laid hands on each, anointed each again with the oil of thanksgiving, and gave the kiss of peace. The liturgy proceeded with the prayer of the faithful, then the liturgy of the eucharist.

---

[6] Geoffrey J. CUMING (ed.): *Hippolytus. A text for students* (Bramcote 1976) 18.
[7] CUMING: *Hippolytus* 19.

The Easter Vigil managed to retain some baptismal character until the thirteenth century even when no baptisms were performed. A blessing of the paschal candle was added to the Vigil liturgy, which had shifted back in time to the early afternoon in the eighth century and as far as Saturday morning by the twelfth. In the twelfth century a blessing of the new fire was instituted as part of the Vigil.[8] Among the Reformers of the sixteenth century, the Lutherans retained Good Friday and Easter, as did the Anglicans, while more radical Reformers rejected all feast days except the Sunday.[9] From the time of the post-Tridentine missal of 1570 up to 1951 very little alteration took place in the Triduum liturgies on the level of Roman liturgical policy. Baroque era texts reflect ritual customs such as processions, benedictions and theatrical pieces. A rite of the elevation of the cross in some localities became the high point, as it were, of the entire Easter celebration.[10]

By the early twentieth century academic research into the ancient sources coupled with the educational and later reform initiatives generated by the Liturgical Movement led to an increasing emphasis on the importance of Easter as the center point of the liturgical year. This was particularly influenced by Odo Casel's theory of the mystery of Christ's presence in the worshiping community.[11] In 1951 the Easter Vigil was returned to its ancient place as the primary vigil feast in the Roman calendar, taking place in the night between Saturday and Easter Sunday. Restored ritual elements included a light-of-Christ procession and the possibility of baptism as well as a renewal of baptismal vows by the assembly. In fact the active role played by the assembled people and the distribution of roles in the liturgy testified to a growing impetus toward general reform of the Roman liturgy to promote active participation. In 1956 the entire Holy Week beginning with Passion/Palm Sunday was renewed in its schedule, along with a number of ancient liturgical customs such as the washing of feet on Holy Thursday.

---

[8] Hansjörg AUF DER MAUR: *Feiern im Rhythmus der Zeit I. Herrenfeste in Woche und Jahr* (= Gottesdienst der Kirche. Handbuch der Liturgiewissenschaft 5) (Regensburg 1983) 84; and Richard M. NARDONE: *The story of the Christian year* (Mahwah 1991) 59-60.

[9] NARDONE: *Story* 101.

[10] AUF DER MAUR: *Feiern* 125.

[11] Odo CASEL: *Gegenwart des Christus-Mysteriums. Ausgewählte Texte zum Kirchenjahr* (Mainz 1986).

As a result of the foundation for liturgical reform set forth in *Sacro-sanctum Concilium* (1963) and the *General Norms for the Liturgical Year* (1969) the originally experimental form of the Vigil was taken a few steps further, using for example a maximum of seven Hebrew Bible readings, not 12 as in the Tridentine missal. The *Rite of Christian Initiation of Adults* was promulgated in 1974 and appeared in the same year in a provisional English translation. The Dutch translation of the rite (*Het doopsel van volwassenen*) by the Nationale Raad voor Liturgie was ready by 1977.[12] The International Committee on English in the Liturgy published the definitive English translation in 1985.

The shift to a concrete baptismal practice within the context of the Easter Vigil is taking place at different rates in different countries. In highly-secularized France, where some experimentation with a renewed catechumenal process took place already in the 1950's, about 11,000 catechumens are preparing for baptism. A sizeable proportion of these come from the working-class and they generally have no cultural background in the Christian faith. In Belgium some parishes have been involved with the catechumenate for a number of years, while in Germany and the Netherlands the rite seems to be at the beginning stages of serious study and implementation. In North America the Rite for the Christian Initiation of Adults has served as the normative practice for adult baptism, as well as providing a catechetical and discernment pattern for baptized adult candidates for full initiation, since the late 1980's. All of the above applies to Roman Catholic practice: while the celebration of Easter night or a pre-dawn vigil has been more recently restored in the practice of reformed churches, the application of baptismal symbolism is not self-evident.[13]

It would be fair to say that the strengthening of the baptismal symbolism of the Vigil liturgy, in other words the dying and rising with Christ in the tomb as represented by baptism in an immersion pool, has yet to substantially influence the general lived experience of the Easter Vigil or the popular festal associations with Easter generally. It is logical that in countries in which cultural Christianity and the expectations of the family influence the decision of parents to have their

---

[12] Jozef LAMBERTS: *Hoogtepunt en bron. Inleiding tot de liturgie* (Averbode/Helmond 1991) 176.

[13] G.F.H. KELLING: *Rond vasten en feesten* (Gorinchem 1992) 111-112 presents a structure and rationale for an Easter daybreak service which, like the Vigil, is not intended to replace Easter Sunday worship.

infants baptized, a baptized but uncatechized adult who expresses interest in the church would start from catechesis and spiritual discernment, if necessary incorporating preparation for confirmation or first eucharist, but not preparation for baptism. Questions have been raised in some quarters concerning the practicability of (re-)introducing an ancient Christian rite, which had developed in a radically different historical and social context, into contemporary worshiping communities, whether in the North Atlantic or elsewhere.[14]

2. THE PASCHAL CENTRALITY OF THE LITURGICAL YEAR

An important component in the post Vatican-II concept of the liturgical year is a shift from a linear concept of the successive feast days and seasons, to the idea that the festal year has a center point: the Paschal mystery, the definitive salvific event of the suffering, death and resurrection of Christ. The Paschal Mystery was the message preached by the earliest Christians. Theologically it constitutes the deep meaning structure or root metaphor of the sacraments, most especially baptism (dying and rising with Christ) and the eucharist (as the memorial of his total self-giving). One principle of the reforms enacted in the *General Norms* involved restoring the central significance of the Paschal Mystery. This had two interconnected results concerning time cycles in liturgical celebration. First, the Sunday took precedence over all saints' days and feast days (apart from several specific dominical feasts) in the new General Roman Calendar of 1969. Secondly, on the yearly cycle the Paschal Mystery, whose summit is celebrated at the Easter Triduum, was more clearly established as the central reference point from which the theological meaning of every other feast of Christ was derived. Each feast of the church year, no matter what its specific historical roots or original intention, was to be interpreted with reference to the foundational paradigm of Christ's suffering, death and resurrection. The logical consequence for liturgical practice would normally be that Easter would be

---

[14] AUF DER MAUR: *Feiern* 141. A 1977 symposium in Austria concluded that at that time "the most pressing task is not to bring about structural change, but to take advantage of the very useful rite we now have. It was felt as a clear defect that the Easter Vigil has too few ties with traditional and new customs, and therefore has still not taken real root among the people." Karl BERG: Introduction to *Celebrating the Easter Vigil* (New York 1983 and Collegeville 1991, originally *Dies ist die Nacht* [Regensburg 1979]) viii.

firmly established as the highest and most significant religious feast day of the entire year. All other feasts would depend theologically upon the Easter event: they would 'radiate' from the meaning-center of the entire festal structure like spokes from the hub of a wheel, each one reflecting certain aspects of the Easter event.

The celebration of the Paschal mystery on a yearly cycle (the Easter Triduum) and on a weekly cycle (the Sunday Eucharistic gathering) anchors the Christian celebration in its Jewish festal antecedents, the Sabbath and the Pascha. In the renewed structure of the liturgical year Easter not only takes priority but also functions as the underlying content of every other major feast. For this reason Christmas, a later feast rooted in the Roman solar calendar, is made to depend structurally and thematically upon the Paschal mystery. In theory the incarnation serves as the chronological precondition for Jesus' death on the cross, but the resurrection gives a retroactively perceived significance to the identity of the baby who was born at Bethlehem.[15]

From a contemporary perspective one might ask whether all this in fact reflects the genuine perception of Christian believers. The answer apparently is No. The real dichotomy exists between Easter and Christmas on the level of experience, the lived experience comprised of personal and collective associations as expressed in festal practice. For many in the northern and western hemispheres Christmas simply seems 'more real' than Easter, more accessible and more integrally a part of that practical experience. The vast majority has had some experience of birth – giving birth or assisting at a birth, rejoicing at a birth in the family – but no one has seen a resurrection. A near-death experience is not resurrection. Resurrection lacks a concrete image as well as clear analogs to lived experience.[16] And an overweening emphasis on the death and resurrection of Christ as the theological justification for his birth seems to demean the profoundly spiritual joy in the birth of a new living creature, a child of God. By extension it trivializes one of the most popularly accessible life-events in which spiritual meaning can still be found and articulated even by marginal Christians or by the unchurched.

---

[15] This might tend to imply that Easter should mark the beginning of the new liturgical year rather than the first Sunday in Advent. One rarely sees this point seriously argued as a suggested reform of the calendar.

[16] Friedrich WINTZER: Auferstehung III, in *Theologische Realenzyklopädie* 4 (Berlin 1979) 540.

By extension family values are traditionally heavily invested in Christmas, a period when in the Northern hemisphere a household more naturally draws together, cozy and comfortable inside on a night which turns dark too early. The inward-turning nesting impulse, as it were, enjoys no counterpart at Easter. Perhaps just such an affirmation of human relational nature holds the potential to satisfy the spiritual hunger evident in the appeal of Christmas, a hunger left unsatisfied by the less tactile death-and-resurrection paradigm of the Easter Triduum.

A further aspect could lie in the observation that contemporary Western Christians in general tend to be 'incarnational' in their faith, rather than redemption-centered and that this tendency persists even after specific forms and habits of worship have disappeared. Perhaps because of its accessibility and its less threatening, less morbid but almost equally dramatic narrative, the Christmas story affirms the often damaged sense of human dignity of alienated Christians. This is far less the case with the story of the Paschal suffering and death of Christ, even when followed by the resurrection, partly because of the heavy overtones of personal guilt and expiation of sin inherent in a redemption/atonement theology of the cross.

3. ADDITIONAL CONTEMPORARY ISSUES IN NORTH ATLANTIC CULTURES

3.1. The date of Easter

In the popular mind Easter tends to be marked as the first of a series of long spring weekends, a seasonal feast consonant with the gradual warming and greening of the earth and increase of light in the Northern hemisphere, a three- or four-day hiatus inviting holiday tourism, particularly conducive to travel southward to even warmer climates. Conveniently located on a Sunday to permit a holiday weekend (a weekend which officially includes Monday in much of Europe) Easter in the North becomes simply the first major spring holiday of the year, an invigorating lift after the winter 'tunnel months' but without the intense emotional investment of Christmas.

A pivotal discrepancy exists between Christmas and Easter in terms of the predictability of their respective positions in the civil calendar. Christmas from its constant position on the 25th of December anchors a constellation of meanings and associations with a defined place in the calendar which forms part of the identity of Christmas: for example, counting a certain number of shopping days before Christmas, or an exact week between Christmas and New Year's. Easter, because its date 'wanders' erratically over a period of five weeks, shifts over the period of early spring, together with its associated meanings and elements, disconnected from a predictable point of reference in the solar calendar. The situation can be confusing enough on the civil calendar since the date of Easter affects holiday periods for schools together with the dates of Ascension, Pentecost Sunday and Monday, and Corpus Christi where this is a civil holiday. In church a parish's liturgy planning also needs to take account of the series of Sundays of the Year, also called Ordinary Time, which breaks off at Ash Wednesday and picks up again after Pentecost, affecting the cycle of lections.

An appendix to *Sacrosanctum Concilium,* the Constitution on the Sacred Liturgy, expressed openness to setting Easter on a fixed date in the conventional Gregorian calendar, generally in early April, with the consent of non-Catholic Christians. While the Reformation churches would have been open to the proposal, the Orthodox did not consent to a fixed Easter date at the vote taken by the World Council of Churches in 1975.[17]

3.2. Inculturation of the Easter Vigil

By 1988 the Congregation for Divine Worship issued a circular letter, On Preparing and Celebrating the Paschal Feasts, which admitted to some lingering concerns regarding the restored Vigil:

> …in some areas where initially the reform of the Easter Vigil was received enthusiastically it would appear that with the passage of time this enthusiasm has begun to wane. The very concept of the Vigil has almost come to be forgotten in some places, with the result that it is celebrated as if it were an evening Mass, in the same way and at the same time as the Mass celebrated on Saturday evening in anticipation of the Sunday.[18]

This suggests a carryover of the habit of attending an anticipated Sunday liturgy on Saturday so as to keep the Sunday clear: church attendance at

---

[17] Adolf ADAM: *The liturgical year* (New York 1981, originally *Das Kirchenjahr mitfeiern. Seine Geschichte und seine Bedeutung nach der Liturgieerneuerung* [Freiburg 1979]) 61.

[18] CONGREGATION FOR DIVINE WORSHIP: *Paschale Solemnitatis* (1988).

Easter can thus be taken care of in such a way as to clear off Easter Sunday for the family, for socializing or for traveling. The intent of the Vigil is to lead into Easter Sunday, not *per se* to substitute for it.

A much deeper issue of inculturation of the Vigil lies in its underlying symbol structures composed of an interrelated network of ritual structure, visual symbols, text, music and other sensory elements characteristic of the Vigil liturgy. Here and there some highly problematic elements show up which suggest unexamined and as yet unresolved layers of Euroamerican normativity, dualism and misogyny.

The first ritual action of the Easter Vigil is the lighting of the new fire, a dramatic, even primordial moment, held in the darkness outdoors in the chill of early spring – that is, in the North. In the Southern hemisphere nature's cycle is in the process of waning, which would permit worshiping communities to make use of natural death symbolism but hardly resurrection. In regions with little discernible seasonal change, or a pattern of rainy and dry seasons, the climatic conditions which occur in March or April can only with difficulty provide symbolic embodiment for the Paschal theology envisioned in the rites.

The verbal expression accompanying the lighting of the fire presents Christ as the light dispelling the darkness, in which light is taken as an unquestioned positive element while darkness symbolizes evil, chaos and danger. This presumes the normativity of a binary either/or split between death and life, and good and evil, none of which has worked traditionally to the advantage of those groups which are represented as the 'bottom-side', the negative identity within the paradigm, particularly women and people of color. The fire in the darkness further symbolizes Christ's victory over death, a central theme of the Vigil celebration, which presumes that death is an enemy to be defeated and conquered, not a natural conclusion to a person's bodily life. If death must be conquered then Jesus' resurrection appearances mean the triumph of the transcendent God not limited by incarnation in a normally fragile and vulnerable human body. This interpretation of resurrection as domination and the defeat of death employs militaristic metaphors which make sense if death is construed as an enemy, but not as a natural and normal occurrence at the waning of the life process. The body, nature, and women all become assimilated to death, the enemy, in this sort of dualistic paradigm.

The tall Easter candle is marked and signed, lighted from the new fire, and carried in solemn procession into the church where it is placed on a stand. Some commentators note that the tall pole-like paschal candle can easily be interpreted as a phallus symbol.[19] The text of the *Exsultet*, a hymn of intense beauty chanted solo in plainsong, echoes the language of vanquishing the enemy and rejoicing over victory. Moreover it employs 'displacement' theology, also known as supercessionism, in which the Hebrew stories of creation, the patriarchs and the liberation from slavery in Egypt are now co-opted and replaced by Jesus, the "true Lamb [who] was slain".[20] Exclusively masculine and monarchical value-laden titles and terms abound: our King, God's throne, the all-powerful Father, eternal Father, the Son who lives and reigns for ever and ever. Redemption and sacrifice themes appear explicitly:

> For Christ has ransomed us with his blood,
> and paid for us the price of Adam's sin to our eternal Father! [...]
> Father, how wonderful your care for us!
> How boundless your merciful love!
> To ransom a slave, you gave away your Son!
> O happy fault, o necessary sin of Adam,
> which gained for us so great a Redeemer![21]

A dualistic gender split appears in the cosmic image of reconciliation, which interestingly echoes the ancient language of the *hieros gamos*, the wedding of a masculine sky deity with an earth goddess:

> Night truly is blessed when heaven is wedded to earth,
> and man [sic] is reconciled with God!

The full list of readings provided for the Vigil liturgy of the word encompasses the scope of Hebrew salvation history from creation up through the prophets. Several of them could be considered problematic for women. The first creation account in Genesis 1:1-2:3 follows a hypnotic rhythmic pattern probably used in ancient cultic worship, but it has parallels in ancient creation myths which speak of creation as an act of form-giving out of, or in defeat of, chaos, formlessness, darkness and

---

[19] Ann Patrick WARE: The Easter Vigil. A theological and liturgical critique, in Marjorie PROCTER-SMITH & Janet R. WALTON (eds): *Women at worship. Interpretations of North American diversity* (Louisville 1993) 83-106, p. 87 writes: "Clearly a phallic symbol, it represents Christ leading the people, enlightening the world. Its form carries the message that a man, Christ, leads, and women are expected to follow. As the lighting of the small tapers indicates, it is from this Light that all other light proceeds."

[20] WARE: Easter Vigil 87.

[21] *The Roman missal. The sacramentary* (Collegeville 1974) 241-242.

water, all womb-images. Genesis 22 can be analyzed from the perspective of sacrifice as a male cultic act to insure patrilineal descent linked to a patriarchal God,[22] even apart from the horrific scene of an innocent young person about to be murdered by his own father, here used as a precursor to the sacrifice/redemption motif applied to Christ as Son of God. Exodus 14 shows a scene of wholesale death of the Egyptian soldiers as the means of liberation for the Hebrews. In Isaiah 54: 5-14 the relation of the people to God is expressed as "a wife married in youth and then cast off", implying a sort of recognizable, if not normative, status of the image.

The liturgy of baptism includes the litany of saints, of whom only seven of the twenty-five named are women,[23] and the blessing of the water which involves the dipping of the Easter candle into the font or pool of water, a visual expression of the masculine symbol penetrating the water as female (and as formless chaos), and rising out as Christ rose from the tomb. The lighted candle is inserted into the water which represents among other things death, the baptismal pool in which candidates will "die and rise with Christ" in baptism. As a result the now-neophytes have been 'reborn', in effect undoing the sinfulness of natural birth from the mother's body by a rebirth "by water and the Spirit" (John 3:5).

3.3. Belief in resurrection

Finally, one cannot underestimate the degree to which diminishing belief in resurrection would undercut the entire festal rationale for the Easter feast: why would people celebrate the resurrection if they do not believe in it? According to the results of the 1991 Europe-wide survey conducted by the European Values Systems Study Group, among respondents of all age groups 70% profess to believe in God, but only 33% believe in resurrection, while 21% believe in reincarnation. In Belgium the figures were lower for each of these: 63% believe in God, 27% in resurrection, and 13% in reincarnation. Among Belgian youth ages 18-24 less than half (45%) believe in God, and 27% in resurrection. In

---

[22] Nancy JAY: *Throughout your generations forever. Sacrifice, religion and paternity* (Chicago and London 1992) xxvii.

[23] Cf. Michael D. WHALEN: In the company of women? The politics of memory in the liturgical commemoration of saints – male and female, in *Worship* 73 (1999) 482-504.

each case, a very significant proportion – more than half of the respondents of all age groups together – of those who believe in God do not accept the idea of resurrection. The survey does not distinguish whether this meant Christ's resurrection, or their own.[24]

4. CONCLUSION

At its most eloquent, Easter expresses, not the sprightly springy optimism of lilies and bunnies and colored eggs, but hope against hope – a deadly serious business, yet profoundly liberating and compellingly necessary. After a century in which two cataclysmic world wars and numerous smaller ones have taken place, the need to speak hope in the face of evil, and to cherish survival snatched from mortal danger, would logically support the festal expression of belief in resurrection. Yet a number of factors militate against the satisfactory festal in-rooting of the renewed form of the Easter liturgy particularly the Vigil, even with its powerful constellation of symbolic, aesthetic and textual multidimensionality. When all of this can successfully be translated into contemporary perceptual categories and made accessible and credible, then the churches will truly be preaching "good news to the poor".

---

[24] Jan KERKHOFS: Waarden-evolutie van jongeren in een postmoderne cultuur, in *Ethische perspectieven* 2 (1992) 3-7, p. 6.

GERARD LUKKEN

INFANT BAPTISM IN THE NETHERLANDS AND FLANDERS
A CHRISTIAN RITUAL IN THE DYNAMIC OF THE ANTHRO-
POLOGICAL/THEOLOGICAL AND CULTURAL CONTEXT

The region in which Dutch is spoken includes both The Netherlands and a section of Belgium, namely the Flemish provinces immediately adjoining the Dutch border.[1] It is striking that within this one language region there are two rather distinct tendencies in relation to infant baptism which can be distinguished among Catholics. In Flanders infant baptism is a deeply felt ritual of life, marking birth, and there are no alternative rituals surrounding that event. There are indeed such alternatives in The Netherlands; there a pluriform practice is developing in the rituals surrounding birth, and the unique place and shape of infant baptism must be sought within this context. In this sense, one can speak of the growth of an adequate and more strict practice of baptism in The Netherlands, while in Flanders on the other hand one must speak much more of a widely inclusive practice of baptism. This contribution is a case study which seeks to approach this variation in the practice of baptism from the perspective of the dynamic relation between anthropology and the theology of liturgy. In this process we will demonstrate how deeply this dynamic anthropological/theological relation is defined by the two contemporary cultural contexts which can be distinguished.

1. TWO DIFFERING TENDENCIES IN THE PRACTICE OF BAPTISM

1.1. Flanders

Birth and Baptism, the thorough study by L. Leijssen, M. Cloet and K. Dobbelaere, appeared in 1996, a product of the *Levensrituelen* research

---

[1] Since 1971 the Belgian Constitution has provided that the country is divided into four language regions, namely the Region of Flanders (Dutch speaking, 55% of the total Belgian population), the Walloon Region (French speaking), the German-speaking cantons, and the Brussels Region (officially Dutch and French-speaking, although most residents speak French).

programme at the Catholic University at Louvain.[2] This study reported that in Flanders in 1993 a high percentage of infants were baptised. In that year, 80.7% of all live-born children there were baptised in the Catholic Church.[3] This high regard for infant baptism was also highlighted in the European Values Research in 1990.[4] Flemings believe it is important to turn to the Church at pivotal moments in life. With this, however, it must be recognised that the demand for baptism does not always arise from religious considerations. Why, for instance, do people still turn to the Catholic Church at these moments, while they no longer take part in the weekend liturgy and even describe themselves as not religious? Apparently popular customs multiply a form of the Catholic ritual of baptism so that it satisfies the need to sacralise the important life-transition that is the birth of a child. That leads to the question of pastoral strategies with regard to infant baptism. It is in this context that the authors of the Louvain collection argue for a liberal policy regarding baptism.[5] It is best that the Church acts to meet the need for sacralisation felt at the time of the birth of a child, while at the same time making use of the opportunity to lay out requirements. The catechesis that takes place in this context is the *moment par excellence* for especially stressing the function of Christian religion in providing meaning in life.[6] However, some doubts are also sounded in the concluding observations to the Louvain collection. The editors of the collection observe there, that in Flanders

---

[2] L. LEIJSSEN, M. CLOET & K. DOBBELAERE (eds): *Levensrituelen. Geboorte en doopsel* (= KADOC-studies 20) (Leuven 1996).

[3] Figures from the Interdiocesan Centre, Religious Statistics Service. Figures for Flanders in the rest of this paper are also derived from information provided by this Service. See A. VAN MEERBEECK: Dopen: ja, waarom niet? Een sociologische verkenning van de betekenis van dopen in Vlaanderen, in LEIJSSEN, CLOET & DOBBELAERE (eds): *Levensrituelen. Geboorte en doopsel* 200 and 216.

[4] A. VAN MEERBEECK: The importance of a religious service at birth. The persistent demand for baptism in Flanders (Belgium), in *Social Compass* (1995) 47-58; A. VAN MEERBEECK: De praktijk van het doopsel. Een doorlichting van de situatie in Vlaanderen, in *Kultuurleven* 64 (1997) 44-51.

[5] In addition to the article VAN MEERBEECK: Dopen: ja, waarom niet?, see particularly J. GOVAERTS: De pastorale begeleiding naar aanleiding van de kinderdoop. Situatie, beleid en vorming, in LEIJSSEN, CLOET & DOBBELAERE (eds): *Levensrituelen. Geboorte en doop* 278-300 and P. PAS: Pastoraal rond het kinderdoopsel, in LEIJSSEN, CLOET & DOBBELAERE (eds): *Levensrituelen. Geboorte en doop* 301-310.

[6] VAN MEERBEECK: Dopen: ja, waarom niet? 215; K. DOBBELAERE: Een minderheidskerk? Enkele sociologische bedenkingen, in *Collationes* 18 (1988) 267-268.

baptism is a 'super-valued sacrament', and pose the question, should the Church in the future profile its rituals more strongly, or is it the case that the Church's rituals connect with a universal experience, the interpretation of which expands the potential for deepening the Christian understanding of the meaning of life? They ultimately favour the latter. In our postmodern society, where 'open stories' play so large a role, with sound guidance and catechesis the way can be opened up for further deepening of Christian faith.[7] Leijssen refers to the proposal of J. De Kesel to replace in certain cases baptism by a 'blessing of the children' in which the birth of a child could be celebrated in a pious and religious manner. Prior to that, De Kesel argues for radicalising the baptismal ritual to emphasize its specific Christian power and expression.[8] Leijssen is however of the opinion that a separation into a blessing of the child as a first step and baptism as a second step is not a good idea. "Who will decide when the ritual must be limited to the blessing of the child and when the second step can be taken?"[9] P. Pas is even more decisive: "In the contact surrounding baptism the Church has the role… of a missionary. That role suits the Church perfectly. It is indeed the peculiar commission of the Church, whatever some may argue." A footnote follows with a reference to De Kesel's book, with the remark, "In this otherwise interesting book the author views this part of pastoral activity as of less value. Yet precisely this pastoral activity in the coming years will be most important." He then concludes, "Statements here about the Church functioning as a religious nursing home imply a terrible arrogance; they would deprive all pastors at the parish level of the courage to continue."[10] It is a passionate plea for a generous baptismal policy.

1.2. The Netherlands

The percentage of Catholic infant baptisms is considerably lower in The Netherlands than in Flanders. In 1993 only 24.7% of all live-born chil-

---

[7] L. LEIJSSEN, M. CLOET & K. DOBBELAERE: Slotbeschouwingen, in LEIJSSEN, CLOET & DOBBELAERE (eds): *Levensrituelen. Geboorte en doopsel* 317-318.

[8] J. DE KESEL: *Omwille van zijn Naam. Een tegendraads pleidooi voor de kerk* (Tielt 1994) 151-155.

[9] L. LEIJSSEN: Sacramentologische reflectie op het kinderdoopsel, in LEIJSSEN, CLOET & DOBBELAERE (eds): *Levensrituelen. Geboorte en doopsel* 271-272.

[10] PAS: Pastoraal rond het kinderdoopsel 310.

dren were baptised, thus 56% less than in Flanders.[11] Moreover, it is striking that a pluriform selection of rituals surrounding birth has gradually developed in The Netherlands. In connection with our subject, it will be important to examine them further.

First of all, one notes the development of new *secular birth rituals*. For a long time there was in The Netherlands, as elsewhere in Western society, rather a paucity of secular rituals accompanying birth. Birth rituals were limited to the choosing of a name for the child by the parents, the registration of the child at the Registry Office by the father under that name, sending birth announcements, lying-in visits to the mother, and distribution and consumption of Dutch rusk with blue aniseed candy sprinkles for a boy and pink for a girl. It could justly be said that Christian baptism was the only richer birth ritual.[12] More highly developed secular rituals did not exist. As Christian baptismal ritual fell out of favour – and particularly in The Netherlands that was increasingly the situation over the past decades – a ritual lacuna gradually formed. It is therefore not surprising that people began to take more interest in secular rituals surrounding the birth of a child. For instance, in 1986 the women's magazine *Viva* devoted an issue to the revival of old rituals surrounding birth, and the creation of new ones.[13] In addition to traditional ritual elements, like the announcement of the birth in the newspaper, sending out cards, registering the name with the Registry Office, the rusks with sprinkles and other sweets, and the maternity visit, other rituals noted were the presentation of jewellery to the child and the mother (for instance, a silver cup, a birth spoon or napkin ring with the name of the child engraved on it, or a charm for the mother's bracelet), the presentation of a savings account by the grandparents, decorative

[11] See KASKI: *Kerncijfers uit de kerkelijke statistiek 1994/1995 van het R.-K. Kerkgenootschap in Nederland* (= Memorandum 291) (Den Haag 1995) 16. KASKI = Katholiek Sociaal Kerkelijk Instituut, Den Haag. Unless otherwise indicated, figures for The Netherlands in the remainder of this paper are also derived from the KASKI.

[12] See G. LUKKEN: Rituelen rond geboorte en doop. Nieuwe ontwikkelingen, in G. LUKKEN & J. DE WIT (eds): *Nieuw leven. Rituelen rond geboorte en doop* (= Liturgie in beweging 1) (Baarn 1997) 9-31.

[13] A. BUYSMAN: Hoe vier je de geboorte van je kind?, in *Viva* 1986, no. 20 (16-5-1986) 6-11; P. DE CLERCK: Orientations actuelles de la pastorale du baptême, in A. HOUSSIAU et al.: *Le baptême, entrée dans l'existence chrétienne* (Bruxelles 1983) 124, note 19, notes that in his documentation he has one proposal for a secular birth celebration, that being from the region of Feurs, in France.

tiles with the child's name and birth date, the planting of a tree to mark the birth (a pear tree for a girl, an apple or nut tree for a boy), and placing a sign in the form of a stork with a baby in front of the new parent's house. A particular case was made for a 'birth party' at which the child would be presented to everyone present. This would be a serious reception, with a guest book, and the introduction of the child to all attending, together with the family.

Recently this same need for birth rituals has been met by what are being called 'maternity parties'.[14] Parents-to-be in the province of Drente receive a brochure on this from Home Care. The 'Maternity Party Bureau' organises one big party for the new parents, where all their acquaintances are invited at the same time to admire the newborn and congratulate the parents. The costs for the standard package, for fifty adults and twenty children under the age of 10, is HFl. 595,00. Parents who are already supporters of the Home Care/Visiting Nurse service receive a 10% discount. Offers like this are slowly spreading across the country.[15] In addition to this ritual with its rather commercial overtones, there are, however, the more wide-ranging rituals of what are termed 'ritual agencies', which are often set up and directed on a freelance basis by theology graduates. The focus of these agencies is broad: they attempt to meet a general human and religious need, and possibly also Christian need, for ritual. For instance, in its brochure the 'Motiev' agency describes its 'Birth Celebration' as "a symbolic manner of including the child in the community and inaugurating a new life, in place of baptism."[16] The female director of another ritual agency notes that all kinds of things can go wrong at a 'birth celebration'. She tells of a couple who did everything they could think of to make the celebration successful: they made sure all the invitations went out, that there were plenty of refreshments, decorations, everything. Still, the parents later felt something had been lacking, although they could not put their finger on what. They ultimately decided that it was because the child, who was, in the end, what the whole thing was supposed to be about, had

[14] See A. VELTHAUSZ: Bij de baby op de borrel, in *De Twentsche courant Tubantia* van 7 juni 1997, 'Leven'-column, p. 1.

[15] See for instance *Thebe Visie* (= publication of the Midden Brabant Care Centre) spring 1999, 13.

[16] 'Motiev. Buro voor rituele vormgeving van belangrijke levensmomenten', Melleveld 15, NL-4724 EK Wouw.

slept through the whole affair in its own room, and nobody had gotten around to see the baby.

> These people wanted something like a baptism, but not in a church. But in that case, you first must understand what a baptism involves, namely the reception of somebody into a certain community. They wanted to have their child formally included in their family and circle of friends. When all the guests were there, they should have brought the child in, and perhaps recited a poem, played some music or lit a candle, just to let it be seen that the child was there. But it's pretty difficult to think of all that by yourself.[17]

The rise of secular birth rituals like this is not surprising. In a study which appeared recently, the Ghent philosopher Jacques De Visscher, a specialist in culture, described the fundamental anthropological categories that play a depth role in the birth of a child, beyond the purely biological level, in a very impressive manner.[18] A child is born into a community. Therefore its birth is accompanied with a whole web of meanings and expectations: a fabric of stories that is the expression of the philosophy of life and world-views of a community. We regard the child as a unique individual and expect that he or she will develop into an inimitable personality. Already before the birth we prepare the new place at home that the child will fill, and initially that place in the family will be a privileged one. All kinds of things can go wrong at the birth: the child must, as it were, be snatched from capricious and dangerous powers of nature. We therefore experience birth as a leaving behind of an absolute bondage to nature, and see the child as in one way or another a gift and a responsibility, as 'ours'. From the beginning, therefore, we mark that child as a human being, as our child. Birth is regarded as a liberation from nature and the reception of the child into the world of humans; it has both a negative and a positive pole. We welcome that child into our world, on the one hand seeking to ward off the destructive powers of nature, and on the other side expressing our desire to make a place for the child in our human world and our history. We give the child a name and express our joy at its arrival in our midst. These com-

---

[17] E. VAN HAAREN: Het gerommel in je hoofd moet naar buiten, in *Hervormd Nederland* 21 december 1996. See also J. VOSSEBELD: Vieren op maat, in *Mara. Tijdschrift voor feminisme en theologie* 9 (1996) 20-21.

[18] J. DE VISSCHER: *Een te voltooien leven. Over rituelen van de moderne mens* (Kampen 1996) 26-47.

mon, basic facts of human life play an unmistakable role in human birth rituals in general. The Louvain study which we have mentioned also refers to these basic facts. Birth is a biological phenomenon which is marked socio-culturally. It is essentially an event which involves the community, because birth is the manner in which the community is perpetuated down through generations. Therefore every culture places it in a socio-cultural context. The new member of the group is acknowledged before the group and by the group in a ritual of naming. The new member's kinship relationships are specified in this way, and the child is acknowledged as a member of the whole community. Thus the ritual of naming is universally the first rite of passage in human life.[19] Indeed, the giving of a name also plays a large role in the new secular birth rituals.

At this point, it is also striking to note that this name-giving is undergoing new developments. For a very long time it was strictly subject to tradition: the child was generally named for a saint, and in any case received a name from the family tradition – perhaps the name of a grandparent, or another family member.[20] Until the 1940s, Johannes, Jan and Cornelis were the most common names for boys in The Netherlands, and Maria, Johanna and Anna the most common names for girls. Since the 1960s, however, the nuclear family has become more important, and broader family traditions that were strongly intertwined with the tradition of certain saint's names have been abandoned. Aesthetic considerations have thus gradually assumed the dominant role. The name must be beautiful and pleasant-sounding.[21] Also, even stillborn children are now given names. People have become conscious that it is very important that this giving of a name to stillborn children should also take on a ritual form.[22] Finally, another whole new development is

---

[19] R. PINXTEN: Geboorte en doopsel. Een visie van een antropoloog en vrijzinnige, in LEIJSSEN, CLOET & DOBBELAERE (eds): *Levensrituelen. Geboorte en doopsel* 47. See also J.M. JASPARD: Geboorte en doopsel vanuit psychofilosofische hoek bekeken, in LEIJSSEN, CLOET & DOBBELAERE (eds): *Levensrituelen. Geboorte en doopsel* 28-45.

[20] M. CLOET: Het doopsel in de nieuwe tijd (ca. 1550-ca. 1800), in LEIJSSEN, CLOET & DOBBELAERE (eds): *Levensrituelen. Geboorte en doopsel* 87-92.

[21] H. STAAL: Kindernamen, in *NRC Handelsblad* 2 november 1999, referring to research by the Meertens Institute and a NIPO survey from 1995.

[22] W. VOGELS: Woord en gebaar rond een doodgeboren kind, in LUKKEN & DE WIT (eds): *Nieuw leven* 90-97. See also G. RAMSHAW-SCHMIDT: Celebrating baptism in stages. A proposal, in M. SEARLE (ed.): *Alternative futures of worship. Baptism and confirmation* (Collegeville 1987) 145-146 (ritual after a miscarriage and when a child is stillborn).

that people can choose to give the family name of the father or of the mother to the child, an innovation related to women's emancipation and equality with men. Secular ritual is evolving in all directions.

But there is still more. Many parents experience the birth of their child as a *religiously* charged event. For instance, a father told how, as he was on his way home after the difficult birth of his first child, he had to stop on the way, so deeply had the event effected him. "Something so beautiful has got to have something to do with religion," he said.[23] Another voice calls so complete a little being a miracle: "There is a driving force behind it, a little piece of God."[24] The Louvain study we have already mentioned repeatedly refers to this general religious experience of the meaning of birth. It is peculiar to The Netherlands, however, that people also express, and create forms for the adequate expression of this broader religious experience in *general religious birth rituals*. Furthermore, it is self-evident that no hard and fast line exists between secular and general religious birth rituals. Whatever the case, it is striking that from the general religious experience of the miracle of birth people do not per se opt for the sacrament of baptism, in which this experience undoubtedly also can be expressed.

In The Netherlands one also finds attempts to shape *specifically Christian birth rituals*. This, to be clear, is the placing of birth in a Christian perspective, and not an express celebration of baptism proper as Christian *re*-birth. One can find explicit suggestions for celebrations of birth of this sort in a study of Th. Kersten.[25] He notes that in these it is important to seek out a suitable Bible story or a passage from other (Christian) sources; a poem or song can also function as an extension of this story. In addition, one can also search for adequate symbols. In that search it appears to be better not to make use of the symbol of water, in order to prevent confusion with baptism. But if someone is considering that, it need not be ruled out entirely. Sytze de Vries has written a song that could function most strikingly in such a Christian celebration of birth. The song speaks of the child who has left the womb to begin life, and from the beginning is connected with his or her Creator and whose

---

[23] L.L. SPRUIT & H. VAN ZOELEN: *Dopen... Ja, waarom eigenlijk? Onderzoek naar de motieven die ouders hebben om hun kind al dan niet te laten dopen in de katholieke kerk* (Hilversum 1980) 77-78.

[24] SPRUIT & VAN ZOELEN: *Dopen... Ja, waarom eigenlijk?* 86.

[25] T. KERSTEN: *Gedoopt voor mensen. Werkboek voor katechese en liturgie* (Nijmegen 1983) 80-81.

destiny is determined by Him.[26] In literal translation the text of the song reads:

> Knit together in my mother's womb,
> a wonder of creation,
> dedicated to the light,
> your love has already shaped my life.

> Long before I could know your Word,
> when the day is just begun,
> You dawned as the Sun
> who will be called my light and life.

> Before I come to that Light,
> You knew me already,
> You have created me,
> and my name is on your lips.

> In the mouth that can hardly speak yet
> the music is already there,
> the song is already to be found,
> that will shatter the silence forever.

> You, whose goodness is sung by little ones,
> let the song of your Name
> comprise my whole life,
> to hold threatening night at bay!

These birth rituals can be performed as self-standing rituals. Particularly the general religious and Christian birth rituals can also function, however, as spurs to and steps toward baptism, whether in the shorter or longer term. In that case one could term them *catechumenal celebrations*. The insight has grown after Vatican II that infant baptism cannot take place without preparation, and this involves particularly the family or milieu in which the child will grow up. Therefore one can speak of there being a certain catechumenate with respect to infant baptism. Thus, after Vatican II what are called 'baptismal instructions' for the parents have very properly been introduced, sometimes individually, sometimes in groups. However, it has not been customary to have rit-

---

[26] See W.M. Speelman: Een lied van een geborene, in *Inzet* 26 (1997) 22-26.

ual moments in this process. Now, if one considers the general religious and Christian celebrations of birth as phases on the way to baptism, one could then think of them as catechumenal celebrations. They could well function as such, if infant baptism follows within a short space of time. But they could likewise be a 'mounting-block' for baptism at a later age, for example when the child enters primary school or when he or she reaches adulthood. Catechumenal celebrations could be experienced as meaningful on the basis of the awareness that there are various degrees of involvement in the church, and from the conviction that one must deal circumspectly with the water of baptism. When people are able to be involved with the core of Christianity in a less decisive way, celebrations other than baptism may be experienced as more adequate, and there might be a preference for a gradual approach to baptism.

Thus it appears that in The Netherlands a pluriform assortment of rituals is slowly developing that stretches from secular birth rituals to catechumenal birth celebrations and baptism itself. Alternative rituals are arising around birth, and it is in the midst of these that Catholics are seeking their own place and shape for infant baptism.

2. ANTHROPOLOGY AND THEOLOGY OF INFANT BAPTISM

It was precisely in the era of the liturgical renewal of the Second Vatican Council in the 1960s that liturgy took an anthropological turn, the way for which, however, had been prepared by the Liturgical Movement at the beginning of the 20th century.[27] Full attention now was given to the anthropological basis of Christian ritual. With regard to infant baptism this meant a revolutionary development. For centuries children had been baptised with an abbreviated version of the ritual for adult baptism. Now, for the first time, a real ritual for infant baptism was designed. The *Ordo baptismi parvulorum* appeared in 1969, and was revised in some particulars in 1973. For the first time the child itself, as such, in its own individuality, became the centre of the ritual. In Dutch-speaking areas this was the impetus for great creativity at the

---

[27] For more detailed information, see G. LUKKEN: *Rituelen in overvloed. Een kritische bezinning op de plaats en de gestalte van het christelijk ritueel in onze cultuur* (Baarn 1999) 311-315.

parish level; a number of new rituals for infant baptism appeared.[28] Attention now focused on the baptismal ritual as a rite of passage accompanying birth. A ritual by Huub Oosterhuis even was headed "Celebration of birth".[29] Birth itself began to play an important role in the ritual. People caught sight of the connections of baptismal ritual with the general secular and religious experiences surrounding birth. This anthropological turn also brought with it increased consideration of the motivations that play a role in infant baptism. As this happened, there was a discovery of the great variation in the meanings assigned to the ritual. Leijssen writes: "We can distinguish... a whole range of interpretations of this event, running from the minimal need to 'do something' at the birth of a child in order to mark the event, to the highest conscious design of a total and deeply-experienced engagement with Christian belief and the church."[30] This can be seen particularly in the research by Van Meerbeeck and by Spruit and Van Zoelen.[31] In this connection Leijssen speaks of a whimsical and *à la carte* approach to ritual at the turning points of life. He remarks that in the present postmodern context one encounters a lot of 'bricolage', which is to say that rites are, as it were, borrowed to fulfil other functions than those for which they were originally intended.[32] And in the concluding observations of the Louvain collection it is remarked that baptism has always been a polysemic ritual, which people sung at a birth in many different symbolic chords.[33] From the perspective of semiotics, one can speak of a multiplicity of assigned meanings being present in the ritual, which can be experienced by participants synchronously, in its fullness, or from which a selection can be chosen. One could also say that the ritual of infant baptism can be appropriated in various ways. The technical term 'appropriation' comes from cultural studies, and goes back

---

[28] For a more comprehensive discussion of these rituals, see R. DE GRAVE & L. GEUDENS: De eigen rituelen van het Nederlandse taalgebied, in *Werkmap voor liturgie* 11 (1977) 110-145; L. MEURDERS: Een lijst van doprituelen, in LUKKEN & DE WIT (eds): *Nieuw leven* 244-268; GOVAERTS: De pastorale begeleiding van de kinderdoop 294-298.

[29] H. OOSTERHUIS: Geboorte vieren, in H. OOSTERHUIS: *In het voorbijgaan* (Baarn 1968).

[30] LEIJSSEN: Sacramentologische reflectie op het kinderdoopsel 269-270.

[31] VAN MEERBEECK: Dopen: ja, waarom niet? 199-216; SPRUIT - VAN ZOELEN: *Dopen... Ja, waarom eigenlijk?*

[32] LEIJSSEN: Sacramentologische reflectie op het kinderdoopsel 273.

[33] LEIJSSEN, CLOET & DOBBELAERE: Slotbeschouwingen 316.

to M. De Certeau.[34] It is used to make a distinction between the peculiar institutional and intended meaning of a ritual, and its meaning as that is experienced in actual practice. In my view, the concept of appropriation can greatly assist in clarifying the tendencies noted in Flanders and The Netherlands. It is clear that in Flanders, with regard to infant baptism as a super-valued sacrament, there are many forms of appropriation. In contrast to that pluriformity through appropriation in Flanders, in The Netherlands there is a pluriformity in the assortment of rituals surrounding birth, which seek an adequate connection with, and seek to be an adequate expression of, the actual practice as it is lived.

All of this now will unquestionably have consequences for the dynamics of the relation between anthropology and the theology of baptism. Where the rituals available have split apart as in The Netherlands, the need to express a peculiar Christian identity in infant baptism in the midst of, and in interaction with these many rituals, will surface more easily, while in Flanders the inclination will be to emphasize the anthropological basis of infant baptism and give this shape in the performance of the ritual itself. It is therefore obvious that infant baptism is preferably performed as a separate birth ritual in the circle of family and friends. The Louvain research emphasized this at many points, and views efforts toward collective baptism in the midst of the congregation as a utopian ideal that is unrealistic in pastoral practice.[35] In contrast to that, among Catholics in The Netherlands one finds ever more voices arguing in favour of performing baptism in the midst of the congregation, a tradition that comes to the fore particularly in Protestant churches, where the peculiar Christian identity of infant baptism has always been emphasized. Furthermore, in the midst of a 'fragmented practice' it is more strongly emphasized that infant baptism is more than just a Christian celebration of birth. Baptism is not just a Christian manner of celebrating birth, but is at the same time a re-birth, a new birth through which the child is taken up into a new community. It is a matter, according to Paul, of tearing loose and reattaching, a grafting into another stem: "For

---

[34] M. DE CERTEAU: *The practice of everyday life* (Berkeley 1984). See also W. FRIJ-HOFF: Toeëigening. Van bezitsdrang naar betekenisgeving, in *Trajecta* 6 (1997) 99-118 and P. POST: De creatie van traditie volgens Eric Hobsbawm, in *Jaarboek voor liturgieonderzoek* 11 (1995) 90 and the literature listed there in note 46.

[35] PAS: Pastoraal rond het kinderdoopsel 302-303, 307; LEIJSSEN, CLOET & DOBBELAERE: Slotbeschouwingen 315-316.

you have been cut from what is by nature a wild olive tree, and grafted, contrary to nature, into a cultivated olive tree" (Rom. 11:24). This being grafted into Christ brings various people from various times and places together onto a new way, irrespective of rank and class. In this, the ethical dimension of infant baptism also is more clearly delineated. The bonds of the child reach further than those of family or clan.

There is thus, as it were, a sliding scale in the relation between anthropology and theology in the liturgy.[36] At the one end, one's point of departure could be the approach which was particularly in the ascendency after Vatican II and that emphasizes the coherence between sacraments and rites of passage. In this perspective the sacraments are seen chiefly as *life*-rituals. As examples, in addition to the Louvain *Levensrituelen* series, one can point to theologians such as Kasper, Ratzinger and Boff.[37] This is a legitimate approach, but it is important to recognise its limits. The fact is, the danger is not merely theoretical that Christian identity and the anthropological basis are so telescoped into one another that the one will lose out at the expense of the other. The identity of the sacrament will then dominate and manipulate the anthropological basis, or the opposite will happen: the anthropological basis will, as it were, swallow up the identity of the sacrament. When one understands the significance of the sacraments too simply in terms of individual life histories, the danger arises that they will close up on themselves. This can lead to subjectivism and privatisation of the sacraments. They will then be seen as only a personal support and comfort in life's critical transitional situations. One remains stuck at the level of the security that the sacrament offers, and they are seen, first and foremost, as family events. But that which is peculiar to a sacrament, that which takes one by surprise in it, is precisely, or in any case should be, that its social dimension is radicalised and universalised. The sacraments are, after all, acts of a new community that breaks through family bonds and knows no ethnic boundaries, a community to whom 'the Jesus

---

[36] LUKKEN: *Rituelen in overvloed* 248-251, 311-316.

[37] W. KASPER: Wort und Symbol im sakramentalen Leben. Eine anthropologische Begründung, in W. HEINEN (Hrsg.): *Bild-Wort-Symbol in der Theologie* (Würzburg 1969) 157-175; W. KASPER: Wort und Sakrament, in *Glaube und Geschichte* (Mainz 1970) 285-310; J. RATZINGER: *Die sakramentale Begründung christlicher Existenz* (Meitingen 1966); L. BOFF: *Die Kirche als Sakrament im Horizont der Welterfahrung* (Paderborn 1972) particularly 142, 380-383, 385; L. BOFF: *Kleine Sakramentenlehre* (Düsseldorf 1976).

affair' happens and must constantly happen. Or, put in other terms, the sacraments place us in the midst of the broad dynamic of Christian sacred history, and therefore, in the midst of the new people of God, who are oriented toward and must focus themselves on the coming of the Kingdom of God, that kingdom of justice and peace which is intended for all. The sacraments are thus about salvation, not as a gift turned in on itself, but as something that reaches much further than the well-being of the individual believer. They aim toward the liberation of mankind. It is the essence of the sacrament that it challenges one to genuine engagement with real problems and with the real world in which we all live. That is the other end of the scale.

Thus it is the case, that the connection between rites of passage and sacraments is not imperative. Baptism as rebirth through water and the Spirit does indeed call up associations in one way or another with birth itself, and that birth can play a large role in the liturgical expression of baptism, but baptism does not have to take place at the moment of birth, or soon after it. Adults can also be baptised. In the first centuries, adult baptism was in fact the normal practice. Baptism is thus decidedly more than a Christian celebration of birth. The relation between anthropology and theology in the ritual is thus not a purely theoretical question. As the foregoing should make clear, it also touches on pastoral practice and the design of baptism itself.

3. Four points that are relevant for both approaches in the anthropology/theology relation

There are four matters which are relevant to both approaches in the relation between anthropology and the theology of infant baptism: the anthropology of children's faith; the course of the process of the birth of a child; the expression of certain biblical baptismal themes in the liturgy of infant baptism itself; and the expression of the liberation of the child from the mystery of evil. These can contribute to a certain more balanced relation between anthropology and the theology of infant baptism.

3.1. Children and faith

Particularly since Vatican II, the question of the relation between faith and baptism has played an important role in the larger question of the identity of baptism. It has correctly been realised that in a completely non-religious environment, the performance of baptism makes no sense. An appeal can be made to 'the faith of the church', but this must have some concrete form in the faith of the parents and in the child's wider environment. The sacrament is not efficacious automatically. Yet in this accent on faith in the environment, there is often no attention paid to children themselves. Children are too easily seen only as a passive being who have not yet come to faith. This vision reflects a narrowly rational human view and a too conceptual/intellectual definition of faith.[38] Even though a child is pre-rational, it is active from the beginning. A child is not a blank slate, but has its own human life, as a child. In any holistic vision of humanity which considers a human being as more than pure consciousness, children must be included in our community. Precisely as a child, children have their own life of faith, hope and love. Faith is more than an acceptance of truth. Faith is also – and first and foremost – trusting oneself to God, a way of being. Children and the mentally handicapped too can in their own manner lead a life of complete dependence on God. Infant baptism can make us aware that the power of grace can be effective beneath the level of rational consciousness. Just as in the parent's expression of love toward the newborn child, in the performance of the sacrament more is happening than we can know. The child also knows, from the very beginning, the constant movement of give and take, of old and new, of dying and rising. In this sense the Paschal Mystery too is experienced by every child from the beginning. And in this sense one can also say that children have an active place in the church community. One could even ask if the child, as child, does not have a peculiar place in the prophetic witness of the church. Whatever the case, there is a full and valuable place for the child in the Christian sacred economy. Scripture itself links children with salvation in a very positive light (Mark 10, 15-15; Luke 9, 47-48, 18, 15-17; Matt. 18, 1-5, 19, 13-15).[39] And did the Lord himself not take the form of a

---

[38] SEARLE: Infant baptism reconsidered 40-43. See also G. LUKKEN: De kinderdoop in de kerk van vandaag, in BLIJLEVENS, BOELENS & LUKKEN (eds): *Dopen met water en geest* 16-18; IDEM: De doop: een onvervangbaar sacrament, in IDEM: *Dopen met water en geest* 105-107; IDEM: De theologie van het doopsel na Vaticanum II 338-348.

[39] RAMSHAW-SCHMIDT: Celebrating baptism in stages 137-138 also refers to the numerous accounts in Scripture in which the central theme is God's saving children, from the narrative of the rescue of the children of Noah through the story of Jairus' daughter.

newborn and growing child? This means that in principle the child is sanctified by the incarnation and from the beginning can really take part in the Christian economy of salvation *as a child.*

3.2. The procedural course of the birth of a child

If one compares the new Roman ritual for infant baptism with that for adult baptism, in a certain sense it appears to be rather thin. The baptism itself features as an instantaneous occurrence. The new official ritual for infant baptism does not have the procedural quality that is so characteristic of adult baptism. This is also true for the rituals that have come into existence at the congregational level in Dutch-speaking areas. I have already mentioned above the possibility of catechumenal celebrations preceding infant baptism. In view of these factors, one can ask whether, particularly in contemporary culture, a further ritualisation preceding baptism is not perhaps desirable. We have a pluriform culture in which Christian faith cannot be assumed any longer. The *corpus christianum* (that is to say, a culture which, in practical terms, coincided with Christian culture) has disappeared. A child has its own 'life of faith', but at the same time it remains true – and is perhaps more true now than ever before – that the family or the immediate environment in which the child is born and grows up is involved in the transmission and experiencing of faith. One might say that this immediate milieu mediates sacramentality in its own particular and irreplaceable way. Translated into classical theological terms, this means that this milieu is an *instrumentum conjunctum* of sacramentality (i.e., an instrument connected with it).[40] Thus we are dealing here with a relation with the child surrounding its birth, given beforehand by nature, in light of sacred history. This relation is not something which takes place purely in one moment. It includes all the events of the child's conception, expectancy, birth and growth as a unique human being with its own name. This given, of the sacramental sacred history dimension of the family, must be translated into the greater *Familia Dei* of the Church. This is only possible if the Church has an eye for the whole of the process by which the child is initiated into the order of salvation. This means that the ritual translation to the larger church

---

[40] Cf. also for what follows, SEARLE: Infant baptism reconsidered 15-24. See also LUKKEN: De theologie van het doopsel na Vaticanum II 338-348.

community must include the whole process that already began before the birth: after all, it was there that the inclusion of the child into the sacred economy already began, and with it the sacramental celebration of the coming of the child. As much as a decade ago A. Scheer already argued for focusing on the whole birth process in the initiation liturgy. The ritual should grow along with all of the events of the birth until they were complete. In the course of his argument Scheer pointed to Eastern liturgy.[41] He did not, however, work out his proposal further in concrete terms for our culture.[42] G. Ramshaw-Schmidt did indeed make such an attempt. He proposes dividing the whole of the initiation of the child into four stages: 1) the pre-catechumenate, with a celebration before the birth and a celebration in which the resolution to baptise the child is spotlighted; 2) the catechumenate, which includes a celebration immediately after the birth and a celebration of the registration of the child's name; 3) purification and illumination, in which are included a ritual in preparation for baptism, and in one ritual, the actual initiation through baptism, confirmation and Eucharist; and 4) the mystagogy, which includes two celebrations in remembrance of the initiation, one in the church, and one in the family. Thus infant baptism would receive a fully developed ritual and the original unity of the initiation would be restored. It is the general conviction in contemporary liturgical studies, that the sacraments of water, unction and table belong together, but how this should be ordered as a practical matter remains controversial. This proposal for making infant baptism a process is an extra argument for the restoration of the original unity of the initiation, in the way this has always been a matter of course in Eastern liturgies. By thus bringing baptism to centre stage, it again comes to be seen as a sacrament of initiation, an insight which can be further sharpened from the perspectives of comparative religion and

---

[41] A.H.M. SCHEER: Zullen we ons kind alsnog laten dopen? Een pleidooi voor een aangepast pastoraat voor doopouders, in *Tijdschrift voor liturgie* 62 (1978) 163-173. For the ritual in Eastern liturgy, see, among others, L. VAN DINTEREN: De doop in de orthodoxe kerken, in LEIJSSEN, CLOET & DOBBELAERE (eds): *Levensrituelen. Geboorte en doopsel* 172-182.

[42] In the new Dutch edition of the Roman ritual of infant baptism, one finds two celebrations which do take into account the nature of infant baptism as a process. An 'Order of service for the blessing of a not yet baptised child', which can precede the baptism, and an 'order of service for the blessing of a woman before or after giving birth' are found there in an 'Appendix'. See NATIONALE RAAD VOOR LITURGIE: *Het doopsel van kinderen* (Zeist 1993) 29-30, 170-196.

the behavioural sciences.[43] An additional advantage of this one initiation would be that the scriptural symbolism of water as the life-giving sign of the Spirit could again be developed.[44]

3.3. The expression of certain biblical baptismal themes in the liturgy of infant baptism itself [45]

In the ritual of adult baptism from after Vatican II, participation in the Paschal Mystery through baptism is a central theme. In it, however, participation in the Paschal Mystery is chiefly seen as the passage of God's people through the water. This interpretation of participation in the Paschal Mystery has most relevance for the active adult baptismal candidate, who is leaving the land of Egypt and passes through the Red Sea on the way to the Promised Land. It is hard to shake off the impression that this image has functioned as the basic model for the new theology of baptism. There is little reference in it to the Paschal Mystery as God's sparing the children of Israel or His sparing his people through the blood of the lamb. One can remark also that the themes of baptism as a new creation, a new birth, a second birth, rebirth, adoption as a child of God, deification, sanctification, indwelling, restoration, incorporation in the body of Christ, illumination and the taking on of the new, imperishable humanity, which are equally as much part of the tradition as the theme of death and resurrection, come to be less central. These are themes which, as it were, are woven around the central theme of the Paschal Mystery, and are all in keeping with the baptismal theology and baptismal liturgy of Scripture and the Early Church. In the new baptismal theology, including that of infant baptism, with regard to the baptismal water the symbolism of death and resurrection is accentuated more than that of the womb and

---

[43] See M. ELIADE: *Das Mysterium der Wiedergeburt. Initiationsriten, ihre kulturelle und religiöse Bedeutung* (Zürich/Stuttgart 1961); J. RIES: Les rites d'initiation à la lumière de l'histoire des religions, in A. HOUSSIAU *et al.: Le baptême, entrée dans l'existence chrétienne* (Bruxelles 1983) 19-34; A.D. THOMPSON: Infant baptism in the light of the human sciences, in SEARLE (ed.): *Alternative futures for worship* 55-102; H. ANDERSON: Pastoral care in the process of initiation, in SEARLE (ed.): *Alternative futures of worship* 103-136.

[44] For this symbolism, cf. M.G. LAWLER: *Symbol and sacrament. A contemporary sacramental theology* (Mahwah 1987) 74-75 and 83 ff.

[45] See particularly SEARLE (ed.): Infant baptism reconsidered, and LUKKEN: De theologie van het doopsel na Vaticanum II 347-348.

the creation. It also should be recognised that by following these other themes, other, less masculine names for God spontaneously arise: God as Womb, the One who gives us birth, the Bosom of mercy, the Source of life, light and strength, the Breath of life, Spirit, Comforter, the One who preserves us. Moreover, many of these themes are closely connected with the contemporary parents' motives for baptism, particularly that of the miraculous experience of birth. The emphasis in post-Vatican II baptismal theology lies strongly on the personal socialisation to adult conversion and adult belief. It is about active participation in the prophetic Church which has succeeded the mass Church.

Finally, it is remarkable that precisely this conviction of the necessity for adulthood and autonomy of the candidate also, to a great extent, is reflected in the Catholic and Protestant tradition of infant baptism precisely as infant baptism. We are not speaking here of the Anabaptists, who rejected infant baptism, nor Protestant theologians following Karl Barth, who likewise are unfavourable to infant baptism. Rather, within the tradition of infant baptism itself, theologically there has constantly been a real difficulty with this infant baptism. One looks as it were for an escape route forward: to a later age. Thus while it is true Luther and Calvin retain infant baptism, they reinterpret confirmation into a rite of personal confession of faith, at a later age. And Catholics, who in general still maintained the practice of infant baptism, gradually began to emphasize the practice, as it actually grew up, of administering confirmation at a later age as a desirable practice. In any case, in general this happened after the Council of Trent: initiation through confirmation and first communion was moved to, at the earliest, the age at which a person was believed to be capable of intellectual and moral discretion (7 or 8 years of age). Confirmation theology itself then has already long been developed as that of the *aetas perfecta*: the age of Christian majority. Confirmation became the rite of passage into adulthood. That is not illegitimate.[46] But at the same time it is the case that in this way the unity of the one initiation is shattered, and one runs into a hidden problem with regard to infant baptism. Christian life is apparently identified with adult life. Children find themselves in the period between

---

[46] See K. DOBBELAERE, L. LEIJSSEN & M. CLOET (eds): *Levensrituelen. Het vormsel* (= KADOC-studies 12) (Leuven 1991); L. LEIJSSEN: La spécificité de la confirmation. Réflexions de théologie sacramentelle (post-moderne), in *Questions liturgiques* 79 (1998) 3-4 and 249-264.

birth and becoming a person, in a sort of preliminary stage to adulthood. Right down to this day both confirmation theology and the liturgical practice of confirmation at a later age (proposals to administer confirmation at graduation from primary school, or, preferably, at an even later age) are often a sign of theological unease with infant baptism. Confirmation must offer, as it were, the real guarantee that infant baptism does make sense. It is therefore not surprising that one encounters baptismal theologies that take post-Vatican baptismal theology to its logical conclusion and argue for the postponement of baptism until the child has turned to God and attained faith.

The themes which are more specifically focused on the child will, however, have to have a place in a fully fledged theology and liturgy of infant baptism. They have the guarantee of Scripture, the Fathers and ancient liturgy. And they would afford more basis for infant baptism as *infant* baptism, both anthropologically and theologically, because they are more adapted to the situation of the child. In the rituals he proposed for review, G. Ramshaw-Schmidt therefore not only gave form to child baptism as a process, but also incorporates the themes concerned.[47] One also finds themes more specifically focused on the child in some of the rituals published in the Dutch-speaking region. This is particularly the case in the 1973 baptismal ritual by J. Nieuwenhuis, 'Ergens komt een kind vandaan', P. Verhoeven's 1996 'Jij leve lang', and Th. Kersten's 1983 'Gedoopt voor mensen'.[48] Further, in rituals of infant baptism the Paschal Mystery should be expressed by interpreting it through the sparing of the children of Israel or God's sparing the Israelites through the blood of the lamb, though certainly in addition to themes of more 'active' participation in the Paschal Mystery. Thus one does not have to exclude the presently dominant interpretation of the pascha as journey (*transitus*); after all, the archetype of the growth of a child is that of giving and taking, falling and getting up again, and also that of earning a place. On the other hand, it would also be wrong to exclude the themes

---

[47] RAMSHAW-SCHMIDT: Celebrating baptism in stages 137-155. One notes in this that the anthropological basis of birth indeed deserves attention in rituals of infant baptism, but that at the same time, infant baptism is about more than a celebration of birth. See G. LUKKEN: Liturgie van de kinderdoop tussen bevestiging en evangelische uitdaging, in *Praktische theologie* 11 (1984) 461.

[48] For these rituals, see MEURDERS: Een lijst van dooprituelen. See also A. GOVAART: Een nieuw doopritueel, in LUKKEN & DE WIT (eds): *Nieuw leven* 43-58.

from infant baptism from adult baptism. It is a matter of different emphases, and not of exclusively reserving the pascha as journey for adult baptism, and the other themes for infant baptism. Expanding upon both types of themes would in no way need to exclude the inter-ference between them.

3.4. Exorcising and liberation from the mystery of evil

After Vatican II, interest in baptism as liberation from original sin ebbed away. For fifteen centuries this element had been strongly emphasized. The emphasis was now placed on positive aspects. The baptismal water was no longer seen purely and only as a means of cleansing, but rather as a way to life and resurrection. The negative pole disappeared from sight. Yet in anthropology water has always been a complex symbol, evoking both death and destruction as well as har-mony, life and resurrection. And today there is still a general human feeling that we must snatch a child away from the capricious and threatening powers of nature and evil forces. It is born into a world in which it is also confronted with the mystery of evil. Over the past decades the consciousness has been breaking through that society is less capable of change than we thought. Time and time again we must avert evil forces that seem to be beyond our comprehension and control. In the second half of the 20th century alone one can think of the 'killing fields' of Cambodia, genocide in Rwanda and the 'ethnic cleansing' in Bosnia-Herzegovina and Kosovo. It does not appear to be sheer chance that in the last few years serious studies are beginning to appear which reflect anew on the concept of original sin.[49] In these this is seen chiefly as the *mysterium iniquitatis,* and as such, not only as the destructive evil outside us, but just as much as an intrinsic wound, an intrinsic fault

---

[49] L. PANIER: *Le péché originel. Naissance de l'homme sauvé* (Paris 1996); G. NIJHOFF: *La confusion des arbres. Essai d'une revalorisation du dogme du péché originel* (Vérossaz 1995). See also M. HEWITT SUCHOCKI: *The fall to violence. Original sin in relational the-ology* (New York 1994); M.S. MULDOON: Forum. Reconciliation, original sin, and mil-lennial malaise, in *Worship* 72 (1998) 445-452; E.J. VAN WOLDE: *A semiotic analysis of Genesis 2-3. A semiotic theory and method of analysis applied to the story of the Garden of Eden* (= Studia Semitica Neerlandica 25) (Assen 1989); J. COURTÉS: Sémiotique et théologie du péché, in H. PARRET & H.-G. RUPRECHT (ed.): *Exigences et perspectives de la sémiotique. Recueil d'hommages pour A.J. Greimas* (Amsterdam/Philadelphia 1985) 863-903; IDEM: *Sémantique de l'énoncé: applications pratiques* (Paris 1989) 177-224.

that all people share with each other, within themselves. On this point too a certain balance between anthropology and theology is possible.

4. Two different cultural contexts as determinants of two differing baptismal practices

It could be argued that the differing approaches in Flanders and The Netherlands are dictated by intrinsic motives. Certain motives will weigh more heavily in the one area than in the other. But such an approach does not take into account the cultural contexts which strongly influence the different forms of practice, and which are not purely an external situation alone, but are just as much determinants that settle infant baptism itself within the particular culture and give it a specific tint. Thus the differing cultures also determine the different ways in which infant baptism is celebrated at this moment in Flanders and The Netherlands. It is a simple fact that rituals are always linked with the total symbolic order of a culture.[50] At several points the Louvain study touches on this cultural background for pastoral choices. For instance, it is noted that rituals are considered as elements of a cultural patrimony that must be accessible for everyone.[51] To my mind, it is formulated in a more explicit way by L. Leijssen:

> Such a low-threshold strategy is in keeping with the pastoral practice of mass Catholicism, typical of a still latent Christian cultural tradition... Those responsible for policy in the Flemish dioceses in general take a rather permissive attitude, and infant baptism is seldom refused. In the pastoral practice surrounding infant baptism the need for serious preparation is stressed in the baptismal instructions, which are sessions of adult catechesis. So long as Christianity is still to a certain degree intertwined with the current culture and has a place in family life, there is a sufficient guarantee that the child can later grow up in faith. To the degree however that secularisation permeates the culture more thoroughly, the demand for a more emphatic Christian motivation will move increasingly into the foreground. Parish priests are seeing that, when baptism is performed on the basis of anthropological motives alone, in the end not much is left of the sacrament.[52]

---

[50] This is also true if the ritual is not inculturated; then it forms a counterculture or occupies only a marginal place in the total symbolic order. See LUKKEN: *Rituelen in overvloed* 115-118.

[51] VAN MEERBEECK: Dopen: waarom niet? 205.

[52] LEIJSSEN: Sacramentologische reflectie op het kinderdoopsel 270-271.

In this context the following answer found in Van Meerbeeck's research, to a question about the motives for asking for baptism, is pertinent:

> Yes, but, o.k., it's more a part of our culture and so, and I'd say, yeah, you live in the shadow of the church tower, we can see it from here too, for instance, and it, it's a part of your life, you know, no matter what you think of it, certainly in Flanders, no matter where you go, but yeah, really we have always, the wife and I, you know, never ever, we never stopped to think about it or talked about it.[53]

It would appear important, then, to examine the two cultures in the one language area a bit more deeply.

4.1. Flanders

Anyone crossing the border from The Netherlands into Flanders is immediately confronted with differences of all sorts. At first sight the landscape appears to continue unchanged, but very quickly one discovers that this is not really the case: the aforestation is different and the fields and pastures are divided up in a much less rectilinear manner. There are considerable differences in the urban and rural planning. The secondary roads in the agricultural areas that lie close to the Dutch border are much narrower. It is striking that everywhere in the agricultural areas and the villages, the electrical supply lines are above ground, not buried. The villages take a different form, what is called 'ribbon development', where houses run for a long distance along the road. Within the villages the streets run less at right angles; they often run off diagonally. On one hand, Dutchmen experience the landscape as beautiful, on the other hand as less tidy. Planning rules are much more permissive than they are in The Netherlands. Right at the border it strikes one that the bricks used in buildings are different, and the style of the houses differs considerably from that in The Netherlands. The free-standing dwellings are more spacious and there seems to be a predilection for little, castle-like towers.

Flanders comes across as a Catholic region: 70% of the people are Catholic, as opposed to 33% in The Netherlands. The royal family in Belgium is Catholic too. There is much that is similar with the Catholic Southern Netherlands, but there are more little parks with

---

[53] VAN MEERBEECK: Dopen: waarom niet? 213.

Marian images and Calvaries, Lourdes grottos and old pilgrimage sites. Despite modernisation, this popular religious culture seems to have sustained itself. In Hoogstraten there appears to be little difficulty in recruiting large numbers of secondary school students to participate in the Sacred Blood procession. There are many traditional folk practices surrounding birth which have been maintained, such as, for instance, the sugar-coated almonds in blue or pink, often in conical bags, tied off with a bow.[54] They are given, when a child is born. One finds all sorts of baptismal presents in the shops. First communion is also celebrated more exuberantly than it is on the average in The Netherlands. Around the time of first communion the stores are chock full of special communion clothing and communion gifts, and after the celebration local photographers show off the pictures of the young communicants in their display windows. From time to time one can participate in a festive blessing of the children on a Sunday afternoon, in which, during the blessing itself, the children are held aloft triumphantly. The norms for raising children are also stricter. Dutch families along the border sometimes send their children to Belgian schools because the discipline there is better. In some places school uniforms are still required, and where that is not the case, dress standards are enforced. Prayer still takes place before lessons begin. Much earlier than in The Netherlands, Flanders had discovered 'seasonal Christians', present only for occasions like Ash Wednesday, Palm Sunday and other festivals of the Church. Flanders has a strong culture of folk festivals and a deeply rooted religious popular culture. In many places the Church in Flanders still functions in conformity with the structures and organisation of a national church. In this, it can rely heavily on the involvement of broadly-based Christian organisations. For years Catholicism has been a dominant political and cultural force.[55] At the same time, it is true that Flanders too is confronted with secularisation and modernisation. As a result, especially since the 1960s there has been a

---

[54] S. TOP: Als de ooievaar komt… Volksculturele facetten van zwangerschap, geboorte en doop (1900-1950), in LEIJSSEN, CLOET & DOBBELAERE (eds): *Levensrituelen. Geboorte en doopsel* 136.

[55] V. DRAULANS & H. WITTE: Identiteit in Meervoud. Nederlands en Vlaams Katholicisme in een veranderende tijd, in *Collationes* 28 (1998) 247-264; 265-280; V. DRAULANS & H. WITTE: Initiatie in de vrijwilligerskerk. Verkenningen in vergelijkend perspectief, in L. BOEVE (ed.): *De kerk in Vlaanderen. Avond of dageraad?* (Leuven 1999) 167-188.

development from a Catholicism rooted in the church to a social-cultural Christianity.[56] The people of God have begun to 'evaporate',[57] but one can still speak of a high degree of cultural Christianity. Secularisation and modernisation thus remain mixed with a Christian infrastructure. In this context Christian rites of passage still always have a rather strong monopoly position. This is referred to explicitly several times in the Louvain study.[58] The Christian rites of passage are very penetratingly characterised as 'buttresses' of a 'Catholicism outside the walls of the church'.[59] Draulans and Witte remark, "Perhaps the monopoly position (of the Church) in the past is today's problem."[60] In this connection they also refer to theories regarding the 'religious market', as put forward by the North American sociologist Rodney Stark, among others. Analogous with market-economic thought, these theories point to the effects of the principle of competition in religion as well. According to this analysis, pluralism and diversity stimulate involvement in the church and encourages an accent on one's own identity, while a monopoly position instead makes the church 'lazy'. The believer can behave rather as a potential customer.[61] This naturally contributes to a permissive practice in the case of rites of passage.

---

[56] See J. BILLIET & K. DOBBELAERE: *Godsdienst in Vlaanderen. Van kerks katholicisme naar sociaal-kulturele kristenheid?* (Leuven 1976); J. BILLIET & K. DOBBELAERE: Les changements internes au pilier catholique en Flandre. D'un Catholicisme d'Eglise à une Chrétienté socio-culturelle, in *Recherches sociologiques* 14 (1983) 141-184; K. DOBBELAERE: Du catholicisme ecclésial au catholicisme culturel, in *Septentrion* 18-3 (1989) 30-35; IDEM: De katholieke zuil nu. Desintegratie en integratie, in *Belgisch tijdschrift voor nieuwste geschiedenis* 13 (1982) 1, 119-160.

[57] K. DOBBELAERE: *Het 'Volk-Gods' de mist in? Over de Kerk in België* (Leuven/Amersfoort 1988).

[58] Van MEERBEECK: Dopen: ja, waarom niet? 204 and 215.

[59] K. DOBBELAERE: De 'overgangsrituelen', steunberen van een 'Katholicisme buiten de muren'?, in J. BULCKENS & P. COOREMAN (eds.): *Kerkelijk leven in Vlaanderen anno 2000* (Leuven 1989) 29-38. See also DOBBELAERE: *Het 'Volk-Gods' de mist in?* 77-78 and L. VOYÉ: Du monopole religieux à la connivence culturelle en Belgique. Un catholicisme 'hors les murs', in *L'Année sociologique* 38 (1988) 135-167.

[60] DRAULANS & WITTE: Initiatie in de vrijwilligerskerk 170.

[61] DRAULANS & WITTE: Initiatie in de vrijwilligerskerk 171, 178-179. See also T. SCHEPENS: De katholieke kerk en de religieuze markt in Nederland, in K.-W. MERKS & N. SCHREURS: *De passie van een grensganger. Theologie aan de vooravond van het derde millennium* (Baarn 1997) 15-26.

4.2. The Netherlands

The Dutch landscape is flat, rectilinear, subdivided in a precise and well-ordered manner. The rural planning favours right angles and the roads tend to run in straight lines. They are also full to bursting. The country is more thickly populated than Flanders; indeed, The Netherlands is the most thickly populated country in Europe. Large parts appear much more strongly urbanised than Flanders. For years the term 'urban agglomerate' has been applied to large areas of the provinces of North and South Holland, but in the last decades this phenomenon of 'urban sprawl' has also spread to the southern Dutch province of Noord-Brabant. The number of daily traffic jams is steadily rising. Until the 1960s The Netherlands had a very quiet and traditional society in which the churches played an important role. They stood proud like robust columns, and Christian rituals for transitional moments in life had a certain monopoly position. The Christian churches imprinted their mark on the society, influencing even secular organisations. People from outside The Netherlands have always been amazed at the division of radio and television among Catholic, conservative and liberal Protestant, and socialist 'columns', but today these are really only the reflection of the earlier traditional society, undergoing severe competition from the 'neutral' commercial broadcasters. In the 1960s a rather abrupt transition took place to an urban, industrialised society. The Netherlands suddenly became a modern, secularised country. Efficiency became the key word. In the course of this transition, the sturdy old columns began to totter.[62] This was accompanied by a rapid increase among those not identifying themselves with any church. The first figures which we have with regard to the unchurched date from 1879. In that year, only 0.3% identified themselves in that way – a minority which could be ignored. The figure grew through the 20th century: in 1960 it reached 21.3%, and in the years following the floodgates opened: 1966, 33%; 1979, 42%; 1987, 49%; 1995, 62%. According to the Social and Cultural Planning Bureau, it can be expected that by the year 2020 it will reach 72%.[63] Especially among the Catholics in The

---

[62] J. THURLINGS: *De wankele zuil. Nederlandse katholieken tussen assimilatie en pluralisme* (Nijmegen/Amersfoort 1971); T. DUFFHUES, A. FELLING & J. ROES: *Bewegende patronen* (Baarn 1982).

[63] SCHEPENS: De katholieke kerk en de religieuze markt in Nederland 16, remarks, "At present the percentage of unchurched people varies, depending on the way the ques-

Netherlands there was, in contrast to Flanders, since the 1960s an acute stream out of the churches.[64] Now, one must not confuse not identifying with a church with a loss of faith. According the 'God in Nederland' survey in 1997, two-thirds of the Dutch still consider themselves as believers, but they are of the opinion that they do not have any need for the church for this.[65] One can conclude that in The Netherlands belonging to a church is in no way something which is done as a matter of course. It is rather a matter of true choice.

Moreover, people were conscious that through the developments on the ground in Dutch society, Christian ritual was gradually losing its monopoly position.[66] One might have expected that the sharp increase among the unchurched since the 1960s would have been accompanied by the rise of alternative birth rituals. That was not immediately the case, however. Precisely in those years, because of the sudden secularisation and modernisation, Dutch society underwent profound 'crisis in ritual'. This particularly involved rites of passage. People doubted whether the ritual marking of the transition from one phase of life to another was of any value. Yet, at the same time, under the influence of the Second Vatican Council, this was precisely the era of great creativity with regard to Christian ritual. There was a search for a new place for Christian ritual in contemporary culture. In this, the forms of Christian

tion is asked, between 40% (according to the Central Statistical Bureau) and 60% (according to the SCP). The precise percentage may be unknown, but there can be no doubt about the increase."

[64] V. DRAULANS & H. WITTE: Initiatie in de vrijwilligerskerk 263, note with regard to this: "For decades, in both Flanders and in The Netherlands, in profiling itself in society the Catholic Church could count on the support of a network of its own organisations and institutions. In Flanders the emancipation also led via this network to emancipation at the level of questions of belief... Precisely this point, the personal appropriation of faith, was absent from the emancipation struggle of Dutch Catholics. The reason for this was the very different social context of Catholicism and the very different type of clerical leadership which corresponded with it." Because of social discrimination against Catholics in The Netherlands, it was necessary to search for an 'identity over against', an emancipation under the leadership of clergy in society in opposition to the threatening environment. When this emancipation was completed, many left the church. In Flanders, in contrast, the clergy provided positive guidance for the secular engagement of the lay believer, which resulted in various generations of laity who remained critically loyal to the church as an institution.

[65] J. PETERS, G. DEKKER & J. DE HART: God in Nederland 1966-1996 (Amsterdam 1997).

[66] LUKKEN: Rituelen in overvloed 191-195.

liturgy were strongly subject to inculturation. To an increasing degree it
was realised that the peculiar identity of Christian ritual was at stake in
our secularised culture. This was also true for the ritual of infant baptism. Beginning in the 1990s, the 'crisis in ritual' in Dutch society has
been broken through, and one can also note great creativity there with
regard to ritual.[67] It was in this context that, within the ritual void, all
sorts of new secular and general religious rituals involving birth arose,
and continue to develop, alongside infant baptism. Within the pluriform situation which has arisen since the 1960s, Catholics, in part stimulated by the renewals of the Second Vatican Council, have tried to give
shape to rites of passage in their own way. This search for a peculiarly
Christian identity for these rituals is undoubtedly strengthened now
that Dutch society is gradually coming to experience a situation of what
has been called 'rituals in abundance'.[68]

5. REMAINING QUESTIONS

Despite the globalisation of our culture and the unification of Europe,
there decidedly remains space for cultural differences and peculiar identities, even right next to each other and within the same language
region. Connected with this, it likewise appears possible to have a pluriform pastoral strategy in adjoining areas within one and the same language region, which will have repercussions for the relation between
anthropology and theology of liturgy. That is, in any case, the situation
with regard to infant baptism in The Netherlands and Flanders. Or,
might one say, that the difference *begins* with infant baptism? It is not
unlikely that one could broaden this out to, for instance, the marriage
liturgy and to other rituals on the axis of life, or the axis of the seasons.
This undoubtedly would deserve further investigation.

A second question is whether the whole matter should be further
nuanced. This appears, indeed, to be the case. On the basis of empirical investigation, Schepens demonstrates that the southern dioceses of
The Netherlands are, in a certain sense, to be characterised as 'lazy

---

[67] See LUKKEN: *Rituelen in overvloed*; P. POST: Alle dagen feest, of: de ritencrisis
voorbij. Een verkenning van de markt, in P. POST & W.M. SPEELMAN (eds): *De
madonna van de Bijenkorf. Bewegingen op de rituele markt* (= Liturgie in perspectief 7)
(Baarn 1997) 10-17.

[68] LUKKEN: *Rituelen in overvloed*.

monopolies'. This is true especially for the most southerly diocese of Roermond, where there is little competition from other religious groups. With the lack of alternatives, as a matter of course people call upon the Catholic Church for baptism, first communion, marriage or funerals when the need arises.[69]

The third question is whether anything can be said about future developments. It would seem we can exclude the possibility that the Dutch practice will shift in the direction of Flemish practice. The prognosis is, after all, that the proportion of the unchurched in The Netherlands will only increase. The question which then remains is, will Flemish practice perhaps develop in the direction of Dutch practice. In December 1999, the Flemish newspaper *De Standaard* published a series of articles on 'Geloven in Vlaanderen' (Faith in Flanders).[70] It is noted that for a long time Flanders, along with Ireland and Poland, was a sort of isolated stronghold, but that in recent years it has secularised at an increasing tempo. The church has lost its monopoly position. At the same time, however, it was confirmed that the church still has a disproportionately strong position with regard to the rites of passage such as baptism, marriage and burial, and that as of yet few alternatives exist. Can it be expected that in Flanders too a pluriform culture with regard to the rites surrounding birth will develop? Opinions are divided on this.[71] For instance, on the one hand it is observed that with respect to membership and participation, the Church in Flanders is presently developing into an organisation which is moving forward on the basis of efforts of volunteer workers, and this is regarded as a positive development.[72] But on the other hand there are arguments for a more careful way of dealing with rites of passage, and with this, for a 'selective'

---

[69] SCHEPENS: De katholieke kerk en de religieuze markt in Nederland 22-25. With regard to first communion, see P. POST & L. VAN TONGEREN: Het feest van de eerste communie. Op zoek naar de identiteit van het christelijk ritueel, in K.-W. MERKS & N. SCHREURS (eds): *De passie van een grensganger. Theologie aan de vooravond van het derde millennium* (Baarn 1997) 249-264.

[70] *De Standaard* 18-19 december 1999, 15; 18-19 december 'Weekend', 14-15, 18; 20 december, 5; 21 december, 6; 22 december, 5.

[71] See S. HELLEMANS: Secularisation in a religiogeneous modernity, in R. LAERMANS (ed.): *Secularisation and social integration. Papers in honor of Karel Dobbelaere* (Leuven 1998) 67-81.

[72] DRAULANS & WITTE: Initiatie in de vrijwilligerskerk; P. VANDE VYVERE: Welke gemeenschap zal welk geloof dragen? De Vlaamse kerk tussen cultuur- en keuzechristendom, in BOEVE: *De kerk in Vlaanderen* 77-99.

retention of elements from the time of mass Catholicism.[73] In any case, Flanders is experiencing a gradual fall in the number of infants baptised (1967, 96.1%; 1993, 80.7%; 1995, 79.1%; 1996, 76.2%).[74] It appears to me that it is not impossible that the situation in Flanders will come to look like the situation in The Netherlands.

[73] DRAULANS & WITTE: Initiatie in de vrijwilligerskerk 181-183; K. DOBBELAERE: Over godsdienst en de kerk in Vlaanderen in 2000, in R. LAERMANS (ed.): *Godsdienst en Kerk in een geseculariseerde samenleving. Een keuze uit het werk van Karel Dobbelaere* (Leuven 1998) 224-225.

[74] The most recent figures for Flanders with regard to infant baptism are those from 1996. Figures for 1998 will become available in early 2001. With regard to The Netherlands the decline was as follows: 1993, 26.7%; 1995, 24.4%; 1996, 23.7%, 1998, 21.7%.

PAUL POST & LOUIS VAN TONGEREN

THE CELEBRATION OF THE FIRST COMMUNION
SEEKING THE IDENTITY OF THE CHRISTIAN RITUAL*

1. INTRODUCTION

Three times between 1966 and 1996 sociologists of religion have conducted extensive research on religiousness in the Netherlands. The report
on the third study also included the results of the 1966 and 1979 studies.[1] The comparison of the information shows a development on the
basis of which one could draw up a balance of thirty years of religion in
the Netherlands. One of the conclusions confirms what everybody
already knew, namely that in the last decades numerous Dutchmen
turned their back on the church and that church attendance has shown
a consistent downward tendency all these years. At the same time it
appears that two-third of the Dutch consider themselves to be religious
and the number of Dutch people that consider religion very important
has actually risen since 1979.[2] Thus, people's religious life and their
ecclesiastical life are increasingly at odds with each other. There is question of a widening gap between religiousness and church. Church and
faith, doctrine and life have drifted increasingly further apart.

One of the striking conclusions from a recent statistical inventarisation of Roman Catholics in the Netherlands is that for years the first
Communion has hardly lost in popularity.[3] Although the average num-

---

* Translated by K. van Tongeren-Kemme. For the greater part this article was first
published in Dutch as: Het feest van de eerste communie. Op zoek naar de identiteit
van het christelijk ritueel, in K.W. MERKS & N. SCHREURS (eds): *De passie van een
grensganger. Theologie aan de vooravond van het derde millennium* (Baarn 1997) 249-264.

[1] G. DEKKER, J. DE HART & J. PETERS: *God in Nederland 1966-1996* (Amsterdam
1997).

[2] The divergence between, on the one hand, decrease in institutional, ecclesiastical
devoutness listed by religious sociologists and on the other hand the interest in religiosity plays a key role in A. VAN HARSKAMP e.a.: *De religieuze ruis in Nederland. Thesen over
de versterving en de wedergeboorte van de godsdienst* (Zoetermeer 1998).

[3] A. GARRITSEN (ed.): *Pius Jaarboek. Almanak Katholiek Nederland 1998* (Houten
1997) 496-499.

Tilburg: communicantje in de wijk Zorgvliet
De traditie van de moderne industriestad

The celebration of the First Communion.

ber of churchgoers per weekend is still decreasing, the number of first Communicants attains about the same high percentage year after year. Apparently, the phenomenon of the first Communion appeals to something that is stronger than the aversion to church and faith and the ecclesiastical disengagement is less than Sunday's church attendance would suggest. And the trend we see in the first Communion also applies to funerals and, to a lesser extent, baptism, initiation and weddings. The participation in these celebrations shows other percentages than those for the weekly church attendance. Evidently, there is still a considerable commitment to church and faith, a commitment which is primarily latent and which shows itself explicitly only now and then.

The nationwide publicity campaign, which was launched by Tilburg council in 1997, shows that the expressiveness of the first Communion has certainly not yet lost any of its meaning. On one of the full-page pictures with which they advertised in the national weekly news-magazines, a first Communicant is prominently present. We assume that this representation is not meant to be controversial; it is true, this would attract attention and bring a lot of publicity, but in the end it would be counterproductive. True enough, the representation is rich in contrast but that was probably the intention. The key figure is a communicant, dressed up in white, a floral wreath on her head and with folded hands. It could hardly be more traditional, and therefore we may presume that the girl is also wearing long white socks and shiny – and especially pinching – patent leather shoes. The advertisement shows the highly appealing effect of the first Communion. In what is traditionally the most Catholic city in the Netherlands, modernity and industry go hand in hand with church customs and habits. Tradition and modernity, nostalgia and progress, religion and industry are combined in one image to support the slogan "Tilburg modern industrial town"; the communicant expresses the tradition of this modern industrial town as the subtitle indicates.

2. Impressions

Everyone who has an affinity with the Roman Catholic tradition in any way, is familiar with the phenomenon of the recurring annual feast of the first Communion. But even complete outsiders are confronted with it, especially in the southern part of the Netherlands. People may be fully non-religious or non-churchgoing, but when the boy or girl next door is going to make their first Communion they are also invited to the feast: they will keep to the code of the feast and attend the party in the afternoon and bring a present or something for the child's money box. In the preceding weeks, too, they may have noticed the advertisements in the newspaper from boutiques offering special communion clothing (in recent years with particular attention to girls' hats), how the various establishments in the area offer special festive arrangements and how special first Communion bikes are recommended.

Preceding the feast, which generally takes place on a Sunday in May, there is a long and extensive preparatory period, which until about twenty years ago was dealt with in class at school. And although the communicants are still recruited from form four of the primary school, the preparation has been almost entirely transferred from the school to the parish. Nevertheless, most schools do devote attention to the subject, although subsequently the teacher faces the problem that there is also a group of children in class who do not participate. A separate preparatory committee, generally consisting of exclusively mothers and volunteers from the parish, have the responsibility and are concerned with the coordination in consultation with the priest. The preparation route starts after New Year, when the parents of the potential candidates receive an invitation. During a special meeting the parents are informed about the date, about the preparatory project and about the series of meetings which the children and/or the parents will be expected to attend; also the parents are asked to assist with all kinds of practical activities such as decorating the church, making the booklets and accompanying the children for a planned excursion to the miller or the bakery.

During the preparatory meetings the children (and the parents) are catechetically initiated into the Christian faith, the special significance of Jesus of Nazareth and the meaning of the eucharist. They make prayers, learn songs and practice small plays. Also a church visit is usually a fixed item where explanation is given about the various images and objects present. On a Sunday preceding the first Communion celebration the communicants are introduced to the parish in a special family service. They are given a prominent place on the sanctuary, their names are written in calligraphy on big sheets which are hung throughout the church and they come forward one by one and announce their own name.

At the communion feast itself the communicants are in the spotlight; they are the centre of attention. The liturgy concentrates on them. For these children the communion feast is the conclusion of the preparatory period with as its climax the receiving of Bread and Wine, which on this day is administered in a special place which provides a good view for everyone, especially for the photographer and the video-team who are hired to prevent a disturbing walking around and flashing camaras. For the occasion the church is exuberantly decorated and outside the flags are waving. All dressed up and in procession the communicants make their entry into the church together with the members of the preparatory committee and the priest. A large part of the seating is reserved for parents, brothers and sisters and grandparents. The rest of the relatives and acquaintances who are invited for the whole day have to find a seat further behind. Fellow parishoners are absent for the most part; after all, the first Communion is especially intended for the family. Because of their personal relationship with one of the children, all those attending show great involvement, especially when the child that brought them there performs in a play, reads a text or sings a song. Apart from this the involvement is very divers. The family of the communicants and a few acquaintances from their neighbourhood usually belong to the parish, but their involvement in the church varies; some take part in parish life on a regular basis, while others may be completely non-church but do not want to withhold their child from making its first Communion. Generally, the rest of the attendants also relate to the ritual in very different ways; one is used to another parish and church, one is disconnected or estranged from the church ritual, or one has never been a churchgoer. Some people are annoyed about the impertinent way the liturgical rituals and the eucharist are dealt with, while others are surprised at the spontaneity and the sometimes chaotic-looking enthusiasm: "that it can also be done in this way". Both someone's ritual behaviour and the reaction to this from others show the background of those present. Some are surprised when a collection plate passes for the second time, or when their neighbour suddenly prays out loud. The same goes for standing and kneeling, answering and taking communion.

3. LITURGICAL SCIENCE APPROACH

Everyone has their own experiences of the first Communion and will recognise many of the impressions described here and can probably add a few from personal observation. It is not our intention to draw a complete picture. This would demand a thorough inventarisation on the basis of a proper empirical research. These impressions do give us a recognisable and representative picture of the current first Communion practice, which subsequently can serve as a model for a wider sketch of the situation of the Christian ritual in the (post) modern culture. The communion celebration offers enough clues to exemplify the direction in which liturgical science is moving and how it deals with questions which can be raised from current liturgical practice. Other rites and feasts on the cycle of year and life can be approached in a similar way.

It is striking that the first Communion has never been the subject of thorough research (at least not in the Netherlands and Flanders),[4] while the various sacraments and divers aspects of the ecclesiastical and liturgical life constantly form the subject of research. However, the impressions of the communion celebration described here show how the first Communion is a striking example of a ritual in which the complexity of the current liturgy is displayed. In recent years there has been a shift in the ritual market and the perception of the ecclesiastical festivals and rituals is liable to various changes.[5] The renewal of the liturgy, which was given a radical impulse at the Second Vatican Council, continues in a dynamic social, ecclesiastical and cultural context which is constantly changing and developing.[6] As a consequence of these shifts we can

---

[4] See H. MEYER: *Eucharistie. Geschichte, Theologie, Pastoral* (= Gottesdienst der Kirche. Handbuch der Liturgiewissenschaft 4) (Regensburg 1989) 560-565, with literature. Furthermore we can mention special issues of liturgical journals; see for instance *Eerste communie. Uitnodiging en uitdaging* (= *Werkmap voor liturgie* 13 (1979) 275-402; 14 (1980) 5-90; *Het vieren van de eerste kommunie* (= Liturgische handreikingen 7) (Breda s.a.); *Doopsel, vormsel, eerste eucharistie, vandaag en morgen* (= *Tijdschrift voor liturgie* 75 (1991) (1-2)); *Als je communie doet* (= *Inzet* 26 (1997) (2)).

[5] Cf. J. PIEPER & P. POST: Rituele veranderingen met betrekking tot de huwelijkssluiting. Een onderzoeksvoorstel, in *Jaarboek voor liturgie-onderzoek* 12 (1996) 136-163, esp. 136-144 and 152-158; P. POST: Alle dagen feest, of: de ritencrisis voorbij. Een verkenning van de markt, in P. POST & W.M. SPEELMAN (eds.): *De Madonna van de Bijenkorf. Bewegingen op de rituele markt* (= Liturgie in perspectief 9) (Baarn 1997) 11-32; IDEM: Rituele dynamiek in liturgisch perspectief. Een verkenning van vorm, inhoud en beleving, in *Jaarboek voor liturgie-onderzoek* 15 (1999) 119-141; G. LUKKEN: *Rituelen in overvloed. Een kritische bezinning op de plaats en de gestalte van het christelijk ritueel in onze cultuur* (Baarn 1999).

[6] Cf. G. LUKKEN: Inculturation et avenir de la liturgie, in *Questions liturgiques* 75 (1994) 113-134; IDEM: Inculturation de la liturgie. Théorie et pratique, in *ibidem* 77 (1996) 10-39; L. VAN TONGEREN: De inculturatie van de liturgie tot (stil)stand

notice differences in ecclesiastical commitment, in the frequency of churchgoing, in the liturgical rituals offered, which have become more varied (in shape and form), in the perception of the sacraments and especially of the eucharist, in views concerning the meaning of initiation into church and faith and incorporation into the community of faith; what was an automatic participation in ecclesiastical life has become a well-reasoned motivation; the liturgy is more clearly embedded in the complexity of pastoral and catechetical activities; the changed perception and design of feasts are also part of this process of change.

Traditional customs (seem to) change and in an altered ecclesiastical-religious and social-cultural context one looks for new designs for the liturgical ritual. At first sight these new designs seem to be at odds with the familiar, traditional customs. When shifts take place within the symbolic practice one is used to, this raises all kinds of questions because one becomes disorientated as a result of the changes. This alienation can be situated within a field of tension in which several dimensions of the ritual interfere; this concerns the interaction between the secular, profane, general religious and Christian or ecclesiastical dimensions which can be distinguished within the ritual. The question about the meaning of the developing liturgy in the (post) modern time, therefore, concentrates on the question regarding the identity of the Christian ritual and the position of sacramentality in our culture. This sets the field of tension which is evoked by the relation between tradition and current events and between continuity and renewal. Many of the aspects mentioned converge in the communion celebration and thus show the complexity of the current liturgy. Therefore, an exploratory study of the feast offers the possibility of showing which objects and questions belong to the central field of research of liturgical science.

4. THE FIRST COMMUNION AS A FEAST

Above all, the first Communion is a feast. The grandeur of this feast may vary. Although no longer as common as it used to be, in the south girls are still dressed up as brides, rooms are hired for the reception and

gebracht? Kanttekeningen bij een Romeins document over liturgie en inculturatie, in *Jaarboek voor liturgie-onderzoek* 12 (1996) 164-186; IDEM: Liturgie in context. De vernieuwing van de liturgie en de voortgang ervan als een continu proces, in *Tijdschrift voor liturgie* 81 (1997) 178-198.

guests are provided with a grand buffet. In the north the feast is generally more modest, but here, too, the first Communion is experienced
and celebrated as a feast. Possibly this is also an important reason why
the first Communion has remained so dominant in the midst of a
process of ongoing secularization. Many families who are increasingly
losing touch with the ritual repertoire of the church still celebrate the
first Communion. The feast is not only a church matter, but has also
got a fixed position in the social order. Because of this, the celebration
of the first Communion is comparable to the important feasts of the
liturgical year and to the (ecclesiastical) celebration of the important
moments in life which are still celebrated on a large scale. Compared
with the recent past the decrease in churchgoing is unarguable; however,
a comparison with the situation before 1850 shows that the current frequency of churchgoing is not at all exceptional. In many ways the dominance of the Christian ritual repertoire in the period between about
1850 and 1950 was an exceptional one. Thus, the abandoning of the
ecclesiastical and liturgical involvement is relative. A suggested crisis is
only relative.[7] There is still great involvement in feasts which take place
in the course of the church year and peoples lives, such as Christmas,
Easter, baptism, first Communion, marriage and funeral. Moreover, a
revival of all kinds of festivities which have a link with church matters is
evident, such as the interest in pilgrimages.

The increasing concentration on the celebration of church feasts
characterises the current churchgoers more and more as feast-day Christians. This development links up with a much broader process that is
going on in our culture and society. All kinds of occasions and events
lead to festive manifestations. Birthdays and jubilees no longer pass by
unnoticed but are lavishly celebrated. Weekends and free days are seized
with both hands as an opportunity to organize festive events for the promotion of the city, the wellbeing of the tradespeople and for the amusement of the population. New rituals are created round birth, marriage,
divorce and funeral. Experts set up specialized agencies which provide
appropriate rituals for any feast. The growing interest in the significance
of a feast and in the design of all sorts of festive rituals ties in with an
important field of research in liturgical science which is also high on the
agenda of many cultural scientists. From the beginning, one of the pil-

---

[7] P. RAEDTS: De christelijke middeleeuwen als mythe. Ontstaan en gebruik van een
constructie uit de negentiende eeuw, in *Tijdschrift voor theologie* 30 (1990) 146-158.

lars of the liturgical scientific discipline has been the study of the historical development and the theological meaning of feasts in relation to their anthropological and cultural setting. This is why, also within the liturgical scientific approach to sacramental theology, the festive ritual holds a key position. Because of the fact that feasts form a vital link within the organisational structure of time, time during the year is arranged in bigger and smaller units which are all marked and distinguished by festivities. By celebrating these feasts and providing them with appropriate rituals and customs, the religious dimension of time in the Christian liturgy is shaped to the rhythm of time.

To approach the first Communion as a feast makes it possible to reflect critically upon the current practice of this feast from a liturgical and theological point of view. A starting point for this reflection can be found in four separate dimensions which determine the feast.[8] First of all, a feast is a break in the everyday rhythm. The daily routine is interrupted. The contrast in relation to the normal routine is typical. A feast day exists only because of a series of ordinary days and, conversely, many days are ordinary or common because a feast day sometimes occurs. If this contrast did not exist we would only have the shallow, everyday rhythm or every day would be a feast day. Secondly, a feast always has a reason or an object; it always celebrates something or someone. An event is so extraordinary or something happens to a person that is so remarkable, you cannot let it pass unnoticed. We celebrate to lift the particular above the day-to-day. The special design of the feast is a third element; there is another rhythm to the day, there are special rules and customs, other (festive) clothes are worn and there are different eating and drinking habits. Each feast has its own ritual game of solemnity and merriment, in which symbolic acts, words and gestures alternate according to fixed patterns or certain rules. Finally, every feast is carried by a solidary group or community. After all, you do not celebrate a feast on your own but with like-minded people, i.e. people who feel an affinity to each other or to the centre of attention. All four aspects mentioned also apply to the celebration of the first Communion and

---

[8] F. TABORDA: *Sakramente. Praxis und Fest* (Düsseldorf 1988); O. MARQUARD: Kleine Philosophie des Festes, in U. SCHUTZ (ed.): *Das Fest. Eine Kulturgeschichte von der Antike bis zur Gegenwart* (München 1988) 413-420; A. SCHILSON: Fest und Feier in anthropologischer und theologischer Sicht. Ein Literaturbericht, in *Liturgisches Jahrbuch* 44 (1994) 3-32; IDEM: Das neue Religiöse und der Gottesdienst. Liturgie vor einer neuen Herausforderung?, in *ibidem* 46 (1996) 94-109; POST: Alle dagen feest.

emphasize its festive character. At the same time a more thorough reflection on these dimensions shows that the communion feast is under strong pressure and is threatened by the changes it is undergoing.

4.1. The contrast

As indicated earlier, a general social tendency towards a growing feast-day culture can be observed, in which every opportunity is taken to turn a normal day into a feast. The ordinary way of life is eliminated as much as possible and transformed into a feast. Because of this the feast may become isolated for it cannot contrast anymore with the usual way of things. It is a characteristic of the feast that it marks a moment in the passing time, which gives it a decisive function. When every day is a feast it loses its embedding in daily life and cannot function as a marking point anymore. Because there are so many feasts the contrast is sought increasingly in the design. Eccentric, exuberant and special inventions must show that one feast differs from the other. It may be good for the environment if you stay quietly at home on a Sunday but you will be looked upon as boring. The most surprising excursions and undertakings are thought of in order to turn a birthday party into a very special day, because the most obvious things have become too common.

The liturgy is also being confronted with this altered feast-day culture. The liturgical structure is intended for a congregation which gathers together every Sunday, week after week. The three-year cycle of readings strengthens this supposition: the congregation is taken by the hand each week by one of the Synoptic Evangelists in a kind of continuing story. This basic pattern is interrupted a few times a year, such as on special feast days and during Lent and Advent. For an ever-growing group of Christians this self-evident weekly rhythm of the liturgy has changed into almost exclusively celebrating the high feasts of the ecclesiastical year and the highlights in life. The contrast with the 'ordinary' Sunday liturgy is gone for them. They have become feast-day Christians, for whom the Christian ritual is identified with feast.

This altered meaning and perception of the liturgical rhythm in the lives of people questions the liturgical practice and requires a reconsideration of the theological meaning of the feasts. Is it possible to celebrate feasts, like Christmas and Easter, in isolation, when they actually form part of a larger entity? What is the meaning of Easter when there is no connection between the resurrection and the theme of the preceding days of the Holy Week, and what about the dynamics of Easter when this is no longer embedded in the perspective of an expected eschatological completion? In other words: by celebrating separate feasts there is a risk that the basic anamnetic structure of the liturgy will disappear and that the coherence will be omitted between the actual feast and the remembrance of the salutary history with a view to a salutary future. Possibly, this calls for a reconsideration of the design of these feasts. For example, a defective Easter can be prevented by combining the themes of Easter, which in the course of time have been spread over several days, back again into one liturgy.[9]

A comparable diagnosis can be made with regard to the celebration of the first Communion which is a one-off occasion for an increasing number of children. In this respect the oft-heard remark that for many children the first Communion is also the last communion is significant. The first Communion assumes a regular participation in the eucharist. If not, the communion feast has no contrast effect and the feast is not raised above the ordinary celebration of the eucharist. The more the first Communion becomes a one-off affair, separate from a regular eucharist practice, the more it will turn into a separate quantity. In many cases the communion feast seems to be transformed into a separate sacrament. In its evolution it has become a new transitional rite of the life-cycle, without it being clear which point of the life-cycle is being marked for a seven-year-old. There is no question of starting school as a *rite de passage* in form four at the age of seven nor can a conscious religious conviction be expected at that age. The idea that the first Communion should complete the initiation into the church presents historical and theological problems, as will be shown in the next paragraph. Moreover, initiation assumes a continuing participation; this involvement however cannot be expected from people for whom the communion feast is a one-off occasion.

4.2. Diversity in objects and causes

Because the eucharist is the most central rite of Christian worship in which the presence of the resurrected Lord is kept alive in celebrating the symbols of bread and wine, it contains a number of themes. The

---

[9] For a concrete design see H. OOSTERHUIS: Dood en opstanding. Een liturgie voor Goede Vrijdag, in *Werkschrift voor leerhuis en liturgie* 2 (1982) (no. 4).

eucharist can be looked upon from a metaphysical or transcendental point of view, but theological or anthropological viewpoints can also be emphasized as well as its ecclesiological meaning. A number of these possible elucidations are embodied in the first Communion. Collectively, they probably come close to the plenitude of the eucharist, but it seems to be asking a bit too much to outline all these aspects during the children's introduction to the eucharist. That is why, usually, only one of the many aspects is enlarged in a first Communion liturgy.

In essence, the first Communion means the first full participation in the eucharist by also joining in the communion rite and receiving bread and wine for the first time. Thus, the eucharist is the centre of the communion feast. Because the perception of the eucharist has been subject to considerable changes over the last decades and because of the fact that from various points of view several levels of significance can be distinguished[10] varying emphasis has also been laid on the celebration of the first Communion. History shows that it has always been very difficult to express the meaning of the eucharist in word and image. According to a more classical theological notion the eucharist is a sacrifice in which, through a consecrating act, bread and wine change into the Body and Blood of Christ. This point of view strongly emphasizes the transformation of the element through transsubstantiation: the priest represents the church and offers the sacrifice on behalf of the congregation.

Through the discovery of the anamnetic structure of the liturgy, nowadays the eucharist is perceived and experienced primarily as a commemorative liturgy by the congregation. In practice however, it appears to be difficult to give shape to the eschatological dimension of the anamnesis. A visionary orientation towards the future often receives too little attention. Mostly one restricts oneself to the connection between the eucharistic meal of the actual liturgy and the life of Jesus on earth. Due to a historicizing bias the remembrance of what once happened eclipses the commemoration of what has to be done today. But "it is not about bringing the past closer, but about bringing the future closer".[11]

---

[10] See G. LUKKEN: Op weg naar eenheid in verscheidenheid. Modellen van gemeenschapsvorming rondom brood en beker, in E. HENAU & F. JESPERS (eds.): *Liturgie en kerkopbouw* (Baarn 1993) 92-104; J. TIGCHELER: De eucharistieviering bijbels herijken, in *Speling* 47 (1995) no. 4, 72-81.

[11] H. VAN WAVEREN: Betlehem in zomer en winter een broodhuis, in *Eredienstvaardig* 13 (1997) 100.

The symbolic character of the eucharist plays an important role. The eucharist is a ritual meal where bread is broken and bread and wine are shared. The breaking and sharing of bread and wine symbolize the imitation of Jesus who lived in complete submission to and in unity with God. The emphasis on the meal or on sharing together shows that these aspects are dominantly present in the first Communion celebrations, sometimes to such an extent that the enclosed ethical appeal becomes moralizing.

At most first Communion celebrations the children are told 'that from now on they fully belong', because by participating in the eucharist they are accepted into the whole sacramental life of the church. This means that the first Communion is considered to be an initiation or a part of it. After baptism and confirmation and through the first Communion one has become a full member of the church. The initiation thus takes place gradually in three stages. This unfolding of the initiation is the consequence of a development, which has grown over time and although it is natural and familiar for us, it can be criticized at the same time, because through this phasing the initial unity of the initiation is lost.

Although we have only inadequate information about the commonplace nature and the spread of infant baptism during the period of the early church and the early Middle Ages, there was a univocal practice up until the early Middle Ages in which the first participation in the eucharist was a continuation of the baptism in one initiation liturgy.[12] Baptismal water was linked with the receiving of the spiritual gifts and with the participation in the eucharist; the separate elements formed a unity. This meant that when the initiation involved children, baptism and first Communion were directly combined. The present-day first Communion was actually a part of the baptismal ceremony for a long time. This did not change until the thirteenth century, when baptism and eucharist were separated. Although the fourth Lateran Council in 1215 did not forbid infant communion, it ruled that one was obliged to communicate at least once a year (Easter) on reaching the age of discretion (*anni discretionis*). The interpretation of when one reached 'the age

---

[12] For a historical description of the relation between baptism and eucharist and the participation of children in the eucharist, see the extensive study by J. HERMANS: *Eucharistie vieren met kinderen. Een liturgie-wetenschappelijke studie over de deelname van het kind aan de eucharistie in het verleden en volgens de huidige kerkelijke richtlijnen* (Brugge 1987).

of discretion' varied, but was somewhere between the ages of seven and twelve. The intention was that one ought to have a fairly reasonable understanding of the meaning of the eucharist. In the sixteenth century the Council of Trent resumed the regulation on the *anni discretionis*. Again, the age was not defined exactly, but in practice it varied from ten to fourteen years old. Following naturally from a eucharistic revitalisation in a period in which the ecclesiastical ritual repertoire was the dominant context,[13] Pope Pius X propagated a more frequent participation in the communion in his decree *Quam singulari*. He especially had the children in mind, for he wanted them to participate in the eucharist earlier in life. As a consequence, the age for making the first Communion was lowered to about seven years old, a practice which is maintained to this very day.

The view of the first Communion as a rite through which one is fully initiated is thus historically explicable, but at the same time remains controversial as regards content;[14] after all, one already becomes a full member of the church through baptism. Adult baptism has no phased initiation; the first participation in the eucharist forms an integral part of the ritual. The distinction is based on the fact that one requires some rationality as a condition for the eucharist. There is nothing anywhere about the level of intellectual comprehension, but insight cannot really be expected from a seven-year-old concerning the content of the eucharist, which is based on predominantly medieval theological concepts. The same is equally true for adults.

In this line of approach, which primarily considers the first Communion as a part of the initiation, a more ecclesiological stress is sometimes placed by emphasizing the admission into a (local) community of faith. The local parish or community is the most concrete form of 'being church' for a child. The parish covers a convenient-sized territory where even a child can become familiar with a group of committed parishioners and with the local customs and practices reasonably quickly. Full admission as a matter of course can best be shaped with the local situation.

---

[13] P. POST: 'An excellent game...': On Playing the Mass, in C. CASPERS, G. LUKKEN & G. ROUWHORST (eds.): *Bread of Heaven. Customs and practices surrounding Holy Communion. Essays in the history of liturgy and culture* (= Liturgia condenda 3) (Kampen 1995) 185-214.

[14] H. MANDERS: Eerste communie een initiatie? Een partiële pastoraal-theologische meditatie, in *Werkmap voor liturgie* 14 (1980) 7-19.

4.3. The design

The liturgy of the communion celebration is strongly child-centered. The whole liturgy is tailored to the world of the child. The design fits in with didactic views and catechetical methods are copied. Regular ingredients are the performing of plays, biblical dramas, dance, music, songs and texts which are presented by several children in the form of a dialogue. In the preparation careful attention is paid to ensuring that every child receives a task. The dramatized elements emphasize the character of the liturgy as a ritual game, but by over-emphasizing this it often turns into a performance. The collective liturgy for everyone present then becomes a spectacle. The intention of the playful design is that children should understand what it is all about, that they should enjoy themselves and that the content of the celebration and of all the subjects discussed during the preparatory period can be communicated with the people present. Because of the special design of the liturgy and the special attention paid to the children, the communion celebration contrasts sharply with common liturgical practice. As a consequence it is very difficult, for the children as well as for the others attending, to correlate this experience with that of other liturgical celebrations.

It has become reality that most children no longer familiarize themselves with the church ritual in a more or less natural way. An inevitable consequence of this is that the communicants need to be provided with an extensive preparatory period in order to let them experience various dimensions of the feast and to give them some insight into its content and meaning. In that sense, the first Communion is comparable to confirmation and marriage. These feasts which are also intensively prepared are, to many people, incidental occasions when church and belief and the liturgical repertoire are briefly in the spotlight. The liturgy on the feast day itself forms the conclusion to the preparatory period which is thus often referred to during the celebration. An additional element of the first Communion and the confirmation is that for the parents these celebrations often mean a renewed or intensified acquaintance with church, faith and liturgy. Consequently, the pastoral objective of these feasts is broadened. They offer the pastors the opportunity to get in direct contact with a group of parents which they would otherwise probably never have met. That is why the preparation of the children is often combined with a form of adult catechesis. Normally, there is no reflection of the content of the adult catechesis in the celebration; here the emphasis lies primarily on the children's preparation.

4.4. The solidary group

Whichever element is given predominance in the celebration of the first Communion, initiation or acceptance always plays a part. Whether this initiation especially concerns the eucharist, the church or the local community, in all cases the celebration itself presupposes the involvement of like-minded people. If not, there is a risk that the celebration will become an isolated moment. In such circumstance the ritual is *ex opere operato*, whereby the celebration becomes an objective in itself. However, for an initiation it is essential that one should be admitted into a group of people who are already initiated and who can subsequently guide the newcomer.

Practice shows that this solidary group is increasingly absent, or that it consists of multicoloured composite subgroups with references of their own. In the liturgy in which a group of children receive communion for the first time, the number of those present who do not communicate increases. An increasing number fulfil the role of onlookers rather than participants. This is caused both by the design of the liturgy, which generally does not stimulate participation, as well as by the fact that many people are present because of their special relationship with the communicants and their family while they themselves have become estranged from church and liturgy. When during the communion celebration the initiation in the local community is emphasized, this presupposes a vital community which is present at the moment when new members are admitted. And although the first Communion is often presented as a big parish feast, it is usually the parishioners who are absent. The first Communion appears to be chiefly a family celebration at which the family, relatives and some friends and acquaintances are the supporting group.

Besides the parents it is especially the members of the preparatory committee who represent the community. It is they who supervise the extensive preparatory period and it is they who almost entirely direct the first Communion liturgy. Although the priest formally performs the ritual, it is the members of the preparatory committee who actually prepare and admit the newcomers on behalf of the parish.

5. The perspective of mystagogy

The current practice of the first Communion shows an explicit appeal to intellectual comprehension. One is free to participate but if one does, a more or less conscious choice is expected. An extensive preparation enables the children to justify their choice at their own level and to interpret the meaning of the eucharist. Society's tendency to rationalize also has repercussions for the liturgy and manifests itself strongly round the first Communion. Faith and liturgy are strongly rationalized through extensive catechetical routes. By means of special projects, the meaning and significance of the eucharist are made understandable to the children and their parents. Attention is paid to the recognisable daily ritual of the meal, to the nescessity of eating and drinking and to the relation between bread and life. Moreover, several projects provide for a more general introduction and initiation into Christianity, church and liturgy. Within that context one visits the church building where various elements of the interior and the furniture are explained. By overemphasizing understanding, insight and rationale, one runs the risk that the ritual has to be constantly accounted for. There is a real danger that overemphasizing this approach will occur at the expense of an essential feature of the ritual and of the liturgy, i.e. the unselfishness and the gratuitousness. One may wonder whether the meaning, the significance and the implications of rites and symbols ought not to be experienced principally by attending actual liturgies. We are then faced with the problem that the first Communion has lost its embedding in a regular liturgical rhythm. One becomes familiar with liturgy by participation, not by learning the rules and principles from a book or through a course. In current first Communion practice there is probably too much emphasis on first wanting to learn and know what we are doing, instead of doing what we do not yet know.[15]

In this connection there is a case for shifting the accent somewhat and seeking inspiration in the early Christian practice of mystagogy. This would mean that not all the attention is exclusively focussed on the preparatory process but that one also puts energy into the follow-up. Then the communion celebration is not so much the conclusion of the preparatory period, but the beginning of a continuing initiation and introduction; a long process of a possibly greater or lesser degree of

---

[15] H. ANDRIESSEN: De eerste communie doen, in *Inzet* 26 (1997) no. 2, 36-41.

commitment is started and marked by a celebration. Since the current liturgy does not provide the scope for such an approach, experimenting with new possibilities is important, for the liturgy itself has also isolated the first Communion. The Sunday after the communion celebration the parish is back to normal again and no trace can be found of a deviating, child-centred design for the liturgy; the services follow their own familiar pattern again and nobody seems to be concerned about a new group of participants who joined them the previous week. The concept of first Communion implies continuance, but this should not be expected solely from the communicants. It is equally the obligation and responsibility of the community to create conditions which make it possible for the newcomers to give shape to this continuance. If they feel unwelcome and unwanted then the community spirit of the parish or community can be criticized.

6. CONCLUSION

The practice of first Communion can be criticized from various angles. But when we look at the shifts that are taking place in the social, ecclesiastical and cultural sphere and in numerous other areas of social life, then at the same time, the communion celebration offers possibilities and chances. Precisely because the communion celebration has maintained its position not only ecclesiastically but also socially, it can be put into a new perspective through the altered context. With reference to the basal anthropological experiences within our culture concerning meals and feasts, the ritual of the first Communion may offer an initial opening to a faithful or religious understanding.[16] The transcendental can thus be opened up and shaped into a ritual articulation. In our perception, appreciation of the initiating character will have to prevail over a maximalistic view in which all theological concepts of sacramentality are interwoven. From time to time, these primary experiences can be regulated and may in later life give one something to hold on to or may be intensified when one gets married, has one's children baptized or has to bid farewell to a relative at a funeral.

---

[16] Cf. J. DE VISSCHER: *Een te voltooien leven. Over rituelen van de moderne mens* (Kapellen/Kampen 1996) 7-25; 95-120.

Ton Scheer

UT DUO SINT…
A THEORY OF ACTS APPROACH TO MARRIAGE LITURGY

1. Introduction

In this study an attempt will be made to determine whether, to what degree and in what way approaches based on the Theory of Acts, particularly as conceived by Paul Ricoeur and John R. Searle, can be applied to a ritual situation.[1] This application is important because the concept of rituality has not been worked out as such in these theories.

A Christian ritual complex has been selected which in practice enjoys considerable interest and regard. It owes its prestige to the fact that it is considered of significance in the creation and construction of the human and religious self of those who are central in this ritual, exchanging vows pledging their lives to each other, and who are bound together by its performance. We are referring to the Christian ritual of marriage.

Such a theory of acts investigation of this ritual is, however, a very complicated affair. In the first place, the ritual is an organic unity of a multitude of actions which are performed by numerous actors. A comprehensive pattern of actions must thus be sought. It will be a challenge to discover the line – and more important, the plot – linking these many and varied actions, which effectuate the fundamental import of this ritual. In the second place, a theory of acts approach, particularly that of Ricoeur, is constructed from the principle of interfering complexity.

2. Interfering complexity

With regard to this latter concept, one proceeds from the assumption that the acts of people can be understood by an outside observer and can be performed by the actors themselves purely as a presentation of

---

[1] P. Ricoeur: *Soi-même comme un autre* (Paris 1990); J.R. Searle: *The construction of social reality* (New York 1995).

the self in perceptibility; these are what are termed basic acts, which give evidence of human actions. Acts can, however, also be conceived as expressions of the desire to be and to give direction to one's own being: this involves acts that express the intentional orientation of the actor, preferably in the form of narrativity. Acts can, however, also be intended as manifestations of the will to be with and for the other; what is meant here are acts that distinguish themselves by their illocutionary character. In addition to these, acts can have the purpose of actualising the aspiration to realise and advance something good; this involves actions that are directed toward the realisation of morality. Further, acts can be the expression and disclosure of the consciousness that performance of being in any way at all ultimately implies responsibility, accountability, acknowledgement and thankfulness in the presence of that which surrounds and transcends mankind: these are acts that are characterised by a religious tenor in general. Finally, acts can refer to the actualisation of the relation to the Other by the naming and calling upon of The Name; what are intended here are acts that have an explicit religious significance, generally derived from established religious traditions.

Human beings possess the possibility of expressing and conveying all of this in the language of the body: the creation of the narrative and the form that they are, radically characterised by contingency and permanency, fate and vocation, isolation and reciprocity, deficit and assets, self and at the same time being other: in other words, human existence as 'drama' – in the sense of act and play – in which the antagony of the tragic cannot be suppressed or excluded.

3. FORMULATING THE QUESTION

We ask now whether these interferences of complexity, and possibly also of intensity, typical of the *agein* of mankind and considered by the philosopher as a 'model', are also reflected in the marriage ritual we have chosen as our example. In this we proceed from the assumption that every ritual complex is constructed according to its *syntagma* (structure) and shaped according to its *paradigma* (content, form) by numerous ritual 'elements', which together form 'components' within the complex ritual, which in turn make up the total ritual 'complex'. The application of the theory of acts model thus demands in advance an analysis of the structure and content of the ritual chosen.

However, until now such ritual analyses have been rather seldom performed. We do possess a number of studies which are characterised by a structuralist approach.[2] The limitation of this approach is, however, that it is precisely the 'acting' of the actor which remains outside of the field of vision, since it is particularly the structure and the generation of the textual meaning that is investigated. Other rituological analyses have turned their attention to the behavioural dimension of the ritual acts.[3] Every ritual can also be characterised as a behavioural order, constructed of elements which are not explicitly, or merely implicitly intended by the actors, while they are indeed the basis for the ritual practice. In this connection reference must be made to the habitual aspect and the repetitive character of ritual acts. Finally, it should be said that there have been a number of empirical theological studies performed into the ritual acts of both leaders and participants in rituals. These especially involve the field of preaching.[4] The principle attention here has been on the conveyance function and the reception of ritual actions, their effect on participants.

In this study we want to focus directly on the acts which are performed by the actors in the ritual in question, and on the relationships which are felt between the acts by the actors, in order to get a perspective on the apparently complex pattern of actions that can be read from the text of the ritual.[5] From what follows it will appear that especially acts of narrativity – toward expression and construction of identity – and acts of illocution – toward the maintenance and encouragement of communication – define the pattern of ritual actions.

4. ACTIONS WITH A PECULIAR STATUS

Taken in itself, this approach tallies well with classical views about liturgy, which first and foremost should be understood as a form of action, and more specifically, ritual action. The Greek roots *ergazomai*

---

[2] G. LUKKEN: *Rituelen in overvloed* (Baarn 1999) 358-360.
[3] M. JOSSUTIS: *Der Weg in das Leben. Eine Einführung in den Gottesdienst auf verhaltenswissenschaftlicher Grundlage* (München 1991).
[4] K.-F. DAIBER *et al.*: *Predigen und hören* 1-3 (München 1980-1992).
[5] An analogous study was performed by J.A. ZIMMERMAN: *Liturgy as language of faith. A liturgical methodology in the mode of Paul Ricoeur's textual hermeneutics* (Boston 1988) also making use of R. Jakobson's theory of communication.

and *agô* and the Latin *agere* express this aspect. It is, moreover, an action that is performed on a large scale and size: with and in front of an audience, the people in a city. With regard to this, rituologists and liturgists observe that rituals must be characterised as exemplary compositions of actions, which are performed with an eye to the realisation of communication in, and for the benefit of the community, and to promote the formation of identity in the persons involved.[6] Precisely this characteristic of exemplariness – as widely recognised, appreciated and affirmed as rituals themselves – differentiates them from ordinary actions and provides them with a unique position with regard to everyday existence: autotopy, with a unique configuration in time and space, design and role behaviour.[7] This autotopic aspect of rituals explains their presentative effect and the repetitive character that is ascribed to them. This is not, however, an exhaustive characterisation of them. They are just as much characterised by and at the same time through their openness and originality of actions, which creates the possibility of giving form to their configuration precisely in and for the *hic et nunc*.

Christian rituality, that is, the liturgy, displays the above characteristics. The liturgical programme itself has developed on the basis of four structuring conditions which form the foundation for the ritual actions of the community and the individual, vid.: the celebration of being (1) according to the conditions of temporality (the permanent cycle that is characterised by the interrelation of past, present and future); (2) according to the conditions of speciality (the advancing rhythm characterised by ascent, advance and recession); (3) according to the conditions of history (ideational and spiritual currents and traditions); (4) according to the conditions of the situation in which and for which it is performed (theme and facticity).[8] Human existence is interpreted there as being in relation to the God of revelation, with Christological and ecclesial implications. Liturgists thus also consider Christian rituals as complexes of actions of and for Christians, for the advancement of their identity in faith, and

---

[6] L.-M. CHAUVET: *Symbole et sacrement. Une relecture sacramentelle de l'existence chrétienne* (Paris 1987).

[7] R.L. GRIMES: *Beginnings in ritual studies* (Columbia 1995); C. BELL: *Ritual. Perspectives and dimensions* (Oxford 1997).

[8] A. SCHEER: Als gemeente geroepen tot vrede, in J.A. VAN DER VEN (ed.): *Toekomst voor de kerk?* (Kampen 1985) 240-256; A. SCHEER: In de liturgie wordt de diakonie tot de genade van ons leven, in J.A. VAN DER VEN & A. HOUTEPEN (eds): *Weg van de kerk* (Kampen 1994) 115-138.

encouraging them in the communication of their faith. They are inclined to consider liturgical actions as the Christian religious acts par excellence.[9] In the perspective of this study, however, this description only has validity if, and so far as, and according to the way in which these rituals fulfil the characteristics that are typical of human actions.

5. MARRIAGE RITUAL

I wish to now apply this positioning of rituality to one of the Christian rituals in particular, namely that of the marriage liturgy. This ritual was chosen because of the fact that I have several times in the past concentrated on the analysis of this ritual complex, in terms of its structure, its nature as an act, and its theme.[10] Before I approach it in the following sections with the aid of the Theory of Acts, there are several complications which must be noted and elaborated. With which ritual complex, precisely, will we actually be dealing? I have chosen the marriage ritual of the Western Catholic tradition, as it was shaped during the liturgical renewal after Vatican II, as it has been published as an official document in Dutch translation, and is assumed to be the guide for contemporary liturgical practice.[11] To what degree or in what ways the last is the case, is a subject for research which falls outside of this study. The post-Vatican ritual, however, raises a number of issues which are not without importance for its interpretation.

In the first place, the ritual is an historical phenomenon, one which has its genesis in Christian antiquity, but which has obtained its ritual shape since the early Middle Ages.[12] Later in the Middle Ages it

---

[9] E.J. LENGELING: *Liturgie. Dialog zwischen Gott und Mensch* (Freiburg 1981).

[10] A. SCHEER: Peilingen in de hedendaagse huwelijksliturgie. Een oriënterend onderzoek, in *Tijdschrift voor liturgie* 62 (1978) 259-317; A. SCHEER: De huwelijksviering 'Vrede voor jou' van H. Oosterhuis, in *Inzet* 8 (1979) No. 5, 16-32.

[11] *Liturgie van de sacramenten en andere kerkelijke vieringen. Orde van dienst voor de liturgische viering van het huwelijk* (Zeist 1996); edited by the Nationale Raad voor Liturgie. Since this study is based upon this official Dutch version, not all texts have been 'normalised' according to the English version of the liturgy, since different translations of the Latin texts can result in differing 'acts'.

[12] Cf. J.-B. MOLIN & P. MUTEMBE: *Le rituel du mariage en France* (Paris 1974); B. KLEINHEYER: Riten um Ehe und Familie, in B. KLEINHEYER & E. VON SEVERUS (eds): *Sakramentliche Feiern II* (= Gottesdienst der kirche. Handbuch der Liturgiewissenschaft 8) (Regensburg 1984) 67-156; R. BURGGRAEVE *et al.* (eds): *Het huwelijk* (= KADOC-studies 24) (Leuven 2000).

underwent considerable development, until in the period after the Council of Trent it received its definitive form.[13] In the liturgical renewal of Vatican II the ritual was subject to a considerable number of alterations.[14]

Secondly, the development of the ritual occurred under the influence of a number of contextual factors: ethnic factors, through which, for instance, Germanic characteristics have remained present; cultural factors, which have, for instance, marked the relation between male and female; social factors, which have defined the place of marriage in society; political factors, which have influenced the position of the institution of marriage in the power relations between church and state; and economic factors, which for centuries have placed the contractual character of marriage in the foreground, and left their traces right down to today's ritual.

Thirdly, we must point to the place of ritual in the liturgical programme. As a ritual which marks the achievement of a step in the path of life, it should be categorised as a ritual of ascent. As such, it belongs to what has been termed the rhythmic structure of liturgy. That does not, however, detract from the fact that characteristics of a conceptual structure are also present, to the extent that, for instance, a particular spirituality with regard to married life (one which changes over time) is woven into it. But, in view of the fact that the circumstances of the concrete situation are always changing and exercise a direct influence on the liturgical actions surrounding the performance of the marriage of the persons involved, with their social ambience, there are also characteristics of a structure reflecting facticity in the liturgical programme.

Fourthly, the marriage liturgy is characterised by a high degree of regulation. This relates to the juridical implications which are involved.[15] In the ritual, particular actions must be done in a particular way, if the performance is to be relied upon to be satisfactory and valid in the public forum. Entering into a marriage follows the system of laws in a society, with all the consequences that entails – one of these being, in par-

---

[13] Cf. J. VAN DE VEN: *In facie ecclesiae. De katholieke huwelijksliturgie in de Nederlanden, van de 13de eeuw tot het einde van het Ancien Régime* (= Miscellanea Neerlandica 22) (Leuven 2000).

[14] A. BLIJLEVENS: Het huidige Romeinse ritueel van de huwelijkssluiting tijdens de eucharistieviering, in A. BLIJLEVENS & E. HENAU: *Huwelijkssluiting. Gelegenheidsverkondiging* (Averbode 1985) 42-76.

[15] *Codex iuris canonici* can. 1095-1123.

ticular, public acknowledgement. This aspect of the marriage liturgy comes all the more to the fore to the degree that the legal systems of the church and society are distinguished from one another, or even diverge.

Fifthly, there is, in opposition to that, the fact that entering into marriage is just as much the *topos* where two persons publicly proclaim their collective intentions for life; they are, however, not merely announcing this to the community, but even more, inaugurating it officially, and initially performing it together, with an eye to the future. As such, marriage is an event with a high personal import, which is written in the memory and casts its shadow over both the future and the past of the partners. Ritually entering into marriage is therefore also experienced as an act of great personal involvement. Their very selves are at stake, and not only as they are now, but even more as they shall be together with and for one another. Ambivalent thoughts and feelings play a large role: farewells and new beginnings, engagement and uncertainty, firm intentions and doubts. The polished surface of the liturgical 'drama' indeed substantially displays the shadow of the tragedy that is peculiar to the experience of human existence.

Finally, it must be mentioned that within the framework of Christian marriage liturgy, actions are taken in the presence of, and in the name of God. As such, these actions are related to taking a solemn oath or making a promise. That is why the entry into marriage takes place within the community of believers. They are the witnesses par excellence. This fact is articulated in the presence and actions of the community's official representative, the pastor of the community. The marriage liturgy is therefore to be understood as a public, legally valid ecclesiastical act.[16]

In the above section we have indicated six general characteristics of the Catholic marriage ritual. With regard to this ritual we pose the question of whether, and if so in what way it fulfils the characteristics that are valid for human actions, in particular those of narrativity and illocution. In the following we offer an overview of the ritual.

6. Research Orientation

Liturgical rituals contribute to the establishment and fostering of both the identity of believers and the communication of faith. We derive the

---

[16] *Codex iuris canonici* can. 1055-1062.

concept of 'identity' from the philosophy of Ricoeur, who couples the development of the 'self' with the concept of 'narrativity'. The 'selfhood' of the person articulates itself in the way in which his or her story comes into being and develops. This points to the permanence of the self. The story is, however, not only a succession of experiences and incidents, but contains an original interpretation from which the singularity of the person's being can be read. Our question is if the ritual actions contain indications of the way in which identity in the form of narratives is manifested and communicated to others.

We derive the concept of 'communication' from J.L. Austin's philosophy of illocutionary language acts, as further developed by J.R. Searle. He defines illocutionary acts as those actions of persons in which audible or written signs are used to express their intentions to reality, doing so in such a manner that others recognise their intentions. In his theory Searle distinguishes five major categories into which all illocutionary language actions can be divided.[17] These categories are: (1) assertive language acts, in which the speaker declares that something is the case; (2) directive language acts, in which the speaker attempts to get the listener to do something; (3) commissive language acts, in which the speaker takes the obligation to do something; (4) expressive language acts, in which the manner of orientation to the other is expressed; and (5) declarative language acts, in which the state of affairs that is expressed in the statement is itself realised. In this study it will be examined if and how these kinds of language acts are apparent in ritual actions, and in what sense they are characteristic of this ritual situation and for the communication pattern going on. The concrete case study, to which these two research orientations will be applied, consists of the liturgical celebration of marriage.

7. THE ORDER OF SERVICE FOR THE MARRIAGE LITURGY

The source is the publication of the official Dutch ritual for the marriage liturgy (1996). There are four orders for the service included there. In the following we examine the first order of service, which bears the title: "The order of service for marriage during the eucharistical celebration."[18] This

---

[17] For a clear discussion of Searle's theory one can be referred to A. DE JONG: *Weerklank van Job. Over geloofstaal in bijbellessen* (Kampen 1990) 46-47.

[18] *Liturgie van de sacramenten en andere kerkelijke vieringen. Het huwelijk* 21-73.

ritual consists of five ritual 'units': the opening ritual, the Liturgy of the Word, the Celebration of Marriage, the Eucharist, and the closing of the service. Here follows an overview of the ritual 'elements' in the order specified:

The opening ritual

(1) The priest moves to the church door.
(2) There he greets the couple and family. He sprinkles Holy Water and speaks the accompanying text.
(3) In procession, with song or organ music, he accompanies them to their places.
(4) Having kissed the altar, he moves to his seat.
(5) The priest and all the congregation make the sign of the Cross.
(6) The priest pronounces the opening words (the confession of sin does not take place).
(7) The Kyrie is sung or spoken.
(8) The Gloria is sung or spoken.
(9) After a silence, the priest speaks the opening prayer.

The Liturgy of the Word

(10) The lector reads the first lesson: Gen. 1, 26-28, 31a.
(11) The cantor sings Psalm 128, 1-6a.
(12) The lector reads the second lesson: Eph. 5, 2a, 21-33.
(13) The choir sings the Alleluia with versicle Ps. 134, 3.
(14) The priest burns incense; the deacon receives the blessing and takes up the Gospels.
(15) The deacon reads the Gospel lesson: Matt. 19, 3-6.
(16) The priest gives the homily.

The Celebration of Marriage

(17) All stand. The witnesses move to places next to the bridal couple. The marriage candle is taken up.
(18) The priest pronounces the words of introduction.
(19) The priest interrogates the bridal couple three times regarding their freedom of action, intention of fidelity and the raising of the children. The couple answer.
(20) The priest speaks the introduction to the marriage vows.
(21) The couple join right hands before the priest, and he lays his stole over their hands.

(22) The groom takes his vows to the bride.

(23) The bride takes her vows to the groom (the exchange of vows can take place as an interrogation).

(24) The priest confirms the marriage vows.

(25) The newlyweds exchange a kiss.

(26) All sing a song of praise.

(27) The priest blesses the rings with Holy Water.

(28) The groom gives the ring to the bride with the accompanying text.

(29) The bride gives the ring to the groom with the accompanying text.

(30) All sing a song of praise.

(31) The marriage candle is lighted.

(32) The general intercessions are spoken, partly by the bridal couple and family members.

(33) The profession of faith is sung or said (if prescribed).

The Eucharist

(34) During the preparation of the gifts a song is sung.

(35) The bridal couple and others present are involved in the preparation of the gifts (bread, wine and other gifts).

(36) The priest speaks the offertory texts.

(37) The priest censes the gifts.

(38) The priest washes his hands, with the accompanying text.

(39) The priest and all present say the "Pray, brethren, that our sacrifice (...)".

(40) The priest speaks the prayer over the gifts.

(41) The priest pronounces the eucharistic prayer, with its peculiar preface and mention of the bridal couple.

(42) The Our Father is said by all.

(43) The bridal couple kneel.

(44) The priest speaks an introduction on the blessing of the marriage.

(45) There follows a moment of silence.

(46) With hands outstretched over the bridal couple, the priest pronounces the marriage blessing.

(47) The people share in the passing of the peace.

(48) The priest performs the *commixtio* and breaks the bread, during which the Agnus Dei is sung.

(49) The priest speaks the invitation to communion.

(50) All pray the "Lord, I am not worthy (...)".

(51) The priest distributes the communion. A communion song is sung. Priest, bridal couple, parents, witnesses and family members receive communion in both forms.

(52) The priest or an other attendant cleanses the objects used.

(53) There is a moment of silence.

(54) The priest speaks the communion prayer.

Closing of the celebration

(55) (optional) Presentation of the marriage Bible.

(56) Announcements are made.

(57) The priest and deacon perform the dismissal.

(58) The priest speaks a four-fold closing blessing over the newlyweds and others present.

(59) (optional) Act of devotion to Mary.

(60) The marriage papers are signed by the witnesses and priest, but not on the altar.

(61) (optional) The priest may present a marriage certificate to the bridal couple.

In the first place, this survey shows that the ritual is built up from five large sections, which follow upon one another successively. The ritual displays the character of a progressive process. History demonstrates that it is precisely this succession that has a considerable value. Before the renewal of the liturgy by Vatican II, the marriage liturgy preceded the celebration of the Mass, and was then the first section of the ritual after the opening rituals.[19] Vatican II has, however, emphatically placed the solemnisation of marriage in the context of the celebration of the Eucharist, and indeed between the Liturgy of the Word and the Liturgy of the Meal. This setting gives a definite significance to the events of the marriage: a separate status, but founded upon what the Council called "the source and high point of Christian life". On the other hand, the context of the celebration of marriage casts light on the Liturgy of the Word and of the Meal, and shows that the celebration of the Eucharist can be adapted and attuned for all situations in human existence.

Further, the survey shows that the order of service is built up from sixty-some 'elements', which all are placed in succession to one another.

---

[19] Readers are generally referred to editions of the *Missale Romanum* and the *Rituale Romanum* which precede the editions of post-Vatican volumes.

We have formulated these elements in such a way that their character as acts is made clear. In the next section we will attempt to further characterise them.

7.1. The opening ritual

(1) The priest walks to the church door. The basic act is walking, which happens with the intention of moving somewhere. This act is however further defined, on the one hand because it is an act of liturgy – in liturgical clothing – and on the other hand by the intention to fetch the bridal couple and receive them.

(2) The priest greets the bridal couple and their families. He bids them a warm welcome. The act of greeting is not filled in textually by the ritual, but alludes to entering into a relation between a host and his guests. Words are exchanged with a phatic purpose, through which the process of communication begins: an expressive language act.

The greeting takes place in a ritual context, which can be seen in the employment of Holy Water – in the form of offering or sprinkling – at the same time speaking a text that refers to the ur-symbolism of water. A connection is made with baptism: "God bless you with the dew of his grace, which you have received by baptism (…)": an expressive language act in the form of a wish. From the very beginning the bride and groom are acknowledged and recognised as having received baptism, a first allusion to the history or the narrative of their religious selves. A ritual situation is thus being created. They are being taken up in the symbolic universe of the liturgy.

(3) All, led by the priest, move in procession to the altar. The basic act is walking, in the form of a solemn entrance into a space in the direction of the centre. The bridal couple, the parents, the witnesses and, if present, their families take their places. The act is accented in a two-fold manner: on the one hand by creating a spatial order with those to be married in the middle, and on the other hand by accompanying the entrance with song or organ music. Both aspects point to the ritual implication of the act of entrance and confer upon it an expressive power.

(4) After having kissed the altar, the priest moves to his place. He performs the basic act of kissing with relation to the altar. The central object with sacred significance forms the first object that is treated with ritual reverence. The space of the church is concentrated around the altar, a symbol that refers to the Eucharist, the centre of the commu-

nity's liturgical life, in particular to the community which is now assembled. In the setting of the marriage liturgy, at the very beginning this manner of dealing with space reveals various aspects of communal identity: people come together, the community acts collectively, they display a differentiated role pattern with regard to the figure of the leader, and it is an eucharistic community.

(5) All stand. Standing upright with the body is one of the basic attitudes of liturgy and refers to active involvement: under*standing* in a religious sense. When standing, all make the sign of the Cross. With this act the community places itself in the name of God. Ritual, liturgical actions, from their very inception, occur in the presence of God. The constative language act and the sign, which is made on the body, have the declarative connotation of a confession: God is named by name, by his Name.

(6) The implicit confession is next made explicit in the citation from II Cor. 13, 13. The closing wish of Paul's letter is transformed into the opening wish of the leader for the community, and has the connotation of a greeting: "The grace of our Lord (…) be with you all." The leader's first contact with the assembled community takes place in the form of the phatic optative: "I wish you…"

The greeting is followed by an address by the worship leader which has an introductory character. This rather extensive language act reveals primarily assertive and constative statements. The leader speaks about the reasons for the gathering – the entry into marriage by N. and N. – about the spatial ambience, and involvement in that; that the Scriptures will be heard and collective prayers raised for those being married. For the rest, the form of the address is free and flexible. The themes being put into words however do not have merely an informational purpose: the art involved is to motivate those present and attune them with what is to transpire. Referentiality and the conative function and directive effects of language are central in all this.

It is notable that the confession of sin is dropped. In its form as an apology, it does not fit with the spirit of this liturgical celebration.

(7) The Kyrie is sung, a song which has a regular place in the order of service. It is regarded as an opening ritual. The function is, however, ambivalent: is its purpose to entreat or to affirm? Opinions differ. In a musical form, it can encourage a festive mood. Then it has an expressive and poetic function.

(8) The Gloria – from the perspective of language, a very complicated hymn of many allusions, of great beauty – is an act expressing and calling

up deep religious feeling, and accentuates the festive nature of the liturgical actions: an expressive language act with poetic power. From this, as an opening ritual, it functions to set the tone, although it has no references to marriage.

(9) The introductory rituals are concluded with a prayer. The priest explicitly calls for participation in this. All pray in silence. It is assumed that all are capable of personally turning to God in language, of entering into communication with God. One can regard this act as the end point, and the climax, of the opening rites of the ritual. The optative to enter into relation with God here receives its first fulfilment. It is a decisive moment in the ritual process. This is confirmed by the act of prayer on the part of the priest, who as *orante* – cf. the gesture – brings the prayers of all into a collective act, in words – *oratio collecta*. The texts provided refer expressly to the event of marriage. They possess an anamnestic (retrospective) and an epicletic (prospective) tendency, as is customary in liturgy. In this moment we stand at the intersection of past and future. The orientation to the future implies the expression of the vulnerable, uncertain and tragic in human existence. The celebration does not exclude this gravity. The formulation of this prayer has a free character. The worship leader chooses his words with deliberation.

7.2. The Liturgy of the Word

(10) All are seated. This is the basic act for listening. It creates the physical condition for being present with the Word. It is a posture which promotes attention through bodily relaxation.

The lector performs the first reading, the first phase in the narrative of the community with respect to the marriage. It involves anchoring the relation between husband and wife in the order of creation: Genesis 1. The lector represents the voice of God, the real teller of the story: "This is the Word of the Lord." This is a declarative language act, which is confirmed by all: "Thanks be to God."

(11) The cantor sings Psalm 128 responsively, about the God-fearing man who is blessed in his wife, children and grandchildren. The mood of the Psalm is optative, a beatitude: a directive language act. The biblical figures are types for the man and woman who are now central to the ritual. Compare this to the marriage blessing, act 46. All endorse what the cantor asserts by joining in the refrain.

(12) The lector performs the second reading, the second phase in the community's narrative with regard to the marriage. This time it is about the anchoring of the relation between husband and wife in the Christian economy of salvation. Christ's love serves the Church as a prototype on which the bond between husband and wife is to be modeled. Marriage is a loving covenant in christological perspective. The reading is to be understood as a pronouncement of God: it has a declarative intent.
(13) The choir sings the Alleluia with versicle Psalm 134, 3. Once again it is a wish directed toward those being married – "That the Lord of creation bless you!" – thus a directive language act.
(14) The priest burns incense, which intensifies the mood by its swirling and odour. The act is a preparation for what is going to come. The deacon approaches the priest and bows to receive his blessing, in order to be worthy to proclaim the gospel. The text has an apologetic tenor: purification, cleansing of the heart (mind) and lips (body); thus a directive language act. The deacon walks to the lectern with the book of the Gospels. The basic act is that of movement to the place of proclamation. There he greets the congregation, announces the reading and censes the evangeliarium. This object, as the Gospel of Jesus Christ, is treated with especial reverence. In the meantime all present stand. Compare act 6.
(15) The reading signifies the third phase of the community's narrative with regard to the marriage. The text, Matt. 19, 3-6, allows Jesus to speak. He refers to the order of creation, the unity in the bond between husband and wife which has its foundation in it and is underscored by it, that this order created by God may not be disrupted by the breaking of the union. The text has a prospective character. It involves the future of the marriage bond, and as a consequence has the tenor of a exhortation or warning. Thus it is a directive language act from the Lord himself, with a conative effect. This reading too is regarded by the congregation as God speaking: this is expressed in the declarative language act, "This is the gospel of the Lord", to which all answer: "Praise to you, Lord Jesus Christ."
     After the reading the deacon kisses the *evangeliarium* (compare with act 5 with regard to the altar) and silently repeats the apology, that through the words of the Gospel our sins (plural) may be wiped away. Once again this is an optative with regard to purification and cleansing, a directive language act.
(16) All are seated. Compare act 12. The priest gives the homily, the most extensive language act of the ritual, in the form of an address. The

instructions in the ritual have a practical and thematic orientation. Three points are made: the starting point should be the Scripture, and in particular the scripture readings; on the basis of these the meaning of Christian marriage should be expounded and the consequences of married life indicated; the personal circumstances of the bridal couple and the others present should be taken into account. The homily is intended to draw the line of the narrative of the community with regard to the marriage through, as it were, to the narrative of those who are present. The art of the homily must be to interweave these two narratives with each other, to integrate them and to interpret them within the situation. The homily is the preeminent act that accomplishes the transition from the Scripture to the celebration of the marriage. It has a clearly referential character, but at the same time attempts through directive and phatic utterance to offer perspective for the future, the realisation of a life plan. The tragedy of human existence does not remain unspoken, but hope, happiness and prosperity are emphasized. Here the leader of the liturgy manifests itself as pastor, exponent of a message full of expectation: a chiefly directive language act.

7.3. The celebration of marriage

(17) All stand. Compare acts 6 and 17. The witnesses are on either side of the bridal couple. From this point, they perform a public act. Their presence and actions are indicators of the place the ensuing acts have in the legal system; thus it is a declarative act. The ritual allows the possibility that one of them holds the marriage candle. This is an object, the significance of which is not yet explained.

(18) The priest presents an introductory address, in which constative language use predominates. It is an assertive language act, in which he invokes the world of official and objective actions: N. and N., you have come before this community of faith and its servant, to receive its seal, in the presence of the Lord, on your desire to enter into marriage. This event follows from your baptism. Now, through this sacrament, the Lord will pour out his blessing on your conjugal love, your intentions of fidelity, and the fulfilment of your conjugal duties. I ask you to bear witness of your intentions before this congregation.

(19) The priest inquires whether those presenting themselves for marriage are acting freely. They answer with "Yes". This is an investigative act and censure with regard to the conditions of freedom, under which

the following acts must be performed. This type of action appears repeatedly in liturgical rituals, when decisions are being taken with regard to the course of future life: baptism, ordination, installation in an office, etc.; these are commissive language acts.

The priest inquires whether they are prepared to remain faithful to one another. The answer is "Yes". This condition is related to the tenet regarding the indissolubility of marriage: again a commissive language act.

The priest inquires whether they are prepared to begin a family and raise the children in the Christian faith. The answer is "Yes". This condition is connected with the moral views regarding responsibility for future generations: again a commissive language act.

These three acts of interrogation make it clear that entering into marriage also has moral implications. It is precisely the norms and values of the community that are the issue here, and as such are manifested in a ritual manner. This is not yet the question of the formal religious intentions and the readiness of those presenting themselves for marriage to fulfil them. The question is also posed to those who are not confessing Christians or members of the Catholic Church, but because of their relation with a baptised Catholic prefer an ecclesiastical blessing on their marriage. It is the institutional context of the liturgical act which here comes to the fore.

(20) The priest introduces the phase of the marriage vows by announcing that N. and N. have publicly demonstrated their readiness to enter into the bonds of marriage. He now bids them to join their right hands, a basic act which points to the physical union of two persons. The *dextrarum coniunctio* is a gesture which the Christian liturgy derived from the Roman legal system for concluding a marriage. Next the priest asks the couple desiring marriage to pronounce their wedding vows here in this community, before family and friends, the church and God: a directive language act. The issue is thus the bridal couple putting into words their intentions with regard to each other. This locution, however, takes place as an illocution with the significance and intention of a marriage vow, but also as an interlocution within the circle of those here present. First the community present here and now are named: that is to say, all, without exception. The performance of a marriage is an act in and before the congregation, an institutional act in accordance with the rules of the community, but also constituting a part of that community. This is now further differentiated. The family and friends have

already been explicitly named on several occasions; they form the first circle around the bridal couple. The Church is also named; it forms the second circle that surrounds them, named in general, and thus more inclusive than the members of this parish who are present. Marriage is an *ecclesia*-wide act, which transcends the boundaries of the local congregation, an act of catholicity according to the prevailing juridic, moral and religious structure. Finally, the community surrounding the bridal couple is designated by the name of God. To marry is to act in the presence of and before God. It is a theologial act, which takes place in the space of the limitless, eternal, omnipresent God, through whom the *hic et nunc* of those being married takes on infinite dimensions. Marriage is a very special act of devotion with a high declarative import. However, the name of God is not elucidated any more specifically, and thus remains open for interpretation.

(21) The bride and groom face each other – a physical approach, symbolising the will to become one – and join their right hands (see above), thereby performing the instruction of the priest. At this moment, however, he does not perform only the purely ceremonial role of guardian of the ritual order, but he also acts as the official witness from and in the name of the community surrounding the bridal couple, as previously specified: a declarative act. This fact is made manifest by his placing his stole over the joined hands of the bridal couple. This item of clothing, which through the whole service visually distinguishes the worship leader with regard to his office from all others present, is now physically brought in contact with the bridal couple, who perform their gesture of union. In this, the office holder presents himself as a qualified witness at the performance of this marriage, within and in the name of the community. The ritual acts are concentrated into an official act in the order of the ecclesiastical institution, according to the rules which apply to the conclusion of a marriage. The placing of the stole is made optional by to the order of service.

(22) The groom faces the bride. The basic act is facing, which has the connotation of establishing contact and approach, from the desire of accomplishing an act with regard to her. It is a language act in the mode of the basic act of speaking.

The first word that is spoken is the name of the bride: he addresses her in her being herself, as the person she is and has become since she was given her name. He says to her, "I take you as my wife", a declarative act in which he reproduces the relationship with her. It is a relationship of intimate approach, accepting and acknowledging in a unique way, namely "as my wife". The acceptance points to the marriage bond with precisely this person. Two aspects demand notice. First, there is the placing of "you" within the plans for life of "I". This is an exclusive placement, so far as the "you" has been chosen out of many, expressed in the word "my". The second aspect is the characterisation of "you" as "wife", the specificity of the wife-being of "you", with all the implications and consequences that it carries with it. The acceptance has an unconditional character; there are no qualifications attached. The groom's act is, to a high degree, illocutionary: opening oneself to provide the other with a place in one's life, and acknowledging her as a partner in and for life, as spouse. The perlocutive effect of the declarative illocution is expressed in the vow which follows upon it: "I promise to remain faithful to you": a commissive language act. I commit myself with regard to you in this sense, that the relationship now being established will endure into the future. There are also two aspects to be noted in this promise. The first is that of the stability and permanence of the relation of being a spouse, expressed in the word "faithful". This is a word with a broad range of connotations, here brought particularly into relation with married life. The second is the unconditionality with regard to the future. There are no limits or provisos. This latter receives specificity in the subsequent four-fold explication: faithful for better, for worse, that is to say, in success and adversity, as these may be present in the course of life; for richer, for poorer, that is to say, in whatever material circumstances may occur in the future; in sickness and in health, that is to say, whatever the physical and psychological conditions are that may affect life. Fidelity is recognised as the characteristic of plans for life, which is exposed to reverses and tragedy, factors which are out of human control but which by this vow are anticipated and figured in, as it were. Faithfulness will, after all, be put to the test. Fourth, the promise of faithfulness is founded in the will to love and cherish the other, "you". At its foundation, married fidelity is guaranteed by the most vital attachment of "I" and "you" in the practice of love. Marriage is entering into a bond of love from the positive affinity of the will that we term love and cherishing, which by virtue of its nature strives for permanence and perfection: "until death do us part". It is clear that at this moment the groom presents his life story to his bride in a public declaration. This story bears the traces of history, to the extent that plans for married life will be marked by successes and reverses; they are realised in the fulfilment of life with the other; the perspective opens on the future to the extent that giving of the self tends to fulfilment and success.

(23) The bride faces the groom, addresses him by name, and speaks the marriage vows with the same words as the groom; compare act 22.

The way in which the marriage vows are carried out makes it clear that the entry into the marriage union is an act on the part of the bridal couple themselves. All others present are witnesses to this; some are even named as such. The act itself is focused directly on the other partner, an illocutionary commissive act with two fundamental movements. First there is the reception or acceptance of the other in her or his otherness, as wife, or husband, respectively. This immediately calls up the second aspect, namely the giving of one's self to the other, which contains within it the readiness not only to respect or accept the other in her or his otherness, but even more, to be integrated with them. This new two-in-one entity will undergo a process of change throughout life. Neither one's own self nor the other's otherness is erased, but an effort is made to transform the duality into a single entity by way of marriage. This receiving of the other and giving of oneself through the illocution with commissive intent is understood as the concentrated life story that the bridal couple exchange with each other with the expectation of realising two life plans, which are now combined in one. This narrative linking of persons is the high point of the ritual, as the stories of the community in God and the interpretation of them by the worship leader now reach their climax in the self-narratives presented by this groom and bride within the community.

This narrative character of marriage vows is considerably weakened by the remark in the ritual that for pastoral reasons the priest may choose to deliver the text of the marriage vow in the form of an inter-rogation, to which those being married answer "Yes, I will". Handled in this way, the official and stated witness in the name of the church com-munity is the one who does the speaking, who performs as the inter-rogator, and the life stories of those being wed are reduced to an official question. The bridal couple are reduced to listeners hearing an official story, which they can only appropriate through giving an affirmative answer to it. In this case, the marriage vow takes on the character of a directive language act, and the roles played in the act shift the accent from the couple being married to the official assisting them. In relation to this, one can ask what kind of pastoral reasons could lead to such a radical reversal of roles in this ritual act, which is intended to be declarative, that is to say, constituent for the events taking place.

(24) The priest confirms the marriage vows by addressing the couple. This is a declarative language act that relates to the preceding actions. He confirms that the church community will henceforth consider them as married, thereby implicitly indicating that the exchange of the vows was a moment of ascent in their existence: they are married and they are acknowledged by the community as being in this state. The marriage has been concluded. This declarative confirmation is followed by an expressive language act with optative intention, which in its themes refers back to the homily, among other things: "May the Lord confirm this joining together of your lives and bless it." This statement makes explicit the religious, theologial context of the marriage act by pronouncing the name of the Lord in a prospective sense: "to bless your life". Finally, the priest literally quotes Matt. 19, a passage from the community's marriage narrative, which once again refers to the continuing bond of marriage, and in which God is denoted as not only the invisible present witness or giver of blessing, but as the one who is the origin of this bond between this man and this woman: "What God has joined together, let no man put asunder." This utterance, at this moment, alludes in a very particular way to the seriousness and the tragedy which lie hidden within this 'drama'. The repetition of this fragment of the Gospel – a saying of Jesus – as the closing of the marriage act plausibly has a high expressive force.

(25) The priest lifts the stole from the hands of the couple. This is a gesture of declarative intent, because it points to the termination of his role as an appointed witness. Next he invites the couple to exchange a kiss, the performance of a basic act that is extremely meaningful at this moment, because that which has been uttered in language is now manifested publicly in the physical act of oral contact, the wedding kiss. It is an act of great expressive power, which, however, is made optional by the ritual.

(26) The priest invites all to praise God. It is the mode of the expressive language act, which is often struck in liturgy and accentuates the celebratory nature of the gathering. Themes such as thanksgiving, praise, and professing God's all-embracing love are sounded, and are placed within the framework of this marriage celebration. All respond to the texts with "We thank God", reminiscent of the acclamations to readings from Scripture. The three-fold laudation emphatically under-

scores what we already noted at the beginning of the ritual, that everything which takes place in the ritual – and in particular the entry into
marriage – happens in the presence of, and oriented to God. The directive language use has the tenor of prayer.

(27) The priest speaks concerning the rings, a directive language act in
the form of a wish that the Lord may bless these rings. Accompanying
this he may, optionally, sprinkle them with Holy Water in the sign of
the Cross. This gesture reinforces the meaning of the text and situates
the objects in a religious ritual context. Compare the function of Holy
Water and incense in acts 2 and 14. At the same time, in assertive language, the priest elucidates the symbolic meaning of the rings: they are
exchanged as a token of live and fidelity, referring back to the marriage
vows already exchanged. The priest then gives the rings to the couple.

(28) The groom places the ring on the bride's ring finger. The act has a
directive connotation, which it is optional for the groom to also put
into words: "Wear this ring as a token of my love and fidelity." The
emphasis is on the word "my": following upon the words of the priest,
the ring is a lasting representation of the groom's self-giving as lover and
his continuing faithfulness. The act of presentation can optionally be
confirmed by the speaking of the name of the Triune God: "In the
name of the Father (…)." This is a declarative language act, that situates
the ritual in the Christian theological sphere.

(29) The bride places the ring on the groom's ring finger. See act 28.

(30) Now a festive song of praise or a song of thanksgiving should be
sung by all. This is an expressive language act by means of singing:
releasing feelings which have been moving the community during the
performance of the marriage. During this song, it is optional for the
couple to light the marriage candle. The ritual indicates that this burning candle is considered to be a sign of the couple's unity of life. This
theme is not, however, put into words.

(32) The general intercessions (or 'prayer of the faithful') are spoken.
The ritual recommends that one or more of the family members should
announce the prayer intentions. The couple can also lead in the prayer.
This recommendation is striking, in view of the fact that those who usually lead prayer – priest, deacons and lector – are present. The participation of the couple and family is particularly prized on this occasion.
The ritual goes still a step further, as the couple themselves can be asked
during the preparations to select and formulate their own intentions. In
this case, the intercessory prayer becomes the last phase of their public

life story, in which they once more look back over their past and look forward to their future in a direct address to God: a powerful and meaningful close to the marriage ritual, which does not pass over the unexpected and tragic that can leave its mark on their lives and the lives of others. It is a perlocutive language act directed prospectively. It involves questions, wishes and intercessions concerning subjects in a state of becoming, in particular the two who have united themselves in marriage, and through God and all present are acknowledged in their highest personal dual bond: an extensive directive language act.

(33) If prescribed, the profession of faith is said. The Rituale characterises this act as a prayer. Strictly speaking, it is an assertive language act, in which everyone for themselves ("I believe...") but together with others speaks out the creed of Christian religion. This act contains no reference to marriage or the marriage ritual, but is part of the general order of service, if it is, for instance, performed during a weekend. There it would precede the prayer of the faithful. In the wedding liturgy it forms the transition into the following part of the ritual, the celebration of the Eucharist.

7.4. The Eucharist

In the following commentary on the ritual of Eucharist attention will be focused on those acts which are especially coordinated with the marriage. The question will be how the celebration of the Eucharist is adapted to or refashioned for this concrete situation.

7.4.1. Offertory

(34) The offertory hymn is sung. The assistants bring the necessary objects to the altar. This act has an introductory function.

(35) The faithful demonstrate their participation by bearing bread and wine or giving other gifts for the needs of the Church and the poor. The ritual makes these acts optional. They are symbols of involvement in the ritual acts and have a primarily expressive nature.

The bride and groom may bring the bread and wine to the altar. This is an expressive act, which is optional. Their action with regard to the elements of bread and wine is highly significant, because from this it would appear that they themselves, from the outset, make a connection between the act of marriage and the Eucharist which follows now.

(36) The priest holds the paten with bread above the altar and repeats a silent prayer, a blessing from God as Creator and giver of the bread;

an offering of this bread, fruit of nature and culture; and a prayer that God will make it the bread of eternal life for us. All respond: "Blessed be God forever." The elevation, prayer and acclamation all have an expressive tenor which accents the central function of the bread as object.

The deacon or the priest pours wine and a little water into the chalice, during the act silently repeating an assertive text (in the Dutch version of the Roman missal), "Water and wine become one. Share Thou [God] our humanity and take us up in your divine life." This is a rendering of the classical concept of the *sacrum commercium*. The text also has a prospective character in the direction of the communion, to the extent that the statement already anticipates the sacramental exchange.

The priest takes the chalice, holds it above the altar, and says words of blessing, offering and prayer suitable for the wine, to which all respond with an acclamation.

The priest bows down – an act of humility, as can also be seen from the text of the silent prayer he repeats: "In the realisation of our powerlessness and guilt, we pray that our offering will be acceptable to you and that we find favour in your eyes." This is an act with a directive intent, with the air of classic apology.

(37) The priest optionally censes the gifts and the altar. See act 14. The action underscores the sacral function of the objects; it is an assertive act, which through the deacon is extended to the actors themselves, the priest and the people. All are placed in the context of a ritual act. The bridal couple, however, receive no special attention. The act is optional.

(38) The priest washes his hands. This is a basic act with a cleansing function, in the perspective of the forthcoming ritual acts, here however with an apologetic connotation, as appears from the text repeated silently: freedom from guilt, freedom from iniquity.

(39) Standing in the middle in front of the altar, facing the community, the priest spreads his hands and brings them together – a gesture of summons and invitation – while speaking a text. In the form of an address, he asks – a directive language act – those present, whom he calls brothers and sisters, to pray that God will accept our offering. All answer this request with the optative, that the Lord may receive it for the praise and honour of his Name and for our (this community and the whole church's) well-being: a directive language act.

(40) The priest says the prayer over the gifts, his hands stretched out in the *orante* attitude. The theme of the prayer is the offering of the bread

and wine, thereby referring to the sealing of the marriage of N. and N. – an assertive act – and passes into the request that the God will watch over, preserve and bring to its fullest development the love that He has awakened in them. It is a directive language act with a prospective tenor, which implicitly takes into account the fortunes, good and bad, which the newlyweds are going to have to share.

7.4.2. Eucharistic prayer

(41) The priest says the eucharistic prayer. After the classic dialogue between the priest and people follows the preface, with the Sanctus.

The preface

It should be noted that the priest may perform the basic act of singing. This is, however, optional. This is true also for those parts of the eucharistic prayer which can be sung at concelebrations by all concelebrants. Singing is considered to be an intensification of, or as increasing the solemnity of speech.

Following upon the introductory dialogue, the first stanza sets the tone for the whole eucharistic prayer: one of thanksgiving and praise, from which the ritual surrounding bread and wine has derived its name. It is a high, expressive language act with assertive, directive and declarative aspects. God is addressed as the holy Father, as almighty and everlasting. It is holy and right, and our joyful duty to thank Him (prospective intent) for his glory (*aequum*, cultic aspect), and in order to find ourselves' salvation and healing (*salutare*, sanctification aspect), at all times and all places (*semper et ubique*).

After this general opening, in the second stanza the preface passes on to specific themes of marriage. In the language of address and announcement, directed to God, a number of assertive statements are made. God has – retrospectively or anamnetically – given the easy yoke (a metaphor that refers to the moral implications) of harmony to the bond between husband and wife. Through the strong bond of peace he has given them a light burden. Both statements refer to the promise of fidelity which the partners have already exchanged with one another. Once again God is termed the source of these interpersonal actions and illocutionary speaking.

In the third stanza it is said that on the basis of fidelity and peace God blesses the worthy love of his people. For instance, he makes his children increase in number in virtuous fruitfulness. Love and fecundity are central in this stanza, two themes which likewise were central in the marriage celebration. The qualifications "worthy" and "virtuous" once again refer to the moral implications of married life and to the development of the self of the partners.

In the fourth stanza the theme of procreation is further developed. In merciful kindness, God provides that the earth is made glad with new life and that his Church, reborn in Christ (a reference to baptism), grows. Looking back at God's ordering of life flows into looking forward for humanity, the world and Church: newness and growth of life.

The closing stanza is coupled to the name of Christ. Through Him we bring God thanks for his love, and together with the angels and saints we praise and laud his mighty deeds with the joyous singing of the Sanctus. The preface thus ends with the expressive language act of thanksgiving and praise, thereby not only taking up again the mode of the opening stanza, but also realising it in the collective doxology of "Holy, holy, holy (...)"

If we survey the text of the preface, it appears it can be characterised as a high anamnesis of God's mighty acts of salvation, with reference to the married lives of man and woman. That is the reason for the narrative colouring of the text. Once again, after Bible reading, proclamation and marriage vows, the story is told, now immediately and exclusively directed toward God in the mode of thanksgiving and praise: directive and assertive, but ultimately predominantly expressive language acts, which issue into the collective singing of "Holy, holy, holy", with the angels and saints. The boundaries of space and time are wiped away and take on infinite dimensions. The preface is one of the most stirring language acts in the Roman liturgy: an act of prayer par excellence, even as the prayer of the faithful, in which the content and situation – here on the basis of the marriage – can be enormously varied.

The praeconsecratory fragments

After the singing of the Sanctus the priest prays in an orante posture. He follows up the central theme of the Sanctus: "Thou truly art holy, our Lord, source of all holiness." This is an assertive language act with the expressive connotation of praise.

The priest folds his hands and extends them over the offerings, while saying: "Bless then these gifts with the dew of your Holy Spirit."

Through a directive language act – in fact an epiclesis – the sung holiness of God is connected with the gifts of bread and wine, referring to the acts of the offertory. The petition involves a form of sanctification, in which the metaphor of moistening (dew; see act 2) by the Spirit is employed, alluding to the image in the incarnation of Jesus Christ (Luke 1, 35). This last is made explicit in the optative: "That they become for us the Body and Blood of Jesus Christ." This incantatory tenor of the eucharistic acts is visualised by the sign of the Cross which the priest makes over the gifts while speaking the words "body" and "blood". The optative refers to the following acts and has a perlocutive effect.

The consecration

The consecration is a rather complicated whole of language and physical acts. The textual component is comprised of a concordant, harmonised version of the Synoptic-Pauline narrative of the Last Supper. The liturgical tradition has gradually shaped the text for, and accommodated it to ritual actions. It is, however, striking that its narrative character has been preserved. In the liturgical actions we identify ourselves with Jesus' actions, or the actions of Jesus are presented in our actions. This reciprocity and its development are manifested in three physical acts: (1) taking up the bread and cup in the hand: the priest appropriates the gestures and words of Jesus, or the acts and words of Jesus appear in the acts of the priest; (2) the lifting up of the bread and cup after the words of consecration. These gestures do not have the import of offering the elements, but of displaying them. The reason for this display lies in the effect of Jesus' words on the bread and wine: they are regarded as the Eucharist, the hallowed symbols of Jesus' Body and Blood, with a presentative significance, thus worthy of veneration; (3) the priest's kneeling after displaying the elements. The gesture does not have the import of humility or a confession of guilt, but of veneration and obeisance. It refers to the presence of someone highly placed and the relation to them. It has its origin in the high Middle Ages and points to the performative effect of the consecratory actions of the priest. The gifts have become Christologised, symbols of Jesus' personal presence in the congregation.

From all this one can infer that the acts of consecration, in their mutual coherence, show a predominately declarative character. What is spoken comes to pass in reality: the anamnestic narrative of Jesus' actions is actualised through the narrative of the community, interpreted by the words and gestures of the priest, in order that all will remember Him. The narrative constitutes the self of the community of Jesus Christ in the *hic en nunc*, in this case on the occasion of a wedding celebration.

The consecration phase is closed with a directive language act by the priest, to proclaim the mystery of the faith. One might expect that the expression *mysterium fidei* refers to the preceding eucharistic event. The acclamation of the people – an assertive language act – expressly refers, however, to the death and resurrection of the Lord Jesus: we proclaim and confess these salvific events until his return. The assertive language act, which is directed to the Lord Jesus, thus must be understood as an actualisation and realisation of the call to remember him in his Passion. At the climax of the anamnesis, the community acts. This also can be seen from what follows.

The post-consecratory fragments

In an *orante* posture, the priest utters a number of prayer fragments. First, in an assertive language act directed to God, he confirms that our remembrance of the Passion mystery results in the offering of the gifts which have become the Eucharist. Then follows an expression of thanksgiving – an expressive language act – in which the community – "we" – shows its gratitude that it may and can celebrate the eucharistic acts, in particular the sharing in the Body and Blood of Christ.

After this anamneticising 'eucharist' the prayer changes course. It follows in the mode of supplication: an extensive directive language act of an epicletic nature. With the connotation of the optative, the community asks God that they may be one through the Spirit. This unity is made more specific in a number of intentions: (1) for the universal church and its leaders, that it may be a community of love; (2) for the bride and groom, who celebrate their marriage this day, thanks to God, that through his grace they may persevere in their love for one another; (3) for the dead, that they may stand in the light of God's countenance; (4) for all of us, so that with all the saints, and in particular with Mary and the apostles, we may share in eternal life and praise and honour God.

The doxology

The yearning for an eschatological expression of praise and honour forms the link to the closing Trinitarian doxology, a high expressive language act during which the priest holds the paten and chalice in an elevated position. The community is focused on God in language and gesture, in expressions of offering and self-giving, in answer to the offering and self-gift of God in the mediation of the eucharistic actions. The doxology has also, however – as does for that matter the whole eucharistic prayer – the assertive connotation of a confession. Thus it is also important that the people respond with the acclamation "Amen". We note that this eucharistic prayer, in both the preface and in one of the prayers, has been adapted for the marriage liturgy.

7.4.3. Ritual of communion

(42) The priest folds his hands and addresses the congregation in a directive language act with a conative tenor to call upon the congregation and urge them to pray the Our Father. This act of prayer is founded on the action of Jesus himself, who not only provided the commission but also the form for this prayer act. Thus it is that the text is also designated as the Lord's Prayer. The congregation makes this model prayer from the Lord its own, and participates in his prayer relation with God, whom He called his Father. An identification with Jesus takes place, through which the self of the Lord transforms the self of the community, inclusive the language they speak. The poetic function of this prayer act can then also be characterised as powerful. The placement of the Our Father at this moment in the eucharistic ritual is common to all great liturgical traditions. The prayer act is a prelude to the eucharistic communion, and disposes the congregation to participate in it.

(43) The embolismus that normally follows the Our Father is omitted. The prayer situation is continued with the blessing that the priest pronounces over the bride and groom. At this point the ritual notes that this marriage blessing may never be omitted. It is one of the essential elements in the marriage liturgy. The couple kneel before the altar, or at the place where they are seated. The basic act of kneeling here connotes an inward attitude of respect and responsiveness to the work of God.

(44) The ritual begins with the invitation by the priest to pray, a directive language act in which he addresses those present, asking that they perform an act of prayer, that God will bless N. and N. Next he confirms

that they have wed each other in Christ, implicitly referring to the wedding ritual. Then he utters the wish that God in love will make them one in heart, and that the eucharistic communion may be salutary for them. These are directive language acts which are to motivate those present to pray.

(45) All present pray for several moments in silence. Compare act 9. The perlocutive and conative statements of the priest are realised in the silent prayer. The prayer act of the Our Father is continued in a silent prayer, the orientation and content of which is defined by N. and N.

Marriage blessing

(46) The priest extends both hands over the couple and pronounces the marriage blessing. It is constructed of seven stanzas. The first three have an anamnestic narrative style and consist primarily of assertive language acts. The first stanza refers to the themes of creation in Genesis 1 and 2, in particular to the creation of man and woman, their equality – woman is placed at the side of man – and their communion of life, not to be separated by anyone. The second stanza refers to Ephesians 5, marriage as sacrament, symbol of the love of Christ for the church. The third stanza refers to the original bond of husband and wife and to God's particular care and blessing for this bond, even when sin had entered the scene in the Fall and unfaithfulness.

The final four stanzas have an epicletic, prospective intent, in the form of supplication, a directive language act with an optative undertone. The fourth stanza asks God to look down on this new couple and bless them with his Spirit, that through love they remain true to one another. Stanza five involves the bride in particular and asks for her the gifts of love and peace, through which she can become the image of the courageous women of the Scriptures. Stanza six concerns the groom in particular. It is asked that the bride will enjoy his trust, that he will acknowledge her as a life partner of equal standing, and will honour her – being co-heir with him of the gift of life – and that he will love her with the love that Christ had for the Church. The seventh stanza asks for the couple, now named by name, the gifts of unity in faith, fidelity, blamelessness and compassionate kindness, according to the example of Christ. Next it is asked that they enjoy the riches and success of parenting and that they may see their children's children, enjoying health and gladness to great old age, and that they will be led by God into the communion of the saints and the joy of the heavenly kingdom. All acclaim this with "Amen".

Surveying the marriage blessing, it appears that, in the form of anamnestic and epicletic wishes and supplications, it comprehensively articulates the ideal life story of the newlyweds, from *prôton* to *eschaton*. The risks, disappointments and defeats which can form the tragic reverse of the married way of life are not stated in so many words, but are heard at the same time in the background, because the ideal image contrasts with the facticity of human failure and with the inevitable difference of being other. It is for this reason that there is the emphasis on unity, acknowledgement and togetherness. The almost moralising import of the sixth stanza, on the role of the man with regard to the woman, is striking: an accent which perhaps is connected with the likewise moralising but woman-unfriendly tone that dominated the classic marriage blessing. Evidently it is difficult to achieve a good balance in these matters. In the ritual the marriage blessing is the end and climax of the community's wedding narrative, after the Scripture reading, proclamation and preface. As such, it is also an essential component of the marriage ritual, even if there is no celebration of the Eucharist.

(47) The priest pronounces the usual greeting of peace: "The peace of the Lord be with you always." He invites the couple and all others to give one another a sign of peace and love. This is a language and physical expressive act, in which the Pax Christi as symbol of the mutual *communio* is manifested, in expectation of the eucharistic communion. For that reason, this act is placed at this point in the Roman ritual of the Eucharist.

(48) The priest takes the Host, breaks it and allows a part to fall into the chalice. While doing this, he prays silently. This is a remnant of the classic commixture ritual in preparation for the communion ritual. Meanwhile the *confractorium* Lamb of God is sung or said – referring to John 1, 29 – for as long as the breaking of the bread is taking place.

Then the priest silently speaks an apology: a supplication to Jesus Christ, Son of God and renewer of the world, to save the priest from evil and iniquity, and to vitalise fidelity to the commandments in love. This is a directive language act in the form of a request for inner purification.

(49) The priest kneels, takes a Host and holds it above the paten. In a clear voice he says to the faithful (as the Dutch version of the missal puts it): "Blessed are those who are invited to the table of the Lord. Behold the Lamb of God, who takes away the sins of the world." This is an assertive language act, directed toward the believers, with the connotation of an invitation.

(50) Next he says in unison with all present, "Lord, I am not worthy
(…)" The ritual with the bread has the significance of the showing and
beholding of the gifts, now become the Eucharist. It is an assertive act
in the manner of a confession, which moreover displays characteristics
of an apology: unworthiness, freeing from sins, healing.
(51) The priest eats of the bread and drinks from the chalice. These are
basic acts of feeding, the foundation of the Eucharist as the action of
taking a meal. All the preceding actions with the gifts of bread and wine
now reach their climax and conclusion: *communio* with the Lord in the
mode of eating and drinking, which also appears in the words that
accompany and interpret the physical acts: "May the Body/the Blood of
Christ bring me to everlasting life." These are the nucleus of a confession – assertive and declarative – with optative connotations. This
declarative character of communicating is seen even more strongly in
the distribution of the consecrated gifts to the participants: "The Body
of Christ", "The Blood of Christ", to which the recipients respond with
the acclamation, "Amen".

The communion ritual in the marriage ritual displays a peculiarity
as compared with the usual celebration of the Eucharist. It is expressly
noted that the couple, their parents, the witnesses and the family
members may receive communion in both forms. The post-Vatican II
liturgy has this procedure on special occasions, if the communion act
can be performed fittingly. In principle, however, it maintains the partial practice of bread communion, even when the classic reasons for
this are no longer applicable. Meanwhile, a communion hymn is being
sung.
(52) After the communion ritual the paten and chalice are cleansed by
an attendant. While this is happening, the priest says silently an apologetic text, which speaks of purity of heart and mediation of salvation, in
the form of a directive language act addressed to God.
(53) The priest can resume his place. The people may remain silent or
sing or say a hymn of praise or a psalm.
(54) The priest says the post-communion prayer. In this prayer,
assertively, there is reference to the marriage concluded by N. and N.,
a gift of God's providence. Further, it is asked, directively, that God
may be their loving guide, and that they – to whom He [God] has
extended the bread and cup – may in love grow to a deep harmony.
The prayer action shows no new elements, and has the character of a
closing.

7.5. Closing of the celebration

(55) The priest may give the marriage Bible to the couple. In doing so, he speaks several assertive and directive words in the form of an address: at this time, now that you have pledged your troth to one another, in the name of the parish may I present you with this marriage Bible, God's gladdening message of liberation and peace. My wish for you is that this book will receive a place in your lives together. The formulation has a rather free character.

(56) Optionally, there follow short announcements to those present, a directive language act.

(57) Then the customary closing benediction for a wedding takes place, a declarative language act, with which the gathering concludes.

(58) The priest faces the people and with his hands extended over the newlyweds and the people, pronounces a blessing in four stanzas. The newlyweds are wished abiding love, harmony and peace as gifts from God in Christ. All respond with "Amen". Next, that they may be richly blessed in their children, may receive the support of friends, and may live in peace with each other; all say "Amen". Third, that they may witness to God's love for the sorrowful, poor and needy, and that they may thankfully welcome them one day in the house of God the Father; all say "Amen". Finally there is the wish for all that the almighty God, Father, Son and Holy Ghost, bless them all, during which the sign of the Cross is made. This closing blessing, accompanied by a laying on of hands – pronounced over the newlyweds and the people – is a threading together of wishes and commissions, a powerful expressive, but also directive language act with regard to the future, whatever it will bring. The sacrifices and reverses which may be in store in life are not specified. The blessing ends in the sign of the Cross, with which the ritual also opened (see act 5), now with a prospective implication – an *inclusio* with which the ritual officially is concluded, as is customary in the Roman liturgy.

(59) The ritual notes yet that in may places it is customary that the bride, possibly together with the groom, goes to an image of Mary, to devote herself to Mary. Sometimes she goes to a representation of the Holy Family. This action is characterised as an act of devotion and has a commissive import. The female slant is noteworthy: this is preferably an act of the bride. Notwithstanding the repeated emphasis on unity, harmony, fidelity, love, the union and bond between the partners, in

this act the otherness of the self appears: unity in diversity. The initial one-status appears to have become a duo-status, in which the otherness of the two selves has not been swallowed up without remainders. Their living and becoming is together.

(60) The ritual has no recessional and parting, which would correspond to the solemn greeting and processional. Compare acts 2 and 3. It ends with the remark that the witnesses and priest sign the marriage papers, a declarative act with which they confirm their official role at the performance of the wedding by signing their name. It is however noted that this act must not take place on the altar, but in the rectory, the sacristy or the church.

(61) A marriage certificate can also be presented. These administrative acts with a public function do not appear to share in the sacrality of the liturgical 'drama'. Ultimately, the ritual has no transition from the inward to the external. It falls silent at the altar, at a distance from the threshold, which must be crossed to once again enter the secular world and begin married life. We are far removed from a marriage liturgy which once extended to encompass the home and departure for the honeymoon, as of old.

8. CHARACTERISATION OF THE RITUAL

Having now analysed and described the marriage ritual in its sequence of 'elements' on the basis of the Theory of Acts, in the following we will attempt to arrive at a further characterisation of the whole. To this end, first the five 'sections' will be successively characterised. We will then close with a consideration of the total ritual.

8.1. The opening ritual

The opening ritual is a rather complex section that allows many variations, because the concrete design is often made optional. It is composed of a number of basic acts such as walking, kissing, standing, and of a number of directive prayer acts and the expressive language acts of greeting and praise. At first sight (and hearing) it seems, then, that there is no great consistency in this section.

The cause of this impression is the ambiguity that lies at the basis of the composition. On the one hand the opening of the ritual is characterised by the specificity of the marriage events. The rituals of greeting and procession, the introductory word and the opening prayer all bear the marks of this, even though these acts differ from each other in their nature because of their expressive, assertive and directive focus. On the other hand the opening of the ritual is constructed of elements from the general ritual of the celebration of the Eucharist: the veneration of the altar, the sign of the Cross, the blessing, the Kyrie and the Gloria, which do not refer to the marriage situation. They are, however, possessed of a declarative and expressive power, certainly if aesthetically they are performed in a musical form. These general elements however make it clear that the order of service for the celebration of Eucharist forms the framework or model, into which the marriage liturgy is fitted.

The most distinctive elements are the ritual of the greeting and procession with accompanying song or music. These acts of reception are performed in a spontaneous and expressive manner. They give shape to the transition from the outside to the inside, from the secular *Umwelt* to the religious ambience.

Notwithstanding the ambiguity in construction mentioned, from its first act the opening ritual situates those present in the universe of Christian rituality. This is evoked by the figure of the worship leader, representative of the ecclesiastical community, through the space, with its design and furnishings, through the procedures with ritual elements such as water and the altar, through the positioning of the *dramatis personae* in the centre, and through the performance of liturgical music and song. Perhaps, though, this ritual world is created most through the language which is spoken: to a large extent derived from Scripture and dictated by liturgical tradition. In this connection, the bridal couple and the others present are not only addressed on the basis of having been baptised, but also and primarily on the basis of their living relationship with God. The performance of the ritual is an action in the Name of the Triune God. This name is uttered declaratively through all the confessions and in almost all the elements. The ritual actions, from the very inception, can be characterised as a religious 'drama' in the Christian sense. The religious language is not only spoken with directive focus on those present, and in particular the bridal couple, but finds its expression explicitly in the prayer of all and in that of the leader, in the name of all. The climax of the opening ritual lies in the public expression of the relation with God in the form of calling upon God. The self of those present speaks to the invisible, not-present Other, Who is represented by means of metaphorical language. In the act of prayer those present manifest them-selves, in the presence of God, as who they are in their deepest being: the people of God. The ritual presupposes that those present have the capac-ity to perform this high religious act. With this act of prayer they are fully introduced into the ritual.

8.2. The Liturgy of the Word

The Liturgy of the word is a clearly structured section, the components of which can be filled in according to choice or with free phrasing according to the circumstances of the wedding performance. Two basic acts are the foundation of the whole: speaking and listening.

The speaking takes place standing, and the listening generally seated. The latter custom is interrupted in the Roman liturgy during the Gospel reading, when out of reverence for the word of Christ himself a standing posture is assumed. Two forms of speaking must be distin-guished. First it takes the form of public reading, and thereafter the form of an address. The act of reading to an audience is regulated, and is performed by the persons appointed for this purpose: the lector and the deacon. By virtue of his office, the latter is particularly related to the Gospel, which is expressed in the blessing he receives with an eye to the act of reading, and in the acts of reverence that he performs with regard to the evangeliarium. The act of publicly addressing the community, which in the *ritualia* is generally termed the homily, is also regulated: it is performed by the main actor in the ritual event.

The equally fundamental act of listening, on the part of the commu-nity, corresponds to the acts of speaking. It demands a high degree of concentration: openness, receptiveness, the desire to participate in com-munication, and the capacity to appropriate for oneself that which is spoken. The self enters into relation with the other, who reveals himself in his speaking, so that change and renewal of life may take place for the building up of the self. Listening is an act of *hermeneuein* in the full sense of the term, in that the text put forward is transformed into a new text in and for the listener.

This linguistic exchange in the ritual takes place on the basis of the vocabulary which is the foundation of Christian identity: the Scrip-tures. The marriage liturgy too has space in which to let them be heard: three readings interspersed with two songs, which are chosen so that they follow on naturally from one another and are components of the great narrative that the community possesses and raises with regard to married life. This is the origin of the fundamental narrative form of the Liturgy of the Word, where marriage is sketched from the all-encompassing narrative of salvation history, retrospectively in the order of creation and election, prospective in the order of realisation and accomplishment. This narrative is presented to the bridal couple, so that they may recognise and acknowledge it for themselves and make it their own, for their own process of becoming. In this form this *narratio* is an act of the community, conceived and composed by the community through a process spanning centuries and actualised in this present. The community likewise understands the story as God's story: "This is the Word of the Lord!" The language action of the community mediates the utterance of God, with all the revelatory and obscuring implications and consequences that follow from that, but also with the commission to lay open the divine story and interpret it for the *hic et nunc*.

The story does not stand by itself, but must be interpreted with an eye to new understanding. That is the foundation of the fundamental act of preaching, which follows the readings. It has the task of bridging and providing continuity. Looking back and looking forward reach their destination in the ritual today, which is focused on how people – in this case, the bridal couple – are to live their lives now. The ritual speaks briefly and in a businesslike manner about the homily. In essence it is, however, an effort to interpret the community's scriptural narrative for the conditions in which people find themselves as today they give form to their married life, actualising and vitalising the text to aid the discovery of religious identity, while at the same time reassessing and renewing the community's narrative so that it promotes the development of religious identity. It is less about the transmission of knowledge with regard to the *depositum fidei* than spiritual guidance, which affords perspective for the future, and assists in understanding the present context that defines married life, with the eventualities and the tragic that is linked to that. Thus the homily is spoken to aid and clarify things for the listening community, which itself does not yet have the opportunity to speak. They nevertheless await the moment of the language action of the bridal couple themselves.

8.3. The marriage celebration

This section is the heart and high point of the whole ritual. It displays a complexity that is a given with marriage in the Catholic tradition. As we noted earlier, almost all the rituals have a secular origin, outside the Church: the answering of questions, the joining of right hands, the exchange of vows, kissing each other, the giving and receiving of rings, the public confirmation that the marriage is constituted, the presence of witnesses. All these acts are, however, performed in the circle of the community and before the face of God. It is a religious, Christian event. The couple to be married are the main actors. Their commissive and declarative statements and acts effectuate a new relation of the union of husband and wife for their lives: being married. All the other acts in this section, in particular the agency of the appointed main witness, are so placed and formed that they provide a matrix for the acts of the bridal couple. Several aspects of this are noteworthy.

First, there is the official style of the performance, related to the legal system. This involves the ordering of the language acts, and their acceptance as givens. One marries by performing acts in this way, and in no other way, by expressing these intentions and ideas, and not any others. In terms of theme and content, no new elements are added; everything has already been put into words during the Liturgy of the Word, especially in the narrative from Scripture and the homily. What must now happen is that it must be appropriated by the couple themselves, *in foro publico*. The public exchange of personal confirmations, vows, intentions of the self, with the other, creates a situation which transcends the other sacramental acts of the liturgy. We encounter here the specificity of the sacrament of marriage, in which the whole selfhood of the individual being married, body and soul, is at stake, in terms of thought, will and deed, in relation to the other – which does not leave the heart unmoved. Marriage is surrounded with powerful emotions, which are channelled by the institutional and ritual actions.

Central to this 'drama' are the bridal couple, surrounded by witnesses: in the middle of the standing community and in the presence of God, the creator of marriage. Here and now they follow in the footsteps of the generations from which they themselves sprang: with the opportunities and risks, prosperity and reverses that will also be their lot, witness to the countless marriage stories of those who preceded them and of all who now stand around them. The central acts of the ritual, in linguistic and physical form, can be understood as the narrative entrance into the reality of marriage: the performance of the story that you are for and with the other, that taking all possible circumstances and stipulations into account, you entrust yourself to the other. Marriage is the giving of your self and the receiving of the other, in which the other's being as other is not only tolerated but acknowledged as the source of self-becoming in mutual exchange. It is not for nothing that the meaning of the act of marriage is expressed with the metaphors of a new beginning, growth and fecundity: the process of self-becoming, of becoming the dual entity, and the triangular relationship with the child.

Moreover, the community's marriage narrative, which it confesses as the narrative of God, is realised in this mutual *narratio*. The marriage act of the man and woman is the personification of the marriage tradition, as it is understood by the religious, Christian community. They actualise the past in their selves, with an eye to the future. In regard to this last, the ritual prefers to speak in terms of union, peace, love and fidelity: prospective statements in the form of a wish, that suggest the successes on the road of life: "May all this be given to you!" In ritual terms, it is asking a blessing.

The marriage ritual is not only an institutional, highly personal and communitarian activity on the part of the bridal couple in the sight of God, it is at the same time the *locus* where what is said occurs. It is a performative activity, in which the status of the persons presenting themselves for marriage undergoes a change: by exchanging this story with one another they are no longer two entities but a couple. This transition in life status is articulated in the ritual: we consider you as husband and wife, as having entered the order of married persons. This performance is emphatically put into words by the appointed witness, and subsequently demonstrated by the newlyweds in the marriage kiss, and finally, with connotations of permanence, visualised in the ritual of the exchange of rings: they bear on their hands the symbols of their union, which they have given each other. Moreover, their new status in the community is manifest in their leading the official prayer of the community, the prayer of intercession. The *narratio* takes the form of supplication, an epicletic looking forward to the future: asking blessing, so that that which is begun may grow and thrive. This prayer, that normally is considered as an answer to the presentation of the word and as the climax of the Liturgy of the Word, is now performed as the fulfilment of the marriage ritual. The newlyweds and others involved – not the official ministrants – appear as the leaders of the community in prayer, as liturgists in the full sense of the word. It is to be regretted that the ritual makes the performance of the prayer in this way optional.

Indeed, in the analysis we have already indicated that the design of diverse rituals in the marriage liturgy can be adapted according to the circumstances. In general – but especially with the exchange of the vows – these alterations weaken and dull the vigour of the ritual actions. It is to be recommended that through pastoral guidance, persons who wish to enter into marriage should be made fully conversant with the actions in the ritual, in order to participate in this major change in their lives as authentically and expressively as possible. Preparation for marriage should involve not only the moral qualities of being married, but also the metaphor and symbolism of the marriage ritual, in the actions of which narrativity, morality and a sense of religion are comprehended.

8.4. The Eucharist

The celebration of the Eucharist that follows the marriage ritual displays in broad outline the design and content of the normal order, as described in the altar missal. If compared to the Liturgy of the Word, it appears that the Liturgy of the Word is both more able to be adapted to the marriage situation, and that that is more easily done. Within the scheme of the Roman liturgy, a number of rituals are refashioned for the situation: participation in the presentation of the gifts, the formulation of the prayer over the gifts, the alterations in the preface and one of the post-consecratory prayers within the eucharistic prayer, the marriage blessing following the Our Father, the performance of the communion and the formulation of the prayer after the communion. Surveying these seven elements, five appear to be language acts on the part of the priest which refer to the theme of marriage. At two points – in the offertory and communion – the newlyweds themselves appear in the ritual 'drama' by bearing and partaking of the gifts: two basic acts that are constitutive for the eucharistic actions. The ritual however makes this special participation by the couple optional. The five language acts of the priest are not adapted for the marriage context purely in terms of content, but moreover fit in harmoniously with the progress of the eucharistic ritual.

From the foregoing it should appear that the celebration of the Eucharist is dominated by the priest's leadership as the main actor, and that in terms of liturgical order it is fixed to a high degree. There is little room for adapting language or physical acts, or for fitting in additional actions for the occasion. This leads to the question of whether such an existing ritual order can be adapted to a sufficient degree, and in particular whether a Eucharist modelled as the first religious meal permits the newlyweds celebrating at the Lord's Table. According to the dynamic of the wedding liturgy this Eucharist should be the crowning of the performance of the marriage and the first manifestation of the couple having been married in the Lord. Three aspects indicate that this only happens to a slight degree. First, the generally appointed language acts of the eucharistic ritual predominate. Secondly, compared with what has been expressed in the ritual actions up to this point, the content of the language acts which are adapted adds no new meanings. Thirdly, one repeatedly encounters an attitudinal dimension which we have termed 'apologetic'. This places the emphasis on humility, falling short and a realisation of guilt, and on asking for forgiveness, cleansing and healing, which are at odds with the spirit of renewal of life, joy and looking ahead which generally pervades the marriage liturgy.

However, the eucharistic ritual does contain one element that is reserved for the marriage liturgy: the marriage blessing that takes place after the praying of the Our Father. This element is peculiar to the Western tradition, and in the post-Vatican liturgical order is considered to be an essential component of the wedding liturgy, even when the Eucharist is not celebrated. It is an act of prayer by all present for the newlyweds and their future, which is put into words by the worship leader. The tenor of this blessing corresponds with what has already been expressed in the ritual. It is worth noting, however, that the newlyweds are mentioned by name both collectively and separately in the prayer, which places special emphasis on their husband/wife relation. With regard to this last, the text of the ritual has not entirely escaped the imbalance that characterised the classic formulation. If formerly the subordination of the woman to the man dominated this prayer – it was then also termed the blessing of the bride – now that is entirely gone and the accent lies on the tasks and responsibilities of the man in relation to the woman and their collective duties and service to society. On the one hand, the text displays narrative characteristics, to the extent that scriptural themes are once again anamnestically brought into relief; on the other hand, the second part is dominated by ethically coloured statements in the optative form, with regard to future married life.

8.5. Closing of the celebration

This section shows a high degree of incoherence. In addition to the dismissal and closing blessing, regular elements in the order of service, it consists of a number of optional acts: the presentation of the marriage Bible – derived from the Reformation tradition –, making announcements to those present, devotions (by the bride, in particular) to Mary – an act of typical Catholic piety –, the signing of the marriage papers by the witnesses and the presentation of the marriage certificate to the couple – acts of church administration. In this whole, the closing blessing stands out as a liturgical language act, directed to the newlyweds and all present, with optative orientation. It is concluded with the sign of the Cross, with which the ritual also opened; thus the ritual process is completed by means of an *inclusio*. All the other acts surround this end point, as it were, without having any structural relation to each other. They can be carried out, or omitted. This optional approach, which is characteristic of the whole marriage liturgy except for the section of the Eucharist, is most manifest in the closing section.

Moreover, it is quite remarkable that the ritual does not provide for acts of recession and farewell or congratulations which would correspond to the greeting and processional at its opening. There is no guided movement from inside to outside. For the closing phase of this ritual, which passes from acts of great festivity in response to religious, ecclesiastical events, this is a structural deficiency. The hospitality, the sense of being witnesses, and the emotional sharing all ultimately fall short of the mark. Is what is involved here perhaps the problem of the difficulty in crossing the threshold between the religious and the secular?

9. EVALUATIVE REMARKS

9.1. In particular

On the basis of the preceding analysis and characterisation of the marriage liturgy, we offer the following comments and draw the following conclusions.

(1) From beginning to end, the ritual must be characterised as a form of religious activity. It takes place in the name of the Triune God.

(2) The ritual bears the characteristics of an institutional activity. This is true particularly for the third 'unit', the marriage ritual, and the fourth 'unit', the Eucharist. These actions proceed according to the regulations of the ecclesiastical institution. The professional character of these actions is represented by the dominant role of the priest/worship leader.

(3) All sorts of illocutionary acts take place in the ritual. The roll of language acts is widely varied, and they often follow one another very quickly. The performance of the ritual demands a high degree of concentration from the participants.

(4) The priest/worship leader fulfils a prominent role in the ritual. His actions during the third 'unit', the marriage ritual, can overshadow those of the bridal couple. This can become problematic for the celebrant of the Sacrament of Marriage.

(5) The first 'unit', the opening, and the fifth 'unit', the closing of the ritual, are complicated in construction and display no clear logic in their structure. It is striking that the design of their 'elements' is often made optional by the ritual.

(6) The second 'unit', the Liturgy of the Word, permits itself to be adapted well to the marriage situation.

(7) The fourth 'unit', the Eucharist, permits some adaptation to the marriage situation, but not more than is given for the Eucharist in the usual order of service. In this regard, the 'elements' of the preface and the marriage blessing fulfil a striking role.

(8) The ritual displays a certain ambiguity as a whole. In the post-Vatican liturgical order, it is structured both with regard to the service for the Eucharist in the *Missale Romanum* and with regard to the order of service for the marriage liturgy of the *Rituale Romanum*. The conditions of the cyclic and rhythmic liturgy are not brought into harmony here.

(9) The Liturgy of the Word/marriage liturgy/marriage blessing structure appears the most desirable ritual sequence for the marriage liturgy.

(10) The apologetic dimension of the ritual acts, particularly with regard to the worship leaders, is at odds with the experience of the participants. It is a relic of the early Middle Ages, that stresses the spirituality of shortcoming and sin and promotes ritual purity.

(11) The legal province, which particularly characterises the third 'unit', the marriage ritual, is the centre of the ritual actions. Here, at the moment that the vows are exchanged, the transition from selfhood to shared otherness occurs.

(12) The uncertainty with regard to realising the idea of marriage gives the ritual acts a strong optative tenor, in the form of wishes and requests directed to God. This characteristic gives the ritual actions not only a moral slant, but also an eschatological, prospective orientation: with each other beginning the continuing journey to completion of life.

9.2. In general

(1) A Theory of Acts analysis, applied to ritual complexes such as the marriage liturgy, should be carried out on the basis of the structural analysis of the ritual. The structure defines the position of the ritual actions and their meaning. Structural analysis in turn should relate to the genetic analysis of a ritual. The historical development clarifies the origin and the growth of a ritual, as well as the influences which have left a continuing mark on it.

(2) A Theory of Acts analysis of ritual actions assumes and implies that investigation is done into acts that are performed by actors. In this study, we have proceeded from a text – an official document – which is a guide for the marriage liturgy. The performance of the actions by the actors themselves has not entered into this study, and requires development of empirical research on the basis of the analysis performed.

(3) The philosophical basis of Theory of Acts analysis does not clarify ritual actions as such. The concept of 'ritual' is, as we have said, ultimately foreign to the model. Rites and rituals illustrate only the way in which people can act. Ritual performance is therefore also to be understood as a form of human action. It is no separate domain in the interfering complexity of the model. It is, however, to be noted that in a ritual like the marriage liturgy, the organised acts of actors can take on all sorts of differentiation, that are given in the model. Does this perhaps say something about the autotopy of ritual and about the relativity of its heterotopy? Those searching for the *proprium* of ritual actions should proceed from their relation of correspondence to human actions in general, to then go in search of the singularities and peculiarities of ritual behaviour.

(4) That which characterises ritual communication is not the fact that a selection takes place in the main sorts of illocutionary acts – assertive, directive, commissive, expressive and declarative. They are all represented. The compressed character of the communication is well worth noting, however: the frequency, the interwovenness and the quick suc-

cession of the acts, which lend an exceptional dynamism and intensity to the ritual actions and place demands on the concentration of the participants. Empirical investigation might reveal that more than a bit escapes their notice. Moreover, ritual communication – for instance in the case of the marriage liturgy – is marked to a great extent by the actions of the appointed leaders, particularly the priest/worship leader. They define the typical, official and ecclesiastical quality of the ritual communication. This can have the result that the community, those present and central figures such as the bridal couple in this case, are consigned to a second level: as listeners and spectators, as consumers or even objects being manipulated. Rituals, however, demand a good balance in communicative power that emanates from the *dramatis personae*, in order not to lurch to the side of a heterotopic, hieratic manner of communicating. Finally, we must point to the working of God, the Star Player par excellence in liturgical communication, who is pointed to and invoked in symbolic and metaphoric representations from beginning to end. He appears as an addressing subject – the One who turns to us – and as the subject of our address – the one to whom we turn. The Theory of Acts analysis of the marriage ritual required the most attention in defining directive acts such as recommendations, requests, wishes, orders and expectations, on the one side directed from God to those present – particularly the bridal couple – and on the other side to God, from those present and the couple. The problem is concentrated in the images and phasing that are employed in preaching and prayer. The central language act of religious Christian ritual – prayer – remains outside the perspective of the Theory of Acts model. This limitation of the philosophical model poses the question to theologians of how to work out the quality of this illocutionary language act.

(5) In our analysis of ritual actions we were most struck by the narrative component, which in this case constitutes the identity in faith of the actors. The community celebrates its *narratio*, both of marriage and more generally, on the basis of Scripture and tradition. Through the words of the leader it actualises the story for the situation in which the participants, and in particular the bridal couple, find themselves. The couple join in to this story and take it to themselves and exchange it with one another in the marriage act. The renewal of their identity to duality-in-unity as a wedded couple means not only the continuation of the intergenerative tradition of marriage, but even more the perspective of realising the ideals for their lives. In the ritual this perspective is inter-

preted through narrative elements in the form of the prayer of intercession, the hymns of praise and blessings, in particular the marriage blessing. The great, anamnestic story of the community condenses and is
personalised in the story of the couple; their story is opened up epiclet-
ically to the future. This narrative structure of ritual actions, which perhaps involves all the actors in different positions, appears to be the
ground for the performativity of the ritual: confirming and renewing
identity, selfhood and solidarity. This is true for all liturgical actions, but
is particularly and especially the case for the performance of marriage,
where two persons, *in foro publico*, are united as husband and wife, from
individuals to become a couple. That their assumption of the *narratio*
for themselves offers possibilities for a successful life but does not guarantee success is sufficiently taken into account in the ritual, and made
manifest in acts of involvement and generosity on the part of those surrounding them: *ut duo sint*. Rituals offer a framework for the possible
and hopeful living of life, but do not perform miracles.

(6) Analysing ritual in the marriage liturgy calls up serious questions.
We have seen that it is marked by a fundamental ambiguity, which is
caused by the insertion of the marriage ritual into the order of service
for the Eucharist. This insertion is only partially successful, which
results in the total ritual complex showing signs of equivocality in 'plot'.
On the one hand, the performance of the marriage is central, and permeates the whole of the ritual action; on the other hand, the celebration
of the Eucharist within the applicable liturgical regulations is so dominant and fixed that they overshadow the 'plot' of the marriage liturgy.
Two possibilities present themselves. In the best case, one might refash-
ion the Eucharist, which is celebrated in the context of the marriage
liturgy, in such a way that it fits in and harmonises with the framework
of marriage rituality, which would demand the possibility of important
adjustments. In the worse case, if such space for eucharistic actions is
not offered or taken, one might omit the Eucharist for rituological and
liturgical studies reasons, such as have been given in this study.

MARTIN J.M. HOONDERT

THE APPROPRIATION OF GREGORIAN CHANT IN THE NETHERLANDS, 1903-1930

1. INTRODUCTION[1]

On November 22, 1903, Pope Pius X issued a *motu proprio* entitled *Tra le sollecitudini*. In it he established that 'traditional' Gregorian plainsong should be given the prime place in Church music. In a second *motu proprio* dated April 25, 1904, the monks of Solesmes were commissioned to prepare new editions of Gregorian plainsong for the hymn books. The new *Graduale* rolled off the Vatican presses in 1908. Upon the publication of the 1903 *motu proprio* the Redemptorist J. Bogaerts wrote a postcard from Rome to M.J.A. Lans, then president of the seminary at Warmond. The text of this postcard, dated January 1, 1904, reads as follows:[2]

> I have just, on New Year's Eve, gotten the *Osservatore Romano* with the expected '*motu proprio*' for church music in Rome, a mettlesome piece. The Pope goes to work most formidably, extolling the traditional songs as the pure ancient reading and easy to perform. That is the music, and no other. Completely disregarding the official edition or the Congregatio Rituum or what Pius IX and Leo XIII had wanted. The *motu proprio* satisfies all the requirements and has all the elements needed to have legal force in Italy. You will certainly note that the Pope has committed a pair of howlers. The papal Congregations can gloat and say to themselves: You wanted to do it without us, Holy Father. You've paid the price for that!

From this postcard it would appear that the plans of Pope Pius X met with opposition, both in Rome itself and among prominent church musicians in The Netherlands.

A new period in the history of Gregorian chant began with the 1903 *motu proprio* and the editions of the new hymn books which followed it.

---

[1] This contribution is based on M.J.M. HOONDERT: *De restauratie van het gregoriaans. Toeëigening van een traditie in Nederland, 1903-1930* (Tilburg 1998) (Thesis for the degree of *doctorandus*, Tilburg Faculty of Theology).

[2] The postcard is in the archive of the Gregoriusvereniging. It was made available to me by Prof. Dr. A. Vernooij.

Since the Council of Trent Gregorian chant had been passed down and sung according to varying editions in which it was adapted to the demands of the time. Melodies were abbreviated and simplified, the placement of texts was altered. The most influential edition was the *Editio Medicaea* from 1614-1615. A reissue of the *Medicaea* was done in 1871, under the influence of the priest and musicologist Fr. X. Haberl, from Regensburg. The use of this *Neo-Medicaea* was earnestly commended by the then Pope Leo XIII. The Gregoriusvereniging, founded in 1878 (although the first volume of their journal, the *Gregoriusblad*, had already appeared in 1876), appointed itself the advocate for the *Neo-Medicaea* in The Netherlands. In many places this book became the hymnal for Roman Catholic choristers. After 1903, however, due to the motu proprio *Tra le sollecitudini*, the Gregoriusvereniging and the *Gregoriusblad* had to alter their stance. In time, the Dutch bishops issued instructions that the new Vatican editions were to be used.

The developments which occurred between the appearance of the *Neo-Medicaea* in 1871 and the *Editio Vaticana* in 1908 are a segment of what is termed the 'restoration of Gregorian plainsong'. In the 19th century musicians and scholars from diverse disciplines discovered that Gregorian music from the centuries after Trent no longer corresponded with what manuscripts from the Middle Ages recorded. An effort began to reconstruct the 'original' Gregorian music. Particularly the monks of the Benedictine abbey at Solesmes, in France, played an important role in this. The restoration of Gregorian music meant not only a new vision of the music itself, but also implied a different view of the past. No longer did one reach back to the results of the Council of Trent, as Haberl did with his edition of the *Neo-Medicaea*, but to sources from the Middle Ages. This altered manner of dealing with the past in turn defined what was meant by concepts such as 'restoration', 'restoring', or 'authentic Gregorian music'.

This contribution describes how the results of the restoration of Gregorian plainsong were received in the practice of church music. In this, the functioning of Gregorian music will not only be considered at the level of designation or stipulation by Church and scholarship, but an attempt will also be made to bring into the picture sung practice, the experience and reception in choirs and parishes, and especially the process of appropriation and assigning meaning. In comparison to other studies, the emphasis in the investigation here will be significantly shifted. Not designation by ecclesiastical authorities and academic institutions, but the specific manner of dealing with Gregorian music that is rooted in the context of Roman Catholics in The Netherlands, will be central.

A very important element in the interaction of designation and appropriation is the insight that it is no longer continuity of culture that is our point of departure, but dynamic and development. Gregorian music was a part of a specific manner of dealing with the past, an activity in which tradition and continuity were construed as components in what could be termed a 'civilizing offensive'. Without further elaborating this here, it can be said that this way of dealing with tradition and the past was closely linked with the identity of Roman Catholics as a social group in Dutch society.

In what immediately follows, the research perspective employed (how the past and tradition are handled; designation and appropriation) will be worked out. This research perspective will be amplified on the basis of an example from ecclesiastical and liturgical history from the 19th century (§2). Next, the history of the restoration of Gregorian plainsong will be sketched in an international perspective (§3). From this international frame of reference the complex interplay of designation and appropriation of the results of the restoration of Gregorian music will be analyzed in the Dutch context (§4). Here use will be made of the journal *Gregoriusblad*. The analysis of the Dutch situation will be limited to the years 1903-1930. The boundaries of this period are on the one hand dictated by the date that the *motu proprio* of Pius X, *Tra le sollecitudini*, appeared, and on the other by the rise of liturgical song, and the discussions connected with it beginning in the fourth decade of the 20th century. A balance will be drawn up in a closing section, and the appropriation of the 'new' Gregorian music in The Netherlands in the period 1903-1930 will be characterized (§5).

2. RESEARCH PERSPECTIVE[3]

2.1. Invention of tradition, identity and group culture

The British historian Eric Hobsbawm has played an important role in shaping the theoretical structure with regard to how groups deal with

---

[3] For a more extensive development of the research perspective, see M.J.M. HOONDERT & P. POST: De dynamiek van het gregoriaans. Een onderzoeksperspectief, in *Jaarboek voor liturgie-onderzoek* 15 (1999) 7-26.

the past. He was the first to formulate the frequently called upon concept of 'invention of tradition'. Hobsbawm's insights have also been applied in liturgical studies in The Netherlands.[4] In 1983 Hobsbawm brought out a collection of articles together with T. Ranger under the title *The invention of tradition*.[5] This collection was the result of a symposium organized by the journal *Past and present*. Hobsbawm wrote the introduction, in which he introduced the concept of 'invention of tradition', and also contributed an article on 'Mass-Producing Traditions' in Europe in the 1870-1914 period.

In the introduction Hobsbawm terms 'invented traditions' "responses to novel situations which take the form of reference to old situations".[6] A 'break in continuity' is characteristic of invented traditions.[7] There is the suggestion of continuity, but this continuity doesn't really exist. It is by this that Hobsbawm distinguishes his concept from the tenacious continuance of traditions. Invented traditions present themselves in a situation of rupture, a vacuum in which something new is created. In order to make this clear Hobsbawm uses words such as invention, creation, innovation and construction interchangeably. What is important for him is that something new has arisen. "Where the old ways are alive, traditions need be neither revived nor invented."[8]

A shift can be detected in the way scholars from various disciplines have handled Hobsbawm's concept. Many researchers who make or made use of the term 'invention of tradition' placed the emphasis on 'invention', on distinguishing real and false traditions. Less attention was paid to the function of invented traditions. By rereading Hobsbawm his insights can be freed from connotations of unmasking manipulation and artificial shaping of myth.

---

[4] P. POST: De creatie van tradition volgens Eric Hobsbawm, in *Jaarboek voor liturgie-onderzoek* 11 (1995) 77-101; IDEM: 'God kijkt niet op een vierkante meter…' of Hobsbawm herlezen…, in C. VAN DER BORGT et al. (eds): *Constructie van het eigene. Culturele vormen van regionale identiteit in Nederland* (Amsterdam 1996) 175-200; IDEM: Rituals and the function of the past. Rereading Eric Hobsbawm, in *Journal of ritual studies* 10/2 (1996[1998]) 85-107; IDEM: The creation of tradition. Rereading and reading beyond Hobsbawm, in J.W. VAN HENTEN & A. HOUTEPEN (eds): *Religious identity and the invention of tradition* (= Proceedings of the 1st Noster Congress, Soesterberg, Jan. 4, 1999. Series: Studies in Theology and Religion) (in the press).
[5] E. HOBSBAWM & T. RANGER (eds): *The invention of tradition* (Cambridge 1983).
[6] HOBSBAWM & RANGER: *Invention* 2.
[7] HOBSBAWM & RANGER: *Invention* 7.
[8] HOBSBAWM & RANGER: *Invention* 8.

Hobsbawm places the process of inventing traditions in the framework of ritualization. To properly understand that concept we must become acquainted with what are termed 'ritual studies'. The book *Ritual theory, ritual practice*, by C. Bell, is a good introduction to this field.[9] In ritual studies, ritual is placed within the broad frame of culture and its study. In the second section of her book Bell locates ritual in social activities in general. Some activities have a privileged status among these social activities. Bell terms the strategies by which this status is obtained 'ritualization':

> Ritualization is a matter of various culturally specific strategies for setting some activities off from others, for creating and privileging a qualitative distinction between the 'sacred' and the 'profane', and for ascribing such distinctions to realities thought to transcend the powers of human actors.[10]

Thus, the end result of ritualization is differentiation, 'privileged contrast'. It is precisely in this that ritualization and construction or invention of tradition cohere. The construction of tradition also leads to differentiation: "(…) a set of distinctions, seen as rooted in the past, which differentiates this group from other groups."[11]

Differentiation, on the basis of a shared past, leads to group identity. In various case studies Hobsbawm demonstrates how in varying historical contexts a sort of legitimizing continuity with the past can be created with the aid of rituals, in order to experience tradition as fixed. It is precisely this suggested continuity and changelessness of tradition from which identity is derived. Identity is created through appropriating collective images of the past and thus constructing what is termed 'authoritative precedent'. Hobsbawm points out that this process of inventing traditions occurs primarily in communities where social structures are weak or have disappeared.[12] It is precisely in this context of instability and change that there arises a need for continuity, for tradition that links the present with the past and in so doing affords a foothold for identity and direction. It is the job of those studying culture to discover and reconstruct the process of how ritual change takes place through the way the past is dealt with, but also to try to under-

---

[9] C. BELL: *Ritual theory, ritual practice* (New York/Oxford 1992).
[10] BELL: *Ritual theory* 13.
[11] BELL: *Ritual theory* 121.
[12] HOBSBAWM & RANGER: *Invention* 4-5.

stand that process in terms of changing contexts – that is to say, to understand why needs arose (and arise), and which patterns play a role in that.[13] The research perspective of invention of tradition which has been set forth above has also found a place in liturgical studies. From a broad perspective it points to the process of historicization and musealization in our culture, and the role of rituals in this. We will not go more deeply into that here, but rather make reference to the numerous publications (and particularly those of Paul Post) on this question which is so important in liturgical studies.[14]

2.2. Designation and appropriation

A complex interplay of designation and appropriation takes place in the process of assigning meaning by means of invented traditions and the appeal to the past.[15] Ritual repertories that are handed down are received in an active way and reinterpreted. The meaning of received ideas and how they are experienced is usually not fixed, but is transformed in a process of appropriation. There is an interchange between production and supply on the one side and consumption and reception on the other. Through paying attention to the context-linked processes of appropriation, a dynamic picture of culture arises. The accent in research shifts: from top-down to bottom-up, in which the community becomes the central focus for the shaping of culture. In place of a lopsided accent on

---

[13] See also P. POST: Zeven notities over rituele verandering, traditie en (vergelijkende) liturgiewetenschap, in *Jaarboek voor liturgie-onderzoek* 11 (1995) 1-30, esp. p. 26.

[14] P. POST: Het verleden in het spel? Volksreligieuze rituelen tussen cultus en cultuur, in *Jaarboek voor liturgie-onderzoek* 7 (1991) 79-124; IDEM: Volksreligieuze rituelen tussen cultus en cultuur, in M. VAN UDEN & J. PIEPER: *Bedevaart als volksreligieus ritueel* (= UTP-Teksten nr. 16) (Heerlen 1991) 47-76; IDEM: Zeven notities; M. HOONDERT: Goede tijden, slechte tijden. Crisis en bloei in liturgie en kerkmuziek, in *Gregoriusblad* 123 (1999) 17-23.

[15] M. DE CERTEAU: *The practice of everyday life* (Berkeley/Los Angeles 1984); R. CHARTIER: *Cultural history between practices and representations* (Cambridge 1988); M. MONTEIRO, G. ROOIJAKKERS & J. ROSENDAAL (eds): *De dynamiek van religie en cultuur. Geschiedenis van het Nederlands katholicisme* (Kampen 1993); G. ROOIJAKKERS: *Rituele repertoires. Volkscultuur in oostelijk Noord-Brabant 1559-1853* (Nijmegen 1994); W. FRIJHOFF: Toeëigening: van bezitsdrang naar betekenisgeving, in *Trajecta* 6 (1997) 99-118; IDEM: *Heiligen, idolen, iconen* (= inaugural lecture, June 1998, Vrije Universiteit, Amsterdam) (Nijmegen 1998).

designation by academic or ecclesiastical authorities, for instance, the emphasis moves to the broad process of production, distribution and consumption of culture, from prescribed order to lived, celebrated, sung practice.

2.3. Dom Prosper Guéranger (1805-1875) and the Christian Middle Ages

In the following the research perspective of invention of tradition will be illustrated on the basis of an example. This example, which is not chosen at random, involves a vision of the Middle Ages held by 19th-century Catholics. Thereby attention is directed on the figure of Dom Prosper Guéranger, who reestablished the Benedictine abbey of Solesmes in 1833 and was moreover an important stimulus for the restoration of Gregorian music. The example will make clear how Guéranger's vision of the Middle Ages arose from specific problems of the 19th century.

One of the most sweeping processes of the 19th century was rising industrialization.[16] Industrialization created urban areas in which labourers lived and worked. This meant shifts from an agrarian society with small communities to an industrial society in which people had to seek their place in large, often complex urban conglomerates. The workers were torn loose from structures rooted in localities which had provided security, meaning and identity. Cultural values in which everyone could participate and which could hold the new forms of society together had to be sought and supplied. On one side these cultural values were supplied by education, through which the workers received a social frame of reference. On the other side a system for interpreting the new social forms was found in nationalism. For Roman Catholics this new system of interpretation was problematic. They were, after all, not only part of the nation, but also of the Roman Catholic Church as an interpretative whole, with universal claims that transcended all nations. The solution for this problem was surprisingly sought by the Church in a strengthening of its own supra-national identity. Particularly in the period 1850-1900 the Church evolved into

---

[16] For what follows, see P. RAEDTS: De christelijke middeleeuwen als mythe. Ontstaan en gebruik van een constructie uit de negentiende eeuw, in *Tijdschrift voor theologie* 30 (1990) 146-158.

a rigid bureaucratic organization with a shared culture that embraced all areas of life, with its own 'national' ideology, ultramontanism. The Church was delineated as a *societas perfecta* with the Pope at its head. By orientation to this 'supra-national nation' believers were wrenched away from local religious connections. This process of up-scaling, analogous to the process of industrialization and the consequences which accompanied it, met with resistance and therefore also had to seek legitimation. This was provided by demonstrating that the 'innovations' were nothing other than reaching back to old traditions. For these Roman Catholic innovators readily reached out to the 19th century image of the Middle Ages: a totally Christian society, in which the Church embraced all aspects of life.[17] This image formed a powerful underpinning for the reorganization of the Roman Catholic Church. In the name of the restoration of the Middle Ages the typically medieval horizontal layers of administration were eliminated in favour of a vertical, strongly hierarchical system of control.

In addition to and beyond rationalizing the administrative structure, the culture of the Catholic Church was homogenized. Through schooling, establishing Catholic labour unions and class-based organizations and the distribution of Catholic publications a Christianization offensive was launched based on the ideal – by now superseded – of a medieval society that was permeated at all levels by faith. This common culture also took shape through the encouragement of neo-Thomism in theology and the standardization of liturgy. This latter led to the disappearance of the neo-Gallican liturgies in France and to the creation of a hymn book with universal claims, the *Neo-Medicaea* of 1871. Finally, popular piety was also homogenized, among other ways by the stimulation of the Marian cultus. As with the reorganization of the administrative structure, for this process of homogenization of Roman Catholic culture it was likewise the case that, accompanied by an appeal to the Middle Ages, what were in fact new forms were introduced. It is characteristic, however, that Catholics themselves in the 19th century spoke of 'restoration' and 'restoring'. The fact that what was happening was a conscious process of innovation was cloaked by the use of these terms.

<hr>

[17] P. RAEDTS: Katholieken op zoek naar een Nederlandse identiteit 1814-1889, in *Bijdragen en mededelingen betreffende de geschiedenis der Nederlanden* 107 (1992) 714.

We must place Prosper Louis Guéranger in this 19th century context.[18] Guéranger was born in 1805, four years after the negotiation of a concordat between the French government and the Roman curia (1801). This concordat meant de facto a return to the situation under the Ancien Régime. The church was again a part of the French state and was chiefly used to guarantee and provide religious legitimization for tranquillity and peace within France. Disappointment however led to opposition, particularly from the younger generation that grouped itself around the priest Hugues-Félicité de Lamennais (1782-1854). De Lamennais and his followers dreamed of the restoration of the medieval Church, on the one hand as an antidote to the confusion of modern times, and on the other to restore the freedom of man. De Lamennais believed that only the Church – as in the past had seemed to be the case – could effectively resist the arbitrariness and tyranny of the monarchs and the state. Only under the leadership of the Pope in Rome could a free and just society be constructed. Guéranger too dreamed of such a supra-national unity under the leadership of the Pope. In a survey of the history of Christianity he wrote, with regard to the crusades:

> If we observe the nationalities of our present-day Europe, divided and mutually at enmity, who shall not then acknowledge the superiority which the peoples of the Middle Ages owed to their sense for the divine; a sense, shared by all, which they loved and understood; a sense that secures the treasures of heaven and at the same time provided a powerful protection for Christian peoples joined together, one in common obedience to the Vicar of Christ, King of the World?[19]

Only at superficial examination does Guéranger's plea for strengthening the papacy appear to share the same starting points as De Lamennais. Unlike De Lamennais, Guéranger was not interested in the human liberties that, according to De Lamennais, could only bloom again if the Church raised its voice against the growing power of the state. The ultramontanism of Guéranger was inspired by the authority and unity

---

[18] For the following, see particularly P. RAEDTS: De katholieken en de Middeleeuwen. Prosper Guéranger OSB (1805-1875) en de eenheid van de liturgie, in R.E.V. STUIP & C. VELLEKOOP (eds): De Middeleeuwen in de negentiende eeuw (Hilversum 1996) 87-109.

[19] Cited from P. DELATTE: Dom Guéranger abt van Solesmes 1805-1875, II (Vaals 1969) 208. (Dutch translation by G. Smeets of: Dom Guéranger, abbé de Solesmes [Paris 1909-1910]).

which surrounded Rome as an aura in the Middle Ages. What made Guéranger unique among the ultramontanists in addition to that was that he was the first to see the potential of the liturgy for again making the unity and authority of Rome visible and tangible to the farthest corners of the Catholic world. In order to realize this ideal of unity under Rome, Guéranger turned his gaze to the past: "Qu'est devenu cette unité de culte que Pépin et Charlemagne, de concert avec les pontifes romaines, avaient établie dans nos Églises."[20] Guéranger's romantic longing for the Middle Ages must be considered as a means to an end that lay in his own time: restoration of the unity of the liturgy through a return to Roman liturgical forms.[21] The Middle Ages themselves played only a subordinate role in this effort. Guéranger wanted to show that the Roman liturgy stood in continuity with the liturgy of apostolic times. The Middle Ages were only an intermediary in this.

For the rest, however, Guéranger did not have a picture in his mind of an unchanging liturgy prescribed in apostolic times. In his view, liturgy is the bearer of tradition, but this tradition is constantly in motion, dynamic and vital. The truth of tradition lies not in its changelessness, but in its being established by the authority of the Pope. From this perspective, even local liturgies might continue to exist, on the condition they were approved by Rome.[22] According to Guéranger, in the early Middle Ages the initiative for the introduction of the Roman liturgy throughout all of Western Europe lay entirely, and already at that date, with the Pope. It is precisely in this vision of the history of liturgy that Guéranger reveals the extent to which his perspective was defined by the problems of his own time. In his view there was no room for observing that in the eighth century the Frankish kings had in fact used the Pope, and that the effort toward unity in the liturgy had first of all served a political purpose for the Franks.

The question is why Guéranger found unity under the leadership of the Pope through the introduction of the Roman liturgy so important.

[20] P. GUÉRANGER: *Institutions liturgiques* I (Paris 1878[2]) lxix-lxx.

[21] This was not, however, true for Gregorian plainsong. Guéranger was of the opinion that the books which were in use in Rome in his own time (among them the Medicaea edition of 1614-15) were worse than the books that circulated in France. See P. COMBE: *Histoire de la restauration du chant grégorien d'après des documents inédits. Solesmes et l'Édition Vaticane* (Solesmes 1969) 19.

[22] On this, see C. JOHNSON: *Prosper Guéranger (1805-1875). A liturgical theologian. An introduction to his liturgical writings and work* (= Studia Anselmia 89 = Analecta liturgica 9) (Rome 1984) 282-283, 290-292, 319, 330-333.

The answer lies in his view of the liturgy. Guéranger emphasized the social dimension of the liturgy: "La liturgie n'est pas simplement la prière mais la prière considérée à l'état social."[23] Precisely in the celebration of the liturgy were Catholics fused together into a social entity. The Church as a supra-national state must express her unity in concrete, social forms. All Catholics all over the world were linked with one another through a common language, Latin, and a universal liturgy, that of Rome. The increasing scaling-up under the influence of industrialization in the second half of the 19th century had need of precisely this new form of solidarity.

With regard to France, Guéranger succeeded in his scheme. Less than forty years after the appearance of his chief work, *Institutions liturgiques* (1840), the Roman liturgy had been introduced everywhere in France. This success was not to be credited to Guéranger's qualities as a scholar. Indeed, his attempt to trace the usages of the Roman liturgy back to apostolic times points rather to an uncritical spirit. Raedts explains Guéranger's success as follows:

> Guéranger was a myth-maker: not only did he provide an extremely clear picture of the past, so that everyone could understand it, but he recounted it in such a way that it could also still be used as a weapon in the present. And the present was the time in which he was really interested; he sought to change the Church of his own day.[24]

It was Guéranger who, by emphasizing the social dimension of the liturgy and by referring back to the idealized situation at the time of Popes in the Middle Ages such as Gregory VII and Innocent III, showed Catholics one way to shape their own supra-national community.

3. The restoration of Gregorian chant

In order to understand the history of the restoration of Gregorian plainsong, we must begin with the instructions regarding liturgy from the Council of Trent (1545-1563). The Council sought to provide an answer to the developments which had been initiated by the Reformation. In the case of the liturgy, this answer was translated into concern

---

[23] Guéranger: *Institutions liturgiques* I, 1. See also Johnson: *Prosper Guéranger* 256-260.
[24] Raedts: De katholieken 105.

for the preservation of tradition, by means of a uniform and centrally regulated liturgy.[25] The liturgy must be stripped of all locally-based additions. In 1570 a missal was published the use of which was obligatory for the entire church. With taking this new book into use for the liturgy of the Mass, the need arose for accompanying music. On October 25, 1577, the composers Giovanni Pierluigi da Palestrina and Annibale Ziolo were commissioned to draw up a hymnal on the basis of the new missal. For reasons which are not clear they never fulfilled this commission. In 1608 Pope Paul V once again commissioned the composition of a hymnal for the Mass. Six musicians were approached for this, but ultimately it was Felice Anerio and Francesco Soriano who were occupied after 1611 with the task. In 1614-15 the new *Graduale* came out in two parts. It was printed on the presses of the Medici, and therefore termed the *Editio Medicaea*.[26]

The *Medicaea* edition was deeply influenced by the times in which it was created, particularly by the humanism of the 17th century and the musical style of the Renaissance. Under the influence of humanism the Latin texts were 'improved' and the relationship between the accents in the words and music was altered. Furthermore the melodies were made more tonal and melismata, considered 'barbaric', were abbreviated or eliminated.

Use of the 1570 missal was made obligatory for the whole of the Western Church. Rome could, however, permit exceptions for churches and orders that could show evidence of a written tradition reaching back more than 200 years. Moreover, Rome did not declare the introduction of the *Editio Medicaea* obligatory, but left this to local bishops.[27] Thus there was no comprehensive standardization. Efforts toward a uniform liturgy were furthermore thwarted by growing objections against Roman/Papal centralism, particularly in France under Louis XIV (1643-1715). In part as a result of the influence of the Enlightenment, after about 1650 people sought freedom, self-fulfilment and autonomy. Under the leadership of the bishops and supported by the king, the French Church went its own way after 1650. This is termed Neo-Gallicanism, a current which expressed itself, among other ways, in

---

[25] H.A.J. WEGMAN: *Riten en mythen. Liturgie in de geschiedenis van het christendom* (Kampen 1991) 312-313.

[26] D. HILEY: *Western plainchant. A handbook* (Oxford 1993) 615-616.

[27] R.F. HAYBURN: *Papal legislation on sacred music 95 A.D. to 1977 A.D.* (Collegeville 1979) 64.

the liturgy. For example, in 1676 a Latin/French missal appeared[28] and new forms of pseudo-Gregorian music were introduced.[29] The Netherlands too had its own tradition of Gregorian hymnals. After about 1700 Amsterdam printers supplied The Netherlands with books of Gregorian chant. These volumes were based broadly on the *Graduale* of Mechelen of 1607 and an Antiphonal of 1617. The Gregorian music in these Amsterdam editions was less 'impaired' than the Gregorian music that the *Medicaea* contained. But here too it can be seen that many melismata *(barbarismi)* have been abbreviated and that the relation between accents in word and music have been altered.[30]

After the period of adjustments and revisions in the Gregorian repertoire, at the beginning of the 19th century there arose a desire to return to 'original' Gregorian music. Diverse factors played a role in this: the need for a generally applicable hymnal in which unity with Rome was expressed; 19th century historicism; and the technical possibility of copying manuscripts.

The wish to return to an 'authentic' form of Gregorian chant is the basis of what we call the 'restoration of Gregorian plainsong'. Two currents can be distinguished in this process of restoration, designated by the names of their centres, Solesmes and Regensburg. Solesmes stands for the Benedictine abbey which was established in 1833 by Dom Guéranger in this town by Le Mans in France. Guéranger and his monks wanted to return to the most authentic Gregorian practice, and began after about 1859 with the study of a large number of manuscripts from the Middle Ages. Regensburg stands for a number of clergy and musicians who had united in the Allgemeiner Cäcilien-Verein, founded in 1868. This association, which we term Caecilianism, sought a deeper and better experience of liturgy. With regard to church music, Caecilianism promoted the music of Palestrina and Gregorian chant, seeing that both genres had been considered by the Council of Trent as the true liturgical music. Regensburg and adherents to this current were therefore less interested in medieval Gregorian manuscripts, but wanted

---

[28] WEGMAN: *Riten en mythen* 346-348.
[29] HILEY: *Western plainchant* 618-621.
[30] A.I.M. KAT: *De geschiedenis der kerkmuziek in de Nederlanden sedert de Hervorming* (Hilversum 1939) 82-115 and 286-287; F. JESPERS: De Noordnederlandse gregoriaanse zangboeken, in *Gregoriusblad* 110 (1986) 209-213; J. VALKESTIJN: Het gregoriaans, in S. GROOT (ed.): *De lof Gods geef ik stem. Inzichten en achtergronden van de vocale muziek in de rooms-katholieke eredienst* (Baarn 1993) 78-79.

to reintroduce the *Medicaea* edition. In the *Medicaea* this current saw Gregorian music as it had been fixed by Rome and adopted for the whole of Christianity. In their view, authenticity coincided with authority. In 1871, under the leadership of Franz Xaver Haberl (1840-1910), in cooperation with the Regensburg publisher Pustet, a reissue of the *Medicaea* came out. Pustet received from Rome a privilege for the printing of Gregorian hymnals for a period of thirty years.

Caecilianism also had its adherents in The Netherlands. For instance, following Haberl's example, M.J.A. Lans, editor in chief of the *Gregoriusblad*, argued strongly for the introduction of the *Neo-Medicaea* in The Netherlands. In order to realize this ideal, in addition to having official books it was necessary to be well organized. In part because of this Lans decided to found the Gregoriusvereniging in 1878. From its earliest years the Gregoriusvereniging was strongly oriented toward Germany. Lans was a proponent of the Pustet edition, on the one hand because it was the official, approved edition, and on the other hand because The Netherlands had an urgent need for books. Lans's efforts for the introduction of the Regensburg books took on an international character with his appearance at the 1882 Congress of Arezzo, for church music. This Congress was entirely dominated by the conflict between Regensburg and Solesmes. On the one side stood Haberl and Lans, and on the other Dom Pothier, who represented Solesmes. In Arezzo Lans propounded a very clear thesis: if one wanted unity, then one must not found this on old manuscripts. After all, on the basis of these manuscripts the first half of the 19th century had already seen many differing editions. Furthermore, the old, restored Gregorian music, with its long melismata and many decorative flourishes, is much too difficult for normal choirs. Lans's international appearance generated considerable sympathy in The Netherlands for the case he argued. It helped advance the introduction of the *Neo-Medicaea*. For the rest, Lans had no doubts about the scholarly quality of the work at Solesmes. His interest was, however, different: Lans wanted to establish unity in the Gregorian practice, and to do this by means of the use of the books that he considered to be most practical, and that had been approved by ecclesiastical authorities.[31]

After the congress at Arezzo the Pope found it necessary to take a clear position in the conflict between Regensburg and Solesmes. In the

---

[31] KAT: *De geschiedenis der kerkmuziek* 252-259.

edict *Romanorum pontificum*, of April 26, 1883, he designated the Pustet edition as the only legitimate and authentic edition. It is true the Pope did not make the use of the *Neo-Medicaea*[32] obligatory, but the pressure on the bishops was certainly very great. In the edict *Quod Sanctus Augustinus*, of July 7, 1894, the Pustet editions were once again emphatically recommended.[33]

When in 1833 Dom Prosper Guéranger reestablished the abbey of Solesmes, he had various goals in mind. Not only did he seek a revitalization of monastic life, he also sought the introduction of the Roman liturgy in France. It was in the context of this Romanization of the liturgy that Guéranger stimulated research into 'authentic' Gregorian chant. Already in the first part of his *Institutions liturgiques* (1840) he had formulated the point of departure for the monks of Solesmes undertaking the restoration of Gregorian plainsong:

> Il est évident que si l'on est quelquefois en droit de croire qu'on possede la phrase grégorienne dans sa pureté sur un morceau en particulier, c'est lorsque les exemplaires de plusieurs Eglises éloigneés s'accordent sur la même leçon.[34]

It was Dom Paul Jausions who after 1856 began the investigation of manuscripts.[35] In 1860 Dom Joseph Pothier (1835-1923) was added to the scriptorium at Solesmes.[36] Pothier put together a *Graduale* with restored melodies and wrote a study on rhythm in Gregorian music:[37] *Mélodies grégoriennes* (1880)[38] and the *Liber gradualis* (1883).[39]

In the year that Pothier published his *Liber gradualis*, the edict *Romanorum pontificum* was issued in Rome. As already described above, this edict was a reaction to the Arezzo Congress on church music in 1882. At this congress an intense conflict had been fought out between the adherents of Regensburg on the one side and those of Solesmes on

[32] HAYBURN: *Papal legislation* 159-161.
[33] HAYBURN: *Papal legislation* 163-165. J.P. SCHMIT: Die Choralbewegung im 19. Jahrhundert, in K.G. FELLERER: *Geschichte der katholischen Kirchenmusik* 2 (Kassel etc. 1976) states incorrectly (on page 258) that this edict made the Pustet edition obligatory.
[34] Cited from COMBE: *Histoire de la restauration* 16.
[35] COMBE: *Histoire de la restauration* 29-33.
[36] COMBE: *Histoire de la restauration* 41.
[37] HILEY: *Western plainchant* 624; COMBE: *Histoire de la restauration* 67-71, 74-76 and 80-82.
[38] J. POTHIER: *Les mélodies grégoriennes d'après la tradition* (Tournai 1880).
[39] *Liber gradualis* (Tournai 1883; second edition 1895).

the other. Solesmes initially appeared to have won this conflict. The Congress approved proposals that favoured the work of Solesmes, and after its conclusion the participants in the Congress were received by Pope Leo XIII and warmly praised. *Romanorum pontificum* therefore came as a complete surprise. However, the edict did leave some room for the work at Solesmes. After all, use of the *Neo-Medicaea* was recommended, not required. Moreover, research into the oldest forms of Gregorian chant was approved.[40] Under the leadership of Dom André Mocquereau (1849-1930), who arrived at Solesmes in 1875, an ambitious project began in 1889: the facsimile publication of a large number of manuscripts of Gregorian hymnals.[41] With this publication, under the title *Paléographie musicale*, Solesmes on the one hand wanted to demonstrate that the melodies of the *Neo-Medicaea* had been mutilated, and on the other that to a large extent the old manuscripts were in agreement with one another and thus could become the basis for a restoration of the melodies for Gregorian plainsong.

On behalf of *Paléographie musicale* and the work of the scriptorium at Solesmes the monks travelled all around Europe in search of suitable manuscripts. By the agency of photography Solesmes could have at its disposal a large collection of manuscripts on the basis of which comparative research and the reconstruction of melodies could take place. A trip to Italy that Mocquereau and his fellow monk Dom F. Cabrol undertook in 1890 was of importance for official acknowledgement of the work at Solesmes. In Rome they made the acquaintance of the Jesuit Fr. Angelo de Santi. They were able to win this influential figure for their vision of the way Gregorian chant should be performed. Pothier's *Liber gradualis* was adopted at various seminaries in Rome. Pope Leo XIII reacted positively to this.[42] Official pronouncements in Rome however remained pro Regensburg, as appears from the edict *Quod Sanctus Augustinus* of July 7, 1894. The continuing monopoly of Pustet, in combination with sentiments arising from the Franco-Prussian War of 1870, out of which the French had come as losers, continued to rankle the French. The Pope found himself in a difficult situation. On the one side he wanted a rap-

---

[40] HAYBURN: *Papal legislation* 172-174.
[41] The history of this publication is discussed in A. KURRIS: Honderd jaar Paléographie musicale, in *Gregoriusblad* 114 (1990) 125-154. See also A. VERNOOIJ: Honderd jaar Paléographie musicale, in *Gregoriusblad* 113 (1989) 131-138. The ambitious project by Solesmes was made possible thanks to new developments in the field of photography.
[42] HAYBURN: *Papal legislation* 179-180.

prochement with Solesmes, not in the least to head off Gallican tendencies. On the other side he was bound by the publisher's privilege that Pustet had obtained for thirty years. That privilege lapsed in 1898.[43] In the meantime Solesmes had brought out a second edition of the *Liber gradualis* (1895) and the *Liber usualis missae et officii* (1896) had appeared, a book which included the most important hymns for the mass and divine office. Only on January 12, 1901, did the Pope make a verbal statement of what should happen now that Pustet's publisher's privilege had expired: the line of Solesmes should be followed. On May 17, 1901, Leo XIII officially notified the third abbot of Solesmes, Dom P. Delatte, of this in the letter *Nos quidem*.[44] Thirty years after the appearance of the *Neo-Medicaea* Rome had changed the direction it looked, from Regensburg to Solesmes. The struggle for the authentic Gregorian chant, a conflict that Schmit characterizes as a conflict between authority and scholarship,[45] had ended.

After the death of Pope Leo XIII in 1903 Rome's altered course was vigorously continued by the new pope, Pius X. When Cardinal Giuseppe Sarto was elected Pope on August 9, 1903, he took as the motto for his new coat of arms *Instaurare omnia in Christo*. This motto was first applied in the area of church music. On November 22, 1903, the feast of Cecilia, the patron saint of music, the Pope issued the motu proprio *Tra le sollecitudini*. In fact, the *motu proprio* only indirectly dealt with Gregorian music. In this document Pius X recommended restored Gregorian chant, not for its own sake, but primarily in an attempt to banish the abuses in polyphony from the Church. Gregorian music was proposed as a model for the often theatrical and worldly polyphonic music.[46] During the congress that was held in Rome in April 1904, to mark the 1300th anniversary of the death of Gregory the Great, it was

---

[43] Various years are given for the ending of Pustet's publisher's privilege. Hiley (*Western plainchant* 620) says 1901, as does Emerson (J.W. EMERSON: Plainchant, in S. SADIE (ed.) *The new Grove dictionary of music and musicians* 14 (London 1980) 830). Schmit (Die Choralbewegung 259) says 1900. To my mind, 1898 is the correct year. The English translation of the edict in question is to be found in HAYBURN: *Papal legislation* 152. The edict is dated October 1, 1868: "His Holiness [...] ordered [...] to allow no similar edition, whether revised or approved, to be printed for the lapse of thirty years; provided that this edition be begun within the year from the date of this decree and be completed as soon as possible."

[44] HAYBURN: *Papal legislation* 182-192.

[45] SCHMIT: Die Choralbewegung 259.

[46] A. VERNOOIJ: Het gregoriaans als liturgische muziek, in *Gregoriusblad* 104 (1980) 3-5.

announced that the Vatican itself would bring out new books.[47] In the *motu proprio* of April 25, 1904, the preparation of this *Editio Vaticana* was assigned to the monks of Solesmes under the supervision of a committee in which, among others, Pothier, Mocquereau and De Santi were members. The committee was chaired by Pothier.[48] Immediately after work was begun the committee was dominated by a difference of opinion between Pothier and Mocquereau. In regard to this, it must be remarked that since 1892 Pothier was no longer resident at Solesmes.[49] He was therefore less well informed about the progress of the research in the scriptorium at Solesmes. The difference of opinion involved two points. First, Pothier and Mocquereau had a different vision on the rhythm of Gregorian music. Pothier began from an oratorical rhythm (*rythme oratoire*) in which the length of the notes was determined by the text. Mocquereau, on the contrary, supported a free musical rhythm (*rythme libre mesuré*). In his view, the notes were to be divided into groups of two or three. It was not the text which was the guide in this, but the image of the notes according to the old manuscripts. The second difference of opinion was over the sources that should be employed in the restoration of the melodies. It was this second conflict that led to a split between Mocquereau and Pothier.[50] Mocquereau, as the representative of Solesmes, strove for an improved version of Gregorian plainsong through return to the oldest sources. Only where these sources were absent might less venerable manuscripts be used. This view, designated the archaeological tendency in the commission, stood opposed to the vision of Pothier. He spoke of a *tradition vivante*:

---

[47] See the anonymous report of this congress in the *Gregoriusblad*: Het 13e eeuwgetijde van den dood van paus Gregorius den Groote, in *Gregoriusblad* 29 (1904) 47-49. The announcement of the *Editio Vaticana* is reported on p. 48.

[48] HAYBURN: *Papal legislation* 255-257.

[49] In 1892 Pothier became prior of Ligugé. Later he became abbot of the monastery of St. Wandrille in Dongelberg, Belgium.

[50] HAYBURN: *Papal legislation* 275. Hayburn cites a letter that Dom P. Combe, a monk at Solesmes, sent him on January 25, 1966: "One believes that generally it is the determination of Dom Mocquereau to wish to introduce the signs in the Vatican Edition [this relates to the symbols that reflected Mocquereau's views on the rhythm of Gregorian chant (M.H.)] which was the cause of the dissension at the sessions of the Vatican Commission, but this is inexact. The cause of these dissensions was the lack of agreement which existed on the subject of the melodic restoration. Dom Mocquereau wished to hold to the manuscripts, assured that it is these which gave the authentic chant and the more beautiful. Dom Pothier, to the contrary, wished to hold equally valuable the usage of the centuries posterior to the golden age of chant, and even those of the present century."

Toujours est-il que la tradition, soit antégrégorienne, soit grégorienne, s'est continuée à travers les siècles, mais à l'état de tradition *vivante*, susceptible par conséquent, comme tout ce que a vie, de recevoir sans cesse des modifications et des accroissements, mais toujours par mode d'*évolution*, non de *révolution*.[51]

The core of the problem lay in the question of what could be accounted as part of the 'legitimate tradition'. Pope Pius X had used this term in the *motu proprio* of April 25, 1904:

What are termed the Gregorian melodies of the Church shall be restored in their perfection and purity according to the oldest codices; in such a way however that the legitimate tradition be expressly taken into account, as this is contained in the codices over the course of the centuries, as well as practical use for contemporary liturgy.[52]

Mocquereau was of the opinion that the only tradition which could be termed legitimate was that which was not in variance with the oldest Gregorian sources. Pothier attached considerable value to the artistic development of Gregorian music. Where choices had to be made in the restoration of melodies, in his view it was not archaeological criteria which were decisive, but artistic.[53] Pothier's tendency received a powerful impetus from a letter he received from Cardinal Rafaello Merry del Val, dated April 3, 1905. The Cardinal indicated that the oldest songs were not necessarily the best for practical use. After all, it was not for nothing that the songs had developed and been adapted to changing circumstances.[54] When Mocquereau heard of this letter he travelled to Rome and asked for an audience with the Pope. Pius X declared to him that he distanced himself from the content of the letter involved. He praised Mocquereau's manner of proceeding.[55] In view of this, a second letter that Cardinal Merry del Val wrote to Pothier, dated June 24,

---

[51] COMBE: *Histoire de la restauration* 292.

[52] *Gregoriusblad* 29 (1904) 57.

[53] HAYBURN: *Papal legislation* 262-263.

[54] *Ibidem* 264: "Indeed one would never find it possible to prove that the most ancient chant is always and necessarily the best to adopt in practice, since art itself and different circumstances of later times have brought about a rational development of the ancient melodies."

[55] COMBE: *Histoire de la restauration* 385. Arriving in Rome, Mocquereau first made a visit to De Santi. Combe writes: "Celui-ci lui révéla qu'il tenait du Pape que la Lettre du cardinal du 3 avril lui avait été arrachée." At the audience the Pope said to Mocquereau: "State fortiter! Pugnate fortiter!"

1905, is remarkable. It instructs that the second edition of the *Liber gradualis* from 1895, Pothier's own work, must be used as the basis for the *Editio Vaticana.* The effect of this letter was that Solesmes felt itself sidelined and declined further cooperation.[56] The Gregorian hymnals which were published after 1905 by the Vatican were entirely the work of Dom Pothier. They did certainly make use of the results of research at Solesmes. For instance, for the *Graduale* of 1908 he introduced over 2000 corrections, as compared with the *Liber gradualis* of 1895, based on the *Liber usualis* of Solesmes.[57] Only after 1912 did the Pope again bring the monks at Solesmes around to lending their cooperation to the *Editio Vaticana.* In 1912 Pothier returned to his abbey in Dongelberg, and the commission was disbanded.[58]

In the years between 1905 and 1912 the scriptorium at Solesmes was not idle. Under the leadership of Dom Mocquereau Solesmes published its own hymnals. In text and melody these books were in full agreement with the *Editio Vaticana.* They had added, however, the rhythmic signs according to Mocquereau's theories: points, horizontal and vertical lines (*episemata*). These volumes, termed rhythmic editions, were published with the approval of Rome. The added signs introduced structure to the Gregorian melodies, simplifying performance. For this reason the books from Solesmes found a ready market.[59]

4. Appropriation of Gregorian chant in The Netherlands, 1903-1930

In order to obtain a picture of the interplay of designation and appropriation of Gregorian plainsong in The Netherlands in the period 1903-1930, the content of 28 volumes of the *Gregoriusblad* will be analyzed. This journal played an important role in the discussion about performance practice for Gregorian chant, and stimulated the use of the new editions of Gregorian hymnals.

In the following section the *Gregoriusblad* is characterized, and a further look is taken at its usefulness as a source. Next the place of

---

[56] Hayburn: *Papal legislation* 264-265; Combe: *Histoire de la restauration* 409-417.
[57] Hayburn: *Papal legislation* 266.
[58] Hayburn: *Papal legislation* 271; Combe: *Histoire de la restauration* 461.
[59] Hayburn: *Papal legislation* 272-285.

Gregorian chant in the *Gregoriusblad* is sketched. Finally the articles regarding Gregorian plainsong are analyzed on the basis of the research perspective outlined in Section 2, above.

4.1. The *Gregoriusblad*

The *Gregoriusblad* was founded in 1876 under the title *Sint Gregorius-blad. Tijdschrift tot bevordering van kerkelijke toonkunst*. From its first volume the journal was under the editorship of several clergy from the various Dutch dioceses, under the leadership of M.J.A. Lans, then teaching at the Hageveld seminary in Voorhout. The reasons that the *Gregoriusblad* was established must have been, on the one hand, the Provincial Council of 1865, and on the other several problems with respect to the performance of Gregorian music in the last quarter of the 19th century.

After the restoration of diocesan hierarchy in The Netherlands in 1853, a Provincial Council was held in 1865 by the bishops of the five Dutch dioceses. Church music was one of the topics at this Council.[60] In *Titulus V, caput VI* of the *Acta* of the Provincial Council church music was extensively discussed.[61] In this chapter, *De cantu ecclesiastico*, it is argued that Gregorian music is the true church music. There was, however, considerable lack of clarity about the way in which it was to be performed. For the purpose of his music lessons at the Hageveld seminary Lans published a small book in 1874: *Handboekje ten gebruike bij het onderwijs in den gregoriaanschen zang*.[62] The publication of this *Handboekje* was the occasion for correspondence with various other priests who were interested in church music. The Roermond seminary professor G. Verzijl suggested that Lans "invite some friends of true church music to a gathering".[63] Collectively they would then be able to decide

---

[60] KAT: *De geschiedenis der kerkmuziek* 240-245; F.P.M. JESPERS: *"Het loflyk werk der Engelen". De katholieke kerkmuziek in Noord Brabant van het einde der zeventiende tot het einde der negentiende eeuw* (Bijdragen tot de geschiedenis van het zuiden van Nederland 78) (Tilburg 1988) 286-289.

[61] The Latin text of this chapter is given by JESPERS: *Loflyk werk* 363-365 (appendix IV). A Dutch translation is to be found in J.J. GRAAF: *Vromer en beter door goeden kerkzang* (Leiden 1880) 70-79.

[62] M. LANS: *Handboekje ten gebruike bij het onderwijs in den gregoriaanschen zang* (Leiden 1874).

[63] Quoted from KAT: *De geschiedenis* 246-247.

what should be done for the improvement of church music in The
Netherlands. A meeting was held at the Hageveld seminary on August
18, 1875. There were nine priests there, including Lans, coming from
the five Dutch dioceses. Among those present was J.J. Graaf, secretary to
the bishop of Haarlem. Graaf is accounted a major stimulator in the
field of church music. In response to the actions of the Provincial Council of 1865, he had already set up an association in the city of Haarlem
with St. Gregory as its patron saint. The purpose of this association was
to arrive at the good performance of church music. In this, Graaf was
well in advance of the developments which would follow after 1876.

At the meeting at the Hageveld seminary mentioned above the idea
arose to publish a journal for church music.[64] After approval from the
Dutch bishops, the first issue of the *St. Gregoriusblad* appeared on January 1, 1876. Two years later, in 1878, the Gregoriusvereniging was
founded. Since the Gregoriusvereniging was established in 1878 the
Gregoriusblad has functioned as the mouthpiece of this association. This
is reflected by the title under which the journal has appeared since
1911: *Sint Gregoriusblad. Tijdschrift tot bevordering van kerkelijke
toonkunst. Officieel orgaan der Nederlandsche Sint Gregorius-vereniging.*
According to its charter, the Gregoriusvereniging set itself the goal of
"promoting sacred and liturgical music according to the spirit of the
Church and with the most punctilious compliance with the laws of the
Church".[65] The promotion and stimulation of particularly Gregorian
music was – and still is – an important aim of the Gregoriusvereniging.
The *Gregoriusblad* can be seen as an intermediary between the official
policy with regard to restoration and the manner of performance of
Gregorian chant, as that is promulgated by Rome and disseminated by
the Gregoriusvereniging on the one side, and the reading public on the
other. As such the *Gregoriusblad* functioned as a sort of 'broker': a link
between supply and demand.[66] The context within which the production, distribution and consumption of culture takes place is made visible in this function which a journal can fulfil as a broker. In this process
our gaze, the research perspective, is again shifted, from top-down to

---

[64] KAT: *De geschiedenis* 247-251; JESPERS: *Loflyk werk* 319-321.
[65] *Gregoriusblad* 3 (1878) 49.
[66] For what now follows, see G.J. JOHANNES: *De barometer van de smaak. Tijd-
schriften in Nederland 1770-1830* (Nederlandse cultuur in Europese context: monografieën en studies 2) (The Hague 1995) 1, 11-15, 198-199.

bottom-up, from vertical to horizontal, from the prescribed order to lived practice. The accent no longer lies on the prescribed rules, but on their appropriation and how they are experienced. It is precisely a journal which can be an important stimulator and indicator of this process of appropriation.[67] In this way, the *Gregoriusblad* on the one side played an active role in promoting the 'new' Gregorian chant, and on the other reflected the degree to which this Gregorian music was appropriated in everyday life.

Moreover, as a journal the *Gregoriusblad* was a platform for contemporary discussion and reforming action. It was precisely its nature as a journal which made a continuous interchange between authors and readers possible. It was, for instance, a driving force behind the reforms in the culture, of which it was at the same time an expression.

4.2. Gregorian chant in the *Gregoriusblad*

The introduction into The Netherlands of the 'new' Gregorian chant according to the *Editio Vaticana* did not take place for some years. While the *Kyriale* had appeared as early as 1905 and the *Graduale* in 1908, it was not until 1915 that the Dutch bishops prescribed the use of the Vatican editions. Prior to this the Gregoriusvereniging and the editors of the *Gregoriusblad* put their all into the effort to extol the new Vatican books and explain the notation and the manner of performance. Many articles appeared in the *Gregoriusblad* which were intended to provide readers with a practical knowledge of the 'new' Gregorian chant. This instruction commenced in 1912[68] with a translation of the introduction to the *Graduale*.[69] An important author was the priest Th.M. Beukers. He wrote a manual for the presentation of Gregorian plainsong according to the Vatican editions, which first

---

[67] FRIJHOFF: Toeëigening.

[68] W.P.H JANSEN & J.A.S. VAN SCHAIK: Bij het einde des jaars, in *Gregoriusblad* 36 (1911) 185-186. "We hope in 1912 and the following volumes to begin more directly providing information regarding the Vatican edition of the Gregorian hymns. What moves us to this, in addition to our own preferences, is the knowledge that the performance of these hymns demands a very special preparation, and the expectation that [...] the Vaticana will presently be taken up in general use."

[69] De uitvoering der Gregoriaansche gezangen volgens de aanwijzingen der Editio Vaticana zelf, in *Gregoriusblad* 37 (1912) 49-53. See also the translation of the preface to the Editio Vaticana in *Gregoriusblad* 37 (1912) 74-79 and 107-109.

appeared in the *Gregoriusblad* and later as a brochure that was much used in courses.[70] Other authors also provided written instruction through the *Gregoriusblad*.

In addition to written instruction through the *Gregoriusblad* courses took place all over the country. Announcements of and reports about these courses appeared in the journal. Particularly for the period in which Caecilianus Huigens was the editor in chief, 1919-1948, the image arises of a very active movement that succeeded in bringing many people together, to get them enthusiastic about Gregorian chant and instruct them in its performance. The many articles in the *Gregoriusblad* worked as a powerful propaganda offensive. What is more, the organization of the Gregoriusvereniging was increasingly tight-knit. In addition to the national association and diocesan departments, choral unions were also created. Several choirs from a local region were united in these. These choral unions organized choir days, also called St. Gregory days, that were reported in the *Gregoriusblad*. Gregorian chant was always a part of these days, and sometimes the only subject.

As well as promotion of the new hymnals and instruction in the notation and manner of performance of the 'new' Gregorian chant, there appeared articles which discussed the relation between Gregorian hymns and the liturgy. Very concrete explanations were given for the *proprium* songs[71] for a given Sunday. A first series of articles appeared in 1914, written by Th. Beukers.[72] In addition to a brief interpretation and translation of the text of the songs involved, Beukers discussed the melody and modality, and offered suggestions for the execution.

Apart from authors who only contributed one article, C. Huigens wrote several articles on diverse songs.[73] Huigens devoted more attention to the liturgy than did Beukers: the significance and history of a

---

[70] Th.M. BEUKERS: Korte leermethode voor de voordracht van het Gregoriaansch volgens de Vaticaansche editie, in *Gregoriusblad* 37 (1912) 53-61, 87-97 and 121-133; IDEM: Handleiding voor het zingen der Vesperpsalmen, Verzen, Lecties, Hymnen, Oratie's, Benedicamus, Epistles, Evangelie's, Ita Missa est volgens de Vaticana, in *Gregoriusblad* 38 (1913) 72-77, 115-126, 156-162, 189-196; 39 (1914) 2-11 and 33-38.

[71] Among *proprium* songs are to be understood songs that are peculiar to a particular Sunday or liturgical feast. These involve the introit, the graduale or tractus, the alleluia, the offertorium and the communio.

[72] See *Gregoriusblad* 39 (1914) 38-40, 101-103, 119-121, 156-157, 173-176, 225-228, 241-243 and 257-259.

[73] See *Gregoriusblad* 46 (1921) 120-130, 133-138, 149-159; 48 (1923) 109-112, 125-130, 141-146; 49 (1924) 67-72 and 50 (1925) 165-169.

particular liturgical feast, the origin and meaning of the texts of the songs.

Huigens and also the other authors expressly approached Gregorian plainsong as a component of the liturgy. In their view, Gregorian chant was the 'most perfect sung prayer'. This special position of Gregorian music placed demands on the attitude and mentality of the choir members. Particularly Huigens emphasized that the choir member occupied an ecclesiastical office:

> The office of church singer is a clerical office, yea, a real ecclesiastical 'ordo' and the singer's official ecclesiastical persona. (…) All too often people regard church music as a means of adorning the service and the choir of singers as a church choral society. No, the office of chorister must become more spiritual, the singers more clerical.[74]

This was laid down in the new bylaws of the Gregoriusvereniging from 1921. There the church choir is described as an 'ecclesiastical fellowship'.[75] The ideal that the Gregoriusvereniging had in mind was a church choir comprised of pious men who fulfilled their duties as singers in cassock and surplice and sang purely Gregorian plainsong, standing next to the altar in the chancel.

4.3. Invention of tradition

Among the reasons for praising the Gregorian plainsong in the Vatican editions, it was emphasized that these were old, traditional songs. In the new editions the melodies had been restored to their original purity. Consequently the terms 'restoration' and 'restored' were frequently used to designate this Gregorian music. This cluster of terms and designations was employed to legitimize the choice of Pope Pius X to publish the Gregorian music according to the standards of scholarly research, particularly that at Solesmes. We encounter references to an old tradition not only in documents which were issued by Rome itself,[76] but also

---

[74] (C. HUIGENS): Rede van P. Caecilianus Huigens op den Katholiekendag, in *Gregoriusblad* 44 (1919) 175-188; the words quoted are found on pp. 179 and 181.

[75] (EDITORS): De nieuwe statuten!, in *Gregoriusblad* 46 (1921) 3-4 and 5-16. See particularly Article 4 of the Huishoudelijk reglement on p. 8.

[76] See, among others, PIUS X: Brief aan Kardinaal Respighi, Vicaris-Generaal van Rome, over de hervorming der gewijde muziek, in *Gregoriusblad* 29 (1904) 6-8; Kardinaal Merry del Val, Z.H. de Paus aan de Nederlandsche St. Gregorius-Vereeniging en de Duitsche St. Caecilia-Vereeniging, in *Gregoriusblad* 29 (1904) 23-24.

in articles by the editors of the *Gregoriusblad*. For instance, Dom J. van Gennep wrote in 1928:

> After spending nearly 600 years in obscurity the true song of the Church, Gregorian chant, is restored to its first purity and like the first, fiery Christian communities we sing the songs of praise to which God's Church Herself added Her words.[77]

The 'new' Gregorian plainsong was particularly solidly anchored in the tradition by coupling it with Pope Gregory the Great himself. Authors wrote that these were the 'ancient' melodies of Pope Gregory which were restored in the Vatican editions.[78] Pius X, who had instructed that this restoration should take place, was placed in the same line as his more illustrious predecessor:

> Pius X: his name shall be mentioned by history in one breath with that of Pope Gregory; the latter brought into being these standard works of ecclesiastical music, and Pius, after they had rested in obscurity for centuries and centuries, awakened them to life again and revealed them to a surprised world in their radiant, glorious beauty.[79]

With regard to the Vatican editions, not only were references made to the Gregorian chant from the distant past, but there were also attempts to introduce a certain continuity between the past and developments in the present. For example, several authors described the transition from the *Neo-Medicaea* to the *Vaticana* not as a break, but as a progressive process from the good to the better:

> If the declaration by Pope Pius IX of the reissued Medicaea as the official song of the Church led to a remarkable rise in interest in Gregorian song, while the recommendation and revision of this edition under Pope Leo

---

[77] J. VAN GENNEP: Gregoriaansche causerieën. Ons groote program, in *Gregoriusblad* 53 (1928) 5-10; quote from p. 6. See also, among others, Th.M. BEUKERS: Korte leermethode voor de voordracht van het Greogriaansch volgens de Vaticaansche editie, in *Gregoriusblad* 37 (1912) 53-61; Gr.L. SERGENT: De Introïtus "Ecce adventi" van Driekoningen, in *Gregoriusblad* 50 (1925) 26-31; C. HUIGENS: Het Gregoriaansch in modern notenschrift, in *Gregoriusblad* 55 (1930) 185-188.

[78] See, among others (EDITORS): Einde 1913, in *Gregoriusblad* 38 (1913) 187-188; J.C.W. VAN DE WIEL: De Gregoriaansche traditie, in *Gregoriusblad* 41 (1916) 142-145; J.A.S. VAN SCHAIK: De beteekenis van het Katholicisme voor de Nederlandsche muziek, in *Gregoriusblad* 50 (1925) 150-155.

[79] W.P.H. JANSEN: Paus Pius X (in memoriam), in *Gregoriusblad* 39 (1914) 205-207, cited from p. 205.

XIII all the more served to promote its practice, the realization of the 'Vaticana' under our presently reigning Pope Pius X has not only restored Gregorian song to its original lustre, but also acquired for it a general sympathy unknown for centuries.[80]

Upon the appearance of the *motu proprio* of November 22, 1903, Lans described the Pope's instructions first of all as a confirmation of the process that had been under way in The Netherlands for over thirty years.[81] Even more fascinating is the comparison that is made by J.J. Graaf between the *Vaticana* and what are termed the Amsterdam editions. In Graaf's opinion, the 'new' Gregorian chant to a great extent corresponded to the melodies as these were to be found in the Amsterdam books.[82] The *Vaticana* thus restored a tradition that for a long time had been peculiar to The Netherlands.

The way in which the past was dealt with in relation to the Vatican editions had as its goal the legitimization of the contemporary choice of Gregorian plainsong according to the insights of Solesmes. It is striking that only a few attempts were made to suggest continuity with this past. Apparently the 'new' Gregorian chant was still experienced too much as a break with the preceding period. It is also striking that hardly any critical questions were asked about the past to which references were being made. Only in one single article, taken over from the Milanese journal *Musica sacra*, was the question asked if 'traditional' Gregorian plainsong was represented only by the Benedictines with their publication based on manuscripts from St. Gallen.[83] Are there, the authors ask, no other

---

[80] J.M.C. DE WOLF: Het "Gloria" van den H. Leo IX, in *Gregoriusblad* 39 (1914) 190-193, cited from p. 192. See also J.A.S. VAN SCHAIK: De uitspraak van het Latijn, in *Gregoriusblad* 39 (1914) 76-80 (esp. p. 80).

[81] M.J.A. LANS: Over de jongste beslissingen van den H. Stoel, in *Gregoriusblad* 29 (1904) 24-27. See also W.P.H. JANSEN & J.A.S. VAN SCHAIK: Bij het einde van den 35sten jaargang, in *Gregoriusblad* 35 (1910) 95-98.

[82] J.J. GRAAF: De introitus van zondag sexagesima, in *Gregoriusblad* 36 (1911) 21-24 (esp. p. 24).

[83] Solesmes made use of manuscripts from the region around St. Gallen. However, manuscripts from other regions were also employed. There was little written in the *Gregoriusblad* about the research into the manuscripts. In 1919 Huigens reported that Solesmes had discovered a new family of manuscripts, namely from the Italian Nontantola. See *Gregoriusblad* 44 (1919) 78: "Nontantola brings us considerably closer to Rome, from which Gregorian song spread across the world." Note that here Huigens expresses a pursuit of 'the song of Rome', as in a similar way Guéranger had sought the 'liturgy of Rome'!

traditions that could be considered 'traditional'?[84] Perhaps the editors of the *Gregoriusblad* dared not permit such questions. After all, by broaching the question of tradition and authenticity one could also come out at the Council of Trent. It is true that it was a less distant past than the time of Gregory the Great, but perhaps it was still sufficient basis for being able to consider the Gregorian music of the *Neo-Medicaea* as 'authentic'. This discussion was not, however, carried on. Perhaps it can also be said that carrying on such a discussion was not in the interests of the Catholics in The Netherlands. What people sought there was unity and a clear Catholic identity. This unity and identity was founded in the past. Which past this was, was of subordinate importance.

In order to deploy the past in the interests of the present, there was need of an authoritative institution that would indicate which past must be considered as legitimate and 'authentic'. People found this authority in the pronouncements of the Pope and the instructions of the Dutch bishops, which were faithfully translated into practice by the *Gregoriusblad* and the Gregoriusvereniging. The authority of the Pope in the case of Gregorian chant was accepted by the leadership of the Gregoriusvereniging, but to all appearances it was not initially a wholehearted acceptance. Many times it was emphasized that the transition to the new Gregorian hymnals was a matter of discipline.[85] In The Netherlands (and elsewhere) people were forced to acknowledge the 'new' Gregorian music as 'better', despite the fact that they were attached to the old books and until that time they had defended these books against every attack and imputation. 'The Pope desires it', was the recurrent watchword.[86] The embodiment of this attitude of obedience was M. Lans, who had still fiercely defended the *Neo-Medicaea* in 1903, but a year later had to yield to authority.

---

[84] *Het 13de eeuwgetijde van den dood van Paus Gregorius den Groote*, in *Gregoriusblad* 29 (1904) 80-82.

[85] See, among others, M.J.A. LANS: *Over de jongste beslissingen van den H. Stoel*, in *Gregoriusblad* 29 (1904) 24-27: "In the Pope's *Motu Proprio* [...] it is formally declared that His Holiness revokes the edicts and recommendations issued by both of his Predecessors [...] with regard to the books with later readings of the notation of Gregorian song, desiring that a transition be made to books with the reading of the notes according to ancient manuscripts [...] This concerns a question of *discipline*, not of *doctrine*" (p. 25).

[86] See, among others, E. FRANSSEN: *In de kathedraal te Roermond*, in *Gregoriusblad* 29 (1904) 90-92. Franssen cites a pronouncement of St. Alphonsus Liguori: "The will of the Pope is also the will of God."

With neither the appeal to the past nor the emphasis on authority and obedience was the issue Gregorian plainsong itself. The undercurrent in both arguments or motives for promoting the 'new' Gregorian chant was the desire for unity with the Pope and solidarity with Rome. Gregorian plainsong was nothing more than a means to this end.

5. BALANCE

In the above, the appropriation of Gregorian plainsong according to the *Editio Vaticana* among the Catholics of The Netherlands in the first decades of the 20th century is described as one of the means or strategies for creating and giving new content to a self-image and group identity. The Gregorian chant prescribed by Rome, which was based on old manuscripts from the Middle Ages, was not only the servant of liturgy and church music, but also of the transformation of Roman Catholic life, which increasingly began to distinguish itself from all ways of life that were considered by the Catholics themselves as profane, secular, Calvinistic, liberal or, in any case, as not specifically Catholic. The 'new' Gregorian chant was a part of and factor in constructing Catholic identity. This function of Gregorian music placed demands on Gregorian chant itself. This was expressed in the constant emphasis on the desired unity in melody, pronunciation of the text and manner of performing Gregorian plainsong. This concern for the quality and the aesthetic of Gregorian chant had the character of a 'civilizing offensive'. The instructional articles in the *Gregoriusblad*, the large number of courses offered and the ceaseless admonitions in the *Gregoriusblad* with regard to abuses, actual or alleged, were expressions of this. This 'civilizing offensive' bore fruit. To a rising degree choirs did begin to conduct themselves as associations of pious men who diligently applied themselves to the performance of Gregorian plainsong, complete with cassock and surplice. If the choir of the 19th century was still more a choral society, in the early years of the 20th century the singers were more and more 'clericalized' and the music was attuned to liturgy according to Roman norms.

Of course there was also resistance to the 'civilizing offensive'. From recurrent admonitions in the *Gregoriusblad* it would appear that many choirs couldn't cope with the 'new' Gregorian plainsong according to the *Editio Vaticana* and that many singers preferred to sing polyphonic masses rather than Gregorian chant of any edition at all. From this last it would appear that there was a difference between the way that from top down Gregorian chant was presented as the liturgical music par excellence, and the way that this music was experienced in the practice of liturgy and church music. The intensity with which Gregorian plainsong was recommended and stimulated makes one suspect that many did not accept these songs as an expression of their own personal religiosity or piety.

In order to legitimize the 'new' Gregorian chant references were repeatedly made to the past, and particularly the person and era of Gregory the Great. Gregorian plainsong was linked with the authority and the services to liturgy and church music of this Pope. The past was deployed in this way in order to carry through an innovation in the present. In this, use was made of the legend that Pope Gregory the Great had played an important role in the creation of Gregorian chant. As early as the second half of the eighth century great authority was conferred on Gregorian plainsong because of its ascription to Gregory the Great.[87] Just as in the eighth century the authority of Gregory the Great was employed to accomplish the introduction of Gregorian plainsong, particularly into the kingdom of the Franks, so at the beginning of the 20th century once again use was made of the legend that Gregory himself had composed an antiphonal. Through scholarly research people tried – or hoped – to track down the hymn book of Gregory the Great, or in any case approach it as closely as possible. In reality, scholars made choices from available manuscripts in which Gregorian music had been set down nearly three centuries after the death of Gregory. The academic research, the results of which were presented in the *Editio Vaticana*, was to a large extent the work of Dom Pothier, who made selections according to his own insights, taking into account musical developments over the course of time (*tradition vivante*) in the process.

It is striking that the authors who extol the 'new' Gregorian plainsong, referring to the early Middle Ages and Gregory the Great, skip over the period from the Council of Trent to the beginning of the 20th century in their argument. During this period Gregorian chant was

---

[87] H. NOLTHENIUS: *Muziek tussen hemel en aarde. De wereld van het Gregoriaans* (Amsterdam 1985) 81-82; M. ZIJLSTRA: *Zangers en schrijvers. De overlevering van het Gregoriaans van ca. 700 tot ca. 1150* (Utrecht 1997) 20-28.

forced into second place in favour of polyphonic church music. More-over, Gregorian plainsong, to the extent it was still sung, was adapted to the musical taste of the times. After a gap of nearly three centuries, at the beginning of the 20th century Gregorian chant was revitalized. The impetus for this had begun already in the second half of the 19th century, in, among others, the Dutch Provincial Council of 1865.

The tension between tradition and innovation, between the *Neo-Medicaea* and the *Editio Vaticana*, was resolved by the construction of continuity. Something which was in fact new was linked with and rooted back into the past. The search by Catholics for their own identity played an important, contextualizing role in this. Through the rise of nation-states in the 19th century, the loyalty of Catholics to the Pope came under pressure. The solution to this question was found in the creation of a supra-national state with the Pope at its head. This context is important for a good understanding of the restoration of Gregorian plainsong. Because of the orientation to Rome, a need was felt for a book of church music prescribed by Rome. Such a collection could make the unity of Catholics worldwide visible – and audible. In the face of this, regional editions of Gregorian hymnals lapsed into discredit. In The Netherlands, for instance, the Amsterdam editions were ousted first by the *Neo-Medicaea* of 1871 and then the *Graduale* of 1908.

Through the analysis of several volumes of the *Gregoriusblad* we have been able to describe and characterize the designation and appropriation of the 'new' Gregorian plainsong. We have seen not only how the *Editio Vaticana* came to be realized and was introduced, but also what role Gregorian chant played in the context of Catholics in The Netherlands at the beginning of the 20th century. The *Gregoriusblad* provides a perspective on the practice of church music and in any case helps us partly visualize the process by which singers, choir directors, organists and churchgoers came to give meaning and significance to the 'new' Gregorian music. From the analysis it appears that in many places the *Editio Vaticana* was studied diligently by choirs. But did the singers also see Gregorian chant as the preeminent liturgical music and as an essential part of their group culture as Catholics? At the level of the singers and churchgoers the appropriation of the 'new' Gregorian plainsong can only be tentatively indicated, however much the *Gregoriusblad* also functioned as the intermediary between institutions and scholars involved with church music on the one side and the practice of liturgy and church music on the other. A complicating, even intangible factor in this is the emotion which Gregorian chant calls up in individuals.[88] The leaders in the field of church music in the Catholic Church at the beginning of this century promoted Gregorian plainsong as the true liturgical music; it was the *musica sacra* par excellence. Perhaps, through the 'new' and 'unusual' nature of *Editio Vaticana*, as compared to the *Neo-Medicaea* and other forms of church music, Gregorian plainsong was indeed experienced in that way. The increased 'clericalizing' of the choirs supports this supposition.

---

[88] For this, see J. JANSSEN: Het moduleren van de stilte. De magie van het gregoriaans, in *Streven* 63 (1996) 11-23.

REGNERUS STEENSMA

THE USE OF IMAGES TO INTENSIFY THE LITURGY IN PROTESTANT CONTEXTS

Liturgical celebrations give shape to the religious orientation towards life, enabling the believer, through his encounters with God and with fellow human beings, to experience an intensification of his existence. There are also various ways in which a liturgical celebration can become a special event, breaking away from customary patterns. One way of intensifying the liturgy is to use visual images.

In the Catholic church there is a long tradition of all sorts of images being used in the church: sculptures, paintings, glass and textile. The subject matter covers the entire gamut of devotional experience: God the Father, Christ, Mary, Bible stories, saints and various symbols. These images serve not only to adorn the church building but also to edify and instruct the church-goers. Normally this takes place in silence: the faithful are surrounded by images which demand and receive their attention to a greater or lesser extent. Sometimes attention is focused on a particular representation during a liturgical celebration, for example in the adoration of the Cross in the Good Friday liturgy and the Mystery play at the Holy Sepulchre on Easter Morning. Showing relics and praying at the fourteen Stations of the Cross might also be included in the list. In some cases the role of an image is emphasized in the opposite way: during Lent crucifixes and images are covered, and sometimes a white Lenten veil is placed between the altar and the nave.[1] In his study of images and their audiences in the Middle Ages, Belting points out that as early as the 13th century mendicant orders aroused deeply felt devotion in church-goers by both preaching and the use of images.[2]

Up to the present day, in certain churches there are celebrations in which an image is the focus of attention. One example is the daily ser-

---

[1] For the function of art in the church building and in the liturgy, see Hans BEL-TING: *Das Bild und sein Publikum im Mittelalter. Form und Funktion früher Bildtafeln der Passion* (Berlin 1995[2]) and Peter VAN DAEL: *Tot lering en verering. Functies van kunst in de Middeleeuwen* (Kampen 1997).

[2] BELTING: *Das Bild* 50.

vice in honour of the Black Madonna in the Polish place of pilgrimage
Czestochowa: an impressive event combining image, sound and movement. Tourist office guides tell us that the Madonna will be shown at
4.00 p.m., and by that time the chapel is packed with pious believers
and curious tourists. At exactly four o'clock the entrance doors are
opened and sixteen clergymen enter the sacred space in procession. To
the sound of trumpet music and Polish hymns in honour of Mary they
advance towards the altar, above which the famous icon of the Mother
of God with the Christ Child is situated. During the procession, a cur-
tain is raised very slowly to uncover the icon and by the time the
singing procession has arrived at the front of the church, the Madonna
can be seen in her entirety. In this imposing setting the attention of the
faithful is focused as keenly as possible on the image of Mary, and their
pious adoration is intensified to a high degree by the hymns, the stately
movement of the priests and, above all, the very slow uncovering of the
icon. The essence of the ceremony is the visual representation in the
form of the icon, whose importance is emphasized by a fixed ritual of
music and gestures. The procession moves straight through the crowd,
who are participants in an all-embracing drama which is performed day
after day.

In recent years, occasionally a work of art has been placed in a
church to play an incidental role during Sunday Mass or another celebration. Friedhelm Mennekes S.J. was a pioneer in this area in the
Catholic church. In 1984 he was involved in placing art works in St
Mark's in Frankfurt-Nied, and later he wrote a detailed report of his
experiences there.[3] Later he had St Peter's of Cologne at his disposal,
and between 1987 and 1995 he frequently hung work by contemporary artists above the main altar there. The form and subject matter
of some of these works led to sharp controversy on more than one
occasion.[4] In the Catholic church, the temporary placement of a
work of art led to an intensification of the role of images in the
liturgy, especially because most of the works do not present a familiar image but a new and often provoking one which challenges the
viewer to take a personal stand. This can be very salutary, but not

    [3] Friedhelm MENNEKES (Hrsg.): *Zwischen Kunst und Kirche. Beiträge zum Thema
Das Christusbild im Menschenbild* (Stuttgart 1985).
    [4] Thorsten NOLTING: Einer von ihnen. Über den kirchlichen Ausstellungsmacher
Friedhelm Mennekes, in *Kunst und Kirche* (1998) Heft 2, 82-85.

every church-goer appreciates it, and in fact the conflicts were not limited to Cologne.[5] This development has also been manifested in Protestant churches, and in the present study I will limit myself to that subject, not only because I am more familiar with it, but also because in the Netherlands few experiments have taken place in Catholic churches.[6]

1. Changes in Protestant Churches

In Protestant churches in the Netherlands, attitudes to the function of visual art in the church were determined for centuries by Calvin and the Heidelberg Catechism. Calvin believed that preaching the gospel should be sufficient and that people who let their eyes wander to look at images would not apply their minds closely enough to doctrine. However, he did recognize that sculpture and painting were gifts of God and did not entirely reject their use in the church, so long as God's majesty was not dishonoured. The judgment of the Heidelberg Catechism (1563) was harsher. Question 98 is: "Should not images in the church be tolerated as books for the lay people?" The answer is: "No, for we must not attempt to be wiser than God, who wishes Christians to be taught not by mute images but by the living preaching of his Word." The expression 'mute images' is understandable as a reaction to the role of images in late mediaeval church buildings and worship, but it is nevertheless a demeaning characterization, which does not do justice to the specific language of images. In fact, practice was not as strict as doctrine. In many churches the figure of Moses was painted on the Table of the Ten Commandments, and many pulpits were decorated with figurative carving, in which allegorical figures and various stories from the Bible were depicted. In the following centuries there was scarcely any change in this attitude.

An important change in views on art in the church can be found in the report *Beginselen van kerkbouw* (Principles of Church-building)

---

[5] A large amount of material on the use (including temporary use) of modern art in Catholic church celebrations can be found in the magazine *Kunst und Kirche*, and also in R. BECK, R. VOLP & G. SCHMIRBER (eds): *Die Kunst und die Kirchen. Der Streit um die Bilder heute* (Munich 1984).

[6] G.D.J. DINGEMANS, J. KRONENBURG & R. STEENSMA (eds): *Kaïn of Abel… Kunst in de kerkdienst: twee vijandige broeders?* (Zoetermeer 1999) is a book about experiments with art in the church service in Protestant churches. It contains not only reports of particular cases but also analyses of experiences from different points of view.

which was accepted by the Synod of the Dutch Reformed Church in 1954. The report makes a plea for visual art in the church, arguing that now there is no question of people venerating images. It praises the didactic value of visual representations of the Bible for modern people, who are so strongly visually oriented, and says:

> Moreover, visual arts can often focus light on the meaning of a figure or an event just as effectively as many a sermon. Visual works of art have the power to make an immediate appeal, without the mediation of rationality: they are able to speak directly to the soul and in that way to reveal unknown things to us. Ecclesiastical, religious art includes both preaching and praise: the visual arts, like architecture, are parallel with the liturgy and are part of the worship service … It is the nature of the artist to acquire deeper insight into the order of things and into life, outside rationality; it is his task to bear witness to that insight in his work. We are now far enough removed from the rationalism of the 19th century to realize that understanding and insight are attainable in other ways than exclusively by means of reason and sermons.

Clearly the Synod spoke very positively about the role of art in the church. It recognized that the artist can acquire deeper insight into the order of things and into life, outside rationality and that he may express that insight in his work. On the other hand, it is talking about 'spiritually justifiable' art, which is edifying for the congregation and the individual. According to the Synod, ecclesiastical, religious art includes both preaching and praise. However, it is not entirely clear whether the Synod was aware of the tension that may arise if the artist expresses his insight into life in his own way, whereas the congregation expects spiritually justifiable art with an edifying effect. That the introduction of free, autonomous art into the church might also be beneficial did not occur to the Synod at that point. However, the plea made in 1954 did result in various forms of visual art being placed in many new churches: glass, sculptures, wall paintings and wall hangings. Most of these works have Bible stories and symbols as their subject matter.

2. THE RELATIONSHIP BETWEEN THE CHURCH AND CONTEMPORARY ART

In recent years, there has been a growing tendency to place a work of art in a church so that it can play an incidental role in a Sunday worship service. In most cases the minister makes reference to the work in his sermon and there is a reciprocal relationship of varying intensity between word and image. In services of this sort the church-goers are brought into very direct contact with the work of art: they have to look at it, because it is in full view at the front of the church and not merely a decoration in the background. Often this way of using visual art leads not only to the intensification of a Bible story, but also to reflection on life and faith.[7]

In our time the relationship between the church and art is different from that of the past. To an increasing extent it has become a relationship between two autonomous partners, in which the church is not subordinate to art nor art to the church. The church is starting to take art seriously, to enter into a dialogue with it and to expect it to contribute its own insights. Art does not proclaim salvation and cannot change reality or redeem, but it can help to reveal reality and in this way it can be a valuable sounding board for the church.

Art can be about all sorts of questions in human life and can express these questions powerfully by visual means. The presence of this sort of art in the church may arouse tension, but that tension can be of assistance in the quest for essential values in life and religion. Art may ask the church if it is approaching modern people in the right way, and the church may expect art to represent reality in a truthful way by artistic means.

Many contemporary works of art confront the viewer with existential questions. Good art is able to focus attention on inward afflictions. The ideas portrayed vary widely: social commitment, the horrors of war, personal fear, doubt and hope. There are always artists looking for the truth, searching for the meaning of life. Art has higher aspirations than adornment; its ultimate purpose is not the concept of beauty. Artists not only have the ability to translate their experience into images; often they have also developed a different and finer sensitivity.

Secondly, art can help to break through the fossilized emotions often linked to Bible stories and to evoke new associations. Many themes are

---

[7] The works of art can be presented in different ways. The ideal way is to have the original work. However, in that case it has to be big enough and hung in such a way that the church-goers can see it clearly. The presence of an original work is sometimes impossible for practical reasons such as problems with transport and insurance costs. In these cases a reproduction of the work in any size desired can be hung. This is less expensive but obviously does not make the same impact as the original work. A third method of presentation is to show slides, which is cheap and provides a large picture, but means that the church has to be darkened.

over-familiar to faithful church-goers and art can contribute to achieving new perceptions. Through art, a story can become more intense and
gain new dimensions. This is also true – perhaps particularly true – of
the central theme of Christ's crucifixion. Some artists identify with his
suffering, for example with his abandonment and loneliness; others see
a sign of new life and hope in Christ's death. Often Christ's suffering is
also related to present-day forms of human suffering such as disease,
hunger, war and exploitation.

Thirdly, there is the meditative aspect, which plays a particularly
important role in abstract art. Forms and colours evoke all sorts of feelings and thoughts: feelings of peace, tranquillity, happiness and security,
but also of unrest, grief, sadness and fear. When looking at paintings
like this, people can daydream, become immersed in themselves. Various artists say that the meaning of their work is mainly to be found in
looking, feeling and experiencing, and not in something words can
explain. These works of art do not pin one down to a single question or
thought, but leave room for personal interpretation.

3. THE ART WORK AS POINT OF DEPARTURE FOR A SERMON

In my study *Mysterie en vergezicht. Over het gebruik van hedendaagse
kunst in de liturgie*,[8] I used twelve examples to describe the function of
works of art in the worship service. They illustrate clearly how an
exchange between word and image can take place in various ways in the
liturgy. Sometimes a sermon contains detailed reflection on the art
work, whereas in other instances there is only an occasional reference to
it. Usually the art work is the point of departure for the sermon. In
some services the minister takes the Sunday gospel or another pre-deter-
mined theme as a starting point and then uses the art work to illustrate
this theme.

If the sermon is based on the work of art, it usually begins with a
description of the feelings and thoughts evoked by the work. Then these
associations are elaborated with the help of examples from everyday life.
Finally the various elements are related to the gospel message. This
method can be illustrated by two examples.

---

[8] R. STEENSMA: *Mysterie en vergezicht. Over het gebruik van hedendaagse beeldende
kunst in de liturgie* (Baarn 1993).

3.1. Hope

In March 1991 the Reformed (Gereformeerde) Church of Burgum (Friesland) held a service in which An Goderie's painting 'Hope' was a central element. This painting shows a seated figure with a door left slightly ajar in the background. We see the figure from the back, so that it is facing the door. Goderie: It is a self-portrait painted after my husband had died. I wanted to show the despair which held me in its sway at that time. But there is a door left ajar, with light streaming in through it. It symbolizes the hope and expectation of light and therefore relief. During the church service the work was hanging on the wall behind the liturgical centre so that it could be seen clearly by the church-goers.

The Rev. J.C. Fockens began his sermon with a description of the feelings the central figure in the painting evoked in him and then pointed out the open door. Then he discussed the two images from a biblical perspective, with particular reference to Psalm 146: The Lord lifts up those who are bowed down.

> An Goderie's painting shows a woman sitting bowed forwards: crooked, bent over, shaken. She is sitting with her back towards the viewer as if to say: stay away for a while. This person has been struck down by grief, has been battered by life, is bowed down by pain. It seems as though for her the door to the future is closed. Nevertheless, the door is ajar; there is still a future. She can open the door wider and go outside into the light. This is the deepest essence of the gospel message: God is opening the door to the light, to the future.

3.2. Communion

On *13 October 1985* Freark van der Wal's painting 'Communion' was hanging in the Reformed church of Kootstertille (Friesland). A large section of the painting consists of a black-and-grey square. This is an upside down table: on a few sides legs are sticking up. On this square outlines of the continents are painted, framed by three grey arched areas resembling church windows.

In his sermon, the Rev. C. Glashouwer pointed out that the work is related to the core of the gospel in the sense that where God is at work things are turned upside down.

> An upside down table, legs sticking into the air here and there, continents projected in mirror image onto the underneath, three arches of light suggesting that the upside down table with the upside down world are located

in a church, and unrest, both by means of the deliberate carelessness of the brushstrokes with which the paint has been applied to the canvas, and also because the table is tilting forwards a little and the world is in danger of sliding off it ... To put it quite simply you might say that wherever God is at work, the usual course of events in the world is turned upside down. For people this is not always easy, but right from the beginning people have been confronted by a God who does not stick to the rules of the world that we take for granted.

I think it is good to take Freark van der Wal's painting seriously and to bear it in mind, for two reasons. The first is that it is good for us to realize, week after week, that God breaks away from the usual course of events and turns things upside down, for the benefit of people in trouble. The second reason for taking the painting seriously is that it draws our attention to the longer-term effects of Communion. If the Lord's Supper is celebrated seriously in the church, it is not without effect in the world. This is sometimes not easy, because the Lord's Supper undermines the established order.

3.3. With leaden wings

Sometimes it is not a single art work that forms the starting point for a church service but an exhibition of several works. On 26 June 1994 the Rev. K. Dijkstra conducted a service in the Reformed Church of Garnwerd (Groningen) which was completely devoted to the exhibition 'With leaden wings', from which ten works were displayed in this church.[9] The preacher had selected four works and devoted time to each, with a few words of introduction, a Bible passage and a hymn, after which he concluded the service with a short period of meditation.

In Jan Smeltekop's painting 'Double Portrait' one can make out two figures embracing each other, or rather closely intertwined. The two figures here are more like two manifestations of the same person than two different persons. The image evokes associations with a person struggling with himself and finding the struggle a burden.

The minister chose the following hymn to accompany this:

My God, armed to the teeth
two men in me wage war:
one wants me

---

[9] For a survey of this exhibition, see R. STEENSMA (ed.): *Met loden vleugels. Zoektocht naar zingeving bij Groninger kunstenaars* (Groningen 1994).

to burn at the right moment with love for Thee,
the other wants to violate your law
and drives me to rebellion.

Come and heal my torn heart
o Lord, by your grace;
it was I myself who resisted.
Restore the oneness of my being
and let him serve and fear Thee
who was once a slave of death.

For this exhibition Geurt van Dijk made an altarpiece in the form of a triptych, with drawings whose predominant theme was transience. The human figures are not an expression of beauty or vitality, but of alienation, defeat and death. They are often vague, faceless figures, in many cases deformed and sometimes reduced to mounds of flesh.

The Bible passage read on this occasion was II Corinthians 4, 7-18: "(…) For while we live we are always being given up to death for Jesus' sake, so that the life of Jesus may be manifested in our mortal flesh (11). (…) Though our outer nature is wasting away, our inner nature is being renewed every day (16)." The hymn was Psalm 103, 6 and 5: "As for man, his days are like grass; (…) As a father pities his children, so the Lord pities those who fear him. For he knows our frame (…)"

4. CHURCH-GOERS' REACTIONS AS STARTING POINT OF THE SERVICE

Sometimes a service is held in which not the minister's associations with a work of art but those of the church-goers function as starting point.

4.1. Walking

On 20 March 1994 a service was held in the Reformed Church of Scharnegoutum (Friesland) in which Gerrit Terpstra's painting 'Walking' played a central part. At the bottom of this work there is a dark prostrate human figure against a somewhat less dark background. Above the figure there is a triangular white area which is marked off on the right by an arrow pointing upwards. It is as though the curved arrow is ordering the figure to stand up. Behind the figure and the triangle there is a large eye. The work expresses a call to stand up, to start walking, to go towards the large white area: the exit. A human being who has been cast down is urged to find a way out. The work was inspired by the resurrection of Lazarus and in that context the 'way out' refers to Christ. A few weeks before the service the work was discussed by a group of church members. The participants had been given a photo of the painting before the meeting so that they had been able to examine it at home without knowing its connection with the story of Lazarus. They had been invited to bring texts which they associated with the work.

One woman brought a painting with a cross radiating light and the text of Hymn 487,[10] in which light is seen as a token of hope from God which renews man and gives him strength. Two women had, independently, chosen a passage from Anne Frank's diary. Both fragments refer to a window through which the imprisoned Anne can see and sometimes feel the outside world. The window represents her longing for freedom and a future.

In the second part of the evening an attempt was made to relate the participants' associations to the story of Lazarus which tells us of hope in a situation in which hope no longer seems possible: light as an element of hope in the darkness. In the story of Lazarus things turn out to be different from what people had thought: there is a widening of perspective. A link is made between the resurrection of Christ and human beings getting on their feet again in situations in which they seem to be weighed down.

A few weeks after the discussion the church service was held. The painting 'Walking' was hung on the pulpit and beside it was a large photo in which the work had been turned around 90°, so that the human figure is standing upright. The work was also printed on the liturgy sheet. The texts and hymns of the service reflected many elements of the contributions made by participants in the group discussion.

The way things were done in Scharnegoutum shows how a work of art can be examined purely on its own merits, by first asking the viewers what associations it has for them, without telling them what the artist has intended. Then these thoughts were put into a biblical perspective and the service was structured around the entire process.

---

[10] *Liedboek voor de kerken. Psalmen en gezangen voor de eredienst in kerk en huis, aangeboden door de Interkerkelijke Stichting voor het Kerklied* (Den Haag/Leeuwarden 1973) 715 (No. 487).

4.2. Kanters – Lucebert – Ter Horst

A surprising experiment took place in May and June of 1995 as a result of the exhibition 'Jezus is boos' (Jesus is angry).[11] A number of ministers who visited this exhibition asked if it would be possible to use this art in church services. Large photos (about 1 x 1 m) were made of three of the works and hung in the churches. These works played a part in ten services. A new element was that during the service those attending were invited to give their response to the works. This invitation was eagerly accepted. Then the minister concluded the service with a short meditation, a prayer and a hymn. The works shown were by Kanters, Lucebert and Ter Horst.

To illustrate what happened, here are a number of quotations from the sermon in the church in Eindhoven (by the Rev. W. Stoker).

> During the preparation someone said of Kanters' work: "It shocks me, Jesus on a coat hanger, it even makes me a bit angry, but a little later I thought, would Jesus not have shocked people then, on the cross?" The strange thing is that for the first believers the cross was also very shocking. To be crucified was demeaning, very humiliating. Now that the cross has become a symbol, we have forgotten the shocking nature of the cross. In the coat hanger and Jesus, Kanters has found a way to evoke the shock and humiliation of that suffering anew. Incidentally – have you noticed the hook on which the coat hanger is hanging? It is in the form of a question mark. This painting expresses self-sacrifice, but at the same time it contains a certain ambiguity, through that question mark. A painting like this does not have only one message, but several. That is also the way St. Mark tells the gospel story: the signs are ambiguous and often people do not understand them. In this painting you might also see a coat hanger on which you can hang Jesus and put him away like an old coat.
>
> Lucebert: during the preparation most people thought it was frightening and bizarre with all its thuggish faces. They are reminiscent of Hieronymus Bosch's misshapen figures. Someone suggested as a title for this work: 'The flight' or 'Beyond Jesus'. This was not far from the mark. The real title is: 'And they turned away from the Cross'. I think this is very close, particularly if you ask yourself: am I not one of those people? You could interpret this as meaning 'for me Jesus is a figure of the past'. The cross is grey, with a battered body, and it hardly seems to have any sym-

---

[11] For a description of this experiment, see R. STEENSMA: 'Jezus is boos' in de kerk-dienst. Reacties op drie hedendaagse kunstwerken tijdens de eredienst, in *Jaarboek voor liturgie-onderzoek* 11 (1995) 223-258.

bolic value left. There is also another way of interpreting the turning away or flight from the cross: as something that occurs again and again, every time you ignore your own faith and deny Christ in your behaviour. I don't know if I see it correctly, but one figure, at the top right, is looking at the cross, and this figure has a halo around his head. Is there someone after all who holds fast to Jesus in spite of all the darkness and gloom?

Ter Horst called his painting: 'King of the Jews'. It is striking that where the body should be hanging there is a large white area. There is another white area at the bottom, with red stripes, and something that looks like a crown of thorns. This painting expresses balance and harmony. But not 'eternal peace'. There is something dynamic in the painting. You can see that the cross is being pushed to the background in favour of the white area. The light of the white area outshines the blackness of the cross. Is the cross connected with the resurrection here? Ter Horst himself says about this: 'Jesus brought a liberating light for others, right across the suffering'.

The responses showed that several people were initially shocked by Kanters' painting, but got more and more used to it. Lucebert frightened people, but made them ask themselves to what extent they themselves turned away from the cross. At first people liked Ter Horst's meditative work, but in the long run it was not as moving as the other two. Because they had the opportunity to react themselves, church-goers were intensely involved with the paintings and after the service they discussed them for a long time. Many people went back into the church to talk to others about the paintings and their own impressions.

The minister concluded his sermon as follows:

> What does this 'dialogue' with art about Jesus mean to us? This is a different way of communicating from what we are used to. The painting communicates with us, not by words but by images. To some people it will mean something, and to others it won't. But isn't this just as true of the sermon? You don't need to agree with the image presented by the painting, but you cannot deny that it confronts you with your own image of Jesus. How much challenge do we dare to take on in exposing our own image of Jesus?

5. A THEME AS STARTING POINT

In the previous section we saw how a work of art can function as a starting point for a service. But it can also be done the other way around: a work of art can be used to clarify a theme.

5.1. Torture

In 1985 Nanko van Dijk painted a Way of the Cross consisting of eight tall narrow works: Last Supper, Temptation, Arrest, Trial, Torture, Golgotha, Death, and Resurrection. In 1986 and 1987 this Way of the Cross hung in a number of churches, particularly in the Passion season. On Sunday 2 March 1986, Last Supper and Torture were hanging in the Reformed Church of Twijzel (Friesland).[12]

The painting of torture is full of drama and horror: Christ is on his knees in humiliation and above him we see the savage faces of soldiers and onlookers. Some have sticks or swords in their hands, and some of the soldiers are wearing caps like those worn by German soldiers in World War II. Van Dijk:

> He who is condemned is less than a dog, like a worm, without rights and desolate, a prey to whim. Whoever strikes him proves he is right.

The painting was hanging on the side wall of the small village church, where it could be seen clearly by half of those present. At the beginning of the sermon, the Rev. Glashouwer invited the church-goers to come out of the pews and stand in a big circle around the two paintings, after which he gave some information about them. He succeeded in fixing the concentration of those present on Jesus' suffering in a particularly gripping way, and then related it to the suffering of the present time. He discussed the painting in depth, interpreting it as an image of contemporary torture. Through the interaction of word and image, the suffering became very real.

> We see the tortured man surrounded by his enemies. They derive pleasure from his suffering and try to make the torture more and more painful. This is appallingly humiliating and degrading. It is difficult to imagine any other sin which could damage self-respect and self-esteem in a more horrible way. Nevertheless, we know that this sin against humanity is not exceptional. The Second World War and present-day television reports have opened our eyes to the terrible cruelty present in human beings – in all of us, I am afraid. But here we are told about Jesus, who of his own free will underwent the worst possible torture, in order that nobody, ever again, will be completely alone. On the other hand, it cannot be denied that this consolation also has a reverse side: it contains a warning. Anyone

---

[12] For a more detailed description of this service, see STEENSMA: *Mysterie en vergezicht* 93-96.

who harms those beneath him, or affronts and injures a fellow human being, contributes at that moment to the suffering of Christ, and affronts and injures Jesus.

5.2. Suffering and light

It is also possible to use a number of art works to illustrate a theme. On Sunday 30 January 1994, a service was held in the Grote Kerk in Leeuwarden in which the theme of suffering and light was pursued by means of works of art, Bible passages and poetry or prose. The works of art themselves were not present in the church but were shown by projecting slides on a large screen. The church was darkened and the readings were given at two lecterns to the left and right of the screen.

> After the poem 'Clair Obscur' by Gerrit Achterberg had been read, six works of art were shown, followed by a brief explanation, a Bible passage and a story mirroring it.
> -Art work 1 and 2: 'Double Cross' by Herbert Falken: the suffering of Christ is continued in the suffering of our time and the image of Christ does not have only one meaning but must be constantly reinterpreted.[13]
> Bible passage: Matthew 25, 31-46: "...Truly, I say to you, as you did it to one of the least of these my brethren, you did it to me..."
> Mirror story: Mother Teresa.
> -Art work 3: 'Diagnosis: brain tumour' by Herbert Falken: a sick person attached to a machine in a hospital.
> Bible passage: Psalm 38: "O Lord, rebuke me not in thy anger, ... There is no soundness in my flesh because of thy indignation..."
> Mirror story: text by Philip Roth.
> -Art work 4: 'Drug addict' by Herbert Falken.
> Bible passage: Romans 7, 13-25: "...Wretched man that I am! Who will deliver me from this body of death? Thanks be to God through Jesus Christ our Lord!"
> Mirror story: the story of Ananias and Sapphira (Acts 5, 1-11).
> -Art work 5: 'Crossed' by Flop Vinken: Christ is crucified (is suffering) on the corners of our streets.[14]
> Bible passage: Hymn 490: "...Here a town was built..."[15]

---

[13] G. ROMBOLD & H SCHWEBEL: *Christus in der Kunst des 20. Jahrhunderts* (Freiburg 1983) 142-147.

[14] R. STEENSMA (ed.): *Jezus is boos. Het beeld van Christus in de hedendaagse kunst* (Zoetermeer 1995) 144-145.

[15] *Liedboek voor de kerken* 719-720 (No. 490).

Mirror story: the poem 'Woninglooze' (Homeless) by J. Slauerhoff.
-Art work 6: 'Suffering and light' by Henk ter Horst: the black beams of
the cross are disappearing behind a white area.[16]
Bible passage: Matthew 16, 21-25, the first warning of the suffering to
come, and 17, 1-9, the Transfiguration on the mountain.
Mirror passage: Hymn 283: "Thou art the meaning of what we are, ..."[17]

After these five parts of the service there was an organ improvisation and
the Our Father was recited by the whole assembly, after which the congregation left the church in silence.

In this service the works of art played a central part; not only was
information given about them, but they remained visible during the
reading of the Bible passages and the mirror stories. The effect was
accentuated by the darkness of the church. The fact that the paintings
were projected on a big screen meant that those attending the service
could see them better than if the original paintings had been there, since
they were smaller in size. On the one hand there was optimal attention
for the works of art, but on the other hand the theme was paramount
and the works of art were used to convey that theme. The works themselves were not the point of departure. Using works of art in this way is
justifiable only if the artist's intention is not violated. The explanation
given should go no further than pointing out what can be seen in the
painting and if necessary making it clearer by quoting the artist.

6. OPPORTUNITIES FOR CHURCH-GOERS TO RESPOND

In the preceding sections it has become clear that there are more ways
than one of responding to works of art. The most usual way is for the
minister to respond in the sermon or other parts of the liturgy. It is also
possible to let the church-goers respond. This can take place in the
period preceding the service – as was the case in Scharnegoutum – or
alternatively just before or during the service, as in the service in Eindhoven.

The Eindhoven service was part of the series of experiments with
three works from the exhibition 'Jesus is angry'.[18] The question asked in

---

[16] STEENSMA: *Jezus is boos* 98-99.
[17] *Liedboek voor de kerken* 430-431 (No. 283).
[18] STEENSMA: 'Jezus is boos' in de kerkdienst 223v.

this study was whether it might be possible to have church-goers respond to a work of art during the service and to incorporate these responses in the service as a whole. The main conclusion is that this is difficult. There is little time, many people find it too difficult to express themselves in the presence of so many other people and in the ambience of the church, and a dialogue is practically impossible, partly because people are sitting in rows of pews. Giving people the opportunity to respond does significantly increase attention for the art works. The best way to enable people to express their associations with them freely and openly is in an informal setting. This can take place in a group discussion a few days before the service or in a meeting just before the actual service. The great advantage of this construction is that people are closely involved with the works of art, can look at them properly and let them sink in for a longer time, and talk to others about them in an informal way. The fact that this takes place in a different room before the actual service need not be a problem. A second positive aspect of this method is that people's responses and feelings, which are sometimes very personal, can be directly incorporated in the preaching of the gospel. The only practical disadvantage is that the 'church service' may be twice as long, but if the discussion is intense, it is unlikely that there will be objections.

In the Reformed Church of Dieren (Gelderland) a new construction was chosen. The service began in the hall beside the church, where the church-goers discussed the art works, first in small groups and then as one whole group. Then everyone went into the church itself. In his report the Rev. F.Z. Ort observes:

> It is now Monday and the services have taken place. The general impression was very positive. At seven o'clock we assembled in the church. There were about 55 members of the congregation. The youngest was twelve, the oldest eighty-six. After a short introduction we let the works have their effect on us as individuals. After a while people took coffee and animated discussions arose in smaller groups. This lasted half an hour. Then all of us examined the works one by one. There was a good discussion; and we took plenty of time for it (an hour). (…)
>
> Then we went into the church. I myself made the 'word collage', which served as a sort of assimilation. As an answer to the last question from the collage with respect to Lucebert's work 'Nooit?' ('Never?') the story in Luke 24 was read. After the silence we praised God with the words of the Magnificat. The prayers included elements of our discussions. Finally faith

in victory was echoed in Huub Oosterhuis's hymn, "that Highest word, written, white on black", as was the question "how might we dare to know who Thou art".

After the service (by then it was quarter past nine) a few elderly ladies came up to me. Their reaction was splendid: "It was interesting, vicar, but I think I'm too old for it. It's a bit too modern." Others had more positive reactions. It had made a deep impression. The best reaction was the fact that nobody had noticed how late it was. This shows how intensely engrossed we were.

7. THE THEMES OF THE ART WORKS

7.1. Intensification

A survey of the art works which have been placed in Protestant churches in the Netherlands in recent years shows that most of these works intensify biblical stories and symbols in some way. In some cases this is achieved by the form, in other cases by relating the story to modern times or interpreting it in a personal way. I will give two examples.

The painting 'Torture' by Nanko van Dijk in the church service at Twijzel is, as has been said above, an image full of drama (see section 5.1). The minister succeeded in fixing the concentration of those present on Jesus' suffering in a particularly gripping way, and then related it to the suffering of the present time, as we can see it on television every day.

The triptych 'Passage' by Jan Grotenberg (Bankraskerk, Amstelveen, Noord-Holland, 1991) shows a cloudy sky with a vertical section in the middle which is lighter: it looks as if the light is about to break through. The three clouds are almost identical except that from left to right the lighter section becomes more pronounced. The minister pointed out that light, both in general and in the painting, has all sorts of connotations, varying from radiant and illuminating to glaring and blinding. In the sermon, examples from the Bible were given of both effects of light, and a connection was made with Jesus as the divine light.

7.2. Contradiction

Sometimes a work of art is shown whose subject matter is at odds with the gospel or even clearly contradicts it. By involving such a work in the liturgy all the same, the minister can illustrate a facet of the Bible message by pointing out the contradiction.

At the exhibition 'Met de dood in de ogen' ('With death in his eyes') in the Grote Kerk in Leeuwarden in 1991, Tom Reeders work 'The burden' was displayed. The work consists of a life-sized skeleton-like human figure made of scrap iron. This figure is connected by steel cables to an iron net in which there are three heavy boulders. According to the artist this is a picture of a human being who is tied to a burden which he carries throughout his life, a life burden from which he is released only at death. For six weeks this work stood beside the pulpit and gave rise to intense discussions about the meaning of life and death and also about suicide. Some church-goers found the confrontation with the image very difficult because of the feelings it aroused in them and some ministers said in their sermons that the work moved them but also aroused contradictory thoughts. It stimulated them to warn against hopelessness and pessimism and to point towards hope in Christ.

A completely different form of contradiction was involved in relation to Christie van der Haak's work 'Resurrection', which hung in the Dom Church in Utrecht during Easter 1992. The specific figurative representation of Christ's resurrection, inspired by Matthias Grünewald's Isenheim altar, caused a few ministers to protest against an image like this. One of them thought it was too compelling and left no room for a different perception of the Resurrection, a perception which does not insist on physical resurrection from death. Another remarked that Grünewald's resurrected Christ is the culmination of a tradition of images which we have recognized as being a mistake, since the moment of the resurrection cannot be seen and cannot be made visible. In his opinion we therefore have no need whatsoever of a representation like this.

7.3. Social criticism

In modern art we often find evidence of reflection on the relationships between people, social problems, the horrors of war, treatment of the environment, coming to terms with recent history, in short, with human existence in its entirety. These subjects are sometimes portrayed in such a way that they express intense expectation and indignation, excitement and distress, solidarity and aversion. Every so often works like this are shown in a church, but much less frequently than art works intensifying a Bible story. In many parishes church leaders are afraid of the discussions and unrest which might result from showing a work of this nature.

In 1980 a triptych by Henk ter Horst called 'Victory over sin, sickness and death' was hung in a church in Assen. On each of the three panels, more than three-quarters of the space is taken up by blue sky: victory means having room, being able to breathe again. On the middle panel there is a big hand which is opening, protecting, pointing towards heaven. At the bottom there are flowers: the resurgence of nature, which time and time again survives the death of winter. Right at the bottom sin, sickness and death are portrayed. Sin is depicted by missile armament, barbed wire, dead fishes, withered plants and malnourished African children. The middle panel shows sickness, both literally and figuratively: cancer cells, a Thalidomide baby, a Down's syndrome child, but also a football-player with a halo, an image of infatuation with sport. There are also two well-dressed gentlemen with piles of money in front of them and behind them a group of people, an image of a blindly following crowd. The third panel shows death, including death as a result of murder and traffic accidents.

There were both positive and negative responses to this work. Many people thought the images were very direct and shocking and said that they made them think differently about the way they lived their lives. Others thought that images causing unrest did not belong in the church, because in their opinion the main reason people come to church is to find peace and consolation. Confrontation with images like these in a church apparently has a stronger tendency to make people think than seeing them on television.

7.4. Emotions

The directness of the images in a work of art sometimes moves people deeply, especially if sorrow, suffering and death are involved. In recent years two exhibitions were held in the Grote Kerk in Leeuwarden for which a side room was set up as a mourning chapel in which a death sculpture was the central feature. In 1987 Werner Knaupp's 'Trace of Life' was placed here. This work consists of twelve wrought-iron corpses in various stages of decomposition. This sculpture confronts the viewer in a harsh and direct way with the total nature of death: all that is left of a human being is an empty shell. It happened several times that visitors, particularly older ones, left the room with tears in their eyes. This work was indirectly involved in the service in that ministers referred to it in their sermons. It was not directly visible to church-goers.

The same is true of the two black steel coffins with two steel chairs behind them which were placed in this room in 1991. They formed a strong contrast with the white walls of the room which was otherwise completely empty. During the time the Gulf War was taking place, a minister preached about death with reference to this work. He described the thoughts and feelings the work had aroused in him and quoted the hymn 'In the middle of life we are surrounded by death'. To counter these thoughts of death and destruction, he pointed to the promise of Isaiah and the hope which was given shape in Christ, a hope which is not a matter of the distant future or the afterlife, but of existence here and now.

7.5. Protests

As far as art in Dutch Protestant churches is concerned a great deal is possible, but every so often a work is placed which several people in the congregation find extremely difficult to accept, a work which in their view oversteps the boundary.

Works depicting naked people are the first to meet with protests. Apparently these works confront people with their own feelings and thoughts about corporality and with their own unsolved hangups in that area. The arguments they use are often that the work is morally offensive and therefore unbiblical.

Anne Feddema's painting 'The Lord's Supper' caused a great deal of commotion. It depicts Christ as an old man, sitting at a table surrounded by clown-like figures and monsters. Beside the table stands a naked figure with both male and female sexual characteristics and a severely deformed head. It is an image full of alienation. For several people the association with the Lord's Supper was the last straw. A minister defended the work in a sermon by pointing out that it invites us to be open to people living at the edge of society and to reflect on the enigma of life. He also pointed out that Christ can sustain us at times when life is a chaos. This work led to deep personal conversations, both in groups and between individuals; however, on two occasions the church council had to address written protests. In both cases the council decided by a large majority that the work should remain in place; one argument used was that it confronted people with themselves in an intense way.

The second reason for works placed in the church to lead to protests is if the works clearly raise political or social issues such as war, nuclear armament, oppression, discrimination, racism, and environmental pollution. Often the argument heard is that people are already confronted with these issues every day on the television and do not need them in the church as well.

M. Bons-Storm pointed out that in this sort of discussion two groups can be distinguished. For one group the gospel is a source of consolation and God is seen as a safeguard for the existing order. Art may illustrate this. For the other group, the gospel is seen primarily as a challenge and God as an opening towards new possibilities, and art may strengthen this. For the group which is looking mainly for consolation, going to church is often an escape from a threatening world: in church old familiar words can be heard and art which disturbs that pattern is felt to be threatening.[19]

8. THE AMBIVALENCE OF A 'FEAST OF SUFFERING'

Of the works taken as examples in the preceding sections, two-thirds have to do with suffering and death. This is no coincidence: in art, images of suffering are very much more frequent than those of happiness. This is true both of religious and of non-religious art. In images of Christ in the 20th century the image of the suffering Christ was also the predominant one, both in works intending to express biblical themes and in those making a statement about human suffering in general through the figure of Christ.

If we ask why this is so, the first point that comes to mind is that in representations of Christ in the past the suffering Christ was also the central figure. In the Middle Ages the cross dominated the church interior, as it still does today in Catholic, Lutheran and Anglican churches. In recent decades an image of the cross has also been introduced into many churches of Calvinist origin. The universal symbol of the Christian faith is the cross, which is a token of suffering and death. In the second place, in a way art is also a reflection of theological ideas, and in theology concepts such as resurrection, ascension and the afterlife are the subjects of many a discussion. Themes like this are difficult to

[19] Cf. R. STEENSMA: *In de spiegel van het beeld. Kerk en moderne kunst* (Baarn 1987) 64v.

express in images, whereas Jesus the man is much easier to portray. In the third place, many images of suffering cause the viewer to wonder if there is not something else besides suffering. Suffering compels us to think about its opposite and calls us to search actively for hope, joy and expectation. In the fourth place, suffering is much easier to depict realistically than happiness. Pictures of happy people easily tend to be perceived as excessively romantic and artificial.

In the Middle Ages suffering was predominant in art; it was a time when because of epidemics and wars death was always very close at hand. In the Renaissance and the Enlightenment suffering became less prominent and beauty and heroism were preferred in human figures. In the 20th century suffering again became predominant. If art is a mirror of culture in a certain period, then suffering must have a very important place in our culture. Every day we see images on television of the suffering caused by the two World Wars, and the suffering of refugees and of people who are starving. People who are not themselves victims of these horrors do know the mental suffering caused by fear, despair, hatred and loneliness, often know some form of physical suffering, and are familiar with deterioration, dying and death. The conclusion can only be that human beings are more deeply moved by images of suffering than by images of happiness; this is true of both the artist who has created the work and the viewer whom it affects.[20]

In 1987 the Institut für Kirchenbau in Marburg organized an exhibition called 'Ecce homo'. Thirty artists were asked to make works portraying their vision of humanity. They were given complete freedom as to whether or not they made any reference to Pilate's words. The catalogue[21] shows 18 works which in some way or another have to do with suffering: suffering in general (4x), Christ's suffering (3x), mental suffering (5x) and sickness, dying and death (6x). Of the other 12, only a few can be characterized as images of hope and happiness.

Günther Maniewski, one of the artists who took part in 'Ecce Homo', asked himself at what moment a human being was truly visible. His answer was:

---

[20] For a more detailed discussion of this subject, see R. STEENSMA: Why does the image of suffering continue to dominate in modern religious art?, in F. BROUWER & R.A. LEAVER (eds): *Ars et musica in liturgia. Celebratory volume presented to Caspar Honders on the occasion of his seventieth birthday on 6 June 1993* (Utrecht 1993) 187-197.

[21] H. SCHWEBEL & H.-U. SCHMIDT (Hrsg.): *Ecce homo. Vom Christusbild zum Menschenbild* (Menden 1987).

When he is completely weak, when his end is near. When it is no longer possible to pretend and only the existential nakedness is recognizable. It is only in a crisis, in a catastrophe, just before death, that the human being can be perceived; but is he then recognized?

If this answer of Maniewski is correct, then we can understand why artists prefer images of suffering to those of happiness, since the former give a sharper and truer picture of human beings.

Within the whole complex of church feasts, those of the Passion have an important place, if not the most important. In Spain, during the Semana Santa there are pious and sorrowful processions in which the participants follow a large crucifix. In some places they practise self-flagellation. For many of those who experience the Passion season intensely, Easter is something of an anticlimax.[22] In The Netherlands, devotion to the Way of the Cross receives extra attention, sometimes through the introduction of a modern Way of the Cross. These religious feasts are accompanied by performances of St. Matthew's Passion in churches and concert halls and on radio and television.

The editors of this collection characterize a **feast** as follows:

> a moment or occasion within the ordering of time and the completion of the course of life at which people, individually, in groups or as a community, give a special ritual form – i.e. a form which breaks away from everyday life – to events which mark personal and social existence, on the basis of a religious and philosophical orientation.

If there is one moment at which ritual form is given to an event marking personal existence on the basis of a religious orientation, it is the funeral, and if we follow this definition, the funeral service must also be regarded as a feast. If we pursue this line further, many church services in which images of suffering play a major role can also be called feasts, even though this may sound like a contradiction in terms. However, it is clear that the more intense the image of suffering is, the more strongly the ambivalence is felt by many attendants.

---

[22] I have borrowed the term 'anti-climax' from Thomas J. STEELE: Foreword, in L. FRANK: *New kingdom of saints. Religious art of New Mexico 1780-1907* (Santa Fe 1992) XV, in which he describes the Passion cult including self-flagellation as practised by the Passion brothers in New Mexico in the 18th and 19th centuries.

9. CONCLUSIONS

The use of contemporary art in the liturgy means breaking away from a number of customary patterns: there is more variation in the form of the liturgy; in Protestant services visual elements are given a place in addition to the traditionally prominent auditory elements; visual art addresses the personal feelings and thoughts of the church-goers, whereby mediation or explanation by a minister is not necessary, in fact often not desirable.

With respect to the relationship between a theme and a work of art, we have seen that in some cases the theme is based on the work of art, but that in others the theme is the starting point and the work of art is an addition. In the latter case the work of art may well intensify the theme, but there is also a considerable danger that the work is used merely as an illustration and is unable to make its own specific impact. In the first case there may be a danger that the question raised or message conveyed by the work of art is too dominant. It is preferable not to force the community to choose, consciously or unconsciously, between peace and provocation, but to give both elements a place.

If we examine the use of contemporary art in the liturgy as described above in relation to the views or criteria given by various authors with respect to the concept of 'feast',[23] then we can conclude that it matches that concept closely. In the first place it creates dynamics between worship and culture; in various, often penetrating, ways church-goers are confronted with aspects of present-day culture, through both the form and the subject matter of the works of art. Secondly, it entails a vigorous process of change and motion. This is especially true in comparison with the historical background of Protestant church services, which were held according to a practically identical pattern for centuries, but it also true of the different facets of services involving art. In the third place, there is close interaction between characterization and familiarization, since much art does not consist of illustrative or meditative images without any commitment, but stimulates reflection and often also challenges the viewer to take a stand, in the light of the gospel. In the fourth place, the use of art is essentially conducted 'from the bottom up'; in no way

---

[23] In particular, I refer the reader to W. FRIJHOFF: Toeëigening. Van bezitsdrang naar betekenisgeving, in *Trajecta* 6 (1997) 99-118 and T. TABORDA: *Sakramente. Praxis und Fest* (Düsseldorf 1988).

is it prescribed or stimulated from 'the top down'. In the fifth place, practice is first and foremost, and not the usual structures of tradition, use of the prayer book, etc. In the sixth place, there is more interplay between the individual and the community than in the past, especially when church-goers are given a chance to speak before or during the service. In the seventh place, the contrast between church and every-day life is revealed in a new way. Evidence of this is the reaction to works of art containing images of discrimination, war, environment etc.; on television such images are normal, but in church people feel uncomfortable with them. This brings a certain ambivalence to these celebrations.

LOUIS VAN TONGEREN

THE SQUEEZE ON SUNDAY
REFLECTIONS ON THE CHANGING EXPERIENCE AND FORM OF SUNDAYS

1. INTRODUCTION

For centuries two elements have defined the Christian celebration of Sunday: Sunday rest and Sunday worship. In a certain sense these two elements suppose one another. Among other ways in which the observance of Sunday as a holy day manifests itself is in Sunday rest, and because Sunday is a day of rest, the possibility is created for observing this day by participating in worship. However, as history demonstrates, these elements do not have to imply each other. Only in the fourth century did Constantine the Great promulgate laws declaring Sunday a day free of labour in the Roman Empire, and subsequently, a day of obligatory rest. Before that time Christians assembled on Sunday for liturgical gatherings, although Sunday as a day of rest did not exist.[1] Both elements together form the Sunday duty or the Sunday obligation,[2] and down to this day define ecclesiastical regulations with regard to Sunday. According to Church law as collected in 1983, Sunday is an obligatory feast day,[3] on which the faithful must "participate in the celebration of the Eucharist; furthermore they should refrain from labour and activity which would be an impediment to the worship which is due to God, to the joy which is peculiar to the Lord's Day, or to the necessary refreshment of spirit and body."[4]

---

[1] For the celebration of Sunday in the period of the early Church and for the relation between Sunday and the Sabbath, see the contribution by G. Rouwhorst in Part III of this collection.

[2] For an historical survey, see P. NISSEN: De geschiedenis van het zondagsgebod, in E. HENAU & A. HAQUIN (eds.): De zondag. Een tijd voor God, een tijd voor de mens (Brussel 1992) 68-83.

[3] Codex iuris canonici (Città del Vaticano 1983) c. 1246 §1 (subsequently abbreviated as CIC).

[4] CIC c. 1247. One can also fulfil the Sunday obligation by participating in the Eucharist on the preceding evening (CIC c. 1248 §1), and anyone who for weighty reasons

In almost all Western countries in the last decades we have witnessed tendencies that have more and more eroded the for centuries familiar image of Sunday as a day of rest that is reserved for worship. Under the influence of various ecclesiastical and social developments church attendance has fallen off, church buildings have been closed and Sunday rest has been disrupted by Sunday becoming increasingly filled with all sorts of activities, which in turn have repercussions for Sunday worship. Sunday is, to be sure, one of the institutions in our Western culture in which traces of the Christian experience of time continue to be preserved, but as a consequence of these developments the Christian character of Sunday is coming more and more under pressure.

It is striking that these developments, and the many, sometimes heated discussions sparked off by changes to laws allowing shop opening on Sunday, the advancing 24-hour economy and 'flexible' working hours in the 1990s have not led to a commensurate development in the amount of theological and liturgical studies literature on the

cannot participate in the celebration of the Eucharist is advised to participate in a celebration of the word; another alternative consists in the person or persons devoting a comparable period of time to prayer, be it individual, or in a family connection (CIC c. 1248 §2).

[5] Without seeking to be exhaustive, reference can be made here to P. JOUNEL: *Le dimanche* (= L'horizon du croyant 12) (Paris 1990); *Zondag vieren. Kerk en liturgie op de eerste dag van de week* (special issue *Tijdschrift voor liturgie* 76 (1992) nos. 1-2); HENAU & HAQUIN: *De zondag*; J. LÓPEZ MARTÍN: *El domingo, fiesta de los cristianos* (Madrid 1992); J. VAN DER VLOET: De antropologische betekenis van de zondag, in *Communio* 19 (1994) 16-26; H. DE DIJN et al.: *De zondag in de postmoderne cultuur* (Leuven 1994); C. POSTHUMUS MEYJES: *Een dag van staken. Zuinig zijn op de zondag* (Zoetermeer 1995); K.-H. BIERITZ: Der Sonntag, in H.-Chr. SCHMIDT-LAUBER & K.-H. BIERITZ (eds.): *Handbuch der Liturgik. Liturgiewissenschaft in Theologie und Praxis der Kirche* (Leipzig/Göttingen 1995[2]) 465-470; W. ZAUNER: Wer mag den Sonntag?, in *Diakonia* 28 (1997) 238-246; *El domingo cristiano* (special issue *Phase* 39 (1999) no. 231); H. WEGMAN: De eerste en de achtste dag. De viering van de zondag, in IDEM: *Voor de lange duur. Bijdragen over liturgie en spiritualiteit* (Baarn 1999) 157-163; L. VAN TONGEREN: De zondag, in M. BARNARD & P. POST (eds.): Ritueel bestek. *Kernwoorden van de Liturgie* (Zoetermeer 2001) 69-76.

Furthermore, a series of diocesan letters and ecclesiastical documents have been appearing for some years now which afford an overview of concerns with regard to the altered experience, significance, function and design of Sunday. See the surveys in P. STEVENS: De heiliging van de zondag. Een voortdurend punt van zorg voor de leiding van de kerken, in HENAU & HAQUIN: *De zondag* 95-99, and in F. SPIERTZ: Gemeenschap vieren in het weekend. Het standpunt van enkele bisschoppen in de tachtiger jaren, in *Tijdschrift voor liturgie* 71 (1987) 168-175. The most recent ecclesiastical document is the apostolic letter of JOHN PAUL II: *Dies Domini* (Città del Vaticano 1998).

topic of Sunday.[5] After all, the shifts which have in a short time changed the appearance of Sunday in many respects demand theological and liturgical reflection regarding the ground and meaning of Sunday, and a thinking through of the implications for the ritual design of Sunday. Before providing some impetus here for this reflection, there will first be a brief description of the changes, in social and liturgical respects, to which Sunday has been subject, and how these developments relate to a changing ecclesiastical context. Next there will be focus on the fact that, through the relationship and interaction between faith and life and between cultus and culture, Sunday has come to stand in a field of dynamic tension as an exponent of this interference. This means that the fundamental dimensions that are decisive for the Christian identity of Sunday must be illuminated from the perspective of this dynamic. Then there must be a consideration of the degree to which the present experience and design of Sunday conflicts with these fundamental dimensions. The Christian identity of Sunday could be strengthened within this area of tension by profiling Sunday as more of a day of rest, and by condensing, optimalizing and differentiating the rituals offered. Moreover, it can be asked if Sunday indeed is as much under pressure on all fronts as is sometimes suggested. Isn't it primarily a specific design or a specific image of Sunday that is crumbling and disappearing? Some dimensions of Sunday have by now taken on a new shape. The challenge this embodies is to perceive this accurately and deal creatively with these new shapes.

2. Social changes with respect to Sunday

Under the influence of Christianity Sunday acquired its own pattern of values, and codes of conduct were established in our culture which in many respects distinguished Sunday from the other days of the week. The most decisive factors were its character as a day without labour and the Sunday obligation. To a great extent social life paused, and church attendance was an organic component of Sunday. We must not, however, idealize the extent to which Sunday church attendance was matter-of-course. This was chiefly connected with the revival in the fortunes of the church in the period from the middle of the nineteenth through the middle of the twentieth century, a period which was definitely not representative of history as a whole.[6] Sunday observance has constantly been a point of concern and attention, and therefore was surrounded with extensive rules and regulations. Throughout history believers have been urged to respect Sunday as a feast day and day of rest.[7] The stereotypical image of Sunday, which until recently was a reality and which still lives on in the memory to mixed feelings, came into being in this period of ecclesiastical boom. Sunday was a special, but also for many a tedious day, dominated by attendance at church (sometimes twice) and otherwise staying at home. The outside world was kept at arm's length and special clothing and a more extensive meal served to increase the festive spirit of the day.

Over the past decades, however, the traditional celebration and ritual design of Sunday has begun to be squeezed.[8] Since the introduction of a free Saturday, Sunday is no longer an isolated island of freedom in the week. Sunday has begun to be a part of an increasingly prominent weekend which must be filled with an increasing number of activities. Sunday is no longer the one point of rest in a busy week filled with labour. The week has been split in two, between four work days and three free days, or, to use the terminology of the tourist industry, between a long weekend and a midweek. Sunday no longer marks the distinction between working hours and leisure – two concepts which have since come to be valued differently. The labour ethic has changed; we no longer live to work, but we work to enjoy our free time. Through various measures, such as reduction of working hours and early retirement, everyone's share in the work process is reduced, and free time has increased considerably. Leisure is no longer primarily intended to recoup one's strength for work, but has become an end in itself, defining our lifestyle to an ever greater degree. One can today rightly speak of a leisure culture, which can now be studied in the separate discipline of leisure studies. Until recently the expression 'time is money' referred to handling time as efficiently as possible and obtaining as high a return as possible on the time available. Today the expression, with a somewhat different twist to it, is also applicable to leisure. Leisure is big business, in which big bucks can be earned. Rising prosperity must, to a large

[6] P. RAEDTS: De christelijke middeleeuwen als mythe: Ontstaan en gebruik van een constructie uit de negentiende eeuw in *Tijdschrift voor theologie* 30 (1990) 146-158.

[7] Cf. the historical survey in NISSEN: De geschiedenis van het zondagsgebod.

[8] For a survey of social developments regarding Sunday, see L. VOYÉ: Over de zondag. Een sociologische benadering, in HENAU & HAQUIN: *De zondag* 8-29.

degree, find its outlet in a prospering free time market. Leisure time has become consumption time, and thereby has been commercialized and entered the economic system. The argument for a 24-hour economy in which the factor of time no longer stands in the way of production and consumption would appear to be only the logical extension of this development.

In 1998, an action with the slogan 'Take time to live' began against the 24-hour economy, initiated by almost all Christian and Jewish religious bodies in The Netherlands, and presently joined by diverse social institutions such as labour unions.[9] In a short time more than 800,000 signatures were collected in support of the action, to send a signal to politicians. The action was a protest against the further expansion of working times and opening hours in shops, and a plea to maintain a common day of rest for the sake of social cohesion and to promote solidarity in society. It is not emphasis on the individual, but on social capital, which is necessary for a liveable society. To the extent that criticism of this social and economic development touches on Sunday, it is primarily directed toward the consequences of Sunday as a collective day of rest. Sunday should be protected as a 'time reservation' in the midst of the other days of the week.[10] Although not formulated as the main goal, ecclesiastical interests also play a role in this action, that church attendance not be further placed in jeopardy by a far-reaching integration of Sunday into the economy.

The debate which has been set in motion by this action has led to further shaping of opinions at a journalistic level in the media, and has sparked off an academic dispute among economists.[11] Aside from the outcome of this campaign and debate, and irrespective of the conclusion which politicians draw from it, the developments as sketched do clearly show that the increasing domination of society by economics also has Sunday in its grip, and in order to obtain a hearing for the 'Take time

---

[9] See the brochure *Neem tijd om te leven. Actie tegen de 24-uurseconomie*, bound into *Een-twee-een*, April 10, 1998. It is not only The Netherlands where such protests are taking place. In Germany, for instance, there has been a similar reaction by the Evangelical Church and the Roman Catholic Church to permitting Sunday shop opening.

[10] So T. BERNTS: De verstoorde zondagsrust, in J. VAN BEVEREN & P. VAN DER PARRE (eds.): *In werkelijkheid is 't anders* (Amsterdam 1995) 29-40, on p. 40.

[11] See Th. VAN DE KLUNDERT (ed.): *Economisering van de samenleving* (Tilburg 1999).

[12] J. GRAAFLAND: Reactie op 'Economisering van de samenleving', in VAN DE KLUNDERT: *Economisering van de samenleving* 74.

to live' campaign it was necessary for the initiators to present their message through economic arguments.[12] Sunday, which until recently was of hardly any interest from the perspective of economics, has since come within reach of consumption and commerce.

That there is considerable importance attached to Sunday as a collective day of rest can also be seen in the new content that Sunday has already taken on. In addition to participation in worship there is a great deal that takes place on Sunday in the sports and social spheres, and this presupposes that people are available and reachable. At the same time, we see that the character of Sunday as a day of rest is otherwise in flux. Sunday is no longer a reservation in time in the sense of a day of rest, but in the sense of a day without work, or of work of a different kind, and through this shows increasing similarity with Saturday. For many households, Saturday and/or Sunday compensate for what one doesn't get around to on regular work days. This includes not only relaxation, entertainment and sports, time for each other and the children (who do not have to be taken to the daycare centre), but also time for housework and shopping.[13] The ironing board is taken out of the closet more often on Sundays now. Or to put it in other terms: Sunday is becoming more like any other day.

3. CHANGES IN SUNDAY LITURGY AND PARTICIPATION IN IT

During the same period in which Sunday was changing shape socially in the ways discussed above, liturgy has also changed radically. Vatican II was the impetus for fundamental renewal in all liturgical books. Yet more radical and far-reaching was the way in which these books were to a large extent set aside, that is to say, the abandonment of prescribed and appointed liturgies. Liturgy was increasingly self-composed, on site – to be sure, on the basis of good models and trustworthy guides – and thereby took on what could be called an experimental character. The subjective aspect entered the stage. The sacrosanct liturgical structure that gave direction to personal faith, that steered experience, and in

---

[13] A. VAN DEN BROEK, W. KNULST & K. BREEDVELD: *Naar andere tijden? Tijdsbesteding en tijdsordening in Nederland 1975-1995* (= Sociale en culturele studies 29) (Den Haag 1999); W. KNULST: *Werk, rust en sociaal leven op zondagen sinds de jaren zeventig* (Tilburg 1999). See also J. ROBINSON & G. GODBEY: *Time for life. The surprising ways Americans use their time* (Pennsylvania 1997).

which one could hide or flee in anonymity, but in which you could also live with conviction, made way for a liturgy from the bottom up. Liturgy started from experience, or at least wanted to connect with it. Those in the pews must feel they were personally addressed by it, so that there was also room left for doubt and uncertainty and for the vulnerability of faith. Liturgy took on a more human format, called 'horizontalism' by its critics, and to increase involvement people were expected to participate. A pluriform selection became available: youth liturgy, children's liturgy, family services and celebrations in Latin or in local languages, with or without Gregorian chant. Some adjudged this subjective liturgy as the kiss of death for the church, and censured it as liturgical tinkering.

In 1966 the possibilities for participating in the Sunday liturgy were expanded through permitting this to be celebrated on the preceding Saturday evening too. This change fit with the social expansion of Sunday into a weekend, and at the same time was a step toward meeting the need to make various options available and expand the opportunity for choice, so that people could also set other priorities for themselves on Sunday without giving up the Sunday liturgy. This expansion was prompted by the need to fulfil the Sunday obligation, and based on the reasoning that the new day began with the setting of the sun. In practical terms this expansion to Saturday evening was made possible by the relaxation of the rules governing the period of abstinence before taking Communion, so that the Eucharist could also be celebrated in the evening and Communion could be received.

Despite the expansion in the possibilities and liturgical selection and despite the more personal character of the liturgy, very quickly a steady decline in church attendance had to be acknowledged. A paradoxical situation presented itself in that to the degree in which people could participate in the liturgy increased, the number who actually participated declined.[14] The improved liturgy which was the aim of Vatican II, since realized, worked out inconsistently: the better the liturgy, the worse the attendance, one might cynically conclude.[15] Initially it was primarily a

---

[14] M. SCHNEIDERS: Een eeuw 'in' de liturgie. Een inleidend overzicht en 'gebruiks-aanwijzing', in P. AL & M. SCHNEIDERS (eds.): *Een soort onschuldige hobby? Een eeuw liturgisch werk van de Norbertijnen in Nederland* (Heeswijk-Dinther 1992) 29.

[15] So A. MÜLLER: Sonntagstheologie von unten. Der Sonntag im Beziehungsfeld zwischen Anthropologie, Soziologie und Theologie, in A. ALTERMATT & TH. SCHNITKER (eds.): *Der Sonntag. Anspruch, Wirklichkeit, Gestalt* (Würzburg/Freiburg 1986) 237.

matter of deserting the church, of people deliberately distancing themselves from church and faith. But soon enough, the habit of not going to church every Sunday also took hold among those who did wish to remain involved with the church. Involvement with the church no longer obviously implied weekly church attendance. The weekly church attendance assumed by the continuous (or semi-continuous) lectionaries is becoming increasingly less a matter of course, which means the use of these schedules must become increasingly relative. Many no longer recognize a Sunday obligation, and it is indeed seen as being at odds with the experience of Sunday as a 'free' day, that is to say a day free of constraints and obligations. If until a few decades ago church attendance was one of the few ways of spending free time on Sunday outside of the home, at the moment the Sunday liturgy has become an increasingly modest competitor within an immensely increased offering in the leisure culture. Liturgy is no longer an obvious component of Sunday, let alone definitive for the meaning of Sunday.

4. INCREASING DISCREPANCY BETWEEN BELIEF AND CHURCH

The shifts which Sunday has undergone in relation to both social and ecclesiastical and liturgical aspects are not to be separated from developments which can be observed across the whole range of church and belief in the context of modern society. Sociological investigations over the last few years have brought into focus the degree to which church life in The Netherlands has been subject to an erosion over the past half-century, and that involvement in the institutional church is steadily shrinking.[16] At the same time, this research brings to light the fact that this receding church involvement is not coupled with a similar decline in belief or religious interest. Two thirds of the Dutch population view themselves as believers, a percentage which has not altered over the last 20 years.[17] Further, the group for whom personal faith has 'great signif-

---

[16] A good overview of the changed significance of worship services and the church over the past decades is afforded by the broadly based research of G. DEKKER, J. DE HART & J. PETERS: *God in Nederland 1966-1996* (Amsterdam 1997). The shifts in the Catholic milieu since the Second World War are extensively described in W. GODDIJN, J. JACOBS & G. VAN TILLO: *Tot vrijheid geroepen. Katholieken in Nederland 1946-2000* (Baarn 1999).

[17] DEKKER, DE HART & PETERS: *God in Nederland* 27.

icance' has even increased over this period, to one third of the population.[18] It is true that their faith has taken on another shape over the course of time, but it has remained a vital factor in the lives of people. The importance that people attach to faith and religion does not translate in equal measure into involvement in the institutional church. Thus one can say there is a growing gap or discrepancy between the experience of belief on the one hand and the church on the other. Church and belief are increasingly estranged from each other. Faith is increasingly a phenomenon that stands outside the structures of the church.[19] Church and society, cultus and culture are to an increasing degree becoming two separate worlds.

Consonant with the general social order, individualizing tendencies play an important role in this. Religion and belief have moved into the private sphere, where religious expression has separated itself from institutional, ecclesiastical practice. Belief is individualized, and does not obviously translate into involvement in a church. One characterizes this trend as "believing without belonging".[20] The emphasis lies on personal experience and on the meaning of belief for one's own life. Central theological themes take a subordinate position in this. Theological dimensions of faith are no longer understood or not experienced as existential, which for many results in their no longer being experienced as real. Faith no longer obviously translates for everyone into themes like grace, salvation, resurrection and the Eucharistic meal or fellowship.

However, there is no lack of religious consciousness or of a feeling for the transcendent. Because philosophies of life and religion enjoy such broad and diverse interest, this shift in the relation between church and belief has led to faith manifesting itself in all manner of forms outside of the traditional framework of the church. Religiosity and a feeling for transcendence no longer obviously translate into the familiar images, formulas and designs, and the vitality of faith and religion can no longer be measured by church attendance figures. There

---

[18] DEKKER, DE HART & PETERS: *God in Nederland* 28-29; 31.

[19] DEKKER, DE HART & PETERS: *God in Nederland* 41.

[20] See J. JANSSEN: Individualiteit en engagement. Religies en relaties in de hedendaagse cultuur, in H. EVERS & J. STAPPERS (eds.): *Het Informatieparadijs* (Nijmegen s.a. [2000]) 64-102, here 76, referring to G. DAVIE: Croire sans appartenir. De le cas britannique, in G. DAVIE & D. HERVIEU-LÉGER (eds.): *Identités religieuses en Europe* (Paris 1996).

are many forms of religiosity to be perceived outside the church.[21] Especially the broad repertory of rituals in our culture serves to make this visible.[22] Frequently these have a religious character and they include elements which comprise reminiscences of classical liturgical ritual patterns, or they may be transformations of the same. Also, with respect to prayer, which is acknowledged as more meaningful than church attendance figures would lead us to suspect, and that also regularly has a place in the life of younger persons,[23] an altered practice is taking shape.[24] Sunday, too, is an exponent of the development observed here.

5. DYNAMIC INTERACTION WITH CULTURE

The shifts which have been described in the social and religious function of Sunday in relation to changes in involvement in the church are only part of a much more sweeping process of transformation that has taken place in the preceding decades in the area of church and society, what has been termed 'secularization'. In recent years individualization has added its peculiar accent to this process, in part under the influence of a social dynamic through which the society has developed in a neo-liberal direction. As a consequence of this, the mass-church with its expectably high degree of participation has disappeared and the great ecclesiastical/social bonds that effectuated this mutual cohesion have disintegrated. The accompanying organizational structures and behavioural patterns have survived. They were part of the emancipation

---

[21] See, for instance, A. VAN HARSKAMP et al.: De religieuze ruis van Nederland. Thesen over de versterving en de wedergeboorte van de godsdienst (Zoetermeer 1998) and J. VERWEIJ: Secularisatie tussen feit en fictie (Tilburg 1998).

[22] See esp. P. POST: Alle dagen feest, of: de ritencrisis voorbij. Een verkenning van de markt, in P. POST & W.M. SPEELMAN (eds.): De Madonna van de Bijenkorf. Bewegingen op de rituele markt (= Liturgie in perspectief 9) (Baarn 1997) 11-32, and G. LUKKEN: Rituelen in overvloed. Een kritische bezinning op de plaats en de gestalte van het christelijk ritueel in onze cultuur (Baarn 1999).

[23] DEKKER, DE HART & PETERS: God in Nederland 21-22; J. JANSSEN, J. DE HART & Ch. DEN DRAAK: Praying as an individualized ritual, in H.-G. HEIMBROCK & H. BOUDEWIJNSE (eds.): Current studies on rituals. Perspectives for the psychology of religion (= International series in the psychology of religion 2) (Amsterdam/Atlanta 1990) 71-85.

[24] See L. VAN TONGEREN: Om zichzelf bewogen? Hedendaagse verschijningsvormen van gebed, in Tijdschrift voor liturgie 84 (2000) 136-154.

process that began in the mid-nineteenth century, crumbling rapidly a century later.[25]

This means that a comparison of the present life of faith, including the practices involving Sundays, with that of the past is problematic. Moreover, it would not be productive, because that period is not an adequate benchmark for the present. A comparison could perhaps bring recent developments into focus and provide explanations for the changes which have taken place, but the past can absolutely never be the source of norms for the present.[26] Such an attempt does justice to neither the past nor the present. Other forces were at work then than are at work today. Questions which present themselves now cannot be answered adequately by citing the past. That would lead to attempts at restoration, or reactionary conduct. The Sunday which was a part of this reference to the past is also a bygone. Just as we no longer can or will return to the primitive and inadequate living conditions of the sod house, a return to a society permeated by religion, with its ideational content, and the experience of Sunday from the first half of the twentieth century, is impossible.

With this we touch upon the subject of inculturation, which for some time now has been the focus of considerable interest in liturgical studies.[27] From this angle of approach the insight has become generally

[25] The rise and fall of this process is comprehensively documented and described in L. ROGIER & N. DE ROOY: *In vrijheid herboren. Katholiek Nederland 1853-1953* (The Hague 1953) and in GODDIJN, JACOBS & VAN TILLO: *Tot vrijheid geroepen.*

[26] For a comprehensive discussion of this, see H. WEGMAN: Liturgie en lange duur, in L. VAN TONGEREN (ed.): *Toekomst, toen en nu. Beschouwingen over de ontwikkeling en de voortgang van de liturgievernieuwing* (= Liturgie in perspectief 2) (Heeswijk-Dinther 1994) 11-38.

[27] A recent, and almost exclusively English-language oriented survey of the literature is given by S. STAUFFER: Worship and Culture. A Select Bibliography, in *Studia liturgica* 27 (1997) 102-128. In any case, the following can be added as a supplement from the abundant literature, CONGREGATION FOR DIVINE WORSHIP AND THE DISCIPLINE OF THE SACRAMENTS: *The Roman liturgy and inculturation. Fourth instruction for the right application of the Conciliar Constitution on the Liturgy (nn. 37-40)* (Rome 1994); G. LUKKEN: *Inculturatie en de toekomst van de liturgie* (= Liturgie in perspectief 3) (Heeswijk-Dinther 1994); J. LAMBERTS (ed.): *Liturgie et inculturation. Liturgy and inculturation* (= Textes et études liturgiques. Studies in liturgy 14) (Leuven 1996); L. VAN TONGEREN: De inculturatie van de liturgie tot (stil)stand gebracht? Kanttekeningen bij een Romeins document over liturgie en inculturatie, in *Jaarboek voor liturgie-onderzoek* 12 (1996) 164-186; G. LUKKEN: Liturgiewetenschappelijk onderzoek in culturele context. Methodische verhelderingen en vragen, in *idem* 13 (1997) 135-148; A. CHUPUNGCO: Liturgy and inculturation, in A. CHUPUNGCO (ed.): *Fundamental liturgy* (= Handbook for liturgical studies 2) (Collegeville 1998) 337-375.

accepted that Christian ritual is closely intertwined with culture, and arises and develops in interaction with the culture(s) surrounding it. According to the present view culture is not defined and carried forward by an elite group of socially prominent individuals, but by various social factors that shape the everyday experiences of life, such as economics, politics, social movements, etc. These themselves are part of the culture too, and through their mutual interactions influence each other, producing changes both in the total picture of the culture and in regard to its component sectors. Liturgy and Christian ritual also have an important place within this constellation of factors. Their development cannot be seen in isolation from the dynamic of the culture of which they are a part. This immediately poses the question of how the Christian heritage that has been passed down, relates to a continuous process of cultural interaction of this sort; what does this mean for the tension between continuity and discontinuity involving Christian ritual and tradition?

One of the many problems that this complex matter calls up involves the definition of the concept of continuity. From a static concept of tradition, continuity will be understood chiefly as the literal citation from the past in the present. In such a concept, the changelessness of ritual forms and their meanings is a guarantee of continuity. A dynamic conception of tradition will, on the other hand, have more of an eye for the interaction between cultus and culture and for the evolution in ritual design and meanings which that implies. It is in this connection that Gerard Lukken argues for a critical/normative analysis of Christian ritual in which past and present are compared not on the basis of literal identification, but in which continuity and discontinuity are assessed on the basis of congruency. By congruence he does not mean the repetition of the same thing in the same culturally defined staging, but of the same thing in a new way, in a different culture.[28] Because Christian rituals are contemporary expressions of fundamental dimensions of faith, they are always inculturated; that was true for the past as much as it is for the present. Changes in the culture will therefore have their repercussions in religious and liturgical expressions of faith. When the analysis of ritual expressions transformed during the course of time is focused on the search for congruency, one must concentrate on underlying values and patterns of values. Further analysis will then be needed to reveal to what degree one is dealing with fundamental or marginal shifts. Subsequently

---

[28] LUKKEN: Liturgiewetenschappelijk onderzoek 142.

it can then be seen that there is perhaps more continuity with the past than the outward manifestations sometimes might lead one to expect. With regard to our topic, this means that Sundays must be approached as inculturated objects, and that the study of Sunday is only possible in its integral context, that is to say, as a component of and in relation to culture. Only then will it be seen if, through the shifts which have been observed with regard to Sunday, the cultural/social value and the religious meaning of Sunday are evaporating, and whether the Christian identity of Sunday is at risk.

6. THE CHRISTIAN IDENTITY OF SUNDAY

The dimensions which have been fundamental from time immemorial may be helpful for an orientation into the Christian identity of Sunday; with an eye to the third millennium they have once again been thoroughly set forth in the apostolic letter *Dies Domini*.[29] Sunday cannot be seen apart from the Sabbath, which has its foundations in the creation, of which it is the completion; the social function of Sunday as a free day is closely linked with this. Because of the Resurrection on the first day after the Sabbath, Sunday is the day of re-creation, the day of resurrection or the weekly Easter. Therefore Sunday is par excellence the day of joy, which is linked with the specific character of Sabbath rest. The presence of the Risen Lord is celebrated in the eucharistic meal. The remembrance of the Living Lord takes on its most condensed form in the eucharistic elements of the bread and wine. As the sacralization of the Sabbath stands in the perspective of the sacralization of time, so Sunday too stamps time and always points forward to the end of time. Sunday is not just the first day, but also the eighth day, and symbolizes ultimate perfection.

A readiness to encounter these dimensions of faith in an open manner is essential for the experience of the richness of the Christian Sunday. If this receptivity is absent, then the Christian Sunday loses its meaning and is perverted into an external and empty ritual, according to an hypothesis of Arno Schilson with regard to Christian feasts, applied there to Sunday.[30] When Sunday is no longer connected with its origins, it is reduced to its social function and in time will inevitably

---

[29] JOHN PAUL II: *Dies Domini*.

[30] A. SCHILSON: Fest und Feier in anthropologische und theologische Sicht. Ein Literaturbericht für B. Neunheuser zum 90. Geburtstag, in *Liturgisches Jahrbuch* 44 (1994) 29.

disappear.[31] In the Christian context, the weekly gathering of the community on Sunday is essential, indeed constitutive. It is essential, because the Sunday celebration is necessary for deepening personal faith; the celebration gives form to the faith that it also presumes.[32] It is constitutive, because when the disciples of Jesus gathered around the eucharistic meal on the day of the Resurrection as a sign of life through death, they bound themselves together into the Christian community. It is this gathering to which they were called together (*ekkaleô*) and thus become the church (*ekklesia*).[33]

As has already been observed, however, experience indicates that weekly church attendance is no longer a matter-of-fact part of belief, and that for many the dimensions discussed here are not necessarily connected with participation in the Eucharist on Sunday. It will have to be considered to what degree this conflicts with the Christian dimensions of Sunday as described, as this tradition has always been summed up in the paired concepts of Sunday rest and Sunday worship attendance. It is an open question how these two elements are manifesting themselves in the present ecclesiastical/social context. In the preceding we have seen that many changes have occurred. But these changes have not so much eliminated the Christian value pattern for Sundays as transformed it. In order to discern that, it is important to see that these elements have entered into new connections with the culture, through which Sunday has attained a different profile. That this has made the Christian celebration of Sunday vulnerable, does not need to be demonstrated. A critical evaluation of liturgical design could contribute to strengthening this profile and its attaining an air of vitality.

7. PROFILING SUNDAY AS A DAY OF REST

From a more general social perspective Odo Marquard argues for the upgrading of Sunday as a necessary and regular reservation in time.[34] He

---

[31] So E. HENAU: De zin van de zondagsheiliging, in HENAU & HAQUIN: *De zondag* 103.

[32] See A. VERGOTE: De zondag. Een culturele verworvenheid, in HENAU & HAQUIN: *De zondag* 39.

[33] See L.-M. CHAUVET: *Symbole et sacrement. Une relecture sacramentelle de l'existence chrétienne* (= Cogitatio fidei 144) (Paris 1990) 190-191.

[34] O. MARQUARD: Kleine Philosophie des Festes, in U. SCHULTZ (ed.): *Das Fest. Eine Kulturgeschichte von der Antike bis zur Gegenwart* (Munich 1988) 413-420, esp. 418-419.

points to the rising feast culture that results in the everyday being eliminated and transformed into feast. Contradictory as it sounds, every day
has become a feast day, because one can only speak of a feast day if there
are also normal days. Furthermore, the inclination to make every day
into a feast leads to a levelling out of the weekly rhythm and a perversion and devaluation of feast.[35] But who will turn earth into heaven,
makes it hell; with this observation Marquard brings down the inclination to total feast, what he terms the *Moratorium des Alltags*. To provide
a counterweight to this trend toward total feast, both the everyday and
Sunday must be surrounded with more care. The need to relieve the
everyday must be reduced, for instance by the further humanization of
labour, and Sunday must be revalued and upgraded as an alleviation and
intermission in the everyday rhythm of living. Sunday is necessary in
order to deal well with the everyday. To the extent that Sunday loses its
strength, the need for total feast becomes greater. Sunday is thus of great
importance for a responsible way of living.

Strictly speaking, any day at random could fulfil this function, and
Sunday is thus negotiable. From the Christian perspective, however, the
dimensions which give the day its content are exclusively connected
with Sunday, and not with any other day of the week. Even though one
might wish to abandon the Christian hegemony of Sunday, it is still not
obvious that any other day could take over this function,[36] however
much the multi-faith society might be justification for a movable day of
rest so that the mutually diverging days of rest of the different faiths
might be respected. There is a good deal of agreement with regard to
making working time and leisure time more flexible, but with regard to
the discussion regarding Sunday it is precisely a collective day of rest
which is being argued, on the ground that this would encourage social
cohesion in a way that dispersed or moveable moments of rest would
not. Because the specific character of Sunday has been so interwoven
with the centuries of history in our Western culture, it cannot now be
easily separated out. At least, that would appear to be the lesson of previous attempts that have been made to break through the traditional
hegemony of Sunday and the week. After both the French Revolution,
at the end of the eighteenth century, and the Russian Revolution at the

---

[35] See also L. VAN TONGEREN: *In het ritme van de tijd. Over de samenhang tussen tijd
en liturgie* (Baarn 1999) 31-33.
[36] See also BERNTS: De verstoorde zondagsrust.

beginning of the twentieth attempts were made to do away with the seven day week and Sunday, but in both cases after several years the revolutionaries were forced to reintroduce the week and Sunday.[37]

Although there are tendencies to which one can point which would make Sunday into a day like any other, and although the pattern of activity on Sunday shows many similarities with that of other days free of labour, the strong feelings surrounding the discussion on the 24-hour economy also demonstrated how much value is attached to Sunday as a counterpoint. This also provided a signal that there are not only inclinations toward the blurring and homogenization of time, but also toward giving it greater depth. Concern for spiritual well-being is no longer exclusively coupled with traditional ecclesiastical/liturgical forms, however, but has entered into connections with forms of relaxation and reflection that promote not only psychic but social and physical well-being: social life, sports, cultural excursions, visits to family and friends – all of which are contemporary, salutary designs for Sunday as a day of rest. Regular participation in the Sunday worship service is for many also an important component in filling in Sunday in a meaningful manner. After all, Sunday church attendance has not disappeared; it has only had to yield its being the obvious component of Sunday. It has been transformed into an option of choice. If for a long time the liturgy was one of the few possibilities for spending free time outside the home on Sunday, at the moment the leisure culture presents an enormous selection with which liturgy must compete.

Despite its new content, Sunday still functions as a day of rest that breaks through the social rhythm of the week. It is a day which is focused on other activities, which are beneficial for body and spirit, and in which people experience the ways that life can be deepened or elevated. In this manner, Sunday can be a window on the transcendent – which is how Alois Müller formulated the most fundamental significance of the Christian Sunday.[38] Seeing Sunday rest not only in relation to labour, as was the case for a long time, creates an opening for approaching free time in other than functional terms. When Sunday rest transcends functionality and becomes 'purposeless' (that is to say,

---

[37] Ph. HARNONCOURT: Der Kalender, in Ph. HARNONCOURT & Hj. AUF DER MAUR: *Feiern im Rhythmus der Zeit* 2/1 (= Gottesdienst der Kirche. Handbuch der Liturgiewissenschaft 6,1) (Regensburg 1994) 40-41.

[38] MÜLLER: Sonntagstheologie von unten.

not directed toward a purpose), it can become a symbol of grace and refer to the transcendent dimension of existence.[39] The concrete design of Sunday is in part determined by history, and therefore for Müller is also in a certain sense relative and secondary. The way in which the Christian celebration of Sunday takes shape in the liturgy is not the only valuable design for Sunday, as though there were no salvation outside the church. The church can not, and may not, impose its will on society any longer, out of a view that proclaims that it has all the answers for all realms.[40] What it can do is to apply its efforts toward a humanization of Sunday, which it is in fact doing by making a substantive contribution to the debate on the 24-hour economy. From a Christian perspective, the importance does not lie in the competition with a secular Sunday but in the concern for retaining Sunday and to guarantee its quality.

For those who see the transformations of the traditional Christian content of Sunday as contemporary congruencies, these no longer appear so great a threat to Sunday. Sunday only appears to be in danger should it be completely offered up to the domination of society by economic concerns, and thus subordinated to production, consumption and commerce on purely rational grounds.

8. SUNDAY LITURGY

The substantive theological dimensions which have been connected with Sunday from time immemorial manifest themselves principally in the liturgical gathering. In the joyous collective celebration of the Eucharist and Resurrection on the first day of the week, believers commemorate the Living Lord with whom they are linked in mutual commitment.[41] For many, participation in the Sunday worship service may not today be the only content for a Christian Sunday, though it still remains a very important one. This does not, however, effect the substantive meaning of

---

[39] MÜLLER: Sonntagstheologie von unten 239-241; HENAU: De zin van de zondagsheiliging 104.

[40] MÜLLER: Sonntagstheologie von unten 245.

[41] Although a tendency can be perceived in the churches of the Reformation toward more frequent celebration of the Lord's Supper, in the ecumenical perspective speaking exclusively of an intrinsic connection between Sunday and Eucharist must be somewhat relativized.

Sunday; that, after all, does not depend on the number of participants. But this development does invite critical reflection on present practice. What strikes one in this, is that to an increasing degree Sunday is being uncoupled from its substantive dimensions. That can be concluded from the shift in the time for the Sunday celebration, and from the changes in the nature and character of this celebration.

As I have already indicated, since 1966 the possibility has existed for celebrating the Sunday liturgy on the preceding Saturday evening. Actually this is not a shift to another day, because according to the old tradition, which continues to live on in Jewish time calculation, a day comprises the period from sunset to sunset. Saturday evening is thus the beginning of Sunday. But in fact many will experience this as a shift, because our experience of time has ingrained in us the sense that a new day begins at midnight. Thus although holding a Sunday celebration on Saturday evening is historically defensible, this does not fit with our present experience of time. Experience shows that over the last few years this period has been pushed further and further up. This has taken place not on the ground of substantive reasons, but of practical considerations. Ever more parishes are offering the opportunity to fulfil the Sunday obligation in the early afternoon of Saturday. The hope is to lower the threshold by adding a more attractive hour. You can go to church at the same time you do your Saturday shopping. Moreover, within various non-affiliated pastoral settings there is a growing tendency to move the Sunday liturgy all the way back to Friday, because of a shortage of pastoral staff on the weekend. This is happening to an increasing extent in nursing homes and prisons because of the limited availability of pastors and the thinner rosters for other staff on Sunday. A shift in time to this extent eliminates both the substantive connection, as well as the experiential connection with Sunday.

The introduction of prayer services and celebrations of the word and communion (termed 'celebrations in the absence of a priest' in various countries) have also fundamentally affected the character of Sunday. The intrinsic link between Sunday and the Eucharist as a sign of the presence of the Living Lord in the midst of the community is lost. Nor is there any positive argument of substance to serve as a foundation for the introduction of these services as an alternative for the Eucharist, but only purely pragmatic considerations. Celebrations of this nature arose because of the problem of insufficient clergy, which ecclesiastical authorities have found no way to solve, and therefore liturgy has been asked to pay the price. By expressly not opting for broader entrance to the clergy, the implicit (but no less deliberate for that) choice has been made to limit opportunities for celebrating the Eucharist. By this, Sunday has indirectly been dropped as the day of the Eucharist. Preserving the traditional priesthood has prevailed over respect for the legitimate desire of the community to celebrate the Eucharist. The alternatives which people in the parish have been forced to choose may well be very meaningful and well designed celebrations in their own right, but they can not do justice to the eucharistic dimension of Sunday, and to the significance of the Eucharist as germ of the community.[42]

The shift in the time of celebration and the replacement of the Eucharist by another sort of celebration are facets that specifically touch upon Sunday. They would seem to be more situation-linked solutions, in order to reach as many people as possible and offer them opportunities to fulfil their Sunday obligation, than powerful expressions of the symbolic character of Sunday. The protection of a familiar custom in a somewhat altered form takes precedence over safeguarding the inherent significance. Apparently we are more attached to the ritual than to that which the ritual expresses.

Although the pastoral motives and interests for introducing these changes with regard to Sunday liturgy are understandable, it is also desirable to take a look at other possibilities that might be able to strengthen the symbolic function of Sunday, while taking into account both the substantive aspects of Sunday and changed circumstances. The revitalization of Sunday liturgy would be indispensable for this.

The first element which appears unavoidable in connection with that is a far-reaching reorganization. With the leadership of various dioceses it can be asked if we, despite the reductions already carried out, still do not have too many church buildings. Does it promote the vitality of a parish

---

[42] I have already tried to show elsewhere that this type of celebration is at the very least open to challenge on theological and historical grounds, and on grounds of content, and in any case does not offer a real alternative for the Eucharist; see L. VAN TONGEREN: De niet-eucharistische viering als een nieuwe vorm van liturgie, in W. LOGISTER et al. (eds.): *Twintig jaar ontwikkelingen in de theologie. Tendensen en perspectieven* (Kampen 1987) 205-219. We do not celebrate Easter by lighting the paschal candle, sharing the light and reading the Easter gospel three days after Easter. It might well be a ritual that refers to Easter, but it is not an alternative for the Easter celebration. In the same way, sprinkling with water can well refer to baptism, but that action is not the celebration of Baptism. Similarly, an isolated communion rite is not the celebration of the Eucharist, even if many do increasingly experience and accept it as such.

to maintain the status quo for as long as possible and attempt, through all
sorts of emergency measures, to keep what is on offer there at the same
level, only to ultimately have to come to the conclusion that capitulation
is unavoidable?[43] One then all too quickly finds oneself caught up in a
negative spiral, which also has its effect on motivation and the image
being projected. Through reorganization the deployment of personnel can
be intensified, in larger teams spanning greater areas, which indeed will
have responsibility for more worship opportunities, but still fewer than
previously. Moreover, the liturgical offerings can be concentrated by this
combining of forces. Reorganization also means a concentration of the
church-goers, and that can have its positive side for everyone involved. A
space three-quarters full is simply more pleasant and inviting than a space
three-quarters empty. One can understand and feel sympathy for many
objections to reorganization, but when the reorganization cannot, in due
time, be avoided any more, why should it have been put off that long?
Postponement does not reduce the objections or pain.

A concentration of strength can moreover be conducive to the necessary improvements in quality. In our world today we have high expectations for quality in all areas of life, while liturgy is generally kept running on dedication, involvement and good intentions.[44] When
compared with social organizations, churches have a far higher percentage of volunteers, the majority of whom are active in the area of liturgy.
This does not mean, however, that the liturgy would not be well served
by a certain kind of professionalization; quite on the contrary! If liturgical ritual is to achieve authority, then the way it is carried out must be
well planned and executed. This requires strong (although invisible)
direction, and places high demands of the broadest nature on those
leading the liturgy. This means not only priests and pastoral workers,
but also lectors, cantors, choir directors and volunteers who lead services
of prayer and evening services. This summary already will indicate that
the roles of the worship leader are many.[45] There is a range of functions

[43] For a reflection on the divers aspects of reorganization and revitalization of the
community of faith, see the various contributions in A. MEIJERS (ed.): De parochie van
de toekomst (= Scripta canonica 2) (Louvain 1998).
[44] In this connection, see also H. GEYER: Gottesdienst im großstädtischen Kontext,
in Pastoraltheologie 87 (1998) 20-34.
[45] The various liturgical, theological (including the theology of clerical offices) and
juridical aspects of both the ordained and lay leader have been the subject of great interest in recent years. See, for example, G. LUKKEN: De voorganger in het spanningsveld

at stake here, all requiring their own competence, and all having their own demands for quality performance. The worship leader is no longer the priest/celebrant who carries out the prescribed rules of the unchanging performance as objectively and neutrally as possible, but with reverence and awe. The ritual has an interplay of functionaries who all must have mastery of their disciplines in combination with their ritual function. For instance, liturgy does not demand a concert pianist, but a professional musician who is able to combine his or her musical gifts with the role of accompanist for congregational singing, and who has developed a liturgical attitude or an instinctive feeling for liturgy. An attitude of this sort is desirable in all worship leaders, so that they know how to speak and how to move in what is generally a large space. Further, there is much asked from the pastors and volunteers who put together the services, in terms of their own creativity and inventiveness. They should have developed a feeling for the golden mean between distance and proximity, between the personal and the involved and sentimental. The demand and need for improving the quality of worship leaders is rising, both in regard to their ritual and their spiritual competence.

Another aspect that is of importance for a vital Sunday liturgy is a further differentiation of what is on offer. The traditional liturgy, as set down in the official books, has proven its value over the centuries and will certainly maintain its place in the liturgical spectrum. Experience shows, however, that there is a need for a more pluriform liturgy; people are frequently different from the basic model assumed by the books. The texts, generally handed down from the early Middle Ages, embody

van de liturgie, in *Tijdschrift voor liturgie* 71 (1987) 259-278; J. SIEMERINK: *Voorgaan in liturgie. Vorming van vrijwilligers* (= Theologie en empirie 14) (Kampen/Weinheim 1993); M. KLÖCKENER & K. RICHTER (eds.): *Wie weit trägt das gemeinsame Priestertum? Liturgischer Leitungsdienst zwischen Ordination und Beauftragung* (= Questiones disputatae 171) (Freiburg/Basel/Wien 1998); G. LUKKEN: Op zoek naar een nieuwe stijl van voorgaan, in *Tijdschrift voor liturgie* 82 (1998) 341-351; *Acteurs et ministères dans la liturgie* (special issue *La Maison-Dieu* (1998) no. 215); P. POST: Leidende kwaliteiten in het spel. Over liturgisch voorgaan, in H. BECK & R. NAUTA: (eds.): *Over leiden. Dynamiek en structuur van het religieus leiderschap* (Tilburg 1999) 57-78; *Praktische theologie* 26 (1999) (2): *Voorganger in de liturgie* (special issue); G. MATTHEEUWS: De voorganger in de eucharistie als sacrament van de ecclesiale Christus, in *Jaarboek voor liturgie-onderzoek* 15 (1999) 95-118. In this connection we must also mention the recent instruction from Rome regarding laity assisting priests in their duties: *Istruzione su alcune questioni circa la collaborazione dei fedeli laici al ministero dei sacerdoti* (Città del Vaticano 1997).

great depth and wisdom, and are often compressed theological tracts. They are, however, hard for many to understand, because they are outside their recognition. That does not say that alternatives are always so successful. Liturgy is more than an expression of one's own emotions and sentiments. Liturgy should also present one with something which transcends the self. That demands an open attitude of receptiveness and a willingness to be addressed, and that is other than liturgy which functions as a ventriloquist's dummy, a mouthpiece for one's own ideas. But it does also assume an existential proximity and recognizability; without this, liturgy becomes a meaningless ritual. When texts or ritual forms are experienced as worn thin or meaningless, why should we not lay them aside (at least temporarily) or modify them? In recent years that has happened, for example, with the use of incense. It was dispensed with by many as a ceremonious and almost magical element, after which it was rediscovered and has received a new role in a different form, now as a sensory support for the prayer of the community.

Following naturally from this is an argument for being more welcoming towards liturgical experimentation. Over the past years, in the continuation of liturgical renewal, there has been a lot of creative and inspiring work done, in which people have searched for contemporary design while retaining respect for tradition. They have searched for a discernable coupling between liturgy and the faith-dimension of personal life. These experiments could be further expanded on the basis of new insights, experiences and sources of inspiration. Pursuant to the often-heard complaint that the liturgy has become extremely verbal, rational and intellectual, one can for instance think of the development of the dimensions of liturgy that appeal to the senses, which so many experience as missing.[46] The use and furnishing of the church building will also play an important role in relation to this. The physical dimension of liturgy can be further developed when the statically designed liturgy in a no less statically used space is broken through.[47] Liturgical ritual is performed on a stage around which the people are gathered in

---

[46] In connection with this, see for instance the much discussed study by A. LOREN-ZER: *Das Konzil der Buchhalter. Die Zerstörung der Sinnlichkeit. Eine Religionskritik* (Frankfurt am Main 1981).

[47] See the reflections and designs of liturgists and architects, collected in response to a public competition for ideas for the structure of Christian worship in the third millennium, in P. POST (ed.): *Een ander huis. Kerkarchitectuur na 2000* (= Liturgie in perspectief 7) (Baarn 1997).

a way that makes it possible to observe all the actions in a glance. Could the liturgy not become more dynamic if, for instance, the altar and the lectern were not presented as one unit, but were in clearly separate locations to which the people make their way during the celebration?[48] Also the use of modern visual art as an integral component of the liturgy could stimulate a different sort of involvement. Experiments have shown that the use of art with liturgy can open up surprising perspectives, and that it produces equally surprising reactions through the sometimes alienating or shocking effect.[49] A final experiment that I would mention here involves the special musical design of a cantata or choral service, which actually already has somewhat of a tradition behind it in some Reformation churches. In Catholic churches a liturgy of this sort is almost unknown. The impetus for this in The Netherlands has been the oratorio-like projects by Huub Oosterhuis, in which large-scale, entirely musical works have been created on the basis of large text units from the Bible, forming the central component of the celebration. If only because of the difficulties in presenting works like this, there exists the danger that such a celebration becomes a performance. However inspiring this type of liturgy can be, it does not encourage the active participation of the community.

The examples given here must not be absolutized, nor are they intended to increase the value of liturgy as entertainment; they can, however, function as a source of inspiration for providing the regular Sunday celebration with an extra stimulus. Both innovative designs of this sort, and improving quality through a concentration of forces, greater differentiation and experimentation can intensify the experience of liturgy and give the Sunday liturgy a more powerful presence.

[48] See S. DE BLAAUW: De (her)inrichting van liturgische ruimten, in *Eredienstvaardig* 15 (1999) 112-116; L. VAN TONGEREN: The re-ordering of church buildings reconsidered (in preparation).

[49] Research on this has been undertaken in The Netherlands by R. Steensma. Various experiments are described and examined in R. STEENSMA: *In de spiegel van het beeld. Kerk en moderne kunst* (Baarn 1987); IDEM: De receptie van de tentoonstelling 'Met de dood in de ogen' in de Grote Kerk te Leeuwarden, in *Jaarboek voor liturgie-onderzoek* 8 (1992) 169-204; IDEM: Hedendaagse beeldende kunst in protestantse kerkdiensten, *Ibidem* 9 (1993) 133-144; IDEM: 'Jezus is boos' in de kerkdienst. Reacties op drie hedendaagse kunstwerken tijdens de eredienst, *Ibidem* 11 (1995) 223-258; IDEM: *Mysterie en vergezicht. Over het gebruik van hedendaagse beeldende kunst in de liturgie* (Baarn 1993); G. DINGEMANS, J. KRONENBURG & R. STEENSMA (eds.): *Kaïn of Abel... Kunst in de kerkdienst: twee vijandige broeders?* (= Religie en kunst 10) (Zoetermeer 1999).

9. CONCLUSION: THE RITE AND THE MYTH OF SUNDAY

In the midst of the commercialization of society and leisure time, and their increasing domination by economic forces, the classic Sunday rest and Sunday observance are being increasingly squeezed. As a day of rest, in the past Sunday perhaps made the labour system possible, or at least legitimized it.[50] One day free of labour made it possible to work the other six days. But at the same time, Sunday as a day of rest relativized the labour pattern through deliberately foregoing work one day per week. In that, Sunday has a critical function as a symbol that points to the rhythms of our life having more purpose than mere functionalism, and to grace. In that way the weekly day of rest structured the transcendent dimension of our being.

Now that faith and religion have withdrawn from the institutional, ecclesiastical context and are privatized and individualized, the observance of Sunday is no longer obviously expressed in participation in a liturgical gathering. The consequence is that the continuity of the liturgical expression and representation of the theological dimensions of Sunday are in decline. On the one hand, this raises questions about the way in which this liturgy is being given shape. On the other hand, it challenges us to go in search in our culture for other manifestations in which the faith or spiritual dimensions of Sunday are present. Various signals can be observed that point to the survival of these themes in other guises in a cultural/social context, so that they have indeed not disappeared from sight. Particularly in the area of the arts, both in the past and present the central themes of Sunday have been and are an inexhaustible source of inspiration. With their archetypical implications, creation, Eucharist, and the paschal triad of suffering, death and resurrection appeal so strongly to existential questions and experiences that they continually inspire artists to contemporary representations. Visitors to museums are confronted with them visually,[51] and visitors at music

---

[50] See V. PEETERS: Zondag zonder arbeid of arbeid zonder zondag, in HENAU & HAQUIN: De zondag 168.

[51] On Easter Monday in 1998, in the Boijmans Van Beuningen Museum in Rotterdam, by way of experiment a well-attended service of 'cultural morning prayer' was held. This service of word, image and prayer was located in the middle of an exhibition displaying a number of enormous tapestries which had recently been created by nine artists. See A. AUGUSTUS-KERSTEN: Liturgie in het hol van de leeuw?, in Eredienstvaardig 16 (2000) 84-88, and M. BARNARD: Een kerkdienst in een museum, in BARNARD & POST (eds.): Ritueel bestek 56-62.

festivals enjoy hearing the motifs worked out in musical form. In these constellations the fundamental dimensions are perhaps stripped of their familiar ritual foundation and design, but the central, substantive Christian motifs live on. The myth is apparently powerful enough; it will find its own way forward, both in the liturgical ritual patterns that have accompanied it throughout the ages, and in new connections with the surrounding culture.

ANDRÉ MULDER, JOS PIEPER & MARINUS VAN UDEN

FROM MYTH TO ACT
MODERN PILGRIMAGE TO SANTIAGO

1. INTRODUCTION

Pilgrimage as a phenomenon is in a state of flux. There is a great deal of activity in this field. Reference can be made to exhibitions, symposia on popular religion and pilgrimages and many publications. The last few years, for instance three voluminous handbooks[1] that describe more than 650 existing or lost holy places in The Netherlands were published and various papers and magazines are continuously interested in pilgrimages. In short: the ritual of pilgrimage is a cultural phenomenon of some significance.

As in former days contemporary pilgrims are concerned about the meaning of their journey and the hardship they may experience on their pilgrimage. In the Middle Ages pilgrims could find consolation in the Christian myth of redemption. Their day to day suffering on the long and dangerous journey to the holy place found a cognitive redefinition, thanks to the religious frame of reference belonging to a Christian pilgrimage. Because they are related to the biblical story, their experiences acquire significance and value, despite everything. The pilgrims raise their frustrations to a higher level by attaching a religious significance to them. Is this also the case today? Is it true, for example, that pilgrims who set out with secular motives, find that there are still other meanings that can begin to play a role as their pilgrimage proceeds? Are complexes of religious significance brought to light by the continual confrontation with Christian cultural elements? Does the 'myth' of Christianity begin to play a role in the interpretation of experiences? Or are other 'myths' involved nowadays?[2]

---

[1] P.J. MARGRY & C. CASPERS (eds.): *Bedevaartplaatsen in Nederland. Deel I: Noord- en Midden-Nederland* (Hilversum/Amsterdam 1997); *Deel II: Provincie Noord-Brabant* (Hilversum/Amsterdam 1998); *Deel III: Provincie Limburg* (Hilversum/Amsterdam 2000).

[2] Our approach of myths concurs with that of V. TURNER: Myth and symbol, in *International encyclopedia of the social sciences* 10 (1968) 567-582, p. 567 and Onno van der HART *et al.*: *Afscheidsrituelen in psychotherapie* (Baarn 1981) where they speak of

Attention for the use of the Christian myth as a meaning giving frame of reference is of special importance when we take the perspective of ritual as a Christian feast. Post discusses the question of the identity of (Christian) rituals in our culture.[3] He takes the concept of feast as a critical perspective for evaluating these rituals. Following Assmann he states that feast is the place of cultural anamnesis. In a feast people connect to the holy past in ritualised myth and give way to collective or cultural anamnesis. Feast is an anamnetic ritual. This means that one of the main features of a Christian feast is that it presents itself as a ritual of anamnesis, wherein aspects of the core story of Christ (passion, death, resurrection, ascension and second coming of Jesus) come to light in the mode of remembering and are connected to the present and the future. Post points at two other central aspects of feast. First, feast transcends the stream of activities in quotidian life, which is dominated by shortage and monotony. In contrast with normal life feast addresses the central issues of human life. Secondly, feast is connected with a group. This aspect points at *communitas* and participating in a group-culture. Transferred to a pilgrimage this perspective leads to the criterion that a pilgrimage is or becomes a Christian feast when the sacred narrative connected with the origins of the pilgrimage or the holy place become part of or dominate the frame of reference of the pilgrims during their pilgrimage. Rephrasing our questions about the use of the Christian myth we might ask: can a modern pilgrimage be interpreted as a Christian anamnetic ritual? We will deal with this question within the framework of the pilgrimage to Santiago de Compostela. Answering the question we also make a few remarks on the other two aspects of feast: contrast and group-involvement.

Nowadays the pilgrimage to Santiago exerts an enormous attraction on many people. Hundreds of thousands travel to Northern Spain to visit the shrine of the Apostle James. It is not easy to find a common denominator for all these pilgrims – maybe the only thing they have in common is the fact that they arrive at Compostela (or wish to arrive: not everyone is going to make it). It is no longer possible – if it ever was the case at all – to speak of 'the' pilgrim on his way to Santiago de

"sacred narratives" and "tribal stories" which relate us to what used to be. In other words, they are frames of interpretation within which experiences may acquire meaning.

[3] P. POST: *Het wonder van Dokkum. Verkenningen van populair religieus ritueel* (Nijmegen 2000) 127-133. See also Part I of this collection.

Compostela. By now we know from various studies that the motives and experiences with regard to the journey to Santiago de Compostela are quite different for the individual pilgrims, as is the way in which they go on a pilgrimage and their possible recordings of the journey in the shape of logbooks or diaries.[4] Furthermore, the journey to Santiago de Compostela may fulfil different functions in the life of a pilgrim and there may also be personal variations in the appropriation of a traditional ritual.[5]

Some years ago we studied diaries and logbooks of pilgrims to Santiago de Compostela. In an attempt to get some grip on this colourful procession of travellers, we introduced a typology that makes it possible to chart the pilgrims' involvement with sacral elements. If we see the pilgrimage as a way of travelling the pilgrim will at least distinguish himself from other travellers because of his focus on a specific sort of destination, namely, a place of pilgrimage. The journey there can be characterised as a sacred journey. We used the involvement with what is sacred, in this case its realisation in the Christian tradition, as a criterion for classification under our typology. The typology presupposes that, though the pilgrims' involvement with the religious domain (things sacred or God) that is part of their pilgrimages may be different for each individual, five types of pilgrims can be distinguished within this plurality, i.e. the religious tourist, the museological-religious tourist, the believing tourist, the quest pilgrim and the true pilgrim.[6]

---

[4] A. DE JONG: Meegaan met pelgrims naar Santiago de Compostela. Verslag van een onderzoeksproject in wording, in J. PIEPER, P. POST & M. VAN UDEN (eds): *Bedevaart en pelgrimage. Tussen traditie en moderniteit* (Baarn 1994) 59-79; A. MULDER: Op zoek naar de ware pelgrim. Over pelgrimage en toerisme, in M. VAN UDEN, J. PIEPER & P. POST (eds): *Oude sporen, nieuwe wegen. Ontwikkelingen in bedevaartonderzoek* (Baarn 1995) 15-51; J. PIEPER & R. VAN UDEN: Op weg naar Santiago de Compostela. Ervaringen van pelgrims, in VAN UDEN, PIEPER & POST (eds): *Oude sporen, nieuwe wegen* 53-83; P. POST: Pelgrims tussen traditie en moderniteit. Een verkenning van hedendaagse pelgrimsverslagen, in PIEPER, POST & VAN UDEN (eds): *Bedevaart en pelgrimage* 7-37; P. POST: Le pélerin moderne. Un rite chrétien entre tradition et (post) modernité, in *Concilium* 266 (1996) 13-24; J. RODING: Hedendaagse pelgrims naar Santiago de Compostela. Over pelgrimage en religieuze identiteit, in M. VAN UDEN, J. PIEPER & E. HENAU (eds): *Bij Geloof. Over bedevaarten en andere uitingen van volksreligiositeit* (Hilversum 1991) 83-103.

[5] E.O. FEINBERG: *Strangers and pilgrims on the Camino de Santiago in Spain. The perpetuation and recreation of meaningful performance* (Princeton 1985).

[6] MULDER: Op zoek naar de ware pelgrim 15-51.

In order to understand the Christian interpretation the pilgrims give to their experiences and the contents of their interpretative frames, other than those relating to Christianity, the examination of diaries and logbooks has been continued. For the time being the corpus of diaries and logbooks to be examined has been limited to the experiences put down in writing by walkers. The long travelling time, the physical hardships and the profound experience of liminality make the experiences of this group of pilgrims to the most intense and lead them to reflect in their travel accounts extensively on nature, meaning, purpose and significance of the journey.[7]

Next we concentrated our attention in this contribution on the type of the quest pilgrim. The reason for this is that we also wanted to gain an insight in interpretative frames placed outside Christianity. In our typology we described this category of travellers as follows:[8]

> The quest pilgrim is the person who partially identifies with sacred aspects, (…) During the journey he is open to transcendental experiences and makes a more or less conscious choice to travel this route to gain new meaning. These pilgrims go the way of the pilgrim, attracted to it by the fact that many have travelled this route before and that it is bound to be meaningful, even though they do not know what a contemporary pilgrim looks like exactly. These travellers hope that their journey will provide them with answers to a number of questions, that they will find solutions to one or more problems. They are, however, somewhat ambivalent towards the experiences during the journey and its outcome. They are not sure if the answers, generated during the journey by the religious-existential experiences they have, comply with their existential questions and can be brought to bear on everyday life. They experience a certain ambiguity in what happens to them. The journey appeals to them and is deeply affecting, but there are questions left. It remains a matter of searching and probing.

What is especially noticeable in this type of pilgrim is the ambivalence towards the experiences that the journey produces and the difficulty of interpreting these experiences. Whereas his maximal involvement allows the true pilgrim to contextualise the experiences and to interpret them with the help of the myth of the Christian faith, with which he comes into contact in various ways during the journey, his lack of complete

---

[7] V. TURNER & E. TURNER: *Image and pilgrimage in Christian culture. An anthropological perspective* (Oxford 1978).

[8] MULDER: *Op zoek naar de ware pelgrim* 33-34.

surrender to the Christian gospel forces the quest pilgrim to find meaning and significance himself in the profound experiences of the journey to Santiago de Compostela. This makes him perfectly suited to help us gain an insight in 'new myths', if any. At the same time, the Christian myth need not be completely absent, though there may be other possible sources of interpretation.

We must opt for an open approach and try to answer the question if, one or more contemporary myths (or parts thereof), completely or partly different from those belonging to the Christian faith, come to light in the way quest pilgrims interpret the experiences related to their journey. In other words: is it possible to find new patterns to interpret experiences connected with their journey within the group of the quest pilgrims?

2. DATA-ANALYSIS: SELECTION, CLUSTERING, DESCRIPTION AND INTERPRETATION OF THE DIARIES

2.1. Selection of diaries

In order to answer our question we first of all made a selection from the corpus of diaries and logbooks of pilgrims to Santiago that we have collected. Among the 37 files available, 13 appeared to be accounts of walkers. We carefully read these files. Following the method that was used to carry out earlier research, these 13 walkers were classified with the help of the typology.[9] The classification of types among these walkers was as follows: one religious tourist, two believing tourists, four quest pilgrims, six true pilgrims. Consequently we have four travel accounts left as research material to deal with our question. In this contribution we will discuss two of them, namely the files of Marijke Schoone and Jan van der Heijden, as these were the most extensive. Once more the files were carefully read. The experiences of these pilgrims were arranged by means of key words. While doing so we used, among other things, key words used in earlier research.[10] Eventually Marijke Schoone's account yielded 23 subjects or key words. The subjects we came across in these letters were: walking, the backpack, the stamp, the sun, encounters on the road, encounters with those who

---

[9] See MULDER: Op zoek naar de ware pelgrim 31-34 for the procedure used.
[10] PIEPER & VAN UDEN: Op weg naar Santiago de Compostela.

stayed at home, evening, water, fatigue, wind, scenery, night, the road, receiving mail, monuments, the body, earth, prayer, the staff, morning, the tent, food and women.

Marijke Schoone, a pedagogue, walked from April 1986 till May 1987 from the Hague to Santiago de Compostela and back again as far as Bruges. Most of the time she travelled on her own. She mostly spent the nights in her tent, but in the winter she stayed in visitors' wings of monasteries, churches and such places. She cooked her own food as often as possible. She kept the people at home or her supporters informed of her experiences by means of circular letters. We have 123 pages of text at our disposal. She wrote while travelling, sometimes there were long intervals. The last letters date from 3, respectively 5 years after the journey. The dates of the letters: 1 May 1986; 3-14 June 1986; 8/9 September 1986; 1 November 1986; 12 November 1986; 1 March 1987; 1 April 1987; 25 April 1987; 4 August 1990; 7 June/12 November 1990; 17 April 1992.

Jan van der Heijden, a former history teacher, covered the route Liege – Santiago de Compostela on foot in 1990. Out on the road he rejects lifts that are offered to him and he travels back by train. He spends the nights in hotels, in private homes, in monasteries, in Gites d'Etapes, out in the open and in refuges. He usually eats where he also spends the night or in restaurants. He wrote his diary while travelling, usually in the afternoon and/or in the evening. We have 85 pages of text at our disposal. These pages yielded 48 subjects. The subjects we found in Van der Heijden's material are: the weather, walking, memories, the stamp, the pilgrim, reflection, being alone, drinking, taking leave, reading, money, the shell, the road, laundry, mail, intention, the backpack, scenery, the people at home, disorientation, the body, animals, travelling, walking, resting, singing, the funeral, clothing, accommodation, mood, surprise, music, fatigue, the church, the staff, situation, leaving, buildings, coincidence, frontier, sleeping, history, shopping, arrival, encounters, food, the pocket knife and *communitas*.

As examples of the material we have at our disposal we show the passages from the two pilgrims' diaries that are part of the subject 'walking'. Between brackets we mention the page numbers in the files.

2.1.1. Marijke Schoone

For Marijke Schoone walking was some undertaking (1.1). Arriving in Santiago is for her "merely the afterbirth". Walking, setting out, that is the main thing. When she shares part of the route with somebody else, she finds that every person has his own rhythm of walking. (1.4). Walking is peaceful (like a Sunday) and enjoying nature (1.6). She also observes that she herself has an alternating rhythm and that she can slowly start to increase the pace (1.9). But first she has to find her ideal rhythm (2.3). From time to time she goes through bad patches, but while she walks she regains her sense of humour (1.9). Walking takes time, as does seeing, hearing and smelling all that she comes across on the road and, not to forget, meeting people (2.4). When she has a stomach-ache, she thinks that walking ("stepping out") is bound to cure it (2.5). Sometimes she has the feeling to be pushed forward (2.6). Sometimes walking on busy roads is dangerous, motorists show no mercy (2.8). But there are also polite drivers (2.11). On some parts of the route "stepping out" is a drudge: "stepping – stopping – stepping – stopping" (3.24). While walking you think of the people at home. Sometimes you walk because you have set yourself an intention (of prayer): ten steps for Willemien (2.8). While walking texts emerge, while walking you generate ideas to combat social problems, such as unemployment (2.10), or about your own future (6.1). You are heading for the unknown (2.11). Time and again stepping out is, figuratively speaking, a matter of falling and getting up again. Getting lost is part of walking (7.21). Later on it appears that walking has become a symbol for life: courageously going on, step by step (10.5). For her walking is a form of prayer and meditation (11.2).

2.1.2. Jan van der Heijden

Jan van der Heijden regularly takes a close look at his walking. He reports whether it was all right, pleasant, perfect, laborious or grinding, whether he was climbing or walking on flat land, whether he was hampered by blisters etc. Good and bad periods alternate, but on the whole he finds it a great and beautiful experience (8). Singing or humming particular songs make light work of walking (7, 10 and 32). Sometimes he calls a stage "a good walk". He notices that gradually the low hills are taking less effort. He always mentions the distances covered, the speed (pace). After a rest the first few metres are the most difficult (16). When the going gets tough, it is sometimes due to the backpack or his walking technique (25, 33, 43). Walking causes him no special problems, because he is well trained, he thinks (54). Walking in the country leads to beautiful experiences (71) and he enjoys it intensely and no two days are the same (49).

2.2. Clustering

Having determined the subjects and having subjected the material to a preliminary arrangement, the researchers, independent of each other, put aside the subjects that contained only superficial religious-existential experiences and clustered the remaining subjects.[11] Comparison of the results showed that the following seven clusters can be formed:

1. Departure and taking leave;
2. Going the road;
2a. Experiences relating to body and walking;
2b. Experiences relating to nature;
2c. Experiences relating to the pilgrim's own path in life;
2d. Experiences relating to other people;
2e. Experiences relating to (religious) culture;
3. Arrival and return.

The seven clusters that were established were then checked as to their relevance against the eleven other files of the pilgrims who walked. From this check it appeared that nearly all the profound religious-existential experiences (insofar present) which the pilgrims described in their files fitted these seven clusters. Consequently these clusters also appear to be relevant to other files, not only the ones that gave rise to them.

Our research is aimed at answering the question in what way experiences are interpreted during the journey. Therefore we excluded categories 1 and 3 from the present analysis. Using the five remaining clusters (2a up to and including 2e) we continued the analysis of the Schoone and Van der Heijden files. Besides, this clustering clearly demonstrates that the threefold structure (separation phase, threshold phase, reintegration phase) ascribed by Van Gennep to rites (of passage) can still be applied to contemporary pilgrimages. The clustering also shows that the phase of liminality (threshold phase) described in detail by Turner[12] indeed leads to probing and wide-ranging experiences.

---

[11] Cf. PIEPER & VAN UDEN: Op weg naar Santiago de Compostela 72-73, for this procedure.
[12] V. TURNER: Pilgrimage and Communitas, in *Studia missionalia* 23 (1974) 305-327; TURNER & TURNER: *Image and Pilgrimage*.

2.3. Description

In our search of profound experiences and (fragments of) old and new myths about pilgrimages we have summarily described the subcategories under 2, 'Going the road', with regard to our two pilgrims.

2.3.1. *The file of Marijke Schoone*

(a) Experiences relating to body and walking

Walking is a physical activity whose pace you must get to know. It is also a sensory activity (seeing, smelling and hearing) that takes up a great deal of time. Sometimes it is a struggle. The backpack puts more and more weight on the shoulders. Walking reduces physical complaints: stomach-ache. Food is an important factor. You must constantly look out for possible places to do your shopping. The journey confronts you with what is physically possible and impossible, with complaints: blisters, stomach-ache, backache, nails that break. You must take well care of yourself to stay healthy and you must react to what your body tells you. Fatigue is a recurring phenomenon: walking, but also communicating in a foreign language is tiring. You learn to live with it.

(b) Experiences relating to nature

The journey is a direct encounter with nature. The sun becomes a partner you cannot always cope with, but the next moment it will talk to you, smile at you and help you. The experience stemming from nature is an intense one. You begin to see animals as your friends. Walking in the country has a soothing effect. You enjoy nature in contrast with towns or crowded camping-sites. The constant changes in scenery are experienced as an adventure. Stepping out and enjoying its beauty. The earth becomes Mother Earth. God is nature's creator.

(c) Experiences relating to the pilgrim's own path in life

"Stepping out", as Marijke calls it, symbolises her own life: falling down and getting up again; life is walking. The route is not fixed, but takes on shape as she walks it. The way she goes is/becomes the Way of God. God does not guarantee a tranquil journey, but he does ensure a safe arrival. St James gradually takes on the shape of a helper, companion and friend on this journey.

Making the journey on foot, taking the road, is what counts. Walking generates ideas, for example about the problem of unemployment, but also about relations, about yourself and your future. Being a pilgrim is stepping out and meditating, silence and talking. It is a way of life. It is an adventure.

(d) Experiences relating to other people

Meeting people feels good. Conversations you have are comforting. Walking is meeting: moving out towards known and unknown people. It is wonderful to experience the hospitality and friendship of people. There is a lot to be learned from people: advice about walking, but also about walking the path of your life. Going on a pilgrimage also means walking with intentions for somebody else.

(e) Experiences relating to (religious) culture

Culture is in contrast to nature: building projects that threaten nature, stinking, unwholesome cities, overcrowded camping-sites, anonymous neighbourhoods. Sometimes does culture contain an element of beauty: the harbour of Rotterdam, certain houses, churches and chapels along the route. The pilgrim's signs along the way are reminiscent of an age-old pilgrim's tradition. The Guardian Angel/St James becomes more and more a friend and helper on your path in life and is finally experienced as God. A pilgrim is poor and faces difficulties on his way. The journey makes you think about all sorts of religious themes: Mary, the shortage of priests, women priests. Experiencing a blessing is comforting. You find that praying remains difficult. Love of people is divine love.

2.3.2. The file of Jan van der Heijden

(a) Experiences relating to body and walking

Jan's body determines his walking. You feel the backpack, at first it is troublesome (painful shoulders), but in the end it becomes part of you. Gradually you learn to bear yourself in such a way that you achieve the best possible way of walking. You feel the heaviness of the weight. You also feel your feet, your nails start to hurt, blisters appear on your toes, there are corns. The awareness of the body becomes so intense that the feet are talked about in loving terms. Furthermore, your own physical condition is measured against that of other people: as an older person he can hold his own condition with younger people in terms of fitness.

Then you discover the necessity of taking rests, taking physical fatigue seriously, eating in time, and the value of taking good physical care of yourself. You feel the road when you go at an even pace. You learn how to cope with walking on different sorts of road surfaces, how to face inclines. Jan notices how fatigue not only takes the edge off his powers of observation, but also off his powers of enjoyment. You discover that the body is the crucial instrument for the pilgrimage, and sometimes fear comes over you that the body will let you down.

The physical activity of walking is subject of daily reflection and is liable to varying classifications. At times it is all right, at other times it is laborious. You learn how to ascend hills. You find that walking makes a good combination with singing or humming, that they are pleasant things to do and make walking easier. When you sing texts, you will appreciate them more. You learn that the available energy is proportional to your attitude. Jan is so taken up by walking, covering distances, his fatigue, etc., that he has little time left to think about things. According to Jan, suffering physical pain is part of going on a pilgrimage. Making a pilgrimage is making an effort (that is why he does not hitchhike). You have to carry your burden.

Undertaking the journey opens your eyes to the value of simple things, for example: resting with no other food than water and bread. The lack of comfort makes you enjoy a simple bed, a tap to wash yourself. Unpretentiousness is part of making the pilgrimage, a pilgrim does not live in luxury. Whether or not food can be found in remote villages is an adventure: going on a pilgrimage is an adventure.

(b) Experiences relating to nature

Walking in the country produces pleasant and pleasurable experiences. The experience of varying scenery leads to insights in yourself: you learn which landscape appeals to you most psychologically. The experiences in the country cause an intense feeling of happiness, especially if you are all by yourself and you can look for miles and miles in all directions. Human interference interrupts these experiences of happiness: traffic, mining, and pollution. When walking in the country you become acutely aware of the necessity of rain for the crops. Observing animals also contributes to feelings of happiness: these encounters can turn out to be intense. But these feelings of happiness may also be disturbed: traffic victims, vicious dogs, the screeching of a crow. Nature is a mirror of life: harmony and dissonance. In a word: reality.

(c) Experiences relating to the pilgrim's own path in life

Jan sees the long way to Santiago as a symbol of his path of life. He reads the Psalms and spiritual literature and compares his experiences with those of others (Aafjes, Post, Andriessen). On arrival in Santiago he reflects on the course his life has taken. Going on a pilgrimage causes a feeling of gratefulness, but it also leads to the question if you are able and allowed to do it just like that: getting away from everyday life without a care. Then there is the anxiety about the return to the normal world. As a pilgrim he does not want to concern himself with this matter. He wants to lead a carefree life, like a shepherd, and he finds that this is exactly what he does.

(d) Experiences relating to other people

Encounters often produce a feeling of gratefulness and happiness in Jan. The journey is also a constant meeting of new people. Often he meets with surprising and spontaneous kindness and hospitality. Meeting fellow-pilgrims and exchanging experiences makes a day to a special day. You share the same destination and sharing the road unites, even though the motives may be different. You belong together, you share things, you are aware of friendship.

(e) Experiences relating to (religious) culture

Jan has questions with regard to his faith. An encounter with a monk also generates questions in him. He realises that he is not a dogmatic believer, but that he is a pilgrim who is open to the mystery of believing. There is also the element of mystery in accidental occurrences. Neither is he a firm believer in the miracles performed by Saint James. His taking part in celebrations sometimes gives him a religious feeling because of the esthetical quality of the singing. Jan notices a cultural difference between Belgium/Northern France and Southern France: in the North people rather keep to themselves. There are also cultural differences between the Spanish and the Dutch. Going on a pilgrimage is plunging into tradition and the performance of rituals in Santiago links you with the millions of people who preceded you.

In the churches it is the music, the singing, the effect of space and the light that move him. He enjoys the beautiful architecture. Churches produce in him feelings of inner harmony and peace. The services in Santiago move him strongly, as do the ones at Lourdes on the way back, for that matter.

2.4. Interpretation

What are the core experiences and the matching interpretations of these two quest pilgrims? Below we will give a so-called consensus interpretation[13] of the material pertaining to Schoone and Van der Heijden that was put together in the clusters.

(a) The body and walking

For the pilgrim the body is the crucial instrument for the journey, the most important tool to make the pilgrimage. Walking determines everything. The pilgrim is faced with his physical possibilities and impossibilities and realises that bodily care is of vital importance in order to make the journey. This includes: taking sufficient rest and in time; taking care of muscles, and especially of the feet; taking care of getting enough to eat and drink. A pilgrim learns to feel and bear pain. Suffering pain is part and parcel of being a pilgrim. This also leads to the experience of unpretentiousness. The basic conditions for the upkeep of the body are a simple bed, rest, water and bread.

(b) Nature

The pilgrim is acutely aware of nature. Both the variety in scenery, as the encounters with all sorts of animals are sources of pleasure. The pilgrim becomes an ally of nature and feels inner resistance against human disruption and pollution of nature. Natural beauty can bring about profound emotions that may lead to experiencing God as the creator of nature.

(c) The personal path in life

Walking leads to silence, meditation and an inner conversation. And these make that the pilgrim experiences travelling the road as a symbol of travelling his own path in life. Walking and all the aspects of, for example, falling down and getting up again, getting lost, fatigue and recovery, are reasons to look back at his own life and to look forward at the future. For Marijke Schoone God becomes a beacon on the route of her pilgrimage, as well as on her own path in life.

(d) Other people

The way of the pilgrim is one of constantly meeting new people. These encounters are informative. When they meet with the people who live

---

[13] See our note 11.

along the route, the pilgrims experience a surprising degree of hospitality. When meeting with fellow-pilgrims they experience feelings of solidarity and friendship, despite all the differences in motives. Experiences with regard to travelling the route are shared.

(e) (Religious) culture

The pilgrim plunges into a tradition, travels an ancient route, performs ancient rituals. On the one hand this leads to religious questions: what does St James mean to me in this day and age? On the other hand, tradition takes on a personal significance: rituals performed in churches along the route lead to experiences of harmony and peace and St James acquires the function of guardian angel who ultimately shows to the way to God. Walking the old pilgrim's route, which leads to a series of encounters and confrontations with people, churches and landscapes, gives also rise to reflection on life, society, environment, faith, church, etc. While travelling the route, the pilgrim is faced with all sorts of 'coincidences', which he sees as so many mysteries.

To sum up, it may be said that there is a strong emphasis on the body/walking and coping with pain; on nature and human interference with it; on the pilgrim's way as a symbol of the path in life; on meeting fellow-humans in hospitality, friendship and solidarity and on the personal faith in confrontation with the Christian tradition of Santiago.

3. CONCLUSION AND DISCUSSION

The first question we address is the role of the Christian myth in the diaries of the pilgrims and in connection with this the question whether the modern pilgrimage to Santiago can be called a Christian feast (at least with regard to the quest pilgrim).

In their most important document about the pilgrimage to Santiago de Compostela, the bishops of Spain declare that the journey undertaken by contemporary pilgrims and tourists often results in surrendering to the myth of Christianity. The bishops say about quest pilgrims that:[14]

---

[14] Quotation from: *'The Road to Santiago.' A Way for the Christian Pilgrimage*, Letter of the Northern Spanish (arch)bishops, dated 24 July 1988, Santiago de Compostela, written in preparation of the second visit of Pope John Paul II to the shrine of the Apostle James.

It is not unusual to see pilgrims set out for St James of Compostela with a vague religious attitude. Sometimes they are going through a deep religious crisis, but they are open-minded and on their Way to Santiago they search for moments for reflection and inner quiet, in a profound longing to find a new purpose in their lives. Frequently the geographical and cultural Way becomes a private path that the soul takes to meet with God, who calls out to it from the deepest recesses of awareness. The external journey was undertaken without any explicit reasons of a religious nature; the greater the distance covered by the pilgrim, the more the Way purified his intentions, to result in a sincere conversion to God and Christ in front of the Shrine of the Apostle, in regaining the faith that had been lost or forgotten in youth or during the transition to University or the world of employment.

The bishops make use of a funnel model for their description: the pilgrim moves from wide to narrow in his orientation. He sets out without a specific religious aim, but ends up as a Christian because of the Christian interpretations that are offered to him along the road. How is this reflected in the experiences of the two quest pilgrims that were subject of our research? To some extent Marijke Schoone may be said to have started moving closer to the Christian tradition. St James and God become companions on the journey and God is also felt to be the creator of nature. Christ, on the other hand, does not appear in her story. Jan van der Heijden remains even more aloof from Christianity. For him faith is first of all a mystery and the esthetical effects of architecture and music move him. The point of view taken up by the bishops could be seen as a matter of hopeful Belief of these Spanish church leaders: it seems to be insufficiently based on at least our empirical data. This modern pilgrimage does not fit an unequivocally Christian frame of interpretation, at least not in the case of this type of pilgrim.

In the Middle Ages pilgrims might have been able to console themselves with a religious frame of reference that was second nature to all of them, but in the case of our quest pilgrim this frame works only partly. The confrontation with the road to Santiago occasionally causes our quest pilgrims to arrive at Christian religious interpretations, more often, though, it leads to experiences that have to do with the body, nature, other people, and self. They do not allow enforced guidance through the Christian frameworks of interpretation offered to them, but they steer by the course of their individuality: their personal 'self' in confrontation with their corporality, other people and nature. Put in another way: for this group of pilgrims their pilgrimage only partially is characterised as anamnesis of the old Santiago-tradition. Stories about St. James and his faith are not providing a dominant frame of reference to cope with their hardship. The analysis of the diaries allows a few remarks on the other two aspects of a feast (group-orientation and contrast). Although the pilgrims travel alone, there are impressive encounters with fellow-pilgrims and with people along the road. Furthermore there is the awareness of thousands of pilgrims who visited Santiago before. Perhaps the most characteristic aspect of the experiences of the pilgrims is the contrast with the quotidian life. Our central conclusion, that there is a strong emphasis on (1) the body, (2) nature, (3) the pilgrim's way as a symbol of the path in life, (4) meeting fellow-humans and (5) reflecting personal faith in confrontation with the Christian tradition of Santiago, could be seen as an increased awareness of five central areas of human life.

The second question we address is the emergence of other, non-Christian myths. In his approach of rituals, the anthropologist Wallace indicated that the cognitive restructuring that can take place during a ritual, depends on the nature of the 'cues' that are offered as the process takes its course.[15] It will be obvious that the 'cues' that pilgrims are offered on their way to Santiago de Compostela, do not only refer to the story of the Christian faith. They meet all sorts of people, they do not only visit chapels, but also bullfight arenas, etc. Yet we did not find any clear outlines of an alternative frame of interpretation. The cases of these pilgrims do not allow us to indicate the presence of alternative myths of a clearly different and circumscribed nature.

Having gone this far, we want to try to explain the significance of our data from a different perspective, and in doing so we refer to the categories that Feinberg[16] uses concerning the various ways contemporary pilgrims appropriate the pilgrimage to Santiago de Compostela. On the one hand there is the motive category: pilgrims take possession of the journey to Santiago with the help of motives and attitudes (penance, religious growth, vows, etc.) that are sanctioned by Christianity. On the other hand there is the performance category: pilgrims take possession of the journey to Santiago by means of the actual travelling of the route, complete with the relevant experiences as to

---

[15] A.F.C. WALLACE: *Religion. An anthropological view* (New York 1966).
[16] See FEINBERG: *Strangers and pilgrims.*

physical condition, geography, nature, etc. It is this performance category which seems to dominate the pilgrimages undertaken by the quest pilgrims. Travelling the road, the physical performance of the ritual using the body, is the main thing. Physically reaching the destination is an important core element of the undertaking. Therefore, the significance of this sort of pilgrimage should not primarily be studied looking at a Christian or ecclesiastical interpretation, nor at a new, different myth. The significance of the pilgrimage must be sought in the personal reflections of the pilgrim, which are generated by performing the ritual act of the pilgrimage with this unique physical instrument: 'his own body'.

This perspective concurs with recent anthropological discussions concerning the description and effects of rituals. Following symbolic and structuralist notions, there is more and more room for performance-oriented or praxis-oriented notions. The assumption is that a ritual is without meaning in the sense that it is not possible to base it on an existing 'meaning', but that the ritual as an act joins the personal intentions of the actor to an existing pattern of activity. Going on a pilgrimage is first of all surrender to a ritual programme, a surrender that leads to various experiences and interpretations. The core of the ritual is the physical aspect, which we also have found. The physical exercise is the crux of the pilgrimage, whether or not surrounded by religious concepts. What applies in our case is that the quest pilgrim keeps searching and that an unequivocal myth seems to remain beyond his reach. The pilgrimage rather raises new questions than that it supplies answers: questions that are closely associated with the acts that characterise the journey to Santiago. An accurate interpretation of the pilgrimage to Santiago has to be sought in the movement from myth to act.

Martin Gertler

WENIG FEIERLICHKEIT AUF DEM BILDSCHIRM
GOTTESDIENSTÜBERTRAGUNGEN IM DEUTSCHEN FERNSEHEN

Erstes Deutsches Fernsehen, eine Mitternachtmesse aus dem Kloster Dinklage an Weihnachten 1998. Das Singen und Beten der Schwestern wirkt intensiv, es gibt keinen Pomp, keine 'triumphierende Kirche', und niemand wirkt abgelenkt, das Medium Fernsehen ergeht sich nicht in Showeffekten. Ein Glanzlicht im von Festglanz und Glimmer überladenen Fernsehprogramm. Ganz allmählich werde ich, der Zuschauer, immer mehr einbezogen, denn die Feierlichkeit wird nicht vorgeführt, sie geschieht, innen. Offenbar eine perfekte Regie, nicht nur weil die Kameras Diskretion und Nähe zugleich herstellen und nahezu wie auf Schienen in der kleinen Kapelle fahren, sondern weil alle Beteiligten ganz bei der Sache sind und wirklich feiern können. Das ist durchaus nicht selbstverständlich – eine Rückblende: Fronleichnam 1998, Katholikentag in Mainz, der ARD-Gottesdienst wird vom Domplatz übertragen, Bischöfe und Prälaten treten auf, zweihundert Sängerinnen und Sänger auf der Bühne, Weihrauch und Würde, eine Menge Latein… Doch die Auftretenden wirken orientierungslos, abgelenkt, ständig damit beschäftigt, Ablauf und drohenden Regen zu bedenken. Was die Kameras übertrugen, waren nicht Sammlung, sondern Zerstreuung, nicht Feiern, sondern Absolvieren. Beides waren Gottesdienstübertragungen an Feiertagen, Sendungen der ARD.

Zu Beginn der neunziger Jahre war die Diskussion aufgekommen, ob mit den Gottesdienstübertragungen im Fernsehen nicht die 'Arkandisziplin', der Geheimnisschutz verletzt würde – so meinte jedenfalls Johann Baptist Metz.[1] Im Falle des Fronleichnamgottesdienstes mochte man Metz beinahe recht geben, doch an Weihnachten war es wieder ganz anders zu erleben.

Wie kann es zu so unterschiedlichen Einschätzungen kommen? Sie beruhen nicht auf subjektiven Standpunkten oder Ideologie, sondern auf benennbaren Gründen.

---

[1] Vgl. J.B. Metz: Kirchliche Kommunikationskultur. Überlegungen zur Kirche in der Welt der Massenmedien, in *Communicatio socialis* 24 (1991) 6.

1. Zuschauer konstruieren ihre Wirklichkeit

Mit kommunikationstheoretischen Überlegungen soll zunächst der Zusammenhang von Agierenden und Rezipienten erhellt werden. Kommunikation ist Handlung und sie ist offenbar unvermeidlich – Menschen kommunizieren, sobald sie miteinander in unmittelbarem oder medial hergestelltem Kontakt stehen, und selbst wenn sie einander ignorieren, ist das Kommunikation. Wegen dieser Schlüsselrolle von Kommunikation wird sie die Perspektive sein, unter der hier mit dem Fest als solchen (der Eucharistiefeier), den Kommunikatoren des Festes (das Fernsehen) und den Mitfeiernden am Bildschirm umgegangen wird.

In Kommunikationsvorgängen werden Vorstellungswelten ausgetauscht, die sich dabei ständig verändern. Kommunikation wird immer dazu dienen, Wirklichkeiten zu konstruieren. Menschen beeinflussen sich gegenseitig durch Kommunizieren, so daß dabei ganz verschiedene 'Wirklichkeiten' (auch Weltanschauungen oder Wahnvorstellungen) entstehen können, wobei "die sogenannte Wirklichkeit das Ergebnis von Kommunikation" ist.[2] Insbesondere die elektronischen Medien dienen heute zunehmend der Wirklichkeitskonstruktion der Rezipienten. Interpersonale und massenmediale Kommunikation haben eine vergleichbar starke Bedeutung bei der Einschätzung von medial berichteten Ereignissen und somit bei ihrer Wirklichkeitskonstruktion.

So ist zu verstehen, daß zum Beispiel das vielfache Auftreten des Papstes im Fernsehen die Folge hat, daß das hierarchische Bild von der Kirche dominiert und das von anderen gewünschte Bild einer Glaubensgemeinschaft, die auf dem Weg zur Erneuerung ist, in den Hintergrund tritt, obgleich das Zweite Vatikanische Konzil dies angestrebt hatte.[3] Wie der Papst oder auch der Priester einer Gottesdienstübertragung im Fernsehen ankommt, hängt nicht so sehr von ihm selbst ab, sondern davon, was man aus ihm macht, in welchem Umfeld er wie dargestellt wird. In ihrer wirklichkeitsbildenden Funktion besteht die Bedeutung des Zusammenspiels interpersonaler und massenmedialer Kommunikation.[4]

---

[2] Vgl. P. Watzlawick: *Wie wirklich ist die Wirklichkeit? Wahn, Täuschung, Verstehen* (München/Zürich 1996) 7.

[3] Vgl. W. Goddijn: De rol van de kerk als communicatiecentrum, in J. Hemels & H. Hoekstra: *Media en religieuze communicatie. Een uitdaging aan de christelijke geloofsgemeenschap.* (Hilversum 1985) 71.

[4] Vgl. J. van den Bulck: *Kijkbuiskennis. De rol van de televisie in de sociale en cognitieve constructie van de realiteit* (Leuven/Amersfoort 1996).

Kommunikationsprozesse hängen von unterschiedlichen Faktoren ab. Einer ist die 'sinnliche Seite': Hören und Sehen. Audiovisuelle Sprache ist einnehmender als das geschriebene oder gesprochene Wort. Diese Medien besitzen Mitteilungsmöglichkeiten für verbal nicht zu erschließende Erfahrungen und Bedeutungen, sprechen die Sprache des Gefühls, des Affektiven und Imaginären. Der Zuschauer hat beim Verfolgen einer Sendung noch die Erlebnisse der letzten Stunden in seinem Erleben präsent; zusammen mit dem gegenwärtigen aktuellen Erleben bilden sie ein diffuses Ganzes. Während auf dem Bildschirm eine Sendung läuft, entsteht eine Art Tauschvorgang mit dem Zuschauer: Er gibt seine diffuse Erfahrung auf zugunsten der vororganisierten Erfahrungsmuster der Sendung. Damit entsteht also weder ein reines Abbild der Fernseherfahrung, noch erweitert sich ausschließlich die eigene Erfahrung des Zuschauers. Es bildet sich etwas Neues aus Elementen beider Prozesse.[5]

Warum verfolgen Zuschauer diese Übertragungen? Neben den Bedürfnissen nach religiöser Beheimatung und Mitfeier spielt auch Orientierungsbedürfnis eine Rolle – die Massenmedien und dabei besonders die Fernsehprogramme steigern die Irritierbarkeit der Gesellschaft und somit auch ihre Fähigkeit zur Erarbeitung von Informationen.[6] Die Sinnzusammenhänge, die in den Medien vorkommen, werden komplexer, die Menschen erleben sich dabei zunehmend Irritationen durch von anderen produzierte Differenzen ausgesetzt – wie im Drama auf der Theaterbühne. Das Erleben dieser Differenzen und Komplexität führt zu dem Bedürfnis nach mehr Halt und weniger Irritation, welches dann aber nicht außerhalb jener Irritationsflächen, sondern genau dort befriedigt werden will, also zum Beispiel durch das zunehmende Verfolgen von Fernsehsendungen.

Davon berichten auch die Einschaltquoten. Daß heute dreimal so viele Zuschauer wie vor fünfzehn Jahren Gottesdienstübertragungen verfolgen, liegt weder daran, daß es damals entsprechend weniger TV-Geräte gegeben hätte, auch hat die Zahl der Alten und Kranken sich nicht inzwischen verdreifacht. Fernsehnutzung ist vielmehr noch selbstverständlicher geworden, die Ausweitung von einst drei auf heute über vierzig empfangbare Programme bietet mehr Anreiz, das Medium zu

---

[5] Vgl. O. NEGT & A. KLUGE: *Öffentlichkeit und Erfahrung. Zur Organisationsanalyse von bürgerlicher und proletarischer Öffentlichkeit* (Frankfurt/M. 1972) 184 ff.

[6] Vgl. N. LUHMANN: *Die Realität der Massenmedien* (Opladen 1996).

nutzen, und: die Entwicklung vom Bildungs- zum Unterhaltungsme-
dium, das immer gleichere und immer oberflächlichere Sendungen wie
vom Fließband ausstrahlt, schafft für die Rezipienten ein Defizit, das
durch primär sinnhaltige Angebote wie Gottesdienstübertragungen aus-
geglichen werden kann.

Damit wird – nebenbei bemerkt – deutlich, welche Verantwortung
die Kirche seit Beginn ihrer Gottesdienstübertragungen trägt und daß
sie dieser Verantwortung durch eine quantitative Reduzierung nicht
gerecht würde. Gottesdienstübertragungen sind folglich unerläßlich,
ebenso pastorale Beheimatungskonzepte wie die Begleitkommunikation
(in Deutschland) und das Omroeppastoraat (in den Niederlanden).

Eine große Rolle spielt ferner der soziale Kontext. Der Rezipient zählt
in der Regel zu den 'Laien', also den Gläubigen ohne Weihepriestertum
in der Kirche. Jeder, der teil hat am kirchlichen Leben, nimmt seinen
Platz in der kirchlichen Hierarchie ein. Heutzutage meint Hierarchie
eigentlich eine Ordnung von Systemen nach dem Maßstab ihrer Effizi-
enz,[7] aber es lebt noch die Vorstellung von einer himmlischen Hierarchie und ihrem Abbild auf Erden, mit der Folge einer Betonung des
Weiheamtes. Dies bedeutet für die Rezipienten der Gottesdienstübertragungen, daß die Beschränkung auf eine passive Rolle bei der Teilnahme
am gottesdienstlichen Geschehen via Fernsehen letztlich der Rolle der
Mehrzahl der wie sonst auch zum Gottesdienst kommenden Gemeinde-
mitglieder entspricht – Symptom einer Versorgungskirche.

Mithilfe bei der Wirklichkeitskonstruktion, Irritationen und ihre
Verarbeitung, sowie die Rollenfestschreibungen in der Kirche sind also
Merkmale des Kommunikationsgeschehens im Falle der Gottesdienst-
übertragungen im Fernsehen.

2. FUNKTIONSWEISEN DES FERNSEHENS

Vom Fernsehen übertragene Bilder bewirken nie genau dasselbe bei den
Zuschauern. Denn die Bilder entstehen nicht auf dem Bildschirm, son-
dern letztlich im Kopf, im Gehirn, in der Vorstellungskraft des
Zuschauers – als Folge der gesendeten Bilder und auf dem Hintergrund
der je eigenen Erfahrungstradition. Eine Fernsehsendung ist wie eine
Komposition: eine Verbindung verschiedener Bildeinstellungen und

---

[7] Vgl. H. PATEE: *Hierarchy theory. The challenge of complex systems* (New York 1973) 5.

Bildabläufe. Totalen und Nahaufnahmen ergänzen sich, bilden für den Zuschauer eine Gesamtschau. Im Medium Fernsehen sorgen die Bilder für die eigentliche Grundorientierung: wo bin ich – kenne ich das Geschehen / die Umgebung – sehe ich Unbekanntes, usw. Wenn Neues, Unbekanntes oder Unerwartetes auftaucht, steigt die Spannung, der Zuschauer wird neugierig. Umgekehrt zeigt sich, daß die Spannung abfällt, wenn Bekanntes erscheint. Mit der Grundorientierung verbunden ist also die emotionale Reaktion beim Rezipienten. Die Einordnung zu diesem Orientierungsvorgang liefert der Ton. Er gibt Hinweise darauf, ob es Grund gibt zur Beunruhigung oder nicht. Die im Ton hörbaren Geräusche lassen in der Vorstellungskraft des Zuschauers neue Bilder aufkommen, die sich aus den Anstößen aus Bild und Ton sowie seiner Erfahrungstradition ergeben. Der Ton steuert mehr als das Bild, denn mit den Ohren kann man Unterschiede erheblich leichter wahrnehmen als mit den Augen.

Die Regie führt mit Zoom-In und Zoom-Out den Zuschauer näher heran zum Geschehen oder von ihm weg. Werden mehrere Personen zugleich gezeigt, kann das einen Zusammenhang suggerieren – in der Gottesdienstübertragung etwa ein Zusammenwirken zwischen Priester und umstehenden Nicht-Priestern. Die Bildauswahl eines einzelnen Agierenden hebt ihn stärker heraus als in einer Gruppenaufnahme. Zeigt die Kamera die Gläubigen in den Bänken und überträgt mit langer Brennweite ein dichtes Bild, wobei Personen im Anschnitt zu sehen sind, entsteht der Eindruck von einer Vielzahl oder Masse. Wählt die Kamera mit kürzerer Brennweite eine kleine Gruppe von Gläubigen aus, die nicht angeschnitten werden und bei denen noch ein oder zwei Plätze frei sind, entsteht möglicherweise der Eindruck, die Kirche sei nur halb gefüllt.

Nahaufnahmen verstärken die Symbolkraft des gezeigten Geschehens, sie erhöhen die Eindringlichkeit der agierenden Person. Hintergrund, Vordergrund, Stimmungen und Farben sind bedeutsam. Weil sich alles nur auf den wenigen Quadratzentimetern des Bildschirms abspielt, weiß der Fernsehmacher, daß jede Einzelheit wichtig ist und den Gesamteindruck mitbestimmt, der in engem Zusammenhang mit der Message steht. Die Kamera wählt aus, verdichtet, kann Zeit raffen und dehnen. Durch die Schnittfolge aneinandergereihte Facetten werden vor dem geistigen Auge des Rezipienten zum Mosaik zusammengesetzt. Der Originalton und die Musik transportieren Atmosphäre, lassen das Bild im Grunde realer wirken.

Zwar haben die Fernsehleute die Aufgabe, möglichst originalgetreu das zu übertragen, was gerade im Kirchenraum passiert. Ausgewählt werden muß aber dabei, was als das Wichtigste von dem Geschehen erkannt worden ist. So entsteht die Wechselwirkung zwischen Gottesdienst und Regie. Besonders gut plazierte und geführte Kameras wecken – so Meyer – "die Illusion, mehr und besser zu sehen als der unmittelbare Teilnehmer am Geschehen".[8] Die gelungene Gottesdienstübertragung an Weihnachten 1998 war deswegen keine Illusion. Es wurden hingegen offenbar entscheidende Faktoren berücksichtigt, die im Folgenden noch deutlich werden.

Das Fernsehen dient dem Zuschauer zur Überbrückung von Raumabständen und damit zur Nähe zu einem Geschehen oder einer Geschichte. Die Annäherung des Rezipienten läßt sich beschleunigen und intensivieren, wenn er in den Kommunikationsvorgang eingebunden wird durch eine Beteiligung. Kontaktaufnahme, aktive Mitgestaltung von zu Hause aus – Beteiligung ist nicht nur eine Frage von Informationsaustausch, sondern impliziert auch Beziehungen zwischen den hauptberuflichen oder bei einer Sendung agierenden Kommunikatoren und den Rezipienten. Über die bei Gottesdienstübertragungen inzwischen üblichen zusätzlichen Kommunikationswege Telefon und Briefpost können die Beziehungen zwischen Agierenden und Rezipienten interaktiv werden, und so können Zuschauer auch wieder einwirken auf künftige Übertragungen. Im Anstoß von Folgekommunikation liegt die weiterführende Kommunikationskraft dieser Sendungen.

3. Liturgie ist Kommunikation

Der Gottesdienst der Gemeinde – Wortgottesdienst und Mahlfeier – kommuniziert die Offenbarung und ihre Geschichte. Er ist ein Abfolge von Ritualen, zu denen Gläubige sich versammeln und die seit Jahrhunderten überliefert wurden und in Maßen auch an die Zeiten angepaßt wurden. Die Rituale formulieren heilsbezogene Erfahrungen und geben sie weiter. Die beiden Kommunikationsaspekte der Liturgie sind die Verkündigung des zukünftigen Heils, das in der Gegenwart

---

[8] H.-B. MEYER: Gottesdienst in audiovisuellen Medien, in *Zeitschrift für katholische Theologie* 107 (1985) 424.

symbolisch dargestellt wird, und die Feier der Gemeinschaft als Träger dieser Zukunft.[9]

Die Eucharistie wird bei Schillebeeckx nach dem Kommunikationsmodell der Offenbarung Gottes in der weltlichen Gestalt als Begegnungsereignis zwischen Gott und dem glaubenden Menschen gesehen.[10] Es läßt die Gemeinde zur Kommunikationsgemeinschaft werden.[11] So hat die Struktur menschlichen Lebens sakramentalen Charakter; umso intensiver, je mehr sich der Mensch auf seine Welt einläßt. Gottes Gegenwart wird dem Menschen dann im symbolischen Ausdruck transparent, nicht in direkter Weise. Gegenständliches, Erlebtes ermöglicht in der Deutung ein Erkennen der Gegenwart Gottes. Auch *Aetatis novae* zieht die grundsätzliche Verbindung vom Lebensalltag zum Heilsgeschehen.[12] Ein solches Sakramentsverständnis, das den Alltag des Menschen einschließt, sieht die Eucharistie als Ort einer Existenzmitteilung in einer erfahrbaren Kommunikationsgemeinschaft. Sie ist Teil dessen, was Offenbarung genannt wird. Offenbarung als Begriff eines Kommunikationsvorganges ist wie jede Kommunikation mit der menschlichen Rezeption verbunden.

Die Feier der Liturgie wird auch verstanden als die Aktualisierung des Neuen Bundes, unter den Zeichen des Sakraments und in der kirchlichen Festlegung vollzogen. So ist sie also nicht nur ein Ritus (ihre Außenseite), sondern die Bezeichnung für das gemeinsame Handeln Christi und der Kirche.[13] Ritualisierte Sprache und Liturgie geben dem Gottesdienst die Freiheit, nicht stets neu begründet werden zu müssen. Ein Schutz für den Gottesdienst, aber auch für den Gläubigen, der in seinem Persönlichsten und Intimsten – seinem Verhältnis zu Gott, seiner persönlichen Lebensproblematik – angesprochen wird, sich aber nicht bloßstellen muß. Er kann mitvollziehen und damit seine Zustimmung geben, muß aber nicht ins Detail gehen, sich nicht auseinandersetzen,

---

[9] Vgl. J.G. HAHN: Liturgie im Fernsehen oder "Fernsehliturgie". Bemerkungen anläßlich einer Fachtagung zum Thema "Liturgie und Massenmedien", in *Communicatio socialis* 15 (1982) 49.

[10] Vgl. E. SCHILLEBEECKX: *Christus, Sakrament der Gottesbegegnung* (Mainz 1960).

[11] Vgl. A. GANOCZY: *Einführung in die katholische Sakramentenlehre* (Darmstadt 1984) 107.

[12] Vgl. *Aetatis novae* (Vatikanstadt 1992) 12 (Nr. 6).

[13] Vgl. Enzyklika *Mediator Dei*, in H. DENZINGER & A. SCHÖNMETZER (Hrsg.): *Enchiridion symbolorum, definitionum et declarationum de rebus fidei et morum* (Barcelona 1973) 3844.

sondern kann von dem profitieren, was seiner Meinung nach ihm persönlich am meisten gibt.

Die Form der Liturgie entspricht der einer gutbürgerlichen Feier – also vorgeformt, festgeschrieben in Ablauf, hierarchischen Rollen, Gesten und Sprache. Spontane und ekstatische Züge, die einem Fest – zumal von Menschen, die nicht bürgerlich oder feudal leben, fühlen und handeln – zukämen, lassen sich bei der Eucharistiefeier nicht finden; sie wären auch nicht in eine *Ordo Missae* oder in eine andere Art Ablaufstruktur oder Regie festlegbar. Gottesdienstliche Sprache hat also funktionale Elemente, die wiederholbar sind, mit wenig Raum für freie Rede. Nicht bodenständige, sondern Hochsprache ist anzutreffen; das erklärt sich schon aus der Lebenswelt derer, die professionell Gottesdienst gestalten und verwalten: Sie sind eher die Wahrer der Tradition und damit die Bewahrer eines Spracherbes als Propheten oder Revolutionäre.[14]

Das zeigt sich auch bei einer Gottesdienstübertragung. Aufgaben und Funktion einer Liturgie, die im Fernsehen übertragen wird, sind nicht grundsätzlich unterscheidbar von denen einer 'normalen' Eucharistiefeier.

4. PARTIZIPATION UND INTENTION

Bereits vor fast 50 Jahren hatte in Deutschland Otto Semmelroth aus der Tatsache, daß ja schon innerhalb der sinnvollen Teilnahme an einer Eucharistiefeier verschiedene Gegenwartsdichten möglich sind, den Schluß gezogen, daß man im Hinblick auf die Zuschauer einer Gottesdienstübertragung im Fernsehen "noch von einer, wenn auch abgeschwächten, aber doch heilsbedeutsamen Teilnahme am Opfer Christi sprechen könne".[15] Semmelroth berücksichtigt dabei, daß nicht nur die aktive Mitfeier der Eucharistie und der Kommunionempfang als übliche und einzig gültige Gottesdienstform für den Katholiken denkbar sind. Die Frage nach einer durch das Fernsehen vermittelten Teil-

---

[14] Vgl. dazu auch die Unterscheidung zwischen Fest und Feier bei W. GEBHARDT: Der Reiz des Außeralltäglichen. Zur Soziologie des Festes, in B. CASPAR & W. SPARN (Hrsg.): *Alltag und Transzendenz* (München 1992).

[15] O. SEMMELROTH: Die Messe im Fernsehen. Theologische Gesichtspunkte, in *Stimmen der Zeit* (1952/53) 445.

nahme an einer Eucharistiefeier, die dort übertragen wird, erörterte kurze Zeit später, 1961, auch Anton Ruf. Er zieht mit dem Begriff *quasi participatio formalis* eine Parallele zum Bild eines abwesenden Geliebten. Auch beim Betrachten dieses Bildes wenden sich die Gefühle ja nicht dem Bild als solchen, sondern dem Abwesenden zu.[16] So kommt Ruf zu dem Schluß, eine Form der Teilnahme am durch das Fernsehen übertragenen Gottesdienst – die *participatio intentionalis activa*[17] – sei möglich, was aus dem Wesen der Eucharistiefeier selbst erwachse, nicht aber aus den Voraussetzungen und Möglichkeiten des Mediums.

Meyer hingegen stellte heraus, daß die personale Kommunikationssituation des Gottesdienstes ein komplexes, situativ bedingtes Geschehen darstelle, dessen Vermittlung durch ein Medium nur eingeschränkt möglich sei. Bedingt durch die Einbahnkommunikation des Mediums bleibe der Zuschauer lediglich Empfänger. Was daheim auf dem Bildschirm sichtbar und hörbar wird, sei stark von der 'Zweitursache' der Apparaturen und derer, die sie handhaben, abhängig.[18] Raum für Partizipation läßt dieser Ansatz nicht. Mit dem Begriff der 'intentionalen Teilnahme' entkamen manche Autoren dem Dilemma, Meyer widersprechen zu müssen. Man verstand 'intentionale Teilnahme' an einer Gottesdienstübertragung als geistig-geistliches Dabeisein in Erkenntnis, Wille und Liebe. So definiert Böhnke den Bezug des Rezipienten zum übertragenen Gottesdienst als "intentionale Teilnahme in Bezug zur Quelle des Glaubens und der Gnade"[19] – die Interaktionsmöglichkeit spielt bei ihm nicht die entscheidende Rolle. Demnach entspricht dem subjektiven Akt des Rezipienten, der auf Teilnahme abzielt, eine objektive Wirklichkeit: die Gegenwart des erhöhten Herrn als die eigentliche Wirklichkeit des Gottesdienstes. Durch sie erwächst eine "Korrelation zwischen der gottesdienstlichen Gemeinde und den Fernsehzuschauern, die geistig-geistlich dabei sind

---

[16] Vgl. A.K. Ruf: Die Fernsehübertragung der hl. Messe. Grundsätzliche Überlegungen über ihre Möglichkeit, ihren Wert und ihre Gestaltung, in *Beiheft 5* zum Werkbuch K. Becker & K.A. Siegel: *Rundfunk und Fernsehen im Blick der Kirche* (Frankfurt/M. 1961) 60.

[17] Ruf: Fernsehübertragung 70.

[18] Vgl. Meyer: Gottesdienst in audiovisuellen Medien 423.

[19] M. Böhnke: Welche Art von Teilnahme ist einem Zuschauer einer Fernsehübertragung von Gottesdiensten möglich?, in *Liturgisches Jahrbuch* 38 (1987) 14.

und nicht nur einer illusorischen Annahme erliegen, sondern in das Gnadenwirken Gottes real einbezogen werden".[20]

Die Frage sowohl nach der Gegenwart als auch der Teilhabe an der Eucharistie kann demnach tiefer ansetzen als bei der Frage nach räumlicher Distanz zum 'sakralen Raum' des Kirchengebäudes, aus dem die Gottesdienstübertragung erfolgt. Die sakramentale Zeichenhaftigkeit könnte also weiterwirken bis in die Krankenzimmer und Wohnstuben hinein. So wird die alte Lehre von der 'geistlichen Kommunion' nach dem Konzil von Trient wieder bedeutsam.[21] Der Unterschied der 'geistlichen' Kommunion zur 'geistlichen und sakramentalen' liegt darin, daß im zweiten Fall – dem üblichen Normalfall – die glaubendliebende Vereinigung mit Jesus (die 'geistliche' Kommunion) dem sakramentalen Empfang vorausgeht und zugleich dessen höchste Frucht ist; es ist also kein wirklich wesentlicher Unterschied, sondern ein Zusammenhang. "Diese Vereinigung 'geistlicher' Art ist, so wie das sie wirkende göttliche Pneuma, etwas absolut Reales und darf nicht mit rein menschlicher Intuition, gedanklicher Verbindung verwechselt werden."[22]

Ob Zuschauer einer Gottesdienstübertragung am Sakrament partizipieren oder nicht, wird letztlich keiner 'definieren' können, der selbst außerhalb des Geschehens und dessen Systems steht. Wie es schon vom Glauben des Erlebenden abhängt, ob er die Inhalte von Schale und Kelch als Hostie und Wein oder Leib und Blut Christi ansieht, bleibt es dem Glauben des Zuschauers überlassen, ob er sich als Teilnehmender erfährt oder nicht. Der kommunikative Kontext der Übertragungen, bei denen Zuschauer stets als 'dabei'-Seiende oder auch Mitfeiernde angesprochen werden, der ganze Aufwand überhaupt, einschließlich der Folgekommunikation mit Telefon- und Briefdienst – all das gibt jedenfalls Anhaltspunkte genug für den Zuschauer, sich als Partizipanten erleben zu dürfen. Seiner Konstruktion von Wirklichkeit kann dabei nicht weniger und nicht mehr Berechtigung zugesprochen werden als jener der Liturgiker im deutschsprachigen Raum, die zum Thema Gottesdienstübertragungen und Teilhabe überwiegend 'ontologisch', nicht aber epistemologisch Stellung bezogen.

[20] BÖHNKE: Teilnahme 10f.
[21] Vgl. DENZIGER & SCHÖNMETZER: *Enchiridion* 1648.
[22] H. VORGRIMLER: *Sakramententheologie* (Düsseldorf 1990) 214.

5. Die unausweichliche Mitfeier

Ziel einer Gottesdienstübertragung im Fernsehen ist also sowohl aus der Einsicht in die Struktur des Mediums als auch aus theologischen Überlegungen eine bestmögliche Teilnahme des Zuschauers, der aus welchen Gründen auch immer nicht im Kirchenraum selbst zugegen ist. Die spezifische Wahrnehmung des Partizipanten in der Kirche ist dabei auch die einer bestimmten Umgebung: Kniebank, Weihrauchgeruch, der Kirchenraum und die anderen Gläubigen. Der Zuschauer dagegen sitzt oder liegt in einem ganz anderen Raum, meist in seiner privaten Umgebung. Er sieht diesen eigenen Raum und muß in seiner geistigen Vorstellung seine wirkliche Umgebung verlassen, sich die Realität der Partizipanten so gut wie möglich zur eigenen Realität machen. Doch er will – weil durch Krankheit oder Alter am Besuch ihrer Ortsgemeinde gehindert – mitbeten,[23] und die 'Mitfeier zu Hause' steht insofern im Lebenskontext des Zuschauers.

Auch eine erste empirisch-theologische Untersuchung von Zuschauerbriefen hat bestätigt, daß sich eine starke Bezugnahme der katholisch sozialisierten Rezipienten auf Mitfeiernde am Übertragungsort und andere Zuschauer zeigt: Sie sind meist Stammseher, verbinden positive Gefühle mit den Übertragungen und auch religiöse Erfahrungen, nahezu jeder vierte Zuschauer realisiert tatsächlich rituelles Handeln während der Sendung, eine wirkliche Mitfeier.[24] Sie drückt sich aus im Vorkommen von Interaktionen, in Form von Gebärden, Gedanken und Worten, die auf die Liturgie als auch auf die Handelnden auf dem Bildschirm bezogen und gerichtet sind.

Mit deutlicher Signifikanz[25] sind diejenigen, die während der Gottesdienstübertragungen mitfeiernd aktiv sind, auch explizit Mitglieder der Kirche:

---

[23] Vgl. hierzu H. BÜSSE, B. JEGGLE-MERZ & M. B. MERZ: *Fernsehübertragungen von Gottesdiensten. Chancen und Risiken* (Freiburg/Brg. 1987) 122.

[24] Vgl. hierzu M. GERTLER: *Unterwegs zu einer Fernsehgemeinde. Erfahrung von Kirche durch Gottesdienstübertragungen* (Köln 1998).

[25] Als Signifikanzniveau gilt: es muß $\leq$.05 sein, der Zusammenhang soll entsprechend Eta, Cramér's V bzw. Phi $\geq$.10 ausmachen.

Tabelle (1): Mitglieder der Kirche und liturgische Aktivität

```
KATHOLIK  Mitglieder der Kirche  by   LITURGIE  Liturgie
          Count  |
                 | nicht ge geäußert
                 | äußert              Row
                 |  ,00  |  1,00  |    Total
KATHOLIK  -----------+---------+---------+
           ,00      |  100  |   23   |    123
          nicht genannt |      |        |    49,2
                    +---------+---------+
          1,00      |   72  |   55   |    127
          katholisch |      |        |    50,8
                    +---------+---------+
          Column      172      78        250
          Total       68,8    31,2      100,0
                                                    Approximate
          Statistic        Value     ASE1   Val/ASE0   Significance
          ---------------------    ----------  ---------  ------------  ----------------
          Phi                       ,26553                             ,00003 *1
```

Liturgisch aktive Zuschauer kommentieren in der Folgekommunikation meist auch die Gottesdienstübertragungen: Kommentare zu den Gottesdienstübertragungen kommen bei 85,9 Prozent (p $\leq$.05, Phi =.13) dieser Kategorie; 78,2 Prozent mit Lob, 16,7 Prozent mit Kritik und 35,9 Prozent mit Vorschlägen.

Ferner beschäftigen sie sich mehr mit sozial-kulturellen Fragen als andere und sind stark von überwiegend positiven Gefühlen bestimmt: Liturgieorientierte zeigen eine signifikante Verbindung zu Affekten (85,9 Prozent; p $\leq$.05, Phi =.26). 65,4 Prozent äußern positive Affekte (p $\leq$.05, Phi =.24), 24,4 Prozent negative Affekte (p $\leq$.05, Phi =.14). Insgesamt eine deutliche Tendenz: positive Gefühle dominieren so sehr, daß eine Wechselwirkung zwischen liturgischem Mitvollzug und einer positiven affektiven Ladung gefolgert werden muß. Daß dieser Schluß berechtigt ist, zeigt auch die folgende Tabelle: Die Zuschauer 'haben' etwas von der Mitfeier.

*Tabelle (2): **Positive Effekte und liturgische Aktivität***

```
            KPOSI_EFF
            Count   |
            Row Pct | nicht ge geäußert
                    | äußert          Row
                    |  ,00  |  1,00  | Total
LITURGIE    -----------+---------+---------+
                ,00  |  112  |   60  |  172
  nicht geäußert     |  65,1 |  34,9 |  68,8
                     +---------+---------+
               1,00  |   34  |   44  |   78
  geäußert           |  43,6 |  56,4 |  31,2
                     +---------+---------+
             Column   146     104     250
              Total   58,4    41,6    100,0
```

Statistic	Value	ASE1	Val/ASE0	Approximate Significance
Phi	,20235			,00138 *1

Positive Effekte spielen also signifikant bei 56,4 Prozent der liturgisch Aktiven (p ≤.05, Phi =.20) eine Rolle. Die aktive Beschäftigung mit der Liturgie, die übertragen wird, führt demnach zu positiven Auswirkungen und zu einer positiven Gefühlslage.

Mehr als drei Viertel äußern sich zu spezifischen Kirchenthemen, was auf die soziale Komponente der Mitfeiernden deutet – Mittun ist für die meisten nicht eine ganz aufs eigene Seelenheil ausgerichtete Praxis, sondern steht in direktem Zusammenhang mit Gemeinde und Kirche.

Tabelle (3): Kirchenbewußtsein und liturgische Aktivität

```
          KIRCHE
          Count  |
          Row Pct | nicht ge geäußert
                  | äußert          Row
                  |  ,00  |  1,00  |  Total
LITURGIE  -----------+---------+---------+
            ,00     |  69   |  103   |   172
          nicht geäußert | 40,1 | 59,9 |  68,8
                  +---------+---------+
            1,00    |  17   |  61    |    78
          geäußert  |  21,8 |  78,2  |  31,2
                  +---------+---------+
          Column     86      164      250
          Total     34,4    65,6    100,0
```

Statistic	Value	ASE1	Val/ASE0	Approximate Significance
Phi	,17869			,00472 *1

Es wäre kaum anders zu erwarten gewesen: zur Kategorie Kirchenbewußtsein besteht ein starker und signifikanter Zusammenhang bei 78,2
Prozent der liturgisch Aktiven (p ≤.05, Phi =.18).

Unter den weiteren Zusammenhängen fällt im übrigen auf, daß überwiegend alleinlebende Menschen liturgische Aktivität thematisierten:
Vor allem Alleinstehende (46,3 Prozent), gefolgt von Zuschauern in
Partnerschaft (39,3 Prozent) und Verwitweten (14,3 Prozent), äußerten
liturgische Aktivitäten.

So zeigte sich bei dieser interdisziplinären Untersuchung an der
Katholischen Universität Nijmegen letztlich das aktive Mittun besonders bei Menschen, die sich auf die religiöse Seite des Lebens orientieren
und sich dabei als Teil einer großen Gruppe, einer Gemeinschaft oder
auch Gemeinde verstehen.

Das Phänomen des Mittuns ist im übrigen nicht nur für Gottesdienstübertragungen typisch, es wurde längst bei Fernsehsendungen
überhaupt registriert und wird auch bezeichnet als 'parasoziale Interak-
tion'. Gemeint ist die Tatsache, daß Zuschauer daheim mitunter einen
Moderator oder Darsteller, der wiederholt auf dem Bildschirm gewesen
ist, während der Sendung ansprechen, als wäre er leibhaftig im Wohn-

zimmer zugegen.[26] Dies drückt auch ein Gefühl der Verbundenheit aus, wie es sich in der Regel bei Menschen in Bezug auf ein konkretes, manchmal aber auch auf ein abgebildetes Gegenüber (z.b. im Hinblick auf Verstorbene oder Darstellungen zur Verehrung von Heiligen) bezieht. So ist die Gottesdienstübertragung kein bloßer Vorgang, wie auch das äußere Zeichen der Eucharistie, sondern eine Handlung, an der die Menschen beteiligt sind. Die Aktivität des Zuschauers, ob sie sich in Gesten des Mitfeierns zeigt oder in seiner anteilnehmenden Aufmerksamkeit, ist eine Tätigkeit des Symbolisierens.

Die These, daß Zuschauer mitfeiern wollen, läßt sich also nicht nur theologisch und empirisch, sondern auch an den grundsätzlich feststellbaren Wirkungen, am Funktionieren des Massenmediums Fernsehen als solchem erhärten; im übrigen haben Radioübertragungen von Gottesdiensten die selbe Rolle für die Hörer: Hier kann mitgefeiert werden, zwar 'nur' innerlich, aber doch wirklich. Die elektronischen Live-Medien führen also zur Aktivität besonders im Sinne des Mittuns (möglicherweise natürlich auch des Umschaltens oder Abschaltens) – Mitfeier wird für den Zuschauer, der eingeschaltet bleibt, damit sozusagen unausweichlich, wird selbstverständlich.

Ähnliches gilt dann auch für den gemeinschaftsbildenden Aspekt. Inzwischen gehört seit Öffnung des 'Internet' für jeden der Begriff der 'virtual reality' zum Sprachgebrauch; er ist damit selbst Realität geworden. Was durch Rundfunk und Fernsehen begann, die das sinnenhafte 'Dabeisein' an ganz anderen Orten erstmals ermöglichten, findet seine Erweiterung bis in den Alltag hinein: Chat-Groups etwa oder per Internet vernetzte Firmenmitarbeiter ohne herkömmliche, gemeinsame Büroräume verknüpfen Individuen und Individualisten online zu expliziten Gemeinschaften, die inzwischen genauso selbstverständlich als Gemeinschaften gehandhabt werden wie klassische Formen.

---

[26] Vgl. hierzu D. HORTON & R. WOHL: Mass communication and parasocial interaction. Observation on intimacy at a distance, in G. GUMPERT & R. CATHEART: *Inter media. Interpersonal communication in a media world* (New York/Oxford 1986) 185ff. Vgl. auch J. MEYROWITZ: *No sense of place. The impact of electronic media on social behaviour* (Oxford 1985), und IDEM: *Die Fernsehgesellschaft. Wirklichkeit und Identität im Medienzeitalter* (Weinheim/Basel 1990).

6. MANGEL AN PROFESSIONALITÄT

Es stellt sich von Jahr zu Jahr mehr die Frage, ob die zuschaueraktivierenden Komponenten solcher Sendungen ihren professionellen Machern eigentlich bewußt sind – und wie dieses Ziel erreichbar wäre. Ein erster Schritt könnte ein Blick in die Zuschauerpost sein: An den Wirkungen von Sendungen und an darüber berichtenden Zuschauerkritiken läßt sich eine Menge ablesen. Die eingangs dargestellten Beispiele einer gelungenen und einer nicht gelungenen Übertragung geben ebenfalls Anhaltspunkte. Warum war die Christmette an Weihnachten so eindrucksvoll, so fesselnd? Offenbar haben die Nonnen von Dinklage nicht nur während der Übertragung selbst ihren Gottesdienst intensiv gefeiert, sondern ihn auch vorher geprobt. So banal es klingen mag: Das Geheimnis einer jeden 'Show' liegt in der präzisen Vorbereitung, in der Probe. Das kennen wir noch aus Meßdienerzeiten: Wenn der Festgottesdienst geprobt war, brauchte man sich nicht ständig zu fragen, wer nun womit an der Reihe war und ob man vielleicht gerade etwas falsch machte. Beim Open-Air-Fronleichnamgottesdienstes hingegen hatte ich, als Regisseur in der Verantwortung, keine Chance mehr: Als die Proben stattfinden sollten, war außer dem Zeremoniar keiner von den geistlichen Herren zu sehen, der Chor suchte wegen Regens das Weite, wir alle kannten also weder die Musik noch das Verhalten der Liturgen am Altar. Es kam, wie es kommen mußte: Die Übertragung mißriet, denn die Kameras schafften Nähe zu einem Geschehen, das keine Nähe vertrug. Die Liturgie wirkte hölzern, absolviert, wie der hundertachtzigste Auftritt einer Laienspielschar.

Die Zuschauer mögen verantwortlich sein für die Wahl der Programme, die Macher sind es für das, was sie produzieren und verursachen. Zu den Machern gehören aber auch im Falle der Gottesdienstübertragungen nicht nur der Regisseur, die Kameraleute und die Toningenieure, sondern mindestens ebenso alle, die da vor den Kameras auftreten: sie verlieren oftmals durch den Lupeneffekt der Kameras. Gerade deshalb kommt es auf ein bewußtes Proben des 'Auftritts' an, denn das Erleben im Saal, in der Masse, ist anders als daheim am Bildschirm. Nah ins Bild gerückt wird gnadenlos enthüllt, ob einer die Erwartungen an seinen Auftritt erfüllt oder nicht. So wird klar, daß das Fernsehen beim Übertragen eines Gottesdienstes nicht gegen eine Arkandisziplin verstößt und auch kein Geheimnis enthüllt, sondern allenfalls die Unangemessenheit, mit der die Beteiligten mit jenem Geheimnis umgehen.

Eine Konsequenz müßte also lauten: Keine Übertragung ohne Probe! Doch wie sollte das durchgesetzt werden – bei 'normalen' Übertragungen aus Pfarreien und Klöstern ist das Proben selbstverständlich, aber wenn wie im Falle der Fronleichnamssendung Bischöfe auftreten, zeigt die Erfahrung, daß sie grundsätzlich nicht zu den Proben erscheinen. Daß sie sich selbst, der Übertragung und den Zuschauern damit schaden, ist ihnen offensichtlich nicht bewußt und es wäre ihnen auch nicht zu vermitteln, denn als Regisseur bekomme ich sie vor der Übertragung einfach nicht zu Gesicht.

Die Stolpersteine liegen aber durchaus nicht immer auf Seiten der Auftretenden. Vielmehr zeigen sich bei näherem Hinsehen fachliche Unzulänglichkeiten bei denen, die die Übertragung realisieren, durchsetzt mit Nebenabsichten, die der Sache nicht gut tun.

Ein Beispiel zum Mangel an Professionalität. Stichwort: Kompetenzmangel. Für eine Serie von drei Gottesdienstübertragungen waren 1999 Vorfilme zu produzieren, in anderthalb Minuten jeweils in den Ort und das Thema des Gottesdienstes einzuführen. Beim ersten Übertragungswochenende gab es am Probentag eine seltsame Konstellation – der Regisseur kam aus Los Angeles angereist, war von Hause aus evangelisch und hatte mit der katholischen Eucharistiefeier ansonsten nichts zu tun gehabt; also nahm bei den Proben der kirchliche Beauftragte das Heft in die Hand und übte mit den Agierenden, bis die Abläufe kameragerecht waren. Wie ein Einzug aussieht, was eine Inzens ist und wie man sie gestalten kann, war dem Regisseur unbekannt. Die seitens des Senders verantwortliche, hauptamtliche Redakteurin hatte ihren Job zwar bei der katholischen Redaktion, war aber ebenfalls evangelisch und weder mit der Liturgie noch den Traditionen, geschweige denn mit der Theologie der Katholiken und den Zuschauererwartungen vertraut. Einer der Vorfilme war ihr gar zu intensiv, wie er mit nahen Bildern in das Thema (Kreuzwallfahrt) einführte: Sie wollte es lieber etwas 'leichter' haben, den Zuschauern ginge es wie ihr selbst, sie müßten sich 'zwischendrin erholen können'.

So wird derzeit generell in Deutschland Programm gemacht: immer leichter statt dichter, schneller und hastiger statt überlegt und nachdenklich, und das unter Berufung auf Zuschauer, die kein Redakteur kennt, auch kein Sender, weil niemand mehr etwas wirklich untersucht, lediglich Einschaltquoten und Einschaltverhalten werden registriert und nach Belieben gedeutet. Für die wirklich überdurchschnittlich erfolgreiche, wöchentliche TV-Serie 'Gottesdienstübertragungen' hat das ZDF in mehr als 20 Jahren nicht eine einzige Untersuchung investiert, die Kirche hat einmal in den 80er Jahren statistisch-bewertend forschen lassen,[27] und auch die erste und bis dato einzige theologisch-empirische Untersuchung zum Thema wertete nicht aktuelle, sondern Zuschauerpost von 1977-1983 aus.[28] Auf Seiten der ARD, des Ersten Deutschen Fernsehens, das nur Anlaßgottesdienste zu Feiertagen überträgt, gibt es schon gar keine Untersuchung und auch kein Konzept, denn immer andere Sender des ARD-Verbundes übertragen die Gottesdienste, ständig wechseln die Redakteure (sie sind meist auch nicht katholisch). Auf beiden deutschen Kanälen zeigt sich also ein konsequentes Chaos.

Es verwundert nicht, daß die Gottesdienstübertragungen selbst noch nach einem Vierteljahrhundert regelmäßiger Ausstrahlungen immer wieder ein Abbild solch komplexer Unstimmigkeiten sind. Fast keiner der Mitarbeiter des größten deutschen Fernsehsenders, weder die zuständige Redakteurin noch die zumeist freiberuflich tätigen Regisseure haben einen fachlichen Background, weder eine spezielle Ausbildung für das Feld der Gottesdienstübertragungen noch theoretisches Rüstzeug durch ein Theologiestudium oder gar eine eigene katholische Sozialisation. Und die gelegentlich vonseiten des kirchlichen Beauftragten vorgetragenen Wünsche nach einer Bildführung, die sich jeweils an Inhalt, Sinn und Symbolik der Liturgie orientiert, werden nur sporadisch realisiert, etwa durch langsame Hinführungen zu einer Darstellung in einem der Kirchenfenster, werden dann aber gleich wieder von schnellen, oftmals harten Schnitten in ihrer Wirkung zunichte gemacht. Alle paar Minuten scheint sich die Crew für einen Moment an ihren Auftrag zu erinnern, um dann wieder in die hastige, dokumentarische Übertragungsweise eines aktuellen politischen Tagesereignisses zurückzufallen.

Die Beschäftigung mit den Gottesdienstübertragungen macht ratlos angesichts des unverständlichen Chaos und der offensichtlichen Professionalitätsmängel. Jede Sportübertragung im Fernsehen funktioniert nach wiedererkennbaren Regeln und richtet sich damit auch an eine wiedererkennbare Zielgruppe – wird in Deutschland eine Eucharistiefeier übertragen, scheint es solche, für eine Sendereihe erwartbaren, Regeln nicht zu geben. Woher rühren solche Probleme? Die übliche Art der Stellenbesetzung bei den Rundfunkanstalten ist vermutlich – außer

---

[27] Vgl. BÜSSE, JEGGLE-MERZ & MERZ: *Fernsehübertragungen von Gottesdiensten.*
[28] Vgl. GERTLER: *Unterwegs zu einer Fernsehgemeinde.*

den mit professioneller Betreuung möglicherweise überwindbaren Darstellerschwächen der Auftretenden – für die mangelnde professionelle Redaktions- und Regiearbeit verantwortlich: Stets werden neu zu besetzende Stellen und Aufgaben erst einmal nur intern, also aus dem Bestand des Senders vergeben – und es reicht dann offenbar, wenn die internen Bewerber 'irgendwie' der Aufgabe gewachsen zu sein scheinen. Dabei dürfte dies gerade für Fachredaktionen nicht zulässig sein – und möglicherweise liegen da auch gerade die Ursachen für die zunehmende Banalisierung des Programms insgesamt und für die zunehmende Entfernung von jeglichen spezifischen Kirchenthemen der Kirchenredaktionen.

Dabei muß es nicht so orientierungslos zugehen, wenn allen erst einmal die Aufgabenstellung klar ist. Zusammen mit den Agierenden vor der Kamera wie auch mit Redaktion, Regisseur und dem gesamten Team lassen sich Grundsätze festhalten, die sich ableiten aus der Tatsache, daß es den Zuschauern ermöglicht werden soll, so gut wie möglich mitzufeiern. Drei Stränge zeichnen sich dafür ab: Das Auftreten der Agierenden vor der Kamera, die Umsetzung in Bild und Ton durch die Regie und eine den Gottesdienst und seine Symbolik unterstützende 'mystagogische' Bildführung.

6.1. Das Auftreten der Agierenden vor der Kamera

Durch den Lupeneffekt der Kameras wird deutlich, ob ein Agierender 'bei der Sache' ist, ob er selbst wirklich betet und singt, oder nicht. Auch die Mikrofone enthüllen gnadenlos, ob der Priester das Vaterunser nur anschiebt und danach nicht mehr selbst mitbetet, oder ob er es persönlich mitvollzieht. Es ist also unerläßlich, auf diese Faktoren alle Mitwirkenden hinzuweisen und sie zu bitten, den Gottesdienst wirklich zu feiern, nicht ihn zu 'absolvieren' und in jedem Augenblick andächtig zu sein.

Neben der Andächtigkeit der Auftretenden ist ihre Blickrichtung von Bedeutung. Selbst wenn es in der katholischen Liturgie gängige Unsitte ist, bei der Fernsehübertragung muß es vermieden werden: das auffordernde Anschauen der Gläubigen in den Kirchenbänken beim Vortragen von Gebeten und Fürbitten. Gebet richtet sich nicht an die anwesenden Menschen, also sollte auch die Ausrichtung des Blickes, der Körpersprache des Vorbetenden dementsprechend sein – geprägt von Innerlichkeit. Genau anders ist es bei den dialogischen Aufforderungen zum Gebet: sie ergehen an die Gemeinde, also darf der Priester nicht suchend im Meßbuch blättern, während er spricht "Lasset uns beten". Einfachste Regeln der Kommunikation werden in den täglich absolvierten Feiern der Gottesdienste verletzt – die Gottesdienstübertragung im Fernsehen macht solche Fehler unvermeidlich sichtbar und kann daher sogar nützlich sein, neu über sein eigenes Auftreten nachzudenken. Insofern sollte eine Durchlaufprobe am Vorabend der Übertragung auch aufgezeichnet und anschließend mit allen Agierenden durchgeschaut werden. Wer dabei feststellt, daß er sich nicht adäquat verhalten hat, was sich in der Nahaufnahme enthüllt, der wird am Übertragungstage mit Sorgfalt seinen Auftritt kontrollieren.

Wie wirklich ist, was wir hören und sehen? Stimmt es denn, daß ein Pfarrer bei einer Übertragung gegebenenfalls unaufmerksam ist, oder wirkt es nur so? Am Bildschirm bekommt das Wirken jedenfalls eine Dominanz gegenüber dem Sein. Wirklich ist, was wirkt… Ein Training der an Gottesdienstübertragungen beteiligten Pfarrer und Regisseure müßte also darauf abzielen, Sein und Wirken optimal zusammenzuführen. Es handelt sich dabei ja nicht um eine Einbahnstraße: das Wirken dürfte wiederum das Sein beeinflussen. Sich an der Wirkung dessen, was man tut, zu orientieren, bedeutet deshalb noch lange nicht, die Zuschauer als willenlose Opfer dieses Tuns zu begreifen. Sie selbst sind es, die ihre Wirklichkeit konstruieren, die Gottesdienst am Bildschirm mitfeiern wollen, und wenn die Leute auf dem Bildschirm offensichtlich wirklich feiern, gelingt auch die Mitfeier daheim besser.

6.2. Die Umsetzung in Bild und Ton durch die Regie

Die Bildführung ist bestimmend für die Wirkung einer Sendung wie auch für die Rolle der Zuschauer. Wenn die Bildauswahl sich auf das Zeigen der Akteure und die Bewegungsabläufe in der Feier konzentriert, wird sie einen dokumentarischen Charakter erzeugen; Zuschauer können dann wie liturgische Beobachter Ablauf und Agieren beobachten und beurteilen. Wenn die Kameras im Kirchenraum 'herumwandern' und die Schönheit der Architektur und einzelne Motive ohne Beziehung zum gerade stattfindenden Gottesdienst vermitteln, wird ein ganz anderer Übertragungscharakter erzeugt: dann sieht der Zuschauer mit den Augen des Touristen. Läßt sich die Kameraführung von Rhythmus und Dynamik der Kirchenmusik leiten, kann aus dem Gottesdienst eine Art geistliches Konzert werden, der Zuschauer wird als Musikliebhaber angesprochen.

Es geht also um die Aufgabenstellung, und danach ist ein partizipatorischer Regiestil gefragt, der konsequent den Zuschauern daheim das Gefühl gibt, die Kirchenbänke seien bis ins Wohnzimmer hinein verlängert worden, und der alle Showeffekte sowie das scheindokumentarische Zeigen von Allem und Jedem vermeidet. Zu unterscheiden sind bei Beobachtung der Praxis derzeit drei unterschiedliche Regieweisen. Zum einen gibt es den Show-imitierenden Ansatz: Man setzt alle technischen Möglichkeiten ein, um einen Gottesdienst so unterhaltsam wie möglich zu übertragen, ständige Umschnitte gehören dazu und eine stets Bewegung suggerierende Krankamera. Zum zweiten findet sich der dokumentarische Ansatz: Es wird anhand des vorgegebenen Ablaufs übertragen, mit möglichst wenig Aufwand und harten Schnitten, dabei läßt man auf alles halten, was sich gerade bewegt oder äußert – und man wird danach immer wieder mal zeigen, was es sonst noch zu sehen gibt in der Kirche. Und schließlich gibt es den partizipatorischen Ansatz: Alle technischen Möglichkeiten und die Art von Bildführung und Schnitten ordnen sich der Aufgabenstellung unter, den Zuschauer daheim so optimal wie möglich mitfeiern, mit dabei sein zu lassen.

Nach dem Dargelegten kann nur der partizipatorische Ansatz unterstützt und entwickelt werden. Verlängerung der Bankreihen bis daheim bedeutet: Die Zuschauer so 'mitsehen' lassen, als wären sie dabei. Wer 'dabei' ist, hat seinen Platz unter den anderen Leuten, schaut sie nur gelegentlich von hinten, höchstens rechts und links an, und blickt ansonsten nach vorn. Eine adäquate Umsetzung der Aufgabenstellung bedeutet: Die Perspektive der Anwesenden in den Bänken ist auch die Kamera-Grundperspektive – nur gelegentliche, sehr dezente andere Blicke sind möglich. Diese 'Einschränkung' ist die Ausrichtung auf das Wesentliche und damit kein Verlust, sondern ein Gewinn für die Zuschauer.

Mit diesen Möglichkeiten läßt sich das Ziel einer zur Mitfeier geeigneten Übertragung erreichen:

(1) Das 'Publikum' wird nie von vorn (außer ggf. in weiten Totalen) gezeigt, sondern nur von hinten bis maximal 90° seitlich. Damit kommt der Zuschauer in die gleiche Perspektive wie die Anwesenden, und diese verlieren ihre ablenkende Wirkung.

(2) Bei Gebeten des Pfarrers bzw. der Gemeinde wird nie der Sprechende einzeln gezeigt, sondern immer mit 'Anschnitt' anderer Anwesender. Damit wird deutlich: es beten stets alle, und Beten

ist keine Ansprache von einer Person an die anderen, sondern eine gemeinsame Ausrichtung.

(3) Ansprachen, wie eine Predigt, werden nicht durch ständiges Weg-schneiden 'geschwächt', sondern durch beständiges Draufbleiben (halbnah), nach anfänglichem Inzoom ohne weitere Brennweiten-veränderungen, wird die Bedeutung des Sprechenden und des Gesagten intensiviert. Zwischenschnitte sind also verfehlt.

(4) Die Annäherung des Inzoom baut Spannung auf und zeigt den Akteur bereits in seinem Ambiente, so daß sich der Zuschauer anschließend ganz auf sein Tun und Sprechen konzentrieren kann. 'Aufzieher', Outzoom hingegen bauen Spannung ab, man verläßt die Szene, Nähe wird beendet; Outzoom sind aber einsetzbar zum Abschluß von Events, z. B. eines Liedes oder des Vaterunsers.

(5) Blenden statt schneiden, denn harte Schnitte sind hart und führen den Zuschauer blitzschnell woanders hin, konsequentes Blenden hingegen beläßt den Zuschauer besser in seiner Mitfeier.

(6) Vorgänge werden nicht 'zerschnitten', das Wechselgebet vor einer Präfation oder auch eine Liedstrophe werden nicht von verschie-denen, unterbrechend umschneidenden Kameras gezeigt, sondern stets in einer einzigen Einstellung.

(7) Die Tonübertragung muß eindeutig und verständlich sein. Die Orgel darf nicht länger den Gemeindegesang übertönen, die Zuschauer sollen jedes Wort verstehen können.

(8) Keine Kräne für Kameras verwenden, jede Showassoziation ist fehl am Platze.

(9) Frontale Rotlichter an den Kameras schon zur Probe, vor allem aber zur Sendung ausschalten lassen, schon hört das Ablenken und das In-die-Kamera-Glotzen der Anwesenden auf.

(10) Es ist für die Zielsetzung nützlich, vier oder fünf Bankreihen, an denen eine Kamera mehrfach seitlich etwas zeigen soll, vorab zu reservieren und mit ausgewählten, mitfeiernden Gemeindemitglie-dern zu besetzen und die dort Plazierten zu bitten, daß sie unbe-irrt von aller Fernsehtechnik aktiv mitsingen und mitbeten mögen. So hilft dieser Trick, die motivierten Zuschauer daheim nicht mit passiven Leuten in den Bänken abzulenken.

Es gibt also einfache, durchaus bei Sendereihen übliche Möglichkeiten, der Gottesdienstübertragung ein wiedererkennbares 'Gesicht' zu geben. Auch dieser Gedanke mag dabei im Hinterkopf bleiben: Gottesdienste sind Feiern, die wiederkehren – und so mag es sinnvoll sein, sie mit je gleichem Instrumentarium medial zu vermitteln.

6.3. Eine 'mystagogische' Bildführung

Neben der mit menschlichen Sinnen wahrnehmbaren Versammlung der Gemeinde und den Aktionen und Interaktionen der Feier wird durch die liturgische Symbolik eine zweite Wirklichkeitsebene angesprochen: die Gegenwart des gekreuzigten und auferstandenen Christus. Der Gottesdienst ist voll von oftmals nicht mehr bekannter Symbolik: So erzählt das mitgetragene Kreuz beim Einzug nicht nur vom Beginn der Feier, sondern auch davon, daß der Gekreuzigte mit einzieht und gegenwärtig ist; Verneigung und Kniebeuge machen deutlich, daß die Gläubigen sich als demütig und erlösungsbedürftig verstehen; Inzens des Altars mit Weihrauch dient der Ehrbezeugung gegenüber Christus, für den der Altar als Opfer- und Abendmahlstisch ein Symbol sein soll; etc.

Solche Symbolik kann das Fernsehen verwässern oder aber bewußt machen – und dabei sogar helfen, sie neu bewußt werden zu lassen und vielleicht sogar neu zu verstehen. Insbesondere der Lupeneffekt der Kameraführung bietet dazu besondere Möglichkeiten. Wenn während des Einzugs die Kamera nicht vorbeiziehende Meßdiener und Priester einfängt, sondern das Vortragekreuz verfolgt, bekommt der Einzug seine symbolische Dimension auch für die Zuschauer daheim am Bildschirm. Zeigt eine Kamera die Kniebeuge der Liturgen und wird diese dabei dann auch noch offensichtlich bewußt vollzogen, erhält die Geste im Zuammenwirken von Liturgen und Regie für die Zuschauer ihre tiefere Bedeutung. Und wenn bei der Altarinzens die Kamera nicht auf das Weihrauchfaß, sondern von ihm weggehend auf ein ggf. vorhandenes Christuszeichen inzoomt, erzählt sie dem Zuschauer die symbolische Bedeutung der Inzens.

Weitere Beispiele lassen sich aufzählen, etwa das Brotbrechen beim Agnus Dei – als Zeichen der Einheit der Getauften im Leib Christi ist sie in den Bankreihen der Kirche kaum noch wahrnehmbar, das Fernsehen hingegen kann durch die Großaufnahme des Brotbrechens den Blick lenken und durch gleichzeitiges Einblenden der singenden Gemeinde – möglichst in einem langsamen Schwenk ohne Anfang und Ende – die gemeinte Aussage dieses liturgischen Elementes aufzeigen. Die Gleichzeitig zweier Bilder sorgt dafür, daß die über Vorgänge hinausgehende Wirklichkeitsdimension der Eucharistiefeier immer wieder in den Blick kommen kann. Beim Sanctus könnte die Kamera von der singenden Gemeinde auf ein Decken- oder Seitengemälde mit einer Darstellung von Gott, Engeln und 'himmlischen Heerscharen' schwenken, um dann von einer zweiten Kamera die noch singende Gemeinde einzublenden: So kann das Einstimmen der Gemeinde in eine 'himmlische Liturgie' angedeutet werden. Wird das Durchblenden einige Zeit gehalten, ergibt sich eine Unschärfe durch die Überlagerung der beiden Bilder, die der Unfaßbarkeit jenes irdisch-himmlischen Brückenschlages gerecht wird; durch das Zurückkommen der Szene schließlich zur feiernden Gemeinde verschwindet die Unschärfe, was wiederum Bodenhaftung verschafft und zeigt, daß eine himmlische Liturgie noch fern ist.

Die Möglichkeit der Bewegung der Kameras kann ebenfalls helfen, tieferliegende Symbolik anzudeuten. Beim Kyrie könnte die Kamera die singende Gemeinde von hinten zeigen und langsam durch den Mittelgang auf das Kreuz zufahren – die Gebetsrichtung wird dadurch herausgestellt, nämlich die Huldigung der Gemeinde an den gegenwärtigen Herrn. Auch eine Rückfahrt kann Aussagen machen: Spricht die Gemeinde das Glaubensbekenntnis oder das Vaterunser und fährt die Kamera dabei vom gebetseröffnenden Priester immer weiter rückwärts, so zeigt sie ständig zunehmend mehr Menschen, die sich diesem Bekenntnis und Gebet angeschlossen haben; und da die Gläubigen von hinten gezeigt werden, kann sich der Zuschauer daheim als einer fühlen, der da eingereiht stehen könnte – er kann mitsprechen, mitbeten.

Die Kameraführung mit ihrem Lupeneffekt und den Möglichkeiten zur Kombination mehrerer Bilder und zur Eigenbewegung wird damit also manchmal sogar zur Voraussetzung, daß der Zuschauer die Symbolik einer Handlung überhaupt wahrnehmen kann. So sorgt eine kompetente Regie für die mystagogische Erschließung der Feier und auf eine nicht nur formale, sondern auch inhaltliche Weise von großer theologischer Bedeutung für die Möglichkeit zur Mitfeier daheim am Bildschirm.

7. Folgerungen für die Gestaltung von Liturgie am Bildschirm

Die Liturgie hat zwar eine vorgegebene Form, diese läßt aber eine Menge Gestaltungsfreiheit. Einerseits schöpfen Gemeinden, aus denen übertragen wird, sie nach ihren eigenen Vorstellungen aus, etwa indem sie musikalische Ereignisse einbauen oder einen speziellen, lokal bedeutsamen Segen mit einer Reliquie.

Daneben können aber auch feste liturgische Bestandteile durch eine kameragerechte Präsentation in ihrer Bedeutung neu erkennbar werden. So zeigt die Auswertung eines Drehbuchs vom 9. September 1990, daß gleich mehrere Chancen dieser Art genutzt wurden. Bei der Begrüßung der Gemeinde erläuterte Pfarrer Hoffsümmer das Kreuzzeichen: "Im Kreuzzeichen wird unser Körper vom Kreuz umfangen. Wir beginnen in der Mitte unseres Geistes, gehen zur Mitte unseres Körpers, und werden dann von beiden Seiten umschlossen. Dann legen wir die Handflächen entspannt und offen aneinander – wir ballen keine Faust." Hier wird eine Chance zur Erläuterung der Symbolik des Kreuzzeichens wahrgenommen, die nicht im Schott-Meßbuch stehen könnte – ritualisiert zur Regelmäßigkeit sind solche Erläuterungen nicht vorstellbar. Die Gottesdienstübertragung im Fernsehen bietet mit ihrer Ausnahmesituation einen guten Anlaß, eine Brücke zu fernstehenden Zuschauern zu schlagen. Ein zweites Beispiel: Statt der üblichen und vorgesehenen Einleitung zum Gebet des Herrn gab der Priester eine Art Regieanweisung an seine Gemeinde: "Wir halten beim Vaterunser unsere Hände wie leere Schalen vor Gott, damit sie uns aus seiner Mitte gefüllt werden." Damit erläuterte der Priester für jene Zuschauer, die möglicherweise nicht wissen, warum der Zelebrant bei den Gebeten stets die Arme ausstreckt, seine eigene bisherige Praxis (etwa beim Hochgebet) und forderte zur Nachahmung auf. Diese Gebetshaltung hat zwar nicht den Stellenwert eines Symbols. Trotzdem kann eine solche 'Regieanweisung' als eine nachahmenswerte Methode gelten, die Zeichensprache am Altar beiläufig zu erläutern, ohne die Ebene der Feier zu verlassen.

Die an Symbolik reiche Liturgie der Eucharistie bietet also jede Menge Chancen, die in Jahrhunderten gewachsene Feier mit Hilfe des Mediums Fernsehen neu zu erklären, ohne daß Erklärungen nötig wären. Von einer Übertragung im Fernsehen dürfte erwartet werden, daß sie sich darum bemüht – die regelmäßigen Sendungen aus 'normalen' Pfarrgemeinden bieten dazu vielleicht noch eher den Raum als Festtags- und Anlaßgottesdienste.

8. MASSNAHMEN

Um Diagnosen und neue Dimensionen soll es hier gehen. Die Diagnose ist klar: Seit Jahrzehnten werden bei den Gottesdienstübertragungen in Deutschland keine stimmigen Rezepte umgesetzt, jeder werkelt nach eigenem Gusto vor sich hin, statt erkennbarer Konzeption zeigt sich Chaos. Die Erwartungshaltung der Zuschauer, mitfeiern zu können, scheint dabei für die TV- und Kirchenleute kein Maßstab zu sein angesichts dessen, was sonntags auf dem Bildschirm angeboten wird. Es stellt sich die Frage, wie die anhaltende Unstimmigkeit überwunden werden kann. Der Schluß liegt zwar nahe, daß eine stimmigere Umsetzung einer noch zu vereinbarenden Gesamtkonzeption durch auf allen Ebenen kompetente Menschen das Bedürfnis der Zuschauer nach Mitfeier besser befriedigen könnte – vielleicht sorgt aber gerade jener Schlingerkurs, die sichtbare Inhomogenität der Übertragungen dafür, daß dieses Bedürfnis nicht so leicht gestillt und damit lebendig erhalten wird? Natürlich könnten eine Menge Maßnahmen getroffen werden, damit eine sachgerechtere Regie das Mitfeiern ermöglicht und diese zugleich auch noch tiefer liegende Bedeutungen liturgischer Handlungen durch entsprechende Kameraführung sichtbar und verstehbar macht. Dennoch kann daraus nicht gefolgert werden, daß solche Maßnahmen automatisch die gewünschten Folgen zeitigen.[29] Alle Maßnahmen beziehen sich wieder auf Kommunikationsvorgänge, die gerade durch Defizite lebendig bleiben und das menschliche Sozialsystem intakt halten sowie auch stören; es zeigt sich aber, daß der menschliche Verstand genau auf diesem Auge 'blind' und nicht geeignet ist, seine eigenen Systeme zu verstehen.[30]

Daher sind die Vorschläge als Bausteine gemeint, die aufgrund einer empirischen Bestandsaufnahme und Reflexion entstanden sind, mit deren Umsetzung aber wiederum neue Wirklichkeiten geschaffen werden würden, auf die die Rezipienten der Gottesdienstübertragungen mit weiteren, anderen, nicht voraussehbaren Wünschen und Erfahrungen reagieren würden, die wiederum zu neuen Maßnahmen führen sollten. Aus konstruktivistischer Perspektive läßt sich immerhin ein epistemologisch verantwortbarer Weg skizzieren, der durch das Kriterium der Viabilität[31] gekennzeichnet ist: Die Brauchbarkeit der Maßnahmen zeigt sich an den Ergebnissen.

---

[29] Vgl. R. RIEDL: Die Folgen des Ursachendenkens, in P. WATZLAWICK (Hrsg.): *Die erfundene Wirklichkeit. Wie wissen wir, was wir zu wissen glauben?* (München/Zürich 1985).

[30] Vgl. J. FORRESTER: Behaviour of social systems, in P. WEISS (Hrsg.): *Hierarchically organized systems in theory and practice* (New York 1971).

[31] Vgl. E. VON GLASERSFELD: Konstruktion der Wirklichkeit und des Begriffs der Objektivität, in *Einführung in den Konstruktivismus* (München/Zürich 1992).

Ergebnisse lassen dann auch den Schluß auf die Brauchbarkeit der Maßnahmen zu. So schließt sich der Kreis mit dem Blick auf die beiden exemplarisch besprochenen Gottesdienstübertragungen im deutschen Fernsehen, zu Fronleichnam und Weihnachten 1998. Der eine Gottesdienst wirkte abschreckend, der andere ansteckend. Beide waren Feiern, nicht spontan, ganz und gar durchgeplant. Gerade deshalb scheint bewußtes, konzeptionelles Vorgehen vonnöten zu sein, gerade deshalb erweist es sich als das Ende der Feierlichkeit, wenn sich die Beteiligten nur mehr darauf verlassen, daß es schon gut gehen wird, wenn man es macht 'wie immer'. Eine Feier ist nie 'wie immer' – schon gar nicht, wenn das Fernsehen sie zu übertragen hat.

WILLEM MARIE SPEELMAN

THE 'FEAST' OF DIANA'S DEATH

> *There is a temptation to rush to canonise your memory; there is no need to do so. You stand tall enough as a human being of unique qualities not to need to be seen as a saint.*
> (From the *Tribute* by Charles Spencer).

1. INTRODUCTION

Sunday morning 31 August 1997 I overheard members of my choir whispering that princess Diana was killed in a car accident in Paris. I remember the feeling of thrill one has when something great is about to happen. That day and that week were filled with questions and guesses. And the TV was on, of course. Only slowly the story about the accident was being composed from many different guesses. And it still has open ends. We are still not sure what the role was of the royal family, the media and the religions in Diana's death: who or what is responsible for her death? It is not that we were looking for the guilty. We simply wanted to know the story of the death of someone who was considered almost a saint. We were not interested in the truth, but in the 'saint's story'. For the death of a saint is the point of her life.

At Sunday the remains of the princess were brought by aeroplane to England. During the flight there was an evening prayer in the St. Paul's Cathedral. I remember a very beautiful 'media-made' moment in that evening prayer: the television juxtaposed shots of the aeroplane landing with the choir singing psalm 130, *de profundis clamavi ad te*. The result was a counterpoint of the descending remains of the princess and the ascending prayers of the people. In the early hours of Monday the coffin was taken to the Chapel Royal of St. James' Palace, where it remained until the night of Friday. During these days thousands of 'ordinary citizens' offered their condolences. From the Chapel Royal the coffin was moved to Diana's apartment at Kensington Palace, where it remained overnight. The bishop of London and the sub-dean of the

Chapel Royal kept a candlelit vigil of prayer over the princess's coffin throughout the night. Saturday, 6 September, was the day of the funeral. We watched it on television. The program began with a long waiting during which the commentator was constantly talking: he told what happened and what was going to happen. At 9.08 am the coffin was borne from Kensington Palace to Westminster Abbey in a slow and impressive two hour-long procession. In the Abbey the funeral service was held at 11.00 am. I particularly remember the last rite, when the coffin was carried outside the church. There was one minute of complete silence during which the Dean was waiting in the west door, before giving the deceased back to the reality outside the church. The camera took a total shot in bird perspective from within the church, so that the door opening appeared as an eye blinding light in which the dean was standing. I remember thinking: is this light from the world or is it from heaven? After that the coffin was driven from London to Althorp, where Diana was buried.

In October my wife and I visited the place in Paris where princess Diana, Dodi Fayed and Henri Paul died, the tunnel with the sculpture of the eternal flame near the Pont de l'Alma along the Seine River. It had spontaneously become a place of pilgrimage. The golden flame was covered with messages from Muslims ('Princess of Islam') and English ('Queen of hearts'). There were also virtual 'places of pilgrimage', Internet sites with information, discussions, pictures etc. One year later there were several programs on the television and Internet sites devoted to princess Diana, her death and the public's reaction to her death. Many experts in theology, psychology and media studies discussed about Diana as a media event and as a 'saint'. The program 'the secular Madonna' revealed that there had been an investigation on the public health effects of the broadcast of the funeral.[1] One of the conclusions was that the broadcast had had a healing effect. The program, it was said, allowed people to reflect their own emotions and thoughts in a distant mirror. Many people said that they cried more about the death of Diana then over the death of their wife or mother: in fact, her near-distant death finally allowed them to cry for their wife or mother.

Now, years later, I am beginning to wonder what had happened. I suspect that Diana has given us the opportunity to celebrate life in her

---

[1] *De seculiere Madonna* was made by Margje de Koning and shown on 20 August 1998 by the Dutch broadcast company IKON.

life and to celebrate death in her death. This celebration of her death was a *mediated* event. "The enormous outburst of emotions felt by an international people" was not only transmitted and intensified but, according to some, even created by the media. The celebration of her death was also a *ritualised* event. The enthusiasm of the happening was channelled through well-known and fixed forms. And just as the canalisation of a river strengthens the stream, the channelled emotions were united in one powerful spirit turning the world into a community and communicating a message of love. In short, what we have experienced in the mediated and ritualised event of Diana's death was a *feast*. The 'feast' of Diana's death gave us the time to become a community and celebrate our faith.

The celebration of our faith in Diana's death took the form of a composition of a saint's story. In such a story not the truth, but meaningfulness is the point. Meaning spouts up from holes in the texture of the endless story of our lives. It can only be grasped when the story reaches an end: when it has become a story with an end, a point. The death of Diana disrupted the story and revealed its meaning.[2] In the making of her story, we try to weave this meaning in the texture of our lives. For some reason, many have explicitly tried to prevent the canonisation of Diana by the media and by the people. Perhaps a canonisation was considered as a continuation of the media making something out of a Diana (and destroying her).

Whatever has happened, the happening worked. It was an effective 'feast'. But why did it work, and what is an effective feast? What role did the mediation and the ritualisation play in the event of Diana's death? And what do we mean when we say that a mediated and ritualised happening 'works'? Let me begin with a description of the happening.

2. THE 'FEAST' OF DIANA

2.1. The image of Diana

Princess Diana was an image. By the time of her death she was the most illustrious subject in the media. On the one hand she was an object chased

---

[2] The tragic of the saint's story is that it can only be construed when the saint is dead; it is thus linked with sacrifice.

by paparazzi eager to catch her image and put it on TV, magazines, covers, cups and spoons, et cetera. On the other hand Diana somehow inverted her role into that of a subject. She became a person who celebrated her life in front of the media. She played with the media in order to be effective in the real world: that of AIDS, homelessness, leprosy, land mines, et cetera. And she played her role remarkably well. Diana became an ambassador of the weak of modern society, combining a glamorous life with works of charity. Some thought that she sold her soul to the media as a post-modern Faust; others thought that she followed the Spirit who breathes where He desires. We all know that her life was far from divine. She was hunted by the media, attacked by her family-in-law and insulted by politicians. But the people loved her. Poor single mothers called this wealthy single mother 'one of us'. The people apparently had no problem with her glamorous life. Why should they? For Diana only did what we all would want to do: she celebrated life. Thus she became a friend, nearby, vulnerable and beautiful. And when her life was attacked, she celebrated being a victim: she became the victim *in persona*.

The image of the victim, standing up to the powerful, was intensified immediately after Diana's death. She was pictured as a victim of the media, especially the gossip papers. It was said that the paparazzi destroyed her life and even killed her. The aggression against the paparazzi had its impact on serious journalists too. Beside the media, the English royal establishment was also held responsible for the victimisation and death of Diana. It was said that the death of Diana in fact solved several problems for this establishment: the shame of a royal 'public fight', the shame of a royal divorce and the problem of a possible marriage between the mother of a future Christian king with a Muslim. The last problem shows that the image of Diana was even put against the background of the religious establishment. Diana became an image of the vulnerable, victimised, chased and outcast woman who stood up as a warm, nearby, faithful, soft, beautiful, young, caring and loving mother against the mighty establishments of media, royalty and politics.[3] By now the image was strong enough to function as an icon, an image of the sacred.[4]

---

[3] Apparently with effect, for the media and the royalty are said to have changed their attitude. See N. HIGHAM: *Media soul searching* and P. REYNOLDS: *Royal Family's changing guard*, both on http://www.bbc.co.uk/diana/.

[4] Jackie LONG: *The making of an icon*, on http://www.bbc.co.uk/diana/, writes: "Diana was our sort of saint, an icon perfect for her time. She made giving glamorous." Rosalind BRUNT: Princess Diana. A Sign of the Times, in J. RICHARDS, S. WILSON & L.

Diana had become an icon, an image of what we believe in and an anti-image of what we distrust. All the more remarkable is the fact that her picture was not broadcast during the funeral until the remains of Diana left the Abbey *after* the funeral service. What the BBC showed us on that day was not the image of Diana, but of the people honouring and commemorating her: the ordinary citizens, the military, the royal family, her blood family, the charity-workers, the church, the media, the politics, 'the world of music' and 'the world of fashion'. The presence of the establishments of the media, royalty, politics and religion can be interpreted as a particularly strong homage, as if everyone acknowledged the integrity of the icon Diana. To a large extent the funeral, as a ritual of homage, functioned as a ritual of reconciliation. We will have a closer look at the organisation of the funeral, especially the procession to the church and the funeral service itself.

2.2. The procession to the church

The procession from the apartment to the Abbey took almost two hours. But it has not been boring, not for a second! At the beginning, before the actual procession, the cameras focused on the gathered people, the Kensington Palace – the start of the procession – and the Westminster Abbey – the end of the procession. For some ten minutes we waited while the cameras showed us the emotional atmosphere (flowers and faces) and the commentator gave us cognitive information. Every minute the Tenor Bell rang 'to watch the time'. Then the procession began, in which the coffin was carried in a cavalcade or cortège.

During the procession the Westminster Abbey opened its doors to invite the 2000 'guests'. The guests were 'personal friends' of Diana: friends from the worlds of politics, music, fashion, media, church, charity and of course her family and her family in law. The commentator mentioned their names and functions, to make public who was there. Further he prepared us for the funeral service. The service would be a service "combining both traditional and modern elements", and was said to be "put together in 48 hours". The cameras showed who were

WOODHEAD (eds.): *Diana. The making of a media saint* (London 1999) 20-39, writes on p. 37: "(…) through its association with Diana, 'icon' has accrued 'indexical' connotations of wished-for democracy and 'symbolic' connotations around celebrity, femininity and the contexts of cultural change. Finally, though, with Diana's death and the entry into the vernacular, 'icon' embraces the numinous again."

there: the coffin, the people, the cortège, the relatives, the guests, the buildings, the flowers, the card from Harry with "Mummy", in short: medial symbols of the environment of Diana. At some moment the male relatives joined the cavalcade: prince Philip, prince William, Charles Spencer, prince Harry and prince Charles. After them 550 (five times 110) charity-workers joined the cortège representing the 110 forms of charity in which the princess had been involved.

Just before the cavalcade reached the church the television crossed the peaceful organ music inside the church over the procession outside the church. It was an extremely slow crossover, in which for a while the two symbols – the world and the church, the profane and the sacred – merged into one another. The fundamental role of the music in this ritual connection will be discussed later. Before the church, in a highly ritualistic manner, the soldiers from the Welsh guard took the coffin on their shoulders and carried it, preceded by an ecclesiastical procession, to the sacrarium. There they put the coffin on a bier between four candles. Then the soldiers left the sacrarium.

2.3. The funeral service

The funeral service, "combining traditional and modern elements", not only revealed who has been there to honour Diana, but was also a portraying of the image of her.

– *Introit with the sentences.* The Introit was a liturgy in itself. We already noticed that the media connected the procession outside the church with the liturgical service through the nexus of the organ music. Before the West door of the Abbey the cortège stopped. In a highly ritual manner the soldiers of the Welsh guard took the coffin on their shoulders and walked to the entrance. Everybody waited in silence. The Tenor Bell rang the minute, the organ played softly and the Bells played the well-known Handel tune as the cue for the beginning. It is difficult to imagine how the cortège has managed to arrive at the Church's entrance at exactly 11.00 am. Then the coffin entered the West door. After a moment of silence the organ stroke up the National Anthem, which was sung loudly by everyone. The choir singing the funeral sentences accompanied the procession to the sacrarium, the relatives laid flowers and the Welsh guard left the sacrarium. Again, the precise timing of the Introit was striking, for the last note of the choral song was sung at the same moment that the last soldiers left the sacrarium.

- *Bidding.* At the high altar the Dean of the Westminster Abbey, Dr. Wesley Carr, spoke the introductory words to the service.
- *Hymn.* As an opening song the congregation sang "I vow to thee, my country".
- *Reading.* Instead of a Scriptural text, the poem "If I should die" was read by Diana's sister Lady Sarah McCorquodale before the coffin. The poem calls to "turn again to life" and to "complete those dear unfinished tasks of mine".
- *Choral singing.* The BBC-singers sang extracts from the *Libera me* from Verdi's *Requiem* during which the camera focused on a stained glass image of the community of saints.
- *Reading.* Diana's sister Lady Jane Fellowes read the poem "Time is too slow for those who wait", which ended with the phrase "but for those who love, time is eternity".
- *Psalm.* The congregation sang psalm 23 in the hymnal version "The King of love my Shepherd is". During the Psalm the camera was looking for symbols and found a mosaic with Christ sharing bread.
- *Reading.* From the lectern the Prime Minister Tony Blair read the ode to love from 1 Corinthians 13.
- *Song.* Elton John then sang a special arrangement of his song *Candle in the Wind* in the nave.
- *Eulogy.* Instead of a sermon, Diana's brother Charles Earl Spencer read a tribute from the pulpit. The camera showed the people, inside and outside, listening to this eulogy in which the media, the politicians and the royal family were reprimanded. After this emotional speech there was much applause.
- *Hymn.* During the song "Make me a channel of your peace" (St. Francis), the camera made a beautiful connection between the highly organised, uniformed boys choir inside and the unorganised, freely dressed people outside, joining in the singing. Again the nexus was the music.
- *Prayers.* The Archbishop of Canterbury, Dr. George Carey led the prayers, from the high altar.
- *Choral singing.* In answer to the prayers the choir sang *An Air from County Derry.*
- *Lord's Prayer.* After this air, the Archbishop led the recitation of the Lord's Prayer, which was joined by the people outside.
- *Blessing.* Then the Archbishop said the blessing.
- *Hymn.* As a closing song the congregation sang the Welsh hymn *Cwm Rhondda* ("Guide me, o Thou great Redeemer").

– *Committal.* The Dean of Westminster said the commendation before the coffin.
– *Exit.* After the commendation the coffin was carried away in a ritual, which was almost as elaborate as the Introit. The soldiers from the Welsh guard had entered the sacrarium, and took the coffin on their shoulders. In a small procession (with the Dean and the cross-bearer) the coffin was carried to the West door, while the choir sang an impressive song from the orthodox funeral service, set to music by John Tavener: "Alleluia. May flights of angels sing thee to thy rest". This text explains why the procession is so small now: after the service we can only bring the body to the grave, may the angels bring Diana's soul to heaven. In the West door the procession halted for one minute in silence. In a total shot of the church in bird perspective over an arch, the camera shot the Dean who was standing on the threshold between the church and the world. The sun was shining, so that the camera gave the impression of an eye blinding light to which the Dean was about to give the body of Diana. The crossover of a portrait of Diana, which itself had been crossed with rays of light, strengthened this impression. This medial 'memorial card' was the only portrait of Diana shown during the entire broadcast. After the silence the Bells set in and the organ began to play, both enthusiastically, as if to say that every body (even the dead) was brought to life again.

2.4. After the funeral

After the service the coffin was driven in an autocade (cortège with cars) to the Spencer family home at Althorp for private burial in sanctified ground on an island in the centre of an ornamental lake. This procession, which went much faster than the procession between Diana's apartment and the church, was far less interesting. The real 'feast' was over.

After the funeral there was a period of mourning. Mourning is usually accompanied with rituals of commemoration. Some remarkable commemorations are mentioned in the introduction to *Diana. The Making of a Media Saint*:

> (…) thirty countries issued Diana commemorative stamps within a month after her death. For a year thereafter, barely a day passed without a story or a picture of Diana in the newspapers. (…) We have seen Italian Christmas

cribs with a painted figurine of Diana lining up with the shepherds and Wise Men, and private shrines to Diana. We have heard Diana's brother ask that Diana should not be turned into a saint, only for him to construct an island shrine to her memory. And we have read the conservative Catholic Paul Johnson confess in *The Spectator* to praying to Diana.[5]

In the same book Jeffrey Richards compares her commemoration with the medieval cult of a saint, including healing miracles, pilgrimages and relics.[6] One year after, there was a series of programs on the TV, sometimes explicitly discussing the sainthood of this 'secular Madonna'. Another year later there was a program about her grave and people visiting it. There appeared to be only little interest for Diana's grave; it had not quite become the popular place of pilgrimage as was expected. But her popularity is still alive. The question of her sainthood will be discussed later.

3. The development of a question to mediated and ritualised events

When the question 'what has happened?' comes up, we will not only have to organise and interpret our memories, but we also need to organise and interpret the question. What do we want to know when we ask what has happened? First of all, it does not seem that we just want to know the facts. People are rarely looking for facts. They usually search for stories. If something happens they need to grasp the event, how trivial it may be, in the form of a story.[7] And they need to understand the *meaning* of that story. Finally, they long to be sure whether and in what sense the story is *true*, which is again not a question of facts but of

---

[5] Richards, Wilson & Woodhead: *Diana* 1.

[6] Jeffrey Richards: The Hollywoodisation of Diana, in Richards, Wilson & Woodhead: *Diana* 59-73, pp. 61-63.

[7] Therefore there is no problem when someone discovers historical 'mistakes' in hagiographies, for they are not mistakes, but rather meaningful reconstructions of history into a story. Pierre Delooz: Toward a sociological study of canonised sainthood in the Catholic Church, in Stephen Wilson (ed.): *Saints and their cults. Studies in religious sociology, folklore and history* (Cambridge 1983), writes: "All saints are more or less constructed in that, being necessarily saints for other people, they are remodelled in the collective representation which is made for them." (Cited in Richards, Wilson & Woodhead: *Diana* 4). See also P. Post: *Het wonder van Dokkum. Verkenningen van populair religieus ritueel* (Nijmegen 2000) 72-87.

meaning. The foregoing is the story as I remember it – again, with the help of the 'mediated memories' of video, books and internet sites. In the following some intriguing moments of the event will be interpreted. And after that the question will be raised in how far and in what sense the happening was true, whereby the influence of the media and the ritual in the telling of the story are important.

4. SOME THOUGHTS ABOUT THE MEANING OF THE EVENT

4.1. The processions

In the organisation of the funeral a pattern can be described of alternation between movement and rest, whereby the places of rest are alternate private and public. See Figure 1. Diana lived a public life, but needed privacy also. The car in which she fled and died was meant to be and was meant to bring her to a place of privacy. In an aeroplane her remains were brought to the Chapel Royal of the St. James' Palace, a public place where the people could honour her and offer their condolences. Then the remains of Diana were brought to the private place of her apartment at Kensington Palace. From her apartment she was brought to the public place of the church. The broadcast of her funeral service was attended by millions of people. From this public place she was brought to the privacy of the grave, which lays in "sanctified ground on an island in the centre of an ornamental lake" and "faces east, toward the rising sun".[8]

Figure 1.

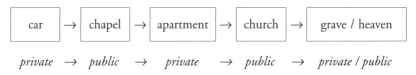

This processional structure, which is religious in character, bears the intention to an accompaniment of the deceased on her path to the grave, which is also the path to heaven. As far as the funeral service is

---

[8] See http://www.royal.gov.uk/main/arr.htm.

concerned, this path begins in the home of the deceased. This may sound confusing, a funeral service beginning in the home of the deceased. But in fact the ritual of the religious funeral service has this processional structure and thus encompasses more than the service in the church itself. The meaning of this processional structure may be catched in the old English word *genesan* (in German *genesen*, in Dutch *genezen*), which means to return or to bring back.[9] It indicates an originally religious service in which someone or something is brought back to the place where she, he or it belongs, and is purified before entering that place. In the case of Diana, her remains were first brought back to her apartment as the place where she belonged in this world. From her home she is brought back to the earth – the place where we all come from – and to heaven – the place to which we believe to belong, our eschatological home. Diana's grave 'on an island', reminding of Avalon in the English mythology, may also be seen as a heavenly place. The transitional places are churches, the intermediaries between earth and heaven, in which we are confronted with God who purifies and saves us and who lets the angels sing us home. We will come back to this phenomenon of *genesan*.

4.2. The cortège

The cortège has been represented in Figure 2. The rectangle represents the coffin borne on a gun carriage, the white circles are the soldiers from the Welsh Guards, the black circles soldiers from the King's Troop, the white ovals horses from the Metropolitan Police and the black ovals horses from the King's Troop.

Figure 2.

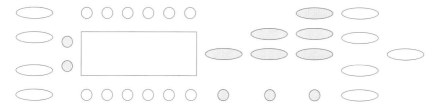

---

[9] The word *genesan* is rooted in the Greek word *neomai*, but translates the Greek *therapeuein*, which means to worship and to cure or recover.

This cortège attracted the attention of millions of people. One might expect that it is not only bearing a dead body, but that it also conveys meaning. The cortège can be divided in four parts. The core is doubtless the coffin with the body of Diana. Next to the coffin the twelve soldiers of the Welsh Guard; then the soldiers and horses of the King's Troop, who carry the coffin on a gun carriage; and last, the horses of the Metropolitan Police. The task of the last is to define the cortège in length and width and to set the course and the tempo. The Welsh Guard is there to carry the coffin. The task of the King's Troop may be to protect the coffin. Thus the cortège shows that something is being carried which is so important that nobody is allowed to come close. But in my opinion there is more to it. Horses and soldiers walk with the dead. On the one hand they accompany the deceased on her path to eternity, thus sharing the expectation of an eternal life. On the other hand they confront themselves with death, carrying it away from the living. Death cannot as it were escape from the cortège to threaten the living. The image of the soldiers around the coffin can be compared with the image of the *candles* around the coffin in the sacrarium, and with the *pillars* around the faithful in the church. Perhaps they have a comparable function, namely to define the sacred space, to indicate the direction, to protect the enclosed and to connect heaven and earth.

When the cortège reached the church the King's Troop and the Police left and were replaced by representatives of the church. The procession in the church is represented in Figure 3. The black circles are the male relatives of Diana. The white circles are members of the Welsh guard. The black squares represent vergers of the Abbey. The white squares liturgical ministers (among whom one cross-bearer, accompanied by two candle-bearers). And the white rectangles are the boys choir. Here the original meaning of a procession as the ecclesiastical community on her way toward the Holy becomes clearer.[10] In the singing choir we may

---

[10] S. FELBECKER: *Die Prozession. Historische und systematische Untersuchungen zu einer liturgischen Ausdruckshandlung* (Altenberge 1995) writes on p. 666: "Wer sich in dieser Weise vorwärtsbewegt, weiß ein Ziel vor sich, das er mit den Vorstellungen von Heil, Heimat, Ankunft, mit etwas Verheißenem verbindet', and on p. 477: 'Wenn die Prozession auch zunächst und am deutlichsten Bewegung ist, so ist sie doch immer auch Schau, sie besteht aus Zeigen und Schauen (...) Der Wunsch, auch das Göttliche zu sehen, bleibt unerfüllt und richtet sich daher auf Ersatzobjekte, auf Spuren des Göttlichen." See also P.J. MARGRY: *Teedere quaesties. Religieuze rituelen in conflict. Confrontaties tussen katholieken en protestanten rond de processiecultuur in 19e-eeuws Nederland* (Hilversum 2000).

recognise the procession as a form of prayer.[11] The deceased is carried by the community (not in order to protect her but to include her) and moves with the community, with the light (candle-bearers), with Jesus (cross-bearer) on the waves of the music toward the Holy.

Figure 3.

4.3. The liturgical order

The order of the liturgical service was said to be a combination between traditional and modern elements. Modern elements in the service can be recognised in the song by a personal friend (Elton John), the poems by Diana's sisters and the eulogy by her brother. Paul Post raises the question how this combination between traditional and modern elements can be valued.[12] Post distinguishes three tracks of rituality: an ecclesiastical, a common religious and a secular track. He sees these three tracks interacting in the funeral service of Diana, thereby considering the reading of 1 Corinthians by Tony Blair as a common religious and the song by Elton John as a secular form of rituality. The question is in how far and in what way the combination can be called an interaction. My first impression was that the service was a traditional liturgy with some modern 'insertions' in it, which did not disturb the traditional order. A closer attention, mainly incited by the question of Post, informs me of the effects of the modern elements.[13]

[11] P. DE HAES: Processie, in *Liturgisch Woordenboek II* (Roermond 1965-1968) 2280-2282.

[12] P. POST: Van Paasvuur tot stille tocht. Over interferentie van liturgisch en volksreligieus ritueel, in *Volkskundig bulletin* 25 (1999) 215-234, p. 224.

[13] Tracing common religious elements in the funeral service is problematic, as the term 'common religious' is too abstract to be recognised as a category. The reading of the ode to love from 1 Corinthians 13, for example, is not a common religious but, although inclusive, a genuine Christian reading. Other religions or philosophies of life may find themselves in

When we compare the given liturgy with the ecclesiastical order in the *Alternative service book* (ASB 1980), we should keep in mind that the order in the ASB gives room for some changes. For example, most funeral services include personal elements such as poems read by relatives or friends, an electronic performance of the deceased favorite music, and an eulogy. What we will be looking for in our comparison is the overall structure. See Figure 4.

Figure 4.

ASB 1980	*Diana's funeral service*
– Sentences	– *Introit with Sentences*
– Collect	– *Bidding*
	– *Hymn*
	– *Poem*
	– *Choral singing*
	– *Poem*
– Psalms	– *Psalm 23*
– Readings	– *Reading 1 Co 13*
	– *Song*
– Sermon	– *Eulogy*
– *Te Deum* or a Hymn	– *Hymn*
– Prayers (*the Lord's Prayer,*	– *Prayers*
Intercessions and a Hymn)	– *Choral singing*
	– *Lord's Prayer*
	– *Blessing*
	– *Hymn*
– Committal	– *Commendation*
	– *Exit*

We may notice that the Collect is missing. This Creed-like prayer, which is to be said by all, has the following words:

the content, but that does not make the text less Christian. The reading itself by the Prime Minister, however, has been an example of re-contextualisation, for Tony Blair read it as if it were his personal political statement. The reading of 1 Corinthians 13, therefore, was not a common religious element, but an interference between the ecclesiastical and the secular.

Heavenly Father,
in your Son Jesus Christ
you have given us a true faith and a sure hope.
Strengthen this faith and hope in us all our days,
that we may live as those who believe in
the communion of saints,
the forgiveness of sins,
and the resurrection to eternal life;
through your Son Jesus Christ our Lord. Amen.

A possible reason for omitting this collect is that it is exclusively Christian and thus maybe offensive to all those who do not believe in Jesus as the Christ and yet attend the service. Instead of this collect, the Dean concludes his bidding with a more inclusive collect, which fits better in the idea of Diana:[14]

Whatever our beliefs and faith,
let us with thanksgiving remember her life
and enjoyment of it;
let us rededicate to God the work of those many charities
that she supported;
let us commit ourselves anew to caring for others;
and let us offer to him and for his service
our own mortality and vulnerability.

A second peculiarity in the funeral liturgy is the reading of 1 Corinthians 13, which is not recommended by the ASB. A possible reason for this choice is, again, that the recommended readings are too Christian to be acceptable for people from other religions, and that this lecture sounds (as Post suggests) more ecumenical. Another reason may be, however, that the ode to love matches perfectly with Diana as we see her, and that this lecture is thus more useful in our painting of her icon. Despite of these differences, we may say that the liturgy of Diana's funeral followed the traditional order. This conclusion was to be expected, of course, for the Dean of a Cathedral will not break the ecclesiastical order, especially in the case of a service in which the Royal family is involved.[15]

---

[14] Diana has not exactly been a traditional Christian, at least not an excluding one. See Paul HEELAS: Diana's self and the quest within, in RICHARDS, WILSON & WOODHEAD: *Diana* 98-118. See also Linda WOODHEAD: Diana and the religion of the heart, *Ibidem* 119-139.

[15] The Netherlands, however, has different experiences with liturgies in which the Royal family is involved. These experiences concern the re-baptism (!) of Princess Irene

The traditional liturgical order creates an atmosphere of unification or, if you prefer, gathering. The unification begins in the spatial gathering in and around the church, directed toward the still empty centre of the sacrarium. The people unify in the movement of the sound, when they sing or listen to the national anthem together. They gather around a content of love and life, when listening to the readings together. They become one, when they pray together. This is what the liturgy is about: a people becoming one unified body appearing in the light of the divine countenance and praying that this deceased human is and will be forever a member of the eternal community of the living and the dead, yet living saints. This is the message of the traditional liturgy. And this is also what the people joining it believe, at least during the ritual.

Modern elements are not only the reading of the poems and the song by a pop-singer, but also the crowd outside attending the ritual in the church via the electronic media (two screens in Hyde Park). The poems, the song and the crowd surrounding the ritual had something to do with Diana as a person. Sisters, friends and ordinary citizens who loved the person of Diana, performed these modern elements in the funeral service, thus accentuating the personal in the traditional liturgy. And the importance of the personal in this service can hardly be overestimated. For if the ritual would have been only traditional, it would have been rather lifeless. The modern elements did not, as has been said, disturb the traditional order, but interacted with it. They moved the old order with moments of breath, nearness and recognition. Some moments of interference 'fitted', as was the case with the poems and the eulogy. Only the pop-song *Candle in the Wind* did not harmonise with the liturgical atmosphere, and yet it neither disturbed the atmosphere. The crowd outside had a very important function, because it was the *pro-fanum* (literally "the place before the temple"), the surrounding real life in which the liturgy is embedded and from which it receives living reality. The interaction with the modern world was nowhere stronger than in the participation of the songs and prayers by people in the crowd. To a certain extent, the people outside were more involved in the service than the people inside. The effect of this interaction was that the people were brought closer to the liturgy and the liturgy was brought closer to the people.

in the Roman Catholic Church (9 January 1964), and the ecumenical Eucharist in the celebration of the matrimony of Prince Maurits and Miss Marilene van den Broek (30 May 1998).

This brings me to another modern element in the service, namely its transmission through the electronic media. The order of the service had been printed in newspapers and can be found still on Internet (http://www.royal.gov.uk), the service was shown on two giant screens in Hyde Park and the whole event was broadcast on television. The broadcast of the service was interacting heavily with the liturgical order. The order of the liturgy itself remained the same, but the presentation and even celebration of the liturgy was influenced strongly by the media of microphone and camera. Some media-made connections have already been noted, such as the organ music crossing over the procession, connecting outside and inside the church. During the service the camera was also making connections: between outside and inside, between songs and stained glass icons, between congregation and individuals, between ordained and ordinary. The effect of this interference between, in Post's words, the ecclesiastical and the secular was an intensification of the connection between the event and the recipient.

In their togetherness the liturgical elements made an icon of princess Diana – leaving the only too human in oblivion and remembering the truly and vulnerably human as sacred (literally 'made inviolable'). This icon of vulnerable beauty was affirmed by the portrait with rays of light shown on the television at the end of the service. But the liturgy also painted a portrait of 'our' philosophy of life. It was already mentioned that a collective subject is being formed during the ritual, a 'we' that carries the ritual and believes in it. This does not mean that every single person in the church, in the crowd and before the television believed and felt the same thing. But it *does* mean that they were indeed concentrated around the ritual and the ritual message: they had become *we*. And this community joined in the celebrated faith of the liturgy. During the ritual the community believed in life after death, that the love with which Diana was gifted is eternal and strong as death, that the Lord – whoever He may be – is our Saviour. Moreover, the community gathered in this liturgy believed in the British identity and in the reconciliation of tradition and modernity. It was the message of this ritual. And during the time of this ritual we, who joined in it, believed in it, whether we do or not!

4.4. The silence, the singing and the timing

The possible reason why a two-hour long procession and a one-hour liturgical service have not been boring, can perhaps be found in the silence with which the whole event was surrounded. The silence was not an absence of sound, but an atmosphere of concentration. The cortège and the camera, the commentator and the crowd were all concentrated and incited an attentive mood in us, the recipients. This mood is a silent mood. And it is this silent mood of which can be said that is 'a fundamental category of rituality'.[16] In ritual there is always a strong concentration on the time of the ritual, its now-moment, more even than on the ritual action. And that is why a ritual, if properly and thus attentively celebrated, is never boring.

A second fundamental category of rituality was met in the music, especially the singing. Music and singing are categories of festivity. Singing changes our everyday speech prosody and gives us a new identity. Music imposes a new order on everyday life, in which everybody is allowed to move together in the same direction, as in dance. In ritual, the singing divides *and* connects the different actors: the leaders (who may act during the song), the choir, the faithful (who join in the singing) and the outsiders (who don't know the melody). But we noticed also other musical functions. Music connects opposites: the organ music inside the church accompanying the procession outside the church, and the liturgical singing of the unorganised people outside with the ordered people inside. Music may even lead the ritual act: the singing choir led the procession in the church defining the procession as movement (striding) and directionality (prayer). This musical-liturgical act is a realisation beforehand of the plea in the final song "May flights of angels *sing* thee to thy rest". Furthermore, to a large extent the singing carried out the ritual process of unification mentioned before. Singing not only transforms individuals into a community, but also founds their faith and directs their thought. Music is a phenomenon that must be followed. Singing the singer follows, with her whole body and mind, the movement of the song and in this movement its content.[17] And finally, the power of a singing community is as strong as a river: here we are, and we are going into that direction!

A third fundamental category is the timing. The ritual concentration on the now-moment of its movement elicits a sense for timing, or in liturgical language: *kairos*, the right time for the right action. The austere

---

[16] POST: Van Paasvuur tot stille tocht 225.

[17] W.M. SPEELMAN: Teksten begrijp je, muziek moet je volgen, in J. MAAS & A. SMEETS: *Werktekeningen. Semiotische constructies in blauwdruk* (Tilburg 1999) 155-167.

timing of Diana's funeral keeps amazing me. The precise timing of the processions, which led for example to the concurrence of the final tones of the Funeral Sentences with the last members of the Welsh guard leaving the sacrarium, has already been mentioned. Anybody involved in liturgical action knows that such perfect timing not only requires practice, but also feeling and trust. What we meet here is the establishing by the ritual of *her* time in *the* time, the ritual time in the time of ritual.[18] When a ritual time is imposed upon the time, there is interference between two parallel time-streams, one of which measured in relative durations, the other in seconds. The ritual art of timing (which in my view is a *musical* art) is the miraculous gift of making one time affirm the other, so that time is intensified. One can even get the idea that the uncontrollable and irreversible time is responding to the holy order of the ritual. When the cortège halted before the church and the Bells rang the hour, I actually wondered whether the time had been "waiting" for the cortège to reach the church. This susceptibility for the magical was also incited by the sun shining at the proper ritual moment.

5. WAS IT TRUE?

Diana is an image, her event a story, and this story reveals us our faith in love and thoughts about life. We believe in love as a vulnerable and beautiful close friend. There is a place for love, and in the end we all belong to this place. Carrying death away from us, we carry the dead toward this eschatological place where we want to be taken ourselves in due course. Now, the question whether or not we as individuals believe in these things indeed, is not very interesting. During the ritual we gather around and join in this faith and thought. Much more interesting is the question whether this story is true, not in metaphysical sense, but in the sense that something or someone can be *true to us*. Is the image of Diana truthful or deceptive? Was the reaction of the people true or illusory? Was it a true funeral or was it a circus? We can only decide on these issues when we understand the role of the media and

---

[18] See H.-G. GADAMER: *Die Aktualität des Schönen. Kunst als Spiel, Symbol und Fest* (Stuttgart 1977) 52 vv. Discussing the temporal structure of the feast, Gadamer distinguishes two fundamental experiences of time: an 'empty' time and a 'fulfilled' time or *Eigenzeit*. One of his conclusions is that we have to learn to sojourn in the *Eigenzeit* of the feast (p. 60).

the ritual in the unfolding of the event and in the making of the icon. Whatever the truth of the event is, it came to us in ritualisations and through the media.

5.1. A media event

When we communicate through the (electronic) media, we believe that the mediated messages refer to a reality. On the other hand, we know that the media-makers influence the messages. Media communicate *reproductions* of reality (images), and reproductions are susceptible to manipulation. Usually that does not make us suspicious, for there is enough truth in the media to believe in, and we are aware of the strategies of illusion. We know that things are not what they seem in the media. And yet we know how to understand this specific manner of communication. Sometimes questions after the reality of a mediated event become important, e.g. in case of advertisements or military news, because we *expect* the messages to be manipulated. But finally we believe that the real truth will come out and be broadcast.

A more persistent question in the communication with the media is that of *authenticity*. Authenticity (literally "done with one's own hand") means personal in the sense that the real person backs the mediated message. Even when it is fully clear to us that the message is fantasy, we demand the play or the illusion to be authentic (*eigentlich*). Our mediated culture demands that the media communicate a 'true illusion'.[19] Watching TV we judge the authenticity of the people who are on it *and* the people who watch 'this sort of thing'. The question is not if the program-maker is capable of creating an effective illusion (which is also important), but if the program-maker is capable of connecting the illusion (which is a quality of media *per se*) with the truth.[20] To be more specific: the question is not whether Diana was an image, she was, but the question is whether that image was authentic, backed by the person

---

[19] The term *true illusion* is taken from a make-up product of *Maybelline*.

[20] Illusion, then, is a form in which truth is expressed. This paradoxical phrase is based on the semiotic difference between expression form and content form. The expression form of the media may be determined by the imaginary (the image or illusion as the material in which the message is conveyed), whereas the content form of this imaginary expression may be a true reality. The medium may be the message, but the expression form of the medium is not the same thing as the content form of the message.

behind it. Was it Diana? Did the media bring out the essence of Diana?[21] I think they did, and I think that Diana indeed agreed with her image. We know or learn to know whether an image has substance or not, and whether there is a truth behind the illusion or nothing.

The primary function of media is, to make an event accessible for people who are not physically there where the event takes place. Decades of practice has taught the media-makers that an event is *not* accessible when it is only transmitted, that is to say, when cameras and microphones are nothing but eyes and ears registering the event. In order to make the event accessible, the media have to join in the movement of the event and become part of it.[22] The effect of media joining in the event is an *intensification* of the event. In the mediation of Diana's funeral we have seen some examples of the media moving with the event. First of all, the movement of the cameras was as slowly as the movement of the procession and service. Furthermore, the zooming in and out of the cameras seemed to move with the patterns of concentration and relaxation necessary to follow the event. We have also seen some examples of a 'medial rhetoric', as one might call it, such as the Dean waiting in the door to the light and the overlapping of Diana's portrait at the end of the service. Another example, which has not been mentioned yet, was the camera placed on the ceiling of the church where we traditionally find the 'eye of God' (centre and highest place of the church). Near the end of the service this camera shot the coffin straight from above in close up and then zoomed out very slowly and very long. The zooming out had a double effect: a farewell to the world and a rising sheer to God. It was as if the camera followed the moving of Diana's spirit. These techniques might be called examples of medial *rhetoric*, for they are reminiscent of musical rhetoric in the seventeenth and nineteenth centuries in which musical figures and moods fulfil, *perform* as it were, the text.[23]

In order to be able to function, the media need to make an image of the event they intend to mediate. The linguist Ferdinand de Saussure

---

[21] W. SANDERS: Gottesdienstübertragung in Hörfunk und Fernsehen der ARD, in *Liturgisches Jahrbuch* 36 (1986) 142-154, quotes Josef Burbach, a director: "[der Fernsehregisseur] muß alles, was das Auge sieht, in mediale Bilder umsetzen und übersetzen, um so zum Wesen vorzustoßen."

[22] This is what reality-TV does: it does not register the event, but moves with the event and becomes part of it.

[23] I here refer to the seventeenth century practice of the *figura* or *Affektenlehre* respectively the nineteenth century practice of the *Leitmotive*.

taught that communication can only work with images (*images acoustiques* in the case of spoken language).[24] This teaching remains true also for the communication of events through the electronic media: that which is communicated is necessarily an image (or a reproduction, as was mentioned above) and not the reality itself. In the case of Diana the media were severely criticised, not for making an image of Diana (i.e. for transforming her into an image) but for their boundless and destructive manner of operation. Making an image of someone does not imply the destruction of the real person. On the contrary, the true imagination implies the preservation of the person's essence in the image. A truthful image is an embodied essence, or else it is an image of nothing. In my opinion, the mediation of Diana's funeral has been a wonderful example of such an imaginative operation. In co-operation the commentator and the cameras represented the event by discussing and showing the coffin, the people, the cortège, the relatives, the guests, the buildings, the flowers, the card from Harry with "Mummy" and the charity-workers as environmental symbols of Diana. Actually, the commentator and cameras made an image of Diana purely by picturing her environment. In other words, they showed Diana in the event, the "Diana" that was alive.

An effect of the mediation of an event is that, whereas some aspects are intensified, others are suppressed. Michael Pokorny has criticised the media for focusing on certain emotions and not showing other:

> (…) the media took the line that we had all reacted the same way and we were all filled with grief. This was clearly false, as there were many and various reactions to the deaths, but the media allowed no dissent from what they deemed to be the official line. This was then promoted to the claim that the whole of Great Britain plus half the world were heartbroken which was a ridiculous claim.[25]

Although this is a sharp observation, one may ask whether the media are to blame for showing only certain emotions and not all. The media moved with the event. The event, however, went in one direction, not in different directions at the same time. What is at stake here is that there

---

[24] F. DE SAUSSURE: *Cours de linguistique générale* (Paris 1972) 97 vv.

[25] See http://www.bbc.co.uk/diana/. The maker of the documentary *The Princess's People* says: "One thing is certain. The way the media covered the event was far from representative. For a short while we forgot to question. Instead we latched on to a very one-dimensional reaction to the tragedy of Diana's death", in A. ALEXANDER: *Queen of (some) hearts*, on http://www.bbc.co.uk/hi/english/static/diana_one_year_on/default.stm.

may be different intentions in the making of television. If one intends to mediate an event, not in a critical reflection but only to make it accessible for recipients, one has to join in the movement of the event. This is the intention in the transmissions of e.g. sporting competitions, liturgical celebrations and artistic performances. In these forms of mediation it is better, in a paraphrase of Mr. Alexander, "for a short while not to question", so that the movement, which is the essential element of these events, is not interrupted. *After* the event there is time (for the movement has stopped, and the spirit rests) for reflection. To be concrete and in contradiction to the critique of Pokorny, I think that the represented reaction of the people was true. Every individual had mixed feelings on that day and some had other feelings than others. But this does not alter the fact that the event of the funeral conveyed feelings of stillness, love and grief. And everybody involved in that event must have felt *also* these conveyed feelings. At a funeral one does not have to feel sad, but if one has the capability to feel at all, one feels the sadness of the event.

To conclude this section, in my view the media succeeded in an authentic mediation of the event. The event was intensified, indeed, but it was balanced enough not to turn it into a circus.

5.2. A ritual event

The funeral of Diana was not only mediated, but also ritualised. To a large extent all funerals are forms of ritualised action. But in this case the ritualisation was very strong. Almost every action in the event, even the Royal Family looking at the flowers, seemed as a performance of a well-defined ritual. This means that even the so-called 'spontaneous' actions were not spontaneous, but calculated (cf. the root-meaning of the word 'rite' as it can be found in *arithmetic* and *rhythm*). We may ask the same question of truth and efficacy regarding this ritualisation. In how far has this ritual been true to us? Did the ritualisation turn the activity into a circus? Was it a play, and if so, was this play meaningful? Was there truth in this ritual?

As was the case in mediation, we also believe to be dealing with reality when we act or communicate through ritual. A ritual act, however, is a specific form of doing.[26] We may *believe* that rituals have an influence

---

[26] See W.M. SPEELMAN: On liturgical enunciation as the transparence of a coming truth, in E. TARASTI (ed.): *On the borderlines of semiotics* (Imatra 1993) 79-91. In this article I argue that liturgy does not have the intention to communicate a message, but

on reality. But we *know* that rituals do not cause things to happen, that they do not work in a technical sense. It may be that the food is better digested if we pay attention to our meal rituals, but even if so, that is not the reason why we perform these rituals. Rituals belong to the domain of the play. They have no sense for those who do not join the ritual.[27] And yet, we expect rituals to be effective in some sense. If we do not have the feeling that the ritual works, that it does something, we will eventually stop performing them. But what is this 'something', in what way are rituals effective, and what kind of truth are they communicating to us?

In my view, an effective ritual transforms the eating into a meal, the burying into a funeral, the drinking into a feast. An effective ritual turns an activity into an event with character (cf. the Greek *rhythmos*). The ritual does so by putting the activity in a perspective, by which the activity is connected with a 'deeper' reality. We have discussed some fundamental categories with which the ritual operates. In the case of the funeral of Diana, the silence, the singing and the timing attracted my attention. But there are also categories that shape the deeper reality with which the activity is to be connected. These categories are the language (text) and the personality (character). In the preparation of a ritual much time and effort is spent on the selection of texts and the character of the wording, for in and through these choices the ritual is put in perspective.

The funeral of princess Diana was ritualised according to the Christian, in this case Anglican tradition. It was built upon typical Christian beliefs, such as the faith in Jesus Christ as the resurrection to life (John 11, 25-26), the Lord's Prayer and the blessing in the name of the Trinitarian God (the Father, the Son and the Holy Spirit). But we have also noticed a shift from the exclusively Christian to a more inclusive religious faith. The liturgy accentuated hope for life after death and faith in love and charity as gifts from eternity. One does not have to be a Christian to believe in these matters. This shift to a more inclusive ritual language gives a perspective matching with the icon of Diana. And this leads me to affirm my original feeling that the ritual 'worked', for

---

to establish a holy order. The effect of this establishment of the holy order, e.g. rain after people have prayed for rain, is suspended to a remote past and an eschatological future. A liturgical celebration, therefore, cannot be evaluated on the basis of its effects.

[27] R. GUARDINI: *Vom Geist der Liturgie* (Freiburg 1957) 89-105.

indeed the liturgy has been able to connect the funeral with a deeper reality that responded to the true Diana. Corresponding to the media, the ritual made an icon of Diana by picturing her spiritual values.

One of the effects of the ritualisation of events is that the ritual 'channels' emotions. Which brings me back to the media critique of Pokorny.[28] Ritual organises the event and the emotions connected to it, such as for example the ritual organising the funeral as a sad event. This does not mean that everybody feels sad during the funeral. On the contrary, organising the sadness into a definite form, the ritual puts the emotion at a certain distance. This distance gives room for emotions. If people feel sad, their emotion is met with a ritual form of sadness and thus canalised. But if they feel something else, they *do not have to* feel sad. The feeling *is there* already, it is given. One can connect his emotions to the ritual form or leave his emotions flow freely in any other direction.

To conclude this and the previous section, in my view the media succeeded in an authentic mediation of the event and the ritual succeeded in putting the event in a truthful perspective. The event of the funeral was intensified, indeed, but it was balanced enough not to turn it into a circus.

6. Is Diana a saint?

In the foregoing, the people's reaction to Diana's death has been described as the making of a saint's story and the painting of an icon. Diana has been treated as a saint, and many people may have thought or still think that she was some kind of a saint. Even those who explicitly tried to prevent her canonisation must have thought that there was a reason to consider Diana a saint of our time. Why do people want to prevent her elevation to a sacred status? Are they perhaps afraid that this will deprive her from her humanity? Anyhow, the discussions about the possible sainthood of Diana may very well be compared with the investigations preparing an official canonisation. And the question of her sacred status remains yet unanswered, until the answer is given by a liturgical practice. Let us have a look at some qualities of sainthood, which may shed light on Diana as a saint.

---

[28] See our note 25.

A saint is first of all a normal human being. What makes this human different from others is, that saints seem to have been touched by the Holy – they are spiritually gifted – and are thus a source of inspiration for us. Saints point us with their lives to the fulfillment of life; their lives show us life in its fullness. Certainly, Diana was a normal human being, but as a human she was a celebrity, an imaginary person in whom we may celebrate life. If Diana was a saint showing us life in its fullness, her sainthood focused on this earthly life here and now, not on a life after death, but indeed on earthly life *beyond* the death of poverty, homelessness, AIDS, land mines, et cetera.

Further, a saint is an intimate friend, dead in her grave and yet living and connecting us with the Holy (cf. Heb 11, 4).[29] Diana was felt to be an intimate friend, now dead, but somehow living and connecting people with something, which might be called holy. As a believer I would say that her life did not connect us with the Holy. But as a scholar one has to go on asking: what do we mean, if not God, with 'the Holy'?

The Holy has a double meaning, both to be found in the Latin word *sanctus*. *Sanctus* comes from *sancire* (to enclose), and refers to an enclosed district (the *fanum*), which is separated from the other places (*pro-fanum*). But Holy does not only mean 'separated', for the Latin word *sanctus* contains also the word *san* (as in the English *sane* and the old-English *genesan*), which refers the Holy as health, wholeness, life in its fullness. And if we understand the Holy in this 'a-theistic' manner, we can admit that Diana connected and connects many people with themselves, their own lives and identities.

Diana was for many of us a source of imagination. And especially here, the media have been helpful. The media gave Diana a lasting identity, a face that will be remembered, a *persona* who will remain a part of our culture. This persona has supported many to develop their own identity. In this commemorative work of the media in co-operation with the people we may even recognize a sort of *anamnesis* (remembrance as a reflection of her life in our lives) and even canonisation (making her life a model for our lives). The ritual, on the other hand, focused on a different, genuinely Christian *anamnesis*: the resurrection to life in Christ. This resurrection was elaborated in the poem "If I should die" as a resurrection by the relatives: "turn again to life". In my opinion these

---

[29] See P. BROWN: *The cult of the saints. Its rise and function in Latin Christianity* (Chicago 1981).

two forms of *anamnesis* do not contradict one another: the making of an icon for our identities in this life and the remembering of our hope to resurrection to life are two sides of one coin.

7. LET US BRING HER HOME

Having tried to measure Diana's sainthood with the help of some qualities, I would like to conclude with the call to bring Diana home. Diana felt that she had a self that could not come out.[30] We split her into two: a real person and an illusionary person. We never knew the real person, whereas the illusionary person lived in papers in an illusive world. Now that the real person is dead, the illusionary person can be released from the illusive and brought back to the earth or heaven where Diana belongs. Bringing her home as in the Old English *genesan*, we move with the funeral processions. Bringing her home we heal her and make her holy by letting her rest.

---

[30] A. MORTON: *Diana. Her true story* (London 1995) 43 (cited in HEELAS: Diana's self 103).

ON THE AUTHORS

- Dr. Marcel BARNARD (1957) is professor for liturgical studies, appointed by the Dutch Evangelical-Lutheran Church, at Utrecht University. He specialized in the relation between liturgy and culture, especially the *artes*. Some publications: *Wat het oog heeft gezien. Verbeelding als sleutel van het credo* (1997); *Liturgiek als wetenschap van christelijke riten en symbolen* (2000); with P. Post (eds.), *Ritueel bestek. Antropologische kernwoorden van de liturgie* (2001).

- Dr. Herman BECK (1953) is professor of the phenomenology and history of religions at the Tilburg Faculty of Theology. His research interest is in the field of religious studies in general and Islam in The Netherlands, Islam in Indonesia and Islam in Morocco in particular.

- Dr. Sible DE BLAAUW (1951) is professor of Early Christian Art and Architecture at the Catholic University in Nijmegen. He explores the relationships between architecture and liturgy, with a major emphasis on Rome before the Council of Trent, and the reception of Early Christian monuments accross the centuries. He recently published a study on the origins and reception of Christian orientation: *Met het oog op het licht. Een vergeten principe in de oriëntatie van het vroegchristelijk kerkgebouw* (2000).

- Dr. Charles M.A. CASPERS (1953) is co-ordinator of the Liturgical Institute in Tilburg (until September 2001), and fellow of the Titus Brandsma Institute in Nijmegen. Most of his publications deal with church history and the history of liturgy, spirituality, and religious culture. He defended a Ph.D. thesis on 'Eucharistic devotion and the feast of Corpus Christi in the Low Countries during the late Middle Ages' (1992). With G. Lukken & G. Rouwhorst he edited *Bread of Heaven. Customs and practices surrounding Holy Communion. Essays in the history of liturgy and culture* (= Liturgia condenda 3) (1995). Together with P.J. Margry, he edited a three-volume lexicon on 'Places of pilgrimage in the Netherlands' (1997, 1998, 2000).

- Dr. Carla DAUVEN-VAN KNIPPENBERG (1950) is associate professor for German literature and culture at the University of Amsterdam. She is working on medieval drama, on the reception of medieval literature and on 'borderline texts' (texts at the border of a genre or at the border of some national literature). Some publications: *Einer von den Soldaten öffnete seine Seite ... Eine Untersuchung der Longinuslegende im deutschsprachigen geistlichen Spiel des Mittelalters* (1990); 'Die "Passion Sainte Geneviève" und das "Donaueschinger Passionsspiel" im Vergleich', in: I. Kasten *et al.* (eds.), *Kultureller Austausch und Literaturgeschichte im Mittelalter* (1998) 271-282.

- Dr. André DROOGERS (1941) is professor of the anthropology of religion at the Vrije Universiteit, Amsterdam. His research interests include popular religion, syncretism, Pentecostalism, play, and qualitative research methods. His publications include: 'Methodological ludism. Beyond religionism and reductionism', in: Anton van Harskamp (ed.), *Conflicts in Social Science* (1996) 44-67; 'Paradoxical views on a paradoxical religion', in: B. Boudewijnse, A.F. Droogers and F.H. Kamsteeg (eds.), *More than Opium. An anthropological approach to Latin American and Caribbean Pentecostal praxis* (1998) 1-34; with S.M. Greenfield (eds.), *Reinventing religions. Syncretism and transformation in Africa and the Americas* (2001).

- Dr. Martin GERTLER (1954) is professor for digital media in Bielefeld and docent for media in the applied theology in Münster. He also is a self-employed mediaproducer (television, audio-visual and interactive productions).

- Dr. Bert Groen (1953) is lecturer at the Institute of Eastern Christian Studies, University of Nijmegen. He has specialized in the liturgy of the sick, Orthodox liturgy and ecumenism.

- Dr. John HELSLOOT (1950) is a researcher at the Department of Ethnology of the Meertens Institute (Royal Netherlands Academy of Arts and Sciences). He specializes in the historical study of calendar rituals. Recent publications: St Nicholas as a public festival in Java, 1870-1920. Articulating Dutch popular culture as ethnic culture, in *Bijdragen tot de Taal-, Land- en Volkenkunde* 154 (1998) 613-637; Die Nationalisierung des Nikolausfestes in den Niederlanden im 20. Jahrhundert. Eine Skizze anhand der Fragebogen des Meertens Instituts von 1943 und 1994, in *Rheinisch-westfälische Zeitschrift für Volkskunde* 45 (2000) 217-244.

- Dr. Jan HOLMAN s.v.d. (1933) studied after his ordination (1959) biblical exegesis at the Catholic University Nijmegen, the Pontifical Institute in Rome and at the Ecole Biblique in Jerusalem. He took a doctorate at the Pontifical Institute with a dissertation on Psalm 139. After having taught Old Testament at the Theological Faculty of Pamplona, the Verbiti Institute at Nemi (Rome), the Missionary Institute London and the Tilburg Faculty of Theology, he retired in 1998. He published studies on Psalms, Prophets, Job, Preacher and Canticles.

- Martin Hoondert M.Div. (1967) studied musicology at the University of Utrecht and theology (liturgy) at the Tilburg Faculty of Theology. He specialized in liturgical music (gregorian chant as well as liturgical music of the 20th century) and is preparing a PhD thesis on inculturation and liturgical music. Besides, he is employed in the national Werkgroep voor Liturgie Heeswijk. He has published several articles about liturgy and liturgical music in the *Gregoriusblad* and the *Jaarboek voor liturgie-onderzoek*.

- Dr. Klaas-Willem DE JONG (1961) studied theology in Kampen and Budapest. He specialized in the liturgy of the reformed churches, especially in its history, and obtained his doctorate at the Free University in Amsterdam. He was ordained protestant minister in 1987. Nowadays he works as such in Alphen aan den Rijn. Some publications: 'Questions à propos de la double épiclèse. Le problème de la double épiclèse, en paticulier dans les prières eucharistiques II-IV', in: *Questions liturgiques* 68 (1987) 256-276; *Ordening van dienst. Achtergronden van en ontwikkelingen in de eredienst van de Gereformeerde Kerken in Nederland* (1996, dissertation); 'Van Forme naar Formulier. Het ontstaan en de ontwikkeling van het klassieke gereformeerde doopformulier in de Nederlandse Reformatie', in: *Jaarboek voor liturgie-onderzoek* 14 (1998) 7-59.

- Dr. Jozef LAMBERTS (1940) is professor of liturgy and sacramental theology at the Faculty of Theology, Catholic University of Leuven. He is chairman of the Liturgical Institute of Leuven and chief-editor of *Questions liturgiques – Studies in liturgy* and of *Tijdschrift voor liturgie*. Some publications: *Hoogtepunt en bron. Inleiding tot de liturgie* (1991); *Op weg naar heelheid. Over bedevaart en liturgie* (1997); (ed.) *Current issues in sacramental theology* (1994); (ed.) *Liturgy and inculturation* (1996); (ed.) *Popular religion, liturgy and evangelization* (1998).

- Dr. Wiel LOGISTER s.m.m. (1938) is professor of fundamental theology at the Tilburg Faculty of Theology. He specialized in the theology of religions (mainly on Christological questions), mariology and eschatology. His recent publications include *Maria – een uitdaging* (1995); *Na de dood. De harde noten van het verrijzenisgeloof* (1997); *Een dramatische breuk. De plaats van Israël in de eerste eeuwen van het christendom* (1997); *Dante – dichter, mysticus, pelgrim* (2000).

- Dr. Gerard LUKKEN (1933) studied at the Diocesan Seminary in Haaren (Noord-Brabant), the Pontificia Università Gregoriana in Rome, and the Institut Supérieur de Liturgie in Paris. He was professor of liturgy and sacramental theology (1967-1994) and director of the Liturgical Institute (1992-1994) at the Tilburg Faculty of Theology. Some publications: *Original Sin in the Roman liturgy. Research into the theology of Original Sin in the Roman sacramentaria and the early baptismal liturgy* (1973, dissertation); with M. Searle, *Semiotics and Church Architecture* (= Liturgia condenda 1) (1993); *Per visibilia ad invisibilia. Anthropological, theological and semiotic studies on the liturgy and the sacraments* (= Liturgia condenda 2) (1994); *Rituelen in overvloed. Een kritische bezinning op de plaats en de gestalte van het christelijk ritueel in onze cultuur* (1999).

- Dr. André MULDER (1959) is staff member at the NBI, School for Higher Education in Theology of Utrecht (The Netherlands). He lectures practical theology and psychology of religion and is mainly interested in the place and function of ritual in a postmodern Christian context. He defended a Ph.D. thesis on cremation liturgy: *Geloven in crematieliturgie. Een pastoraalliturgisch onderzoek naar hedendaagse crematieliturgie in een rooms-katholieke context* (2000).

- Dr. Rein NAUTA (1944) is professor of pastoral psychology and psychology of religion at the Tilburg Faculty of Theology. He published on subjects as religious leadership, festivity and ritual, guilt and shame, conversion. In 1995 he published *Ik geloof het wel* (*Do I believe? –* An introduction into the psychology of religion). Presently he is preparing a book on the psychology of the pastor.

- Dr. Jos PIEPER (1953) is associate professor of psychology of religion at the Theological Faculty of the University of Utrecht (The Netherlands) and the Catholic Theological University of Utrecht. His main interests are the fields of religion and mental health and religious rituals. Some publications: with P. Post & M. van Uden, *The modern pilgrim. Multidisciplinary explorations of Christian pilgrimage* (= Liturgia condenda 8) (1998); with H. van der Ven, 'The inexpressible God. God images among students of Dutch Catholic secondary schools', in: *Journal of empirical theology* 11-2 (1998) 64-80.

- Dr. Paul POST (1953) studied in Utrecht and Rome. Since 1994 he is professor of liturgical studies at the Tilburg Faculty of Theology and director of the Liturgical Institute located in Tilburg. His main interests are in the field of liturgy, theory and method of liturgical studies, the interference of ritual and liturgical studies, the anthropological dimensions of liturgy, popular religion (pilgrimage), Christian art (iconography, church architecture), and (post)modern developments in ritual and liturgy. Recent books: (ed.), *Een ander huis. Kerkarchitectuur na 2000* (1997); with J. Pieper & M. van Uden, *The modern pilgrim* (1998); *Het wonder van Dokkum. Verkenningen van populair religieus ritueel* (2000); with M. Barnard (eds.), *Ritueel bestek* (2001); with L. van Tongeren (eds.), *Devotioneel ritueel* (2001).

- Dr. Susan K. ROLL (1952) is asssociate professor of liturgy and systematic theology at Christ the King Seminary, Buffalo, New York. A specialist in the liturgical year and the women's liturgical movement, she received the Ph.D. with top honors in 1993 from the Catholic University of Louvain, Belgium. She is the author of *Toward the origins of Christmas* (= Liturgia condenda 5) (1995) and co-editor of *Revisioning our sources. Women's spirituality in European perspectives* (1994) and *Women, ritual and liturgy* (2001). She wrote more than forty articles in the fields of liturgy, sacraments and feminist theology.

- Dr. Els ROSE (1972) works as a lecturer at the Catholic Theological University of Utrecht and is co-ordinator of the Liturgical Institute in Tilburg (from September 2001). In 2001, she achieved her doctoral thesis *Communitas in commemoratione. Liturgisch Latijn en liturgische gedachtenis in het Missale Gothicum (Vat.reg.lat. 317)* (Diss. Utrecht 2001) from the Faculty of Arts of Utrecht University.

- Dr. Gerard ROUWHORST (1951) is professor in the history of liturgy at the Catholic Theological University of Utrecht. His research focusses particularly on the liturgical traditions of Syriac-speaking churches and on the relation between early Christian and Jewish ritual traditions. He published several studies dealing with the history of Christian worship.

- Dr. Ton SCHEER (1934) is professor of liturgy at the Theological Faculty of the Catholic University of Nijmegen. He published studies on the history of liturgy, and the theory of liturgical practice.

- Dr. Jan SMELIK (1961), studied musicology at the University of Utrecht. He was researcher for the Priority Programme 'Dutch Culture in European Context' of the Netherlands Organization for Scientific Research (NWO). In 1997 he received his doctorate at the University of Groningen. Some publications: 'The Gospel Hymn in the Low Countries', in: G. Harinck & H. Krabbendam (eds.), *Sharing the Reformed tradition. The Dutch-North American exchange, 1846-1996* (1996) 79-96; *Één in lied en leven. De stichtelijke liedcultuur bij Nederlandse protestanten tussen 1866 en 1938* (1997, dissertation).

- Dr. Willem Marie SPEELMAN (1960) is a scholar in musical and liturgical sciences. He works as a research assistent at the Liturgical Council of the Dutch Roman Catholic Episcopal Conference. Some publications: 'The plays of our culture. A formal differentiation between theatre and liturgy', in: *Jaarboek voor liturgie-onderzoek* 9 (1993) 65-81; *The generation of meaning in liturgical songs* (= Liturgia condenda 4) (1995, dissertation); 'The Sacrament is the message. On the mediation of liturgy through the electronic media', in: *Questions liturgiques* 81 (2000) 265-277.

- Dr. Regnerus STEENSMA (1937) is director of the Institute for Liturgical Studies of the State University Groningen. He wrote books and articles about the furnishing of historical churches, contemporary churchbuilding and the relation between art and liturgy.

- Dr. Gérard P.P. VAN TILLO (1937) is a professsor in the sociology of religion at the Faculty of Humanities at the University of Amsterdam. Some publications: *De kwalitatieve dimensie. Een methodologisch perspectief voor de godsdienstsociologie* (1987); *Onthullingen. Spiritualiteit sociologisch benaderd* (1994).

- Dr. Louis VAN TONGEREN (1954) is lecturer in liturgical studies at the Tilburg Faculty of Theology. He specialized in liturgical studies and the history of liturgy. He published in several collections and reviews on subjects concerning early medieval aspects of the liturgy, and contemporary liturgical practices. Recently he published *Exaltation of the Cross. Toward the origins of the Feast of the Cross and the meaning of the Cross in early medieval liturgy* (= Liturgia condenda 11) (2000).

- Dr. Marinus VAN UDEN (1952) is professor of clinical psychology of religion at the University of Nijmegen and the Tilburg Faculty of Theology. He also works as a clinical psychologist-psychotherapist in Heerlen (The Netherlands). His main interest is the field of religion, world view and mental health. Some publications: with P. Post & J. Pieper, *The modern pilgrim* (1998); 'Psychotherapy and religious problems', in: *Archiv für Religionspsychologie* 23 (2000) 243-252.

INDEX OF NAMES